DATE DUE

FOR REFERENCE

Do Not Take From This Room

*International Encyclopedia of the
Social Sciences, 2nd edition*

International Encyclopedia of the Social Sciences, 2nd edition

VOLUME 9
**WAGE AND PRICE CONTROLS–Z-TEST
ANNOTATED BIBLIOGRAPHY
INDEX**

William A. Darity Jr.
EDITOR IN CHIEF

MACMILLAN REFERENCE USA
A part of Gale, Cengage Learning

GALE
CENGAGE Learning

Detroit • New York • San Francisco • New Haven, Conn • Waterville, Maine • London

International Encyclopedia of the Social Sciences, 2nd edition

William A. Darity Jr., Editor in Chief

© 2008 Gale, Cengage Learning

For more information, contact
Macmillan Reference USA
A part of Gale, Cengage Learning
27500 Drake Rd.
Farmington Hills, MI 48331-3535
Or you can visit our Internet site at
gale.cengage.com

For permission to use material from this prod-uct, submit your request via Web at http://www.gale-edit.com/permissions, or you may download our Permissions Request form and submit your request by fax or mail to:

Permissions Department
Gale 27500 Drake Rd.
Farmington Hills, MI 48331-3535
Permissions Hotline:
248-699-8006 or 800-877-4253 ext. 8006
Fax: 248-699-8074 or 800-762-4058

Since this page cannot legibly accommodate all copyright notices, the credits constitute an extension of the copyright notice.

While every effort has been made to ensure the reliability of the information presented in this publication, Gale does not guarantee the accuracy of the data contained herein. Gale accepts no payment for listing; and inclusion in the publication of any organization, agency, institution, publication, service, or individual does not imply endorsement of the editors or publisher. Errors brought to the attention of the publisher and verified to the satisfaction of the publisher will be corrected in future editions.

LIBRARY OF CONGRESS CATALOGING-IN-PUBLICATION DATA

International encyclopedia of the social sciences / William A. Darity, Jr., editor in chief.—2nd ed. v. cm. Rev. ed. of: International encyclopedia of the social sciences / David L. Sills, editor. c1968–c1991.
Includes bibliographical references and index.
ISBN 978-0-02-865965-7 (set hardcover : alk. paper)—ISBN 978-0-02-865966-4 (v. 1 hardcover : alk. paper)—ISBN 978-0-02-865967-1 (v. 2 hardcover : alk. paper)—ISBN 978-0-02-865968-8 (v. 3 hardcover : alk. paper)—ISBN 978-0-02-865969-5 (v. 4 hardcover : alk. paper)—ISBN 978-0-02-865970-1 (v. 5 hardcover : alk. paper)—ISBN 978-0-02-865971-8 (v. 6 hardcover : alk. paper)—ISBN 978-0-02-865972-5 (v. 7 hardcover : alk. paper)—ISBN 978-0-02-865973-2 (v. 8 hardcover : alk. paper)—ISBN 978-0-02-866141-4 (v. 9 hardcover : alk. paper)—ISBN 978-0-02-866117-9 (ebook : alk. paper)
1. Social sciences—Dictionaries. 2. Social sciences—Encyclopedias. I. Darity, William A., 1953– II. Title: Encyclopedia of the social sciences.
H40.A2I5 2008
300.3–dc22

2007031829

0-02-865965-1 (set)   0-02-865970-8 (v. 5)
0-02-865966-X (v. 1)   0-02-865971-6 (v. 6)
0-02-865967-8 (v. 2)   0-02-865972-4 (v. 7)
0-02-865968-6 (v. 3)   0-02-865973-2 (v. 8)
0-02-865969-4 (v. 4)   0-02-866141-9 (v. 9)

This title is also available as an e-book.
ISBN 978-0-02-866117-9; 0-02-866117-6
Contact your Gale representative for ordering information.

Printed in the United States of America
3 4 5 6 7 8 14 13 12 11 10 09 08

Editorial Board

Contents

VOLUME 1

Introduction	XI
List of Articles	XVII
List of Contributors	XLV
Thematic Outline	CXXIII
Abortion–Cognitive Dissonance	1

VOLUME 2

Cohabitation–Ethics in Experimentation

VOLUME 3

Ethnic Conflict–Inequality, Gender

VOLUME 4

Inequality, Income–Marxism, Black

VOLUME 5

Masculinity–Nyerere, Julius

VOLUME 6

Oaxaca, Ronald–Quotas, Trade

VOLUME 7

Rabin, Yitzhak–Sociology, Micro-

VOLUME 8

Sociology, Parsonian–Vulnerability

VOLUME 9

WAGE AND PRICE CONTROLS

Examples of rulers and governments attempting to control prices and wages can be found in distant history, but comprehensive wage-price controls or similar voluntary programs for anti-inflation purposes are really a twentieth-century development. Simple microeconomic analysis suggests that controls that set prices and wages too low will create product or labor shortages. However, under wartime circumstances, governments have sometimes been willing to allow shortages and rationing. And in peacetime, the rationale for wage-price controls was for many years centered on the idea that prices and wages, especially the latter, could be administered.

In the United States and other countries, wage-price controls were enforced to varying degrees during the two world wars. The United States also imposed controls during the Korean and Vietnam wars. Voluntary wage-price programs were initiated during the Kennedy-Johnson and Carter administrations. After World War II, various European countries adopted "incomes policies" similar to the voluntary programs later installed in the United States. Controls during the two world wars and the Korean War were part of larger schemes aimed at diverting resources for military purposes. Beginning in the 1960s, attempts to influence or control wages and prices had a more general macroeconomic justification.

American participation in World War I was relatively brief but involved a diversion to military purposes of perhaps a fifth of the nation's gross domestic product (GDP). Large corporations had developed by that time, so control administrators could interact with the heads of these firms. The idea developed that controls could be achieved by involving a few key captains of industry. Just as successful corporations engaged in internal planning, so too could the national economy be planned and—in wartime or other emergencies—controlled. As might be expected, in competitive industries—such as foodstuffs and coal—World War I controls did produce temporary shortages. However, formal ticket-based consumer-rationing schemes were not adopted and reliance instead was placed on patriotic appeals to reduce demand. Unions expanded during the war, and government pushed for industrial peace and production uninterrupted by strikes. In some instances, notably involving the railroads, the authorities seized enterprises when labor strife was threatened.

The World War I experience with controls on wages, prices, and resource allocation tended to reinforce notions of the practicality and virtue of national economic planning. These ideas carried over into the New Deal during the Great Depression and—when World War II arrived—into a cadre of individuals to staff wartime economic planning agencies and, in particular, wage-price control programs. Because of its duration and scale, World War II controls were more extensive than in World War I. Military expenditures exceeded 40 percent of GDP at the peak of the war.

Agencies were established to control prices, wages, and more general resource allocation. Formal ticket-based rationing of consumer goods applied to food, gasoline, and other products. The result was a retarding of officially measured inflation. In some cases, however, black markets developed for goods in short supply. The economic meaning of price indexes based on official prices at which goods were not freely available can be debated. However, the

overall system of controls was justified on the basis of fairness, wartime resource needs, and appeals to patriotism.

Unions had already become powerful during the New Deal, and a pattern arose that carried on into the postwar wage-price programs. Specifically, the wage authorities—the War Labor Board in World War II—established a standard for pay, albeit one laden with exceptions. Price controls—under the Office of Price Administration—were then largely based on markups over costs. In a relatively closed economy, interindustry goods purchases and their costs largely net out, making labor a major cost element. During World War II, the pay standard was based on the "Little Steel Formula," a wage settlement reached with smaller steel firms. When strikes occurred during World War II for pay above the standard, enterprises were sometimes seized and workers were sometimes threatened with conscription. Inflation and labor disputes were repressed sufficiently so that when the war ended and decontrol commenced, there was a wave of strikes and a burst of measured inflation.

Although federal controls ended, local rent controls lingered in some local jurisdictions, notably New York City. The wage authorities during World War II had tended to allow exceptions to the standard for fringe benefits such as pensions. As a result, pensions and health insurance gained a foothold at the employer level, which expanded after the war into a company-based system of social insurance.

The World War II experience led to public expectations that wars meant consumer goods shortages. Hence, when the Korean War began in 1950, a surge in consumer buying and hoarding led to a jump in inflation and, eventually, a reinstatement of wage-price and resource allocation controls by the Truman administration. In broad terms, the controls followed the World War II model, with a price authority and a wage authority. The program was again generally based on control of pay, with price controls largely to be achieved by allowable markups over costs. However, the overall program was less extensive than before, partly because peak military expenditures during the Korean War were about 15 percent of GDP, a substantially lower ratio than in the earlier conflict.

Presidential authority during the Korean War was also more limited than in World War II. An attempt by President Truman to seize the steel industry during a labor dispute was rebuffed by the U.S. Supreme Court. When President Eisenhower took office in early 1953, the Truman-era wage-price controls were quickly dismantled. Decontrol did not lead to a sharp surge in inflation, in part because the anticipatory price surge had occurred before controls were imposed. Under Eisenhower, activity in the wage-price area was largely limited to exhortations aimed at moderate wage settlements and price behavior.

In the period after the Korean War, a theoretical base developed in academia for wage-price interventions, encouraged in part by the observation of European incomes policies. Such European policies typically involved centralized wage settlements though a tripartite negotiation between employer federations, union federations, and government. With unions at their peak in the United States, notions developed of wage-push inflation and resulting wage-price spirals. These concepts were combined with empirical studies of the "Phillips curve," which depicted an unpleasant trade-off between wage inflation (and therefore price inflation) and the unemployment rate.

Essentially, the idea was that if wages could be made less "pushy" through some form of governmental intervention, the nasty trade-off of the Phillips curve could be repositioned to allow lower unemployment at a given inflation rate. Later, when the idea of a permanent Phillips curve was replaced by that of a non-accelerating inflation rate of unemployment (NAIRU), the same argument could still be advanced. Intervention aimed at making wages less pushy could lower the NAIRU. There were notions of "key" union pay settlements, which were then imitated elsewhere in the union sector and which spilled over into nonunion pay adjustments. If the key union settlements could be moderated, pay setting would be less inflationary.

The incoming Kennedy administration—whose economists were Keynesians with a focus on lowering unemployment—was particularly receptive to this concept. Under the Bretton Woods fixed exchange-rate system, the United States was committed to maintaining the value of the dollar relative to other currencies and the value of gold relative to the dollar. By the early 1960s, there was a dollar surplus and concern about the dwindling gold stock. Holding down inflation was seen as needed to defend the dollar by maintaining American cost competitiveness in world markets. But absent some other policy instrument, inflation moderation was also seen as requiring a higher level of unemployment than President Kennedy wanted. As a result, the Council of Economic Advisors under Kennedy (and later Johnson) put forward voluntary wage-price "guideposts," with its wage standard to be based on the trend rate of productivity (seen as a little over 3 percent per annum) and prices to be based on markups.

Steel was again the center of a major dispute. The Kennedy administration intervened in a steel labor negotiation and achieved what it believed was a moderate pay settlement. When the industry subsequently raised its prices, President Kennedy demanded and ultimately received a price rollback. The guidepost program became more elaborate as time went on. But it eventually was

overcome by demand pressures in the labor market and union demands for wage increases above the standard, and it basically faded away.

Inflation became a political issue in the early years of the Nixon administration. In August 1971, President Nixon announced an end to the Bretton Woods system, disengaged the dollar from gold, and imposed a ninety-day wage-price freeze. Thereafter, mandatory controls on wages and prices were imposed, which then passed though a series of phases of varying intensity. The most elaborate was Phase II, which featured a tripartite Pay Board and a Price Commission. This model was subsequently imitated in Britain and Canada.

Although the Vietnam War was in progress, the Nixon controls were not part of a larger scheme to redirect resources to the military. Indeed, the peak ratio of military expenditures to GDP during the Vietnam War was about 10 percent—and that peak had already occurred under Johnson. Moreover, because of earlier ongoing cold war military spending, the ramp-up of such spending to accommodate the Vietnam War was less dramatic than in prior wartime situations.

The initial pay standard after the freeze was based on productivity plus an allowable rate of inflation, with price controls built—as before—on permissible cost markups. Some shortages occurred during the Nixon controls, notably involving meat and gasoline. The Nixon program was largely ended under President Ford in the spring of 1974, except for elaborate controls on oil prices. Ford replaced formal wage-price controls with a program of anti-inflation exhortation coordinated by a Council on Wage and Price Stability (COWPS). This program featured promotion of much-ridiculed WIN buttons ("Whip Inflation Now") and various announced "inflation alerts."

President Carter continued COWPS and returned in 1978 to a Kennedy-Johnson-type program of voluntary wage-price restraints, termed "guidelines" rather than guideposts. A wage standard of 7 percent was announced with various exceptions. Academics in the 1970s had toyed with using the tax code to reward employers and/or workers for complying with such pay standards or penalizing those who did not. Reflecting this academic work, the Carter administration proposed an elaborate (and probably unworkable) program of "real wage insurance," which would have used tax rebates to protect complying workers from inflation above 7 percent.

Subsequently, a tripartite Pay Advisory Committee was established with a vague charter to support the 7 percent target. Congress never enacted the Carter tax program, and the Reagan administration quickly abandoned wage-price interventions altogether, relying on tight monetary policy at the Federal Reserve to reduce inflation. The mandatory controls on oil prices that Carter had inherited

from Nixon and Ford led to very unpopular gasoline shortages, contributing to Carter's defeat by Reagan in the 1980 presidential election.

Post-Korean wage-price interventions were based heavily on notions of wage-push and wage-price spirals. But starting in the mid-1950s, the union share of the workforce had begun to decline, a process that accelerated during the Reagan years and continued thereafter. In much of the developed world, similar union declines occurred. Thus, the intellectual rationale for wage-price interventions—mandatory or voluntary—largely has disappeared. In addition, wars after the Korean War have not entailed large shares of GDP. Absent the earlier military or macroeconomic justifications, it is unlikely that such programs will be used in the future.

The era of wage-price controls, guideposts, and guidelines, with its accompanying notions of dangerous wage-push pressures and wage-price spirals that needed to be restrained, has left a mark on macroeconomics. Contemporary economists often explain the concept of the NAIRU in language from the era of extensive unionization and collective bargaining. Low unemployment is often said to lead workers to "demand" higher wages or refuse to "accept" wage offers by employers. In fact, the conversion of labor markets to nonbargained pay determination has created what past proponents of mandatory or voluntary wage-price programs had once hoped to achieve. The U.S. economy in the 1990s and thereafter operated with a relatively low NAIRU and without the inflationary tilt feared to exist in the period beginning in the 1950s. Given this institutional change, it is likely that the rhetorical legacy of mandatory and voluntary wage-price programs will eventually also disappear.

SEE ALSO *Carter, Jimmy; Cold War; Deregulation; Economic Crises; Eisenhower, Dwight D.; Great Depression; Inflation; Johnson, Lyndon B.; Kennedy, John F.; Korean War; Monetarism; Natural Rate of Unemployment; New Deal, The; Nixon, Richard M.; Phillips Curve; Prices; Regulation; Rent Control; Statism; Supreme Court, U.S.; Truman, Harry S.; Unions; Vietnam War; World War I; World War II*

BIBLIOGRAPHY

Conner, Valerie Jean. 1983. *The National War Labor Board: Stability, Social Justice, and the Voluntary State in World War I*. Chapel Hill: University of North Carolina Press.

Edelman, Murray, and Robben W. Fleming. 1965. *The Politics of Wage-Price Decisions: A Four-Country Analysis*. Urbana: University of Illinois Press.

Goodwin, Crauford D., ed. 1975. *Exhortation and Controls: The Search for a Wage-Price Policy, 1945–1971*. Washington, DC: Brookings Institution.

Manning, Thomas G. 1960. *The Office of Price Administration: A World War II Agency of Control*. New York: Henry Holt.

Mitchell, Daniel J. B. 1980. The Rise and Fall of Real Wage Insurance. *Industrial Relations* 19 (Winter): 64–73.

Mitchell, Daniel J. B., and Christopher L. Erickson. 2005. Not Yet Dead at the Fed: Unions, Worker Bargaining, and Economy-wide Wage Determination. *Industrial Relations* 44 (October): 565–606.

Rockoff, Hugh. 1984. *Drastic Measures: A History of Wage and Price Controls in the United States*. New York: Cambridge University Press.

Rockoff, Hugh. 2004. Until It's Over, Over There: The U.S. Economy in World War I. Working Paper 10580, National Bureau of Economic Research.

Sheahan, John. 1967. *The Wage-Price Guideposts*. Washington, DC: Brookings Institution.

Ulman, Lloyd, and Robert J. Flanagan. 1971. *Wage Restraint: A Study of Incomes Policies in Western Europe*. Berkeley: University of California Press.

U.S. Joint Economic Committee. 1982. *Final Report on the Anti-Inflation Guidelines By the Pay Advisory Committee, 1979–80*. Washington, DC: U.S. Government Printing Office.

U.S. National War Labor Board. 1948. *Termination Report of the National War Labor Board*. 3 vols. Washington, DC: U.S. Government Printing Office.

U.S. Office of Economic Stabilization, Department of the Treasury. 1974. *Historical Working Papers on the Economic Stabilization Program, August 15, 1971 to April 30, 1974*. 3 vols. Washington, DC: U.S. Government Printing Office.

Daniel J. B. Mitchell

WAGES

Wages are remuneration for labor services, in the form of either cash or some other mechanism of compensation. Wages have been the subject of extensive empirical and theoretical inquiry, the focus of which has included causes and consequences of wage variation, implications of evolving labor market conditions, and the effects of wage increases on productivity and growth. Generally, these studies approach such questions through the prism of two alternative labor market circumstances: perfectly competitive markets, in which consumers and producers have no market power to affect prices, and imperfectly competitive markets.

THE LABOR MARKET UNDER PERFECT COMPETITION

Traditionally, economic analysis is predicated on the assumption that labor markets are perfectly competitive. For this to be reasonable, three criteria must hold: There must be no barriers to entry; agents must have complete information; firm and labor mobility must be costless. When these conditions obtain, wage rates of a given quality are determined by the intersection of the labor supply and demand curves. The labor demand curve reflects the marginal productivity of labor confronting profit-maximizing firms. The labor supply curve reveals the willingness of utility-maximizing individuals to supply labor at each conceivable wage. The intersection of these two curves determines the market clearing wage rate, at which all persons willing and able to work will find employment. In this framework, the wage rate is a market price that effectively allocates labor across alternative (and competing) uses.

One vein of the empirical work mentioned above is essentially rooted in this perfectly competitive framework. For instance, there is a tradition of fairly straightforward examination of inter-temporal wage patterns implicitly interpreted through the lens of perfect competition. Katz and Autor (1999) examine longitudinal wage data in the United States, revealing several interesting patterns. The ratio of wages of those in the ninetieth percentile of workers to those in the tenth percentile has grown substantially in recent decades. Large wage disparities have also been detected by education and experience levels. Nonetheless, wage gaps between white and black males and males and females overall have narrowed.

There is, however, no consensus regarding the causes of these structural changes. An often-cited theory explains wage differentials as a result of investments in human capital (e.g., through education, health, or training). Becker (1964) formalized this idea by demonstrating that greater human capital expenditures could account for empirically observed patterns of wage variation via their impact on the marginal revenue product of labor. This theory received empirical support from Mincer (1974), whose estimates of the returns to education were positive and increasingly significant with controls for years of experience in the labor market.

Numerous studies question this explanation of observed wage differences. For instance, Pritchett (2001) shows that education has contributed very little to economic growth. He speculates that, among other possibilities, this might reflect the irrelevance of knowledge transmitted through formal schooling (in terms of the skills actually required in the workplace). From a slightly different perspective, some (e.g., Spence [1974]) have argued that education contributes little directly to labor market productivity, but instead serves as a kind of signal for ability that allows employers to sort high and low ability workers.

Another avenue for wage variation generally approached through the framework of perfect competition is immigration. LaLonde and Topel (1991) consider

the impact of newly arrived immigrants on the wages of workers born in the United States as well as those who had immigrated to the United States earlier. They find that immigration has a negative, but small, impact on the wages of earlier immigrants and native-born workers who represent close substitutes (i.e., low skilled workers) for these more recent arrivals. This relationship attenuates as the tenure of earlier immigrants in the United States increases. Others (e.g., Borjas [2003]) have disputed these findings, claiming that they stem from the failure to control for the migration of native-born Americans to other cities and states.

A DEPARTURE FROM A PERFECTLY COMPETITIVE LABOR MARKET

The other major theoretical and empirical tradition focuses on possible market failure resulting in involuntary unemployment (a situation where workers willing to work at the prevailing market wage rate cannot find employment). Efforts to explain such failures have centered on two major theoretical possibilities: market failure rooted in the purposeful decisions of optimizing agents and failure as a consequence of government intervention.

The former possibility (failure stemming from the actions of optimizing agents) has received considerable research attention. To begin with, there is the obvious potential for a "menu costs" type situation: Firms may resist adjusting wages to a new equilibrium level if the transaction costs associated with doing so are sufficiently high. Another possibility that has attracted more interest is commonly referred to as "efficiency wages" (e.g., Akerlof and Yellen [1986]). This is the idea that wages might be set above market equilibrium for the purpose of inducing higher worker productivity and efficiency.

Several specific motivations for efficiency wages have been suggested. First, they might reduce shirking and increase the financial penalty associated with termination. Shapiro and Stiglitz (1984) demonstrate that in the face of limited monitoring resources firms are willing to pay efficiency wages for these reasons. Efficiency wages might also lessen turnover costs by rendering workers less likely to quit their jobs (more experienced workers tend to be more productive than new employees, whose training can also be costly). Particularly in the setting of lower income countries, higher wages can improve the health and overall well-being of workers (through greater food and health consumption), potentially raising their productivity. Finally, efficiency wages can help firms avoid adverse selection by encouraging more skilled (and thus more productive) workers to apply for jobs.

Another potential source of market failure comes from the timing of wage contracts. In essence, contracts offer a specified wage payment over some fixed interval of time during which there might be shifts in labor supply or demand (and hence in the fundamental equilibrium wage that would prevail in an unfettered market). However, such contractual agreements can prevent adjustment in wages toward these new equilibrium conditions (a situation referred to as "wage stickiness").

State intervention is another major reason that equilibrium conditions in the labor market may fail to obtain. For instance, a legally mandated minimum wage (a kind of price floor) may result in labor market disequilibrium if that minimum wage level is binding in the sense that it exceeds the equilibrium level that would emerge in its absence. Most empirical and theoretical work on the subject suggests that minimum wages that are binding in this sense yield, ceteris paribus, lower employment levels. However, a few studies (e.g., Card and Krueger [1994]) have received a great deal of attention for reaching the opposite conclusion. Card and Krueger (1994) examine the effects of an April 1992 minimum wage increase (from $4.25 to $5.05 an hour) by exploiting the fact that the increase was implemented earlier in some states than others. Employment levels before and after the change showed no signs of the decline anticipated in the face of an increase in the minimum wage: Employment levels actually increased. However, Card and Krueger (1994) have received a great deal of methodological criticism.

SEE ALSO *Becker, Gary; Employment; Labor Demand; Labor Force Participation; Labor Market; Labor Supply; Signals*

BIBLIOGRAPHY

Akerlof, George A., and Janet L. Yellen, eds. 1986. *Efficiency Wage Models of the Labor Market*. Cambridge, U.K. and New York: Cambridge University Press.

Becker, Gary. 1964. *Human Capital: A Theoretical and Empirical Analysis, with Special Reference to Education*. New York: National Bureau of Economic Research.

Borjas, George. 2003. The Labor Demand Curve is Downward Sloping: Reexamining the Impact of Immigration on the Labor Market. *Quarterly Journal of Economics* 118 (4): 1335–1374.

Card, David, and Alan Krueger. 1994. Minimum Wages and Unemployment: A Case Study of the Fast Food Industry in New Jersey and Pennsylvania. *American Economic Review* 84 (4): 772–793.

Katz, Lawrence F., and David H. Autor. 1999. Changes in the Wage Structure and Earnings Inequality. In *Handbook of Labor Economics*, vol. 3a, eds. Orley Ashenfelter and David Card, 1463–1555. Amsterdam: North-Holland. http://economics.harvard.edu/faculty/katz/papers.html.

LaLonde, Robert, and Robert Topel. 1991. Labor Market Adjustments to Increased Immigration. In *Immigration, Trade, and the Labor Market*, 167–199. Eds. John Abowd and Richard Freeman. Chicago: University of Chicago Press.

Mincer, Jacob. 1974. *Schooling, Experience, and Earnings.* New York: National Bureau of Economic Research.

Pritchett, Lant. 2001. Where Has All the Education Gone? *The World Bank Economic Review* 15 (3): 367–391.

Shapiro, Carl, and Joseph Stiglitz. 1984. Equilibrium Unemployment as a Worker Discipline Device. *American Economic Review* 74 (3): 433–444.

Spence, A. Michael. 1974. *Market Signaling: Informational Transfer in Hiring and Related Screening Processes.* Cambridge, MA: Harvard University Press.

Mai Noguchi Hubbard

WAGES, COMPENSATING

Adam Smith was the first to suggest that persons in dangerous or unpleasant jobs should be paid a high wage. His example was extreme: public executioner. Smith reasoned that despite the black hood that conceals the executioner's identity, people would not want that job unless they were paid additional compensation above the average wage for the community. Economists have since used the term *compensating wages* to refer to this additional compensation. The compensating wage hypothesis holds that compensating wages are generated in competitive labor markets to equalize the net benefit (wage minus risk) workers derive from safe and dangerous jobs. If true, the hypothesis and corresponding empirical estimates of the amount of compensating wages for different levels of risk have implications for occupational safety and health policy, workers' compensation, and statistical estimates of the value of life.

Evidence for compensating wages is undeniable in high-profile and dangerous jobs such as iron workers constructing tall buildings, airline pilots, bounty hunters, ocean fishers, and coal miners. But these jobs comprise only a fraction of all jobs, and the associated risks are obvious. It is not clear that compensating wages are generated across all dangerous jobs throughout the economy. (See Mason 1995 for a critique of compensating wage differentials.)

The hypothesis requires that workers be mobile, informed about job hazards, rational, and risk averse. Most debate about the hypothesis has to do with mobility and information. Job attachment increases with age, marriage, and children in the family, but jobs can become more or less dangerous over time, and attached workers may not change jobs. In addition, some workers, especially poor ones, may not have much mobility if the only choice is between a dangerous job or none at all. Information is also problematic. Vehicle crashes and assaults are frequently overlooked by the public as likely job hazards, yet together they are responsible for 40 percent of all fatal injuries. The frequency of vehicle crashes helps explain why relatively low-wage occupations such as gardeners, construction laborers, traveling sales workers, pizza delivery drivers, garbage collectors, and farm workers face excessively high death rates. The rate of assaults helps explain why clerks in convenience stores and fast-food restaurants, as well as gas-station attendants, also face high death rates. In addition, even the strongest advocates for the hypothesis acknowledge that due to lack of information, compensating wages are unlikely to be paid for occupational diseases, yet job-related diseases cause roughly 60,000 deaths per year in the United States, compared to 5,000 injury deaths.

The empirical evidence with large data sets is mixed. The best evidence supporting the hypothesis derives from U.S. Bureau of Labor Statistics data on fatality rates across industries. But these industry data conflate blue-collar with white-collar jobs, and death rates across industries are correlated with historical interindustry wage differentials. For more than 100 years and within many developed countries, wages for blue-collar workers have been high in transportation, construction, and manufacturing, and low in services, wholesale, and retail trade, independent of job hazards. Studies suggest that when interindustry wage differentials are accounted for, evidence supporting the hypothesis evaporates.

Despite the controversy, virtually all economists agree on one point: More information regarding job hazards would help "the market" generate compensating wages. One idea would require firms to include hazard information and fatality rates on job application forms the same way food manufacturers list fat content on packaged food.

BIBLIOGRAPHY

Leigh, J. Paul. 1995. Compensating Wages, Value of a Statistical Life, and Inter-Industry Differentials. *Journal of Environmental Economics and Management* 28: 83–97.

Mason, Patrick L. 1995. Race, Competition, and Differential Wages. *Cambridge Journal of Economics* 19 (4): 545–568.

Viscusi, W. Kip, and Joseph E. Aldy. 2003. The Value of a Statistical Life: A Critical Review of Market Estimates throughout the World. *Journal of Risk and Uncertainty* 27 (1): 5–76

J. Paul Leigh

WAGES, NOMINAL

SEE *Nominal Wages.*

WAGNER'S LAW

SEE *Public Sector.*

WALD TEST

SEE *Specification Tests.*

WALDEN

SEE *Thoreau, Henry David.*

WALKER, ALICE

SEE *Womanism.*

WALL STREET

Wall Street refers to the geographical concentration of financial service providers that constitutes New York's financial district. Its heart is the narrow thoroughfare of the same name in Lower Manhattan that is home to the New York Stock Exchange. The term carries a wide spectrum of meanings that intersect geography, finance, and political economy.

The origins of Wall Street can be traced to the brushwood barricade erected by Peter Stuyvesant along the northern boundary of the New Amsterdam community of Dutch settlers in Lower Manhattan in 1653. The "wall" was meant to protect the early settlers against attack from Lenape Indians, New England colonists, and the British (who dismantled it in 1699). The subsequent growth and lore of local merchants and financiers imbued this simple geographic setting with its modern significance—the story of the formation of a world financial center, the powerful headquarters of U.S. financial capital.

THE RISE OF A FINANCIAL CENTER: FINANCE AND GEOGRAPHY

Wall Street's early history as a financial market began with gatherings of securities and commodities traders during the Revolutionary War. These curbstone and coffeehouse traders first developed financial techniques for loans and shares out of the needs of mercantile trade, a rudimentary copy of the 1600s Dutch exchanges. The consolidation of the New York exchange accelerated with U.S. government demands for new sources of capital to bail out securities issued to finance the Revolutionary War. The first

Continental Congresses in New York issued $80 million in government bonds under Alexander Hamilton to redeem war debts at face value. Speculators seeking to profit on leaked news of the bailout plan set up operations at the east end of the street to broker insider trading of the government paper.

Wall Street's development during the eighteenth century was shaped by trade in government debt and state-licensed monopolies. During the nineteenth century, railroad shares and bonds fueled the market and its proliferation of trading instruments. Early institutional development was characterized by the monopolization of trading activity that excluded informal curb participants and curtailed the growth of rival exchanges. On May 17, 1792, twenty-four stockbrokers signed the "Buttonwood Agreement" (so named for the sycamore tree on Wall Street under which the signing is said to have taken place). The accord restricted membership and formalized rules for the loosely associated "Brokers for the Purchase and Sale of Public Stock" who conducted their exchange auctions out of the Tontine Coffee House. The financial turbulence of the War of 1812 prompted creation of the New York Stock and Exchange Board (NYSEB) in 1817. The board turned a handsome profit by financing the Erie Canal. It further restricted membership, enforced full commissions and secrecy, and moved member brokers into rented office space. The measures served to snuff out competition from rival curbstone exchanges, such as the 1835 Commercial Exchange Association.

The 1840s to the 1860s produced growth in securities issues associated with railroad stock (first listed in 1830). A major speculative boom driven by Civil War finance (1861–1865) spawned demand for new manufacture and mining and a swelling trade in government debt. This activity fueled persistent attempts to establish rival exchanges to the NYSEB, which culminated in the formation of the Open Regular Board in 1864. Unable to remove the Open Board from the trading arena, the NYSEB was forced to merge with it in 1869. This merger created the New York Stock Exchange as it is now known, with its 1,060 founding members. Subsequent challenges by rival exchanges, such as the Consolidated Stock and Petroleum Exchange (CSPE) founded in 1885, provoked aggressive response by the NYSE, which outlawed CSPE dealings and in 1900 ordered Western Union to stop supplying quotation services to all rival exchanges in New York City (Doede 1967, p. 14).

Financial turbulence in conjunction with the growing concentration of wealth on Wall Street prompted congressional reaction with the Pujo hearings in 1907. Wall Street was implicated in the monopolistic practices of the money trusts that facilitated industrial concentration under the control of a small number of corporations. During the

1920s, Wall Street flourished as a financial center, promoting the rise of large corporations with dispersed ownership and professional management along with a dramatic concentration of capital.

The fragile foundation of this accumulation of financial claims became apparent with the Black Thursday stock market crash of October 24, 1929, and the Black Tuesday sell-off panic that began on October 29. The collapse in equity prices came at the height of Wall Street's reputation and prompted a wave of regulatory legislation, from the 1933 Bank Act to the creation of the Securities and Exchange Commission in 1934. In the world of finance, Wall Street's characteristic business activity had produced a speculative financial frenzy that put short-term capital gains before enterprise, setting the stage for a debt-deflation crisis that brought down more than nine thousand banks and triggered the onset of the Great Depression in the 1930s. From this historical episode, major debates ensued about the role of financial markets in the development process.

Viewed from the perspective of the efficient markets hypothesis, Wall Street is the archetype of a highly competitive, efficient capital market whose prices reflect all relevant information. It is impossible to beat the market, and capital is optimally allocated to productive firms. Viewed from the financial instability school of thought, however, Wall Street is predisposed to speculative excess, where the larger constellation of private credit-creating institutions serve the interests of financial accumulation, distorting the allocation of productive capital in debilitating waves of crisis and bankruptcy. Contemporary reference to the "Wall Street View," coined by Hyman Minsky, derives from this interpretation of the Great Depression's speculative overleveraging and collapse in world capital markets. Laissez-faire finance, absent regulation and supervision, produces destabilizing real economic performance.

Throughout the 1930s Wall Street exchanges shrunk from losses. Trading during the post–World War II golden age was lackluster until the end of the 1950s. In perspective, NYSE trading for all of 1950 was 525 million shares, which was equivalent to just two hours of an average day's trading volume in 2005. Wall Street emerged by securing its geographic and financial monopoly over U.S. capital markets. The dense area of real estate demarked by Wall and Broad Streets came to include the New York and American stock exchanges, member firms, over-the-counter firms, government securities dealers, major banks and trust companies, the New York Federal Reserve Bank, and countless insurance, utility, mercantile, and commodity exchanges. The NYSE became the symbolic hub for U.S. financial capital. The amount of new capital Wall Street actually provisioned for "Main Street," however,

proved to be quite low—less than 1 percent of gross domestic product (GDP). It is not new capital but retrading existing capital that defines Wall Street's key development role. Following the 1970s, speculative financial leveraging of accumulation returned to Wall Street, exploding trading volumes, where the banking system was engaged to secure profits on capital gains from asset price run-ups on financial claims. The resulting market volatility made more observers receptive to the financial instability hypothesis.

THE POLITICAL ECONOMY OF FINANCE CAPITAL

In the world of political economy, Wall Street signifies the epicenter of U.S. and global financial capital. In the tradition of imperialist extension, Wall Street is seen as having the power to create or undermine nations in accordance with U.S. national interest. Wall Street speculators, most notably J. P. Morgan, played a decisive role in Panama's secession from Colombia and its birth as a nation in 1903 to ensure huge profits from the construction of the Panama Canal and U.S. controlling interest in the Canal Zone (Diaz Espinoza 2001). Morgan's Wall Street partnership bought up the worthless stock of the failed French Canal Company in 1900 and dispatched Nelson Cromwell to convince the U.S. government to purchase the company's rights and equipment at an exorbitant price. When Colombia's refusal to ratify the Hay-Herran Treaty threatened Washington's rights to build the canal, Wall Street financiers funded an uprising by Panamanian nationalists, causing President Theodore Roosevelt to deploy U.S. troops to the region.

Nineteenth-century political critique faulted Wall Street for advancing the monopoly powers of national capital and imperialist extension. Modern variants of this viewpoint examine in greater detail the evolving technology of financial institutions in promoting "accumulation by dispossession" (Harvey 2003, p. 147), where predatory asset redistributions are produced in the context of speculation-induced economic crises. Attention concentrates on the wave of financialization that occurred after 1973. Transactions involved stock promotions, Ponzi schemes, international debt-pushing and repayment servitude alongside speculative raiding conducted by hedge funds. The global reach of Wall Street's agenda and contribution to financial instability is captured in the reference to the "Wall Street–Treasury–IMF complex." This highlights the desire of large brokerage firms to have access to capital markets throughout the world through enforcement of complete capital account convertibility, while the International Monetary Fund (IMF) asserts its role as an international lender of last resort in the wake of impending crises.

The destruction of Manhattan's World Trade Towers on September 11, 2001, made evident that Wall Street's financial nexus had assumed symbolic dimensions as the center of U.S. financial power and was vulnerable to attack. A previous episode had occurred on September 6, 1920, when a bomb was exploded outside the NYSE building, killing thirty-three people. The post 9/11 geography of money produced a diaspora of the financial industry out of its concentrated center in Lower Manhattan. The disaster dislocated fifty thousand financial service employees to new office space in Midtown Manhattan and nineteen thousand across the river to New Jersey. Over thirteen million square feet of class A office space were completely destroyed, and insurance industry claims from property and life topped $40 billion.

Wall Street's financial dominance continues despite encroaching competition by rival exchanges trading with new electronic technologies. In 2006 the NYSE acquired Archipelago Holdings, a rival exchange based entirely on electronically traded funds. The resultant public corporation, NYSE Group, took on the all-electronic NASDAQ to consolidate its control in the Internet trading world, where member "seats" and "trading floor" no longer signify geographic reference when accounting for revenue streams. The NYSE Group's subsequent merger with Euronext produced the first transatlantic bourse.

SEE ALSO *Casino Capitalism; Corporations; Economic Crises; Efficient Market Hypothesis; Federal Reserve System, U.S.; Financial Instability Hypothesis; Financial Markets; Great Depression; Hedging; Investment; Market Fundamentals; Random Walk; Regulation; September 11, 2001; Speculation; Stocks; Transaction Taxes*

BIBLIOGRAPHY

Darity, William A., Jr. 1992. Financial Instability Hypothesis. In *The New Palgrave Dictionary of Money and Finance*, eds. M. M. Peter Newman and John Eatwell, vol. 2, 75–76. London: Macmillan.

Diaz Espinoza, Ovidio. 2001. *How Wall Street Created a Nation: J. P. Morgan, Teddy Roosevelt, and the Panama Canal*. New York: Four Walls Eight Windows.

Doede, Robert W. 1967. The Monopoly Power of the New York Stock Exchange. PhD diss., University of Chicago.

Geisst, Charles R. 2004. *Wall Street: A History; From Its Beginnings to the Fall of Enron*. Oxford and New York: Oxford University Press.

Harvey, David. 2003. *The New Imperialism*. Oxford and New York: Oxford University Press.

Henwood, Doug. 1997. *Wall Street: How It Works and for Whom*. London and New York: Verso.

Kindleberger, Charles Poor. 1974. *The Formation of Financial Centers: A Study in Comparative Economic History*. Princeton

Studies in International Finance, no. 36. Princeton, NJ: International Financial Section, Princeton University.

Pohl, Nicole. 2004. Where Is Wall Street? Financial Geography after 09/11. *Industrial Geographer* 2 (1): 72–93.

Wachtel, Howard M. 2003. *Street of Dreams—Boulevard of Broken Hearts: Wall Street's First Century*. London and Sterling, VA: Pluto.

Joseph Ricciardi

WALLERSTEIN, IMMANUEL
1930–

Immanuel Wallerstein has been one of the most influential and prolific American sociologists in the post–World War II (1939–1945) period. He obtained his B.A. (1951), M.A. (1954), and PhD (1959) from Columbia University in New York City. In his early years as an assistant professor of sociology there, Wallerstein was primarily a political sociologist. His expertise in Africa's independence movements led to his meeting social theorist Frantz Fanon (1925–1961) while doing fieldwork in the region. The political and revolutionary activity sweeping the African continent in the late 1950s and early 1960s caused Wallerstein to question the traditional focus on the nation-state as a meaningful unit of analysis, particularly in those areas of the world where such entities were an obvious byproduct of prolonged colonialism and imperialism. In the late 1960s, Wallerstein politically sided with students in their anti–Vietnam War (1957–1975) protests against university administrators, a confrontation that resulted in his book *University in Turmoil* (1969) and his decision to leave Columbia to join the Department of Sociology at McGill University in Montreal. It was during his tenure there, and inspired by French economic historian Fernand Braudel's (1902–1985) long-term vision of historical processes, that he published the first volume of *The Modern World-System* (1974), which has been translated into thirteen languages. In combination with Volume 2 (1980) and Volume 3 (1989), the trilogy has had a significant impact in the fields of sociology, political economy, history, geography, and more recently, anthropology and comparative literature.

Wallerstein's main thesis in these and other studies is that capitalism is a specific socioeconomic system, characterized by an axial division of labor resulting from intense yet unequal bulk trade linkages between different zones, which he labeled the *core, periphery,* and *semiperiphery*. This capitalist world-system emerged in sixteenth-century Europe and subsequently expanded to incorporate more

areas (e.g., various minisystems and world empires not characterized by the same primacy of ceaseless capital accumulation). In the context of the colonialism and imperialism that unfolded from 1492 until the early twentieth century, the entire world became interlinked through these trade patterns constitutive of unequal exchange. The latter was also a major concern of the Latin American dependency school, which in the 1960s argued that the unequal power relationships reproduced through world trade mechanisms in the context of imperialism were the result of the relationship between *metropolis* and *periphery*. By stressing the importance of economic cycles and the commodity chains of leading sectors, however, Wallerstein espoused the idea that the upward and downward social mobility of specific polities was possible (as demonstrated, for example, by Spain, South Korea, and Taiwan).

Wallerstein also argued against the modernization or developmentalist school, dominant in the 1960s, which assumed that every country could achieve upward social mobility as long as it implemented the correct policies. For Wallerstein, the growth of world trade does not alter the fact that it is essentially a polarizing zero-sum game, reproducing and expanding poverty and inequality on a world scale. The crucial Wallersteinian concept of semiperiphery was introduced to clarify this idea theoretically: the three zones in which different political entities (nation-states, principalities, etc.) are located contain divergent practices (in terms of life expectancy, standard of living, labor control, production of items for sale on the world market, and political regimes) precisely because of their hierarchical location within the capitalist world-economy.

Unlike the orthodox Marxists' focus on the nation-state, Wallerstein and other world-system analysts (e.g., Samir Amin) conceptually regard free labor and slavery as coexisting within the same mode of production. Using the world-economy as the sole unit of analysis, Wallerstein insists that labor control and production for trade are historically, relationally, and therefore mutually constitutive: only because wage remuneration in the periphery, which mostly exports raw materials for the world market, is so low, is wage remuneration so relatively high in the core, where value-added products are exported.

After joining the Sociology Department at the State University of New York at Binghamton, Wallerstein created the *Fernand Braudel Center for the Study of Economies, Historical Systems, and Civilizations* in 1976 and its scholarly journal, *Review*. There he systematically wrote on cycles and trends of the world-economy, commodity chains, hegemony, antisystemic movements, households, racism and sexism, and the geoculture from a world-system perspective. One key historical event was the 1848 world revolution, in which spontaneous antisystemic

(especially socialist and nationalist) movements organized themselves politically in order to obtain state power. Their eventual success in turn led to the 1968 world revolution, engineered by different antisystemic movements from the New Left. Wallerstein claims that 1968 put an end to faith in universal progress and related classical liberal paradigms, which coincided with the beginning of American decline because of its loss of significant economic superiority to Western Europe and Japan and its political-military defeat in Vietnam.

Beginning in the 1980s, Wallerstein argued that the United States was from 1945 onward in de facto collusion with the Soviet Union, and he characterized the latter not as a communist experiment but as a typical powerful semiperipheral state that embraced protectionism (as opposed to the typical state located in the core in favor of free trade). Similarly, World War I (1914–1918) and World War II are interpreted as one major war to determine which state would succeed England as hegemon, the primus inter pares in the core zone that temporarily benefits from unprecedented financial, political, and ideological capital. From the late 1980s onward, Wallerstein predicted ever more crisis in the world-system due to a gradually falling rate of profit linked to increasing pressures from antisystemic movements, environmental constraints, democratization, and wage increases concurrent with urbanization. In this period he agreed with most of the studies written by his colleague, Andre Gunder Frank. But in the early 1990s, Frank, who was attempting to trace world-system economic cycles to as far back as 5000 BCE, began to criticize his former collaborator as being Eurocentrist. He also argued, contra Wallerstein, that the modern world-system was not so much in terminal crisis as experiencing yet another transition towards East Asian hegemony.

Starting in the 1990s, Wallerstein's writings focused more on the changing geoculture of the modern world-system. Since his term as president of the International Sociological Association (1994–1998), his scholarly contributions have been particularly geared towards unthinking nineteenth-century paradigms and critically reflecting upon the structures of knowledge production in the academic realm of the world-system. These efforts are best illustrated by his chairing of the Gulbenkian Commission on the Restructuring of the Social Sciences (1993–1995) and his publishing of *The End of the World as We Know It* (1999) and *The Uncertainties of Knowledge* (2004). Not unlike the later years of sociologist Pierre Bourdieu (1930–2002), Wallerstein's increased scholarly recognition—reflected in his move to Yale University in 2000—coincided with an increasing engagement in the political field. Evidence of this can be found in his public interventions at the World Social Forum with regard to potential strategies that progressive movements may consider (see

Utopistics [1998]) and in his desire to engage with a broader audience through public lectures and various biweekly commentaries (posted on the Internet as of October 1998). One of his lasting contributions has been the creation of the Political Economy of the World System Section of the American Sociological Association, which has continually increased its membership over the years and for which he is often the keynote speaker.

BIBLIOGRAPHY

PRIMARY WORKS

Wallerstein, Immanuel. 1969. *University in Turmoil: The Politics of Change.* New York: Atheneum.

Wallerstein, Immanuel. 1974. *Capitalist Agriculture and the Origins of the European World-Economy in the Sixteenth Century.* Vol. 1 of *The Modern World-System.* New York: Academic Press.

Wallerstein, Immanuel. 1980. *Mercantilism and the Consolidation of the European World-Economy, 1600–1750.* Vol. 2 of *The Modern World-System.* New York: Academic Press.

Wallerstein, Immanuel. 1989. *The Second Great Expansion of the Capitalist World-Economy, 1730–1840s.* Vol. 3 of *The Modern World-System.* San Diego, CA: Academic Press.

Wallerstein, Immanuel. 1998. *Utopistics, or Historical Choices of the Twenty-first Century.* New York: New Press.

Wallerstein, Immanuel. 1998–2006. Commentaries. Fernand Braudel Center. http://www.binghamton.edu/fbc/cmpg.htm.

Wallerstein, Immanuel. 1999. *The End of the World As We Know It: Social Science for the Twenty-first Century.* Minneapolis: University of Minnesota Press.

Wallerstein, Immanuel. 2004. *The Uncertainties of Knowledge.* Philadelphia: Temple University Press.

Eric Mielants

WALRAS, LÉON
1834–1910

Marie Esprit Walras was born on December 16, 1834, in Évreux (Upper Normandy, France) to Auguste (1801–1866) and Louise-Aline Sainte-Beuve (1811–1893). Despite having no university degree, Léon Walras was offered a professorship at the University of Lausanne on November 12, 1870. He officially occupied the chair of political economy from October 20, 1871 to 1892, when he retired early for health reasons. His political and social economy is best examined through the trilogy of works titled *Éléments d'économie politique pure* (*Elements of Pure Economics or the Theory of Social Wealth,* 1874–1877, 1889, 1896, 1900), *Études d'économie sociale* (*Studies in Social Economics or the Theory of Distribution of Social Wealth,* 1896), and *Études d'économie politique appliquée* (*Studies in Applied Economics or the Theory of Production of*

Social Wealth, 1898). Walras died at his home in Clarens (Vaud, Switzerland) on January 5, 1910.

Founder of the School of Lausanne, Walras is one of the economists whose contributions have decisively influenced the development of economic theory. Almost simultaneously with, but independently from, Carl Menger (1840–1921) and Stanley Jevons (1835–1882), Walras introduced the concept of marginal utility (*rareté*) and took an important step toward the mathematization of economics. In his view, mathematics is not only one of the possible forms of expressing economics but also is the form necessarily required for a rigorous formulation of economic laws.

However, Walras's most original and important contribution is the analysis of price determination by means of the interactions between the various markets that make up an economy. The modern analysis of the existence, uniqueness, and stability of general equilibrium had been inspired by Walras's *Pure Economics.* In the 1950s modern theorists, with the use of advanced mathematics, specified the hypotheses enabling them to rigorously prove the existence of a price system equalizing supply and demand on each market—that is, the existence of a general equilibrium. In this perspective, the Walrasian *tâtonnement* (groping) was interpreted as a process of convergence of prices towards equilibrium, a representation of how markets actually work. Nevertheless, in the early 1970s enthusiasm chilled. It was proven that in a general equilibrium framework aggregate excess demand functions have an arbitrary nature, while specific assumption must be made to obtain uniqueness and stability results. To simplify matters rather drastically, as every change in the price system affects one's income and purchasing power, the aggregate excess demand functions that result behave capriciously. In others words, income effects prevent the groping process from leading to equilibrium. So, the correspondence between the hypothesis of the *homo oeconomicus* and the convergence towards equilibrium does not hold, and the *tâtonnement* process cannot be interpreted as the process that allows economic equilibrium to be reached.

Modern developments of general equilibrium have been inspired by Walras's theory of value in exchange (pure economics), while his theories of production and distribution of social wealth (applied and social economics) have been neglected. But from the perspective of the history of economic thought it is not possible to assert that pure economics is separable from the other two parts of the Walrasian triptych (applied economics and social economics) or that pure economics only is worthy of scientific consideration. Thanks to the publication of Walras's collected writings (1987–2005), historians of economic thought now rarely discuss Walras's works referring only

to pure economics, even though there is still no consensus on the relationships between these three components of Walras's political and social economy.

Nevertheless, the actual and fundamental controversy about Walras's writings involves the meaning of general equilibrium theory and what it is supposed to refer to. Most scholars considered Walras's general equilibrium theory as an attempt to represent the actual working of nineteenth-century capitalism, even though they disagreed on its heuristic value. For most critics, the general equilibrium theory is simply inadequate for this task, both in Walras's and in modern versions. Others instead find in Walras's writing some elements pertinent for the understanding of real markets. Finally, some argue that one can learn more from the differences between model and reality than from their alleged similarities.

However, if one takes Walras's philosophy of science seriously, a different point of view emerges: general equilibrium does not refer to actual market working or other economic facts but to the social wealth considered in itself. Pure economics does not aim at representing, in a more or less faithful and simplified manner, the contingent reality but rather at grasping the essence of the reality which does not yet completely exist, a reality in its becoming. For Walras, general equilibrium is the perfect, ideal form, towards which economic systems are evolving but are not yet realized. This ideal form is described in Walras's *Elements of Pure Economics*, but in his other writings he often referred to the economic and social phenomena that were right before his eyes: one might cite the essays on money and credit, monopolies, and railroads, but also on salaries, tax system, and real estate. These studies are definitely far from being an apology of the market as a self-driven and self-regulating mechanism. Instead, they represent a long list of cases requiring State intervention. The State has to organize the economy in order to approach the ideal form represented by general equilibrium but it is also destined to produce as a monopolist where too much competition kills competition.

Finally, three different Léon Walras have to be considered. The first is a neoclassical icon, the founder of neowalrasian economics, but known by economists at best as the author of *Elements of Pure Economics* only. The second is the founder of the School of Lausanne and the father of general equilibrium as a formalized invisible hand. The third, unknown to economists and only recently discovered by historians of thought, is a critic not only of the capitalism of his time, but of market economy in itself.

SEE ALSO *Economics, Neoclassical; Equilibrium in Economics; General Equilibrium; Lausanne, School of; Marginalism; Mathematical Economics; Stability in Economics; Tâtonnement; Walras' Law*

BIBLIOGRAPHY

Jaffé, William, ed. 1965. *Correspondence of Léon Walras and Related Papers.* 3 vols. Amsterdam: North Holland.

Walras, Léon. 1987–2005. *Auguste et Léon Walras: Œuvres Économiques Complètes.* Vols. 5–14, ed. Pierre Dockès, Pierre-Henri Goutte, Claude Hébert, Claude Mouchot, Jean-Pierre Potier, and Jean-Michel Servet. Paris: Economica.

Roberto Baranzini

WALRAS' LAW

Walras' law is a powerful modeling tool that is used by economists when they undertake general equilibrium analysis. It captures the interdependence between markets implied by the budgetary constraint that all individual transactors (i.e., a single person, a household, a firm, or the government) must take into account when they formulate purchase and sales plans.

It is assumed that no individual transactor in a market economy is so misguided as to suppose that he or she can acquire something for nothing. This being the case, the plan to purchase (or sell) something necessarily implies the plan to sell (or purchase) something of equal value. In the language of economics, each individual must satisfy his or her budget constraint. Consequently, for each individual the total value of the planned supply must exactly equal the total value of the planned demand. This means that there can be neither an excess of demand over supply (excess demand) nor an excess of supply over demand (excess supply) at the level of the individual.

It follows by simple aggregation that there can be no excess demand or excess supply in the aggregate whether one is summing over the individuals as individuals or as participants in various markets, and this must be true whether or not prevailing market prices are such as to equate demand with supply for each specific commodity. In other words, the aggregate market value of supply equals the aggregate market value of demand for any set of prices, not just the equilibrium set of prices. This proposition sometimes is called Walras' law but more commonly is known as Walras' identity.

Walras' identity implies that if there is ever an excess of demand over supply for any single commodity, there must be a corresponding excess of supply over demand for at least one other commodity; otherwise the aggregate value of commodities that agents wish to supply could not be equal to the aggregate value of commodities that agents wish to demand. Another way to put this is to say that the aggregate value of the excess demands and the excess supplies over all the markets must equal zero and that this applies whether or not all the markets are in equilibrium.

This proposition is one of a number of logical implications of Walras' identity that is given the name *Walras' law*. Léon Walras explicitly formulated and drew upon this proposition in his attempt to explain how general economic equilibrium may be established in a market economy (Walras [1926] 1954).

Walras' law is a statement that refers to all markets taken together (that is, it refers to the aggregation of the markets for final goods and services along with the markets for raw materials, labor, money, and bonds) and should not be confused with a proposition known as Say's law, or at least one version of it (Sowell 1972), which claims that there never can be an excess supply of final goods and services taken alone. Although Walras' law asserts the logical impossibility of oversupply in all markets taken together, it does not rule out the possibility of there being an oversupply in a particular market, such as the market for final goods and services, taken alone.

Walras' identity and Walras' law are valid whether or not market prices equate demand with supply for each and every commodity, and because of this they have implications for both equilibrium and disequilibrium situations. Those implications are of such fundamental importance in modeling interdependence between markets that they often have been used by writers to define Walras' law.

Equilibrium in a market is a situation in which the price of the commodity is such that the supply of the commodity is equal to the demand for it. Now, suppose a set of prices has been established that will equate demand with supply in every market except the nth market. Because there can be neither excess supply nor excess demand in the aggregate, it follows that if all but one of the markets in an economy are in equilibrium, that other market also must be in equilibrium. Thus, to demonstrate that a situation of general equilibrium holds, it suffices to show that $n-1$ markets are in equilibrium. This implication of Walras' law plays an important role in models of markets and models of asset portfolios.

In regard to the implications of Walras' law for disequilibrium, the law implies that regardless of the price that is set, the aggregate value of excess demands in the system equals the aggregate value of excess supplies. This carries the implication that an excess supply in any one market must be matched by an equal value of excess demand in some other market or markets. To put this statement slightly differently, if there is a disequilibrium in any one market, at least one other market must also be in disequilibrium.

This implication of Walras' law leads many to be concerned about the theoretical grounding of John Maynard Keynes's theory of unemployment, which seems to suggest that the labor market can be in disequilibrium even if all other markets are in equilibrium. An important contribution to this debate was made in 1965 by Robert Clower, who pointed out that in Walrasian analysis the excess demands and supplies are measured as differences between planned or "notional" demands and supplies, not between actual or "effective" demands and supplies. Clower suggested that Walrasian analysis is not appropriate for modeling situations in which there is involuntary unemployment (an excess supply of labor) because this excess supply in the labor market will result in household incomes that are lower than what the households were counting on when they formulated their expenditure plans. As a result the excess supply in the labor market will be matched by only a notional and not an effective excess demand for commodities.

Although in this situation certain prices will be at disequilibrium levels, no process of bidding them away from those inappropriate levels may get started, and so it can be argued that unemployment persists because the market signals that are presupposed in much general equilibrium analysis are not transmitted. Consideration of issues such as these has led to the development of non-Walrasian approaches to economics. In particular, in 1971 and 1976 Robert Barro and Herschel Grossman formalized the ideas of Clower and others and laid the foundations for a non-Walrasian macroeconomics.

SEE ALSO *Barro-Grossman Model; Economics, New Classical; Economics, New Keynesian; General Equilibrium; Macroeconomics; Market Clearing; Prices;* Tâtonnement; *Walras, Léon*

BIBLIOGRAPHY

Arrow, Kenneth J., and F. H. Hahn. 1971. *General Competitive Analysis*. San Francisco: Holden-Day.

Barro, Robert J., and Herschel I. Grossman. 1971. A General Disequilibrium Model of Income and Employment. *American Economic Review* 61 (1): 82–93.

Barro, Robert J., and Herschel I. Grossman. 1976. *Money, Employment and Inflation*. New York: Cambridge University Press.

Clower, Robert. 1965. The Keynesian Counter-Revolution: A Theoretical Appraisal. In *The Theory of Interest Rates*, eds. F. H. Hahn and F. P. R. Brechling, 103–125. London: Macmillan.

Patinkin, Don. 1987. Walras' Law. In *The New Palgrave: A Dictionary of Economics*, vol. 4, eds. John Eatwell, Murray Milgate, and Peter Newman, 863–868. London: Macmillan.

Sowell, Thomas. 1972. *Say's Law: An Historical Analysis*. Princeton, NJ: Princeton University Press.

Walras, Léon. [1926] 1954. *Elements of Pure Economics*. Trans. William Jaffe. London: Allen and Unwin.

Robert Dixon

WALTZ, KENNETH
1924–

Kenneth Neal Waltz, born and raised in Ann Arbor, Michigan, is best known for developing the *neorealist* or *structural realist* approach to the study of international relations. A central figure in the development of international relations scholarship in the post–World War II (1939–1945) era, Waltz has also made notable contributions to the understanding of nuclear weapons proliferation and its consequences. Waltz received his bachelor's degree from Oberlin College in 1948 and his graduate degrees from Columbia University in the 1950s. He retired from teaching in the mid-1990s and, as of 2005, was serving as Emeritus Ford Professor of Political Science at the University of California at Berkeley and as an adjunct professor of political science at Columbia University.

Waltz's earliest contribution, presented in *Man, the State, and War: A Theoretical Analysis* (1954), organizes the primary causes of war into three distinct *images* or levels of analysis. The first image considers human nature and whether it can be developed and constrained in such a way as to minimize the likelihood of war. The second image emphasizes domestic political factors as the source of interstate conflicts. Finally, the third image identifies as the key causes of war the structure of the international system and, in particular, the absence of any centralized arbiter to settle disputes among countries, a condition known in international relations as *anarchy*. Through these levels of analysis, Waltz seeks to isolate and therefore better understand the root causes of conflict among countries.

Waltz's most influential work is *Theory of International Politics* (1979), in which he elaborates the principal tenets and predictions of *neorealism*. Sometimes called *structural realism*, neorealism emphasizes third-level causes of conflict among countries. As a result of anarchy, states can trust only themselves to secure their survival. Therefore, they must always be suspicious of others, making cooperation with other countries limited and infrequent. In Waltz's view, even though states must strive for security, they do not intrinsically seek boundless power or territory; therefore, once their security needs are met, most states will accept the status quo and avoid conflict with other states. States whose ambitions exceed these legitimate security needs can be contained by the systemic balance of power.

Beginning in the 1980s, Waltz's research turned increasingly to the implications of nuclear proliferation. The leading *nuclear optimist*, Waltz argues that, given the destruction any nuclear exchange would entail, an increase in the number of states with nuclear weapons makes the international system more stable and armed conflict less likely. In effect, nuclear proliferation obligates states to be more restrained and careful in their relations with other countries. *Nuclear pessimists*, on the other hand, contend that the proliferation of nuclear weapons destabilizes international relations. Together with Scott D. Sagan, Waltz coauthored *The Spread of Nuclear Weapons: A Debate* (1995), which elaborates the debate between nuclear pessimists and optimists in the context of the cold war's superpower nuclear standoff. Sagan and Waltz reissued their book in 2002 with an expanded discussion of proliferation in India and Pakistan, and of the threat of nuclear weapons being acquired by terrorists.

SEE ALSO *Casino Capitalism; International Relations; Market Fundamentals; Realism, Political*

BIBLIOGRAPHY

Sagan, Scott D., and Kenneth N. Waltz. 2002. *The Spread of Nuclear Weapons: A Debate Renewed.* New York: W. W. Norton.

Waltz, Kenneth N. 1979. *Theory of International Politics.* New York: McGraw Hill.

Gerald M. DiGiusto

WANT CREATION

Introductory economics textbooks assume consumers are sovereign in the market. The preferences of consumers are supposed to be authentic, self-generated. Consumers' preferences are supposed to determine what producers supply. But this is an age in which producers increasingly contest that sovereignty. With powerful corporations, costly information, pervasive advertising, and persuasive salesmanship, consumers are less independent, their preferences less authentic. Created wants do not arise spontaneously from individual preferences but from advertising and salesmanship. John Kenneth Galbraith described such want creation as "the revised sequence" (Galbraith 1967, p. 212).

Of course, the traditionally accepted sequence still operates. Information about what is wanted still flows from consumers to producers, from the demand side of the product market to the supply side. Not all wants are created by producers. Sovereign consumers have not lost their power. But they do have to share it. Producers no longer respond passively to consumer whim, if they ever wholly did. The sovereignty of the consumer is being challenged on a widening front. A significant flow of information is now going in the other direction. A revised sequence has been established in which information flows from producer to consumer, from the supply side of the product market to the demand side. Supply has begun to create demand. Consumer wants have begun to depend

on producer production. Galbraith coined the phrase "the dependence effect" to describe consumption that depends on production (Galbraith, 1969, p. 143).

THE SIGNIFICANCE OF WANT CREATION

Want creation reduces the authenticity and the urgency of consumer preferences. It undermines much of neoclassical economics. It cuts the hearts out of microeconomic and welfare theory, changes macroeconomic theory, and forces a reconsideration of the benefits of globalization. If taken seriously, want creation would revolutionize textbook economics, where it is still largely ignored.

In microeconomic theory, want creation means that the price mechanism is not the only way markets reach equilibrium. Excess supply of consumer goods may or may not be eliminated by a decline in the market price. It may also be eliminated by an increase in advertising and salesmanship and other alterations in the flow of information from producer to consumer—all intended to shift the demand curve to the right instead of moving downward along the demand curve toward a lower price and higher quantity demanded. Excess demand for consumer goods, likewise but in reverse, may or may not be eliminated by the price mechanism. That is, advertising, salesmanship, and information management may be adjusted downward, instead of price being adjusted upward, to clear the excess demand from the market. Want creation introduces indeterminacy and producer discretion into the market adjustment process (Waller and Robertson 1998).

In welfare theory, want creation destroys the presumption of market optimality. To the extent that wants are created so that producers can profit by supplying them, equilibrium in the product market does not represent optimal consumer utility in the form of consumer surplus. In fact, consumer surplus loses its meaning when consumer wants are created by producers. Furthermore, if workers supply their work in order to buy the products that meet the wants created by the producers who hire them, how can it be said that human welfare is served?

In macroeconomic theory, want creation replaces more orthodox consumption functions with the demonstration effect (Duesenberry 1949). When the desirability of new goods and services is demonstrated to consumers, short run consumption permanently shifts up to include the new item. This makes the average and marginal propensities to consume the same in the long run, even if the marginal propensity is less than the average propensity in the short run. Of course, in the United States, want creation has made the pressure to consume so intense that the marginal and average propensities are both close to unity.

When wants are created, it is questionable to what extent underdeveloped countries benefit from globalization when it opens them up to the advertising, salesmanship, and information management exercised by the powerful corporations of developed countries (Dugger 1998).

Applied to a wide range of economic doctrines, want creation is a subversive concept.

Among the economists seriously discussing want creation are Robert H. Frank, who is linking individual preferences to social emulation (Frank 1985, 1999), and Juliet B. Schor, whose work is more focused on manipulation by advertisers (Schor 1991, 1998).

SEE ALSO *Consumer; Consumer Protection; Consumerism; Consumption; Functionings; Galbraith, John Kenneth; Hidden Persuaders; Needs; Relative Income Hypothesis; Subliminal Suggestion; Wants; Welfare Economics*

BIBLIOGRAPHY

Duesenberry, James S. 1949. *Income, Saving and the Theory of Consumer Behavior*. Cambridge, MA: Harvard University Press.

Dugger, William M. 1998. Thorstein Veblen and the Upper Class. In *Thorstein Veblen in the Twenty-First Century*, ed. Doug Brown, 73–84. Cheltenham, UK: Edward Elgar.

Frank, Robert H. 1985. *Choosing the Right Pond: Human Behavior and the Quest for Status*. New York: Oxford University Press.

Frank, Robert H. 1999. *Luxury Fever: Why Money Fails to Satisfy in an Era of Excess*. New York: Free Press.

Galbraith, John Kenneth. 1967. *The New Industrial State*. Boston: Houghton Mifflin.

Galbraith, John Kenneth. 1969. *The Affluent Society*. 2nd ed. Boston: Houghton Mifflin.

Schor, Juliet B. 1991. *The Overworked American: The Unexpected Decline of Leisure*. New York: Basic Books.

Schor, Juliet B. 1998. *The Overspent American: Upscaling, Downshifting, and the New Consumer*. New York: Basic Books.

Waller, William, and Linda Robertson. 1998. The Politics of Consumption and Desire. In *Thorstein Veblen in the Twenty-First Century*, ed. Doug Brown, 28–48. Cheltenham, U.K.: Edward Elgar.

William M. Dugger

WANTS

In economics, the term *want* refers to a wish or desire to own goods and services that give satisfaction. More generally, the concept involves the endless succession of material wants exhibited by all human beings. Material wants are the desires of consumers to obtain and use various goods and services that provide utility. Usually, wants are backed by effective demand—ability and willingness to pay.

Nature has made lavish the distribution of its natural resources and this has brought about an endless desire for many things even though they may not necessarily be basic needs (food, clothing, and shelter). As basic needs and wants are satisfied, other wants will arise. For this reason, human wants are unlimited: The satisfaction of one want leads to another. At the same time, the means (natural, human, and manufactured) used in satisfying them are limited (scarce).

The study of economics begins with a consideration of scarcity. *Scarcity* refers to a situation in which goods and services are limited in supply, and thus the full demand for those goods and services cannot be met. Because people have unlimited wants—and thus want more than they have or can purchase with their incomes—what they have is never enough, even if they are wealthy. And given that people do not have everything they want, they must use their limited time and income to select those things they want most and forgo the rest. The choices they make and the manner in which the choices are made explain much of why the real world is what it is. A choice is simply a comparison of alternatives. When you choose one thing, the lost benefits of the next best alternative represent the *opportunity cost* of your choice.

The rapid introduction of new products whets our appetites and extensive advertising persuades us that we need countless items we might not otherwise buy. For instance, not too long ago, we did not want light beer, videocassette recorders, fax machines, or compact discs—because they did not exist. The overall objective of all economic activity is to attempt to satisfy material wants, both longstanding and newly created.

The wants of consumers (goods and services) become available through business activities. It is, then, business that produces the food, clothing, shelter, furniture, household utensils, and so on that we all need. It supplies us with all our means of transportation, from the simple bicycle to the sophisticated airliner. It provides all our entertainment, from children's comics to the television programs beamed to us from satellites in space.

Wants expressed as effective demand reflect major economic decisions by states, corporate institutions, and multilateral institutions, and are significantly affected by forces emanating from either the world market or domestic markets. For instance, domestic pricing mechanisms influence the investment decisions of individuals, as well as corporate economic factors. Examples can be found in the stock exchange process, in which decisions to buy or sell stocks are influenced by stock values.

In practical terms, wants for goods emanate from consumers, and thus producers produce what consumers need; if they do not, they may go out of business. Furthermore, if production is undertaken in order to sup-ply the wants of mankind, then demand must be the basic force in economics. Every individual demands goods and services and when all the individual demands are put together, the resulting composite demand is what industry must meet if people are to achieve satisfaction. Demand for goods that are not to our personal taste, or are less fashionable or less well promoted through advertisement will be weaker. Tastes and preferences, as well as publicity, thus play some part in determining the total want for a commodity or service.

At the national level, the overall want of countries may differ, depending on their level of development (technological, human, and material), income, state of peace or war, and natural resources. For example, a war-torn country will have a constant need to import arms. Because nature has not equitably distributed its resources over the surface of the earth, nation-states depend on one another for those goods for which they have the least comparative cost advantage. The exchange between nations of such resources is an obvious solution to national shortages.

Nations may have diverse wants (perhaps reflected in development programs and projects), but few resources. This scarcity of resources comprises a huge constraint, and thus nations may be forced to drop some of their white elephant projects and arrange their programs in order of importance pending the availability of funds. With scarcity, which ensures that nations' wants exceed what they can actually produce, potential demand will obviously exceed potential supply. As a result, the shortfall in supply of a nation's wants will be made up by other nations.

More significantly, national wants determine the level of international trade and what categories of goods (wants) will be imported. For instance, for years the United States stockpiled its own oil resources for strategic reasons and instead used cheap supplies from Venezuela and the Middle East. Similarly, Great Britain has allowed its own cotton industry to run down in the face of competition from the newly industrialized countries of the Far East, whose cheap labor and skillful exploitation of new technology have made them more economical than Lancashire. This economic philosophy of wants has been criticized for being excessively laissez-faire.

Wants are driven by self-interest, and in most cases involve a clash of interests. For example, nations may go to war to protect their own "national interest" despite the obvious consequences. Another difficulty connected with the satisfaction of human wants is that people and nations are spread around the world in a very haphazard way, making it impossible to evenly satisfy human wants; furthermore, one person's wants may be another person's needs and vice versa. In addition, the means of fulfilling wants are inherently limited, as the world at any given

time can only produce a limited amount of goods and services due to the limited resources at its disposal.

Wants as an economic desire never cease; they grow in spiral-like movements of business activity. We engage in business activity so that we can satisfy human wants. When we do satisfy these wants, the very act of satisfaction consumes the useful goods or services created and we must start the process again in order to supply a further batch. The process goes from wants through enterprise, production, distribution, and marketing to consumption and satisfaction, and back to wants again.

SEE ALSO *Consumption; Demand; Functionings; Needs; Needs, Basic; Scarcity; Trade; Utility, Objective; Utility, Subjective; Want Creation*

BIBLIOGRAPHY

Anderton, Alain. 2000. *Economics*. 3rd ed. Lancashire, U.K.: Causeway Press.

Anyaele, Johnson Ugorji. 2003. *Comprehensive Economics*. Rev. ed. Lagos, Nigeria: Johnson Publishers.

Boyes, William, and Michael Melvin. 2006. *Fundamentals of Economics*. 3rd ed. Boston: Houghton-Mifflin.

Culyer, A. J. 1985. *Economics*. New York: Basil Blackwell.

Forster, Bruce, and Geoffrey Whitehead. 2003. *Economics: A Business Text*. London: ICM Publishers.

Sloman, John. 2006. *Economics*. 6th ed. London: Pearson Education.

Whitehead, Geoffrey. 1994. *Business Studies*. 2nd ed. London: Butterworth-Heinemann.

Cajetan Nnaocha

WAR

In general, war is the outbreak of armed hostilities within, between, or among states or other political groups and communities, in which strategic, political, economic, and other important outcomes are decided mainly by the use of military force. In international law, war is a legal condition of open and declared hostility between or among states, wherein diplomatic relations are automatically severed (if an official state of war is declared) and states may use any military force deemed appropriate or effective, subject only to the laws of war and perhaps to notions of "just war." According to the Bismarckian *realpolitik* ("realistic politics") school of international relations, war as organized political violence is the ultimate "self-help" device in the power politics of an anarchic world consisting of sovereign states. The "Iron Chancellor" Otto von Bismarck (1815–1898), architect of Germany's "reunification from above" during the nineteenth century, recog-

nized the importance of war's nation-building function, declaring in the German Bundestag that "It is not by speeches and resolutions that the great questions of the time are decided … but by iron and blood" (Barash and Webel 2002, p. 58).

According to the most illustrious "philosopher of war," Carl von Clausewitz, a nineteenth-century Prussian army officer best known for his treatise *On War*, war is "not a mere act of policy, but a true political instrument, a continuation of political activity by other means" (Clausewitz [1832] 1976, p. 87). In other words, war is fundamentally a continuation of a country's peacetime diplomacy by other, more violent methods, rather than a complete break with it. It is not an act of senseless fury and violence, but an orchestrated military action with a particular strategic goal in mind—namely, disarming one's opponents to the point where they cannot resist one's demands. This conception of warfare as essentially political in nature is in accord with Clausewitz's general definition of war as "an act of force to compel the enemy to do our will." War, he wrote, is "nothing but a duel on a larger scale" ([1832] 1976, p. 75). In contrast, Marxist and neo-Marxist writers emphasize the socioeconomic causes of war, claiming that mankind has been historically in a state of almost perpetual warfare due to the economic interests of the dominant social classes. Since the rise of class-divided society in the Early Bronze Age (c. 3500–2000 B.C.E., war has been promoted by powerful members of the socially dominant classes who are seeking—out of sheer economic self-interest or imperialist ambition—to gain colonies, export markets, or natural resources abroad; political and economic spheres of influence; regional or global domination; and so on. The American Socialist leader Eugene Debs (1855–1926) told an antiwar rally in 1917: "Wars throughout history have been waged for conquest and plunder.… The master class has always declared the wars; the subject class has always fought the battles" (Zinn 2005, p. 27).

Quincy Wright (1890–1970), a pioneering peace and conflict researcher, considered a war to have taken place either when it was formally declared or when a certain number of troops—at least 50,000 as a minimum—were involved. Other writers have defined wars by the number of deaths incurred, focusing on a minimum of 1,000 combat-related fatalities—either per war or per year of the conflict (see Singer and Small 1972; Eckhardt 1991). Reality is, of course, much more complicated than such definitions of war. In the War of the Bavarian Succession (1778–1779), for instance, after an official state of war had been declared, the Prussian and Austrian armies marched against each other in the field, but not a single shot was fired in anger and, as a result, no one died. In contrast, during the Korean War (1950–1953), in which nearly 3 million people—mostly innocent civilians—were

killed, including more than 54,000 Americans, there was neither an official declaration of war nor the signing of a peace treaty, and the whole conflict was euphemistically labeled a "U.N. police action." In the First Gulf War (1990–1991), not only was an official state of war never declared, nor a peace treaty signed at the end of the hostilities, but diplomatic relations with Iraq were not severed by most of its adversaries.

The sheer wastefulness of warfare in terms of human, economic, environmental, and social losses has been appalling, even without the use of nuclear weapons. For example, during the Thirty Years' War (1618–1648) a third of Germany's population was killed. At least 9 million soldiers and more than 1 million civilians died during World War I (1914–1918), with approximately 20 million more people perishing during the war-driven influenza epidemic of 1918. During the Battle of the Sommes in 1916, the joint British-French forces tried for five months to break through German lines, gaining a mere 120 square miles at a cost of 420,000 British and nearly 200,000 French soldiers; the Germans lost 445,000. Military deaths in World War II (1939–1945), during which nuclear bombs were dropped on the Japanese cities of Hiroshima and Nagasaki, were about 17 million, but civilian deaths—at approximately 35 million—were many times greater than in World War I. Of the 2.9 million Americans who served in the military during the undeclared Vietnam War, more than 58,000 were killed, 3,000 became missing in action, and more than 300,000 were wounded or maimed. Yet these casualty figures convey very little of that war's horrors, both for those who fought in the war and especially for the peoples of Indochina. In Vietnam itself, the economy and natural environment were devastated, and well over 3 million Vietnamese were killed, more than two-thirds of them civilians. Overall, at least 3.5 billion people are believed to have died as a direct or indirect result of the more than 14,500 wars that have been waged during the 5,000 years since the dawn of human civilization (Beer 1981).

The direct and indirect costs of warfare, and especially the tragic loss of human life, have elicited harsh criticism of war throughout the ages. The ancient Greek historian Plutarch (46-120) complained in the first century C.E. that "the poor go to war, to fight and die for the delights, riches, and superfluities of others" (Plutarch 1948, p. 167) According to Benjamin Franklin (1706–1790), one of America's founding fathers, "there never was a good war or a bad peace" (quoted in Barash and Webel 2002, p. 12). Ernest Hemingway, a badly wounded World War I veteran and author of the famous antiwar novel *A Farewell to Arms*, agreed: "Never think that war, no matter how necessary, nor how justified, is not a crime" (Hemingway 2003, p. 233). And the famous British philosopher and pacifist Bertrand Russell warned at the beginning of the twentieth century that "either man will abolish war, or war will abolish man" (Russell 1915).

The march of technology has radically altered the scope and nature of war over the centuries. Technological progress has increased the need to mobilize the entire nation for military-industrial and other production in support of the war effort (the war's "home front"), but has also made civilian populations a legitimate target for the military in what is often referred to as "total war," a twentieth-century invention. The technological ability to use lethal weapons at a distance has escalated from primitive warfare's bow and arrow to today's supersonic jet and intercontinental ballistic missile, both of which can deliver deadly munitions at a speed of thousands of miles per hour and with pinpoint accuracy. This quantum leap has been matched by similar technological advances in destructive power, from the swords and spears of medieval combat to the massive explosive force of the thermonuclear bomb—measured in millions of tons (megatons) of TNT and capable of completely obliterating even the world's largest cities.

In the age of nuclear and other weapons of mass destruction, some commentators suggest that their sheer destructiveness has made war obsolete, because no rational goal could be achieved by using such doomsday weapons that are endangering the very existence of mankind and indeed the survival of all life on the planet. For example, the total U.S. nuclear arsenal in 1990 was about 3,200 megatons of TNT, whereas the entire explosive power detonated by all militaries in World War II was approximately three megatons—including the two atomic bombs dropped on Hiroshima and Nagasaki in August 1945, which had the explosive force of 12 and 20 kilotons, respectively. Some scholars believe that the detonation of as little as 100 megatons of TNT, a tiny fraction of the world's stockpiles of nuclear arms, could trigger a "nuclear winter"—the prolonged darkening and cooling of the planet (temperatures could plummet as much as 50 degrees Fahrenheit). After a nuclear exchange, the huge quantities of smoke and soot generated by the resulting firestorms would rise into the upper atmosphere and absorb incoming solar heat and light, thereby making the Earth cold, dark, and eventually uninhabitable (Sagan and Turco 1990). Even though wars are still taking place, causing immense destruction and misery, the threat of nuclear Armageddon has fostered powerful peace and antiwar movements that are not only deterring the nuclear-weapon powers from using or even testing their strategic arsenals, but also instilling the increasingly widespread belief that war is an illegitimate method for settling grievances.

SEE ALSO *Arms Control and Arms Race; Civil-Military Relation; Conflict; Deterrence; Deterrence, Mutual; Militarism; Military; Military Regimes; Military-Industrial Complex; Peace; Weapons Industry*

BIBLIOGRAPHY

Barash, David P., and Charles P. Webel. 2002. *Peace and Conflict Studies*. Thousand Oaks, CA: Sage.

Beer, Francis A. 1981. *Peace Against War: The Ecology of International Violence*. San Francisco: W. H. Freeman.

Clausewitz, Carl von. [1832] 1976. *On War*. Princeton, NJ: Princeton University Press. Originally published as *Vom Kriege*.

Eckhardt, William. 1991. War-related Deaths Since 3,000 B.C. *Peace Research* 23: 80–85.

Hemingway, Ernest. 2003. *Hemingway on War*. Ed. and intro. Sean Hemingway. New York: Scribner.

Plutarch. 1921. *Plutarch Lives; Parallel Lives*, Vol. 10: *Agis and Cleomenes. Tiberius and Gaius Gracchus. Philopoemen and Flamininus*. Trans. Bernadotte Perrin. Cambridge, MA: Harvard University Press (Loeb Classical Library).

Russell, Bertrand. 1915. War and Non-Resistance. *Atlantic Monthly* 116 (2): 266–274. http://fair-use.org/atlantic-monthly/1915/08/war-and-non-resistance.

Sagan, Carl, and Richard Turco. 1990. *A Path Where No Man Thought: Nuclear Winter and the End of the Arms Race*. New York: Random House.

Singer, J. David, and Melvin Small. 1972. *The Wages of War, 1816–1965: A Statistical Handbook*. New York: Wiley.

Wright, Quincy. 1964. *A Study of War*. Chicago: University of Chicago Press.

Zinn, Howard. 2005. *Just War*. Milano: Edizioni Charta.

Rossen Vassilev

WAR, SPANISH-AMERICAN

SEE *War of 1898.*

WAR AND PEACE

War and Peace by Leo Tolstoy (1828–1910) is arguably the world's greatest epic novel. Written and published in the monthly *Russkij Vestnik* from 1863 to 1869, the work depicts the years leading up to and including Russia's wars with Napoleon from 1805 to 1812. The novel immortalizes the quiet heroism and spiritual strength of the Russian people in a time of national crisis and historical transition. *War and Peace* began as a social novel called *The Decembrists* about a Russian Decembrist returning from Siberian exile in the 1850s. As Tolstoy worked he realized that in order to describe his hero he would first need to understand his formative years during the Napoleonic wars. A lasting trace of this original conception is the character of Pierre Bezukhov, the hero of the original novel (named Pyotr Labazov) and a main protagonist in *War and Peace*. What began as a contemporary social study grew into a vast, vivid tableau of early-nineteenth-century Russian life that goes beyond historical fact to capture the emotional, psychological, and moral fabric of the time.

TOLSTOYAN WISDOM IN *WAR AND PEACE*

War and Peace reflects the deep imprint of French culture on nineteenth-century Russian life, not least in the aristocratic characters' frequent use of French. And yet just as the vast Russian countryside in the novel engulfs the invading French army, so Tolstoy's massive literary landscape assimilates French and other cultural influences into a synthetic creation that encompasses all of life.

In *War and Peace* characters are born, they marry, they decay, and they die. These events occur on a clock that ticks on with slow, implacable calm. This has led some readers to sense in the novel a spirit of fatalism. But *War and Peace* is also a freshly inspiring vision of the world's physical plenitude and of the meaningful moral choices it offers. Many of the novel's greatest scenes, such as Natasha Rostova's first ball, the Rostovs' wolf hunt, and Prince Andrei's vision of the "lofty infinite sky" as he lay wounded on the battlefield at Austerlitz, are among the most enthralling moments in world literature.

Almost all of the main protagonists in *War and Peace* find happiness in a balanced, mature view of the world as a place where joy and tragedy, moral choice and providential design, are present in equal measure. These characters discover that their individual lives are both finite and full of possibility, both solitary and also part of an organic tapestry of human evolution and history. Only Prince Andrei is unable to reconcile his noble ideals with reality. He is the novel's one tragic hero.

If there is an overt ideological thesis in *War and Peace*, it is that great men do not move history but are its slaves and that free will is an illusion, albeit a necessary one to help us get through everyday life. Tolstoy takes particular aim at Napoleon, who arrogantly believes that he shapes events; at historians who accept the great man theory of historical evolution; and at all manner of strategists, military and otherwise, who believe that rational planning affects the outcome of events.

In Tolstoy's novel those characters who live spontaneously are wise and productive because they are in sync with the forces of history and nature. Kutuzov defeats Napoleon not because of strategic planning (he sleeps before the Battle of Austerlitz while his military strategists quibble) but because he instinctively senses the inevitable course of events. Pierre grows wise and finds happiness

after he gives up his Utopian schemes and accepts the world in its beautiful unpredictability.

THE NOVEL IN AN AGE OF SOCIAL UNREST

Tolstoy's initial work on *The Decembrists* and the early drafts of *War and Peace* occurred when he was growing concerned about the impending Great Reforms of Alexander II, begun in 1861. Tolstoy, an aristocrat, believed that the centuries-old system of aristocratic privilege and serfdom, while imperfect, was superior to the chaos—political, social, and spiritual—that the reforms would unleash. Tolstoy's social conservatism is evident in the work's idealized depiction of the landlord–peasant relationship at the beginning of the century. According to prominent Soviet scholar Viktor Shklovsky, Tolstoy distorts historical facts to further his ideological agenda. A prominent example of this described by Shklovsky is the author's suppression of the real reason that Princess Marya's peasants at Boguċharovo rebel in book three, part two, when she offers to take them with her to Bald Hills: because they believed that, by staying at Boguċharovo, they would be freed by Napoleon. Rather, Tolstoy's portrayal of the peasants gives the impression that their uprising was a senseless, isolated event, motivated by their eccentricity instead of their deep-seated dissatisfaction with the social status quo.

Although Shklovsky and some other scholars rightly discover strains of social conservatism in the novel, they reduce the great epic to a web of self-serving artistic illusions. A more likely source of Tolstoy's idealized portrayal of the peasant–landlord relationship is the author's life-long attraction to the ideals of national unity, social harmony, and universal fellowship of human beings. We may read *War and Peace* as Tolstoy's heroic attempt to create for his discordant Russian society of the 1860s a mythical past in which Russians were secure in their collective identity and unified in their response to a national crisis.

FORM OF THE WORK

When it first appeared, *War and Peace* was a radical departure from the traditional form of the European novel. The work combines elements of the psychological novel, historical novel, family chronicle, epic, and Bildungsroman. It has astonished and confounded readers with its deluge of detail, its vast array of characters who seem to appear and disappear at random, and its inclusion of historico-philosophical essays throughout. Scholars differ about whether the work's idiosyncratic form was intended or "a splendid accident," as American writer and critic Henry James called it. Twentieth-century scholars suggest that the novel's unconventional form intends to show that real life, like history, does not unfold in neat, narrative pat-

terns. Other scholars argue that despite its strangeness the work contains concealed artistic patterns and unifying aesthetic principles.

Despite its sprawling canvas (approximately 365 chapters, or 1,500 pages in the original publication), *War and Peace* focuses the reader's deepest sympathies on Pierre Bezukhov and the novel's other four main aristocratic protagonists: Prince Andrei Bolkonsky, Nikolai Rostov, Natasha Rostova, and Princess Marya Bolkonskaya. Tolstoy presents their journeys with extraordinary lifelike realism, and he describes how their personal destinies become intertwined with the encroaching forces of war and history.

So interconnected do the "peace" and "war" sections of the novel become that it appears virtually impossible to disentangle them. Power politics, schemes, and stratagems are as present in the St. Petersburg drawing rooms as on the battlefield, and characters are as apt to achieve spiritual illumination in the throes of war as in the joys of family life. The "peace" of the novel's title refers not only to peacetime but also to the spiritual tranquility characters seek amid the confusion of modern life.

FUTURE IMPACT

War and Peace has inspired generations of Russian writers and artists, who have tried to recreate Tolstoy's expansive vision and have regarded Tolstoy's masterpiece as a model for recording the unique destiny of the Russian people. Among the works that *War and Peace* has influenced are Mikhail Sholokhov's novel *The Quiet Don* (1928–1940), Boris Pasternak's *Doctor Zhivago* (1957), and Vasily Grossman's *Life and Fate* (1959). Sergei Prokofiev's operatic version of *War and Peace*, a masterpiece in its own right, beautifully transports to the stage the deep patriotic currents of Tolstoy's novel, as well as the majestic calm of Tolstoy's omniscient narrative voice. Tolstoy's novel remains required reading in Russian schools, and ordinary Russians frequently can recite by heart passages from their adored classic. Even Joseph Stalin, infamous for his ability to harness the power of art for political purposes, recognized the potency of *War and Peace* when he ordered the book to be included in a propaganda series called "Books for Victory" during World War II (1939–1945).

SEE ALSO *Aristocracy; Conservatism; Feudalism; Landlords; Monarchism; Napoléon Bonaparte; Naturalism; Peace; Peasantry; Planning; Stability, Political; Stalin, Joseph; Utopianism; War*

BIBLIOGRAPHY

Berlin, Isaiah. [1953] 1993. *The Hedgehog and the Fox: An Essay on Tolstoy's View of History.* Chicago: Ivan R. Dee.

Christian, R. F. 1962. *Tolstoy's "War and Peace": A Study*. Oxford: Clarendon Press.

Clay, George R. 1998. *Tolstoy's Phoenix: From Method to Meaning in* War and Peace. Evanston, IL: Northwestern University Press.

Eikhembaum, Boris. 1982. *Tolstoi in the Sixties*. Trans. Duffield White. Ann Arbor, MI: Ardis.

Feuer, Kathryn B. 1996. *Tolstoy and the Genesis of* War and Peace, eds. Robin Feuer Miller and Donna Tussing Orwin. Ithaca, NY: Cornell University Press.

Morson, Gary Saul. 1987. *Hidden in Plain View: Narrative and Creative Potentials in "War and Peace"*. Stanford, CA: Stanford University Press.

Shklovsky, Viktor. 1996. *Lev Tolstoy*. C.I.S.: Raduga Publisher.

Tolstoy, Leo. [1863–1869] 1996. *War and Peace*. Trans. Louise and Aylmer Maude. Ed. George Gibian. New York: Norton.

Andrew D. Kaufman

WAR CRIMES

The notion of crimes of war has been known in the Western legal tradition since classical antiquity. For the ancient Greeks it was part of Hellenic customary law that provided some basic if ill-defined norms for the protection of civilians, suppliants, and prisoners in warfare between the Greek states. While this notion has persisted as the "laws and customs of war," it was only with the incipient development of a body of international law at the end of the nineteenth and beginning of the twentieth centuries that it began to take shape in its modern form as a central category in the body of norms whose aim is to regulate the violence of armed conflict. The "laws and customs of war," as the name indicates, apply only in the context of armed conflict. As the dual terminology "laws" *and* "customs" also implies, in the modern period these norms are regarded as having a dual basis. On the one hand, they are defined by the body of statutory law that has developed since the first Hague Conventions adopted around the beginning of the twentieth century. On the other hand, such conventions represent only one source of the international law of armed conflict. The codifications do not exhaust this body of law, which also arises from the customs and usages of warfare as reflected in the practices of nations.

Three major phases of development of the notion of war crimes in the modern period can be identified. The first begins with the adoption of the Hague Conventions of 1899 and 1907, regulating the conduct of hostilities and the employment of various kinds of weapons and modes of warfare. Most immediately relevant to war crimes is the 1907 Hague Convention IV on "The Laws and Customs of War on Land" and particularly its provisions defining the limits of military necessity and limiting the violence that may be employed against cities and other civilian targets (Articles 22–28). While the treatment of prisoners of war is addressed in the Hague Conventions, it was the Geneva Convention of 1929 that provided the basic legal framework for this subject in the pre–World War II (1939–1945) era. While the distinction between "Geneva law" and "Hague law" was widely regarded as fundamental in earlier periods, it has, as we will see, largely ceased to have any relevance in the contemporary period.

The experience of "total war" in the European and Asia-Pacific theaters in World War II involved the total destruction of major civilian centers, the displacement of entire populations, industrialized murder, civilian deaths in the tens of millions, and devastation on a scale hitherto unimagined. Total war led to a widespread recognition that the laws of war had to be revised so as to reflect the exigencies of a new age. The first major step in this direction was taken by the victorious Allies in the creation of two international criminal tribunals in Nuremberg and Tokyo to try German and Japanese military and civilian leaders for crimes against peace, war crimes, and crimes against humanity. The definition of "war crimes" in the Nuremberg Charter provided an important and expansive definition of the scope of such criminal conduct:

> Violations of the laws or customs of war. Such violations shall include, but not be limited to, murder, ill-treatment or deportation to slave labor or for any other purpose of civilian population of or in occupied territory, murder or ill-treatment of prisoners of war or persons on the seas, killing of hostages, plunder of public or private property, wanton destruction of cities, towns or villages, or devastation not justified by military necessity.

For the first time governmental and military leaders were held criminally responsible as individuals and punished by the Nuremberg and Tokyo tribunals for their roles in planning, instigating, ordering, or perpetrating such war crimes. In addition, building upon the Nuremberg and Tokyo Charters, the Allies created a legal framework for national war crimes tribunals that convicted thousands of Japanese and German war criminals of war crimes. This step marks the decisive move into the contemporary age of individual accountability for war crimes and other violations of international law regulating armed conflict.

During the same period in the aftermath of World War II, the four Geneva Conventions of 1949 and the Genocide Convention of 1948 also represent major landmarks in the development of the contemporary legal framework regulating armed conflict. The Geneva Conventions of 1949 greatly expanded and refined this framework and also made decisive contributions to the law of war crimes. Particularly

grave violations falling within the category of war crimes were designated as "grave breaches" of the conventions. These include: wilful killing; torture or inhuman treatment; biological experiments; unlawful deportation or transfer, taking of hostages, etc. (The 1977 Protocol 1 to the 1949 conventions greatly expands the category of grave breaches, particularly by including various limitations on the conditions under which civilian targets may be made the object of attack.) Further, for the first time the coverage of this body of law was extended to noninternational conflicts. That is, previously war crimes by definition involved violations committed in time of war or serious armed conflicts between nations. The hitherto seemingly inviolable principle of national sovereignty had protected governments from interference with what they did within their own territory to their own citizens. The development of the category of "crimes against humanity" represented one important prong in limiting this principle, and Article 3 of the 1949 Geneva Conventions represented another. The coverage of the 1949 conventions as to war crimes was extended further by the two 1977 protocols to the 1949 conventions, the first covering international conflicts the second internal ones.

Common Article 3, so called because it is found in all four of the 1949 conventions, extends basic minimum protections of international law to purely internal conflicts and thus brings the notion of war crimes into the sphere of the kinds of internal conflicts that have been so prevalent in the post–World War II era. Common Article 3 provides:

> In the case of armed conflict not of an international character occurring in the territory of one of the High Contracting Parties, each party to the conflict shall be bound to apply, as a minimum, the following provisions:
>
> 1. Persons taking no active part in the hostilities, including members of armed forces who have laid down their arms and those placed hors de combat by sickness, wounds, detention, or any other cause, shall in all circumstances be treated humanely, without any adverse distinction founded on race, colour, religion or faith, sex, birth or wealth, or any other similar criteria.
>
> To this end the following acts are and shall remain prohibited at any time and in any place whatsoever with respect to the above-mentioned persons:
>
> (a) Violence to life and person, in particular murder of all kinds, mutilation, cruel treatment and torture;
>
> (b) Taking of hostages;
>
> (c) Outrages upon personal dignity, in particular, humiliating and degrading treatment;

> (d) The passing of sentences and the carrying out of executions without previous judgment pronounced by a regularly constituted court affording all the judicial guarantees which are recognized as indispensable by civilized peoples.

The third phase in the development of the body of law defining and punishing war crimes began with the creation of the Ad Hoc International Criminal Tribunals for Rwanda and the former Yugoslavia (ICTR and ICTY) in 1993–1994. Whereas war crimes had not been punished by international tribunals since Nuremberg and Tokyo, the ICTY and ICTR ushered in an age of the institutionalization of such prosecutions, reaching fulfillment in the creation of the permanent International Criminal Court (ICC) in the Hague in 2002. All three of these bodies have made important contributions to the definition, jurisprudence, and punishment of war crimes, as have the so-called international "hybrid tribunals" in East Timor, Kosovo, Bosnia, Sierra Leone, and Cambodia.

The statutes of all three of these international criminal tribunals include war crimes as one of the major categories of violations of international law within the jurisdiction of these courts. (See, e.g., ICTY Statute Articles 2 and 3; ICC Statute Article 8.) The Appeals Chamber of the ICTY has clarified the relations between the categories of "grave breaches," other violations of the "laws and customs of war" defined by the Hague and Geneva Conventions, and common Article 3. It has ruled that all of these norms are war crimes and that the previous distinction between "Hague law" and "Geneva law" is no longer relevant. (See, e.g., the Tadic Jursidiction Decision, para. 87, and the Celebici Appeals Judgment, paras. 132–133.)

The statute of the ICC makes this clear in Article 8 by specifying that the category of war crimes includes grave breaches and "other serious violations of the laws and customs of war applicable in international armed conflict" as well as common Article 3 and other "serious violations of international law applicable in non-international armed conflict." The category of war crimes has thus expanded to encompass a very wide range of offenses committed in international or internal conflicts. These offenses have also become much more clearly defined than in previous eras. In particular, the jurisprudence of these courts has provided authoritative discussions and definitions of the elements of these offenses. This represents an important contribution to the interpretation and applications of such crimes because the post–World War II trials had left them largely undefined. Most recently, the ICC has promulgated the Elements of Crimes, which also includes definitions of each of the key components of all major crimes of war. As the ICC assumes an ever more prominent role in the application of international humanitarian law, its definitions of

the elements of war crimes is likely to prove to be of decisive influence.

SEE ALSO *Genocide; Holocaust, The; War; World War II*

BIBLIOGRAPHY

Detter, Ingrid. 2000. *The Law of War*, 2nd ed. Cambridge, U.K.: Cambridge University Press.

Neier, Aryeh. 1998. *War Crimes: Brutality, Genocide, Terror, and the Struggle for Justice*. New York: Times Books.

David Cohen

WAR OF 1898

The Spanish-American War of 1898 presented a series of opportunities and consequences for both nations. For example, Spanish historiographers have evaluated the war as a disaster after which Spain experienced decades of disarray and disorder. For Cuba, the Philippines, Hawaii, and Puerto Rico the year 1898 represented a transition from colony to nation status, although not without fierce opposition from resistance fighters such as Emilio Aguinaldo and leaders such as Queen Liliuokalani of Hawaii who fervently protested foreign encroachment on their sovereignty. Moreover, U.S. historians have debated whether to describe the war as an "accidental" conflict, a war for territorial expansion, or an inevitable war induced by public opinion. In the end, as "benevolent" victors, most Americans believed that they had acted as humanitarian benefactors on behalf of their neighbor Cuba.

A major cause of disarray on the island had been the appointment by Spain of Valeriano Weyler y Nicolau as the governor of Cuba in 1896, a period of heightened insurgency. His cruelty captured the attention of American newspapers dominated by William Randolph Hearst's sensationalist *New York Journal* (the Yellow Press). Governor Weyler disturbed humanitarian observers by establishing "reconcentration" camps that were designed to confine the peasants in detention facilities and thus isolate the insurgents, who theoretically would remain outside the quarantined areas. Although unintended, conditions in the camps caused the malnutrition of hundreds of thousands. The estimates of those who died from disease and hunger approach 321,934.

In 1898 a private letter written by the Spanish foreign minister, Enrique Dupuy de Lome, who was stationed in Washington, characterized U.S. President William McKinley as "a would be politician." Cuban revolutionaries intercepted the communiqué and offered it to the American print media. Portions of the infamous "de Lome letter" were published throughout the United States.

The primary event that justified going to war occurred in the middle of the controversy about Governor Weyler and the danger to American investments on the island. Americans labeled it "fiendish treachery" on February 15, 1898, when the American battleship *USS Maine* suddenly and without warning exploded in Havana Harbor. Out of a complement of 354 officers, 266 perished in the explosion. The *Maine* had been situated in what had been recognized as Spanish waters. The cause of the destruction of the *Maine* was uncertain. Nonetheless, on March 28 a report of the U.S. Naval Court of Inquiry determined that the explosion had been caused by a mine planted by Spanish operatives. On April 19, after a short period of deliberation, Congress voted for the immediate outbreak of hostilities against the Spanish forces in Cuba by a margin of 311 to 6 in the House and 42 to 35 in the Senate.

The first battle of the war occurred halfway across the world from Cuba, on the high seas in Manila Bay in the Philippines. The famous orders at Manila Bay to "fire when ready" were issued by the commander of the Asiatic Squadron, Commodore George Dewey. Dewey transferred the fleet from Hong Kong to the Philippines when briefings arrived on April 24. Dewey's strategy included the broadsiding of the Spanish fleet, which had been caught by surprise and ultimately proved obsolete compared with the U.S. fleet. In Cuba the American forces first landed at Guantánamo Bay and then at San Juan Hill (the site of Teddy Roosevelt's dangerous assault with the American volunteer force known as the Rough Riders), El Caney, and Santiago de Cuba. The Spanish surrendered at Santiago de Cuba on August 12. Overall, the United States lost 379 troops in combat and an estimated 5,000 as a result of disease and tropical conditions.

The war concluded with the Treaty of Paris, which was signed on December 10, 1898. The Cuban government was denied the opportunity or right to participate in the peace negotiations. Congress followed the cessation of hostilities with the Platt Amendment, guaranteeing the right of the United States to intervene militarily in Cuba any time internal disarray attracted its attention.

In the aftermath of the war the United States acquired Hawaii, Guam, the Philippines, Cuba, Puerto Rico, and the Wake Islands. Those territorial acquisitions allowed the United States to penetrate foreign markets, most importantly China, and end a decade of economic depression. The United States elected to maintain a naval station at Guantánamo Bay that proved to be a vital security installation. Securing Cuba had been a longtime priority because of its proximity to American shores and former control by a European government. President McKinley delivered the Imperial Gospel speech in 1899, in which he offered a justification for conquering foreign territories that seemed reasonable to business advocates,

the military, and imperialist patriots: "to uplift, civilize and Christianize them." Seemingly overnight America became a world colonial power.

SEE ALSO *Colonialism; Concentration Camps; Guantánamo Bay; Imperialism*

BIBLIOGRAPHY

Perez, Louis. 1998. *The War of 1898.* Chapel Hill: University of North Carolina Press.

Pratt, Julius W. 1951. *Expansionists of 1898: The Acquisition of Hawaii and the Spanish Islands.* New York: P. Smith.

Schoonover, Thomas. 2003. *Uncle Sam's War of 1898 and the Origins of Globalization.* Lexington: University Press of Kentucky.

Jonathan Jacobs

WAR ON DRUGS

SEE *Drug Traffic.*

WAR ON POVERTY

The war on poverty of the John F. Kennedy (1917–1963) and Lyndon B. Johnson (1908–1973) administrations grew out of the civil rights movement of the 1950s and continued from 1964 to 1981. It had antecedents, beginning with the 1941 state of the union address of President Franklin Delano Roosevelt (1882–1945), in which he enunciated "freedom from want" as one of four fundamental human rights. This pronouncement was taken as a program by Governor W. Averill Harriman (1891–1986) in New York state from 1954 to 1958.

A more direct antecedent had developed in New York City in 1946 at the Lafargue Psychiatric Clinic at the Saint Philip's Episcopal Church in Harlem, where Shelton Hale Bishop (1889–1962) served as rector. The clinic was named for Paul Lafargue (1842–1911), a medical doctor and the son-in-law of Karl Marx (1818–1883). Its director was psychiatrist Frederic Wertham (1895–1981). Thurgood Marshall (1908–1993) and Kenneth B. Clark (1914–2005) were members of this church. Wertham, Marshall, and Clark collaborated to help the NAACP win the 1954 U.S. Supreme Court case, *Brown v. Board of Education of Topeka*, which outlawed segregation in public schools.

MOBILIZATION FOR YOUTH

Three years later, an organization called Mobilization for Youth was incorporated on the Lower East Side of New York City by the Henry Street Settlement House with the collaboration of the Columbia University School of Social Work. In 1959 the National Institute of Mental Health (NIMH), which had just received increased allocations from Congress, provided a two-year planning grant, and Columbia sociologists Richard A. Cloward (1926–2001) and Lloyd Ohlin were retained as consultants. Cloward and Ohlin had developed an extension of Durkheim-Merton alienation/anomie opportunity theory in sociology, and in 1960 they published *Delinquency and Opportunity*, in which they argued that delinquents behaved in unapproved ways precisely because they had accepted approved social goals but found no socially approved means by which they could attain those goals, and so resorted to unapproved means. To motivate delinquents to adopt not only the goals but the approved means, opportunity must be provided. In support of this idea, Leonard S. Cottrell Jr. (1899–1985) of the Russell Sage Foundation testified on March 10, 1960, before a subcommittee of the House Appropriations Committee that delinquency was not so much a matter of curing sick individuals but of curing sick communities.

Mobilization for Youth's final planning report, "A Proposal for the Prevention and Control of Delinquency by Expanding Opportunity," was presented December 9, 1961, and was submitted to the NIMH for funding. The NIMH, the President's Committee on Juvenile Delinquency and Youth Crime (PCJDYC), the U.S. Department of Labor and other federal agencies, the New York City government, and the Ford Foundation subsequently funded Mobilization for Youth for $12.5 million for three more years. In April 1962 Mobilization for Youth submitted "Youth in the Ghetto: A Study of the Consequences of Powerlessness and a Blueprint for Change" to the PCJDYC review committee, headed by Cottrell. This committee recommended that one million dollars be granted to the program. The city of New York, under Mayor Robert Wagner (1910–1991), then allocated $3.5 million from its antipoverty funds. The Department of Labor under the Manpower Development and Training Act granted another half million dollars for job training aspects of the program. The initial directors were Cloward and George A. Brager (d. 2003).

In his first race for the office of New York City mayor in 1977, Edward Koch coined the terms *poverty pimp* and *povertician* to refer to Raymon Velez of the South Bronx. Velez, born in Puerto Rico in 1930, had developed beginning in 1968 a network of organizations in the South Bronx funded by the Office of Economic Opportunity (OEO). He had earned a BA in history and political science from Inter-American University of Puerto Rico, after which he became a school teacher. Immigrating to New York, Velez became a social worker. On the basis of his antipoverty network, which provided needed social services and jobs to residents of Puerto Rican neighborhoods,

he gained popularity and turned this social and economic success toward politics. Velez became the "boss" of South Bronx politics, securing the election of many Puerto Ricans to city, state, and federal office. In the 1980s he was elected to the New York City Council, a step downward in his estimation, and served only briefly. This evidently was a slap at Democratic primary opponent, Herman Badillo, whom Velez supported. The rise of Puerto Rican political power in the South Bronx was attained at the expense of Jewish politicians who previously had controlled the area. Changing demographics accounted for the transition.

THE FEDERAL ANTI-POVERTY PROGRAM OF THE KENNEDY-JOHNSON ADMINISTRATIONS

In the presidential election campaign of 1960, John F. Kennedy promised a "war against poverty and degradation" and "an economic drive on poverty" to address the high and persistent unemployment of the 1957–1958 and 1959–1960 recessions. His thought on this issue was based largely on John Kenneth Galbraith's (1908–2006) *The Affluent Society* (1958), especially chapter 23, "The New Position on Poverty." Upon Kennedy's election, the president's Council of Economic Advisors and the Budget Bureau immediately advocated a tax cut, accompanied by an increase in spending as a Keynesian economic remedy for the recession. The result would be a deliberate increase in the federal deficit. This was an attempt to establish Keynesian economic theory as a viable basis for government economic policy. The president accepted this advice.

The particular cabinet departments and programs involved in the spending increases and tax cuts were determined in other ways. In March 1961 Kennedy called a President's Conference on Juvenile Delinquency, chaired by his brother Robert F. Kennedy (1925–1968), the new attorney general. Based upon the recommendations of the March conference, the PCJDYC was established on May 11, 1961. The PCJDYC was to finance projects seeking a solution to juvenile delinquency. Robert Kennedy selected his friend David Hackett as executive director.

In September 1961 Congress passed the Juvenile Delinquency and Youth Offenses Act, which authorized demonstration and training programs in finding "the most effective ways of using total resources to combat juvenile delinquency in local communities." It authorized an expenditure of $10 million over three years for the program. In 1962 the committee gave planning grants to agencies in sixteen cities. The act also funded Mobilization for Youth in late 1961 to develop a plan of action to curb juvenile delinquency on New York's Lower East Side. Cloward then lent his principal assistant, sociologist James A. Jones (1932–1992), to Kenneth Clark to

design a similar program for Harlem. Clark and Jones in 1962 established Harlem Youth Unlimited Inc. (HARYOU), of which Jones became research director. Harlem Congressman Reverend Adam Clayton Powell Jr. (1908–1972), the new chairman of the House Education and Labor Committee, formed a rival Harlem organization, Associated Community Teams (ACT). He then insisted that HARYOU be merged with ACT, and when this was accomplished, Clark resigned. He was replaced by ACT executive director Livingston Wingate (1916–1995), Powell's assistant.

In December 1962 President Kennedy asked his Council of Economic Advisors chairman, Walter W. Heller (1915–1987), to pull together all available information on the poverty issue. Heller assigned this task to council member Robert J. Lampman (1920–1997). He and Heller suggested that Kennedy read socialist Michael Harrington's (1928–1989) *The Other America: Poverty in the United States* (1962), along with Leon Keyserling's (1908–1987) *Poverty and Depression in the United States* (1962). Harrington was considered a "responsible radical," because he was a follower of former Trotskist Max Schactman, whose tactic was to "bore from within." This meant that instead of running Socialist Party candidates for elective office, the party would support Democratic Party candidates. Harrington, thus, had been a well-known worker for left and liberal organizations and journals throughout the 1950s. In July 1959, he wrote an article on poverty for *Commentary Magazine,* and it was from this article that the book *The Other America* grew. In an approving commentary of Galbraith's book *The Affluent Society* (1958), he noted the existence of 50 million impoverished people in the United States, about one quarter of the total population. Poverty persisted from generation to generation, helped by what Oscar Lewis called a "culture of poverty," a non-Marxist idea. It was precisely this idea that recommended him to the Kennedy administration, because it undercut left leadership of the anti-poverty struggle. Harrington's entire body of work thus led to an eager anticipation of the book, and accounted for the wide extent of its positive reception. That he had worked for Catholic organizations did not hurt his acceptance by the president, even though he had lapsed from the faith by then. After Lampman reported that the U.S. poverty rate was increasing, Kennedy directed Heller to include a "war on poverty" in the 1964 White House legislative package for Congress.

On the day after Kennedy's November 22, 1963, assassination in Dallas, Heller met with President Johnson and suggested to him that a war against poverty might be a good way to begin his presidency. Johnson agreed. In his 1964 state of the union address, titled "The War on Poverty," he called on Congress to enact a package of measures embodying programs that would eliminate

poverty "in our lifetimes." On February 1, 1964, Johnson appointed Kennedy's brother-in-law and Peace Corps director Sargent Shriver to head a Task Force on Poverty.

THE EQUAL OPPORTUNITY ACT

David Hackett and Richard Boone of PCJDYC suggested that their community action model should be the vehicle for this war on poverty. Other departments proposed programs over which they had jurisdiction. At this point, the Budget Bureau, headed by economists Kermit Gordon (1916–1976) and Charles L. Schultze, became involved. Budget Bureau staff member William B. Cannon wrote a memorandum suggesting that the community action program begin with ten demonstration areas across the country, and that a development corporation be established in each. Schultze suggested similarly that poverty funds be allocated to "pockets of poverty," rather than uniformly across the country. He also suggested using the term *action program*, from Cannon's memo, rather than *development corporation*. Someone added *community* to *action program*, and the community action title of the proposed legislation was born. The task force developed the plans for an organization to conduct the "war on poverty," and submitted them to the president on March 15, 1964; he then disbanded the group. The next day, on the basis of the task force report, Johnson delivered a message to Congress calling upon it to enact legislation creating such an agency. He stated that the program would not consist of top-down planning from Washington, but would involve the talents of people from all over the country, at every level of society. He also called for the establishment of an office of equal opportunity. In testimony before Congress in 1964, Shriver listed 137 people who had participated in writing the legislation. On August 29, 1964, Congress passed, and Johnson signed into law, the Equal Opportunity Act of 1964. The act created the OEO, and on August 30, 1964, Congress gave the OEO $947.7 million for ten programs.

The OEO was initially lodged in the Office of the President, but subsequently became an independent agency. Shriver was named director of the OEO and served until 1968. Economist and AFL-CIO lobbyist Hyman H. Bookbinder, a member of Shriver's 1964 task force, became associate director.

The Equal Opportunity Act also created an OEO Advisory Committee of fourteen, which was appointed by President Johnson on January 29, 1965. Perhaps the most important arm of the OEO administrative structure, although it had no program responsibilities, was the Office of Research, Plans, Programs, and Evaluation, which might be called the "war room" of the war on poverty. Here were placed those economists who had actual experience in administering economic planning.

The first director of this office was Joseph A. Kershaw (1913–1978), who served from 1964 to 1966. He was succeeded by Robert A. Levine (1966), Robinson G. Hollister (1966–1968), and Walter Williams (1968–1969). Levine attempted to establish a five-year plan to end poverty that proposed a national negative income tax program to replace Aid to Families with Dependent Children (AFDC). The OEO funded the New Jersey Negative Income Tax demonstration project to estimate the cost of the program.

The war on poverty required for its success a definition of poverty and a means of measuring it. In March 1965, Kershaw and the Office of Research, Plans, Programs, and Evaluation used the work of economist Mollie Orshansky of the Social Security Administration to establish such a definition. Two months later, the OEO officially adopted the Orshansky poverty thresholds as a working definition of poverty.

The unique feature of the Equal Opportunity Act was Title II: the Rural and Urban Community Action Program. The OEO divided the country into seven to ten regions, each with a regional director. Fieldworkers in the Washington headquarters traveled to regions to help establish and monitor the operation of community action agencies located in the major cities of each region. In addition, the OEO funded national organizations to facilitate theoretical and empirical research on the issue of poverty. Chief among these were the Harvard-MIT Joint Center for Urban Studies, the National Association for Community Economic Development, the Institute for Research on Poverty, the Urban Institute, the Center for Community Economic Development, and the National Rural Center.

THE INSTITUTE FOR RESEARCH ON POVERTY

The Institute for Research on Poverty was established at the University of Wisconsin by Lampman, who was considered the leading expert on the economics of poverty. Its first director was Harold W. Watts (1966–1971). By 1985, with the OEO no longer in existence, oversight of the Institute for Research on Poverty had shifted to the assistant secretary of Health and Human Services for Planning and Evaluation. By 1996 the institute was no longer the national poverty center, but only one among several area poverty centers. The Center for Community Economic Development in Cambridge, Massachusetts, was codirected in 1971 by Geoffrey P. Faux, who had been director of the OEO Economic Development Division from 1967 to 1970. The National Rural Center was established in 1975, with F. Ray Marshall as president and director. When President Jimmy Carter named Marshall his secretary of labor in 1977, John M. Cornman replaced him.

Half of the OEO's community action program funds went to prepackaged national programs such as Head Start. The other half went to local initiative programs developed by the community action agencies themselves.

New York City, where the theory and operational model for the war on poverty had been developed, now received feedback from the federal government. In 1962 Mayor Wagner had created a Council on Poverty and an Anti-poverty Operations Board. Surgeon Arthur C. Logan (1909–1973) was the first chairman of the community action program under Wagner. Wagner was defeated in 1965 by former congressman John V. Lindsay (1921–2000), who in 1966 established a Mayor's Task Force on Poverty, headed by Mitchell Sviridoff (1918–2000). The task force recommended the establishment of a superagency comprised of all agencies having any responsibility for providing services to the poor. On September 15, 1966, Lindsay established the Human Resources Administration, which included the Community Development Agency and the Manpower and Career Development Agency, among other agencies. The Community Development Agency was designated the New York City community action agency under the OEO. Sviridoff served as head of the Human Resources Administration from 1966 to 1967.

New York's Community Development Agency was headed by George Nicolau from 1966 to 1967. He was replaced by Major Owens in 1968, and Owens served until 1973. In 1968 the agency wrote a grant proposal to NIMH for a Brownsville Community Council economic advocacy planning project. The NIMH funded the proposal, its first grant to a community action agency to conduct economic advocacy planning, and the Brownsville Advocacy Planning Agency was born. The agency's staff included graduate students in economics from Yale and Columbia universities.

A participant in the 1949 founding of the NIMH, and a member of its advisory board at the time of this grant, was Eli Ginzberg (1911–2002), director of the Conservation of Human Resources Project of Columbia Business School. His staff at Columbia in 1956 consisted of two economists and four psychologists and social psychologists. The grant to the Brownsville Community Council was a departure, as advocacy planning was developed largely by architects and city planners. Columbia's School of Architecture, for example, was responsible for the creation of the Architect's Renovation Committee of Harlem and the East Harlem Studio of the Real Great Society Uptown. In the 1950s the NIMH had established a unit to finance outside research. In response to Johnson's war on poverty, the NIMH established centers for minority group and urban mental health problems. It was the conjuncture of these institutions and forces that enabled the grant to the Brownsville Community Council in 1968.

Robert Kennedy resigned as attorney general and was elected senator from New York in 1964. In 1966 he and Jacob Javits (1904–1986), the senior senator from New York, introduced the Kennedy-Javits Amendment to the Equal Opportunity Act, creating a new Title I-D, the special impact program (SIP). This title caused a shift in the OEO toward community-controlled business development through community development corporations. The community development corporations were designed as community holding companies or community trusts. To administer the new program, the OEO established the Economic Development Division, under which the Bedford-Stuyvesant Restoration Corporation in Brooklyn, New York, and the Hough Area Development Corporation in Cleveland, Ohio, were funded in 1966 as the first two community development corporations in the nation.

In 1967 the Edith Green Amendment placed a ceiling of 33 percent for representatives of the poor on a city's community action agency. In the meantime, Kenneth Clark in 1967 founded the Metropolitan Applied Research Center and served as president until 1975. The Metropolitan Applied Research Center received a grant of $190,000 from the Field Foundation. In 1970 the center and Howard University, with an $860,000 Ford Foundation grant, established the Joint Center for Political Studies in Washington, D.C., with Howard law professor Frank D. Reeves (1916–1973) as director.

From 1968 to 1969, New York's community action program guidelines made advocacy planning the highest project-funding priority, leading to the funding of the Pratt Institute's Center for Community Development; Harlem Commonwealth Council's (HCC) Commonwealth Holding Company, Inc., a subsidiary, with the Black Economic Research Center in Harlem as a major consultant; and the Brownsville Advocacy Planning Agency. These organizations were intended to provide economic expertise and advocacy for their respective communities in dealing with the City Planning Commission and other relevant city, state, and federal agencies in developing and locating commercial, industrial, and service enterprises.

The Ford Foundation, a major partner of the federal and city governments in the war on poverty, provided grants for advocacy planning to the Black Economic Research Center from 1968 through 1980. The center developed the theory that the major economic problem of black Americans was not labor market inequality but capital market inequality, which included access to the major stock and commodity exchanges, as well as to the Treasury Department, which represented capital interests, on a communal basis. Current capital reallocation was necessary, and the first stage of such a transfer was social capi-

tal, including infrastructure, and educational facilities with financing for operations.

Current income redistribution was also deemed necessary, along with future nondiscrimination in markets to maintain the gains achieved. These developments were a direct confrontation of the theory upon which the war on poverty was based—that a change of unmeasurable internal states of being could result in a measurable diminution of poverty in a finite and short period. It also confronted the theories of economists Gary S. Becker, Theodore Schultz (1902–1998), and Milton Friedman (1912–2006), which defined lifetime earnings as capital stock, human capital, and focused on future income distribution and not current income redistribution. This polemic was one of the sources for the development of the reparations argument in the black community. Reparations as a large lump sum would enable the purchase of capital assets by the residents of black communities, and avoid the necessity for politically impossible capital expropriation. This concept, which had been a tenet of black nationalist doctrine since the 1920s, began to gain academic and social respectability at the Black Economic Development Conference in Detroit in 1969.

DEVELOPMENTS UNDER NIXON AND LATER ADMINISTRATIONS

The election of Richard M. Nixon (1913–1994) as president in 1968 heralded the demise of the OEO and the war on poverty. In April 1969, Donald H. Rumsfeld was appointed OEO director with the charge to dismantle the agency. He selected Richard B. Cheney as his assistant. Howard Phillips was appointed as OEO director in 1973 to succeed Rumsfeld. However, court decisions forced the administration to expend the funds appropriated, because the Equal Opportunity Act had a ten-year life by law. In 1970 amendments to the Equal Opportunity Act created SIP Title VII. Title VII funds went to, among other entities, the Federation of Southern Cooperatives, which created surplus-earning entities in rural areas of southern states. OEO programs were transferred to the Department of Health, Education, and Welfare, and to the Department of Labor. By the time Nixon resigned on August 8, 1974, the war on poverty was essentially over.

The coup de grâce occurred from 1974 to 1976 during the Gerald R. Ford (1913–2006) administration. Funding for OEO programs could now be legally cut, and the OEO was actually abolished by the Headstart, Economic Opportunity, and Community Partnership Act of January 4, 1975, which created the Community Services Administration (CSA), the name suggesting a retreat from community action by citizens to government provision of services to citizens in communities. For the horizontal relationships among equal citizens uniting to achieve a commonly determined purpose at the neighborhood level was substituted the old vertically hierarchical relationship between the rulers and the ruled.

From 1977 to 1981 the Carter administration attempted to resurrect the war on poverty by increasing funding for the CSA and enacting legislation expanding the SIP emphasis. Chief among the new institutions established by Congress was the National Consumer Cooperative Bank, signed into law in 1978 and opened for business in 1980, and the Rural Development Loan Fund, established in 1981. Both had boards of directors consisting of representatives elected by residents of low-income communities. The National Consumer Cooperative Bank made federally subsidized below-market-rate loans to consumer and producer cooperatives in largely urban areas. From the Community Economic Development Act of 1981, the Rural Development Loan Fund was to consist of all remaining funds from Part A of Title III of the Equal Opportunity Act and the funds from Title VII community development credit unions. It was located in the CSA, and provided one-percent interest rate loans for rural business purposes.

The OEO, the Rockefeller Brothers Fund, and the Ford Foundation had earlier financed the development of the idea for these financial institutions. Edward K. Hamilton and Belden Hull were hired as consultants by the National Rural Center and the Opportunity Funding Corporation (established in 1970) to design the bank as an experiment in development finance. The Opportunity Funding Corporation was an OEO demonstration project in community capital development, led by John Gloster, a former Atlanta insurance executive. The National Rural Center invited experts from Europe, Canada, and the United States to a conference at the University of Wisconsin to provide ideas on a design. The final design drew upon the Treasury Department's new Federal Financing Bank, established in 1973. This design was negotiated largely at the Treasury Department with an interagency task force appointed by President Carter.

With Carter's defeat by Ronald Reagan (1911–2004) after one term, however, the fate of the war on poverty was sealed. The Equal Opportunity Act was repealed on October 1, 1981. The Community Development Block Grant was established in 1981, ensuring that federal funds would not go directly to neighborhoods but would be filtered through established political groups at the state and municipal levels. Then CSA was abolished, although the Rural Development Loan Fund was allowed to remain.

Despite these developments, the national advocacy groups for community development corporations continued the battle against poverty, financed as before the war on poverty by religious organizations, universities, private foundations, and unsystematically by federal, state, and

local government. The war on poverty had degenerated from a massed frontal assault into a guerrilla war. In addition, the surpluses generated from the operation of community development corporations and cooperatives were plowed back into operations to help finance operations and expand capital equipment. And the national financial institutions still existed. As of 2005, at least 80 percent of counties in the United States still had community action agencies or community development corporations.

CONCLUSION

The war on poverty involved socially well-placed individuals using social science ideas to create new institutions in low-income communities, and at the national level to assist these local institutions. These individuals and institutions then engaged in actions that created historic events. The social science ideas reflected Keynesian economic theory, as well as opportunity theory in sociology and social psychology, and the political science theory of urban politics that maintained that urban neighborhood communities should be self-governing, independent political entities.

The new institutions created were, at the first level, community social service agencies in poor communities. The organizations responsible for these creations were private religious organizations, universities, and foundations. Using these community organizations as models, the federal, state, and local governments transformed their structures to replicate those of the private social service agencies for these functions, and wrote these changes into law. These practices thereby became obligatory for the nation as a whole and, importantly, became familiar to the large portion of the electorate who were neither poor nor involved in service to the poor.

SEE ALSO *Culture of Poverty; Great Society, The; Johnson, Lyndon B.; New Deal, The; Poverty; Poverty, Indices of; Roosevelt, Franklin D.; Welfare State*

BIBLIOGRAPHY

Altshuler, Alan A. 1970. *Community Control: The Black Demand for Participation in Large American Cities.* Indianapolis, IN: Pegasus.

Aponte-Parés, Luis. 1998. Lessons from El Barrio—The East Harlem Real Great Society/Urban Planning Studio: A Puerto Rican Chapter in the Fight for Urban Self-determination. *New Political Science* 20 (4): 399–420.

Beck, Bertram M. 1969. Organizing Community Action. *Proceedings of the Academy of Political Science* 29 (4): 162–178.

Bellush, Jewel, and Stephen M. David. 1972. *Race and Politics in New York City: Five Studies in Policy-Making.* New York: Praeger.

Brager, George A., and Francis P. Purcell, eds. 1967. *Community Action against Poverty: Readings from the Mobilization Experience.* New Haven, CT: College and University Press.

Clark, Kenneth B. 1965. *Dark Ghetto: Dilemmas of Social Power.* New York. Harper & Row.

Clark, Kenneth B. 2006. *Notable New Yorkers: Kenneth Clark.* Columbia University Libraries Oral History Research Office. http://www.columbia.edu/cu/lweb/digital/collections/nny/clarkk/index.html.

Dentler, Robert A. 1973. Eulogy on a Laboratory: The Center for Urban Education. *Urban Review* 6 (5–6): 3–7.

Domhoff, G. William. 2005. The Ford Foundation in the Inner City: Forging an Alliance with Neighborhood Activists. *Who Rules America?* http://sociology.ucsc.edu/whorulesamerica/power/ford_foundation.html.

Eisenberg, Pablo. 2000. Time to Remove the Rose-Colored Glasses. National Housing Institute 25th Anniversary Essays. *Shelterforce* online 110 (March/April). http://www.nhi.org/online/issues/110/eisenberg.html.

Elsberry, James W. 1972. EDO 92637: A Final Report of the Brownsville Community Council's Advocacy Planning Unit. ERIC (Educational Resources Information Center).

Farmer, James. [1985] 1998. *Lay Bare the Heart: An Autobiography of the Civil Rights Movement* (chap. 28). Fort Worth: Texas Christian University Press.

Fisher, Gordon M. 1992. The Development of the Orshansky Poverty Thresholds and Their Subsequent History as the Official U.S. Poverty Measure. Poverty Measurement Working Paper. U.S. Census Bureau. *Social Security Bulletin* 55 (4): 3–14.

Fisher, Gordon M. 2000. *Reasons for Measuring Poverty in the United States in the Context of Public Policy: A Historical Review, 1916–1995.* 1999; rev. 2000. Washington, DC: U.S. Department of Health and Human Services. http://aspe.hhs.gov/poverty/papers/reasmeaspov.htm.

Hamilton, Charles V. 1991. *Adam Clayton Powell, Jr.: The Political Biography of an American Dilemma.* New York. Atheneum.

Harrington, Michael. 1962. *The Other America: Poverty in the United States.* New York: Macmillan.

Henry Street Settlement Records. Social Welfare History Archives. University of Minnesota Libraries, Minneapolis.

Johnson, Lyndon B. 1967. Statement by the President Upon Appointing the National Advisory Council on Economic Opportunity, March 4. American Presidency Project, John Woolley and Gerhard Peters, eds. Santa Barbara: University of California. http://www.presidency.ucsb.edu/ws/index.php?pid=28679.

Kershaw, Joseph A. 1970. *Government against Poverty.* Washington, DC: Brookings Institution.

Kremen, Gladys Roth. 1974. *MDTA: The Origins of the Manpower Development and Training Act of 1962.* Washington, DC: U.S. Department of Labor, History Office. http://www.dol.gov/oasam/programs/history/mono-mdtatext.htm.

Levine, Robert A. 1974. Gift of Personal Statement to the Lyndon Baines Johnson Library, September 30.

Levine, Robert A., Harold Watts, Walter Williams, et al. 2004. A Retrospective on the Negative Income Tax Experiments: Looking Back at the Most Innovative Field Studies in Social Policy. USBIG Discussion Paper 86.

Levitan, Sar A. 1969. The Community Action Program: A Strategy to Fight Poverty. *Annals of the American Academy of Political and Social Science* 385 (1): 63–75.

Meier, August, and Elliott Rudwick. [1973] 1975. *CORE: A Study in the Civil Rights Movement, 1942–1968.* Urbana: University of Illinois Press.

Mitchell, Todd, and Stuart J. Eisendraft. 2002. Community and Migrant Health Centers. In *Encyclopedia of Public Health*, ed. Lester Breslow. New York: Macmillan.

Montagna, Joseph A. 2006. *Urban Renewal in New Haven.* New Haven, CT: Yale-New Haven Teachers' Institute.

Moynihan, Daniel P. 1970. *Maximum Feasible Misunderstanding: Community Action in the War on Poverty.* New York: Free Press.

Myers, Jim. 2002. RFK's Childhood Pal Carries On—Alone: David Hackett's Commission on Delinquency and Youth Crime Faded, But His Ideas and His Ideals Didn't. *Youth Today* 11 (3). http://www.youthtoday.org/youthtoday/aajune2002/story2.html.

Perry, Stewart E. 1987. *Communities on the Way: Rebuilding Local Economies in the United States and Canada.* Albany: State University of New York Press.

Pogrebin, Robin. 1995. Saying Farewell to Roy Wingate. *City Weekly*, July 11.

Pritchett, Wendell E. 2001. The Brownsville Community Council and the Politics of Black Power. Paper presented at the Annual Conference of the Organization of American Historians, Los Angeles, April 24.

Putnam, Israel. [1970] 1976. Poverty Thresholds: Their History and Future Development. In *Documentation of Background Information and Rationale for Current Poverty Matrix*, comp. Mollie Orshansky, 272–278. Washington, DC: U.S. Department of Health, Education, and Welfare.

Report on Juvenile Delinquency. 1960. Hearings before the Subcommittee of the Committee on Appropriations, House of Representatives, Eighty-Sixth Congress, Second Session. Washington, DC: U.S. Government Printing Office.

Saxton, Wolfgang. 1995. Livingston Leroy Wingate, 79, Judge and Harlem Civic Leader. *New York Times*, June 2.

Schlesinger, Arthur M., Jr. 1965. *A Thousand Days: John F. Kennedy in the White House.* Boston: Houghton Mifflin.

Schwartz, Joel H. 1985. Tenant Power in the Liberal City, 1943–1971. Chap. 4 in *The Tenant Movement in New York City, 1904–1984*, ed. Ronald Lawson. New Brunswick, NJ: Rutgers University Press.

Smith, Muriel. 1973. Community Development in New York City. *Community Development Journal* 8 (3): 139–144.

Sundquist, James L., ed. 1969. *On Fighting Poverty: Perspectives from Experience.* New York. Basic Books.

Taylor, Jessamy. 2004. The Fundamentals of Community Health Centers. National Health Policy Forum: Background Paper. http://www.gwumc.edu/sphhs/healthpolicy/ggprogram/BP_CHC_08-31-04.pdf.

Time. 1965. Poor No More. 86 (25) December 17.

Union Settlement Association Records. Rare Books and Manuscripts Division. Columbia University Libraries, New York.

Julian Ellison

WARFARE, NUCLEAR

Nuclear warfare consists of armed conflict between states in which one or more sides employ nuclear weapons. Because no war since World War II has involved nuclear weapons, how such a conflict would be triggered and executed is largely a matter of theoretical speculation. Furthermore, the sophistication and destructive scale of the nuclear weapons used against Japan pale in comparison to modern weapons. A nuclear war between two nuclear states would result in the deaths of hundreds of thousands, if not millions, of people. The areas surrounding locations hit with nuclear weapons would be highly contaminated with radioactive fallout. In addition, depending on the number of weapons used, such a war could have long-term devastating effects on the earth's ecosystems and atmosphere. Because today only a few countries possess nuclear weapons, the number of conflicts that could conceivably escalate to nuclear war is limited. These countries include the United States, Russia, China, Great Britain, France, Israel, Pakistan, India, and most likely North Korea. Proliferation to additional countries remains a continual problem for international security.

The destructive power of nuclear weapons makes nuclear warfare fundamentally different from traditional conventional warfare. The single fifteen-kiloton bomb dropped on Hiroshima, for example, destroyed 80 percent of the city, immediately killing between 66,000 and 80,000 people and injuring roughly 70,000. As Wilfred Burchett (1945), the first journalist to report on the devastation, put it: "Hiroshima does not look like a bombed city. It looks as if a monster steamroller has passed over it and squashed it out of existence." The city of Hiroshima estimates that the total killed from the explosion and subsequent radiation poisoning is over 240,000. Nagasaki saw high casualties as well, with 39,000 immediately killed and 25,000 injured, and many others who later died due to radiation poisoning.

How nuclear weapons would be used in war, and whether a nuclear war between two nuclear powers could even be won, has been a central problem facing military strategists and planners. Because of the devastating effects of nuclear weapons, they are less useful in battle than conventional weapons. However, because such weapons exist and because no country can be sure of what another's

intentions would be in the event that they were to gain a dominant nuclear advantage, the major nuclear powers have continued to develop nuclear war strategies. That said, nuclear powers have shown extreme caution when conflict develops with other nuclear powers, out of fear that a minor crisis could escalate into an unwanted nuclear war; this was displayed during the 1962 Cuban missile crisis. Nuclear powers have also been reluctant to use their nuclear capabilities in conflicts against a non-nuclear power, as with the United States in Vietnam or Israel in its 1973 war with Egypt and Syria.

COUNTERFORCE, COUNTERVALUE, AND MUTUAL ASSURED DESTRUCTION

Nuclear strategy makes distinctions between *counterforce* and *countervalue*. Counterforce strategies are intended to affect an opponent's capabilities, whereas countervalue capabilities affect an opponent's will. Counterforce targets an opponent's armed forces and military-industrial installations, limiting the opponent's ability to retaliate in a counterattack. A country that struck first in a nuclear war would most likely employ a counterforce targeting strategy. Countervalue strategies target an opponent's cities—that is, things of human and emotional value. A country that feared a nuclear attack by an opponent would threaten a countervalue retaliation with the hope that even the possibility of its opponent losing one city would be enough to deter a nuclear first strike. Of course, for a countervalue deterrent to be effective, the country being deterred must believe that at least some of its opponent's nuclear arsenal would survive a first strike. It also must believe that the damage that that remaining arsenal could deliver would outweigh the benefits gained from striking first. With nuclear weapons it is oftentimes difficult to distinguish between what constitutes a counterforce and what constitutes a countervalue target. Military targets are often found in population centers and given the large radius of damage caused by a nuclear attack it is extremely difficult to target the one without hitting the other. For example, when U.S. war planners began looking for military-industrial targets across the Soviet Union after 1945, every sizeable Soviet city was deemed to contain military targets.

The logic behind counterforce and countervalue, as well as first-strike versus second-strike capabilities, is encompassed in the idea of *mutual assured destruction* (MAD). MAD describes a state of affairs in which both sides' nuclear forces are such that a sufficient percent would remain after an attack that it would still be possible to bring about the near total destruction of the attacking state. The hope of MAD was that this mutual suicide pact would prevent either side from ever being tempted to use nuclear weapons. In order for MAD to be viable, however,

it required the United States and the Soviet Union to stockpile large quantities of nuclear weapons and to develop targeting lists of single targets that would be hit multiple times. In addition, U.S. and Soviet force structures were designed to survive a possible first strike. Achieving this involved spending on difficult-to-target nuclear forces, such as submarines, hardened missile silos, and continually in-flight bomber fleets.

MAINTAINING A STRATEGIC BALANCE

Those who wanted to maintain a strategic nuclear balance put emphasis on developing less-accurate, single large warheads that would be unable to hit anything smaller than area targets. Such missiles would be effective against countervalue targets, which do not require precise accuracy to be effective; but would be less effective hitting silos or airfields.

It was feared, however, that a number of innovations and weapons systems could disrupt this strategic balance. Such a disruption could lead one side to perceive a "window of opportunity" in which they would be tempted to launch a preventive war before new technological innovations either restored the balance or shifted first-strike advantage to the opponent. For example, declarations of "bomber gaps" or "missile gaps" by United States politicians, particularly in the late 1950s and early 1960s, led many to fear that (alleged) Soviet advantage could lead to a devastating first strike. The development of multiple independently targeted reentry vehicles (MIRVs), which are intercontinental ballistic missiles (ICBMs) carrying multiple warheads that can be individually programmed to hit separate targets, was also seen as destabilizing, as one missile could target multiple ICBM silos. This offensive advantage, it was feared, could tempt one country to launch a preemptive attack out of fear that it would suffer a debilitating blow if it were not the one to attack first.

Another potential innovation capable of disrupting strategic balance is some form of missile defense system. While an effective missile defense system could protect a country from nuclear annihilation, it would also provide it with an overwhelming first-strike advantage, as its opponent would be unable to retaliate, regardless of the number of surviving nuclear forces. There would also be an incentive to strike sooner rather than later, as military history has shown that all defenses are eventually penetrable.

Arms control agreements between the United States and the Soviet Union during the Cold War were primarily designed to stabilize the strategic balance between the two sides. By limiting each side's ability to gain first-strike advantage, the hope was that neither side would be tempted to carry out a preemptive first strike. The Anti-Ballistic Missile (ABM) Treaty, Strategic Arms Limitation Talks

(SALT I and II), the Strategic Arms Reduction Treaties (START I and II), and the Strategic Offensive Reduction Treaty (SORT) were all designed to provide a framework in which the United States and the Soviet Union (now Russia) could maintain a nuclear balance without engaging in a costly and potentially dangerous arms race.

CURRENT CONCERNS AND FEARS

Since the end of the Cold War, fears of a nuclear exchange between the United States and Russia have subsided. However, a number of concerns still remain. India and Pakistan, which both officially declared their nuclear status with a series of tests in 1997, have a long history of conflict, specifically over the contested Kashmir region. This history of conflict, their contingent border, and an underdeveloped command and control system, make a nuclear exchange (either intentional or accidental) a very real possibility.

It is also feared that a "rogue" state could develop a nuclear weapon and be able to hold the world hostage by threatening to use it against a major world city if its demands were not met. While the world could easily retaliate if such a threat were carried out, the question remains whether there would be a willingness to risk giving up an important city in the first place. It is this potentiality that has led world leaders to take aggressive stances (with mixed success) against such potential proliferators as North Korea, Iraq, Iran, and Libya.

The final fear is that a terrorist organization would be able to acquire a nuclear device by stealing, buying, or being given it from a country's arsenal. This is a particularly difficult scenario because normal countervalue threats would not have a very strong deterrent effect on a small, decentralized, apocalyptic terrorist organization.

SEE ALSO *Cold War; Defense; Defense, National; Deterrence, Mutual; Disarmament; Proliferation, Nuclear; World War II*

BIBLIOGRAPHY

Allison, Graham T. 2004. *Nuclear Terrorism: The Ultimate Preventable Catastrophe.* New York: Times Books.

Burchett, Wilfred. 1945. The Atomic Plague. *London Daily Express*, September 4.

Larsen, Jeffrey A., and James M. Smith, eds. 2005. *Historical Dictionary of Arms Control and Disarmament.* Lanham, MD: Scarecrow Press.

Paul, T. V. 1995. Nuclear Taboo and War Initiation in Regional Conflicts. *Journal of Conflict Resolution* 39 (4): 696–717.

Quester, George H. 2000. *Nuclear Monopoly.* New Brunswick, NJ: Transaction Publishers.

Schelling, Thomas C. 1966. *Arms and Influence.* New Haven, CT: Yale University Press.

Waltz, Kenneth N. 1990. Nuclear Myths and Political Realities. *American Political Science Review* 84 (3): 731–745.

York, Herbert F. 1970. ABM, MIRV, and the Arms Race. *Science* 169 (3942): 257–260.

David R. Andersen

WARREN, EARL
1891–1974

As the fourteenth Chief Justice of the United States, Earl Warren presided over a Supreme Court that handed down landmark rulings in the areas of race relations, school prayer, political representation, and criminal justice. Warren was born to Scandinavian immigrants in Los Angeles, California, on March 19, 1891. He was raised in Bakersfield, where his father worked for the Southern Pacific Railroad, and he himself worked a variety of summer jobs with the railroad. He put himself through school, earning both his undergraduate and law degrees at the University of California at Berkeley.

Warren began his political career as the district attorney of Alameda County, California. He went on to serve as California's attorney general, and in 1942 he was elected governor. During his state service, Warren supported the evacuation of persons of Japanese ancestry from the West Coast during World War II. Throughout the remainder of his political career, Warren publicly defended his action, which stands in stark contrast to his role as one of the staunchest civil libertarians ever to serve on the U.S. Supreme Court.

Warren sought the Republican presidential nomination in 1948 and 1952. In 1948 he was chosen as Thomas Dewey's running mate, but the Dewey–Warren ticket was defeated. In 1952, the Republican nomination, and the presidency, went to General Dwight D. Eisenhower. Following the unexpected death of Chief Justice Fred Vinson in the summer of 1953, President Eisenhower appointed Warren to fill the vacancy.

On the Supreme Court's docket for the 1953 term was *Brown v. Board of Education*, a group of cases challenging the racial segregation of public primary and secondary schools. At the time, one-third of the states and the District of Columbia maintained segregated schools by law, often with vast disparities in school funding and facilities for black and white students. The Warren Court handed down a unanimous ruling in the *Brown* cases in May 1954, declaring that "separate educational facilities are inherently unequal." A year later, in *Brown II*, the Court ordered that public schools be desegregated "with all deliberate speed." In subsequent decisions, the Warren Court struck down racial segregation in public buildings, transportation, housing, and recreational facilities. The

Brown decisions were not the only Warren Court rulings that impacted public education. In *Engel v. Vitale* (1962) and *Abington School District v. Schempp* (1963), the Court ruled that state-sponsored prayer and Bible reading in public schools were establishments of religion in violation of the Constitution.

During the 1960s the Warren Court instituted a constitutional revolution in criminal justice. In a series of decisions, the Court used the Fourteenth Amendment to apply many of the guarantees of the Bill of Rights—the protections against self-incrimination and double jeopardy, the right to counsel, the right to a jury trial and to confront witnesses—to the states. Some of these protections were encapsulated in what became known as the Miranda warnings. According to the Court's decision in *Miranda v. Arizona*, criminal suspects who are in custody must be informed of their constitutional rights, and they must waive those rights before any questioning may occur.

The Warren Court significantly altered the system of political representation in the United States as well. The first half of the twentieth century saw substantial population shifts from rural to urban areas, yet many state legislatures did not redraw representational districts to reflect these shifts. In a previous decision the Court had declined to address the apportionment issue, describing it as a "political thicket" that the Court should avoid. But in its 1962 ruling in *Baker v. Carr*, the Court rejected this reasoning, opening the door to a series of decisions establishing the "one person, one vote" principle for political representation and applying this principle at the congressional, state, and local levels. After leaving the Court, Warren described *Baker v. Carr* as the most important decision handed down during his tenure.

Warren resigned from the Court in 1969 and was replaced as Chief Justice by Warren E. Burger. He died on July 9, 1974, following a series of heart attacks, and was buried in Arlington National Cemetery.

SEE ALSO Brown v. Board of Education, *1954;* Brown v. Board of Education, *1955; Civil Liberties; Concentration Camps; Eisenhower, Dwight D.; Incarceration, Japanese American; Judicial Review; Supreme Court, U.S.; Warren Report*

BIBLIOGRAPHY

Cray, Ed. 1997. *Chief Justice: A Biography of Earl Warren.* New York: Simon & Schuster.

Schwartz, Bernard. 1983. *Super Chief, Earl Warren and His Supreme Court: A Judicial Biography.* New York: New York University Press.

Malia Reddick

WARREN REPORT

Warren Report is the abbreviated, unofficial name of the Report of the President's Commission on the Assassination of President John F. Kennedy. This commission's unofficial, commonly used name is the Warren Commission because it was chaired by Earl Warren, chief justice of the U.S. Supreme Court. President Kennedy was assassinated in Dallas, Texas, on November 22, 1963. President Lyndon B. Johnson established the Warren Commission on November 29, 1963. The Warren Report was published on September 27, 1964.

Shortly after Kennedy's assassination, there was widespread speculation that Kennedy's assassination was the result of a conspiracy, probably involving the Communist governments of Cuba and/or the Soviet Union. President Johnson was concerned that widely held conspiracy beliefs might undermine the legitimacy of the American presidency and detrimentally affect American foreign policy. Johnson hoped that a presidential commission that carefully investigated Kennedy's assassination and published a well-researched conclusion would dismiss or discourage irresponsible, groundless, alternative explanations of Kennedy's assassination. He assumed that the public credibility of the Warren Commission's investigation and report depended on the objectivity, integrity, and expertise of the commission's members.

Consequently, Johnson appointed Democrats and Republicans, current or former members of all three branches of the U.S. government, and senators and representatives to the commission. With Chief Justice Warren as its chairman, the commission also included Democratic Representative Hale Boggs of Louisiana, Republican Representative Gerald R. Ford of Michigan, former World Bank president and Kennedy adviser John McCloy, former CIA director Allen W. Dulles, Democratic Senator Richard Russell of Georgia, and Republican Senator John Sherman Cooper of Kentucky. During its ten-month investigation, the Warren Commission received testimony from 552 witnesses, reports from the FBI, CIA, Secret Service, and other federal agencies, tests on ballistics, and information from officials in Texas.

The major finding of the Warren Report was that Kennedy's assassination was not the result of a conspiracy. The report found that Lee Harvey Oswald acted alone in killing Kennedy and wounding Governor John Connally of Texas. The report concluded that Oswald fired three bullets from the Texas School Book Depository. One bullet hit Kennedy in the back, went through his throat, and struck Connally. A second bullet fatally struck Kennedy in the head. A third bullet missed Kennedy's car entirely.

The Warren Report also stated that there was no evidence to prove that there was a second gunman who shot at the motorcade from a different location. The report

rejected the idea that Jack Ruby, who shot and killed Oswald shortly after Oswald's arrest, was part of a conspiracy to silence Oswald. Chapter 8 of the Warren Report detailed what the commission regarded as lax, inadequate, and outdated practices by the Secret Service in planning and protecting Kennedy's trip to Dallas. In particular, the report noted the Secret Service's use of its outdated security plan for Franklin D. Roosevelt's 1936 visit to Dallas as the basis for Kennedy's visit, its inadequate coordination with Dallas officials in planning and conducting security for Kennedy's visit, and the lack of a bulletproof cover for Kennedy's car in Dallas. The Secret Service also failed to thoroughly search all buildings, rooftops, and windows along the motorcade route before the motorcade began.

By the late 1960s, independent researchers and the American public increasingly doubted the findings of the Warren Report, especially its "lone gunman" and "single bullet" theories. The first two well-known books challenging the Warren Report were Edward J. Epstein's *Inquest* and Mark Lane's *Rush to Judgment*, both published in 1966. Lane's book was also made into a documentary. Epstein especially challenged the feasibility of the "single bullet" and "lone gunman" theories, and Lane asserted that Oswald did not assassinate Kennedy. In general, both books criticized the Warren Commission for intentionally ignoring or rejecting important evidence that threatened its anticonspiracy bias.

By the 1970s, with the Watergate scandals and Richard M. Nixon's forced resignation from the presidency, more Americans were willing to believe that government officials and agencies, especially the military, FBI, and CIA, engaged in conspiracies, cover-ups, and abuses of power. The congressional investigation of Watergate was followed by highly publicized congressional investigations of the FBI and CIA, including allegations that the CIA was connected to assassination conspiracies directed against foreign leaders. Most significantly, the 1979 report of the House Select Committee on Assassinations (HSCA) rejected part of the Warren Report and concluded that a total of four shots were fired, one of which was fired by a second gunman from Dealey Plaza's grassy knoll.

During the 1980s and 1990s, the number and variety of conspiracy theories rejecting the Warren Report increased. Some theorists claimed that Kennedy was killed by organized crime because gangsters were angry that Kennedy had betrayed them by allowing the Justice Department to vigorously prosecute them and by failing to overthrow Fidel Castro. Others asserted that wealthy, right-wing extremists in Texas hired assassins to kill the president. Oliver Stone's 1991 film *JFK*, based on Louisiana attorney James Garrison's investigation of Kennedy's assassination, implied that a government conspiracy that included the CIA, the military, and Johnson killed Kennedy.

Partially to refute this film, Gerald Posner researched and wrote *Case Closed: Lee Harvey Oswald and the Assassination of JFK* (1993). Posner criticized some of the Warren Commission's efforts as too hasty and incomplete, but he generally reaffirmed the Warren Report's conclusions, especially the "lone gunman" and "single bullet" theories. Shortly after Posner's book was published, Harold Weisberg countered with *Case Open: The Omissions, Distortions, and Falsifications of* Case Closed (1994), which rejected the Warren Report and Posner's defense of it. It is unlikely that there ever will be a definitive, widely shared public acceptance of the Warren Report.

SEE ALSO *Kennedy, John F.*

BIBLIOGRAPHY

Oglesby, Carl. 1992. *Who Killed JFK?* Berkeley, CA: Odonian Press.

Posner, Gerald L. 1993. *Case Closed: Lee Harvey Oswald and the Assassination of JFK.* New York: Random House.

President's Commission on the Assassination of President John F. Kennedy. 1964. *The Warren Commission Report.* New York: St. Martin's Press.

Weisberg, Harold. 1994. *Case Open: The Omissions, Distortions, and Falsifications of* Case Closed. New York: Carroll and Graf.

Sean J. Savage

WARS, CIVIL

SEE *Civil Wars.*

WARSAW PACT

The Warsaw Pact was signed on May 14, 1955, in order to create an organization of Central and East European Communist states. It is different from the Warsaw Convention, signed in 1929, which is an international convention regulating liability for commercial airlines transporting persons, luggage, or goods.

The formal name of the Warsaw Pact was the Treaty of Friendship, Co-operation, and Mutual Assistance. It was created for two reasons: first, to counter the threat from the North Atlantic Treaty Organization (NATO), an alliance established six years earlier; and second, in reaction to the admission of West Germany into NATO. The initial members of the Warsaw Pact were the Soviet

Union, Albania, Bulgaria, Czechoslovakia, East Germany, Hungary, Poland, and Romania. Yugoslavia was the only Communist state not to sign the treaty. Albania withdrew from the pact in 1968. Despite being initially created to counter the threat of NATO, in practice the pact was a tool of the Soviet Union, used to strengthen its hold over its satellite countries. In contrast to NATO, the Warsaw Pact was completely subordinated to a single power. The pact allowed the Soviet Union to impose its military and political agenda on Central and East European countries through the use of both its military and economic power. The pact was supposed to last for only twenty years and become void if any of the members decided to drop out. Nonetheless, the agreement was renewed in 1975 for another ten years, despite Albania's unilateral withdrawal from it seven years earlier.

PRINCIPLES

The signatory parties of the Warsaw Pact agreed to abstain from violence or from the threat of violence in international relations. The treaty established the goals of the members, which included world peace and security, and global disarmament. Countries also had to confer with each other on matters of international affairs and agreed that in the event of outside aggression against one member, all member countries would defend the threatened country together. However, the Soviet Union also wanted to use the Warsaw Pact as a bargaining tool with non-Communist European countries. This is evidenced by the concluding article of the pact, which stipulated that the agreement would lapse in the event of an East-West collective security pact.

The treaty, signed in 1955, was supplemented by numerous bilateral treaties between the Soviet Union and satellite countries. Among other things, these treaties gave Soviet troops the right to be on the soil of signatory countries. Some countries, such as Poland, allowed the stationing of Soviet troops on their soil under the 1945 Potsdam Agreement and through a separate bilateral treaty. Hungary also had a bilateral agreement with the Soviet Union. Soviet troops prevented Hungary's 1956 attempt to secede from the organization and crushed liberal movements in Czechoslovakia that emerged in what came to be known as the "Prague Spring." Czechoslovakia only signed its bilateral treaty with the Soviet Union *after* the Soviet invasion and was essentially forced to accept the "Brezhnev Doctrine," which limited the sovereignty of the Communist states and granted the right of Soviet intervention.

The extent to which the Soviet Union maintained a military presence in the satellite countries depended on its assessment of each individual member's risk of defecting from the organization were it to be pressured to allow Soviet troops on its soil. Thus, when the bilateral agreement with Romania expired in 1958, it was not renewed, because of Romania's wish to avoid the presence of Soviet troops, even for temporary purposes such as maneuvers. Soviet troops were stationed in Bulgaria, on the other hand, though only for temporary purposes, such as military exercises.

Even though the Warsaw Pact allowed for military alliances outside the Communist-bloc countries and functioned as an instrument of Soviet policy, it had no provisions concerning activities outside the European continent.

ORGANIZATION

The Political Consultative Committee (PCC) was the highest governing body of the Warsaw Treaty Organization. Its permanent members were the Communist Party's first secretaries and the premiers and foreign ministers of member countries. The PCC had managerial authority over the cultural, political, and economic spheres of the entire organization. However, its most important function was deciding when a crisis met the criteria for executing the provisions of the military clauses. In practice, the PCC's power could be limited, as shown by the 1968 invasion of Czechoslovakia, which was not decided on by the PCC.

The secretary general of the organization was always a Soviet general or Soviet foreign ministry official and control was always held in Moscow. The Committee of Defense Ministers (CDM), which decided on directives communicated to national defense planners in member nations, was subordinate to the PCC and was also located in Moscow.

THE END OF AN ERA

Even though NATO and the Warsaw Pact were created to counter each other's dominance, the member countries never engaged each other in armed conflict, though they did engage in "proxy wars." In December 1988, Mikhail Gorbachev, then leader of the Soviet Union, declared that the Brezhnev Doctrine would be abandoned and that the Soviet Union's satellite countries could do as they wished. Soon after, a number of political changes swept across Central and Eastern Europe, leading to the end of Communism. After 1989 the Warsaw Pact started losing the support of its members. In January 1991, Czechoslovakia, Hungary, and Poland announced they would withdraw all support within six months. Bulgaria followed suit in February 1991. The Warsaw Pact was officially dissolved at a meeting in Prague on July 1, 1991.

SEE ALSO *Brezhnev, Leonid; North Atlantic Treaty Organization*

BIBLIOGRAPHY

Michta, Andrew A. 1992. *East Central Europe after the Warsaw Pact: Security Dilemmas in the 1990s.* New York: Greenwood Press.

Lewis, William J. 1982. *The Warsaw Pact: Arms, Doctrine, and Strategy.* New York: McGraw-Hill.

Dagmar Radin

WASHINGTON, GEORGE
1732–1799

George Washington was the first president of the United States of America. He was born in Westmoreland County, Virginia, on February 22, 1732. Washington's father, Augustine Washington, died in 1743 and his older half brother, Lawrence Washington (1718–1752), was subsequently responsible for George Washington's upbringing and training as a surveyor and tobacco planter. Lawrence also nurtured Washington's interest in military service.

Partially because of his protégé relationship with Thomas Fairfax (1691–1782), a Virginia planter influential with British nobility, and his replacement of Lawrence as district adjutant in 1752, Washington was promoted to the rank of colonel in the Virginia militia in 1754. Shortly before the outbreak of the French and Indian War (1756–1763), Washington led a military expedition to the westernmost boundaries of Virginia because French troops and their Indian allies threatened British-claimed territory. He ordered his men to build Fort Necessity in this area but soon abandoned the fort because of superior French and Indian forces in 1754. After the arrival of British troops, Washington became an aide to British general Edward Braddock (1695–1755). Washington distinguished himself in combat, especially in the campaign against Fort Duquesne, and was elected to Virginia's House of Burgesses in 1758.

In 1759 Washington married Martha Custis (1731–1802), a wealthy widow, and increased his ownership of land and slaves. He was active in local politics, but he mostly focused on his agricultural and financial interests. Washington had admired Britain's army, aristocracy, and mixed system of government since childhood. But he gradually concluded during the 1760s and early 1770s that new British taxes and regulations reflected "taxation without representation" and their implementation by British troops and officials increasingly violated Americans' legal rights as British subjects. While he was occasionally disturbed by the more extreme rhetoric and behavior of revolutionary leaders in Boston, Washington eventually became committed to the cause of rebellion and then independence. He concluded that the American colonies must become a separate nation in order to protect their liberty, self-government, and economic interests.

In 1774 Washington was elected as a delegate to the first Continental Congress. John Adams (1735–1826), a delegate from Massachusetts, became acquainted with Washington. Adams was impressed by Washington's military service and political status in Virginia. Wanting to increase national, and especially southern, support for the American Revolution against Britain, Adams secured Washington's appointment as general and commander-in-chief of the Continental Army in 1775. Washington then traveled to Massachusetts and assumed command on July 3, 1775. After placing artillery to threaten British ships in Boston Harbor, Washington forced the British to evacuate Boston on March 17, 1776.

Until the British surrender at Yorktown, Virginia, in 1781, Washington's strategy was to continue the American military and political effort until the British government decided to end the war as too costly. Washington generally avoided large-scale, prolonged battles and relied on surprise attacks, like the Battle of Trenton (1776), and tactical retreats to limit American casualties. During the Revolutionary War, Washington gained a national reputation among Americans for his endurance, integrity, and strength of character in the cause for independence. He struggled to maintain discipline, order, and professional military standards among American troops. Although Washington was critical of Congress for not providing enough pay and supplies for his troops, he always yielded to Congress's civilian supremacy over his military command. After the Treaty of Paris officially ended the war in 1783, Washington voluntarily surrendered his commission as commander-in-chief to Congress and returned to Mount Vernon, his plantation in Virginia.

After the Revolutionary War, Washington struggled to improve his neglected finances. Like other planters, however, Washington suffered from the disruption of prewar trading relationships with the British Empire, high inflation, and trade barriers that states imposed against each other. The weak national government of the Articles of Confederation was unable to solve or alleviate these economic problems. Washington was also troubled by Shays's Rebellion in Massachusetts in 1786 and other events that indicated that the nation might dissolve into anarchy, disunity, and political radicalism.

In his personal life, Washington had no legally recognized children, although he may have fathered a child with Venus, his half brother's slave. He was an Anglican (or Episcopalian) but was not a frequent churchgoer. Like many upper-class Americans in the late eighteenth century, Washington was a deist who perceived God to be

impersonal and rational. Nevertheless, his private and public statements reveal his belief that God, or Providence, had a special destiny for the American nation. Later in his life, Washington expressed the need for religion to promote civic virtue.

Washington was known for treating his slaves more humanely than other slave owners. He encouraged marriage among his slaves and refused to break up slave families by selling them to other planters or investing in the "breeding" of slaves. As he became older, Washington became more troubled by the moral dilemma and economic burden of slave ownership. Nonetheless, Washington accepted the institution of slavery, and his wife inherited his slaves after his death.

Washington reluctantly returned to public life and was elected as a Virginia delegate to the Constitutional Convention in Philadelphia in 1787. Washington's fellow delegates unanimously elected him to preside at the convention. As president of the convention, Washington maintained order during the debates and rarely expressed his political opinions. Washington's judicious reticence further enhanced his reputation among delegates as a dignified, virtuous, self-restrained national leader who could be entrusted with executive power. Alexander Hamilton (1755/57–1804) was a delegate from New York who served as a staff officer for Washington during the war and revered him. Hamilton shrewdly promoted the common assumption that Washington would be the first president in order to gain delegate support and later ratification for the strong presidency that he explained and advocated in *The Federalist Papers.*

George Washington was unanimously elected president in 1789 and inaugurated in New York City, the nation's first capital under the Constitution. John Adams was elected vice president, and Washington's first cabinet included Thomas Jefferson (1743–1826) as secretary of state and Alexander Hamilton as secretary of the treasury. Washington was unanimously reelected in 1792 and inaugurated in Philadelphia in 1793. He disliked the growing partisan and policy conflicts between the Federalists and Anti-Federalists, especially between Hamilton and Jefferson, and warned the nation of the dangers of partisanship in his farewell address of 1796. Washington struggled to be nonpartisan during his first term but became a Federalist during his second term, partially because of the criticism of his presidency and policies from Anti-Federalist newspapers and politicians.

George Washington's interpretation and use of presidential powers established several important precedents for the American presidency. First, Washington established the belief that a president should limit himself to two terms of office, a practice that continued until President Franklin D. Roosevelt (1882–1945) was elected

to a third term in 1940. The Constitution was amended in 1951 to formally limit a president to two elected terms. Washington had previously rejected the suggestion that he be appointed as a monarch or president with a life term of office. He later rejected a request that he run for a third term.

Second, Washington believed that a president should only veto bills that he regarded as unconstitutional. Consequently, he vetoed only two bills during his presidency. It was not until the presidency (1829–1837) of Andrew Jackson (1767–1845) that a president actively vetoed bills because of political or policy differences with Congress.

Third, while Washington believed that a president should be self-restrained and generally defer to Congress on domestic legislation, he also asserted that a president should exercise more discretionary and dominant power in foreign and defense policies. He interpreted the president's power to "receive Ambassadors" in Article II of the Constitution to mean that the president alone can decide whether to recognize a new foreign government as legitimate for a regular diplomatic relationship with the U.S. government. Fourth, after a frustrating experience with the Senate in negotiating a treaty with the Creek Indians, Washington began the precedent of a president initiating and conducting treaty negotiations and only seeking the Senate's "advice and consent" afterward for ratification. Likewise, he refused to provide diplomatic correspondence pertaining to the Jay Treaty to the House of Representatives because the Constitution did not require him to do so. This was an early example of *executive privilege,* that is, the president's limited, unwritten constitutional right to withhold information from Congress.

Washington also developed the president's symbolic role as the head of state who represents all Americans both nationally and internationally. He contributed to this role by occasionally visiting the various states and issuing proclamations. He proclaimed Thanksgiving as a national holiday in 1789. More importantly, he proclaimed American neutrality between the warring governments of Britain and France in 1793. Washington also insisted that all of his cabinet members publicly support his policies. For example, Washington forced the resignation of Secretary of State Edmund Randolph (1753–1813) in 1795 because he suspected Randolph of being pro-French, despite American neutrality.

Although Washington usually deferred to Congress on domestic legislation, he relied on Alexander Hamilton, his first secretary of the treasury and closest adviser, to formulate and promote legislative passage of his economic program, which included a national bank, a hard currency, and tariffs and excise taxes to liquidate Revolutionary War debts and provide adequate revenue to

maintain a national army. Because of Article II's "take care" clause, Washington believed that a president should exercise broad, discretionary powers to enforce federal laws. This belief was especially evident in Washington's firm, decisive suppression of the Whiskey Rebellion of 1794. Washington personally led troops during part of their expedition to western Pennsylvania to end mob violence against the collection of the federal excise tax on whiskey.

Despite the efforts of Hamilton to persuade Washington to remain in office, Washington publicized his farewell address on September 19, 1796. In addition to warning the public about how partisan conflict threatened liberty, order, civic virtue, and national unity, Washington stated that future American foreign policy must continue to avoid "permanent alliances" with foreign governments that endangered American independence, liberty, and peace. Shortly after John Adams was inaugurated as president on March 4, 1797, Washington returned to Mount Vernon.

During his retirement, Washington busied himself with improving his finances and repairing buildings on his plantation. In 1798 Washington accepted a commission as a lieutenant general from President Adams and the Senate. He avoided public statements on politics and refused to undermine Adams's authority as president. He was dismayed that the Federalist Party became bitterly divided between pro-Adams and pro-Hamilton factions and that war with France seemed more likely.

Washington returned home after inspecting his fields on December 12, 1799, and became ill with a severe cold. Further weakened by the use of bloodletting as a medical treatment, Washington died on December 14, 1799. General Henry Lee's (1756–1818) funeral oration, delivered before Congress on December 26, 1799, popularized Washington's historical and patriotic reputation as "the father of his country." The nation's new capital city was named after Washington, as were many towns, counties, schools, and a state. The most nationally prominent artistic dedications to George Washington include the Washington Monument in Washington, D.C., and an enormous sculpture of his face on Mount Rushmore in South Dakota. His birthday was celebrated as a separate national holiday but was more recently incorporated as part of Presidents' Day in February.

SEE ALSO *American Revolution; Constitution, U.S.; Presidency, The; Slavery*

BIBLIOGRAPHY

Flexner, James T. 1974. *Washington: The Indispensable Man.* New York: Mentor.

McDonald, Forrest. 1974. *The Presidency of George Washington.* Lawrence: University Press of Kansas.

Phelps, Glenn A. 1993. *George Washington and American Constitutionalism.* Lawrence: University Press of Kansas.

Wiencek, Henry. 2003. *An Imperfect God: George Washington, His Slaves, and the Creation of America.* New York: Farah, Straus and Giroux.

Sean J. Savage

WASHINGTON CONSENSUS

The phrase *Washington Consensus* has come to refer to a neoliberal economic agenda for developing countries and carries the implication that the Washington, D.C.–based public organizations concerned with development agree on the appropriateness of this agenda. *Neoliberal* refers to the ideas about the virtues of free markets and small, regulatory states emanating from the Mont Pelerin Society and developed primarily by Milton Friedman and Friedrich von Hayek, and to some extent implemented by Ronald Reagan, Margaret Thatcher, Augusto Pinochet, and the New Zealand Labour government during the 1980s.

The phrase had more modest beginnings. It was coined in a 1990 article by the British economist John Williamson, who had spent years working in a Washington, D.C., think tank, the Institute for International Economics. Williamson noticed that during the second half of the 1980s Latin American countries experienced a major change in economic policy norms. Previously, Latin American governments tended to think that import substitution, state enterprises, and inflationary finance constituted the core of development strategy, and that macroeconomic stabilization, free trade, and a framework-providing state were only appropriate for the already-developed countries. In the wake of the 1980s debt crises, both Latin American governments and the Washington organizations "saw the light" and concluded that what was appropriate for the developed countries was also appropriate for them.

Williamson's list of what he considered to be generally accepted policy priorities in Washington and in Latin America by the late 1980s included the following:

1. Keep budget deficits small.

2. Shift public expenditure priorities from non-merit subsidies to expenditures that are pro-growth and pro-poor, like spending on basic health, education, and infrastructure.

3. Construct a tax system that combines a broad tax base with moderate marginal tax rates.

4. Liberalize interest rates (meaning that while independent central banks should fix the base rate, commercial lenders should be free to set whatever the market can bear on top of base rate).

5. Maintain a competitive exchange rate via an "intermediate" regime, between fixed and free-floating.

6. Liberalize trade.

7. Liberalize inward foreign direct investment—but without pursuing comprehensive capital account liberalization.

8. Privatize state enterprises.

9. Ease sectoral barriers to entry and exit.

10. Provide the informal sector with the ability to gain property rights at acceptable cost.

After Williamson published his list, champions of neoliberalism deployed the phrase *Washington Consensus* for their own purposes. They detached it from Williamson's policy list by adding elements like low taxes, a minimal state, and rapid liberalization of cross-border financial flows ("opening the capital account"). They also detached it from its regional origin, implying that it applied to all developing countries, including those "in transition" from socialism to capitalism. In this newly fundamentalist form it coursed through the echo chamber of the Washington-based organizations, including the International Monetary Fund, the World Bank, the U.S. Treasury, USAID, and think tanks; through transatlantic components including *The Financial Times*, *The Economist*, and the U.K. Treasury; and into finance and development ministries in many developing countries.

"Stabilize, deregulate, open up, and privatize" became the slogan of technocrats and political leaders through the 1980s, and it inspired a wave of reforms that had transformed the policy landscape of much of the developing world by the early 1990s. The common denominator was the drive to extend private property rights geographically and "vertically," to types of assets not previously privately owned, and in this way expand profit opportunities for global firms facing declining profits at home. The reforms accelerated the "financialization" of the world economy and the shrinkage of the economic sovereignty of the state. Yet economic performance of most developing countries remained disappointing. Many countries that adopted this approach to a high degree had worse performance than during the era of "bad" import-substituting industrialization, and worse performance than those that adopted it to a small degree. In particular, many countries that followed the neoliberal prescription of "economic growth with foreign savings"—which entailed opening the economy to free flows of finance—were hit by financial crises through the 1990s.

In response a new consensus, sometimes called the *Augmented Washington Consensus*, began to emerge by the mid-1990s (see Williamson 2003). It said that neoliberal policies would not have lasting effects where institutions were unfriendly to markets, an argument in line with the major thrust in development economics over the 1990s to assert the role of institutions in affecting transaction costs and thereby economic performance. "Get the prices right" had to be supplemented with "get the institutions right." The new "good governance" agenda called for reforms in the civil service (the budget office, the central bank, the customs bureaucracy), the judiciary, the financial sector (the accountancy profession, the rights of minority shareholders, credit registries), systems of primary education and primary healthcare, and microcredit.

The Augmented Washington Consensus retained the neoliberal premise that the state was the problem and the market the solution, and the aim was to make markets work better and to extend surrogate markets into the state. The word *reform* was reserved for changes in this direction. Many champions hoped that financial reforms would strengthen regulation sufficiently so that opening the capital account could again become a top global priority. Issues of equity, income distribution, technology, firm-level capabilities, and industrial policy remained firmly off the radar screen.

However by the late 1990s some parts of the "international development community," notably the United Nations' General Assembly and the United Nations Development Programme (UNDP), began to unite around an action agenda that emphasized poverty reduction and investment in primary health and primary education. This perspective was spelled out in the Millennium Declaration and in the Millennium Development Goals adopted by the UN in 2000. Critics of neoliberalism took advantage of the new discussion to declare that the Washington Consensus was dead and had been replaced by a "Post 'Washington Consensus' Consensus," which held that "countries should be given scope to experiment, to use their own judgment, to explore what might work best for them" (Stiglitz 2004, p. 12).

A more open-minded stance toward policy experimentation is surely a good thing. But pragmatism is not a strategy. At the operational levels of the Washington-based organizations and in the most powerful agencies in developing countries—finance ministries as distinct from development ministries—the Washington Consensus is far from dead, if only because nothing coherent has emerged to replace it. Development technocrats find it a huge advantage to be able to use the Washington Consensus one-size-fits-all approach; whatever the coun-

try, they know what the government should be doing. Certainly the Millennium Development Goals are an add-on rather than an alternative because they assume that the core microeconomic reforms of the Washington Consensus are necessary conditions for achieving the goals. In short, reports of the death of the Washington Consensus are greatly exaggerated, whether for better or for worse.

SEE ALSO *Neoliberalism*

BIBLIOGRAPHY

Seccareccia, Mario, ed. 2002–2003. Beyond the Washington Consensus: Overhauling the Neo-Liberal Reforms. *International Journal of Political Economy* 32 (4). (Spec. issue.)

Stiglitz, Joseph. 2004. The Post Washington Consensus Consensus. Initiative for Policy Dialogue Working Paper. New York: Initiative for Policy Dialogue, Task Force on Governance of Globalization, Columbia University.

Williamson, John. 1990. What Washington Means by Policy Reform. In *Latin American Adjustment: How Much Has Happened?* Ed. John Williamson, 7–20. Washington, DC: Institute for International Economics.

Williamson, John. 2003. The Washington Consensus and Beyond. *Economic and Political Weekly* 38 (15): 1475–1481.

Robert H. Wade

WATER RESOURCES

The planet Earth is inherently short of freshwater, the proportion of which is as little as 3 percent of all available water. The remaining 97 percent of water is saline and is stored in the oceans. Of the 3 percent of water that is freshwater, only 0.3 percent flows through surface water systems such as rivers and lakes; the remaining 2.97 percent is frozen in glaciers and ice caps or held in the ground.

This inherent scarcity has been worsened by the accelerated diversion of water for agricultural, commercial, industrial, and residential uses, which has increased greatly in response to a growing world population that reached 6.5 billion people in 2006. As much as 95 percent of that growth has taken place in the water-deficit developing world, predominantly in Asia and Africa. Among all human uses, agriculture tends to use 70 percent of the available freshwater. According to experts, 1 ton of grain requires 1,000 tons of water. As agriculture increasingly is becoming dependent on irrigation, especially in Asia, the most populous continent, the availability of water for industrial, commercial, and municipal uses has been shrinking.

WATER SCARCITY AND THE HUMAN CONDITION

The impact of dwindling water supplies on humankind is evident worldwide. According to a 2006 report by the United Nations Development Program, over 1 billion people are without clean drinking water and over 2.4 billion lack basic sanitation. Access to clean drinking water is lowest in Africa, and Asia has the largest number of people without basic sanitation. The human toll of the inaccessibility of water and sanitation runs as high as 2 million child deaths a year (United Nationals Development Program 2006). In all, in the early years of the twenty-first century 12 million people died each year from drinking contaminated water.

In 2003 the United Nations World Water Development Report estimated that $110 billion to $180 billion would be needed each year to provide safe drinking water to the poor in developing countries. Although an annual outlay of that size for water resource development seems prohibitive for low-income nations, the economic benefits of such an outlay would be two to three times as large. Recognizing those benefits, the United Nations Millennium Development Project planned to widen the access of the poor to safe drinking water by 50 percent by 2015. The economic benefits of increased access to safe drinking water in terms of health, longevity, and time saved in fetching water range from $300 billion to $400 billion a year.

PRICING AND PRIVATIZATION OF WATER

International development agencies such as the World Bank and the Asian Development Bank (ADB) plan to broaden the access of the poor to safe water by pricing water use and privatizing water resources. Water pricing means consumers will pay the fees, taxes, or charges for water supplies they use. It has been argued that water privatization can meet the water needs of the poor effectively. In 2005 Segerfeldt pointed out that public water systems in developing countries tend to serve wealthy and middle-class households, whereas the poor are left to draw from municipal water mains. However, 80 percent of the poorest parts of the population in fifteen developing countries are not served by municipal water supplies (Segerfeldt 2005). Although privatization is intended to bring the entire water supplies and treatment systems of developing countries into the private market, in the first decade of the twenty-first century only 3 percent of the poor worldwide were served by private-sector water supplies.

Critics see water privatization as a "global water grab" with disastrous outcomes in places such as Cochabamba, Bolivia. Between 1989 and 1999 the proportion of Bolivian households connected to the public water system

fell from 70 percent to 60 percent. Water was available only sporadically; 99 percent of the wealthier households were receiving the subsidized water, whereas in some poorer suburbs less than 4 percent were receiving water.

FATE OF PRIVATIZATION IN INDIA AND CHINA

In 2002 Vandana Shiva blamed the World Bank and the ADB for creating water markets to benefit multinational corporations (MNCs). Privatization, she argued, is preceded by a hike in water tariffs to "secure private sector investment in risky countries" (Shiva 2005). The tariff increase, Shiva asserted, exceeds by ten times the "full cost recovery," although this is rationalized by privatization supporters. Using the case of her native India, Shiva stated that private operators will harvest public investment of 1 trillion rupees for private gains through water privatization in India (Shiva 2005).

Pricing and privatization of water are intended to rationalize water use. In light of worldwide extreme income inequalities, however, it is feared that privatization will save water by diverting it from the poor to the rich and from rural areas to urban centers. In 2005 Shiva argued that the best way to conserve water is to make a radical shift from water-intensive chemical farming to organic farming, along with a reversal in export-led agricultural production, which amounts to exporting "virtual water" to the rich consumers of the North at the expense of the poor in the South.

Like India, China is poor in freshwater supplies, the per capita availability of which is one-fourth of the world average (Yu and Danqing 2006). The pollution of rivers and groundwater from industrialization and urbanization has exacerbated the water shortage. In the first decade of the twenty-first century, two-thirds of Chinese cities had an insufficient supply of freshwater and 110 of them had critically inadequate access to freshwater.

Beijing's plan to meet the water needs of urban centers angered Chinese rural residents. On July 6, 2000, thousands of farmers in the Yellow River Basin in eastern China clashed with police over a government plan to recapture runoff from a local reservoir for cities, industries, and other uses (Postel and Wolf 2001). The incident took place in Shandong, the last province through which the Yellow River runs before reaching the sea. Worldwide water disputes have been occurring in the downstream regions of overtapped river basins (Postel and Wolf 2001). The Yellow River has been running dry in its lower reaches on and off since 1972, and its dry spell grew to a record 226 days in 1997. As a result, per person use of water in China, which already was severely low, fell by 1.7 percent in seven years (Yu and Danqing 2006).

WATER CONFLICTS

The Indus Basin Intrastate water shortages have spilled over into interstate water conflicts. In the first decade of the twenty-first century India and Bangladesh were worrying about alleged Chinese attempts to divert the waters of Yarlung Zangbo River (which in India is called Brahmaputra, and in Bangladesh Jamuna) into the Yellow River. The Yarlung Zangbo passes through the Tibet Autonomous Region into the Indian states of Arunachal Pradesh and Assam and into Bangladesh. Even starker conflicts have been simmering between India and Bangladesh over the Ganges River and between India and Pakistan over the Jhelum River. In the 1960s and early 1970s India unilaterally constructed a barrage (dam) on the Ganges River at Farakka, near the border with Bangladesh, to divert more river water to the port of Calcutta (Postel and Wolf 2001). That diversion left Bangladesh with significantly less water for irrigation during the dry season, causing increased migration of its population across the border into the Indian states of West Bengal (Postel and Wolf 2001) and Assam. Although the Indus River Basin Treaty between India and Pakistan of the 1960s has held, the growing water and power needs of each nation are fueling the conflicts as never before. The major conflict between Islamabad and New Delhi has erupted over the controversial construction of Bhagliar Dam over the Jhelum River in the disputed territory of Jammu and Kashmir; that conflict was being arbitrated by the World Bank.

Euphrates and Jordan River Basins Euphrates and Jordan River Basin nations have long argued over their shared surface water systems. Syria and Iraq experienced a reduction of almost 50 percent in the average flow of the Euphrates after the 1970s (Allan 1998). Both countries have been anticipating additional reductions in the flow of Tigris as well. The Euphrates and Tigris rivers originate in Turkey, which has diverted their water by building dams. In the case of the Jordan basin, the river system rises in four tributaries (Lowi 1995): the Yarmouk in Syria, the Banias in Israeli-occupied Syria, the Hasbani in Lebanon, and the Dan in Israel. The Banias, Hasbani, and Dan meet in northern Israel to form the Upper Jordan River, which flows into Lake Tiberias, and then the Lower Jordan. Israel has become the upstream riparian basin on the Upper Jordan system, and Syria is upstream on the Yarmouk. Jordan and the Palestinians, as downstream riparian basins vis-à-vis both Israel and Syria, have remained in the worst positions in the basin (Lowi 1995).

About one-half of Israel's annual supply of groundwater and one-quarter of its total renewable supply of freshwater originate in two subterranean basins in the West Bank (Lowi 1995). By virtue of its occupation of the West

Bank, Israel has been controlling water in the territory. The result has been that approximately 80 percent of West Bank water is exploited in Israel and by Israeli settlers in the territory, leaving only 20 percent for the Palestinian population (Lowi 1995). Although Lowi does not think that water disputes alone could cause active conflict between Israel and the countries of the Jordan River Basin, Adel Darwish (2003) and John Bulloch and Darwish (1993) believe that water disputes underlie the political conflict in the region. King Hussein of Jordan and the late Egyptian President Anwar Sadat, each of whom signed peace treaties with Israel, vowed never to go to war with Israel except to protect water resources (Darwish 2003). Bulloch and Darwish (1993) claim that water was the hidden agenda for past conflicts and has been a major obstacle to a lasting peace in the region. The Six Day War, they argue, started because Syrian engineers were working to divert part of the water flow from Israel. The Israeli leader Ariel Sharon backed up their argument by saying: "People generally regard 5 June 1967 as the day the Six-day war began. That is the official date. But, in reality, it started two and a half years earlier, on the day Israel decided to act against the diversion of the Jordan" (quoted in Darwish 2003).

POSSIBLE SOLUTIONS

It is feared that global warming will cause further stress in the already water-short nations of Asia, Africa, and the Middle East. Although bilateral and multilateral water-sharing mechanisms are important to ensure critical water supplies, the significance of conservation and further development of water resources cannot be overemphasized. There are a number of technological means to augment water resources, including but not limited to cloud seeding, desalination, wastewater reuse, rain harvesting, and importing water from relatively wet zones (Postel and Wolf 2001). Of equal importance are a shift from water-intensive chemical farming to less water-intensive farming methods and a reversal in export-led agricultural production, which amounts to the export of virtual water from the water-short South to the water-surplus North (Shiva 2005).

SEE ALSO *Agricultural Industry; Arab-Israeli War of 1967; Gender; Global Warming; Inequality, Political; Irrigation; Needs; Nutrition; Poverty; Poverty, Indices of; Privatization; Public Health; Sharon, Ariel; Women and Politics*

BIBLIOGRAPHY

Allan, Tony. 1998. *Avoiding War over Natural Resources.* Global Policy Forum. http://www.globalpolicy.org/security/docs/resource2.htm.

Bulloch, John, and Adel Darwish. 1993. *Water Wars: Coming Conflicts in the Middle East.* London: Victor Gollancz.

Darwish, Adel. 2003. Analysis: Middle East Water Wars. BBC News, May 30. http://news.bbc.co.uk/2/hi/middle_east/2949768.stm.

Lowi, Miriam R. 1995. *Water and Power: The Politics of a Scarce Resource in the Jordan River Basin.* Cambridge, U.K., and New York: Cambridge University Press.

Postel, Sandra L., and Aaron T. Wolf. 2001. Dehydrating Conflict. *Foreign Policy* 126: 60–67. http://www.edcnews/Reviews/Postel_Wolf2001.pdf.

Segerfeldt, Fredrik. 2005. *Water for Sale: How Business and the Market Can Resolve the World's Water Crisis.* Washington, DC: Cato Institute.

Shiva, Vandana. 2002. *Water Wars: Privatization, Pollution and Profit.* Cambridge, MA: South End Press.

Shiva, Vandana. 2005. Water Privatization and Water Wars. ZNet Daily Communications. http://www.Zmag.org/Sustainers/Content/2005–07/12Shiva.cfm.

United Nations. 2003. First UN World Water Development Report, 2003: *Water for People, Water for Life.* United Nations: World Water Assessment Program. Paris: UNESCO Publishing.

United Nations Development Program. 2006. Human Development Report 2006: *Beyond Scarcity: Power, Poverty, and the Global Water Crisis.* Washington, DC: UNDP.

Yu, Au Loong, and Liu Danqing. 2006. *The Privatization of Water Supply in China.* Amsterdam, Netherlands: Transnational Institute. http://www.tni.org/books/waterchina.pdf.

Tarique Niazi

WATERGATE

The Watergate scandal involved Richard M. Nixon (1913–1994) during his second term as president of the United States. The scandal led to his impeachment and resignation from office.

In June 1971 a former employee of the U.S. Department of Defense, Daniel Ellsberg, gave *The New York Times* a secret government history of the Vietnam War (1957–1975) known as the Pentagon Papers. These revealed, among other things, a secret bombing campaign against neutral Cambodia. The White House issued an injunction against publication on the grounds of national security, but the injunction was declared unconstitutional by the U.S. Supreme Court, which saw it as a form of prior restraint in violation of the First Amendment. In response, Nixon directed aides to find damaging information about his perceived political enemies. By September 1971, a special investigative group known as "the plumbers" was hired by Nixon's assistant for domestic affairs, John Erlichman, to burglarize the office of Ellsberg's psychiatrist, which was located in the Watergate office complex in Washington, D.C.

On the night of June 17, 1972, a security guard working at the Watergate Hotel noticed a piece of tape between the door of the basement and the parking garage. Upon investigation by the Washington police, five men were discovered and arrested for breaking into the headquarters of the Democratic National Committee, located in the Watergate complex, in a failed attempt to place listening devices and take photographs of committee documents. Later, one of the burglars, James W. McCord Jr., was found to be in possession of phone numbers belonging to E. Howard Hunt (1918–2007) and G. Gordon Liddy, former employees of Nixon's reelection committee. At his arraignment, McCord identified himself as a former employee of the Central Intelligence Agency.

In attendance on the day of McCord's arraignment were *Washington Post* reporters Bob Woodward and Carl Bernstein, who began what became one of the most significant journalistic investigations of the twentieth century. A then-unknown individual with close ties to the White House, dubbed Deep Throat by Woodward, provided the journalists with information and assistance that helped them follow the story from an insignificant burglary to a cover-up orchestrated by the Nixon administration. Thirty years later, Deep Throat's identity was revealed when former FBI agent Mark Felt admitted that he had been Woodward's source.

In 1972 the Federal Bureau of Investigation established that the Watergate Hotel break-in stemmed from a spying effort conducted on behalf of the Nixon reelection effort. Despite this finding, Nixon won reelection in a landslide over the Democratic candidate Senator George McGovern in November 1972. By January 1973, however, the original burglars, along with Hunt and Liddy, went to trial, pleading guilty in a failed attempt to shield those above them from further inquiry. When the presiding judge, John Sirica (1905–1992), threatened thirty-year sentences, the defendants began cooperating with the prosecution. As the investigation broadened, the U.S. Senate established a committee, chaired by Senator Sam Ervin (1896–1985), to investigate the Watergate break-in.

By May 1973 two of Nixon's White House aides, H. R. Haldeman (1926–1993) and John Ehrlichman (1925–1999), resigned amidst growing evidence of their knowledge of the events. Both would later go to prison for their role in the Watergate break-in and cover-up. The Watergate hearings were broadcast live on television from May to August 1973, and were immensely popular, with dire consequence for the Nixon administration's approval ratings. As a result of these investigations, it was revealed that Nixon had recorded all his phone calls and conversations in the Oval Office. When Congress requested these tapes as part of the investigation, the president refused to turn them over. In an attempt to save himself from further

political embarrassment and possible criminal indictment, Nixon directed Attorney General Elliot Richardson (1920–1999) to instruct special counsel Archibald Cox (1912–2004) to drop the subpoena for the White House tapes. When Cox refused, Nixon ordered Richardson to fire Cox. When the attorney general refused, Nixon fired both Richardson and his deputy in what is now known as the "Saturday night massacre." A young solicitor with the attorney general's office, Robert Bork, assumed the role of attorney general. Bork then fired Cox, but was pressured to name another prosecutor, Leon Jaworski (1905–1982).

Citing executive privilege, Nixon refused to comply with the subpoena for the White House tapes, creating a constitutional conflict between the president and Congress. In July 1974 the U.S. Supreme Court unanimously ruled, in *United States v. Nixon*, that the president had to turn over the tapes to the committee. According to the Court, the president had no "unqualified" privilege of immunity. Less than one week later, a review of the tapes proved Nixon's role in the conspiracy to cover up the Watergate break-in. On one tape, Nixon and Haldeman, the White House chief of staff, directed the CIA to obstruct the FBI and the Justice Department's investigation into the break-in. It then became clear that the president and his aides had broken the law by orchestrating a cover-up, using the CIA to block the FBI investigation, lying to Congress, and destroying documents related to the investigation. Another scandal erupted when it was disclosed that an eighteen-minute gap had been found on one of Nixon's tapes. The gap was explained as an accident by Rose Mary Woods (1917–2005), Nixon's secretary.

In July 1974 the House Judiciary Committee passed the first of three articles of impeachment against the president for obstruction of justice, abuse of power, and contempt of Congress. Two additional articles of impeachment did not pass the committee: one for federal income tax evasion, and another for the authorization and subsequent concealment from Congress of American bombing operations in Cambodia. Throughout the ordeal, Nixon steadfastly proclaimed his innocence. On August 8, 1974, after consulting prominent members of Congress on the likelihood of the committee indictment being affirmed by the full House, Nixon became the first U.S. president to resign from office. Vice President Gerald R. Ford (1913–2006) assumed the presidency. Ford pardoned Nixon of all charges related to the Watergate break-in and cover-up on September 8, 1974.

In the aftermath of the Watergate affair, the media became more confident and aggressive in their coverage of Washington politics. Investigative journalists began looking into the public and private lives of politicians as never before. As a result, there have been numerous "gates" since Watergate, each referring to another scandal at the highest

levels of government. Additionally, Congress passed numerous "good government" bills in the years following the Watergate scandal. These addressed such issues as campaign finance reform, disclosure of campaign contributors and expenses to the Federal Election Commission, ethics in government, and a greater role for Congress in the appointment of independent counsels. Nixon continued to proclaim his innocence in the Watergate affair until his death in April 1994.

SEE ALSO *Democratic Party, U.S.; Government; Government, Federal; Impeachment; Nixon, Richard M.; Republican Party; Vietnam War*

BIBLIOGRAPHY

Kutler, Stanley. 2002. *Abuse of Power.* New York: Touchstone.

Schudson, M. 2005. *Watergate in American Memory.* New York: Basic Books.

Woodward, Bob, and Carl Bernstein. 2005. *All the President's Men.* New York: Pocket Press.

James Freeman

WATSON, JOHN B.

SEE *Behaviorism; Psychotherapy; Tolman, Edward.*

WAVES, LONG

SEE *Long Waves.*

WEAK AXIOM OF REVEALED PREFERENCE

SEE *Revealed Preference.*

WEAK SEPARABILITY

SEE *Separability.*

WEALTH

Throughout their history, human beings have been trying to improve the conditions of their existence. Ever since their early days, they sought to understand nature and dominate it. They discovered tools, salt, and fire, all of which made life better and easier. Possession of these "things" became a necessity. Wealth then meant all the things that are useful for satisfying needs and ensuring the well-being of their holder. This way of understanding wealth has not changed very much, for even today the *Merriam-Webster Collegiate Dictionary* defines wealth as "the stock of useful goods having economic value in existence at any one time," or to be more precise: "All property that has a money value or an exchangeable value." The modern definition reflects the popular understanding that wealth is synonymous with the acquisition and accumulation of real (physical) and financial assets. Material wealth, it seems, has always been important in the lives of individuals, from ancient to modern societies.

However, history of economic thought tells us that early civilizations in Mesopotamia, Egypt, and Greece had a positive attitude to knowledge, and many philosophers regarded it as the basis for wealth and empowerment. All the achievements in terms of progress (technical and other) were the result of the skills acquired through knowledge. The "light of fire" was a reflection of the "light of thought." Modern economic theory also recognizes what we call "human capital" (health, education, and knowledge in general) is an important element of wealth. The subtlety of the modern view is that wealth is not only created—it is also inherited. Because wealth can often be transferred from parents to heirs without impediments, some rich people may not be particularly knowledgeable and some great minds may not be particularly rich. People naturally reject poverty and have a desire to get rich and live comfortably. Therefore, not only will they question the unequal distribution of wealth, they will also try—by whatever means available—to change the status quo. Poverty makes people feel oppressed, disobedient, difficult to govern, and ready for revolt. The extremists would claim that a life of deprivation is not worth living. Tensions over the distribution of wealth existed even in ancient societies. Class struggle, according to Karl Marx ([1867–1910] 1956), is a dynamic force of change in all class societies.

ORIGIN AND EVOLUTION OF THE CONCEPT

In ancient societies, when human needs were basic and wealth meant getting the goods from nature to satisfy their "natural" needs, there were no quarrels about being or wanting to be rich. Increased wealth simply translated into increased consumption and improved well-being. Wealth was necessary and everyone approved of it. Social values encouraged the ability to gather and/or produce more goods. The consensus came to an end when the distinction could be made between what was necessary (natural) and what had become luxurious or superfluous

(artificial). Luxurious consumption, which could be afforded by only some people, was condemned on moral and religious grounds as waste, ostentation, or vanity. The desire for luxury, it was argued, has no limits and requires excessive riches. In turn, the pursuit of excessive wealth makes people selfish, greedy, dishonest, and morally corrupt. The rise of private property is justified by the need to ensure continuous control over the flow of resources or goods that satisfy these needs, whether natural or artificial. Greek philosophers such as Plato and Aristotle opposed both extreme poverty and excessive wealth. Poverty was considered by most as a debilitating state, whereas the desire for excessive wealth led to a state of unhappiness. To avoid these extremes, many philosophers recommended moderation. The ideal state of well-being is that where the individual learns how to control and limit his or her desires and needs. Wealth therefore became associated with wisdom and virtue. The same idea was later integrated into religious thought as "the wealth of the soul"; an inner dimension that can be achieved through moderate use of material wealth. (For an excellent review of the ancient thought on the subject, see Perrotta 2003.)

However, as pointed out by Cosimo Perrotta, even though many ancient thinkers praised modesty and the simple, natural lifestyle, most would still prefer wealth and reject poverty. Material wealth, after all, "contributes to the life according to nature" (Perrotta 2003, p. 210). The rejection of poverty is also found in ancient eastern civilizations. For instance, ancient Indian thinkers believed that life on earth was only a transitory state, but they still wanted it to be a good life; an opportunity to "perform good deeds" and achieve "prosperity on earth." According to Balbir Sihag, "[a]ncient thinkers in India put heavy emphasis on keeping a proper balance between spiritual health and material health" (2005, p. 2). Chanakya Kautilya, one of India's ancient thinkers and a contemporary of Aristotle, "considered poverty as a living death and concentrated on devising economic policies to achieve salvation from poverty without compromising with ethical values" (Sihag 2005, p. 1).

Islamic thought did not consecrate poverty either. It advocated the circulation of wealth through voluntary alms giving, *sadaqa*, and required giving, *zakat*, from the rich to the poor. In fact, Arabs, both before and after Islam, believed that wealth included a part that must be given away. In Islam, the poor and the needy have a claim on, a recognized right to, a portion of the property of the rich. The Qur'an refers to the community of the believers as "those upon whose wealth there is a recognized right for the beggar and the deprived" (surat 70: 24–25). Based on this philosophy, the Muslims sought to build a "community that regulates its flow of money and goods in the right direction … that practices generosity as reciprocation for God's bounty, that observes the haqq [i.e., the rec-ognized right] inhering in the good things of this world, that purifies and maintains its wealth by giving up a portion of it in alms, and that takes ample account of the kinsman as well as … the poor stranger" (Bonner 2005, p. 404). The final goal is to achieve a virtuous life on earth—the moral well-being that the ancient Indian thinkers talked about.

MODERN VIEWS

The idea that wealth must be shared equitably was also expressed later by modern thinkers such as Adam Smith, Marx, and John Maynard Keynes. Smith, for instance, considered the unequal distribution of wealth as "the great and most universal cause of the corruption of our moral sentiments" ([1776] 1976b, p. 61). Smith defined wealth in terms of production of goods and services for the purpose of satisfying the needs of society as a whole. He argued that because workers are the main factor of production, they should have their fair share: "[n]o society can surely be flourishing and happy, of which the far greater part of the members are poor and miserable. It is but equity, besides, that they who feed, cloath and lodge the whole body of the people, should have a share of the produce of their own labor as to be themselves tolerably well fed, cloathed and lodged" ([1776] 1976b, p. 96).

Keynes also was in favor of spreading wealth and against its concentration in the hands of the capitalist class. He considered scarcity, which is artificially created by the capitalist, to be "one of the chief social justifications of great inequality of wealth." (Keynes 1936, p.373). Therefore, he sought to eliminate "the cumulative oppressive power of the capitalist to exploit the scarcity-value of capital" because, he argued, "interest today rewards no genuine sacrifice, any more than does the rent of land. The owner of capital can obtain interest because capital is scare just as the owner of land can obtain rent because land is scarce. But whilst there may be intrinsic reasons for the scarcity of land, there are no intrinsic reasons for the scarcity of capital" (1936, p. 376).

The artificial scarcity preoccupied Marx as well, who argued that "[i]t is quite simply the private ownership of land, mines, water, etc. by certain people, which enables them to snatch, intercept and seize the excess surplus-value over and above profit … contained in the commodities of these particular spheres of production …" ([1867–1910] 1968, p. 37) In other spheres of production such as manufacturing, Marx rose against the exploitation of the working class and called for a community based on social justice.

Whereas Smith and early thinkers defined wealth either as production (of goods and services) or as consumption, Marx considered it as the creation of value and distinguished between use value (goods and services pro-

duced for own needs) and exchange value (goods and services produced for sale). Marx wrote:

> [a] commodity, such as iron, corn, or a diamond, is therefore … a use value, something useful. This property of a commodity is independent of the amount of labor required to appropriate its useful qualities. … Use values become a reality only by use or consumption: they also constitute the substance of all wealth, whatever may be the social form of that wealth. In the form of society we are about to consider, they are, in addition, the material depositories of exchange value. ([1867–1894] 1992, p. 44)

Exchange value, in contrast, exists only when the product is sold. As Marx put it, "a thing can be useful, and the product of human labor, without being a commodity. Whoever directly satisfies his wants with the produce of his own labor, creates, indeed, use values, but not commodities. In order to produce the latter, he must not only produce use values, but use values for others, social use values" ([1867–1894] 1992, p. 48).

If some authors have argued that all members of society should enjoy the benefits of increased wealth, others wanted to exclude the lower classes. In ancient times, the opposition to increased consumption was part of the general criticism of luxury, the desire to get rich, and selfishness. In modern times, the justification has been that consumption by lower classes takes away resources from investment—the key to accumulation. However, one must remember that consumption is what sets apart the different members of society. After all, as the popular adage says, "you are what you eat (consume)," that is, consumption sets your social status. Therefore, we should understand that "[t]he authors hostile to increased consumption … nearly always conceal (or reveal) a social motive: they are opposed to the rise of the lower classes and fear that their subordination may come to an end. They appear to be concerned about the destiny of the world, but are often concerned merely about the loss of their own privileges" (Perrotta 2003, p. 179).

Thorstein Veblen (1899) saw in the exclusion of the lower classes a means of guaranteeing the power and maintaining the social status of what he called the "leisure class," for it is through this power relationship that wealth is truly valorized. Preventing the poor from having access to increased consumption is important in the process of valorizing wealth. The logical step therefore is to prevent them from having access to increased wealth, that is, to keep wealth scarce and concentrated in the hands of the leisure class. This is done through what Veblen (1899) called "conspicuous consumption" and "industrial sabotage." Technology speeds up the production process and increases the total amount of goods and services, thus con-

tributing to eliminate scarcity by gradually shifting luxury consumer goods from being exclusively consumed by the leisure class to being widely available to the lower classes. As pointed out by Charles Clarke,

> this tendency must be kept in check, and it is done so by the process Veblen labeled industrial sabotage. Industrial concentration and monopoly are necessary in order to keep profits high.… Thus at the micro level industrial concentration generates scarcity, while at the macro-economic level this is done by keeping the value of money higher than it need be, i.e., keeping interest rates too high. (2002, p. 419)

INTERNATIONALIZATION OF WEALTH AND POVERTY

Advocates of globalization, including the World Trade Organization (WTO), have been arguing that inequality will fall as economies become more integrated and flows of capital and commodities more liberalized. The conclusions of the globalization-equality thesis are based on the neoclassical economic theory according to which free trade (one aspect of globalization) will bring about convergence in commodity prices, whereas factor mobility (another aspect of globalization) will equalize factor incomes by raising the income of the abundant factor and lowering that of the scarce factor. In the context of trade between developed and developing countries, one should expect that incomes of the working poor (the abundant factor) will rise and that returns to capital or even the incomes of highly skilled workers (the scarce factor) will fall. Globalization, therefore, will reduce inequality.

However, this is in sharp contrast with what is observed on the ground. At the national level, available evidence indicates that inequality between the rich and the poor—whether measured by income or by wealth—has been rising in most cases. The United Nations Development Program (UNDP) found that "a study of 77 countries with 82% of the world's people shows that between 1950s and 1990s inequality rose in 45 of the countries and fell in 16.… In the remaining 16 countries either no clear trend emerged or income inequality initially declined, then levelled off" (2001, p. 17). At the international level, according to the UNDP, the average GDP per capita from various regions as a ratio to that of high-income OECD countries declined between 1960 and 1998, and "in sub-Saharan Africa the situation has worsened dramatically: Per capita income, around 1/9 of that in high-income OECD countries in 1960, deteriorated to around 1/18 by 1998" (UNDP 2001, p. 16). The UNDP summarized its results on world inequality by stating that the ratio of the income of the world's richest 10

percent to that of the poorest 10 percent has increased from 51:1 to 127:1 between 1970 and 1997.

A study by the World Institute for Development Economics and Research reported that

> [t]he figures for wealth shares show that the top 10 percent of adults own 85 percent of global household wealth, … [The corresponding figure for the top 1 percent of adults is 40 percent of global wealth]. This compares with the bottom half of the distribution which collectively owns barely 1 percent of global wealth. Thus the top 1 percent own almost forty times as much as the bottom 50 percent. The contrast with the bottom decile of wealth holders is even starker. The average member of the top decile has nearly 3,000 times the mean wealth of the bottom decile, and the average member of the top percentile is more than 13,000 times richer. (Davies et al. 2006, p. 26)

The unequal distribution of wealth between nations via trade flows was the main argument of the dependency theory in the 1950s. Raul Prebisch (1950) and others have documented this inequality as a transfer of wealth from developing to developed countries in the form of declining terms of trade. Others have argued that underdevelopment (and therefore poverty) is a by-product of the development of Europe and other industrial countries (Darity 1992; Rodney 1972). James Galbraith (2002), on the other hand, showed that the rise in inequality that began in the early 1980s coincided with a sharp increase in real interest rates, an event that had dramatic effects on poor countries, which were forced to adopt austere policies that resulted in more poverty.

Wealth and poverty are not mutually exclusive. They coexist in a dialectical manner; they are both the result of one thing: the unequal distribution of value created in all the stages of production. The mechanisms underlying this unequal distribution have to do with the power relationships leading to the appropriation of profits made from the production and sale of commodities, whether at the national or the global level. The market mechanism cannot bring about social justice. To achieve some form of democratic wealth, redistribution through public intervention is necessary.

SEE ALSO *Aristotle; Class Conflict; Economics, Stratification; Globalization, Social and Economic Aspects of; Human Capital; Inequality, Income; Inequality, Wealth; Inheritance; Interest Rates; Islam, Shia and Sunni; Justice, Social; Keynes, John Maynard; Markets; Marx, Karl; Plato; Poverty; Power; Prebisch-Singer Hypothesis; Profits; Property; Slavery; Smith, Adam; Surplus; Underdevelopment; Veblen, Thorstein; World Trade Organization*

BIBLIOGRAPHY

Bonner, Michael. 2005. Poverty and Economics in the Qur'an. *Journal of Interdisciplinary History* 35 (3): 391–406.

Clarke, Charles M. A. 2002. Wealth and Poverty: On the Social Creation of Scarcity. *Journal of Economic Issues* 36 (2): 415–421.

Darity, William, Jr. 1992. A Model of "Original Sin": Rise of the West and Lag of the Rest. *American Economic Review* 82 (2): 162–167.

Davies, James B., Susanna Sandstrom, Anthony Shorrocks, and Edward N. Wolff. 2006. *The World Distribution of Household Wealth.* Helsinki: World Institute for Development Economics and Research.

Galbraith, James K. 2002. A Perfect Crime: Inequality in the Age of Globalization. *Daedalus* (Winter): 11–25.

Keynes, John Maynard. 1936. *The General Theory of Employment, Interest, and Money.* London: Macmillan.

Marx, Karl. [1867–1910] 1968. *Capital.* Vol. IV. Moscow: Progress Publishers.

Marx, Karl. [1867–1910] 1992. *Capital.* Vol. I. New York: International Publishers.

Perrotta, Cosimo. 2003. The Legacy of the Past: Ancient Economic Thought on Wealth and Development. *European Journal of History of Economic Thought* 10 (2): 177–229.

Prebisch, Raul. 1950. *The Economic Development of Latin America and Its Principal Problem.* Santiago: United Nations Economic Commission for Latin America.

Rodney, Walter. 1972. *How Europe Underdeveloped Africa.* London: Bogle-L'Ouverture.

Sihag, Balbir S. 2005. Kautilya on Ethics and Economics. *Humanomics* 21 (3–4): 1–28.

Smith, Adam. [1759] 1976a. *The Theory of Moral Sentiments.* Oxford: Oxford University Press.

Smith, Adam. [1776] 1976b. *An Inquiry into the Nature and Causes of the Wealth of Nations.* Oxford: Oxford University Press.

United Nations Development Program (UNDP). 2001. *Human Development Report.* Oxford: Oxford University Press.

Veblen, Thorstein. 1899. *The Theory of the Leisure Class.* New York: Macmillan.

Hassan Bougrine

WEALTH OF NATIONS

SEE *Smith, Adam.*

WEAPONRY, NUCLEAR

The advent of the nuclear weapons age began on July 16, 1945, when the United States tested its first nuclear device in New Mexico at the Alamogordo Bombing Range, now

known as the White Sands Missile Range. The successful nuclear explosion, named Trinity, was the end result of the Manhattan Project, a three-year, $1.9 billion ($26.9 billion in 2005 dollars) effort that brought hundreds of the world's top scientists together to develop a weapon to be used in the United States' war efforts against Japan and Germany. Nuclear weapons have been used in warfare on two occasions: on Hiroshima, Japan, on August 6, 1945, and on Nagasaki, Japan, on August 9, 1945. Both bombs were dropped by the United States. As of 2006, eight nations were known to possess nuclear weapons: the United States, Russia, the United Kingdom, France, China, Israel, India, and Pakistan. It is possible that North Korea also possesses a nuclear weapon. In 2003 North Korea claimed to have had successfully developed nuclear weapons. While North Korea has not tested a device, most intelligence estimates believe it is likely that it has nuclear capabilities. South Africa once possessed nuclear weapons but dismantled them in 1993 (see Cirincione, Wolfsthal, and Rajkumar 2005).

Nuclear weapons require *fissionable* materials. When a fissionable atom absorbs a neutron, it will split and release additional neutrons. In a nuclear chain reaction, those neutrons are absorbed into other fissionable atoms that subsequently split and release additional neutrons into other atoms. Nuclear explosions are the result of the rapid release of energy that comes from an uncontrolled nuclear chain reaction.

The two fissionable elements used in nuclear weapons are uranium and plutonium. Uranium is found in nature, but the specific fissionable isotope, uranium-235, constitutes only 0.7 percent of all natural uranium. A nuclear weapon, however, requires uranium-235 to make up over 90 percent of the sample. In order to achieve such a high concentration, the uranium must go through an enrichment process that separates uranium-235 from the more common uranium-238 isotope. This has most commonly been achieved with centrifuges, but other methods, such as gaseous diffusion and electromagnetic isotope separation, have also been successful. Plutonium is not found in nature but is a product of the highly radioactive waste from a controlled chain reaction of uranium, usually performed in a nuclear reactor. To extract plutonium from this waste, a sophisticated chemical process is used. For a country seeking to establish a nuclear weapons program, these large-scale industrial and technical processes can be prohibitive.

Critical mass is the smallest amount of fissionable material that is needed to maintain a nuclear chain reaction. How much uranium or plutonium is needed to reach critical mass depends on various elements of weapon design, such as the shape of the fissile core (gun-type or sphere) or the effective use of reflectors to capture errant neutrons. Most estimates are that between 12 to 60 kilograms of weapons-grade uranium and 4 to 10 kilograms of plutonium are needed. In addition, the efficiency and yield of a weapon can be increased by adding a fusion fuel "booster," such as lithium-6, as found in thermonuclear weapons.

THE EFFECTS OF A NUCLEAR EXPLOSION

The effects of a nuclear explosion are devastating. The majority of damage is caused by three main elements: blast effects, thermal heat, and ionizing radiation. For example, the bomb that was dropped on Hiroshima, a uranium-type device known as Little Boy, had a yield of 12.5 kilotons of TNT. Of the 76,000 buildings in Hiroshima, 48,000 were completely destroyed and another 22,000 were damaged. According to one study of the Hiroshima bombing, the temperature at the site of the explosion reached 5,400 degrees Fahrenheit and "primary atomic bomb thermal injury was found in those exposed within [2 miles] of the hypocenter" (quoted in Rhodes 1986, p. 714). The heat was so intense that people within a half mile of the fireball were reduced to bundles of smoking char. The number of deaths in Hiroshima due to the bomb is estimated to be 140,000, with an additional 60,000 dying from radiation effects over the next five years.

Since these early devices, the yield of nuclear weapons has grown considerably. Although never deployed, on October 30, 1961, the largest nuclear bomb ever tested was the Soviet Union's "Tsar Bomba," which had a maximum yield of 100 megatons. More commonly, modern nuclear weapons have yields ranging between one and 5.5 megatons.

For a one-megaton device, the damage would be even more widespread than at Hiroshima and Nagasaki. According to Ansley J. Coale (1985), the shockwaves from a one-megaton blast would destroy modern multistory buildings within 2.9 miles and unreinforced brick and wood buildings within 4.2 miles of impact. Damage to brick and wood buildings would be substantial up to 8.5 miles from the blast. Heat would cause third-degree burns to exposed skin and set fire to clothing within 4.2 miles. The gamma rays produced from such a blast would be almost immediately lethal to any exposed person within 2.5 miles. People exposed at a slightly greater distance (2.7 miles) would have about a 50 percent mortality rate within a month of the explosion. Finally, a nuclear explosion that makes contact with the ground (as opposed to an airblast) would create tremendous amounts of radioactive fallout that could spread over an area as far as 1,000 square miles downwind from the explosion. Estimates of what percentage would be killed in a one-megaton blast on an urban population vary from 11 percent to 25 percent of

the total population, with an additional 16 to 25 percent injured. Of course, in a nuclear exchange between advanced nuclear weapons states, multiple bombs would likely be assigned to single targets, resulting in even higher levels of devastation.

DELIVERY METHODS

The three main methods of delivery involve ballistic missiles, aircraft, and submarines. Delivery methods are tied to larger strategic and tactical issues related to nuclear deterrence. Nuclear states, such as the United States and the Soviet Union during the cold war, are concerned that a first-strike nuclear attack from another country could be so damaging that it would successfully eliminate any possibility for retaliation. As a result, states design their nuclear forces in such a way that a sufficient number of weapons would remain to respond with a devastating second strike. Many argue that the sole purpose of any nuclear weapon is to deter other states from ever using one. Some also fear that a terrorist organization could gain possession of a nuclear weapon and smuggle it into a major urban center.

Intercontinental ballistic missiles (ICBMs) are launched from reinforced below-ground silos and have ranges of more than 8,000 miles. Often, ICBMs are equipped with multiple warheads—multiple, independently targeted reentry vehicles (MIRV)—capable of hitting multiple targets. Shorter-range ballistic missiles, which could more easily be used in tactical or battlefield scenarios, have largely been eliminated from the arsenals of major nuclear states.

The appeal of aircraft and submarines is their mobility, as well as an enemy's consequent difficulty in targeting them. Heavy-duty bombers, primarily equipped with up to twenty short-range attack missiles capable of hitting multiple targets, have the ability to penetrate enemy territory and withstand a great deal of abuse. Submarines carrying strategic nuclear missiles can remain below the surface for long periods and can launch missiles capable of hitting specific targets over distances of hundreds of miles. The possession of a nuclear-equipped submarine fleet gives a country a very credible second-strike deterrent.

Since the end of the cold war, both the United States and the former Soviet Union have worked to decrease their nuclear arsenals. However, many fear that tensions between other nuclear states, such as India and Pakistan, and the ongoing threat of further proliferation could result in the future use of nuclear weapons.

SEE ALSO *Defense; Defense, National; Deterrence, Mutual; Disarmament; Proliferation, Nuclear; World War II*

BIBLIOGRAPHY

Barnaby, Frank. 2003. *How to Build a Nuclear Bomb and Other Weapons of Mass Destruction.* London: Granta.

Campbell, Christopher. 1984. *Nuclear Weapons Fact Book.* Novato, CA: Presidio Press.

Cirincione, Joseph, with Jon B. Wolfsthal and Miriam Rajkumar. 2005. *Deadly Arsenals: Tracking Weapons of Mass Destruction.* Washington, DC: Carnegie Endowment for International Peace.

Coale, Ansley J. 1985. Nuclear War and Demographers' Projections. *Population and Development Review* 11 (3): 483–493.

Nuclear Weapons Data. *Bulletin of the Atomic Scientists.* http://www.thebulletin.org/nuclear_weapons_data.

Rhodes, Richard. 1986. *The Making of the Atomic Bomb.* New York: Simon and Schuster.

Schwartz, Stephen I., ed. 1998. *Atomic Audit: The Costs and Consequences of U.S. Nuclear Weapons Since 1940.* Washington, DC: Brookings Institution Press.

David R. Andersen

WEAPONS INDUSTRY

The fusion of militarism and industrialism was made possible by the Industrial Revolution. In the early industrializing nations of Europe and North America, military leaders harnessed new sources of energy to facilitate transportation (e.g., steam-powered trains and ships) and new means of communication (e.g., the telegraph). This did not require a distinctly militarized industrial sector, only the ability to commandeer commercial goods to feed, clothe, and transport significantly larger military forces. Industrialism also gave rise to the invention of uniquely military end-items and the emergence of large industrial concerns, including defense firms and state-owned armories and shipyards, to produce them. In the twentieth century, this refinement of military goods would give rise to defense firms and the military-industrial complexes (van Creveld 1989).

The fusion of industrialism and militarism facilitated colonialism and conquest. European empires expanded dramatically in the latter half of the nineteenth century, and settler nations such as the United States, Australia, and South Africa completed the conquest of entire continents. Even as they conquered and displaced indigenous peoples, nations such as the United States did *not* become "warrior" societies. Rather, based on technological advantages afforded by industrialism, European powers and settler nations enjoyed distinct military advantages, often against much larger military forces. To compete on the international stage, military and political leaders in Germany, Japan, and Russia induced industrial develop-

ment in the late nineteenth and early twentieth centuries. These top-down industrialization programs, driven by military priorities, were among the least democratic totalitarian regimes of the twentieth century.

During World Wars I (1914–1918) and II (1939–1945), the industrial capacity of leading economic powers was harnessed to perpetrate an unprecedented slaughter of soldiers and civilians. This industrialization of warfare transformed the battlefield and military organization. Equally important was the social transformation. The mass industrial wars of the twentieth century demanded total mobilization of the armed forces and the economy. In the United States, the iconic Rosie the Riveter called attention to the large number of women contributing to the war effort during World War II, many of whom had not previously worked outside the home. A similar trend unfolded among the industrialized nations fighting industrialized wars. Although the World War II mobilization temporarily redefined the roles of men and women in factories and offices, gender segregation persisted during the war and was reasserted at the war's end (on the U.S. case, see Milkman 1987). These mass industrial wars also transformed the risks and casualties among civilians. Improved record keeping and social control allowed states to identify, transport, incarcerate, and in some cases, slaughter millions of civilians (the Holocaust being a spectacular example). For these wars, industrial targets in densely populated areas became prominent targets. World War II was especially lethal (Kolko 1994): Large portions of London and several Soviet cities were decimated by German attacks; Dresden and Tokyo were consumed in firestorms and Berlin reduced to rubble; and two Japanese cities (Hiroshima and Nagasaki) were destroyed by atomic bombs.

THE WEAPONS INDUSTRY IN THE COLD WAR ERA

In the course of the cold war (1948–1989), the United States and the Soviet Union built and maintained large weapons industries. The sustained fusion of industrialism and militarism in the postwar United States prompted President Eisenhower to warn the nation and the world about the dangers of the military-industrial complex (Eisenhower 1961). As Eisenhower had warned, the weapons industry distorted technological development and diverted scarce human and physical resources.

During the cold war, a "wall of separation" grew between the defense and civilian sectors of the economy (Markusen and Yudken 1992). Defense-oriented firms and diversified corporations that garnered defense contracts were among the fastest growing and most profitable firms. For the Soviet Union, overinvestment in the military was exacerbated by the war in Afghanistan and costly military and diplomatic commitments around the globe. These chronic fiscal strains contributed to the collapse of the Soviet Union—and with this collapse a dramatic reduction in the size and the scope of the military-industrial complex in successor states. In the twenty-first century, the U.S. arsenal is increasingly reliant on state-of-the-art science and technology. In addition to nuclear weapons, chemical and biological weapons are also produced through sophisticated scientific processes. Even "conventional" forces are being transformed by new sensing, computing, and communication devices being assembled to create an electronic battlefield. Space may become militarized as well. If satellites capable of destroying moving missiles or stationary targets are deployed, highly automated weapons far removed from earth would be at the center of the war and would pose the greatest threat to human life.

CONTEMPORARY DYNAMICS AND THREATS POSED BY THE WEAPONS INDUSTRY

The collapse of the Soviet Union and the end of the cold war raised hopes that the military-industrial complex would be dismantled. In the early 1990s, global military expenditures and arms sales fell as expected. But a resurgence in military spending began in the late 1990s, with the nations of the Middle East figuring prominently. The United States has also increased defense spending since the mid-1990s, to $475 billion in 2005 ($30 billion higher than in 1988). In 2005, the United States accounted for 48 percent of all military spending in the world, an unprecedented level of concentration (Stockholm International Peace Research Institute 2006a).

The resurgence of the military-industrial complex goes beyond the spike in arms production and sales. The changing organizational structure of the military-industrial complex is an equally important—perhaps more important—aspect of this resurgence. When defense spending declined in the 1990s, leading defense firms did not "beat swords into ploughshares." They redoubled efforts in the shrinking defense market. A round of mergers, acquisitions, and reorganizations occurred: The number of firms declined because of these mergers, and the surviving firms were much larger (see Markusen and Costigan 1999). Whereas the top five firms accounted for 22 percent of the world's arms sales in 1990, their share doubled (44%) by 2003. With the top five firms accounting for most of the increase, the top twenty firms commanded 57 percent in 1990, and their share of arm sales jumped to 74 percent by 2003 (Stockholm International Peace Research Institute 2006b). Not only are arms sales concentrated in fewer firms, but these firms are concentrated in the United States and a handful of nations.

The increased privatization of national security is also a cause for concern. Private firms have provided construction, logistics support, and so forth to military organizations for centuries. But the growth in the size and range of activities has been notable. The concentration of arms sales in a handful of enormous transnational corporations also concentrates scientific and technical expertise. Governments are growing reliant on corporations (often distant corporations) to plan and coordinate essential national security functions. In addition, corporate mercenaries have played a direct role in toppling governments and in the prisoner abuse committed by the United States during the wars in Afghanistan and Iraq (Isenberg 2004). These mercenaries and the corporations employing them rarely face criminal charges. They not only operate with impunity but also shield the government employing them from democratic scrutiny. In a world in which five firms control more than 40 percent of all arms sales and the top twenty firms account for nearly 75 percent, many governments have lost a measure of control over defense policies. The increased reliance on mercenaries further reduces democratic control and oversight.

Citizens forced to make sacrifices, serve in mass armies, and experience directly the horror of war often question the necessity of fighting. But citizens insulated from the horrors of war often cheer on technological marvels that kill thousands of people and destroy distant cities. Citizens of powerful nations often fail to empathize with the suffering caused by the highly scientific and distant slaughter perpetrated in their name. This callousness is reinforced by the role of major arms-producing corporations. These corporations sell military goods and defense planning to governments around the globe; they also supply mercenaries to fight on the battlefield and interrogate prisoners. By ceding so much control to the insulated corporations of the weapons industry, governments are more distant from their own people and contribute to removing military policies from public scrutiny and democratic oversight. At the dawn of the twenty-first century, our challenge is to restore democratic oversight in a realm dominated by enormous corporations and government bureaucracies.

SEE ALSO *Cold War; Deterrence, Mutual; Eisenhower, Dwight D.; Holocaust, The; Industrialization; Industry; Militarism; Military; Military Regimes; Military-Industrial Complex; Union of Soviet Socialist Republics; War; Weaponry, Nuclear; Weapons of Mass Destruction*

BIBLIOGRAPHY

Eisenhower, Dwight. [1961] 1992. President Eisenhower's Farewell Address to the Nation. In *The Military-Industrial Complex: Eisenhower's Warning Three Decades Later*, eds. Gregg Walker, David Bella, and Steven Sprecher, 361–368. New York: Peter Lang.

Hooks, Gregory. 1991. *Forging the Military-Industrial Complex: World War II's Battle of the Potomac*. Chicago: University of Illinois Press.

Isenberg, David. 2004. Profit Comes with a Price. *Asia Times On-line*, May 19. http://www.atimes.com/atimes/Middle_East/FE19Ak01.html

Kolko, Gabriel. 1994. *Century of War: Politics, Conflicts, and Society Since 1914*. New York: New Press.

Markusen, Ann, and Sean Costigan, eds. 1999. *Arming the Future: A Defense Industry for the 21st Century*. New York: Council on Foreign Relations Press.

Markusen, Ann, and Joel Yudken. 1992. *Dismantling the Cold War Economy*. New York: Basic Books.

Milkman, Ruth. 1987. *Gender at Work: The Dynamics of Job Segregation by Sex During World War II*. Urbana: University of Illinois Press.

Stockholm International Peace Research Institute (SIPRI). 2006a. *SIPRI Yearbook 2006: Armaments, Disarmament and International Security*. New York: Oxford University Press.

Stockholm International Peace Research Institute (SIPRI). 2006b. *Concentration Ratios*. http://www.sipri.org/contents/milap/milex/aprod/concentration_ratios.html

Van Creveld, Martin. 1989. *Technology and War: From 2000 B.C. to the Present*. New York: Free Press.

Gregory Hooks

WEAPONS OF MASS DESTRUCTION

Weapons of mass destruction (WMD) have been used throughout history. While there are definitional ambiguities, all conceptions of WMD imply societally unacceptable levels or forms of destruction. Despite international efforts to curb their spread, concerns over WMD use have increased since the 1990s.

DEFINITIONS AND HISTORIC USES OF THE TERM

The term *weapons of mass destruction* was first used in a London *Times* article (December 28, 1937) in reference to the German aerial bombardment of Guernica, Spain, during the Spanish Civil War (1936–1939): "Who can think without horror of what another widespread war would mean, waged as it would be with all the new weapons of mass destruction?" (p. 9). While the Luftwaffe (the German air force) used only "conventional" weapons in the attack, subsequent definitions have emphasized weapons whose materials and effects violate a societal boundary of what is considered "acceptable" in wartime.

The United Nations Security Council Commission for Conventional Armaments (August 12, 1948) defined WMD as "atomic explosive weapons, radioactive material weapons, lethal chemical and biological weapons, and any weapons developed in the future which have characteristics comparable in destructive effect to those of the atomic bomb or other weapons mentioned above." Since the Iraq War beginning in 2003, the United States has used the term to refer to chemical, biological, nuclear, and, increasingly, radiological (CBNR) weapons. This remains the most common use of the term, although sometimes it is defined more broadly to include any weapons, including conventional weapons, capable of inflicting mass casualties.

WEAPONS OF MASS DESTRUCTION AND WARFARE

Chemical weapons include such agents as mustard, sarin, and VX nerve gases, as well as chlorine, hydrogen cyanide, and carbon monoxide. Most chemical weapons are designed to attack the nervous system. They were first used in modern times during World War I (1914–1918) when the French used tear gas during the first month of the war, and during the Second Battle of Ypres (1915) when Germany used chlorine gas in its attack against French and Algerian troops. By the end of the war, more than one million casualties and ninety thousand deaths were attributed to chemical warfare use by all sides. During World War II (1939–1945) the Nazis used hydrogen cyanide and carbon monoxide in the extermination camps, killing millions. More recent chemical attacks include the U.S. use of Agent Orange during the Vietnam War (1957–1975); Iraqi president Saddam Hussein's use both of sarin gas against Iran during the Iran-Iraq War (1980–1988) and of multiple chemical agents against the Iraqi town of Halabja in 1988, killing up to five thousand Kurds; and Aum Shinrikyo's sarin gas attacks in Matsumoto (1994) and on the Tokyo subway (1995) in Japan.

Biological weapons are weapons of germ warfare; they include a large number of living agents such as anthrax, botulinum toxin, plague, ricin, smallpox, and typhus. A subclass of biological weapons that could be directed specifically at agriculture includes mad cow disease and swine fever. Although used throughout history, biological weapons have seen limited use in attacks in modern times due to difficulties in creating effective dispersal mechanisms. Exceptions include Japan's use of biological agents during the Sino-Japanese War (1937–1945) and World War II, including a 1943 attack on Changde, China, that involved an attempt to spread bubonic plague. In 1984 members of the Rajneeshee cult infected a salad bar with salmonella in The Dalles, Oregon, sickening nine hundred, and anthrax was disseminated through the U.S. postal system in 2001, killing five.

Nuclear weapons produce their destructive effects through nuclear fission from chain reactions involving uranium or plutonium or from nuclear fusion (the so-called hydrogen bomb). Considered the most destructive of all WMD, nuclear weapons have been used on two occasions, both at the end of World War II. The bombing of Hiroshima, Japan, on August 6, 1945, killed some 80,000 civilians immediately and another 60,000 from radiation by the end of the year. The attack on Nagasaki three days later ultimately killed 100,000.

Radiological weapons, unlike nuclear weapons, have no blast effect. They derive their destructive power from radiation alone and typically depend on an explosive device to disperse the radiation, although radioactive material could also be sprayed from crop duster planes. Radiological weapons have never been used, but Iraq is believed to have tested them in 1987 for possible use against Iran. The plan was abandoned after it was found that the radioactivity dissipated within a week of the weapon's manufacture.

WMD CONTROL

Due largely to their ability to indiscriminately kill and inflict harm on civilian populations even when the intended target is military, WMD, unlike conventional weapons, have traditionally encountered societal opprobrium. This has led to a number of international agreements to limit their development and use.

The Nuclear Non-Proliferation Treaty (1970) seeks to prevent the spread of nuclear weapons and weapons technology beyond the states already known to possess them. A total of 187 parties have joined the treaty. At least nine countries are known or suspected to possess nuclear weapons as of 2006 (the United States, Russia, Great Britain, France, China, India, Pakistan, Israel, and North Korea). The Comprehensive Nuclear-Test-Ban Treaty seeks to deter development of nuclear weapons by banning all nuclear explosions. The treaty was opened for signature in 1996. As of 2006, the treaty had 176 members but would not come into force until all forty-four nations conducting nuclear research or possessing nuclear power reactors signed and ratified the treaty; eleven ratifications were still necessary in 2006.

The 1925 Geneva Protocol bans the use of biological weapons, and the 1975 Biological and Toxin Weapons Convention bans their "development, production, stockpiling, acquisition, or retention" except for "prophylactic, protective or other peaceful" purposes. The convention has been signed by 162 countries. The United States, Russia, North Korea, and Syria are known or believed to possess biological weapons.

The Chemical Weapons Convention (1997) prohibits the "development, production, acquisition, stock-

piling, transfer, and use" of chemical weapons and requires all signatories to destroy their chemical weapons and chemical-weapons production facilities. The convention was signed by 140 nations; some seventeen nations are known or believed to maintain chemical weapons stockpiles.

Despite efforts to curb WMD proliferation, real concerns remain. One major concern involves their acquisition by rogue states or terrorist organizations. As of 2006, North Korea's and Iran's nuclear programs were deemed threatening, and the terrorist organization Al-Qaeda was believed to be seeking some level of WMD capability.

SEE ALSO *Hussein, Saddam; Iraq-U.S. War; Terrorism; Terrorists; Weaponry, Nuclear*

BIBLIOGRAPHY

Comprehensive Nuclear-Test-Ban Treaty. 1996. http://www.ctbto.org.

Convention on the Prohibition of the Development, Production, and Stockpiling of Bacteriological (Biological) and Toxin Weapons and on Their Destruction. 1975. http://disarmament2.un.org/wmd/bwc/.

Convention on the Prohibition of the Development, Production, Stockpiling, and Use of Chemical Weapons and on Their Destruction. 1997. http://disarmament.un.org/wmd/cwc/.

Macfarlane, Allison. 2005. All Weapons of Mass Destruction Are Not Equal. Massachusetts Institute of Technology, Center for International Studies. http://web.mit.edu/cis/pdf/ Audit_6_05_Macfarlane.pdf.

Times. 1937. Archbishop's Appeal. December 28: 9.

Treaty on the Non-Proliferation of Nuclear Weapons. 1970. http://disarmament2.un.org/wmd/npt/.

United Nations Security Council Commission for Conventional Armaments. August 12, 1948.

Weapons of War: Poison Gas. 2002. FirstWorldWar.com. http://www.firstworldwar.com/weaponry/gas.htm.

Donna J. Nincic

WEAVER, ROBERT C.
1907–1997

Robert Clifton Weaver's career as economist and presidential advisor spanned the New Deal to the War on Poverty. He produced two major treatises on the economic status of African Americans, *Negro Labor* (1946) and *The Negro Ghetto* (1948), and an influential textbook in urban planning and policy, *The Urban Complex* (1964). Weaver was the first U.S. Secretary of Housing and Urban Development (HUD) and the first African American to hold a cabinet-level position.

Born in Washington, D.C., on December 29, 1907, Weaver earned his doctorate in economics in 1934 from Harvard University. From 1933 through 1944, he held a sequence of advisory positions in the administration of President Franklin D. Roosevelt, including Advisor on Negro Affairs to Secretary of the Interior Harold Ickes (1934–1938) and chief, Negro Manpower Service, War Manpower Commission (1942–1944). From 1961 to 1966, under Presidents John F. Kennedy and Lyndon B. Johnson, he was Administrator of the Housing and Home Finance Administration. President Johnson appointed Weaver the first secretary of HUD in 1966, a post he held until 1968.

Although most of his career was spent in government, Weaver was a consistent critic of government's failure to end—and occasional duplicity in—the subjugation and segregation of the black population. In *Negro Labor*, Weaver detailed the participation of government agencies and trade unions in the exclusion of black workers from defense industry jobs. In *The Negro Ghetto*, Weaver explained how the Federal Housing Authority's (FHA's) lending practices reinforced local efforts to exclude African Americans from moving into white communities. Weaver argued that segregation would result in deteriorating housing quality and, eventually, to anger, the degradation of social relationships, and increased violence. In essence, he predicted the urban uprisings of the 1960s in 1948.

Walter B. Hill, in "Finding Place for the Negro: Robert C. Weaver and the Groundwork for the Civil Rights Movement" (2005), and Charles and Dona Hamilton, in "Social Policies, Civil Rights and Poverty" (1986), credit Weaver with the creation of a forerunner of modern affirmative action—the minimum percentage clause. This clause, which was inserted into Public Works Administration contracts for low-cost housing, prohibited discrimination on the basis of race or religion and identified, as prima facie evidence of discrimination, a contractor's failure to hire a minimum percentage of black workers, based on the number of skilled black craftsmen in the locality.

Weaver outlined his vision of how to revitalize these urban centers in *The Urban Complex* and in *Dilemmas of Urban America* (1965). Weaver sought to revitalize urban centers through comprehensive, regional planning. Despite the black community's perception that urban renewal meant "Negro removal," Weaver remained an advocate of the use of eminent domain, government subsidies, and tax incentives to replace deteriorating, low-cost housing in urban centers. Weaver believed urban renewal projects created the opportunity to replace segregated ghettos with integrated communities. Later, in a 1985 article, "The First Twenty Years of HUD," Weaver acknowledged the difficulty of realizing this vision.

Following his tenure at HUD, Weaver served as president of Baruch College, City University of New York, and as a Distinguished Professor of Urban Affairs at Hunter College. He died in July 17, 1997, at the age of eighty-nine. In 1999, Congress renamed the HUD headquarters in his honor.

SEE ALSO *Discrimination, Racial; General Equilibrium; Ghetto; Johnson, Lyndon B.; Kennedy, John F.; New Deal, The; Poverty; Roosevelt, Franklin D.; Segregation; Segregation, Residential; Urban Renewal; Urban Studies*

BIBLIOGRAPHY

Hamilton, Charles V., and Dona C. Hamilton. 1986. Social Policies, Civil Rights and Poverty. In *Fighting Poverty: What Works and What Doesn't*, eds. Sheldon H. Danziger and Daniel H. Weinberg. Cambridge, MA: Harvard University Press.

Hill, Walter B., Jr. 2005. Finding Place for the Negro: Robert C. Weaver and the Groundwork for the Civil Rights Movement. *Prologue* 37 (1): 42–51. http://www.archives.gov/publications/prologue/2005/spring/weaver.html.

Weaver, Robert C. 1946. *Negro Labor: A National Problem*. Port Washington, NY: Kennikat Press, 1969.

Weaver, Robert C. 1948. *The Negro Ghetto*. New York: Harcourt, Brace, Jovanovich.

Weaver, Robert C. 1964. *The Urban Complex: Human Values in Urban Life*. New York: Doubleday.

Weaver, Robert C. 1965. *Dilemmas of Urban America*. Cambridge, MA: Harvard University Press.

Weaver, Robert C. 1985. The First Twenty Years of HUD. *The Journal of the American Planning Association* 51 (Autumn): 463–474.

Cecilia Conrad

WEBB, BEATRICE AND SYDNEY

SEE *Fabianism.*

WEBER, MAX
1864–1920

Max Weber helped establish sociology as a social scientific discipline at the beginning of the twentieth century. In *Economy and Society: An Outline of Interpretive Sociology* (1920) he analyzed modern bureaucracies, the structure of stratification, origins of the city in the West, types of political domination, the genesis of modern legal systems, the importance of religion for social life, and other topics. Perhaps no sociologist, before or since, has displayed his intellectual range and sophistication.

EARLY YEARS

Weber was born on April 21, 1864, in Erfurt, Germany. A gifted child, Weber became politically astute at a young age. His father, a lawyer and politician, entertained prominent people in his salon and the young Weber participated in their discussions.

Weber's parents were mismatched. His father, a hedonist who enjoyed bourgeois living, ruled the household absolutely. His mother, while loving and affectionate, adhered to strict Calvinist standards of hard work, ascetic behavior, and personal morality. Weber's wife, Marianne, later reported that he believed he needed to choose between his parents. This dilemma became a source of emotional agony throughout his life. Indeed, his sociological writings may constitute an attempt at working through this inner conflict.

During the 1880s and 1890s, Weber became a successful lawyer and college professor. He had political aspirations. According to Marianne, a distant cousin whom he married in 1893, Weber lived an ascetic life, strictly regulated by the clock. On completing each task he immediately took on a new one. He was chronically overworked, which may have contributed to his eventual collapse.

In 1897 his mother planned a visit with Max and Marianne that his father opposed. Father and son clashed and parted without reconciliation. Shortly thereafter, the old man died. Within weeks, Weber suffered a complete nervous breakdown. At that time, before psychotherapy, the only treatment for such ailments was rest. Weber resigned his teaching position and remained incapacitated for five years. In 1903 Max and Marianne toured America, witnessing its vitality. The trip seemed to rekindle his ability to work.

MAJOR CONTRIBUTIONS

In 1904 Weber posed a simple question: "In what sense are there 'objectively valid truths' in those disciplines concerned with social and cultural phenomena?" ([1904] 1949, p. 51). His subsequent writings provide an answer to this query.

Weber's first goal was to show that objective social scientific research is possible, a controversial position at that time and one that remains divisive. He insisted that sociologists should not infuse research with their personal values, economic interests, or political agendas. As he put it, research should be value free, as unbiased and objective as possible.

This goal carries an important implication: Sociology should not be a politically committed discipline. Rather, Weber distinguished between "what ought to be," the sphere of values, and "what is," the sphere of science. Science, Weber said, cannot tell people either how to live or what public policies to adopt. Objective social scientific knowledge can, however, provide them with information necessary to make such decisions ([1904] 1949, p. 54).

In order to achieve this goal, Weber argued that sociologists should apply a "rational method" to their work; that is, they should use clear concepts and systematic observations and then make logical inferences ([1920] 1946a, p. 143; [1904] 1949, p. 105). But this task is difficult. After all, researchers participate in social life, which means they often approach topics with preconceived opinions. Moreover, any specific study only provides a partial picture, which can imply taking sides. The solution to these difficulties is for scholars to critically evaluate and replicate research. Although this practice is imperfect (since human beings are imperfect), it leads to a self-correcting process that produces research findings that are as objective as possible. Given accurate information, Weber argued, sociologists can sometimes suggest strategies for achieving policy goals and possible consequences. At that point, values intrude, since the problem becomes what is to be done. Weber addressed this issue in his essay "Politics as a Vocation," where he described politics as a process by which competing interest groups seek to affect public policies and the state as monopolizing the use of force in implementing them. The political problem of evaluating and applying scientific findings to practical matters is perennial in modern societies.

Another implication of Weber's argument for value-free sociology is that the new discipline reflected an ongoing historical process that he called rationalization, in which social life becomes methodically organized based on the use of reason and observation. Weber saw that this process permeates every sphere of modern life: education, work, law, economy, and family. The sciences, of course, including sociology, are the archetypal methodical disciplines. They provide new ways of understanding and controlling our environment, natural and social, opening up dizzying new possibilities. Industrialization, capitalism, democracy, and scientific advance are linked historically, leading to improved lives for most people. For example, they have straight teeth, better diets, and—the ultimate gift—longer lives. All reflect the process of rationalization. In modern societies, then, people look for explanations based on reliable knowledge. They seek solutions to problems rather than accepting fate. This orientation becomes generalized to every sphere: Anyone who uses modern technology learns to approach problems methodically, rather than by relying on magical thinking. But the impact can be disquieting, even frightening, because choices sometimes must be made between competing moral imperatives.

Weber, like many others, feared the impact of rationalization on social life. Knowledge based on reason and observation destroyed magical explanations that had provided meaning for people throughout history. In his essay "Science as a Vocation," he mused about the "disenchantment of the world" that characterizes modern societies ([1920] 1946a, p. 139). This evocative phrase suggests that humans have passed from an enchanted world of mystery and spirituality into one that is colder, more heartless, perhaps bereft of moral guidance. In a rationalized world, Weber lamented, there are no longer simple answers to the fundamental questions of human existence.

Weber's second goal was to understand the origin of modern societies. He confronted this issue in his most important book, *The Protestant Ethic and the Spirit of Capitalism* (1904–1905), and subsequent studies in the sociology of religion. They constitute an exercise in historical hypothesis testing in which Weber constructed a logical experiment using ideal types as conceptual tools.

Ideal types are concepts that identify the essential characteristics of a social phenomenon in the purest form possible. As he put it, they are designed "to be perfect on logical grounds," which has the "merit of clear understandability and lack of ambiguity" ([1920] 1968, p. 6). Empirical observations, of course, will deviate from the ideal (or pure form). By providing a common point of comparison, however, ideal types set up a logical experiment. They function like a control group in an experiment, and observed variations reflect the impact of causal forces (a stimulus in an experiment) that can be discovered.

In *The Protestant Ethic* and other studies, Weber explained why capitalism arose in Western Europe and helped to usher in modern life by using ideal types to systematically compare Western Europe in the seventeenth and eighteenth centuries with China and India. What distinguished Europe, he found, was not the level of technology, a free labor force, or other factors. Rather, the West became unique due to the rise of the culture (or spirit) of capitalism as an unintended consequence of the Protestant Reformation.

The Protestant Ethic opens with a then-common finding: "Wherever capitalism ... has had a free hand" a relationship existed between Protestantism and economic success ([1904–1905] 1958a, p. 25). Why might this be so?

Weber began his answer by describing the "spirit of capitalism" as it existed in the eighteenth century: (1) work is an end in itself; (2) economic success reflects personal virtue; (3) a methodically organized life is inherently proper; and (4) immediate pleasure should be postponed in favor of future satisfaction. Although expressed as ideal types, these cultural values could be observed in the writ-

ings of Benjamin Franklin and others at that time, and can be observed today as well. Weber argued that such values became historically significant as religious asceticism (self-denial) emerged from the monastery and convent into everyday life. The modern world is rationalized (in Weber's sense) to the degree that ordinary people organize their lives in light of values like these.

Such values originated in the peculiar beliefs of the protesting faith groups. In *The Protestant Ethic*, Weber examined Puritanism as the ideal type. Puritan life was dominated by unusual ethical norms, which could be observed in pastoral directives: people should work hard, take a methodical approach to everyday life, and use their possessions for purposes that enhance the glory of God. The believers' underlying motive was purely religious: to ensure they were among the elect going to heaven. The unintended impact, however, was that many of those adhering to such norms became successful, even rich. Moreover, because these religious principles displayed what he called an "elective affinity" with other historical changes occurring at about the same time—the rise of science, democracy, and industrialization—they spread and became secular values. Together, Weber argued, these interrelated changes produced modern rationalized capitalist societies, with their improved lives and potential for disenchantment.

Weber's third goal was to develop a set of concepts that would be useful for describing and understanding modern societies. This conceptual map comprises the opening sections of *Economy and Society*.

The "types of social action" illustrate both his theoretical intent and his interpretation of the modern world. According to Weber, people's actions can be classified in four ways. *Instrumentally-rational action* occurs when means and ends relate to each other based on knowledge. The model for instrumentally-rational action is scientific knowledge. Because it is based on reason and observation, science avoids self-deception and thus becomes effective in solving problems. *Value-rational action* is based on values. It always involves demands that people believe compel them to act. Parents educating children; soldiers obeying orders; citizens supporting or opposing abortion; all behave rationally in being faithful to their values. As the examples imply, value-rational action constitutes an end in itself, not a reflection of economic interest. *Traditional action* is "determined by ingrained habituation" ([1920] 1968, p. 25). In contexts where people are subject to fate, they regulate behavior by custom, often religiously sanctified. *Affectual action* is determined by emotions, and it occurs in all times and places. The parent slapping a child and the basketball player punching an opponent are examples.

Weber argued that traditional action occurs typically in preindustrial societies, where choices are limited (because knowledge is limited) and people have little control over their lives or environment. In such situations, the family usually constitutes both a productive and a consumptive unit, which means that people make economic, legal, and most other decisions in the light of tradition. Tradition (or custom) nearly always precludes the logical evaluation of means and ends based on reason and observation.

Understanding modern societies, Weber said, requires the distinction between instrumentally-rational and value-rational action, although they are interrelated in practice. The pervasiveness of instrumentally-rational action reflects the process of rationalization. People use values, however, to channel behavior. For example, they emphasize increasing knowledge, individual autonomy, protecting life, and equal opportunity, among other fundamental moral guides. In such contexts, bureaucracies become the means of administration. Their common objective is to create and enforce rules efficiently, fairly, flexibly, and competently in order for government to operate in the public interest or companies to produce goods and services. In their pure (or ideal type) form, bureaucracies constitute a model of instrumentally-rational action. Ideally, administrators obtain positions based on qualifications, personal and official affairs are kept separate, decision-rules are based on reason and knowledge, and rules are applied uniformly.

In the real world, of course, human beings comprise bureaucracies, which means they do not meet these standards perfectly. For example, corruption occurs and rules are not always applied uniformly—who one knows often makes a difference. Moreover, bureaucratic procedures (following the rules) sometimes become more important than the goals they are designed to achieve—an irrational result. The ideal type, however, provides a point of comparison, a way of evaluating people's performance in bureaucratic organizations.

Still, Weber was pessimistic about the future. The ability to obtain "objectively valid truths" about both natural and social phenomena has radically increased human understanding and improved people's lives. But it also stripped the supernatural of its ability to explain the meaning of life. At the same time, Weber showed in *The Protestant Ethic* that while the religious roots of the spirit of capitalism have died out, Puritanism bequeathed to modern people "an amazingly good, we may even say a pharisaically good, conscience in the acquisition of money" ([1904–1905] 1958a, p. 176). The Puritan, he wrote, wanted to work hard for the glory of God; we are forced to do so. But for what reason? In a disenchanted world, this question becomes hard to answer. In this context, Weber feared, the culture of capitalism, combined with capitalist social, economic, and political institutions, would place people in a bureaucratic "iron cage" from which there

might be no escape and for which there is no longer a religious justification. This possibility led to Weber's last, sad lament: "specialists without spirit, sensualists without heart; this nullity imagines that it has attained a level of civilization never before achieved" (p. 183).

COMMENTARY

The problem of objectivity remains one of the most vexing in sociology. On the one hand, some reject the goal, arguing that sociology must be politically engaged. Among the classical theorists, both Karl Marx and Émile Durkheim embraced this position, although in quite different ways. Many early American sociologists also held this view and some continue to do so in the twenty-first century. The idea is that an activist discipline can be a force for good, liberating people from oppression. On the other hand, the logic of Weber's argument suggests that a discipline committed to political change would produce unreliable knowledge and, hence, become politically irrelevant. Many, perhaps most, sociologists agree that the goal of objectivity should animate the discipline, even though its achievement can be difficult.

The "Protestant Ethic" thesis became controversial immediately and remains so today. A typical criticism is that capitalism has existed in some form throughout history. This is correct, but not Weber's point. He distinguished between the traditional enterprises of a few "adventurer capitalists," who sought windfall profit sufficient to last a lifetime, and a modern rationalized capitalist economy, which is based on the mass production of consumer goods in an environment where everyone strives to make money as an ethical duty. A more accurate criticism is that Weber missed the existence of functional equivalents to the protestant ethic in other parts of the world, such as China and Japan. This assessment provides a simple example of how the social sciences can be self-correcting. *The Protestant Ethic* also became important because its logic suggested some of the limitations of Marx's analysis. Marx argued that political and economic interests guide action. Weber agreed but added that ideas and values function like railroad switchmen: They determine the tracks along which interests push action. For example, people sometimes vote against their economic interests because of their values. In fact, in today's rationalized world, people lead methodical lives and use reason buttressed by knowledge to achieve their values.

Weber and Marx constitute opposing poles among the classical sociologists. Both were structuralists, emphasizing the importance of understanding the context in which people make decisions. But while Marx posited the existence of historical laws of development in which feudalism led inevitably to capitalism and the latter to communism, Weber replied that history has no direction.

Rather, as it occurs, history is messy and disorderly. Observers see patterns only in retrospect. Capitalism, he pointed out, arose in the West based on a series of unpredictable historical accidents, such as the Protestant Reformation. Both stressed the importance of human decision making, but again in different ways. Marx argued that inequality would increase to unsustainable levels in capitalist societies. In this context, he claimed, alienated people who did not own the means of production would rebel and usher in a new, communal society. Marx was wrong. Writing a half-century later, Weber saw that capitalism combined with industrialization to produce a middle class. He worried instead about the possibility of reason run amok: In a "disenchanted" world, "rationalized" bureaucracies would oppress people, creating conformists without a sense of ethical responsibility.

Although Weber may have been too pessimistic, the historical process of rationalization creates huge dilemmas that are not easily resolved. It is secularizing, thus frustrating a deeply felt human need for what Weber called "theodicies," ways of understanding and coping with suffering and evil. It is individuating, which leads to a paradox: People come to value both individual autonomy and communal bonds. And it is liberating, as so many areas previously determined by fate become opportunities for choice—by individuals, the state, or both. For example, one of the benefits of modernity is the gift of long life and an increasing ability to control the circumstances of death. In this context, what ethical criteria should individuals use in making end of life decisions? As interest groups offer their competing solutions, how should policy makers evaluate the political, economic, and ethical considerations surrounding this dilemma? The simple answer provided by tradition—thou shall not kill—becomes difficult to maintain when individuals' right to life must be balanced against their freedom and autonomy. Moral imperatives collide. Weber saw this essential feature of modern capitalist societies perhaps more clearly than any other classical sociologist.

Toward the end of his life, Weber seemed to find release from his psychic wounds.

Marianne reported that his ability to work became steadier and sleep more regular. He began teaching for the first time in more than twenty years, giving two of his most famous lectures: "Science as a Vocation" and "Politics as a Vocation." He also reworked his explanation of the origins of capitalism and began composing the conceptual map that frames the substantive portions of *Economy and Society*. During the summer of 1920 Max Weber developed pneumonia. He died on June 14; he was only fifty-six years old.

SEE ALSO *Capitalism; Protestant Ethic; Tawney, R. H.*

BIBLIOGRAPHY

Becker, Howard. 1967. Whose Side Are We On? *Social Problems* 14 (2): 239–247.

Bellah, Robert N. 1985. *Tokugawa Religion: The Cultural Roots of Modern Japan*. New York: Free Press.

Berger, Peter L. 1977. Toward a Critique of Modernity. In *Facing Up to Modernity*, ed. Peter L. Berger. New York: Basic Books.

Buroway, Michael. 2005. 2004 Presidential Address: For Public Sociology. *American Sociological Review* 70 (1): 4–28.

Swatos, William H., and Lutz Kaelber. 2005. *The Protestant Ethic Turns 100*. Boulder, CO: Paradigm Publishers.

Turner, Jonathan H., Leonard Beeghley, and Charles Powers. 2002. *The Emergence of Sociological Theory*, 5th ed. Belmont, CA: Wadsworth.

Weber, Marianne. [1926] 1975. *Max Weber: A Biography*. New York: Wiley.

Weber, Max. [1904] 1949. "Objectivity" in Social Science and Social Policy. In *The Methodology of the Social Sciences*, trans. Edward A. Shils and Henry A. Finch. New York: Free Press.

Weber, Max. [1904–1905] 1958. *The Protestant Ethic and the Spirit of Capitalism*, trans. Talcott Parsons. New York: Charles Scribner's Sons.

Weber, Max. [1913] 1951. *The Religion of China: Confucianism and Taoism*, trans. and ed. Hans Gerth. Glencoe, IL: Free Press.

Weber, Max. [1916–1917] 1958. *The Religion of India: Sociology of Hinduism and Buddhism*, trans. Hans Gerth. Glencoe, IL: Free Press.

Weber, Max. [1920a] 1946. Politics as a Vocation. In *From Max Weber: Essays in Sociology*, eds. Hans Gerth and C. Wright Mills. New York: Oxford University Press.

Weber, Max. [1920b] 1946. Science as a Vocation. In *From Max Weber: Essays in Sociology*, eds. Hans Gerth and C. Wright Mills. New York: Oxford University Press.

Weber, Max. [1920c] 1968. *Economy and Society: An Outline of Interpretive Sociology*, eds. Guenther Roth and Claus Wittich. New York: Bedminster Press.

Weber, Max. [1922–1923] 1946c. The Social Psychology of the World Religions. In *From Max Weber: Essays in Sociology*, eds. Hans Gerth and C. Wright Mills. New York: Oxford University Press.

Leonard Beeghley

WECHSLER INTELLIGENCE SCALE FOR CHILDREN (WISC)

SEE *Flynn Effect*.

WEDDINGS

SEE *Marriage*.

WEIGHT

Body weight is most commonly measured in kilograms or pounds. *Body mass index* (BMI) is a frequently used measure and serves as an index of weight-for-height calculated in kg/m². BMI is often used to stratify individuals into categories ranging from underweight to severely obese. One critique of BMI is that it does not distinguish between muscle and fat mass (Kraemer et al. 1990). Anthropomorphic measures (e.g., waist circumference) enhance measurement accuracy by examining distribution of excess weight around the abdominal region. Negative health consequences are associated with a waist circumference > 102 centimeters for men and > 88 centimeters for women (NIH 1998). Total body fat percentage is also used to measure excess weight and can be calculated by skin-fold caliper, hydrostatic weighing, or bioelectrical impedance testing.

Statistics compiled by the Centers for Disease Control and Prevention (CDC) indicate that in 2006 two-thirds of adults in the United States were overweight and 32.2 percent met the criteria for obesity. Moreover, obesity prevalence rates among children and adolescents have tripled since the mid-1980s (Ogden et al. 2003). Average BMI is increasing across demographic groups, and recent reports suggest that 45 percent of non-Hispanic black adults and 30 percent of non-Hispanic white adults are obese (CDC 2006). These trends are alarming because obesity is the second leading cause of preventable death and a risk factor for chronic illness, including type 2 diabetes, hypertension, and coronary heart disease.

Although the causes of obesity are not fully understood, it is viewed as a chronic disease influenced by genetic, environmental, behavioral, and cultural factors. Research suggests that genetic influences account for a significant amount of variability in BMI. Findings from twin studies suggest that up to 70 percent of variation in BMI can be accounted for by genetic factors, while adoption studies have produced more conservative heritability estimates of 20 to 30 percent (Bouchard 2002). However, genetic influences do not account for the dramatic and steady increase in the prevalence of obesity (Brownell 1994). Environmental factors, such as the widespread availability of calorie-dense foods and urban development not conducive to physical activity (e.g., lack of parks and busy intersections), also have contributed significantly to the rise in obesity.

SOCIAL CONSEQUENCES OF WEIGHT

A thin physique continues to be the accepted ideal in Western cultures despite a steady increase in the prevalence of overweight and obesity. Fashion models and popular cultural icons have become increasingly thin since the 1960s (Wolf 1991). Dissatisfaction with body weight has become the norm, especially for women (Rodin et al. 1985). In fact research suggests that 52 percent of men and 66 percent of women in the United States are dissatisfied with their weight (Garner 1997), and some women report dieting even when their weight is at or below normal (Rodin et al. 1985). However, there are racial differences on satisfaction with weight (Gluck and Geliebter 2002). Relative to white females, African American females report less concern about dieting and fatness (Rucker and Cash 1992). In addition, compared to overweight white females, overweight African American females are more satisfied with their bodies and feel more attractive (Stevens et al. 1994). While the overwhelming majority of women desire to lose weight, it is somewhat different for males. Although a substantial percentage (88%) of men who are dissatisfied with their weight do desire to lose weight, 22 percent of men who express dissatisfaction with their bodies actually wish to gain weight (Garner 1997). This is most likely due to the muscular ideals that are portrayed for male physiques (Drewnowski and Yee 1987; Frederick et al. 2005).

Weight-related stigmatization is prevalent in Western cultures, and data suggest that there has been an increase in weight bias since the mid-twentieth century (Latner and Stunkard 2003). Of the many conditions that are stigmatized in Western culture, it has been suggested that the stigma associated with being overweight may be the most debilitating and harmful (Sarlio-Lahteenkorva et al. 1995). Overweight individuals perceive stigmatization from co-workers, strangers, friends, and spouses (Friedman et al. 2005). Obesity also negatively affects employment (Rothblum et al. 1990) and socioeconomic status (Puhl and Brownell 2001). In addition data suggest that weight-based stigmatization negatively impacts the mental health of obese individuals (Friedman et al. 2005) and may contribute to overeating behaviors (Ashmore et al. 2007).

WEIGHT AND MENTAL HEALTH

Studies examining obesity and mental health have yielded mixed results. Earlier studies reported no significant mental health differences between community samples of obese and healthy-weight individuals (Wadden and Stunkard 1985). More recently, data from the National Health and Nutrition Examination Survey revealed a 1.5-fold higher risk for major depression among obese individuals relative to healthy-weight cohorts. Results suggested that severely obese individuals were at greatest risk for depression (Onyike et al. 2003). Several reviews suggest that the risk for major depression is particularly significant among the severely obese and those seeking surgical treatment for weight loss (see Wadden and Sarwer 2006), suggesting that extreme obesity is related to increased depression.

TREATMENT

Management of obesity is a major health-care challenge. There is a range of available treatments, including lifestyle modification, pharmacotherapy, and bariatric surgery. Typically, a step-care approach is taken with the least invasive intervention attempted first. Most treatments produce some initial weight loss; however, behavioral and pharmacological interventions have been largely unsuccessful in the long-term maintenance of weight loss among the severely obese (NIH 1998). Behavioral and pharmacological treatments for obesity typically result in a 5 to 15 percent weight reduction when successful, though patients often have higher weight-loss goals (Foster et al. 1997). According to the National Heart, Lung, and Blood Institute, surgical intervention is an option when BMI > 40 or > 35 in the presence of comorbid conditions (e.g., hypertension, diabetes). Follow-up studies of weight-loss surgery patients demonstrate 49 percent maintenance of excess weight loss over a fourteen-year period and resolution of many medical comorbidities (Pories 1995).

SEE ALSO *Anthropology; Anthropology, Biological; Body Image; Body Mass Index; Disease; Obese Externality; Obesity; Overeating; Self-Esteem; Undereating*

BIBLIOGRAPHY

Bouchard, Claude. 2002. Genetic Influence on Body Weight. In *Eating Disorders and Obesity: A Comprehensive Handbook*, eds. Christopher G. Fairburn and Kelly D. Brownell, 16–21. New York: Guilford.

Brownell, Kelly D. 1994. Get Slim with Higher Taxes. *New York Times*, December 15.

Centers for Disease Control and Prevention (CDC): National Center for Health Statistics. National Health and Nutrition Examination Survey. http://www.cdc.gov/nchs/nhanes.htm.

Drewnowski, Adam, and Doris K. Yee. 1987. Men and Body Image: Are Males Satisfied with Their Body Weight? *Psychosomatic Medicine* 49: 626–634.

Foster, Gary D., Thomas A. Wadden, Renee A. Vogt, and Gail Brewer. 1997. What Is a Reasonable Weight Loss? Patients' Expectations and Evaluations of Obesity Treatment Outcomes. *Journal of Consulting and Clinical Psychology* 65 (1): 79–85.

Frederick, David A., Daniel M. T. Fessler, and Martie G. Haselton. 2005. Do Representations of Male Muscularity

Differ in Men's and Women's Magazines? *Body Image* 2 (1): 81–86.

Friedman, Kelli E., Simona K. Reichamn, Philip R. Costanzo, et al. 2005. Weight Stigmatization and Ideological Beliefs: Relation to Psychological Functioning in Obese Adults. *Obesity Research* 13 (5): 907–916.

Garner, David M. 1997. The 1997 Body Image Survey Results. *Psychology Today* 30: 75–84.

Gluck, Marci E., and Allan Geliebter. 2002. Racial/Ethnic Differences in Body Image and Eating Behaviors. *Eating Behaviors* 3 (2): 143–151.

Kraemer, Helena C., Robert I. Berkowitz, and Lawrence D. Hammer. 1990. Methodological Difficulties in Studies of Obesity, I: Measurement Issues. *Annals of Behavioral Medicine* 12: 112–118.

Latner, Janet D., and Albert J. Stunkard. 2003. Getting Worse: The Stigmatization of Obese Children. *Obesity Research* 11: 452–456.

National Institutes of Health (NIH). 1998. Clinical Guidelines on the Identification, Evaluation, and Treatment of Overweight and Obesity in Adults: The Evidence Report. *Obesity Research* 6 (2): 51S–209S.

Ogden, Cynthia L., Margaret D. Carroll, and Katherine M. Flegal. 2003. Epidemiologic Trends in Overweight and Obesity. *Endocrinology and Metabolism Clinics of North America* 32: 741–760.

Onyike, Chiadi U., Rosa M. Crum, and B. Lee Hochang, et al. 2003. Is Obesity Associated with Major Depression? Results from the Third National Health and Nutrition Examination Study. *American Journal of Epidemiology* 158: 1139–1147.

Pories, W. J. 1995. Who Would Have Thought? An Operation Proves to be the Most Effective Therapy for Adult-Onset Diabetes Mellitus. *Annals of Surgery* 222: 339–352.

Puhl, Rebecca, and Kelly D. Brownell. 2001. Bias, Discrimination, and Obesity. *Obesity Research* 9: 788–805.

Rodin, Judith, Lisa R. Silberstein, and Ruth Striegel-Moore. 1985. Women and Weight: A Normative Discontent. *Psychology and Gender: Nebraska Symposium on Motivation* 32: 267–307.

Rothblum, Esther D., Pamela A. Brand, Carol T. Miller, and Helen A. Oetjen. 1990. The Relationship between Obesity, Employment Discrimination, and Employment-Related Victimization. *Journal of Vocational Behavior* 37: 251–266.

Rucker, C. E, and T. F. Cash. 1992. Body Images, Body-Size Perception, and Eating Behaviors among African-American and White College Women. *International Journal of Eating Disorders* 12: 291–299.

Sarlio-Lahteenkorva, Sirpa, A. Stunkard, and A. Rissanen. 1995. Psychosocial Factors and Quality of Life in Obesity. *International Journal of Obesity* 6: 1–5.

Stevens, June, Shiriki K. Kumanyika, and Julian E. Keil. 1994. Attitudes toward Body Size and Dieting: Differences between Elderly Black and White Women. *American Journal of Public Health* 84: 1322–1325.

Wadden, Thomas A., and David B. Sarwer. 2006. Behavioral Assessment of Candidates for Bariatric Surgery: A Patient-Oriented Approach. *Obesity* 14: 53S–62S.

Wadden, Thomas A., and Albert J. Stunkard. 1985. Social and Psychological Consequences of Obesity. *Annals of Internal Medicine* 103: 1062–1067.

Wolf, Naomi. 1991. *The Beauty Myth: How Images of Beauty Are Used Against Women.* New York: Morrow.

Kelli Friedman
Cara O'Connell

WELFARE

Welfare is typically a term that denotes varying kinds of social spending allocated by governments following industrialization in nation-states. Prior to industrialization, most governments left assistance for the underprivileged to landlords in feudal systems, private organizations, and (primarily) the Catholic Church. Such "poor relief" became known as "welfare" following government intervention in such provisions.

The pairing of government and poor relief can be traced in part to responses to natural disasters—such as earthquakes, fires, and floods—that led monarchical governments to feed people and rebuild homes in order to preserve order. This definition of welfare—providing assistance to those who are otherwise unable to feed, house, or clothe themselves—remains the primary guide to most countries and scholars who study and implement welfare programs. Thus "welfare" is commonly considered to include redistributive policies and programs that enable the disadvantaged to reach some minimal level of existence within a nation-state.

Many nation-states now provide varying levels of housing assistance, income supplementation, in-kind goods and service provision, and public education as part of the welfare state. The programs and policies to provide these aspects of a minimal human existence can vary. For example, income supplementation can consist of cash payments, tax credits, or child-care subsidies. Similarly, in-kind goods and services can include vouchers for food, free or subsidized medical care, and free job training or referral services. Each nation (and in federal systems such as the United States, each state) makes decisions regarding: (1) the financial commitment to make to these programs; (2) the kinds of programs to provide to its poor; and (3) who is eligible to receive aid under the programs.

The comparative welfare-state literature and the public-policy literature have determined that several factors interact in producing fiscal outcomes and programmatic decisions made at the national level. Most of this work has focused on comparing European nations with other developed democracies such as Canada, Australia, and the United States. Other work has also compared Western

nations such as these with Asian democracies such as Japan and socialist states such as the former Soviet Union, Cuba, and China. The primary findings from these examinations focus on three types of variables to explain and predict both the level of funding and the kinds of programs that are developed: (1) the system of political institutions in place; (2) the attitudes among the citizenry and policymaking bodies toward the poor; and (3) the level of racial/ethnic heterogeneity within the polity.

The political system comparisons proceed at the national level and focus first upon whether federal systems or unitary systems tend to provide greater redistribution to the poor. In particular, the federal system of the United States has been frequently cited as one reason why the United States lags so far behind most other similarly situated nations in terms of social welfare provision. The United States stands alone among OECD (Organization for Economic Cooperation and Development) nations, for example, in its dependence on private health care as 35 percent of total health expenditures. Far smaller and less-developed nations in Europe and in Asia provide universal or near-universal public health coverage. In addition to these systemic differences, comparative welfare-state experts focus on the types of institutional arrangements that may produce different kinds of welfare program provision. For example, states with proportional representation systems have over the course of history had greater influence from left-of-center ideological parties working in coalition governments; winner-take-all electoral systems require far less coalition politics and therefore depress the influence of parties that would seek greater redistribution when they lose elections.

Both systems and institutional arrangements are shaped by the parties that enter power and whether they are required to respond to the electorate in their policymaking decisions. In cases where the electorate plays a significant role in determining the allocation of power, political parties reflect to a large degree mass public opinion regarding the views of the poor. In countries where the electorate views the poor as "trapped in poverty," more generous and comprehensive welfare programs exist. Where the majority of the electorate views the poor as "lazy," less generous and comprehensive welfare programs exist. Where moves toward less generous and comprehensive programs succeed, the burden continues to fall on private relief organizations (including religious organizations), as it did prior to industrialization. Although there is a direct correlation between public opinion and welfare policy, such a correlation is also shaped by both the institutional arrangements and the degree of racial/ethnic heterogeneity in the country.

In addition to institutional arrangements and mass public opinion, the degree of racial/ethnic heterogeneity plays a unique role in the provision of welfare benefits at the national level. Racial/ethnic animus has been examined at length in more diverse societies as a factor that depresses the likelihood of generous or comprehensive welfare policy. However, a strict breakdown between ethnically diverse countries and homogenous nations does not explain the variation. In fact, it is those countries with both racial/ethnic diversity and a concentration of poverty among the ethnic/racial minorities that leads to an "anti-solidarity" effect: Both the mass electorate and the parties that represent them are less likely to provide welfare benefits to a subset of the population that is perceived to be undeserving.

In the United States, for example, race- and income-based disparities in the provision of health-care coverage have existed since the founding of the American welfare state with the Social Security Act of 1935, which exempted select industrial sectors employing large numbers of African Americans from old-age salary replacement and medical coverage programs. While federal and state legislation has since outlawed the exclusion of citizens on the basis of race from such programs, race- and income-based disparities in program participation persist.

The cross-national analyses of welfare provision generally tend to focus on states that are capable of providing welfare benefits domestically, whether through capitalist or socialist economic systems. Much less attention has been given in such analyses to the role of international or global organizations that attenuate dire situations in countries that are incapable at the national or local level of providing such services. A separate literature contends with the role of international organizations such as the World Health Organization, the International Monetary Fund, and the United Nations in the provision of welfare benefits to developing nations. Future comparative research can and should integrate these literatures to comprehensively determine the relevant weights of the three factors identified above—the system of political institutions, mass public opinion, and racial/ethnic heterogeneity—to examine how the outcomes of welfare policymaking serve to further stabilize and strengthen democracy, or serve to undermine it.

SEE ALSO *Great Depression; Great Society, The; International Monetary Fund; National Health Insurance; New Deal, The; Racism; Socialism; United Nations; Welfare State; World Health Organization*

BIBLIOGRAPHY

Colombo, Francesca, and Nicole Tapay. 2004. Private Health Insurance in OECD Countries: The Benefits and Costs for Individuals and Health Systems. OECD Health Working Paper No. 15. http://www.oecd.org/dataoecd/34/56/33698043.pdf.

Esping-Anderson, Gøsta. 1990. *Three Worlds of Welfare Capitalism*. Princeton, NJ: Princeton University Press.

Feldman, Stanley, and John Zaller. 1992. The Political Culture of Ambivalence: Ideological Responses to the Welfare State. *American Journal of Political Science* 36 (1): 268–307.

Hacker, Jacob. 2006. Inequality, American Democracy, and American Political Science: The Need for Cumulative Research. *PS: Political Science and Politics* 39: 47–50.

Hancock, Ange-Marie. 2004. *The Politics of Disgust: The Public Identity of the "Welfare Queen."* New York: New York University Press.

Lieberman, Robert. 2005. *Shaping Race Policy: The United States in Comparative Perspective*. Princeton, NJ: Princeton University Press.

Pontusson, Jonah. 2006. The American Welfare State in Comparative Perspective: Reflections on Alberto Alesina and Edward L. Glaeser, *Fighting Poverty in the US and Europe. Perspectives on Politics* 4: 315–326.

Skocpol, Theda. 1995. *Social Policy in the United States: Future Possibilities in Historical Perspective*. Princeton, NJ: Princeton University Press.

Vreeland, James Raymond. 2003. *The IMF and Economic Development*. New York: Cambridge University Press.

Ange-Marie Hancock

WELFARE ANALYSIS

Welfare economics is the study of how a society can best use its scarce endowments—for example, its natural resources, technical know-how, stock of physical and human capital, and so forth—to maximize the well-being of its members. When the principles of welfare economics are used to evaluate a specific policy issue, it is known as *welfare analysis*. This entry describes the main features of welfare analysis, focusing on its intellectual foundations and practical challenges, as well as controversies surrounding its use.

Two policy examples will help clarify what welfare analysis is. First, psychologists have shown that the academic achievement of underprivileged children is significantly improved by enrollment in prekindergarten programs. These programs are, of course, expensive to run. Will society be better off if prekindergarten is freely and universally provided? Second, as of 2007, high gas prices have caused U.S. policymakers to consider opening the Arctic National Wildlife Refuge in Alaska for energy exploration. Would the benefits to society from the increase in domestic energy sources outweigh the environmental implications of this decision?

Neither of these questions has an obvious answer, although each can invoke varying opinions from different members of society. The task of welfare analysis is to assemble information to aid in determining whether the proposed policy action would on balance be beneficial to society. Economists use two fundamental concepts to aid in this process. The first is *consumer sovereignty*, which has its roots in the philosophy of individualism. Consumer sovereignty has two related consequences for welfare analysis: it implies that the individual is the best judge of what is good or bad for his or her well-being, and that a proposal can only be judged by examining the sum of its impacts on individuals. The latter gives rise to the second fundamental concept, the *compensation criterion*, as originally proposed by John Hicks (1939) and Nicholas Kaldor (1939). Almost any policy action will involve winners and losers. The compensation criterion suggests that a policy is desirable if those who gain from the action gain enough in aggregate that they would be able to compensate the losers for their losses. Thus welfare analysis is a matter of measuring changes in individuals' well-being as they see it as a result of a policy change, and determining whether the sum of the individual gains is greater than the sum of the individual losses.

This view of welfare analysis might more accurately be described as the neoclassical interpretation in that it is intentionally silent on issues of fairness, justice, and other notions of equity. Said another way, neoclassical welfare analysis focuses narrowly on maximizing the size of the well-being pie rather than providing prescriptions on how it should be divided. Implicitly, distributional questions are left to other mechanisms. A wider view of welfare analysis requires specific judgments on what is fair and just and hence is more difficult to implement. Nonetheless there have been efforts by political economists past and present to cast welfare analysis in a wider light. Prominent among these is the work of Amartya Sen, who advocates the use of mild interpersonal comparisons—based, for example, on the ability of people to freely choose their lifestyle—in conjunction with neoclassical criteria. The work of Sen and others notwithstanding, the narrow view of welfare analysis as described above has tended to dominate the operational use of the technique.

The operational challenge of neoclassical welfare analysis is to assess changes in well being from an action. Because a person's well being cannot be objectively measured, economists use money proxies in their stead. A prime example of this is *willingness to pay*, which measures how much money a person would pay out of their income to secure (or prevent) an action. This measure is valid and useful even if the payment is not actually made. The magnitude of the payment, if accurately assessed, provides a sense of the relative importance of the action under consideration. Techniques for measuring individuals' willingness to pay have a long history in economics, beginning with Alfred Marshall (1930) and including seminal works

by Robert Willig (1976), Michael Hanemann (1978), and Jerry Hausman (1981).

The principles of welfare analysis (if not always the techniques) are widely accepted by economists. Nonetheless, they can be controversial among noneconomists. Three of the main points of contention deserve mention in closing. First, some object on ethical grounds to the use of money measures to gauge the value of public policy issues related to, for example, human health and the environment. Second, based as it is on the notion of individualism, welfare analysis does not readily admit notions of collective responsibility. Finally, welfare analysis tends to be silent on the subject of income distribution. Nonetheless, welfare analysis is often the only means available to policymakers of organizing complex and conflicting points of view; as such, it will likely continue to play a role in policy decisions.

SEE ALSO *General Equilibrium; Hicks, John R.; Pareto, Vilfredo; Pareto Optimum; Rawls, John; Sen, Amartya Kumar; Social Welfare Functions; Theory of Second Best*

BIBLIOGRAPHY

Hanemann, Michael. 1978. A Theoretical and Empirical Study of the Recreation Benefits of Improving Water Quality in the Boston Area. PhD diss. Harvard University, Cambridge, MA.

Hausman, Jerry. 1981. Exact Consumer's Surplus and Deadweight Loss. *American Economic Review* 71: 662–676.

Hicks, John. 1939. The Foundations of Welfare Analysis. *Economic Journal* 49: 696–712.

Kaldor, Nicholas. 1939. Welfare Propositions of Economics and Interpersonal Comparisons of Utility. *Economic Journal* 49: 549–552.

Marshall, Alfred. 1930. *Principles of Economics*. London: Macmillan.

Sen, Amartya. 1998. The Possibility of Social Choice. *American Economic Review* 89: 349–378.

Willig, Robert. 1976. Consumer's Surplus without Apology. *American Economic Review* 69: 589–597.

Daniel J. Phaneuf

WELFARE ECONOMICS

Welfare economics is a normative branch of economic theory that attempts to assess the implications of laws and institutions, including market outcomes, for human well-being. Welfare economics begins with John Stuart Mill's "canons of taxation," in which he applies rule-utilitarian ethics to suggest guidelines for taxation that might reduce its bad impacts. Nevertheless, A. C. Pigou's *Economics of*

Welfare (1920) can be thought of as the founding book of welfare economics. Among the propositions of welfare economics there would be a broad consensus, for example, that (1) in the absence of externalities, competitive equilibria are efficient, and (2) with few exceptions, taxes, monopoly power, and externalities tend to move the economy predictably away from an efficient allocation of resources.

THE UTILITARIANISM OF MILL AND PIGOU

The ideas of Mill and Pigou are utilitarian in the narrow sense that they assume the following:

1. Acts, laws, rules, and institutions should be evaluated on the basis of their consequences rather than on some intrinsic rightness or wrongness; that is, nothing is good unless it does somebody some good.

2. Good and bad subjective states of mind are the consequences that should be considered in the assessment.

3. For a particular individual, the degree to which good states of mind are attained, and bad states avoided, can be expressed by a number (called utility).

4. Moreover, this number can be compared between individuals and cumulated over the population; and so this cumulative number can be made the objective of public policy.

This narrow utilitarianism would imply, among other things, that efficiency depends on the distribution of income as well as the allocation of resources. Many economists found this undesirable, on the grounds that one ought to be able to assess the efficiency of resource allocation apart from the distribution of income, as indeed Mill had suggested. This led them to reject the fourth assumption. For this purpose, Vilfredo Pareto had proposed the criterion that bears his name: An allocation of resources is said to be "Pareto optimal" if no one person can be made better off without making another person worse off. Without interpersonal comparability of utility, however, no discrimination can be made among Pareto optimal allocations as to which is better or worse.

Moreover, to some, the third assumption also seemed implausible. In place of numerical or "cardinal" utility, they held that individual decisions and well-being are based on a system of *preferences*. The "good states of mind" are the ones that the person prefers (which may not correspond to pleasure and pain), and therefore the vectors of consumption goods and services that produce the states of mind can be placed in an order from better to worse, from that individual's point of view, but the ordering does not

correspond to any unique numerical measure. As Paul A. Samuelson (1948) observes, however, the preferences could in principle be reconstructed from ("revealed" by) the observed choices of the individuals. The revision of welfare economics without the last two assumptions is known as the "new welfare economics."

INDIFFERENCE CURVES

A preference system can be visualized by a map of "indifference curves." Beginning from a particular vector of consumer goods, such as "one coffee and two doughnuts," the indifference curve corresponding to that vector is the boundary between all of the vectors preferred to "one coffee and two doughnuts" and those to which "one coffee and two doughnuts" is preferred. If one assumes that this boundary is well-defined, it forms a curve with the property that, taking any two vectors along the curve, the individual feels no preference for one over the other. Thus, for example, if "one coffee and two doughnuts" and "two coffees and one doughnut" are on the same curve, then the individual can be said to be indifferent between the two, and accordingly the curve is called an indifference curve. The preference map can also be represented by any one of an infinite array of "utility indices," provided that, comparing two consumption vectors, the higher number is assigned to the one that is preferred. In this case, however, the only valid conclusions of the analysis are those that do not depend on the specific utility index numbers used.

Francis Ysidro Edgeworth addressed the efficiency of allocation of goods in a pure exchange economy using the indifference curve approach (1995). First, assume that the total quantities available of two goods, good x and good y, are X and Y as shown in Figure 1. If the coordinates of a point in the interior of the diagram are x_0, y_0, then those are the quantities of the two goods allocated to individual j, and the quantities allocated to individual k are $X - x_0$, $Y - y_0$. Thus, the indifference curves for individual j are oriented to the x, y axis and are shown by curves 1, 2, 3, while the indifference curves for individual k are inverted and are illustrated by curves i, ii, iii. The points of tangency of two indifference curves, shown by the *contract curve LM*, are all Pareto optimal allocations of the two goods between the two individuals. In general, then, there will be infinitely many Pareto optima. A shift from one Pareto optimum to another trades off one person's preferences against those of the other person.

To visualize this trade-off, one assigns a numerical index u_j to each indifference curve 1, 2, 3 and a numerical index u_k to each indifference curve i, ii, iii. One must keep in mind that these arbitrary indices of utility cannot be compared as between the two individuals nor added. Figure 2 shows a diagram with u_j on the horizontal axis and u_k on the vertical axis. Any combination of utility

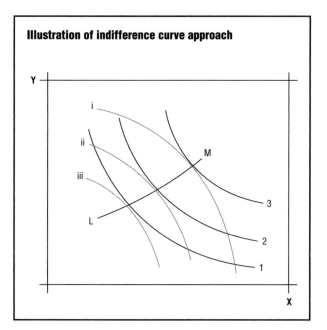

Figure 1

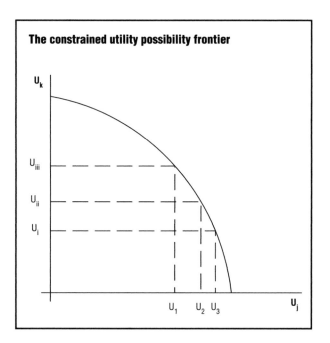

Figure 2.

indices (indifference curves) on or beneath this curve are attainable when X and Y are produced, while none of the combinations beyond the curve are attainable. This is called the *constrained utility possibility frontier* corresponding to the production of X and Y.

Suppose one carries out the same exercise for each technically efficient, feasible set of outputs X, Y. One

would then trace the outer limit of all of the constrained utility possibility frontiers obtained in this way. This outer limit is the grand utility possibility frontier or simply the *utility possibility frontier*. With an appropriate change in the definitions of u_1, u_2, ... u_{iii}, one may take Figure 2 as illustrative of the utility possibility frontier. Every point on this frontier has the properties that (1) the two goods produced are allocated between the two persons in a Pareto optimal way; and (2) production is technically efficient—that is, no reallocation of resources can increase the production of one good without reducing the production of the other; and (3) therefore, production and allocation is Pareto optimal over all possible allocations of resources and consumer goods. With appropriate mathematical notation, this conception can be extended to very large numbers of distinct goods and services and a very large population of agents.

SELECTING ALLOCATIONS

Two issues remain in this analysis. First, how does one choose the "best" among the points on the frontier? Second, for many practical problems, one must choose between two allocations, at least one of which is not Pareto optimal. How may one do that?

Taking these questions in reverse order, the new welfare economics answers the second question with a cost–benefit analysis based on the "Kaldor-Hicks compensation test," named after Nicholas Kaldor (1939) and John R. Hicks (1939). One may illustrate this compensation test with an example of property on the banks of a river. John Doe owns land on the banks of Flowing River, while Richard Roe owns downstream property, including both banks. Roe builds a dam, entirely on his own property. The impoundment of Flowing River floods Doe's property. In this sequence, Roe is the gainer and Doe the loser in clear senses. But can one say that Roe's benefits exceed Doe's costs?

To answer this question, one considers whether Roe could allocate some of his benefits to compensate Doe and still be a gainer on net? This is the Kaldor-Hicks test, and if the answer is yes, then building the dam is a *potential Pareto improvement*. That is, if the dam is built, there is a distribution of income that would leave everyone in society better off than they were without the dam. But another, equally reasonable, compensation test asks: Could Doe compensate Roe for ceasing and desisting from dam building, so that Roe would be better off than he would be if the dam were built? This is the Scitovszky test—named after Tibor de Scitovszky (1941)—and if the answer is yes, the world without a dam is potentially Pareto superior to the world with the dam. The two tests would be equivalent if benefits and costs were independent of the distribution of wealth, but, as Hicks noted,

they are not. If the dam is built, and compensation is not paid, then wealth is redistributed and a new situation created. From the new situation, it might be a potential Pareto improvement to return to the original position. In practice, there is likely to be little difference between the two, because the impacts of the shifting income distribution is likely to be small relative to the impact of a project, and the Kaldor-Hicks test is the one usually used.

THE SOCIAL WELFARE FUNCTION

Is it possible, then, to choose one among the allocations on the utility possibility frontier that is the optimum of optima? For example, some might prefer an allocation with a more equal distribution of income or one in which certain "basic needs" are more thoroughly met, or that satisfy other conditions. Ideally, one might hope to express some consensus of such conditions in a *social welfare function* that would indicate which allocations are socially preferable to other allocations independently of their technical feasibility. Visualizing this social welfare function as a set of *social indifference curves*, and superimposing it on the grand utility possibility frontier, results in Figure 3. In this figure, the grand optimum allocation of resources could be identified with point *V*. Further, following Samuelson (1956), the utility index could be made an index of real income. Remember that any numbers that correspond to indifference curves and assign larger numbers to the more highly preferred curves can be used as utility index numbers. In general, an index of real income will have this property. Therefore, suppose the axes meas-

Figure 3

ure the real incomes, R_j and R_k, of the two individuals. With this interpretation, the curvature of the social indifference curves could express one's attitudes toward income equality, so that, for example, social indifference curves tightly curved around the 45-degree line would express a strong preference for equal incomes.

This ideal was set back by the Nobel laureate research of Kenneth J. Arrow (1951), in his general (im)possibility theorem. Arrow showed that, if we require some reasonable-seeming conditions on the social welfare function, such as the requirement that it generate transitive preferences, there could be no social welfare function that would satisfy them all. For a system of majority rule, for example, Arrow adapted a paradox attributed to the marquis de Condorcet (1972) to show that (imposing his other conditions) voting outcomes could always be cyclical rather than transitive. But Arrow also extended this to any (nonmajoritarian) social welfare rule, and in the context of his theorem, it is equally impossible to say that a market outcome defines a social welfare optimum.

Arrow's theorem has spawned a large literature of reconsideration. Sometimes the conditions he proposed for a social welfare function can seem less self-evidently appropriate on further consideration. For example, one of the conditions is "nondictatorship," mathematically expressed; but in some simple models of majority rule, the median person is a "dictator" in Arrow's mathematical sense, although not on a conventional understanding of dictatorship. Thus, much of the controversy has centered on the refinement of Arrow's conditions, and there is a large variety of possibility and impossibility theorems. All the same, Arrow's discussion raised enough doubts about the concept of a social welfare function that it has been little used since the mid-twentieth century.

NEW UTILITARIAN APPROACHES

The new welfare economics is utilitarian only in the broader sense in that it accepts assumptions (1) and (2) above. But the narrower utilitarian approach is not dead. Game and decision theorists reformulated utility theory so that an objective numerical measure of utility can be based on observations of risk-averse behavior. In social philosophy, John Rawls (1971) renewed the social-contract theory, arguing that public policy should promote the interests of the least-favored individual. One interpretation of this is that it demands interpersonal comparison of utility and supplies a social welfare function based on the minimax principle. Drawing on the reformulation of utility theory and Rawls's social-contract approach, John C. Harsanyi (1975) argued that social welfare could after all be based on a summation of individual utilities. Like Harsanyi, Amartya Sen (1985) admits interpersonally comparable utilities, at least as a logical possibility, and he

has proposed conditions less limiting than Arrow's that allow the possibility of a consistent majoritarian social welfare function. Sen, however, rejects what he describes as the welfarism of both the old and the new welfare economics, by which he means the supposition that the goodness of a social system depends only on the welfares of individuals in those social systems. In addition, Sen would have data on the capacities and perhaps freedoms of individuals reflected in the normative evaluation of economic society.

For many welfare economists, inequality in the income distribution is something to be avoided, but that cannot be completely avoided because of the sacrifice of production that would result. But inequality is not a simple thing in itself. Anthony Atkinson has made important contributions to the measurement of inequality and incorporation of inequality in discussions of policy issues such as taxation and fiscal policy. In 2001, Atkinson addressed "The Strange Disappearance of Welfare Economics." Atkinson does not suggest that welfare judgments are disappearing from economics. Quite the contrary. For Atkinson, "welfare economics" comprises systematic and critical thinking in normative economics, and he notes with regret the de-emphasis of welfare economics from graduate programs and from the current research literature. The result, he suggests, is a proliferation of ill-considered value judgments in economic research, including a good deal of prejudice and confusion. Atkinson illustrates this with examples from recent macroeconomics, a field which perhaps has never been rich in careful thinking on value issues. For Atkinson, then, welfare economics has never been more needed, although this field of study receives far less attention than it did two generations ago. On the whole, nevertheless, welfare economics is a highly developed branch of economic theory that supplies tools for applications in cost–benefit analysis, but that also raises unsettled questions for future research.

SEE ALSO *Arrow Possibility Theorem; Arrow, Kenneth J.; Paradox of Voting; Pareto, Vilfredo; Pareto Optimum; Samuelson, Paul A.; Social Welfare Functions; Utilitarianism*

BIBLIOGRAPHY

Arrow, Kenneth J. 1951. *Social Choice and Individual Values.* New York: Wiley.

Atkinson, Anthony B. 2001. The Strange Disappearance of Welfare Economics. *Kyklos* 54 (2/3): 193–206.

Condorcet, Marie-Jean-Antoine-Nicolas de Caritat, Marquis de. 1972. *Essai sur l'application de l'analyse à la probabilité des décisions rendues à la pluralité des voix* [Essay on the application of analysis to the probability of majority decisions]. New York: Chelsea Publishing. (Orig. pub. 1785.)

Edgeworth, Francis Ysidro. 1995. *Mathematical Psychics.* Mountain Center, CA: James and Gordon. (Orig. pub. 1881.)

Harsanyi, John C. 1975. Can the Maxim in Principle Serve as a Basis for Morality? A Critique of John Rawls's Theory. *American Political Science Review* 69 (2): 594–606.

Hicks, John R. 1939. Foundations of Welfare Economics. *Economic Journal* 49 (196): 696–712.

Kaldor, Nicholas. 1939. Welfare Propositions of Economics and Interpersonal Comparisons of Utility. *Economic Journal* 49 (195): 549–552.

Mill, John Stuart. 1987. *Principles of Political Economy.* Ed. William Ashley. Fairfield, NJ: A. M. Kelley. (Orig. pub. 1909.)

Pareto, Vilfredo. 1971. *Manual of Political Economy.* Trans. Ann S. Schwier. Eds. Ann S. Schwier and Alfred N. Page. New York: A. M. Kelley. (Orig. pub. 1906.)

Pigou, A. C. 1920. *The Economics of Welfare.* London: Macmillan.

Rawls, John. 1971. *A Theory of Justice.* Cambridge, MA: Harvard University Press, Belknap Press.

Samuelson, Paul A. 1948. Consumption Theory in Terms of Revealed Preferences. *Economica* 15 (60): 243–253.

Samuelson, Paul A. 1956. Social Indifference Curves. *Quarterly Journal of Economics* 70 (1): 1–22.

Scitovszky, Tibor de. 1941. A Note on Welfare Propositions in Economics. *Review of Economic Studies* 9 (1): 77–88.

Sen, Amartya. 1985. *Commodities and Capabilities.* Amsterdam: North-Holland.

Roger A. McCain

WELFARE STATE

The welfare state is a set of government programs aimed at ensuring citizens' welfare in the face of the contingencies of life in modern, individualized, industrialized society. All welfare states provide direct state assistance to the poor in cash (e.g., social assistance) and in kind (e.g., housing and social services), as well as social insurance against the financial consequences of certain biological risks (illness, incapacity to work, childbirth, child-rearing, old age) and occupational risks (unemployment, accident, or injury). Whereas social assistance—in the United States popularly termed *welfare*—entails redistribution from the non-poor to the poor, social insurance rarely does so and instead can be understood primarily as redistribution across the individual life course, from periods of employment to periods of inability to work. (Prominent exceptions would be the U.S. public pension system, Social Security, and the German social health insurance scheme, both of which are moderately redistributive across classes.) Usually, this latter type of social protection is available only to persons who have been employed and hence contributed to the relevant social insurance scheme.

In most welfare states, substantial efforts are also made to mitigate socioeconomic inequalities in primary income distribution through secondary redistribution, that is, government spending on social programs funded by progressive income taxation together with tax expenditures (tax deductions for social-insurance or charity contributions, as well as negative income taxation for the working poor). Historically, such reductions in socioeconomic inequality have been pursued to achieve four objectives: (1) to reduce the costs of production for employers, especially through unemployment, health, and pension schemes; (2) to maintain social peace, that is, to forestall both radical unionism within the factory, primarily via accident insurance, as well as threats to private property from leftist or rightist political radicalism in society as a whole; (3) to secure equality of economic opportunity, seen as conducive both to social peace and to economic growth; and (4) to enrich the status of citizenship beyond civil and political equality by including a social dimension, as articulated by T. H. Marshall in 1950. Countries pursuing this goal of social citizenship—with the exception of the United States, virtually all members of the Organization for Economic Cooperation and Development (OECD)—consider equally funded and free public education to be an essential component of their pursuit of equality of opportunity and hence of their welfare state in a broader sense.

WELFARE REGIMES

Beyond these shared traits, welfare states differ in many dimensions. Early classification schemes of the 1960s and 1970s, such as that of Harold Wilensky, ranked welfare states in linear fashion according to their "generosity" measured in only one dimension, aggregate spending levels. In 1990 Gøsta Esping-Andersen's groundbreaking book *The Three Worlds of Welfare Capitalism* proposed a new typology based on essential differences among welfare states that are not quantitative but qualitative. He preferred the term *welfare regime*, which focuses the analysis on the patterns of interaction of institutions governing primary and secondary distribution in the context of a nation's historically rooted political economy, to the term *welfare state*, which is typically viewed as working against or independent of market forces. First, welfare regimes differ according to their degree of "decommodification," or "the degree to which individuals and families can uphold a socially acceptable standard of living independently of market participation" (p. 37); this dimension includes not only the benefit levels but also the eligibility terms and coverage levels of a country's social welfare schemes. Second, welfare regimes differ in terms of their

impact on social stratification, that is, their degree of redistribution, poverty reduction, and income equalization. Finally, they differ based on the priority given to the role of the state, market, and family respectively in protecting against welfare risks. Esping-Andersen's widely accepted typology distinguishes among three types of welfare regimes: liberal (e.g., the United Kingdom, the United States, Australia), social-democratic (e.g., Sweden, Norway, the Netherlands), or corporatist (e.g., Germany, Austria, Italy). Not only Esping-Andersen but also subsequent research on the "varieties of capitalism" by Peter Hall and David Soskice (2001) have demonstrated that a country's system of social protection forms an integral part of its political economy; thus a leading field of contemporary welfare research takes this holistic regime perspective, looking for institutional *elective affinities* between a country's variety of capitalism ("liberal," "coordinated," etc. [Hall and Soskice 2001]) and variety of welfare regime (e.g., Ebbinghaus and Manow 2001).

Liberal Regimes Of the three types of welfare regime, the liberal regimes redistributes income the least. Countries of this type provide minimum benefits to the poor and devote most of their expenditure to social-insurance schemes focused on the middle classes. The public schemes are not intended to be the beneficiaries' sole source of income in time of need, but instead to be a "safety net," or one pillar beside the second and third pillars of occupational plans and individual savings. In the liberal welfare world, individual performance in the *market* is considered to be the primary source of welfare, hence generous tax expenditures subsidize employee benefits and individual savings accounts in the pension and health areas. Citizens' welfare is *commodified*: they have weak or no constitutionally inscribed social rights, and high levels of socioeconomic inequality are tolerated. Citizens' welfare is best guaranteed, in the liberal worldview, through economic growth and opportunity rather than state provision; this is best achieved when minimal state taxation of private wealth fosters maximum investment and when minimal state benefits foster maximum self-reliance. Particularly in the United States, the more generous welfare states of Western Europe are viewed more as hammocks than safety nets, whereas the U.S. social net is seen by most Europeans as a sieve.

Conservative Regimes Conservative welfare regimes redistribute moderately, having as their main goals the preservation of social status achieved in the labor market and the realization of social citizenship rights. They provide equally funded and free public education, moderate benefits to the poor, and generous social-insurance schemes for employed persons, in which benefits are linked to contributions and both are linked to the income

level attained. In the conservative welfare world, the *family* is considered to be the primary source of welfare. Hence both the tax system and social-insurance benefits are designed to support the family breadwinner.

Social-Democratic Regimes Social-democratic welfare regimes redistribute extensively and are by far the most successful in achieving long-term reductions in socioeconomic inequality, particularly across generations, as Walter Korpi and Joakim Palme demonstrate in their 1998 study. These regimes integrate antipoverty and social insurance programs in schemes open to all citizens. The schemes are designed to achieve decommodification, that is, to grant social citizenship—the right of meaningful participation in social life—independent of employment status. The *state* is responsible for achieving a considerable degree of distributional equality.

Although Esping-Andersen's typology still prevails in welfare state (or welfare regime) research, it has been criticized for overlooking certain dimensions. First, Ilona Ostner and Jane Lewis (1995) have pointed out that this hegemonic typology fails to account for gender discrimination in welfare states, most of which were based on the now-outdated male breadwinner model. Ann Orloff (1993) has developed a new welfare state typology based on the criterion of whether welfare states reinforce the traditional family system and women's inferior labor-force position or promote new, equal roles for both sexes. Second, in comparing Esping-Andersen's ideal-types to specific national experiences, many scholars have found the typology to be based too narrowly on the experiences of Britain, Germany, and Sweden and only partially applicable to other countries. In addition to ongoing debates about the classification of individual countries such as France, Ireland, or the Netherlands within Esping-Andersen's scheme, scholars have proposed supplementary ideal-types: Francis Castles and Castles and Deborah Mitchell (1993) distinguish an "antipodean" "wage-earners" welfare regime in Australia and New Zealand characterized by minimum wage legislation, compulsory arbitration and a protectionist consensus; Maurizio Ferrera (1996) and Giuliano Bonoli (1997) contend that a distinct Latin rim welfare regime (resembling the conservative one) exists in Italy, Spain, and Greece, where family and informal networks are important suppliers of welfare; Bob Deacon (2000), Nick Manning (2004), and Jolanta Aidukaite (2004) have documented the emergence of a postsocialist welfare regime (resembling the liberal one) in eastern Europe; and finally, some, such as Catherine Jones (1993) and Elmar Rieger and Stephan Leibfried (2003), have investigated and posited the existence of East Asian welfare regimes, based on "Confucian" values.

HISTORICAL ORIGINS

As the "logic of industrialization" school correctly observes, the historical origins of welfare state development lie in the consequences of the Industrial Revolution and attendant societal modernization—specifically, urbanization, industrialization, and economic liberalization—in the mid- to late nineteenth century. As Ferdinand Tönnies (2001) explains, these developments uprooted western Europe's inhabitants from premodern, static communities that had provided for mutualist social protection through the family, community, parish, feudal lord or guild, and thrust them into an individualized, comparatively anonymous urban society in which the satisfaction of basic needs was commodified, that is, had to be purchased with wages from employment. In the early decades of this societal modernization (from the late nineteenth century through World War I [1914–1918]), social unrest, epidemics, slum formation, violent labor conflicts, and radical political movements were rampant. Initially, bourgeois philanthropic associations attempted to mitigate this malaise but within a few decades realized they were overwhelmed. At the same time, the working classes' sacrifice and service to their states as soldiers in the two world wars earned them sociopolitical recognition and rights in many European countries.

As Walter Korpi (1983, 1993) among others have noted, three factors converged to move political coalitions of bourgeois and working-class parties across Europe to grant workers social and political rights and institute generous welfare-state programs during the period 1918–1949: (1) workers' newly won political power, organized in Social-Democratic and Labor parties and in some places accompanied by popular uprisings; (2) bourgeois elites' fear of the political radicalization of impoverished workers as had occurred in the revolutions in Russia (the Soviet Revolution of 1917) and Germany (Adolph Hitler's ascent to power in 1933)—a fear exacerbated by the Great Depression of 1929 to 1939 and by the witnessing of Hitler's destruction of the Continent during the five years thereafter; and (3) strong national identities in newly unified nation states, forged and strengthened in the two world wars. Benjamin Veghte (2004) notes that in the United States, where the first two factors were largely absent, the working-class movement was much weaker and unable to achieve social citizenship rights for a variety of reasons. An ambitious welfare state (the New Deal) was introduced during this period, in 1935, but not based on social rights; rather, it largely excluded most of the poor population, such as agricultural workers and southern African Americans. Theda Skocpol's research (1990) has revealed that the New Deal welfare state was not completely new, but rather followed in the footsteps of a generous Civil War pensions scheme that served millions of beneficiaries (Skocpol 1996). In Britain the Beveridge Report of 1942 highlighted the need for a welfare state to avoid the breakdown of society in the postwar period, and this became the blueprint for the welfare state introduced in postwar Britain.

PUBLIC-PRIVATE MIX

As noted above, prior to the formation of the modern nation-state, most types of social welfare were provided by collective, private forms of provision such as those offered by feudal hierarchies, guilds, and the church. In the course of urbanization, societal modernization, and the ascendance of liberal political and economic ideology since the late eighteenth century, free-market individualism undermined these traditional collectivist forms of private welfare provision, creating the modern "social question." After the mid-nineteenth century, modern collectivist private welfare solutions such as solidaristic union/professional initiatives as well as bourgeois or church-based charitable ventures filled the vacuum, followed by welfare *state* initiatives from the 1880s in Germany, Belgium, and—since World War I—in most other western nations. In most Western countries, then, since the mid-twentieth century the welfare *state* has been the primary instrument of welfare provision.

This has not been the case in many non-Western countries, however, nor in several liberal welfare regimes, most notably the United States. Interestingly, most countries with weak welfare states evince high rates of religiosity and associated church-based welfare provision and religiously inspired philanthropy. As Leibfried and Mau note,

> The history of religiosity in European and other countries which developed strong welfare states shows that the need for religious reassurance in one's social existence has become less pressing when greater security is provided by the secular institutions of public policy. In other parts of the world, however, where state power has remained weak, the social institutions of religions—for example Islamic charities in Arabic countries, Hinduist castes in India and familial networks in East and Southeast Asia—remained the main provider of social security. (2007, p. xxv)

Secular welfare states may thus be viewed as functional alternatives to religiously inspired and/or organized private welfare provision. Empirically, as Pippa Norris and Ronald Inglehart (2004), and Elmar Rieger (2005) have observed, the revival of evangelical Protestantism in recent decades strongly correlates with the erosion of social security guarantees through the welfare state.

Non-profit, religiously inspired forms of welfare provision are not the only form of private provision to survive and thrive complementarily to and in tension with the

modern welfare state. Profit-oriented, market-based provision has done so as well, most strongly in the liberal welfare regimes of Great Britain, Switzerland, the United States, and Australia. These countries were pioneers in private, insurance-based provision, both for individuals and employees. Such welfare provision differs markedly from public provision in both its distributive dynamics (redistributing not across income classes but across the individual life course from economically self-sufficient to risky/dependent life phases) and its financial logic (calculated on actuarial rather than solidarity principles). This realm of social provision, much of which is subsidized by the government in the form of tax deductions (from the government's perspective: "tax expenditures"), was overlooked in comparative welfare state research until the appearance of Martin Rein and Lee Rainwater's (1986) pathbreaking analysis of the interplay of public and private welfare provision in OECD countries. Still today, however, most comparative research does not interpret the state-subsidized employee and individual benefits sphere, even though—as Willem Adema (1999, p. 30) and Jacob Hacker (2002, p. 338) have documented—in some countries such as the United States it makes up one-third of (public and private) social spending. Even Esping-Andersen's (1990) research on the liberal welfare regime type, which theorizes the interaction between the state and the market, overlooks the magnitude and significance of private provision, thus misconstruing the U.S. system as "residual" and "means-tested." Adema (1998, 1999, 2005) and Hacker (2002) have corrected this misinterpretation, pointing out that if U.S. employee and individual benefits are included in social spending data, the U.S. welfare system evinces a share of GDP *roughly equal* to the OECD average. The key difference between public (direct) and private (tax expenditure) welfare state expenditure is that the former tends to be redistributive and focus on alleviating poverty, whereas the latter focuses on helping the middle classes provide for their own economically precarious life episodes.

THEORIES OF DEVELOPMENT

In the 1960s and early 1970s, the best comparative work on the welfare state found a country's prevailing political culture—often termed *national values*—to be causally significant in shaping its welfare state institutions and their degree of generosity (e.g., Rimlinger 1966, 1971). This ideational approach was displaced in the 1970s by functionalist and modernization theories, most prominently that of a "logic of industrialization" (Wilensky 1975). In light of the universal dissolution of pre-modern mechanisms of social protection—namely, the family, church, feudal hierarchy, guild and local community—all industrializing countries faced similar social problems, and

hence developed similar modern instruments to secure a healthy and productive workforce. In this view, differences in welfare state spending levels are attributable not to political-cultural or other qualitative cross-national differences, but to a country's level of economic development as well as the age structure of its population and degree of maturation of its welfare state. Ultimately, the school claimed, all countries would converge toward an institutionally similar, generous welfare state. Since the 1980s, *power-resources* as well as polity-centered (and closely related *new-institutionalist*) explanations have proven more convincing. The power-resources approach, articulated by Korpi (1983) and Evelyne Huber and John Stephens (2001), argues that the social and political balance of power between labor and capital has determined the level of spending and in particular the degree of redistributiveness of welfare states. Research on the correlation between the partisan composition of governments and their levels of welfare state expenditure has largely corroborated the power-resources interpretation: Manfred G. Schmidt (1982, 1996), Castles and Herbert Obinger (2007), and indeed recently also Wilensky (2002) himself have found strong statistical evidence that where left-of-center ("social democratic," "labor" or "democratic") parties have ruled, levels of government social spending and redistribution have been much higher on average than in cases where right-of-center, free-market-liberal ("liberal," "conservative," or "republican") parties have reigned. This "parties matter" explanation enriches the power-resources interpretation, moreover, by showing that the left-right dichotomy does not explain partisan influence fully: Christian-democratic and center parties, historically common in continental Europe, correlate with moderate social spending, that is, more generous than the free-market-liberal parties and less generous than the leftist parties.

Willem Adema and Maxime Ladaique (2005) have demonstrated that when the tax system and private benefits are also taken into consideration, liberal welfare regime expenditure approximates that of the other two regime types. This suggests that Wilensky's "logic of industrialization" explanation of welfare state growth was correct, according to which a high level of economic development has driven all Western countries to converge toward a uniform, generous welfare state. Castles and Obinger (2007) rebut Adema and Ladaique, however, arguing that while the much greater private welfare spending of liberal welfare regimes often puts them on a par with conservative and social-democratic welfare regime expenditure, the latter are far more redistributive across income categories, making for a fundamentally different type of welfare state. Regarding the causes of welfare state development, they find that while the levels of economic development and economic growth best explain the increase in overall (public cum private) welfare spending,

power resources—measured in terms of partisan incumbency—best explains the growth in the more redistributive, direct *state* welfare spending.

The polity-centered and new-institutionalist approaches adamantly dispute the explanatory power of class. They attribute the scale and type of welfare state expansion and retrenchment to state-structural factors such as the nature of the party system and civil service and the influence of policy intellectuals and reformist associations on these, as in the work of Skocpol (1985); Margaret Weir, Orloff, and Skocpol (1988); and Dietrich Rueschemeyer and Skocpol (1996); the lack of constitutional "veto points," as in the work of Ellen Immergut (1989) and George Tsebelis (2002); and "feedback effects" of (pre-)existing institutions and policies, as in the work of Paul Pierson (1993).

Both theory and comparative data on public opinion on the welfare state have improved since the 1990s, giving ideational approaches an empirical basis and rendering them worthy of causal reconsideration alongside the power-resources and new-institutionalist explanatory approaches. Indeed, Clem Brooks and Jeff Manza (2006) have found that national social policy preferences exert a strong and measurable influence on welfare state spending as well as on cross-national variation therein, after controlling for other factors such as institutional feedback effects. Mau and Veghte (2007) find strong relationships between welfare regimes and social policy attitudes across OECD countries. Further, Veghte, Greg M. Shaw, and Robert Y. Shapiro (2007) have revealed that social policy preferences and issue prioritizations themselves are contingent and malleable in response to issue framing—for example, of military over social security—by political elites. Given the availability of new transnational datasets on both public opinion and party platforms, more research into public opinion on welfare state issues and its relation to the aforementioned causal factors, and incorporation of this dimension into welfare state theory, can be expected.

SOURCE OF FUNDING

Scholars used to distinguish between contribution-based (the Bismarckian, German model) and tax-based (the Beveridge, English model) funding of welfare state programs, but in practice these two models have converged, as most social-insurance schemes are funded by a mixture of employer/employee contributions and subsidies from general state revenues. Contribution-based schemes, which are funded and administered independent of the government budget and in which members have vested benefits, have historically tended to be more generous and less susceptible to retrenchment than tax-funded schemes, which legislators can cut back when tax revenues are scarce or an antiwelfare state party comes to power.

WELFARE STATE CRITIQUE AND REFORM

After expanding steadily during the "Golden Age" of welfare-state development in the 1960s and early 1970s, most Euro-American welfare states suffered a critical shock from the oil crises and recession of the mid-1970s and the deindustrialization and high unemployment rates that followed. Not only did these factors deprive the welfare state of its financial bases in both tax revenues and employer/employee contributions, the welfare state itself was widely considered to have contributed to the economic collapse by draining the economy of investment income and burdening it with bureaucratic regulations, as well as undermining individual initiative and the will to work through excessive benefits that fostered dependency. Further, the decline in industrial and the rise in service sector employment, as well as increasing individualization, disintegrated the working classes, which historically had directly or indirectly been the main driving force and constituency of welfare state development in all OECD countries except the United States. Overall, the rapid and sharp rise in the absolute and relative amount of government spending devoted to the welfare state, together with the declining popular support for the latter, led many observers by the mid- to late 1970s to perceive a "crisis of the welfare state" (Flora 1981; Offe 1984). If some degree of retrenchment were not implemented, the welfare state threatened to bring Western economies to a standstill. Conservatives won national elections in Britain (Margaret Thatcher), the United States (Ronald Reagan), and West Germany (Helmut Kohl), in the early 1980s and were reelected in the mid-1980s, all running on anti-welfare-state platforms. Ever since, conservatives in most other OECD countries have tried to scale back welfare-state benefits as well as restrict eligibility to those "truly in need." This has proven extremely difficult, given that in democratic systems, once citizens and/or interest groups have acquired benefits, they mobilize strongly to retain them. As Pierson observes, "Retrenchment is generally an exercise in blame avoidance rather than 'credit claiming.' First, the costs of retrenchment are concentrated, whereas the benefits are not. Second, there is considerable evidence that voters exhibit a 'negativity bias,' remembering losses more than gains. As a result, retrenchment initiatives are extremely treacherous" (1994, p. 18). Due to this "conservative welfare function" (Rieger and Leibfried 2003), benefits in most welfare states (with the exceptions of New Zealand and Switzerland) have been scaled back very little in OECD countries despite extended periods of neoliberal governance.

What welfare state reformers have been able to achieve is a tightening of eligibility criteria, moving away from the model of the welfare state as provider of benefits to persons unable to work and toward an *activating* wel-

fare state that provides an incentive to work by targeting benefits (and/or providing more generous benefits) to persons working or actively seeking employment, while further decreasing the number of inactive citizens by scaling back employment and wage regulation and postponing the retirement age.

Many scholars have also criticized the welfare state for its focus on the male breadwinner and the attendant discriminating effects on social groups long denied equal opportunity in the labor market, such as women, ethnic minorities, and the disabled. Feminist scholars have called attention to the fact that such welfare-state subsidizing of the higher earner (breadwinner) in a family, particularly pronounced in conservative welfare states, reinforces the gendered division of labor within the family. Others have criticized citizenship requirements in many welfare state programs for their discriminatory effects on noncitizens, who are in most cases ethnic minorities.

TRENDS IN THE EARLY TWENTY-FIRST CENTURY

The most important developments affecting welfare states are not their internal dynamics but changes in their fiscal, economic, and societal environments. Over the past quarter century, deindustrialization has brought about a dramatic and enduring decline in the proportion of skilled middle-class workers, transforming many of them from employees who pay into the system into long-term unemployment beneficiaries—especially in the conservative welfare regimes of continental Europe, with their generous unemployment schemes.

At the same time as these costs have risen, since the 1990s economic globalization has given new credibility to threats by the owners of capital to leave countries that tax corporations and/or wealthy individuals excessively (Genschel 2005), placing strong external restrictions on the national welfare states to finance themselves through taxation. Further, as Jef van Langendonck (1997), Esping-Andersen (1999), and Peter Taylor-Gooby (2004) have shown, the demographic challenges of population aging and a vast increase in single-parent families have created new social risks which the traditional welfare state—based on the male breadwinner—was not designed to handle. As a result of these developments, most welfare states have experienced a decline in contributions and an increase in demand for benefits, posing a formidable challenge to their sustainability and suggesting the need for welfare state reforms to adapt to these new social conditions.

The main response to this second crisis of the welfare state since the late twentieth century has been privatization. Such privatization entails three principle shifts: first, from publicly guaranteed outcomes to defined contributions; second, from mandatory to voluntary provision

against future risks; and third, from the group solidarity to the individual actuarial principle. Such privatization promises to lessen the fiscal burdens incurred by public social insurance schemes for the health and pension needs of the imminently retiring baby boom generation by increasing copayments and restricting eligibility and benefits, while simultaneously offering all individuals the opportunity to save individually for their future security needs via tax-deductible contributions to publicly regulated, individual private pension plans. This should also lessen the burden on corporations posed by the non-wage labor costs entailed in employer and employee contributions to public social-insurance schemes, increasing the international economic competitiveness of Western economies in the era of globalization. The biggest disadvantage of such privatization is that it necessarily entails a shift from universal to partial coverage of the population in need, with a tendency to exclude precisely those who need social protection the most, because they lack the surplus income required to voluntarily save for their and their families' future risks. Finally, corporations, which have long provided tax-deductible employee benefit plans to their employees, have moved from defined benefit to defined contribution plans, i.e. from occupational pension plans which guaranteed a specific payout in retirement based on a formula for years of service and salary earned, to plans which collect employer and employee contributions in interest-bearing individual retirement accounts which are transferable from one job to the next, but may or may not suffice to meet—in combination with one's public pension—a person's retirement needs.

A final challenge to the welfare state at the outset of the twenty-first century is posed by immigration. As Wim van Oorschot (2000), Michael Bommes and Andrew Geddes (2000), Carsten Ullrich (2002), Knut Halvorsen (2007), and van Oorschot and Wilfred Uunk (2007) have shown, national solidarity communities that long provided the normative foundation for European welfare states are now being threatened by real and/or perceived increases in ethnic/national heterogeneity, as evidenced by political debates throughout western Europe in the first decade of the century. Regarding the United States, Korpi (1983), Martin Gilens (1999), and Veghte (2004) have argued that racial, ethnic and religious heterogeneity have always limited development of a solidarity community and hence a redistributive welfare state. Now, scholars such as Alberto Alesina and Edward L. Glaeser (2004) are asking if, as citizens increasingly tend to distinguish between "we" and "they," the welfare consensus and commitment to publicly institutionalized solidarity in western Europe is still sustainable. Keith Banting and Will Kymlicka (2004) have determined, however, that clear evidence of a negative association between the influx of migrants and support for the welfare state is lacking. The

structure of countries' political institutions mediates and conditions the effects of immigration on welfare state development, and at the cross-national level other factors are likely more decisive. Nevertheless, as Leibfried and Mau (2007) observe, politicians may use ethnic and sociocultural divisions within a society to position themselves in public debates about distributional conflicts, leading to restrictive effects on welfare state policies.

While the threats from increasing immigration seem formidable, most welfare states are showing signs of successful adaptation to the challenges posed by economic globalization. Comparative research by Fritz Scharpf and Vivien Schmidt (2000) on the effects of globalization on Western welfare state development has revealed that welfare regimes differ in their capacity to adjust to the fiscal and competitiveness constraints constituted by increasing global product and capital market integration. Social-Democratic and liberal welfare regimes in Scandinavian and Anglo-American countries respectively, though fundamentally different, have proven better suited to successful adaptation to the challenges of economic globalization than have the conservative welfare regimes of continental Europe.

Moreover, Elmar Rieger and Stephan Leibfried (2003) argue convincingly that strong welfare states will not only survive the era of globalization, but have themselves historically paved the way for it. Since World War II (1939–1945) and continuing under conditions of intensified economic globalization since the 1990s, strong welfare states have provided political leverage in capitalist democracies such as Germany for leaders to embrace exposure to the risks of international competition in foreign economic policy, whereas countries with weak welfare states such as the United States have tended toward protectionism. As Sven Steinmo (2002) has shown, the Swedish case in particular demonstrates that a generous welfare state, with some recalibration over the past decade, can co-exist over the long term with a thriving, open and internationally competitive national economy.

A half century ago, one of the fathers of modern social policy, the Swedish Nobel prize-winning economist Gunnar Myrdal (1898–1987) argued that a transition from the welfare state to a "welfare world" would eventually transpire. Today, a budding field of welfare state research—pioneered by Deacon, Michelle Hulse, and Paul Stubbs (1997); Nicola Yeates (2002); Lutz Leisering (2004); and John Meyer (2004); and pursued in the journal, *Global Social Policy* (launched in 2001)—traces the emergence of "global social policies" emanating from supranational and global nongovernmental organizations and governmental institutions such as the ILO, World Bank, World Trade Organization, or United Nations. At the crossroads of the "world society," international relations, welfare state and area studies literatures, this research examines how welfare concepts, programs, and models are becoming globalized.

Many eminent welfare state scholars, however, such as Abram de Swaan (1997), Claus Offe (2003), Fritz Scharpf (1999, 2002), and Wolfgang Streeck (1995, 2000), are skeptical concerning the prospects of transnational social policy. Historically, as Stein Rokkan elaborated in his seminal 1974 essay, welfare states have developed in the wake of processes of state-building, nation-building, and democratization, that is, in democratic nation-states. This process took several centuries to evolve and was a rocky road paved by multiple wars and, in many countries, revolutions. Transnational social policy is unlikely to develop until something equivalent to the public sphere and solidarity community of the nation-state evolves on the transnational level, that is, a shared willingness to redistribute income across national boundaries.

The closest thing to such a transnational polity and solidarity community on the horizon is the European Union, formerly the European Community. For the first four decades of its existence, the European Community pursued economic integration without political or social integration. Since the last decade of the twentieth century, however, the European Union is slowly but discernibly moving toward such political and social integration, yet, as Franz-Xaver Kaufmann (2001) has noted, continues to evince a strong reticence with regard to all issues of interpersonal income redistribution. Leibfried (2005) and Obinger, Leibfried, and Castles (2005) observe that rather than employing centrally administered, mandatory, redistributive "hard" social policies, as national welfare states had done, the European Union has relied thus far on courts and markets and on "soft policy," that is, governance measures with which compliance is not enforced by legal sanctions, but simply encouraged through the "open method of coordination." As Leibfried and Mau (2007) have observed, beyond its borders Europe is the leading advocate of transnational social policy as propagated by global institutions such as the WTO, the WHO, and ILO, and may one day serve as an organizational model inspiring for example the NAFTA, MERCOSUR and ASEAN countries to pursue transnational social policies in their respective regions. The debates on the evolution of European social policy can be followed above all in the *Journal of European Social Policy* (since 1991) and increasingly in the *Journal of European Public Policy* (since 1994), which explores the interaction between central and nation-state social policy in the European Union.

SEE ALSO *Beveridge Curve; Conservatism; Democracy; Family; Globalization, Social and Economic Aspects of; Great Depression; Hitler, Adolf; Income Distribution; Insurance; Liberalism; National Health*

Insurance; Nazism; Political Science; Recession; Risk; Socialism; Welfare; World War II

BIBLIOGRAPHY

Adema, Willem. 1999. Net Social Expenditures. *Labor Market and Social Policy Occasional Papers*, No. 39. Paris: OECD.

Adema, Willem, and Marcel Einerhand. 1998. The Growing Role of Private Social Benefits. *Labor Market and Social Policy Occasional Papers*, No. 32. Paris: OECD.

Adema, Willem, and Maxime Ladaique. 2005. Net Social Expenditure, 2005 Edition. More Comprehensive Measures of Social Support. *Social, Employment and Migration Working Papers*, No. 29. Paris: OECD.

Aidukaite, Jolanta. 2004. The Emergence of the Post-Socialist Welfare States—The Case of the Baltic States: Estonia, Latvia and Lithuania. PhD diss., Stockholm University.

Alesina, Alberto, and Edward L. Glaeser. 2004. *Fighting Poverty in the US and Europe.* Oxford: Oxford University Press.

Banting, Keith G., and Will Kymlicka. 2004. Do Multiculturalism Policies Erode the Welfare State? In *Cultural Diversity versus Economic Solidarity*, ed. Philippe van Parijs, 227–284. Brussels: Deboeck Université Press.

Bommes, Michael, and Andrew Geddes, eds. 2000. *Immigration and Welfare: Challenging the Borders of the Welfare State.* London and New York: Routledge.

Bonoli, Giuliano. 1997. Classifying Welfare States: A Two-Dimensional Approach. *Journal of Social Policy* 26 (3): 351–372.

Brooks, Clem, and Jeff Manza. 2006. Social Policy Responsiveness in Developed Democracies. *American Sociological Review* 71 (3): 474–494.

Castles, Francis G. 1985. *The Working Class and Welfare: Reflections on the Political Development of the Welfare State in Australia and New Zealand, 1890-1980.* Wellington, New Zealand: Allen and Unwin.

Castles, Francis G., and Deborah Mitchell. 1993. Worlds of Welfare and Families of Nations. In *Families of Nations: Patterns of Public Policy in Western Democracies*, ed. Francis G. Castles, 93–128. Aldershot, U.K. and Brookfield, VT: Dartmouth.

Castles, Francis G., and Herbert Obinger. 2007. Social Expenditure and the Politics of Redistribution. *Journal of European Social Policy* 17 (3): 206–222.

Deacon, Bob. 2000. Eastern European Welfare States: The Impact of the Politics of Globalisation. *Journal of European Social Policy* 10 (2): 146–161.

Deacon, Bob, Michelle Hulse, and Paul Stubbs. 1997. *Global Social Policy: International Organizations and the Future of Welfare.* London and Thousand Oaks, CA: Sage.

De Swann, Abram. 1997. The Receding Prospects for Transnational Social Policy. *Theory and Society* 26 (4): 561–575.

Ebbinghaus, Bernhard, and Philip Manow, eds. 2001. *Comparing Welfare Capitalism: Social Policy and Political Economy in Europe, Japan and the USA.* London and New York: Routledge.

Esping-Andersen, Gøsta. 1990. *The Three Worlds of Welfare Capitalism.* Cambridge, U.K.: Polity Press; and Princeton, NJ: Princeton University Press.

Esping-Andersen, Gøsta. 1999. *Social Foundations of Postindustrial Economies.* New York: Oxford University Press.

Ferrera, Maurizio. 1996. The Southern Model of Welfare in Social Europe. *Journal of European Social Policy* 6 (1): 17–37.

Flora, Peter. 1981. Solution or Source of Crisis? The Welfare State in Historical Perspective. In *The Emergence of the Welfare State in Britain and Germany 1850–1950*, ed. Wolfgang Mommsen in collaboration with Wolfgang Mock, 343–389. London: Croom Helm.

Genschel, Philipp. 2005. Globalization and the Transformation of the Tax State. In *Transformations of the State?* Eds. Stephan Leibfried and Michael Zürn, 53-71. Cambridge, UK: Cambridge University Press.

Gilens, Martin. 1999. *Why Americans Hate Welfare: Race, Media, and the Politics of Anti-Poverty Policy.* Chicago: University of Chicago Press.

Hacker, Jacob S. 2002. *The Divided Welfare State: The Battle over Public and Private Social Benefits in the United States.* Cambridge, UK: Cambridge University Press.

Hall, Peter A., and David Soskice, eds. 2001. *Varieties of Capitalism. The Institutional Foundations of Comparative Advantage.* Oxford and New York: Oxford University Press.

Halvorsen, Knut. 2007. Legitimacy of Welfare States in Transitions from Homogeneity to Multiculturality: A Matter of Trust? In *Social Justice, Legitimacy and the Welfare State*, eds. Steffen Mau and Benjamin Veghte 239–259. Aldershot, U.K.: Ashgate.

Howard, Christopher. 1997. *The Hidden Welfare State: Tax Expenditures and Social Policy in the United States.* Princeton, NJ: Princeton University Press.

Howard, Christopher. 2007. *The Welfare State Nobody Knows: Debunking Myths about U.S. Social Policy.* Princeton, NJ: Princeton University Press.

Huber, Evelyne, and John D. Stephens. 2001. *Development and Crisis of the Welfare State: Parties and Policies in Global Markets.* Chicago: University of Chicago Press.

Immergut, Ellen M. 1989. Institutions, Veto Points and Policy Results: A Comparative Analysis of Health Care. *Journal of Public Policy* 10 (4): 391–416.

Jones, Catherine. 1993. The Pacific Challenge. In *New Perspectives on the Welfare State in Europe*, ed. Catherine Jones, 198–217. London and New York: Routledge.

Kaufmann, Franz-Xaver. 2001. Der deutsche Sozialstaat im internationalen Vergleich. In: *Geschichte der Sozialpolitik in Deutschland seit 1945*, Vol. 1: *Grundlagen der Sozialpolitik* ed. Bundesministerim für Arbeit und Sozialordnung [BMA] und Bundesarchiv. Baden-Baden: Nomos.

Korpi, Walter. 1983. *The Democratic Class Struggle.* London and Boston: Routledge and Kegan Paul.

Korpi, Walter. 1993. American Exceptionalism in Social Policy Development. Review of *Protecting Soldiers and Mothers: The Political Origins of Social Policy in the United States*, ed. Theda Skocpol. *Contemporary Sociology: An International Journal of Reviews* 22 (6): 779–781.

Korpi, Walter, and Joakim Palme. 1998. The Paradox of Redistribution and Strategies of Equality: Welfare State Institutions, Inequality, and Poverty in the Western Countries. *American Sociological Review* 63 (5): 661–687.

Langendonck, Jef van, ed. 1997. *The New Social Risks* [*Les Nouveau Risques Sociaux*]. Hague: Kluwer Law International.

Leibfried, Stephan. 2005. Social Policy: Left to the Judges and the Markets? In *Policy-Making in the European Union*, eds. Helen Wallace, William Wallace, and Mark A. Pollack, 243–278. Oxford: Oxford University Press.

Leibfried, Stephan, and Steffen Mau. 2007. Introduction. In *Welfare States: Construction, Deconstruction, Reconstruction*, eds. Stephan Leibfried and Steffen Mau, xi–lxii. Cheltenham, U.K. and Northampton, MA: Edward Elgar.

Leisering, Lutz. 2004. Social Policy Learning und Wissensdiffusion in einer globalisierten Welt. Working Paper No. 6. Universität Bielefeld. http://www.uni-bielefeld.de/ soz/Forschung/Projekte/socialworld/pdf/working%20paper% 206.pdf.

Lipset, Seymour Martin. 1996. *American Exceptionalism: A Double-Edged Sword*. New York: Norton.

Manning, Nick. 2004. Diversity and Change in Pre-Accession Central and Eastern Europe since 1989. *Journal of European Social Policy* 14 (3): 211–232.

Marshall, Thomas Humphrey. 1950. *Citizenship and Social Class, and Other Essays*. Cambridge, U.K.: Cambridge University Press.

Mau, Steffen, and Benjamin Veghte, eds. 2007. *Social Justice, Legitimacy and the Welfare State*. Aldershot, U.K. and Burlington, VT: Ashgate.

Meyer, John W. 2004. World Society, the Welfare State, and the Life Course. Working Paper No. 9. Universität Bielefeld. http://www.uni-bielefeld.de/soz/Forschung/Projekte/ socialworld/pdf/working%20paper%209.pdf.

Myrdal, Gunnar. 1960. *Beyond the Welfare State: Economic Planning and its International Implications*. New Haven: Yale University Press.

Norris, Pippa, and Ronald Inglehart. 2004. *Sacred and Secular: Religion and Politics Worldwide*. Cambridge, U.K. and New York: Cambridge University Press.

Offe, Claus. 1984. *Contradictions of the Welfare State*, ed. John Keane. Cambridge, MA: MIT Press.

Offe, Claus. 2003. The European Model of "Social" Capitalism: Can it Survive European Integration? *Journal of Political Philosophy* 11 (4): 437–469.

Oorschot, Wim van. 2000. Who Should Get What, and Why?: On Deservingness Criteria and the Conditionality of Solidarity among the Public. *Policy & Politics* 28 (1): 33–48.

Oorschot, Wim van, and Wilfred Uunk. 2007. Multi-level Determinants of the Public's Informal Solidarity towards Immigrants in European Welfare States. In *Social Justice, Legitimacy and the Welfare State*, eds. Steffen Mau and Benjamin Veghte, 217–238. Aldershot, U.K.: Ashgate.

Orloff, Ann. 1993. Gender and the Social Rights in Citizenship: The Comparative Analysis of Gender Relations and Welfare States. *American Sociological Review* 58: 303–328.

Ostner, Ilona, and Jane Lewis. 1995. Gender and the Evolution of European Social Policies. In *European Social Policy:*

Between Fragmentation and Integration, eds. Stephan Leibfried and Paul Pierson, 159–193. Washington, DC: Brookings Institution.

Pierson, Paul. 1993. When Effect Becomes Cause: Policy Feedback and Political Change. *World Politics* 45 (4): 595–628.

Pierson, Paul. 1994. *Dismantling the Welfare State? Reagan, Thatcher, and the Politics of Retrenchment*. Cambridge, U.K. and New York: Cambridge University Press.

Pierson, Paul, and Stephan Leibfried. 1995. Multitiered Institutions and the Making of Social Policy. In *European Social Policy: Between Fragmentation and Integration*, eds. Stephan Leibfried and Paul Pierson, 1–40. Washington, DC: Brookings Institution.

Rein, Martin, and Lee Rainwater, eds. 1986. *Public/Private Interplay in Social Protection: A Comparative Study*. With Ellen Immergut, Michael O'Higgins, and Harald Russig. Armonk, NY: M. E. Sharpe.

Rieger, Elmar. 2005. The Wondrous Politics of Global Ideas. *Global Social Policy* 5 (1): 8–14.

Rieger, Elmar, and Stephan Leibfried. 2003. *Limits to Globalization: Welfare States and the World Economy*. Trans. Benjamin W. Veghte. Cambridge, U.K.: Polity.

Rimlinger, Gaston V. 1966. Welfare Policy and Economic Development: A Comparative Historical Perspective. *Journal of Economic History* 26 (4): 556–571.

Rimlinger, Gaston V. 1971. *Welfare Policy and Industrialization in Europe, America, and Russia*. New York: Wiley.

Rokkan, Stein. 1974. Dimensions of State Formation and Nation Building. In *The Formation of National States in Western Europe*. Ed. Charles Tilly, 562–600. Princeton, N.J.: Princeton University Press.

Rueschemeyer, Dietrich, and Theda Skocpol, eds. 1996. *States, Social Knowledge, and the Origins of Modern Social Policies*. Princeton, NJ and New York: Princeton University Press and Russell Sage Foundation.

Scharpf, Fritz W. 1999. *Governing in Europe. Effective and Democratic?* Oxford and New York: Oxford University Press.

Scharpf, Fritz W. 2002. The European Social Model: Coping with the Challenges of Diversity. *Journal of Common Market Studies* 40 (4): 645–670.

Scharpf, Fritz W., and Vivien A. Schmidt, eds. 2000. *Welfare and Work in the Open Economy*. Oxford and New York: Oxford University Press.

Schmidt, Manfred G. 1982. *Wohlfahrtsstaatliche Politik unter bürgerlichen und sozialdemokratischen Regierungen: ein internationaler Vergleich*. Frankfurt/Main and New York: Campus.

Schmidt, Manfred G. 1996. When Parties Matter: A Review of the Possibilities and Limits of Partisan Influence on Public Policy. *European Journal of Political Research* 30 (2): 155–183.

Skocpol, Theda. 1985. Bringing the State Back In: Strategies of Analysis in Current Research. In *Bringing the State Back In*, eds. Peter B. Evans, Dietrich Rueschemeyer, and Theda Skocpol, 3–37. Cambridge, U.K. and New York: Cambridge University Press.

Skocpol, Theda. 1996. *Protecting Soldiers and Mothers: The Political Origins of Social Policy in the United States.* Cambridge, MA: Harvard University Press.

Steinmo, Sven Holger. 2002. Taxation and Globalization: Challenges to the Swedish Welfare State. *Comparative Political Studies* 35 (7): 839–862.

Streeck, Wolfgang. 1995. From Market Making to State Building? Reflections on the Political Economy of European Social Policy. In *European Social Policy*, eds. Stephan Leibfried and Paul Pierson, 389–431. Washington, DC: Brookings Institution.

Streeck, Wolfgang. 2000. Competitive Solidarity: Rethinking the "European Social Model". In *Kontingenz und Krise: Institutionenpolitik in kapitalistischen und postsozialistischen Gesellschaften*, eds. Karl Hinrichs, Herbert Kitschelt, and Helmuth Wiesenthal, 245–261. Frankfurt/Main: Campus.

Taylor-Gooby, Peter. 2004. *New Risks, New Welfare: The Transformation of the European Welfare State.* Oxford and New York: Oxford University Press.

Tönnies, Ferdinand. 2001. *Community and Civil Society* [*Gemeinschaft und Gesellschaft*], ed. Jose Harris, trans. Jose Harris and Margaret Hollis. Cambridge, U.K. and New York: Cambridge University Press.

Tsebelis, George. 2002. *Veto Players: How Political Institutions Work.* Princeton, NJ: Princeton University Press.

Ullrich, Carsten G. 2002. Reciprocity, Justice and Statutory Health Insurance in Germany. *Journal of European Social Policy* 12 (2): 123–136.

Veghte, Benjamin. 2004. *Why Did the Working and Lower Classes in the United States not Successfully Mobilize for a Redistributive Welfare State? An Exploratory Study of Constraints on Political Mobilization.* Working Paper No. 1. Bremen: Graduate School of Social Sciences at the University of Bremen. https://www.gsss.uni-bremen.de/index.php?id=bveghte.

Veghte, Benjamin, Greg M. Shaw, and Robert Y. Shapiro. 2007. Social Policy Preferences, National Defense and Political Polarization in the United States. In *Social Justice, Legitimacy and the Welfare State*, eds. Steffen Mau and Benjamin Veghte, 145–168. Aldershot, U.K.: Ashgate.

Weir, Margaret, Ann Shola Orloff, and Theda Skocpol, eds. 1988. *The Politics of Social Policy in the United States.* Princeton, NJ: Princeton University Press.

Wilensky, Harold L. 1975. *The Welfare State and Equality: Structural and Ideological Roots of Public Expenditures.* Berkeley: University of California Press.

Wilensky, Harold L. 2002. *Rich Democracies: Political Economy, Public Policy, and Performance.* Berkeley: University of California Press.

Yeates, Nicola. 2002. Globalization and Social Policy: From Global Neoliberal Hegemony to Global Political Pluralism. *Global Social Policy* 2 (1): 69–91.

Benjamin W. Veghte

WELFARE SYSTEM
SEE *Social Welfare System.*

WELLS-BARNETT, IDA B.
1862–1931

Ida Bell Wells-Barnett gained a national reputation in the 1890s as a pioneering crusader against lynching. Her long career spanned a wide variety of venues, including schoolroom, settlement house, municipal court, electoral politics, home, church, and social club. Journalism, however, was her calling. Her publications, many of them too militant or sharply worded to find a substantial receptive audience, remain her greatest legacy.

The eldest of eight children, Ida was born into slavery in Holly Springs, Mississippi, fifty miles southeast of Memphis. Her parents died in the yellow fever epidemic that swept through the Mississippi River Valley in 1878, leaving sixteen-year-old Ida to care for five siblings. She quickly secured a teaching position, made possible by her education at Shaw University in Holly Springs. Between 1880 and 1882 she relocated to Memphis, taking along two sisters and leaving her other siblings in the care of relatives.

Wells found her teaching career in Memphis unsatisfying, and she soon discovered a far more rewarding form of pedagogy: journalism. She published her first newspaper article in a church weekly in 1883, and began sending articles about black women to major African American publications in eastern cities. By 1885, writing as "Iola," she was among the few African American women writing about politics, and in 1889 she became co-owner of the Memphis *Free Speech and Headlight.* Her straightforward criticism in 1891 of the Memphis school board's neglect of black children and exploitation of black female teachers led to a decision not to renew her teaching appointment.

Wells's uncompromising journalism reflected her general approach to race relations. At the age of twenty-two, she sued a railroad after being thrown off the train for refusing to ride in a segregated car. In 1892 three Memphis black grocers were lynched after a conflict with a white competitor envious of their success. Wells later recalled that the event "changed the whole course of my life" (DeCosta-Willis 1995). Her unsigned attack on the lynching eschewed the cautious convention observed by southern black spokesmen who paired their criticism of lynching with ritualized reminders that the black community should not accept criminal behavior within its ranks. Wells understood that lynching was meant less to punish depravity (which white southerners expected from "their Negroes") than to punish the more dangerous sin of a black person not accepting his place.

Wells left Memphis immediately, probably expecting the mob attack on her newspaper the following day. She spent the next three years in eastern cities and Great Britain, lecturing and writing (now under the name "Exile"). Drawing on statistics compiled from careful research, she demonstrated that less than a third of lynching victims had even been accused of rape. Lynching, she argued, had less to do with the honor of white womanhood than "an excuse to get rid of Negroes who were acquiring wealth and property and thus keep the race terrorized and 'keep the nigger down' " (DeCosta-Willis 1995, p. xiii). Her charge that liaisons between white men and black women constituted the true threat to racial purity stirred even greater controversy.

Wells visited Chicago in 1893 to protest the exclusion of African Americans from the World's Columbian Exposition. Characteristically, she took a more militant position that most of her peers, advocating a boycott of the "Colored American Day" granted by the fair managers to placate the protesters. She relocated to Chicago permanently two years later, marrying prominent attorney Ferdinand Barnett. Over the next three decades she wrote less, putting her energies into the woman suffrage movement, local politics, and social work. In 1910 she founded the Negro Fellowship League as a venue for "missionary work" and "social work" on the city's South Side. Facing competition first from the city's black YMCA (1913) and then Urban League (1915), the Fellowship League shifted to a focus on politics and had only a minor presence by the time black southerners began moving to Chicago in large numbers in late 1916.

Wells-Barnett, who attended the founding meeting of the NAACP in 1910 in New York, never established herself as a major figure in African American institutional life. Although conventionally middle class in style, manners, and religious observance, she had limited patience with polite diplomacy during a generally cautious era of black politics.

Although she effectively mobilized black voters briefly through the Alpha Suffrage Club (established in 1913), Ida B. Wells was more adept at analytical and rhetorical provocation than organization. She understood in the 1890s what W. E. B. Du Bois (1868–1963) would famously enunciate four decades later in *Black Reconstruction* (1935): that African American success and dignity were less likely to win equal citizenship than to provoke the violence necessary to keep "the Negro" in his place.

SEE ALSO *Journalism; Lynchings; Militants; Resistance; White Supremacy*

BIBLIOGRAPHY

PRIMARY SOURCES

Wells, Ida B. 1892. *Southern Horrors: Lynch Law in All Its Phases.* Chicago: Donohue and Henneberry.

Wells, Ida B., Frederick Douglass, I. Garland Penn, and Ferdinand L. Barnett. [1893] 1999. *The Reason Why the Colored American Is Not in the World's Columbian Exposition,* ed. Robert W. Rydell. Urbana: University of Illinois Press.

Wells-Barnett, Ida B. 1895. *A Red Record: Tabulated Statistics and Alleged Causes of Lynchings in the United States, 1892–1893–1894.* Chicago: Donohue and Henneberry.

Wells-Barnett, Ida B. 1899. *Lynch Law in Georgia.* Chicago pamphlet, distributed by Chicago Colored Citizens.

Wells-Barnett, Ida B. 1900. *Mob Rule in New Orleans: Robert Charles and His Fight to the Death.* Chicago pamphlet.

Wells-Barnett, Ida B. 1917. *The East St. Louis Massacre: The Greatest Outrage of the Century.* Chicago: The Negro Fellowship Herald Press.

Wells-Barnett, Ida B. 1922. *The Arkansas Race Riot.*

Wells-Barnett, Ida B. 1991. *Selected works of Ida B. Wells-Barnett.* Comp. Trudier Harris. New York: Oxford University Press.

SECONDARY SOURCES

DeCosta-Willis, Miriam, ed. 1995. *The Memphis Diary of Ida B. Wells.* Boston: Beacon Press.

Grossman, James. 1997. "Social Burden" or "Amiable Peasantry": Constructing a Place for Black Southerners. In *American Exceptionalism?: U.S. Working-class Formation in an International Context.* Eds. Rick Halpern and Jonathan Morris, 221–243. New York: St. Martin's Press.

Holt, Thomas C. 1982. The Lonely Warrior: Ida B. Wells-Barnett and the Struggle for Black Leadership. In *Black Leaders of the Twentieth Century,* eds. John Hope Franklin and August Meier, 38–61. Urbana: University of Illinois Press.

Schechter, Patricia A. 2001. *Ida B. Wells-Barnett and American Reform, 1880–1930.* Chapel Hill: University of North Carolina Press.

James Grossman

WELTANSCHAUUNG

Weltanschauung is a German word that often is translated as "worldview" or "world outlook" but just as frequently is treated as a calque or left untranslated. A Weltanschauung is a comprehensive conception or theory of the world and the place of humanity within it. It is an intellectual construct that provides both a unified method of analysis for and a set of solutions to the problems of existence. The concept of a Weltanschauung has played an important role in the development of psychoanalysis, critical theory, and nineteenth- and twentieth-century hermeneutics.

Weltanschauung is connected closely to the work of Wilhelm Dilthey (1833–1911), who wanted to provide for the human sciences what Immanuel Kant (1724–1804) had provided for the natural sciences. Kant had established the possibility of objective and certain knowledge for natural science (*Naturwissenschaft*) in his *Critique of Pure Reason* (1781). Dilthey intended to fashion a critique of reason on behalf of the historical human or cultural sciences (*Geisteswissenschaft*). For Dilthey the goal of natural science was causal explanation, whereas the goal of human sciences was to achieve understanding by means of interpretation. Every interpretation, he reasoned, takes place within a larger understanding of the world (i.e., a Weltanschauung), which itself is historically conditioned. Thus, interpreters of human history and culture must recognize their immersion in a particular historical situation and tradition and in that process come to terms with the finitude of their perspective. The irony of Dilthey's historicist conclusions lies in the fact that they undermine his original goal of establishing universal validity for judgment in the human sciences. This split or contradiction resulted in differing orientations to the concept of the Weltanschauung among thinkers such as Freud, Husserl, Heidegger, and Gadamer.

For Sigmund Freud (1856–1939) the age of modernity was the coming into being of the rational or scientific Weltanschauung and the subsequent decline or eclipse of alternative religious or philosophical Weltanschauungen. The scientific Weltanschauung sees both the natural world and the cultural world as being ultimately transparent to the power of human cognition. Therefore, it consciously supplants world outlooks that place certain phenomena beyond the reach of human understanding. In Freud's view psychoanalysis represented the last contribution to the criticism of nonscientific Weltanschauungen (for instance, by tracing the origin of religion to the persistence of the wishes and needs of childhood into maturity). The arrival of the scientific Weltanschauung, which Freud described as still being in its infancy, would resolve the paradox left behind by Dilthey. This was a historically conditioned view of the world, but because it represented the endpoint or terminus of human cognition, it could provide objective and certain knowledge for all human activities and endeavors.

A more direct successor to Dilthey was Edmund Husserl (1859–1938). In rejecting the strong claims of scientific rationalism, Husserl argued that objects are experienced by the observer only from within an intentional horizon of consciousness, or "life-world" (*Lebenswelt*). In other words, objects are not located in objective or autonomous space and time; they do not exist outside a detached observer who can come to know them objectively and finally. For Husserl meaning does not exist "out there" but resides only where subject and world meet. The goal is to strip away the preconceptions of history and science so that consciousness can understand the object as it really is.

Husserl, however, like Freud, ignored the historical nature of Dilthey's account. The very possibility of ahistorical meaning was challenged by Husserl's successors in phenomenology and hermeneutics, including Martin Heidegger (1889–1976) and Hans Georg Gadamer (1900–2002).

Heidegger emphasized the finitude of all historical and cultural interpretation at the expense of ahistorical accounts. For Heidegger hermeneutics, as the theory and practice of interpretation, must remain cognizant of different Weltanschauungs operating in certain historical contexts. One can know an object only from within one's peculiar and historically conditioned Weltanschauung or (Heidegger's favored term) *Weltbild* (world-picture). As interpreters of the world around them, people always find themselves within a particular language and culture. People cannot bracket the presuppositions of their Weltanschauung in order to explicate reality; in fact, those presuppositions become part of the very existence that demands explication.

Hans-Georg Gadamer, whose 1975 work *Truth and Method* represents the major thrust of contemporary hermeneutics, extended the Heideggerian critique of ahistorical interpretation in many ways. For Gadamer understanding involves an interpretive dialogue with the Weltanschauung in which one finds oneself. People's modes of understanding (their "methods") are at one and the same time the means of interpretation and objects that require interpretation. Gadamer reconnects to the historicist conclusions of Dilthey with his assertion that understanding can be achieved only with reference to the Weltanschauung in which that understanding is taking place. Unlike Dilthey and Heidegger, however, Gadamer posits that there can be no final interpretation of reality because new life-worlds or world pictures will cause future interpreters to see and experience the world differently.

SEE ALSO *Freud, Sigmund; Hermeneutics; Ideology; Philosophy; Political Theory*

BIBLIOGRAPHY

Dilthey, Wilhelm. 1996. *Selected Works*. Vol. IV: *Hermeneutics and the Study of History*, eds. Rudolf A. Marrkkreel and Frithjof Rodi. Princeton, NJ: Princeton University Press.

Freud, Sigmund. 1933. Lecture XXXV: A Philosophy of Life. *New Introductory Lectures on Psycho-Analysis*. Trans. W. J. H. Sprott. New York: W. W. Norton.

Gadamer, Hans-Georg. 1975. *Truth and Method.* London: Sheed & Ward.

Heidegger, Martin. 1962. *Being and Time.* Trans. John Macquarrie and Edward Robinson. New York: Harper.

David W. McIvor

WEST BANK

SEE *Palestinians; Intifada, The.*

WEST INDIES

SEE *Caribbean, The.*

WESTERN COLLABORATIVE GROUP STUDY

SEE *Personality, Type A/Type B.*

WESTMINSTER MODEL

SEE *First-past-the-post.*

WHISTLE-BLOWERS

In a definition typical of those found in the research literature, Janet P. Near and Marcia P. Miceli in 1985 described whistle-blowers as organization employees, current or former, who report practices they consider unethical or illegal to someone with the power to take action. Although the public and many journalists may consider whistle-blowing to include only those cases in which the whistle-blower has alerted external audiences to the misconduct, for example, of someone in the media or in law enforcement, researchers in the field since the mid-1980s have tended to extend the definition to include both internal and external audiences. For example, an employee at a nuclear power plant might alert only a manager in a superior position in the authority hierarchy to a safety violation or concern. Researchers refer to this as "internal whistle-blowing." Alternatively, the individual employee could go directly to a mass-media outlet or to law enforcement with their observations. This is termed "external whistle-blowing." In the prototypical case, it has been found that employees with serious concerns tend to take them first to their superiors in the employing organization, and only when they find the senior managers to be inert or complicit in the perceived wrongdoing do they take the matter to external agencies that might be able to intercede (Glazer and Glazer 1989; Miethe and Rothschild 1994).

A GROWING PHENOMENON

In the late twentieth century and the early twenty-first century the extent of whistle-blowing grew greatly, with studies reporting substantial cases in Canada, Australia, South Africa, the United Kingdom, and Europe in addition to the United States, and worldwide attention paid to whistle-blowers in the mass media has been expanding. One analysis of previous research studies of whistle-blowing in the United States found that approximately 37 percent of employees observe in their workplaces some type of wrongdoing that troubles them (Miethe and Rothschild 1994). This rate, however, can vary considerably by occupational grouping. Among internal auditors, people who are trained to discover financial fraud and whose jobs require them to look for it, 82 percent say they have observed wrongdoing (Near and Miceli 1985). A large survey of federal employees found the rates of observing misconduct to range from 7 percent to 45 percent, depending upon the agency and the occupation involved (U.S. Merit Systems Protection Board 1993). The proportion of those who say they have observed serious misconduct in the workplace varies greatly by the opportunity for such observation in one's occupation.

Of those who do say they have observed misconduct, most remain silent, although this too can vary considerably by country, occupation, and type of employer. Across six U.S. studies of employers, the average rate of silence among those who said they did observe serious misconduct in their places of work was 58 percent (Miethe and Rothschild 1994), while a later international review of the research literature shows that the rate of those who remain silent can vary from 25 percent to 91 percent (Maria 2006). These numbers imply that there is considerable room for growth in this whistle-blowing phenomenon if more individuals felt free to voice their concerns. Undeniably, interviews with these silent observers indicate two main reasons so many employees hold back from voicing their concerns at work: (1) they fear retribution from their employer, and (2) they suspect that their reportage would not effect organizational change in any case (Rothschild and Miethe 1999).

THE WHISTLE-BLOWER'S EXPERIENCE

Research findings quite clearly show that observers of misconduct do put themselves in jeopardy by reporting or disclosing the misconduct, whether they stay inside the organization or go outside the organization with their disclosures. Indeed, employer retaliation against whistle-blowers is the rule, not the exception, and some whistle-blowers are so devastated by the reprisals they suffer that they cannot reclaim their lives (De Maria 1999; Alford 2001). A nationwide study of whistle-blowers from all occupations and regions of the United States found that among those employees who stayed within their employing organization, reporting their observations and concerns only to those above them in the organizational hierarchy, the following occurred as a result of their disclosures:

- 69 percent were fired or forced to retire from their jobs,

- 64 percent saw their job performance evaluations decline abruptly,

- 68 percent had their work more closely monitored by supervisors,

- 64 percent felt they had been blacklisted from getting another job within their field.

For each of these items, the rate of retaliation was 10 to 15 percentage points higher for those who went outside of the employing organization with their concerns (Rothschild and Miethe 1999). In many cases, the reprisals that follow the reportage are experienced as traumatic. Some 84 percent said the experience gave rise to "severe depression or anxiety," 78 percent said they learned from it "distrust of others," 69 percent said they suffered a "decline in physical health," 66 percent said they suffered "severe financial decline," and 53 percent said the experience harmed their "family relations." Many former whistle-blowers describe their experiences as giving rise to a political and personal transformation by which they now see themselves as exceedingly moral and their former employers (and in many cases, large organizations in general) as corrupt (Rothschild and Miethe 1999).

Statistical analysis of the data indicates that no special gender, age, educational attainment, years of employment, or method of reporting can insulate individuals from organizational retaliation should they choose to disclose the organizational misconduct. Validity of the claim also provides no insulation. Indeed, the data show that retaliation against whistle-blowers is most severe and certain when the observed wrongdoing is systemic and central to the way the organization conducts its business and accumulates its profit (Rothschild and Miethe 1999).

FEDERAL AND STATE LAWS

Federal and state laws that would protect whistle-blowers from retaliation and that would thereby encourage the disclosure of organizational practices that injure the public are not comprehensive, and even where they do seem to be applicable, they are frequently not enforced (see Government Accountability Project 1996 for a review of these). It is not easy for the whistle-blower, generally unemployed, to mount a successful legal claim against a former employer with vastly greater legal resources. The Sarbanes-Oxley Act of 2002 provides the most substantial legal protection for whistle-blowers, but it applies only to those who would disclose corporate misconduct that, if proven, would materially affect the valuation of a publicly traded company. The *qui tam* suits filed under the provisions of the False Claims Act have proven most effective at gaining large awards for whistle-blowers, but this act applies only to those employees whose employers were defrauding the federal government, again covering only a portion of the potential whistle-blowers.

As organizations grow larger in scope and more complex operationally, effective oversight from outside agencies becomes more difficult, and often the only people who are in a position to detect when the organization is defrauding or endangering the public are key employees themselves. The U.S. Congress has recognized the public's interest in protecting whistle-blowers so abuses of the law or the public trust can come to light, and parliaments in other nations have recognized the same. But the extent of persistent retaliation against whistle-blowers and the extent of employees who choose to remain silent in the face of abuses at work suggests that more needs to be done.

BIBLIOGRAPHY

Alford, C. Fred. 2001. *Whistleblowers: Broken Lives and Organizational Power.* Ithaca, NY: Cornell University Press.

De Maria, William. 1999. *Deadly Disclosures: Whistleblowing and the Ethical Meltdown of Australia.* Kent Town, Australia: Wakefield.

Glazer, Myron Peretz, and Penina Migdal Glazer. 1989. *The Whistleblowers: Exposing Corruption in Government and Industry.* New York: Basic.

Government Accountability Project. 1996. *Courage without Martyrdom: The Whistleblower's Survival Guide.* Washington, DC: Author.

Maria, William. 2006. Brother Secret, Sister Silence: Sibling Conspiracies against Managerial Integrity. *Journal of Business Ethics* 65 (3): 219–234.

Miethe, Terance D., and Joyce Rothschild. 1994. Whistleblowing and the Control of Organizational Misconduct. *Sociological Inquiry* 64 (3): 322–347.

Near, Janet P., and Marcia P. Miceli. 1985. Organizational Dissidence: The Case of Whistle-Blowing. *Journal of Business Ethics* 4 (1): 1–16.

Rothschild, Joyce, and Terance D. Miethe. 1999. Whistle-Blower Disclosures and Management Retaliation: The Battle to Control Information about Organizational Corruption. *Work and Occupations* 26 (1): 107–128.

U.S. Merit Systems Protection Board. 1993. *Whistleblowing in the Federal Government: A Report to the President and the Congress of the United States.* Washington, DC: U.S. Government Printing Office.

Joyce Rothschild

WHITE, WALTER
1893–1955

Walter White, author and chief executive of the National Association for the Advancement of Colored People (NAACP) between 1929 and 1955, was born in Atlanta, Georgia. According to the *New York Times* obituary of March 22, 1955, "Mr. White, the nearest approach to a national leader of American Negroes since Booker T. Washington, was a Negro by choice" (p. 31). White had blond hair, blue eyes, and a complexion that was light enough to "pass" for white. But if ever White questioned his racial identity, the 1906 Atlanta race riot made clear to him that he was African American. During this pogrom, a white mob threatened to attack his family home, and at the age of thirteen he determined that he could never be part of a race that carried within it such a ghastly hatred. His aspect and the riot were central to his life and career as an advocate for race advancement.

Upon his graduation from Atlanta University in 1916, White helped to found the Atlanta branch of the NAACP. He joined the national staff in January of 1918, and for the next eight years his primary responsibility was conducting undercover investigations of lynchings and race riots. He investigated forty-one such instances. Passing for white, White tricked whites into giving him candid accounts of the recent violence, which the NAACP would then publicize. "I Investigate Lynchings," which appeared in the July 1929 issue of *American Mercury*, is White's account of his investigative exploits. *Rope and Faggot*, published in 1929 and still considered authoritative, is his detailed analysis of the extent and causes of lynching.

When James Weldon Johnson (1871–1938) retired from the NAACP in 1929, White was elevated to the position of secretary. During both the Franklin Roosevelt (1882–1945) and Harry Truman (1884–1972) administrations, White's style of working for political gain by ral-

lying enlightened elites achieved stunning results. His close friendship with Eleanor Roosevelt (1884–1962), who joined the NAACP board of directors following her husband's death, gave him direct access to the White House. He orchestrated massive support in Congress for an antilynching law, which was defeated only by filibustering southern Democratic senators. White also organized Marian Anderson's (1897–1993) historic Easter 1939 concert at the Lincoln Memorial in Washington, D.C., including a sponsoring committee studded with New Deal officials. In 1941 White collaborated with A. Philip Randolph's (1889–1979) March on Washington movement, which pressured President Roosevelt into issuing Executive Order 8802 banning racial discrimination in defense industries. White persuaded President Truman to appoint a civil rights commission, which produced the report *To Secure These Rights* in 1947.

During White's tenure as NAACP secretary, the association launched a series of legal suits designed to ensure equality between the races in education. This effort culminated in the Supreme Court's 1954 *Brown v. Board of Education* decision, which declared unconstitutional the doctrine of "separate but equal."

During World War II (1939–1945), White promoted the idea that an allied victory should lead to both the dismantling of European colonialism and racial equality for African Americans. He pursued these goals in 1945 as one of three NAACP consultants to the U.S. delegation to the founding conference of the United Nations in San Francisco and again in 1948 as a consultant to the U.S. delegation to the UN General Assembly meeting in Paris. Yet his friendship with Eleanor Roosevelt and alliance with President Truman precluded White from advocating the more expansive definition of human rights favored by W. E. B. Du Bois (1868–1963) and Paul Robeson (1898–1976) that included economic and social as well as political rights.

White's twenty-six year marriage to Gladys Powell, an African American, ended in divorce in 1948. The following year he married Poppy Cannon, a white woman born in South Africa. Many in the NAACP objected and called for White's resignation. Eleanor Roosevelt threatened to resign from the board of directors should White be dismissed, thereby saving his position. He remained NAACP executive secretary until his death (he had been in declining health for several years) but with diminished powers.

Walter White's importance lay in his organizational skills and leadership style. His abilities to successfully cultivate ties with people of influence both in and out of government and to popularize and publicize the association and its program were instrumental to placing civil rights on the national agenda.

SEE ALSO *Harlem Renaissance; National Association for the Advancement of Colored People (NAACP)*

BIBLIOGRAPHY

Janken, Kenneth Robert. 2003. *WHITE: The Biography of Walter White, Mr. NAACP.* New York: New Press.

New York Times. 1955. Walter White, 61, Dies in Home Here. March 22: 31.

White, Walter. 1948. *A Man Called White: The Autobiography of Walter White.* New York: Viking.

Kenneth R. Janken

WHITE NOISE

There are uncertainties in dynamics of social and natural processes. Basic approaches of statistical analysis model these processes based on theoretical derivations or empirical observations. The primary goal in statistical modeling is to extract as much underlying information of the processes as possible and let the residuals approximate a realization of white noise. White noise is one of the fundamental stochastic processes in many fields. Mathematically, it has a constant spectrum, which is the same as the white light we observe through our eyes.

White noise has been utilized to mask distraction of undesirable sound in the environment. Financial analysts have applied white noise to model stock markets. In fact white noise has been used for audio synthesis, impulse response, art, sensory deprivation, sleeping aid, and more. White noise is a basic form of stochastic process that provides the foundation for almost all useful statistical models used in natural and social sciences.

Let $\{Z_t\}$ be an equally spaced time series (a sequence of random variables) with a mean of zero and finite autocovariance

$$\gamma(t, s) = E(Z_t Z_s), \qquad (1)$$

where $E(X)$ is the expected value (mean) of random variable X and t, s donate the time. If $\{Z_t\}$ has a nonzero mean, without loss generality, it can be subtracted from the time series to get a time series with a zero mean. The expected value of a discrete random variable X is defined as

$$E(X) = \sum_{\text{all } x} x P(X = x), \qquad (2)$$

where $P(X = x)$ is the probability mass function of X. For a continuous random variable, its expected value is

$$E(X) = \int_x x f(x)\, dx, \qquad (3)$$

where $f(x)$ is the density function of X.

If the autocovariance function $\gamma(t, s)$ of time series $\{Z_t\}$ is only a function of $|t - s|$, then $\{Z_t\}$ is a (weak) stationary process. White noise is the simplest stationary process with

$$\gamma(t, s) = \begin{cases} \sigma^2 & t = s \\ 0 & t \neq s \end{cases} \qquad (4)$$

where $\sigma^2 = E(Z_t^2)$ is the variance of Z_t.

White noise plays an important role not only in physical sciences such as in signal processing, but also in almost all statistical analysis of time series observed from social and economic activities. For example, according to George Box, Gwilym M. Jenkins, and Gregory C. Reinsel in their 1994 book *Time Series Analysis: Forecasting and Control,* the widely used Autoregressive and Integrated Moving Average (ARIMA(p,d,q)) models in time series analysis are generated by the white noise innovations $\{Z_t\}$ through the following expression:

$$\phi(B)(1 - B)^d Y_t = \theta(B) Z_t \qquad (5)$$

where Y_t is the time series under study, $\varphi(B) = 1 - \sum_{l=1}^{p} \alpha_l B^l$, $\theta(B) = 1 + \sum_{j=1}^{q} \beta_j B^j$, B is the back shift operator defined as $BY_t = Y_t - Y_{t-1}$, d is an integer, and Z_t is the Gaussian white noise with mean zero and variance σ^2. From expression (5) we can see that Y_t of ARIMA(0,0,0) is the white noise.

ARIMA(0,1,0) denotes a random walk model, which is a model of unit root and widely used in modeling financial markets. ARIMA(p,0,0) becomes an autoregressive model of order p (AR(p)), ARIMA(0,0,q) is a moving average model of order q (MA(q)), and ARIMA(p,0,q) is ARMA(p,q). For a proper range of the parameters α_l and β_j the Y_t in ARMA(p,q) is stationary and invertible (Box, Jenkins, and Reinsel 1994).

Many methods have been proposed to estimate the parameters in ARIMA models from observed time series. A crucial step in model diagnosis is to check, through a battery of tests and plots, if the residuals from the models are consistent with white noise (Box, Jenkins, and Reinsel 1994).

In general there are two types of techniques in analyzing time series. The first type is based on direct modeling such as ARIMA models, which are called time domain techniques (Box, Jenkins, and Reinsel 1994). The second type, according to M. B. Priestley in the 1981 publication *Spectral Analysis and Time Series,* is in the frequency

domain that utilizes the spectrum of a stationary process. The spectrum is defined as

$$f(\omega) = \sum_{k=-\infty}^{\infty} \gamma_k e^{-ikw} = \gamma_0 + 2\sum_{k=1}^{\infty} \gamma_k \cos(k\omega) \quad (6)$$

where $\gamma_k = \gamma(t, t + k)$ and $i = \sqrt{-1}$. For a stationary ARMA(p,q) process, the spectrum is $f(\omega) = \sigma^2 |\theta(e^{-i\omega})|^2 |\varphi(e^{-i\omega})|^{-2}$, where $|.|$ is the norm of a complex number.

For white noise, its spectrum is

$$f(\omega) = \gamma_0 = \sigma^2, \quad (7)$$

a constant for all value of frequency ω. That is, the plot of the spectrum of white noise is flat against ω. The spectrum of white noise can be estimated through the periodogram of finite observations with length n. Let g_k be the sample autocovariance computed from the n observations of a stationary time series $\{Y_t\}$:

$$g_k = \sum_{t=k+1}^{n} (y_t - \bar{y})(y_{t-k} - \bar{y})/n, \quad (8)$$

where $\bar{y} = \sum_{t=1}^{n} y_t/n$. Then, the periodogram ordinates are

$$I(\omega) = g_0 + 2\sum_{k=1}^{n-1} g_k \cos(k\omega). \quad (9)$$

usually computed at the Fourier frequencies $\omega_j = 2\pi j/n$. The plot of the periodogram ordinates gives a visual examination of the underlying spectrum of the process. For a sample of white noise, its $I(\omega)$ is distributed as $\sigma^2 \chi_2^2/2$, where χ_2^2 is a chi square random variable with 2 degrees of freedom. Note that $I(\omega)$ is an unbiased estimator of $f(\omega)$, but not consistent (Priestley 1981). Many techniques were proposed to construct unbiased and consistent estimators of $f(\omega)$ using functions of $I(\omega)$, and many tests on white noise can also be constructed via periodogram ordinates $I(\omega)$ (Priestley 1981).

White noise is not only the driving force for classic ARIMA models, it also plays a fundamental role in the popular Generalized Autoregressive and Conditional Heteroscedastic (GARCH) models in financial analysis, in vector cointegration models for economic time series, and in long memory time series models such as in Autoregressive Fractional Integrated Moving Average (ARFIMA(p,d,q)) models with d being a non-integer. White noise is the core of statistical analysis. However, some realizations of simple deterministic chaotic systems may exhibit white noise like sequences. The study of chaos requires new techniques and concepts that are beyond the classic approaches of time series analysis.

SEE ALSO *Autoregressive Models; Cointegration; Randomness; Regression; Regression Analysis; Residuals; Unit Root and Cointegration Regression*

BIBLIOGRAPHY

Box, George E. P., Gwilym M. Jenkins, and Gregory C. Reinsel. 1994. *Time Series Analysis: Forecasting and Control.* 3rd ed. Englewood Cliffs, NJ: Prentice Hall.

Priestley, M. B. 1981. *Spectral Analysis and Time Series.* London: Academic Press.

Dejian Lai

WHITE PRIMARY

Following Reconstruction (1865–1877), white southerners employed various tactics to minimize the economic, political, and social opportunities of former slaves and their descendents. The white primary, which limited blacks' political influence, was one. A primary is an election within a political party to select the party's nominees for public offices. Late in the 1800s states began to replace party conventions with primaries as nominating devices. The primary became a "white" primary as participation in it was denied to voters of color. Along with poll taxes and literacy tests, white primaries were "Jim Crow" laws, practices used in the South in the late 1800s and early 1900s to marginalize African Americans politically.

The white primary had significant discriminatory potential because the Democratic Party was virtually the only political institution involved in selecting public officials in the South. The Republican Party had virtually disappeared there; much of its numeric strength was contributed by black voters, whose numbers dwindled in the face of discriminatory voting laws and practices. By denying black voters the option of participating in Democratic Party nominations, they were left with few avenues for effective electoral involvement.

The creation of white primaries could be accomplished in several ways. First, the state could statutorily exclude African American voters from primaries. Alternatively, the Democratic Party itself could adopt rules that either denied the opportunity of party membership to black voters or prohibited black voters from casting ballots in primaries. White primaries could also be effectively created by using other discriminatory practices to disqualify black citizens from involvement in elections.

The black electorate was substantially reduced during this period by requiring prospective voters to pass literacy tests, pay poll taxes, and the like. Because most southern blacks had a rudimentary education at best and because of

the pervasive impoverished circumstances in which they lived, these policies were potent barriers to voting by black citizens. It was not particularly necessary to reinforce these devices with statutory white primaries. Moreover, some recognized that the Fourteenth and Fifteenth Amendments to the U.S. Constitution might prevent enforcement of laws that overtly denied to African Americans the right to vote.

Nonetheless, additional efforts to exclude black voters from nomination and election processes were desired by Southern whites. The Democratic Party at the county and state levels began to impose rules that prohibited participation of black voters in party affairs. Texas, however, took this further. There, as in some other southern locations, Democratic factions occasionally relied on black votes to gain and retain official power. A San Antonio faction sought to weaken one of its rivals that used that practice by convincing the state legislature to adopt a statute prohibiting black voter participation in primaries. The Texas legislature passed just such a law in 1923. Two years earlier the U.S. Supreme Court had decided *Newberry* v. *United States* (1921), which sprang from a Michigan election for a U.S. Senate seat. In *Newberry* the Court held that Congress could not regulate campaign spending in congressional primaries because primaries were not elections under Article I, Section 4 of the U.S. Constitution. Texas proponents of a statutory white primary thus reasoned that prohibitions of racial discrimination in the Fourteenth and Fifteenth Amendments would not apply to their primaries.

The equal protection clause of the Fourteenth Amendment requires that states offer "equal protection" to all persons in their jurisdictions; it is a prohibition against a state acting in discriminatory fashion. The Fifteenth Amendment simply provides that citizens may not be denied the right to vote on the basis of race, color, or previous status as slaves; it overtly guarantees African Americans the right to vote in elections. The Court's ruling in *Newberry* evaded these guarantees by holding that primaries were not a part of the electoral process.

Once the Texas statute was in place, a black El Paso doctor, L.A. Nixon, attempted to vote in a Democratic primary and was turned away. He sued Herndon, the election judge who prevented his voting, and claimed that his Fourteenth and Fifteenth Amendment rights had been violated. The U.S. Supreme Court decided *Nixon* v. *Herndon* in 1927, evaluating its issues solely within the context of the Fourteenth Amendment; the Texas law was held to clearly violate the equal protection clause. No consideration was given to the relevance of the Fifteenth Amendment to the case, nor was the question of whether federal laws applied to party primaries taken up.

Texas responded to the decision by repealing the offending statute and passing a new law permitting a party's state executive committee to determine the qualifications for political party membership. The Texas Democratic Party then passed a resolution affirming the right of qualified white Democratic voters to participate in the party's primaries, but no one else. In a subsequent primary Nixon again attempted to vote and was again turned away. He sued once more, and the Supreme Court took up his claim in the case of *Nixon* v. *Condon* (1932).

The logic of Texas's new law was that the Fourteenth Amendment specifically prohibited state action that is discriminatory, but the rule barring voting by black citizens was one adopted by the Texas Democratic Party, a private association. Since the rule was made and enforced by a private entity, proponents contended, the Fourteenth Amendment did not apply. The Court, however, disagreed, pointing out that the power to exclude black voters had been given to the party by the state and that the state was using the party to accomplish racial discrimination in voting, thereby violating the equal protection clause.

The Texas legislature then enacted a statute compelling political parties to employ the primary to nominate candidates and giving to parties complete responsibility for the actual conduct of the primary without state direction or supervision. When black voters were prevented from voting under this statute, yet another lawsuit resulted. This time the outcome was different. The Supreme Court ruled in *Grovey* v. *Townsend* (1935) that since operation of the primary was totally in the hands of a private entity and since political parties could be viewed as "voluntary associations for political action," a party might exclude African American voters without violating the equal protection clause. In these situations parties were not considered agents or instrumentalities of the state and could determine their own procedures as nonpublic institutions.

The Court's ruling in *Townsend* might have ended the debate as to the legal legitimacy of white primaries for some time; however, an unrelated Louisiana lawsuit revived the issue. Primary officials in New Orleans were charged with election fraud in the course of conducting an election for a seat in the U.S. House of Representatives, a violation of federal law. Because there was no competition for the seat in the general election, the primary outcome was tantamount to election. The embattled election officials defended themselves by invoking *Newberry* and asserting that federal law applied only to general elections. In *United States* v. *Classic* (1941), however, the Supreme Court held that the Constitution created a right to voter participation even in primaries when it gave to "the people in the several states" the authority to select their dele-

gates to the House of Representatives, provided that the primaries are an integral part of electoral procedure. *Classic* thus reversed the Court's position in *Newberry*, but it made no reference to *Grovey*.

Black voters, though, saw in *Classic* a stepping-stone to link white primaries to constitutional prohibitions against voter discrimination based upon race. A black Houston dentist, Lonnie E. Smith, had been refused a ballot in the 1940 primary by S. E. Allwright, an election judge. Smith sued and invoked the Court's finding in *Classic*, and the Court sided with him and overruled *Grovey* in so doing. The Court noted the state's authority to regulate political parties and primaries and concluded that primaries were thus a mechanism for electing public officeholders. *Smith* v. *Allwright* (1944) thereby struck down the white primary as an unconstitutional infringement of black voters' rights.

The impact of white primaries as a delimiter of black voting is not clear, for their specific effects must be disentangled from those of other discriminatory practices and laws. Although it is apparent that African American participation in elections declined during the period white primaries were operated, some analysts assert that literacy tests and poll taxes were principally responsible for the decline in black voting. Similarly, the impact of white primaries' demise is not obvious; some argue that eliminating the white primary did little to stimulate black voter participation. However, the percentage increase in black voter registration from 1940 to 1947, during which time the white primary was outlawed, is matched only by the increase in black voter registration from 1960 to 1969, when the Voting Rights Act of 1965 was first implemented.

Dismantling the complete array of discriminatory devices was necessary to stimulate widespread African American involvement in politics in the South. If nothing else, litigating the status of primaries in the framework of American elections was essential to making their public role apparent not only to the legal community and to political elites but also to private citizens. Given the almost universal adoption of primaries as nomination devices across the nation, these lessons were as important to nonsoutherners as they were to voters in the South.

SEE ALSO *Democratic Party, U.S.; Discrimination; Discrimination, Racial; Equal Protection; Jim Crow; Politics, Black; Politics, Southern; Poll Tax; Reconstruction Era (U.S.); South, The (USA)*

BIBLIOGRAPHY

Bell, Derrick. 2004. *Race, Racism, and American Law*, 5th ed. New York: Aspen Publishers.

Key, V. O., Jr. [1949] 1984. *Southern Politics in State and Nation*, A New Edition. Knoxville: University of Tennessee Press.

Klarman, Michael J. 2004. *From Jim Crow to Civil Rights: The Supreme Court and the Struggle for Racial Equality*. New York: Oxford University Press.

Kousser, J. Morgan. 1974. *The Shaping of Southern Politics: Suffrage Restriction and the Establishment of the One-Party South, 1880–1910*. New Haven, CT: Yale University Press.

Lawson, Steven F. 1976. *Black Ballots: Voting Rights in the South, 1944–1969*. New York: Columbia University Press.

Stanley, Harold W. 1987. *Voter Mobilization and the Politics of Race: The South and Universal Suffrage, 1952–1984*. New York: Praeger.

CASES

Newberry v. *United States* 256 U.S. 232 (1921)

Nixon v. *Herndon* 273 U.S. 536 (1927)

Nixon v. *Condon* 286 U.S. 73 (1932)

Grovey v. *Townsend* 295 U.S. 45 (1935)

United States v. *Classic* 313 U.S. 299 (1941)

Smith v. *Allwright* 321 U.S. 649 (1944)

James F. Sheffield Jr.

WHITE SUPREMACY

White supremacy—the belief in the superiority of the white race, especially in matters of intelligence and culture—achieved the height of its popularity during the period of European colonial expansion to the Western Hemisphere, Africa, and Asia stretching from the late 1800s to the first half of the twentieth century. White supremacists have based their ideas on a variety of theories and supposedly proven facts; the most prominent of these include the claims of pseudoscientific racist academic research that attempted to correlate inferiority and pathological behavior with categories of racial phenotypes, especially head size in the case of eugenics. White supremacist belief has also been justified by the Biblical Hamitic hypothesis, which viewed blacks as the descendants of Ham who would be cursed for life. There is a direct correlation between the rise of imperialism and colonialism and the expansion of white supremacist ideology justifying the changing international order, which increasingly saw Europeans assuming political control over peoples of darker skin color through military force and ideological means, such as religion and education. It is important to note that the range of those considered "white" expanded considerably in the twentieth century. For example, in the United States, not all ethnic groups with white skin were initially considered white. It was not until well into the

twentieth century that the Irish and Italians, for example, were considered white. By the end of that century, the United States federal government had also expanded its definition of whites to include Arabs.

Various groups and institutions have used varieties of white supremacist thinking to organize followers socially and politically, often with the purpose of policing racial barriers. This activism has included, but not been limited to, the physical elimination of nonwhite populations (especially through violence), preventing cross-racial marriage, and maintaining racial segregation. The most well known examples of institutionalized white supremacy were "Jim Crow" segregation in the United States, apartheid in southern Africa, and the Nazi German state under Adolph Hitler, which sought a "final solution" through the extermination in gas chambers of millions of Jews and gypsies, and under which various racial medical experiments were carried out.

The academic field of anthropology has been most closely associated with theories of racial difference, including white supremacy. As anthropology developed as a field in Europe and North America in the 1800s, its epistemological foundations actually provided scholarly legitimacy to the practice of categorizing human beings according to race. In the twentieth century it was also the field that amassed the primary evidence to refute white supremacist thinking. Of particular note as regards this latter phase was the work of Franz Boas, whose fieldwork among North American indigenous peoples provided evidence to refute ideas that races and cultures could be placed in hierarchies that ranged from primitive to sophisticated, with the white race at the top.

After World War II (1939–1945), and the carnage caused by Nazi racial ideology, effort was invested by social scientists to refute white supremacist ideology. Of particular note was the "Statement by Experts on Problems of Race" that the then new United Nations sponsored and had published in the early 1950s. The list of scholars who supported the document comprised the most prominent thinkers on issues related to race at the time, including E. Franklin Frazier, Claude Levi-Strauss, Julian S. Huxley, Gunnar Myrdal, Joseph Needham, and Theodosius Dobzhansky. The central point of the Statement was that race was not based on biological difference and was actually a social construction because all the supposedly different human races belonged to the same species of Homo sapiens.

Due to publications such as the Statement and the mapping of the human genome (which provided additional evidence that there are few significant genetic differences between races), biological justifications for white supremacy popular during the first half of the twentieth century declined in prevalence in the second half.

Similarly, by the end of the century all states that had officially declared themselves to be white supremacist had been eliminated. However, white supremacist ideology was resuscitated by a number of social transformations that were particularly evident by the last decade of the twentieth century. These included the end of Communist states in eastern Europe, increased immigration to Europe and North America by nonwhite groups, and the growth of technologies to facilitate rapid transnational communication. White supremacy was deployed by various groups as an organizing tool. In eastern Europe, groups in the former Communist societies used it to create new identities in the wake of communism's demise, and eastern Europe quickly became the center of neo-Nazi activism. In the United States, groups such as the World Church of the Creator and so-called citizen militias invoked religious and nationalist mythology to rally their believers against the increased power of racialized groups and the presence of illegal immigrants from Latin America. The expansion of the Internet was useful to these hate groups because it facilitated the exchange of documents and enabled the organization of adherents over vast distances. It also allowed some European white supremacy activists to obviate European antiracist propaganda laws that had been enacted after World War II.

The persistence of white privilege, even in societies where nonwhites are the majority, has meant that white supremacy and its consequences have not ceased to be sources of social scientific research. A notable event in the growth of "white studies" was the conference "The Making and Unmaking of Whiteness," held at the University of California, Berkeley in April 1997. This yielded, four years later, a volume of the same name published by Duke University Press.

In the United States the legal scholar Cheryl Harris, the historian David Roediger, and the American Studies scholar George Lipsitz are among those whose work in white studies has been influential. Melissa Steyn, the South African, has also been a prominent thinker in the area.

White studies is best contextualized as another stage in the evolution of humanities and social science research on the functioning of social systems. One of the most prominent themes in the study of whiteness is identity formation. The argument for doing white studies, and putting it on par with other more established areas of ethnic studies such as black studies, is that the adoption of white identity and the related ideology of white supremacy confer privilege at the expense of others who cannot or will not invest in them.

SEE ALSO *Frazier, E. Franklin; Genomics; Hierarchy; Immigration; Inequality, Racial; Levi-Strauss, Claude; Myrdal, Gunnar; Nazism; Racism; Whiteness*

BIBLIOGRAPHY

Boas, Franz. [1945] 1969. *Race and Democratic Society*. New York: Biblo & Tannen.

Brander Rasmussen, Birgit, ed. 2001. *The Making and Unmaking of Whiteness*. Durham, NC: Duke University Press.

Montagu, Ashley. 1972. *Statement on Race*. 3rd ed. New York: Oxford University Press.

Steyn, Melissa E. 2001. *"Whiteness Just Isn't What It Used to Be": White Identity in a Changing South Africa*. Albany: State University of New York Press.

Mark D. Alleyne

WHITENESS

Whiteness refers to the nature and social impact of white racial identity. "White" is best understood as a position in a racialized social structure; that is, it is a label that is meaningless outside of a social system where racial categories influence access to social, political, and economic resources and in the absence of other socially constructed identities such as "black" or "Asian."

Historically, the subject of whiteness was overlooked by mainstream social science in favor of an emphasis upon the "problems" of immigrants and minorities. When whiteness was taken into consideration, it was not as the focus of study, but as the mainstream or baseline against which other groups were compared. One significant exception to this line of thought was presented in African American sources such as the works of W. E. B. Du Bois and those compiled by the editors of *Ebony* magazine (1966) and David Roediger (1998). That this literature was overlooked is perhaps best understood as a reflection of the historical marginalization of the contribution of African American writers to the study of race relations.

Whiteness studies emerged in the late 1980s and early 1990s in such fields as history, sociology, critical legal studies, cultural studies, anthropology, and education. In sharp contrast to earlier work in the field of race and ethnic relations, whiteness studies involves an *explicit* focus upon the socially constructed nature of white racial identity and the role of whiteness in the reproduction of racism and racial inequality. This serves to emphasize that whites are an important racial collectivity and that it is important to understand how whites perform as racial actors (see Lewis 2004). Seminal early works included Roediger's *The Wages of Whiteness* (1991), Ruth Frankenberg's *White Women, Race Matters* (1993), and Peggy McIntosh's "White Privilege" (1988); these works were the vanguard of a large body of literature that flourished after 1995. Why whiteness studies emerged when it did is best explained by a combination of factors, includ-

ing the continuing challenge to white supremacy in the post–Civil Rights era, the changing racial demography of the United States, the decline of white ethnic identities, and intellectual trends that emphasized the social construction of race and the examination of identities.

MAJOR CONTRIBUTIONS

Major ideas and concepts that emerged from the field of whiteness studies are (1) the importance of white racial invisibility and white privilege, (2) the social and political impact of whiteness, and (3) the historical evolution of whiteness. White racial invisibility is the observation that for most white Americans under most circumstances, white racial identity has little or no social meaning. This "hidden" nature of whiteness is closely connected to the fact that white understandings and practices have historically constituted the social and cultural mainstream of American society. In essence, to be white is to be not different, to be "just like everyone else." White invisibility is also linked by many writers to white privilege, the unearned and invisible benefits (e.g., being viewed as an individual) that whites experience in everyday life (McIntosh [1988] 2002).

A second core insight of whiteness studies has emphasized the effect of white invisibility on racial politics and the reproduction of racial inequality. The hidden nature of whiteness has made it more difficult for many whites to understand the experiences of racial minorities and the persistence of racial inequality. This has led to the emergence of what many writers have termed *color-blind racial ideology* (see Bonilla-Silva 2001), the claim that racism is a thing of the past and that race no longer matters in American society. From the color-blind perspective, racial inequality is due to the failure of individuals to take advantage of opportunities for mobility. Carried to an extreme, it even leads to the claim that white Americans experience significant race-based economic and cultural victimization (see McKinney 2005).

The social and political effects of whiteness have also been studied at the institutional level. As Cheryl Harris observed in "Whiteness as Property" (1993), whiteness can be viewed as "property" in that it has historically embodied social and economic benefits for whites. The historian Ira Katznelson, in *When Affirmative Action Was White* (2005), chronicled how New Deal and other mid-twentieth-century programs widened the economic gap between white Americans and peoples of color. Other writers have highlighted how the government's urban, housing, and fiscal policies have resulted in the systematic and unequal accumulation of wealth by white Americans.

A third focus of whiteness studies has been on the evolution of whiteness. Much of this analysis has been historical, as scholars such as David Roediger (2005), Noel

Ignatiev (1995), and Matthew Frye Jacobson (1998) have traced how immigrants from Ireland and southern and eastern Europe initially faced both discrimination and an uncertain racial status but later "became" white and were absorbed into the dominant racial group. This argument is not universally accepted, as other writers (e.g., Guglielmo 2003) have asserted that groups such as Italians were "white on arrival," and that their whiteness made it easier to be accepted into American society. What is less contentious is that European immigrants learned what it *meant* to be white in the United States, especially with respect to establishing themselves in contrast to African Americans.

Another element of the evolution of whiteness has involved the construction and reconfiguration of racial boundaries and the meaning of whiteness. As Ian Haney Lopez has documented in *White by Law* (1996), the question of who was (and who was not) white was socially contested and was frequently adjudicated by the courts. With the passage of time, white ethnic identities and intragroup boundaries have dissipated, leading to the emergence of a more generic white, European American identity (see Doane 1997). Future changes may continue to redefine whiteness. As Eduardo Bonilla-Silva asserted, social and demographic forces may lead to the expansion of "white" identity to include some Latino and Asian American groups, as well as persons claiming a multiracial identity (2003).

CRITIQUE AND FUTURE DIRECTIONS

While relatively new, whiteness studies is not without its critics. One charge leveled at whiteness studies, and at the study of racial groups and categories in general, is that the attention paid to whiteness tends to essentialize it as an objective and omnipotent social force. Whiteness studies has frequently been guilty of viewing whites as a homogeneous, monolithic social entity where certain qualities are ascribed to all whites. Clearly, while whiteness involves a shared social context that influences individual and group behavior, there are significant intragroup differences that determine how whiteness is perceived and experienced (see, for example, Hartigan 1999). In addition, as Margaret Andersen observed in "Whitewashing Race" (2003), authors writing on whiteness have tended to emphasize white identity and privilege while deflecting attention from key issues of power, inequality, and racism.

Whiteness studies faces many challenges in the future. Clearly, whiteness cannot be understood in isolation—apart from racism and racial inequality. It is also essential to study the complexity of whiteness; that is, to explore how variations in factors such as class and situation produce differences in the social role of whiteness. Equally important is the need to keep abreast of changes in the nature and expression of whiteness. Past studies have highlighted moments when whites, both individually and collectively, became racially self-conscious actors, especially as a defense in the face of perceived challenges or threats from other groups (e.g., anti–Civil Rights movement backlash, various anti-immigrant movements). As U.S. society and its institutions become more diverse, the social and political meaning of whiteness will continue to evolve. If the field of whiteness studies is to make a meaningful contribution to understanding race and ethnic relations, then it must successfully confront these issues.

SEE ALSO *Racialization; Racism; Whites*

BIBLIOGRAPHY

Andersen, Margaret. 2003. Whitewashing Race: A Critical Perspective on Whiteness. In *White Out: The Continuing Significance of Race*, eds. Ashley W. Doane and Eduardo Bonilla-Silva, 21–34. New York: Routledge.

Bonilla-Silva, Eduardo. 2001. *White Supremacy and Racism in the Post–Civil Rights Era*. Boulder, CO: Lynne Rienner.

Bonilla-Silva, Eduardo. 2003. "New Racism," Color-Blind Racism, and the Future of Whiteness in America. In *White Out: The Continuing Significance of Race*, eds. Ashley W. Doane and Eduardo Bonilla-Silva, 271–284. New York: Routledge.

Doane, Ashley W. 1997. Dominant Group Identity in the United States: The Role of "Hidden Ethnicity" in Intergroup Relations. *Sociological Quarterly* 38 (3): 375–397.

Du Bois, W. E. B. [1920] 1969. *Darkwater*. New York: Schocken.

Editors of *Ebony*. 1966. *The White Problem in America*. Chicago: Johnson.

Du Bois, W. E. B. [1935] 1956. *Black Reconstruction in America*. New York: Russell.

Frankenberg, Ruth. 1993. *White Women, Race Matters: The Social Construction of Whiteness*. Minneapolis: University of Minnesota Press.

Guglielmo, Thomas A. 2003. *White on Arrival: Race, Color, and Power in Chicago, 1890–1945*. New York: Oxford University Press.

Haney López, Ian F. 1996. *White by Law: The Legal Construction of Race*. New York: New York University Press.

Harris, Cheryl I. 1993. Whiteness as Property. *Harvard Law Review* 106: 1707–1791.

Hartigan, John. 1999. *Racial Situations: Class Predicaments of Whiteness in Detroit*. Princeton, NJ: Princeton University Press.

Ignatiev, Noel. 1995. *How the Irish Became White*. New York: Routledge.

Jacobson, Matthew Frye. 1998. *Whiteness of a Different Color: European Immigrants and the Alchemy of Race*. Cambridge, MA: Harvard University Press.

Katznelson, Ira. 2005. *When Affirmative Action Was White: An Untold History of Racial Inequality in Twentieth-Century America*. New York: W. W. Norton.

Lewis, Amanda. 2004. "What Group?" Studying Whites and Whiteness in the Era of "Color-Blindness." *Sociological Theory* 22 (4): 623–646.

McIntosh, Peggy. [1988] 2002. White Privilege: Unpacking the Invisible Knapsack. In *White Privilege: Essential Readings on the Other Side of Racism*, ed. Paula Rothenberg. New York: Worth.

McKinney, Karyn D. 2005. *Being White: Stories of Race and Racism*. New York: Routledge.

Roediger, David R. 1991. *The Wages of Whiteness: Race and the Making of the American Working Class*. London: Verso.

Roediger, David R., ed. 1998. *Black on White: Black Writers on What It Means to Be White*. New York: Schocken.

Roediger, David R. 2005. *Working toward Whiteness: How America's Immigrants Became White*. New York: Basic.

Ashley ("Woody") Doane

WHITENING

From the 1400s to the 1900s European colonialism and imperialism exported an ideology of white superiority throughout the world, rationalizing European ascendancy over indigenous, inferior-raced peoples fit for conquest, exploitation, and domination. From this history a white-dominated sociopolitical order has been constituted, normalized, and maintained. As a result whiteness and the process of "whitening" have emerged as both ideal and practice. Significantly whiteness as an ideal communicates ideas about superiority with respect to moral or intellectual and aesthetic worth. Although conceptually distinct, there is a psychological tendency to conflate the two, and attempts at whitening, by both individuals and nations, have sought to capitalize on a supposed white superiority in both respects.

WHITENING AS AN INDIVIDUAL IDEAL

The elevation of whiteness both justifies the material and psychological privileging of whiteness and reinforces the white ideal. Unsurprisingly this has encouraged individuals to adopt a variety of strategies aimed at whitening physical appearance. Skin lightening is a prominent example, and the United States is instructive in examining how this strategy emerged historically.

The institution of U.S. slavery was undergirded by powerful rules maintaining racial differentiation, including those regarding hypodescent. According to the "one-drop rule," individuals with any ascertainable "Negro blood" were considered black, a determination that served slaveholders' property interests in slaves while reinforcing the ideological fiction of white purity and superiority. Slaveholders also instigated tension between lighter- and darker-skinned blacks through colorism, differentiating among blacks to prevent their alliance in potential revolts. Lighter-skinned slaves were often "privileged" as house servants relative to darker "field" slaves, for example, receiving less-violent treatment and greater opportunities for education, skilled labor, and even manumission.

In this extreme racialized context, enslaved African Americans began applying lye and other harsh cleaning products to lighten their skin. Other household concoctions included applying lemon juice, bleach, and even urine to the skin and swallowing arsenic wafers. Advancements in modern medicine encouraged more scientifically "legitimate" methods, researched and developed by the medical community. Whitening products began appearing during the nineteenth century, and by the early twentieth century hundreds of unique brands were available.

In the early twenty-first century skin whitening is a global, multibillion-dollar industry that includes major cosmetics corporations, including L'Oreal, Maybelline New York, and Lancôme Paris. L'Oreal alone made $14 billion on skin whitening products in 2003. In the United States and elsewhere, consumers of whitening products include not only blacks but also other people of color and darker-complexioned whites. Typical products include soaps, creams, and ointments that often contain mercury, topical corticosteroids, or hydroquinone, each of which disrupts melanin production in the skin. Although touted as safe by regulators, side effects of such products range from permanent spots and splotchiness to disfigurement and even poisoning. Indeed whitening products are often made in third world countries, imported legally and illegally, and sold on Internet domains to avoid regulations and critical resistance.

Reinforced by popular media and persistent disparate treatment, marketing of the white beauty ideal extends beyond skin whitening to include hair straightening, hair weaving, and colored contact lenses. Increasingly popular are more permanent and medically intrusive procedures, such as plastic surgery. Consider, for example, the use of rhinoplasty among black and Jewish Americans and the growing prevalence of eyelid surgery among Asian Americans. Even strategies such as marrying "lighter" and distancing oneself from dark-skinned people and communities, both literally and through self-classification, are considered forms of whitening by some scholars.

WHITENING AS A NATIONAL PRACTICE

Significantly the whiteness ideal has not only influenced individuals but has also become the basis of large-scale state policies seeking to whiten national populations. Many Latin American countries in particular—including Brazil, Venezuela, Cuba, Argentina, Uruguay, and Colombia—enacted collective whitening strategies during the nineteenth and twentieth centuries. Such efforts typically revolved around promoting white European immigration (often while restricting immigrants of color) and encouraging "race mixing," or miscegenation, as a way of gradually lightening the total population. Brazil offers one of the best-examined cases of a whitening ideology influencing national goals.

Portugal colonized Brazil beginning in the sixteenth century, dominating the indigenous population and instituting the importation of 3.6 million enslaved Africans over three centuries. Brazil's racial composition was dramatically altered both directly via slavery and via the mixed-race children born of frequent unions (often violent and coerced) between Portuguese colonizers and African and indigenous women. By the end of the eighteenth century blacks and their descendants formed a majority of the Brazilian population.

Brazil's largely mixed-race population was problematized in the nineteenth century, as Europe's burgeoning race "science" reached the nation. Such theories validated the white political and economic domination characteristic of colonial nations by asserting the superiority of the white race, associated with progress and advancement, while deeming other, darker races as inferior and backward. The views of Count Arthur de Gobineau of France were exemplary of such thinking. For Gobineau, Brazil epitomized the perils of miscegenation, which in his view had produced a degenerate people, dooming the country to perpetual underdevelopment.

As a way out of such fatalistic predictions, Brazil turned to the project of whitening, or *blanqueamiento*, as a national solution. Brazilian eugenicists proposed a theory of "constructive miscegenation" based on the belief that white genes were stronger and would "dominate" and "purify" colored blood. Miscegenation was rearticulated as an assurance that Brazil could achieve a whitened population over several generations and the inferior features of African and indigenous ancestry overcome. To further hasten the process of national whitening, Brazil encouraged, recruited, and subsidized European immigration to fill postslavery labor needs while simultaneously prohibiting black (both African and American) and Asian immigration. The Brazilian government attempted to lure European immigrants, both directly and through landowners, by paying transportation costs, exempting tax payments and military service, and offering loans, grants, and other material incentives. European immigration promised to whiten the population both by literally increasing the number of whites in the country and through ensuing miscegenation.

While Brazil's first census in 1872 documented 37 percent of the population as white, by the 1890s more than 1.2 million Europeans had immigrated, bolstering the percentage to 44 percent. Mass European immigration halted with the onset of World War II, but by 1940 fully 64 percent of Brazil's population was white. From 1940 onward the brown, mixed-race population increased, while the black population steadily declined.

Of Latin American nations, Argentina was perhaps the most "successful" with respect to whitening, virtually eliminating the Afro-descendant racial group. Colombia offers a unique comparison. When European immigration proved unattainable, elites sought the next best thing—interregional migration as a means of whitening. For example, elites from the Colombian region of Cauca encouraged the migration of neighboring Antioqueños, emphasizing their European- and "Yankee-like" qualities and appearance.

Predominantly white countries, while not instituting explicit whitening policies, have attempted to maintain the national dominance of whiteness. For instance, the United States, Canada, and Australia all maintained discriminatory immigration policies, privileging white European immigrants and limiting or excluding immigrants of color until the late twentieth century. Historically the United States engaged in other legal efforts to firmly differentiate between whites and people of color, particularly blacks, including codifying racial designations through rules of hypodescent, limiting nonwhite citizenship, barring miscegenation, and enacting legalized segregation. Additionally, although some early immigrants, including the Irish and Italians, were originally discriminated against as nonwhite "races," white elites eventually extended what has come to be known as the "wage of whiteness" to such groups in an effort to manage changing demographics and diminish the likelihood of cross-racial coalitions. Clearly practices such as these serve to entrench the racial structure that privileges whiteness both nationally and globally.

In the early twenty-first century the ideology of white superiority persists, although its expression may be less explicit. Nonetheless, as long as whiteness is maintained as a privileged status, materially and psychologically, whitening, as both ideal and practice, will also persist.

SEE ALSO *Black Face; Blackness; Colorism; Preference, Color; Racism; Whiteness; Whites*

BIBLIOGRAPHY

Andrews, George Reid. 1980. *The Afro-Argentines of Buenos Aires, 1800–1900*. Madison: University of Wisconsin Press.

Appelbaum, Nancy. 1999. Whitening the Region: Caucano Mediation and "Antioqueño Colonization" in Nineteenth-Century Colombia. *Hispanic American Historical Review* 79 (4): 631–667.

Dos Santos, Sales Augusto. 2002. Historical Roots of the "Whitening" of Brazil. Trans. Laurence Hallewell. *Latin American Perspectives* 29 (1): 61–82.

Eichberg, Sarah L. 1999. Bodies of Work: Cosmetic Surgery and the Gendered Whitening of America. PhD diss., University of Pennsylvania, Philadelphia.

Gilman, Sander. 1998. *Creating Beauty to Cure the Soul: Race and Psychiatry in the Shaping of Aesthetic Surgery*. Durham, NC: Duke University Press.

Graham, Richard, ed. 1990. *The Idea of Race in Latin America, 1870–1940*. Austin: University of Texas Press.

Haney López, Ian F. 1996. *White by Law: The Legal Construction of Race*. New York: New York University Press.

Helg, Aline. 1995. *Our Rightful Share: The Afro-Cuban Struggle for Equality, 1886–1912*. Chapel Hill: University of North Carolina Press.

Herring, Cedric, Verna Keith, and Hayward Derrick Horton, eds. 2004. *Skin/Deep: How Race and Complexion Matter in the "Color-Blind" Era*. Urbana: University of Illinois Press.

Kaw, Eugenia. 1993. Medicalization of Racial Features: Asian American Women and Cosmetic Surgery. *Medical Anthropology Quarterly* 7 (1): 74–89.

Mire, Amina. 2000. Skin-Bleaching: Poison, Beauty, Power, and the Politics of the Colour Line. *New Feminist Research* 28 (3–4): 13–38.

Russell, Kathy, Midge Wilson, and Ronald Hall. 1992. *The Color Complex: The Politics of Skin Color among African Americans*. New York: Anchor Books.

Skidmore, Thomas E. 1974. *Black into White: Race and Nationality in Brazilian Thought*. New York: Oxford University Press.

Stepan, Nancy. 1991. *"The Hour of Eugenics": Race, Gender, and Nation in Latin America*. Ithaca, NY: Cornell University Press.

Telles, Edward E. 2004. *Race in Another America: The Significance of Skin Color in Brazil*. Princeton, NJ: Princeton University Press.

Wade, Peter. 1997. *Race and Ethnicity in Latin America*. Chicago: Pluto Press.

Wright, Winthrop. 1990. *"Café con leche": Race, Class, and National Image in Venezuela*. Austin: University of Texas Press.

Jennifer C. Mueller
Rosalind Chou

WHITES

The issue of whiteness is intimately tied to the issue of social construction. Whiteness is a social construction that serves to empower some and disenfranchise others. The fact of the social construction is often masked as a referent to biological categories. As Grace Elizabeth Hale points out, "Long before they [whites] conceived of regional differences, early Americans linked skin color to the origins of peoples, using it to distinguish various nationalities and ethnicities of African, Native Americans, and Europeans" (Hale 1998, p. 4). David Roediger suggests that "the term *white* arose as a designation for European explorers, traders, and settlers who came into contact with Africans and the indigenous people of the Americas" (Roediger 1991, p. 21). The early uses of the term *white* were to distinguish Native Americans and Africans from Europeans.

According to Karyn McKinney, "Before it became popular to write of the 'social constructions of whiteness,' African American scholars, such as W. E. B. Dubois, James Baldwin, and Ralph Ellison had recognized race as a social rather than biological trait, and the fact that one 'becomes,' rather than is born, white." Ellison and other black scholars also highlighted the observation that the quickest way for an immigrant to "become" white, and thus feel "instantly American," was to learn to deride African Americans (McKinney 2005, p. 11).

The historical boundaries of whiteness continue to change over time. As Matthew Frye Jacobson (1998) has noted, the historical construction of whiteness was tied to the political notion of "fitness for government," and the process of defining who was or was not white occurred largely as a result of legal decisions in the determination of citizenship (Haney-López 1996). Furthermore, Joe Feagin, Hernán Vera, and Pinar Batur suggest:

> Those called "whites" in the United States and across the globe are really not white in skin color but rather are some shade of brown, tan, pink, or mixture thereof. These truer-to-life skin colors, however, are not generally associated with the qualities—such as purity, innocence, and privilege—to which "white" skin is often linked. White people do not exist in the flesh; they are a social construction. (Feagin et al. 2001, p. 2)

THE WAGE OF WHITENESS

W. E. B. Du Bois (1868–1963) considered the economic aspects of embracing the ideology of whiteness. He brilliantly developed a concept for analyzing class—the *psychological wages of whiteness*. This concept spearheaded contemporary scholarship on the process of immigrants embracing the category of white in America. The psychological wage of whiteness meant that:

The white group of laborers, while they received a low wage, was compensated in part by a sort of public and psychological wage. They were given public deference and titles of courtesy because they were white. They were admitted freely with all classes of white people to public functions, public parks, and the best schools. The police were drawn from their ranks and the courts, dependent on their votes, treated them with leniency as to encourage lawlessness. Their vote selected public officials, and while this had small effect upon the economic situation, it had great effect upon their personal treatment and the deference shown them (DuBois [1935] 1969, pp. 700–701).

As Noel Ignatiev suggests:

> The hallmark of racial oppression [is the reduction of] all members of the oppressed group to one undifferentiated social status, a status beneath that of any member of any social class within the dominant group.... It follows, therefore, that the white race consists of those who partake of the privileges of the white skin in this society. Its most wretched members share a status higher, in certain respects, than that of the most exalted persons excluded from it. (Ignatiev 1995, p. 1)

McKinney further notes that "in the United States whiteness is so central a social reality, so 'normal,' that most whites of all ages rarely examine the reality of their white identities and privileges. For most whites, including scholars and commentators, even the term 'American' seems to conjure up the image of a white person" (McKinney 2005, p. xii).

HOW THE IRISH AND JEWS BECAME WHITE

The Irish became white, according to Ignatiev, when they immigrated to America "in the eighteenth and nineteenth centuries [because] they were fleeing caste oppression and a system of landlordism that made the material conditions of the Irish peasant comparable to those of an American slave" (Ignatiev 1995, p. 2). The Irish, upon arrival, found themselves thrown into the neighborhoods, status, and categorization of African Americans. They quickly discovered the importance of skin color and adopted the ideology of a racial hierarchy that was pervasive in America. The Irish made a conscious choice to enter the white race.

To the Irish, embracing the country's racial ideologies offered the benefit of a degree of privilege and citizenship that was not provided to African Americans. Becoming white meant that they were not restricted to working and selling their goods in segregated areas. "It meant that they were citizens of a democratic republic and they could vote, live where they wanted to live, and spend without racially imposed restrictions. In becoming white the Irish ceased to be Green" (Ignatiev 1995, p. 3).

The Irish did not just become white because they wanted to be white; Brodkin suggests that they were assisted and supported by Jacksonian Democrats and the white elite. The willingness of the Irish to participate in organized racial violence against African Americans also contributed to their being accepted into the white racial hierarchy (Brodkin 1998, p. 65). According to Roediger, the Irish worker embraced white supremacy and thus gained popularity in America: "The success of the Irish in being recognized as white resulted largely from the political power of Irish and other immigrant voters" (Roediger 1991, p. 137).

The techniques utilized by the Irish to become white resemble the ways in which American Jews became white. For the Jews, becoming white was based on the assistance of the federal government and their willingness to embrace the white racial hierarchy and ideology. According to Brodkin, who is Jewish, all the members of her family had to learn the ways of whiteness through years of socializing with whites. "The myth that Jews pulled themselves up by their own bootstraps ignores the fact that it took federal programs to create the conditions whereby the abilities of Jews and other European immigrants could be recognized and rewarded rather than denigrated and denied" (Brodkin 1998, p. 50). Jews embraced the country's racial hierarchy, and they received aid from federal programs set in place after World War II (1939–1945). Many of the programs were designed to discriminate against African Americans who had served in the war. Jews became white and enjoyed the benefits of federal programs such as the GI Bill, the Federal Housing Administration, and the Veterans Administration. These programs overlooked and denied benefits to African Americans. And like other white ethnic groups had done in the past, to prove their commitment to embracing their white status, Jews engaged in racial violence that targeted African Americans and other people of color.

CRITIQUING "WHITE"-NESS

Brodkin and Ignatiev attribute becoming white to acquiring political, social, and economic acceptance, as well as assimilating into the American lifestyle. However, Eduardo Bonilla-Silva points out, "When race emerged in human history, it formed a social structure (a racialized social system) that awarded systemic privileges to Europeans (the peoples who became 'white').... Since actors racialized as 'white'—or as members of the dominant race—receive material benefits from the racial order, they struggle (or passively receive the manifold wages of whiteness) to maintain their privileges" (Bonilla-Silva 2003, p. 9). Those who

have become white, such as the Irish, Jews, and some white Latinos, go on to embrace the white racial hierarchy and ideology of the dominant society.

Joe Feagin similarly points out:

> In its use for human groups, the word "white" was originally defined by the English colonist mainly in contrast with "black".... White defined who the European Americans were, and who they were not. Whiteness was indeed a major and terrible invention, one that solidified white thinking into an extensive and racialized either/or framework and that came to symbolize for whites the "ownership of the earth" and "civilization." (Feagin 2006, pp. 14–15)

"Moreover," according to Feagin, "whites are collectively so powerful that they pressure all new immigrants groups, including immigrants of color, to collude in the white-racist system by adopting not only general white ways of doing and speaking … but also the white racial frame and its view of the racial hierarchy of U.S. society" (Feagin 2006, p. 292). New immigrants who come into the United States strive to speak, dress, and act white based upon the white racial hierarchy that decides who is white and who is nonwhite. Furthermore, buying into the cultural attributes of whiteness includes internalizing and supporting antiblack sentiment.

Chris Cuomo and Kim Hall suggest that because of the role of whiteness "in justifying and maintaining racism and colonialism in the United States (and, now, most of the world), whiteness is uniquely located on the racial map. For whites to fail to consider whiteness as a historical, constructed, and dynamic category is to risk treating it as normal (rather than normalizing), uniform (not immeasurably variable), paradigmatic (instead of fundamental to racism), and given (rather than dutifully maintained)" (Cuomo and Hall 1999, p. 3). In the early years of the twenty-first century, the historical techniques of becoming white are being adopted by new Latino immigrants who, for the purpose of reaping the benefits of whiteness, classify themselves as white.

SEE ALSO *Race; Racism; Whiteness*

BIBLIOGRAPHY

Bonilla-Silva, Eduardo. 2003. *Racism without Racists: Color-blind Racism and the Persistence of Racial Inequality in the United States*. Lanham, MD: Rowman and Littlefield. 2nd ed., 2006.

Brodkin, Karen. 1998. *How Jews Became White Folks and What That Says about Race in America*. New Brunswick, NJ: Rutgers University Press.

Cuomo, Chris, and Kim Hall. 1999. *Whiteness: Feminist Philosophical Reflections*. Lanham, MD: Rowman and Littlefield.

Du Bois, W. E. B. [1935] 1969. *Black Reconstruction in America: An Essay Toward a History of the Part Which Black Folk Played in the Attempt to Reconstruct Democracy in America, 1860–1880*. New York: Atheneum.

Feagin, Joe. 2006. *Systemic Racism: A Theory of Oppression*. New York: Routledge.

Feagin, Joe, Hernán Vera, and Pinar Batur. 2001. *White Racism: The Basics*. 2nd ed. New York: Routledge.

Hale, Grace Elizabeth. 1998. *Making Whiteness: The Culture of Segregation in the South, 1890–1940*. New York: Vintage.

Haney-López, Ian F. 1996. *White by Law: The Legal Construction of Race*. New York: New York University Press. Rev. ed., 2006.

Ignatiev, Noel. 1995. *How the Irish Became White*. New York: Routledge.

Jacobson, Matthew Frye. 1998. *Whiteness of a Different Color: European Immigrants and the Alchemy of Race*. Cambridge, MA: Harvard University Press.

McKinney, Karyn D. 2005. *Being White: Stories of Race and Racism*. New York: Routledge.

Roediger, David R. 1991. *The Wages of Whiteness: Race and the Making of the American Working Class*. New York: Verso.

Ruth Thompson-Miller

WHOLESALE PRICE INDEX

The Wholesale Price Index (WPI) measures average price changes over time in the stage prior to the final demand, covering therefore the flow of goods and services from the wholesaler to the retailer. Available on a daily, weekly, monthly, or quarterly basis, this index supplies information constructed from the point of view of gross transactions at the purchaser's prices, information that is useful to understand, anticipate, or coordinate the economic activity, particularly in large-scale industrial economies. Because there is a short interval between the inquiries and the public release of the indexes (the norm being divulgation two weeks after the end of the month or the quarter), the information provided by the synthesis-numbers allows producers, traders, and government officials to gauge, at a glance, the current tendencies of economic evolution. This practical and utilitarian nature is further reinforced by the fact that the Wholesale Price Index captures price movements in advance to the retail level, and is likely to foreshadow subsequent changes in the price of goods and services purchased by consumers. In vertical, integrated markets this time advance tends to be shorter in circumstances of price increases and longer in price decreases.

Historically, the revolution in transportation and communications of the late nineteenth century paved the way for the appearance of this kind of aggregate measure-

ment of prices. The connection between the network of enterprises and businessmen working out in distant regions became reinforced through the public diffusion of economic statistics such as prices composites, aggregate index of commodities, and wholesale price indices published by several U.S. newspapers. At the beginning of the twentieth century important nongovernmental institutions also set up solid reputations in the release of weekly and daily series of index numbers. The first official initiatives came out almost simultaneously in the United States (1902) and in Europe (United Kingdom, 1903), in response to parliamentary investigations into the effects of laws and tariffs on domestic prices. Japan saw the establishment of a Wholesale Price Index of Tokyo City in 1897, through the initiative of the Bank of Japan.

A major drawback of these pioneer undertakings was the proliferation of methods for computing the average price of the commodities, and also the limited coverage given by price quotations. The introduction of a system of weighting, combined with an enlarged sample of goods taken from widely distributed markets, under the responsibility of the United States Bureau of Labor Statistics in 1914 marked a new phase in the credibility of governmental agencies. Up to the present time, the formula that closely approximates the computation procedures in use around the world for weighting the "basket of commodities" comprised in the Wholesale Price Index is some variant of the index formula suggested by Etienne Laspeyres in 1871. Thanks to these developments, the scope of the Wholesale Price Index is additionally extended from a micro benchmark indicator and a reference for escalating purchase and sales contracts to a macroeconomic indicator for the formulation of fiscal and monetary policies, and to a deflator used to adjust economic time series.

SEE ALSO *Inflation; Price Indices; Prices*

BIBLIOGRAPHY

Diewert, W. Erwin. 1988. The Early History of Price Index Research. NBER Working Paper No. W2713. http://www.nber.org/papers/w2713.pdf.

Peltzman, Sam. 2000. Prices Rise Faster Than They Fall. *Journal of Political Economy* 108 (3): 466–502.

Nuno Luís Madureira

WICKSELL EFFECTS

The term *Wicksell effects* was introduced by Joan Robinson (1953, p. 95) during a debate in the theory of capital (see Kurz and Salvadori 1995, chapter 14). There is a distinction between *price Wicksell effects* and *real Wicksell effects*

(henceforth, PWE and RWE). A PWE relates to a change in relative prices corresponding to a change in income distribution, given the system of production in use. A RWE in addition takes into account the problem of the choice of technique. The "changes" under consideration refer to comparisons of long-period equilibria.

Knut Wicksell (1954; 1934, pp. 147–151) discussed these effects within an "Austrian" framework of the analysis, which conceives of production as a one-way avenue of finite length leading from the services of original factors of production, in particular labor, via some intermediate products to consumption goods. Before Wicksell they had been studied by the classical economists, especially David Ricardo (*Works* I, pp. 30–43), who wrote that relative prices depend on income distribution because of the "variety of circumstances under which commodities are actually produced" (*Works* IV, p. 368). This in conjunction with the fact that "profits [are] increasing at a compound rate … makes a great part of the difficulty" (*Works* IX, p. 387). Ricardo also tackled the problem of the dependence of the chosen technique on distribution in his disquisitions on rent and on machinery (1951–1973). The classical economists and Karl Marx typically conceived of production as a *circular flow* where commodities are produced by means of commodities.

The source of PWEs can be illustrated by expressing the ratio of the prices of two commodities, *A* and *B*, by means of their "reduction to dated quantities of labour" (Sraffa 1960, chapter VI). Call p_a and p_b the prices of one unit each of two commodities, w the wage rate per unit of labor (paid *post factum*), and r the rate of interest (or profits). Then we have

$$\frac{p_a}{p_b} = \frac{wl_{a0} + (1 + r)wl_{a1}}{wl_{b0} + (1 + r)wl_{b1}}$$

$$\frac{+ (1 + r)^2 wl_{a2} + \dots}{+ (1 + r)^2 wl_{b2} + \dots}$$

$$\frac{+ (1 + r)^n wl_{an} + \dots}{+ (1 + r)^n wl_{bn} + \dots}$$

(On the RHS of the equation w could be eliminated.) Obviously, l_{a0} (l_{b0}) gives the amount of labor expended directly on the last stage of producing one unit of commodity a (b); l_{a1} (l_{b1}) the amount expended directly on the last but one stage; and so on. Whereas with the Austrian concept each series is finite, with the classical circular flow concept it is infinite. Because for a given system of production the rate of interest and wages are inversely related (as has already been established, albeit imperfectly, at the

time of the classical economists), a change in distribution typically affects the prices of the two commodities differently: It all depends on how the total amounts of labor expended are distributed over time—whether or not relatively much labor is expended in early periods of time and little in later ones. Because with a rise of w and the corresponding fall of r the size of each term in each of the reduction equations (except the first one) is pulled in different directions, the overall effect of a change in distribution on relative prices depends on how the time patterns of the labor inputs compare with one another, with compound interest as a magnifier.

With a choice of technique, a change in the real wage rate may prompt cost-minimizing producers to change the methods of production to produce the various commodities. This brings us to the concept of RWE. In order to be able to compare the new situation with the original one, it has to be assumed that in both situations the same net output is produced; typically the economy is taken to be in a stationary state both before and after the change. The questions to be answered are: (1) which technique will be chosen in the new situation?; (2) what will then be the level of the other distributive variable and the set of normal prices?; and, most importantly, (3) is it possible to say anything definite about how the two situations compare with one another?

To illustrate RWEs, we may refer back to the equation above, but now A and B stand for two different processes of production of a *given* commodity available to producers. In competitive conditions the method chosen will be the one that allows one to produce the commodity at lower unit costs and thus a lower price.

Marginalist theory, of which Austrian theory is but a variant, maintains that both effects are positive. A *positive PWE* means that with a rise (fall) in the rate of interest, consumption goods will become relatively more (less) expensive compared with capital goods. The reason given is that consumption goods are said to be produced more capital intensively than are capital goods, because consumption goods emerge at the end of the production process, whereas capital goods are intermediate products that gradually "mature" towards the final product. The higher (lower) the rate of interest, the less (more) expensive the intermediate products in terms of a standard consisting of a (basket of) consumption good(s). At the macro level of a stationary economy (in which the net product contains only consumption goods), this implies that with a rise in the rate of interest, the value of the net social product rises relatively to the value of the aggregate of capital goods employed. Clearly, seen from the marginalist perspective, a positive PWE with regard to the relative price of the two aggregates under consideration involves a negative relationship between the aggregate

capital-to-net output ratio on the one hand and the interest rate on the other. Let $K/Y = \mathbf{x}\mathbf{p}(r)/\mathbf{y}\mathbf{p}(r)$ designate the capital-output ratio, where $\mathbf{x}$ is the row vector of capital goods, $\mathbf{y}$ the row vector of net outputs, and $\mathbf{p}(r)$ the column vector of prices (in terms of the consumption vector) which depends on r); then the marginalist message is:

$$\frac{\partial(K/Y)}{\partial r} \leq 0 \qquad (\mathrm{I})$$

Because for a given system of production the amount of labor is constant irrespective of the level of the rate of interest, the ratio of the value of the capital goods and the amount of labor employed, or capital-labor ratio, K/L, would also tend to fall (rise) with a rise (fall) in the rate of interest:

$$\frac{\partial(K/Y)}{\partial r} \leq 0 \qquad (\mathrm{II})$$

This is the first claim marginalist authors put forward. The second is that RWEs are also positive. A *positive RWE* means that with a rise (fall) in the rate of interest, cost-minimizing producers switch to methods of production that generally exhibit higher (lower) labor intensities, "substituting" for the "factor of production" that has become more expensive—"capital" (labor)—the one that has become less expensive—labor ("capital"). Hence (II) is said to apply also in this case. The assumed positivity of the RWE underlies the marginalist concept of a demand function for labor (capital) that is inversely related to the real wage rate (rate of interest).

Careful scrutiny of the marginalist argument has shown that it cannot be sustained generally: There is no presumption that PWEs and RWEs are invariably positive. In fact, there is no presumption that techniques can be ordered monotonically with the rate of interest (Sraffa 1960). As Mas-Colell (1989) stressed, the relationship between K/L and r can have almost any shape. The finding that PWEs and RWEs need not be positive challenges the received doctrine of the working of the economic system as it is portrayed by conventional economic theory with its reference to the "forces" of demand and supply.

SEE ALSO *Cambridge Capital Controversy; Capital*

BIBLIOGRAPHY

Kurz, Heinz D., and Neri Salvadori. 1995. *Theory of Production: A Long-Period Analysis.* Cambridge, U.K., Melbourne, and New York: Cambridge University Press.

Mas-Colell, Andreu. 1989. Capital Theory Paradoxes: Anything Goes. In *Joan Robinson and Modern Economic Theory*, ed. George R. Feiwel, 505–520. London: Macmillan.

Ricardo, David. 1951–1973. *The Works and Correspondence of David Ricardo*, 11 vols., ed. Piero Sraffa with Maurice H. Dobb. Cambridge, U.K.: Cambridge University Press.

Robinson, Joan V. 1953. The Production Function and the Theory of Capital. *Review of Economic Studies* 21: 81–106.

Sraffa, Piero. 1960. *Production of Commodities by Means of Commodities: Prelude to a Critique of Economic Theory.* Cambridge, U.K.: Cambridge University Press.

Wicksell, Knut. [1893] 1954. *Value, Capital, and Rent.* London: Allen and Unwin. Reprint 1970. New York: Kelley.

Wicksell, Knut. [1901] 1934. *Lectures on Political Economy.* Vol. 1. Trans. E. Classen, ed. Lionel Robbins. London: George Routledge and Sons.

Heinz D. Kurz

WIDOW'S CRUSE

The term *widow's cruse* was first used in economics by John Maynard Keynes (1930, p. 139) in the presentation of his fundamental equations. Keynes argued that enterprise macroeconomic profits, as he defined them there, or what we would now call "business retained earnings," moved up one-to-one with increases in investment and increases in consumption out of profits. Thus, Keynes argued that "however much of their profits entrepreneurs spend on consumption, the increment of wealth belonging to entrepreneurs remains the same as before. Thus profits, as a source of capital increment for entrepreneurs, are a widow's cruse which remains undepleted however much of them may be devoted to riotous living" (p. 139). Keynes was then making a reference to the Old Testament story (1 Kings 17) in which a widow was assured that her barrel of meat and jar of oil would never be depleted.

The analogy was later picked up by Nicholas Kaldor (1956), when he presented his Keynesian theory of income distribution and growth. Both Keynes (1930) and Kaldor (1956) assumed full employment. For both of them, lower propensities to save would lead to an increase in prices relative to costs, and this would entail higher profits in the static case of Keynes and higher profit share and profit rates in the dynamic case of Kaldor.

In the meantime, another version of the widow's cruse was put forward by Michał Kalecki (1942), without the full-employment assumption, based on adjustments through quantities (real output and employment) rather than prices. Kalecki's equation reads that *Profits = Investment + Consumption Out of Profits*, under the classical assumption that wages are all spent. Taking the public sector into account, government deficit should be added to the right-hand side. Kalecki's equation has given rise to the aphorism—attributed to Kalecki, but which can be found in Kaldor (1956, p. 96)—that "capitalists earn what they spend, and workers spend what they earn." This aphorism shows the asymmetry in capitalist relations:

Capitalists can always decide to spend more (provided banks accept to finance additional investment), whereas workers cannot decide to earn more, because this depends on the employment they are offered by entrepreneurs. Modern versions of this quantity-adjusting theory can be found in the so-called Kaleckian models of growth, which show that a decrease in the propensity to save leads to higher rates of output growth and higher rates of profit.

The widow's cruse is the price-adjusting equivalent of the quantity-adjusting paradox of thrift. With output adjusting through the multiplier, the short-run version of the paradox of thrift asserts that individual efforts to increase saving will be useless, and that, instead, output will fall, as was outlined by Keynes in 1936. But this is simply the quantity analogue of the mechanisms he was describing in 1930 as the "Danaid jar," which can never be filled up, or the "banana parable," whereby a thrift campaign in a banana-producing economy will lead only to rotten bananas, heavy business losses, large unpaid bank loans, and destroyed wealth.

The widow's cruse is just as relevant now as it was at the eve of the Great Depression. Mainstream economists and right-wing think tanks are still chanting the virtues of household savings and government budget surpluses, without realizing that household expenditures have sustained the U.S. economic boom and that government deficits add to business profits. The issue of public pension-funds finance is also related to the widow's cruse, which implies that such funds can only be financed as a pay-as-you-go redistribution mechanism: If one attempts to save too much, the savings will vanish like the rotten bananas.

BIBLIOGRAPHY

Kaldor, Nicholas. 1956. Alternative Theories of Distribution. *Review of Economic Studies* 23 (2): 83–100.

Kalecki, Michał. 1942. A Theory of Profits. *Economic Journal* 52 (June–September): 258–267.

Keynes, John Maynard. 1930. *The Treatise on Money.* Vol. 1. London: Macmillan.

Marc Lavoie

WILLIAMS, ERIC
1911–1981

Eric Eustace Williams was chief minister, premier, and prime minister respectively of Trinidad and Tobago from 1956 to 1981. He was also one of the Anglophone Caribbean's first professionally trained historians. Several outstanding self-trained historians preceded him. Edward

Wilmot Blyden (1832–1912) of Saint Thomas, J. J. Thomas (1840–1889) of Trinidad, J. A. Rogers (c. 1883–1966) of Jamaica, Theophilus A. Marryshow (1887–1958) of Grenada, C. L. R. James (1901–1989) and George Padmore (1903–1959) of Trinidad, and Norman Eustace Cameron (1903–1983) of Guyana were among his precursors and contemporaries. Most of these men had no university training or had studied subjects other than history. When Eric Williams graduated first among the firsts at Oxford University in 1935 and went on to obtain his D.Phil. there in 1938, he ushered in a new era in Anglophone Caribbean historical scholarship.

Williams grew up in Port of Spain, the son of a minor civil servant. He had a distinguished academic record from childhood and won an island scholarship, the ultimate achievement of high school excellence. This entitled him to a free university education, and he broke with tradition by choosing to read history, rather than the law or medicine favored by scholarship winners before and after him. Along the way Williams experienced an unusually eclectic array of influences. C. Augustin Petioni, later a pioneer of Marcus Garvey's (1887–1940) Universal Negro Improvement Association and a leader of the Caribbean independence movement in the United States, was a friend of his father. So was T. A. Marryshow, a pioneer journalist and the "father of West Indian federation." Williams's brilliance in elementary school brought him the long-standing patronage of Englishman J. O. Cutteridge, arguably the most important figure in the era of colonial education in Trinidad, but a man much disliked in nationalist circles. At Queens Royal College in Port of Spain, C. L. R. James, later one of the outstanding intellectual figures of his generation, was both Williams's teacher and a fellow member of the school's cricket team.

While at Oxford, Williams interacted extensively with James, Padmore, and their coterie of Pan-Africanist (and often Marxist) radicals. He interested himself in the affairs of various nationalist groups, including those of Indian students. As an Afro-Caribbean person in England he inevitably came into contact with racism.

In 1939 Williams began teaching at Howard University, America's most prestigious African American university at the time. Here he interacted with a cast of brilliant scholars, among them Alain Locke (1886–1954), Ralph Bunche (1886–1954), Rayford Logan (1897–1982), and E. Franklin Frazier (1894–1962). Williams distinguished himself even in this distinguished crowd. Two Rosenwald fellowships enabled him to pay research visits to the non-English speaking territories of the Greater Antilles. He won the *Journal of Negro History's* prize for best article of 1940. His first book, *The Negro in the Caribbean*, appeared in 1942 in a series edited by Locke. His second, *The Economic Future of the Caribbean*, coedited with Frazier, was published in 1944. In 1944 his magnum opus, *Capitalism and Slavery*, was published by the University of North Carolina Press.

Capitalism and Slavery, a revised version of Williams's doctoral dissertation, assured him a position of preeminence in Caribbean historiography. It demonstrated in exhaustive detail how the unprecedented profits generated by the slave trade in Africans provided the economic wherewithal for the Industrial Revolution in England. Williams argued that the productive forces unleashed by the Industrial Revolution in turn eventually made slavery itself obsolete. For the new industrial and technological age, slavery had become an outmoded form of production and a brake on development. Slavery was abolished in the British Empire as a result of these economic forces. The abolitionist "saints" of British historiography were not primarily responsible for abolitionism. Theirs was a secondary role, which, happily for them, happened to coincide with the economic necessity of the time. *Capitalism and Slavery* was hailed as a masterpiece in some quarters and as an unwarranted attack on cherished orthodoxy in others. The battle over this book has never subsided.

Williams's book was doubtless influenced by his very unique attributes. Here was an Afro-Caribbean colonial who had beaten the best that the mother country had to offer, in the most prestigious of English universities. He had also indulged actively in the radical anticolonial activity of the time. He acknowledged C. L. R. James as the source of the thesis that underlay his book. James's *The Black Jacobins* (1938) had posited a similar idea for the French colonial empire, and Williams had helped James work on this book. Williams's years in the United States, while he revised his dissertation, were also a period of constant contact with Caribbean and African American radicals, as well as with such establishment institutions as the Anglo-American Caribbean Commission and the Organization for Strategic Services, a U.S. espionage agency (for both of which Williams worked). Williams was a full-time official for the Anglo-American Caribbean Commission (later the Caribbean Commission) from 1946 to 1955. In this capacity he crisscrossed the Caribbean and researched a huge swath of Caribbean economic and social life. This complemented his already deep knowledge of the area's history. There was probably no one else who could rival his historical and contemporary knowledge of the area.

The excellence of *Capitalism and Slavery* and Williams's many articles in scholarly journals did not open the door to major publishers. The University of North Carolina Press required him to pay a considerable subsidy, which he was able to raise only after several months of effort. It would be a quarter of a century before another major publisher would do the first printing on any of his

books. Various subsequent publishing proposals came to naught. His manuscript on *Education in the British West Indies* remained unpublished for years until he published it in Trinidad in 1950. Between 1944 and 1969 Williams nevertheless authored or edited nine important works, all published directly or indirectly through his own efforts. Some were published under the auspices of his Historical Society of Trinidad and Tobago. Some were published by the press of the Peoples National Movement (PNM), the political party that took him to political power in Trinidad in 1956. In 1969 André Deutsch published Williams's autobiography, *Inward Hunger*, the first of his books to be initially released by a major publisher in twenty-five years.

Williams wrote history with a passion matched by few professional historians. For him history was a tool of the anticolonial struggle and a stepping stone to politics. His *Historical Society of Trinidad and Tobago* brought history to the masses in the early 1950s. He spread the society's work with the same energy that had characterized his efforts to promote *Capitalism and Slavery*. (He bought copies from the publishers and resold them himself through a network of friends and helpers). His *Education in the British West Indies* (1950) was a manifesto for a Caribbean university. His *History of the People of Trinidad and Tobago* (1962) was an independence gift to his nation written, in between his political duties, in one month.

The professional Anglophone historians who followed Williams were often ambivalent toward his historical activism. Elsa Gouveia, the doyenne of the first generation of indigenous historians at the University of the West Indies, vitriolically denounced his *British Historians and the West Indies* (1964) for substituting "new shibboleths for old." Williams envisaged this work as an exposé of the "prejudices of metropolitan historians."

Williams's last major work, *From Columbus to Castro* (1970), was a survey textbook for university students. He had worked on it for years. It was vintage Williams, with a lively dogmatic style and a heavy bias toward economic history. It reflected his strengths in the colonial period, but was less detailed on the twentieth century.

Williams's many important works do not provide a complete picture of his historical activity. He published voluminously in academic and popular publications, and issued many of his political speeches as pamphlets. The *Caribbean Historical Review*, published under the auspices of his Historical Society of Trinidad and Tobago, released four issues between 1950 and 1954.

SEE ALSO *Anticolonial Movements; Capitalism; Industrialization; James, C. L. R.; Plantation; Plantation Economy Model; Slavery*

BIBLIOGRAPHY

PRIMARY WORKS

Williams, Eric. 1942. *The Negro in the Caribbean*. Washington, DC: Associates in Negro Folk Education.

Williams, Eric. 1944. *Capitalism and Slavery*. Chapel Hill: University of North Carolina Press. Rev. ed. 1994, with new introduction by Colin A. Palmer.

Williams, Eric. 1950. *Education in the British West Indies*. Port of Spain, Trinidad: Guardian Commercial Printery.

Williams, Eric, ed. 1952. *Documents on British West Indian History, 1807-1833*. Port of Spain, Trinidad: Trinidad Publishing.

Williams, Eric, ed. 1954. *The British West Indies at Westminster: Extracts from the Debates in Parliament*. Port of Spain, Trinidad: Historical Society of Trinidad and Tobago.

Williams, Eric. 1962. *History of the People of Trinidad and Tobago*. Port of Spain, Trinidad: PNM Publishing Company.

Williams, Eric. 1963. *Documents of West Indian History*. Port of Spain, Trinidad: PNM Publishing Company.

Williams, Eric. 1964. *British Historians and the West Indies*. Port of Spain, Trinidad: PNM Publishing Company.

Williams, Eric. 1969. *Inward Hunger: The Education of a Prime Minister*. London: Deutsch.

Williams, Eric. 1970. *From Columbus to Castro: The History of the Caribbean, 1492–1969*. London: Deutsch.

SECONDARY WORKS

Frazier, E. Franklin, and Eric Williams, eds. 1944. *The Economic Future of the Caribbean*. Washington, DC: Howard University Press. Reprinted 2004. Dover, MA: The Majority Press.

Martin, Tony. 2003. Eric Williams and the Anglo-American Caribbean Commission: Trinidad's Future Nationalist Leader as Aspiring Imperial Bureaucrat. *Journal of African American History* 88 (3): 274–290.

Palmer, Colin. 2006. *Eric Williams and the Making of the Modern Caribbean*. Chapel Hill: University of North Carolina Press.

Solow, Barbara L., and Stanley L. Engerman, eds. 1987. *British Capitalism and Caribbean Slavery: The Legacy of Eric Williams*. Cambridge, U.K.: Cambridge University Press.

Sutton, Paul K., ed. 1981. *Forged from the Love of Liberty: Selected Speeches of Dr. Eric Williams*. Port of Spain, Trinidad: Longmans Caribbean.

Tony Martin

WILMINGTON RIOT OF 1898

American history is filled with violent racial conflict, oftentimes justified by the perpetrators as necessary to protect (or avenge) honor, life, or property. The Wilmington Riot of 1898 was not an act of spontaneous

violence. Rather, the events of November 10, 1898, were the culmination of a long-range plan by Democratic Party leaders to win control of the city of Wilmington and North Carolina. The party leadership used the concept of white supremacy to regain power lost as a result of a Populist and Republican coalition known as Fusion. Fusionists gained control of the General Assembly in 1894, and, in 1896, elected Daniel Russell as the state's first Republican governor since 1877. In 1897 Fusionists made sweeping changes to the city's charter and state government in favor of African Americans and middle-class whites. Wilmington, the state's largest city, sustained a complex, wealthy society for all races, with African Americans holding elected office and working in professional and mid-range occupations vital to the economy.

Furnifold Simmons led the State Democratic Party campaign of 1898. Josephus Daniels of the Raleigh *News and Observer* noted that Simmons used a three-prong attack to win the election: men who could write, speak, and "ride." Men who could write created propaganda for newspapers. Men such as Alfred M. Waddell gave fiery speeches to inflame white voters. Men who could ride, known as Red Shirts, intimidated blacks and forced whites to vote for Democratic Party candidates. Democrats from across the state took special interest in securing victory in Wilmington. A group of white businessmen, called the "Secret Nine," planned to retake control of the city and mapped out a citywide plan of action.

Further fueling the Democratic Party's agitation was an article by Alex Manly, editor of the *Wilmington Record*, the city's African American newspaper. Manly challenged white taboos regarding interracial sexual relationships, and his article became a tool used by Democrats to further anger whites. Democrats won the election, and the next day a group of whites passed a series of resolutions requiring Alex Manly to leave the city and close his paper, and called for the resignations of the mayor and chief of police. A committee of men led by Waddell was selected to implement the set of resolutions, called the White Declaration of Independence. The committee presented its demands to a Committee of Colored Citizens (CCC)—prominent local African Americans—and asked for compliance by the next morning, November 10, 1898.

Waddell met a crowd of men at the Wilmington Light Infantry (WLI) Armory at 8:00 a.m. on the tenth. Delayed response from the CCC and growing tensions led to a march by Waddell and as many as 2,000 whites to the *Record* printing office where they broke in and burned the building. By 11:00 a.m., violence had broken out across town at an intersection where groups of blacks and whites argued. Shots rang out and several black men fell dead or wounded—both sides claimed the other fired the first shot with two "witnesses" providing conflicting testimony.

Governor Russell called out the WLI, a home guard militia unit, and they marched into Brooklyn to calm the riot where they participated in skirmishes and killed several black men.

During the riot, members of Waddell's committee plus George Rountree, John D. Bellamy, and others worked to facilitate a coup d'etat to overthrow the municipal government. By 4:00 p.m., elected officials were forced to resign under pressure and were replaced by men selected by leading Democrats. Waddell was elected mayor by the newly seated board of aldermen. Additionally, leading African Americans and white Republicans were banished from the city over the next days. Besides the primary target of Alex Manly, men selected for banishment fit into one of three categories: African American leaders who were open opponents to white supremacy, successful African American businessmen, and whites who benefited politically from African American voting support. No official count of dead can be ascertained due to a paucity of records. At least 14 and perhaps as many as 60 men were murdered.

State and federal leaders failed to react to the violence in Wilmington. No federal troops were sent because President William McKinley received no request for assistance from Governor Russell. The U.S. Attorney General's Office investigated, but the files were closed with no indictments in 1900. African Americans nationwide rallied to the cause of Wilmington's blacks and tried to pressure President McKinley into action. However, many leading blacks were split on the best solution to the "Negro problem" and no nationwide campaign materialized.

Democrats solidified their control over city government through a new city charter in January 1899. Waddell and the board of aldermen were officially elected in March 1899 with no Republican resistance. The new legislature enacted the state's first Jim Crow legislation regarding the separation of races in train passenger cars. A new suffrage amendment that disfranchised black voters was added to the state constitution by voters in 1900. The Democratic legislature overturned Fusion and placed control over county governments in Raleigh. New election laws limited Republican power in the 1900 election. Democrats controlled local and statewide affairs for the next seventy years after victory in 1898.

Inside Wilmington, out-migration following the violence negatively affected the ability of African Americans to recover. Black property owners were a minority of the overall black population before the riot, and property owners were more likely to remain in the city. An African American collective narrative developed to recall the riot and place limits on black/white relationships for future generations. White narratives claimed that the violence was necessary to restore order, and their narrative was perpetuated by most historians.

Wilmington marked a new epoch in the history of violent race relations in the U.S. Several other high profile riots followed Wilmington, most notably Atlanta (1906), Tulsa (1921), and Rosewood (1923). All four communities dealt with the aftermath of their riots differently. Whites in Tulsa and Atlanta addressed the causes and some effects of violence and destruction soon after their events; Wilmington whites provided compensation only for the loss of the building housing Manly's press.

SEE ALSO *Democratic Party, U.S.; Jim Crow; Race Relations; Race Riots, United States; Racism; Republican Party; Terror; Tulsa Riot; Violence; White Supremacy*

BIBLIOGRAPHY

Cecelski, David S., and Timothy B. Tyson, eds. 1998. *Democracy Betrayed: The Wilmington Race Riot and Its Legacy.* Chapel Hill: University of North Carolina Press.

Crow, Jeffrey J., and Robert F. Durden. 1977. *Maverick Republican in the Old North State: A Political Biography of Daniel L. Russell.* Baton Rouge: Louisiana State University Press.

Edmunds, Helen. 1951. *The Negro and Fusion Politics in North Carolina, 1894–1901.* Chapel Hill: University of North Carolina Press.

Prather, H. Leon, Sr. 1998. *We Have Taken a City: Wilmington Racial Massacre and Coup of 1898.* Cranbury, NJ: Associated University Press. (Orig. pub. 1984.)

Umfleet, LeRae S. 1898 Wilmington Race Riot Commission Report. May 31, 2006. http://www.ah.dcr.state.nc.us/1898-wrrc/.

LeRae S. Umfleet

WILSON, WILLIAM JULIUS
1935–

William Julius Wilson is an African American sociologist who is most noted for his work in urban sociology and his study of the black urban underclass. He was born December 20, 1935, in Derry Township, Pennsylvania, and he received a BA from Wilberforce University, an MA from Bowling Green State University, and a PhD from Washington State University. He began his professional career at the University of Massachusetts at Amherst, where he wrote his first book on the African American community. He continued his research and wrote his most influential treatise while a professor at the University of Chicago. As of the mid-2000s he was Lewis P. and Linda L. Geyser University Professor at Harvard University.

In his book *The Declining Significance of Race: Blacks and Changing American Institutions* (1980) Wilson posits that although past racial oppression created an urban black underclass, the black class structure is now parallel to that of whites. Therefore, blacks' life chances are now more a function of their economic class status than of race relations with whites. Consequently, race-specific programs such as affirmative action improve the life chances of middle-class blacks who are in the position to take advantage of the programs. Although Wilson does not deny the existence of racism, he suggests that programs designed to lessen the effects of poverty on all races, rather than race-specific policies, would better serve the needs of the urban black underclass, and are more likely to receive political acceptance.

Jack Niemonen (2002) argued that Wilson's historical analysis was underdeveloped, and that his concentration on aggregate labor market inequality underscores the effect of persistent racism and discrimination in the workplace. In addition, Wilson (1980) noted other reactions to his work. Political conservatives embraced Wilson's theory as evidence of social pathology in the black community and as support for discontinuance of affirmative action–type programs. They attributed problems of the inner city such as high crime rates, poverty, and high rates of female-headed families to underclass culture and welfare policies. Sociologists criticized Wilson for his disregard of racism when segregation in housing and education still hampered opportunities for blacks, as well as for the perceived public-policy implications of his treatise. They sought evidence to counter Wilson's claims of the existence of an underclass, and argued that social problems in the inner cities were caused by racism (summarized in Wilson 1980; 1987).

Wilson (1987) rejects liberal claims of racism and conservative claims of welfare policies and social pathology as the cause for inner-city social problems. Instead, he offers as explanation the economy-driven factors of urban black male unemployment, the male marriageable pool index (MMPI), social isolation, and negative concentration effects (negative consequences of the spatial and social isolation of impoverished African Americans). He also acknowledges some negative behaviors of ghetto inhabitants such as drug pushing and diminished work ethic, but continues to reject racism or social pathology as the cause (Wilson 1996). He posits that the global economy has a negative "domino effect" on the urban poor: When urban jobs are lost to suburbia and foreign countries, spatial and skills mismatch occurs, the tax base in the cities dwindle, public services such as education suffer, working- and middle-class blacks flee the city, and poorly educated blacks who possess no job skills eventually aban-

don their job searches for public assistance, and/or work in the illegal economy (Wilson 1996).

Critics argue that Wilson's application of John Kain's (1968) spatial mismatch hypothesis is limited for the following reasons: Residential segregation enhances the effect of spatial mismatch; employers' decisions determine black employment in local jobs; there are numerous methodological inconsistencies; and because of the lack of black human capital and the simultaneous existence of immigrant social capital (Niemonen 2002). Another researcher, Michael Stoll, points out that racial discrimination contributes to the disparity between employment rate of suburban black males who reside in close proximity to available jobs and that of comparably educated white males (Stoll 1998). Others explain that the diminished work ethic earlier noted is a function of the lack of structural opportunities available to the black inner-city poor (Gould 1999) and the negative perception of employers towards inner-city black men (Kirschenman and Neckerman 1991). Mark Gould contends that if educational and employment opportunities become more available to the urban underclass, their attitudes towards work are likely to change as well (1999).

Finally, Wilson (1999) addresses the growing schism between the elite class and the dwindling middle class. He maintains that the middle and working classes, regardless of racial group, fail to see that racial division not only worsens the conditions of the black urban poor, it also exacerbates the political and economic disparity between the elite and nonelite classes. He recommends a grassroots multiracial coalition and affirmative opportunity programs based on merit that are neither race nor class specific.

Overall, Wilson's major contribution to social science has been his illumination of the devastating effect that the global economy has had on the urban black community. Yet, his focus on class averts attention away from his agenda of improving the life chances of the ghetto inhabitants, as well as from the persistent racism and discrimination experienced by this group and other African Americans. Nevertheless, his scholarship redirected the academic community's attention to the plight of the black urban poor.

SEE ALSO *Poverty; Social Exclusion; Sociology, Urban; Spatial Theory; Underclass; Urban Studies*

BIBLIOGRAPHY

PRIMARY WORKS

Wilson, William J. 1980. *The Declining Significance of Race: Blacks and Changing American Institutions.* Chicago: University of Chicago Press.

Wilson, William J. 1987. *The Truly Disadvantaged: The Inner City, the Underclass, and Public Policy.* Chicago: University of Chicago Press.

Wilson, William J. 1996. *When Work Disappears: The World of the New Urban Poor.* New York: Knopf.

Wilson, William J. 1999. *The Bridge over the Racial Divide: Rising Inequality and Coalition Politics.* Berkeley: University of California Press.

SECONDARY WORKS

Gould, Mark. 1999. Race and Theory: Culture, Poverty, and Adaptation to Discrimination in Wilson and Ogbu. *Sociological Theory* 17 (2): 171–200.

Kain, John F. 1968. Housing Segregation, Negro Employment, and Metropolitan Decentralization. *The Quarterly Journal of Economics* 82 (2): 175–197.

Kirschenman, Joleen, and Kathryn M. Neckerman. 1991. "We'd Love to Hire Them, But…": The Meaning of Race for Employers. In *The Urban Underclass,* eds. Christopher Jencks and Paul E. Peterson, 203–232. Washington, DC: The Brookings Institution.

Niemonen, Jack. 2002. *Race, Class, and the State in Contemporary Sociology: The William Julius Wilson Debates.* Boulder, CO: Lynne Rienner Publishers.

Remnick, David. 1996. Dr. Wilson's Neighborhood. In *The Devil Problem,* 250–274. New York: Random House.

Stoll, Michael. 1998. When Jobs Move, Do Black and Latino Men Lose? The Effect of Growth in Job Decentralisation on Young Men's Jobless Incidence and Duration. *Urban Studies* 35 (12): 2221–2239.

Yolanda Y. Johnson

WILSON, WOODROW
1856–1924

Thomas Woodrow Wilson was the twenty-eighth president of the United States of America. He served as president from March 4, 1913, until March 3, 1921. Wilson was born in Staunton, Virginia, on December 28, 1856, and died in Washington, D.C., on February 3, 1924.

Wilson was the son of a prominent Presbyterian minister and grew up in Georgia and South Carolina. Wilson attended Davidson College in North Carolina and was graduated from Princeton University in 1879. He studied law at the University of Virginia and earned a PhD in political science from Johns Hopkins in 1886. He later taught at Princeton and became its president in 1902.

Well-known for his support of progressive causes and his academic reforms at Princeton, Wilson was elected governor of New Jersey as a Democrat in 1910. Wilson attracted favorable national attention from progressive Democrats for his eloquence, integrity, and opposition to machine politics and from southern Democrats for his support of a "states' rights" position that argued that Southern states should be free to pursue their own policies

of racial segregation. Supported by former Democratic presidential nominee William Jennings Bryan, Wilson received the Democratic presidential nomination of 1912. Calling his progressive platform *the New Freedom*, Wilson emphasized a more competitive, decentralized economy, lower tariffs, and states' rights. Wilson was elected president with 42 percent of the popular vote when most voters divided their support between Republican president William H. Taft and Theodore Roosevelt, the Progressive Party's nominee and a former Republican president.

Wilson revolutionized the rhetorical role of the American president by personally addressing Congress about his legislative proposals and, later, conducting national speaking tours to promote his foreign policy. Wilson, however, also strengthened racial segregation in Washington, D.C., and admired the romanticized portrayal of the Ku Klux Klan in the silent film *Birth of a Nation*. In domestic policy, Wilson secured passage of major economic reform legislation. The Federal Reserve Act of 1913 decentralized and stabilized the national money supply by broadly distributing federal bank notes among several reserve banks. The Federal Trade Commission Act of 1914 promoted consumer protection and regulated interstate business behavior in order to eliminate, punish, and deter anticompetitive practices. Promoted by Wilson in order to prevent a national railroad strike, the Adamson Act of 1916 required an eight-hour workday for railroad workers.

Having adopted some of the Progressive Party's 1912 platform through his legislation, Wilson was narrowly reelected in 1916 after he secured California's electoral votes. His neutrality in World War I (1914–1918), summarized by the campaign slogan "He Kept Us Out of War," also helped his reelection. After Germany resumed unrestricted submarine warfare in 1917 and tried to form an anti-American alliance with Mexico, Wilson secured a declaration of war from Congress on April 6, 1917.

Wilson believed that U.S. military and diplomatic efforts should be devoted to making World War I the "war to end all wars" and the war "to make the world safe for democracy." In a speech to Congress on January 8, 1918, Wilson announced his Fourteen Points as the basis for establishing a just, lasting peace in Europe. These principles and objectives included national self-determination, freedom of the seas, and the creating of a League of Nations to enforce the peace after World War I. Unfortunately for Wilson, Britain and France opposed major elements of the Fourteen Points, especially national self-determination, which threatened their empires. Nonetheless, the League of Nations was included in the Treaty of Versailles of 1919, which officially ended World War I. For his diplomatic efforts, Wilson received the Nobel Peace Prize of 1919.

Some of Wilson's critics perceived his egotistical, self-righteous refusal to compromise with Republican senators, especially Henry Cabot Lodge, to be the primary reason why the Senate rejected an active role for the United States in the League of Nations. While conducting a national speaking tour to increase public support for the League of Nations, Wilson suffered a severe stroke on October 2, 1919. The extent and nature of Wilson's physical and mental disability were kept hidden from the vice president, cabinet, Congress, and the press by his second wife, Edith Wilson. As the Republicans prepared for landslide victories in the 1920 presidential and congressional elections, the nation experienced a Red Scare, labor disputes, and high inflation. After he left the White House in 1921, Wilson continued to live in Washington, D.C., until his death in 1924.

SEE ALSO *League of Nations; Nobel Peace Prize; United Nations; World War I*

BIBLIOGRAPHY

Blum, John Morton. 1956. *Woodrow Wilson and the Politics of Morality*. Boston: Little, Brown.

Knock, Thomas J. 1992. *To End All Wars: Woodrow Wilson and the Quest for a New World Order*. New York: Oxford University Press.

Link, Arthur S. 1954. *Woodrow Wilson and the Progressive Era, 1910–1917*. New York: Harper. Reprint, Norwalk, CT: Easton Press, 1989.

Sean J. Savage

WINNER-TAKE-ALL SOCIETY

In conventional labor markets, reward is proportional to absolute performance, which in turn is generally modeled as proportional to human capital—an amalgam of talent, experience, education, training, and other factors that affect productivity. Thus, in the classic piece-rate scheme, a worker who assembles 101 widgets in a week gets paid 1 percent more than a coworker who assembles only 100. In contrast, a winner-take-all market is one in which small differences in performance often translate into very large differences in economic reward.

The winner-take-all perspective urges us to look first to the nature of the positions people hold, rather than to their personal characteristics. An economist under the influence of the human capital metaphor might ask: Why not save money by hiring two mediocre people to fill an important position instead of paying the exorbitant salary required to attract someone unusually good? Although

that sort of substitution might work for jobs involving routinized tasks and flexible staffing arrangements, it often will not be feasible in the professions. Two average surgeons or CEOs or novelists or quarterbacks are often a poor substitute for a single gifted one. The result is that for positions for which additional talent has great value to the employer or the marketplace, there is no reason to expect that the market will compensate individuals in proportion to their human capital. For these positions—ones that confer the greatest leverage or "amplification" of human talent—small increments of talent have great value and may be greatly rewarded as a result of the normal competitive market process.

Technology has greatly extended the power and reach of the planet's most gifted performers. The printing press let a relatively few gifted storytellers displace millions of village raconteurs. Now that we listen mostly to recorded music, the world's best musicians can be everywhere at once. The electronic newswire has allowed a small number of syndicated columnists to displace a host of local journalists. And the proliferation of personal computers enabled a handful of software developers to replace thousands of tax accountants.

The dependence of economic reward on performance ranking is nothing new; what is new is the rapid erosion of the barriers that once prevented the top performers from serving broader markets. The global marketplace has been fostered by the reduction in trade barriers, vast improvements in information transmission and processing, the almost universal adoption of English as the language of business, and the emergence of a common popular culture.

Winner-take-all markets can be wasteful to the extent that they induce contestants for high rank to engage in costly and mutually offsetting investments to obtain positional advantage. In such cases, "positional arms control" schemes may reduce waste and improve economic efficiency. Such schemes range from market-specific policies, such as steroid bans for athletes and caps on the tax deductibility of executive compensation, to more general policies such as progressive income taxation.

BIBLIOGRAPHY

Frank, Robert H., and Philip J. Cook. 1995. *The Winner-Take-All Society*. New York: Free Press.

Marshall, Alfred. 1920. *Principles of Economics*. 8th ed. London: Macmillan.

Rosen, Sherwin. 1981. The Economics of Superstars. *American Economic Review* 71 (5): 845–858.

Robert H. Frank
Philip J. Cook

WINNER'S CURSE

The winner's curse story begins in 1971 when Edward Capen, Robert Clapp, and William Campbell, three petroleum engineers, wrote an article in which they claimed that oil companies suffered unexpectedly low returns "year after year" in early Outer Continental Shelf (OCS) oil lease auctions. OCS auctions are common value auctions where the value of the oil in the ground is essentially the same to all bidders. Bidders have their own estimate of the (unknown) value at the time that they bid. Even if these estimates are unbiased, bidders must account for the informational content inherent in winning the auction: the winner's estimate of the common value is (one of) the highest estimates. If bidders ignore this *adverse selection effect* inherent in winning the auction, it will result in below normal or even negative profits. The systematic failure to account for this adverse selection effect is referred to as the winner's curse: you win, you lose money, and you curse. (Unfortunately, many economists, particularly theorists, characterize the winner's curse as the difference between the expected value of the item conditional on the event of winning and the unconditional, naive expectation, using the term to refer to bidders fully accounting for this difference, rather than failing to do so and losing money as a consequence.)

Similar claims regarding a winner's curse have been made in a variety of other contexts: book publication rights, professional baseball's free agency market, corporate takeover battles, and real estate auctions (see chapter 1 in John H. Kagel and Dan Levin's 2002 book *Common Value Auctions and the Winner's Curse*). These claims have traditionally been greeted with a good deal of skepticism by economists as they imply that bidders repeatedly err, thus violating basic notions of economic rationality. It is exceedingly difficult to support claims of a winner's curse with field data because of data reliability problems and plausible alternative explanations.

The ambiguity inherent in interpreting field data, and the controversial nature of the winner's curse, provided the motivation for experimental investigations on the subject. Initial experiments conduced by Max H. Bazerman and William F. Samuelson in 1983 showed that inexperienced bidders are quite susceptible to the winner's curse in a corporate takeover game. John H. Kagel and Dan Levin found similar results in 1986 in first-price sealed-bid common value auctions. Subsequent experiments have focused on the robustness of the phenomena and features of the environment that might attenuate its effects. Does the commonly known presence of an "insider" who knows the true value of the item attenuate the winner's curse? (No, it does not.) Do open outcry (English) auctions in which bidders with higher value estimates gain information as a consequence of lower valued

bidders dropping out attenuate the winner's curse? (Yes, to some extent, but this experience does not transfer into doing better in sealed-bid auctions.) Are subjects who have learned to avoid the winner's curse in auctions with relatively few (four) bidders able to avoid it in auctions with larger numbers of rivals (seven) with its more severe adverse selection effect? (No, they are not.) Thus, although bidders are able to avoid the winner's curse with enough experience, this learning appears to be context specific, so that it does not easily generalize to related environments.

Research has also focused on key public policy issues. As theory predicts, public information that is correlated with the common value raises seller's revenue in first-price sealed-bid auctions in the absence of a winner's curse (i.e., for experienced bidders), but contrary to the theory lowers revenue for less experienced bidders who still suffer from a winner's curse. English auctions, where public information is released endogenously, have the same effect. Finally, there are striking parallels between laboratory outcomes and anomalous findings from field data, along with experiments in which experienced industry executives in the laboratory suffer to the same extent from the winner's curse as do student subjects, which lead most scholars and a number of other observers to believe that the winner's curse is alive and well both inside and outside the laboratory (Kagel and Levin, 2002).

SEE ALSO *Adverse Selection; Auctions; Economics, Experimental; Expected Utility Theory; Rationality*

BIBLIOGRAPHY

Bazerman, Max H., and William F. Samuelson. 1983. I Won the Auction but Don't Want the Prize. *Journal of Conflict Resolution* 27 (4): 618–634.

Capen, Edward C., Robert V. Clapp, and William M. Campbell. 1971. Competitive Bidding in High-Risk Situations. *Journal of Petroleum Technology* 23: 641–653.

Kagel, John H., and Dan Levin. 1986. The Winner's Curse and Public Information in Common Value Auctions. *The American Economic Review* 76 (5): 894–920.

Kagel, John H., and Dan Levin. 2002. *Common Value Auctions and the Winner's Curse.* Princeton, NJ: Princeton University Press.

John H. Kagel
Dan Levin

WIZARD OF OZ

The book *The Wonderful Wizard of Oz* (1900) and its film adaptation *The Wizard of Oz* (1939) quickly became a foundational element in American popular culture with countless idiomatic allusions, cultural references, and pervasive merchandizing. Lyman Frank Baum wrote seventeen sequels comprising the Oz series, though none repeated or surpassed the popularity of the first book. The film launched actress Judy Garland's stardom; she won an Academy Award and made the song "Somewhere Over the Rainbow" popular and famous, earning it recognition as the number one song of the twentieth century. Since the 1950s, the film has aired continuously on network and cable television. These airings, with few exceptions, became an annual tradition and continued through 2002. Sidney Lumet directed an African American stage version in 1978; *The Wiz* starred pop-music icons Diana Ross and Michael Jackson as Dorothy and the Scarecrow, respectively. In 1998 *The Wizard of Oz* ranked sixth out of one hundred in an American Film Institute poll; it was the highest ranked musical in the genre of fantasy and family movies. Through the first half decade of the 2000s, it continued to generate academic and mainstream books, journal articles, CD music releases, videocassette releases, websites, blogs, merchandizing, and a remastered digital DVD release.

Baum was born on May 15, 1856, in Chittenango, New York. He suffered a stroke and died on May 5, 1919. Many biographies exist detailing his life and work. The success of the Oz books prompted a musical adaptation for the stage. *Oz* (1902) became very popular and toured for nine years. The film *The Wizard of Oz* was adapted from Baum's first book, other books in the series, and stage scripts.

The basic storyline details the adventures of a young girl named Dorothy as a tornado transports her and her dog to the magical land of Oz, where she encounters and befriends interesting characters and experiences a range of adventures, some of which are frightening, even gruesome, and others humorous. The characters most remembered are Dorothy; her dog Toto; the Munchkins; the Scarecrow; the Tin Man; the Cowardly Lion; the Wizard of Oz; Glinda, the Good Witch of the North (Glinda is from the South in the book); and the main villain, the Wicked Witch of the West. The film is mostly true to the original books, though one key difference is that the land of Oz and the Emerald City are real places in the books, but the film indicates that these places are fantasy and only exist in Dorothy's dream, which occurs as a result of a bump on the head. This notion is portrayed through the contrast of the dual-tone sepia segments, which depict real-life Kansas, and the Technicolor® segments, which depict the land of Oz. Also, the same actors who play the role of the farm hands play the roles of the major land of Oz characters.

The most noted dialogue that has worked its way into American popular culture includes the sayings: "Toto, I've

got a feeling we're not in Kansas anymore," "Follow the yellow brick road," and "Pay no attention to the man behind the curtain." The first line has appeared in many variations in movies, television sitcoms, and skits. One of the most famous yellow brick road references is pop singer Elton John's 1973 album *Goodbye Yellow Brick Road.* "The man behind the curtain" has been used in reference to conspiracy theories and political scandals, including the Kennedy assassinations, Watergate, Iran-Contra, and suspicions of voter fraud in the 2000 U.S. presidential election.

There have been several scholarly interpretations of the story and film, including Daniel Dervin's 1978 Freudian interpretation, in which Dorothy's journey is symbolic of a sexual coming of age; Darren John Main's 2000 Jungian interpretation, in which Dorothy's journey is emblematic of archetypal spiritual journeys; and Lynette Carpenter's 1985 analysis, which presents the film as embodying U.S. isolationist tendencies during the dawn of World War II. The most acclaimed interpretation is Henry M. Littlefield's 1964 view of the story as allegory for the gold versus silver standard debate, political populism, and William Jennings Bryan's presidential run. For Littlefield, "*The Wonderful Wizard of Oz* has provided unknowing generations with a gentle and friendly Midwestern critique of the Populist rationale.... [L]ed by naive innocence [Dorothy] and protected by good will [Glinda], the farmer [Scarecrow], the labourer [Tin Man] and the politician [Bryan in particular] approach the mystic holder of national power [the Wizard] to ask for personal fulfilment" (pp. 57–58).

Another Populist perspective exists between the film and the New Deal. The lyricist for all the songs in the film was E. Y. "Yip" Harburg (1896–1981), who wrote the Great Depression anthem "Brother, Can You Spare a Dime?" He also helped shape most of the story. Harburg claimed that the Emerald City represented the New Deal. In 1990 Francis MacDonnell extended this interpretation, stating that the Wizard represents New Deal president Franklin D. Roosevelt. In the same way that the Wizard shows Dorothy and her friends that they always had the qualities they were in search of, President Roosevelt demonstrated that the American people held the solutions to their problems and restored their self-confidence.

BIBLIOGRAPHY

Carpenter, Lynette. 1985. There's No Place Like Home: The Wizard of Oz and American Isolationism. *Film and History* 15 (5): 37–45.

Dervin, Daniel. 1978. Over the Rainbow and Under the Twister: A Drama of the Girl's Passage through the Phallic Phase. *Bulletin of the Meninger Clinic* 42: 51–57.

Dighe, Ranjit S. 2002. *The Historian's Wizard of Oz: Reading L. Frank Baum's Classic as a Political and Monetary Allegory.* Westport, CT: Praeger.

Hearn, Michael Patrick. 2000. *The Annotated Wizard of Oz: Centennial Edition.* New York: W. W. Norton.

Littlefield, Henry M. 1964. The Wizard of Oz: A Parable on Populism. *American Quarterly* 16 (Spring): 47–58.

MacDonnell, Francis. 1990. "The Emerald City was the New Deal": E. Y. Harburg and *The Wonderful Wizard of Oz. Journal of American Culture* 13 (Winter): 71–75.

Main, Darren John. 2000. *Spiritual Journeys along the Yellow Brick Road.* Tallahassee, FL: Findhorn Press.

Nathanson, Paul. 1991. *Over the Rainbow : The Wizard of Oz as a Secular Myth of America.* Albany: State University of New York Press.

Jeff Williams

WOLF, ERIC
1923–1999

Anthropologist Eric Robert Wolf was born in Vienna, Austria, in 1923 and died in Irvington, New York, in 1999. The son of an Austro-Russian marriage, Wolf passed a cosmopolitan childhood in Vienna and the Sudetenland before being sent to school in England as Adolf Hitler's (1889–1945) destruction loomed. After emigrating with his parents to New York, he served in World War II (1939–1945). After the war, Wolf completed his undergraduate degree at Queens College (1946) and a PhD at Columbia University (1951), both in anthropology. Along with returning veterans such as Morton Klass (1927–2001), Robert F. Murphy (1924–1990), Stanley Diamond (1922–1991), and others, Wolf formed the Mundial Upheaval Society to discuss the influence of classical social theory, especially Marxism, in the social sciences. During early fieldwork in Puerto Rico and Mexico, Wolf combined Marxian and Weberian frameworks with Middle European political-economic debates arising from the 1917 Russian Revolution, examining the praxis of grounded power relations. From this work emerged contributions to anthropologist Julian Steward's (1902–1972) *People of Puerto Rico* (1956), and Wolf's classic *Sons of the Shaking Earth* (1959), which synthesized archaeological and ethnohistorical knowledge of Mesoamerican civilization within a class-sensitive framework. Wolf also authored or coauthored groundbreaking articles that addressed the history and sociology of cultural forms—for example, the Virgin of Guadalupe, *compadrazgo*, corporate communities, and Santa Claus—as these forms build liens of redistribution across class, caste, and nation. In early publications as in later ones, Wolf

served as a translator of European social thought into American anthropology.

Over a long and distinguished teaching career at the universities of Illinois, Virginia, Chicago, and Michigan, and at Lehman College at the City University of New York Graduate Center, from which he retired in 1992, Wolf was a prolific and iconoclastic scholar, publishing more than one hundred articles, and editing many journal issues and books. In addition to *Sons of the Shaking Earth*, his books include: *Anthropology* (1964), *Peasants* (1966), *Peasant Wars of the 20th Century* (1969), *The Human Condition in Latin America* (1972, with Edward Hansen), *The Hidden Frontier* (1974, with John Cole), and the magisterial *Europe and the People Without History* (1982), followed by *Envisioning Power* (1999). *Pathways to Power*, edited with his wife, the anthropologist Sydel Silverman, appeared posthumously in 2001. All illustrate coherent themes central to his scholarship: connections between intellectual histories and social movements and broad political economic trends; ties binding specific cultural forms to class-inflected power relations; and embedded local class relations that play out articulations of global history. Thus, the daily political and social lives of family, community, faction, religious-ethnic group, state, and nation may appear as somewhat autonomous, but in Wolf's writings they all serve as termini of concrete international processes. His work underlines the historical depth of these interconnections within and across shifting national boundaries of modernity, and he insists on the historical incorporation of the small-scale societies anthropologists conventionally study into larger webs of power, exploitation, and occasionally resistance. It is Wolf's enduring achievement to have enabled individuals to understand such societies in new ways, as dependent on connections of political economy and culture.

In *Anthropology*, Wolf labeled his field "the most scientific of the humanities, the most humanist of the sciences" (1964, p. 88). Later texts carried humanist scientific study into the interstitial connections throughout modern history. His synthetic intelligence and highly comparative method enabled Wolf to produce books that remain beacons of social scientific clarity in anthropology. *Peasant Wars of the Twentieth Century* (1969) illuminated the limited, class-fragmented, and constrained agency of the peasants who helped to topple and transform regimes in Mexico, Russia, China, Vietnam, Algeria, and Cuba, too often at their own expense. *Europe and the People Without History* (1982) showed that the bands, tribes, and villages once considered classical anthropological subjects were actually products of the socioeconomics of the modern capitalist world. After its publication, anthropologists could never again work in the "ethnographic present." It was Wolf's accomplishment, as the subtitle of his last

book forcefully proclaims, to have oriented his field toward *Building an Anthropology of the Modern World.*

SEE ALSO *Anthropology; Anthropology, U.S.; Culture; Humanism; Marxism; Mintz, Sidney W.; Peasantry; Politics; Revolution*

BIBLIOGRAPHY

Ghani, Ashraf. 1995. Writing a History of Power: An Examination of Eric R. Wolf's Anthropological Quest. In *Articulating Hidden Histories: Exploring the Influence of Eric R. Wolf*, eds. Jane Schneider and Rayna Rapp, 31–48. Berkeley: University of California Press.

Schneider, Jane. 1995. Introduction: The Analytic Strategies of Eric R. Wolf. In *Articulating Hidden Histories: Exploring the Influence of Eric R. Wolf*, eds. Jane Schneider and Rayna Rapp, 3–30. Berkeley: University of California Press.

Wolf, Eric R. 1964. *Anthropology*. Englewood Cliffs, NJ: Prentice-Hall.

Wolf, Eric R. 2001. Introduction: An Intellectual Biography. In *Pathways of Power: Building an Anthropology of the Modern World*, 1–10. Berkeley: University of California Press.

Rayna Rapp

WOMANISM

An ongoing concern for black feminists has always been that their specific experiences have been elided within a discourse that is biased towards a white, Anglo-American perspective. It is a view clearly enunciated by Audre Lorde's essay "An Open Letter to Mary Daly" (1984) in which she castigates the radical feminist philosopher for her misrepresentation of black women in her book *Gyn/Ecology* (1978), which Lorde claimed, "dismissed my heritage and the heritage of all other noneuropean women" (69).

But in 1983, in which Lorde published her address to Daly, the writer Alice Walker published what was to prove an extremely influential essay, "In Search of Our Mothers' Gardens" (1983) in which her central concern was to formulate a definition of black feminism from within African American culture itself. Whereas Lorde argued that Daly portrayed black women only as victims, ignoring their power as active agents capable of combating their own oppression, Walker focused on precisely those positive aspects, developing a feminist terminology drawn from everyday discourse used in the black community.

Although the term *womanist* is now synonymous with Walker's essay and book by the same title, it was not new to the English language. According to the *Oxford English Dictionary*, the term *womanism* first appeared in 1863, indicating "advocacy of or enthusiasm for the rights, achievements, etc. of women." In the context of second wave feminism, however, "womanism" has become

INTERNATIONAL ENCYCLOPEDIA OF THE SOCIAL SCIENCES, 2ND EDITION

more specifically aligned with the black feminist movement. Walker's use of the term "womanism" therefore etymologically relates directly not to its prior usage in the nineteenth century but to the colloquial term *womanish*, which Walker defines as "Opp. of 'girlish,' i.e., frivolous, irresponsible, not serious." A "womanish" girl is wilful, inquisitive, and wise beyond her years, refusing to accept rules and limitations imposed by others.

However, although Walker draws the concept of womanism from, and defines it through, a black cultural context, she intends it to be inclusive rather than exclusive, offering four increasingly poetic understandings of the word that stress its connectedness to wider experiences of feminism. Although she begins with the black folk usage of "womanish," her second description expands the term to designate any woman, of any color, whose primary identification is with other women, either sexually or nonsexually. Nevertheless, a womanist is not a separatist but someone who is a "universalist," committed to "wholeness of entire people, male *and* female" (xi). She thus harmonizes two contradictory subject positions: a dedication to personal freedom along with an acknowledgment of the innate interconnectedness of peoples and genders. Walker's third definition stresses this balance between separation and association, identifying a womanist as someone committed to sensual gratification but also political struggle; to herself and to the wider community within which she is situated.

It is for this reason that "womanism" has become a widely used term within feminist theory, for it allows black women to articulate their feminism without relinquishing an attachment to black culture and racial politics. The subtle distinction between feminism and womanism is best summed up by Walker's final definition: "Womanist is to feminist as purple to lavender" (xii), and is exemplified in a speech delivered over a hundred years earlier. When Sojourner Truth, speaking at the Women's Convention in Akron, Ohio in 1851, proclaimed 'ain't I a woman?,' she asserted her rights not only as a woman, but also as an African American, an ex-slave, and a political campaigner.

SEE ALSO *Feminism; Feminism, Second Wave; Inequality, Racial; Truth, Sojourner*

BIBLIOGRAPHY

Lorde, Audre. 1984. An Open Letter to Mary Daly. *Sister Outsider,* ed. Audre Lorde. 66–71. Freedom, CA: The Crossing Press.

Walker, Alice. 1983. In Search of Our Mothers' Gardens. In *In Search of Our Mothers' Gardens: Womanist Prose.* New York: Harcourt.

Sarah Gamble

WOMB ENVY
SEE *Oedipus Complex.*

WOMEN

A definition of "woman" that applies cross-culturally, one that includes the definitions offered by societies that are not part of our own Western/industrial tradition, will inevitably include some allusions to female physiology and to cultural constructions that include women's reproductive role, spiritual role (or its absence), domestic role, work role, and role in the care of children, assigning varying degrees of importance to each. The definition of womanhood may or may not be related to a society's definition of manhood, and may or may not be related to other gender categories that a society might recognize—which can be as many as five.

Furthermore, the definition of "woman" and "womanhood," when viewed from a cross-cultural perspective, will vary depending upon three variables. The first variable is the society's recognition of the specific stages of the female life course. Societies differ in how they identify and define the physical and psychological maturational stages of a woman's individual development. Some stages that we may readily identify in our own society (such as getting a driver's license) do not exist or are ignored, while other developmental events are given exaggerated attention and some are of such importance that they are accorded ceremonial recognition. The second variable, the society into which the individual is born (or of which she may become a member by a choice made later in life), will provide a variety of cultural expectations, some of which every individual female member is expected to meet and some of which only a chosen few may achieve. The third variable consists of the time period in the history of a particular society in which the individual finds herself. These three variables are not necessarily independent but can interact with each other to provide the specific definition of what it means to be a "woman" for a female individual of a particular age, in a specific society, and at a particular moment in history.

THE FIRST VARIABLE: THE LIFE COURSE

In all societies, the infant's sex is noted at birth, and in some societies, a female identity may lead to immediate infanticide. Yet often the baby is viewed as virtually neuter, in contrast to our own society, in which even the tiniest infant garments are gendered. Recognition of the individual's gender can begin at various stages early in the life course, but by the time signs of adolescence appear, the individual has been assigned. Although some societies

did not particularly note menarche or other evidences of adolescence, in many traditional societies, mere girls could only "be made into women" by means of an elaborate ritual. In these societies, only the initiated conformed to the definition of "woman." Such ceremonies, sometimes celebrated individually at the time of menarche and sometimes celebrated for groups of girls at the approximate onset of their adolescence, took a variety of forms. Some were elaborate, involved considerable expense for the family of the girl, engaged the entire community, and took months to complete. In other societies, the observance was brief, involved only a few female relatives, and was somewhat private.

In the ceremony of the Bemba of east Africa as reported by Richards (1956), men actually had specific roles to perform in the initiation. In many other societies, men are banned from even seeing the ritual. Among the Bemba, there were tests of competence for the initiates, and it was believed that their roles as food providers would be performed with the appropriate, womanly attitude after the completion of the long, elaborate ceremony. (In contrast, our own educational system typically focuses on transmitting skills and tends to neglect training for the proper attitude toward work.) Several ceremonies performed in other traditional societies included a painful genital operation, but most female initiation rites provided instruction, often regarding sexual activity, as well as a period of seclusion during which the initiate had to observe a number of taboos. These rites were typically followed by feasting, receiving gifts and new clothes, and being declared beautiful and ready for marriage negotiations to begin.

The life course of women can be viewed as discontinuous even if no ritual activity creates a major change in what it means to be a woman. Thus the end of virginity, menarche, the arrival of children, and menopause are one and all irreversible phases of womanhood that are not only physical but also have psychological and cultural meaning. The recognition or lack of recognition a society provides for these physiologic milestones in the lives of women varies cross-culturally. Thus, for example, as reported by Meigs (1984), the Hua of Papua New Guinea were a society in which not only the physiological changes characteristic of the female life course but also culturally constructed changes without a biological basis created a fluid definition for Hua womanhood. The body of Hua women and girls were believed to be filled with a vital essence that was both polluting and to some degree dangerous to men and that was transmitted to men through each act of sexual intercourse and through the food that women handled, prepared, and served. The essence was drained from women's bodies in the act of childbirth. Thus an older woman, the mother of several children, became as pure as a man, while aging men became impure

like women. Because many older women were pure like men, they could have access to the great men's house, which was forbidden to women and children. Unlike them, she might have participated in male activities and had access to secret male knowledge. Thus among the Hua, the meaning of womanhood was not based only on physiological changes that characterize the female life course but depended on the culturally constructed definitions assigned to these female life courses stages.

THE SECOND VARIABLE: SOCIETY

In many societies the definition of womanhood is shaped by the view that women are physically weaker and intellectually inferior to men, as well as spiritually underendowed. In some societies the definition must take account of the fact that women are viewed as naturally lecherous and wanton. Rape, wife abuse, and even murder are viewed as justifiable responses to these female tendencies. Women's sexual impulses are corrupting to men and constantly threaten the honor of the family, requiring the unremitting vigilance of a brother or a husband. Women of childbearing age in such societies must be restrained by perpetual chaperonage, by the alert supervision of elder female kin, and by confinement, an enforced claustration, lived in the company of other women.

In spite of the negative valuation that was part of the definition of women in many societies, there was also evidence of envy by men. Among the Inuit of the central Arctic, women's lives were confined to the igloo during the long winter. Unconfined, the men ranged freely from the camp to hunt and fish, yet they envied the shelter and warmth of the women's indoor life. An attempt to imitate women that may have been based on envy was the periodic self-inflicted bleeding practiced by the men of several Melanesian societies. In a private ritual, a man would scrape his penis to induce bleeding, an imitation of women's menstruation, which was believed to provide strength and well-being. An example of a positive valuation of women comes from the traditional Native American societies of the Gulf region, where there were separate languages for men and women and men felt the women's language was more beautiful than their own.

Women's Economic Role Whether or not the men of a particular society envy women, or whether or not the members of a society subscribe to a definition of womanhood that attributes inferiority to women, or whether or not members of a society have a more egalitarian view of the sexes, womanhood is inevitably defined in part by the work women perform (unlike our own society, where it would be unusual for a definition of womanhood to include references to specific vocations.) Thus among the traditional Iroquois of New York State, raising the crops

upon which the people's livelihood depended was the work of women. A man working in the gardens was either too old and too frail for male activity or he was a prisoner of war compelled to perform humiliating, inappropriate work. Thus, for example, the Iroquois "made women" out of the defeated Delaware by making them work in their gardens. Yet the productivity of the Iroquois women was revered. Female spiritual beings represented the crops, and ceremonial activity celebrated the cultivated foods provided by women, not the hunting and warfare of the men.

Competence in woman's work was valued so highly in many traditional societies that it overshadowed sexual attractiveness in the choice of a wife. Thus, among the Iroquois and the traditional Inuit, an older competent woman might be viewed as a desirable wife for a far younger man. Productivity, diligence, and highly developed female skills were among the qualities that were accorded the privilege of being a "manly hearted woman" among the North Piegan, a Canadian Blackfoot tribe, according to Lewis (1970). Although most married women in this society served as lower or "slave wives," the "manly hearted woman" was the "sit-by wife." She was not masculine, as the title might suggest; instead she excelled in women's work and was therefore an economic asset. She was the favorite wife, actively sexual and outspoken. Lower wives were beaten mercilessly for such behavior in traditional times.

As reported by Elam (1973), the traditional Hima, east African herders, further illustrate how the work women perform and their sex life define womanhood in a particular society. In traditional times, Hima girls joined the herders with their cattle outside the village. They acted as assistants to the men in activities such as milking. They were physically active and free to move about the landscape and were expected to be chaste until marriage. The wife, in contrast, was confined to the hut. Unlike girls, she was heavily clothed and her diet and lack of physical activity were intended to make her fat, which was viewed as sexually attractive. Fat and desirable, she was expected to grant sexual favors to numerous men, including her father-in-law. Unlike girls, she was forbidden to milk, bleed, or slaughter cattle. In her life as a woman, she was by definition confined, and her work consisted of making butter and curd and keeping the milk jugs clean.

Women's Spirituality In many societies, the definition of womanhood that pertains to most of a woman's life, the childbearing years, appears to exclude the possibility of spirituality. Thus among the traditional !Kung of southern Africa, pregnancy and lactation were viewed as incompatible with trance, since such spiritual activity could harm the unborn child or the nursing infant. In parts of North America, a woman could become a shaman, and a spiri-

tual being would enable her to attain special powers. But in many societies only a man could be a shaman. Among the Navajo, it was believed that the evil powers of witchcraft were inaccessible to a woman of childbearing age. Thus the ability to exert spiritual power or the absence of this ability is noted in the definition of womanhood in many societies. In contrast, spiritual attributes are typically not part of a definition of womanhood in our own society.

THE THIRD VARIABLE: HISTORIC FACTORS

A society's definition of womanhood inevitably evolves to reflect historical changes. This is as true for our own society as it is cross-culturally. In the later twentieth century, historical changes have created a redefinition of womanhood in the Western/industrial world that is almost as dramatic as the redefinition of womanhood created by the end of colonialism and the spread of globalization in those parts of the world that are not part of our own tradition. An example of such changes is offered by Draper (1975) in her description of the !Kung of southern Africa. Their traditional way of life had continued into the mid-twentieth century, and although aware of the outside world (a world that mistakenly believed they were extinct), they had retained a traditional definition of womanhood. The women of the !Kung sustained the life of the small, migratory camps with their food-gathering activities. Each day that the women set out into the Kalahari Desert, they were successful in harvesting the vegetable foods that constituted the major portion of the !Kung diet. While collecting, the women also gathered information about the movement of animals, which they provided to the men to help them in their hunting. The hunting activities of the men, though less frequently successful than the gathering activities of the women, received a great deal of cultural attention and provided the food that was harder to obtain, made up less of the diet, and was more highly valued. Although the gathering activities of women were not accorded particular recognition, women had the right to be outspoken, and the relationship between men and women was markedly egalitarian. These traditional circumstances have been attributed to women's economic importance. And this in turn was made possible by a benign environment, in which women were not threatened by enemy neighbors or wild animals that might have made male protection necessary. Their autonomy made possible the traditional !Kung women's role as the "major breadwinners."

Dramatic and rapid changes occurred when the !Kung became sedentary, living on the outskirts of the villages of herders, who now controlled the region. !Kung women became housewives. The open camps were

replaced by huts which isolated women from relatives and neighbors. Their economic importance was a thing of the past, as was their autonomy. Wife abuse was now a problem. This vastly oversimplified history of the !Kung during the later twentieth century illustrates how a particular society's definition of womanhood can undergo dramatic change. Although still living in their homeland, their new circumstances totally altered how "woman" was defined.

CONCLUSION

The definition of "woman" is only partially based on the physical traits that differentiate the sexes. Superimposed on physiological reality is the possibility that a society may recognize more than two genders. In addition, the definition a culture constructs for the term "woman" may change during different stages of the life course, for example, by not including the category "uninitiated female adolescent" as part of the definition of "woman." Different societies also vary on which aspect of womanhood the culture stresses in its definition. Is it her economic role? Is it her maternal role? Is it her sexual role? Is it her domestic role? (For a review of the interrelationships of these factors, see Brown 1973.) Or perhaps it is her physical or mental inferiority and lack of spirituality compared to men. Historical changes can alter a society's definition. And all of these possible aspects of a society's definition of "woman" can be interdependent and influence each other. The cross-culturally applicable definition of any concept is inevitably complicated, but the necessary ingredients of the varied definitions can be identified.

SEE ALSO *Anthropology; Cultural Relativism; Femininity; Feminism; Feminism, Second Wave; Gender; Gender, Alternatives to Binary; Matriarchy; Patriarchy; Rites of Passage; Rituals; Womanism; Women and Politics; Women's Liberation; Women's Movement; Work and Women*

BIBLIOGRAPHY

Brown, Judith K. 1973. The Subsistence Activities of Women and the Socialization of Children. *Ethos* 1: 413–423.

Draper, Patricia. 1975. !Kung Women: Contrasts in Sexual Egalitarianism in Foraging and Sedentary Contexts. In *Toward an Anthropology of Women*, ed. Rayna R. Reiter, 77–109. New York: Monthly Review Press.

Elam, Itzchak. 1973. *The Social and Sexual Roles of Hima Women: A Study of Nomadic Cattle Breeders in Nyabushozi County, Ankole, Uganda.* Manchester, U.K.: Manchester University Press.

Lewis, Oscar. 1970. Manly-Hearted Women among the North Piegan. In *Anthropological Essays*, ed. Oscar Lewis, 213–230. New York: Random House.

Meigs, Anna. 1984. *Food, Sex and Pollution: A New Guinea Religion.* New Brunswick, NJ: Rutgers University Press.

Richards, Audrey. 1956. *Chisungu: A Girls' Initiation Ceremony among the Bemba of Northern Rhodesia.* New York: Grove.

Judith K. Brown

WOMEN AND DEVELOPMENT
SEE *Gender and Development.*

WOMEN AND POLITICS

From an international perspective, the scholarship of women and politics focuses on issues of women's participation and representation in governmental institutions, the legal right over decisions concerning reproduction and sexuality, and the effects of globalization on women's work and social movements.

POLITICAL PARTICIPATION AND REPRESENTATION

Issues of participation and representation of women in politics (political empowerment) are centered in the ideology of the Enlightenment period of the mid-eighteenth century and, therefore, the idea that equal political participation and representation of women in local, state, and federal governments will challenge gender inequality. American feminists were at the forefront of this movement arguing in the 1920s and then in the 1970s for suffrage and equal treatment, respectively. The United Nations (UN) promoted the importance of political empowerment for women as evidenced by the UN's observance of a Decade for Women (1976–1985); the UN's agenda for the political empowerment of women set forth in *The Beijing Declaration and Platform for Action* (1995); a UN treaty based on *The Universal Declaration of Human Rights* and embodied in Article 25 of *The International Covenant on Civil and Political Rights* (1976); and the convening of delegates at the *Convention on the Elimination of all Forms of Discrimination Against Women* (1967) to discuss the political rights of women around the world. The liberal political theory that informs the UN's politics embodies the ideas that (1) political systems are undermined and illegitimate when women are underrepresented; (2) the representation of women in politics contributes to an inherently more democratic multiparty system; (3) gender reform lies in legal reform; (4) "special treatment" (e.g., maternity leave) reproduces gender inequality; (5) a "critical mass" of women represented in governments ensures gender equality; (6) states should legally protect women from discrimination in all areas of

social life; and (7) women have a civil right to representation and their political participation serves as role model behavior and influences the status of women outside the political body.

Critics of the idea that representation and participation challenge gender equality argue that (1) women's participation and representation do not necessarily translate into a representation of women's interests, (2) feminist priorities need to be reinforced in structures and networks (with non-governmental organizations and women's committees within legislative bodies) in order for change to occur and (3) the presence of women in politics does not ensure a feminist political platform. All women, in other words, are not feminists. As a response to the underrepresentation of women in politics, quotas ensuring the participation of women have been suggested and imposed (e.g., France established party laws in 2000). In 2004, the Inter-Parliamentary Union reported that only 15.6 percent of governmental bodies around the world were represented by women. Women represented 6.8 percent in the Arab States, 18.6 percent in the United States, and 39.7 percent in the Nordic states.

RIGHTS OVER REPRODUCTION AND SEXUALITY

The political struggle over rights to abortion, contraception, and the female body has characterized feminist movement around the world. In the United States this is characteristically exemplified by the legalization of abortion in 1974 (*Roe v. Wade*). In the Middle East, North Africa, India, and parts of Southeast Asia, the political struggle over reproduction and sexuality is framed in discourses about the high incidents of female genital mutilation, honor crimes, sex trafficking, bride burning, marital rape, and sexual abuse.

In the Middle East and North Africa (MENA), feminists argue, family law (called in the region "personal status law"), as well as criminal law is informed by traditional and patriarchal cultural norms, thereby legitimizing the violation and control over women's bodies and rights. In neo-Islamic states, such as Iran, religious scholars are increasingly informing the legal code. Global feminists have argued that laws in MENA have allowed for violence against women, statutory discrimination, and disproportionate punishment for women. Women's movements in MENA are demanding political equality, the ability to contract and register their own marriages, a right to divorce, and justice in cases of rape or sexual abuse. Not only the state, but families and local communities have great control over women's sexuality and reproductive rights. "Honor killings"—the murder of a woman by a male family member for a violation of the social norms of sexuality—exemplify the control family has over the sexu-

ality of daughters. Sometimes the families, including mothers, gather and plan the murder of a daughter. Feminists in the region, scholars of women in MENA, as well as global feminists recognize the role of family and community over the control of women and seek to criminalize behavior such as "honor killings" that are often treated as private rather than public matters.

GLOBALIZATION

The effect of globalization on the status of women is a central theme in the study of contemporary women worldwide. Globalization is defined as the movement toward global capitalism and culture. Scholars have explored the negative and positive effect of globalization on women cross-culturally. Critics of globalization point to policies that buttress the industrialized monetized sector of the economy, thereby favoring work performed by men at the expense of informal modes of work performed by women, particularly in the developing countries. According to this perspective, public subsidies that support social programs for women and children are diminished as nations struggle to pay off high interest loans to industrialized nations.

In Latin America, as a response to the weakening economic position of women, political collectivities of women have organized around the demand for greater provision of public services such as running water, electricity, transportation, day care and health services (all sorely lacking in squatter settlements in which poor women live). The women have also protested against the rising price of food. Often these women defend their right to a decent living on the basis of their status as "mothers," "housewives," or both. These types of social collectivities have been criticized by feminists who favor "equality" and "no special treatment" over supporting women in their traditional roles. Conversely, women activists engaged in informal social movements sometimes separate themselves, by way of identification, from woman activists who are more concerned with mainstream political participation and representation ("equality" and "no special treatment"). Since the period of advanced economic globalization, Latin American women have mobilized along with men in labor unions; yet, unions, it has been argued, continue to be regarded as a male sphere where women only serve as supplementary workers.

Other scholars believe there are positive effects to globalization such as women's political representation (in formal governmental institutions), the liberalization of traditional gender roles, and increased education. As a result of these positive effects, they argue, the political presence of women has increased dramatically in the beginning of the twenty-first century. For example, in January 2007 in Chile's presidential run-off Michelle

Bachelet was elected the first female president of Chile. Other Latin American women have made inroads into state power. The Brazilian constitution of 1988 formed The Council on the Condition of Women (subsequently named The National Council on Women's Rights), which implemented a family planning program; extended maternity leave; facilitated the establishment of a special police force to end sexual abuse and domestic violence; ended the prohibition of abortion; and successfully promoted a women's agenda.

The democratization and the rise of civil society often attributed to globalization further increased Latin American opposition groups. In 1988, Chilean women fought against President Augusto Pinochet's (1915–2006) military authoritarian rule and demanded the recognition of human rights. The Mothers of the Plaza del Mayo in Argentina played a decisive role in the defeat of the dictatorship there. On the basis of their status as mothers, sisters, daughters, The Mothers of the Plaza del Mayo protested the disappearance of their sons, brothers, and husbands.

The UN's Human Development Program has recognized the need for a broad understanding of gender that includes not only the role of politics, but economics and cultural interpretations of women's and men's roles on the lives of women throughout the world. Consequently, in 1995 they created the Gender Empowerment Measure, which measures gender equality/inequality on the basis of decision-making power, and political and economic participation.

SEE ALSO *Feminism; Feminism, Second Wave; Gender Gap; Inequality, Gender; Participation, Political; Poll Tax; Rape; Representation; Reproductive Rights;* Roe v. Wade; *Sexual Harassment; Sexuality; Suffrage, Women's; United Nations; Women; Women's Liberation; Women's Movement; Work and Women*

BIBLIOGRAPHY

Kahne, Hilda, and Janet Z. Giele, eds. 1992. *Women's Work and Women's Lives: The Continuing Struggle Worldwide.* Boulder, CO: Westview Press.

Nelson, Barbara J., and Najma Chowdury, eds. 1994. *Women and Politics Worldwide.* New Haven, CT: Yale University Press.

Sawer, Marion. 2002. The Representation of Women in Australia: Meaning and Make Believe. In *Women, Politics and Change,* ed. Karen Ross. New York: Oxford University Press.

Tinker, Irene. 1992. *Persistent Inequalities: World Development.* Chicago, IL: University of Chicago Press.

Women for Women's Human Rights. 2005. *Gender, Sexuality and the Criminal Laws in the Middle East and North Africa: A Comparative Study.* Istanbul, Turkey: Women for Women's Human Rights.

Vaso V. Thomas

WOMEN'S LIBERATION

The term *women's liberation* in twentieth-century discourse has been used interchangeably with feminism, women's rights, and the women's movement. A more precise focus on the term *women's liberation* raises the question, "Liberation from what?" The response that feminists have offered is liberation from the oppressive practices of patriarchy and women's second-class social status that have been a part of the structure of traditional and modern societies. The concept of women's liberation was popularized by the early stages of the Second Wave of the women's movement, by the United Nations' (UN) decade of focus on women (1975 to 1985), and more recently by UN-sponsored events like the 1995 Beijing Conference on Women. Because women constitute 50 percent of the world's population, the potential for coalitions across nations, ethnicities, ages, classes, religions, and sexualities is significant for all people. These UN events, which included governmental and nongovernmental agency representatives, have offered opportunities for international networking to supporters of the women's movement. The term *liberation* draws insights from Marxist and liberal democratic theories, which argue that societies work best when all adult persons are free and able to participate fully in public life. But what counts as women's liberation shifts over time.

HISTORIC OVERVIEW

Historically, the women's movement can be divided into three waves, which begin with the issue of suffrage. Setting the stage for the First Wave were some key political writings in Western societies that articulated the centrality of individuals in the state. These include the eighteenth-century work of Mary Wollstonecraft (1759–1797), *A Vindication of the Rights of Woman;* the nineteenth-century work of John Stuart Mill (1806–1873) with Harriet Taylor (1807–1858), *On the Subjugation of Women,* which compares women's situations to slavery; and the work of the German socialist Friedrich Engels (1820–1895), *Origins of the Family, Private Property, and the State,* shaped by his work with the political philosopher Karl Marx (1818–1883), which argues that women's oppression begins with the division of labor in the family.

The women's movement has developed in a variety of world cultures in complex ways, but an understanding of the Western tradition offers a context from which to examine some of the key issues. For those influenced by U.S. politics, the First Wave began with the Seneca Falls Convention in New York in 1848, when activists involved in the abolition of slavery met to talk about women. It ended in 1920 with a U.S. constitutional amendment that granted women the vote. The Second Wave began with

the civil rights struggles in 1962 and included a push for an equal rights amendment, workplace equity, educational opportunities, and policies that supported women's participation in public life. During this period women's studies programs were established as challenges were made to traditional discipline-based theories and epistemologies. In the early 1980s the New Right began to gain momentum just as feminist goals were shifting from legal rights to cultural issues and as multiculturalism was gaining greater recognition. These developments gave rise to the Third Wave of feminism in the 1990s, which has gained momentum since the beginning of the twenty-first century.

The Seneca Falls Convention was organized by Lucretia Mott (1793–1880) and Elizabeth Cady Stanton (1815–1902), with the abolitionist Frederick Douglas (1817–1895) and various Quakers in attendance. The issues in the First Wave were laid out at the convention in the Declaration of Sentiments, which called for women to have access to education, to their own salaries, to courts, to property, to child custody, to employment, to professions, and to the right to vote, which was the most controversial resolution. It would take from 1848 to 1920 for this last resolution to be achieved in the United States. The struggles for women's equality in European societies followed similar historical paths.

THE SECOND WAVE

The Second Wave of American feminism grew out of the civil rights movement of the 1960s and the New Left. During the early stages activists readily employed the term *women's liberation* as a way of explaining that the problem women faced as a group was similar to that of other oppressed groups. Second Wave consciousness-raising groups helped women move from seeing themselves as ineffective individuals in a fair society to identifying the structural patterns of sex bias that turned women as a group into second-class citizens. Women were in need of liberation from patriarchy and the cultural, legal, and political practices that flowed from patriarchy to subjugate them. As the civil rights movement progressed and the women's movement gained supporters, four key categories became the base for critical analysis: race, class, gender, and sexuality. The removal of their accompanying social ills—racism, class privilege, sexism, and heterosexism—would liberate societies from oppressive practices and unjust institutional structures. Feminists argued that women's liberation would result in the liberation of men because gender roles would be more open and individuals could assume them according to their talents and tastes instead of the shape of their bodies.

The Second Wave of feminism was supported by a variety of local and national political organizations that pressed for such rights as to continue work while pregnant and to have access to information about birth control, to abortion, to health care for pregnant women, and to legal protection from domestic violence, rape, sexual harassment, and economic discrimination. Concerns over women's health, reproductive choices, and body image came to the foreground as the issues of health and medical practices were scrutinized for sex or gender bias. Groups used lobbying, demonstrations, community-based organizations, and litigation and were loosely linked together through national-level organizations like the National Organization for Women (NOW), founded in 1966.

Betty Friedan (1921–2006), one of the NOW founders, raised a key question about women's liberation in her book *The Feminine Mystique*: "Who knows what women can be when they are finally free to become themselves?" (Friedan 1963, p. 378). Her critical review of women's roles as housewives helped citizens see how women were restricted in their ability to develop into full persons. Coalitions between the women's movement and the New Left, the anti–Vietnam War campaigns, the black liberation movement, and the ecological movement produced a variety of feminist theories and analyses, each of which explained liberation differently. Liberal feminism sought legal rights on a par with men's rights; socialist and Marxist feminism sought economic equity; radical feminism sought liberation and recognition for women-based theories, cultures, and sexualities; eco-feminism sought to explain how the subjugation of women is connected to the subjugation and abuse of nature; and postmodern feminism sought linguistic equities.

As the Second Wave of the women's movement progressed, pejorative nicknames like *women's libber* emerged as some social groups began to resist the changes. While there were feminists who wore the label *libber* or *radical* proudly, embracing the popular adage that "feminism is the radical notion that women are people," others found that the labels hindered other types of political work. Feminists fought against the stereotype of themselves as man haters and humorless. While women as a group were oppressed, many also belonged to privileged groups: whites, elites, developed nations, majority religions, and heterosexual dyads. Since the term *liberation* could be understood as liberation from men or from slavery, other terms were employed to discourage these misunderstandings. Instead of using the term *women's liberation*, many political activists and scholars refer to this concept with the terms *feminism* or *gender equity*.

Groups within the feminist movement who focused on rights put their energies into legislation, gaining political office, protests, and litigation. Others were concerned with cultural transformations and focused on reframing language, what counted as the canon in art and literature,

everyday life activities, the division of labor in the household, and images of women presented in schools and the media.

"The personal is political" was a phrase that articulated the ways all women could be involved in this process of change, and personal choices were seen as manifestations of political commitments. The genuineness of a political commitment was indicated in the details of how one lived one's life. Those who were vegetarian were expected not to wear leather shoes. Those who believed women were equal to men were expected to refer to adult females as "women," not as "girls." Hence a notion of political connection between individual actions and political beliefs was advocated, and this led to a form of "political correctness" in that one's personal behavior was to match one's ethical commitments. Progressive activists would point out such inconsistencies in each others' actions in order to discourage patriarchal practices. Such actions examined and corrected speech practices to alert citizens to inconsistencies between political commitments and personal utterances. Calling adult women "girls" or referring to women as "chicks" could elicit public criticism. The Second Wave established inclusive speech practices for both genders that are now accepted in the society as a whole.

Affirmative action programs were put in place to recruit women and minorities into schools and the workplace, and watchdog agencies were created to be sure that such policies were followed. Sexism and racism were scrutinized, and citizens became aware that they needed to be careful about engaging in these types of behaviors. Some of these programs and the scrutiny associated with them have diminished with the rise of the New Right and its critiques of affirmative action, abortion policies, and other limits on corporate interests. The New Right resurrected the term *political correctness* to suggest that feminists and their allies had unduly politicized issues that were best left to individuals or corporations to work out as they thought best. Drawing from the ways in which *politics* has been treated as a negative term, the new use of *political correctness* permitted a quick negative label for social practices (especially related to affirmative action, protections for equal political and economic access for women and ethnic minorities, and inclusive language practices) that the political right wanted to eliminate from social policy.

Because rights in the United States are focused on limits to government action, U.S. politics has focused on how states have prevented women's access to contraceptives and abortion as well as preventing corporations from discrimination in employment and educational opportunities on the basis of gender or sex. The New Right in the United States has developed an antiabortion component to their political agenda with a "pro-life" argument based on the protection of what they call the unborn. This position builds on the general interests of the New Right in gender politics. Antifeminists have attempted to reduce women's liberation to women's individual opportunity and even to "bra burning" by making the claim that Second Wave feminists burned bras. However, the occurrence of this event cannot be found by those who study the movement even though it was reported in the media. Reducing a movement to "bra burning" was probably a confusion with the anti–Vietnam War movement that burned draft cards, an illegal activity that did serve as civil disobedience. While burning draft cards is illegal, there is no such law against burning bras; discussions about bra burning are designed to trivialize women's liberation. The central issues of the Second Wave movement were equal access to education, employment opportunities, and health care.

Internationally, gender issues have included a struggle over women's identities as wife and mother with a primary location in the modern private sector as opposed to women's identities as political citizens with economic roles in modern societies that include but are not limited to their roles within the family. Because the world economy depends on women's economic contributions to the economies of nations, the limitation of women to the private sector of the home has disappeared as an economic factor even though the issue remains alive as an emotional factor in some political ideologies or religious interpretations. These issues were debated at the 1995 UN Conference on Women in Beijing, China, where representatives from major religions, the political right and left, and other sectors discussed what is required to liberate women.

In an international context, the key issues for feminists remain women's access to educational opportunities, including educational levels comparable to those offered to men, employment and pay opportunities that afford a living wage and are comparable to the pay men receive, and access to health care. In some nations women continue to struggle for equality with men in suing for divorce and custody of their children. Government policies vary on reproduction regulation, including abortion. In some nations abortion is limited to early stages or conditions that depend on the life of the mother. In others, such as China with its one-child policy, abortion can be encouraged and supported up to later stages of pregnancy. While some would reduce women's liberation to access to reproductive health technologies, women's liberation depends on access to general health care, education, and wages that will reduce women's poverty and the devastation that comes when women are unable to provide for themselves, their families, and their children.

As the political climate developed in the 1980s and 1990s, feminists no longer had to contend with the prob-

lems of invisibility or of not being taken seriously. Nonetheless, while they were taken seriously in the 1990s, they were targeted by the New Right as a source of social ills. Internationally, a New Right, neoconservative feminism emerged that emphasized the role of women as wives and mothers. In the United States these activists are often part of the "pro-life" movement that has opposed abortion and worked to counter the effects of *Roe v. Wade*. They have argued that women did not need and would not benefit from the individual protection that could be granted through social and political rights that are the same as those granted to men. At the same time, among Western feminists, tighter alliances were built with the gay and lesbian movements, so issues of sex and reproduction remained important in the struggle over what counts as women's liberation.

THE THIRD WAVE

In the 1990s postmodern analyses came to the foreground with a focus on the politics of language and culture and an emphasis on everyday political transformations as well as notions of difference. These shifts placed greater emphasis on culture and language as mechanisms for change at local levels. As the children of the Second Wave of feminism began to reach adulthood, they became activists with a new agenda that embraced the postmodern turn to language and cultural issues but also focused on mentoring, leadership, art, and new articulations of feminine and feminist identities. Rebecca Walker, the daughter of the Second Wave activist and novelist Alice Walker (b. 1944), is an example of a Third Wave activist. Building on Second Wave feminism, these activists and academics raise new questions such as that found in Leslie Heywood and Jennifer Drake's *Third Wave Agenda*: "Which personal? And whose politics? How to think 'sisterhood' in terms of difference and hybridity?" (Heywood and Drake 1997, p. 23). Examinations of multiple identities, complex articulations of feminine and feminist, coalition politics, and everyday practices became even more important than party affiliations and legal reforms. Retaining a loyalty to womanist perspectives and multicultural understandings, feminists continued to argue that each woman must gain the opportunity to tell her own story and speak for herself.

As academic feminism moved from the Second Wave feminists, who had drawn on empirical evidence to substantiate gender bias, to Third Wave academics, who drew more from postmodern theoretical frameworks, linguistic playfulness became a form of politics. Third Wave feminists have focused on reinventing women's identities, languages, and symbols while framing their own articulations of feminist politics. In this context *women's liberation* means the freedom to select the context for political change, the ability to frame the issues in response to both

contemporary and local contexts, and the means by which various surprising reversals, including linguistic turns, might liberate.

Women's liberation is a part of the women's movement, which includes access to education and political office; health care benefits, including reproductive health benefits; legal rights for women; employment access; protection from rape, domestic violence, and sexual harassment; access to professions and professional development; and protections from unwanted medical interventions and practices that put men in charge of women's lives. The democratization of nation-states depends on women's liberation because 50 percent of the population of a nation—women—cannot be denied equal participation and rights if a democracy is to emerge. Such denial undercuts democratization.

Women's liberation has come to mean liberation from patriarchal practices. However, the ways liberation might take place and what practices count as patriarchal are matters for political debate, and women, like men, differ in their assessment of their own needs. While there are similarities in women's situations, different contexts and values create different understandings of what women's liberation requires and how it might best be achieved. These differences offer important political insights for social justice and the development of strong democratic societies.

SEE ALSO *Affirmative Action; Civil Rights; Civil Rights Movement, U.S.; Feminism; Feminism, Second Wave; Gender; Gender Gap; Inequality, Gender; Left Wing; Liberation; Politics; Politics, Gender; Reproductive Politics; Reproductive Rights; Right Wing; Sexism; Social Movements; Vietnam War; Women and Politics; Women's Movement*

BIBLIOGRAPHY

Basu, Amrita, with C. Elizabeth McGrory, eds. 1995. *The Challenge of Local Feminisms: Women's Movements in Global Perspective*. Boulder, CO: Westview.

Friedan, Betty. 1963. *The Feminine Mystique*. New York: Norton.

Harding, Sandra G. 1991. *Whose Science? Whose Knowledge? Thinking from Women's Lives*. Ithaca, NY: Cornell University Press.

Heywood, Leslie, and Jennifer Drake, eds. 1997. *Third Wave Agenda: Being Feminist, Doing Feminism*. Minneapolis: University of Minnesota Press.

hooks, bell. 2000. *Feminism Is for Everybody: Passionate Politics*. Cambridge, MA: South End.

Jaggar, Alison M. 1983. *Feminist Politics and Human Nature*. Totowa, NJ: Rowman and Allanheld.

Meyers, Diana Tietjens, ed. 1997. *Feminist Social Thought: A Reader*. New York: Routledge.

Rossi, Alice S., 1973. *The Feminist Papers: From Adams to de Beauvoir.* New York: Columbia University Press.

Seager, Joni. 2003. *The Penguin Atlas of Women in the World.* 3rd ed. New York: Penguin Books.

Eloise A. Buker

WOMEN'S MOVEMENT

The women's movement has often been called one of the most important social movements of the twentieth century. Its most basic goals are to improve women's social, economic, and political conditions by facilitating personal transformations, introducing new ideas to public discourse, and exerting pressure on policymakers. In addition to voting, it has been a key form of women's political participation, joined only recently by greater numbers of women in political office. Beyond these basic features, however, there is considerable diversity among specific women's movements around the world.

First, not all types of political engagement by women would be considered a women's movement. As Karen Beckwith emphasizes, the term *women's movements* refers to any kind of systematic organizing by women, including that of a nonfeminist nature (Beckwith 2000). Women's movements are thus distinct from *women in social movements*, who are female participants in social movements that may or may not focus on gender issues. They are also a broader phenomenon that includes but is not equivalent to *feminist movements*, which engage women—and some men—through a more explicitly gendered lens that seeks to understand and overcome women's subordination.

Second, women's movements themselves vary enormously across countries and over time. They appear during different waves of feminism, originate in various kinds of other social movements, espouse a range of different issues of concern, and interact in numerous ways with global and regional trends. In addition, they are situated within a variety of social, economic, and political contexts that shape their emergence, development, and prospects for success. As such, many analysts are skeptical of universalizing claims about women's mobilization. When studying "the women's movement," therefore, they seek to understand the diverse conditions under which women organize as women—rather than with men—to achieve social, economic, and political change.

WAVES OF FEMINISM

Although women's movements are not synonymous with feminist movements, the two frequently overlap. As a result, one common starting point for analyzing women's movements is to position them in relation to waves of feminism. Due to important differences in context, the timing and character of these waves vary significantly across countries. In the western world, the "first wave" is generally associated with the mobilization of women's groups across many countries in the late nineteenth and early twentieth centuries. The main focus of these movements was to attain basic rights for women, including the right to vote, the right to employment, the right to receive equal pay, and the right to retain their own nationality upon marriage to men of other nationalities. Focused on equality, these campaigns largely sought to gain rights for women that were already guaranteed to men. However, in many cases these movements overlooked crucial issues of race and class, devoting most of their attention to rights for white and upper-class women.

The "second wave" of feminism, often dated in the West to the 1960s and 1970s, embraced a much wider range of theories and issues. Initially inspired by the need to dispel the "feminine mystique," or the idea that women found their life's fulfillment in being married and raising children, second-wave groups began to question women's roles in the private sphere and to point to the social construction of gender roles. Drawing on ideas introduced by writers such as Simone de Beauvoir, they made a distinction between the terms *sex* and *gender*, using *sex* to refer to biological differences between male and female and *gender* to denote social differences between masculine and feminine. Although sex and gender were related, second-wave feminists emphasized that the relationship was imperfect, as men could be feminine and women could be masculine. Women's groups developed these ideas in a number of different directions: Some stressed the universality of women's oppression, some sought to revalue the "feminine," and still others aimed to break down the distinction between the public and the private through slogans such as "the personal is political." Despite this diversity, the shared feature of all these efforts was to focus on women as women, rather than as individuals who aspired to a male standard.

The feminist project of defining the terms *women* and *women's issues*, however, was not without controversy. On the one hand, activists disagreed as to the coherence of "women" as a group. Many called attention to race- and class-based exclusions that were implicit in discourse on "universal" female oppression that in fact reflected the experiences of women from dominant racial and class groups. Others noted that accounts of the sexual division of labor, and especially women's experiences as mothers, tended to assume that all women were heterosexual, thus overlooking—and marginalizing—the experiences of lesbians. On the other hand, feminists prioritized a wide range of women's issues that implied distinct—and even conflicting—visions of the status quo and prescriptions

for change. Whereas some aimed to undermine patriarchy by promoting women's status in the public sphere, others sought to foster a "women's culture" by revaluing women's labor inside the home, raise awareness of women's experiences through consciousness-raising, and theorize patriarchy by pointing to the power that men exercised over women through violence and coercion.

The "third wave" is a more contested concept, existing in an uneasy relation to the term *postfeminism*. Both notions are generally taken to refer to ideas that emerged in the West in the 1990s and continue to develop through the present day. This wave is largely characterized by a focus on difference, both between women and men and among women themselves. At the same time, it aims to break down binary categories by emphasizing the fluid and relational aspects of identity and experience. As such, it questions traditional approaches to conceptualizing sex and gender by exploring intersections between race, class, and gender; uncovering the assumptions of heterosexuality that underpin analysis of women in relation to men; and probing the possibility that gender may cause sex rather than sex causing gender. In this sense, the third wave incorporates a number of ideas articulated by feminists of color, lesbian feminists, and postmodern feminists. However, because these theories stress the contradictions and multiplicities inherent in definitions of women and women's issues, they have paradoxical effects on women's movements: They help build coalitions with other movements for social justice, but also undermine the prospects for mobilizing by women as women for social, economic, and political change.

ORIGINS OF WOMEN'S MOVEMENTS

Many scholars draw on the wave analogy to identify major shifts in feminist theorizing and their relation to concentrated periods of mobilization by women's groups. This approach has its critics, however, who point out that women are active politically between waves and are not always inspired initially by feminist concerns. Indeed, despite the widespread belief that women's movements emerge in cycles as women become more educated and politically informed, evidence from around the world suggests that women's movements often have their origins in various other kinds of social movements. In these cases, women gain a shared sense of gender oppression through discrimination they experience in the course of their participation in other campaigns for social justice. These include movements for civil rights, revolution, nationalism, independence, and human rights. Similar consciousness-raising also occurs in authoritarian regimes, where the creation of state-led women's organizations aims to control women's political activity but sometimes provides

an official platform for women's organizing. Many women's movements nonetheless hesitate to label themselves "feminist" on the grounds that the term has various negative associations as "bourgeois," "Western," "forced emancipation," and even "man-hating." Further, few movements succeed at incorporating all women due to differences among women that remain important, including nationality, race, class, religion, region, language, and sexual orientation.

ISSUES OF WOMEN'S MOVEMENTS

Given their distinct origins and relations to waves of feminism, women's movements around the world focus variously on a wide range of issues. These concerns fall into six broad categories: women's legal rights, violence against women, reproductive choice, sexual freedom, employment opportunities and discrimination, and women's political participation and representation. Legal rights include such issues as rights in marriage, the right to divorce, and the right to own and inherit property. Violence against women refers to practices such as rape, domestic abuse, female genital cutting, sexual slavery, and sex trafficking. Reproductive choice encompasses access to contraception, the right to abortion, and the right to not be subjected to forced sterilization. Sexual freedom involves the right to express one's own sexuality and claims for the same privileges conferred on heterosexual couples. Employment opportunities and discrimination include rights to equal pay, access to all jobs, provision of maternity leave, and freedom from sexual harassment. Women's political participation and representation, finally, comprise the rights to vote, join political parties, participate in civil society, and run for political office. Individual movements rarely cover all these issues, and specific movements address particular issues in a variety of different ways. In addition, some groups mobilize to preserve rather than undermine women's traditional status as mothers and inside the home.

GLOBAL AND REGIONAL WOMEN'S MOVEMENTS

Despite their emergence and development in specific contexts around the world, women's movements inform and reflect broader global and regional trends. Women's organizing has always had an international dimension, reaching back more than 100 years to the early suffrage campaigns and activism for world peace. In the last thirty years, however, women's movement activism has grown exponentially in relation to developments beyond national borders. At the global level, international conferences have placed new issues on national political agendas and facilitated networking among women's groups around the world, even as they have been marked in some

instances by sharp conflicts among women in developed and developing nations. At the regional level, transnational organizing has become increasingly important as a means for spreading new ideas across national borders, fostering policy diffusion and solidarity among politically marginalized groups. Despite their long history, women's movements are thus constantly being reborn, reinventing themselves, and taking on new forms in order to politicize women's concerns, however these are identified and defined.

SEE ALSO *Abortion Rights; Equality; Family Planning; Femininity; Feminism; Feminism, Second Wave; Gender Gap; Inequality, Gender; Interest Groups and Interests; Masculinity; Politics; Politics, Black; Politics, Gender; Politics, Gay, Lesbian, Transgender, and Bisexual; Reproductive Rights; Social Movements; Stepford Wives; Suffrage, Women's; Women and Politics; Women's Liberation*

BIBLIOGRAPHY

Alvarez, Sonia. 2000. Translating the Global: Effects of Transnational Organizing on Local Feminist Discourses and Practices. *Meridians: Feminism, Race, Transnationalism* 1 (1): 29–67.

Basu, Amrita. 1995. *The Challenge of Local Feminisms: Women's Movements in Global Perspective.* Boulder, CO: Westview Press.

Beauvoir, Simone de. 1952. *The Second Sex.* New York: Alfred A. Knopf.

Beckwith, Karen. 2000. Beyond Compare? Women's Movements in Comparative Perspective. *European Journal of Political Research* 37 (4): 431–468.

Friedan, Betty. 1963. *The Feminine Mystique.* New York: Dell Publishing.

Rich, Adrienne. 1977. *Of Woman Born: Motherhood as Experience and Institution.* New York: Virago.

Mona Lena Krook

WOMEN'S RIGHTS MOVEMENT

SEE *Women's Movement.*

WOMEN'S STUDIES

Women's studies is an interdisciplinary academic field that concentrates on the experiences and aspirations of women. Although women's studies departments and programs in the United States and around the world are reflective of their locations within educational institutions and their larger social context, a common thread is the claim that women's experiences have been underrepresented or misrepresented in more traditional academic disciplines that claim to capture the human experience. This has been found by some critics to be the case in traditional disciplines that purport to speak about human nature but consider only the social location of men or take men as the universal subject, casting women as either substitute or inferior men.

WOMEN'S STUDIES AS CRITIQUE AND CORRECTIVE

Arguing that women are human too and that the academic is also political, women's studies is founded on critical terrain, offering critiques of traditional disciplines and correctives to their representations or exclusions of women. Thus, a women's studies program may offer courses in education, literature, history, political science, philosophy, psychology, ethnic studies, biology, medicine, religious studies, and international relations, among other fields, centralizing women and the theoretical frameworks of feminism within each of those fields. Further, the misrepresentation of women's experiences in academic disciplines is thought by some to reflect a generalized societal devaluation of women's experience and social roles and thus to be part of the oppression of women. In this way the purpose of women's studies is shaped by its relationship with women's movements inside and outside the academy. The field has developed around the idea that the personal is political, meaning that gender identity and the subjectivities of individuals are shaped through the political structures of a gendered social system.

In these ways the field of women's studies is a critique and a corrective as well as a self-reflexive and politically engaged discipline that functions with a commitment to social transformation within education and the wider society in which it exists. Since their inception women's studies programs have operated from the often contradictory position of educating for social change and existing within traditional academic institutions that tend to favor neutral and disinterested knowledge production.

EARLY COURSES AND PROGRAMS

The first women's studies courses were offered in the United States in 1965 at the New Orleans Free School, the University of Chicago, Barnard College, Spelman College, and the Free University of Seattle. The earliest women's studies program was established in 1970 at San Diego State University, and the Women's Resource and Research Center was established at Spelman in 1981. Influenced by the civil rights, women's, and New Left movements and the inception of African American,

American, and ethnic studies, early women's studies courses were guided by a vision of a world free from sexism, racism, class bias, ageism, and heterosexual bias.

The scope of the field has expanded continuously, increasing from 150 women's studies programs in the United States in the period 1970–1975 and three cross-disciplinary journals in 1972 to the growing number of courses, programs, departments, academic conferences, and journals of the first decade of the twenty-first century. In 2006 there were over seven hundred degree-granting women's studies departments in the United States with approximately seventeen doctoral programs, including the Africana Women's Studies program at Clark Atlanta, the Graduate Certificate Program at Howard University, and the earliest doctoral program at Emory University; more than two hundred fifty women's departments in sixty countries worldwide, with approximately twenty-five doctoral programs; and over forty scholarly journals and dozens of annual national and international conferences. The U.S. National Women's Studies Association (NWSA) was founded in 1977, and Women's Worlds: International Interdisciplinary Congress on Women was founded in 1981 with conferences held since that time in locations ranging from Haifa, Israel, to Seoul, South Korea.

METHODOLOGY AND STRATEGIES

The primary methodological approach of women's studies is derived from feminist analysis, a complex field of study that questions the foundations of traditional male-centered knowledge. Feminists have interrogated the masculine—also known as the patriarchal, androcentric, and phallocentric—biases and exclusions of prevailing social relations, institutions, and political structures to understand why women consistently experience gender-based oppressions that are manifested differently in accordance with the context. From home, to schools, to the workplace, to neighborhood streets, to war zones feminists have demonstrated the ways in which women, by virtue of being female, are barred disproportionately and systemically from the privileges enjoyed by men. At the same time feminist analysis documents women's political agency and resistance to oppressive circumstances. This has been particularly true of black feminist traditions.

To rectify structurally derived inequalities between men and women, one set of approaches feminists have offered consists of strategies to oppose existing masculine structures. Feminist oppositional solutions have taken a number of forms, from proposing equity in the workplace, government, and home to more profoundly transformative solutions of challenging masculinist epistemologies with feminist ways of knowing. Whereas man has dominated the social and human sciences, feminists

have proposed woman as a replacement, a supplement, or the basis for structural transformation.

A number of concerns about the transformative potential of feminist oppositional strategies have been articulated within feminist debates. Proposing woman as an oppositional category immediately raises the question of whether gender is the primary identification of all women everywhere, casting doubt on the core of much of feminist politics. Racialized women, lesbians, disabled women, working-class and poor women, and women outside North America and Western Europe have been the most insistent voices against homogenizing women into hegemonic categories, thus contributing to the plurality of feminist analyses.

The long tradition of black feminist thought, for instance, has reconceptualized feminism by demanding attention to race, to diaspora communities, and to the construction of womanhood outside the United States. Debates about difference, or multipositionality, within women's studies programs continue, revolving around the ways in which race, class, nation, ability, age, and other social locations modify gender. Not only was the notion of woman challenged, the entire notion of a core focus or single identity was challenged by debates that demanded intersectional, plural, and culturally attentive approaches to feminism that are simultaneously antisexist and antiracist. For women's studies programs that primarily have focused on the experiences of white women the challenge is to integrate a racial analysis; for programs within historically black colleges and universities the challenge is to integrate a gender analysis into already established racial analyses.

DEBATES WITHIN WOMEN'S STUDIES

Starting from their initial questioning of man as the legitimate grounds of knowing, feminism and women's studies debate the proper subjects and objects of the field. In this sense feminist and women's studies debates are both reflective of and a challenge to broader debates within the social sciences about conventional criteria of knowledge production, disciplinary configurations of relevance, verifiability and falsifiability, the separation of subject from object, and the criteria of objectivity and universality as necessary features of legitimate knowledge production. With the "crisis of reason" comes the instability of feminist claims to know, and feminism is both oppositional to and implicated in conventional epistemological discourses. In fact, the very immersion of feminism in patriarchal practices is seen a factor in the critical effectiveness of feminism and thus the transformative potential of the field of women's studies.

These debates manifest themselves in a variety of ways in women's studies programs. Pedagogically, the field of women's studies has attempted to create inclusive, non-hierarchical, and open learning environments that do not privilege hegemonic voices or experiences. In this regard peer facilitation, experiential knowledge, and self-reflection are emphasized in many women's studies programs. Epistemologically, women's studies programs offer feminist theory and methodology courses in interdisciplinary and politically engaged knowledge production. This means that women's studies programs provide courses that centralize women's experiences as well as methods of reading the social through feminist theory. Normatively, women's studies courses tend to highlight the value biases of feminist theory and demonstrate the hidden values of knowledge that is said to be neutral and disinterested. Institutionally, women's studies programs are often in an uneasy alliance with academia, on the one hand attempting to offer transformative curricula and on the other hand finding it necessary to offer courses and programs that are recognizably legitimate in comparison with other liberal arts degree programs. Additionally, women's studies departments often seek models of departmental governance that maintain some of the ideals of feminist organizing while operating within the larger institutional framework. Finally, the field of women's studies continues to nurture its relationship with women's movements and community activism beyond the academy.

Beyond women's studies programs and departments, feminist analysis has found its way into many traditional disciplines and departmental appointments. In light of the mainstreaming of feminist analysis, the question arises whether women's studies as an autonomous field has outlived its utility in the academy. At the same time there are qualitative differences between working as a feminist scholar within a discipline that does not centralize the project of academic and social transformation and working within an interdisciplinary women's studies department that is intended to transform the entire educational experience from the classroom to departmental governance.

As women's studies programs have increased their legitimacy within the academy, acquired departmental status, increased their number of tenure-track appointments, and developed doctoral programs, the negotiations about remaining transformational and autonomous have continued. In that context the field of women's studies is dynamic, worldly, and continuously engaged with the central epistemological and normative debates that animate much of the social sciences.

SEE ALSO *Gender; Gender Gap; Gender Studies; Women; Women and Politics; Women's Liberation; Work and Women*

BIBLIOGRAPHY

Boxer, Marilyn J. 1982. For and about Women: The Theory and Practice of Women's Studies in the United States. *Signs* 7 (3): 661–695.

Brown, Wendy. 1997. The Impossibility of Women's Studies. *Differences: A Journal of Feminist Cultural Studies* 9 (3): 43–64.

Carby, Hazel. 1982. White Woman Listen! Black Feminism and the Boundaries of Sisterhood. In *The Empire Strikes Back: Race and Racism in 70s Britain*, ed. Centre for Contemporary Cultural Studies. London: Hutchinson.

Cruikshank, Margaret, ed. 1982. *Lesbian Studies: Present and Future.* Old Westbury, NY: Feminist Press.

Grosz, Elizabeth. 1993. Bodies and Knowledge: Feminism and the Crisis of Reason. In *Feminist Epistemologies*, eds. Linda Alcoff and Elizabeth Potter. New York: Routledge.

Guy-Sheftall, Beverly, with Evelyn Hammonds. 1997. Whither Black Women's Studies. *Differences: A Journal of Feminist Cultural Studies* 9 (3): 31-45.

hooks, bell. 1981. *Ain't I a Woman: Black Women and Feminism.* Boston: South End Press.

Hull, Gloria T., Patricia Bell Scott, and Barbara Smith, eds. 1982. *All the Women Are White, All the Blacks Are Men, but Some of Us Are Brave: Black Women's Studies.* Old Westbury, NY: Feminist Press.

Lowe, Marian, and Margaret Lowe Benston. 1991. The Uneasy Alliance of Feminism and Academia. In *A Reader in Feminist Knowledge*, ed. Sneja Gunew, 48–60. New York: Routledge.

Mohanty, Chandra T., Anne Russo, and Lourdes Torres, eds. 1991. *Third World Women and the Politics of Feminism.* Bloomington: Indiana University Press.

Parmar, Ratibha, and Valerie Amos. 1984. Challenging Imperial Feminism. *Feminist Review* 17: 3–19.

Riviere, Rebecca, and Anita Nahal. 2005. Finding Our Place: Women's Studies at Howard University. *NWSA Journal* 17 (2): 150–155.

Sheridan, Susan. 1991. From Margin to Mainstream: Situating Women's Studies. In *A Reader in Feminist Knowledge*, ed. Sneja Gunew, 61–72. New York: Routledge.

Wiegman, Robyn, ed. 2002. *Women's Studies on Its Own: A Next Wave Reader in Institutional Change.* Durham, NC: Duke University Press.

Liz Philipose

WOODSTOCK

Although the Woodstock Music and Arts Festival is a celebrated symbol of the "hippie" counterculture, it did not initiate the counterculture, nor did it mark its end. Nevertheless, Woodstock is a useful reference point for discussions of this significant social phenomenon. By 1969, the "hippie" movement had emerged as a group of primarily young people, who not only were opposed to

the Vietnam War but also wore distinctive and colorful clothing, engaged in illegal drug use, and enjoyed rock and roll music.

In early 1969, business associates John Roberts and Joel Rosenman met record executive Artie Kornfield and festival promoter Michael Lang, and the four decided to produce the largest music festival to date. Although not fully immersed in the counterculture, they sought to produce a festival that would appeal to that group. To promote the festival they formed Woodstock Ventures, named after the town in Ulster County, New York, where Bob Dylan lived. Woodstock Ventures advertised the festival in the alternative and college media, hired a crew to assist with production, and booked the most significant bands of that era. Their most difficult concern was finding a site to hold a large, three-day music and art festival, which would also allow attendees to camp. Woodstock Ventures eventually found a site in Sullivan County, New York. They leased land from a local dairy farmer named Max Yasgur. Although Sullivan County residents expressed trepidation about the concert and especially the influx of "hippies," Yasgur resisted this pressure and allowed the festival to occur.

Woodstock started on Friday, August 15, 1969, and on that day, approximately 400,000 (some estimated closer to one million) people, many without tickets, arrived at the festival gate. Fans waited hours in line, and when they entered, it was clear that they were not prepared for three days of camping. To make matters worse, it had rained considerably during the weekend, soaking the festival grounds. The promoters also did not adequately prepare for the throngs of attendees, and eventually they agreed to waive admissions fees.

Woodstock is the quintessential symbol for the "hippie" counterculture. Illegal drug use was extensive and open. While most of the fans maintained control, a small percentage of them overindulged, though there was also a "freak-out tent" to calm them down. Woodstock included a self-contained market, in which fans sold food, artwork, jewelry, and clothing to one another. The artists, promoters, and fans were more concerned about music and art than about politics, but the undercurrent of progressive activism was inescapable. The musicians and fans expressed support for social justice and intense opposition to the Vietnam War.

Woodstock attracted considerable media attention, which brought the "hippie" counterculture into the mainstream, and, as a result, the festival became part of the American cultural imagination. Although the festival was only one of many crucial events during a time of social and cultural upheaval, intellectuals, the press, popular entertainment, and the advertising industry have made Woodstock into the symbol of the cultural and political ideals of the late 1960s. Supporters of the social changes brought about by the 1960s cite the ability of the festival to overcome tremendous obstacles as an example of the success of the "hippie" subculture and progressive politics. Conversely, opponents of these changes deride Woodstock as an example of the chaos and lawlessness the 1960s wrought on American society.

Although in the early 1970s many experts predicted the end of the "hippie" movement, the spirit of Woodstock has not disappeared from the American cultural scene. Throughout the 1970s, 1980s, and early 1990s, the Grateful Dead, which had been at the forefront of the "hippie" movement and performed at Woodstock, played thousands of shows throughout the United States. A new generation of fans, known as *Deadheads*, many of whom were not born when Woodstock occurred, followed the band to different cities. Like Woodstock, Grateful Dead concerts featured illegal drug use, expression of progressive views, and vibrant economic activity. This subculture was so significant that University of North Carolina, Greensboro, sociologist Rebecca Adams set out to study Deadheads by attending shows and conducting field research on the fans (Adams 1998). During the 1990s a second generation of musicians and fans maintained the Woodstock spirit. So-called *jam bands*, such as Phish, have developed their own followings, especially after the 1995 death of Grateful Dead band-leader and "hippie" icon Jerry Garcia. Since 2002, the Bonnaroo Music and Arts Festival has occurred every June in Manchester, Tennessee. Although this festival only attracts 90,000 to 100,000 people and is generally well organized, it is strikingly similar to Woodstock. An eclectic selection of bands entertains fans; there is widespread and open illegal drug use; progressive political views abound; and people sell food, art, and clothing.

SEE ALSO *Popular Music; Rock 'n' Roll; Youth Culture*

BIBLIOGRAPHY

Adams, Rebecca G. 1998. Inciting Sociological Thought by Studying the Deadhead Community: Engaging Publics in Dialogue. *Social Forces* 77 (1): 1–25.

Makower, Joel. 1989. *Woodstock: The Oral History*. New York: Doubleday.

Steven Tauber

WORK

It may seem that everyone knows what *work* means—most people have engaged in activities that they call *work*, and they know that institutions and social structures are

sustained through the work of large numbers of individuals in society. Yet, a closer examination reveals that the concept of work has a long and contested history. Peter David Anthony, for example, characterizes work as anything that gives people "moral responsibility" and "spiritual significance." He writes that "if life has any meaning, work has meaning because life is work" (1980, p. 419). Along the same lines, Sean Sayers notes that "the experience of being without a job is profoundly demoralizing and unfulfilling" (1988, p. 731). In contrast, Herbert Applebaum argues that "work in the modern world is purely instrumental. It is a mere means to gain a living, not an activity of value in itself, not a means of self-expression" (1992, p. 573). Paul Thompson (1983) characterizes work as a loss of autonomy and an experience of being confined by the scheduling and disciplining of others. As Nona Glazer summarizes, work is "a problematic concept" (1993, p. 33).

Common to the various debates on the meaning of *work*, however, is the recognition that in the contemporary social and economic system, work has an economic and moral function. As Arlene Kaplan Daniels notes, in modern industrialized society, "the most common understanding of the essential characteristic of work is that it is something for which we get paid" (1987, p. 403). In addition, the recognition of an activity as work gives it a "moral force and dignity": "To work and earn money is also to gain status as an adult" (p. 404).

Many of the ways in which we think about work in relation to pay and value have been influenced by the writings of Karl Marx (1818–1883). Marx noted that the process of exchange makes all the different types of labor homogeneous; this homogeneous labor, which produces commodities, is called *abstract labor*. Value is measured in terms of abstract labor, which in turn is measured in terms of the time necessary to produce a commodity vis-à-vis another commodity (Bottomore 1991a, p. 565). In this way, Marx described value as "not something intrinsic to a single commodity apart from its exchange from another" (Bottomore 1991a, p. 566). Marx constructs value as a *social relation* rather than a description of a thing (Rubin 1972, p. 70). Under capitalism, labor—or work—itself becomes a commodity that is bought and sold. One of the central ways that we organize our understanding of work is in terms of the jobs people do. Jobs are classified into sectors, such as agricultural, industrial, manufacturing, managerial, and service, according to the main activities involved. Around the world, jobs are deeply stratified by gender. For example, women tend to predominate in agricultural employment in Asia, sub-Saharan Africa, the Middle East, and North Africa. Women in most parts of the world hold many of the jobs in the service sector, such as community, social, and personal services, whereas men dominate in the business and financial sectors (Elder and Schmidt 2004).

Not all labor, or work, is valued equivalently. Work done by engineers, financiers, and managers is well paid, while the service jobs in which many women, people of color, and recent migrants are employed are precarious and poorly paid. According to the International Labour Organization (ILO), 1.39 billion people (almost 50 percent of the world's workers) do paid work but earn less than two dollars per day. These people form the *working poor*, who are employed yet simultaneously live below the poverty line (ILO 2004).

Many scholars have focused their analyses on how work is deeply stratified in terms of gender. Peta Tancred notes that it is often assumed that "women are born with certain 'natural' skills which require neither talent nor training, and which are merely part of their 'natural,' 'feminine' behaviour" (1995, p. 17). Jane Aronson and Sheila Neysmith document the experiences of home-care workers who do work that is similar to that which would otherwise have been assumed by female relatives. Although home-care workers are paid, their work is accorded little status and assumed to require little skill (Aronson and Neysmith 1996, p. 61).

Feminist theorists also provide vivid illustrations of the ways in which individuals are expected to re-create particular versions of masculinity and femininity as part of their jobs. Lisa Adkins, for example, discusses the jobs of catering assistants within a leisure park, where women are required to have the "right" appearance to be employed. This "right" appearance includes being "attractive and looking fresh" and not looking "weird" or "too butchy" (Adkins 1995, pp. 105–106). Adkins's study provides an illustration of the ways in which occupations are segregated not only by sex (i.e., biological femaleness or maleness) but more importantly by gender (i.e., appropriate manifestations of masculinity and femininity).

Jobs, and the organizations within which they are situated, do not just require individuals to conform to stereotypical notions of femininity and masculinity. As Jennifer Pierce notes, gendered structures shape "workers' practices at the same time that … workers participate— wittingly or not—in the reproduction of gender relations" (1995, pp. 2–3). Gender is a continual process, being actively created and resisted within organizational structures. The ways in which women and men both reproduce and re-create a variety of gender norms through their jobs is illuminated in Elaine Hall's analysis of interactions between table servers and customers. Hall demonstrates the ways in which expectations of behavior conforming to stereotypical notions of masculinity and femininity are not universally held, but rather are contextually developed. For example, both female and male table servers

think that the public expects waitresses to be more friendly than waiters and "cross-sex interactions to be more friendly than same-sex interactions" (Hall 1993, p. 460). Female customers, however, are seen only by the waiters, and not by waitresses, to be friendly. Friendliness is, in this case, not a component of femininity across contexts, but rather a gendered process developed within the particular work role assigned to waitresses (termed by Hall a *service script*) (1993, p. 461).

In addition to the gendered nature of work, only certain activities are labeled as *work* in the first place, depending on the social context. An activity such as sewing a shirt can be paid work, unpaid work, or leisure, depending on the context. This raises the questions of how certain activities get labeled as *work* and how some are deemed worthy of remuneration. Feminist theorists have noted that the strong economic orientation in conventional understandings of work fails to recognize much of the "work" that women do in our societies. Domestic chores and childcare are seldom recognized as work, even though they require more effort, commitment, and skill than many paid jobs. In fact, a lot of work is difficult to classify in terms of payment. Marjorie DeVault (1991) describes the work that goes into feeding a family, which involves not only cooking but also planning, provisioning, and being attentive to family members' nutritional needs and individual tastes. Many of these activities are not only unpaid, they *cannot* be paid for. For example, if one were to make a detailed list of the activities that are involved in finding a place to live in a new city, one would find that many of the activities (such as figuring out where like-minded people live; balancing such factors as the size, brightness, and proximity of the apartment; and reconciling the needs of various family members) cannot be done by others, even for pay. These activities require *emotion work* (Daniels 1987).

As Deanne Messias and colleagues argue, "attempts to define work in terms of economic activity are met with the problems of having to determine where noneconomic housework ends and economic activity begins" (1997, p. 307). Given that women more often than men assume primary responsibility for family work (Pierce 1995) and that women are significantly more likely to be employed in jobs requiring emotion work (Wharton 1993), much of women's work is not only unpaid, but also cannot be paid for. Writers have called these tasks *tailoring work* and note that it is such invisible work that sustains many of our social structures. Daniels, for example, argues that "the normative expectation in every industrialized society is that women will coordinate public and purchased services with the private requirements of their families [and] … this tailoring is … part of the invisible work in social life" (1987, p. 405). Glazer provides illustrations of the tailoring work that women do through her analysis of the growth of self-service and self-care in the American retail

and health-care industries. Self-service in shopping, for example, translates into considerable work for the customer. This work, done by women, involves gaining knowledge about goods, locating and evaluating items, and transporting goods to the home. The tailoring work involved in shopping is constructed as leisure (Glazer 1993, pp. 49–102). In a similar way, cost-cutting measures in health care involve a "work transfer" where women learn and do high-technology health care at home, which includes providing food, changing linen, bathing, toileting, keeping detailed records, and administering medication. This care is treated as "routine housekeeping" rather than being recognized as skilled work integral to the U.S. health-care system (Glazer 1993, p. 179).

The discussion above illustrates the political nature of the concept of *work* and the ways in which different definitions of work signify gender, race, and class hierarchies within society. It can be seen that only certain activities are labeled as *work*, depending on the social context. William Ronco and Lisa Peattie, for example, ask what distinguishes *work* from a *hobby* and reveal the fuzziness of these categories. They conclude that "the distinction between 'work' and 'hobby' is thus not inherent in the activity; it lies in the social context in which the activity is carried out" (1983, pp. 13–18). The consequence of the social labeling of only certain activities as *work* is that these activities hold higher financial and normative status in contemporary society. Given the importance of unpaid, family, and emotion work, conventional definitions of work need to be constantly challenged.

SEE ALSO *Clock Time; Work and Women; Work Day*

BIBLIOGRAPHY

Adkins, Lisa. 1995. *Gendered Work: Sexuality, Family, and the Labor Market.* Buckingham, U.K.: Open University Press.

Anthony, P. D. 1980. Work and the Loss of Meaning. *International Social Science Journal* 32 (3): 416–426.

Applebaum, Herbert. 1992. *The Concept of Work: Ancient, Medieval, and Modern.* Albany: State University of New York Press.

Aronson, Jane, and Sheila M. Neysmith. 1996. You're Not Just in There to Do the Work: Depersonalizing Policies and the Exploitation of Home Care Workers' Labor. *Gender and Society* 10: 56–77.

Bottomore, Tom. 1991a. Labour Power. In *The Dictionary of Marxist Thought*, ed. Tom Bottomore, 565–571. 2nd ed. Oxford: Blackwell.

Bottomore, Tom. 1991b. Value. In *The Dictionary of Marxist Thought*, ed. Tom Bottomore, 296–301. 2nd ed. Oxford: Blackwell.

Daniels, Arlene Kaplan. 1987. Invisible Work. *Social Problems* 34: 403–415.

DeVault, Marjorie L. 1991. *Feeding the Family: The Social Organization of Caring as Gendered Work*. Chicago: University of Chicago Press.

Elder, Sara, and Dorothea Schmidt. 2004. *Global Employment Trends for Women*. Employment Strategy Paper 8. Employment Trends Unit. Geneva: International Labour Organization.

Glazer, Nona Y. 1993. *Women's Paid and Unpaid Labor: The Work Transfer in Health Care and Retailing*. Philadelphia: Temple University Press.

Hall, Elaine J. 1993. Smiling, Deferring, and Flirting: Doing Gender by Giving Good Service. *Work and Occupations* 20 (4): 453–466.

International Labour Organization (ILO). 2004. *World Employment Report 2004–05: Employment, Productivity and Poverty Reduction*. Geneva: ILO. http://www.ilo.org/public/english/employment/strat/wer2004.htm.

Messias, Deanne K. H., Eun-Ok Im, Aroha Page, et al. 1997. Defining and Redefining Work: Implications for Women's Health. *Gender and Society* 11 (3): 296–323.

Pierce, Jennifer. 1995. *Gender Trials: Emotional Lives in Contemporary Law Firms*. Berkeley: University of California Press.

Ronco, William, and Lisa Peattie. 1983. *Making Work: Self-Created Jobs in Participatory Organizations*. New York: Plenum Press.

Ronco, William, and Lisa Peattie. 1988. Making Work: A Perspective from the Social Sciences. In *On Work: Historical, Comparative, and Theoretical Approaches*, ed. R. E. Pahl, 709–721. New York: Blackwell.

Rubin, Isaak I. 1972. Basic Characteristics of Marx's Theory of Value. In *Essays on Marx's Theory of Value*, 63–75. Trans. Miloš Samardžija and Fredy Perlman. Detroit, MI: Black and Red.

Sayers, Sean. 1988. *The Need to Work: A Perspective from Philosophy on Work: Historical, Comparative, and Theoretical Approaches*, ed. R. E. Pahl, 709–721. New York: Blackwell.

Tancred, Peta. 1995. Women's Work: A Challenge to the Sociology of Work. *Gender, Work, and Organization* 2 (1): 11–20.

Thompson, Paul. 1983. *The Nature of Work: An Introduction to Debates on the Labour Process*. London: McMillan.

Wharton, Amy. 1993. The Affective Consequences of Service Work: Managing Emotions on the Job. *Work and Occupations* 20: 205–232.

Kiran Mirchandani

WORK AND WOMEN

The term *work*, generally implying some sort of activity or achievements, acquired specific connotations due to the development of capitalist productive relations (Williams 1976), particularly since the Industrial Revolution in the late eighteenth and early nineteenth centuries in Britain. Under capitalism it is the payment of wages that makes clear the distinction between work and nonwork. The notion of work came to be associated with some sort of paid employment, so that time spent outside waged employment is not considered "work" but leisure time. For example, taking care of one's own household and children—a job typically done by women—is usually considered nonwork because it is a non-wage-generating activity. In fact, the dichotomy of work versus nonwork can be best understood if we look at how women's work has evolved through centuries in our society.

Though a single basis of comparison cannot be regarded as absolute in comparing historically what constitutes women's work across different cultures, studies have demonstrated that historically women in many so-called developed and developing countries have actively taken part in forms of work that are generally regarded as non-productive or non-income-generating. For example, women in Asia, Africa, and Latin and North America engaged in a wide variety of jobs (e.g., raising livestock, processing food, fetching water and fuel, sewing, selling homemade pottery, child rearing and housekeeping) that may not have always conformed to the clear-cut distinction of work and nonwork produced by the discourses of capitalism (Kessler-Harris 2003). Although in the gendered division of labor women generally had the bulk of domestic work, this was considered vital to the survival of the family and the society. In the wake of capitalist economy, while women continued to engage in various subsistence crafts or family labor systems, the emergence of a male-dominated waged workforce diminished women's visible role as productive workers. Women's housework gained a pejorative connotation and was seen as segregated from the public (i.e., male) capitalist economy. As many of women's traditional tasks (e.g., cloth manufacturing and spinning) became mechanized and production sites moved to factories, women's work increasingly became coterminous with nonproduction that cannot be evaluated in monetary terms. Women who did enter the wage labor market because of family responsibilities were either assembling goods at home for subcontractors or working in factory jobs that were considered low status and attributed less value in relation to work done by men.

Thus according to Deborah Simonton (1998), the advent of capitalism and industrialization resulted in creating a distinction between the public (men's) world and the private (women's) world. Household work came to be exclusively a women's activity, and the private world of home the ideal place for women. Women came to be identified more as mothers or caregivers and not as economic contributors to the family. As Elisabeth Prügl and Eileen Boris (1996) note, women, being identified with nurturing and caring, were separated from waged workers, and men

were considered the ideal waged workers and main bread-winners of their families. This role of women in society gained wider life even outside Europe, in many countries of Asia and Africa because of British colonization. However, this social role had different implications for middle-class and working-class women, and was gendered and racialized. For example, for women of the rising bourgeoisie in Victorian and Edwardian England, working outside the home was not considered "respectable," and home was considered a woman's proper place. However, working-class women were forced to work for financial reasons, although mainly as seamstresses, spinners, weavers, or domestic servants—jobs that are traditionally considered women's work. These jobs were perceived as less skilled and inferior to men's work and were paid less as well. Vis-à-vis class, the public/private divide had a racial dimension as well. For example, in the late nineteenth century, many African American women migrants who settled in the United States had no other option but to work as domestic servants in burgeoning urban middle-class families. Being racially excluded from most occupations, these women had to go out of their homes to earn a living for their families.

A major change in women's role in society in the United States, Britain, and continental Europe came with the two world wars (1914–1918 and 1939–1945). At the outset of each war, as men left their jobs to enlist, the supply of workers declined, resulting in labor shortages. The crisis of war unsettled the prescribed and dominant gender and class codes, and this, compounded by economic pressures, made possible the entry of women into the public workplace.

Women started entering into jobs that were previously considered men's domain, not only in manufacturing and agriculture, but also in banks and offices. Professions and careers also opened up in academia, medicine, law, and engineering. As women demonstrated their abilities to do skilled and highly mechanized work, they cast doubt on the dominant assumptions about women's physical abilities and social role. New work opportunities instilled in women a sense of confidence and individualism so that domestic work was no more the ultimate goal in their lives. For a significant number of women, paid work outside the home came to represent economic and social mobility, and they were ready to balance work and home without giving up one or the other.

Deborah Simonton (1998) notes that in spite of the significant achievements made in the workplace in the post–World War II era, attitudes toward women's roles at work and home have continued to be patriarchal and gendered. Household work and child rearing are still considered to be women's major role, and women's paid work is mostly seen as neglect of home and family. Marriage and the arrival of children thus mark an end to many women's

prospering careers in countries around the world. At the same time, certain jobs such as nursing and teaching are stereotyped as "women's jobs" because they are assumed to be closely related to women's "natural" caring and mothering roles; predictably, these jobs do not enjoy the same high social status as other official or clerical jobs belonging to the domain of men. Coupled with this, women in the workplace are expected to be polite, docile, apolitical, hardworking, and contented with a lower wage. Women are seen as casual or temporary workers, a reserve army of labor to be drawn on when needed and sent back when not required.

Economic restructuring and globalization since the 1980s have made women's positions at home and in the labor market more gendered and unequal. As pointed out by Prügl and Boris (1996), women's unpaid work at home has increased, as they need to compensate for care that was previously provided by the state. At work, because of the limited options in the formal sectors that consist of regulated, organized economies and protected workers, more and more women are forced to take up jobs in the informal sectors, where jobs are unregulated, part-time, low-paid, with no benefits or social protection and highly contingent in nature. Women's share of informal sector employment thus remains high in many countries, through their involvement in self-employment, subcontracting production, family enterprises, and home-based labor. While these jobs contribute not only to families' survival but to national income as well, they often go unrecognized or are considered peripheral and a mere extension of household work. For instance, women carpet weavers in Turkey or home-based garment sewers in Bangladesh who sew sweatshirts at home for multinationals are hardly recognized as "workers," although their work provides important bases for national economic development.

The rise of sweatshops and home-based industrial labor in developing as well as industrialized countries has further disadvantaged women's role in the labor market, as they force women into particular niches, with low pay, low skills, and poor working conditions. Often this involves doing repetitive, highly routinized, and regulated jobs on assembly lines; some believe that women are well-suited to these jobs because of their supposed inherent docility and dexterity and ability to do monotonous and labor-intensive jobs. Many labor-intensive, light manufacturing industries such as the garment, footwear, and electronics industries employ women rather than men because they make higher profits with a female workforce.

A further impact of globalization can be felt through the process of racialization of women's work as well: Caribbean or Filipino women as domestic workers, Chinese or South Asian women as garment workers.

Indeed, studies indicate that a large number of women of color are clustered in low-income sectors in countries such as Canada or Britain (Sassen 1998; Jackson 2002). These women, especially immigrant women in developed countries, are low paid, receive no benefits, and are left with little in the way of social security, labor standards, or other state guarantees. Thus women of color are systemically excluded from the better paid, secure, and the more desirable jobs in the labor markets. Despite a major increase in women's labor-force participation, the intersectionalities of gender, class, and race continue to stereotype the women's labor force and affect the employment trajectories of women in the capitalist world economy.

SEE ALSO *Discrimination, Wage, by Gender; Gender; Gender Gap; Inequality, Gender; Inequality, Political*

BIBLIOGRAPHY

Jackson, Andrew. 2002. *Is Work Working for Workers of Colour?* Ottawa: Canadian Labour Congress.

Kessler-Harris, Alice. 2003. *Out to Work: A History of Wage-Earning Women in the United States.* 20th anniversary ed. New York: Oxford University Press.

Prügl, Elisabeth, and Eileen Boris. 1996. Introduction. In *Homeworkers in Global Perspective: Invisible No More,* eds. Eileen Boris and Elisabeth Prügl, 3–17. New York and London: Routledge.

Sassen, Saskia. 1998. *Globalization and its Discontents.* New York: New Press.

Simonton, Deborah. 1998. *A History of European Women's Work: 1700 to the Present.* London and New York: Routledge.

Williams, Raymond. 1976. *Keywords: A Vocabulary of Culture and Society.* 2nd ed. London: Fontana.

Srabani Maitra

WORK DAY

The current concept of the work day did not exist prior to the modern age. Before the Industrial Revolution work was an integral part of life. What we know today as leisure and work were mixed thoroughly. As late as the colonial period in American history daily work schedules were casual, set by custom rather than by contract, law, or the clock.

The work day in colonial America traditionally ran from dawn to dusk six days a week. However, meals and rest breaks customarily accounted for two and a half to three hours of that long day. In addition, the work day was casual, interspersed with non-work activities such as conversations, household chores, games, and simple idleness.

THE SEPARATION OF WORK AND LIFE

As the marketplace became increasingly rationalized and the factory system grew, competition forced labor to become more efficient. Work increasingly was purged of its nonproductive elements. The clear division between work and life fundamental to the modern definition of the work day emerged in the United States around the turn of the nineteenth century. Impersonal market forces transformed casual preindustrial work patterns. Wages replaced older kinds of traditional compensations such as masters' support of and guarantees given to apprentices and journeymen.

Having to pay daily wages, masters, managers, and contractors tried to increase profits by intensifying work effort and expanding the customary dawn-to-dusk work day to the limits of human endurance. By the 1830s traditional artisanal republican workshops were well on their way to being replaced by what commonly was called a "bastard system of production." As manufacturing was increasingly rationalized, what Karl Marx called in his *Communist Manifesto* the "motley feudal ties" ([1894] 1906) that had connected owner to operative fell away, replaced by impersonal market relations that often exploited workers in a kind of wage slavery that many, including Walt Whitman, likened to the experience of African Americans in the American South.

ATTEMPTS TO REDUCE THE WORK DAY

Initially workers struggled against the advent of modern work discipline. Gradually, though, as E. P. Thompson showed, workers accepted the division of work from life, but then began a new "fight … about" time (Thompson 1967, p. 85). For over a century workers attempted to reduce the working day, week, year, and life to reclaim in their leisure the conviviality, creativity, equality, independence, and citizenship that characterized the essential republican virtues that once had been part of their jobs. The historians David Roediger and Philip Foner conclude that "the length of the workdays … has historically been the central issue raised by the American labor movement" (Roediger and Foner 1989, p. vii).

William Heighton articulated a worker vision of *continual* work reduction that endured for over a century. In a pamphlet circulated during the 1827 carpenters' strike in Philadelphia for a ten-hour day, Heighton called for the work day to be reduced from "12 to 10, to 8, to 6, and so on" until "the development and progress of science have reduced human labor to its lowest terms" (Heighton 1827).

Organizing across craft lines and hoping to influence customary standards and new contracts, workers pressured politicians to pass ten-hour laws for government

employees. Various cities and states considered or passed such legislation. The process culminated in 1840 with President Martin Van Buren's executive order granting the ten-hour day to manual workers under government contract.

After the Civil War labor turned its attention to the eight-hour day. As Karl Marx observed, the issue "ran with the seven-leagued boots of the locomotive from the Atlantic to the Pacific, from New England to California" (Marx 1906, p. 329). The eight-hour day became an important political issue, finding a place in the Omaha platform of the Populists and the Bull Moose platform. The Democratic and Republican platforms in 1932 called for reductions in the work day to below eight hours. Some of the most dramatic and significant events in the history of labor, such as the strikes of 1886, the Haymarket disaster, and the steel strike of 1919, concerned the length of the work day. During Woodrow Wilson's administration, the eight-hour day became the national norm and Congress passed laws regulating the work day of children, women, and workers in hazardous occupations.

In the Great Depression, continuing their commitment to the "progressive shortening of the hours of labor," unions supported the introduction of the Black-Connery bill setting the work day at six hours as a remedy for unemployment. The bill nearly passed Congress in 1933 and continued to be a key political issue until it was refashioned as the Fair Labor Standards Act and passed in 1938. The Fair Labor Standard Act set the standard work day at eight hours instead of six. Since then no advance has been made. No new laws reducing the work day have been passed. Labor seems to have lost interest. Now there is some evidence that the work day is lengthening and the eight-hour norm giving way. Overtime is growing. Salaried employees' work days have lengthened. The work day in newly industrializing nations are at nineteenth-century U.S. levels (Hunnicutt 1996).

EXPLANATIONS OF THE LENGTH OF THE WORK DAY

Trying to account for the length of the work day historically through the use of traditional economic models of supply and demand is unrewarding. The oldest relevant economic model, dating back to the mercantilists of Thomas Jefferson's day, is an economic paradox. Unlike all other goods and services, the supply curve of labor was long understood to be "backward-bending." For generations economists predicted that above a certain wage rate workers would offer increasingly less of their time to work; the work day would shrink naturally as workers chose to "buy back" their lives instead of continuing to work to purchase new, less desirable (by comparison) goods and services.

That theory was a good fit with the declining work day of the nineteenth and early twentieth centuries. However, economists such as Lionel Charles Robbins tried to amend labor supply theory in the 1920s, arguing that the substitution effect of higher wages offsets the income effect: A wage raise increases the cost of an additional hour of leisure, making the workers' choice between additional, more expensive leisure and new purchases indeterminate. Whatever labor supply theory was tested for the remainder of the twentieth century, however, in most longitudinal studies the correlation between the work day and wages and unemployment (unemployment rates are understood as a proxy for the demand for labor) was found to be insignificant.

Indeed, in 1998 Dora Costa argued that the length of the work day has not decreased as much for the highest-paid workers as it has for the lowest-paid. Economists such as Juliet Schor (1991) agree, demonstrating that salaried employees' work days have lengthened well beyond eight hours in corporate cultures that pressure workers to expand the work day to extreme limits. Observing these developments, some might theorize with Karl Marx that the expanding work day reflects the capitalist tendency to maximize surplus value and hence profits by lengthening the work day. Others may understand the progressive shortening of the hours of labor as a fundamental threat to capitalism. As Herbert Marcuse observed in 1966:

[A]utomation threatens to render possible the reversal of the relation between free time and working time: the possibility of working time becoming marginal and free time becoming full time. The result would be a radical transvaluation of values, and a mode of existence incompatible with the traditional culture. Advanced industrial society is in permanent mobilization against this possibility. (Marcuse 1966, p. vii)

For whatever reason, the century-old vision of industrial progress as consisting of both higher wages for the finer things in life and shorter work days to enjoy them seemed to have been lost at the turn of the twenty-first century.

SEE ALSO *Great Depression; Industrialization; Labor; Management; Mercantilism; Populism; Work; Work Week; Working Class; Working Day, Length of*

BIBLIOGRAPHY

Costa, Dora. 1998. *The Unequal Work Day: A Long-Term View.* NBER Working Paper No. W6419. Cambridge, MA: National Bureau of Economic Research.

Heighton, William. 1827. *An Address to the Members of Trade Societies and to the Working Classes Generally*. Philadelphia: Historical Society of Pennsylvania Archives.

Hunnicutt, Benjamin Kline. 1996. *Kellogg's Six-Hour Day*. Philadelphia: Temple University Press.

Marcuse, Herbert. 1966. *Eros and Civilization: A Philosophical Inquiry into Freud*. Vintage: New York.

Marx, Karl. [1894] 1906. *Capital: A Critique of Political Economy*, ed. Frederick Engels. New York: Modern Library.

Roediger, David, and Philip Foner. 1989. *Our Own Time: A History of American Labor and the Working Day*. New York: Greenwood Press.

Schor, Juliet. 1991. *The Overworked American: The Unexpected Decline of Leisure*. New York: Basic Books.

Thompson, E. P. 1967. Time, Work Discipline, and Industrial Capitalism. *Past and Present* 38 (1): 56–97.

Benjamin Hunnicutt

WORK WEEK

Annual hours of paid work increased substantially in much of the second half of the twentieth century due to more hours in a work week and more weeks worked. Economic sociologist Juliet Schor has sparked a national debate about work and time use with her best-selling books. For instance, in 1991 Schor reported that on average, men worked 43 weekly hours in 1969 and 43.8 hours in 1987. The corresponding increase for women was 35.2 to 37 hours. According to a study by Peter Kuhn and Fernando Lozano 18.5 percent of American men worked over 50 hours per week in 2001 (2005). In addition, with the increasing number of service sector jobs in the United States, "shift workers" have become more prevalent. A shift worker is at work during something other than a typical nine to five business day. According to numerous studies, workers keeping odd hours are more likely to have sleep difficulties and health problems.

The work week is also longer for many Americans due to urban expansion and increased commute times. In order to purchase larger houses in upscale neighborhoods with strong schools, many Americans have moved farther from their employer, therefore spending more time traveling to work each day. This trend suggests that Americans have less leisure time, and live with a rather frenetic pace of life. A number of surveys report that Americans would prefer shorter work weeks, but they do not want a lower standard of living. Increased time on the job generates income for the family, but a longer work week and commute further reduce the time workers have with their families.

Some statistics counter Schor's findings. The *Current Employment Statistics* compiled by the U.S. Department of Labor's Bureau of Labor Statistics reveal a decline in the length of the work week across all private sector jobs, from nearly thirty-nine hours in the mid-1960s to thirty-four hours in the early twenty-first century. This change is largely fueled by sharp decreases in average weekly hours in retail and services, sectors that have expanded substantially over the last half of the twentieth century, and that employ many part-time workers. In contrast, weekly hours worked in manufacturing have stayed fairly constant at forty-one hours during this time period. In addition, many professional and managerial employees are expected to work more hours than a standard full-time schedule.

Changes in the work week arise from a number of factors, including company policies. During recessions, firms regularly lay off workers (sometimes closing entire plants) to cut costs and manage inventories. The recession of the early 1980s saw many layoffs, but during the economic recovery that followed, firms did not rehire many workers. Instead, many firms added more overtime for existing workers. Indeed, there has been a general increasing trend in average manufacturing overtime from 2.5 hours in 1960 to 4.6 hours in 2000.

Largely due to higher health costs, benefits as a share of compensation have generally increased over time as well. According to the U.S. Department of Labor's Bureau of Labor Statistics' *National Compensation Survey*, at the beginning of the twenty-first century benefit costs comprised nearly 30 percent of total compensation. Benefits are fixed costs for employers, because they are paid once for each worker, and are not dependent upon how many hours an employee works. Therefore, high benefits costs deter businesses from adding workers.

Throughout the 1900s workers were increasingly paid on salary rather than with an hourly wage. This coincided with increased educational attainment, more professional occupations, and fewer manufacturing jobs. Salaried workers are required to work enough hours to keep their jobs, and the company culture reveals these expectations. For an employer, the cost of an additional hour of work from an hourly worker is the wage or the overtime wage. For salaried workers, the additional cost is zero. Salaried employees work longer hours in order to finish projects, to fit in the company culture, or to be productive enough to earn a promotion.

The structure of compensation has also changed, in that seniority-based pay is less common while pay for performance is more prevalent. Piece rates were the first form of incentive compensation, where employers tied pay to the amount a worker produced. Economist Edward Lazear presented the success of a piece rate system instituted at Safelite Glass, where both productivity and profit improved substantially. When workers face

schemes that tie their compensation to productivity, they have a clear incentive to put forth more effort and work longer hours (2000).

Government policies have also contributed to longer work weeks. For instance, caps on employer contributions to social security, unemployment insurance, and other business costs are based upon employee salary levels. In order to eliminate the funding gap for Social Security, it is possible employer contribution caps may be removed. But these sorts of tax caps clearly suggest that having fewer workers (even highly-paid workers) can lessen a company's tax burden. This is an incentive not to hire more workers, but to keep existing employees working more hours. In addition, the Fair Labor Standards Act dictates overtime pay eligibility. Around the turn of the twenty-first century, more occupations became ineligible for overtime pay. Exempt workers include computer professionals, administrative workers, and some salespersons—all are occupations that employ many American workers. Thus, the cost to a company for an additional hour of work is further reduced.

The structure of the work week has also changed as a standard nine to five schedule became less common in the twentieth century. Some employers offer "flex time," which is a schedule that involves some variable hours that workers can choose, according to their preferences. This is particularly valuable to employees with family commitments. Other nontraditional arrangements include the extended and compressed work week. The extended work week spreads the same amount of hours over more days, with shorter shifts. This is compared to the more common compressed work week, which includes longer shifts over fewer days. One particularly popular arrangement is four ten-hour days from Monday through Thursday, yielding an extended weekend. It seems that some employers understand workers' desires to have flexible leisure time without sacrificing their standard of living.

In order to increase earnings, many workers have more than one job. According to the Bureau of Labor Statistics (2002), 7.8 million Americans (5.7 percent of the labor force) had multiple jobs in 2001, and the most frequently cited reasons for this were to earn extra money (35.4 percent of respondents) and meet expenses or pay off debt (27.8 percent). Schor states that workers are caught in a cycle of ever more spending and ever more working to cover their expenses. Labor economic theory generally assumes that workers select their optimal number of hours, but Schor argues that this is not the case. Instead, employers set the hours they expect from workers and their employees adjust accordingly.

SEE ALSO *Labor; Leisure; Vacations; Work; Work Day; Working Day, Length of*

BIBLIOGRAPHY

Kuhn, Peter, and Fernando Lozano. 2005. *The Expanding Workweek? Understanding Trends in Long Work Hours among U.S. Men, 1979–2004.* NBER Working Paper No. 11895.

Lazear, Edward P. 2000. Performance Pay and Productivity. *American Economic Review* 90 (5): 1346–1361.

Schor, Juliet B. 1991. *The Overworked American: The Unexpected Decline of Leisure.* New York: Basic Books.

Schor, Juliet B. 1998. *The Overspent American: Upscaling, Downshifting, and the New Consumer.* New York: Basic Books.

U.S. Department of Labor. Bureau of Labor Statistics. 2002. *Issues in Labor Statistics.* September, Summary 02–07. Washington, D.C. http://www.bls.gov/opub/ils/pdf/opbils50.pdf.

U.S. Department of Labor. Bureau of Labor Statistics. 2006. *Current Employment Statistics.* Washington, D.C. ftp://ftp.bls.gov/pub/suppl/empsit.ceseeb2.txt.

U.S. Department of Labor. Bureau of Labor Statistics. 2006. *National Compensation Survey.* Washington, D.C. http://www.bls.gov/ncs/ebs/sp/ebsm0004.pdf.

Sherrilyn M. Billger

WORKING CLASS

The capitalist class structure consists of two main classes: the capitalist class, owners of means of production, and the working class, owners of labor power. The relations between these classes are complementary and contradictory. Complementary, because capitalists need workers to produce the wealth they accumulate, and workers' economic survival depends on capital investments: Lacking access to means of production, it is only through the sale of their labor power that workers and their families subsist. Their class interests are, however, inherently contradictory: It is in capitalists' interest to lower production costs—that is, wages, pensions, health plans, and so on—to increase profits and facilitate capital accumulation. It is in workers' interest not only to attain good wages and benefits but, eventually, to overthrow capitalism and take over the means of production, thus ending their exploitation by the capitalist class: The working classes are bound to become the capitalists' "gravediggers" (Marx and Engels [1848] 1998).

HISTORICAL CHANGES AND THE WORKING CLASS

Karl Marx (1818–1883) and Friedrich Engels (1820–1895) wrote in the nineteenth century, when class differences were stark and the large and growing working class was composed of manual, mostly male workers.

Since then and up to World War II (1939–1945), workers lived close to the factories, in dense working-class communities. These conditions facilitated workers' awareness of shared experiences and interests, and the formation of trade unions that enhanced workers' economic and political power (Marx [1847] 1969, pp. 172–173). The concentration of capital and emergence of large-scale industry resulted in the spacial concentration of workers, giving "this mass a common situation, common interests. This mass is thus already a class as against capital, but not yet for itself. In the struggle … this mass becomes united, and constitutes itself as a class for itself. The interests it defends become class interests. But the struggle of class against class is a political struggle" (p. 173).

During the nineteenth and the first half of the twentieth centuries there were in the United States and Europe numerous instances of violent class struggles and widespread working-class mobilization and organizing under socialist, Communist, and anarchist banners: "social and cultural identities were forged by the categories of class and strata; everyday life, aesthetic expressions, and cognitive mappings articulated with production relations" (Aronowitz 1992, p. 23). In 1917 successful revolution in Russia seemed to confirm Marx and Engels's prediction about the revolutionary role of the working class.

After World War II, however, the world's economic and political conditions changed, partly as a result of the cold war and anticapitalist struggles in Asia, Africa, and Latin America. In the advanced capitalist countries, the working classes abandoned anticapitalist politics in exchange for steady employment and a good standard of living. Changes in the forces of production altered the economic and the occupational structures, decreasing the proportion of manual, "blue-collar" workers employed on farms and in the industrial, manufacturing sector. The proportion of workers employed in the service sector and in nonmanual, "white-collar" clerical, professional, and managerial jobs increased, thus giving rise to theories that conceptualized the top echelons of such jobs as a new class. Typical of such views is the "professional managerial class" (PMC) thesis put forth by John and Barbara Ehrenreich (1979). The PMC owes its existence to "the expropriation of the skills and culture once indigenous to the working class" (p. 2) and acts, with some degree of class awareness, in ways detrimental to the working class, leading to, for example, "the reorganization of the productive process, the emergence of mass institutions of social control, and the commodity penetration of working class life" (p. 18). Although professionals and managers may make decisions adversely affecting the working class, it remains open to debate whether such decisions reflect their own antiworking class intentions, or the objectives of the capitalist employers for whom they work. More important is the contention that the PMC is guilty of expropriating the workers' skills and culture and that this expropriation constitutes a sufficient basis for considering them a social class. Historically, the development of capitalist industrialization has entailed the progressive deskilling of the working class and the emergence of a complex division of labor that includes deskilled masses of workers and layers of intermediate workers (foremen, managers, engineers, administrators, etc.), which embodied the power of capital and its ability to deskill and control the organization and pace of the labor process (see Braverman 1974 for a thorough analysis of these processes). The PMC is found not only in factories, of course, but also in all institutions where high-ranking salaried employees are the visible face of capitalist or of institutional power over rank-and-file workers. The view that the PMC is a "class for itself," acting autonomously against the working class, overlooks the significance of its intermediate location, as employees who carry out the mandates of their bosses. The PMC can be viewed more appropriately as a strata within the propertyless class, occupying a "contradictory class location" between the capitalist class and the proletariat—that is, foremen, technocrats, bottom and top managers, and so on—and between the petty bourgeoisie and the proletariat—that is, semiautonomous employees such as teachers, professors, scientists, and so on (Wright 1978, p. 84). In other words, the PMC occupies the top layers in the social stratification of the working population; it is not a class but a social strata within the working class, objectively defined as the class of relatively privileged propertyless workers whose power and economic resources depend on their continued employment. Loss of a job can reduce them to poverty or near poverty because, barring individual exceptions, the members of the PMC do not own capital and depend on their salaries for their economic survival (Gimenez 1978).

In the last twenty-five years the rise and widespread use of information technologies and the increasing mobility of capital resulting in deindustrialization, downsizing, and outsourcing have further changed the occupational composition of the working classes, as well as their conditions of employment: Stable, relatively well-paid blue-collar and white-collar employment is becoming scarce, while contingent and temporary employment is increasing among low-skilled and highly skilled professional workers. Long-standing racial, ethnic, and gender conflicts—which have excluded women and nonwhite workers from well-paid, stable jobs and led to disproportionate female and nonwhite poverty—eventually in the last decades of the twentieth century spurred social movements for civil rights and equal opportunity for all. The politics of class, particularly in the United States, was replaced by identity politics.

ISSUES IN WORKING-CLASS SCHOLARSHIP AND POLITICS

The changing occupational composition of the working class, the decline in workers' anticapitalist struggles and union membership, and the dominance of identity politics challenge the validity of the Marxist concept of the working class and its revolutionary potential. If narrowly defined as composed only of "productive workers," that is, blue-collar workers producing surplus value (Poulantzas 1973, pp. 30–31), it would seem the working class is dwindling away within advanced capitalist countries. Reducing the working class to only skilled, craft workers, André Gorz argues that organizational and technological changes that have practically abolished skilled work have rendered obsolete the working class as a class composed of knowledgeable workers capable of taking over control of the means and the process of production; we must, therefore, bid "farewell to the working class" (Gorz 1982, p 46). If broadly defined, in terms of political allegiances, the working class could include everyone mobilized in struggles against the state. Rosa Luxemburg (1871–1919), for example, celebrated the spontaneous rising of the laboring masses composed of factory workers, rural proletarians, policemen, military personnel, and bank employees (Luxemburg [1906] 2004, p. 180). Historian E. P. Thompson (1924–1993) offered a dialectical understanding of the working class. Emphasizing process and agency, and arguing that class is a historical phenomenon, not a structure or a category, he states that "the working class was present at his own making" (Thompson 1966, p. 9). It is in the midst of struggles, as people sharing similar experiences become aware of common interests and enemies, that the working class "makes itself," that "class happens" (p. 9). Thompson acknowledges, however, that common experiences, the basis for the emergence of class consciousness, are "determined by the productive relations into which men are born—or enter involuntarily. Class consciousness is the way in which these experiences are handled in cultural terms" (pp. 9–10). As culture (that is, institutions, value systems, beliefs, traditions, and so on) varies historically and cross-culturally, class consciousness, though it reflects an economically determined experience, is itself undetermined in its content; class struggles, it follows, can be fought under a variety of ideological legitimations.

Like Marx, who stressed the need to distinguish between changes at the level of production and the ideological ways in which individuals become conscious of those changes and engage in political struggles (Marx [1859] 1970, p. 21), Thompson differentiates between the determining role of productive relations and the contingent, cultural, or ideological forms that class consciousness might take. In Marx and Engels's *Communist Manifesto* (1848), however, class consciousness—that is,

workers' awareness of their economic and political interests as a class that can succeed only by abolishing all classes, in the struggle to overthrow the economic and political power of the capitalist class—seems to flow unproblematically from the experiences of the working class. Capitalists require, in their economic and political struggles, the support of the working class; capitalists educate the proletariat and supply it with the political and economic know-how to fight and defend its interests as a class (pp. 18–19). Late-twentieth- and early-twenty-first-century capitalists, however, through the mass media and the democratization of consumption, seem to have established firm ideological control over workers' consciousness, an unsurprising development because "the ideas of the ruling class are in every epoch the ruling ideas" (Marx and Engels [1845–46] 1947, p. 39). The lack of working-class mobilization and revolutionary upheavals in advanced capitalist social formations, and the successes of globalized capitalism, have undermined, among some academics and most left-leaning activists, the traditional Marxist analysis of the working class as the only revolutionary class, the only class capable of challenging the rule of capital (Marx and Engels [1848] 1998, p. 20).

The working classes of the twenty-first century are far less class conscious (in the sense indicated in the *Manifesto*) than they were a century ago. Recent social movements, the effects of racial, ethnic, and gender oppression and exclusion, have centered around inequality rather than exploitation. In their work, African American, Latino, and feminist scholars have examined the connections between class, gender, and race and have expanded the concept of working-class politics to include issues related to racial, ethnic, and gender oppression and discrimination (see, for example, Collins 1993; Davis 1981). In the United States the impact of these social movements on the social sciences and on politics was profound. It led to a bifurcation in political practice and in scholarship between those who give primacy to working-class politics and class analysis, and those who prioritize identity politics and race, gender, and ethnicity as structures of inequality independent from social class, and as equally determinant of individuals' life chances as social class. A new social science perspective emerged in the late 1980s: the "race, gender, and class" trilogy, popularized by a journal originally called *Race, Sex & Class*. This perspective is enshrined in countless articles, anthologies, and books (see, for example, Landry 2007). Within this perspective, the role of class, ostensibly given equal visibility, is often minimized, for class is often reduced to income, and/or to another identity.

Another effect of the bifurcation in politics and scholarship mentioned above is the rise of cultural politics and the rejection of class politics and scholarship as forms of economic determinism or class reductionism. The cul-

turalization of politics can be traced in the new academic and political language: policies about diversity, multiculturalism, identity, inclusion of "diverse" (a euphemism for women and nonwhites) populations in educational institutions and the workplace, the value of "multiculturalism" and "cultural diversity," and so on have replaced, to a large extent, earlier concerns with the economic, racial, and gender discrimination. This discourse obfuscates the class divisions within the "diverse" populations, and the working-class basis of many of the grievances (for example, low wages, segregated labor markets and employment, exclusion from opportunities for upward mobility and access to higher education, etc.) that fueled the social movements of the late 1960s and early 1970s. The grounds for the emergence of political solidarity across gender and racial/ethnic differences remain as overlooked, in the context of cultural politics, as the poverty, powerlessness, and economic insecurity of white male workers. This is why, in the absence of a discourse on class that could contribute to undermine racial and gender antagonisms, "many Americans have displaced their resentments resulting from what Sennet and Cobb called the 'hidden injuries' of class, to patriotism … nationalism … racism and sexism" (Aronowitz 1992, p. 67).

The philosopher Charles Taylor explored the potential conflict between universalizing democratic politics, which equalize all citizens under the law, and the political affirmation of gender, racial, and ethnic differences as sources of dignity and claims for recognition, rather than second-class citizenship. A positive, rather than negative, public evaluation of difference is the objective of what Taylor calls "the politics of recognition" (Taylor 1992). The feminist philosopher Nancy Fraser offers a clear statement of these divisive issues:

> Demands for "recognition of difference" fuel struggles of groups mobilized under the banners of nationality, ethnicity, "race," gender and sexuality … group identity supplants class interest as the chief medium of political mobilization. Cultural domination supplants exploitation as the fundamental injustice. And cultural recognition displaces socioeconomic redistributions as the remedy for injustice and the goal of political struggle. (Fraser 1995, p. 64)

Arguing that justice requires both redistribution and recognition, Fraser identifies important problems inherent in the changes necessary to remedy these injustices, whether such remedies support or challenge the status quo. Measures that seek only to redistribute income to different groups require the preservation of group identities, thus provoking negative reactions from the excluded (for example, whites' critique of reverse discrimination). Though those groups may strive toward the public affir-

mation of their identities' worth and dignity, changes in the allocation of respect will remain superficial, because of the endemic struggles triggered by redistribution. But, transforming identities through deconstruction of the categories currently used to define difference would be just as problematic, for this would deprive groups of the identities that today mechanisms of redistribution and inclusion use to identify those who benefit from such policies (pp. 86–91). Although preserving the cultural and economic status quo is inherently problematic, "… the scenario that best finesses the redistribution-recognition dilemma is socialism in the economy plus deconstruction in the culture," which "to be psychologically and politically feasible requires that people be weaned from their attachments to current cultural constructions of their interests and identities" (p. 91). In reality, these struggles are intertwined, as the feminist philosopher Iris Young argues in her critique of Fraser's analysis: economic relations presuppose cultural understandings and cultural and political recognitions are a means toward economic and political justice (Young 1997, p. 148). But these struggles so far appear to be remarkably ineffective in mobilizing the U.S. working class as a class, despite its worsening economic situation. As long as workers tend to perceive themselves primarily in terms of group identities rather than common class location—a situation strengthened by the official political discourse, within which any mention of class and class interests is deemed undesirable, almost "un-American"—perhaps only mass unemployment and household bankruptcies on a scale not seen since the Great Depression might create the material conditions for the emergence of working-class political leaders, simultaneously with the rise in workers' receptiveness to their views.

Class struggles in Latin America, as in China and Vietnam, have included workers and peasants in political mobilizations under socialist and nationalist banners. For Chairman Mao Tse-tung (1893–1976), national struggles were class struggles; he set in opposition to the ruling classes the masses of "enlightened" workers, farmers, and intellectuals (Mao 1966, p. 10). Some scholars argue, however, that the proletarianization of the middle strata and peasantries has not happened, and that the working class has no privileged role to play. Anticapitalist struggles, in their view, encompass a variety of conflicts between capitalism and sectors of the population inside and outside the working class (for example, conflicts around war and peace, environmental pollution, land management, and so on) (Laclau and Mouffe 1987, pp. 103–104).

Marxist social scientists, however, continue to study the working class and the changes in its size, racial, gender, and occupational composition, giving equal importance to individuals' relationships to the means of production, skills and credentials, and location in the authority structure (Wright 1997, pp. 17–26). Examining

the transformation of the U.S. class structure between 1960 and 1990, Wright concludes that there has been a decline in the proportion of skilled workers (from 13.46% of the labor force in 1960 to 12.77% in 1990) and unskilled workers (from 44.59% to 41.38%). The working class as a whole, skilled and unskilled, declined from 58.05 percent to 54.15 percent (p. 99). In terms of race and gender, "by a large margin, the American working class now predominantly consists of women and racial minorities" (p. 69). Changes in the racial and gender composition of the working class contribute to the persistence of racial/ethnic and gender conflicts within the U.S. working class and the extent to which issues of racial, ethnic and gender oppression are the most salient and important aspect of workers' consciousness in the United States.

The meaning of the decline in the size of the working class in the United States and other advanced capitalist countries remains an unresolved and unresolvable issue in Marxist theory. For some (for example, Gorz 1980; Laclau and Mouffe 1987) it signals a reversal of the proletarianization process and an end to the revolutionary role of the working class. Others, however, point out that the proletarianization process worldwide proceeds unabated, and that as the size of the working class declines in the wealthy countries, proletarianization is intensifying in the rest of the world (Arrighi 1990; Wright 1997, pp. 109–110). Another issue subject to conflicting interpretations is the rise in the proportion of propertyless but expert, professional salaried workers, placed in "contradictory locations within class relations" (Wright 1997, p. 20). Is this an indicator of the future demise of the working class, the rise of a new class (for example, a "professional managerial class," according to Ehrenreich and Ehrenreich 1979), or of the rise of a new working class? On the basis of the analysis of the effects of capitalist development upon the characteristics of the labor force that Marx presents in the *Grundrisse* (Marx [1857–1868] 1953), Nicolaus (1973) reaches this conclusion: The working class fated to lead the revolution is not the impoverished, unskilled, and pauperized working class but the educated, expert, credentialed working class that develops as capitalists develop the forces of production to such an extent that

> the creation of real wealth comes to depend less on labor-time and on the quantity of labor expended, and more on the power of the instruments which are set in motion during labor-time, and whose powerful effectiveness itself is not related to the labor-time immediately expended in their production, but depends rather on the general state of science and the progress of technology. (Marx [1857–1868] 1953, cited in Nicolaus 1973, p. 328)

Marx depicts a time in which the development of the forces of production empowers workers, when

> the cornerstone of production and wealth is neither the labor which man directly expends, nor the time he spends at work, but rather the appropriation of its own collective productive power.... As soon as labor in its direct form has ceased to be the great wellspring of wealth, labor-time ceases and must cease to be its measure. (Marx [1857–1868] 1953 cited in Nicolaus 1973, p. 329)

Perhaps Nicolaus's inferences are correct, for it is possible today to observe a bifurcation in the development of the working class: on the one hand, growth in the exploited, poor, and relatively powerless proletariat whose labor fuels the industrialization of Asian and Latin American countries while being the source, through migration, of cheap manual labor and services in the wealthy countries; and on the other hand, growth in the numbers of "the well-fed proletarian, scientifically competent, to whom an eight hour day would presumably appear as a waste of time" (Nicolaus 1973, p. 329). These are issues that can be resolved only by the outcome of current and future political struggles, not by theoretical fiat or the exegesis of scholarly texts.

SEE ALSO *Bourgeoisie; Capitalism; Employment; Employment, White Collar; Lumpenproletariat; Proletariat; Underemployment; Unemployment*

BIBLIOGRAPHY

Aronowitz, Stanley. 1992. *The Politics of Identity: Class, Culture, Social Movements.* New York: Routledge.

Arrighi, Giovanni. 1990. Marxist Century—American Century: The Making and Remaking of the World Labor Movement. *New Left Review* 179: 29–63.

Braverman, Harry. 1974. *Labor and Monopoly Capital: The Degradation of Work in the Twentieth Century.* New York: Monthly Review Press.

Collins, Patricia H. 1993. Toward a New Vision: Race, Class, and Gender as Categories of Analysis and Connection. *Race, Sex, and Class* 1 (1): 25–45.

Davis, Angela Y. 1981. *Women, Race, and Class.* New York: Random House.

Ehrenreich, John, and Barbara Ehrenreich. 1979. The Professional-Managerial Class. In *Between Labour and Capital*, ed. Pat Walker, 5–45. Brighton, U.K.: Harvester.

Fraser, Nancy. 1995. From Redistribution to Recognition? Dilemmas of Justice in a "Post-Socialist" Age. *New Left Review* 212: 64–93.

Gimenez, Martha E. 1978. The Professional/Managerial Class: An Ideological Construct. http://www.colorado.edu/Sociology/gimenez/work/pmg.html.

Gimenez, Martha E. 1999. Latino Politics—Class Struggles: Reflections on the Future of Latino Politics. In *Latino Social Movements: Historical and Theoretical Perspectives*, eds. Rodolfo D. Torres and George Katsiaficas, 163–180. New York: Routledge.

Gorz, André. 1980. *Farewell to the Working Class: An Essay on Post Industrial Socialism*. Boston: South End Press.

Laclau, Ernesto, and Chantal Mouffe. 1987. Post-Marxism Without Apologies. *New Left Review* 166: 79–106.

Landry, Baht. 2007. *Race, Gender, and Class: Theory and Methods of Analysis*. Upper Saddle River, NJ: Prentice Hall.

Luxemburg, Rosa. [1906] 2004. The Mass Strike, the Political Party, and the Trade Unions. In *The Rosa Luxemburg Reader*, eds. Peter Hudis and Kevin B. Anderson, 168–199. New York: Monthly Review Press.

Mao Tse-tung. 1966. *Quotations from Chairman Mao Tse-tung*. Peking: Foreign Languages Press.

Marx, Karl. [1847] 1969. *The Poverty of Philosophy*. New York: International Publishers.

Marx, Karl. [1857–1868] 1953. *Grundrisse der Kritik der Politischen Okonomie* (*Rohentwurf*) [Fundamental traits of the critique of political economy (rough copy)]. Berlin: Dietz.

Marx, Karl. [1859] 1970. *A Contribution to the Critique of Political Economy*. New York: International Publishers.

Marx, Karl, and Frederick Engels. [1845–1846] 1947. *The German Ideology*. New York: International Publishers.

Marx, Karl, and Friedrich Engels. [1848] 1998. *The Communist Manifesto*. New York: Monthly Review Press.

Nicolaus, Martin. 1973. The Unknown Marx. In *Ideology in Social Science: Readings in Critical Social Theory*, ed. Robin Blackburn, 306–333. New York: Vintage Books.

Poulantzas, Nicos. 1973. On Social Classes. *New Left Review* 78: 27–54.

Taylor, Charles. 1992. *Multiculturalism and "The Politics of Recognition."* Princeton, NJ: Princeton University Press.

Thompson, Edward P. 1966. *The Making of the English Working Class*. New York: Vintage Books.

Wright, Erik Olin. 1978. *Class, Crisis, and The State*. London: Verso.

Wright, Erik Olin. 1997. *Class Counts: Comparative Studies in Class Analysis*. Cambridge, U.K.: Cambridge University Press.

Young, Iris. 1995. Unruly Categories: A Critique of Nancy Fraser's Dual Systems Theory. *New Left Review* 222: 147–160.

Martha E. Gimenez

WORKING DAY, LENGTH OF

In countries where hours of work are the subject of collective agreements, the pattern of reference for the length of the working day is often given by governmental legislation that limits working hours. The concept of "normal hours" or "legal hours" (France) is used to describe the limit beyond which overtime becomes payable. Although this legal, institutional, and focal time sets the basic rules for entrepreneurial activity, it does not provide an accurate indicator for the amount of time effectively supplied by individuals. The pervasiveness of practices such as overtime, part-time, moonlighting, sick leave, and remuneration systems such as piece rates, hourly wages, or monthly salary, all contribute towards extending or shrinking job hours across offices, shops, and manufacturers. If common sense generally recognizes the working day as something typical that can be calculated as the work time accomplished during a twenty-four-hour period or as the total work-time accomplished in one week, statistical analysis prefers instead to draw this measurement over the full cycle of the year to capture the global picture of work effort. Two main variables are generally considered: "average hours of work per person employed," which describes actual hours in the work-post, whether paid or unpaid; and "market hours," which describes hours at work, plus paid off-time (e.g., vacations, holidays, sick leave, and maternity leave).

In terms of free workers who receive payment, the peak of human effort seems to have been historically reached by the middle of the nineteenth century, a time when working hours attained an annual level of between 3,150 to 3,650 hours per year (61 to 70 hours per week). Such harsh conditions resulted from a long-term trend to cut leisure time in the form of breaks and holidays, and from a short-term tendency to expand work time in factory and cottage industries. In western Europe and the United States, men, women, and children experienced the repetition of a twelve-, fourteen-, or even sixteen-hour day, six days a week, fifty-two weeks a year. This was also a period of habituation to the economy of time revealed by mechanical clocks, supervisor's discipline, and fines.

From 1880 onwards, most workers saw the achievement of the ten-hour day, and only a few who worked in the more competitive industries such as textiles, leather, food-processing, paper, chemicals, and energy production exceeded this limit. In spite of these achievements the spark of industrial agitation and strikes continued thereafter ignited by the demand for higher pay and shorter hours, in what came to be known as the "eight-hour day movement." The bulk of unions' and workers' voluntary associations joined this demand, and both businessmen and governments were preemptively forced to review work schedules.

By 1920 the eight-hour day was recognized by law in the main industrialized countries. Further reductions in work time took the form of reducing the work week from six to five-and-a-half days, and later to five days. After that,

the downward trend continued through small incremental decreases instead of drastic changes. Thanks to the extension of vacations, holidays, sick days, personal leave, and earlier retirement, substantial improvements were added to the standard of living and the leisure time of workers. The decline in labor time became visible not only in the typical working day, but in all aspects of people's lives.

For much of the 1950s and 1960s, the primary beneficiaries of fewer working hours were the less educated and lower paid workers. Studies regarding American occupations revealed that individuals with a college education worked longer hours than people with a less formal education. To a lesser extent, those with larger incomes followed the same path of an extended working time. Hence, the upper echelons benefited from the productivity gains brought about by the golden age of economic development through increases in money instead of increases in leisure.

According to sociologist Juliet Schor (1991), the trade-off of more money for less leisure time, endemic of senior executives and professionals, soon filtered down to the less well-off segments of society, wedging millions of Americans into a work-and-spend cycle and an unremitting shortage of free time. Schor estimates that between 1969 and 1987, the average employed person was on the job for an additional 163 hours per year, the equivalent of an extra month. The additional month is attributable to both longer weekly schedules and to more weeks at work, revealing an overturn in the process of incremental decreases of the working day. The causes are twofold: On the supply side, people changed the extension of vacations, holidays, sick days, personal leave, and single jobs for more money; on the demand side, enterprises preferred to pay for overtime rather than increase the fringe benefits required by a larger staff. Schor then concludes that individual choices and economic constraints contributed to the contemporary outcome of the overworked American.

Recent studies have confirmed the tendency to augment working hours, even though this is a phenomenon restricted to a particular group of countries, such as the United States, Sweden, and Hungary. The main pattern of industrializing nations still runs in the direction of a shorter working time or through a stabilization of the average hours of work per person employed, which at present is between 1,500 and 2,000 hours per year.

The increased flexibility of working hours established by a number of arrangements has contradictory effects over the length of the working day: On the one hand, it contributes to the extent of full-time employment through overtime, evening, night, and weekend working; on the other hand, it contributes to shorter hours through the growth of part-time employment. While the United States currently matches the first case, the Japanese evolution fits well into the second.

SEE ALSO *Clock Time; Labor; Leisure; Regulation; Vacations; Work; Work Day; Work Week*

BIBLIOGRAPHY

Atack, J., and Fred Bateman. 1992. How Long Was the Workday in 1880? *The Journal of Economic History* 52 (1): 129–160.

Costa, Dora L. 2000. The Wage and the Length of the Work Day: From the 1890s to 1991. *Journal of Labor Economics* 18 (1): 156–181.

Evans, John M., Douglas C. Lippoldt, and Pascal Marianna. 2001. *Trends in Working Hours in OECD Countries (Labour markets and Social Policy Occasional Papers No. 45.* OECD Publishing. http://www.oecd.org/LongAbstract/0,2546,en_2649_37457_1885449_1_1_1_37457,00.html.

Schor, Juliet B. 1991. *The Overworked American: The Unexpected Decline of Leisure.* New York: Basic Books.

Nuno Luís Madureira

WORKPLACE RELATIONS

In 1957 economist Gary Becker, in his seminal work on workplace discrimination, noted that employees may interact, and hence have professional workplace relations, with their managers and coworkers as well as customers of the firm. Workers and managers at a firm typically interact through institutions designed to assist firms in carrying out their objectives. These institutions govern performance evaluation, compensation, and discipline. The design and functioning of these systems is studied by human resource professionals and management scholars to evaluate a range of questions, including whether diverse workers are treated fairly and if a firm's compensation practices promote productivity and firm loyalty. In his 2003 work Paul Levy provided a thorough review of this literature. Marketing researchers and practitioners explore the link between customers and representatives of a firm. Their inquires are aimed at identifying the services customers expect from a firm's workforce, how they are best provided, and if customers prefer workers based on race, ethnicity, gender, and factors related to workplace efficiency, such as experience. Social scientists following the pioneering 1952 work of the psychologist Kurt Lewin study the nature of associations between persons in small groups to enrich their understanding of how coworkers interact and influence firm performance. This essay provides an overview of this area of inquiry with emphasis placed on the questions being explored and the insights fostered by prior research.

WHY WORK GROUPS

A worker's productivity, the output he or she generates per unit of time, depends on the skills and knowledge he or she possesses, called human capital, along with the technological resources available at the work site. Human capital can be acquired through additional schooling, improvements to health, and learning on the job owing to participation in formal job training programs and learning-by-doing through experience. Accumulation of human capital is often a costly and time-consuming process since more highly skilled workers command higher wages, educational materials and instructional time must be paid for, and learning time results in lost production. Nevertheless, firms are willing to finance acquisition of human capital for members of their workforce if the additional knowledge advances worker productivity enough to expand firm profits. However, the breadth of knowledge needed to successfully complete assignments in the workplace has increased since the late twentieth century due to advances in technology and greater globalization along with more complex legal and reporting requirements. Therefore managers have become increasingly uneasy with the prospects that an employee, in isolation, can meet the challenges of the modern workplace.

Managers can organize workers into work groups, also referred to as work teams, that are responsible for completing tasks for the firm rather than assigning duties to an individual. Work groups consist of individuals who are truly interdependent in that they must coordinate their efforts or work together to complete the tasks assigned to the team. Work groups are necessary because of the range of knowledge and talents needed to solve the problems that must be overcome to produce goods and services in a profitable manner. Managers recognize that workers possess different types of skills, talents, backgrounds, and experiences; that they are heterogeneous. The fundamental idea promoting the organization of workers into work groups is that employees with complementary skills can be clustered to enhance the productivity of the firm's workforce if they are willing to readily share skills and expertise. Thus the breadth of talents needed to complete work does not need to be embedded in a single worker but can be obtained across the members of a work group. A product development work team might be composed of researchers, market analysts, accountants, sales personnel, legal counsel, secretaries, and communications specialists. However, worker heterogeneity may present obstacles to effective work group functioning.

WORK GROUP DIVERSITY AND COWORKER RELATIONS

Managers often construct diverse work groups by selecting members with different demographic characteristics, including race, ethnicity, and gender. They believe that diverse groups will promote better work team performance by incorporating a wider range of ideas and perspectives into the decision-making process. However, when group members are dissimilar, conflicts among them are more likely to arise, weakening group cohesion, which harms skill sharing and productivity (see Patrick L. Mason's 1995 article for a discussion of the relationship between workplace diversity and discrimination). Social psychologists attribute this to work group members identifying with a subgroup of workers who share a particular demographic trait to a greater extent than to the entire work team. Social psychologists have developed a number of theories to explain why persons in a particular demographic group form such strong allegiances and engage in prejudiced behavior toward persons outside of their group. The litany of theories includes social identity theory (Tajfel and Turner 1986), realistic conflict theory (Sherif 1966), and group position theory (Blumer 1958). These theories hold that biased perceptions and poor treatment across groups is motivated by a desire to maintain or improve the standing of the group a person is affiliated with relative to other groups. Two decades of experimental research by psychologists reviewed by Marilynn Brewer and Rupert Brown in 1999 reveals that social identification with a group elicits liking, trust, and cooperation toward members of that group that are not extended to persons outside of their group.

In 1906 the anthropologist William Sumner coined the term *in-group* to describe a subgroup ascribed high social status in a society. In 1985 the Nobel Prize–winning economist Arthur Lewis asserted that high social status groups often maneuver and shape legal, political, and educational institutions to obtain economic status and privilege. He referred to subgroups with both social and economic power as dominant groups, while subaltern groups are composed of persons lacking economic privilege and social standing. Relations between coworkers associated with dominant and subaltern subgroups can be particularly troublesome for firms seeking to establish harmonious, highly productive work groups since dominant group members may feel little pressure to share skills with members of the subaltern group. Meanwhile members of the subaltern group may be compelled by their weak political and economic position to cooperate extensively with persons in the dominant group. Therefore status and power differentials may set in motion behaviors that foster economic inequality and tense workplace relations.

Gordon W. Allport's 1954 contact hypothesis theory and Leon Festinger's 1957 dissonance theory suggest that bringing diverse groups into greater contact with one another can be an effective way to reduce tensions, alter preconceived perceptions, and ultimately improve cross-group sharing, leading to better firm performance. Work

site policies to improve workplace relations between diverse subgroups are likely to be an expanding presence in the United States due to the growing diversity of the labor force.

BIBLIOGRAPHY

Allport, Gordon W. 1954. *The Nature of Prejudice*. Reading, MA: Addison-Wesley.

Becker, Gary S. 1957. *The Economics of Discrimination*. Chicago: University of Chicago Press.

Brewer, Marilynn B., and Rupert J. Brown. 1999. Intergroup Relations. In *The Handbook of Social Psychology*, vol. 2, eds. Daniel T. Gilbert, Susan T. Fiske, and Gardner Lindzey. Boston: McGraw-Hill.

Festinger, Leon. 1957. *A Theory of Cognitive Dissonance*. Evanston, IL: Row, Peterson.

Levy, Paul E. 2003. *Industrial/Organizational Psychology: Understanding the Workplace*. Boston: Houghton Mifflin.

Lewin, Kurt. 1952. *Field Theory in Social Science*. New York: Harper and Row.

Lewis, Arthur W. 1985. *Racial Conflict and Economic Development*. Cambridge, MA: Harvard University Press.

Mason, Patrick L. 1995. Race, Competition, and Differential Wages. *Cambridge Journal of Economics* 19 (4): 545–568.

Sherif, Muzafer. 1966. *Group Conflict and Co-Operation: Their Social Psychology*. London: Routledge and Kegan Paul.

Sumner, William. 1906. *Folkways*. New York: Ginn.

Tajfel, Henri, and John C. Turner. 1986. The Social Identity Theory of Intergroup Behavior. In *Psychology of Intergroup Relations*, eds. Stephen Worchel and W. G. Austin. Chicago: Nelson.

Arthur H. Goldsmith

WORLD BANK, THE

Conceived in 1944 at a meeting of the Allied powers in Bretton Woods, New Hampshire, the World Bank was created as a counterpart to the International Monetary Fund (IMF). Located side-by-side in Washington, D.C., the World Bank was designed to provide development assistance to countries in need, while the IMF was set up to serve as a lender-of-last-resort for countries struggling with balance-of-payment crises. Together, these twin entities have come to symbolize the kinds of post–World War II multilateralism and institution-building known as the Bretton Woods system. Both the World Bank and the IMF are owned and governed by 184 member countries, which make up the client base of each organization.

Formally, the World Bank is run by a board of governors and a board of directors, which jointly represent the views of all the member countries. The founders of the World Bank vested predominant ownership and control in the wealthier countries, as embodied in a weighted voting system that gives more power to those countries that contribute the most financial resources or quota, which is the amount each member pays according to a percentage of its gross national product (GNP). The World Bank is thus clearly divided between those countries that primarily give funds and those that mostly receive them. The formula used to determine country quotas is based on measurements of national income, foreign reserves, and international trade. Some technical changes in the formula have occurred through the years, while the most important revisions have come about as a result of fierce political negotiations.

Although the World Bank's early work centered on the reconstruction of war-torn Europe, over the years it has primarily focused on the welfare of developing countries. At the same time, it has evolved into a far more complex institution. The World Bank has acquired five main affiliates, which now operate under the banner of the World Bank Group: the International Bank for Reconstruction and Development (IBRD); the International Development Association (IDA); the International Finance Corporation (IFC); the Multilateral Investment Guarantee Agency (MIGA); and, the International Centre for Settlement of Investment Disputes (ICSID).

The IBRD focuses on middle-income and creditworthy developing countries, while the IDA targets poverty reduction in the poorest countries in the world economy. For example, the IDA provides interest-free loans and some grants for programs aimed at enabling poor countries to meet the United Nations' Millennium Development Goals (MDGs), which were adopted in 2000 in an effort to halve world poverty rates by the year 2015. The role of the IFC is to promote sustainable private-sector investment in developing countries, and MIGA's mission is to promote foreign direct investment (FDI) in developing countries. Finally, ICSID provides facilities for the arbitration of disputes between member countries and investors who qualify as nationals of other member countries. Recourse to ICSID conciliation and arbitration is entirely voluntary.

A common depiction of the World Bank nowadays is that of an international organization that is overstretched and undernourished, and one that faces several conflicting challenges. These include the general decline in resources available for official development assistance, a rapidly expanding development agenda, and increasing competition from private lenders and other bilateral and nongovernmental aid agencies. The World Bank has also been subject to mounting criticism from nonstate actors, who are demanding the adoption of new policies that would greatly increase transparency, accountability, and self-

evaluation. Much of this has to do with the marked changes that have occurred in the international political economy since the World Bank's inception more than sixty years ago.

FROM PROJECT LENDING TO STRUCTURAL ADJUSTMENT

Up until the late 1960s, the World Bank was largely committed to project lending, meaning that its loans were used for investment in physical assets and infrastructure. Such projects were concrete, finite, and usually tied to a given sector, such as hydroelectric energy or railroad transport. This all changed when Robert McNamara assumed the World Bank presidency in 1968. McNamara placed poverty alleviation and the development process itself at the top of his agenda. He shifted the World Bank's mission toward country programming and a region-by-region deployment of project work that was no longer tied to just one sector. It was also during this period that conditionality for World Bank lending was tied more closely to a given country's effort to promote the satisfaction of basic needs among the poorest segment of the population. One of McNamara's strongest legacies was a massive allocation of in-house financial support for development research.

By 1973, when he began his second term as president, McNamara had linked growth with poverty reduction and strongly supported a shift from project lending to loans that would enable the developing countries to undertake structural adjustment programs geared toward policy reform and export promotion. These structural adjustment loans (SALs) would offer incentives for reform progress, as well as disincentives for reformers that lagged. The coinciding of the SALs and the 1973 oil price shocks would delay their widespread implementation until the 1980s, however, because the oil shocks generated excess international liquidity and low-cost private lending alternatives for many developing countries. As a result of these alternative lending sources, the World Bank's client countries were less receptive to the policy coaching and reform guidance that were a condition for disbursement of the SALs. McNamara served as president of the World Bank until 1981.

The advent of the 1982 debt crisis revealed the excesses of the previous decade's borrowing spree, as well as the inability of the World Bank and the IMF to motivate debt-burdened developing countries to sustain the kinds of macroeconomic policy reforms that had been built into the SALs. With the end of the cold war in the late 1980s, and after a full decade lost to policy mismanagement and false starts on the reform front in Africa and Latin America, SALs became most important for these regions. The World Bank embraced a new wave of neo-classical economic orthodoxy and openly promoted the virtues of liberalization.

The 1989 Baker Plan for developing-country debt restructuring signaled another shift in which the World Bank would play a major role. The idea, which met with debatable success, was to use multilateral lending to encourage private international banks to offer fresh loans to those highly indebted middle-income countries that were prepared to undertake further policy reforms. This period also saw the expansion of the World Bank's mandate to include new issue areas like environmental protection, women and development, private-sector reform, and deeper involvement in social service delivery. In 1990 the World Bank's annual *World Development Report* focused on poverty reduction, reviving earlier commitments that had surfaced during the McNamara era.

THE GLASS IS STILL HALF EMPTY

On December 31, 1991, then World Bank president Lewis Preston inserted the following reminder into each staff member's Operational Manual: "Sustainable poverty reduction is the Bank's overarching objective." This became a main benchmark by which the World Bank was judged as it approached its fiftieth anniversary in 1994. For many critics, the World Bank's shortcomings on this count were more notable than its achievements. "Fifty years is enough" became one of the retorting slogans from within a tightly knit community of global nongovernmental organizations (NGOs) that had been monitoring the World Bank's track record. Even a former career economist at the World Bank, William Easterly, would go on to publish a highly critical best-selling book, *The Elusive Quest for Growth* (2002), a patently blunt analysis of the weak link between World Bank lending and positive developmental outcomes in client countries over the lifetime of the bank.

Apart from its lackluster record on sustainable poverty reduction, the World Bank's branching out into other issue areas has run up against measurement and financing constraints. On the question of measurement, with each passing decade it has become more difficult to firmly assess and hold the institution accountable for the multiplicity of goals that have been pursued. The need to prioritize policy preferences and establish reliable evaluation indicators is one part of this problem; the other lies on the side on internal leadership. Rather than directly tackle those institutional weaknesses that have long been identified as impeding the World Bank's performance, Paul Wolfowitz, who was appointed World Bank president in 2005, has narrowly focused on the elimination of corruption within client borrowers. In the meantime, although the 2015 deadline for reaching the Millennium Development Goals is rapidly approaching, the World

Bank risks lagging further behind in its ability to play a key poverty reduction role.

On the question of financing, the World Bank faces two main constraints. First, there is a growing divergence between voting rights and the contributions made to IBRD equity by shareholders, as the share of retained earnings has risen while the share of paid-in capital has declined over the years. In short, the major shareholders have used their control rights to allocate portions of IBRD net income in ways that serve their interests over those of the institution as a whole. Second, the continuation of a stagnating loan portfolio in nominal terms, and a declining one in inflation-adjusted terms, is likely to curtail the bank's net income from lending operations and make its profitability increasingly dependent on financial trading. Part of this is a generational shift, whereby the dependence of middle-income countries on official assistance has greatly declined, leaving the IBRD with a dwindling client base. An obvious but highly controversial solution would be to shift these funds to the IDA, where the borrowing demands from poorer country members are still on the rise. While the IBRD is still the most important institution of the World Bank Group, and while it is obviously reluctant to cede financial power, the IDA is gaining ground in a de facto manner.

In sum, since the 1980s, the work of the World Bank has mainly affected the poorer developing countries, yet the structure of representation on the board of directors has changed little since it was established at Bretton Woods in 1944. This imbalance raises crucial stakeholder issues, for the World Bank's own research suggests that policy reform commitments will be upheld when governments actively participate in the identification and formulation of these very programs. On these grounds alone, the argument favoring internal reform of the World Bank's governance structure is a compelling one.

DEVELOPMENT AGENCY VERSUS DEVELOPMENT BANK

For all its shortcomings, it is important to note that the World Bank has successfully changed its profile from that of a development bank proper to the world's leading development agency. This partly reflects the long-term payoff from the financing of development research. Indeed, the World Bank has become one of the most important sources of knowledge for development and poverty reduction. The influence of the policy research generated in-house by the World Bank is overwhelming, both in terms of quality and quantity. Lending and operations, loan proposals, and assessment of the outcomes are still an important part of the bank's daily workload, but it also undertakes research in over 150 countries and brings together the world's largest concentration of development specialists.

A key criticism nowadays is that the legitimacy and credibility of the World Bank's expertise is drawn through a circular process between the knowledge it produces and the audiences that legitimize this knowledge. The World Bank Institute (WBI), created in 1955 to train policymakers in development economics, has become increasingly influential. In 1999 the WBI created the Global Development Network (GDN) with the aim of building research capacities in the Global South. But the GDN's doubters point to its rationalist tendency, which portrays research as scientific and independent from its social context. This is captured by the GDN slogan: "Better Research, Better Policy, Better World." However, neither its ideas nor its research are neutral. Partnerships with the South have enabled the World Bank to pair up with institutions that share its core ideas while arguably excluding other viewpoints. At a time when critics are calling for a more open and inclusive debate about development strategy, the World Bank seems increasingly resistant to an open exchange of this nature.

SEE ALSO *Corruption; Developing Countries; Development; Development Economics; Globalization, Social and Economic Aspects of; International Monetary Fund; Loans; Needs, Basic; Poverty; Structural Adjustment; Transparency*

BIBLIOGRAPHY

Birdsall, Nancy, ed. 2006. *What Next for the World Bank?* Washington, DC: Center for Global Development.

Easterly, William. 2002. *The Elusive Quest for Growth: Economists' Adventure and Misadventures in the Tropics.* Cambridge, MA: MIT Press.

Kapur, Devesh, John P. Lewis, and Richard Webb. 1997. *The World Bank: Its First Half Century.* Washington, DC: Brookings Institution Press.

Pincus, Jonathan R., and Jeffrey A. Winters, eds. 2002. *Reinventing the World Bank.* Ithaca, NY: Cornell University Press.

Woods, Ngaire. 2006. *The Globalizers: The IMF, and the World Bank, and Their Borrowers.* Ithaca, NY: Cornell University Press.

Carol Wise

WORLD HEALTH ORGANIZATION

The World Health Organization (WHO) was established in 1948 when its constitution entered into force. WHO

was created to be the United Nations' specialized agency for health. The WHO's mission is "the attainment by all peoples of the highest possible level of health" (WHO Constitution, Article 1).

International health cooperation began in the mid-nineteenth century, and the need for an international health organization was discussed in the latter half of that century. The first half of the twentieth century witnessed the creation of various types of health organizations, both regional (e.g., Pan American Sanitary Bureau, 1902) and international (e.g., Office International de l'Hygiène Publique, 1907; Health Organization of the League of Nations, 1923). WHO's establishment consolidated international health activities in one organization, membership in which was open to all states. In 2005, 192 states were WHO members.

The WHO Constitution's preamble defines *health* as the "state of complete physical, mental, and social well-being and not merely the absence of disease or infirmity." This definition empowers WHO to work on virtually all aspects of communicable and noncommunicable diseases. The WHO Constitution also stipulates that the enjoyment of the highest attainable standard of health is a fundamental human right, and the concept of a "right to health" has helped shape WHO policies.

WHO has three governing organs—the World Health Assembly (WHA), Executive Board (EB), and Secretariat. The WHA is the supreme policy-making body and is made up of representatives from all WHO member states. It meets annually to establish policy for the organization and to make other decisions important to WHO's operations, such as approving the budget. The EB acts as the WHA's executive organ and is comprised of representatives from thirty-two WHO member states who are technically qualified in the health field. The Secretariat, headed by a director general appointed by the WHA, is responsible for the technical and administrative aspects of WHO policy implementation.

WHO's headquarters are in Geneva, Switzerland, but there are also regional offices in the Americas, Europe, the eastern Mediterranean, Africa, Southeast Asia, and the western Pacific. WHO representatives working at the country level provide support to WHO headquarters and regional offices.

Since its establishment, WHO has focused much of its effort on improving health conditions, systems, and policies in developing countries. WHO efforts in this regard have followed two basic approaches. First, WHO has implemented "vertical" programs targeting specific diseases, such as disease eradication efforts. The second approach involves "horizontal" strategies that seek to improve health-system capacities with respect to multiple threats that populations face. WHO's efforts to ensure universal access to primary health care services provide an example of a horizontal approach.

WHO achieved some success in both vertical and horizontal strategies during the first few decades of its existence. In the late 1970s WHO completed the worldwide eradication of smallpox, an achievement widely regarded as one of the most important public health successes of the twentieth century. WHO also helped developing countries increase childhood immunization rates. Vertical strategies did not, however, always work. For example, WHO's campaign to eradicate malaria, initially started in the 1950s, did not succeed.

At approximately the same time that WHO successfully eradicated smallpox, it launched the seminal Health for All by the Year 2000 initiative, a horizontal campaign to provide all people, especially those in developing countries, with access to primary health care services. In addition to advancing the concept of the "right to health," the Health for All effort increased attention to the social determinants of poor health (e.g., poverty, limited education, and racial and gender inequities), which cannot be managed through medical technologies, such as vaccines, but only through social policies linking health with the pursuit of broader social or distributive justice.

These achievements were followed in the 1980s and 1990s by crises that revealed the weaknesses of and problems in WHO. The 1980s witnessed the explosion of HIV/AIDS into a global health problem, particularly for developing countries and especially sub-Saharan Africa. Responsibility for the global response to HIV/AIDS was eventually taken from WHO's Global Programme on AIDS in 1996 and assigned to a newly created entity, the Joint United Nations Programme on AIDS (UNAIDS). Nevertheless, HIV/AIDS continued to spread globally and, according to UNAIDS, has become one of the worst pandemics in human history.

In the 1990s WHO struggled with the emergence and reemergence of many new and old communicable diseases, a phenomenon made more challenging by the acceleration of globalization that occurred after the end of the cold war. The 1990s also saw WHO trying to address increased morbidity and mortality in the developing world caused by noncommunicable diseases, especially those related to tobacco consumption. WHO's responses to these mounting global health threats were undermined by leadership and institutional problems at WHO headquarters and regional offices. The failure of WHO member states to achieve the goals of Health for All by the Year 2000 was painfully apparent as the twentieth century came to a close.

Efforts in the latter half of the 1990s and the early 2000s to renew and reinvigorate WHO and its mission have achieved some success, returning credibility and

influence to the organization. Key achievements include the successful WHO global response to the 2003 outbreak of severe acute respiratory syndrome (SARS); the adoption of the Framework Convention on Tobacco Control in 2003 as part of the global strategy to reduce tobacco-related diseases; and the adoption in 2005 of the new International Health Regulations, which represent a significant development for global health governance and for WHO's authority and responsibility concerning the international spread of disease. WHO has also been active in addressing the benefits and costs globalization presents to health policy, assessing potential synergies and conflicts between health and international trade law (especially within WHO), working with nongovernmental organizations in health-centered public-private partnerships, advancing health components of the UN's Millennium Development Goals, and pursuing disease eradication (e.g., Global Polio Eradication Initiative).

SEE ALSO *Health in Developing Countries; Public Health*

BIBLIOGRAPHY

Fidler, David P. 2005. From International Sanitary Conventions to Global Health Security: The New International Health Regulations. *Chinese Journal of International Law* 4 (1): 1–68.

Goodman, Neville M. 1971. *International Health Organizations and Their Work*. 2nd ed. London: Churchill Livingstone.

Luca Burci, Gian, and Claude-Henri Vignes. 2004. *World Health Organization*. The Hague: Kluwer Law International.

Siddiqi, Javed. 1995. *World Health and World Politics: The World Health Organization and the UN System*. Columbus: University of South Carolina Press.

Tomasevski, Katarina. 1995. "Health." In *United Nations Legal Order*, vol. 2, eds. Oscar Schachter and Christopher C. Joyner, 859–906. Cambridge, U.K.: Cambridge University Press.

World Health Organization. http://www.who.int.

David P. Fidler

WORLD HEALTH REPORT

SEE *Health in Developing Countries.*

WORLD INSTITUTE FOR DEVELOPMENT ECONOMIC RESEARCH (WIDER)

SEE *Deininger and Squire World Bank Inequality Database.*

WORLD MUSIC

The term "world music" was first circulated in ethnomusicology (the study of music in or as culture) and entered Western popular culture as a category of musical commodity in the 1980s. It is a packaging of music "from the outside" into popular music primarily intended for Western consumers. In this sense, world music generally connotes non-Western music traditions (e.g., singing-storytelling in Mali, *qawwali* in Pakistan, and Aboriginal music in Australian); music that combines Western and non-Western elements (e.g., Nigerian *jùjú* and Afrobeat, Paul Simon's collaborations with South African musicians); and non-mainstream music from folk traditions or ethnic groups within Western societies (e.g., Irish folk music, salsa in New York, Indian *bhangra*—fusion of folk music with Western popular music—in London). The term is intended to exclude other marketing categories (e.g., classical, rock), but its boundaries have never been clearly delineated, and what is considered world music has changed over time, affected by shifting patterns of Western musical interests.

At least since the 1960s, ethnomusicologists have used the term world music to denote all music (e.g., folk, art, popular) of all the world's peoples. The "world" qualifier stresses the inclusion of non-Western music. In practice, studies of world music have tended not to include Western art (classical) music, so the term, as used in ethnomusicology, tends to refer more to music outside of that tradition.

Music scholar Timothy D. Taylor recounts the entry of world music into popular discourse in *Global Pop: World Music, World Markets* (1997). In response to growing sales of non-Western music recordings, representatives of independent record companies, broadcasters and concert promoters met in London in 1987 to discuss marketing the music. They determined that record stores were reluctant to stock the music because it was not clear under which heading it should be sold: The existing rubrics of folk, ethnic and international were not clearly defined, differentiated or adequately promoted. Following ethnomusicologists, the group decided to term the emerging niche *world music*. The term entered the music press and spread internationally. In 1990 *Billboard* magazine created a world music chart, and in the 1990s catalogues and guidebooks to world music appeared, such as *World Music: The Rough Guide*.

Whereas ethnomusicologists introduced the term world music as an inclusive term, in music promotion and distribution the term is used to distinguish it from other existing categories such as pop, rock, classical, and jazz. Yet the precise boundaries of the world music category are unclear and somewhat fluid, as the following examples illustrates. Filipina singer Banig sings in a Western pop

style with English lyrics, and as Timothy Taylor observes in *Global Pop*, she is classified as a world music artist. Swedish band Ace of Base, French Canadian Céline Dion, and German singer Nena are all categorized as pop music rather than world music, regardless of which language they use. World music is sometimes defined as "roots music," meaning that it is perceived as explicitly connecting with or continuing a people's tradition or heritage. Thus, while Nena and the German band Kraftwerk are not classified as world music, German Heimatmusik (music associated with the countryside) is categorized as world music. In addition, the content of world music racks in stores is shaped more by trends in Western music purchasing than a systematic attempt to represent all the world's music. The swelling of the Celtic music subcategory within world music in the 1990s was due to North Americans exploring their (vaguely defined) Celtic heritage and not, for example, a change in the overall makeup of the music of the world.

THE POPULARITY OF WORLD MUSIC IN WESTERN CULTURES

There has been Western interest in world music as far back as Westerners have encountered other cultures. For example, the Middle Eastern santur was a blueprint for the European pianoforte, and the banjo was descended from a Northwest African lute adapted by Africans in the Caribbean. During the twentieth century there was an acceleration of outside influences on music. Examples include the "Latin invasion" of the 1930s and 1940s (audible in the music of Duke Ellington and Dizzy Gillespie); the popularity of calypso in the 1940s and 1950s (the Andrew Sisters and Harry Belafonte); Brazilian *bossa nova* in the 1950s; and South African vocal music in the 1960s (The Tokens's "The Lion Sleeps Tonight").

During the 1960s and 1970s there was a surge in popularity of folk and folk-rock music, stimulating an unprecedented interest in world folk music recordings. Folkways Records and Elektra Records's Nonesuch Explorer Series began to meet this growing demand. Several British and American popular musicians incorporated world musical elements into their music, for example, George Harrison (Indian *sitar* and *ragas*), Led Zeppelin (Arabic melodies) and the Clash (reggae rhythm).

George Harrison, and Paul Simon later (with *Graceland*), not only incorporated world influences, but "curated" the music like ethnomusicologists. The musicians went into the field (Harrison to India, Simon to Africa), "discovered" the music, and presented it to the Europe and North American market, often performing with world musicians. World music was introduced to listeners by familiar musical personalities with star appeal.

David Byrne, Peter Gabriel, and Mickey Hart followed in this vein. Ethnomusicologist Steven Feld argues that the Western experience of world music in the 1980s was largely shaped by "pop star collaboration and curation" (Feld 2000, p. 149). As world music grew in popularity, an increasing number of record labels started marketing it.

Pop-star collaboration and curation continued into the 1990s; however, other channels of distribution also emerged. In the late 1990s and 2000s the Internet became a leading means of distributing world music. With the Internet, the term world music is perhaps less crucial to marketing because consumers can also search online by country of origin, musician, or instrument. But the category shows no signs of disappearing. The world music category is prominently used in Web sites and sold in the cosmopolitan cities of Europe, North America, Australia, and elsewhere. Also, chain coffee shops increasingly sell recordings of world music, such as the Hear Music CDs in Starbucks.

SEE ALSO *Ethnology and Folklore; Ethnomusicology; Globalization, Anthropological Aspects of; Indigenismo; Internet; Music; Music, Psychology of; Popular Music*

BIBLIOGRAPHY

Bohlman, Philip V. 2002. *World Music: A Very Short Introduction.* Oxford: Oxford University Press.

Broughton, Simon, Mark Ellingham, and Richard Trillo, et al., eds. 1999. *World Music: The Rough Guide.* London: Rough Guides/Penguin.

Feld, Steven. 1994. Notes on "World Beat." In *Music Grooves: Essays and Dialogues*, eds. Charles Keil and Steven Feld, pp. 238–246. Chicago: University of Chicago Press.

Feld, Steven. 2000. A Sweet Lullaby for World Music. *Public Culture* 12(1): 145–71.

Frith, Simon, ed. 1989. *World Music, Politics, and Social Change: Papers from the International Association for the Study of Popular Music.* Manchester, U.K.: Manchester University Press.

Guilbault, Jocelyn. 1997. Interpreting World Music: A Challenge in Theory and Practice. *Popular Music* 16(1): 31–44.

Meintjes, Louise. 1990. Paul Simon's *Graceland*, South Africa, and the Mediation of Musical Meaning. *Ethnomusicology* 34 (1): 37–73.

Mitchell, Tony. 1993. World Music and the Popular Music Industry: An Australian View. *Ethnomusicology* 37 (3): 309-38.

Sweeney, Philip. 1992. *The Virgin Directory of World Music.* New York: Henry Holt.

Taylor, Timothy D. 1997. *Global Pop: World Music, World Markets.* New York: Routledge.

Paul D. Greene

WORLD TRADE ORGANIZATION

The World Trade Organization (WTO) is the international organization that oversees trade among member nations and acts as a forum for governments to negotiate trade agreements and settle trade disputes under a system of rules and procedures. Its aim is to increase world trade by lowering barriers to the international sale of goods and services, including intellectual property. The WTO was formed on January 1, 1995, replacing the postwar multilateral trading order under the General Agreement on Tariffs and Trade (GATT) with a more formal institutional arrangement. Headquartered in Geneva, Switzerland, the WTO as of November 2006 had 150 members, the latest addition being Vietnam. As of this date Russia was the largest state that was not yet a member. The governing principles of the WTO's global trading system were described by Director General Pascal Lamy in 2006: "Built up stone by stone over the past 50 years, this system is founded on the idea that prosperity depends on efficiency, stability, predictability, and equity in international trade" (Lamy 2006).

THE SUCCESSOR TO THE GATT

In some respects, the WTO is a new organization, growing out of globalization, but the idea of an international trade institution dates at least to the period immediately following World War II (1939–1945). The Bretton Woods Conference of 1944, near the end of World War II, proposed the creation of an International Trade Organization to complement the International Monetary Fund and Bank for Reconstruction and Development (World Bank) in order to stabilize the postwar world economy and promote trade. The member states of the United Nations (UN) agreed to the creation of the International Trade Organization (ITO) at the UN Conference on Trade and Employment in Havana, Cuba, in 1948. The ITO charter covered trade in goods and services and included rules on employment, commodity agreements, restrictive business practices, and investment. The organization failed to materialize, however, when the U.S. Senate rejected the implementing agreement.

GATT, a part of the proposed ITO, survived as a treaty agreement among twenty-three of the fifty signatory states of the ITO to set tariffs (or customs duties) to mutually agreed-upon levels without discrimination among members under a *generalized system of preferences.* This system called for treating goods from all countries on the same level as that of the *most-favored nation (MFN)* and allotted *national treatment* to both domestic and imported goods once they had entered the market. Certain exceptions to the *nondiscrimination principle* were allowed—for example, for regional trading arrangements or special access to developing countries—because these types of arrangements expanded regional trade and accorded with the goal of expanding global trade. These principles and exceptions were incorporated into the WTO. Tariff levels were agreed on through an intergovernmental negotiating forum facilitated by the small GATT secretariat, but the system did not provide for any enforcement mechanisms or dispute-settlement procedures, and it dealt almost entirely in trade in goods. Services and intellectual property were later addressed under separate agreements—the General Agreement on Trade in Services (GATS) and the Agreement on Trade-Related Aspects of Intellectual Property Rights (TRIPS)—that were also incorporated into the WTO. GATT also contained provisions against unfair competitive practices, such as dumping and subsidies, that are also part of WTO fair-trade rules.

Two major industries were given special treatment under the postwar system—agriculture, which was not covered by GATT, and textiles and apparel, which was regulated under a quota system set up by a separate multilateral agreement, the Multifiber Agreement, until 2005. Eight rounds of multiyear trade negotiations were completed under GATT. The WTO was created at the conclusion of the eighth round, known as the Uruguay Round (1986–1995).

INSTITUTIONAL FRAMEWORK AND DISPUTE-RESOLUTION MECHANISMS

Unlike GATT, the WTO has an extensive institutional structure. It comprises the Ministerial Conference, the General Council, and a Secretariat with various bodies, committees, divisions, and working groups on specific issues. The General Council is the WTO's highest decision-making body and meets on a regular basis. Its members are official government representatives, the ambassadors to the WTO, from all member states. The Ministerial Conference comprises the trade or commerce ministers of the member states and meets approximately every two years; the Sixth WTO Ministerial Conference met in Hong Kong, China, on December 13–18, 2005. The Ministerial Conference issues declarations and decisions outlining the broad mandate of the WTO. A recurrent desire expressed in these declarations has been for greater cooperation and coherence between the IMF, World Bank, and WTO on global economic policy making and development.

The structure of the WTO was created by the legal texts of the Uruguay Round of trade negotiations, which include approximately sixty agreements, annexes, decisions, and understandings incorporating GATT, GATS, and TRIPS and covering trade in goods, services, intellec-

tual property, dispute settlement, and transparency through reviews of governments' trade policies. The agreements negotiated under GATT and the WTO provide the legal ground rules for international commerce, binding governments much like commercial contracts. Like any contract, disputes between parties are likely to arise, and for this reason a new dispute-settlement process was written into the WTO agreements and have become a central pillar of the global trading system. Within this system, a member country can file a dispute against another country or group of countries that it believes is violating a rule of the agreements or failing to live up to its obligations under the agreements.

The procedure resembles a court or tribunal, with formal consultations, mediation, and a panel set up to hear the arguments, examine the legal obligations of the parties, and prepare a report for the Dispute Settlement Body (consisting of all WTO members) to adopt or reject. It also includes an appeals process based on legal interpretation heard by a permanent Appellate Body composed of seven individuals of high legal standing without governmental affiliations. Members of the Appellate Body have four-year terms and can uphold, modify, or reverse the panel's legal findings or conclusions. Rulings are adopted by the Dispute Settlement Body automatically unless there is a consensus against the panel or appeals report (not a consensus in favor of the report) and are binding; if a state loses a dispute, it must comply with the report recommendations and state its intention to do so within thirty days. In cases of nonimplementation, the parties negotiate compensation pending full implementation. The Dispute Settlement Body monitors implementation of the report rulings and recommendations (if adopted) and has the power to authorize retaliatory action by the harmed country against the country violating its treaty obligations. By July 2005 a total of 332 cases had been brought before the WTO. A typical dispute may take up to sixty days for consultations, up to a year for panel review without an appeal, or a year and three months with an appeal. For any given dispute, the panel's report is normally presented to the parties within six months (or three months when the issue involves perishable goods).

THE DOHA ROUND

Trade negotiations among member states continue under the WTO, as under GATT, on a multiyear, multilateral basis. As of May 2007 the ninth round of global trade negotiations, the Doha Round, was still ongoing. Doha Round negotiations began in 2001 and are considered by many as much more difficult than earlier rounds. Several reasons are commonly used to explain this difficulty: (1) It goes deeper and farther than other rounds in addressing for the first time such issues as agricultural subsidies and

bureaucratic border requirements and documentation, making for political complexity. (2) It makes greater attempts at fair trade by making economic development more central to the international trading system. (3) The membership has grown so much in size and socioeconomic diversity that negotiating outcomes based on the practice of consensus has become much more difficult. (4) It faces strong opposition to globalization by various nonprofit associations representing labor, the environment, and other constituencies. The WTO has been a focus of globalization debates among intellectuals and policy makers and a target of antiglobalization protests by civil society groups.

CONTROVERSY AND 1999 SEATTLE PROTESTS

The WTO has come to represent the institutionalization of globalization, with its positive trade expansion effects as well as its negative effects on communities, local industry, and human rights. The adverse effects of globalization have given rise to a global social movement with active published criticism and consistent protests by activists at WTO Ministerial meetings as well as the annual World Bank–IMF conferences. The first protest of significant size and impact took place at the WTO Ministerial meeting in Seattle from November 29, 1999, to December 3, 1999. An estimated 50,000 protesters from around the world included human rights groups, students, environmental groups, religious leaders, labor-rights activists, others demanding fair trade with less exploitation, and various protectionist groups demanding a nationalist response to maintain domestic industries and preserve communities without foreign influence. While the majority were nonviolent protestors, a small group clashed violently with police, leading the Seattle police and the National Guard to declare a state of emergency that included curfews, arrests, teargas, pepper spray, and rubber bullets fired at nonviolent protestors. Many found the violation of the right of free speech for the purpose of free trade and the ensuing police actions unacceptable. Enormous public protests ensued, ultimately causing the resignation of the Seattle police chief and succeeding in disrupting the meeting, which collapsed. Over 500 related events took place between February 18, 1999, the day the Ministerial location in Seattle was announced, and mid-December 1999, after the WTO had departed. Over 1,400 organizations signed a letter stating their opposition to the WTO. According to the text of the letter, protesting organizations accused the WTO of

> principally to pry open markets for the benefit of transnational corporations at the expense of national and local economies; workers, farmers, indigenous peoples, women and other social

groups; health and safety; the environment; and animal welfare. In addition, the WTO system, rules and procedures are undemocratic, un-transparent and non-accountable and have operated to marginalize the majority of the world's people. (WTO History Project)

At the root of the protests are many fundamental differences in the perspectives of developing and industrialized nations, as well as labor unions and some domestic industry in developed countries, on the current reality of free trade and how it affects them. The protests have drawn attention to the democratic deficit within the WTO and to the social issues globalization can adversely impact. However, long-term legislative impact on the WTO itself remains unclear.

SEE ALSO *Diplomacy; Free Trade; General Agreement on Tariffs and Trade; Globalization, Social and Economic Aspects of; International Monetary Fund; Protest; Social Movements; Trade; Uruguay Round; World Bank, The*

BIBLIOGRAPHY

Bhagwati, Jagdish. 2005. *In Defense of Globalization*. Oxford: Oxford University Press.

Jackson, John H. 1998. *The World Trade Organization: Constitution and Jurisprudence*. London: Royal Institute of International Affairs.

Lamy, Pascal. 2006. Partnership and Global Prosperity. Speech made on June 5, 2006, in Montreal, Canada, for the International Economic Forum of the Americas. http://www.wto.org

Scott, Jeffrey J., ed. 2000. *WTO after Seattle*. Washington, DC: Institute for International Peace.

Stiglitz, Joseph E. 2003. *Globalization and Its Discontents*. New York: Norton.

Stiglitz, Joseph E. 2006. *Making Globalization Work*. New York: Norton.

Thomas, Janet. 2000. *The Battle in Seattle: The Story behind and beyond the WTO Demonstrations*. Golden, CO: Fulcrum.

Wallach, Lori, and Michell Sforza. 1999. *Whose Trade Organization? Corporate Globalization and the Erosion of Democracy: An Assessment of the World Trade Organization*. Washington, DC: Public Citizen.

WTO History Project, University of Washington. http://depts.washington.edu/wtohist/index.htm

Anastasia Xenias

WORLD WAR I

World War I (1914–1918), known as "The Great War" at the time, marked a profound political, economic, and social shift in international relations. Historian Eric Hobsbawm has referred to 1914 as the *de facto* beginning of the twentieth century.

The triggering cause of the war was the assassination of Archduke Franz Ferdinand, the Habsburg heir, on June 28, 1914, in Sarajevo by Bosnian Serb nationalists. This matter might have stayed an internal dispute in Austria-Hungary, but other states quickly took sides. Germany, the Ottoman Empire, and Austria-Hungary made up the Central Powers. Russia stood up for the Serbs, and was joined by France and Great Britain in the Triple Entente.

According to one interpretation of World War I, a rigid alliance structure drew reluctant states into what would otherwise have been a localized conflict. Many of the belligerents did have alliances binding them to a particular side. For example, both Britain and France had pledged to defend Belgian neutrality, which was violated at the beginning of the war by German invasion. However, all of the belligerents also had compelling national interests for participating in World War I, including concerns about national insurgency and perceptions of the European balance of power.

Nationalism drew belligerents into World War I in two ways. Russia defended Serbia at least partly in the name of pan-Slavism, or solidarity among Slavic peoples. The Ottoman Empire had a different concern. Like its Habsburg counterpart, the Ottoman Empire comprised a variety of national groups, all ruled by a single dominant national group. The spread of democracy and other egalitarian movements in Europe challenged the legitimacy of the old empires. Over the course of the nineteenth century, the Ottoman Empire experienced various national uprisings, including those by Greeks, Serbs, Bulgarians, and Armenians. By helping the Habsburgs resist nationalist insurgency, the Ottomans hoped to avert future problems of their own.

In addition, many states were concerned about the changing European balance of power. The pentagonal balance created at the 1815 Congress of Vienna had been relatively successful, both in keeping European conflicts manageable and protecting the interests of Austria-Hungary, Britain, France, Germany (previously called Prussia), and Russia. By 1914, however, several of these states were not content with the existing balance of power.

For example, Germany was a latecomer to imperialism, a process dominated by France and Britain, and therefore perceived itself at a disadvantage in both power projection and resource extraction. Although overseas imperialism offered limited possibilities by the early 1900s, Germany began to pursue a policy (*Drang nach Osten*) of increased economic and political influence in eastern Europe, thus "colonizing" the region. German leaders argued that this would balance French and British power.

France and Britain, however, did not perceive themselves as at an advantage vis-à-vis Germany. Germany had benefited tremendously from the Industrial Revolution, especially since its natural resource base was well suited to industrial production. In 1870, Germany ranked third in industrial production behind Britain and France. By 1914, Germany led them both by a substantial margin. Britain and France feared that Germany's economic trajectory would soon render moot efforts at power balancing. To avoid German hegemony as a *fait accompli*, the other great powers would need to act quickly.

Russia, too, had balance-of-power concerns regarding Germany, with which it shared a tense history. The *Drang nach Osten* interfered with Russia's domestic economy and trade with its neighbors. Furthermore, Russia had been at an enduring geopolitical disadvantage because it lacked warm water ports (i.e., ones in which the water does not freeze), which limited its military and commercial expansion. Defeating the Central Powers could mean Russian access to Germany's Baltic ports and the Mediterranean Sea via Turkish straits.

THE WORLD AT WAR

Once the war began, its course was horrifyingly unique to European experience. Germany expanded the aggression outside of Austria-Hungary by implementing the Schlieffen Plan, a military strategy designed to prevent Germany from fighting on two fronts simultaneously. The existence of such a plan reflected the influence of prevailing social attitudes on military doctrine. The popularity of ideas such as Social Darwinism, a perversion of Charles Darwin's concept of natural selection then applied to human social interaction, bred a pan-European "cult of the offensive," or fanatical confidence in initial aggression as the guarantor of victory. Darwin argued that organisms with traits well suited to their environment would be the most likely to survive and reproduce. The Social Darwinist ideal twisted this commentary to argue that powerful groups had the ability, even the right, to dominate weaker ones and to mold human relations as they saw fit. As a result, states generated extremely aggressive military grand strategies—their overall plans for using the military instrument of foreign policy. For example, Germany's Schlieffen Plan called for the speedy conquest of France, via neutral Belgium, so German forces could then focus on an eastern front against Russia, which would mobilize relatively slowly for geographic and technological reasons.

The reality of World War I looked very little like the Schlieffen Plan. In early August 1914, Germany attacked Belgium. Reinforced by troops from Britain and France, Belgium tenaciously resisted German invasion. Russia, having anticipated conflict with Germany and availing itself of technological advances such as railroads, mobilized faster than Germany had anticipated. Within weeks, Germany found itself caught in a two-front war.

This conflict was unlike any Europe had seen before. A popular slogan claimed that soldiers marching off in August 1914 would be "home before the leaves fall from the trees," but even after months the two sides had made little progress toward their war aims. Various conditions of the war made territorial conquest difficult. In the west, the extremely flat terrain of Southwestern Belgium provided little natural shelter. This encouraged trench warfare, the digging of passageways open to the surface, from which soldiers could attack with at least minimal cover. The introduction of barbed wire assisted in this process and in holding territory. Capturing territory from the trenches was difficult. Instead, World War I became a war of attrition, in which victory would be defined by exhausting the enemy's resources rather than by superior mobility and territorial conquest. Military engagement frequently ended in deadlock, as when the 1916 German attack at Verdun preempted an Entente offensive on the Somme, but did not achieve the larger goal of crippling the French. Later that year, Britain launched its first major offensive of the war, at the Somme. In four months the Entente lost some 600,000 men while gaining only a few miles of territory. For years, neither side had an enduring battlefield advantage, although both expended unprecedented amounts of materiel and human lives. At least twenty million soldiers were killed or wounded during the war.

Military leaders introduced destructive new technologies, attempting to break the trench stalemate. Machine guns allowed for tremendous firepower and resulted in devastating casualties, as did tanks and submarines as new weapons platforms. Poison gas, introduced by Germany at Ypres in 1915, was difficult to control in deployment and undetectable until its effects were irreversible; gas caused pain, burns, other physical trauma, and death. These conditions eventually generated a sense of futility and ennui among many soldiers, and caused mutiny late in the war, such as that of the French army in 1917. One of the lasting consequences of these battle conditions was the emergence of "shell shock" (today known as post-traumatic stress disorder), which disabled thousands of soldiers who had survived the fighting.

On the eastern front, armies enjoyed greater mobility but suffered staggering casualties in the face of the technological innovations. In 1917 Russia withdrew from the conflict because of the Bolshevik Revolution. Britain and France appealed to the United States, which had been supplying their war effort for some time, to take Russia's place. Although President Woodrow Wilson (1856–1924) had campaigned on a no-war platform, the economic significance, in particular of Britain and France, finally persuaded him to change his position. With the declaration

of war by the U.S. Congress on April 6, 1917, the United States formally allied itself with Britain and France.

The new influx of American resources and personnel, beginning in earnest in the summer of 1918, was too much for Germany. Recognizing that Germany could not win a war of attrition against this energetic, well-supplied new enemy, the German navy mutinied, popular revolution led the Kaiser to abdicate, and the new government agreed to an armistice on the Entente's terms. The agreement was signed on November 11, 1918, at 11: 00 a.m. For many Germans, the Entente victory seemed illegitimate. Germany had not been outmaneuvered on the battlefield and victorious Entente troops did not capture Berlin. Rather, the Entente seemed to have won by calling in outsiders to the dispute; this said nothing about Germany's prowess vis-à-vis France and Britain.

Beginning in January 1919, the former belligerents met in Paris to formulate the peace treaty, known as the Treaty of Versailles after the palace in which it was signed. President Wilson attended the conference, to the surprise and consternation of many of his counterparts, making him the first sitting U.S. president to visit a foreign country. Two major goals of the treaty were to render Germany harmless and to avoid future problems with national insurgency. To achieve the first goal the victors implemented a number of programs targeting Germany, including reparation payments, disarmament, and neutralization of territory. To achieve the second goal, the victors promoted national self-determination for European ethnic groups, redrawing the map of eastern Europe so that the political boundaries more closely matched the homelands of ethnic groups.

SEE ALSO *Colonialism; Darwinism, Social; Genocide; Imperialism; Isolationism; Monarchy; Nationalism and Nationality; Ottoman Empire; Patriotism; Post-Traumatic Stress; Revolution; Russian Revolution; War; Wilson, Woodrow; World War II*

BIBLIOGRAPHY

Ferro, Marc. 1973. *The Great War, 1914–1918.* Trans. Nicole Stone. London: Routledge & K. Paul.

Fussell, Paul. 1975. *The Great War and Modern Memory.* New York: Oxford University Press.

Kennedy, David M. 1980. *Over Here: The First World War and American Society.* New York: Oxford University Press.

Keylor, William R. 2001. Germany's Bid for European Dominance (1914–1918). In *The Twentieth-Century World, an International History.* 4th ed. New York: Oxford University Press.

Van Evera, Stephen. 1984. The Cult of the Offensive and the Origins of the First World War. *International Security* 9 (1): 58–107.

Lisa L. Ferrari

WORLD WAR II

World War II was a military conflict from 1939 to 1945 that engulfed much of the globe. It is considered to have been the largest and deadliest war in world history, killing 62 million people on the battlefield, in massive bombings of civilians in cities, and by genocide. There were two hostile camps—the Axis Powers of Germany, Italy, Japan, Romania, Bulgaria, Hungary, Croatia, Slovakia, Finland (cobelligerent), Thailand, and others; and the Allied Powers of the British Empire and Commonwealth (including India, Canada, Australia and New Zealand), France, the United States, the Soviet Union, China, the Netherlands, Norway, Belgium, Poland, and others. The global reach of the empires of France, Italy, and Britain meant that non-European areas became directly involved with battles fought in Africa, the Middle East, Europe, and Asia. Organized civilian resistance movements in occupied countries (notably Yugoslavia, France, and Greece) made important contributions to the Allied war effort. The economic effects of the war have been estimated at $1 trillion in 1945 (approximately $10.5 trillion in 2005 terms). It is the only time in history that nuclear weapons were used (by the United States against Japan). The end of World War II resulted in the partitioning of Europe into East (ruled by Communist governments under the sphere of influence of the Soviet Union aligned under the Council for Mutual Economic Assistance, or Comecon, and the Warsaw Pact) and West (with democratic governments receiving economic reconstruction aid through the U.S. Marshall Plan aligned under NATO), the U.S. occupation of Japan, and new international organizations such as the United Nations, the International Monetary Fund, and the World Bank. The immediate postwar era also saw the rise of European integration efforts with the formation of the European Coal and Steel Community and the European Economic Community, which would develop into the European Union by the end of the century, and the beginning of the cold war between the United States and the Soviet Union that would mark the second half of the twentieth century.

EXPANSIONISM AND ECONOMIC CONDITIONS

Territorial expansion of Germany and Italy began before any military hostilities. The most noted example of territorial demands made by Hitler's Germany is Czechoslovakia (where Germans comprised one-third of the population), followed by German-speaking Austria. But the Reich sought further expansion. Many in Germany never accepted the creation of Poland following World War I, and they focused territorial demands on the Polish Corridor, a narrow strip of land separating East Prussia from Germany that allowed Poland access to the Baltic

Sea, but also sought broader territory that would expand Germany to a common border with Russia. In 1935 Germany regained the Saar region, in March 1936 it reoccupied the Rhineland, and in 1937 it achieved *Anschluss* (union) with Austria. Italy's fascist leader, Benito Mussolini, also hoped to acquire territory, particularly at the expense of France, Albania, and Greece, to create a New Roman Empire. In 1934 Italy moved against Abyssinia on the border of Italian Somaliland and Ethiopia. Territory was also an important factor in the war in Asia. One of the most often cited reasons for Japan's aggression in Asia is that nation's need for the raw materials naturally lacking in its own territory. Thus Japan, the only burgeoning industrial economy in Asia at the time, invaded first Manchuria, then other areas throughout the Asian mainland, and finally the Western Pacific in order to secure necessary natural resources such as oil and iron ore.

The economic effects of the Treaty of Versailles and the Great Depression were important factors in radicalizing German politics. In April 1921 Germany was presented with a reparations bill of $33 billion by the victorious allies of World War I. Reparations payments hobbled the weakened German economy, causing rapidly rising inflation and a dramatically depreciating currency. France refused Germany's request for a postponement, Germany defaulted on the war reparations in 1923, and the French army occupied part of the Ruhr (the German industrial zone). Hyperinflation ensued as the German currency, the mark, plummeted to 4 billion marks to the dollar (from 75 marks to the dollar in 1921 and 18,000 in January 1923), eliminating life savings and making salaries worthless. Groceries cost billions of marks (wheelbarrows of currency were needed for a single loaf of bread) and hunger riots broke out. In September 1923 the German government resumed reparations payments, inciting bitter popular resentment and paving the way for extremist political groups such as the Nazi Party (National Socialist Party).

IDEOLOGY, NATIONALISM, AND MILITARISM

Under the terms of the Treaty of Versailles, the German army was allowed to remain intact and was not forced to admit defeat by surrendering. The German general staff supported the idea that the army had not been defeated on the battlefield and could have fought on to victory were they not betrayed at home (the *Dolchstosslegende*, or "stab-in-the-back legend") by German politicians who signed the November 1918 armistice (the "November Criminals"). The theory became very popular among Germans: Adolf Hitler, a World War I veteran, became obsessed with this idea, laying blame firmly on Jews and Marxists for undermining Germany's war effort. The Nazi

Party won 230 of 608 seats in the Reichstag (German parliament) in January 1933; within six months Hitler was elected chancellor. The Nazis pledged to first restore Germany to its rightful place in Europe, and then to seek world power.

Racism and anti-Semitism characterized the Nazi Party, which organized official boycotts of Jewish shops and professional men and the opening of the first concentration camp in Dachau, outside Munich, in March 1933. In September 1935 the Nuremberg Laws relegated Jews to separate, second-class status and prohibited intermarriage and sexual relations with Aryan Germans. In November 1938 Nazis orchestrated a nationwide pogrom on Jews following the murder of a German diplomatic assistant in the German embassy in Paris by a French Jew. Jewish homes, shops, and 191 synagogues were destroyed and 20,000 Jews were arrested on *Kristallnacht* ("Night of Broken Glass"). German anti-Semitism culminated in the Holocaust.

Although technically an absolute monarchy under Emperor Hirohito, Japan was politically dominated by a group of militaristic generals in charge of the most powerful army in Asia at the time. Japanese militarism was accompanied by racism, toward both Europeans and other Asians, especially Chinese and Koreans. Anyone who was not Japanese was considered inferior and treated as such. One example of Japanese violent racism is General Shiro Ishii's Unit 731 experiments in Pingfan in Harbin, China, in which as many as 10,000 Chinese, Korean, and Russian prisoners of war and civilians were subjected to brutal experiments in vivisection, germ warfare, and weapons testing.

APPEASEMENT

Britain and France followed an early policy of accommodation and compromise in Germany's favor in the hope of avoiding another war, known as the "policy of appeasement"; many thought the Treaty of Versailles imposed unreasonable demands on Germany. In June 1935 the Anglo-German Naval Agreement was signed, signaling Britain's unwillingness to defend the Versailles settlement. In March 1936 German military reoccupation of the Rhineland (demilitarized under the Versailles Treaty) met with no opposition from France and thus successfully challenged France's willingness to defend the Versailles settlement. In January 1937 Hitler publicly broke with the Treaty of Versailles.

Neville Chamberlain, the prime minister of Britain from 1937 to 1940, is known for adopting a policy of appeasement in an attempt to preserve the peace and buy time for any major rearmament. In September 1938 Britain, France, and Italy agreed at the Munich Conference to grant Czechoslovakia's Sudetenland to Germany. In

return, Hitler gave Chamberlain his personal word on future cooperation. The Munich Pact is considered the height of appeasement. On his return to London, Chamberlain stated: "We regard the agreement signed last night [Munich Pact] and the Anglo-German Naval Agreement as symbolic of the desire of our two peoples never to go to war with one another again.... My good friends, for the second time in our history, a British Prime Minister has returned from Germany bringing peace with honor. I believe it is peace for our time.... Go home and get a nice quiet sleep." Chamberlain resigned in 1940 and was replaced by Winston Churchill, who led Britain to the end of the war. The Molotov-Ribbentrop Pact of nonaggression signed by Germany and the Soviet Union in 1939 is also considered by some historians as an act of appeasement or as an attempt by Joseph Stalin to buy time to prepare for an impending German attack on the Soviet Union.

U.S. ENTRY INTO THE WAR

Since 1940 the United States had allowed the covert operation in China of the American Volunteer Group, or "Chennault's Flying Tigers," to assist the Chinese war effort. The Flying Tigers destroyed an estimated 115 Japanese aircraft, sunk numerous Japanese ships, and participated in the Burma land campaign. U.S. president Franklin D. Roosevelt cut exports of oil and scrap iron to Japan in 1941. Japan planned and executed a strike on Pearl Harbor, Hawaii, on Sunday, December 7, 1941, to cripple the U.S. Pacific fleet and consolidate oil fields in Southeast Asia. The attack on Pearl Harbor achieved military surprise and severely damaged the U.S. navy, and it remains the largest military attack on U.S. soil.

Following the Japanese attack on Pearl Harbor, Hitler declared war on the United States on December 11, 1941, in the hope that Japan would assist Germany by attacking the Soviet Union (it did not). Pearl Harbor, in conjunction with Hitler's declaration of war, gave Roosevelt the domestic support he needed to join the war in Europe and Asia without meaningful opposition from Congress. Many historians consider this an important turning point of the war in Europe, marking the formation of a grand alliance of powerful nations (the United Kingdom, the United States, and the Soviet Union) against Germany.

POSTWAR DIVISION, OCCUPATION, AND RECONSTRUCTION

After World War II, Europe was informally partitioned into Western Europe and Eastern Europe under the NATO and Warsaw Pact military alliances and the Marshall Plan and Comecon economic arrangements. Germany was formally divided into the states of the Federal Republic of Germany (F.D.R., or West Germany) and the German Democratic Republic (G.D.R., or East Germany). Allied troops remained in Germany for decades following the war. Following German reunification in October 1990, the new united Germany still had Soviet troops stationed in its eastern provinces.

The U.S. Marshall Plan intended to rebuild the European economy and promote European unity while thwarting the political appeal of communism. For Western Europe, economic aid ended the dollar shortage and stimulated private investment for postwar reconstruction. The Marshall Plan required European states to work together to utilize the funds, an obligation that later facilitated the formation of the European Economic Community.

The Council for Mutual Economic Assistance (COMECON, Comecon, CMEA, or CEMA) was formed in 1949 as an economic organization of Communist states. Its original members were the Soviet Union, Bulgaria, Romania, Hungary, Czechoslovakia, Albania, the German Democratic Republic, and Poland. Albania, Hungary, Czechoslovakia, Bulgaria, and Romania, which were allied with the Axis Powers during the war, came under the Soviet sphere of influence, with their Communist governments joining the Soviet-led Comecon economic and trade area, as did Poland. In 1950 East Germany joined Comecon. (Other members included Mongolia [1962], Cuba [1972], and Vietnam [1978]. Yugoslavia [1964] was an associate member; other Communist countries or Soviet-friendly governments were observers.) Comecon members had common approaches to state economic ownership and planned management, and political regimes that espoused the ideologies of Marxism-Leninism. In 1949 the ruling Communist parties of the founding states were also linked internationally through the Cominform, the Communist Information Bureau, which established information exchanges between members. The East European members of Comecon were also militarily allied with the Soviet Union in the Warsaw Pact.

In Asia, the U.S. military occupation of Japan led to Japan's democratization. China's civil war continued during and after World War II, culminating in the establishment of the Communist People's Republic of China. Europe's Asian colonies India, Indonesia, and Vietnam started toward independence.

LEGACY OF WORLD WAR II

One of the most important legacies of World War II was the creation of a set of international institutions to provide for international governance of global security and monetary relations. Postwar security and economic institutions were created exclusively by the victorious Allied Powers and reflected the postwar power structure. The term *United Nations* was first coined by Roosevelt during

the war to refer to the Allies. On January 1, 1942, the Declaration by the United Nations committed the Allies to the principles of the Atlantic Charter and pledged them not to seek a separate peace with the Axis Powers. Thereafter, the Allies used the term *United Nations Fighting Forces* to refer to their alliance. The United Nations institutions were created during the war itself to govern international relations after the war.

The initial ideas for a global security organization were first elaborated at wartime Allied conferences in Moscow, Cairo, and Tehran in 1943. During August to October 1944 representatives from France, Britain, the Soviet Union, China, and the United States met in Dumbarton Oaks in Washington, D.C., to prepare plans for an organization that would maintain peace and security, and economic and social cooperation. The formal monetary conference predated the security conference: The United Nations Monetary and Financial Conference of July 1 to 22, 1944 (called the Bretton Woods conference), took place in Bretton Woods, New Hampshire, with 730 delegates from 45 Allied countries. It established the Bretton Woods system of international exchange-rate management that remained in place until the mid-1970s, and it produced two separate institutions (called the Bretton Woods institutions) to monitor, regulate, and facilitate international monetary affairs and finance in the post–World War II era. The World Bank and the International Monetary Fund, both headquartered in Washington, D.C., have had lasting influence on the international political economy since their inception. The International Monetary Fund was entrusted with overseeing the global financial system by monitoring exchange rates and balance of payments, providing liquidity, and offering technical and financial assistance. The World Bank, or International Bank for Reconstruction and Development (IBRD), was entrusted with providing finance such as grants or loans at preferential rates, technical assistance, and advice to countries for the purpose of economic development and poverty reduction, and for encouraging and safeguarding international investment. Although the World Bank's activities have evolved to focus on developing countries, the first loan issued by the World Bank was approved on May 9, 1947, to France in the amount of $250 million for postwar reconstruction; this remains its largest loan to date in real terms. World Bank loans and grants provide financing to countries that have no access to international capital markets.

The United Nations Conference on International Organizations opened at the Fairmont Hotel in San Francisco on April 25, 1945, with fifty nations and some nongovernmental organizations represented. Initially referred to as the United Nations Organization, the UN was comprised of several administrative bodies (General Assembly, Secretariat, Economic and Social Council,

Trusteeship Council, and the International Court of Justice to adjudicate disputes among nations), the most prominent of which is the Security Council, where members resolve action on issues of war and aggression. (For example, all UN peacekeeping operations must be approved by the Security Council.) The United Nations Charter was signed on June 26, 1945, and the UN, headquartered in New York City, came into existence in October 1945 after the charter had been ratified by the five permanent members of the Security Council and a majority of signatory states. It replaced the League of Nations, which had been founded after World War I and had proved ineffective at preventing war and securing peace and order. The structure of the UN reflected the World War II victory, with the most powerful Allies—the United Kingdom, France, the United States, the Soviet Union, and China—holding the only permanent seats in the UN Security Council with veto power over decisions. The World Bank and International Monetary Fund came into existence a few months after the UN, in December 1945 following international ratification of the Articles of Agreement (called the Bretton Woods agreements).

Another legacy of World War II saw the development and use of many new technologies, including long-range missiles, jet aircraft, radar, and atomic (nuclear) weapons. Nuclear weapons were created in the top-secret Manhattan Project in the United States (with assistance from the United Kingdom and Canada) by an international team that included émigré scientists from Central Europe, initially out of fear that Germany would develop them first. (The Soviet Union became the second nuclear power in 1949.) Nuclear weapons have only been used twice in the history of warfare, both in the closing days of World War II by the United States against Japan, the first on August 6, 1945, on the Japanese city of Hiroshima, and the second on August 9, 1945, on the Japanese city of Nagasaki. Each use comprised the dropping of a single airborne atomic bomb (atom bomb, A-bomb, or simply "the bomb"). The bombs killed an estimated 200,000 people (mostly civilians) instantly, and twice as many later through the effects of radiation. The advent of nuclear weapons came only weeks after the signing of the UN Charter, providing immediate impetus to concepts of arms limitation and disarmament. The first resolution of the first meeting of the UN General Assembly on January 24, 1946, was "The Establishment of a Commission to Deal with the Problems Raised by the Discovery of Atomic Energy," which called upon the commission to make specific proposals for "the elimination from national armaments of atomic weapons and of all other major weapons adaptable to mass destruction."

World War II atrocities and genocide in both Europe and Asia led to a consensus that nations must work to prevent such tragedies in the future. Another early objective

of the United Nations was to create a legal framework for considering and acting on complaints about human rights violations. The UN Charter obliges all member nations to promote "universal respect for, and observance of, human rights" and to take "joint and separate action" to that end. The Universal Declaration of Human Rights was adopted by the UN General Assembly in 1948 as a common standard of achievement for all.

World War II resulted in a fundamental shift in global power from the weakened British Empire to the United States and the Soviet Union. Almost immediately following World War II, a protracted geopolitical, ideological, and economic struggle emerged between two of the most powerful Allied Powers—the United States and the Soviet Union. The struggle was called the cold war because it did not involve direct armed conflict between the United States and the Soviet Union, although each formed an opposing military alliance in Europe and engaged in the biggest arms race (including nuclear weapons) in history. The cold war lasted from about 1947 to the collapse of communism in the late 1980s, the fall of the Berlin Wall in 1989, and the dissolution of the Soviet Union in 1991.

The North Atlantic Treaty Organization (NATO, or the North Atlantic Alliance, Atlantic Alliance, or Western Alliance) was established with the signing of the North Atlantic Treaty on April 4, 1949, in Washington, D.C., for the purpose of collective security of the members, binding each to a military alliance with all the others. The treaty avoids identification of an enemy or concrete measures of common defense, but the implied adversary was the Soviet Union. This marked a significant change in the isolationist tendencies of the United States and signaled the lasting involvement of the United States in European security affairs. It also formally divided the World War II Allies in the West from the Soviet Union by creating a new military alliance composed largely of World War II Allied Powers. The original members of NATO were the United States, France, Britain, Belgium, Luxembourg, Netherlands, Portugal, Norway, Denmark, and Iceland (West Germany was not incorporated until 1955, after the formation of the Warsaw Pact).

In 1955 the Warsaw Pact (Warsaw Treaty, or Treaty of Friendship, Cooperation, and Mutual Assistance) was established as a military organization of Eastern and Central European Communist states to counter the threat perceived by NATO. Its members consisted of the Soviet Union, Bulgaria, Czechoslovakia, Hungary, Poland, Romania, East Germany (in 1956), and Albania (which withdrew in 1968). Similar to the NATO members, the Warsaw Pact signatories pledged to defend each other if one of them was attacked. It is noteworthy that the members of the Warsaw Pact consisted of Axis Powers as well

as Allied Powers (the Soviet Union and Poland). The Warsaw Pact officially dissolved in 1991. Although not a member of NATO, the Axis Power Japan became allied with the United States. Although not a member of the Warsaw Pact, the Allied Power China was friendly to the Soviet Union. Countries such as Yugoslavia, Switzerland, Austria, India, Sweden, and Finland conspicuously maintained their neutrality by participation in the Non-Aligned Movement.

SEE ALSO *Defense; Deterrence, Mutual; Disarmament; Pearl Harbor; Warfare, Nuclear; Weaponry, Nuclear*

BIBLIOGRAPHY

Bundy, McGeorge. 1988. *Danger and Survival: Choices About the Bomb in the First Fifty Years.* New York: Random House.

Churchill, Winston S. 1948–1953. *The Second World War.* 6 vols. Boston: Houghton-Mifflin.

Gaddis, John Lewis. 1997. *We Now Know: Rethinking Cold War History.* Oxford: Clarendon Press; New York: Oxford University Press.

Gaddis, John Lewis, ed. 1999. *Cold War Statesmen Confront the Bomb: Nuclear Diplomacy Since 1945.* New York: Oxford University Press.

Gilbert, Martin. 1988. *Atlas of the Holocaust.* New York: Pergamon Press.

Keegan, John, ed. 1978. *Who Was Who in World War II.* New York: T. Y. Cromwell.

Keegan, John. 1989. *The Second World War.* London: Hutchinson.

Kimball, Warren F. 1992. *America Unbound: World War II and the Making of a Superpower.* New York: St. Martin's Press.

Overy, Richard J. 1995. *Why the Allies Won.* New York: W. W. Norton.

Shirer, William L. 1959. *The Rise and Fall of the Third Reich.* New York: Simon and Schuster.

Tohmatsu, Haruo, and H. P. Willmott. 2004. *A Gathering of Darkness: The Coming of War to the Far East and the Pacific.* Lanham, MD: SR Books.

Watt, Donald Cameron. 1989. *How War Came: The Immediate Origins of the Second World War, 1938–1939.* New York: Pantheon.

Young, Robert. 1996. *France and the Origins of the Second World War.* New York: St. Martin's Press.

Anastasia Xenias

WORLD-SYSTEM

The great French historian Fernand Braudel coined the term *économie-monde* (world-economy). The hyphen is important; it signifies that he did not mean that his "economy" covered the whole world, merely that it was effec-

tively *a* world. Braudel's major work, *The Mediterranean and the Mediterranean World in the Age of Philip II* (1972–1973) on the sixteenth century, inspired the American founder of "world-systems theory," Immanuel Wallerstein (b. 1930).

According to Wallerstein, if we exclude small-scale societies, which he calls mini-systems, where a complete economic division of labor is accompanied by a single culture, we have only *world*-systems. Of these there are just two variants. The *world-empire* has many cultures but a single political superstructure (and a division of labor). The *world-economy* possesses a single economic division of labor. Unlike the mini-system and the world-empire, it has both many cultures and many political units. The capitalist world-economy started in sixteenth-century northwestern Europe and has continued to exist ever since, unlike other (non-capitalist) world-economies and world-empires. Capitalism is a system given over to the unlimited accumulation of capital through exchange. It is driven by the search for profit. Profit comes from unequal exchange (a term pioneered in the Latin American context), whereby goods produced under monopolistic conditions in the core are traded for other goods produced in the periphery under competitive conditions; that is, non-monopolistic ones, in many countries. The former goods enjoy a cost advantage over the latter. This is because the sale price is high relative to the cost of production, whereas, in contrast, peripheral producers are forced to sell cheaply, close to or at the cost of production. (*Surplus value*, for Wallerstein, is the difference between cost of production and sale price of a product.) Goods produced under competitive conditions in the peripheral zones of the capitalist world-economy tend to flow to countries located in the core of the capitalist world-economy. Profits are highest to producers located in this core. The states located in the core are used by leading capitalists to prop up the system. Trade within this system, in which they enjoy a marked, historically unprecedented freedom of maneuver, benefits the latter unequally.

Wallerstein likens his interest in the historical development of the capitalist world-economy, seen as a single "unit of analysis," to that of the astronomers in the single planetary system, the laws of motion of which they set out to discover. It is the world-system as a whole that interests him. This overall system determines what goes on in any particular part. Nation-states are only one institution among others in the capitalist world-economy. What goes on in them is determined less by the character of a particular nation-state and far more by this state's position within the capitalist world-economy.

From 1540 the geographical area of northwestern Europe emerged as the "core." Eastern Europe and Iberian America were reduced to peripheral status in relation to this core. Mediterranean Europe settled into an intermediate position, becoming semiperipheral, midway between core and periphery within the system. Its trade, state structure, and forms of labor exploitation reflected this intermediate position, just as in the cases of the core and the periphery. Subsequent phases of development saw industrial capitalism appear in the core; the European world-economy spread to encompass the entire globe; and changes within the core, semiperiphery, and periphery. The periphery includes most of Asia and Africa, the semiperiphery at various times Japan, the United States, Germany, and Russia. After 1945 the United States assumed a leading role in the whole system, closely followed by, among others, Soviet Russia. The USSR, although nominally a socialist state, could not, in Wallerstein's judgment, possibly have been one. There is just one capitalist world-economy to date, and there can as yet be no socialist systems. Socialism awaits the qualitative change of the whole system, which, following deepening crises, will eventually assume the form of a world government. This revolution is preparing itself mainly in the periphery of the capitalist world-economy.

WORLD-SYSTEMS ANALYSIS

Capitalism requires a world economy. This is because it requires capitalists to be free of political interference—that is, free to accumulate; capitalists also require a large market, so cannot inhabit a mini-system. It is the continuous accumulation that has provided the system with its dynamism over five hundred years. Competition between capitalists is continuous. The division of labor, implying the exchange of basic goods and significant flows of capital and labor, alone binds the system together. It can do so because of the expansive properties of capitalism that have enabled capitalism to survive and grow continuously. (Noncapitalist world-economies have not survived.) Capitalists, to flourish, need to be able to evade states hostile to their interests and to pressure other states into pursuing policies favorable to those interests. They need a multistate world-system. Profit comes from state-supported quasi-monopolies. Capitalists in the core can charge high prices but producers in the periphery are in no position to do so.

Core countries are few. Peripheral ones are many. The semiperipheral countries (e.g., South Korea, India, and Brazil) aim to move up to the core and to avoid falling down into the periphery. They have a mix of activities—some are core-like, some are periphery-like—whereas in core and periphery countries, core and periphery activities are respectively preponderant. Surplus value flows in the core from the working class to the employers, but it also flows from the periphery to the core in world-system terms via trade. Analysts detect long cycles of expansion

and recession over about sixty-year periods (known as Kondratieff cycles). These occur as quasi-monopolies become exhausted. Recovery from recession does not bring the world-economy back to where it was before the cycle started. "Secular" or long-term trends are visible. Eventually these create problems for the system.

Cultural phenomena are interpreted by Wallerstein in terms of his world-system model. Subsequent to the publication of his historical-sociological trilogy (*The Modern World-System*, 1974, 1980, 1989), Wallerstein has treated these phenomena in response to the criticism that he had neglected them. The world-system, he argues, now has a "geoculture." Central to it is "centrist liberalism." Principles of universalism (equality of opportunity, meritocracy) applicable to the managerial cadres are offset and balanced by de facto particularisms—of race, nation, ethnicity, gender, and religion. These legitimate the various divisions within the capitalist world-system—for example, states promote "nations"; the core-periphery division encourages divisions of "race"; and households placed at a lower level in the world occupational hierarchy socialize their young into consciousness of ethnic identity and uphold the mainly unpaid labor of their female members through sexism. These particularistic definitions involve lines of social division that are drawn and redrawn in the workforce as divisions within the capitalist world-economy change: changes in the position of countries in the long-term cycles and in overall tendencies toward crisis, and adaptive responses to particular crises of the system as a whole. Semiproletarian households that predominate in the periphery today effectively subsidize capitalists in the core (where truly proletarian households fully supported by wage labor predominate). Such households permit workers and their families to survive through means of support other than wage labor, such as subsistence and petty trading, thus allowing wages to fall below what otherwise would be necessary to ensure the survival of the whole household.

Just as the modern world-system of today has a single culture, the content of which was initiated by the ideals of the French Revolution, so too it has an interstate system. Here again, this system follows in its workings the patterns visible in the world-economy to which it is bound of necessity. The actions of states influence the workings of the capitalist world-economy through their relations to their capitalists and to foreign states, especially in other "zones," and their relative strengths and weaknesses vis-à-vis each other are determined by their relative economic success as taxing and military entities.

Wallerstein and his colleague Terence K. Hopkins built a successful research school, the Fernand Braudel Research Center at the State University of New York, Binghamton. Fellow analysts include Samir Amin, Christopher Chase-Dunn, Giovanni Arrighi, Albert J.

Bergesen, and, notably, André Gunder Frank, whose metropolis-satellite model was effectively replaced by the world-system. A list of former students produces a series of illustrious names in American social science, many of whom, with others who are not world-systems scholars, have attempted to synthesize the world-system approach with ideas from other traditions. World-systems analysis should not be seen in isolation.

World-systems analysis and orthodox Marxism overlap in many ways, despite significant differences. Marxists of the stature of Rosa Luxemburg (1871–1919) (see *The Accumulation of Capital*, [1913] 1951); V. I. Lenin (1870–1924), whose analysis bears some striking resemblances to Wallerstein's; and N. I. Bukharin (1888–1938) (see *Imperialism and the Accumulation of Capital*, [1924] 1972) struggled with the problem of imperialism, as did J. A. Hobson. (It should also be noted that the non-Marxist scholar Oliver Cromwell Cox's *The Foundations of Capitalism* (1959) anticipated Wallerstein's conception in certain noteworthy ways.)

The central issue dividing orthodox Marxism from world-systems theory is whether analysis should focus on class relations within a given national mode of production, pivoting on the wage contract. The defense of this position has been made by Robert Brenner (1977) and has led to the charge that Wallerstein's is a neo-Smithian Marxism—a charge with which other critics like Theda Skocpol (who argues for a degree of state autonomy allegedly denied by Wallerstein) have some sympathy (1977). Wallerstein's dating of the origins of the capitalist world-economy means that he cannot subscribe to these tenets, and his conception of the role of states in monopolies, of the world-system in which states are contained as the relevant totality, and of the historical variety of forms of labor control (not just wage labor) necessarily denies them too. The issue dividing Marxists from non-Marxists is the primacy to be accorded to economic relations: Are they primary or not? And how are states and culture to be understood relative to economic matters? Whatever the answers to these profound, complex questions, Wallerstein and his colleagues have opened up questions previously considered closed. In their scholarship, fact and theory are brought into a fruitful relationship, as in the days before modern social science replaced historical sociology with the abstract "science" of society.

SEE ALSO *Cox, Oliver C.; Imperialism; Skocpol, Theda; Wallerstein, Immanuel*

BIBLIOGRAPHY

Amin, Samir. 1974. *Accumulation on a World Scale: A Critique of the Theory of Underdevelopment*, trans. Brian Pearce. New York: Monthly Review Press.

Balibar, Etienne, and Immanuel Wallerstein. 1991. *Race, Nation, Class: Ambiguous Identities*, trans. (of Balibar) by Chris Turner. London and New York: Verso.

Braudel, Fernand. 1972–1973. *The Mediterranean and the Mediterranean World in the Age of Philip II*, 2 vols., trans. Siân Reynolds. London: Collins.

Brenner, Robert. 1977. The Origins of Capitalist Development: A Critique of Neo-Smithian Marxism. *New Left Review* 104 (July–August): 25–92.

Frank, André Gunder. 1978. *World Accumulation, 1492–1789*. New York: Monthly Review Press.

Hopkins, Terence K., and Immanuel Wallerstein, eds. 1982. *World-Systems Analysis: Theory and Methodology*. Beverly Hills, CA: Sage.

Skocpol, Theda. 1977. Wallerstein's World Capitalist System: A Theoretical and Historical Critique. *American Journal of Sociology* 82 (5): 1075–1090.

Wallerstein, Immanuel. 1974. *The Modern World-System, 1: Capitalist Agriculture and the Origins of the European World-Economy in the Sixteenth Century*. New York: Academic Press.

Wallerstein, Immanuel. 1980. *The Modern World-System, 2: Mercantilism and the Consolidation of the European World-Economy, 1600–1750*. New York: Academic Press.

Wallerstein, Immanuel. 1989. *The Modern World-System, 3: The Second Era of Great Expansion of the Capitalist World-Economy, 1730–1840s*. San Diego, CA: Academic Press.

Ian Varcoe

WORSHIP

The term *worship* refers to a complex of acts whereby humans express their devotion and reverence toward a deity (in theistic religions) or toward a transcendent yet nondivine being (in nontheistic religions). Arguably, as soon as human individuals become conscious of their utter dependence on a supernatural power and express their devotion to him, her, or it, worship is born. While this private worship is undoubtedly valid, conventionally *worship* refers to the public and corporate acts of devotion performed in an organized religion. Furthermore, the three pronouns—in the masculine, feminine, and neutral genders—used above to refer to the deity (alternatively, deities) or the transcendent but nondivine being(s) indicate the diverse ways they are conceived, either as personal (male and female) or impersonal, as singular (monotheistic) or as plural (polytheistic). This entry focuses on worship rendered to a personal deity, male or female, in theistic religions.

Studies of religion have shown that there is a reciprocal relationship between worship and belief and that in this relationship the former is prior to the latter. The first human reaction to the presence of the *tremendum et fascinans*—to use Rudolf Otto's (1869–1937) expression for the sacred—is not to formulate beliefs about it but to worship it in awe and devotion. This worship eventually gives rise to theological reflections and beliefs, which in turn shape and regulate the rituals in which worship is carried out.

One of the most fundamental forms of worship is sacrifice. These rituals are performed publicly, in the open air or in religious buildings, and privately, among family. Religious officials generally preside at public sacrifices, whereas the male head of the household often, but not always, presides over worship in family settings. In Daoism and Buddhism, for instance, worship, including sacrifices, may be undertaken by women as representatives of the family. Various objects are offered to the one God, gods, spirits, ancestors, demonic beings, or any other transcendent being. In *bloodless sacrifices*, food and drink, such as fruits, grains, and baked goods, milk and milk products, water, alcoholic beverages, and flowers, are offered. Inanimate objects are offered too, including clothing, jewelry, coins, precious stones, and precious metals. In *blood sacrifices*, domesticated animals and, less often, humans are ritually slain, and their blood is sprinkled on the altar or on the fields to maintain the cosmic order or promote fertility. The sacrificial rite may be a simple act of lifting up the offering, killing or burning the animal, and the libation of its blood. Eventually, the rite can become highly complicated, requiring performance by religious experts. The intentions of sacrificial worship are described as fourfold: praise, thanksgiving, supplication, and expiation. Sacrifices are offered regularly (daily, weekly, monthly, at the beginning of seasons, and yearly) and extraordinarily (for special joyful events or on dangerous occasions) and at various sacred sites, both natural (e.g., trees, mountains, rivers, and stones) and constructed (e.g., temples, pagodas, and churches).

Ritual worship varies greatly from religion to religion, from age to age, and from place to place. In Vedic practice and later Hinduism, the central sacrifice is the offering of fire, personified as the god Agni and the symbol connecting Vedic understandings of the person, society, and the cosmos. In addition, worship of deities through the offering of foods, service, and gestures of respect toward the deities (*pūjā*), later amalgamated into devotional (*bhakti*) Hinduism, is one of the most pervasive forms of Hindu worship. This worship takes a variety of forms, from simple gestures, such as offerings of water, foods, and flowers, recitation of mantras, singing of songs, and the waving of camphor before the image of the deity, to more elaborate gestures, such as offering hospitality to the god, invocations, bathing and dressing the image, and carrying the enthroned image in procession. Central to this *pūjā* is the experience of "auspicious seeing" (*darsana*), in which the devotee "sees" the god or goddess and is "seen" by those who are granted favors by the deity, symbolized by the returning of the sacred food (*prasāda*).

In ancient Israel, sacrifices at the Jerusalem Temple, officiated by the priestly class, played a pivotal role in the religious life of the people until the destruction of the Temple in 70 CE. In terms of ritual, in pre-Rabbinic Judaism a distinction is made between *burnt offerings* ("holocaust"), in which the sacrificial animal is totally burned up, and *peace* or *communion offerings*, in which only parts of the sacrificial animal are burned, with the animal's blood poured out or smeared on the altar and some parts of the animal consumed by the people in a sacrificial meal. In *expiatory sacrifices*, the sacrificial animal is burned up and no part of it is eaten. Ancient Israel also practiced bloodless sacrifices consisting of the offering of agricultural products. These sacrifices, blood and bloodless, were made daily and on solemn festivals, such as Passover, Shavu'ot, Yom Kippur, and Sukkot. With the destruction to the Temple, the whole Jewish sacrificial system came to an end, and new forms of worship arose with the emergence of the rabbis as spiritual leaders.

According to Christianity, the Jewish sacrificial system and worship reached their culmination in Jesus's death on the cross, which is seen as the perfect and definitive sacrifice, bringing about the redemption of the world. Jesus's life, ministry, death, and resurrection are made efficaciously present (not repeated) in the sacraments—there are seven of these in the teaching of the Roman Catholic Church. Of them, the highest is the Eucharist, the perfect sacrifice, in which Jesus's body and blood are believed to be physically and really present and the spiritual benefits of Jesus's sacrifice on the cross are imparted to his followers and constitute the church as his mystical body. Christian worship is often called *liturgy*, that is, the whole public worship of the mystical body of Jesus Christ, head and members.

Islam is in principle opposed to sacrifice. Consonant with its fundamental belief in the unity of God (*tawhīd*) and in Muhammad (c. 570–632) as the final prophet, Islam emphasizes worship as "service" (*'ibadah*) to God and veneration of the Prophet. This worship/service constitutes the so-called Five Pillars of Islam: the confession of faith (*shahada*), ritual prayer (*salat*), fasting (*sawm*) during the month of Ramadan, the pilgrimage (*hajj*) to Mecca, and almsgiving (*zakat*).

Whereas sacrifice occupies an important place in theistic religions, it is by no means the only form of worship. In all the religions examined above, the reading and studying of the scripture constitutes an essential part of worship. In Hinduism, the study of the sacred books is combined with ascetic (*tapas*) and meditation (*yoga*) practices. In Judaism, after the destruction of the Temple and in the subsequent Diaspora, a class of nonpriestly leaders called *rabbis* sought to construct a system of worship in which the study of the Torah is a central mode of honoring God. This Torah piety also provides insights into the commandments (*mitsvot*) that govern the lives of devout Jews. To replace the Temple sacrifices, the rabbis composed prayers for the use of their synagogues (such as the Prayer of Eighteen Blessings) and introduced the practice of reciting Deuteronomy 6:4–9 and 11:13–31 and Numbers 15:37–41 (the *shma'*). Worship is conducted in the presence of the Torah scroll, and the leader of the worship stands in front of the ark housing it. Another innovation is the public reading of the Torah and exposition of scripture. In Christian liturgy, scriptural readings, from the Old and New Testaments, are incorporated into the liturgy and are often followed by a homily. In Islam, the Qur'an is the object of ubiquitous veneration and devotion. Wrapped in silk, it is stored as the most sacred object in the room and must not be handled in a state of ritual impurity.

The reading of sacred scripture also plays a key role in other religions, such as Sikhism and Buddhism. The Ādi-Granth, draped in silk and placed on a cot under an awning, is the central object of worship in every Sikh *gurdwārā*, and offerings of money, flowers, and food are made to it. On special occasions there is nonstop recitation by a relay of readers. In Buddhism, the simplest act of devotion is homage in front of the image, usually of the Buddha, accompanied by an offering of flowers, incense, and candles. In this ritual the devotee, particularly in the Theravada tradition, takes refuge in the *three jewels*, that is, the Buddha, the *dhamma* (teaching), and the *samgha* (community). Because of the emphasis on the Buddha's teaching, one important component of Buddhist liturgy is the recitation and chanting of the sacred texts, such as the *tipitaka*. In Tibetan Buddhism, the reading by a monk of a specific text, often a version of the *Prajñāpāramitā* in 100,000 verses or 8,000 verses, is done if possible once a year in each household to insure blessings for the family.

In addition to the official liturgy, other acts of worship, conventionally referred to as *popular religion* or *devotion*, play a no less important role in the piety of the faithful. Among these are fasting (e.g., during Ramadan for Muslims, during Lent for Christians, on certain festivals for Jews, and throughout the year for Buddhists), pilgrimage (e.g., the hajj for Muslims, circumambulation in Tibetan Buddhism, visits to sacred places for Hindus, Buddhists, and Christians), meditation (in yoga, Zen Buddhism, and Daoism), ancestor worship (in Confucianism) and the feeding of hungry ghosts (in Buddhism), veneration of saints (in Roman Catholicism and Orthodoxy), the cult of relics and images (in Roman Catholicism and Buddhism), life-cycle rituals (the *samskāra* in Hinduism and the sacraments in Christianity), the sanctification of time by means of the Liturgy of the Hours and the sacred calendar, the taking of vows, healing and exorcism, and so on.

Worship is the lifeblood of religion. Ever-changing and yet permanent, this universal phenomenon represents the response, both of the individual and the community, to the presence of God or a supernatural being. While historical and theological studies of worship have revealed much of its nature and developments, much still remains controversial, especially regarding the origins of worship and sacrifice, the relation between worship and ideology, the social dimensions of worship and devotion, the role of goddesses and women in worship, the relation between worship and personal cultivation in meditation, the relation between the local and translocal traditions of practice, and the impact of postmodernism and globalization on worship.

SEE ALSO *Buddha; Buddhism; Christianity; Church, The; Hinduism; Islam, Shia and Sunni; Jainism; Jesus Christ; Judaism; Lay Theories; Muhammad; Nation of Islam; Religion; Rituals; Sikhism; Supreme Being; Symbols*

BIBLIOGRAPHY

Beyer, Stephan. 1973. *The Cult of Tārā: Magic and Ritual in Tibet.* Berkeley: University of California Press.

Bradshaw, Paul, ed. 2002. *The New Westminster Dictionary of Liturgy and Worship.* Louisville, KY: Westminster John Knox.

Cragg, Kenneth, and R. Marston Speight, eds. 1980. *Islam from Within: Anthology of a Religion.* Belmont, CA: Wadsworth.

Faure, Bernard, ed. 2003. *Chan Buddhism in Ritual Context.* London and New York: Routledge Curzon.

Fink, Peter, ed. 1990. *The New Dictionary of Sacramental Worship.* Collegeville, MN: Liturgical Press.

Lopez, Donald, Jr., ed. 1997. *Religions of Tibet in Practice.* Princeton, NJ: Princeton University Press.

Phan, Peter C. 2004. *Being Religious Interreligiously: Asian Perspectives on Interfaith Dialogue.* Maryknoll, NY: Orbis.

Rodrigues, Hillary. 2003. *Ritual Worship of the Great Goddess: The Liturgy of the Durgā Pūjā with Interpretations.* Albany: State University of New York Press.

Schipper, Kristofer. 1993. *The Taoist Body.* Trans. Karen C. Duval. Berkeley: University of California Press.

Wainwright, Geoffrey, and Karen B. Westerfield Tucker, eds. 2006. *The Oxford History of Christian Worship.* Oxford: Oxford University Press.

Peter C. Phan

X

X-CRISE

X-Crise is an acronym for the Centre de Renseignements et d'Informations Sociales et Économiques, an association created by alumni of France's elite École Polytechnique; this association was later known as the Centre Polytechnicien d'Études Économiques (CPEE). X-Crise was formed in 1931 by Gérard Bardet, manager of the Bardet company, who became CPEE's general secretary; André Loizillon, whose career in industry spanned companies from Shneider to Shell and who was CPEE's treasurer for a while and a member of X-Crise's transport workshop; and John Nicoletis, a consulting engineer and manager specializing in less-developed countries. X-Crise's purpose was to examine the causes of the world economic crisis and propose possible solutions. From a membership of about twenty *Polytechniciens* in October 1931, it grew to close to two thousand members (not all *Polytechniciens*) in 1939, the year the association disbanded. As an open, tolerant, and scientific think tank, X-Crise gathered together liberals (in the French sense of the word; i.e., market-oriented economists) like Clément Colson, Jacques Rueff (both teachers at the Ecole Polytechnique), Alfred Sauvy, and Henri Michel; socialists personalities like John Nicoletis, the tireless Jean Coutrot, Jules Moch (a socialist deputy and close relative of Charles Spinasse's), and the French historian Marc Bloch; and centrists such as Gérard Bardet, Auguste Detoeuf (Alsthom's founder), and André Loizillon.

X-Crise was not a research center as one finds in universities. It was a network of *Polytechniciens*, graduates considered to be part of the elite of the French nation, together with some non-*Polytechniciens*, all united around a mission: to get France out of economic crisis through intervention both in government, as experts in macroeconomics, and in industry, as managers skilled in the scientific organization of work. But if some of these *Polytechniciens* had already applied the scientific organization of work to their own firms, none of them, initially, was expert in macroeconomics. Hence, X-Crise organized meetings and published working papers in the École Polytechnique's bulletin. Small workshops were created to focus on particular topics like econometrics (Fischman and Lendjel 2000b), transport, finance, foreign experiences, and the study of the present state of the economy. Their members were volunteers; while they published many reports in X-Crise's bulletin, they were never academic researchers trying to obtain intellectual fame in France and abroad. Yet because X-Crise's aim was also to help *Polytechniciens* become France's macroeconomics experts, X-Crise became a magnet for innovative economic studies.

Two bodies of economic work that were very innovative for France in the 1930s have to be mentioned here: Maurice Potron's (Abraham-Frois and Lendjel 2004), and the economic models of François and Georges Guillaume and François Moch (brother of the socialist deputy Jules Moch). Indeed, as early as 1911 Maurice Potron applied Perron-Frobenius's theorems to a Leontief-type model, in order to find the conditions for the existence of a "satisfactory economic regime." He also laid the foundations of input-output analysis in work published in 1912. The works of the Guillaume brothers and of François Moch provided one of the first economic models in France. The Guillaume brothers' model (Guillaume 1932; Fischman and Lendjel 2000a) can be considered a draft of the French

national accounting system. Moch's model (Moch 1933–1934; Fischman and Lendjel 1999), designed to explain the positive consequences of a cut in working hours on the level of economic activity, presented some Keynesian arguments. Firstly, it pointed out the important role of demand as an economic motor; secondly, it demonstrated the need for the state to intervene in order to get the economy out of a downward economic spiral; and, thirdly, it made an argument quite close to the acceleration principle of R. F. Kahn that Keynes used. Guillaume and Moch attempted also to test their theoretical models with statistical facts. This led Moch to elaborate an econometric "method" of interpreting economic cycles.

Even in X-Crise, these works did not have a large audience. But they have had a great impact on subsequent thinking, as have other X-Crise writings and debates. Indeed, as Michel Margairaz wrote, there is "no doubt X-Crise has eased Ecole Polytechnique's conversion to economics, as well as [that of] the State experts to macroeconomics, more or less explicitly inspired by Keynesianism" (Margairaz 1995, p. 181). In fact, before, during, and after World War II, some of X-Crise's members—such as Charles Spinasse, Georges Boris, Jacques Branger, Jean Coutrot, Georges Guillaume, Louis Rosenstock-Frank, Alfred Sauvy, Jean Ullmo, Robert Gibrat, Lucien Romier, Robert Loustau, Gérard Bardet, Auguste Detoeuf, Louis Vallon, and François Divisia—had high positions in the country's administration, especially in ministries in charge of economic matters. For example, X-Crise members served in the Ministry of National Economy (MEN in French)—a true instrument of political economy—in 1936; in the Vichy government in the public works department, in communications, and in the ministry of production; and, finally, in General De Gaulle's administration.

SEE ALSO *Economics, Keynesian; Potron, Maurice*

BIBLIOGRAPHY

Abraham-Frois, Gilbert, and Emeric Lendjel. 2004. *Les œuvres économiques de l'abbé Potron.* Paris: L'Harmattan.

Brun, Gérard, ed. 1982. *X-Crise, Centre Polytechniciens d'Etudes Economiques: De la récurrence des crises économiques: Son cinquantenaire, 1931–1981.* Paris: Economica.

Desaunay, Guy. 1965. X-Crise: Contribution à l'étude des idéologies d'un groupe de Polytechniciens durant la grande crise économique (1931–1939). Doctoral thesis, the Sorbonne.

Fischman, Marianne, and Emeric Lendjel. 1999. X-Crise et le débat sur la réduction du temps de travail. In *La réduction du temps de travail: L'espace des possibles*, eds. Laurent Cordonnier and Nicolas Vaneecloo, 33–56. Special issue of the *Cahier Lillois d'Economie et de Sociologie.*

Fischman, Marianne, and Emeric Lendjel. 2000a. X-Crise et le modèle des frères Guillaume. In *Les traditions économiques françaises: 1848–1939*, eds., Pierre Dockès, Ludovic Frobert, Gérard Klotz, Jean-Pierre Potier, and André Tiran, 369–382. Paris: C.N.R.S. Editions.

Fischman, Marianne, and Emeric Lendjel. 2000b. La contribution d'X-Crise à l'émergence de l'économétrie en France dans les années trente. *Revue Européenne des Sciences Sociales* 38 (118): 115–134.

Guillaume, Georges, and Edouard Guillaume. 1932. *Sur les fondements de l'économique rationnelle.* Paris: Gauthier-Villars.

Margairaz, Michel. 1995. Les autodidactes et les experts: X-Crise, Reseaux et parcours intellectuels dans les années 30. In *La France des X: Deux siècles d'histoire de l'Ecole polytechnique*, eds. Bruno Belhoste et al., 169–184. Paris: Economica.

Moch, François. 1933–1934. Sur l'évolution des systèmes économiques. Parts 1–3. *Bulletin du C.P.E.E.* 7 (October–November): 24–39; 8–9 (December): 34–44; 10 (February): 18–27.

Marianne Fischman
Emeric Lendjel

XENOPHOBIA

Xenophobia is discrimination against and hatred of foreigners, targeting outsiders and strangers or more often those who are in effect part of one's own society but are perceived as incommensurably different from the majority population. The most pointed, long-term, and widely documented case of xenophobia is that of anti-Semitism, which culminated in the mass murder of six million European Jews and countless others during World War II (1939–1945). A new form of xenophobia that grew in western Europe and North America during the late twentieth century and early twenty-first century is Islamophobia, which targets migrant Muslim communities with or without citizenship.

CAUSES AND CHARACTERISTICS

Anti-Semitism and other forms of xenophobia often are said to be related to the innate characteristics of a given culture or a consequence of economic malaise and political turmoil in select societies. The typical example given for such an assertion is Germany. These explanations are not only insufficient, they also lead to normalization of the hatred and violence commonly associated with institutionalized practices of exclusion and discrimination. The problem of hatred of foreigners and intolerance for ethnic, religious, racial, and cultural difference must instead be put into the larger context of dominant political movements and ideologies with a transnational dimension.

There are observable links between migration, racism, discrimination, ethno-religious stereotyping, and xenophobia. Increased ethno-religious and racial diversity

in societies makes the reality of the heterogeneity of human communities more obvious. In the absence of political, legal, social, and economic mechanisms to ensure mutual respect and to mediate relations across differences, xenophobia and various related forms of racism become manifest. Particularly among European societies that received substantial numbers of immigrants after World War II both as workers and as asylum seekers, migrants with a different skin color or religion became the targets in violent internal disputes about authentic national identity. This indicates that despite the en masse elimination of Jews from Europe, xenophobia did not loosen its grip across the Continent. Still, xenophobia was by no means an exclusively European phenomenon. In an era when first nation-state politics and then neoliberalist policies increased societal and economic inequalities, and societies grappled with the changing realities of their multiethnic, multireligious, or multiracial makeup and often arbitrarily carved national borders, a marked increase was seen in discrimination and violence directed toward migrants, refugees, and minorities on a global scale.

XENOPHOBIA AND RACISM

Although racism and xenophobia are distinct phenomena, they are closely interrelated. Racism generally implies value-laden distinctions based on presumed or aggrandized differences in physical characteristics, such as skin coloration, hair type, facial features, and body type. Xenophobia, by contrast, is the perception that people and communities identified as "other" are foreign to a given community or society, that they lack the capacity for integration, and that they can bring harm to the authentic identity of the majority. Racism is an ideological construct; it assigns a certain race or ethno-religious group a position of power and privilege on the basis of the group's physical and cultural attributes. It involves the establishment and sustenance of hierarchical relations in which the self-appointed superior race exercises domination and control over others. Xenophobia too refers to attitudes, prejudices, and behavior that reject, exclude, and vilify its targets based on the belief that they are perpetual outsiders who cannot be included or trusted. Consequently it is sometimes difficult to make a clear distinction between racism and xenophobia because they exhibit similar motivations for exclusive behavior designed to demean others and the exercise of political violence. However, there is one element missing in racism that is often present in xenophobia: religious identity. Manifestations of xenophobia occur not only against people with different physical characteristics but also against those of similar background who are believed to hold different and presumably dangerous and hostile religious convictions.

INITIATIVES AGAINST XENOPHOBIA

Even in societies with a long history of legalized discrimination, it is possible to take measures to alleviate or at least curtail the culture of hatred aimed at those deemed essentially unassimilable. The Roll Back Xenophobia campaign established in South Africa in 1998 is a succinct example of how political will and determination can produce a widely visible and national effort to confront systematic incidences of xenophobic hostility and violence. The campaign began as a joint initiative between national and international institutions: the South African Human Rights Commission, the National Consortium on Refugee Affairs, and the office of the United Nations High Commissioner for Refugees. It emphasized broad, multifaceted, and synchronized activities by the government, civil society organizations, and communications media, including information campaigns by national and local governments, retraining of the police force, strengthening of labor rights protections for migrant workers, sensitization of trade union officials, awareness raising by religious organizations, reinstitution of codes of conduct for civil servants, and the inclusion of migration- and refugee-related concerns in primary, secondary, and tertiary education. These measures, in the larger context of the antiapartheid movement in the country, were suggestive of a tidal wave of change in South Africa in terms of how its citizens began to deal with differences that had violently divided the society in the past.

Another example that points in a positive direction is reforms made in Canadian immigration policies beginning in the 1980s. Immigration and refugee policy discussions are rarely separable from general debates on racial, interethnic, and interreligious relations within host communities. Therefore strong border controls are often advocated as necessary for dealing with and controlling the status of racial, cultural, or ethno-religious minorities by the dominant culture. Still, while immigration controls have historically discriminated between nationalities, ethnicities, and religions, the Canadian example proved that it is possible to alleviate at least the overt marks of racism or xenophobia via institutional reforms and policy changes.

Xenophobia is clearly observable when immigration procedures target particular ethno-religious groups for exclusion or lack transparency or when the immigration process itself is made so grueling for select groups that it can act as a deterrent. With regard to refugee applications, for instance, the systematic use of detention often singles out specific nationalities or ethno-religious groups more than others. Meanwhile many refugees have no choice other than to use irregular entry, increasingly at the hands of smugglers. Thus they run the risk that their irregular

migration will be held against them in their asylum claim, and if they gain entry, they will be set apart from other minorities and mainstream society. This tension has been clearly observable in European Union (EU) policies regarding refugees and asylum seekers. In this regard the establishment of the European Monitoring Centre on Racism and Xenophobia (EUMC) in Vienna by the European Union in 1997 and the successive creation of the European Union Agency for Fundamental Rights on March 1, 2007, were important initiatives to develop regional institutional mechanisms for monitoring and countering xenophobia. They kept records of the racial and xenophobic discrimination and violence directed toward migrants and other ethno-religious minorities in Europe. They also identified and highlighted examples of good practices in challenging and remedying xenophobic policies.

The global nature of violence and discrimination against migrants, refugees, and settled ethno-religious minorities has also been increasingly acknowledged by the post–World War II international human rights community. By 2007 there had not yet been wide acceptance by signatory states of the basic rights and entitlements for unauthorized migrants recognized in the United Nations 1990 International Convention for the Protection of the Rights of All Migrant Workers and Members of Their Families. However, under the International Labor Organization Conventions related to migrant workers, undocumented migrants are entitled to equal treatment with respect to rights related to their present or past employment, including issues of remuneration, social security, and other benefits as well as trade union membership and exercise of trade union rights. The undocumented migrants and refugees remain especially vulnerable because they were either unwilling, out of fear of being deported, or unable to seek protection from authorities when confronted with xenophobic violence.

RESURGENCE OF RIGHT-WING POLITICS

Increasingly after the 1980s Europe witnessed growth in racism and xenophobia that began to swamp its politics. In June 2004 elections for the European Parliament, twenty-five representatives of ten neo-Nazi and extreme right-wing parties from seven member states won seats. Although xenophobia and the growth of neo-fascist and far-right parties in Europe had long been held in check by the memory of the atrocities of Adolf Hitler's Germany, subsequent developments suggested that the situation had started to change and new forms of counteraction needed to be developed. In Austria the radical right-wing Freedom Party, led by Jörg Haider, won an unprecedented 27 percent of the vote in national elections in 2001 and

ascended to power. The EU, of which democratic Austria is a member, immediately imposed diplomatic sanctions, citing the Freedom Party's long history of xenophobia and Nazi sympathies. Meanwhile although the EU categorically denounced Haider's anti-immigration agenda, its own member nations also instituted policies that excluded nonwhite immigrants from entering the Continent. While Austria markedly tightened its immigration and asylum rules in the aftermath of the Yugoslav crisis, several European countries also introduced new legislation restricting immigration and asylum, citing the need to respond to growing xenophobia in European societies and thus inadvertently blaming the immigrants and refugees for the societal reaction against them. In addition although the rise of the right in British politics during the late 1990s and the early 2000s was not a revival of the classic fascism of the 1930s, the xenophobic and racist tendencies embodied by the new movement had similar characteristics. Furthermore skinheads, neo-Nazis, and other xenophobic movements that emerged in the aftermath of German unification exhibited a shift in anti-Semitic and antiforeigner violence and demonstrated an increasing connection to local and ideological networks with aggressive elements. These European movements found support in national politics to an extent that would have been unimaginable in the 1970s. Following Haider's success in Austria, in Italy's May 13, 2001, general election Umberto Bossi and his religious and xenophobic Northern League party became a full governing partner in the center-right coalition led by Silvio Berlusconi. The league was the party most loyal to Berlusconi's government until 2006, and it held the three ministries of Labor and Social Affairs, Justice, and Institutional Reforms and Devolution.

The increase in xenophobic sentiments toward migrant and refugee populations in European societies was examined by data compiled from four waves of Eurobarometer surveys in twelve countries between 1988 and 2000. The resultant analysis showed a substantial rise in antiforeigner, xenophobic sentiments and fears between 1988 and 2000 in all twelve core European countries. The analysis also proved that antiforeigner sentiment is much more pronounced in places with greater support for right-wing extremist parties and fascist movements. According to these findings, the impact of individual-level socioeconomic characteristics such as education remained stable over the years, but the effect of political ideology increased. In this context, formation of civil society organizations such as the European Coalition of Cities against Racism constituted an important step toward combating xenophobia in Europe. Linked with the International Coalition of Cities against Racism, an initiative launched by UNESCO in 2004 to establish a network of cities interested in sharing experiences in order to improve poli-

cies to curtail racism, discrimination, and xenophobia, a ten-point plan of action was formulated by the European coalition. These comprised areas such as increased competence of city authorities in education, housing, and employment as well as cultural and sport activities for combating racism and xenophobia and suggested practical policies that city authorities might develop. To the same end of combating xenophobia, the United Nations World Conference against Racism, Racial Discrimination, Xenophobia, and Related Intolerance (WCAR), held in September 2001 in Durban, South Africa, was a gathering that provided nongovernmental organizations (NGOs) representing minority populations and historically oppressed groups an opportunity to speak against their governments over human rights violations.

ISLAMOPHOBIA

After the World Trade Center bombings in the United States in 2001, there emerged an alarming surge in racism and xenophobic actions against people of Arab background and Muslim faith across Europe and North America. This phenomenon, called Islamophobia, denoting fear of Islam and Muslims, made life particularly difficult for Arab and Muslim Americans after the September 11 attacks. Many were harassed at work, had their property vandalized, and were subjected to regular security checks. Although public leaders, including President George W. Bush, called for tolerance, the Council for American-Islamic Relations (CAIR) in Washington, D.C., counted some 1,700 incidents of abuse against Muslims in just the 5 months following September 11. In response to these developments in 2004 the United Nations held a conference called Confronting Islamophobia: Education for Tolerance and Understanding at its New York headquarters. Attended by more than 600 delegates, the event was part of the progressive initiative organized by the United Nations Department of Public Information seeking to improve awareness of xenophobia.

Criticisms of Islam and anti-Muslim political rhetoric have been intertwined with cultural and ethnic hostility that extends even to secularized immigrants from traditionally Muslim societies. As early as 1997 the Runnymede Trust in the United Kingdom issued a report on Islamophobia, revealing widespread hatred of Islam and Muslims across all sections of British society. Similarly the November 2005 riots in which minority ethnic youths in France took part exposed a deeply entrenched racism in the country. Both the riots and the response to them, which involved the invocation of emergency law, the imposition of curfews, and the deployment of thousands of police, brought into the open the xenophobic aspects of France's secular republicanism. These events were fol-

lowed by the debate over the publication of Danish cartoons of the Prophet Muhammad, based on the assumption that Muslims do not have any experience of freedom of speech or do not believe in the concept. In the United States and Canada the growing threat to civil liberties and the resultant alienation experienced by many Muslims or citizens of immigrant background from traditionally Muslim societies also constituted direct examples of xenophobia. In Britain the 2005 London bombings led to new antiterrorist legislation advanced by the government of Prime Minister Tony Blair, ultimately scapegoating past policies of multiculturalism and targeting Muslim communities as a whole.

Immigration has historically been associated with xenophobia. In periods of high unemployment and global dislocation, immigrants easily become the targets of political leaders who accuse them of criminality, lack of morals, making excessive demands on public services, and creating undue competition for scarce employment. Meanwhile the danger represented by the rebirth in eastern Europe of highly aggressive forms of nationalism; the growth of xenophobia in western Europe both as increased anti-Semitism and as Islamophobia and racism against people of Asian, African, and Caribbean background; and the increase in the strength of the extreme right and xenophobic politics in the United States suggest that xenophobia cannot be eradicated purely by procedural democracy or welfare state policies. Lack of respect for difference and of the political will for negotiating national identities in the face of change constitute challenges that feed reformulations of xenophobia even at the very bastions of pluralism and tolerance.

SEE ALSO *Anti-Semitism; Borders; Discrimination; Hate Crimes; Immigration; Islam, Shia and Sunni; Nativism; Phenotype; Prejudice; Racism; Religion; Third World; United Nations*

BIBLIOGRAPHY

Arendt, Hannah. 1951. *Antisemitism*. Part 1 of *The Origins of Totalitarianism*. New York: Harcourt, Brace.

Davies, Merryl Wyn, Ashis Nandy, and Ziauddin Sardar. 1993. *Barbaric Others: A Manifesto on Western Racism*. London and Boulder, CO: Pluto.

Halliday, Fred. 2002. *Two Hours That Shook the World: September 11, 2001*. London: Saqi.

Macedo, Donaldo, and Panayota Gounari, eds. 2006. *The Globalization of Racism*. Boulder, CO: Paradigm Publishers.

Turner, Bryan S. 2006. *Vulnerability and Human Rights*. Philadelphia: Pennsylvania State University Press.

Wistrich, Robert S. 1999. *Demonizing the Other: Antisemitism, Racism, and Xenophobia*. Jerusalem: Harwood Publishers.

Nergis Canefe

Y

YELTSIN, BORIS
1931–2007

Boris Nikolaevich Yeltsin was the founding father of the post-Communist Russian state, and the man responsible for giving shape to contemporary Russian democracy. His life reflected the sufferings and achievements of the Soviet era, and also came to symbolize the chaos and confused aspirations of the capitalist democracy that came after. Yeltsin was born on February 1, 1931, in the village of Butka some 250 miles east of Yekaterinburg (called Sverdlovsk at the time). In that year the region was engulfed by Stalin's savage struggle to force peasants off their individual plots and into collective farms. Yeltsin's family was comparatively prosperous and therefore, as *kulaks* (rich peasants), were exiled to the east. With the countryside in chaos, in 1932 Yeltsin's father, Nikolai Ignatevich, moved to work on a construction site in Kazan. Two years later Ignatevich was arrested as a "deku-lakised kulak," or someone allegedly retaining the kulak mentality, and sentenced to three years hard labor, a fact that Yeltsin kept secret until 1994. The family moved to Berezniki in the Perm region to work on the construction of a giant potassium processing plant. The hard conditions worsened following Russia's entry into World War II in 1941, but the young Boris thrived at school, taking up numerous sports and excelling at volleyball.

In 1949 at the age of 18, Yeltsin became a student in the civil engineering department of the Urals Polytechnical Institute in Sverdlovsk, the city he made his home for the next 36 years. He divided his time between intense bouts of study and sporting activities, travelling the country as captain of the volleyball team. He met his future wife, Naina Girina from Orenburg, at this time. Yeltsin graduated in June 1955, and then gained practical experience on a building site. He was a hard but fair task master, imposing enormous demands on himself and fellow workers. In 1957, newly married, Yeltsin took charge of the construction of the Sverdlovsk Textile Kombinat, a major project that he completed on time. In 1959 Yeltsin joined the Communist Party of the Soviet Union (CPSU), but only in 1966 did he leave active civil engineering to head the Construction Department of the Regional Party Committee (Obkom, the acronym of the Oblast [Regional] Committee of the Communist Party). Yeltsin refused many of the perks that went with the job, but he was driven by his characteristic "obsessive ambition."

In November 1976 Yeltsin made it to the top, becoming Obkom First Secretary over a region with a population of nearly five million, covering an area the size of England. He was an innovative and demanding leader, but never strayed from Party orthodoxy. At the Twenty-Sixth Party Congress in March 1981 Yeltsin was elected a member of the Central Committee (CC).

In March 1985 Mikhail Gorbachev came to power committed to reform. In April 1985 Gorbachev brought Yeltsin to Moscow as head of the CC's Construction Department. In December of that year Yeltsin was appointed head of the Moscow Party Organization and with it, shortly afterwards, candidate membership of the Politburo, the Communist Party's highest body. Yeltsin ran Moscow in a confrontational manner, firing those whom he considered resistant to change, but his talk of "social justice" and condemnation of elite privileges and corruption won him enormous popularity.

At the CC plenum of October 21, 1987, Yeltsin criticized the slowness of reforms and Gorbachev personally, and announced that he would resign from the Politburo. Facing a barrage of condemnation, Yeltsin was removed from leadership of the Moscow Party but was appointed head of the state construction agency, Gosstroi. Cast out of the political establishment, Yeltsin placed himself at the head of the anti-Soviet revolution. He skillfully exploited the new democratic opportunities, being elected by acclaim in March 1990 a deputy from Moscow to the new Russian Congress of People's Deputies (CPD). On May 29th, he narrowly defeated orthodox contenders to become chair of the new Russian parliament. He sponsored Russia's declaration of state sovereignty on June 12, 1990, signaling the end of the Soviet Union and of Gorbachev's attempts to reform communism from within. Elected Russia's first president on June 12, 1991, Yeltsin exploited his democratic legitimacy to defeat the attempted hard-line coup of August 18 to 21, 1991. A meeting of the presidents of Ukraine, Belarus, and Russia near Minsk on December 8, 1991, announced the disintegration of the Union of Soviet Socialist Republics. Russia was now independent, and Yeltsin its leader.

Yeltsin's impetuous and determined character stamped the new state. Throughout his leadership he remained committed to market-oriented liberal, democratic, and Westernizing policies, although the way these policies were implemented was often at odds with the goal. In Yeltsin's typical campaigning style, economic "shock therapy" was launched in January 1992, allowing the liberalization of prices. His failure to build consensus with parliament led to a breakdown in relations that ended with the forced dissolution in September and violence in October 1993.

The new constitution of December 12, 1993, provided for a strong presidency with weak oversight powers by parliament and the courts. Yeltsin used his powers to drive through market reforms, including a crash privatization program that allowed a few to become very rich (the so-called oligarchs), while the mass of the population became much poorer. Yeltsin's decision to invade the breakaway republic of Chechnya in December 1994 caused untold suffering, and contravened several articles of the constitution. In federal relations, Yeltsin encouraged the development of segmented regionalism whereby regional leaders were able to enjoy an enormous devolution of authority as long as they remained loyal to him personally. Only by allying with the oligarchs was Yeltsin able to win a second term in 1996, but at the price of mortgaging the state to big business. The fall in oil prices precipitated the partial default of August 1998, provoked by the failure to collect enough taxes to service the growing budget deficit. On December 31, 1999, Yeltsin transferred power to his hand-picked successor, Vladimir Putin. He entered political retirement, offering critical support for the new president. Yeltsin left Russia a democratic, federal, market-oriented society, but all of these were deeply flawed in their operation. Yeltsin laid the foundations for a free society, but it would be up to his successors to build on what he had started.

SEE ALSO *Democracy; Democratization; Economies, Transitional; Gorbachev, Mikhail; Putin, Vladimir; Stalin, Joseph; Union of Soviet Socialist Republics*

BIBLIOGRAPHY

Aron, Leon. 2000. *Yeltsin: A Revolutionary Life.* New York: St. Martin's Press.

Breslauer, George W. 2002. *Gorbachev and Yeltsin as Leaders.* Cambridge, U.K.: Cambridge University Press.

Medvedev, Roy. 2000. *Post-Soviet Russia: A Journey Through the Yeltsin Era.* Trans. and ed. George Shriver. New York: Columbia University Press.

Morrison, John. 1991. *Boris Yeltsin: From Bolshevik to Democrat.* New York: Dutton.

Shevtsova, Lilia. 1999. *Yeltsin's Russia: Myths and Reality.* Washington, DC: Carnegie Endowment for International Peace.

Yeltsin, Boris N. 1990. *Against the Grain: An Autobiography.* Trans. Michael Glenny. New York: Summit Books.

Yeltsin, Boris N. 1994. *The Struggle for Russia.* Trans. Catherine A. Fitzpatrick. New York: Belka Publications Corp., Times Books.

Yeltsin, Boris N. 2000. *Midnight Diaries.* Trans. Catherine A. Fitzpatrick. New York: PublicAffairs.

Richard Sakwa

YIELD

In economics and finance the word *yield* is used to describe the interest rate on a bond. In fact, the words *yield* and *interest rate* are used interchangeably and mean the same thing. There are several ways of calculating interest rates, with the most important being the *yield to maturity*, also known in many contexts as the *internal rate of return*. Economists consider the yield to maturity as the most accurate measure of the interest rate, and this is what they have in mind when they talk about interest rates.

The yield to maturity is the interest rate that equates the present value of payments received from a debt instrument with its cost (its value today). As an example, consider a simple, one-year loan. Assuming that you borrowed $1,000 for a year and you are required to repay the principal of $1,000 one year from now along with an interest payment of $100, then (according to the definition) the yield to maturity is given by

$$\$1000 = \frac{\$(1000 + 100)}{1 + i}, \qquad (1)$$

where $\$1,000$ is the value of the loan today and $\$(1,000 + 100)/(1 + i)$ is the present value of the payments received from this instrument. Solving equation (1) for i yields $i = 0.10$ (or 10%). In this case, the yield to maturity is the same as the *simple interest rate*, the latter being calculated as the ratio of the interest payment to the principal, $\$100/\$1,000$.

Although for simple loans, the yield to maturity equals the simple interest rate, this is not the case for other debt instruments. To calculate the yield to maturity on an n-year coupon bond with market price P, coupon payment C, and face value F, the following formula is used (see Mishkin and Serletis 2007, Chapter 4, for more details):

$$P = \frac{C}{1 + i} + \frac{C}{(1 + i)^2} + \cdots + \frac{C}{(1 + i)^n} + \frac{F}{(1 + i)^n}. \qquad (2)$$

If P, C, F, and n are all known, then the above equation could be solved for the yield to maturity on the n-year bond (also known as the n-year interest rate), i. It should be noted that the yield to maturity is different from the coupon rate of interest, the latter being the ratio of the yearly coupon payment to the bond's face value, C/F. In fact, when the coupon bond sells at its face value ($P = F$), the yield to maturity is the same as the coupon rate; when the bond sells at a discount from face value ($P < F$), the yield to maturity is greater than the coupon rate; and when the bond sells at a premium from face value ($P > F$), the yield to maturity is less than the coupon rate. Equation (2) also shows that the yield to maturity and the price of a coupon bond are negatively related; when the yield to maturity increases, the price of the coupon bond falls, and when the yield to maturity falls, the price of the coupon bond rises.

As already noted, the yield to maturity can be calculated by solving equation (2) for i, if P, C, F, and n are known. But this equation is difficult to solve algebraically, especially for high values of n. However, the same answer can be obtained using a financial calculator. Consider, for example, an eight-year, 10 percent coupon bond, with a face value of $\$1,000$, selling for $\$900$. Set a Texas Instruments BA-35 solar calculator in FIN mode by pressing the MODE key until the word FIN appears on the screen, and clear it by pushing the 2nd key and then the CE/C key. To find the yield to maturity:

1. Enter 900 and push the PV key.
2. Enter 1000 and push the FV key.
3. Enter 8 and push the N key.
4. Enter 100 and push the PMT key.

5. Push the CPT key and then the %i key.

The answer is 12.01 (or 12.01%).

Because of difficulties in calculating the yield to maturity, other less accurate measures of the interest rate have also come into common use in economic and finance. Two such measures are the *current yield* and the *yield on a discount basis*. The current yield is calculated as the ratio of the bond's yearly coupon payment, C, to the bond's current market price, P. That is,

$$\text{Current yield} = \frac{C}{P}.$$

The current yield is the best approximation to the yield to maturity for coupon bonds, and changes in the current yield always signal changes in the same direction for the yield to maturity.

In the case of discount bonds, the interest rate is usually quoted as a *yield on a discount basis*. Discount bonds are bonds that sell at a discount from face value and involve no periodic coupon payments (this is why they are also known as zero-coupon bonds). Treasury bills and long-term zero-coupon bonds are examples of discount bonds. Consider, for example, a ninety-day Treasury bill with a face value F selling at a price P. The yield on a discount basis (also known as *discount yield*) is usually calculated as follows:

$$\text{Discount yield} = \frac{F - P}{F} \times \left(\frac{\text{Days in year}}{\text{Days to maturity}} \right).$$

A related concept is the *yield curve*. The yield curve, published in the financial pages of most newspapers, shows the yield to maturity, i, as a function of the term to maturity, n. When the yield curve is upward sloping (the most typical case), the yield to maturity on long-term bonds (or, equivalently, the long-term interest rate) is greater than the yield to maturity on short-term bonds (the short-term interest rate); when the yield curve is downward sloping (referred to as an inverted yield curve), the spread between long- and short-term interest rates is negative; and when the yield curve is flat, short- and long-term interest rates are the same.

Early investigations into the yield curve looked at whether the slope of the yield curve can help predict future short-term interest rates and the level of economic activity. It was found that the yield curve does not always help predict future short-term interest rates—see, for example, Shiller, Campbell, and Schoenholtz (1983) and Mankiw and Summers (1984). More recent research based on better testing procedures, however, supports the view that the slope of the yield curve contains useful information about future interest rates over the short run and the long run, but not over the intermediate term—see, for

example, Fama (1984) and Campbell and Shiller (1991). Moreover, research over the past twenty-five years has documented a relationship between the slope of the yield curve and the overall level of economic activity; it has been shown that the slope of the yield curve is a good predictor of future economic activity. More recently, Estrella and Trubin (2006) offer practical guidance regarding the use of the yield curve as a forecasting tool in real time.

SEE ALSO *Capital; Economics; Finance; Financial Instability Hypothesis; Financial Markets; Hedging; Interest Rates; Liquidity Premium; Loans; Overlending; Yield Curve*

BIBLIOGRAPHY

Campbell, John Y., and Robert J. Shiller. 1991. Yield Spreads and Interest Rate Movements: A Bird's Eye View. *Review of Economic Studies* 58: 495–514.

Estrella, Arturo, and Mary R. Trubin. 2006. The Yield Curve as a Leading Indicator: Some Practical Issues. Federal Reserve Bank of New York. *Current Issues in Economics and Finance* 12 (July/August): 1–7.

Fama, Eugene. 1984. The Information in the Term Structure. *Journal of Financial Economics* 13 (4): 509–528.

Mankiw, N. Gregory, and Lawrence H. Summers. 1984. Do Long-Term Interest Rates Overreact to Short-Term Interest Rates? *Brookings Papers on Economic Activity* 1: 223–242.

Mishkin, Frederic S., and Apostolos Serletis. 2007. *The Economics of Money, Banking, and Financial Markets*, 3rd Canadian ed. Toronto: Addison Wesley.

Shiller, Robert J., John Y. Campbell, and Kermit L. Schoenholtz. 1983. Forward Rates and Future Policy: Interpreting the Term Structure of Interest Rates. *Brookings Papers on Economic Activity* 1: 173–217.

Apostolos Serletis

YIELD CURVE

The yield curve is a graph depicting the relationship between yield and the length of time to maturity for debt securities with comparable degrees of risk. The horizontal scale measures years to maturity, while the vertical axis presents yield to maturity. This relationship is also called the term structure of interest rates.

The shape of the yield curve plays a critical role in the decisions of individuals and corporations, and in the conduct of monetary policy by central banks, such as the U.S. Federal Reserve Bank. Individuals choosing between an adjustable and fixed-rate mortgage, and corporations deciding whether to issue short- or long-term debt, can make sensible decisions only if they understand the factors that shape the yield curve. Central banks, which operate in the short-term market, need to understand the likely effect of their activities on long rates.

Generally, the yield curve approximates one of three shapes. The curve may display the lowest yields on short-term issues, then rise and become relatively flat in the longest maturities, forming an ascending curve. Alternatively, yields may be highest on short-term securities, forming a descending (or inverted) curve. Sometimes, yields are the same for all maturities. Three economic theories—the expectations, liquidity-preference, and institutional or hedging pressure theories—explain the shape of the yield curve.

THE EXPECTATIONS THEORY

For expectations theorists, the shape of the yield curve is a reflection of investors' anticipations of future interest rates. Suppose that lower rates are likely in the future. Long-term bonds will appear more attractive than short-term ones if both maturities sell at equal yields. Long-term bonds allow an investor to earn a relatively high rate for a longer time period than shorter issues permit. Short-term bond investors risk having to reinvest their funds later at lower yields. Also, since bond prices move inversely to interest rates, buyers of long-term bonds realize capital appreciation if yields decline.

If investors act in accordance with these expectations, they will tend to bid up prices (force down the yields) of long-term bonds and sell short-term securities, causing their prices to fall (yields to rise). These operations will produce a descending yield curve with short-term issues yielding more than long-term bonds. Similarly, the expectations theory predicts the yield curve will be upward-sloping when investors expect interest rates to rise. The yield curve will be flat when no change is expected in rates.

THE LIQUIDITY-PREFERENCE THEORY

The liquidity-preference theory agrees that expectations are important but argues that short-term issues are more liquid and thus inherently more desirable to investors than longer-term bonds. Short-term issues can be converted into cash on short notice without appreciable loss in principal. Long-term issues tend to fluctuate in price with unanticipated changes in interest rates and hence ought to yield more than shorts by the amount of a risk premium.

If no premium were offered for holding long-term bonds, most individuals and institutions would prefer to hold short-term issues. Borrowers, however, prefer to issue long-term debt to assure themselves of a steady source of funds. This leaves an imbalance in the pattern of supply

and demand for the different maturities. Thus, even if interest rates are expected to remain unchanged, the yield curve should be upward-sloping, since the yields of long-term bonds will be augmented by risk premiums necessary to induce investors to hold them. The "normal relationship" is assumed to be an ascending yield curve.

THE INSTITUTIONAL OR HEDGING-PRESSURE THEORY

Liquidity is critical for some investors, but not for others. Commercial banks care about liquidity and prefer short-term issues, but liquidity is not important for life insurance companies and pension funds, which typically hedge against risk by purchasing long maturities.

That is precisely the thrust of the hedging-pressure argument. Different groups of investors have different maturity needs that lead them to concentrate their security purchases in restricted segments of the maturity spectrum. Flows of funds to particular investors, as well as changes in those preferences, will then influence the curve independent of expectations. So will the preference of international investors recycling Petro and Sino dollars. In 2005 foreigners invested over $350 billion in U.S. Treasury bonds while they were net sellers of Treasury bills, depressing the yields of long-term U.S. bonds.

EMPIRICAL STUDIES OF THE YIELD CURVE

Empirical studies of the yield curve suggest that all three theories have an influence on the shape of the yield curve. Expectations of future rates are important, but so are liquidity and institutional considerations. The average shape of the yield curve is ascending, suggesting that holders of long-term bonds do earn (il)liquidity premiums. The yield curve also appears to be a predictor of future economic activity. Inverted yield curves, while not invariably followed by a recession, have preceded all recessions experienced in the United States during the last forty years. Such a signal is consistent with the logic of the expectations theory. An inverted curve suggests that investors expect lower future rates. Recessions usually lower rates by lowering business loan demand and encouraging expansionary monetary policy.

SEE ALSO *Capital; Expectations; Financial Instability Hypothesis; Financial Markets; Hedging; Liquidity Premium; Loans; Overlending; Yield*

BIBLIOGRAPHY

Bodie, Zvi, Alex Kane, and Alan J. Marcus. 2005. *Investments.* 6th ed. New York: Irwin/McGraw-Hill. See Chapter 15, "The Term Structure of Interest Rates."

Rubenstein, Mark. 2006. *A History of the Theory of Investments.* New York: John Wiley. See pp. 218–219.

Burton G. Malkiel

YORUBA

SEE *Negro; Santería.*

YOUTH CULTURE

The term *youth culture* is used generally in reference to the ways adolescents set themselves apart from the adult culture. Although age-based cultural differences have existed since the beginnings of recorded history, it was only in the 1950s, after the crystallization of "teenagers" as distinct social personae with their own music, lifestyles, fads, and characteristic slang, that the concept of a "youth culture" as separate from adult culture materialized in North American and European society. Before then anyone reaching the age of puberty was expected to conform to the norms of the larger adult culture.

The emergence of an autonomous youth culture was heralded in fictional form by the American novelist J. D. Salinger (1919–) in his still popular and controversial novel *The Catcher in the Rye,* published in 1951. Salinger provided the first portrait of the new teenage persona—a portrait that was shortly thereafter enshrined in all kinds of media (magazines, songs, television programs, and movies), taking on a social life of its own. Since the mid-1950s youth culture has evolved independently and primarily through lifestyle designations associated primarily with youth-generated musical trends and styles (rock and roll, disco, punk, and rap). This is why cultural historians tend to characterize the evolving forms of youth culture with terms such as the *hippie era,* the *disco era,* the *punk era,* and the *hip-hop era.* Each era is in fact marked by its own pattern of symbolism, ritual, slang, and overall lifestyle (clothing and body decorations) derived from attendant musical styles.

The study of youth culture in the social and human sciences has become a major academic enterprise since the 1960s. Three major cultural theories have come forth relating specifically to youth, as separate from the psychology of adolescence. One of these posits that any youth trend is perceived initially by the adult culture as subversive or transgressive, constituting a sign of impending apocalyptic danger or threatening societal values, but which gradually dissipates and blends into the larger cultural mainstream. Known as "moral panic theory," the concept was proposed by Stanley Cohen (1972) in his

insightful study of mods and rockers in the mid-1960s. An early twenty-first century crystallization of moral panic surfaced as a result of the trend of many youths to "network socially" on the Internet at sites such as MySpace and Friendster.

Another main theory is that youth culture has become the default form of all North American and European culture, spreading throughout the social landscape independently of age. As the social critic Thomas Frank (1997) has skillfully argued, youth has become a social and economic commodity since the 1960s. Because youth sells, trends in the adolescent world quickly become the cultural norm, dictating look, taste in music, and fashion.

A third major theory of youth culture is that it constitutes a form of carnivalesque theater in which the sacred, perceived to be anything authoritative, rigid, or serious, is "profaned" or mocked simply for the sake of it. This theory has been inspired by the work of the social critic Mikhael Bakhtin (1986). It would explain why, for example, emerging youth forms of culture seem to fly in the face of the adult official "sacred world" while at the same time not posing any serious subversive political challenge to it.

SEE ALSO *Culture; Street Culture*

BIBLIOGRAPHY

Bakhtin, Mikhael M. 1986. *Speech Genres and Other Late Essays.* Trans. Vern W. McGee. Austin: University of Texas Press.

Cohen, Stanley. 1972. *Folk Devils and Moral Panics: The Creation of the Mods and Rockers.* London: MacGibbon and Kee.

Danesi, Marcel. 2003. *My Son Is an Alien: A Cultural Portrait of Today's Youth.* Lanham, MD: Rowman and Littlefield.

Danesi, Marcel. 2006. *Perspectives on Youth Culture.* Boston: Pearson Education.

Frank, Thomas. 1997. *The Conquest of Cool.* Chicago: University of Chicago Press.

Hebdige, Dick. 1979. *Subculture: The Meaning of Style.* London: Methuen.

Palladino, Grace. 1996. *Teenagers: An American History.* New York: Basic Books.

Marcel Danesi

YOUTH RISK BEHAVIOR SURVEY
SEE *Research, Cross-Sectional.*

YOUTHS
SEE *Adolescent Psychology.*

YUGOSLAVIAN CIVIL WAR

The civil wars in Yugoslavia after 1991 involved the most severe violence in Europe since the Greek civil war (1946–1949), generating almost 70,000 battle-deaths and displacing many refugees. Many claimed that the cold war had contained nationalism in Europe, and that its end would unleash a wave of sectarian conflict. Paradoxically, this failed to materialize in most socialist states except for Yugoslavia, where the Soviet Union had only minimal direct influence, previously considered a relatively successful case of multi-ethnic political integration.

The Federal Republic of Yugoslavia was torn apart by demands for autonomy from the relatively more prosperous republics of Slovenia and Croatia and the increasing assertiveness of Serbia under Slobodan Milošević (1941–2006). Slovenia's declaration of independence in June 1991 led to a minor violent confrontation with the Yugoslav National Army (JNA) but was quickly settled. Whereas independence was relatively uncontroversial for the ethnically homogenous Slovenia with undisputed borders, Croatia was much more contentious due to its large Serb population. The increasingly Serb-dominated JNA seized control over much of Croatia, and violent conflict escalated with the siege of Vukovar in August-November 1991. A January 1992 United Nations' (UN) peace plan brought combat to an end but perpetuated Serb control over much of Croatia. Later that year violence erupted between Croats, Serbs, and the Muslim dominated central government in Bosnia, leading to a protracted war with many atrocities. An International Criminal Tribunal (ICT) was set up in 1993 to investigate allegations of war crimes in the former Yugoslavia. Although fighting in Bosnia formally was carried out by autonomous militias, the Milošević and Franjo Tuđman governments of Serbia and Croatia are believed to have provided extensive support, and the ICT has brought charges against official representatives of both.

The inability of the UN to contain the conflict in Bosnia led NATO and the United States to take a more active role in 1994. The United States brokered a settlement agreement between the Bosnian Croats and the central government and provided military assistance to Croatia. In a military offensive in mid-1995, Croatia reconquered most of the Serb-held areas, and NATO bombardment forced the Serbs to sign the Dayton peace agreement in late 1995. The growing inability of Milošević to control events outside Serbia proper in turn

promoted violence among the Albanian majority in the formerly autonomous Kosovo province. The main Albanian opposition leader Ibrahim Rugova (1944–2006) had advocated a strategy of nonviolent resistance, which had succeeded in keeping Kosovo quiet but brought few Serb concessions and did not prevent extensive repression.

Following an influx of arms during the chaos in Albania in 1997, the Kosovo Liberation Army (KLA) turned to violent confrontation. Although the KLA was militarily much weaker than the JNA and the immediate Serb response was increased repression, the escalating violence, with a large outflow of refugees and allegations of atrocities, prompted NATO to start bombing Serbia in March 1999. Faced with prospects of a ground invasion, Milošević agreed to NATO demands in June, and a UN protectorate was established in Kosovo. Although Milošević had survived previous mass demonstrations calling for his resignation in 1991 and 1996, he was finally forced to leave in October 2000 after attempts to dispute an opposition electoral victory, and Serbia has not engaged in conflict with its neighbors since his ouster. The perceived success of the KLA inspired an Albanian armed uprising in Macedonia in 2001, but outside involvement prevented the conflict from escalating.

SEE ALSO *Civil Wars; Croats; Genocide; Milosevic, Slobodan; Muslims; North Atlantic Treaty Organization; Serbs; Tito (Josip Broz); United Nations; War Crimes; Warsaw Pact; World War I*

BIBLIOGRAPHY

Bass, Gary J. 2000. *Stay the Hand of Vengeance: The Politics of War Crimes Tribunals.* Princeton, NJ: Princeton University Press.

Bertsch, Gary K. 1971. *Nation-Building in Yugoslavia: A Study of Political Integration and Attitudinal Consensus.* Beverly Hills, CA: Sage.

Kaplan, Robert D. 1993. *Balkan Ghosts: A Journey through History.* New York: St. Martin's.

Ramet, Sabrina P. 2002. *Balkan Babel: The Disintegration of Yugoslavia from the Death of Tito to the Fall of Milošević.* 4th ed. Boulder, CO: Westview.

Woodward, Susan L. 1995. *Balkan Tragedy: Chaos and Dissolution after the Cold War.* Washington, DC: Brookings Institution.

Kristian Skrede Gleditsch

YUNUS, MOHAMMED

SEE *Grameen Bank; Nobel Peace Prize.*

Z

ZAPATA, EMILIANO
1879–1919

Leader of the Mexican Revolution of the early twentieth century, Emiliano Zapata was born on August 8, 1879, in Anencuilco in the southern state of Morelos and died in an ambush on April 10, 1919. Zapata was the revolution's leading advocate of agrarian issues and one of Mexico's most renowned and mythological heroes. The iconic image of Zapata dressed in a broad sombrero with a black mustache and cartridge belts across his chest appears commonly across Mexico. Contemporaries and subsequent scholars have alternatively interpreted Zapata as a bandit or a social revolutionary. The division between rural supporters who viewed Zapata as their champion and urban dwellers who denounced him as the Attila of the South points to persistent social divisions that run through the country.

The Zapata family had long been privileged leaders of their community, but under the dictatorship of Porfirio Díaz they had begun to lose their lands and their class status eroded. Recognizing Zapata's organizing skills, his community elected him to a leadership position in 1909. When legal negotiations for land titles with landowners collapsed, Zapata led community members to occupy haciendas. He had become an armed revolutionary, and his followers were known as Zapatistas.

Zapata initially joined forces with Francisco Madero, who launched a revolution against Díaz in 1910. When Madero disposed the dictator in 1911, Zapata asked the new president to return communal lands. Madero, however, insisted on following institutional procedures and demanded that Zapata's Liberation Army of the South dis-

arm. Zapata refused, arguing that they could gain their goals only through the pressure of armed force. This led Zapata to break from Madero and demand more radical reforms. On November 25, 1911, Zapata issued his Plan of Ayala (named after his local municipality), which denounced Madero as a tyrant and dictator worse than Díaz unwilling to make the necessary deep-seated changes that the revolutionaries demanded. Zapata called for a continued revolution to overthrow Madero.

The Plan of Ayala's most important thrust was a demand for agrarian reform, including a return of communal lands and expropriation of hacienda lands—without payment if the owners refused to accept the plan. The plan led to Zapata's most famous slogan "Tierra y Libertad" (Land and Liberty), which was borrowed from and reflected the ideological influence of the anarchist Ricardo Flores Magón. Over the next decade the plan became the guiding principle for Zapata's forces.

In February 1913, when General Victoriano Huerta assassinated Madero in a military coup, Zapata allied with Venustiano Carranza's Constitutionalist Army to defeat the new dictator. After Huerta's disposal, Zapata unified forces with Pancho Villa at a convention in Aguascalientes to continue the battle against the more moderate Carranza. Together, Zapata and Villa occupied Mexico City. Zapata, however, was more interested in local issues in Morelos than governing the country. His alliance with Villa quickly broke down, and Carranza recaptured the capital. Carranza convoked a constitutional assembly that elected him president. Even though he did not invite Zapata to the assembly, the latter's Plan of Ayala influenced Article 27 of the progressive 1917 constitution that codified an agrarian reform program. No significant dis-

tribution of land occurred, however, until Lázaro Cárdenas's populist government in the 1930s.

Zapata fought on despite overwhelming odds. With his prospects for victory declining and desperately short of weapons, Zapata was lured into an ambush on April 10, 1919, at the Chinameca hacienda in Morelos. Revealing their fear of Zapata's leadership and symbolism, government troops riddled his body with bullets and then dumped his corpse in Cuautla's town square. Supporters refused to accept Zapata's death, claiming that someone else had taken his place and that he had escaped to the mountains. With Zapata gone, the Liberation Army of the South began to fall apart.

After his martyrdom Zapata was incorporated into the pantheon of Mexican revolutionary leaders, even though he most certainly would oppose the policies of many subsequent political leaders. Although over the years Zapata's name was invoked for a variety of political causes, his name and image gained renewed interest in 1994 with the Zapatista Army of National Liberation (EZLN) uprising in Chiapas. Although Chiapas was isolated from the Mexican Revolution and Zapata never organized in that area, the neo-Zapatistas fought for many of the same issues that their namesake had almost a century earlier. Paralleling the situation in Morelos, indigenous communities in Chiapas had lost their lands to large landowners and faced a corrupt and repressive regime with a political stranglehold on local communities. Zapata's slogan "Land and Liberty" summarized their ongoing struggle and pointed to how few of Zapata's dreams had been realized.

SEE ALSO *Chiapas; Mexican Revolution (1910–1920); Villa, Francisco (Pancho)*

BIBLIOGRAPHY

Brunk, Samuel. 1995. *Emiliano Zapata: Revolution and Betrayal in Mexico.* Albuquerque: University of New Mexico Press.

McLynn, Frank. 2001. *Villa and Zapata: A History of the Mexican Revolution.* New York: Carroll and Graf.

Womack, John, Jr. 1968. *Zapata and the Mexican Revolution.* New York: Knopf.

Marc Becker

ZAPATISTAS

SEE *Zapata, Emiliano.*

Z-D MODEL

The Z-D model refers to the analysis contained in chapter 3, "The Principle of Effective Demand," of John Maynard Keynes's *The General Theory of Employment, Interest, and Money* (1936). It was in this early chapter that Keynes first unveiled what he considered a revolutionary new approach, defining the range of possible levels of employment that could (and in the West in the 1930s, did) characterize a market economy in equilibrium. At this early stage of his book, his task was to outline the path his argument was to take. He used what has since become known as the Z-D model to accomplish this task.

Keynes's model is based on the expectations of producers and demanders as to how much employment-generating aggregate activity they can profitably either engage in (the producers) or purchase the output of (the demanders) in the *short period*. The short period is defined by the time necessary to realize the results of the aggregate of producers' decisions (whether these were maximally profitable or not) for demand and supply. Crucially, demand for consumer goods can be known within this period, but the demand for investment goods cannot, since the value of such goods to demanders depends on an expectation of return over a longer time horizon than just the short period. In practice, this reduced to the assumption that the following are fixed: (1) the existing level of technology; (2) capital and labor; (3) the existing propensity to consume or save out of income; and (4) the expectations of the return on newly produced investment (what Keynes termed *long-period* expectations).

With this in mind, we can understand Keynes's basis for declaring—as he did many times after the *General Theory* was published—that his theory of short-period employment is most easily understood under the assumption that short-period expectations are always fulfilled; that is, given their assumptions, producers' output *is* the profit-maximizing one for each of them in this situation. Notice this leaves the state of long-term expectations, and so the level of investment, as given, and not necessarily at the level required for full employment.

A *Z* or *aggregate supply function* is then posited to capture producers' short-period expectations as to what level of production and employment will be profitable, given the relevant *ceteris paribus* conditions (above) and their expectations of demand (which can be assumed to be correct in equilibrium). Thus *Z* is a function of the proceeds producers expect, given the costs of producing a level of output. Hence: Let *Z* be the aggregate supply price of the output from employing *N* men, the relationship between *Z* and *N* being written $Z = \Phi(N)$, which can be called the *aggregate supply function* (Keynes 1936, p. 23).

Similarly, a *D* or *aggregate demand function* is posited to represent the sectoral demands, namely, the consump-

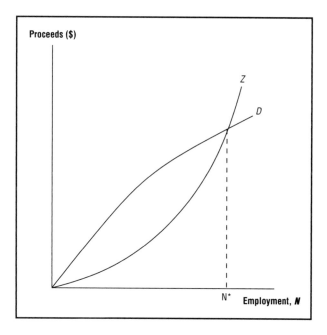

Proceeds ($)

Employment, *N*

N*

Zero Population Growth

and the volume of investment become the keys to what level of employment a market economy will generate in short-period equilibrium (i.e., the time frame in which we live).

SEE ALSO *Aggregate Demand; Aggregate Demand and Supply Price; Aggregate Supply; Economics, Keynesian; Investment; Keynes, John Maynard; Long Period Analysis; Propensity to Consume, Marginal; Propensity to Save, Marginal; Returns, Diminishing; Short Period*

BIBLIOGRAPHY

Chick, Victoria. 1983. *Macroeconomics After Keynes: A Reconsideration of the General Theory.* Cambridge, MA: MIT Press.

Darity, W. A., and J. K. Galbraith. 2005. *Macroeconomics.* Delft, The Netherlands: VSSD.

Keynes, John Maynard. 1936. *The General Theory of Employment, Interest, and Money.* London: Macmillan.

Michael S. Lawlor

ZEN

SEE *Buddhism.*

ZERO MARGINAL PRODUCT OF LABOR

SEE *Labor, Surplus: Conventional Economics; Lewis, W. Arthur.*

ZERO POPULATION GROWTH

The term *zero population growth* encompasses both an urgent call to reduce the number of human beings and a neutral description of anticipated future demographic conditions. In either case, social scientists have not debated whether the world will reach zero population growth but when, at what level, and with what costs or benefits along the way.

Population growth has periodically preoccupied theorists since ancient times, but fears of overpopulation emerged in earnest in response to the unprecedented demographic expansion that accompanied the post–1650 global agricultural revolution. (From 50 million in 1000 BCE, the earth's population increased slowly to 545 million in the year 1650, and then more than doubled to 1.2 bil-

tion function for goods and services by households (later in the chapter, D_1), and the demand for newly produced capital by investors (D_2). Hence: Similarly, let D be the proceeds that entrepreneurs expect to receive from the employment of N men, the relationship between D and N being written $D = f(N)$, which can be called the *aggregate demand function* (Keynes 1936, p. 23).

Due to diminishing returns to employment, N, in the short period, we may expect the supply function, $\Phi(N)$, to rise at an increasing rate in N. We also expect D_1 to rise at a constant and eventually less-steep rate than $\Phi(N)$ as N increases (with growing output) because the household marginal propensity to consume (χ) is less than one (or, amounting to the same thing, the marginal propensity to save out of increased income is positive); and that D_2 is fixed by long-term expectations as to the amount a community is currently willing to spend on investment. Thus, where the increasingly rising Z function intersects a constantly rising total D function, employment will be determined.

This is the point of expected profit maximization. To the left of the intersection, producers can expect to make increased profits by employing more workers; to the right, the expected proceeds do not justify the additional expected cost.

"Hence the volume of employment in equilibrium depends on (i) the aggregate supply function, Φ, (ii) the propensity to consume, χ, and (iii) the volume of investment, D_2. This is the essence of the General Theory of Employment" (Keynes 1936, p. 29).

Thus does Keynes stake out his question. Those factors that determine the marginal propensity to consume

lion in 1850 [Kremer 1990, p. 683]). At the turn of the nineteenth century, the British economist and pastor Thomas Malthus (1766–1834) famously argued, "Population, when unchecked, increases only in a geometrical (exponential) ratio. Subsistence (the food supply) increases only in an arithmetical ratio" (Malthus [1798] 1959, p. 5). During much of the nineteenth century, leading European classical economists, especially John Stuart Mill (1806–1873), incorporated Malthusian precepts and argued that population growth leads to diminishing economic returns as poorer land is brought under cultivation and an excess of workers drives down wages. Yet Thomas Jefferson (1743–1846) and other American intellectuals dismissed the notion of a population-resources problem as inapplicable to their imagined wide-open and egalitarian nation.

THE MALTHUSIAN ERA

The closing of the American frontier, as declared by the U.S. Census Bureau in 1890, engendered a Malthusian revival (that is, calls for immediate zero population growth). Moreover, as immigration to the United States surged and a pseudoscience of race matured, the desire to limit total population growth became intimately related to anxiety among many elite, white Americans that native-born Americans were having fewer children than non-white immigrants. A trans-Atlantic eugenics movement sought to breed a better population by encouraging more births among the genetically "fit" and discouraging them among the "unfit." The mixture of eugenics and Malthusianism contributed to the passage of restrictive immigration laws in the United States in the 1920s.

During the 1930s, Malthusian concerns abated. Birthrates in the industrialized world, in response to the Great Depression, continued to decline. For the first time, the prospect of zero population growth in the wealthy European and North American nations seemed a possibility. One group of economists, led by Great Britain's John Maynard Keynes, overturned the classical economists on the matter of population growth; they argued that population growth spurs economic progress by creating more consumers and economies of scale. Many economists and demographers, however, disagreed. They continued to espouse the traditional view that a smaller population would be good for the economy; in their view, the economy could grow through higher consumption per person rather than through a sheer increase in numbers.

After World War II (1939–1945), overpopulation concerns reemerged. A few social scientists and policymakers suggested that the war had been caused by population-resource pressures in the Axis nations. Many more became alarmed by the skyrocketing rates of population growth in the developing or Third World, which resulted from better hygiene and public health, and by the baby boom in the United States and other wealthy nations (from 1945 to 1964). Two best-selling books of 1948, Fairfield Osborn's *This Plundered Planet* and William Vogt's *Road to Survival,* briefly generated a revival of radical Malthusian ideas.

The postwar Malthusian resurgence was undercut somewhat by optimism that modern science would alleviate resource scarcity by better extracting natural resources and even creating new ones from scratch. In particular, atomic power and the Green Revolution in agriculture (the higher yields produced by crop breeding and pesticides) promised nearly unlimited energy and food supplies. In addition, while many postwar intellectuals concluded that population growth in the developed world caused aesthetic problems (e.g., more garbage and less parkland) as well as cultural concerns (e.g., more conformity and less privacy), they doubted whether it engendered true resource scarcity.

Still, in the 1950s and early 1960s, most social scientists continued to espouse a moderate anti-population-growth position, if not the strident Malthusians's goal of a rapid transformation to zero population growth. The dominant paradigm within the demography profession was *demographic transition theory.* This was the idea that industrialization and economic development first drive population increase because medical and sanitary improvements lower mortality well before cultural norms of (copious) childbearing shift. In the next stage, however, birthrates drop in response to the new gender and economic arrangements that accompany modernization. Eventually, population decreases. Demographers concluded, however, that waiting for modernization to run its course was not sufficient; population expanded too rapidly in the early stages and the resulting poverty actually blocked the further progress of modernization. They reached a consensus that direct intervention (e.g., family planning aid) was needed to induce the transition to lower birthrates. In a seminal 1958 study of India, two American economists, Ansley Coale and Edgar Hoover, predicted that lower birthrates would substantially increase incomes in that nation. The Coale-Hoover thesis informed efforts to invest in family planning programs for the developing world. In the 1950s, the American philanthropic sector (especially the Population Council, founded by John D. Rockefeller III [1906–1978] in 1952) took the lead in promoting such programs and fostering population-related research.

THE ZERO POPULATION GROWTH MOVEMENT PEAKS

The United States government did not articulate an official anti-population-growth policy, but it did incorporate

population-resource concerns into cold war geopolitical strategies. The idea that population growth generated conditions conducive to communism was fundamental to the development of foreign aid programs to the Third World as well as diplomatic efforts to promote international resource conservation. In the mid-1960s, the U.S. government began providing direct technical assistance and grants for family planning programs overseas and at home.

By the late 1960s, the peak of the annual global population growth rate (about 2.1 percent from 1965 to 1970; Cohen 1995, p. 54), famine in Africa, and burgeoning mass environmentalism propelled an organized zero population growth movement, the high-water mark of postwar Malthusianism. The fear now was that population growth—in both the developing and developed worlds—would ruin the world's ecological systems, not merely threaten the food supply. In 1969, the American biologist Paul Ehrlich (b. 1932), author of *The Population Bomb* (1968), spearheaded the creation of the group Zero Population Growth. This organization created widespread awareness of the putative population problem and generated significant publicity. *The Limits to Growth*, a widely debated 1972 study by a team of Massachusetts Institute of Technology (MIT) researchers, used a crude algorithm of resources, pollution, and population to predict the collapse of the world system in 100 years. Most proponents of zero population growth primarily emphasized education and the need for voluntary reductions in fertility (and to a lesser degree, promoted public policies such as the elimination of tax benefits for families and the legalization of abortion rights). A small but vocal minority, however, reduced the staying power of the population movement by calling for such radical measures as involuntary sterilizations of women after they had given birth to a certain number of children.

As the 1970s began, the U.S. government briefly accelerated its engagement with the population question beyond the question of funding for contraception, but ultimately abandoned the issue all together. President Richard Nixon offered a special message to Congress endorsing a gradual transition to zero population growth. In 1972, after meeting for two years, the Commission on Population Growth and the American Future, chaired by Rockefeller, called for several moderate measures to hasten the arrival of zero population growth in the United States. Nixon, however, immediately distanced himself from the commission's final report, and in particular its call for abortion rights (the Supreme Court would not decide the epochal case of *Roe v. Wade* until January 1973). Personally opposed to abortion, the president was also embracing a political strategy of appealing to Catholic and culturally conservative voters.

Wider forces than presidential politics ensured the rapid demise of the zero population growth movement. Ascendant conservatives, led by Julian Simon, celebrated the purported economic and cultural benefits of steady population growth (1990). In addition, the birthrate decreased noticeably in the early 1970s, which took some of the sting out of the zero population growth movement's critique. Many opponents of the zero population growth movement accused it—unfairly, for the most part—of seeking to primarily regulate the fertility of racial minorities. Other critics insisted that blaming population growth for environmental and social ills was a copout compared to attributing primacy to technology run amok and the inequalities of capitalism.

TOWARD ZERO POPULATION GROWTH

By the late 1970s, the Malthusian moment had passed in the United States. Domestic and overseas family planning policies had become institutionalized, but policymakers no longer seriously considered intervening to reduce the birthrate. The environmental movement largely abandoned its support for zero population growth due to an anti-immigration stigma increasingly attached to this position. China's adoption in 1979 of a one-child policy, which engendered myriad human rights violations (even though in many locales, especially the cities, the policy merely codified existing trends), further increased the stigma surrounding population policy. At the 1984 World Population Conference, the U.S. delegation famously declared that population growth was a neutral phenomenon. In the early twenty-first century a few Malthusians around the world continue to argue that population growth, especially in wealthy, high-consumption nations, is a major cause of global warming and will eventually have ruinous consequences for the worldwide standard of living and the environment. Some economists continue to argue that the transition to lower fertility leads to a *demographic dividend* for developing nations. But demands that world leaders act to slow down population growth are few and far between.

The United States has become something of a demographic outlier. Currently, the global population increases by about 80 million, or 1.2 percent, per year, but developing nations account for virtually all of that growth (*World Population Prospects: The 2006 Revision* 2007). Many industrialized nations such as Japan and Italy are headed toward zero population growth and should actually be in decline in fifty years. In contrast, in the United States, high levels of immigration and relatively high birthrates among immigrants and the U.S.-born alike have put the nation of 304 million (in 2007) on a path toward 570 million in 2100, according to the U.S. Census Bureau's

middle-range projections (*Methodology and Assumptions for the Population Projections of the United States: 1999 to 2100* 2000). Some experts fear the possible geopolitical consequences of this demographic trajectory, such as a further dependence on foreign oil. But most experts celebrate the supposed economic benefits of steady population growth. Perhaps the greatest demographic fear in the United States is of an aging crisis. That is, many social scientists worry that Americans are not having enough babies (future workers) to pay the imminent Social Security bill of the baby boom generation.

Assuming that fertility declines continue on their present course, the United Nations Population Division predicts the earth's population will reach 9.2 billion in 2050 (from nearly 7 billion in 2007) and then crest soon thereafter (*World Population Prospects: The 2006 Revision* 2007). Since the 1970s, the zero population growth movement has faded into near irrelevancy, but if early twenty-first-century trends hold, zero population growth will nonetheless be achieved in the not-too-distant future.

SEE ALSO *Abortion; Baby Boomers; Club of Rome; Cold War; Contraception; Demographic Transition; Demography; Eugenics; Famine; Green Revolution; Immigration; Jefferson, Thomas; Keynes, John Maynard; Limits of Growth; Malthus, Thomas Robert; Malthusian Trap; Overpopulation; Population Control; Productivity; Reproductive Politics;* Roe v. Wade; *Stationary State; Third World; Welfare State*

BIBLIOGRAPHY

Coale, Ansley J., and Edgar M. Hoover. 1958. *Population Growth and Economic Development in Low-Income Countries: A Case Study of India's Prospects.* Princeton, NJ: Princeton University Press.

Cohen, Joel E. 1995. *How Many People Can the Earth Support?* New York: W. W. Norton.

Commission on Population Growth and the American Future. 1972. *Population and the American Future.* Washington, DC: General Printing Office.

Critchlow, Donald T. 1999. *Intended Consequences: Birth Control, Abortion, and the Federal Government in Modern America.* New York: Oxford University Press.

Easterlin, Richard A. 1996. *Growth Triumphant: The Twenty-first Century in Historical Perspective.* Ann Arbor: University of Michigan Press.

Ehrlich, Paul R. 1968. *The Population Bomb.* New York: Ballantine Books.

Kremer, Michael. 1990. Population Growth and Technological Change: One Million BC to 1990. *Quarterly Journal of Economics* 108 (August): 681–716.

Malthus, Thomas Robert. [1798] 1959. *Population: The First Essay.* Foreword by Kenneth E. Boulding. Ann Arbor: University of Michigan Press.

Meadows, Donella H., et al. 1972. *The Limits to Growth: A Report for the Club of Rome's Project on the Predicament of Mankind.* New York: Universe Books.

Osborn, Fairfield. 1948. *This Plundered Planet.* Boston: Little, Brown and Company.

Simon, Julian L. 1990. *Population Matters: People, Resources, Environment, and Immigration.* New Brunswick, NJ: Transaction Publishers.

United Nations, Department of Economic and Social Affairs, Population Division, 2007. *World Population Prospects: The 2006 Revision.* United Nations: New York. http://www.un.org/esa/population/publications/wpp2006/wpp2006.htm.

U.S. Census Bureau, Population Division. 2000. *Methodology and Assumptions for the Population Projections of the United States: 1999 to 2100.* Population Division Working Paper No. 38. Washington, D.C. http://www.census.gov/population/www/documentation/twps0038.pdf.

Vogt, William. 1948. *Road to Survival.* New York: William Sloan Associates.

Derek S. Hoff

ZERO-SUM GAME

"Zero-sum game" describes a situation in which two "players" with strictly opposed interests each make a decision that results in one player's winning equaling the opposing player's loss. Many recreational games, such as chess, poker, and tic-tac-toe, are zero-sum because for one player to win, the opposing player(s) must lose.

The notion of zero-sum games originated in a branch of applied mathematics known as game theory, which has enjoyed extensive application in the social sciences. John von Neumann (1903–1957), a mathematician, is usually credited with creating game theory, and he first explicated the theory of zero-sum games in his seminal work with Oskar Morgenstern, *Theory of Games and Economic Behavior* (1944). Game theory is essentially a study of conflict situations between two or more opponents or players. Each player in the game situation must decide on a course of action, or *strategy*, and the strategy each player chooses affects the outcome for all players in the game. The outcome, or solution, to a zero-sum game specifies how each player should move, and if each player moves accordingly, then the resulting payoff is known as the *value* of the game (Kelly 2003).

The easiest class of games to analyze is *two-person* zero-sum games, and these games typically receive the most scholarly attention among those who study zero-sum games. In *Theory of Games*, von Neumann and Morgenstern focus their attention on *two-person* zero-sum

games and show that in this type of game situation there always exists a solution that allows each player to avoid the worst possible outcome. To arrive at this solution, both players base their course of action on what they expect their opponent's action will probably be. Keeping their opponent's likely course of action in mind, both players attempt to minimize the opponent's maximum payoff, thereby maximizing their own minimum payoff. In doing so, the outcome of the game ends up being that both players obtain the best payoff they possibly can, given the nature of the game, and neither is able to do any better. This outcome is known as the *equilibrium* of the game, and this point can be thought of as the outcome in which neither player has any regrets about the course of action chosen. This method of play is known as the *minimax theorem*, and von Neumann and Morgenstern showed that all two-person zero-sum games have a minimax solution.

All zero-sum games can be classified as having either *perfect information* or *imperfect information*. In a game with perfect information, each player in the game is fully aware of all previous moves in the game, meaning that each player knows what actions the opponent has already taken. In tic-tac-toe, for example, after the "X" player's move, the "O" player knows exactly where the "X" player has placed an "X." In games of perfect information, there is always at least one optimal or best possible strategy for each player. However, the existence of a best possible strategy does not guarantee that a player will win or even be able to identify that strategy. Using the best possible strategy only guarantees that both players will minimize their losses, regardless of whether they win. But there may also be so many viable strategies to choose from that it becomes impossible to determine what the best strategy is.

When applying the minimax theorem to zero-sum games with perfect information, it is possible to achieve the equilibrium point, or the point that represents the outcome that results from both players using their best possible strategy, also known as the *saddle point*. All zero-sum games with perfect information have at least one saddle point, and the saddle points can be determined using the minimax theorem. However, on some occasions the minimax theorem does not necessarily have to be used to determine a game's saddle points. Occasionally, one player has strategies available that *dominate* the other strategies. A strategy is considered *dominant* if it yields a player a better outcome than any other strategy, despite the actions taken by the opponent. When a strategy is dominated by another, then the dominated strategy is said to be *inadmissible* because, if players are trying to get the best possible outcome, then it cannot make sense to choose a dominated strategy (Kelly 2003).

In games with imperfect information, the players are not fully aware of their opponent's prior moves. This

means that each player must choose an action without knowing what action the opponent has taken or may be taking simultaneously. A simple example of this would be the game rock-paper-scissors. While there may not be one best possible strategy, it is still possible to find a minimax solution to two-person games of imperfect information. This solution can be obtained by using *mixed strategies*. Using a mixed strategy means that a player uses one strategy sometimes, another strategy at other times. The player assigns each strategy a particular probability of being used and chooses a strategy based on these probabilities. When mixed strategies are in equilibrium, meaning that neither player can do better by deviating from these strategies, the strategies are sometimes called *minimax mixed strategies* (Kelly 2003).

Analysis of zero-sum games has been applied to a variety of social science disciplines, but it has probably enjoyed most extensive application in the fields of economics and political science. In political science, for example, most elections can be thought of as zero-sum games given that for one candidate to win, the opposing candidate must lose. Also, when considering the distribution of political resources, some scholars believe that for one group to gain political resources, others must lose resources, thus implying a zero-sum nature to political competition. However, the application of zero-sum games to political and economic phenomena is necessarily limited given that most conflict situations are not zero-sum. In many conflict situations, competitors do not have strictly opposed interests; it is often possible for both players in a game to win, as sometimes is the case with economic competition, or for both players to lose, as can happen with pollution or arms races (McCain 2004). Because of the dearth of real-world zero-sum situations, and thus zero-sum's limited applicability, most game theoretic applications in the social sciences are not zero-sum.

SEE ALSO *Elections; Electoral Systems; First-past-the-post; Game Theory; Information, Asymmetric; Information, Economics of; Mixed Strategy; Politics; Social Science; Strategic Behavior; Strategic Games; Voting Schemes*

BIBLIOGRAPHY

Dixit, A. K., and B. Nalebuff. 1991. *Thinking Strategically: The Competitive Edge in Business, Politics, and Everyday Life.* New York: Norton.

Kelly, A. 2003. *Decision Making Using Game Theory: An Introduction for Managers.* Cambridge, U.K., and New York: Cambridge University Press.

McCain, R. A. 2004. *Game Theory: A Non-Technical Introduction to the Analysis of Strategy.* Mason, OH: Thomson/South-Western.

Von Neumann, J., and O. Morgenstern. 1944. *Theory of Games and Economic Behavior*. Princeton, NJ: Princeton University Press.

Monique L. Lyle

ZIMBARDO, PHILIP
1933–

Few psychologists are as famous as Philip George Zimbardo. Zimbardo is known both for his flamboyant behavior (e.g., he is rumored to have worn a black cape decorated with a *Z*) and for his research, teaching, and promotion of psychology. His work has had a meaningful impact on the social sciences and the general public. Zimbardo received his PhD from Yale University in 1959. He became a professor at New York University in 1960 and in 1968 joined the faculty at Stanford University, where he remained until his retirement in 2003. This entry discusses just a few of Zimbardo's important contributions.

Zimbardo obtained fame in 1971, when he conducted what has become known as the Stanford Prison Experiment (SPE). Zimbardo randomly assigned twenty-four normal college students to the roles of prison guard and prison inmate in a mock prison set up in the basement of the Stanford psychology building. The experiment was to last two weeks but was terminated after six days because some participants became the role they were assigned to play; some guards acted sadistically and aggressively toward inmates, whereas some inmates exhibited depressive-like symptoms, anxiety, and extreme anger. Zimbardo's experiment led him to conclude that the behavior of guards and inmates in real prisons is created more by their roles than by their personalities.

Zimbardo's SPE is a classic in psychology. It revealed the power that situations and roles can have in shaping behavior. Zimbardo frequently speaks on this topic and has even pointed out parallels between his experiment and the 2004 Abu Ghraib prison abuse scandal. Zimbardo's experiment, however, is not without its critics. Some critics (including Zimbardo) contend that it was blatantly unethical because of the extreme stress placed on inmates, whereas other critics challenge the conclusions of the SPE because of its methodology (e.g., the data collection was limited; guards were given instructions on how to behave).

Although Zimbardo is most known for his SPE, he has contributed to psychology in other important ways. After the SPE, Zimbardo and colleagues embarked on a program to investigate debilitating shyness. His research led to over thirty publications on this topic alone and to the creation of a shyness clinic. Zimbardo is also an instrumental voice in promoting psychology to the general public. He has authored a popular introductory to psychology textbook, *Psychology and Life*, that was in its eighteenth edition in 2007. In 1990 he narrated the PBS television series *Discovering Psychology*, which discussed almost every area of psychology in an understandable and engaging format. This series introduced many people for the first time to the fascinating world of psychology. Its 2001 updated edition is frequently used in high schools and universities. The possible highlight of Zimbardo's career came in 2002, when he was elected president of the American Psychology Association, the largest worldwide association for psychologists with over 150,000 members.

Few psychologists are as well known as Zimbardo. The mere mention of his name to others in psychology might lead to stories of his flamboyant behavior or to an engaging discourse about the ethics and conclusions of the SPE. Regardless of what comes to mind when one thinks of Zimbardo, it is difficult to discount the positive impact his research, teaching, and promotion have had on psychology and society.

SEE ALSO *American Psychological Association; Ethics in Experimentation; Experiments; Experiments, Human; Hierarchy; Prisons; Psychology; Punishment; Role Theory; Shyness; Social Psychology*

BIBLIOGRAPHY

Fromm, Erich. 1973. *The Anatomy of Human Destructiveness*. New York: Holt.

Haney, Craig, Curtis W. Banks, and Philip G. Zimbardo. 1973. Study of Prisoners and Guards in a Simulated Prison. *Naval Research Reviews* 9: 1–17.

Reicher, Stephen, and S. Alexander Haslam. 2006. Rethinking the Psychology of Tyranny: The BBC Prison Study. *British Journal of Social Psychology* 45: 1–40.

Brian P. Meier

ZIONISM

Zionism is the modern movement whose goal is the restoration of the Jewish people to the region on the eastern shore of the Mediterranean commonly known (at least until the establishment of the Jewish State of Israel in 1948) as Palestine or Zion. Not all of its adherents have been Jews. It draws, however, on ancient motifs sustained in Jewish collective memory, religion, and culture (and to some extent in the Christian West more generally), relating the telos of world-historical redemption and the com-

ing of the Messiah to the restoration of the Jews to their ancient homeland and the building of the third, and eternal, holy Temple in Jerusalem. Since its inception in the nineteenth century, Zionism has been an ideologically multifaceted and internally contentious movement, and its fortunes have changed in complex relation with European anti-Semitism and with colonialism beyond Europe's borders.

It is certainly difficult, and may be impossible, to present a summary account of Zionism, along with its bases of support and the sources of opposition to it, that is genuinely objective—not only because the movement continues to inspire intense passions, both positive and negative, but because its premises rest on accounts of history, geography, and nationality that are themselves fundamentally contested. Thus, Palestine refers to an ancient Roman province, to a British protectorate in the period of late European colonialism, and to the place claimed as a homeland by those residents of the region who have come to understand themselves as forming part of a non-Jewish, Palestinian nation. Speaking of the land as Zion reinforces the centrality of the region to Christian as well as Jewish sacred history and eschatological expectations. Even the notion that the Jewish people the world over constitute a single nation, central to Zionism and accepted as well by some competing Jewish movements prior to World War II (1939–1945), has not been universally accepted by Jews in the modern period.

ANCIENT AND MEDIEVAL ROOTS

Zionism draws on a rich and powerful repository of memorial resources preserved through Jewish generations, which profoundly inform ritual and expressions of religious yearning. Memorial literature that has been continuously studied since the destruction of the First and then the Second Temples in Jerusalem mourns their loss, enjoins their memory, and promises their restoration. The model of return from exile, as noble adventure and divinely sanctioned, is prefigured in the chronicles of the return from Babylonian exile led by Ezra and Nehemiah. Portions of the Babylonian Talmud detailing the correct procedures for fulfillment of commandments and strictures that relate only to times when the Jews live in Israel and the Temple stands continued to be studied, both in commemoration of the past and in anticipation of a redeemed future.

Nearly all this commemoration took place not only in the absence of Jewish sovereignty, but outside the land. At least since the destruction of the Second Temple in 70 CE, and continuing throughout the Christian era until the twentieth century, Jewish communities have been found overwhelmingly outside the imagined national homeland. This condition is itself subject to differing designations

with various ideological implications. The Hebrew and Yiddish terms *galut* or *goles*, commonly translated as *exile*, stress the element of loss inherent in location outside the homeland. On the other hand, the scattered Jewish communities are also commonly described as being in *diaspora*, an ancient term originally applied to colonies of Greek settlers throughout the Mediterranean. A thriving Jewish diaspora existed prior to the destruction of the Second Temple, and some recent scholarship has stressed the sustainability and creativity of Jewish and other diasporas.

Along with the memory of the land, its reality was preserved throughout the Middle Ages by the reports of occasional pilgrims, including famous Jewish artists and thinkers, such as the twelfth-century philosopher-poet Judah HaLevi. Extremely pious Jews sought to die, or at least to be buried, in the soil of Zion. Small settlements of religious mystics were established in Jerusalem and the Galilee during the early modern period. During the late seventeenth century, the false messiah, Sabbatai Zevi (1626–1676), raised hopes of immediate restoration of the Jews to Zion; Jews across the Western world sold their worldly goods and prepared for the journey that never came.

MODERN ZIONISM

The modern movement of Zionism, understood in large part as a mobilization to "actualize" these ancient hopes and dreams, is inseparable from key aspects of modern European history, including the dissolution of the ancien régime; the rise of secularism and religious pluralism; and the effort to create one-to-one alignments between ethnic collective identities and territorially defined nation-states. As part of the first aspect, Jewish communities were simultaneously freed of historic restrictions on movement, settlement, and employment, and deprived of their historic self-governing character. As part of the second, the *haskalah*, or "Jewish Enlightenment," sparked a profound internal critique and resistance to traditional modes of communal authority, based as it was on patriarchy, family, and class prestige, and mastery of religious law and lore. Meanwhile, chauvinist nationalisms in Europe spawned the modern variety of Jew-hatred that went by the "scientific" name of *anti-Semitism*. This inspired Zionism as a response, claiming that the only possible place for the Jewish people in a modern world of nation-states was together, preferably in its own historical homeland.

Starting in the late nineteenth century, various Zionist manifestos appeared. In Eastern Europe, Leon Pinsker's (1821–1891) *Autoemancipation*, which was inspired by a wave of pogroms in 1881 and argued that the Jews would neither be safe nor free so long as they remained in an "abnormal" situation as guests and strangers, was published in 1882. In 1896 the Viennese

journalist Theodor Herzl (1860–1904), who came to be canonized as the founder of Zionism, published his *The Jewish State*, arguing that the Jews would never be free nor gain respect until they ceased being a scattered minority. Ahad Ha'am (1856–1927), who argued that Zion should serve as a spiritual center for the renewal of world Jewry, did not carry the day, but his vision may be seen as a remarkable prediction of the relation between Jewish Israel and the Jews of the diaspora at the start of the third millennium. Intellectuals such as Judah Magnes (1877–1948) and Martin Buber (1878–1965), concerned with the ethical demand to acknowledge the presence and humanity of the Arab inhabitants of Palestine, argued early in the twentieth century for a binational solution to what came increasingly to be understood as a conflict between two nationalist movements struggling for control of the same land. The Revisionists, led by Vladimir Jabotinsky (1880–1940), contended that such reconciliation was impossible and that the conflict might well be a fight to the death, one that the Jews must at all costs win. Meanwhile the most popular variant of Zionism as a popular movement was Socialist Zionism, itself subject to bitter contention, though all of its adherents believed both that the way to revive the Jewish people was through the renewal of Jewish labor in the Jewish land and that the Zionist effort was consistent with the worldwide movement of the working class. Zionist ideology emphasized the close attachment between the people and the land in modern practice, not only in historical memory; and Zionist strategy prior to World War II involved substantial efforts to purchase land in Palestine.

WORLD WAR II AND POSTCOLONIALISM

World War II affected the Zionist movement in profound ways: It seemed to offer convincing proof that there was no safe future for Jews in diaspora, and it led to mass immigration by refugees and survivors to what was, until the late 1940s, still commonly called *Palestine* even by Jews. The establishment of the State of Israel in 1948 and the ensuing war marked a new phase in the history of the movement and the controversies surrounding it. Many Zionists understood themselves as anticolonialists, both because the Jews worldwide whom they sought to redeem could plausibly be understood as being "internally colonized" by various powerful nations and empires, and because the Zionist pragmatic and military effort involved resistance as well as collusion with the British protectorate. Palestinians displaced during the 1948 war known in Israel as the War of Independence were neither allowed by Israel to return to their homes, nor absorbed into surrounding Arab countries, thus exacerbating and perpetuating the Israeli-Palestinian conflict. The Soviet Union,

after initially voting in the United Nations for recognition of Israel, came to be aligned with the Arab States and with the Palestinian movement, while much of the world came to see Israel and Zionism as opposed to postcolonial liberation struggles.

Consistent both with the Zionist ideal of worldwide Jewish peoplehood and with the reality of vastly different Jewish communities in various parts of the world, the mass absorption of a large percentage of the world's Jews has been problematic and controversial. In the decades following World War II, the majority of the Jews of North Africa and the Middle East emigrated to Israel, as did a large percentage of the Jews of Eastern Europe and, somewhat later, the Soviet Union. Tensions arose and persist among these major immigrant groups. In the latter decades of the twentieth century, the secular Zionist goal of shaping the "new Jew," free of supposed religious obscurantism and the supposed neuroses of diaspora, was challenged both by movements to retain rather than jettison traditional Jewish cultures and by an increasingly popular and militant combination of Zionist-exclusive territorialism and fervent religious orthodoxy. Moreover, a number of scholars and commentators have argued that by the end of the twentieth century, the era of "post-Zionism" had come, meaning that the fundamental goal of establishing and securing a Jewish state had been achieved, but that it was no longer feasible or necessarily desirable to persist in the attempt to gather in all of the world's Jews.

BIBLIOGRAPHY

Ben-Ari, Eyal, and Yoram Bilu, eds. 1997. *Grasping Land: Space and Place in Contemporary Israeli Discourse and Experience.* Albany: State University of New York Press.

Benvenisti, Meron. 1986. *Conflicts and Contradictions.* New York: Villard.

Herzl, Theodor. [1896] 1997. *The Jews' State.* Trans. Henk Overberg. Northvale, NJ: Jason Aronson.

Vital, David. 1975. *The Origins of Zionism.* Oxford: Clarendon.

Zerubavel, Yael. 1995. *Recovered Roots: Collective Memory and the Making of Israeli National Tradition.* Chicago: University of Chicago Press.

Jonathan Boyarin

ZOMBIES

The word *zombie* refers to the "living dead" and originally derives from Central Africa. In Kongo, the cadaver or spirit of a deceased person is called *nzambi*. But the belief in the existence of the "living dead" is widespread, and the term has also been subject to much cross-cultural appropriation, decontextualization, and recontextualization.

Popular discourses associate zombies with the Caribbean Voodoo religion. For example, Haitians believe that malevolent sorcerers sometimes gain control of the bodies of their victims by robbing them of the component of the soul that contains personality, character, and willpower (*tibon ange*) or by raising them from their graves. The sorcerers then lead their innocent victims in a comatose trance, under cover of night, to distant places where they must toil indefinitely as slaves. The Haitian conception has informed the image of zombies in mass-mediated popular culture as the macabre figure of a corpse in tattered rags, entirely subservient and beholden to the authority of some unknown master. Zombies are portrayed as docile, with glassy empty eyes, and as being without will, memory, and emotion.

A controversial theory by ethnobiologist Wade Davis (1988) suggests that there may well be an ethnobiological basis for reports of the zombie phenomenon in Haiti. He refers to a case of zombification that was verified by a team of physicians. In 1962 Clairvus Narcisse was pronounced dead at a hospital, and buried eight hours later. But Clairvus reappeared in 1980, claiming that his brother had made him a zombie because of a land dispute. Davis argues that Clairvus was mistakenly diagnosed as dead, buried alive, and taken from the grave. Clairvus claimed that following his resurrection from the grave, he was forced to work as a slave with other zombies. He escaped after two years and spent the next sixteen years wandering about the country, fearful of his vengeful brother. Among the various preparations used by Haitian sorcerers, Davis identified a fish containing tetrodotoxin, an extremely potent neurotoxin that induces a complete state of peripheral paralysis and imperceptibly low metabolic levels. Davis postulates that the Haitian belief in zombies could be based on rare instances where an individual receives the correct dosage of the poison and is misdiagnosed as dead. Davis describes zombification as a form of punishment imposed by Bizango secret societies. These societies are arbiters of social life, protect community resources such as land, and use poison and sorcery as weapons.

Other scholars regard the belief in zombies as purely mythical. From a neo-Marxian perspective, the image of zombies as people who are dehumanized and left only with the ability to work is seen as a symbolic commentary on the historical processes of enslavement, colonialization, and proletarianization.

In many parts of Africa, zombies are recognized as an integral aspect of witchcraft discourses, particularly where these address social inequalities. Throughout the Cameroon, *nouveau riches* are imagined as witches who no longer eat their victims but change them into zombies. For example, the concept of *nyongo* emerged amongst the Bakweri after German and British colonists arrogated their land, resettled them on reserves, and allowed strangers to profit from the new economic opportunities. The Bakweri suspected prosperous outsiders of forming witch associations, taking deceased kin from their graves, and transporting the zombie spirits by lorry to Mount Kupe, where they worked on invisible plantations. These beliefs are informed by traumatic memories of the slave trade and of forced labor, as well as by perceptions of wealthy absentee landlords.

In Malawi, witchcraft discourses constitute an argument about the morality of accumulation. Accumulation is endowed with moral adequacy when entrepreneurs make their constitutive relations visible by supporting their kin financially, and by redistributing wealth through patronage, gift giving, and feasting. It is perfectly legitimate when entrepreneurs, who are motivated by these concerns, use medicines to protect their businesses. By contrast, accumulation that is motivated by individualism and greed is morally despised. In this situation, entrepreneurs are said to achieve prosperity at the cost of human lives. Zombies are believed to reside with them, to protect their money, and to attract customers to their businesses. Zombies thus serve exactly the same purposes as medicines, but are an index of morally disreputable witchcraft.

In South Africa, images of witches and zombies have multiple symbolic meanings, but capture the desire to dominate and the fear of being dominated. These images resonate with those of elderly women who control the work of their daughters-in-law, and of white industrialists who employ black laborers. The deployment of zombies in a nocturnal "second world" echoes the daunting experiences of young brides who leave their natal households for those of their husband's family, and of migrants who leave the countryside for alien industrial and mining centers. The smallness of zombies alludes to the diminutive status of these persons, and the idea that their tongues are cut suggests unquestioning obedience.

SEE ALSO *Vodou*

BIBLIOGRAPHY

Davis, Wade. 1988. *Passage of Darkness: The Ethnobiology of the Haitian Zombie.* Chapel Hill: University of North Carolina Press.

Isak Niehaus

Z-TEST

In scientific and social investigations, researchers may need to make decisions through statistical-hypothesis testing guided by underlying theory and empirical observa-

tions. The *Z*-test is one of the most popular techniques for statistical inference based on the assumption of normal distribution. Many social and natural phenomena follow the law of normal (Gaussian) distribution, which was discovered by Carl F. Gauss (1777–1855), a German mathematician, in the early nineteenth century. The normal distribution is one of the fundamental statistical distributions used in many fields of research, and it has a bell-shaped density function with μ (mean) representing the central location and σ^2 (variance) measuring the dispersion. The normal density function is

$$\frac{1}{\sqrt{2\pi}\,\sigma}\,e^{-\frac{1}{2}(x-\mu)^2/\sigma^2}. \tag{1}$$

A general normal random variable X with a mean of μ and variance σ^2 can be rescaled into the standard normal random variable Z with mean 0 and variance 1 using

$$Z = \frac{X - \mu}{\sigma}, \tag{2}$$

where σ is the standard deviation of X. The observed value of Z is called the Z score. Almost all introductory statistics books provide the table for the probability of $\{Z \le c\}$ or its variants for many convenient values of c (Agresti and Finlay 1997). These values are available in all statistical software packages.

Statistical hypothesis testing and inference on the population mean are usually performed through a sample of random variables observed from the population. Let X_1, X_2, …, X_n be n independent and identically distributed normal random variables with a mean of μ and a variance of σ^2, such as the gas mileages of a particular type of vehicle, the annual average income of households in a city, or the vital signs of patients under various treatments. Denote the sample mean $\sum_{i=1}^{n} X_i / n$ as $\bar{X}$. Then

$$Z = \frac{\bar{X} - \mu}{\sigma/\sqrt{n}} \tag{3}$$

is distributed as the standard normal random variable, where $\sigma/\sqrt{n}$ is the standard deviation of $\bar{X}$. This result provides the base for a one-sample Z-test on the mean (μ) of the study population when σ^2 is known. To test the null hypothesis H_0: $\mu = \mu_0$ (for example, to test if the mean gas mileage [μ] is 25 [μ_0] miles per gallon for a particular type of vehicle), one can form the Z-test statistic as

$$Z = \frac{\bar{X} - \mu_0}{\sigma/\sqrt{n}}. \tag{4}$$

One would reject the null hypothesis H_0 in favor of the alternative H_a: $\mu \ne \mu_0$ (the two-sided Z-test) when the observed value of Z is significantly different from 0. In many situations, one may be interested in a one-sided alternative (H_a: $\mu < \mu_0$ or H_a: $\mu > \mu_0$).

In rejecting or accepting the null hypothesis, one could commit two types of errors. The type I error (α) is the probability of rejecting the null hypothesis when it is true, and the type II error (β) is the probability of accepting the null hypothesis when it is false. The *p*-value is the probability of the test statistic as contradictory to H_0 as the observed Z value. A detailed study on statistical hypothesis testing is given by Erich Lehmann and Joseph P. Romano (2005). For the two-sided Z-test, one may reject $\mu = \mu_0$ in favor of $\mu \ne \mu_0$ if the observed Z value of the test statistic satisfies

$$|Z| = \left| \frac{\bar{X} - \mu_0}{\sigma/\sqrt{n}} \right| > 1.96. \tag{5}$$

The type I error for this test is less than 0.05. The upper bound of the type I error is called the *size*, and $1-\beta$ is called the *power* of the test. For a test, if the *p*-value is less than the size, one may reject the null hypothesis H_0. A commonly used size is 0.05. For the two-sided Z-test with size 0.05, the critical region is $\{|Z| > 1.96\}$. The Z-test is closely related to the constructing of confidence intervals. For example, the 95 percent confidence interval for the mean μ is

$$(\bar{X} - 1.96\sigma/\sqrt{n}, \bar{X} + 1.96\sigma/\sqrt{n}) \tag{6}$$

for the two-sided estimation. If $X_1, X_2 \ldots, X_n$ are not independent and identically normally distributed, under some conditions, the central limit theorem shows that

$$Z = \frac{\bar{X} - \text{Mean}\,(\bar{X})}{\sqrt{\text{Var}\,(\bar{X})}} \tag{7}$$

is approximately standard normal when n is large (typically $n \ge 30$). That is, one can still use the Z-test when n is large.

In many applications, the standard deviation of the population is unknown. In these cases, one can replace σ with the sample standard deviation s and form a test statistic as

$$t = \frac{\bar{X} - \mu_0}{s/\sqrt{n}}, \tag{8}$$

where

$$s^2 = \frac{1}{n-1} \sum_{i=1}^{n} (X_i - \bar{X})^2 \tag{9}$$

is the sample variance. The test follows the *t*-distribution of $n-1$ degrees of freedom. As n increases, t converges to Z. Hence, even when the standard deviation is unknown, the Z-test can be used if n is large. In fact, the estimates of parameters from many parametric models, such as regres-

sion models, are approximately normally distributed. The
Z-test is therefore applicable for statistical inference of
these parameters. When comparing the means (μ_1 and μ_2)
of two normally distributed populations, $N(\mu_1, \sigma_1^2)$ and
$N(\mu_2, \sigma_2^2)$, one can construct a two-sample Z statistic for
testing $H_0: \mu_1 - \mu_2 = \mu_0$:

$$Z = \frac{\bar{X} - \bar{Y} - \mu_0}{\sqrt{\sigma_1^2/n + \sigma_2^2/m}}, \qquad (10)$$

where $\bar{X} = \sum_{i=1}^{n} X_i/n$, $\bar{Y} = \sum_{i=1}^{m} Y_i/m$ and X_i, Y_i are independent random samples from these two populations
respectively.

The two-sample Z-test can be carried out in the same
way as the one-sample Z-test. Similar to the case of the
one-sample Z-test, the two-sample Z-test corresponds to
the two-sample t-test when the population variances are
replaced by their sample variances. However, when n and
m are large, there is not much difference between the two-
sample Z-test and the two-sample t-test. The two-sample
t-test is a special case of Analysis of Variance (ANOVA),
which compares the means of multiple populations. For a
small sample size, it is preferable to use nonparametric
methods instead of the Z-test, particularly when it is difficult to verify the assumption of normality.

SEE ALSO *Student's T-Statistic; Test Statistics*

BIBLIOGRAPHY

Agresti, Alan, and Barbara Finlay. 1997. *Statistical Methods for the Social Sciences*, 3rd ed. Upper Saddle River, NJ: Prentice Hall.

Lehmann, Erich L. 1986. *Testing Statistical Hypotheses*, 2nd ed. New York: Wiley.

Dejian Lai

Bibliography

This annotated bibliography is the product of the efforts of the Board of Editors to identify works in the social sciences published from 1960 onward that have had a major academic or sociopolitical impact or that represent exceptional creativity and originality. By no means do the Board of Editors claim that this list encompasses all works of merit published in the social sciences since 1960. Additional article citations are listed under a separate heading in each subject section.

ANTHROPOLOGY AND ARCHAEOLOGY

Ali, Tariq. *The Clash of Fundamentalisms: Crusades, Jihads, and Modernity.* London: Verso, 2002. Responding to Huntington's argument in *Clash of Civilizations,* Ali presents a scathing indictment of U.S. imperialism and of fundamentalism in both Islam and the Christian right.

Appadurai, Arjun. *Modernity at Large: Cultural Dimensions of Globalization.* Minneapolis, MN: University of Minnesota Press, 1996. Appadurai, while engaged in an important meditation of the idea of "modern," examines the effects of globalization on identity, lifestyle, culture, and political thought.

Behar, Ruth. *Translated Woman: Crossing the Border with Esperanza's Story.* Boston: Beacon Press, 1993. Researching in Mexico, anthropologist Behar went to a cemetery near the town of Mexquitic and attempted to photograph a Mexican-Native American woman placing flowers on the graves of her children. The woman, to whom Behar assigned the name Esperanza, bargained with Behar. If Behar and her husband would serve as godparents to one of her living children, Esperanza would tell her story to Behar, providing intimate details of the life of women in Mexquitic. The result is Behar's moving portrait of suffering and abuse. This work crystallizes the possibilities associated with subject and observer being collaborators in ethnographic projects.

Behar, Ruth. *The Vulnerable Observer: Anthropology That Breaks Your Heart.* Boston: Beacon Press, 1996. Behar advocates a more personal approach to anthropology in which the line between observer and subject is not so easily drawn. She addresses the methodological issues inspired by her earlier study, *Translated Woman,* that pushed toward a more collaborative, negotiated relationship between subject and observer. She maintains that "anthropology that doesn't break your heart just isn't worth doing."

Davies, Charlotte Aull. *Reflexive Ethnography: A Guide to Researching Selves and Others.* London: Routledge, 1999. A comprehensive guide to the relationship between the theory and practice of ethnographic research emphasizing the necessity of a self-critical stance by the researcher. Reflexive ethnography pushes researchers to be open about their biases and perspectives and to recognize that their presence can have an impact on the events that they observe and record. It rejects the notion that it is possible to achieve absolute detachment and objectivity in conducting ethnographic research.

Diop, Cheikh Anta. *Civilization or Barbarism: An Authentic Anthropology.* Translated by Yaa-Lengi Meema Ngemi. Edited by Harold J. Salemson and Marjolijn de Jager. Chicago: Lawrence Hill Books, 1991. Diop presents archaeological and historical evidence to support his assertion that Egypt was a black civilization, and that Greek civilization is indebted to Egyptian learning and accomplishments. The study argues for the centrality of African cultural production in world history.

Dumont, Louis. *Homo Hierarchicus: An Essay on the Caste System.* Translated by Mark Sainsbury. Chicago: University of Chicago Press, 1966. In a now classic study, Dumont reviews ethnographic data and explores the structure of hierarchy embedded in Hindu religious texts that constitute the ideological foundations of the Indian caste system.

Freeman, Derek. *Margaret Mead and Samoa: The Making and Unmaking of an Anthropological Myth.* Cambridge, MA:

Harvard University Press, 1983. Freeman advances a provocative refutation of the conclusions reached by anthropologist Margaret Mead in her famous study of the transition from childhood to adulthood in Samoa.

Kleinman, Arthur. *Patients and Healers in the Context of Culture: An Exploration of the Borderland between Anthropology, Medicine, and Psychiatry.* Berkeley: University of California Press, 1981. Kleinman outlines what he calls "a theoretical framework for studying the relationship between medicine, psychiatry, and culture." He focuses on illness experiences, practitioner-patient interactions, and the healing process, seeking to demonstrate how biological and sociocultural aspects of human behavior interact to influence illness and health.

Lévi-Strauss, Claude. *La Pensee Sauvage.* Paris: Plon, 1962. The noted French anthropologist presents his theories of culture and mind and his thoughts on history and social change.

Lévi-Strauss, Claude. *Mythologiques.* 4 vols. Paris: Plon, 1964–1971. Lévi-Strauss's complex series of works provide a frame for the analysis of myths and explores their importance in understanding human thought and social relationships.

McClaurin, Irma. *Women of Belize: Gender and Change in Central America.* New Brunswick, NJ: Rutgers University Press, 1996. In a postcolonial critique of gender relations in Belize, McClaurin asks how women find unity to organize themselves for the purposes of self-improvement and collective social change. Across all ethnic groups in one village, an economic-sexual dynamic was uncovered, where female dependence on men restricted women's physical and social mobility. Focusing in depth on three Belizean women of different ethnicities, McClaurin found that participation in organizations focused on traditional women's concerns helped women overcome marginalization.

Mintz, Sidney. *Caribbean Transformations.* Chicago: Aldine, 1974. This volume collects in one place several of anthropologist Mintz's most important articles on Caribbean society. Tracing the history of the region, Mintz analyzes the long-term sociocultural impact of slavery and the plantation system.

Moore, Henrietta L. and Todd Sanders, eds. *Anthropology in Theory: Issues in Epistemology.* Malden, MA: Blackwell, 2006. Contains 57 articles centering on anthropological theory and epistemology in the twentieth century. The articles provide an overview of the resurgence of the study of anthropology, new directions within the discipline, and how anthropology contributes to debates and theory in other social sciences.

Ong, Aihwa and Donald E. Nonini, eds. *Ungrounded Empires: The Cultural Politics of Modern Chinese Transnationalism.* New York: Routledge, 1997. A collection of essays exploring modern Chinese transnational capitalism and the complexity of the Chinese experience of modernity, identity, and diaspora.

Prashad, Vijay. *Everybody Was Kung Fu Fighting: Afro-Asian Connections and the Myth of Cultural Purity.* Boston: Beacon Press, 2001. Prashad analyzes historical evidence of centuries of cultural and political interaction between blacks and Asians around the world, seeking to reject notions of multiculturalism and the primacy of a white majority in favor of a model of polyculturalism. Prashad also presents four ways of thinking about race, exploring ways in which race

has been conceptualized in the past and conjecturing on implications for the future.

Prashad, Vijay. *The Karma of Brown Folk.* Minneapolis: University of Minnesota Press, 2000. Prashad discusses how some American political groups have pointed to the success of South Asian immigrants as an example of successful assimilation and proof that the U.S. offers a level playing field (i.e. South Asians as a "model minority"). Prashad counters this with an argument about America's selective immigration policy in the late twentieth century that focused on welcoming professionals from Asia.

Sahlins, Marshall. *Culture and Practical Reason.* Chicago: University of Chicago Press, 1976. Sahlins rejects the notion that, unlike other societies, Euro-American peoples can be understood strictly in terms of rational, utilitarian choices. He uses various examples to argue that a society cannot be understood without reference to symbols and meanings unique to its culture.

Sahlins, Marshall. *Stone Age Economics.* Chicago: Aldine-Atherton, 1972. By focusing on aboriginal, precolonial communities, Sahlins raises questions about the conditions of prosperity. He proposes that societies with low levels of material wants and the capacity to meet those wants while having substantial time for leisure are "the original affluent societies." Thus, Sahlins breaks the conventional link between affluence and consumerism in a major contribution to the field of economic anthropology.

Sheriff, Robin E. *Dreaming Equality: Color, Race, and Racism in Urban Brazil.* New Brunswick, NJ: Rutgers University Press, 2001. Sheriff lived in a primarily black ghetto in Rio de Janeiro for over a year compiling research on the lives of black Brazilians, exploring their perceptions about issues of race and racism in Brazil—a nation often formally described as a "racial democracy."

Said, Edward. *Orientalism.* New York: Pantheon, 1978. Perhaps Said's most influential work, *Orientalism* examines European and U.S. representations of the peoples and societies of the Middle East. The author argues that traditional Euro-American scholarship on the region has created a stereotype of its cultures as irrational, unchanging, violent, and morally degenerate. Such negative stereotypes of the Arab "Orient" and its peoples have long been exploited to justify Euro-American economic and political domination of the Middle East, and they continue to inform both popular attitudes and public policy toward the region.

Said, Edward. *Culture and Imperialism.* New York: Knopf, 1993. Said explores the relationship between imperialism and developments in popular culture that both reflected and reinforced the supremacist principals that supported imperialist projects.

Scott, David. *Conscripts of Modernity: The Tragedy of Colonial Enlightenment.* Durham, NC: Duke University Press, 2004. Scott argues for a need to reconceptualize the past in evaluating postcolonial history, viewing the transition from colonialism to postcolonialism not as "romance" but rather as tragedy, with important implications for the anticolonial utopias that have experienced conflict and disillusionment.

Singleton, Theresa A., ed. *"I, Too, am America": Archaeological Studies of African-American Life.* Charlottesville: University Press of Virginia, 1999. The volume consists of an important

set of essays that examines what has been learned about the lives of African Americans in the colonial period based upon archaeological findings.

Stocking, George W. *Race, Culture and Evolution: Essays in the History of Anthropology.* New York: Free Press, 1968. A collection of essays centering on issues of scientism, racism, and a history of the interaction between anthropology and other social science disciplines.

Trouillot, Michel-Rolph. *Silencing the Past: Power and the Production of History.* Boston: Beacon Press, 1995. A collection of five essays probing the meaning and interpretation of history, and considered an important contribution to the anthropology of history. Trouillot cites as one example the significance of the Haitian Revolution, which has not been widely accepted as one of the most important revolutions in world history. Yet, as Trouillot persuasively asserts, that revolution founded an independent black state at a time when the vast majority of blacks in the western hemisphere were enslaved. Trouillot concludes that those wielding power determine which accounts of history are considered authoritative.

Twine, France Winddance. *Racism in a Racial Democracy: The Maintenance of White Supremacy in Brazil.* New Brunswick, NJ: Rutgers University Press, 1997. Twine provides an important ethnographic study on race in Brazil, based on three years she spent in a Northern Brazilian town, that comprehensively challenges the notion that racism is of marginal importance there. She argues that Brazilians define racism with sufficient narrowness so that both everyday acts of racial indignity as well as general patterns of racial inequality often go unchallenged or are attributed to class disparity.

Wade, Peter. *Race and Ethnicity in Latin America.* London: Pluto Press, 1997. Wade's major study analyzes racial and ethnic systems of classification in Mexico, Central America, and South America.

Williams, Brackette. *Stains on My Name, War in My Veins: Guyana and the Politics of Cultural Struggle.* Durham: Duke University Press, 1991. Study of cultural, ethnic, and class conflict in Guyana. Since independence in 1966, the nation-building process in Guyana has shown how a colonial past shapes the way citizens think and act in the postcolonial context. Williams finds that political rivalry is ethnically entrenched, each group claiming superiorities over the other ethnic groups using Anglo-European standards.

Yelvington, Kelvin, editor. *Trinidad Ethnicity.* Knoxville: University of Tennessee Press, 1993. A collection of twelve essays exploring issues of ethnicity, class, color, and gender in Trinidad, one of the most demographically diverse nations in the world.

ARTICLES

Appadurai, Arjun. "Is Homo Hierarchicus?" *American Ethnologist* 13, no. 4 (1986): 745–761.

Appadurai, Arjun. "Disjuncture and Difference in the Global Cultural Economy." *Public Culture* 2, no. 2 (1990): 1–24.

Baker, Lee. "Franz Boas Out of the Ivory Tower." *Anthropological Theory* 4, no. 1 (2004): 29–51.

Blakey, Michael L. "The New York African Burial Ground Project: An Examination of Enslaved Lives, a Construction of Ancestral Ties." *Transforming Anthropology* 7, no. 1 (1998): 53–58.

Bochner, Arthur P. "Narratives Virtues." *Qualitative Inquiry* 7, no. 2 (2001): 131–157.

Caton, Hiram. "The Mead/Freeman Controversy is Over: A Retrospect." *Journal of Youth and Adolescence* 29, no. 5 (2000): 587–605.

Jarrett, Robin. "Growing Up Poor: The Family Experiences of Socially Mobile Youth in Low-Income African American Neighborhoods." *Journal of Adolescent Research* 10, no. 1 (1995): 111–135.

Jones, Rhett. "Black/Indian Relations: An Overview of Scholarship." *Transforming Anthropology* 10, no. 1 (2001): 2–16.

Lewis, Herbert. "Boas, Darwin, Science, and Anthropology." *Current Anthropology* 42, no. 3 (2001): 381–406.

Shankman, Paul. "The History of Samoan Sexual Conduct and the Mead-Freeman Controversy." *American Anthropologist* 98, no. 3 (1996): 555–567.

ARTS, MEDIA, AND POPULAR CULTURE

Bogle, Donald. *Toms, Coons, Mulattoes, Mammies, and Bucks: An Interpretive History of Blacks in American Films.* New York: Viking, 1973. Film historian Bogle's first book examines blacks in American films dating back to the era of silent movies. In analyzing their work, Bogle endeavors to reconstruct the cultural and social context of the day for each film produced. Throughout the study, he discusses the stereotypes that black actors were forced to perpetuate—noting, of course, that these films provided black actors with the opportunity for work.

Bourdieu, Pierre. *Distinction: A Social Critique of the Judgment of Taste.* Translated by Richard Nice. Cambridge, MA: Harvard University Press, 1994. Originally published as *La distinction: critique sociale du jugement,* 1979. Using evidence from a survey of more than 1,000 subjects from Paris and two other French towns, Bourdieu argues that taste functions to legitimize social differences and to orient individuals to their sense of social status and belonging. Class differences, Bourdieu asserts, can be discerned from tastes in food, including choice of food as well as preparation, presentation, and even understanding of the effects of that choice on matters of health and well-being. Bourdieu explores the relationship between economic and social conditions, arguing that people attempt to enhance class characteristics by imposing their own classifications and symbolism onto common social experiences.

Carby, Hazel V. *Reconstructing Womanhood: The Emergence of the Afro-American Woman Novelist.* New York: Oxford University Press, 1987. Carby seeks to reconstruct the social, political, and literary contexts in which the earliest novels by African American women writers were produced. She explores the marginalization of black women in history, as well as the racist undercurrents of the women's suffrage movement, in which white women saw themselves as the "ideal of true womanhood."

Frith, Simon. *Sound Effects: Youth, Leisure, and the Politics of Rock'n'Roll.* New York: Pantheon, 1981. Asserting that the

sociology of rock is the sociology of youth, Frith discusses rock music's meanings, production, and consumption.

Gans, Herbert J. *Popular Culture and High Culture: An Analysis and Evaluation of Taste.* New York: Basic Books, 1974, revised, 1999. Gans describes his study as "an argument for cultural democracy and an argument against the idea that only the cultural expert knows what is good for people and society." He discusses the multiplicity of "taste cultures" in America and opposes philosophies that suggest that such tastes can or should be improved.

Gilroy, Paul. *The Black Atlantic: Modernity and Double Consciousness.* Cambridge, MA: Harvard University Press, 1993. The black Atlantic is a space where a rich cultural synthesis has occurred in the aftermath of the disasporization of African peoples; the black Atlantan is a person forcibly removed from his home country but never fully accepted or absorbed in the new one. This displacement prompts the "double consciousness" described by W. E. B. Du Bois and acknowledged in Gilroy's title, with implications for an understanding of the work of black artists and intellectuals ranging from Frederick Douglass, Du Bois, and Richard Wright, to modern-day figures like rock musician Jimi Hendrix and novelist Toni Morrison. Gilroy argues for "an explicitly transnational and intercultural" approach to the study of black identity.

Hall, Stuart. *Encoding and Decoding in the Television Discourse.* Birmingham, UK: University of Birmingham, 1973. Analyzes media influence in relation to genre using the specific example of the Western television programming and violence. Hall argues: "[In] part what the production of the Western genre/code achieved was the transformation of a real historical west, selectively, into the symbolic of mythic 'West.'"

Hall, Stuart. *Representation: Cultural Representation and Signifying Practices.* Thousand Oaks, CA: Sage, 1997. Hall examines how visual images and language work as "systems of representation." He discusses the use of photography in national identity, the construction of masculine and feminine identity in popular culture and entertainment, and the popularization of radical movements in the mass media.

Hobsbawm, Eric J. and Terence O. Ranger, eds. *The Invention of Tradition.* Cambridge: Cambridge University Press, 1983. Six essays outline what Hobsbawm describes as the universal practice of inventing traditions during periods of rapid social change, largely for political purposes and for "the inculcation of beliefs, value systems and conventions of behavior."

hooks, bell. *Black Looks: Race and Representation.* Boston: South End Press, 1992. Twelve essays examine the black experience in America, exploring images of blacks promoted by advertisers and the media.

Jones, Le Roi (Amiri Baraka). *Blues People: Negro Music in White America.* New York: William Morrow, 1963. Baraka's classic history traces black music from slavery to contemporary jazz, noting the evolving consciousness of black identity as expressed in these works. The blues, a staple of black American music, grew out of the encounter between African and American cultures in the South to become an art form uniquely connected to both the African past and the American soil.

Lott, Eric. *Love and Theft: Blackface Minstrelsy and the American Working Class.* New York: Oxford University Press, 1993. Lott's important historical and cultural study examines the origins of blackface minstrelsy in America, focusing on its design as entertainment for white, male, working-class audiences. Lott asserts that minstrelsy helped to define and give voice to various working-class ideologies, centering his discussion on those involving race, class, and gender.

McLuhan, Marshall and Quentin Fiore. *The Medium Is the Massage: An Inventory of Effects.* New York: Bantam, 1967. With a title that offers a pun on McLuhan's famous statement "the medium is the message," this photomontage seeks to convey McLuhan's declared belief that instead of neutrally presenting content, "all media work us over completely. They are so pervasive in their personal, political, esthetic, psychological, moral, ethical, and social consequences that they leave no part of us untouched, unaffected, unaltered. The medium is the massage."

Rose, Tricia. *Black Noise: Rap Music and Black Culture in Contemporary America.* Middletown, CT: Wesleyan University Press, 1994. Rose received the American Book Award for this study, considered an outstanding treatment of rap music in its cultural contexts. The author examines the historical evolution of rap, its technological innovations, and the racial, cultural, and sexual politics of the genre.

Sollors, Werner. *Beyond Ethnicity: Consent and Descent in American Culture.* New York: Oxford University Press, 1986. Examines ethnicity in American literature and its implications for an understanding of American culture. Surveying a variety of works from all periods of American history, Sollors focuses on what he describes as the tension between "descent," the concern for one's heritage, and "consent," the desire to choose one's own life course and identity.

Szwed, John. *Space Is the Place: The Lives and Times of Sun Ra.* New York: Pantheon, 1997. A sympathetic portrayal of the twentieth-century jazz composer, musician, and orchestra leader Sun Ra (born Herman "Sonny" Blount), whose idiosyncratic temperament and wild claims of space travel were perplexing to many. Szwed explores Sun Ra's concerns with mysticism, Egyptology, and Afrocentrism, tracing his early career and artistry against the background of the emerging civil rights movement in the U.S.

Williams, Raymond. *Marxism and Literature.* Oxford: Oxford University Press, 1977. Williams insists that literature be analyzed in terms of the intentional choices of the writer at each stage of construction, and the grounding of those choices in the conflict of social forces then prevalent. The critic must reconstruct these dynamics and perceive the creative work as a production rather than a finished object.

Williams, Raymond. *Television: Technology and Cultural Form.* London: Fontana, 1974. Williams notes that television, with its centralized transmission for the purpose of a privatized reception, reinforces and extends particular cultural standards. Central to his study of technology and culture is an exploration of cultural assumptions regarding the use of television, and the political and economic structures that influence the creation and growth of new technologies.

ARTICLES

Gates Jr., Henry Louis. "Black London: After Three Generations Being Black Has Finally Become A Way of Being British." *The New Yorker* (28 April and 5 May 1997).

DEMOGRAPHY

Boserup, Ester. *Population and Technological Change: A Study of Long-Term Trends.* Chicago: University of Chicago Press, 1981. Boserup challenges Malthusian theories, positing that technological progress is induced by the pressure generated by population growth.

Croll, Elizabeth, Delia Davin, and Penny Kane, eds. *China's One-Child Family Policy.* New York: St. Martin's Press, 1985. A compilation of essays contributed by a number of well-known writers on Chinese social demography. The collection traces the origins of China's controversial one-child policy, assessing problems associated with the policy along with future prospects.

Mamdani, Mahmood. *The Myth of Population Control: Family, Caste and Class in an Indian Village.* New York: Monthly Review Press, 1972. Challenging the premise that poverty and underdevelopment in less affluent nations are the result of overpopulation, Mamdani analyzes the relationship between family size and family wealth in Manupur, India.

Schumacher, E. F. *Small is Beautiful: Economics as if People Mattered.* New York: Harper and Row, 1973. A collection of essays that rejects larger populations, larger scale, economic growth and mechanization as indicators of human social progress.

Simon, Julian L. *The Ultimate Resource.* Princeton, NJ: Princeton University Press, 1981. Simon responds to contemporary concerns about diminishing resources, environmental degradation and overpopulation with an optimistic treatise on what he describes as "the ultimate resource," human intelligence. He supports his arguments with an abundance of empirical data to highlight human resourcefulness in addressing a variety of serious problems.

ARTICLES

Anderton, Douglas L., Andy B. Anderson, John Michael Oakes, and Michael R. Fraser. "Environmental Equity: The Demographics of Dumping." *Demography* 31, no. 2 (1994): 229–248.

Arnold, Fred and Liu Zhaoxiang. "Sex Preferences, Fertility, and Family Planning in China." *Population and Development Review* 12, no. 2 (1986): 221–246.

Black, Dan, Gary Gates, Seth Sanders, and Lowell Taylor. "Demographics of the Gay and Lesbian Population in the United States: Evidence from Available Systematic Data Sources." *Demography* 37, no. 2 (2000): 139–154.

Bollen, Kennet A., David Guilkey and Thomas Mroz. "Binary Outcomes and Endogenous Explanatory Variables: Tests and Solutions with an Application to the Demand for Contraceptives in Tunisia." *Demography* 32, no. 1 (1995): 111–131.

Bumpass, Larry L. "What's Happening to the Family? Interactions Between Demographic and Institutional Change." *Demography* 27, no. 4 (1990): 483–490.

Das Gupta, Monica. "Selective Discrimination Against Female Children in Rural Punjab, India." *Population and Development Review* 13, no. 1 (1987): 77–100.

Lutz, Wolfgang, Warren Sanderson, and Sergei Sherbov. "The End of World Population Growth." *Nature* 412 (2001): 543–545.

Qian, Zhenchao. "Breaking the Racial Barriers: Variations in Interracial Marriage Between 1980 and 1990." *Demography* 34, no. 2 (1997): 263–276.

ECONOMETRICS AND STATISTICS

Anselin, Luc. *Spatial Econometrics: Methods and Models.* Boston: Kluwer, 1988. A significant textbook presenting Anselin's techniques for analyzing spatial processes.

Baltagi, Badi H. *Econometric Analysis of Panel Data*, 3rd edition. Hoboken, NJ: Wiley, 2005. A standard text on panel data written by one of the architects of this form of econometrics. Baltagi addresses basic issues in estimation and hypothesis testing.

Fisher, Franklin M. *The Identification Problem in Econometrics.* New York: McGraw-Hill, 1966. Includes Fisher's analysis of the concepts of block recursiveness and near identifiablility.

Granger, Clive W. *Modeling Nonlinear Economic Relationships.* New York: Oxford University Press, 1993. Granger provides a foundational work on specification and estimating systems of equations in economics that are characterized by nonlinearities, particularly in macroeconomics.

Granger, Clive W., and Paul Newbold. *Forecasting Economic Time Series.* New York: Academic Press, 1977. Granger and Newbold outline various models useful to economists analyzing and predicting time series. Their text is considered a classic in econometrics.

Johnston, J. J. *Econometric Methods.* New York, McGraw-Hill, 1963. A standard text on econometrics for undergraduate study, highlighted by what is considered a fine survey of matrix algebra for statistics. A fourth edition, with co-author John DiNardo (published 1996) updates methods and theory.

Pagan, Adrian and Aman Ullah. *Nonparametric Econometrics.* London: Cambridge University Press, 1999. Pagan and Ullah review a great deal of literature written over a period of five decades on the evolution of nonparametric and semi-parametric statistics. Their text breaks new ground in teaching and research methods.

Pindyck, Robert S. and Daniel L. Rubinfeld. *Econometric Models and Economic Forecasts.* New York: McGraw-Hill, 1976. Includes highly regarded sections on time series and forecast models.

Theil, Henri. *Principles of Econometrics.* New York: Wiley, 1971. Theil's classic study includes an explanation of his methods in applying index number theory to consumer demand.

ARTICLES

Blackwell, David. "Discounted Dynamic Programming." *Annals of Mathematical Statistics* 36, no. 1 (1965): 226–235.

Durbin, J. and G. S. Watson. "Testing for Serial Correlation in Least Squares Regression." *Biometrika* 58, no. 1 (1971): 1–19.

Hausman, Jerry A. and William E. Taylor. "Panel Data and Unobservable Individual Effects." *Econometrica* 49, no. 6 (1981): 1377–1398.

Lucas, Robert E., Jr. "Econometric Policy Evaluation: A Critique." *Carnegie-Rochester Series on Public Policy* 1 (1976): 19–46.

Oaxaca, Ronald and M.R. Ransom. "On Discrimination and the Decomposition of Wage Differentials." *Journal of Econometrics* 61, no. 1 (1994) 5–21.

Pagan, Adrian. "Three Econometric Methodologies: A Critical Appraisal." *Journal of Economic Surveys* 1, no. 1 (1987): 3–24.

Phillips, P. C. B. "Testing for a Unit Root in Time Series Regression." *Biometrika* 75, no. 2 (1988): 335–346.

Rao, C. Radhakrishna. "The Theory of Least Squares When the Parameters are Stochastic and its Application to the Analysis of Growth Curves." *Biometrika* 52, no. 3–4 (1965): 447–458.

ECONOMIC DEVELOPMENT

Amin, Samir. *Accumulation on a World Scale: A Critique of the Theory of Underdevelopment.* 2 vols. Translated by Brian Pearce. New York: Monthly Review Press, 1974. Amin contends that accumulation of capital within advanced capitalist countries impedes development within peripheral societies. Underdevelopment must therefore be considered historically as a part of a heterogeneous world system which is shaped by capitalism, such that "development is possible for the countries of the periphery only if they break out of the world market."

Barro, Robert J. and Xavier Sala-i-Martin. *Economic Growth.* Cambridge, MA: MIT Press, 2004. Barro and Sala-i-Martin provide a comprehensive guide to both recent developments in the theory of economic growth and the empirical conclusions about the growth process that can be drawn from large, cross-country data studies.

Boserup, Ester. *The Conditions of Agricultural Growth: The Economics of Agrarian Change Under Population Pressure.* Chicago: Aldine, 1965. Boserup outlines a theory of economic development in "primitive" (non-chemical, non-mechanized) food production centering on population pressure which prompts the adoption of more intensive methods and accompanying adjustments in land use and time allocation. She argues that the long-term effect of intensification is a dramatic rise in productivity in agriculture.

Boserup, Ester. *Women's Role in Economic Development.* New York: St. Martin's Press, 1970. Boserup examines work by women in developing countries of Latin America, Africa, and Asia, commenting on the declining role of women in agriculture, income and opportunity disparities among men and women in more "modern" sectors of the economy, and gendered competition for jobs. This is a foundational text for the field of gender and economic development.

Chenery, Hollis, Sherman Robinson, and Moshe Syrquin. *Industrialization and Growth: A Comparative Study.* New York: Oxford University Press, 1986. The authors explore the relationship between industrialization and economic growth, highlighting quantitatively and empirically the conditions or policies that are most likely to foster industrial development. Special attention is paid to the impact of the industrialization process on income distribution.

Elson, Diane, ed. *Male Bias in the Development Process.* Manchester: Manchester University Press, 1991. Important collection of essays centering on male bias in development theory and practice.

Emmanuel, Arghiri. *Unequal Exchange: A Study of the Imperialism of Trade.* Translated by Brian Pearce. London: Monthly Review Press, 1972. Emmanuel seeks to explain why terms of trade for developing countries are so consistently unfavorable, contending that inequality between nations in the international capitalist economy is maintained largely because capital is mobile and labor is immobile.

Goldsmith, Raymond W. *Financial Structure and Development.* New Haven, CT: Yale University Press, 1969. Ambitious study of the relationship between financial structure and economic growth and development in thirty-five nations.

McKinnon, Ronald. *Money and Capital in Economic Development.* Washington, DC: Brookings Institution, 1973. McKinnon's study on policy for economic development centers on distortion in the domestic capital markets of underdeveloped nations. His analysis centers on the phenomenon he labels "financial repression," government policies that keep interest rates banks offer to customers too low and rates they charge to borrowers too high.

Mishan, E. J. *The Costs of Economic Growth.* New York: Praeger, 1967. By focusing on the disamenities of economic growth—for example, increased pollution and increased congestion—Mishan contends, somewhat like Schumacher, that economic growth can be accompanied by declines in human welfare.

Nelson, Richard R. and Sidney G. Winter. *An Evolutionary Theory of Economic Change.* Cambridge, MA: Harvard University Press, 1982. The authors outline "an evolutionary theory of the capabilities and behavior of business firms operating in a market environment," constructing and analyzing models that track "the response of firms and the industry to changed market conditions, economic growth, and competition though innovation." Their study is a rare and creative extension of Joseph Schumpeter's framework for analyzing the process of economic development.

Sen, Amartya K. Y. *Development As Freedom.* New York: Anchor, 1999. The Nobel Prize–winning economist argues that the absence of material want, educational opportunity, and civil and political liberties are constituent aspects of his notion of freedom. Greater freedom is, for Sen, economic development which should be the social objective rather than mere economic growth, i.e. increases in per capita income.

Shaw, Edward S. *Financial Deepening in Economic Development.* New York: Oxford University Press, 1973. Shaw argues for a policy of financial liberalization in developing countries, urging for the importance of private savings and increased reliance on financial systems to spark economic development.

ARTICLES

Alesina, Alberto and Dani Rodrik. "Distributive Politics and Economic Growth." *Quarterly Journal of Economics* 109, no. 2 (1994): 465–490.

Acemoglu, Daron and Jaume Ventura. "The World Income Distribution." *Quarterly Journal of Economics* 117, no. 2 (2002): 659–694.

Besley, Timothy, Stephen Coate, and Glenn Loury. "The Economics of Rotating Savings and Credit Associations." *American Economic Review* 83, no. 4 (1993): 792–810.

Birdsall, Nancy, David Ross, and Richard Sabot. "Inequality and Growth Reconsidered: Lessons from East Asia." *The World Bank Economic Review* 9, no. 3 (1995): 477–508.

Easterly, William and Ross Levine. "What Have We Learned from a Decade of Empirical Research on Growth? It's Not Factor Accumulation: Stylized Facts and Growth Models." *The World Bank Economic Review* 15, no. 2 (2001): 177–219.

Fafchamps, Marcel. "Ethnicity and Credit in African Manufacturing." *Journal of Development Economics* 61, no. 1 (2000): 205–235.

Findlay, Ronald. "The Terms of Trade and Equilibrium Growth in the World Economy." *American Economic Review* 70, no. 3 (1980): 291–299.

Harris, John R. and Michael P. Todaro. "Migration, Unemployment and Development: A Two Sector Analysis." *American Economic Review* 60, no. 1 (1970): 126–142.

Kremer, Michael. "The O-Ring Theory of Development." *Quarterly Journal of Economics* 108, no. 3 (1993): 551–575.

Krugman, Paul. "Trade, Accumulation, and Uneven Development." *Journal of Development Economics* 8, no. 2 (1981): 149–161.

Krugman, Paul. "The Myth of Asia's Miracle." *Foreign Affairs* 73, no. 6 (November/December 1994): 62–78.

Lewis, W. A. "Economic Development with Unlimited Supplies of Labour." *Manchester School of Economic and Social Studies* 22, no. 2 (1954): 139–191.

Lucas, Robert E., Jr. "On the Mechanics of Development." *Journal of Monetary Economics* 22 (1988): 3–42.

Myint, Hla. "Adam Smith's Theory of International Trade in the Perspective of Economic Development." *Economica* 44, no. 175 (1977): 231–248.

Pritchett, Lant. "Divergence Big Time." *Journal of Economic Perspectives* 11, no. 3 (1997): 3–17.

Sarkar, Prabirjit. "The Singer-Prebisch Hypothesis: A Statistical Evaluation." *Cambridge Journal of Economics* 10, no. 4 (1986): 355–371.

Weisskopf, Thomas. "The Impact of Foreign Capital Inflow on Domestic Savings in Underdeveloped Countries." *Journal of International Economics* 2, no. 1 (1972): 25–38.

ECONOMICS

Arrow, Kenneth J. and Frank Hahn. *General Competitive Analysis.* San Francisco, CA: Holden Day, 1971. The authors provide a definitive analysis of the model of general equilibrium in economics.

Baran, Paul A. and Paul M. Sweezy. *Monopoly Capital: An Essay on the American Social Order.* New York: Monthly Review Press, 1966. In an influential work that informed the New Left critique of the U.S. economy, the authors argue that American capitalism has entered a monopoly phase resulting in persistent overproduction and attendant social ills.

Barro, Robert J. and Herschel I. Grossman. *Money, Employment and Inflation.* Cambridge, UK: Cambridge University Press, 1976. The authors present their macroeconomic model where, in the absence of instantaneous price adjustments, a condition of general non-market clearing or "general disequilibrium" prevails. This enables them to provide a potential explanation for stagflation, the condition of simultaneously rising prices and unemployment.

Bates, Timothy. *Race, Self-Employment, and Upward Mobility: An Illusive American Dream.* Baltimore: Johns Hopkins University Press, 1997. Bates compares self-employment among Asian and African Americans, arguing that such employment and steadily rising economic success is open only to those who are highly educated and/or possess significant personal wealth and resources.

Bharadwaj, Krishna. *Classical Political Economy and the Rise to Dominance of Supply and Demand Theories.* Calcutta: Orient Longman, 1978. Bharadwaj provides a provocative analysis of the demise of classical political economy (CPE) and the coming to prominence of the marginalist school. She argues that the assumptions of context of CPE were too readily mobilized on behalf of the interests of labor to meet with ongoing acceptance by the defenders of capitalism and, hence, fell into disfavor with the emergence of the more politically palatable supply and demand theories.

Card, David and Alan Krueger. *Myth and Measurement: The New Economics of the Minimum Wage.* Princeton, NJ: Princeton University Press, 1995. Card and Krueger refute the notion that the minimum wage decreases job opportunities for members of the low-wage labor force.

Davidson, Paul. *Money and the Real World.* London: Macmillan, 1972. Davidson isolates and explicates the core of Keynes's monetary theory to argue against the notion of neutrality of money and against the idea that the macroeconomy self-adjusts to full employment.

Fine, Ben. *Social Capital Versus Social Theory: Political Economy and Social Science at the Turn of Century.* New York: Routledge, 2001. Fine offers a vigorous critique of social capital, discussing the relationship between economics and other social sciences.

Fine, Ben. *The World of Consumption: the Material and Cultural Revisited.* New York: Routledge, 2002. Fine analyzes how the study of consumption has grown exponentially over the past 20 years, and examines what he terms "economic imperialism," globalization, commodities markets, and the consumer society.

Folbre, Nancy. *The Invisible Heart: Economics and Family Values.* New York: New Press, 2001. Featuring a pun on Adam Smith's "Invisible Hand" theory, Folbre's *Invisible Heart* contends that free markets and corporate individualism greatly hinder the ability of society to look upon the less fortunate with compassion. The author takes government and the private sector to task for "regressive taxation" and a lack of social responsibility, arguing for a redistribution of wealth.

Foley, Duncan and Miguel Sidrauski. *Monetary and Fiscal Policy in a Growing Economy.* New York: Macmillan, 1971. The authors provide a comprehensive presentation of their two-sector monetary model of economic growth.

Frenkel, Jacob A. and Harry G. Johnson. *The Monetary Approach to the Balance of Payments*. Toronto: University of Toronto Press, 1976. The authors bring together documents of a research theory on the balance of payments and test them using empirical methods.

Friedman, James. *Oligopoly and the Theory of Games*. Amsterdam: North-Holland Publishing Co., 1977. Friedman applies game theory systematically to the problem of oligopoly, a small number of sellers in a market who must anticipate the reactions of their rivals in making their own decisions about how to price their product.

Fudenberg, Drew and David Levine. *The Theory of Learning in Games*. Cambridge, MA: MIT Press, 1998. The authors present an alternative to traditional thinking about game theory.

Fudenberg, Drew and Jean Tirole. *Game Theory*. Cambridge, MA: MIT Press, 1991. Provides an introduction to non-cooperative game theory, which studies the behavior of agents when confronted with the knowledge that each agent's best choice is dependent upon forecasting an opponent's choice. The authors apply their findings and theories to political science as well as economics.

Galbraith, John Kenneth. *The New Industrial State*. London: H. Hamilton, 1967. Galbraith advances his notion that the United States is no longer a free-enterprise economy or society, and that large corporations control a structured state that creates demand that was previously non-existent through advertising.

Harcourt, Geoffrey C. *Some Cambridge Controversies in the Theory of Capital*. Cambridge, UK: Cambridge University Press, 1972. An entertaining explication of the sometimes heated exchanges, originally centered on disputes over the theory of capital, that took place between faculty in the two Cambridges (University of Cambridge in England and Massachusetts Institute of Technology in the U.S.). At the base were two competing and somewhat incompatible views of the economic system. While clearly allied with the Cambridge, England side of the debate, Harcourt provides an accurate description of the positions taken by both sets of disputants and the issues at stake.

Helpman, Elhanan and Paul Krugman. *Market Structure and Foreign Trade: Increasing Returns, Imperfect Competition, and the International Economy*. Cambridge, MA: MIT Press, 1987. Helpman and Krugman offer a theory of trade in market conditions that are less-than-perfect. The authors explore trade patterns, welfare, and the role of multinational corporations.

Kemp, Murray C. *The Pure Theory of International Trade*. Englewood Cliff, NJ: Prentice-Hall, 1964. Kemp's classic study analyzes numerous ramifications of non-monetary models of trade between nations, including several original results of his own.

Leijonhufvud, Axel. *On Keynesian Economics and the Economics of Keynes: A Study in Monetary Theory*. New York: Oxford University Press, 1968. Constructing an interpretation of Keynes's General Theory that may be legitimately called "Austro-Keynesianism," Leijonhufvud attributes to an intractable coordination problem the theoretical onus of the failure of macroeconomy to self-adjust to full-employment.

Lewis, W. Arthur. *Growth and Fluctuations 1870–1913*. Boston: Allen & Unwin, 1978. Lewis, the Nobel Prize winner in economics in 1979, presents evidence from the late 19th and early 20th centuries that growth in countries exporting primary products was dependent on their capacity to trade with countries that were centers of manufacturing activity.

Lewis, W. Arthur. *The Evolution of the International Economic Order*. Princeton, NJ: Princeton University Press, 1978. Lewis's Janeway lectures are the vehicle for his argument that the terms of trade operate to the disadvantage of "tropical" countries because of their comparatively low levels of productivity in agriculture.

Mills, Edwin. *Urban Economics*. Glenview, IL: Scott, Foresman, 1972. Mills utilizes economic theory to analyze urban difficulties and issues. An economic history of urban areas in the U.S. is offered, along with basic theoretical models that amplify the histories. Mills also discusses urban policy in the housing market, transportation, and within local government.

Newell, Allen and Herbert A. Simon. *Human Problem Solving*. Englewood Cliffs, NJ: Prentice-Hall, 1972. By examining the answers reached to problems with independently known optimal solutions by human subjects in laboratory settings, Newell and Simon construct a theory of actual human problem solving. The work explored here provides the foundation for Nobel Prize–winning economist Simon's further development of the notion of "satisficing" behavior and his investigations into the possible resemblance between human intelligence and artificial intelligence.

Olson, Mancur. *The Logic of Collective Action: Public Good and the Theory of Groups*. Cambridge, MA: Harvard University Press, 1965. Olson unveils his original theory of group and organizational behavior that can be applied across many social sciences. Olson contends that most organizations produce an output that is analogous to a public good and is available to all participants in the organization or the society, regardless of how much individual effort they have put into its making, the "free rider" problem.

Robinson, Joan. *Economic Philosophy*. Chicago: Aldine Press, 1962. Robinson reviews and analyzes the philosophical and ideological influences on economic theories and concepts, including in-depth critiques of value theory and utility theory.

Rosenberg, Nathan. *Inside the Black Box: Technology and Economics*. Cambridge University Press, 1983. Rosenberg attempts to unpackage precisely what economists mean by the concept of technology, its relationship to theories of economic growth and development, and the difficulties involved in assessing the eventual performance of new technological processes and their impact on productivity.

Schor, Juliet B. *The Overworked American: The Unexpected Decline in Leisure*. New York: Basic Books, 1993. Schor details data that show Americans spend increasingly more time at work and less time with families or at leisure. Schor blames both the pursuit of profits among corporations and the pursuit of higher pay and benefits among workers. Schor offers solutions in the form of a more minimal approach by workers and business operators.

Sen, Amartya K. Y. *Collective Choice and Social Welfare*. San Francisco: Holden-Day, 1970. A monograph discussing the

theory of social choice, which the author helped devise with Kenneth Arrow. Sen's work focuses upon the inequalities within individual rights and the availability of information relating to individual conditions. This text influenced researchers to look at basic welfare, at times apart from traditional economic models of analysis.

Sen, Amartya K. Y. *Inequality Reexamined.* Cambridge, MA: Harvard University Press, 1995. Sen discusses the importance of governments paying attention to their poorest citizens. Sen argues that governments have the capability to not only prolong the lives of the poor but can extend significant opportunities for their betterment. For such writing and other texts like it, Sen won the Nobel Prize for economics in 1998.

Sraffa, Piero. *Production of Commodities By Means of Commodities: Prelude to a Critique of Economic Theory.* Cambridge, UK: Cambridge University Press, 1960. This slim volume represents the culmination of Sraffa's attempt to develop a model that characterizes "general equilibrium" for an economy with the attributes of the system of classical political economy. This contrasts sharply with the general equilibrium features of a neoclassical economy of the type examined by Arrow and Debreu or Arrow and Hahn. Central to Sraffa's framework is the condition of a uniform rate of profit in all activities. Sraffa is the key figure in the resuscitation of classical political economy in theoretical economics and in the emergence of what has been labeled Neo-Ricardian economics.

Taylor, Lance. *Structuralist Macroeconomics.* New York: Basic Books, 1983. With inventive formalizations of the analysis of the Latin American structuralist school, Taylor advances applicable models to address the macroeconomic problems confronting developing countries.

Theil, Henri. *Economics and Information Theory.* Amsterdam: North-Holland, 1967. In an innovative work, Theil applies the principles of information theory and the principle of entropy to develop an array of index numbers with appealing properties.

Williamson, Oliver E. and Sidney G. Winter. *The Nature of the Firm: Origins, Evolution and Development.* New York: Oxford University Press, 1993. A series of essays marking the fiftieth anniversary of the publication of economist Ronald H. Coase's landmark paper entitled "The Nature of the Firm." This text gives an overview of the volume, republishes Coase's original paper, and discusses a host of issues stemming from the transaction cost economic field.

ARTICLES

Akerlof, George. "The Market for 'Lemons:' Quality Uncertainty and the Market Mechanism." *Quarterly Journal of Economics* 84, no. 3 (1970): 488–500.

Ando, Albert and Franco Modigliani. "The 'Life Cycle' Hypothesis of Saving: Aggregate Implications and Tests." *American Economic Review* 53, no. 1 (1963): 55–84.

Arrow, Kenneth J., Hollis B. Chenery, B. S. Minhas, and Robert M. Solow. "Capital-Labor Substitution and Economic Efficiency." *Review of Economics and Statistics* 43, no. 3 (1961): 225–250.

Arrow, Kenneth J. "The Economic Implications of Learning by Doing." *Review of Economic Studies* 29, no. 3 (1962): 155–173.

Basu, Kaushik and Pham Hoang Van. "The Economics of Child Labor." *American Economic Review* 88, no. 3 (1998): 412–427.

Bertrand, Marianne and Sendhil Mullainathan. "Are Emily and Greg More Employable Than Lakisha and Jamal? A Field Experiment in Labor Market Discrimination." *American Economic Review* 94, no. 4 (2004): 991–1013.

Bhagwati, Jagdish. "The Proofs of the Theorems of Comparative Advantage." *Economic Journal* 77 (1967): 75–83.

Blanchard, Olivier, Peter Diamond, Robert Hall, and Janet Yellen. "The Beveridge Curve." *Brookings Papers on Economic Activity* 1 (1990): 1–60.

Borjas, George. " Long-Run Convergence of Ethnic Skill Differentials: The Children and Grandchildren of the Great Migration." *Industrial and Labor Relations Review* 47, no. 4 (1994): 553–573.

Buchanan, James. "Public Finance and Public Choice." *National Tax Journal* 28, no. 4 (1975): 383–394.

Darity, William A., Jr. and Patrick L. Mason. "Evidence on Discrimination in Employment: Codes of Color, Codes of Gender." *Journal of Economic Perspectives* 12, no. 2 (1998): 63–90.

Diamond, Peter A. "National Debt in a Neoclassical Growth Model." *American Economic Review* 55, no. 5 (1965): 1126–1150.

Dornbusch, Rudiger, Stanley Fischer, and Paul A. Samuelson. "Comparative Advantage, Trade, and Payments in a Ricardian Model With a Continuum of Goods." *The American Economic Review* 67, no. 5 (1977): 823–839.

Fleming, John M. "Domestic Financial Policies Under Fixed and Under Floating Exchange Rates." *IMF Staff Papers* 9 (1962): 369–379.

Flood, Robert P. and R. J. Hodrick. "On Testing for Speculative Bubbles." *Journal of Economic Perspectives* 4, no. 2 (1990): 85–102.

Frey, Bruno and A. Stutzer. "What Can Economists Learn from Happiness Research?" *Journal of Economic Literature* 40, no. 2 (2002): 402–435.

Friedman, Milton. "The Role of Monetary Policy." *The American Economic Review* 58, no. 1 (1968): 1–17.

Galbraith, John Kenneth. "Power and the Useful Economist." *American Economic Review* 63, no. 1 (1973): 1–11.

Harsanyi, John C. "Games with Incomplete Information." *American Economic Review* 85, no. 3 (1985): 291–303.

Jones, Ronald W. "The Structure of Simple General Equilibrium Models." *Journal of Political Economy* 73, no. 6 (1965): 557–572.

Kregel, Jan Allen. "Ricardo, Trade, and Factor Mobility." *Economia Internazionale* 30 (1977): 215–225.

Krueger, Anne. "The Economics of Discrimination." *Journal of Political Economy* 71, no. 5 (1963): 481–486.

Krueger, Anne. "The Political Economy of the Rent-Seeking Society." *American Economic Review* 64, no. 3 (1974): 291–303.

Krugman, Paul and Lance Taylor. "Contractionary Effects of Devaluation." *Journal of International Economics* 8, no. 3 (1978): 445–456.

Loury, Glenn C. "Market Structure and Innovation." *Quarterly Journal of Economics* 93, no. 3 (1979): 395–410.

Lucas, Robert E. Jr. "Expectations and the Neutrality of Money." *Journal of Economic Theory* 4, no. 2 (1972): 103–124.

Mundell, Robert A. "A Theory of Optimum Currency Areas." *American Economic Review* 51, no. 4 (1961): 657–665.

Muth, John F. "Rational Expectations and the Theory of Price Movements." *Econometrica* 29, no. 3 (1961): 315–335.

Neal, Derek and William Johnson. "The Role of Premarket Factors in Black-White Wage Differences." *Journal of Political Economy* 104, no. 4 (1996): 869–895.

Oaxaca, Ronald. "Male-Female Wage Differentials in Urban Labor Markets." *International Economic Review* 14, no. 3 (1973): 693–709.

Pasinetti, Luigi. "A Mathematical Formulation of the Ricardian System." *Review of Economic Studies* 27, no. 2 (1960): 78–98.

Pasinetti, Luigi. "Rate of Profit and Income Distribution in Relation to the Rate of Economic Growth." *Review of Economic Studies* 29, no. 4 (1962): 267–279.

Poole, William. "Optimal Choice of Monetary Policy Instruments in a Simple Stochastic Macro Model." *Quarterly Journal of Economics* 84, no. 2 (1970): 197–216.

Riach, Peter and Judith Rich. "Field Experiments of Discrimination in the Market Place." *The Economic Journal* 112, no. 483 (2002): 480–518.

Samuelson, Paul A. and Robert M. Solow. "Analytical Aspects of Anti-Inflation Policy." *American Economic Review* 50, no. 2 (1960): 177–194.

Sato, Ryuzo. "Fiscal Policy in a Neo-Classical Growth Model: An Analysis of Time Required for Equilibrating Adjustment." *Review of Economic Studies* 30, no. 1 (1963): 16–23.

Sims, Christopher A. "Money, Income and Causality." *American Economic Review* 62, no. 4 (1972): 540–552.

Tobin, James. "A General Equilibrium Approach to Monetary Theory." *Journal of Money, Credit and Banking* 1, no. 1 (1969): 15–29.

Tobin, James. "Money and Economic Growth." *Econometrica* 33, no. 4 (1965): 671–684.

Uzawa, Hirofumi. "Production Functions with Constant Elasticities of Substitution." *Review of Economic Studies* 29, no. 4 (1962): 291–299.

Varian, Hal. "A Model of Sales." *American Economic Review* 70, no. 4 (1980): 651–659.

EDUCATION

Anderson, James. *Education of Blacks In the South, 1860–1935*. Chapel Hill: University of North Carolina Press, 1988. Anderson reviews the history of southern black education from Reconstruction to the Great Depression, shedding new light on, among other issues, the commitment of blacks to education, the importance of the Tuskegee experiment, and the role of philanthropies.

Bowen, William G. and Derek S. Bok. *The Shape of the River: Long-Term Consequences of Considering Race in College and University Admissions*. Princeton: Princeton University Press, 1998. A foundational work on the impact of affirmative action in college admissions. Bowen and Bok provide a detailed analysis that shows the benefits of the policy in terms of opportunities provided to large numbers of African Americans, and in terms of later benefits to society. The authors found that black students who completed highly selective colleges and universities are more likely than their white peers to attend graduate or professional school and to select careers where they can make direct contributions to their communities.

Bowles, Samuel and Herbert Gintis. *Schooling in Capitalist America: Educational Reform and the Contradiction of Economic Life*. New York: Basic Books, 1976. These frequent collaborators argue that the American system of formal education is designed to prepare young people to take their "appropriate" place in a hierarchical workplace and, hence, reinforces and perpetuates preexisting inequalities.

Coleman, James S. *The Adolescent Society: The Social Life of the Teenager and its Impact on Education*. Glencoe, IL: Free Press, 1961. Analysis of the culture and social systems of American high schools. Coleman's highly regarded study relies on the results of questionnaire surveys administered to students in ten high schools representative of varied social and economic strata of urban/suburban/rural Illinois in the late 1950s. It exposes adolescent isolation and recognizes that teens expect more from interactions with their peers than from relations with adults. Points to the need for educators to take into account teenagers' view of the importance of positive social status among their peers in the design and objectives of secondary-school education.

Coard, Bernard. *How the West Indian Child Is Made Educationally Subnormal in the British School System: The Scandal of the Black Child in Schools in Britain*. London: New Beacon for the Caribbean Education and Community Workers' Association, 1971. Long before his long-term imprisonment in Grenada in the aftermath of the collapse of the New Jewel Movement and the U.S. invasion, Bernard Coard employed interviews and statistical data to prepare a major study of discrimination against children of Caribbean origin in British schools in the 1960s. Coard found that children of West Indian origin were overrepresented systematically in slow learner and mentally handicapped classes.

Delpit, Lisa. *Other People's Children: Cultural Conflict in the Classroom*. New York: New Press, 1995. Nine essays focusing on learning issues faced by African-American students. Delpit challenges the assumption that good teaching looks the same in every context, explaining that poor cross-cultural communication has repeatedly caused teachers to mislabel the learning abilities and general attitudes of their students. Examples of different approaches are found in a study of Papua New Guinea village elementary schools; of cultural conflict in Alaska schools; and in a discussion of ways to reconcile curricula with local needs.

Fiske, Edward B. and Helen Ladd. *Elusive Equity: Education Reform in Post-Apartheid South Africa*. Washington, DC: Brookings Institution Press, 2004. Describes South Africa's "post-apartheid strategies for transforming its education system in the context of the nation's history," and evaluates

that country's success in "promoting a more racially equitable system." The study focuses on school governance, funding, and curriculum for the period 1994–2002.

Freire, Paolo. *Pedagogy of the Oppressed*. New York: Continuum, 1970. Freire proposes that oppressed peoples must be encouraged and taught to think more critically and to be persuaded to take action against their oppressors. He criticizes much of Western society (especially its system of public education) and capitalism, calling for a communal approach to liberation.

Jencks, Christopher, et. al. *Inequality: A Reassessment of the Effect of Family and Schooling in America*. New York: Basic Books, 1972. The analysis of "the dynamics of adult inequality" is at the core of this work and has to be seen in the historical context of the 1960s War on Poverty and its programs designed to guarantee equality of opportunity. For Jencks, the origins of inequality pervade America's economic, social, political, and cultural institutions; thus, reforming the educational system alone would not fix the problem. The authors demonstrate that there is no evidence that larger school budgets or racial integration reduce learning inequalities as they are tested and measured by standard tests of verbal ability, reading comprehension, and math skills. The failure of such programs, Jencks concluded, was due to an "inadequate conceptualization of equality," not lack of resources.

Jencks, Christopher and Meredith Phillips, editors. *The Black-White Test Score Gap*. Washington, DC: Brookings Institution Press, 1998. The Jencks and Phillips edited volume includes a set of 15 papers commissioned in preparation of a series of workshops convened to assess "general knowledge of cognitive skills and schooling." The studies revealed that test score gaps between blacks and whites contribute both to subsequent racial disparities in educational attainment and in income. The papers seek to explore comprehensively the reasons for the racial gap in test score performance and to arrive at solutions to close the gap.

Kane, Thomas J. *The Price of Admission: Rethinking How Americans Pay for College*. Washington, DC: Brookings Institution Press, 1999. Kane employs empirical data and analysis to review federal education policy designed to make college more accessible to students, arguing that removing certain barriers within the admissions process of institutions may have a more significant impact than merely increasing student financial aid.

Lewis, Amanda. *Race in the Schoolyard: Negotiating the Color Line in Classrooms and Communities*. New Brunswick, NJ: Rutgers University Press, 2003. Lewis examines how race is perceived among students, teachers, and parents in elementary schools. Lewis aims to show how racial classification in even the most seemingly mundane aspects of schooling can have a profound effect on students, and argues that cultural differences between black and white students are not seen neutrally.

Margo, Robert. *Race and Schooling in the South, 1880–1950: An Economic History*. Chicago: University of Chicago Press, 1990. Based on census data and school district records, the work describes and analyzes in eight chapters the experience of black men in the American economy. The author looks at a variety of economic factors, pointing to connections between investments in education and taxation, racial discrimination, and professional mobility to shed light on the costs of segregation.

Oakes, Jeannie. *Keeping Track: How Schools Structure Inequality*. New Haven, CT: Yale University Press, 2005. Described as one of the most influential works on American education, Oakes's study demonstrates that tracking (orienting and grouping students based on presumed ability) is a reflection of underlying social, ethnic/racial, and gender inequalities and perpetuates preexisiting disparities.

Silberman, Charles S. *Crisis in the Classroom: The Remaking of American Education*. New York: Vintage, 1971. In the author's own words, this book is about "the crisis in the classroom—the public school classroom, the college classroom, the national 'classroom' created by the mass media and by the operation of the American political system—as both a reflection of and a contributor to the larger crisis of American society."

Tatum, Beverly Daniel. *Why Are All the Black Kids Sitting Together in the Cafeteria?: A Psychologist Explains the Development of Racial Identity*. New York: Basic Books, 1997. Tatum explains why and how black students need to come together in an environment in which racial stereotypes are not necessarily overt. She implores white students to ignore the privilege of their skin color and work to combat racial injustice and intolerance.

Valencia, Richard R. (ed.). *The Evolution of Deficit Thinking: Educational Thought and Practice*. London: Falmer Press, 1997. Defines "deficit thinking" (blaming poor and minority students and their families for the students' school issues/failures while leaving unquestioned the role of educational institutions) and its consequences on policies and education practices.

Williams, Heather. *Self-Taught: African American Education in Slavery and Freedom*. Chapel Hill: University of North Carolina Press, 2005. Williams writes a comprehensive history of education among African Americans in the United States. She discusses the idea of "agency" among educated blacks, who partnered with others to advance the educational opportunities of their race in America.

Wolf, Alison. *Does Education Matter? Myths About Education and Economic Growth*. London: Penguin, 2002. Wolf presents an iconoclastic study in which she calls into question beliefs widely held by economists and other social scientists that increased educational attainment in a society raises the rate of economic growth. She explicitly addresses the paradoxical condition that increased education for individuals appears to increase their personal income prospects but increased education across a population does not seem to be associated with higher average per capita income.

ARTICLES

Behrman, Jere and Nancy Birdsall. "The Quality of Schooling: Quantity Alone is Misleading." *American Economic Review* 73, no. 5 (December 1983): 928–946.

Berg Dale, Stacy and Alan Krueger. "Estimating The Payoff To Attending A More Selective College: An Application Of Selection On Observables And Unobservables." *Quarterly Journal of Economics* 117, no. 4 (2002): 1491–1527.

Card, David and Alan Krueger. "School Quality and Black-White Relative Earnings: A Direct Assessment." *Quarterly Journal of Economics* 107, no. 1 (1992): 151–200.

Coleman, James S. "Equality of Educational Opportunity." *Equity and Excellence in Education* 6, no. 5 (1968): 19–28.

Currie, Janet and Duncan Thomas. "Does Head Start Make a Difference?" *American Economic Review* 85, no. 3 (1995): 341–364.

Dickens, William T. "Genetic Differences in School Readiness." *Future of Children* 15 (2005): 55–69.

Dreze, Jacques and Geeta Kingdon. "School Participation in Rural India." *Review of Development Economics* 5, no. 1 (2001): 1–24.

Fordham, Signithia and John U. Ogbu. "Black Students School Success: Coping with the 'Burden of "Acting White."'" *The Urban Review* 18, no. 3 (1986): 176–206.

Fryer, Roland and Steven Levitt. "Understanding the Black-White Test Score Gap in the First Two Years of School." *Review of Economics and Statistics* 86, no. 2 (2004): 447–464.

Hoxby, Caroline. "Does Competition Among Public Schools Benefit Students and Taxpayers?" *American Economic Review* 90, no. 5 (2000): 1209–1238.

Jensen, Arthur S. "How Much Can We Boost IQ and Scholastic Achievement?" *Harvard Educational Review* 39 (1969): 1–123.

Pritchett, Lant. "Where Has All the Education Gone?" *World Bank Economic Review* 15, no. 3 (2001): 367–391.

Resnick, Lauren B. "The 1987 Presidential Address: Learning In School and Out." *Educational Researcher* 16, no. 9 (1987): 13–20, 54.

Resnick, Lauren B. "From Aptitude to Effort: A New Foundation for Our Schools." *Daedalus* 124, no. 4 (1995): 55–62.

Rodgers, William and William E. Spriggs. "What Does the AFQT Really Measure: Race, Wages, and Schooling and the AFQT Score." *Review of Black Political Economy* 24, no. 4 (1996): 13–47.

Rouse, Cecilia. "Private School Vouchers and Student Achievement: An Evaluation of the Milwaukee Parental Choice Program." *Quarterly Journal of Economics* 113, no. 2 (1998): 553–602.

GEOGRAPHY

Feldman, Maryann P. *The Geography of Innovation.* Boston: Kluwer Academic, 1994. Feldman analyzes and theorizes about the tendency of technological innovations to occur in clusters both temporally and spatially.

Harvey, David. *Explanation in Geography.* London: Edward Arnold, 1969. Classic text in which Harvey explains the methodology and philosophy of geographical studies.

Harvey, David. *Social Justice and the City.* Baltimore, MD: Johns Hopkins University Press, 1973. Harvey argues that the field of geography must cease to remain neutral to urban poverty and other societal ills, contending that capitalism destroys living space to fuel its own growth. The book is an iconic example of the then-emerging field of "Marxist geography."

Massey, Doreen. *Spatial Divisions of Labor: Social Structures and the Geography of Production.* London: Macmillan, 1984. Massey argues that social inequality arises from the uneven nature of the capitalist system, which creates gross injustices and divisions between the affluent and the poor.

Rose, Gillian. *Feminism and Geography: The Limits of Geographical Knowledge.* Minneapolis, MN: University of Minnesota Press, 1993. Radical work arguing that capitalism represents the male species equating women with property. Rose also discusses her observations regarding bodies located in spaces and, subsequently, spaces mapped onto bodies.

ARTICLES

Alesina, Alberto and Enrico Spolaore. "On the Number and Size of Nations." *Quarterly Journal of Economics* 112, no. 4 (1997): 1027–1056.

Krugman, Paul. "Increasing Returns and Economic Geography." *Journal of Political Economy* 99, no. 3 (1991): 483–499.

HISTORY AND HISTORIOGRAPHY

Allen, Theodore W. *The Invention of the White Race: Racial Oppression and Social Control.* London: Verso, 1994. Compelling study of immigration, race, class, and privilege. Allen published a second volume in 1997, subtitled: "The Origin of Racial Oppression in Anglo-America."

Anderson, Perry. *Passages From Antiquity to Feudalism.* London: New Left Books, 1974. One of the foremost contemporary Marxist theorists, Anderson has been acknowledged as an authority on leftist politics and history. He charts the socio-political evolution of Europe and its economies from antiquity through the feudal system in this study.

Anderson, Perry. *Lineages of the Absolutist State.* London: New Left Books, 1974. Anderson continues the analysis developed in *Passages From Antiquity to Feudalism*, focusing on historical materialism as he traces the rise of the absolutist state.

Cantor, Norman F. *In the Wake of the Plague: The Black Death and the World It Made.* New York: Free Press, 2001. Cantor chronicles the advent of the plague with a biomedical survey, speculation as to its origins, and a record of the devastation it caused, including a mortality rate of 40 percent of the population. The author discusses fears of a Jewish conspiracy, the political effects on lineage and genealogy, and the possibility that a variety of anthrax was partly responsible for the large number of deaths.

Caro, Robert A. *The Power Brokers: Robert Moses and the Fall of New York.* New York: Knopf, 1974. Chronicles the career of New York's longtime public works commissioner Robert Moses. Caro details the building projects Moses planned, organized, and completed during his career. He also examines the enormous power that public authority commissions—which are funded by their own taxes and managed by unelected bureaucrats—have in the nation's big cities.

Carrington, Selwyn H. H. *The Sugar Industry and the Abolition of the Slave Trade, 1775–1810.* Gainesville: University of Florida Press, 2002. Drawing from a wealth of primary source material and statistical data, Carrington presents a detailed examination of the political economy of sugar production in the British West Indies. His analysis of an economic system in decline has important implications for

the debate about factors leading to Britain's abolition of the slave trade in 1807.

Constable, Pamela and Arturo Valenzuela. *A Nation of Enemies: Chile Under Pinochet.* New York: Norton, 1991. A social and political portrait of Chile from the middle of the 1960s to the early 1990s, examining the origins and results of the dictatorship under Pinochet that led to deep divisions in Chilean society and the "nation of enemies" alluded to in title.

Curtin, Philip D. *The Atlantic Slave Trade: A Census.* Madison: University of Wisconsin Press, 1969. Curtin's ground-breaking study assesses and analyzes the numerical dimensions of the Atlantic slave trade. The author surveyed existing literature, slave import figures, shipping records, and other primary documents to provide compelling new estimates of the number and distribution of slaves transported during a period of more than four centuries beginning in the 1400s.

Diamond, Jared. *Guns, Germs, and Steel: The Fates of Human Societies.* New York: Norton, 1997. Diamond's study, which won him the 1998 Pulitzer Prize in nonfiction, offers a thought-provoking theory of how the peoples of Europe and Asia were able to conquer those of the Americas, Africa, and Australia. His thesis is not that Europeans and Asians are genetically or otherwise superior but that immunological history (an "unequal germ exchange") proved decisive in shaping the international disparities in economic development that are present in the contemporary world.

Diop, Cheikh Anta. *The African Origin of Civilization: Myth or Reality?* Edited and translated by Mercer Cook. New York: Lawrence Hill, 1974. Classic study in which Diop presents historical, archaeological, and anthropological evidence to show that the ancient Egyptians were phenotypically black, and that the earliest forms of civilization can be traced to sub-Saharan Africa.

Diop, Cheikh Anta. *Precolonial Black Africa.* Translated by Harold Salemson. New York: Lawrence Hill Books, 1987. Diop offers a comparative analysis of the political and social systems of Europe and black Africa, tracing their development from antiquity to the formation of modern states.

Dirks, Nicholas B. *Castes of Mind: Colonialism and the Making of Modern India.* Princeton: Princeton University Press, 2001. Dirks maintains that the long-term British colonial rule of India required a deliberate and calculated manipulation of the Indian caste system, noting that Britain used the caste system as a means of organizing and controlling the various social groups and hierarchical layers of Indian society.

Fogel, Robert and Stanley Engerman. *Time on the Cross: The Economics of American Negro Slavery.* 2 vols. Boston: Little, Brown, 1974. Fogel (winner of the 1993 Nobel Prize in Economics) and Engerman contend that slavery was a robust economic institution prior to the Civil War and that the slaves themselves—on average—fared slightly better than free white farm laborers. The authors were careful to make clear that they were not passing a moral judgment on slavery, but rather analyzing the institution from an economic viewpoint.

Foucault, Michel. *Madness and Civilization: A History of Insanity in the Age of Reason.* Translated by Richard Howard. New York: Pantheon, 1965. In a study considered by many to be his masterpiece, Foucault traces the evolution of the human concept of madness from the middle ages through the eighteenth century.

Goldin, Claudia. *Understanding the Gender Gap: An Economic History of American Women.* New York: Oxford University Press, 1990. Seminal study of the economic history of working women in the United States.

Higman, Barry W. *Slave Populations of the British Caribbean 1807–1834.* Baltimore, MD: Johns Hopkins University Press, 1984. Important demographic study of slavery in the English-speaking Caribbean, examining economic, social, and environmental factors to establish, as Higman declared, "what was *typical* of the slave population after 1807 and also to establish the limits of the *possible.*"

Hochschild, Adam. *King Leopold's Ghost: A Story of Greed, Terror and Heroism in Colonial Africa.* Boston: Houghton Mifflin, 1998. Often compared to Hitler and Stalin, King Leopold of Belgium exploited the Congo for personal gain in the rubber industry. Hochschild recounts Leopold's conquest of the Congo in 1885, noting that the barbaric war, and the violence with which Leopold ruled his colony, drew the outraged attention of the world.

Ignatiev, Noel. *How the Irish Became White.* New York: Routledge, 1995. A study of the change in status of Irish immigrants to the United States in the early 1800s. While the Irish were initially discriminated against, Ignatiev asserts that they became "white" in order to improve their position economically and politically in a competitive society. The Irish ousted blacks, sometimes using violence, from shared neighborhoods and from widely held lower-class jobs.

Inikori, Joseph. *Africans and the Industrial Revolution in England: A Study in International Trade and Economic Development.* NY: Cambridge University Press, 2002. Details the expansion of Atlantic commerce and its impact on the emergence of the industrial revolution in England, noting the pivotal role of Africans (especially enslaved Africans) in this history.

Jalal, Ayesha. *The Sole Spokesman: Jinnah, the Muslim League, and the Demand for Pakistan.* Cambridge, UK: Cambridge University Press, 1985. An important and provocative study of the factors leading to the creation of Pakistan in 1947, including the role of the leader of the Muslim League in India and first Prime Minister of Pakistan, Mohammed Ali Jinnah.

Lewis, David Levering. *When Harlem Was in Vogue: The Politics of the Arts in the Twenties and Thirties.* New York: Knopf, 1981. Lewis analyzes the phenomenon known as the Harlem Renaissance, detailing the social, cultural, and historical influences that shaped the artistic achievements for which this period and place have been celebrated. He seeks to reexamine the Renaissance from the perspective of a variety of important participants: not only the black authors, artists, and musicians whose works were "in vogue," as the title suggests, but also whites who were writers, artists, wealthy patrons, or otherwise influential in race matters.

Lewis, David Levering. *W. E. B. Du Bois: Biography of a Race, 1868–1919.* New York: Holt, 1994. Lewis won the Pulitzer Prize for this first part of a two–volume biography. In 2000, he completed the companion volume, *W. E. B. Du Bois: The Fight for Equality and the American Century, 1919–1963.*

Lipton, Merle. *Capitalism and Apartheid: South Africa 1910–1986.* Aldershot, U.K.: Wildwood House, 1986. Lipton explores the evolution of the relationship between economics and politics in South Africa, citing a growing divergence in the interests of capitalists and the policies of the apartheid state.

McDougall, W. A. *The Heavens and the Earth: A Political History of the Space Age.* New York: Basic Books, 1985. Exploring the space race from the end of World War II through the Apollo 11 moon landing in 1969, the author comments on the implications of this drive into space for public policy at various levels.

McGuire, James W. *Peronism Without Peron: Unions, Parties, and Democracy in Argentina.* Stanford: Stanford University Press, 1997. Substantial analysis of Peronism and democratic instability in twentieth-century Argentina.

Mintz, Sidney W. *Sweetness and Power: The Place of Sugar in Modern History.* New York: Viking Penguin, 1985. Arguing that sugar was both a part of, and an agent in, the rapid modernization of European life, Mintz speculates about the political, cultural, and social significance of sugar consumption. He reveals that sugar was used primarily by the wealthy as a spice, medicine, and decoration as late as the sixteenth century, and only later assumed its modern role as a sweetener and preservative.

Nove, Alec. *Economic History of the USSR.* London: Allen Lane, 1969. Nove presents an economic history of the Soviet Union, beginning with the state of the Russian economy in 1913 and tracing his analysis through Krushchev's fall.

Ortiz, Paul. *Emancipation Betrayed: The Hidden History of Black Organizing and White Violence in Florida From Reconstruction to the Bloody Election of 1920.* Berkeley: University of California Press, 2005. Ortiz provides the first major study of white political violence in the state of Florida in the early part of the 20th century as the central mechanism to disenfranchise the state's black electorate.

Parsa, Misagh. *Social Origins of the Iranian Revolution.* New Brunswick, NJ: Rutgers University Press, 1989. Sociologist Parsa analyzes events in Iran during the revolutionary period of 1977–1979, focusing on the major participants while seeking to construct what he calls "a broad theory of revolution and political conflict."

Post, Ken. *Arise Ye Starvelings: The Jamaican Labour Rebellion of 1938 and Its Aftermath.* The Hague, London: Institute of Social Studies Series, 1978. Post investigates the actions taken in 1938 by workers and peasants involved in the labor rebellion in Jamaica. The author declares that his aim is "to develop a Marxist concept of political practice by showing its necessary relations to material and mental production."

Prunier, Gerard. *The Rwanda Crisis: History of a Genocide.* New York: Columbia University Press, 1995. Prunier briefly traces the history of Rwanda from pre-colonial times, through German and Belgian colonial regimes, independence in the 1950s, to the political coup of 1973 and refugee crisis that followed, focusing his analysis and exploration on events leading to the tragic genocide of the 1990s.

Rodney, Walter. *How Europe Underdeveloped Africa.* London: Bogle-L'Ouverture, 1972. Rodney identifies European colonialism and its present-day repercussions as the fundamental cause of African economic underdevelopment.

Sheridan, Richard B. *Doctors and Slaves: A Medical and Demographic History of Slavery in the British West Indies, 1680–1834.* Cambridge: Cambridge University Press, 1985. Sheridan examines slavery in the British West Indies, analyzing the sharp differences between the slave workforce in the American south, which increased in number by natural means, and that in the Caribbean, where slaves could not reproduce or endure long enough to maintain a steady population.

Thompson, E. P. *The Making of the English Working Class.* New York: Pantheon Books, 1963. Highly regarded social history tracing the emergence of the modern industrial working class in England.

Wiencek, Henry. *An Imperfect God: George Washington, His Slaves, and the Creation of America.* New York: Farrar, Straus and Giroux, 2003. Wiencek explores the complex personality of the first president of the United States with a special focus on the evolution of Washington's response to the moral dilemma presented by slavery.

Williams, Eric. *From Columbus to Castro: The History of the Caribbean, 1492–1969.* London: Deutsch, 1970. Important study by historian Williams (first Prime Minister of Trinidad and Tobago), focusing on the history of sugar and its production in the Caribbean. Williams begins with Columbus, who brought sugarcane from the Canary Islands to the Caribbean on his second voyage to the New World, and ends his analysis with Fidel Castro and his rule of Cuba.

ARTICLES

Cuenca Esteban, Javier. "The Rising Share of British Industrial Exports in Industrial Output, 1700–1851." *Journal of Economic History* 57, no. 4 (1997): 879–906.

Cutler, David M., Edward L. Glaesar, and Jacob L. Vigdor. "The Rise and Decline of the American Ghetto." *Journal of Political Economy* 107, no. 3 (June 1999): 455–506.

Suzuki, Masao. "Success Story? Japanese Immigrant Economic Achievement and Return Migration, 1920–1930." *Journal of Economic History* 55, no. 4 (1995): 889–901.

Wynter, Sylvia. "Seville and the Conversion Experience of Bartolome de Las Casas." *Jamaica Journal* 17, no. 2 (1990): 25–32.

INTERNATIONAL RELATIONS, ORGANIZATION, AND LAW

Allison, Graham. *Essence of Decision: Explaining the Cuban Missile Crisis.* New York: Little, Brown, 1971. Allison's landmark work examines the 1962 nuclear weapons crisis between the United States and Soviet Union by applying the events of the situation to three decision-making models in order to help explain group behavior in organizations. This work introduced the term "groupthink" to the academic and mainstream lexicon and is required reading in many areas of study.

Anaya, S. James. *Indigenous Peoples in International Law.* New York: Oxford University Press, 1996. A highly regarded overview of the historical, contemporary and emerging international law related to indigenous peoples.

Barnet, Richard J. *Intervention and Revolution: The United States in the Third World.* New York: World Publishing Company,

1968. Barnet traces the history of United States covert intervention in foreign revolutions in the 20th century. In addition to discussing events ranging from Franklin D. Roosevelt's blocking of a proposed constitutional amendment requiring a national referendum on sending troops overseas to the Truman Doctrine and the war in Vietnam, Barnet gives detailed attention to the role taken by the U.S. Central Intelligence Agency in foreign political developments.

Birnie, Patricia and Alan E. Boyle. *International Law and the Environment.* New York: Oxford University Press, 1992. Authoritative study of the primary principles of international law concerning protection of the environment.

Bill, James A. *The Eagle and the Lion: The Tragedy of American-Iranian Relations.* New Haven: Yale University Press, 1988. Bill analyzes the slow erosion of diplomatic, political, and economic ties between the United States and Iran, beginning in 1835. His detailed study explains the complicated set of circumstances that yielded American hostage crises in Iran and Lebanon in the 1970s and 1980s, and the Iran-*contra* affair. Bill concludes that the strained relationship is a catastrophic foreign policy failure.

Buzan, Barry. *People, States and Fear: The National Security Problem in International Relations.* Chapel Hill: University of North Carolina Press, 1983. Buzan argues for a rethinking of political and military relations, so that security is seen as a quality of interdependence rather than as an attribute of individual nations.

Eatwell, John and Lance Taylor. *Global Finance at Risk: The Case for International Regulation.* New York: The New Press, 2000. Economists Eatwell and Taylor recap the reasons for and outcomes of a series of international economic crises dating to 1970, building a case for the establishment of a powerful regulatory agency called the World Financial Authority. The proposed agency would oversee international investment, implement policy, and act as an enforcement mechanism.

Galanter, Marc. *Competing Equalities: Law and the Backward Classes in India.* Berkeley: University of California Press, 1984. Galanter provides an extensive, empirically based study of India's affirmative action programs.

Gilpin, Robert E. *The Political Economy of International Relations.* Princeton, NJ: Princeton University Press, 1987. Gilpin examines the influence of politics on the international economy, advocating the need for a strong central power like the United States in fostering international economic cooperation.

Huntington, Samuel. *The Clash of Civilizations and Remaking of World Order.* New York: Simon & Schuster, 1996. Huntington argues that the world need not be viewed as a collection of states, but as a set of "zones" of civilizations that are destined for conflict based on clashes of identity. Huntington posits that western civilization should most worry about Islam and its theories of cultural superiority combined with the inferiority of their collective power on the world stage.

Mamdani, Mahmood. *Good Muslim, Bad Muslim: America, the Cold War, and the Roots of Terror.* New York: Pantheon, 2004. Mamdani discusses the way many Americans view Muslims, noting that Muslims who support the West are labeled secular and "good," while Muslims who disagree with Western policies are pejoratively considered fundamentalist and "bad." The tenets of terrorist organizations such as al-Qaeda, writes Mamdani, are based in politics and not religion, a critical difference ignored by the West. More importantly, Mamdani insists that Americans must understand the role of the U.S. government in creating some of these radical movements not only in the Middle East, but also in Africa and Asia.

Rueschemeyer, Dietrich, Evelyne Huber Stephens, and John D. Stephens. *Capitalist Development and Democracy.* Chicago: University of Chicago Press, 1992. Focusing on the economies and societies of advanced industrial countries and nations in Latin America and the Caribbean, the authors contend that capitalist development is associated with democracy because it transforms class structure, empowering the working and middle-classes and making it more difficult for elites to exclude them.

Roorda, Eric Paul. *The Dictator Next Door: The Good Neighbor Policy and the Trujillo Regime in the Dominican Republic.* Durham, NC: Duke University Press, 1998. Reviewing the optimistic 1930s American foreign policy of encouraging emerging nations in the Western Hemisphere to adopt the principles of self-government, Roorda explains and analyzes the rise of the brutal dictator Rafael Trujillo and its influence on other Latin American strongmen. Roorda's work concludes by examining the change in American policy in the 1950s and 1960s and Trujillo's ultimate demise.

ARTICLES

Barnett, Michael N. and Martha Finnemore. "The Politics, Power, and Pathologies of International Organization." *International Organization* 53, no. 4 (1999): 699–732.

Chan, Steve. "In Search of Democratic Peace: Problems and Promise." *Mershon International Studies Review* 41, no. 1 (1997): 59–91.

Cox, Robert W. "Ideologies and the New International Economic Order: Reflections on Some Recent Literature." *International Organization* 33, no. 2 (Spring 1979): 257–302.

Conway, Patrick. "IMF Lending Programs: Participation and Impact." *Journal of Development Economics* 45, no. 2 (1994): 365–391.

Haas, Peter. "Introduction: Epistemic Communities and International Policy Coordination." *International Organization* 46, no. 1 (1992): 1–35.

Krugman, Paul. "Competitiveness: A Dangerous Obsession." *Foreign Affairs* 73, no. 2 (July/August 1994).

Kuran, Timur. "Now Out of Never: The Element of Surprise in the East European Revolution of 1989." *World Politics* 44, no. 1 (1991): 7–48.

Nagar, Richa, Victoria Lawson, Linda McDowell, and Susan Hanson. "Locating Globalization: Feminist (Re)readings of the Subjects and Spaces of Globalization." *Economic Geography* 78, no. 3 (2002): 257–284.

LINGUISTICS

Chomsky, Noam. *Aspects of the Theory of Syntax.* Cambridge, MA: MIT Press, 1965. The noted linguist first reveals his controversial theories of language in this study, introducing such concepts as Deep Structure and Universal Grammar.

Chomsky also attempts to clarify the distinction between grammar and meaning.

Chomsky, Noam *Knowledge of Language: Its Nature, Origin, and Use.* New York: Praeger, 1985. Chomsky considers two major conceptual shifts in the study of language: the beginning of the modern study of generative grammar, and a theoretical process utilized to study contemporary perspective on traditional questions. Chomsky also posits that the study of language can offer universal insights to the workings of the human mind.

Derrida, Jacques. *Of Grammatology.* Translated by Gayatri Chakravorty Spivak. Baltimore, MD: Johns Hopkins University Press, 1976. Spivak translates Derrida's revolutionary theories about structuralism, psychoanalysis, and deconstruction. Derrida's ideas led students of the humanities, literature, and philosophy to reconsider traditional views of their areas of study.

Foucault, Michel. *Archaeology of Knowledge & the Discourse on Language.* Translated by Rupert Swyer. London: Tavistock, 1972. Challenging study of the connections between knowledge, language, and action, providing insight into Foucault's development of theories posited in previous books. An appendix reprints "The Discourse on Language," Foucault's investigation into the ways in which society manipulates language for purposes of politics and power.

Heidegger, Martin. *On the Way to Language.* Translated by Peter D. Hertz. New York: Harper and Row, 1971. Heidegger elaborates on his phrase "Language is the House of Being" by presenting a dialogue with a Japanese acquaintance followed by four lectures concentrating upon Heidegger's main themes of the importance and significance of linguistics in understanding the human mind.

Heidegger, Martin. *Poetry, Language, Thought.* Trans. Albert Hofstadter. New York: Harper & Row, 1971. This collection of seven essays by Heidegger examines his interest in poems, poetry, and poets (as well as painters and prose authors) not as an artistic or cultural critic, but from his particular point of view known as "ontological knowledge." Heidegger's aim is to focus on art as a guide in the "investigation of Being."

METHODOLOGY

Blaug, Marc. *The Methodology of Economics: Or, How Economists Explain.* Cambridge, UK: Cambridge University Press, 1980. Blaug's classic work on the nature of economic explanation and interpretation contains a review of methodology literature and an examination of the philosophy of science, followed by case studies of economic problems and questions. The author concludes with thoughts on the difficulties and opportunities presented by modern economics.

Caldwell, Bruce. *Beyond Positivism: Economic Methodology in the Twentieth Century.* London: Routledge, 1994. Caldwell provides an overview of philosophical theories and approaches within economics that is readily understood by non-specialists. Caldwell concludes by arguing for a new approach in studying economic philosophy called methodological pluralism.

Friedman, Milton. *Essays in Positive Economics.* Chicago: University of Chicago Press, 1966. The Nobel Prize–winning economist discusses various topics such as methodology of positive economics, price theory and monetary economics in this collection of essays. Friedman also touches on the relationship between welfare and taxes, exchange rates, and inflation.

Gleick, James. *Chaos: Making a New Science.* New York: Penguin, 1988. A former science writer for the *New York Times,* Gleick here engagingly writes about the complicated and often obtuse subject of chaos theory, the study of seemingly random patterns of science that make up natural phenomena. Gleick profiles dozens of scientists dedicated to the study of chaos theory, highlighting their ideas and research.

PHILOSOPHY OF SCIENCE

Althusser, Louis and Etienne Balibar. *Reading Capital.* Translated by Ben Brewster. London: New Left Books, 1970. The prominent French philosopher, Louis Althusser, offers a structuralist reading of Marx that rejects historicist and humanist readings of Capital.

Derrida, Jacques. *Specters of Marx: The State of the Debt, The Work of Mourning & the New International.* Translated by Peggy Kamuf. New York: Routledge, 1994. Derrida writes of the impact of the fall of the Berlin Wall on Marxism and economic theory's future in two expanded lectures. Derrida argues that phrases such as "new world order" and "the end of history" (which categorized the fall of Communism) are merely old debates attempting to extinguish the "spirit" of Marxism.

Foucault, Michel. *The Order of Things: An Archaeology of the Human Sciences.* New York: Pantheon, 1971. Foucault introduces his archaeological method, presenting the idea that "in any given culture and at any given moment there is only one *episteme* (a system of instinctual knowledge) that defines the conditions of possibility of all knowledge." Foucault then attempted "to dig up and display the 'archaeological' form or forms which would be common to all mental activity," tracing these forms throughout historic cultures.

Heidegger, Martin. *Being and Time.* Translated by John Macquarrie and Edward Robinson. London: Blackwell, 1962. Heidegger felt that it was man's primary duty to define the word "being." He was driven to "pose anew the question" in this study by his belief that man—in the classical Greek period—had hastily applied the assumption that truth was whatever was intellectually perceived as correct. For Heidegger, it was not enough to say simply that something existed. He devoted most of his lifetime to addressing this difficult problem of metaphysics. Heidegger's work is essential to studies of ontology.

Kuhn, Thomas. *The Structure of Scientific Revolutions.* Chicago: University of Chicago Press, 1962. One of the most important philosophical works of the mid-twentieth century, Kuhn's analysis of the research process utilized by scientific inquirers and their psychological make-up has influenced academic work and study in diverse fields since its publication. Kuhn may best be remembered for his use in this book of terms such as "paradigm shift" and "normal science."

Lakatos, Imre. *The Methodology of Scientific Research Programmes.* Edited by John Worrall and Gregory Currie. Cambridge,

UK: Cambridge University Press, 1978. A wide array of papers written by Lakatos are compiled into two primary sections: the first concentrating on the philosophy of the physical sciences, the second containing many previously unpublished essays on the philosophy of mathematics.

Popper, Karl. *The Logic of Scientific Discovery.* New York: Basic Books, 1959. A classic text on the scientific method. Introduces Popper's solution to the problem of induction, and articulates his view of "falsifiability" as the determining criterion of scientific knowledge.

Popper, Karl. *Objective Knowledge: An Evolutionary Approach.* Oxford, UK: Clarendon Press, 1972. Collection of essays attempting to define Popper's theories of epistemology and explain his realist's approach to such topics as logic, history, and physics.

Sartre, Jean-Paul. *Being and Nothingness: An Essay on Phenomenological Ontology.* Translated by Hazel E. Barnes. New York: Philosophical Library, 1956. The famed French existentialist examines man, the being who questions being, and concludes that he is both his body occupying a place in the world — that is, an object among objects — and a subject or a consciousness reflecting on objects. Sartre contends that all consciousness is consciousness of *something.* Since it is basically a negating — or distinguishing — function (saying that this chair, for instance, is *not* this table), consciousness produces the concept of nothingness; man is the being by whom negation is introduced into an otherwise complete world.

Sartre, Jean-Paul. *Search for a Method.* Translated by Hazel E. Barnes. New York: Knopf, 1963. Sartre contends that existentialism and a study of the individual's role in history is central to an understanding of Marxism.

POLITICAL SCIENCE

Aldrich, John Herbert. *Why Parties? The Origin and Transformation of Political Parties in America.* Chicago: University of Chicago Press, 1995. Aldrich examines the origins and development of political parties in America, noting how the party system offers a solution to three primary problems of democracy: limiting the number of candidates seeking office; mobilizing voters; and achieving consensus to accomplish political goals.

Almond, Gabriel A. and Sidney Verba. *The Civic Culture: Political Attitudes and Democracy in Five Nations.* Princeton, NJ: Princeton University Press, 1963. Writing during an era that saw the formation of several new democracies around the world, Almond and Verba argue that such governments thrive not only when their structures and institutions are democratic, but also when their ideals are supported by an egalitarian culture. The authors define this culture as one "based on communication and persuasion, a culture of consensus and diversity, a culture that permitted change but moderated it."

Bahro, Rudolf. *The Alternative in Eastern Europe.* Translated by David Fernbach. London: New Left Books, 1978. Bahro provides a class analysis of the hierarchical character of the "actually existing socialism" in Eastern Europe prior to the collapse of the Soviet Union. Some identify this work as the origin point for the eco-socialist movement in Germany.

Cohen, Cathy J. *The Boundaries of Blackness: AIDS and the Breakdown of Black Politics.* Chicago: University of Chicago Press, 1999. Cohen explores the impact of the AIDS epidemic on the African American community, analyzing the responses of black leaders to this crisis.

Dahl, Robert A. *Democracy and Its Critics.* New Haven, CT: Yale University Press, 1989. Dahl defends democracy against arguments that democratic government has elements of coercion and that true democracy is impossible due to the inevitable presence of a social elite. The author maintains that a wide distribution of wealth is necessary for meaningful political democracy and proposes greater civic participation by the random incorporation of groups of citizens within the structure of government.

Dahl, Robert A. *Polyarchy: Participation and Opposition.* New Haven, CT: Yale University Press, 1971. Dahl's study is concerned with two main variables of democracy: competition among various political individuals and forces, and participation among those citizens afforded the right to participate in the democratic process. Dahl argues that a "polyarchy," or a system including the greatest number of participants, should be the goal of the ideal society.

Dahl, Robert A. *Who Governs? Democracy and Power in an American City.* New Haven, CT: Yale University Press, 1961. Dahl examines the city of New Haven in this seminal study of political power dynamics in local government. This book is considered essential for those studying urban politics and/or political systems.

Dawson, Michael C. *Behind the Mule: Race and Class in African-American Politics.* Princeton, NJ: Princeton University Press, 1994. Examines the importance of race and class in shaping African American political opinion.

Hinich, Melvin J. and Michael C. Munger. *Ideology and the Theory of Political Choice.* Ann Arbor: University of Michigan Press, 1994. Important study of the relationship between ideology and voter behavior.

Hirschman, Albert O. *Exit, Voice and Loyalty: Responses to Decline in Firms, Organizations, and States.* Cambridge, MA: Harvard University Press, 1970. Hirschman maintains that business corporations typically operate at merely a "satisfactory level," as opposed to maximum efficiency, which in turn leads to a deterioration in times of weaker competition. He outlines the concepts of "exit" and "voice" as consumer options when businesses operate at unsatisfactory levels, applying this same theory to the two-party political system in the United States.

Iyob, Ruth. *The Eritrean Struggle for Independence: Domination, Resistance, Nationalism, 1941–1993.* Cambridge, UK: Cambridge University Press, 1995. The first comprehensive analysis of Eritrea's political history in the aftermath of its difficult fight for independence from Ethiopia. Iyob traces the roots of Eritrean nationalism and, in the context of regional and global circumstances, analyzes competing political forces within the nation.

Kariel, Henry. *The Decline of American Pluralism.* Palo Alto, CA: Stanford University Press, 1961. Kariel uses Nietzsche's idea of the impossibility of humans grasping final social and political truths as a base to argue that political scientists must work to question established truths about pluralism as well as to actively create a new democracy catering to all citizens.

Kariel, Henry. *Open Systems: Arenas for Public Action.* Itasca, IL: Peacock, 1969. Student protests against the Vietnam War, urban decay and violence, government scandals and a backlash against traditional reliance on established institutions inform Kariel's critique of traditional methods within the study of political science, and his argument of the need for a more egalitarian democracy.

Laclau, Ernesto. *Emancipation(s).* New York: Verso, 1996. Laclau's collection of essays focus on the postmodern political world and the various and competing interests that attempt to be heard, recognized, and rewarded in western democracies. The author argues that certain changes occurring in the twentieth century completely altered previous definitions of "emancipation."

Laclau, Ernesto and Chantal Mouffe. *Hegemony and Socialist Strategy: Towards a Radical Democratic Politics.* New York: Verso, 1985. Laclau and Mouffe provide a Gramscian analysis and critique of socialism as actually practiced during the post–World War II period.

Lukes, Steven. *Power: A Radical View.* New York: Macmillan, 1974. Lukes offers a radical assessment on political power by examining its conceptual, empirical, and moral implications.

Mamdani, Mahmood. *Citizen and Subject: Contemporary Africa and the Legacy of Late Colonialism.* Princeton, NJ: Princeton University Press, 1996. Mamdani explains the unequal distribution of power that exists in many post-colonial African countries as legacies of a system that allowed urban residents, or "citizens," more rights and privileges than those people in rural areas, the "subjects." Eventually, as colonial governments withdrew, collapsed, or were overthrown, repressed "subjects" began struggling with the "citizens" for power, beginning conflicts throughout the African continent.

Mamdani, Mahmood. *When Victims Become Killers: Colonialism, Nativism, and the Genocide in Rwanda.* Princeton, NJ: Princeton University Press, 2001. Continues Mamdani's research into the aftermath of post-colonial systems of government in Africa. The author claims that the distinction made by the formerly ruling Belgians between the Tutsi and the Hutu was a fundamental reason for the eventual genocide in Rwanda.

Marcuse, Herbert. *One-Dimensional Man: Studies in the Ideology of Advanced Industrial Society.* Boston: Beacon Press, 1964. This work was a major influence upon many of the student movements of the mid-to-late 1960s in the United States and Europe. Marcuse synthesizes the works of Marx and Freud to argue that man lives in a deficient society dominated by capitalism. He gives particular attention to the military-industrial complex in the United States, which he criticizes as the cause of a wealth of unnecessary spending and irreparable environmental damage.

McClain, Paula D. and Joseph Stewart Jr. *"Can We All Get Along?": Racial and Ethnic Minorities in American Politics.* Boulder, CO: Westview Press, 1995. Comparative survey of the political status and experience of four major groups in the U.S.: African Americans, Latinos, Asian Americans, and American Indians.

Nkrumah, Kwame. *Neo-Colonialism: the Last Stage of Imperialism.* London: Nelson, 1965. Nkrumah's political and philosophical contributions to Pan-Africanism earned him the title "Greatest African." In this essay, Nkrumah discusses the effects of imperialism on the continent and the forces that might prevent a new freedom for Africans, particularly in Ghana.

Polsby, Nelson W. *Community Power and Political Theory.* New Haven, CT: Yale University Press, 1963. Polsby studies communities in which a social and economic elite dominate each community's political institutions, contradicting the prevailing stratification theory and arguing for a new pluralism.

Pressman, J. L. and Aaron Wildavsky. *Implementation: How Great Expectations in Washington are Dashed in Oakland, or, Why it's Amazing that Federal Programs Work at All.* Berkeley, CA: University of California Press, 1973. The authors examine the difficulties inherent in implementing a political or governmental policy, even when attempted by public servants with the best of intentions.

Schlozman, Kay and J. T. Tierney. *Organized Interests and American Democracy.* New York: Harper and Row, 1986. Examines the impact of well-organized and powerful lobbying groups on the U.S. federal government.

Skocpol, Theda. *States and Social Revolutions: A Comparative Analysis of France, Russia, and China.* New York: Cambridge University Press, 1979. This comparative analysis studies three nations that underwent significant social revolution, and how each movement was fomented by factors involving state structures, international events, and class relations.

Swain, Carol M. *Black Faces, Black Interests: The Representation of African Americans in Congress.* Cambridge, MA: Harvard University Press, 1993. Challenges the notion that only African Americans can represent black interests effectively in Congress. Swain argues for black and white representatives to form coalitions to better serve their constituents.

Verba, Sidney, Kay Schlozman and Henry E. Brady. *Voice and Equality: Civic Voluntarism in American Politics.* Cambridge, MA: Harvard University Press, 2006. The authors examine the level of political participation among various strata of the American population, analyzing the impact and class and income on political involvement.

Wildavsky, Aaron. *The Politics of the Budgetary Process.* New York: Little, Brown, 1964. Classic study outlining the relationship between political dynamics and the formal U.S. federal budgetary process.

Wolfinger, Raymond and Steven J. Rosenstone. *Who Votes?* New Haven, CT: Yale University Press, 1980. Wolfinger and Rosenstone analyze U.S. Census Bureau surveys of over 90,000 Americans in 1972 and again in 1974. The authors study ever-increasing levels of voter apathy in the United States, showing that education, age, and residential mobility explain almost all of the differences among American voters' rates of turnout. Wolfinger and Rosenstone were the first to demonstrate what is now a common assumption among students of elections: higher voter turnout would not affect the results of elections.

ARTICLES

Alderich, John H. "Rational Choice and Turnout." *American Journal of Political Science* 37, no. 1 (February 1993): 246–278.

Bachrach, Peter and Morton Baratz. "Two Faces of Power." *American Political Science Review* 56, no. 4 (1962): 947–952.

Bacharach, Peter and Morton Baratz. "Decisions and Nondecisions: An Analytical Framework." *American Political Science Review* 57, no. 3 (1963): 632–642.

Denzau, Arthur T. and Michael C. Munger. "Legislators and Interest Groups: How Unorganized Interests Get Represented." *The American Political Science Review* 80, no. 1 (March 1986): 89–106.

Huber, Evelyne, Charles Ragin and John D. Stephens. "Social Democracy, Christian Democracy, Constitutional Structure, and the Welfare State." *The American Journal of Sociology* 99, no. 3 (1993): 711–749.

Huntington, Samuel P. "The Clash of Civilizations?" *Foreign Affairs* 72, no. 3 (1993): 22–49.

Lindblom, Charles E. "Still Muddling: Not Yet Through." *Public Administration Review* 39, no. 6 (November–December 1979): 517–526.

PSYCHOLOGY

Allport, Gordon. *Pattern and Growth in Personality.* New York: Holt, Rinehart and Winston, 1961. In a foundational study, Allport constructs a theory of individual personality that emphasizes sociocultural factors as determinants.

Aronson, Elliot. *The Social Animal.* San Francisco, CA: Freeman, 1972. Aronson presents a lucid introduction to the world of social psychology, maintaining that the purpose of his study is to "spell out the relevance that sociopsychological research might have for some of the problems besetting contemporary society." His study offers insight into the challenges involved in applying experimental methods to social psychological queries.

Eagly, Alice H. and Shelly Chaiken. *The Psychology of Attitudes.* Orlando, FL: Harcourt Brace Jovanovich, 1992. An important overview of attitude research from a psychological perspective. Noting the lack of relation between attitude and action, Eagly and Chaiken stress that social contexts, and the ways in which social norms and expectations complicate laboratory findings, must be considered in the research of social psychologists.

Fanon, Frantz. *The Wretched of the Earth.* 1961. Translated by Constance Farrington. New York: Grove, 1963. Fanon's now classic study of the meaning, necessity, and inevitability of violence in the process of liberation extends his exploration of the psychological impact of colonialism on the colonized and the colonist.

Flavell, John H. *The Developmental Psychology of Jean Piaget.* London: Van Nostrand, 1963. Explores Piaget's development system of analyzing intellectual growth. Flavell asserts that his purpose is to "speak clearly for Piaget to anyone who has reasons to listen to what he has to say who has some background and sophistication in psychology or related disciplines."

Gardner, Howard. *Frames of Mind: The Theory of Multiple Intelligences.* New York: Basic Books, 1983. Gardner argues that intelligence is a psychological construct, and that there are not just two basic forms of intelligence—math/music and verbal—but rather many forms, including linguistic, spatial, and bodily kinetic, which the author defines according to specific criteria.

Gilbert, Daniel T., Susan T. Fiske and Gardner Lindzey. *The Handbook of Social Psychology.* 4th edition. Boston: McGraw-Hill, 1998. Considered the standard reference work in the field of social psychology. The first edition of the Handbook, edited by Carl Murchison, was published in 1935. The Handbook explores development, socialization, intrapersonal process, self and identity, and language and social interaction, while showing the breadth and depth of social psychology as a discipline.

Gilligan, Carol. *In A Different Voice: Psychological Theory and Women's Development.* Cambridge, MA: Harvard University Press, 1982. Groundbreaking study in which Gilligan rejects the notion that women are inferior to men in the realm of moral reasoning. The author proposes that women's psychological development—especially their identity and moral development—have long been judged erroneously by standards set by and for men. Men and boys, the study argues, tend to define themselves as separate beings and solve moral problems in accordance with abstract principles, while women tend to describe themselves as living in connection with others, and to consider interpersonal relationships when resolving human problems. Gilligan argues that both separation and connection are human experiences, and that men and women tend to take different—and valid—approaches to defining and solving moral problems.

Grier, W. H. and P. M. Cobb. *Black Rage.* New York: Basic Books, 1968. Examines black life from the perspective of psychiatry. Addressing the heritage of slavery, psychiatrists Grier and Cobb analyze what they call the "inter-psychic dynamics of blacks in America that are traced to slavery."

Hersen, Michel, ed. *Comprehensive Handbook of Personality and Psychopathology.* 3 vols. Hoboken, NJ: Wiley, 2005. Describes the major theories of personality. Volumes 2 and 3 summarize the major classifications of psychological disorders in adults and children as well as the most common treatment methods.

Kahneman, Daniel and Amos Tversky, eds. *Choices, Values, and Frames.* Cambridge, UK: Cambridge University Press, 2000. This volume is comprised of academic papers from a diverse group of journals, and includes original chapters written by the editors. Together they examine new perspectives on decision and value, the fundamental categories of choice.

Lacan, Jacques. *The Four Fundamental Concepts of Psychoanalysis.* New York: Norton, 1978. Lacan's study is based on a year-long seminar he conducted with the goal of introducing "a certain coherence into the major concepts on which psychoanalysis is based."

Milgram, Stanley. *Obedience to Authority: An Experimental View.* New York: Harper and Row, 1974. Outlines the results of Milgram's controversial 1960s laboratory experiments on human conformity and aggression. Milgram postulated that the "most fundamental lesson" of his study is that "ordinary people, simply doing their jobs, and without any particular hostility on their part, can become agents in a terrible destructive process. Moreover, even when the destructive effects of their work become patently clear, and they are asked to carry out actions incompatible with fundamental standards of morality, relatively few people have the resources needed to resist authority."

Ross, Lee and Richard E. Nisbett. *The Person and the Situation: Perspectives of Social Psychology*. Philadelphia, PA: Temple University Press, 1991. Important study of situational theory in social psychology. Ross and Nisbett explore the power of situations, the subjective nature of perception and interaction, and the concept of tension systems.

Schachter, Daniel. *Searching for Memory: The Brain, the Mind, and the Past*. New York: Basic Books, 1996. The numerous neurological and cognitive factors that have been shown to affect memory are analyzed in discussions of amnesia, inaccurate recall, the forms of memory, and recovering memory of past sexual abuse.

ARTICLES

Costanzo, Philip R., John D. Coie, Judy F. Grumet, and Douglas Farnhill. "A Reexamination of the Effects of Intent and Consequence on Children's Moral Judgments." *Child Development* 44, no. 1 (Mar 1973): 154–161.

Dickens, William T. and J. R. Flynn. "Heritability Estimates Versus Large Environmental Effects: The IQ Paradox Resolved." *Psychological Review* 108, no. 2 (2001): 346–369.

Haney, C., C. Banks and P. G. Zimbardo. "Interpersonal Dynamics in a Simulated Prison." *International Journal of Criminology and Penology* 1 (1973): 69–97.

Krieger, Nancy. "Does Racism Harm Health? Did Child Abuse Exist Before 1962? On Explicit Questions, Critical Science, and Current Controversies: an Ecosocial Perspective." *American Journal of Public Health* 93 (2003): 194–199.

Sellers, Robert M. and J. A. Shelton. "The Role of Racial Identity in Perceived Discrimination." *Journal of Personality and Social Psychology* 84, no. 5 (2003): 1079–1092.

SOCIAL ISSUES AND POLICY

Clotfelter, Charles and Philip J. Cook. *Selling Hope: State Lotteries in America*. Cambridge, MA: Harvard University Press, 1989. The authors explore the business of state lottery commissions throughout the U.S., analyzing the history of the lottery, the various games and players, marketing schemes, and public policy issues over the role and involvement of state government.

Des Forges, Allison L. *Leave None to Tell the Story: Genocide in Rwanda*. New York: Human Rights Watch, 1999. Des Forges, the principal author, and her collaborators utilize government documents and other sources to detail an extensive and authoritative account of the Rwandan genocide.

Folbre, Nancy. *Who Pays for the Kids? Gender and the Structures of Constraint*. New York: Routledge, 1994. Feminist economist Folbre examines the unequal distribution of the "costs of caring" between men and women, analyzing individual choice within structures of constraint based on gender, age, sex, nation, race and class. She compares political movements, policies, and programs in the United States, Europe, and Latin America and the Caribbean.

Frank, Robert H. and Philip J. Cook. *The Winner-Take-All Society: Why the Few At the Top Get So Much More Than the Rest of Us*. New York: Penguin, 1996. Frank and Cook examine the market forces that combine to create great income disparity, with the spoils going to the ultimate "winner" in economic contests. The authors argue that this phenomenon is not confined to the fields of entertainment and professional athletics, but permeates almost every other endeavor.

Friedan, Betty. *The Feminine Mystique*. New York: Norton, 1963. Friedan's classic study helped launch the modern women's movement by debunking the myth of the post-war woman—a content homemaker who deferred her own ambitions and interests to take care of her family. Friedan was the first writer to analyze how the perpetration of this stereotype belied the complexity of most women's lives. With the publication of the book, she became one of the women's movement's most visible proponents, participating in the founding of the National Organization for Women (NOW) in 1966 and lobbying incessantly for such causes as the passage of the Equal Rights Amendment and legalization of abortion.

Galanter, Marc. *Competing Equalities: Law and the "Backward Classes" in India*. Berkeley, CA: University of California Press, 1984. Galanter critically reviews the government of India's policy of affirmative action toward scheduled castes (Dalits or "untouchables") and tribals.

Greer, Germaine. *Sex and Destiny: The Politics of Human Fertility*. New York: Harper and Row, 1984. Greer analyzes social institutions centering on human reproduction, commenting on the influence of European and American thought on fertility in the developing world. The noted and controversial feminist depicts sexual freedom as a step backward in modern society, informing the reader that the modern world is decidedly opposed to reproduction. Greer also objects to contemporary attitudes toward sex and children, asserting that children are treated as commodities.

Harrington, Michael. *The Other America: Poverty in the United States*. New York: Macmillan, 1962. Harrington's classic work has been called the seminal treatise on poverty in the United States. He argued that an underclass of poor existed in America and was neglected by the rest of society. This underclass lived in a "culture of poverty" that made it difficult for its members to escape their condition. Harrington's study drew the attention of President John F. Kennedy and led to the programs comprising the "War on Poverty."

Harvey, Philip. *Securing the Right to Employment: Social Welfare Policy and the Unemployed in the U.S.* Princeton, NJ: Princeton University Press, 1989. Harvey examines the history of federal and state welfare and other entitlement programs designed to assist the unemployed, analyzing the effectiveness and results of these policies.

Hernnstein, Richard J. and Charles Murray. *The Bell Curve: Intelligence and Class Structure in American Life*. New York: The Free Press, 1994. Hernnstein and Murray argue that genetically determined intelligence—rather than economic background, family dynamics, discrimination, and so on—dictates academic levels of achievement, employment, income, and behavior, including patterns of criminality. The authors contend that social stratification increasingly is based upon levels of intelligence, which they also argue varies systematically by race and gender, with important implications for public policy.

Irelan, Lola M., ed. *Low-Income Life Styles.*Washington, DC: U.S. Department of Health, Education and Welfare, 1968. *Low-Income Life Styles* is a U.S. government document that epitomizes the influence and impact of Oscar Lewis's construction of the idea of the "culture of poverty" on social policy.

Jacoby, Russell and Naomi Glauberman, eds. *The Bell Curve Debate: History, Documents, Opinions.*New York: Times Books, 1995. The editors present an anthology of book reviews, essays, and other writings penned in reaction to the various controversies about race and intelligence raised by the publication of *The Bell Curve.*

Massey, Douglas S. and Nancy A. Denton. *American Apartheid: Segregation and the Making of the Underclass.* Cambridge, MA: Harvard University Press, 1993. The authors explore the persistence, causes, and consequences of residential segregation in American cities.

Nesiah, Devanasan. *Discrimination with Reason? The Policy of Reservations in the United States, India, and Malaysia.* Oxford, UK: Oxford University Press 1997. Nesiah provides a comparative analysis of government-mandated reservations (or affirmative action) policies on behalf of historically excluded groups in three nations.

Rainwater, Lee and W. L. Yancey, eds. *The Moynihan Report and the Politics of Controversy.* Cambridge, MA: MIT Press, 1967. Rainwater and Yancey's book includes the full text of Daniel Moynihan's controversial internal memorandum at the Department of Health, Education and Welfare, "The Negro Family: The Case for National Action," and documents representing the reaction to it.

Ryan, William. *Blaming the Victim.*New York: Pantheon, 1971. Ryan confronts and challenges conventional thinking about the root causes of poverty, particularly the "culture of poverty" hypothesis. Instead of viewing the poor as agents of their own social dysfunctionality, Ryan argues that their condition is due to structural factors that entrap them.

Schor, Juliet B. *The Overspent American: Upscaling, Downshifting and the New Consumer.* New York: Basic Books, 1998. Schor examines the spending patterns and motivations of American consumers, analyzing the influence of media and marketing on the modern American lifestyle. She also offers comparative profiles of individuals who purposely live as minimalists and reject popular culture.

Skocpol, Theda. *Protecting Soldiers and Mothers: The Political Origins of Social Policy in the United States.* Cambridge, MA: Belknap Press, 1992. A detailed case study in social policy and history that analyzes the period between the 1880s to the 1920s in the United States. Skocpol examines the interrelation between government, interest groups, culture, and unions in formulating public policy. She also addresses the key influence of women in the advocacy of welfare programs and other social policies.

Skrentny, John David. *The Ironies of Affirmative Action: Politics, Culture, and Justice in America.* Chicago: University of Chicago Press, 1996. Important study of the development and evolution of affirmative action policies in the United States.

Stacey, Judith. *Brave New Families: Stories of Domestic Upheaval in Late Twentieth-Century America.* New York: Basic Books, 1990. Stacey studies the lives of two family networks in California's Silicon Valley to highlight the evolution of the modern nuclear family.

Struyk, Michael and Raymond J. Fix, eds. *Clear and Convincing Evidence: Measurement of Discrimination in America.*Washington DC: The Urban Institute Press, 1992. Contributors analyze the results of auditing (two individuals matched on all relevant characteristics except the one being tested) to measure discrimination in America.

Wilson, William Julius. *The Truly Disadvantaged: The Inner City, the Underclass and Public Policy.* Chicago: University of Chicago Press, 1987. Wilson's defining work argues that the rise of urban poverty in the latter half of the twentieth century can be traced to major shifts in the American economy during that same period.

ARTICLES

Borjas, George J. "The Economics of Immigration." *Journal of Economic Literature* 32, no. 4 (1994): 1667–1717.

Cook, Philip J. and J. H. Laub. "The Unprecedented Epidemic in Youth Violence." *Crime and Justice* 24 (1998): 27–64.

McLanahan, Sara and Karen Booth. "Mothers-Only Families: Problems, Prospects, and Politics." *Journal of Marriage and the Family* 51, no. 3 (1989): 557–580.

SOCIOLOGY

Bonilla-Silva, Eduardo. *Racism Without Racists: Color-Blind Racism and the Persistence of Racial Inequality in the United States.* Lanham, MD: Rowman and Littlefield, 2003. Short answer surveys and polling data indicate dramatic improvements in racial attitudes in the United States over the past half-century. Bonilla-Silva argues that such findings are plagued by "social desirability" effects and self-censorship on the part of respondents. Instead he undertakes a set of in-depth, open-ended interviews with college students at a major midwestern university conducted by same-race interviewers. He uncovers a set of beliefs that he refers to as "color-blind racism." Bonilla-Silva argues that, while explicit racism is taboo, it has been replaced by a perspective in which whites claim that their racial position places them at a social disadvantage.

Braverman, Harry. *Labor and Monopoly Capital: The Degradation of Work in the Twentieth Century.* New York: Monthly Review Press, 1975. Braverman applies Marxist theory to argue that technology upgrades in industry are used by owners of capital to reduce the number of employees needed and to reduce the skill level (and value) of remaining employees.

Burawoy, Michael. *Manufacturing Consent: Changes in the Labor Process Under Monopoly Capitalism.* Chicago: University of Chicago Press, 1979. Burawoy's sociological study of industry seeks to determine why workers routinely submit to their own exploitation. The author's research included ten months of labor as a machine operator in a Chicago factory. Burawoy compares his findings with those of Donald Roy, who studied the same factory 30 years earlier.

Burawoy, Michael *The Politics of Production: Factory Regimes Under Capitalism and Socialism.* New York: Verso, 1985. Burawoy provides the major comparative sociological study of the conduct of factory production in capitalistic and socialistic societies.

Coleman, James S. *Foundations of Social Theory*. Cambridge, MA: Harvard University Press, 1990. Considered a landmark in sociological theory, Coleman's study provides a framework relating the behavior of individuals to organizational behavior and to society as a whole.

Collins, Patricia Hill. *Black Feminist Thought: Knowledge, Consciousness and the Politics of Empowerment*. Boston: Unwin Hyman, 1990. Revised. New York: Routledge, 2000. Collins provides a history and outline of contemporary black feminist thought through the use of source material that includes music, literature, oral history, and academic research. Her work is built upon three main tenets: that oppressions are interconnected; that the need for self-definition has required women of color to create alternative worldviews; and that externalities such as standards of beauty and success have been racialized in favor of white women. She then examines how race intersects with gender to create narrowly defined roles for African American women.

Gans, Herbert J. *The Urban Villagers: Group and Class in the Life of Italian-Americans*. New York: Free Press of Glencoe, 1963. This is the classic sociological study of Italian Americans living in Boston's working-class West End in the late 1950s and early 1960s.

Gouldner, Alvin Ward. *The Future of Intellectuals and the Rise of the New Class*. New York: Seabury Press, 1979. Drawing on Marxist theory, Gouldner contends that the "New Class," the intellectuals and the intelligentsia, have risen to power by asserting cultural authority.

Hall, Stuart and Paul du Gay, eds. *Questions of Cultural Identity*. London: Sage, 1996. A collection of essays from various contributors on the implications of the decline in traditional patterns of social and cultural identity.

Hall, Stuart and Tony Jefferson, eds. *Resistance Through Rituals: Youth Subcultures in Post-War Britain*. London: Hutchinson, 1976. The authors advance an important sociological analysis of post-war youth subculture in urban Britain.

Harvey, David. *The Limits to Capital*. Chicago: University of Chicago Press, 1982. Harvey provides a highly regarded analysis and extension of Marx's critique of political economy in light of developments in the twentieth century.

Lieberson, Stanley. *A Piece of the Pie: Blacks and White Immigrants Since 1880*. Berkeley, CA: University of California Press, 1980. Lieberson is concerned with the origins of group-based inequality in America, which he dates back to the arrival of "new" European immigrants in the late nineteenth and early twentieth centuries. Both the European immigrants and American-born blacks were competing for "a piece of the pie," including housing and work, as they moved from rural to urban environments. Studying a number of explanations for the European immigrants' greater economic success since the Hayes-Tilden Compromise of 1876, he dismisses cultural explanations and discusses residential segregation, labor market discrimination, and the timing of migration to urban areas as critical factors.

Oliver, Melvin L. and Thomas M. Shapiro. *Black Wealth/White Wealth: A New Perspective on Racial Inequality*. New York: Routledge, 1995. An instant classic, Oliver and Shapiro's study of race, wealth, and inequality provides the empirical case that shows that wealth disparity—rather than income disparity—is central to understanding racial inequality in the United States.

Silberman, Charles. *A Certain People: American Jews and Their Lives Today*. New York: Summit, 1985. Silberman combines exhaustive research with personal interviews to study lifestyle patterns among Jewish Americans.

Steinberg, Stephen. *The Ethnic Myth: Race, Ethnicity and Class in America*. New York: Atheneum, 1981. Steinberg rejects the view that culture and ethnicity are the primary determinants of economic success for minority groups in America, contending that locality, class conflict, and other socioeconomic factors are of much greater consequence.

Telles, Edward E. *Race in Another America: The Significance of Skin Color in Brazil*. Princeton, NJ: Princeton University Press, 2004. Telles presents a detailed sociological study and statistical analysis of race and color in Brazil, tracing the dimensions and mechanisms of discrimination while proposing a host of policy initiatives.

Walker, Pat, ed. *Between Labor and Capital*. Boston: South End Press, 1979. This anthology of essays centers on the theory of the emergence and potential rise to dominance of a third class in advanced capitalist society, the professional-managerial class.

Williams, Raymond. *Culture and Society, 1780–1950*. New York: Columbia University Press, 1958. Williams outlines the historical tension between definitions of culture as art and "culture as a whole way of life" and argues for the latter.

ARTICLES

Bonacich, Edna. "A Theory of Ethnic Antagonism: The Split Labor Market." *American Sociological Review* 37, no. 5 (1972): 547–559.

Bonacich, Edna. "A Theory of Middleman Minorities." *American Sociological Review* 38, no. 5 (1973): 583–594.

Burawoy, Michael. "The Extended Case Method." *Sociological Theory* 16, no. 1 (1998): 4–33.

Coleman, James S. "Social Capital in the Creation of Human Capital." *American Journal of Sociology* 94 (1988): S95–S120.

Feagin, Joe. "The Continuing Significance of Race: Antiblack Discrimination in Public Places." *American Sociological Review* 56, no. 1 (1991): 101–116.

Granovetter, Mark. "Economic Action and Social Structure: The Problem of Embeddedness." *American Journal of Sociology* 91, no. 3 (1985): 481–510.

Inglehart, Ronald and Wayne E. Baker. "Modernization, Cultural Change, and the Persistence of Traditional Values." *American Sociological Review* 65, no. 1 (2000): 19–51.

Stacey, Judith. "Can There Be a Feminist Ethnography?" *Women's Studies International Forum* 11, no. 1 (1988): 21–27.

Zuckerman, Harriet. "The Sociology of Science." *Handbook of Sociology*. Thousand Oaks, CA: Sage Publications, 1988.

Index

Page numbers are referenced according to volume number followed by a colon and the page number(s) on which that subject appears in the volume. Boldface page numbers refer to the main entry on the subject. Italic page numbers refer to illustrations and figures. Page numbers followed by the letter t indicate a table on that page.

A

AA (Alcoholics Anonymous), 1:22

AAA (Agricultural Adjustment Act; U.S. 1933), 5:494, 6:667

AAA (American Anthropological Association), 1:**92–93**

AAAP (American Association for Applied Psychology), 1:102

AAI (Adult Attachment Interview), 1:196

Aaron, Cooper v. (1958), 2:316

ABB (African Blood Brotherhood), 1:316, 328

Abbas, Mahmoud, 6:104, 106

Abbasid caliphate, 1:160

Abbott, Andrew, 8:6

Abbott, Robert S., 1:501

Abductions, alien, 8:507–508

Abdullah I, King of Jordan, 3:530–531

Abdurahman, Abdullah, 2:15

Abington School District v. Schempp, 9:33

Abkhazians, 5:418

Abolition of slavery

described, 7:544–545

Douglass, Frederick, 2:438–440

Haiti, 3:406, 407–408

as liberation, 4:429

Lincoln, Abraham, 4:451

Sharp, Granville, 7:494

slave trade, 7:539

Truth, Sojourner, 8:462

vindication, 8:618

Aboriginal rights. *See* Indigenous rights

Aborigines. *See* Natives

Abortion, 1:**1–3**

birth control, 1:302, 303

Catholic Church, 1:1–2, 8:594

conservatism, 2:86

contraception, 2:114

death and dying, 2:247, 248

eugenics, 3:21–22

family planning, 3:88, 89

out-of-wedlock births, 1:308

reproduction, 7:178

reproductive politics, 7:180, 181, 182

Roe v. Wade, 7:270–272

surplus population, 8:238–239

Abortion rights, 1:**3–4**

biological determinism, 2:326

left wing, 4:403

reproductive rights, 7:182, 183

Roe v. Wade, 7:270–272

Abrahamic religion. *See* Monotheism

Abramoff, Jack, 2:180

Abramovich, Roman, 1:572

Abramson, Lyn, 4:388

Absentee landlords, 4:**347–348**

Absentee ownership, 8:596

Absentee Ownership (Veblen), 8:596

Absolute and comparative advantage, 1:**5–6**

Absolute and competitive advantage, 1:5*t*, 3:448–449

Absolute income hypothesis, 1:**6–7**, *7*

consumption function, 2:109

life-cycle hypothesis, 4:442

relative income hypothesis, 7:153, 154

Absolute monarchy. *See* Monarchism; Monarchy

Absolute surplus value, 7:155

Abstinence, reproductive politics, 7:180, 181

Abstract labor, 9:122

Absurdism, 8:338

Abuse, corporal punishment as, 2:134–136

Abuse, drugs of. *See* Drugs of abuse

Abuse of dominance, 1:143

Abyssinia, 9:148

Academic achievement. *See* Educational achievement

Academic freedom, 1:105–106, 8:532

Academic journals. *See* Professional journals

Acceptance and rejection, 7:**149–150**

peer cliques, 6:197–198

peer effects, 6:198–200

Acceptance and rejection, *continued*
  peer influence, 6:202
Access consciousness. *See*
  Consciousness
Accidents
  law and economics, 4:367–368
  normal accident theory, 1:9
  preindustrial workplace, 1:8
  vehicle, 9:4
  vulnerability, 8:657
Accidents, industrial, 1:**8–9**, 9*t*
Accommodation, child development,
  1:506
Accommodationism, 1:535
Accountability, 1:**9–12**
  Central Intelligence Agency, U.S,
    1:484
  civil-military relation, 1:547
  community power studies, 2:44
  cooperatives, 2:125
  ethics, 2:632
  institutional investors, 4:136
  international nongovernmental
    organizations, 4:98–99
  monetary policy, 6:295
  parliaments and parliamentary
    systems, 6:146
  recall, 7:102–103
  referendum, 7:121
  transparency, 8:434–435
  volunteer programs, 8:639–640
Accounting, growth. *See* Growth
  accounting
Accounting costs vs. opportunity
  costs, 6:47
Acculturation, 2:169, 170, 3:466, 467
Accumulation, primitive. *See* Primitive
  accumulation
Accumulation of capital, 1:**12–14**
  bourgeoisie, 1:360–361
  capitalist mode of production,
    1:446
  class conflict, 1:569
  classical economics, 2:504
  described, 1:431
  development economics, 2:344
  golden rule of, 3:346
  low and high culture, 2:205
  Lucas, Robert E., Jr., 4:510
  Luxemburg, Rosa, 4:522
  managerial capitalism, 1:442
  primitive accumulation,
    6:463–464
  Robinson, Joan, 7:267
  surplus labor, 4:308, 309, 310

The Accumulation of Capital
  (Luxemburg), 1:12–13, 446, 4:522,
  6:464
The Accumulation of Capital
  (Robinson), 1:13
Accumulation on a World Scale (Amin),
  1:110
Achenbach, Thomas, 1:504
Achenbach System of Empirically
  Based Assessment (ASEBA),
  1:504–505
Acheson, Dean, 1:550
Achievement, 1:**14–15**
  overachievers, 6:87–88
  social status, 7:622
  upward mobility, 8:533, 535
  See also Educational achievement
Achievement gap, racial, 1:**15–17**,
  7:17
  Clark, Kenneth B., 1:561
  educational, 6:33–34, 48
  IQ controversy, 4:140–141
  Jencks, Christopher, 4:184
  oppositional culture, 6:48
  qualifications, 6:649–650
  race and education, 7:17
  schooling oppositionality, 6:50
  standardized tests, 8:96–98
  Steele, Claude M., 8:130–131
  stereotype threat, 8:135–136
  teacher expectations, 8:290–291
  tracking in schools, 8:409–410
  unequal education, 2:537–539,
    540–545
Achievement tests, underachievers,
  8:484
ACLU (American Civil Liberties
  Union), 1:547
ACOTA (African Contingency
  Operation Training and Assistance),
  1:38
Acquaintance rape. *See* Rape
Acquired immunodeficiency syndrome
  (AIDS). *See* AIDS (Acquired
  immunodeficiency syndrome)
Acquisitions. *See* Corporate strategies
The Acquisitive Society (Tawney),
  8:272
ACRI (African Crisis Response
  Initiative), 1:**37–38**
ACT (Associated Community Teams),
  9:25
Act of the Suppression of Trade in and
  Circulation of Obscene Literature
  and Articles of Immoral Use (U.S.
  1873), 7:180

Act of the Suppression of Trade in and
  Circulation of Obscene Literature
  and Articles of Immoral Use (U.S.
  1973), 3:89
Act to Prohibit the Coming of
  Chinese Persons in the United
  States (U.S. 1892). *See* Geary Act
  (U.S. 1892)
Act utilitarianism, 8:553
Acting white, 1:**17–18**, 6:165–166,
  7:434–435
Action, affirmative. *See* Affirmative
  action
Action, collective. *See* Collective action
Action, covert. *See* Covert action
Action, preventive. *See* Preventive
  action
Action, social. *See* Behavior
Action-awareness merging, 3:157
Active learning, 8:294–295
Activism, 1:**18**
  American Indian Movement,
    1:98–99
  black nationalism, 1:315–318
  black politics, 6:324–325, 326
  Black Power, 1:320–322
  blackness, 1:328–329
  Bonacich, Edna, 1:352–353
  Brown v. Board of Education
    (1954), 1:374–375
  Buddhism, 1:385
  buraku, 1:389
  caste, 1:463
  Castro, Fidel, 1:464
  Chávez, César, 1:493–494
  Chomsky, Noam, 1:529
  civil rights movement, U.S.,
    1:551–552
  Coloreds (South Africa), 2:15
  Congress of Racial Equality, 2:75
  constitutional courts, 2:93
  cooperatives, 2:125
  dalits, 2:221
  Davis, Angela, 2:242–243
  death and dying, 2:248
  disability, 2:377, 378
  dissidents, 2:411–412
  Du Bois, W. E. B., 2:459–460
  gay, lesbian, transgender, and
    bisexual politics, 6:329–332
  internal colony, 2:14
  Love Canal, 4:504–505
  Lynd, Staughton, 4:528–529
  Mankiller, Wilma, 4:586
  Mexican Americans, 5:124
  militarism, 5:165

mobilization, 5:213–214
pacifism, 6:101–102
peace movements, 6:182–185
Pettigrew, Thomas F., 6:234–235
political participation, 6:154
social, 7:603–607, 9:56
sociology, 7:664
Spock, Benjamin, 8:61–62
Weber, Max, 9:57
Woodstock, 9:121
See also Protest
Activism, judicial, 1:**18–19**,
    4:223–225, 226–228
Actometers, 3:537–538
Actor-observer effect, 1:206
Actuarial tables, 3:366
Ad Hoc International Criminal
    Tribunals, 9:22
Ad hoc specification, 8:599
Ad valorem tariffs. *See* Tariffs
ADA (Americans for Democratic
    Action), 7:277
Adam Smith and Laissez-Faire (Viner),
    4:335
Adams, Abigail, 8:215
Adams, Creighton, 8:614
Adams, J. Stacy, 3:179
Adams, James Truslow, 1:96
Adams, John
    checks and balances, 1:495
    conservatism, 2:84
    Declaration of Independence,
        U.S., 2:254
    Democratic Party (U.S.), 2:286
    federalism, 3:114
    Hamilton, Alexander, 3:414
    Jefferson, Thomas, 4:182
    judicial review, 4:223
    Washington, George, 9:36, 38
Adamson Act (U.S. 1916), 9:102
Adaptation
    child development, 1:506
    Darwin, Charles, 2:228–229
    developmental regulations, 1:24
    emotion regulation, 2:573
    environmental determinism, 2:327
    evolutionary psychology, 3:33–34
    genetic determinism, 2:329, 330
    medical anthropology, 1:131
    murder, 5:339–340
    organizational, 6:71
    personality, 6:218–219
    social equilibrium, 3:232
    social intelligence, 4:75

Adaptation in Cultural Anthropology
    (Alland), 1:131
The Adapted Mind (Cosmides and
    Tooby), 5:440
Adaptive expectations, 1:**19–20**
    cobweb cycles, 1:591–592
    Lagrange multipliers, 4:334
    Lucas, Robert E., Jr., 4:510
    static expectations, 3:53
ADB (Asian Development Bank),
    9:40–42
Addams, Jane, 7:661, 8:542
Addiction, 1:**20–22**
    alcohol, 1:21, 71–72
    Becker, Gary S., 1:270
    classical conditioning, 1:574
    diathesis-stress model, 2:358
    dopamine, 2:437
    drug tolerance, 8:385
    drugs of abuse, 2:452
    nature *vs.* nurture, 5:446
    rational, 6:56
    Schachter, Stanley, 7:342
    self-constrained behavior, 1:273,
        274
    smoking, 7:559
Adema, Willem, 9:70
Adenauer, Konrad, 2:84
ADHD (Attention-
    deficit/hyperactivity disorder),
    1:**197–200**, 7:391
Adi Granth, 9:155
Adjustment, structural. *See* Structural
    adjustment
Adjustment speed. *See* Flexibility
Adkins, Lisa, 9:122
ADL (Anti-Defamation League),
    3:431
Adler, Alfred
    Freud, Sigmund, 3:215
    inferiority complex, 4:18–19
    lifestyles, 4:445
    Napoleon complex, 5:366
Administration, public, 6:**603**
    metropolitan regions, 7:132–133
    regions concept, 7:130
    technotopia, 8:312–313
Administrative law, 1:**22–23**
Adolescent Development (Bandura),
    1:248
Adolescent Health Longitudinal
    Survey. *See* National Longitudinal
    Study of Adolescent Health
Adolescent psychology, 1:**24–27**
    body image, 1:346

child development, 1:505–508
developmental psychology, 2:349
Erikson, Erik, 2:625
hope, 3:502
identity, 3:552, 553–554, 555
loneliness, 4:486
maturation, 5:36
peers, 6:198–200, 201–202
psychological depression, 2:307,
    308
Rosenberg's Self-Esteem Scale
    (RSES), 7:288
self-constrained behavior,
    1:273–274
social cognitive map, 7:575–576
suicide, 8:222
teacher-child relationships,
    8:291–292
youth culture, 9:167–168
Adolescents
    acting white, 1:17–18
    depression, 8:656–657
    gambling, 3:249
    National Longitudinal Study of
        Adolescent Health, 5:405–407
    National Longitudinal Survey of
        Youth, 5:407–408
    obesity, 9:58
    smoking, 5:391
    video games, 8:611–612
    See also Children; Youth culture
Adoption
    childlessness, 1:510
    children, defined, 1:511
    heredity, 3:461
    nature *vs.* nurture, 5:446
    same-sex marriage, 4:620–621
Adoption of technology. *See*
Technology, adoption of
Adorno, Theodor W.
    alienation, 1:75
    authoritarian personality,
        6:220–221
    authority, 1:214
    critical theory, 2:176, 177
    culture, 2:203
    Davis, Angela, 2:242
    Enlightenment, 2:597
    Habermas, Jürgen, 3:401
    Holocaust, 3:496, 497
    narratives, 5:371
    social theory, 7:628
    Veblen, Thorstein, 8:597
    See also Frankfurt School

ADR (American Depositary Receipts), 2:624

Adrain, Robert, 4:392

Adult Attachment Interview (AAI), 1:196

Advanced Micro Devices, 5:139

Advanced Pricing Agreement (APA), 8:428

Advanced Research Projects Agency, U.S. (ARPA), 4:104

Advantage, absolute and comparative, 1:5–6, 5*t*, 3:199–200, 448–449

The Adventures of Obadiah Oldbuck (Töppfer), 2:23

Adverse selection, 1:27–28, 4:51, 9:103

Adversus omnes haereses (Irenaeus), 6:78

Advertising, 1:28–29
    campaigning, 1:423–424
    classical conditioning, 1:574
    coffee industry, 1:595–596
    color preference, 6:433
    consumer protection, 2:103
    consumption, 2:107–108
    corporations, 2:140
    hidden persuaders, 3:472–473
    lexicographic preferences, 4:422
    lifestyles, 4:445
    message-based persuasion, 6:229
    persuasion, 6:227, 228
    social values, 8:582
    subliminal suggestion, 8:201–202
    television, 8:320
    want creation, 9:14
    See also Marketing

Advertising, the Uneasy Persuasion (Schudson), 1:28–29

Advocacy, public interest. *See* Public interest advocacy

Aesthetic Theory (Adorno), 2:177, 3:189

Aesthetics, 1:29–30
    critical theory, 2:177
    literature, 4:463
    Lukacs, Georg, 4:515

AFDC (Aid to Families with Dependent Children), 4:118, 9:26

Affect and emotion, 2:571–572

Affection, 5:455

Affectual action, 9:56

Affinal family, 3:86, 87

Affirmative action, 1:30–32
    African Americans, 1:31, 35
    black capitalism, 1:439–442

black immigrants, 3:566–567
California Civil Rights Initiative, 1:416
caste, 1:458
creamy layer, 2:161
crowding hypothesis, 2:182
dalits, 2:221, 222
diversity, 2:420
Dred Scott v. Sanford, 2:446
equal opportunity, 2:612–613
Great Society, 3:373, 374
Jencks, Christopher, 4:184
Moynihan, Daniel Patrick, 5:304
passing, 6:166
quotas, 6:668–671
race-blind policies, 7:35–36
race-conscious policies, 7:37
social policy interventions, 4:118–119
Supreme Court decisions, 3:373, 392–393
urban poverty, 6:411
Weaver, Robert C., 9:53
women's liberation, 9:114

Affirmative Discrimination (Glazer), 3:327

Affluence. *See* Wealth

The Affluent Society (Galbraith), 2:106, 3:246, 473, 9:25

Afforestation, 2:262

Afghan-Soviet War (1980s), 7:606–607

Afghanistan
    Al Jazeera, 1:69–70
    bin Laden, Osama, 1:298, 299
    Bush, George W., 1:399
    Central Intelligence Agency, U.S, 1:483
    counterterrorism, 2:155
    deviance, 2:353
    femininity, 3:118
    invasion of, 1:451
    mercenaries, 9:51
    national defense, 2:261
    NATO, 5:546
    Taliban, 8:262–263
    USSR invasion, 8:512
    vindication movements, 8:619

AFL (American Federation of Labor), 4:302, 8:515

AFL-CIO, 4:302, 8:515–516

Aflaq, Michel, 3:532, 8:521

Africa
    AIDS/HIV, 1:65–66
    anthropology, 3:29

banana industry, 1:246
black nationalism, 1:316, 317, 318
Black Power, 1:321
Boer War, 1:348–350
brain drain, 1:367
census, 1:477
civil-military relation, 1:547
civil wars, 1:554
clash of civilizations, 1:559
clientelism, 1:579
coffee industry, 1:594, 595
Columbus, Christopher, 2:20, 22
communism, 2:36
cotton industry, 2:151, 152, 153–154
coups d'etat, 2:156
decolonization, 2:255–256, 257
demographic transition, 2:292
dependency theory, 2:299, 300
developing countries, 2:335–337
development and ethnic diversity, 2:343
development economics, 2:344
diamond industry, 2:356–357
Diop, Cheikh Anta, 2:368–370
dowry and bride price, 2:440–441
drought, 2:448
East Africa, 1:139
famine, 3:165
fatherhood, 3:106–107
global warming effects, 3:330
import substitution, 3:593
indirect rule, 3:617–618
international relations, 3:166
Kaunda, Kenneth, 4:250–251
Kenyatta, Jomo, 4:255–256
land fertility, 3:131
land reform, 4:343, 344
left wing, 4:404
neocolonialism, 5:466–468
North
    AIDS/HIV, 1:65
    anticolonial movements, 1:139
    Islamic fundamentalism, 3:237–238
    population aging, 3:306
    veils, 8:602–604
Pan-African Congresses, 6:112–115
peacekeeping and conflict management, 1:37–38
population aging, 3:306
poverty, 6:405–406

refugees, 7:126

regions, 7:132

reincarnation, 7:145, 146

reproductive politics, 7:182

Rhodes, Cecil, 7:239–240

Rodney, Walter, 7:269–270

rotating savings and credit associations, 7:286

rural development, 2:342

slave-gun cycle, 7:540–542

slave mode of production, 7:532

slave trade, 7:537–539

socialism, 7:638–641

sub-Saharan

 AIDS/HIV, 1:65, 66

 anticolonial movements, 1:140

 Green Revolution, 3:378

 population aging, 3:306

surplus labor, 4:309

telecommunications industry, 8:316

toxic waste, 8:408

tribes, 8:450

underdevelopment, 8:490–491

Verdoorn's law, 8:608

virgins, 8:629

water resources, 9:40

women's work, 9:124, 125

zombies, 9:180, 181

See also African sociology; Pan-Africanism; South Africa; West Africa

Africa, scramble for. *See* Imperialism

Africalogy, 1:47

African American studies, 1:**32–34**

Drake, St. Clair, 2:442–443

Du Bois, W. E. B., 2:457–460

Hurston, Zora Neale, 3:526, 527

African Americans, 1:**34–37**

acting white, 1:17–18

addiction, 1:21

affirmative action, 1:31, 35

African burial grounds, 1:393–394

archaeology of slave lives, 7:529–531

assimilation, 1:190–191

benign neglect, 1:283–284

bigotry, 1:295–296

Birth of a Nation (film), 1:304–306

black capitalism, 1:439–442

black conservatism, 1:310–311

black liberalism, 1:312

black middle class, 1:313–314

black nationalism, 1:315–318

Black Panthers, 1:318–320

Black Power, 1:320–322

black towns, 1:325–326

blackface, 1:326–327

blackness, 1:328–330

blues, 1:342–343

Boas, Franz, 1:345

body image, 1:346

Bracero Program, 1:365

Brimmer, Andrew, 1:371–372

Brown v. Board of Education (1954), 1:373

burden of acting white, 6:49–50

California Civil Rights Initiative, 1:416

caste, 1:460

child development, 1:507

Chisholm, Shirley, 1:522

cities, 1:541

citizenship, 1:543

civil rights movement, U.S., 1:551–552

Clark, Kenneth B., 1:560

cohabitation, 2:1

colonialism, 2:12

colorism, 2:17–18

comic books, 2:24

Congress of Racial Equality, 2:75

cooperatives, 2:125–126

corporal punishment, 2:135

correspondence tests, 2:141–143

crime and criminology, 2:173

critical race theory, 2:174–176

crowding hypothesis, 2:181, 182

culture of poverty, 2:206

Davis, Angela, 2:242–243

Defender, 1:501

Democratic Party (U.S.), 5:497

desegregation, 2:313–315

deviance, 2:354

diaspora, 2:356–357

digital divide, 2:366

Diop, Cheikh Anta, 2:369, 370

discrimination, 2:388–391, 393–396

disease, 2:408

divorce and separation, 2:427

drugs of abuse, 2:455–456

economics, 7:6

economists, 5:387–390

education, 7:16–18, 69–75, 351, 354–355

education achievement, 6:33–34, 48

employment discrimination, 3:327

ethnic enterprises, 3:4–5

families, 3:191–192

female-headed families, 3:116–117

gentility, 3:300–301

ghettos, 3:312–313

gifted and talented, 3:*316,* 316–317, 316*t*

hard-core unemployed, 3:422–423

Head Start, 3:437

Herskovits, Melville J., 3:466–467

hip hop, 3:480–481

hypertension, 3:538–540

identity politics, 6:335

immigration, 3:564–567

imprisonment, 3:596–597

inner-city, 1:36

integration, 4:56–61

internal colony, 2:13–15

interracial marriage, 4:616–619

interracial sex, 7:468–470

intersectionality, 4:114–115

jazz, 4:176–178

Jim Crow, 4:198–201

John Henryism, 4:207–208, 6:87–88

Kerner Commission Report, 4:257, 258

liberation, 4:430, 435, 436

low and high culture, 2:205

lynchings, 4:526–527, 9:76–77

metropolitan regions, 7:135

middle class, 1:35, 36

military, 5:169

Mill, John Stuart, 5:178

minorities, 5:191, 192

minstrelsy, 5:195

model minority, 5:221–222

Moynihan, Daniel Patrick, 5:304–305

Moynihan Report, 5:305–306

Multidimensional Inventory of Black Identity, 5:318–319

Muslims, 5:348

Myrdal, Gunnar, 1:93–96

National Survey of Black Americans, 5:415–416

naturalization, 5:444

New Deal, 5:496–497

obesity, 9:58

occupational status, 6:27

Olympic Games, 6:40

oppositional culture, 6:48

out-of-wedlock births, 1:307, 308

parent-child relationships, 6:133

African Americans, *continued*
  passing, 6:165–166
  phenotype, 6:245
  politics, 2:430, 6:323–326,
    7:18–21
  poll tax, 6:352
  prisons, 6:476
  psychology, 7:21–23
  qualifications, 6:649–650
  quotas, 6:671
  race, 7:6
  race-blind policies, 7:35–36
  race-conscious policies, 7:36–38
  racism, 4:7, 7:41–42, 44–46
  rape, 7:65
  Reconstruction Era, U.S., 7:112,
    113–115
  reparations, 7:166–168
  Republican Party (U.S.), 7:186,
    187
  resegregation of schools,
    7:201–202
  residential segregation, 7:384
  restitution principle, 7:213–215
  returns to education, 7:66
  Robeson, Paul, 7:265–266
  rock 'n' roll, 7:268–269
  role models, 7:273–274
  Roosevelt, Franklin D., 7:283
  Sambo, 7:312–314
  school desegregation, 2:316–318
  school segregation, 7:386–388
  segregation, 7:381–382
  self-fulfilling prophecies,
    7:414–415
  self-hatred, 7:416
  separate-but-equal, 7:445–447
  slavery hypertension hypothesis,
    7:546–547
  smoking, 7:560
  social demography, 2:296
  social welfare system, 7:633
  socioeconomic status, 3:566*t*
  sociologists, 1:323–325
  Southern politics, 6:339–349
  stereotype threat, 8:135–136
  street culture, 8:172–173
  Tally's Corner, 8:263–264
  terminology, 5:459
  Tuskegee syphilis study,
    8:472–473
  Uncle Tom, 8:482–483
  underclass, 8:486–487
  unequal education, 2:537–539
  upward mobility, 8:534

  urban poverty, 6:410–411
  urban renewal, 8:536–537
  urban riots, 8:538–539
  urban studies, 8:542–543
  veils, 8:602
  Vesey, Denmark, 8:608–610
  vindication movements,
    8:618–619
  voting patterns, 8:649–650
  voting rights, 8:651–654
  wage discrimination, 2:400–401,
    405–406
  Weaver, Robert C., 9:53–54
  weight, 9:59
  white primary, 9:83–85
  whitening, 9:89–91
  women's work, 9:125
  See also Black Marxism; Harlem
    Renaissance; Slavery
African Blood Brotherhood (ABB),
  1:316, 328
African burial grounds, 1:**393–394**
African Commission on Human and
  Peoples' Rights, 6:63
African Commune of Bad Relevant
  Artists, 1:309
African Contingency Operation
  Training and Assistance (ACOTA),
  1:38
African Crisis Response Initiative
  (ACRI), 1:**37–38**
African diaspora, 1:**38–41**, 2:356–357
  African burial grounds, 1:393–394
  archaeology of slave lives,
    7:530–531
  black immigrants, 3:565–566
  black Marxism, 4:642
  black nationalism, 1:317
  blackness, 1:328, 330
  dance, 2:223
  Diop, Cheikh Anta, 2:369
  Drake, St. Clair, 2:442
  Du Bois, W. E. B., 2:460
  Herskovits, Melville J., 3:466–467
  Hurston, Zora Neale, 3:527, 528
  Inikori, Joseph, 4:37–38
  Pan-African Congresses,
    6:112–115
  Rastafari, 7:66–68
  See also Pan-Africanism
African National Congress (ANC),
  1:**41–43**, 140, 148, 314
  Kaunda, Kenneth, 4:250, 251
  liberation movements, 4:431–432
  Mandela, Nelson, 4:580–581

  Mandela, Winnie, 4:581–582
African nationalism. *See* Pan-
  Africanism
African Party for the Independence of
  Guinea and the Cape Verde Island.
  See Partido Africano da
  Independéncia de Guinea e Cabo
  Verde (PAIGC)
African Political Organization (APO),
  2:15
African socialism, 2:11, 4:250,
  7:**638–642**
African sociology, 7:**664–666**
  black immigrants, 3:565–566
  blackness, 1:328
  census, 1:477
  Creole, 2:167, 168, 169
  diaspora, 2:356–357
  digital divide, 2:367
  Turner, Victor, 8:468–471
African studies, 1:**43–45**
  Afrocentrism, 1:32, 46–48
  Diop, Cheikh Anta, 2:368–370
  Herskovits, Melville J., 3:466–467
  Turner, Victor, 8:468–471
African Studies Association, 1:43
African Union, 6:62
Africville (Canada), 1:**45–46**
Afrikaners, 1:42
Afro American Reality Company,
  3:424
Afro-Carribeans, 9:97
Afro-Cubans, 1:329, 6:80–81
Afro-Orientalism, 1:44
Afrocentrism, 1:**46–48**
  African American studies, 1:32,
    43–45
  African studies, 1:43–44
  black nationalism, 1:315–318
  Black Power, 1:321–322
  blackness, 1:329
  civilization, 1:558
  Diop, Cheikh Anta, 2:369–370
Aftalion, Albert, 1:591, 6:97
Afterlife
  death and dying, 2:247, 248
  heaven, 3:445–446
  hell, 3:457–459
  terror, 8:326
  See also Reincarnation
Against Oneself and against One's People
  (Bahro), 1:237
Agamben, Giorgio, 2:63
Age and aging, 3:306–308
  childlessness, 1:510

death and dying, 2:248

dementia, 2:271–272

memory in psychology, 5:78

midlife crisis, 5:148–150

morbidity and mortality, 5:290–291

overlapping generations model, 6:93, 94

political attitudes, 1:103

population, 3:306–307

population studies, 6:382

wage discrimination, 2:401–402

welfare state, 9:72

Age discrimination, 3:308

  civil rights, 1:549

  race, 2:406

  wage, 2:401–402

Age Discrimination in Employment Act (ADEA) (U.S. 1967–1968), 2:402

Age-specific fertility rate (ASFR), 3:127

Ageism. *See* Age discrimination

Agencies, for development, 9:139

The Agency. *See* Central Intelligence Agency, U.S. (CIA)

Agency in psychology, 6:**586–587**

Agency theory

  cultural anthropology, 1:121

  organizations, 6:69

Agenda setting, 1:**48–49**, 202–203, 4:375

Agent Orange, 8:614

Agent-principal models. *See* Principal-agent models

Agglomerative clustering, 1:585

Aggregate demand, 1:**49–51**

  aggregate supply, 1:54

  Keynes, John Maynard, 4:259, 260

  Z-D model, 9:172–173

Aggregate demand and supply price, 1:**51–53**, 9:172–173

Aggregate production function, 8:619–620

Aggregate supply, 1:**53–55**, *54,* 9:172–173

Aggression, 1:**55–57**

  alpha-males, 1:83–84

  Bandura, Albert, 1:248, 249

  Freud, Sigmund, 3:214

  Hamilton's rule, 3:414–415

  hypertension, 3:540

  instrumental, 1:55, 83

  just war, 4:235, 236

self-constrained behavior, 1:273–274

social information processing, 7:600

sociobiology, 7:654–655

type A/type B personality, 6:222–223

video games, 8:611–612

Aghion, Philippe, 1:215

Aging and Society (Riley), 3:306

Agitators (English activists), 4:414

Aglietta, Michel, 1:447

Agnew, Spiro, 4:370, 371, 5:506, 8:538

Agnosticism, 1:**57**, 8:340

The Agony of Education (Feagin, Vera, and Imani), 2:317

Agoraphobia, 1:146

Agostini v. Felton (1997), 1:535

Agrarian economy. *See* Agricultural economics

Agreement on Trade-Related Aspects of Intellectual Property Rights (TRIPS), 9:143

Agreements, trade. *See* Trade

Agribusiness, 1:**58**, 6:667–668

Agricultural Adjustment Act (U.S. 1933), 5:494, 6:667

Agricultural Adjustment Act (U.S.1938), 6:668

Agricultural economics, 1:**58–59**

  Boserup, Ester, 1:357–358

  Chicago School, 1:502

  civil wars, 1:554

  cobweb cycles, 1:591

  collectivism, 2:11

  development economics, 2:344

  dual economy, 2:457

  farm quota system, 6:667–668

  farm subsidies, 8:203–204

  knowledge society, 4:283, 284

  Kuznets hypothesis, 4:295, 297

  Ladejinsky, Wolf, 4:327–328

  land reform, 4:341–345

  landlords, 4:345, 346

  latifundia, 4:352–354

  Lenin, Vladimir Ilitch, 4:411

  loans, 4:473

  NAFTA, 5:541

  peasantry, 6:195–196

  populism, 6:383

  primitive communism, 2:37–38

  sharecropping, 7:490–492

  slavery, 3:161–162

  subsistence agriculture, 8:204–206

See also Plantation economy model

Agricultural industry, 1:**59–63**

  African Americans, 1:34–35

  Appalachia, 1:150, 151

  bananas, 1:245–247

  Boserup, Ester, 1:357

  Bracero Program, 1:364–365

  business cycles, 1:403

  Chávez, César, 1:493–494

  coffee, 1:594

  collective, 1:61

  contango, 2:112

  cotton, 2:151–153

  cross of gold, 2:181

  deforestation, 2:263–264

  division of labor, 2:423

  drought, 2:447–448

  environmental impact, 1:59

  famine, 3:97–99

  farm subsidies, 8:203–204

  fertile crescent, 3:125–126

  feudal mode of production, 3:133–134

  food crisis, 3:164

  Great Depression, 5:494

  Green Revolution, 3:164–165, 378

  history, 3:162–163

  import substitution, 3:593

  industrialization, 1:61–62

  irrigation, 4:153–154

  labor, 4:301

  land fertility, 3:131–132

  migrant labor, 5:154–155

  Moore, Barrington, 5:278

  New Deal, 5:496

  Operation Bootstrap, 6:44–45

  organic, 9:41

  Ottoman Empire, 6:84

  peanuts, 6:188–189

  peasantry, 6:74–75, 195–196

  plantations, 6:277–278, 278–279

  rural development, 2:341–342

  rural sociology, 8:8–9

  sharecropping, 7:490–492

  slash-and-burn, 3:130

  slavery, 3:131

  subsistence, 3:97–99, 4:420–421, 8:204–206

  swidden, 5:425

  tea, 8:288

  tenancy system, 1:34

  urban sprawl, 8:540

  Vaisyas, 8:568

Agricultural industry, *continued*
  water resources, 9:40, 41, 42
Agricultural Labor Relations Board
  (ALRB), 1:494
Agricultural unions, 6:74
Agriculture. *See* Agricultural industry
Agriculture, subsistence. *See*
  Subsistence agriculture
AHA (American Historical
  Association), 1:268
Ahluwalia, Montek, 4:296
AICT (Automated information and
  communication technologies),
  2:217
Aid, foreign. *See* Loans
Aid to Families with Dependent
  Children (AFDC), 4:118, 9:26
AIDS (Acquired immunodeficiency
  syndrome), 1:**63–65**
    contraception, 2:115
    developing countries, 1:65–67,
      3:442
    gay, lesbian, transgender, and
      bisexual politics, 6:329–330
    India, 5:393
    medicine, 5:63
    reproductive politics, 7:182
    self-constrained behavior, 1:274
    World Health Organization, 9:140
    See also HIV (Human
      immunodeficiency virus)
AIDS/HIV in developing countries,
  impact of, 1:64, **65–67**
Aidukaite, Jolanta, 9:68
Ainsworth, Mary, 1:**67–68**, 195–196,
  363, 507
Ainsworth-Darnell, James, 6:48
Ain't I a Woman (Friedan), 3:268
Air pollution, 6:360, **361–363**
Air Quality Act (U.S. 1967), 6:362
Air transport aviation, 1:232–233
Aircraft
    history, 1:232
    nuclear weapons, 9:49
    See also Aviation industry
Airline Deregulation Act (U.S. 1978),
  1:233
Airline industry. *See* Aviation industry
Aisbett, Kate, 1:249
AIT (Aryan Invasion Theory), 1:185
Aitken, A. C., 3:286
Aitken's estimator. *See* Generalized
  least squares
Ajzen, Icek, 3:403
Akayesu, Jean-Paul, 3:297
Akenson, Donald, 2:357

Akerlof, George A., 1:**68–69**,
  4:313–314
al-Fatah. *See* Fatah
Al Jazeera, 1:**69–70**, 161
Al-Qaeda, 1:**86**, 8:629
    bin Laden, Osama, 1:299
    Bush, George W., 1:399, 400
    Central Intelligence Agency, U.S,
      1:483, 484
    counterterrorism, 2:155
    defense, 2:259, 261
    diamond industry, 2:355
    domino theory, 2:435
    Iraq-U.S. War, 4:146
    Qadhafi, Muammar al, 6:648
    September 11, 2001, 7:452–453
    social movements, 7:606–607
    suicide bombers, 8:224–225
    Taliban, 8:263
    terrorism, 8:329–330
al-Rifai, Zaid. *See* Rifai, Zaid al-
al-Tali, Wasif. *See* Tali, Wasif al-
Al Thani, Hamad bin Khalifa, 1:69
Alabama
    civil rights, 1:550
    Confederate States of America,
      2:66
    cooperatives, 2:125–126
    gerrymandering, 3:309
    King, Martin Luther, Jr., 4:268
    Tuskegee syphilis study,
      8:472–473
Alaska, Creole, 2:168
Alaska Land Act (U.S. 1980), 1:451
Alaska Natives, 1:21, 5:423
Albania, Warsaw Pact, 9:35
Alberti, Leon Battista, 3:517
Albright, Madeleine, 5:470
The Alchemy of Race and Rights
  (Williams), 5:372
Alchian, Armen, 2:519
Alcohol, 2:452–455
    See also Alcoholism; Spirits
      industry
Alcohol myopia. *See* Steele, Claude M.
Alcoholics Anonymous (AA), 1:22
Alcoholism, 1:21, **70–71**, 2:173,
  8:131–132
Alembert, Jean le Rond d', 8:635
Alesina, Alberto, 9:72
Alexander, Jeffrey, 8:6
Alexander I, Tzar, 5:365, 368
Alexander II, Tzar, 8:628, 9:20
Alexander VI, Pope, 2:20
Alexandria (Egypt), 1:533

Alexis, Marcus A., 5:387, 388
Algarin, Miguel, 5:552–553
Algebra, matrix. *See* Matrix algebra
Alger, Horatio, 1:**72–73**, 8:534, 535
Algeria
    anticolonial movements, 1:139,
      140
    The Battle of Algiers (film),
      1:257–258
    Black Power, 1:321
    Bourdieu, Pierre, 1:358, 359
    De Gaulle, Charles, 2:265
    decolonization, 2:257
    Fanon, Frantz, 3:99–100,
      8:625–626
    nationalist movement, 1:139,
      8:625–626
    OPEC, 6:65
    veiling, 8:603, 604
Algerian National Liberation Front,
  3:100
Algerian Revolution. *See* Battle of
  Algiers
Algerian War (1954–1962),
  1:257–258
The Algerians (Bourdieu). *See* Sociologie
  de l'Algérie
Algiers, Battle of (1957), 1:257–258
Algonquins, 5:426
Ali, Muhammad (Egyptian military
  leader), 1:73
Ali, Muhammad (U.S. boxer),
  1:73–74, 5:216
Ali, Noble Drew, 5:379
Ali ibn Abi Talib, 4:154, 156–157
Alien abductions, 8:507–508
Alienated work, 3:79
Alienation, 1:**75–76**
    cities, 1:540
    civil society, 1:553
    class consciousness, 1:572
    communalism, 2:30, 31
    division of labor, 2:424
    Fromm, Erich, 3:222–223
    labor, 4:301
    The Lonely Crowd (Riesman),
      4:487
    Lukacs, Georg, 4:516
Alienation-anomie, 1:**76**
Aliens Act (U.S. 1798), 3:578
Aliens (immigrants). *See* Immigrants
Alighieri, Dante. *See* Purgatory
Alinsky, Saul, 1:493
All-African People's Conference
  (1958), 1:140

All Our Kin (Stack), 5:462

Allais, Maurice, 2:249, 3:284, 5:519, 6:93

Alland, Alexander, 1:131

Allegiance. *See* Loyalty

Allen, Robert, 2:13, 15

Allen, Roy G. D., 6:57

Allen v. State Board of Elections (1969), 8:651

Allende, Salvador, 1:**77–78**, 483, 7:234–235

Alley Life in Washington (Borchert), 8:264

Alliance for Progress (U.S.), 1:303, 6:45

Alliances, 1:**78–81**
  Chávez, César, 1:493–494
  coalition, 1:586–587, 587–588
  Cold War, 2:4–5
  Cuba, 2:186–187
  defense, 2:258
  kinship, 1:128
  League of Nations, 4:385–386
  marriage, 4:615
  multilateralism, 5:320–321
  Southern bloc, 8:34–35
  Spanish Civil War, 8:43–44
  trilateralism, 8:453–454

Allied Social Sciences Association (ASSA), 5:387, 388

Alliger, George, 4:379

Alliot-Marie, Michèle, 2:262

Allison, Graham T., 2:185, 3:170–171

Allison, Luther, 1:343

Allocation, time. *See* Time allocation

Allport, Gordon W., 1:**81–82**
  contact hypothesis, 2:111–112, 9:136–137
  personality, 6:217
  prejudice, 6:438

Allwright, S. E., 9:85

Allwright, Smith v. (1944), 9:85

Alma-Ata Declaration (1978), 3:442

Almon, Shirley, 4:334

Almond, Gabriel A., 1:**82**, 6:301, 327, 8:606

Alonso, William, 8:541

Alpert, Richard, 4:390, 391

Alpha-females, 1:83

Alpha-males, 1:**83–85**, 7:479–480

Alpha Suffrage Club, 9:77

ALRB (Agricultural Labor Relations Board), 1:494

The Alternative (Bahro), 1:237

Alternative lifestyle, 8:583

Alternative vote, 8:**643–645**, 644t

Alternatives to multiple genders. *See* Binary gender, alternatives

Althusius, Johannes, 2:278

Althusser, Louis, 1:**86–87**, 3:82
  capitalist mode of production, 1:447
  class, 1:564
  class conflict, 1:570–571
  class consciousness, 1:572
  cultural studies, 2:199
  discourse, 2:387
  empiricism, 2:579
  gaze, 3:263–264
  humanism, 3:518
  ideology, 3:559
  Poulantzas, Nicos, 6:404
  science, 7:358
  structuralism, 8:183
  subjectivity, 8:199

Altman, Dennis, 6:329

Altruism, 1:**87–88**
  evolutionary theory of kinship, 4:273–274
  Hamilton's rule, 3:414–415
  well-being, 3:292–293

Altruism and prosocial behavior, 1:**88–89**
  Becker, Gary S., 1:271
  bequests, 1:287
  cooperation, 2:122–123
  cultural group selection, 2:191
  emotion and affect, 2:572
  empathy, 2:573–574
  individualism, 3:619–620
  League of Nations, 4:385
  moral philosophy, 6:254–255t
  norm of reciprocity, 7:107
  perspective-taking, 6:227
  rationality, 7:79
  reciprocity, 7:105–107
  sellouts, 7:434, 435
  sociobiology, 7:654
  in vivo transfers, 3:598

Alumina, 1:261

Aluminum, 1:261

Aluminum oxide. *See* Alumina

Alves, Rubem, 4:435

Alzheimer's disease, 1:**89–90**, 2:271–272, 3:307

Ambar, Malik, 1:39

Ambedkar, B. R., 1:**90–92**, 3:255
  Buddhism, 1:383
  caste, 1:459–460, 463
  dalits, 2:221

Jinnah, Mohammed Ali, 4:204
  Sanskritization, 7:324

Amendments, U.S. Constitution. *See* Constitution, U.S.

America in Midpassage (Beard and Beard), 1:268

American Anthropological Association (AAA), 1:**92–93**

American Association for Applied Psychology (AAAP), 1:102

American Bar Association, Nader's Raiders, 5:360

American Capitalism (Galbraith), 3:246

American City Government (Beard), 1:268

American Civil Liberties Union (ACLU), 1:547

American Civil War. *See* U.S. Civil War

American Civilization (James), 4:168

American Depository Receipts (ADR), 2:624

An American Dilemma (Myrdal), 1:**93–96**
  benign neglect, 1:283
  Bunche, Ralph Johnson, 1:388
  Clark, Kenneth B., 1:560
  cumulative causation, 2:207
  Herskovitz, Melville J., 3:467
  Myrdal, Gunnar, 5:351
  National Economic Association, 5:389

American Directory of Certified Uncle Toms, 8:483

American dream, 1:**96–97**
  energy sector, 2:592
  immigrants, 3:575
  Japanese Americans, 4:173, 174

American Economic Association, 1:97, 4:337, 5:388

American Ethnological Society, 1:92

American exceptionalism, 1:107

American Federation of Labor (AFL), 4:302, 8:515

American Government and Politics (Beard), 1:268

American Historical Association (AHA), 1:268

American History and Its Geographic Conditions (Semple), 2:328

American Independent Party, 2:430

American Indian Movement, 1:**98–99**
  Black Panthers, 1:319
  Mankiller, Wilma, 4:586
  Means, Russell, 5:53

American Indians. *See* Native Americans

American Liberty League, 2:85

American Medical Association
abortion, 1:3
attention-deficit/hyperactivity disorder, 1:198
Social Security Act (U.S. 1965), 3:372

American Muslim Mission, 5:381

American National Election Studies (ANES), 1:**100**

The American Occupational Structure (Blau and Duncan), 1:332, 2:463

The American People and Foreign Policy (Almond), 1:82

American Political Science Association (APSA), 1:**100–101**, 105, 6:314

American Politics: The Promise of Disharmony (Huntington), 3:526

American Popular Culture and High Culture in a Changing Class Structure (Gans), 2:204

American Psychiatric Association, attention-deficit/hyperactivity disorder, 1:197

American Psychological Association (APA), 1:**101–102**, 8:572

American Psychological Society (APS), 1:102

American Revolution, 1:**103–105**
Americanism, 1:108
Appalachia, 1:149–150
conservatism, 2:83
Daughters of the American Revolution, 2:241
Declaration of Independence, U.S., 2:254
decolonization, 2:255
desegregation, 2:315
Franklin, Benjamin, 3:190
going native, 3:338
Iroquois, 4:151
Jefferson, Thomas, 4:179–180
liberty, 4:439
slavery, 7:543–544
Washington, George, 9:36

American Sociological Association (ASA), 1:**105–107**, 3:549

American sociology. *See* Sociology, American

American sociology, post-Parsonian. *See* Post-Parsonian American sociology

The American Spirit (Beard and Beard), 1:268

American Telegraph and Telephone Company (AT&T), 8:314, 315

An American Tragedy (Dreiser), 1:96

The American Voter (Campbell, Converse, Miller and Stokes), 1:100, 425

Americanism, 1:**107–108**
Daughters of the American Revolution, 2:241–242
Disney, Walt, 2:410
tradition, 8:420–421

Americanization, 3:327, 331

Americans for Democratic Action (ADA), 7:277

Americans with Disabilities Act (U.S. 1990), 4:347

Americas. *See* Central America; Latin America; North America; South America

AmeriCorps, 5:414

AmeriCorps Act (U.S. 1993), 1:580

Ames, Aldrich H., 1:483

Ames, Jessie Daniel, 4:526

Amhara, 8:630

L'ami des hommes (Mirabeau), 1:558

Amicus curiae briefs, 1:48

Amin, Idi, 1:**109–110**, 5:341, 554

Amin, Samir, 1:**110–111**, 5:466, 8:490, 506

Amir, Yigal, 7:1, 2

Amnesty, cartels, 1:145

Amnesty International, 1:547

Amniocentesis, 3:294

Amphetamines, 2:453

Amsterdam, Morey, 1:417

Amygdala, 1:573

Anabaptists, 1:531, 533

Anabolic steroids, 2:452, 454

Anafranil. *See* Clomipramine

Analytic behaviorism. *See* Logical behaviorism

Anarchical Society (Grotius), 5:489

Anarchism, 1:**111–112**
centrism, 1:488
international relations, 4:99
left wing, 4:403
Levellers, 4:414, 415
libertarianism, 4:438
lumpenproletariat, 4:517
Social Darwinism, 2:233

Anasazi, 6:426

Anastasi, Anne, 8:484

ANC (African National Congress). *See* African National Congress (ANC)

Ancestor worship, 9:155

Ancestry. *See* Kinship

Ancient Law (Maine), 1:127

Ancient liberty, 4:439

The Ancient Near East (Hallo and Simpson), 3:125–126

Ancient Regime and the Revolution (Tocqueville), 2:84

Ancient Times (Breasted), 3:125

And We Are Not Saved (Bell), 2:175

The Andaman Islanders (Radcliffe-Brown), 1:127

Andersen, Margaret, 9:88

Anderson, Barbara, 1:130

Anderson, Benedict, 4:429, 5:378–379

Anderson, Craig, 8:612

Anderson, Elijah, 1:325, 8:172, 264

Anderson, James, 1:145

Anderson, Kay, 5:464

Anderson, Marian, 9:81

Anderson, Perry, 1:**112–113**
class, 1:564
feudal mode of production, 3:134
hegemony, 3:455
transitional conjunctures, 2:77–78

Anderson, Rudolf, 2:184

Andropov, Yuri, 1:370, 8:512

ANES (American National Election Studies), 1:**100**

Angell, James Rowland, 3:233

Anger, 2:572, 3:540

Anglicanism, 1:531, 533, 534, 2:114

Anglo-American alliance, 1:79, 80

Anglo-Boer War. *See* Boer War

Anglo-Chinese War (1839–1842), 6:46

Anglo-French Treaty of Commerce (1860), 2:134

Anglo-German Naval Agreement (1935), 9:148–149

Anglo-Portuguese trade, 8:**413–414**

Anglo-Saxons, eugenics, 5:430

Angola
African socialism, 7:641
civil wars, 1:554, 555
Cuba, 2:187

Animal Farm (Orwell), 1:390

Animals
behaviorism, 1:275, 276
Columbus, Christopher, 2:21
conditioning, 1:572–573, 574
consciousness, 2:80
domesticated, 3:162–163
fertile crescent, 3:125–126
learned helplessness, 4:387–388

pollution, 6:360

primates, 6:459–461

reinforcement theories, 7:147

sexual selection theory, 7:479–480

shock experiments, 3:62

Thorndike, Edward, 8:358

Tolman, Edward, 8:386–387

Animism, 1:**113–114**, 6:367, 7:487

Animus. *See* Taste for discrimination

Annales school, 3:304, 482, 483

Annexation, 1:**115–116**, 4:340–341, 5:126–129

Annulment, 2:426

Anocracy, 1:555

Anomie, 2:466

Anorexia nervosa, 8:491–492

See also Body image; Undereating

Anselm, Saint, 8:231

Antarctica, global warming, 3:328

Anthem (Rand), 6:7

Anthony, Peter David, 9:122

Anthony, Susan B., 2:439, 440, 3:120

Anthrax, 1:301–302, 9:52

Anthropological Essays (Lewis), 4:418

Anthropology, 1:**116–125**

applied, 1:116–117

biological, 1:118

cultural, 1:124

linguistic, 1:118–119

public health, 1:131

public *vs.*, 1:132–133

United States, 1:137

caste, 1:457–460, 461–463

cooperation, 2:122–123

creationism *vs.*, 2:163

critical medical, 1:131

cultural, 1:119–124, 2:202–203

landscape, 2:192–193

relativism, 2:193–196

U. S., 1:137–138

dance, 2:223–225

demographic transition, 2:292

ethnology and folklore, 3:17

ethnomusicology, 3:20

Evans-Pritchard, E. E., 3:29–30

feminist, 1:121

four-field, 1:116–122, 124

functionalism, 3:232–233

globalization, 3:330–332

hybridity, 3:535, 536

Islamic fundamentalism, 3:237

nation-states, 3:332

history, 1:136–137

identity, 3:554–555

interpretive, 1:121, 3:265–266

Johanson, Donald, 4:206–207

kinship, 4:271–273

Kroeber, Alfred Louis, 4:289–291

Le Guin, Ursula K., 4:407

Leakey, Richard, 4:386–387

magic, 4:554–555

Marx, Karl, 4:631–633

material culture, 5:12–17

matriarchy, 5:28–30

midwifery, 5:151–154

polytheism, 6:367–368

primates, 6:460–461

primitivism, 6:465–466

reflexivity, 7:122–123

reincarnation, 7:145–146

reproduction, 7:178–179

Sahlins, Marshall, 7:308–309

social science, 7:616

sociology, 3:231

structuralism, 8:182–183

symbols, 8:249–253

topography, 8:389–390

totemism, 8:397–398

tribalism, 8:448–449

tribes, 8:449–450

violence, 8:623

virgins, 8:630

Wolf, Eric, 9:105–106

See also specific fields of anthropology; Ethnography

Anthropology, biological, 1:117–118, **125–127**

African burial grounds, 1:393–394

Boas, Franz, 1:344–345

race, 7:8–11

Anthropology, British, 1:**127–128**

Malinowski, Bronislaw, 4:566–567

Radcliffe-Brown, A. R., 7:47

Anthropology, cultural. *See* Ethnography

Anthropology, linguistic, 1:118–119, **129–130**

Chomsky, Noam, 1:527–529

consciousness, 2:78

conversational analysis, 2:118–120

Creole, 2:167–168

creolization, 2:169

cultural relativism, 2:194–195

dance, 2:224

Diop, Cheikh Anta, 2:369, 370

discourse, 2:387

Dravidians, 2:442–443

ethnicity, 3:9

hybridity, 3:536

race, 7:8–11

Roma, 7:277–279

semiotics, 7:436–438

Anthropology, medical, 1:**130–132**

Anthropology, physical. *See* Biological anthropology

Anthropology, practicing. *See* Public anthropology

Anthropology, public, 1:**132–134**

Anthropology, race and, 7:8–13

Boas, Franz, 1:344–345

Du Bois, W. E. B., 2:458–460

Herskovits, Melville J., 3:466–467

Hurston, Zora Neale, 3:526–528

Latino National Political Survey, 4:355

Anthropology, social. *See* Ethnography

Anthropology, urban, 1:**134–136**

case method, 1:453

human ecology, 3:510

metropolitan regions, 7:132–135

street culture, 8:173–174

Anthropology, U.S., 1:**136–138**

Benedict, Ruth, 1:282

Boas, Franz, 1:344–345

Castaneda, Carlos, 1:456–457

Lévi-Strauss, Claude, 4:416–417

Lowie, Robert, 4:507–508

Mead, Margaret, 5:47

Mintz, Sidney W., 5:195–196

Montagu, Ashley, 5:273–274

Anthropology (Wolf), 9:106

The Anthropology of Food (Pottier), 3:163

Anthropometrics, 3:162

Anti-Ballistic Missile Treaty, 9:31

Anti-cholinesterases, 2:272

The Anti-Christ (Nietzsche), 5:503

Anti-Defamation League (ADL), 3:431

Anti-Federalist Papers, 2:91

Anti-Federalists. *See* Federalism

Anti-intellectualism, 4:**64–66**

Anti-intellectualism in American Life (Hofstadter), 4:64

Anti-Reelectionist party, 8:617

Anti-Semitism, 1:**141–143**, 4:195–196

Arendt, Hannah, 1:173

Aryans, 1:185–186

Christianity, 1:530

fascism, 3:104

Hitler, Adolf, 3:486–488

Anti-Semitism, *continued*
infidels, 4:23
Jewish diaspora, 4:190
loans, 4:472
Nazism, 5:448–450, 9:148
racial attitudes studies, 1:204
racial slurs, 7:42
Social Darwinism, 2:233–234
xenophobia, 9:158, 159, 160
Zionism, 9:179
See also Holocaust; Jews; Pogroms
Anti-terrorism initiatives. *See*
Counterterrorism
Anti-Untouchability Act (India 1955),
1:91
Anti-Zionism, 1:141
Antianxiety drugs, 1:147, 147*t*
Anticipated reactions, rule of, 5:518
Anticolonial movements, 1:**139–141**
black nationalism, 1:315–316,
317
Black Power, 1:321
Bose, Subhas and Sarat,
1:356–357
Cabral, Amílcar, 1:415–416
civilization, 1:558
commonwealth, 2:29
communalism, 2:31
communism, 2:34
Cuba, 2:185–186
Du Bois, W. E. B., 2:458–460
Ho Chi Minh, 3:491–492
Indian National Army, 3:610–611
Indian National Congress, 3:611
Jefferson, Thomas, 4:180
Kenyatta, Jomo, 4:256
Kimathi, Dedan, 4:266
Latin American revolutions, 7:233
Le Duc Tho, 4:398
liberation, 4:429
Lumumba, Patrice, 4:517–518
Machel, Samora, 4:532–533
Mau Mau, 5:36–38
Mossadegh, Mohammad,
5:296–297
Pan-African Congresses, 6:113
Pan-Africanism, 6:115
postcolonialism, 6:392–393
reggae, 7:127, 129
resistance, 7:208
revolution, 7:229
revolution of rising expectations,
7:231–232
self-determination, 7:405–406
treaty federalism, 8:445–446

Zionism, 9:180
See also Colonialism
Anticommunism. *See* Communism
Antidepressants, 1:147
See also Psychotropic drugs
Antiglobalization movement. *See*
Globalization
Antihypertensive drugs, 3:540
Antinomies of Antonio Gramsci
(Anderson), 3:455
Antioch (Syria), 1:533
Antipersonnel mines, 1:176
Antiquities Act (U.S. 1906), 7:169
Antiretrovirals, 1:66
Antisatellite weapons, 1:178–179
Antiterrorism. *See* Counterterrorism
Antitrust, 1:**143–144**
agribusiness, 1:58
deregulation, 2:309
litigation, 4:465
Antitrust regulation, 1:**144–145**
corporations, 2:140
described, 7:143
labor law, 4:303
monopoly, 5:264, 265
Antiwar movements. *See* Peace
movements
Antonelli, Giovanni, 2:269, 270
Antwerp bourse, 3:180
Anxiety, 1:**145–147**, 146*t*
John Henryism, 4:207–208
luck, 4:512
panic, 6:122–123
performance, 3:179
phobia, 6:262–263
social, 6:262, 7:563–564
terror, 8:326–327
terror management theory,
8:327–328
Anxiety, separation. *See* Separation
anxiety
Anxiety, social. *See* Social anxiety
Anxiety disorders, 1:145
Aoun, Michel, 4:397
AP (Associated Press), 4:213
APA (Advanced Pricing Agreement),
8:428
APA (American Psychological
Association), 1:**101–102**, 8:572
APA Publication Manual, 1:102
Apache, 5:425
Apanovitch, Anne Marie, 2:252
Apartheid, 1:**147–149**
black middle class, 1:314–315
Boer War, 1:350

Coloreds (South Africa), 2:16–17
commonwealth, 2:29
diamond industry, 2:355, 356
direct action, 2:372
divestiture, 2:421
ethnicity, 3:10
liberation, 4:430
Machel, Samora, 4:533
Mandela, Nelson, 4:580–581
Mandela, Winnie, 4:581–582
race, 7:5
racial inequality, 4:6–7
repression, 7:174
school segregation, 7:386
as segregation, 7:382
townships, 8:405–407
white supremacy, 9:86
Apartment buildings, 1:170
APC (Average propensity to consume),
1:6–7
Apeal (Walker), 8:618
Apes. *See* Primates
APO (African Political Organization),
2:15
Apocalypto (film), 3:516
Appadurai, Arjun, 3:331
Appalachia, 1:**149–152**
Appalachian Regional Development
Act (U.S. 1963), 1:151
An Appeal to the World (Du Bois),
1:550
The Appeals of Communism (Almond),
1:82
Appeasement, 1:**152–154**, 489, 537
Appelbaum, Richard, 1:351, 352
Appetitive conditioning, 1:573
Apple Computer, video games, 8:611
Applebaum, Herbert, 9:122
Appleby, R. Scott, 1:82
Applewhite, Marshall Herff, 2:188
Applied anthropology
biological, 1:118
cultural, 1:124
description, 1:116–117
linguistic, 1:118–119
public health, 1:131
public *vs.*, 1:132–133
United States, 1:137
Applied Anthropology in America
(Partridge and Eddy), 1:137
Applied economics, School of
Lausanne, 4:361–362
Apportionment, 1:**154–155**
black politics, 6:325
elections, 2:557, 558, 560–562

electoral college, 2:559–560

Southern politics, 6:345–346

Appreciation, currency. *See* Currency appreciation and depreciation

Appreciation and Interest (Fisher), 3:151

Apprenticeship, 8:514

Appropriations, 1:**155**

Approximation, method of successive, 6:43

Approximation Theorems of Mathematical Statistics (Serfling), 4:349

APS (American Psychological Society), 1:102

APSA (American Political Science Association), 1:**100–101**, 105, 6:314

APT (Arbitrage pricing theory), 3:141

Apt illustration, 1:454

Aquaculture, 3:152, 153

Aquinas, Saint Thomas. *See* Thomas Aquinas, Saint

Arab Common Market, 1:159

Arab-Israeli War of 1967, 1:**156–159**, 161

Hussein, King of Jordan, 3:531

Hussein, Saddam, 3:533

Nasser, Gamal Abdel, 1:154, 5:377

Thant, U., 8:334

two-state solution, 8:477

Arab League, 1:154, **155–156**

Arab nationalism. *See* Pan-Arabism

Arabian Peninsula, 1:159

Arabic language, 1:159

Arabica coffee. *See* Coffee industry

al-Arabiyya, 1:70

Arabs, 1:**159–161**

African diaspora, 1:39

Ben-Gurion, David, 1:283

biased policing, 6:290

bigotry, 1:296

Darfur, 2:226–227

Hussein, King of Jordan, 3:531

Hussein, Saddam, 3:531–533

Nasser, Gamal Abdel, 5:376

nationalism, 1:160, 3:531

Palestinian diaspora, 6:108–110

wealth, 9:45

whiteness, 9:86

Zionism, 9:180

See also Palestinians; Pan-Arabism

Arafat, Yasir, 1:**161–162**

Black September, 1:323

Palestine Liberation Organization, 6:103–104

Palestinian Authority, 6:105–106

Rabin, Yitzhak, 7:1

Arámbula, José Doroteo Arango. *See* Villa, Francisco

Arawak. *See* Taino

Arawak dialect, 3:258

Arbenz, Jacobo, 7:234

Arbitrage and arbitrageurs, 1:**162–163**

efficient market hypothesis, 2:548–549

selling long and selling short, 7:432–433

spot market, 8:67–68

Arbitrage pricing theory (APT), 3:141

ARCH (Autoregressive conditional heteroscedasticity), 1:229–230, 8:587

Archaeological Insights into the Custer Battle (Scott, Fox, Connor, and Harmon), 1:259

Archaeological Perspectives on the Battle of the Little Bighorn (Scott, Fox, Connor, and Harmon), 1:259

Archaeology, 1:**163–170**

African burial grounds, 1:393–394

Battle of the Little Big Horn, 1:259

classical, 1:165–166

colonial, 1:167

creationism *vs.*, 2:163

cultural resource management, 2:196–197

culture-historical, 1:166–167

description, 1:117

Johanson, Donald, 4:206–207

Leakey, Richard, 4:386–387

material culture, 5:12–13

Native American burial grounds, 1:395

post-processual, 1:168–169

prehistoric, 1:117, 166

processual, 1:167–168

race, 7:11

repatriation, 7:169

Schliemann, Heinrich, 7:346–347

settlement, 7:464

slave lives, 7:529–531

underwater, 1:117

Archaeology, History, and Custer's Last Battle (Fox), 1:259

Archaeology of Knowledge (Foucault), 3:182

Archaeology of slave lives, 7:**529–531**

Archer, Margaret, 3:314

Archetypes, 4:229–231

Architecture, 1:**170–172**

cultural resource management, 2:196, 197

Hinduism, 3:479–480

history, 8:631

Jefferson, Thomas, 4:182–183

material culture, 5:14

modernism, 5:229

Moses, Robert, 5:296

Shinto, 7:497

urban studies, 8:542

Archytas, 1:232

Arctic, global warming, 3:328

Are We Civilized? (Lowie), 4:507

Arendt, Hannah, 1:**173**, 6:274

anti-Semitism, 1:142

architecture, 1:172

Holocaust, 3:497

narratives, 5:370

New School for Social Research, 5:501

Arens, W., 1:427

ARFIMA (Autoregressive fractional integrated moving average) model, 9:83

Argentina

authoritarianism, 1:214

cattle industry, 1:471

concentration camps, 2:64

corporatism, 2:141

coups d'etat, 2:156

Falkland Islands war, 3:80–81

job guarantee, 4:206

Mothers of the Plaza del Mayo, 9:110, 112

Peronism, 6:214–215

populism, 6:384

whitening, 9:90

Argonauts of the Western Pacific (Malinowski), 1:127

Arguments with English Marxism (Anderson), 1:113

Argyle, Michael, 5:530

Arian churches, 1:533

Ariès, Philip, 2:248

Arif, Abdul Salam, 3:532

ARIMA (Autoregressive moving average) model, 1:229, 8:42–43, 517–518, 9:82–83

Aristippus of Cyrene, 1:111

Aristocracy, 1:**173–174**

checks and balances, 1:495

landlords, 4:345, 346

latifundia, 4:352–354

Aristocracy, *continued*
    rentier class, 1:566
    republicanism, 7:188
Aristotle, 1:**174–175**, 495, 2:82
    abortion, 1:1
    aesthetics, 1:30
    animism, 1:114
    behaviorism, 1:275
    biological determinism, 2:325
    classical conditioning, 1:572
    consciousness, 2:80
    economic rhetoric, 2:496
    family values, 3:96
    freedom, 3:196
    happiness, 3:415
    hermeneutics, 3:464
    justice, 4:237
    labor theory of value, 4:323
    Lafargue, Paul, 4:330
    law, 4:365
    leisure, 4:408
    markets, 4:606–607
    monetary theory, 5:246
    monotheism, 5:270
    narratives, 5:370
    naturalism, 5:441
    necessities, 5:451
    Occam's razor, 6:20
    oligarchy, 6:37
    politics, 6:319, 320
    relative deprivation, 7:152
    representation, 7:171
    representative and participatory
      democracy, 2:284
    republicanism, 7:188
    rhetoric, 7:237
    symbolic logic, 4:481
    theater, 8:336
    universalism, 8:526
    universities, 8:531
    wealth, 9:45
Arithmetic mean. *See* Mean
Arius, 2:132
Arizona, Miranda v. (1966), 2:461,
    9:33
Arkansas
    African burial grounds, 1:394
    civil rights, 1:550, 551
    Clinton, Bill, 1:579, 581
    Confederate States of America,
      2:67
    desegregation, 2:314
    school desegregation, 2:316
Arkwright, Richard, 3:77

Armed forces. *See* Military
Armenia, 2:30, 3:296
Armies. *See* Military
Arms control, 1:**175–180**, 9:31–32
    Carter, Jimmy, 1:451
    Cold War, 2:5
    League of Nations, 4:385
    United Nations role, 8:525
    See also Disarmament
Arm's length price. *See* Transfer pricing
Arms race, 1:**175–180**
    defense, 2:258, 259
    differential equations, 2:364
    disarmament, 2:379–380
    linear systems, 4:456
Armstrong, Anne, 3:123
Armstrong, David, 5:442
Armstrong, Louis, 1:550, 4:176, 177
Army. *See* Military
Army Air Force (U.S.), unidentified
    flying objects, 8:507
Army Corps of Engineers (U.S.),
    5:433
Arneson, Richard, 3:234
Arnheim, Rudolf, 5:501
Arnold, Kenneth, 8:507
Arnold, Matthew
    culture, 2:203
    literature, 4:463
    resistance, 7:208–209
Aronowitz, Stanley, 4:302
Aronson, Elliot, 1:**180–181**, 3:133
Aronson, Jane, 9:122
Aronson, Joshua, 1:15
Arouet, Francois Marie. *See* Voltaire
ARPA (U.S. Advanced Research
    Projects Agency), 4:104
Arquilla, John, 2:259
Arranged marriage. *See* Endogamy;
    Marriage
Arrhenius, Svante August, 3:378
Arrighi, Giovanni, 4:309
Arrow (musician), 1:419
Arrow, Kenneth J., 1:**181–182**
    choice in economics, 1:524–525
    elections, 2:557
    equilibrium, 2:620–621, 3:283
    health economics, 3:440
    Hurwicz, Leonid, 3:529, 530
    majority voting, 4:558–559, 562
    mathematics in the social sciences,
      5:26
    neoclassical growth model, 5:465
    paradox of voting, 6:127

    research and development,
      7:199–200
    rules *vs.* discretion, 7:293
    social welfare functions, 7:630,
      9:66
    state enterprise, 8:109
    technological change, 1:491
    utility function, 8:556
    Uzawa, Hirofumi, 8:562, 563
    voting schemes, 8:654–655
    wage discrimination, 2:403
Arrow-Debreu-McKenzie theory,
    3:173
Arrow-Debreu Model, 1:**182–183**
    Debreu, Gerard, 2:249
    mathematics in the social sciences,
      5:27
Arrow impossibility theorem. *See*
    Arrow possibility theorem
Arrow possibility theorem, 1:181–182,
    183–185
    paradox of voting, 6:127
    social welfare functions, 7:630
Arrow War (1856–1860), 6:46
Art, visual. *See* Visual arts
The Art of Loving (Fromm), 3:223
The Art of Political Manipulation
    (Riker), 7:249
Arthur, Chester A., 5:447
Articles of Agreement of the
    International Monetary Fund
    (IMF). *See* International Monetary
    Fund (IMF)
Articles of Confederacy (U.S.), 3:113
Articles of Confederation
    confederations, 2:68
    Constitution, U.S., 2:90–91
Artifacts. *See* Material culture
Artifacts, organization theory, 6:70
Artificial intelligence
    behaviorism, 1:278–279
    cognition, 1:598
    social intelligence, 4:75
    theory of mind, 8:348
Artificial life, Occam's razor, 6:20
Artisanal mining, 3:342–343
Artisans, labor unions, 8:514
Arts
    aesthetics, 1:29–30
    decorative, 8:630
    folk, 8:632–633
    graphic, 8:632
    naturalism, 5:442
    orientalism, 6:75–76
    See also Visual arts

Arts and Crafts movement, 1:171
Aryan Invasion Theory (AIT), 1:185
Aryan Nations movement, 1:185–186
Aryans, 1:**185–186**
  biological determinism, 2:325
  census, 1:477
  concentration camps, 2:63
  cultural relativism, 1:123
  Dravidians, 2:443
  Gobineau, Comte de, 3:335–336
  Hitler, Adolf, 3:486–488
  Nazism, 5:449
  race and psychology, 7:21
  Social Darwinism, 2:234
  See also White supremacy
ASA (American Sociological
  Association), 1:**105–107**, 3:549
Aśoka, Emperor of India, 1:383
Asad, Talal, 1:128
Asante, Molefi Kete, 1:32, 46–47, 318
Ascending-bid auctions, 1:206
Asceticism, Nirvāna, 5:504
Asch, Solomon, 1:**186–187**, 5:501
  conformity, 1:186–187, 217, 2:71
  Milgram, Stanley, 5:161
  peer influence, 6:201
  social influence, 7:595
Ascribed social status, 1:60
ASEBA (Achenbach System of
  Empirically Based Assessment),
  1:504–505
ASFR (Age-specific fertility rate),
  3:127
Ashcroft, Georgia v. (2003), 8:653
Ashcroft v. Free Speech Coalition
  (2002), 6:13
Ashdown, Paddy, 4:427
Ashkenazi Jews, genetic testing, 3:295
Asia
  AIDS/HIV, 1:65–66
  anticolonial movements,
    1:139–140
  banana industry, 1:245
  brain drain, 1:367
  Buddhism, 1:383–384
  casino capitalism, 1:455
  cattle industry, 1:470
  Central, AIDS/HIV, 1:65
  civil wars, 1:554
  clientelism, 1:579
  coffee industry, 1:594
  Columbus, Christopher, 2:19
  communism, 2:36
  corporations, 2:140
  cotton industry, 2:151, 152, 153

coups d'etat, 2:156
crony capitalism, 2:180
decolonization, 2:255–256
demographic transition, 2:292
dependency theory, 2:299, 300
developing countries, 2:335–337
development economics, 2:344,
  345, 346
domino theory, 2:434
dowry and bride price, 2:440–441
export promotion, 3:67
geography, East Indies, 2:476
global warming effects, 3:330
gold industry, 3:343
Green Revolution, 3:164–165
Kuznets hypothesis, 4:297
land reform, 4:343, 344
latifundia, 4:353
legal systems, 4:405
microelectronics industry, 5:138
Raj, 7:55–57
regions, 7:132
Silk Road, 7:511
sociology of cities, 1:541
telecommunications industry,
  8:315
tourism, 8:565
trade liberalization, 4:428
underdevelopment, 8:490–491
water resources, 9:40
women's work, 9:124, 125
See also South Asia
Asian-African Conference, 5:541–542
Asian American politics, 6:**321–323**
Asian Americans
  addiction, 1:21
  interracial marriage, 4:616–619
  metropolitan regions, 7:135
  minorities, 5:191
  model minority, 5:220–221,
    220–222
  occupational status, 6:27
  parent-child relationships, 6:133
  public opinion, 7:20–21
  race, 7:5, 23
  settlement, 3:563–564
  socioeconomic status, 3:566t
  See also Chinese Americans;
    Japanese Americans
Asian Development Bank (ADB),
  water resources, 9:40–42
Asian Drama (Myrdal), 3:164, 5:351
Asian immigrants, 3:**562–564**
  California Civil Rights Initiative,
    1:416

Chinese diaspora, 1:515–519
ethnic enterprises, 3:4–5
Japanese American incarceration,
  3:599–601
model minority, 5:221, 222
railway industry, 7:53
regulation, 3:573–574, 578, 579
settlement, 3:578
socioeconomic status, 3:566t
See also Japanese Americans
Asians, choice in psychology, 1:526
Asiatic mode of production,
  1:**187–188**, 2:35–36, 5:219
Asimov, Nanette, 2:318
ASPA (American Political Science
  Association). *See* American Political
  Science Association
Aspects of the Theory of Syntax
  (Chomsky), 1:527–528
Aspira, 4:357
ASQ (Attributional Style
  Questionnaire), 6:54
Asquith, Herbert, 4:428
ASSA (Allied Social Sciences
  Association), 5:387, 388
Assassination
  Central Intelligence Agency, U.S,
    1:484
  Gandhi, Indira, 3:253
  Lumumba, Patrice, 4:518
  Rabin, Yitzhak, 7:1
  Warren Report, 9:33–34
Assault, 9:4
ASSC (Association for the Scientific
  Study of Consciousness), 2:81
Assembly line, Ford Motor Company,
  1:217–218, 3:168
Asset pricing, 3:141
Assets
  capital, 5:403, 8:551–552
  intangible, 5:398–399
  liquidity, 4:459–460
Assimilation, 1:**188–191**
  Black Power, 1:321
  Cherokees, 1:497
  child development, 1:506
  Chinese Americans, 1:514–515
  Chinese diaspora, 1:516, 517
  Coloreds (South Africa), 2:15, 16
  creolization, 2:169
  ethnic enterprises, 3:6
  ethnicity, 3:10
  Hermandez v. Texas, 3:465
  immigrants, 3:570, 574, 575, 578,
    579

Assimilation, *continued*
  indirect rule, 3:617
  Jews, 4:190, 191–192, 196
  malinchistas, 4:564–565
  multiracial meritocracy, 5:100
  Park, Robert E., 6:141–142
  Park School, 6:143
  petty bourgeoisie, 1:362
  Quebecois movement, 6:661–663
  race relations, 7:29, 32, 33
  racial slurs, 7:41
  Roma, 7:278
  self-hatred, 7:417
  sellouts, 7:134–135
  See also Melting pot
Assistance, public. *See* Public assistance
Assisted death, 1:191–192
  bioethics, 1:301
  morality, 2:248
  See also Euthanasia and assisted
    suicide
Assisted suicide. *See* Euthanasia and
  assisted suicide
Associated Community Teams (ACT),
  9:25
Associated Country Women of the
  World, 6:74
Associated Press (AP), 4:213
Association for the Advancement of
  Psychology, 1:249
Association for the Scientific Study of
  Consciousness (ASSC), 2:81
Association of Black Sociologists,
  1:324
Association of Coffee Producing
  Countries, 1:595
Associationism, 2:80, 81, 8:358
Associations, voluntary
  (organizations), 1:193–194
  cooperatives, 2:123
  international nongovernmental
    organizations, 4:96–99
  social theory, 7:628
Associations (psychology)
  classical conditioning, 1:572–574
  Mill, John Stuart, 5:178, 179
  Pavlov, Ivan, 6:178–179
  person memory, 6:216
  priming, 6:462
Assumptions, organization theory,
  6:70
Assyriology, 1:165
Astronomy, ordinary least squares,
  4:393
Astroturf NGOs, 5:520

Aswan Dam, 5:376
Asylum, political. *See* Political asylum
Asylums (Goffman), 3:337
Asymmetric information, 4:28–30
  Akerlof, George A., 1:68–69
  distortions, 2:414
  economics of information,
    4:30–32
  predatory pricing, 6:428–429
  signals, 7:507–508
  Stiglitz, Joseph E., 8:146
  trade barriers, 1:255
  zero-sum game, 9:177
Asymmetric returns to scale,
  7:223–224
Asymmetry, loss functions, 4:497–498
Asymptotic estimators. *See* Properties
  of estimators (asymptotic and exact)
Atari, 8:611
Athabaskans, 5:425
Athanasius of Alexandria, 1:532,
  2:132
Atheism, 1:194–195, 8:340
Athens (city-state), 1:544
Atkinson, Anthony, 8:530, 9:67
Atkinson, John, 1:14–15
Atkinson, Ti-Grace, 3:121
Atlanta (GA), 2:42, 3:524–525
Atlantic slave trade, 1:39–40
Atlas Shrugged (Rand), 6:7
ATM (Automated teller machines),
  1:490
Atrocities. *See* Genocide; War crimes
AT&T (American Telegraph and
  Telephone Company), 8:314, 315
Atta, Mohammed, 1:299
Attachment Q-Sort, 1:196
Attachment theory, 1:195–197
  Bowlby, John, 1:363
  child development, 1:507
  children, 1:511
  empathy, 2:574
  infant-mother, 1:76, 195–196
  Oedipus complex, 6:28–29
  parent-child relationships, 6:132
  relationship satisfaction, 7:151
  role models, 7:274
  romance, 7:281
  self-representation, 7:427
  separation anxiety, 7:447–448
  socialization, 7:647–648
  teacher-child relationships,
    8:291–292
  traumatic bonding, 8:441–442
Attention, cognition, 1:598

Attention, selective, 7:391
Attention-deficit/hyperactivity
  disorder (ADHD), 1:197–200,
  7:391
Attitude object, 1:200
Attitudes, 1:200–201
  bigotry, 1:295–296
  classical conditioning, 1:574
  cognitive dissonance, 1:600
  conformity, 2:71, 72
  differential equations, 2:365
  disability, 2:375–376
  Guttman scale, 3:398–399
  interracial marriage, 4:617
  Jung, Carl, 4:230
  Kelley, Harold, 4:252–253
  lay theories, 4:374
  Likert scale, 4:447–448
  looking-glass effect, 4:495
  message-based persuasion, 6:229
  misanthropy, 5:198
  misogyny, 5:203–204
  mood, 5:275
  norms *vs.,* 5:536
  persuasion, 6:228
  political, 1:202–204
  polling, 6:353–355
  prejudice, 6:438–440
  relationship satisfaction, 7:151
  rumors, 7:296
  sample surveys, 8:244–245
  self-consciousness, 7:400–402
  self-identity, 7:418
  Sherif, Muzafer, 7:495
  similarity/attraction theory,
    7:213–214
  sleeper effects, 7:550
  social cognition, 7:573–574
  social judgment theory,
    7:601–602
  social psychology, 7:609
  stereotypes, 8:136–139
  xenophobia, 9:158–161
Attitudes, behavioral, 1:201–202,
  3:403
Attitudes, political, 1:202–204
Attitudes, racial, 1:204–205
  colorism, 2:17–18
  political science, 7:19–20
  race-conscious policies, 7:37
Attiyah, Abdulah, 6:64
Attlee, Clement, 4:327
Attraction, personal. *See*
  Similarity/attraction theory

Attraction theory. *See* Similarity/attraction theory

Attribution, 1:**205–206**
  decision-making, 2:252
  Jones, Edward Ellsworth, 4:210–211
  Kelley, Harold, 4:253
  optimism/pessimism, 6:54
  over-attribution bias, 6:88–89
  person memory, 6:215
  person perception, 6:206
  self-justification, 7:421
  self-serving bias, 7:429
  social cognition, 7:571, 573
  trait inference, 8:424

Attributional Style Questionnaire (ASQ), 6:54

Attrition, sample. *See* Sample attrition

Attucks, Crispus, 2:315

Atwater, Lee, 4:371

Auclert, Hubertine, 3:119

Auctions, 1:**206–208**, 8:579–580, 9:103–104

Audits, for discrimination, 1:**208–210**

Auerbach, Alan, 6:93

Augmented Washington Consensus, 9:39

Augustine, Saint, 1:1, 4:235

Auletta, Ken, 8:485

Aum Shinrikyo, 1:302

Aumann, Robert, 3:173, 284

Austen-Smith, David, 1:17

Austin, Hudson, 3:383

Austin, John, 1:129, 8:38, 56

Australia
  ballots, 1:242
  bauxite industry, 1:261
  blood and bloodline, 1:336
  cattle industry, 1:470, 471
  census, 1:476
  Chinese diaspora, 1:516, 518
  citizenship, 1:543
  clash of civilizations, 1:559
  commonwealth, 2:29
  consumption, 2:107
  Cook, James, 2:121–122
  cultural resource management, 2:196
  cultural tourism, 2:202
  desegregation, 2:315
  drought, 2:448
  gender gap, 2:142
  global warming effects, 3:330
  gold mining, 3:339–340, 342
  land claims, 4:340–341
  legal systems, 4:406
  multiculturalism, 1:543
  Royal Commissions, 7:291
  Stolen Generations, 8:158–159
  urban sprawl, 8:540
  Vietnam War, 8:614
  whiteness, 9:90

Australian ballots. *See* Ballots

Australian Business Round Table on Climate Change, 3:329

Austria
  annexation by Germany, 1:115, 153
  banking industry, 1:252
  central banks, 1:477
  codetermination, 1:593
  corporatism, 2:141
  latifundia, 4:352–353
  Napoleonic Wars, 5:365, 367–369
  World War II, 9:148
  xenophobia, 9:160

Austria-Hungary, 2:63, 9:145

Austrian economics, 1:**210–212**
  capitalism, 1:439
  competition, 2:51
  conservatism, 2:84
  gold standard, 3:345
  Hayek, Friedrich August von, 3:435
  libertarianism, 4:438
  Mises, Ludwig Edler von, 5:202–203
  neoliberalism, 5:474
  Wicksell effects, 9:94–95

Austro-Marxism, 1:**212–213**, 3:476

Autarky, 1:253, 293, 444, 2:300, 3:624

Auténtico Party. *See* Partido Revolucionario Cubano (PRC)

Authenticity, leadership, 4:382

Authoritarian personality, 2:64, 6:**220–221**

The Authoritarian Personality (Adorno, Levinson, and Sanford), 1:214, 3:189, 6:220–221

Authoritarianism, 1:**213–214**
  authoritarian personality, 6:220–221
  civil-military relation, 1:547–548
  civil wars, 1:554, 555
  clash of civilizations, 1:559
  communism, 2:34
  conformity, 2:72
  conservatism, 2:84
  constructivism, 2:97
  corporatism, 2:141
  cult of personality, 6:221–223
  democracy research, 7:191
  dependency, 2:297
  description, 3:354
  dissidents, 2:411
  Hall, Stuart, 3:409–410
  Holocaust, 3:496, 497
  military regimes, 5:174–176
  monarchies, 5:237–238, 238–240
  Palestinian Authority, 6:105–106
  parent-child relationships, 6:131, 132–133
  parenting styles, 6:135, 137
  political culture, 6:301
  political psychology, 6:309
  political stability, 8:73–74
  prejudice, 6:440
  state capitalism, 1:443, 444
  USSR dissolution, 8:513
  women's movement, 9:117
  See also Dictatorship; Totalitarianism

Authority, 1:**214–215**
  Baumrind, Diana, 1:260
  charismatic, 6:68
  consensus, 2:82
  decentralization, 2:250–251
  firms, 3:149
  law, 4:363
  leaders, 4:375–377
  legal, 1:214
  legitimate, 1:214, 3:353–354
    destructive obedience, 6:2–3
    nationalism, 5:417
  Milgram, Stanley, 5:161–162
  Mills, C. Wright, 5:180–181
  political philosophy, 6:257–258
  postnationalism, 6:398
  rational-legal, 6:68
  traditional, 1:214, 6:68

Autism
  Bettelheim, Bruno, 1:290
  classical conditioning, 1:574
  social intelligence, 4:75
  theory of mind, 8:347–348

Autobiography (Malcolm X), 1:317

Autobiography (Mill), 8:553

Autocephaly, 3:376

Autocorrelation function, partial. *See* Time series regression

Autocracy, 1:**215–216**
  civil wars, 1:555
  cult of personality, 6:221–223

Autocracy, *continued*
democracy, 2:273, 274, 275
dictatorship, 2:359–360
Machiavelli, Niccolò, 4:533–534
oligarchy *vs.*, 6:36
parent-child relationships, 6:131
political stability, 8:73
Russian Federation, 7:303
Autocratic government, 3:354
Autoemancipation (Pinsker), 9:179
Autoeroticism, 3:213
Autogenocide, 3:297
Autokinetic effect, 1:**216–217**
Automated information and communication technologies (AICT), 2:217
Automated teller machines (ATM), 1:490
Automation. *See* Machinery
Automobile industry, 1:**217–224**
asymmetric information, 1:68–69
Ford Motor Company, 1:217–218, 219, 220–221, 223, 3:167–169
General Motors, 1:218, 219, 220–221, 3:167, 285–286
labor unions, 1:220, 3:168, 285–286
mass production, 1:217–218, 3:77
Nader, Ralph, 5:359
post-WWII, 3:168–169
Autonomy, 1:**224–225**
Allport, Gordon W., 1:81
Bettelheim, Bruno, 1:290
Bourdieu, Pierre, 1:358
capitalist mode of production, 1:447
children's rights, 1:512
civil society, 1:552, 553
communalism, 2:30
community power studies, 2:42, 43
cooperatives, 2:124
cultural rights, 2:197
decentralization, 2:250–251
empire, 2:576
ethics, 2:632–633
Kant, Immanuel, 4:248, 249
liberalism, 4:425
liberation, 4:429
liberty, 4:439–440
petty bourgeoisie, 1:362
politics, 6:320
privacy, 6:477

representative and participatory democracy, 2:284
self-determination, 1:224–225
separatism, 7:450–451
technophobia, 8:311
Autopoetic systems, social system, 7:626
Autor, David, 9:4
Autoregressive conditional heteroskedasticity (ARCH) model, 1:229–230, 8:587
Autoregressive fractional integrated moving average (ARFIMA) model, 9:83
Autoregressive latent trajectory analysis, 3:391–392
Autoregressive models, 1:**226–230**, 9:83
cointegration, 2:3
econometrics, 2:480–482
error-correction mechanisms, 2:627
real business cycles, 1:408–409
trends, 8:447–448
vector, 1:229, 8:598–600, 601
vector autoregression, 1:408–409
Autoregressive moving average (ARIMA) model, 1:229, 8:42–43, 517–518, 9:82–83
Autotelic experience, 3:158
Avant-garde theater, 8:338
Average and marginal costs, 1:**230–231**, *231*
Average propensity to consume (APC), 1:6–7
Average revenue, described, 7:226
Average variability, 8:590
Aversion, risk. *See* Maximin principle; Risk; Risk neutrality
Aversion therapy. *See* Psychotherapy
Aversive conditioning, 1:573, 4:387–389
Aviation industry, 1:**232–234**
Carter, Jimmy, 1:451
consumer protection, 2:102
nationalization, 5:419
technological change, 1:490
transportation industry, 8:436–438
Avoidance, tax. *See* Tax evasion and tax avoidance
Avoiding Social and Ecological Disaster (Bahro). *See* Logik der Rettung (Bahro)
Awareness. *See* Consciousness
Awareness, control groups, 8:574

Axelrod, Robert, 3:32
Axis (World War II), 1:79
Axis Rule in Occupied Europe (Lemkin), 3:296
Ayahuasca, 3:410, 412
Ayres, Clarence E., 4:337
Azande, 7:122–123
Azerbaijan, 2:30
Aztecs, 3:515, 516, 6:426, 427
Azzam, Abdullah, 1:70, 298

B

Baa Baa Black Sheep (nursery rhyme), 5:550
Ba'ath Party (Iraq). *See* Hussein, Saddam
Baba: Men and Fatherhood in South Africa (Richter and Morrell), 3:106–107
Babbage, Charles, 2:424
Babcock, Barbara, 7:258
Babies. *See* Children; Infants
Baby boomers, 1:**235–236**
demographic transition, 2:291
Kennedy, John F., 4:255
social demography, 2:296–297
Babylonia, 1:206, 4:190, 193–194
Bacchanalia, 2:189, 6:20
Bach, Johann Sebastian, 1:575
Bach, Robert L., 4:359–360
Bachelier, Louis, 1:228, 2:548
See also Efficient market hypothesis (EMH)
Bachrach, Peter, 1:48, 2:219, 5:518
Back to Africa movement, 1:41, 316, 3:258
See also Repatriation
Backus, David K., 5:491
Backward conditioning, 1:573
Backward countries. *See* Developing countries
Backwardation, 1:450, 2:113
See also Carrying cost; Contango
Backwards Classes (India), 1:458, 459, 2:161, 222
Backwash effects, 1:**236–237**
Bacon, Francis, 7:362, 363
Badenhorst, L. T., 3:127
Badillo, Herman, 9:25
Bagehot, Walter, 1:478, 4:410, 485
Baghdad Conference (1960), 6:65
Bahrain, Gulf Cooperation Council, 3:397
Bahro, Rudolf, 1:**237–238**, 392
Bailey, Ron, 2:14–15
Bainbridge, William, 2:61, 188, 3:241

Baird, Eisenstadt v. (1972), 3:90, 7:271
Bajari, Patrick, 1:207–208
Baker, Ella. *See* Student Nonviolent
    Coordinating Committee
Baker, Lee, 1:133
Baker Plan, 9:138
Baker v. Carr (1962), 9:33
Bakhtin, Mikhail
    hybridity, 3:535–536
    linguistic anthropology, 1:130
    narratives, 5:371
    otherness, 6:82–83
    youth culture, 9:168
Bakke, California v. (1978). *See*
    Grutter decision (1978)
*Bakke, Regents of the University of
    California v.* (1978). *See Grutter*
    decision
Bakr, Ahmad Hasan al-, 3:532
Bakunin, Mikhail, 1:111, 4:517
Bakweri, 9:181
Bal, Mieke, 5:371
Balance, cognitive balance. *See*
    Cognitive dissonance; Equilibrium
    in psychology
Balance of payments, 1:**238–241**, 239*t*
    currency appreciation and
        depreciation, 2:210
    currency devaluation and
        revaluation, 2:211–212
    foreign reserves, 7:202–203
    Hume process, 3:520–521
    international economics, 2:508
    trade deficit, 8:415–416
Balance of power
    civil-military relation, 1:547–548
    Cold War, 2:4–5
    constitutions, 2:94
    corruption, 2:144
    defense, 2:257–259
    developing countries, 2:335–336
    domino theory, 2:434–436
    ethnic fractionalization, 3:6, 7
    game theory, 3:251
    history, 9:146
    Iran-Iraq War, 4:143
    Kissinger, Henry, 4:274, 275
    League of Nations, 4:385
    Morgenthau, Hans, 5:295
    multilateralism, 5:321
    mutual deterrence, 2:334–335
    political realism, 7:96–97
    politics, 6:320
    republicanism, 7:188
    Trilateral Commission, 8:452–453

Balance of trade, 1:**241–242**
    balance of payments, 1:238–240
    central banks, 1:478
    currency appreciation and
        depreciation, 2:210
    described, 8:411–412
    exports, 3:67, 68–69
    Hume process, 3:520–521
    J-Curve, 4:179
    trade surplus, 8:417–418
Balance sheet effect, 2:210
Balanced reciprocity. *See* Reciprocity
Balances, checks and. *See* Checks and
    balances
Balassa-Samuelson effect, 3:349
Balbir Sihag, 9:45
Baldwin, Alfred, 6:131
Baldwin, David, 5:412
Baldwin, James, 9:91
Baldwin, Stanley, 1:489
Balen, Frank van, 3:116
Bales, Robert, 3:386
Balfour-Paul, H. G., 3:126
Balibar, Etienne, 1:447
Balkan War, concentration camps,
    2:64
Balkanization, of labor markets, 5:515
Ball, John, 3:301
Ball family, 4:528
Ballet. *See* Dance
Balliol College, 8:528
Ballots, 1:**242–243**, 2:561
Balseros, 3:571
Balzac, Honoré de, 5:442
BAM (Black Arts Movement). *See*
    Black Arts Movement (BAM)
Bambaataa, Afrika, 3:480–481
Bamboozled (film), 1:**243–245**, 7:314
Banana Boat Song, 1:418
Banana industry, 1:**245–247**
Banana parable, 1: **247–248**
Banditos. *See* Villa, Francisco
Bands, autocracy, 1:216
Bandura, Albert, 1:**248–249**
    cognition, 1:597
    reciprocal determinism, 2:331
    social leaning perspective,
        7:602–603
    socialization, 7:647
    time orientation, 8:368
Bangladesh
    Grameen Bank, 3:362–363
    land reform, 4:343, 344
    Raj, 7:55
    water resources, 9:41

Banig, 9:141–142
Banjo (McKay), 3:426
Bank Act (U.S. 1933), 1:252
Bank Charter Act (U.K. 1944), 4:485
Bank of England, 1:477, 4:410, 6:31
    history, 1:251
    Lombard Street, 4:485
    quantity index, 6:658
    Ricardo, David, 7:243
    Soros, George, 8:31
Bank of Latin America, 6:31
Bank runs. *See* Economic crises; Panics
Banking, 1:**249–250**
    bourgeoisie, 1:360
    coordination failure, 2:128
    development, 9:139
    endogenous money, 5:257
    Federal Reserve System,
        3:110–111, 112–113
    Great Depression failures,
        3:367–369, 370, 5:496
    herd behavior, 3:459–460
    Hilferding, Rudolf, 3:476
    international economic order, 4:93
    investment, 8:605
    lender of last resort, 4:409–410
    loans, 4:472
    merchant, 6:31
    New Deal, 5:496
    offshore, 3:504, 6:30–33
    panics, 6:124–125
    secrecy laws, 6:32
    technological change, 1:490
    Vatican, 8:593
    See also Central banks
*Banking in the Early Stages of
    Industrialization, A Study in
    Comparative Economic History*
    (Cameron and Patrick), 1:19
Banking industry, 1:**250–254**
    black capitalism, 1:440, 441
    casino capitalism, 1:455
    central banks, 1:478
    development economics, 2:345
    Keynes, John Maynard, 4:261
    lender of last resort, 4:409–410
    loans, 4:473
    Rothschilds, 7:289
    savings and loan crisis,
        overlending, 6:94
    Soros, George, 8:31
Banks, central. *See* Central banks
Banks, commercial. *See* Banking
    industry
Banks, Daniel, 1:98

Bans. *See* Regulation

Banting, Keith, 9:72

Bantu Authorities Act (South Africa 1951), 1:148

Bantus, 6:12

BAPA (Bilateral Advanced Pricing Agreement), 8:428

Baptism, 1:457, 531

Baptists, Christian fundamentalism, 3:236

Bar charts. frequency distributions, 3:207–208, *208*

Baraka, Amiri, 1:309

Baran, Paul, 2:299, 3:621, 5:266, 8:488, 489–490

Baratz, Morton, 1:48, 2:219, 5:518

Barbados, 1:330, 393

Barbaresi, William J., 1:198

Barbarism, 8:595–596

Barbiturates, 2:454

Barchas, Jack, 1:248

Bards. *See* Storytelling

Bargaining
interest-based, 5:457
positional, 5:457
solution, Nash, 5:373
See also Negotiation; Screening and signaling games

Bargh, John, 2:249

Baring, Francis, 4:410

Barkow, Jerome, 5:440

Barnett, Ross, 1:551

Barnett, William A., 4:459

Barone, Enrico, 8:108

Baroque architecture, 1:171

Barrès, Maurice, 2:84

Barriers to trade, 1:254–255
automobile industry, 1:221–222
bilateral trade, 8:414–415
common market, 2:29
customs union, 2:215
export penetration, 3:66
exports, 3:68
import penetration, 3:590, 591
tariffs, 8:265–266
tea industry, 8:289
trade liberalization, 4:427–428
trade quotas, 6:672–673

Barro, Robert J., 1:255–256, 9:13
bequests, 1:287
Ricardian equivalence, 7:240, 241

Barro-Grossman model, 1:**255–256**

Barrows, 1:166

Barrows, Harlan, 5:433

Bartering. *See* Trade

Barth, Fredrik, 1:128

Barthes, Roland, 2:199, 5:371, 6:398, 399

Bartlett, Frederic Charles, 1:597

Bartley, Robert L., 2:85

Basal ganglia, 6:18

Basel Accord (1988), 1:253–254

Basel Accord (2004), 1:254

Basel Ban Amendment. *See* Toxic waste

Basel Convention. *See* Toxic Waste

Basic ecclesial communities (BEC), 4:436

Basic needs, 5:**455–456**
malnutrition, 4:567–568
Maslow, Abraham, 5:451
self-determination theory, 7:407–408

Basic Needs Approach (BNA), 5:456

Basic real wages, 3:218

Basle Committee on Banking Supervision, 6:33

Basle Concordant (1988), 6:30

Bass, Bernard, 4:376, 377, 378

Bastiat, Frédéric, laissez-faire, 4:335, 336

Bates, John E., 8:321, 322

Bates, Robert, 1:595

Bates, Timothy, 2:182

Ba'th Arab Socialist Party. *See* Hussein, Saddam

Batista, Fulgencio, 1:464, 465, 2:185, 186
See also Cuban Revolution

La battaglia di Algeri (film). *See The Battle of Algiers* (film)

Battista, Robert J., 4:317

Battle of Algiers (1957), 1:257–258

The Battle of Algiers (film), 1:**257–258**

Battle of Goose Green (1982), 3:81

Battle of the Little Big Horn (1876), 1:**258–259**, 5:426, 7:522

Battle of the Sommes (1916), 9:18

Battle of Waterloo (1815), 5:366, 368

Batur, Pinar, 9:91

Baudelaire, Charles, 7:92

Baudrillard, Jean, 2:97, 203–204, 5:32, 8:597

Bauer, Bruno, 3:587
See also Imperialism

Baum, Lyman Frank, 9:104–105

Bauman, Zygmunt, 2:320, 3:496

Baumgarten, Alexander, 1:30, 48

Baumgartner, Frank, 3:609–610

Baumol, William J., 3:148, 6:653

Baumol-Tobin model, 8:378

Baumrind, Diana, 1:**260–261**, 6:132–133, 135–136, 137

Bauxite industry, 1:**261**

Bavaria. *See* Germany

Bavelas, Alex, 5:479

Baxter, James, 5:530

Bay of Pigs, 1:**262**
Castro, Fidel, 1:465
Central Intelligence Agency, U.S, 1:483
Cold War, 2:5
Cuba, 2:186
Kennedy, John F., 4:254
Khrushchev, Nikita, 4:264

Bayes, Thomas, 1:262, 265, 4:13

Bayes-Nash equilibrium, 5:375

Bayes' theorem, 1:**262–263**, 265–266, 6:486

Bayesian calculations, game theory, 3:251

Bayesian econometrics, 1:262, **263–266**, 6:487–488

Bayesian inference, 1:262, 4:**13–14**, *14*, 8:122

Bayesian statistics, 1:**266–267**
Bayes' theorem, 1:263
Dawes, Robyn, 2:244
limits in probability, 6:487–488

Bazerman, Max H., 9:103

BBC (British Broadcasting Company). *See* Television

BEA (U.S. Bureau of Economic Analysis), 4:331–332, 6:658

Beale, Calvin, 1:61

Bear market. *See* Bull and bear markets

Beard, Charles, 1:**268–269**, 5:500, 6:311–312

Beard, Mary, 1:**268–269**

Bearden, Jim, 5:476

Beat Zen. *See* Buddhism

Beauty
aesthetics, 1:30
feminine, 3:118–119
whitening, 9:89

Beauty contest metaphor, 1:**269–270**

Beauvoir, Simone de, 3:120
femininity, 3:118
gender, 3:267
sex *vs.* gender, 9:116

BEC (Basic ecclesial communities), 4:436

Bechtel, William, 7:119

Beck, E. M., 4:526

Beck, Ulrich, 2:149, 8:657
Becker, Gary S., 1:**270–272**
    age discrimination, 2:402
    Chicago School, 1:502
    consumer, 2:101
    discrimination, 2:388–390,
        398–399
    female-headed families, 3:115
    marginal product of labor, 4:306
    National Economic Association,
        5:389
    o-ring theory, 6:77
    optimizing behavior, 6:56
    positive social science, 6:389
    race, 7:14
    time allocation, 8:363, 364
    wages, 2:400, 403, 405, 9:4
    War on Poverty, 9:28
    workplace relations, 9:135
Becker, George, 4:321
Becker, Gordon, 8:580
Becker, Howard, 3:266, 4:445, 8:7
Becker, Robert, 6:52
Beckwith, Karen, 9:116
Bedouins, virgins, 8:630
Beef industry. *See* Cattle industry
Bees, vanilla industry, 8:583
Beggar-thy-neighbor, 1:**272–273**
    currency devaluation and
        revaluation, 2:211
    J-Curve, 4:179
    product dumping, 2:462
Begin, Menachem, 1:283
Beginnings: Intention and Method
    (Said), 7:310
Behaim, Martin, 2:20
Behavior
    altruism and prosocial, 3:414–415
    attitudes, 1:204–205
    butterfly effect, 1:414
    Child Behavior Checklist,
        1:504–505
    crime and criminology,
        2:170–174, 172–173
    culture of poverty, 2:206
    Darwin, Charles, 2:229–232
    Exit, Voice, and Loyalty
        (Hirschman), 3:43–45
    flight, 6:123
    genetic determinism, 2:329–330
    habits, 3:402–404
    habitus, 3:404–406
    herd, 3:459–460, 4:201–202
    heredity, 3:461
    ideal type, 3:546–547

ingratiation, 4:34
lifestyles, 4:445
lying, 4:524–525
morality, 5:283–286
mystification, 5:353–355
natural selection, 5:440–441
neuroscience research, 5:484–485
nonverbal, 5:530–531
optimizing, 6:55–56
    golden rule in growth
        models, 3:346
    objective functions, 6:6
panic, 6:122–123
pluralistic ignorance, 3:560–561
political, 8:606
prosocial, 1:88–89
rationality, 7:79
reflection problem, 7:121–122
rumors, 7:296
self-control, 7:402–404
self-defeating, 7:404–405
self-identity, 7:418
social experiments, 7:590–592
social psychology, 7:609
spatial, 5:530
temperament, 8:321–322
theory, 8:344–345
trait inference, 8:424
trait theory, 8:425–426
visual, 5:530
See also Conformity; Strategic
    behavior
Behavior, herd. *See* Herd behavior
Behavior, optimizing. *See* Optimizing
    behavior
Behavior, prosocial. *See* Altruism and
    prosocial behavior
Behavior, satisficing. *See* Satisficing
    behavior
Behavior, self-constrained, 1:**273–274**,
    2:572–573, 574
Behavior, strategic. *See* Strategic
    behavior
Behavior in Public Places (Goffman),
    3:337
Behavior-status link. *See* Role theory
Behavioral attitudes, 1:**201–202**,
    3:403
Behavioral economics, 2:**499–502**
    Becker, Gary S., 1:270–271
    economic psychology, 2:495
    Hamilton's rule, 3:414, 415
    happiness, 3:415–419
    lexicographic preferences,
        4:422–423

microeconomics, 5:133–136
neuroeconomics, 5:483–484
poverty, 6:407
strategic behavior, 8:162–163
Behavioral genetics, 5:446
Behavioral political science,
    6:312–314, **315–316**
    Easton, David, 2:476–477
    Lasswell, Harold, 4:351
    Merriam, Charles Edward, Jr.,
        5:101–102
    Miller, Warren, 5:180–181
    opinion polls, 6:356
    spatial theory, 8:44–45
Behavioral therapy. *See* Psychotherapy
Behaviorial Risk Factor Surveillance
    System (BRFSS), 8:657
Behaviorism, 1:**274–281**
    Chomsky, Noam, 1:527, 528
    classical conditioning, 1:572–574
    cognition, 1:596–597
    cognitive dissonance, 1:600
    consciousness, 2:81
    described, 1:274–275
    developmental psychology, 2:350
    functionalism, 3:231
    genetic determinism, 2:329
    habits, 3:402, 403
    history, 1:275–276
    Hull, Clark, 3:505–506
    leadership, 4:379
    mental health, 5:86
    objections to, 1:279–280
    parent-child relationships,
        6:131–132
    philosophical, 1:274, 275,
        277–279
    prediction, 6:430
    psychological, 1:276–277
    reinforcement theories, 7:146–148
    Skinner, B. F., 7:525–527
    Skinner box, 7:528
    smoking, 7:559–560
    social leaning perspective,
        7:602–603
    tastes, 8:268
    taxes, 8:282–283
    Thorndike, Edward, 8:358–359
    Tolman, Edward, 8:386–387
Behemoth (Hobbes), 3:493
*Behemoth : The Structure and Practice
    of National Socialism* (Neumann),
    5:482
Behind the Label (Bonacich and
    Appelbaum), 1:351

Beijing Declaration and Platform for Action (UN), 9:110, 114
Being Black, Living in the Red (Conley), 8:534
Being seen vs. seeing, 3:263
Belafonte, Harry, 1:418
Belarus, 2:30
Belgian Congo. *See* Congo
Belgium
    air pollution, 6:362
    colonialism, 3:568, 569
    common market, 2:28
    compulsory voting, 2:59
    Lumumba, Patrice, 4:517–518
    Mobutu, Joseph, 5:215–217
    national debt, 5:386
    neutrality, 5:488, 490
    unemployment compensation, 2:49
    World War I, 9:145–147, 146
Belief systems
    attitudes, 1:202
    cultural relativism, 1:123
    evolution of, 1:119
    referential, 3:386
    status, 3:386
    See also Lay theories
Beliefs. *See* Attitudes
Beliefs, false. *See* Lay theories
Belize, 3:257–258
Bell, Alexander Graham, 8:314
Bell, Buck v. (1927), 8:141
Bell, Daniel, 2:60, 3:240, 4:283–284
    futurology, 3:241
    neoconservatism, 5:468
    post-Parsonian American sociology, 8:6
Bell, Derrick, 1:374, 375, 377, 5:372
    social status, 7:621
    See also Critical race theory
Bell, John, 7:542
Bell, Wendell, 8:541
Bell curve. *See* Normal distribution
The Bell Curve (Herrnstein and Murray), 1:15–16, 2:326, 3:160, 4:73, 7:22
Bell System, 6:651, 8:314
Bellamy, Edward, 8:312, 561
Bellamy, John D., 9:99
Bellecourt, Vernon, 1:98
Belmont Report, 3:60–61, 4:33, 43
Belonging, 3:385, 6:61
Belzoni, Giovanni, 1:165
Bem, Daryl, 1:600
    See also Self-perception theory

Bemba, 9:108
Ben-Gurion, David, 1:**282–283**
Benartzi, Shlomo, 2:252–253
Bendix, Reinhard, 1:563
Benedict, Ruth, 1:120, **281–282**, 5:455
    Boas, Franz, 1:345
    Cox, Oliver C., 2:158
    cultural relativism, 2:195
    determinism, 2:323
Benedict XVI, Pope, 7:280
Benefits, employee, 9:128
Bengal, famine, 3:164
Benhabib, Jess, 6:51–52
Benign neglect, 1:**283–284**
    Central Intelligence Agency, U.S, 1:484–485
    culture of poverty, 2:206
    Moynihan, Daniel Patrick, 5:304–305
    Moynihan Report, 5:306
Benin, 1:38, 3:275
Benjamin, Judah P., 1:**284–285**
Benjamin, Walter, 2:177, 203, 5:370–371
Bennett, Rolla, 8:609
Bennett, William, 2:326
Benston, Kimberly, 1:309
Bentham, Jeremy, 1:**285–286**
    distributive justice, 4:239
    happiness, 3:415
    Kant, Immanuel, 4:249
    laissez-faire, 4:335
    law and economics, 4:367
    liberalism, 4:425
    marginalism, 4:597
    Mill, John Stuart, 5:178
    objective utility, 8:557
    panoptic gaze, 3:262
    rhetoric, 7:238
    subjective utility, 8:558
    utilitarianism, 8:553–554
    utility function, 8:554–555
Benz, Carl, 1:217
Benzodiazepines, 1:147, 2:454
Bequests, 1:**286–288**
    black middle class, 1:314
    inheritance, 4:35
    life-cycle hypothesis, 4:442, 443
    in vivo transfers, 3:597
Bereavement, 3:239
Berelson, Bernard, 1:202
Berg, Ivar E., 1:**288–289**
Berger, Peter, 2:96, 3:403, 6:69–70, 7:162

Berghe, Pierre van den, 2:201
Bergman, Gustav, 4:457
Bergmann, Barbara R., 2:181, 403
    See also Crowding hypothesis
Bergson, Henri, 2:7, 22, 23
Berkeley, George, 2:578, 3:521, 547
Berle, Adolf A., 1:361, 442, 5:495
Berle and means. *See* Managerial capitalism
Berlin, Isaiah, 4:424, 439–440
Berlin Wall, 1:**289**
    Cold War, 2:5
    decisive events, 2:254
    iron curtain, 4:150
Berlusconi, Silvio, 1:558, 2:84, 9:160
Bernadotte, Folke, 1:387
Bernal, Maestro, 2:20
Bernanke, Ben, 1:252, 3:370, 380
Bernard, H. Russell, 1:138
Bernoulli, Daniel, 5:519, 8:331
    See also Expectations; Expected utility theory; Von Neumann-Morgenstern utility
Bernoulli, John, 8:331
Bernstein, Carl, 4:215, 9:43
Bernstein, Eduard, 1:446, 3:74
Bernstein, Irwin, 1:83
Bernstein, Jared, 6:99
Berreman, Gerald, 1:460, 462
Berry, Wendell, 2:39
Bertrand, Marianne, 2:142
Bertrand's paradox, 2:419
Besant, Annie, 5:460
Best, Lloyd. *See* Lewis, W. Arthur
Best linear unbiased estimator (BLUE), 5:521
Beta distribution. *See* Probability distributions
Betances, Ramón Emeterio, 1:355
Béteille, André, 1:458
Bettelheim, Bruno, 1: **290–292**, 4:171, 172
Between Facts and Norms (Habermas), 2:179, 3:401
Bevan, Aneurin, 4:327
Bevan, Nye. *See* Bevan, Aneurin
Beverages, alcoholic. *See* Spirits industry
Beveridge, William H., 1:292, 3:227, 8:16
Beveridge curve, 1:**292**
Beveridge model. *See* Welfare state
Beveridge Report (1942), 9:69
Bevin, Ernest, 4:327
Beyond a Boundary (James), 4:168

Beyond Human Scale (Ginzberg), 3:324

Beyond Interpretation: The Meaning of Hermeneutics for Philosophy (Vattimo), 3:463

Beyond Left and Right (Giddens), 3:314

Beyond the Melting Pot (Glazer and Moynihan), 3:327

Beyond the Nuclear Family Model (Leñero-Otero), 3:87

Beyond the Pleasure Principle (Freud), 3:210, 215

Bhabha, Homi, 3:536

Bhagavad Gita, 1:185, 8:568

Bhagwati, Jagdish, 1:**292–293**, 367, 368, 3:583, 8:510

Bharatiya Jana Sangh (BJS), 8:569

Bharatiya Janata Party (BJP), 2:76, 77, 8:569

Bhindranwale, Jarnail Singh, 7:509

Bhopal. *See* Disaster management

Bhutto, Zulfikar Ali, 7:644

BIA (Bureau of Indian Affairs), 1:99, 5:428

Bian, Yanjie, 8:534

Bias
    attributional, 1:206
    cross-sectional research, 7:189
    documentary studies, 2:434
    ethnographic research, 7:193–194
    internal validity, 8:574
    media, 1:529
    mobilization of, 5:518
    mortality, 8:574
    over-attribution, 6:88–89
    politics, 7:20
    professional journals, 5:105
    racial inequality, 4:6
    rites of passage, 7:258
    skill, 8:300–302
    social cognition, 7:570
    standardized tests, 8:96–98
    survey methods, 5:117
    survey research, 7:197
    teacher expectations, 8:291

Bias, selection. *See* Selection bias

Bias, self-serving. *See* Self-serving bias

Bias, simultaneity. *See* Simultaneity bias

Bias, simultaneous equation. *See* Simultaneous equation bias

Bias, statistical. *See* Properties of estimators (asymptotic and exact)

Bias, urban. *See* Urban bias

Bias crimes. *See* Hate crimes

Biased policing, 6:**289–291**
    discrimination, 2:390
    integration, 4:61
    racial democracy, 2:282

Bible
    Christianity, 1:530–531
    The Church, 1:532
    creationism, 2:161–163
    fundamentalism, 3:234–235, 236
    hell, 3:457–458
    Jesus Christ, 4:187, 188
    Jews, 4:194

Bicameralism, 1:**294**
    Congress, U.S., 2:73
    Constitution, U.S., 2:91
    constitutions, 2:95
    Diet (Japan), 2:360

Bickle, Alexander M., 2:93

Bid-ask spreads, 8:**69–70**

Bid-rent theory, 8:541

Bidding
    auctions, 1:206–208
    winner's curse, 9:103–104

Big band music. *See* Swing music

Big Brother. *See* Cult of personality

Big push. *See* Threshold effects

Bigamy. *See* Marriage

Bigotry, 1:**295–296**, 2:405
    See also Prejudice; Racism

Biko, Steve, 1:148, 545, 4:430

Bilal, 1:39

Bilateral Advanced Pricing Agreement (BAPA), 8:428

Bilateral monopoly. *See* Monopoly

Bilateral trade, 8:**414–415**
    Anglo-Portuguese trade, 8:413
    import promotion, 3:592

Bilateralism, 1:**296–297**, 2:211

Bilingual Education Act 9U.S. 1968), 3:372

Bill of Rights, U.S., 1:**297–298**, 9:33
    Church and state, 1:534–536
    civil liberties, 1:546–547, 548
    civil rights, 1:548
    Constitution, U.S., 2:91, 92
    due process, 2:461
    liberty, 4:440

Bimetallism, 3:151, 344–345

Bimodal distribution, 1:488

bin Laden, Osama, 1:70–71, **298–300**
    Bush, George W., 1:399
    national defense, 2:261
    September 11, 2001, 7:452–453

Binary gender, alternatives, 3:270–272, 6:663

Binary operations. *See* Symbols

Binford, Lewis, 1:167, 168

Binge eating, 6:89–90

Bingham, Hiram, 1:166

Binnig, Gerd, 5:361

Biobanks, 3:295

Biodeterminism. *See* Biological determinism

Bioeconomics, overfishing, 6:91

Bioethics, 1:**300–301**, 7:178–179, 183

Biological anthropology, 1:117–118, **125–127**
    African burial grounds, 1:393–394
    Boas, Franz, 1:344–345
    race, 7:8–11

Biological determinism, 2:**325–327**, 3:353
    cultural group selection, 2:191–192
    empathy, 2:574
    essentialism, 2:630–631, 631
    evolutionary psychology, 3:33
    gender preference, 6:434
    genetic determinism, 2:329
    intelligence, 4:72–73
    IQ controversy, 4:139–142
    maturation, 5:34, 35
    race, 7:2–7, 8–11, 23
    racial inequality, 4:5
    racialization, 7:43
    Scarr, Sandra Wood, 7:340–341
    temperament, 8:321–322
    twin studies, 8:473–475

Biological life, gender, 3:268, 9:107–110

Biological needs, 3:232, 5:451, 455

Biological weapons, 1:301–302, 9:52

Biological weight. *See* Body image; Body mass index; Obese externality; Obesity; Overeating; Undereating; Weight

Biology
    alpha-males, 1:83–84
    consciousness, 2:81
    contemporary human, 1:118
    creationism *vs.*, 2:163
    evolutionary, 3:352–353, 5:367
    psychological depression, 2:307
    violence, 8:627–628
    See also Sociobiology

Biomedicine. *See* Medicine

Biopsychosocial model, addiction, 1:22

Bioterrorism, 1:**301–302**, 2:155, 8:330

Bipolar disorder. *See* Manias; Manic depression; Schizophrenia

Biracial classification, 1:36

Biracials. *See* Multiracials; Race mixing

Birdwhistell, Raymond, 2:32, 5:530

Birmingham (AL), civil rights, 1:550

Birth. *See* Childbirth

Birth, sex ration at, 3:366

Birth control, 1:**302–303**
    demographic transition, 2:291
    out-of-wedlock births, 1:308
    population control, 6:377–378
    reproduction, 7:178, 179
    reproductive politics, 7:180, 181, 182
    reproductive rights, 7:182, 183
    See also Contraception; Family planning

Birth of a Nation (film), 1: **304–306**, 3:347, 9:102

The Birth of Pleasure (Gilligan), 3:320

The Birth of the Clinic (Foucault), 3:182

Birth rates. *See* Births

Birth strike. *See* Demographic transition

Births
    baby boomers and, 1:235
    crude, 3:127
    Green Revolution, 3:378
    See also Multiple births

Births, multiple. *See* Multiple births

Births, out-of-wedlock, 1:**306–308**

Bisexuals. *See* Gay, lesbian, transgender, and bisexual politics

Bishop, Maurice, 3:381–383

Bishop, Shelton Hale, 9:24

Bismarck, Otto von, 1:297, 3:587, 9:17

Bismarckian model. *See* Welfare state

Bissell, Richard, 1:267

Bittker, Boris, 7:213–214

BJP (Bharatiya Janata Party), 2:76, 77, 8:569

BJS (Bharatiya Jana Sangh), 8:569

Black, Donald, 8:6

Black, Duncan, 1:184, 524

Black, Earl, 6:339, 340

Black, Fischer, 3:142

Black, John D., 3:246

Black, Merle, 6:339, 340

Black Americans. *See* African Americans

Black Americans in Affluent Suburbs (Ogbu), 6:34

Black Arts Movement (BAM), 1:**309–310**

Black Arts Repertory Theatre/School, 1:309

Black Bourgeoisie (Frazier), 3:192

Black Brazilian Front. *See* Frente Negra Brasileira

Black capitalism, 1:**439–442**
    black conservatism, 1:311
    black liberalism, 1:312
    black nationalism, 1:316
    diamond industry, 2:355
    ethnic enterprises, 3:4–5
    internal colony, 2:13
    middleman minorities, 5:147–148

Black Caribs. *See* Garifuna

Black codes. *See* Jim Crow

Black colleges, 1:32

Black-Connery Bill, 9:127

Black conservatism, 1:**310–311**
    black liberalism, 1:312
    black nationalism, 1:318
    development, 2:86

Black Death. *See* Disease; Nursery rhymes; Public health

Black dysfunctionality hypothesis, 3:327

Black Economic Development Conference, 9:28

Black enterprise. *See* Black capitalism; Ethnic enterprises

Black face
    Jim Crow, 4:198–199
    minstrelsy, 5:195
    Sambo, 7:313, 314

Black Folk Then and Now (Drake), 2:442

Black Identities (Waters), 1:191

Black immigrants, 1:313, 315, 316, 3:**564–567**, 566t

Black inferiority. *See* White supremacy

The Black Jacobins: Toussaint L'ouverture and the San Domingo Revolution (James), 4:168, 9:97

Black liberalism, 1:**312–313**

Black Manhattan (Johnson), 3:423

Black market. *See* Informal economy

Black Marxism, 4:**641–643**
    black liberalism, 1:312
    Harlem Renaissance, 3:426
    Harris, Abram L., Jr., 3:426–427
    James, C. L. R., 4:168

Black Marxism: The Making of the Black Radical Tradition (Robinson), 1:310

Black Metropolis: A Study of Negro Life in a Northern City (Drake and Cayton), 2:181

Black middle class, 1:35, 36, **313–315**, 3:192
    educational achievement, 6:34
    internal colony, 2:13
    quotas, 6:671
    schooling, 7:351

Black Muslims. *See* Nation of Islam (NOI)

The Black Muslims in America (Lincoln), 5:379

Black nationalism, 1:**315–318**
    back to Africa movement, 3:258
    black capitalism, 1:439
    black liberalism, 1:312
    black Marxism, 4:642
    Black Panthers, 1:319
    Black Power, 1:321
    blackness, 1:329
    Garvey, Marcus, 3:258–259
    James, C. L. R., 4:168
    Malcolm X, 4:563–564
    Muhammad, Elijah, 5:310
    Pan-African Congresses, 6:112–115
    Rastafari, 7:66–70

Black Panther Party for Self-Defense (BPP). *See* Black Panthers

Black Panthers, 1:**318–320**
    black nationalism, 1:317
    Black Power, 1:321
    civil rights movement, U.S., 1:552
    Davis, Angela, 2:242
    NAACP, 5:385

Black politics, 6:**323–326**
    black Marxism, 4:641–642
    Chisholm, Shirley, 1:522
    Coloreds (South Africa), 2:15–17
    Defender, 1:501
    Harris, Abram L., Jr., 3:427
    public opinion, 7:18–20
    Southern politics, 6:343–346

Black Power, 1:**320–322**
    Black Arts Movement, 1:309
    black liberalism, 1:312
    black nationalism, 1:315–318
    Black Panthers, 1:318–320, 319–320
    black politics, 6:324–325
    blackness, 1:328–329

calypso, 1:418
    civil rights movement, U.S., 1:552
    Congress of Racial Equality, 2:75
    Forman, James, 3:174–175
    Haitian Revolution, 3:408
    Harris, Abram L., Jr., 3:427
    ideology, 1:35–36
    internal colony, 2:13
    Kerner Commission Report, 4:258
    King, Martin Luther, Jr., 4:269
    law and order, 4:369
    liberation theology, 4:435
    Malcolm X, 4:563–564
    NAACP, 5:385
    Olympic Games, 6:40
    Pan-African Congresses,
        6:112–115
    Rastafari, 7:66–67
    reggae, 7:129
    Rodney, Walter, 7:269–270
    self-determination, 7:407
*Black Power: The Politics of Liberation
    in America* (Carmichael and
    Hamilton), 1:317, 2:13
Black Reconstruction (Du Bois), 9:77
Black Seminoles. *See* Osceola
Black September, 1:**322–323**
    Hussein, King of Jordan, 3:531
    Hussein, Saddam, 3:533
    Palestine Liberation Organization,
        6:103
Black Skin, White Masks (Fanon),
    2:257, 3:99, 262, 4:430
Black sociologists, 1:**323–325**, 7:667
Black Star Line, 3:258
Black studies. *See* African American
    studies
Black towns, 1:45–46, **325–326**, 328
Black underclass. *See* Underclass
Black-white achievement gap. *See*
    Racial achievement gap
The Black-White Test Score Gap
    (Jencks), 4:184
Black women
    feminism, 9:119
    gender, 3:268
    women's studies, 9:119
The Black Worker (Harris), 5:389
The Blacker the Berry … (Thurman),
    2:17
Blackface, 1:**326–327**
    Bamboozled, 1:243, 244
    Birth of a Nation (film), 1:305
Blackfoot tribe, 9:109
Blacklisting. *See* Discrimination

Blackman, Garfield, 1:419
Blackmun, Harry, 7:271
Blackness, 1:**328–330**
    Bamboozled, 1:243
    black nationalism, 1:315–318
    blackface, 1:326–327
    Boricua, 1:355, 356
    Coloreds (South Africa), 2:15–16
    colorism, 2:17–18
    Creole, 2:168
    defined, 5:514
    Diop, Cheikh Anta, 2:368–370
    Fanon, Frantz, 3:99–100
    Haiti, 2:468–469, 3:406–408
    immigrants, 3:565, 580
    Latino National Political Survey,
        4:355
    Memín Pinguín, 5:73–74
    Mexican Americans, 5:119–120
    moreno/morena, 5:293–294
    mulatto escape hatch, 5:310–312
    mulattos, 5:312–313
    mutiracials, 5:332–333
    phenotype, 6:243–245
    race, 7:2–7, 8–11, 13
    Sambo, 7:312–314
    trigueño, 8:452
    Uncle Tom, 8:482–483
Blacks. *See* African Americans;
    Blackness
Blackstone, William, 1:285, 495
Blair, Tony, 1:**330–331**
    Bush, George W., 1:399
    centrism, 1:489
    Conservative Party (U.K.), 2:88
    Labour Party (U.K.), 4:326
    Liberal Party (U.K.), 4:423
    Thatcher, Margaret, 8:335
    xenophobia, 9:161
Blair House Accord (1992), 8:69
The Blair Revolution (Mandelson and
    Liddle), 4:326
Blaming the victim. *See* Culture of
    poverty
Blanchard, Kenneth, 4:379, 380
Blanchot, Maurice, 3:182
Bland, Bobby "Blue," 1:343
Blank slate. *See* Tabula rosa
Blanquemiento. *See* Whitening
Blatchford, Herb, 1:98
Blatz, William, 1:67
Blau, Judith, 2:318, 4:524
Blau, Peter M., 1:**331–332**
    class, 1:563

Duncan, Otis Dudley, 2:463
    intergenerational transmission,
        4:88
    post-Parsonian American
        sociology, 8:7
Blaug, Mark, 2:493
Blauner, Robert, 2:13–14, 15, 7:30
Blaxploitation, 2:24
Blecker, Robert, 5:540
Blended family, 3:93
Blinder, Alan S., 1:333, 2:478, 6:1
Blinder-Oaxaca decomposition
    technique, 1:**332–334**, *333,* 2:478,
    6:1–2
Bliss, Chester Ittner, 6:483
BLKARTSWEST, 1:309
Bloc Québécois, 6:663
Bloc vote, 1:**334–335**, 2:560, 8:655
Bloch, Ernst, 8:81–82, 561–562
Bloch, Marc, 2:323, 3:482
Bloch, Maurine, 2:223
Block, Jeanne Humphries, 6:135
Block, Ned, 2:79, 3:231
Block clustering, 1:586
Block grants, 8:536, 537, 9:28
Block recursive models. *See* Recursive
    models
Block voting. *See* Bloc vote
Blockades. *See* Embargoes
Blocking, 3:55, 56
Blogs. *See* Internet
Blomberg, S. Brock, 1:406
Blood and bloodline, 1: **335–337**
    monarchies, 5:238, 239
    mutiracials, 5:332–333
    passing, 6:165
    racial classification, 7:40
    See also Kinship; Race
Blood Diamond (film), 2:356
Blood pressure, high. *See*
    Hypertension
Blood sacrifice, 9:154
Bloody legislation. *See* Primitive
    accumulation
Bloom, Alan, 2:38
Bloom, Allan, 5:318
Bloom, Harold, 2:310
Blount, William, 3:585
BLS (U.S. Bureau of Labor Statistics).
    See U.S. Bureau of Labor Statistics
    (BLS)
BLUE (Best linear unbiased
    estimator), 5:521
Blue collar and white collar,
    1:**337–341**, 338*t,* 9:130

Blue collar and white collar, *continued*
  credentialism, 2:166
  crime and criminology, 2:171–172
  crowding hypothesis, 2:182
  labor law, 4:303
  middle class, 5:144
  Mills, C. Wright, 5:182
  white collar employment, 2:583–585, 584*t*
  See also Working class
Blue Grass Boys (musical group), 1:341
Blue Vein Society, 2:17
Bluegrass, 1:**341–342**
Blues, 1:**342–343**, 3:425, 426
The Bluest Eye (Morrison), 2:17
Bluestone, Barry, 2:14
Blumenbach, Johann Friedrich, 1:126, 7:3, 21, 39
Blumer, Herbert, 1:**343–344**, 4:75–76, 8:7, 17
Blundell, Richard, 4:322
Bluntschli, Kaspar, 3:335
Blyden, Edward Wilmot, 1:41, 7:639, 9:96–97
  See also African socialism; Pan-Africanism
Blythe, William Jefferson, Jr. *See* Clinton, Bill
BMI (Body Mass Index), 1:**347–348**, 347*t*, 6:4, 9:58
BNA (Basic Needs Approach), 5:456
Board, institututional review. *See* Institutional review board
Board of Education, Brown v. (1955). *See Brown v. Board of Education* (1955)
Board of Education, Brown v. (1954). *See Brown v. Board of Education* (1954)
Board of Education (Niagara Falls, NY), 4:504–505
Board of Governors of the Federal Reserve System, 3:111, 112
Board of Trade (Chicago), 3:180
Boas, Franz, 1:**344–346**, 2:328
  American Anthropological Association, 1:92
  Benedict, Ruth, 1:281
  cultural anthropology, 1:119–120
  cultural relativism, 2:194, 195
  culture, 2:203
  dance, 2:223, 224, 225
  ethnology and folklore, 3:18
  Herskovits, Melville J., 3:466

Hurston, Zora Neale, 3:526
Kroeber, Alfred Louis, 4:290
linguistic anthropology, 1:129
Lowie, Robert, 4:507
public anthropology, 1:133
race, 7:10
racist paradigms, 3:426
research methods, 1:137–138
white supremacy, 9:86
Boat people, 8:615
Bobo, Lawrence, 1:324
Bodhisattva. *See* Buddhism
Bodily Communication (Argyle), 5:530
Bodin, Jean, 6:367
Body dysmorphic disorder, 6:17–18
Body image, 1:28, **346–347**
Body language, 5:530
Body Mass Index (BMI), 1:**347–348**, 347*t*, 6:4, 9:58
Body-mind connection. *See* Mind-body connection
Body Shop, 2:137
Body-soul connection, 1:114
Body Techniques (Mauss), 2:223
Body weight. *See* Weight
Boehm, Christopher, 1:84
Boeing Company, 1:233
Boer War, 1:**348–350**, 2:63, 7:240
Bogardus, Emory, 1:189–190
  See also Assimilation
Boggs, Hale, 9:33
Böhm-Bawerk, Eugen von, 3:476, 4:518
  Austrian economics, 1:211
  capital, 1:430
  ordinality, 6:57
  property rights, 8:627
  time preference, 8:369
Böhm-Bawerk's average period of production, 3:151
Böhm-Bawerk's Criticism of Marx (Hilferding), 3:476
Boldrin, Michele, 6:52
Boley, OK, 1:326
Bolívar, Simón, 1:494, 7:235
Bolivarian Revolution, 7:235
Bolivia
  class conflict, 1:569–571
  drug traffic, 2:450, 451
  land reform, 4:342
  Latin American revolutions, 7:234
  water resources, 9:40–41
Boll weevils. *See* Southern Bloc
Bollen, Kenneth, 3:391
Bollerslev, Tim, 1:229–230, 8:587

Bollinger, Gratz v. See Grutter decision (1978)
Bollinger, Grutter v. See Grutter decision (1978)
Bollywood, 3:140
Bolshevik Party. *See* Bolshevism
Bolshevik Revolution. *See* Russian Revolution
Bolshevism, 1:**350–351**
  Chinese Revolution, 1:520
  convergence theory, 2:117
  Lenin, Vladimir Ilitch, 4:410–411
  Leninism, 4:411–412
  Russian Revolution, 7:303–304
  Stalin, Joseph, 8:86
  Stalinism, 8:87
  Trotsky, Leon, 8:456
Bolton, Doe v., 1:4
Bolton, John, 8:509–510
Boltvinik, Julio, 5:454
Bombers, suicide. *See* Suicide bombers
Bommes, Michael, 9:72
Bonacich, Edna, 1:**351–353**
Bonald, Louis de, 2:83
Bonaparte, Napoléon. *See* Napoléon Bonaparte
Bond, Charles, 4:525
Bond, Julian, 5:383
Bond, Rod, 2:72
Bondage, 8:566
Bonding, traumatic. *See* Traumatic bonding
Bonds
  central banks, 1:479, 480
  description, 3:142
  international trade, 3:147
  investors, 4:134
  risk-return tradeoff, 7:256
  stocks *vs.,* 8:155, 156
  yield, 9:164–165
Bonilla, Frank, 4:357
Bonilla-Silva, Eduardo, 7:36, 43, 44, 9:88, 92
Boninsegni, Pasquale, 4:362
Bonnaroo Music and Arts Festival (TN), 9:121
Bonnichsen v. United States (2004), 1:395
Bonoli, Guiliano, 9:68
Book of Going Forth by Day, 3:458
Book of the Dead. See Book of Going Forth by Day
Bookbinder, Hyman H., 9:26
Boole, George, 4:481

Boom, economic. *See* Economic growth

The Boondocks (comic strip), 1:452

Boone, Daniel, 1:149

Boone, Richard, 9:26

Booth, John Wilkes, 8:551

Bootstrap method, 1:**353–354**, 2:241, 629

Bootstraps. *See* Alger, Horatio

Bop music, 4:177

Borchert, James, 8:264

Borda, Jean-Charles, 1:524

Borda's rule, 1:184

Border Protection, Anti-terrorism, and Illegal Immigration Control Act (U.S. 2005), 1:365

Borderlands. *See* Borders

Borders, 1:**354–355**
  Berlin Wall, 1:289
  Bracero Program, 1:364–365
  counterterrorism, 2:155
  international law, 3:360
  Iran-Iraq War, 4:143
  maquiladoras, 4:591–592
  regions, 7:131
  secession, 7:373–374
  society, 7:650
  two-state solution, 8:477

Bordo, Michael, 1:253

Borel, Émile, 6:490

Boricua, 1:**355–356**, 4:356–357, 8:261

Boris, Eileen, 9:124–125

Borjas, George, 3:581

Bork, Robert, 9:43

Borlaug, Norman, 2:342

Borofsky, Rob, 1:133

Borrowing. *See* Loans

Bortkiewicz, Ladislaus von, 4:324, 484, 8:576

Bos, Henny M. W., 3:116

Bose, Rash Behari, 3:610

Bose, Sarat Chandra, 1:**356–357**

Bose, Subhas Chandra, 1:**356–357**, 3:610, 611

Boserup, Ester, 1:**357–358**

Bosnia and Herzegovina
  Bosnian nationalism, 5:418
  Clinton, Bill, 1:580
  refugees, 7:126

Boss Platt and His New York Market (Gosnell), 3:351

Bossa nova, 4:178

Bosses, political. *See* Political bosses

Bossuet, Jacques-Bénigne, 2:421

Boston (MA), burial grounds, 1:393

Botha, P. W., 1:147

Botswana, 1:66, 3:6

Botta, Paul Emile, 1:165

Boudin, Louis, 1:212

Bounded rationality, 5:473, 6:55–56, 71
  See also Rationality

Bouniatian, Mentor, 6:97

Bourassa, Robert, 6:662

Bourdieu, Pierre, 1:**358–359**
  aesthetics, 1:30
  class, 1:564
  conspicuous consumption, 2:89
  constructivism, 2:97
  consumption, 2:107
  cultural capital, 2:189, 190
  cultural distinctions, 2:412–413
  habits, 3:403
  habitus, 3:404–406
  leisure class, 1:566
  lifestyles, 4:445–446
  low and high culture, 2:204
  neoliberalism, 5:474
  orthodoxy, 6:79
  practice theory, 6:418–419
  social capital, 7:564, 566
  urbanity, 8:544
  vacations, 8:565

Bourgeois mode of production. *See* Capitalist mode of production

Bourgeoisie, 1:**360–361**
  Anderson, Perry, 1:113
  capitalist mode of production, 1:445
  civil society, 1:553
  as class, 1:562
  communism, 2:34–35
  consumption, 2:106
  dependency theory, 2:299
  Fromm, Erich, 3:222–223
  hegemony, 3:455, 456
  as leisure class, 1:565
  Lenin, Vladimir Ilitch, 4:411
  lumpenproletariat, 4:516, 517
  nouveaux riches *vs.,* 5:548
  Rousseau, Jean-Jacques, 7:290, 291
  women's work, 9:125
  See also Middle class

Bourgeoisie, petty, 1:**361–362**, 563, 7:411

Bourguiba, Habib, 1:139

Bovenkerk, Frank, 2:142

Bovine spongiform encephalopathy (BSE), 1:471, 3:164

Bowen, Gary L., 8:571

Bowen, Natasha K., 8:571, 572

Bowlby, John, 1:67, **363**, 7:427, 8:291

Bowling for Columbine (film), 3:80

Box, George P., 8:115
  autoregressive models, 1:229
  cointegration, 2:3
  white noise, 9:82

Box-Cox transformation. *See* Regression analysis

Boxing, Muhammad Ali, 1:73–74

Boycotts. *See* Protest

Boyd, Richard, 7:98–99
  See also Realist theory

Boyer, Elizabeth, 3:121

Boyer, Jean-Pierre, 8:609

Boyer, Robert, 1:447

Boykin, A. Wade, 1:506

Boynton v. Virginia (1960), 2:615

BPP (Black Panther Party for Self-Defense). *See* Black Panthers

BR (British Railways), 7:54

Bra burning, 9:114

Bracero Program, 1:**364–366**
  Chávez, César, 1:494
  critical race theory, 2:175
  Latin American immigrants, 3:579, 4:359
  maquiladoras, 4:591
  Mexican Americans, 5:122, 124
  migrant labor, 5:154

Braddock, Edward, 9:36

Braddon-Mitchell, David, 3:231

Bradley, Gifford Weary, 1:206

Bradley, Milliken v. (1974). *See* *Milliken v. Bradley* (1974)

Bradley, Robert A., 5:432

Bradonlini, Andrea, 8:530

Bradshaw, Jonathan, 5:455

Brady Handgun Violence Prevention Act (U.S. 1993), 1:580

Brahmins, 1:**366–367**
  affirmative action, 1:31
  Ambedkar, B. R., 1:91
  caste, 1:457–458, 459, 461, 462
  Kshatriyas, 4:291
  Vaisyas, 8:567–568

Braidwood, Robert, 3:125

Brain
  classical conditioning, 1:573, 574
  cognition, 1:598
  dopamine, 2:436–437
  dreaming, 2:445

Brain, *continued*
lobotomy, 4:475–476
See also Neuroscience
Brain damage, alcoholism, 1:71
Brain drain, 1:**367–368**, 3:565–566, 4:284
Brain gain, 1:368
Brain scans, neuroeconomics, 5:483–484
Brain tax, 1:368
Brain waste, 1:368
Brainard, William C., 8:379–380
Brainstorming, 2:9
Branch Davidians, 2:188
Brandeis, Louis, 3:114, 4:465
Branding. *See* Advertising
Brands. *See* Advertising
Brandt Report, 2:339
Braque, Georges, 8:632
Braudel, Fernand, 2:323, 5:466, 9:151–152
Braun, Volker, 1:237
Braunstein, Elissa, 3:275
Brave New World (Huxley), 5:98–99, 8:561
Bray, George A., 2:407
Bray, Margaret, 3:173
Brazel, Mac, 8:507
Brazelton, T. Berry, 1:**368–369**
Brazil
Anglo-Portuguese trade, 8:413
automobile industry, 1:221
bauxite industry, 1:261
black nationalism, 1:318
blackness, 1:329
capital controls, 1:432
cattle industry, 1:471
coffee industry, 1:594–595
colorism, 2:18
compulsory voting, 2:59
corporatism, 2:141
cotton industry, 2:153
Creole, 2:168
decolonization, 2:256
Freire, Paulo, 3:202
gold mining, 3:342–343
integration, 4:62
land reform, 4:342, 343, 344
miscegenation, 5:200
mulatto escape hatch, 5:310–312
nonrenewable natural resource use, 5:438
pardo, 6:130
phenotype, 6:244
positivism, 6:390

race, 7:5
race and education, 7:18
racial democracy, 2:282–283
racial inequality, 4:7
slavery, 1:60
whitening, 9:90
women, 9:109, 111
BrCA gene, 3:294–295
Breaks, tax. *See* Tax relief
Breast cancer, genetic testing, 3:294–295
Breasted, James Henry, 3:125
Brecher, Jeremy, 5:540
Breeding, selective. *See* Eugenics
Breen, Richard, 8:535
Brehm, Jack, 1:600, 7:85–86
Brenner, Robert, 2:78, 3:134, 9:153
Brent, Margaret, 8:215
Brentano, Franz, 2:80
Bretton Woods Agreement, 1:273, 3:112, 9:137
description, 9:150
Keynes, John Maynard, 3:200
wage and price controls, 9:3
See also Exchange rates; Gold standard; International Monetary Fund (IMF)
Breuer, Josef, 3:209
Brewer, Dominic J., 5:391
Brewer, John, 2:89
Brewer, Marilynn, 9:136
Brezhnev, Leonid, 1:**369–370**
career, 8:512
Carter, Jimmy, 1:451
Cold War, 2:5
communism, 2:36
gulags, 3:396
Russian Federation, 7:302
Brezhnev Doctrine, 9:35
BRFSS (Behaviorial Risk Factor Surveillance System), 8:657
Bribery, 1:**370–371**, 2:144, 145
Brickman, Philip, 7:577
Brickner, Richard, 3:497
Bride price. *See* Dowry and bride price
Brides, virgin, 8:629–630
Bridewells, 8:567
Bridging theory, 1:168
Bridgman, Sturges v. (U.K. 1879), 1:589
Briggs, Cyril, 1:316
Brimmer, Andrew, 1:**371–373**
Brinkman, Richard, 1:391
Britain, 1801-. *See* United Kingdom (U.K.)

Britain, pre-1801. *See* England
British anthropology, 1:**127–128**
Malinowski, Bronislaw, 4:566–567
Radcliffe-Brown, A. R., 7:47
British Broadcasting Company (BBC). *See* Television
British Columbia, alternative vote, 8:644, 644*t*
British Conservative Party. *See* Conservative Party (U.K.)
British Guiana. *See* Guyana
British Parliament. *See* Parliament, U.K.
British Railways (BR), 7:54
British South Africa Company (BSAC), 7:240
British Telecommunications, 8:315
British Virgin Islands, offshore banking, 6:32
Broadcasting, censorship, 1:475–476
Broadcasting Act (Canada 1991), 1:476
Broca, Paul, 7:21
Brodkin, Karen, 9:92
Bronfenbrenner, Urie, 1:506, 3:511
Brookings Insitution, OPEC, 6:66
Brooks, Clem, 9:71
Brooks, Stephen G., 8:510
Brooks, Van Wyck, 3:300
Brothers. *See* Sibling relationships
Brown, E. Cary, 3:370
Brown, George, 8:656–657
Brown, H. Rap, 4:369, 370
Brown, Harry G., 3:151
Brown, Jerry, 1:494
Brown, Joseph, 2:67
Brown, Linda, 1:374
Brown, Lyn Mikel, 3:320
Brown, Malcolm, 7:45
Brown, Michael, 4:504
Brown, Oliver L, 1:374
Brown, Ron, 1:580
Brown, Rupert, 2:72, 9:136
Brown, Sterling, 3:426
Brown decision. *See Brown v. Board of Education* (1954)
Brown II decision. *See Brown v. Board of Education* (1955)
Brown v. Board of Education (1954), 1:**373–377**
black liberalism, 1:312
Brown v. Board of Education (1955), 1:377
child development, 1:507
civil rights, 1:550, 551

Clark, Kenneth B., 1:560, 561
desegregation, 2:313–314
equal protection, 2:615
gifted and talented education, 3:317
Hernandez v. Texas, 3:464
Houston, Charles Hamilton, 3:505
Jim Crow, 4:198, 201
judiciary, 1:19, 4:227
Marshall, Thurgood, 4:625–626
race, 7:16, 17
separate-but-equal, 7:447
Southern politics, 6:342
Supreme Court decisions, 8:234, 9:32–33
unequal education, 2:537
White, Walter, 9:81
See also School desegregation; School segregation
Brown v. Board of Education (1955), 1:**377–378**, 6:342, 7:16
Browne, Robert S., 5:388
Browning, Barbara, 2:224
Browning, Christopher, 3:497
Brownsville Advocacy Planning Agency, 9:27
Broz, Josip. *See* Tito, Josip Broz
Bruce, Thomas, 7:168–169
Bruce Church Incorporated, 1:494
Bruch, Hilde, 1:346
Brudney, Jeffrey L., 8:638–640, *639*
Brumberg, Richard, 4:441
Brumfitt, J. H., 8:636
Brunswik, Egon, 1:425
Bry, Theodor de, 3:261
Bryan, William Jennings, 7:187, 9:102, 105
cross of gold, 2:180, 181
Democratic Party (U.S.), 2:287
populism, 6:383, 384
See also Scopes Trial
Bryce, James, 2:273, 3:113
Brzezinski, Zbigniew, 4:285
BSAC (British South Africa Company), 7:240
BSE (Bovine spongiform encephalopathy), 1:471, 3:164
BSO (Black September Organization). *See* Black September
Bubble, internet. *See* Internet Bubble
Bubbles (economics), 1:**378–379**
bull and bear markets, 1:385–386
Cantillon, Richard, 1:429
capital flight, 1:434

economic crises, 2:483, 484
Law, John, 4:366
panics, 6:124–125
Ponzi schemes, 6:369
South Sea Bubble, 8:33–34
speculation, 3:380, 8:54–56
Buber, Martin, 2:31, 9:180
Buchanan, James, 3:144
dirigiste, 2:373–374
laissez-faire, 4:337–338
marginal product of labor, 4:307
Buck, Carrie. *See* Human sterilization
Buck v. Bell (1927), 3:21, 8:141
Buckley, William F., Jr., 2:85, 5:414
Buckminsterfullerenes, 3:229
Buddha, 1:**379–381**
Brahmins, 1:366
Buddhism, 1:381–385
middle way, 5:146
monotheism, 5:271
Buddhism, 1:**381–385**
Brahmins, 1:366–367
Buddha, 1:379–381
caste, 1:459–460
Chinese diaspora, 1:516
culture, 7:159
dalits, 2:221–222
demography, 7:161
divine right, 2:422
heaven, 3:446
hell, 3:458
Hinduism, 3:478
Jainism, 4:166
Kammatic, 5:504
legal systems, 4:406
Mahāyanā, 5:504, 505
martyrdom, 4:629
middle way, 5:145, 146
missionaries, 5:205
monotheism, 5:271
mysticism, 5:352
nirvāana, 5:504–505
reincarnation, 7:145
scripture reading, 9:155
Shinto, 7:496
sin, 7:519
theism, 8:341
Theravada, 5:504
Tibetan, 9:155
worship, 9:154
Budget deficit, national debt, 5:386–387
Budgeting. *See* Finance
Budig, Michelle J., 3:116

Bueno de Mesquita, Bruce, 6:37
Buffon, Georges, 1:126
Bùi, Tín, 8:614
Buick, 3:285
Build-to-order manufacturing, 1:223
Building and Anthropology of the Modern World (Wolf), 9:106
Building codes, 1:170–171
Buiter, Willem, 6:93
Bukharin, Nikolai. *See* Bukharin, Nikolay
Bukharin, Nikolay, 1:361, 446, 3:134, 588, 9:153
Bulgaria, 5:544, 9:35
Bulimia nervosa, 6:89–90
See also Body image; Overeating
Bull and bear markets, 1:**385–387**, 450
Buller, David, 3:34
Bullins, Ed, 1:309
Bullion, 7:243
Bulloch, John, 9:42
Bullying. *See* Harassment
Bulman, Ronnie J., 7:577
Bulnes, Francisco, 4:219
Bulow, Bernhard von, 3:335
Bulow, Jeremy, 1:207, 5:545
Bunche, Ralph Johnson, 1:93, **387–388**, 5:383
Bundy, McGeorge, 2:183
Bunyoro, Lost Counties of, 6:12
Burakmin, 1:**388–389**
Buraku, 1:**388–389**
Buraku Liberation League (Japan), 1:389
Burawoy, Michael, 1:454, 8:5
Burch, William, Jr., 8:9
Burchett, Wilfred, 9:30
Burden, tax. *See* Tax incidence
Burden of acting white, 6:49–50
Burden of proof process, 3:386
Burdian's ass. *See* Conundrum
Bureau of American Ethnology, 1:92
Bureau of Indian Affairs (BIA), 1:99, 5:428
Bureau of Investigation, U.S. (BOI). *See* Federal Bureau of Investigation (FBI)
Bureau of Labor Statistic (U.S.). *See* U.S. Bureau of Labor Statistics
Bureaucracy, 1:**389–391**
bureaucrat, 1:391–392
capital controls, 1:432
Central Intelligence Agency, U.S, 1:480–482

Bureaucracy, *continued*
    corruption, 2:144, 145
    ideal type, 3:547
    leaders, 4:377
    managerial class, 4:578, 579
    Mills, C. Wright, 5:181–182
    Moore, Barrington, 5:278
    political sociology, 8:3
    rational-legal authority, 6:68
    Royal Commissions, 7:291–292
    secrecy, 7:376
    state capitalism, 1:443, 444
Bureaucracy (Mises), 1:392
Bureaucrat, 1:**391–392**
    bureaucracy, 1:389–391
    corruption, 2:144, 145
    lobbying, 4:474
    technocrat *vs.,* 8:297–298
Bureaucratic authoritarianism, 1:214
The Bureaucratic Experience
    (Hummel), 1:391, 392
Bureaucratic politics model, 3:171
Bureaucratization, gaze, 3:263
Burger, John, 3:138
Burger, Warren E., 9:33
Burgess, Ernest W., 1:541, 2:296,
    8:541
Burial grounds, 1:**392–393**
Burial grounds, African, 1:**393–394,**
    7:531
Burial grounds, Native American,
    1:**394–396,** 7:169
Burke, Edmund, 1:**396–397**
    conservatism, 2:83, 84, 86
    Conservative Party (U.K.), 2:87
    leaders, 4:375–376
    Levellers, 4:414–415
    liberalism, 4:426
    Malthus, Thomas Robert, 4:570
    political parties, 6:306
    representative and participatory
        democracy, 2:284
    resistance, 7:208
    right wing, 7:247, 248
*Burlington Northern and Santa Fe
    Railway v. White* (2006), 7:216
Burma. *See* Myanmar
Burnham, James, 1:390, 392, 2:85
Burnham, Walter Dean, 5:498, 8:648
Burns, Arthur F., 4:288
Burns, Nancy, 8:606
Burr, Aaron, 1:**397–398,** 3:414
Burt, Ron, 5:476
Bus Boycott (South Africa, 1955). *See*
    Apartheid; Townships

Buses. *See* Transportation industry
Bush, George H. W., 1:**398–399**
    Bush, George W., 1:399
    Clinton, Bill, 1:579, 581
    disaster management, 2:384
    Great Society programs, 3:373
    Iran-Contra affair, 4:143
    law and order, 4:371
    Muhammad Ali, 1:74
    NAFTA, 5:541
    Republican Party (U.S.), 7:187
    rules *vs.* discretion, 7:293
    schooling, 7:353
    Southern strategy, 8:37
    unequal education, 2:538
Bush, George W., 1:**399–400**
    autocracy, 1:216
    Bracero Program, 1:365
    Castro, Fidel, 1:467
    Central Intelligence Agency, U.S,
        1:485
    Church and state, 1:535
    civilization, 1:558
    Clinton, Bill, 1:580
    computers, 2:60
    conservatism, 2:86
    contraception, 2:114
    Cuba, 2:187
    digital divide, 2:366
    domino theory, 2:435
    education in the U.S., 2:542
    electoral college, 2:560
    Fahrenheit 9/11 (film), 3:79–80
    Great Society programs, 3:373
    Hussein, Saddam, 3:535
    illegal immigrants, 5:431
    Iraq-U.S. War, 4:146–148
    judicial appointments, 3:139
    military-industrial complex, 5:174
    Nader, Ralph, 5:360
    national service programs, 5:413
    NATO, 5:546
    neoconservatism, 5:468, 469
    Palestinian Authority, 6:106
    Republican Party (U.S.), 7:187
    schooling, 7:354
    September 11, 2001, 7:453
    state capitalism, 1:445
    tax cuts, 3:380
    unequal education, 2:538
    unilateralism, 8:509–510
    vindication movements, 8:619
    Voting Rights Act (U.S. 1965),
        8:650

Bush, Rasul v. (2004), 3:394
Bush v. Vera (1996), 8:653
Bushman, Richard, 3:301
Business, 1:**400–403**
    Chinese diaspora, 1:517
    community power studies, 2:42,
        44, 45
    cooperatives, 2:123–126
    diversity, 2:419–420
    enterprise, 2:598–599
    entrepreneurship, 2:604–605
    government relationship,
        5:495–496
    inventories, 4:126–129
    leadership, 3:524–525
    management, 4:574–575
    modernism, 5:229
Business cycles
    Cantillon, Richard, 1:429
    difference equations, 2:362
    economic crises, 2:483–485
    employment, 2:582
    insurance, 4:50
    inventories, 4:128–129
    investment, 4:132–133
    Kondratieff, 9:153
    Mises, Ludwig Edler von, 1:211
    Mitchell, Wesley Clair, 5:206–207
    monetary policy, 6:295
    Prebisch-Singer hypothesis, 6:424
    price *vs.* quantity adjustment,
        6:453–454
    recession, 7:103–105, 103*t*
    Russian economics, 7:300, 301
    shocks, 7:500
    unemployment, 3:227, 8:498, 502
    Verdoorn's law, 8:608
Business cycles, empirical literature,
    1:**403–405,** 406–412
Business cycles, political, 1:**406–407,**
    479, 4:492–494
Business cycles, real, 1:**407–409**
    bubbles (economics), 1:378–379
    bull and bear markets, 1:385–386
    business cycle theories, 1:412
    economic depression, 2:304
    Keynesian economics, 2:512
    lagging, leading and coincident
        indicators, 4:331
    long run, 4:492–494
    models, 1:403–405
    political business cycles, 1:406,
        407
    quantity index, 6:658–659
Business cycles, theories, 1:**409–413**

cobweb cycles, 1:591

economic depression, 2:304

Kalecki, Michał, 4:247

long run, 4:492–494

Business Cycles (Mitchell), 1:410

Business Cycles (Schumpeter), 1:438, 4:260

Business Cycles and Economic Policy (Lundberg). *See Konjunkturer och ekonomisk politik* (Lundberg)

Business elites

public policy, 6:72

Veblen, Thorstein, 8:596, 597

Business ethics, 2:**633–635**

bribery, 1:370–371

bubbles (economics), 1:379

corruption, 2:143

crony capitalism, 2:180

Ponzi schemes, 6:368–369

See also Corporate social responsibility (CSR)

Business mergers. *See* Corporate strategies

Business Networks and Economic Development in East and Southeast Asia (Hamilton), 1:516

Business trusts, 1:144

Busing. *See* School desegregation

Butler, Dino, 1:99

Butler, Judith, 3:269, 6:208, 395

Butler, Rab, 2:87

Butler, Rhett Barnwell, 2:243

Butler, Robert N., 3:308

Butterfield, Paul, 1:343

Butterfly effect, 1:**413–414**, 7:63–64

Buttonwood Agreement, 9:7

Buvinic, Mayra, 3:274

Buying power. *See* Purchasing power

Buzan, Barray, 5:412

Bwa kayman, 8:634

Byrd, James, Jr., 1:296, 3:431, 4:527

Byrne, David, 9:142

Byrnes, James F., 1:481

C

CA (Conversational analysis), 2:**118–121**

Cabanis, Pierre, 1:275

Cable television. *See* Television

Cabral, Amílcar, 1:**415–416**, 5:507

African sociology, 7:665

Black Power, 1:321

blackness, 1:330

non-alignment, 5:513

Cacioppo, John T., 5:452–453

CAFE (Corporate Average Fuel Efficiency Standards), 1:223

Cagan, Philip, 1:20

Cairnes, J. E., 5:514

Cairns, Robert. *See* Social cognitive map

Caja Laboral, 2:125

Cajun, 2:168

Calabresi, Guido, 4:367

Calas, Jean, 8:636

Caldeira, Gregory, 1:48

Caldwell, Ben, 1:309, 310

Caldwell, John C., 2:291, 294, 295

Calendars, 1:583–584

Calhoun, John, 2:84, 429

Calibration, 1:403, 404–405

California

Chávez, César, 1:493–494

Chinese diaspora, 1:516

civil rights, 1:549

digital divide, 2:366

gold mining, 3:339–340

Mexican Americans, 5:125–126

Native Americans, 5:424

occupational regulation, 6:23

Proposition 187, 5:430–431

racial identification, 3:549

recall, 7:102

referendum, 7:120

Silicon Valley, 7:510–511

tax revolts, 8:278, 279

California, Miller v., 6:13, 8:652–653

California, Rochin v. (1952), 2:461

California Agricultural Labor Relations Act (1975), 1:494

California Civil Rights Initiative, 1:**416–417**

black conservatism, 1:311

race, 7:11

race-blind policies, 7:35, 36

racial identification, 3:549

California v. Bakke (1978). *See Grutter* decision (1978)

A Call to Civic Service (Moskos), 5:414

Callaghan, James, 4:327

Calle, Alfonso de la, 2:20

Callender, James IT., 3:245

Calles, Plutarco Elías, 6:156

Calley, William, 8:614–615

Calvet de Magalhães, José, 2:370–371

Calvin, John, 1:531

Calvinist churches. *See* Reformed churches

Calypso, 1:**417–419**

Calypso Rose (musician), 1:419

Cambodia

civil wars, 1:554

concentration camps, 2:64

ethnic conflict, 3:2

genocide, 3:298

Khmer Rouge, 4:262–263

Killing Fields, 4:265

Kissinger, Henry, 4:275

Pol Pot, 6:289

United Nations role, 8:524

Vietnam War, 8:615

Cambridge capital controversy, 1:**419–421**

capital, 1:431

marginal product of labor, 4:307

neo-Ricardian economics, 2:520, 521

Pasinetti, paradox, 6:165

physical capital, 6:264

Robinson, Joan, 7:267

two-sector models, 8:476

Cambridge School, neoclassical growth model, 5:465

Cambridge University, 1:419, **421–423**

Cameron, Charles, 8:610

Cameron, David, 2:88

Cameron, Norman Eustace, 9:97

Cameron, Rondo, 1:253

Cameroon, 3:107, 9:181

Camp David Accords (1979), 1:451

Campaign reform. *See* Congress, U.S.; Elections

Campaign spending, Supreme Court decisions, 9:84

Campaigning, 1:**423–424**

constituency, 2:90

Internet, 4:107–119

law and order, 4:369, 370, 371–372

mobilization, 5:213–214

primaries, 6:458–459

race, 7:20

representative and participatory democracy, 2:285

Southern politics, 6:343–344

Campbell, Angus, 1:100, **424–425**

Campbell, Donald, 1:**425–427**

Campbell, Howard, 8:448–449

Campbell, John, 2:110

Campbell, Joseph, 2:247

Campbell, Ming, 4:427

Campbell, William, 9:103

Campbell-Bannerman, Henry, 4:428

Can Capitalism Survive? (Schumpeter), 2:164

Canada
    aboriginal peoples, 5:423
    alternative vote, 8:644, 644*t*
    banking industry, 1:251, 252, 253
    blood and bloodline, 1:336
    cattle industry, 1:471
    censorship, 1:475–476
    census, 1:476
    Chinese diaspora, 1:518
    commonwealth, 2:29
    Cook, James, 2:121
    corporate social responsibility, 2:137
    day care, 2:246
    divorce and separation, 2:426–427
    East Indian diaspora, 2:473–474
    economics
        full capacity, 3:224
        goodwill, 3:350
        NAFTA, 5:540–541
        national income accounts, 5:400
        negative income tax, 5:456–457
    educational accountability, 1:10
    history
        Africville, 1:45–46
        Great Depression, 3:368
        whiteness, 9:90
    income maintenance experiments, 3:605, 607
    indigenous rights, 3:616
    labor, 4:302
    land claims, 4:340–341
    legal systems, 4:406
    loyalists, 4:508–509
    multiculturalism, 1:543
    national health insurance, 5:395
    natives, 5:429
    peasant organizations, 6:74
    political science
        gerrymandering, 3:309
        NATO, 5:544–546
        voting patterns, 8:650
    Quebecois movement, 6:661–663
    society, 7:650, 652
    tax credits, 8:274–275
    treaty federalism, 8:446
    urban sprawl, 8:540
    xenophobia, 9:159
Canada, Figueroa v. (2003), 3:309
Canada, Harper v., 3:309

Canada Child Tax Benefit (CCTB), 8:274
Canadian Radio-Television and Telecommunications Commission, 1:475–476
Canary Islands, 1:39, 2:20
Candidates, ranking, 8:643–645, 644*t*
Candide (Voltaire), 8:635
Canguilhem, Georges, 3:182
Cannabis. *See* Marijuana
Cannibal Talk (Obeyesekere), 1:428
Cannibalism, 1:**427–428**
Cannon, Poppy, 9:81
Cannon, William B., 9:26
Canon law. *See* Roman Catholic Church
Cantillon, Richard, 1:**428–429**, 4:489
Cantor, Nancy, 4:74–75
Cantor, Norman, 5:550
Cantwell v. Connecticut (1940), 1:534
Capabilities, 2:348
    functionings, 3:233–234
    nominal income, 5:511
Capacity, full, 3:**223–225**
Cape Colony. *See* Africa
Cape Verde Island, 1:415
Capen, Edward, 9:103
Capital, 1:**429–431**
    accumulation, 1:12–14, 3:346
        bourgeoisie, 1:360–361
        capitalist mode of production, 1:446
        class conflict, 1:569
        classical economics, 2:504
        described, 1:431
        development economics, 2:344
        golden rule, 3:346
        low and high culture, 2:205
        Lucas, Robert E., Jr., 4:510
        Luxemburg, Rosa, 4:522
        managerial capitalism, 1:442
        Robinson, Joan, 7:267
        surplus labor, 4:308, 309
    Cambridge capital controversy, 1:419–421
    community power studies, 2:43
    constant, 1:446
    cultural, 2:189–190, *190*
        conspicuous consumption, 2:89
        consumption, 2:107
        cultural distinctions, 2:412–413
        curriculum, 2:214

        gentility, 3:301
        habitus, 3:404–406
        leisure class, 1:566
        low and high culture, 2:204–205
        nouveaux riches, 5:548
        practice theory, 6:419
        tracking in schools, 8:410
        urbanity, 8:544
    diminishing returns, 7:218, 219
    economic
        gentility, 3:301
        nouveaux riches, 5:548
        venture, 8:604–605
        vintage models, 8:619–621
    equity markets, 2:623–624
    fixed, overproduction, 6:97
    goodwill, 3:350
    Hilferding, Rudolf, 3:476
    human, 3:506–510
        Becker, Gary S., 1:270, 271
        Berg, Ivar E., 1:288
        blue collar and white collar, 1:337
        Castro, Fidel, 1:466
        described, 1:429
        health economics, 3:440–441
        intergenerational transmission, 4:89
        Jencks, Christopher, 4:184
        labor economics, 2:514
        managerial capitalism, 1:442–443
        mobility, 5:210
        population studies, 6:382
        returns to education, 7:65–66
        soft skills, 8:21–22
        unemployability, 8:496
        wealth, 9:44
        winner-take-all society, 9:102–103
        workplace relations, 9:136
    initial public offering, 4:38–39
    Keynes, John Maynard, 4:261
    leverage, 4:415–416
    marginal product of labor, 4:307
    neo-Ricardian economics, 2:520–521
    optimal growth, 6:51–53
    overlapping generations model, 6:93
    physical, 6:264–265
        development economics, 2:344–345
        human, 3:506–509

primitive communism, 2:37
psychological, 6:580–582
Ricardo, David, 7:244–246
Rybczynski theorem, 7:305–306
social, 7:564–567
 African Americans, 1:36
 cultural capital and, 2:190
 described, 1:430
 habitus, 3:404–406
 network analysis, 5:481
 political sociology, 8:4
 voluntary assocations, 1:193
symbolic, 1:359, 6:419
venture, black capitalism, 1:440–441
Wicksell effects, 9:94–95
Capital: A Critique of Political Economy (Marx), 3:79, 82, 133
 accumulation of capital, 1:12
 economic value, 8:576
 social formation, 3:177
 underdevelopment, 8:489
Capital, financial. *See* Money
Capital (Marx), 1:437, 445, 571, 4:324
 determinism, 2:324
 Lafargue, Paul, 4:330
 Marxian economics, 2:516–517
 relative surplus value, 7:154
Capital account. *See* Balance of payments; Currency appreciation and depreciation
Capital accumulation. *See* Accumulation of capital
Capital adequacy agreements, 6:30
Capital and Growth (Hicks), 3:472
Capital and Interest (Böhm-Bawerk), 1:211
Capital asset pricing model. *See* Finance
Capital asset pricing model (CAPM), 3:141, 7:256
Capital assets
 national income accounts, 5:403
 user costs, 8:551–552
Capital Control, Financial Regulation, and Industrial Policy in South Korea and Brazil (Nembhard), 1:252
Capital controls, 1:**431–434**
 balance of payments, 1:238–240
 capital flight, 1:436
 central banks, 1:480
 trade liberalization, 4:428
Capital flight, 1:**434–436**
 capital controls, 1:432

hot money, 3:504
 money laundering, 5:263
Capital goods. *See* Capital
Capital goods, vintage models, 8:619–621
Capital measurement. *See* Cambridge capital controversy; Capital
Capital punishment
 death-qualified jurors, 4:233
 jurisprudence, 4:232–233
 jury selection, 4:234
 lynchings, 4:526, 527
 morality, 2:247, 248
 rape, 7:65
 Southern politics, 6:348
Capital theory. *See* Capital
Capital-to-labor ratio, golden rule in growth models, 3:346
Capitalism, 1:**437–439**
 African socialism, 7:641
 alienation, 3:222–223
 anarchism, 1:111–112
 Bonacich, Edna, 1:352
 bourgeoisie, 1:360–361
 business, 1:400, 401
 casino, 1:455–456
 Castro, Fidel, 1:465
 centrism, 1:489
 Chinese diaspora, 1:517
 cities, 1:541
 citizenship, 1:543
 civil society, 1:553
 civilization, 1:558
 class, 1:562
 class conflict, 1:568, 569, 570, 571
 class consciousness, 1:571, 572
 classical economics, 2:502–504
 common land, 2:27
 communism, 2:34, 35
 consumption, 2:106–107
 convergence theory, 2:117
 cooperation, 2:123
 corporations, 2:139–140
 corporatism, 2:141
 Cox, Oliver C., 2:158–159
 creative destruction, 2:163–164
 critical theory, 2:176–178
 crony, 2:180
 culture, 2:203
 curriculum, 2:214
 De Soto, Hernando, 2:319–320
 decolonization, 2:256
 democratization, 2:289

dependency theory, 2:299, 300
deregulation, 2:308–309
developing countries, 2:335
development economics, 2:345
development in sociology, 2:347
dirigiste, 2:372–374
division of labor, 2:424
dual economy, 2:456–457
economic crises, 2:484, 485
economic depression, 2:302–303, 304
enterprise, 2:598–599
entrepreneurship, 2:604–605
exploitation, 3:64, 65, 8:576
factory system, 3:78–79
feminism, 3:122
feudal mode of production, 3:134
Galbraith, John Kenneth, 3:246
Heilbroner, Robert, 3:456–457
Hilferding, Rudolf, 3:476
immigration, 3:581, 582
imperialism, 3:586–589, 8:489
industrial, 1:238, 3:300, 620–622
internal colony, 2:14
intersectionality, 4:114
Kalecki, Michał, 4:246–247
Keynes, John Maynard, 4:260, 262
labor theory of value, 4:323–324
labor *vs.*, 4:301, 302
Lafargue, Paul, 4:330
laissez-faire, 4:337–338
land fertility, 3:131
latifundia, 4:352, 353, 354
Lefebvre, Henri, 4:401
leisure, 4:408
Lenin, Vladimir Ilitch, 4:411
Leninism, 4:412
liberalism, 4:425
liberation movements, 4:432–433
liberation theology, 4:434
liberty, 4:439
long period analysis, 4:489–491
lumpenproletariat, 4:516
Luxemburg, Rosa, 4:522–523
Machinery Question, 4:536–537
managerial firms, 3:148
Mandel, Ernest, 4:579–580
market socialism, 7:644–646
Marxian economics, 2:516
Marxism, 4:638–641
Marxist competition, 2:55–56
middle class, 5:143–145
mobility, 5:209–211

Caritat, Marie Jean Antoine de. *See* Condorcet, Marquis de
Carlaw, Kenneth, 7:223
Carlos, John, 6:40
Carlyle, Thomas
  collective wisdom, 2:9
  leadership, 4:378
  Schumpeter, Joseph, 2:163–164
Carmichael, Stokely, 4:269, 5:385
  law and order, 4:369, 370
  race relations, 7:30
  See also Black nationalism; Black Power
Carnap, Rudolf, 1:275, 278, 279, 280, 4:481, 6:9
Carnegie, Andrew, 2:233, 3:183
Carnival (festival), 1:417, 419
Carolene Products, United States v. (1938), 2:615
Carpenter, Lynett, 9:105
Carpenter, Ray, 1:83
Carpetbaggers, 7:113
Carr, Baker v. (1962), 9:33
Carranza, Venustiano, 5:130–131, 8:618, 9:171
Carrero, Jaime, 5:552
Carriacou, Grenadian Revolution, 3:381–383
Carrying capacity, overpopulation, 6:95
Carrying cost, 1:**449–450**
  contango, 2:112
  liquidity premium, 4:460
Carson, Kit, 5:447
Carsten, Janet, 4:273
Cartels
  amnesty, 1:145
  antitrust, 1:143
  banking industry, 1:253
  bauxite industry, 1:261
  drug traffic, 2:451
  energy industry, 2:588
  gender gap, 3:282–283
  Hilferding, Rudolf, 3:476
  imperfect competition, 2:52
  shipping industry, 7:498, 499
  state capitalism, 1:444
Carter, Gregg L., 8:538
Carter, Howard, 1:165
Carter, James Earl. *See* Carter, Jimmy
Carter, Jimmy, 1:**450–452**
  Castro, Fidel, 1:467
  conservatism *vs.,* 2:86
  Cuba, 2:187
  Democratic Party (U.S.), 2:288

disaster management, 2:384
  Federal Reserve System, 3:112
  Great Society programs, 3:373
  income maintenance experiments, 3:606
  Iranian Revolution, 4:144
  Kissinger, Henry, 4:275
  Love Canal, 4:504
  Muhammad Ali, 1:74
  wage and price controls, 9:3
  War on Poverty, 9:26, 28
Carter, Prudence, 6:48, 50
Carter, Robert, 5:384
Carter, Vernon, 1:62
Cartesianism. *See* Descartes, René
Cartoons, 2:409–410
  See also Comic books
Cartoons, political, 1:**452**, 5:377–378
Carver, Charles S., 2:129, 6:54–55
Carver, George Washington. *See* Peanut industry
Casablanca Group, 6:62
Casanova, Jose, 7:162
Case Closed (Posner), 9:34
The Case for Black Reparations (Bittker), 7:213–214
Case method, 1:**453–454**
Case method, extended, 1:453, **454–455**
Case Open (Weisberg), 9:34
Case studies. *See* Case method
Casey, Planned Parenthood of Southeastern Pennsylvania v. (1992), 1:4
Cash. *See* Money
Casino capitalism, 1:**455–456**
Casino Capitalism (Strange), 1:455
Casinos, Native American, 5:428
Caspi, Avshalom, 1:25
Cass, David, 6:51
Cassady, Ralph, Jr., 1:206
Cassava, 3:258
Castaneda, Carlos, 1:**456–457**, 7:443
Caste, 1:**457–460**
  affirmative action, 1:31
  Ambedkar, B. R., 1:90–92
  Brahmins, 1:366–367
  Buddha, 1:381
  Buddhism, 1:383
  buraku, 1:388–389
  colorism, 2:18
  Congress Party, India, 2:76, 77
  Cox, Oliver C., 2:157, 158
  creamy layer, 2:161
  dalits, 2:221–222

dowry and bride price, 2:441
  East Indian diaspora, 2:473
  hierarchy, 3:474
  Hinduism, 3:478
  India, 3:254
  integration, 4:61
  Jajmani matrix, 4:167
  Jinnah, Mohammed Ali, 4:204
  Kshatriyas, 4:291–292
  left and right, 4:401
  mobility, 5:209
  Ogbu, John U., 6:34
  quotas, 6:670
  Raj, 7:56–57
  Sanskritization, 7:323–324
  servitude, 7:463
  Sudras, 8:212–213
  tribe, 8:450–451
  tribes, 8:449
  Vaisyas, 8:567–568
Caste, anthropology of, 1:**461–463**
Caste, Class, and Race: A Study in Social Dynamics (Cox), 2:158
Castells, Manuel, 3:240, 6:86, 8:543
Castles, Francis, 9:68, 70, 73
Castles, Stephen, 3:581, 582
Castration. *See* Human sterilization
Castration, globalization, 6:30
Castro, Fidel, 1:**463–468**
  Bay of Pigs, 1:262
  Central Intelligence Agency, U.S, 1:484
  communism, 2:36
  Cuban Missile Crisis, 2:183, 184
  Cuban Revolution, 2:185–187
  Guantánamo Bay, 3:393
  Latin American immigrants, 3:571
  Latin American revolutions, 7:234
  Latinos, 4:359
  non-alignment, 5:513
  socialism, 7:638
Castro, Raúl, 2:185, 186
Catastrophe theory, 1:*468,* **468–470,** *469*
Catastrophism, 1:166
Catastrophizing. *See* Psychotherapy
The Catcher in the Rye (Salinger), 9:167
Catchings, Waddill, 8:488
Categorization, social. *See* Social categorization
Catholic Church. *See* Roman Catholic Church

Catholicism. *See* Coptic Christian Church; Greek Orthodox Church; Roman Catholic Church

Cato the Elder, 4:352

Cattle industry, 1:**470–471**

Caucasians. *See* Race and psychology; Whites

Cauchy distribution. *See* Probability distributions

Caucus for a New Political Science, 6:314

Caucus of Black Economists. *See* National Economic Association

Caudill, William, 1:131

Causality, 1:**471–473**
  controlled experiments, 3:58–59
  cross-sectional research, 7:189–190
  econometrics, 2:480–482
  essentialism, 2:630
  experiments, 3:55–58
  Granger, 8:598
  locus of control, 4:478
  longitudinal data, 2:238
  loss functions, 4:501–502
  multifinality, 5:319–320
  Myrdal, Gunnar, 5:351
  path analysis, 6:168
  philosophy of science, 6:261
  regression analysis, 7:138–141
  survey methods, 5:117
  theory, 8:344–345

Causation
  cumulative, 1:94
  over-attribution bias, 6:89
  vector autoregression, 8:598–600

Causation, cumulative. *See* Cumulative causation

CAVE (Content analysis of verbatim explanations), 6:54

Cave paintings, 8:630–631

Caves, Richard, 2:601

Cayman Islands, offshore banking, 6:32

Cayton, Horace R., 1:324, 2:181

CBA. *See* Cost-benefit analysis (CBA)

CBCL (Child Behavior Checklist), 1:**504–505**

CBR (Crude birth rate), 3:127

CCC (Civilian Conservation Corps), 5:413, 494

CCC (Committee of Colored Citizens), 9:99

CCCS (Centre for Contemporary Cultural Studies), 2:199, 7:209

CCP (Chinese Communist Party). *See* Communist Party (China)

CCTB (Canada Child Tax Benefit), 8:274

CD (Compact discs), 8:622

CDBG (Community Development Block Grants), 8:537, 9:28

CDC (Centers for Disease Control and Prevention)
  AIDs, 1:63–65
  HIV, 3:489

CDM (Committee of Defense Ministers), 9:35

Ceci, Stephen, 3:160

Ceilings, rent. *See* Rent control

Celebration riots. *See* Riots

Cell lines, immortalization, 3:307

Cell phones. *See* Cellular technology

Cells, replicative senescence, 3:307

Cells, stem. *See* Stem cells

Cellular technology, 8:**306–308**

Celtic music, 9:142

Celts, human sacrifice, 3:515

Cemeteries. *See* Burial grounds

Censoring, left and right, 1:**473–474**, 2:464

Censoring, sample, 1:**474–475**

Censorship, 1:**475–476**
  Al Jazeera, 1:69, 70
  comic books, 2:24
  fascism, 3:103
  journalism, 4:212
  polling, 6:354–355
  repression, 7:174

Census, 1:**476–477**
  black immigrants, 3:565
  Cherokees, 1:498
  Current Population Survey, 2:212–213
  Integrated Public Use Microdata Series, 4:53–56
  measurement, 5:54–55
  metropolitan regions, 7:133
  Mexican Americans, 5:124–125
  multiracial movement, 5:331
  mutiracials, 5:331
  pardo, 6:130
  quantification, 6:656
  race, 7:4, 5
  race mixing, 7:28
  racial classification, 7:40
  racial identification, 3:549
  Raj, 7:56
  Royal Commissions, 7:291
  social demography, 2:296

socioeconomic status, 7:656–657

Survey of Income and Program Participation, 8:243–244

Census Bureau (U.S.). *See* U.S. Census Bureau

Center for Health, Environment, and Justice, 4:505

Center for Human Resource Research, 5:407

Center for Political Studies. *See* Pollsters

Center for Responsive Politics, 1:423

Center for the Study of Responsive Law, 5:359

Center for Urban Research and Learning, 1:18

Center-periphery. *See* Dependency theory

Centers for Disease Control and Prevention (CDC)
  AIDS, 1:63–65
  HIV, 3:489

Central African Republic, 1:38

Central America
  coffee industry, 1:594, 595
  Columbus, Christopher, 2:20
  cotton industry, 2:151
  decolonization, 2:255
  Garifuna, 3:257–258
  Latin American immigrants, 3:572
  political regions, 7:132
  See also specific countries

Central Asia, AIDS/HIV, 1:65

Central banks, 1:**477–480**
  bubbles (economics), 1:379
  dirty float, 2:375
  economic sterilization, 8:139–140
  endogenous money, 5:256–257
  exchange rates, 3:37–40
  exogenous money, 5:258–259
  foreign reserves, 7:202–203
  Hamilton, Alexander, 3:413
  history, 1:251, 252, 253
  inflation, 4:24, 26
  liquidity trap, 4:461–462
  Lombard Street (Bagehot), 4:485
  monetary base, 5:243–245
  monetary policy, 6:293–296, 294*t*
  neutral rate of interest, 4:78
  nominal interest rates, 4:87
  open market operations, 6:42–43
  quantity index, 6:658
  role, 1:250
  rules *vs.* discretion, 7:294
  supply of money, 5:260–261

yield curve, 9:166

Central Intelligence (Warner), 1:482

Central Intelligence Agency, U.S.
(CIA), 1:**480–486**
  Allende, Salvador, 1:77–78
  Bay of Pigs, 1:262
  Cuban Missile Crisis, 2:184
  hallucinogens, 3:411
  history, 1:480–482
  Hussein, Saddam, 3:532
  interrogation, 4:111, 113
  Lumumba, Patrice, 4:518
  national defense, 2:260
  purpose, 1:482–485
  September 11, 2001, 1:485

Central Intelligence Group (CIG),
U.S. *See* Central Intelligence
Agency, U.S. (CIA)

Central limit theorem, 1:**486–487**
  large sample properties, 4:349
  law of large numbers, 4:373

Central planning. *See* Planning

Central Selling Organization (CSO),
2:355, 356

Central state materialism, 1:278

Central tendencies, measures of,
1:**487–488**, 5:51, 217–218

Central tendency, measures of, 8:592

Centralism, democratic. *See*
Democratic centralism

Centre de Renseignements et
d'Informations Sociales et
Économiques. *See* X-Crise

Centre for Contemporary Cultural
Studies (CCCS), 2:199, 7:209

Centre Polytechnicien d'Études
Économiques (CPEE). *See* X-Crise

Centrism, 1:**488–489**, 578

CEPAL (Comisión Económica para
América Latina). *See* Economic
Commission for Latin America and
the Caribbean (ECLAC)

Ceramics. *See* Pottery

Cerebellum, 1:573, 574

Cernea, Michael, 1:124

Certification, occupational, 6:23

Cervantes, Miguel de, 6:149

Césaire, Aimé, 3:336

Césaire, Suzanne Roussy, 3:336

Ceylon. *See* Sri Lanka

Cézanne, Paul, 8:632

CFCs (Chlorofluorocarbons), 3:378

Chador. *See* Veils, in Middle Eastern
and North African cultures

Chain-weighting, 6:658

Chakrabarty, Dipesh, 2:597, 8:355,
356

Chalcolithic period, 3:125

Challenge-skill balance, 3:157

Challenger (space shuttle), 3:388, 6:76

Chalmers, David, consciousness, 2:79

Chalybäus, Heinrich, 3:454

Chamberlain, Arthur Neville. *See*
Chamberlain, Neville

Chamberlain, Houston, 1:185,
3:335–336

Chamberlain, Joseph, 1:349

Chamberlain, Neville, 1:**489–490**,
9:148–149
  appeasement, 1:153
  Churchill, Winston, 1:537

Chamberlin, Edward, 2:57
  experimental economics, 2:505
  monopolistic competition, 2:56

Chambers, Whittaker, 2:85

Chambliss, William, labeling theory,
4:299

Champernowne, David, 3:218, 5:435,
6:249

Champollion, Jean Francois, 1:165

Chance. *See* Randomness

Chandler, Alfred Dupont, Jr., 1:442,
3:148

Chaney, James, 4:527

Chang-Lin Tien, 1:416

Change
  attitude, 1:200–201
  conservatism, 2:83
  cultural, 1:122
  developmental psychology,
    2:349–351
  flexibility, 3:156–157
  global warming rate, 3:328
  growth curve analysis, 3:390–392
  institutional, 5:545, 6:70
  life events and stress, 4:443–444
  marginalism, 4:596–597
  period effects, 6:209–210
  See also Social change

Change, technological, 1:**490–492**
  checks and balances, 1:496
  described, 8:302
  determinism, 2:332
  division of labor, 2:423–425
  labor demand, 4:313
  legacy effects, 4:405
  Luddites, 4:513–515
  Machinery Question, 4:536–537
  progress, 8:298–302
  rentier class, 1:566–567

  social aspects, 1:490
  surplus labor, 4:310–311
  technological determinism, 2:332
  technological progress, 8:298–302
  vintage models, 8:619–621

Change To Win (CTW) coalition,
8:516

*Changes in Bodily Form of Descendants
of Immigrants* (Boas), 1:345

Channel Islands, 2:63

Chaos and Time Series Analysis
(Sprott), 1:492

Chaos theory, 1:**492–493**
  butterfly effect, 1:413–414
  catastrophe theory, 1:468–469
  randomness, 7:63–64
  system analysis, 8:256

Chapais, Bernard, 1:83

Chaplinsky v. New Hampshire (1942),
7:42

Chappell, David L., 5:497

Characters, fictional, 3:137

Charaibs. *See* Garifuna

Charcot, Jean-Martin, 3:306

Charismatic authority, 6:68

Charismatic leadership, 2:360,
4:376–377, 381–382

Charitable foundations, 3:**183–185**
  institutional investors, 4:134
  international nongovernmental
    organizations, 4:96–99

Charlemagne, 1:533, 3:498, 8:593

Charles I, King of England, 4:414

Charleston (SC), African burial
grounds, 1:393

*Charlotte-Meklenburg Board of
Education, Swann v.* (1971), 2:314

Charmes, Jacques, 3:275

Charnes, Abraham, 2:240

*A Charter for the Social Sciences in the
Schools* (Beard), 1:268

Chartism, 3:483

Chavannes, Jean-Baptiste, 3:407

Chávez, César, 1:**493–494**
  civil rights movement, U.S., 1:552
  migrant labor, 5:155

Chávez, Hugo, 1:**494–495**
  Castro, Fidel, 1:466
  class conflict, 1:571
  developing countries, 2:336
  Latin American revolutions, 7:235
  populism, 6:384

Chavinism. *See* Jingoism

Chavis, Benjamin F., Jr., 5:383–384

Cheaters, 7:108

Chebyshev, Pafnuty, 8:588
Checks and balances, 1:**495–496**
    Central Intelligence Agency, U.S,
      1:484–485
    civil-military relation, 1:547–548
    Congress, U.S., 2:73
    Constitution, U.S., 2:91
    constitutional courts, 2:93
    corruption, 2:144
    judiciary, 4:226–227
    Locke, John, 4:477
    republicanism, 7:188
Chemical weapons, 9:52–53
    hallucinogens, 3:411
    World War I, 9:146
Chemical Weapons Convention
    (1997), 9:52–53
Cheney, Dick, 9:28
Chernenko, Konstantin, 8:512
Chernobyl. *See* Disaster management
Cherokee Nation, 1:496, 497, 4:586
Cherokee Preservation Foundation,
    1:498
Cherokees, 1:**496–499**
    Appalachia, 1:149
    Mankiller, Wilma, 4:586
    Sequoyah, 7:453–455
Chesneaux, Jean, 1:188
Chesson, Harrell, 8:369
Cheung, N. S., 7:491
Chevalier, Michel, 2:134
Chevra Kaddisha, 3:239
Chi-square, 1:**523–524**, 6:192
Chiang Kai-shek, 1:**499**, 520, 521
Chiapas, 1:**500–501**
    latifundia, 4:354
    Latin American revolutions, 7:235
    Zapata, Emiliano, 9:172
Chicago *Defender* (newspaper),
    1:**501–502**
Chicago (IL)
    Board of Trade, 3:180
    Chicago School, 1:502–503
    Defender, 1:501
    Haymarket Square riot, 3:437
    jazz, 4:176
    Moving to Opportunity, 5:303
Chicago School, 1:**502–503**
    American sociology, 7:667
    case method, 1:453
    conservatism, 2:85
    human ecology, 3:510
    Janowitz, Morris, 4:171, 172
    Lasswell, Harold, 4:351

Merriam, Charles Edward, Jr.,
    5:101–102
    neighborhoods, 5:463
    neoliberalism, 5:474
    Park, Robert E., 6:140, 141
    Park School, 6:142, 143
    race, 7:14
    race relations, 7:29–30
    regions, 7:130
    schools in sociology, 8:11
    social demography, 2:296
    socioeconomic status, 7:655–656
    sociology, 7:661
    Stigler, George Joseph, 8:144
    urban poverty, 6:410–411
    urban studies, 8:541
    See also University of Chicago
Chicano movement. *See* Mexican
    Americans
Chicanos. *See* Mexican Americans
Chicken (game), 3:252
Chief Joseph, 1:**503–504**
Chiefdoms, autocracy, 1:216
Child Behavior Checklist (CBCL),
    1:**504–505**
Child care. *See* Day care
Child development, 1:**505–508**
    achievement, 1:14
    attachment theory, 1:195–197
    Baumrind, Diana, 1:260
    Bettelheim, Bruno, 1:290–291
    Bowlby, John, 1:363
    Brazelton, T. Berry, 1:368–369
    Child Behavior Checklist,
      1:504–505
    day care, 2:246
    developmental psychology,
      2:349–351
    economic psychology, 2:495
    emotion and affect, 2:571–572
    emotion regulation, 2:573
    equilibrium, 2:622–623
    Erikson, Erik, 2:625–626
    infants, 1:25
    Maccoby, Eleanor, 4:531–532
    maturation, 5:34–36
    moral domain theory, 5:279–280
    Oedipus complex, 6:28–29
    parenting styles, 6:137–138
    peer effects, 6:198–200
    perspective-taking, 6:226
    Piaget, Jean, 6:268–271
    psychological depression, 2:306,
      307
    resiliency, 7:205–206

Scarr, Sandra Wood, 7:340–341
    school readiness, 7:87–88
    self-concept, 7:399
    self-representation, 7:426–427,
      427*t*
    socialization, 7:646–648
    Spock, Benjamin, 8:61–62
    stages of, 1:511–512, 8:77–79
    stunted growth, 8:187–189
    teacher-child relationships,
      8:291–292
    temperament, 8:322
    theory of mind, 8:346–348
Child labor, 1:**508–510**
    children's rights, 1:512
    diamond industry, 2:356
    employment, 2:581
    labor law, 4:303
    migrant labor, 5:155
    sweatshops, 8:247–248
    trade liberalization, 4:428
Child pornography, 6:13
Child-rearing, personality, 1:120
Child study movement. *See*
    Maturation
Child support. *See* Divorce and
    separation
Child Tax Credit, U.K. (CTC),
    8:274–275
Child Tax Credit, U.S. (CTC), 8:274
Childbearing. *See* Childbirth
Childbirth
    cultural meaning, 9:108
    medicalization, 5:431
    midwifery, 5:151–154
    outside of marriage, 3:91–92, 91*t*,
      115
    rites of passage, 7:258–259
Childbirth, natural, 5:**431–432**
Childcare, women's work, 9:124
Childe, V. Gordon, 1:167
Childlessness, 1:**510–511**, 4:19–20
Children, 1:**511–512**
    aggression, 1:55–56
    Child Behavior Checklist,
      1:504–505
    child development, 1:505–508
    child labor, 1:508–509
    Chinese Americans, 1:514
    Clark, Kenneth B., 1:560
    cohabitation, 2:1–2
    corporal punishment, 2:134–136
    day care, 2:245–246
    demographic transition,
      2:291–292

divorce and separation, 2:428
Erikson, Erik, 2:625–626
essentialism, 2:631
family structure, 3:92, 93
fatherless, 3:107
gambling, 3:249
gifted and talented, 3:315–318
hearsay, 3:444–445
homelessness, 3:499
hope, 3:502
language, 1:528–529
lying, 4:523–524, 525
maturation, 5:34–36
mental health, 5:85
migrant labor, 5:155
National Education Longitudinal
    Study, 5:390–392
obesity, 6:4, 9:58
out of wedlock, 8:486
parent-child relationships,
    6:131–133
peer effects, 6:198–200
post-traumatic stress, 6:403
poverty statistics, 3:92, 92t
psychological depression, 2:306
rights, 1:512–513
Rosenberg's Self-Esteem Scale
    (RSES), 7:288
school readiness, 7:87–88
separation anxiety, 7:447–448
single-adult families, 3:94
social information processing,
    7:599–600
social skills interventions, 4:120
socialization, 7:646–648
Spock, Benjamin, 8:61–62
Stolen Generations, 8:158–159
suicide, 8:222
tax credits, 8:273, 274
television, 8:319–321
theory of mind, 8:346–348
type A/type B personality, 6:224
video games, 8:611–612
The Children of Sánchez (Lewis), 4:418
Children's rights, 1:**512–513**
child labor, 1:508–509
described, 1:511
Chile
Allende, Salvador, 1:77–78
architecture, 1:170
Central Intelligence Agency, U.S,
    1:483, 484
Chicago School, 1:502–503
concentration camps, 2:64
copper industry, 2:131

Kissinger, Henry, 4:275
Latin American revolutions,
    7:234–235
Chiluba, Frederick, 4:251
Chimpanzees. *See* Primates
Chin, Vincent, 1:514
China
AIDS/HIV, 1:65, 66
birth rate, 3:127
Central Intelligence Agency, U.S.,
    1:483
Chinese Americans, 1:513
Chinese diaspora, 1:516–517
clash of civilizations, 1:559
demography, 2:294
drought, 2:448
economics
    aquaculture, 3:152
    automobile industry, 1:221,
        223
    banana industry, 1:246
    bauxite industry, 1:261
    beggar-thy-neighbor, 1:273
    blue collar and white collar,
        1:339
    bull and bear markets, 1:386
    Chinese diaspora, 1:518
    collectivism, 2:11
    copper industry, 2:130, 131
    corporations, 2:140
    cotton industry, 2:152
    crony capitalism, 2:180
    currency devaluation and
        revaluation, 2:212
    economic growth, 2:490–491
    foreign reserves, 7:202
    free trade, 3:196
    labor supply, 4:320
    Ladejinsky, Wolf, 4:328
    land reform, 4:342, 343, 344
    life-cycle hypothesis, 4:443
    microelectronics industry,
        5:139
    nonrenewable natural
        resource use, 5:438
    saving rate, 2:108
global warming, 3:330
history
    anticolonial movements,
        1:139
    Bush, George H. W., 1:398
    Chinese Revolution,
        1:519–521
    concentration camps, 2:64

feudal mode of production,
    3:134
India, 5:542
interwar years, 4:122
irrigation, 4:152
Mao Zedong, 4:587–590
Opium Wars, 6:45–46
peaceful coexistence,
    6:186–188
repression, 7:175
Silk Road, 7:511
state, 8:103–104
Sun Yat-sen, 8:225–226
visual arts, 8:631
Hmong, 3:490–491
international relations, 1:451
Khmer Rouge, 4:263
Korean War, 4:289
latifundia, 4:353
occupational hazards, 6:22
political science
    borders, 1:355
    Chiang Kai-shek, 1:499
    civil disobedience, 1:546
    communism, 2:35–36
    democratization, 2:288
    divine right, 2:422
    Little Red Book, 4:467–468
    Maoism, 4:590–591
    Marxism, 4:639
    merit, 5:95–96
    one-party states, 6:41–42
    regions, 7:131
    reproductive politics, 7:181
    socialism, 7:638
population growth, 6:380
religion
    Buddhism, 1:383, 384
    monotheism, 5:271
sociology
    birth control, 1:303
    multiracial meritocracy,
        5:100–101
    peasant organizations, 6:74
    population control, 6:378
    virgins, 8:630
    working class, 9:132
state capitalism, 1:443
suicide, 8:223
theater, 8:337
United Nations membership,
    8:522
water resources, 9:41
China and the Chinese Overseas
    (Gungwu), 1:516

Chinese Americans, 1:**513–515**
  race, 7:5
  settlement, 3:563, 579
Chinese Communist Party (CCP). *See* Communist Party (China)
Chinese diaspora, 1:**515–519**, 3:563
Chinese Exclusion Act (U.S. 1892). *See* Asian immigrants; Chinese Americans
Chinese immigrants
  cultural identity, 5:464
  oppression, 5:513
Chinese Revolution, 1:**519–522**
  Mao Zedong, 4:588–590
  Sun Yat-sen, 8:225–226
Chippewa Indians, Mille Lacs, 5:428
Chips, computer. *See* Microelectronics industry
Chiquita, 1:245
Chisholm, Shirley, 1:**522–523**
Chlorofluorocarbons (CFCs), 3:378
Cho, Sumi, 2:174
Chodorow, Nancy, 5:5–6, 6:29, 7:593, 8:5–6
Choi, Incheol, 2:252
Choice
  Arrow possibility theorem, 1:183–184
  maximin principle, 5:38–39
  neuroeconomics, 5:483–484
  opportunity costs, 6:47
  rational, 5:484
  reproductive, 9:117
  social
    leaders, 4:376
    theory, 8:654
    topology, 8:391
    voting schemes, 8:654
  Tiebour, 5:391
  women's liberation, 9:114
Choice, constrained. *See* Constrained choice
Choice, economic. *See* Choice in economics
Choice, pro-. *See* Pro-choice/pro-life
Choice, psychological. *See* Choice in psychology
Choice, public. *See* Public choice theory
Choice, social. *See* Social choice
Choice in economics, 1:**524–525**
  choice in psychology, 1:525–526
  constrained, 2:95–96
  consumer, 2:101
  decision-making, 2:249–251

happiness, 3:416
  lexicographic preferences, 4:422–423
  lifestyles, 4:445, 446
  McFadden, Daniel L., 5:44–45
  revealed preference, 7:224–225
  Tobin, James, 8:378
  trade-offs, 8:418–419
Choice in psychology, 1:**525–526**
  cognitive dissonance, 1:599–600
  decision-making, 2:249–251
  Lazarsfeld, Paul Felix, 4:375
  lexicographic preferences, 4:422–423
  rational choice theory, 7:74–76
  reactance theory, 7:85–86
  self-constrained behavior, 1:273–274
  sociometry, 8:18–20
Cholesky, André-Louis, 1:526
Cholesky decomposition, 1:**526–527**
Cholinesterase inhibitors, 1:90
Chomsky, Noam, 1:**527–529**
  behaviorism, 1:277
  public intellectuals, 4:69
  Skinner, B. F., 7:527
  television, 8:320
Choquet expected utility, 5:519
Chorionic villus sampling, 3:294
Chow, Gregory, 1:**529–530**
Chow test, 1:**529–530**
Christ. *See* Jesus Christ
Christaller, Walter, 3:304, 8:541
Christian Coalition, 2:86
Christian Democracy, 2:84, **276–277**
Christian Democratic Party (Chile), 1:77
Christian fundamentalism, 3:234, **236–237**
  anti-intellectualism, 4:65
  conservatism, 2:86
  contraception, 2:114
  corporal punishment, 2:135
  creationism, 2:162
  politics, 7:160–161
  religiosity, 7:163
  reproductive rights, 7:183
  right wing, 7:248
  Scopes trial, 7:366
  Southern politics, 6:347, 348
  Truth, Sojourner, 8:462
Christian right. *See* Right wing
Christian socialism, 4:403, 7:**642–643**
Christianity, 1:**530–532**
  abortion, 1:1–3

Arabs, 1:159
Aristotle, 1:175
Buddhism, 1:384, 385
caste, 1:459
Christian socialism, 7:642–643
The Church, 1:532–534
civilization, 1:557, 558
clash of civilizations, 1:559
Columbus, Christopher, 2:20, 21
conservatism, 2:84
Coptic Christian Church, 2:132
creationism, 2:161–163
cults, 2:188
heaven, 3:445–446
hell, 3:457, 458
Holy Roman Empire, 3:498
infidels, 4:22
Jews, 4:195, 221–222
Lebanese civil war, 4:396, 397
liberation theology, 4:434–436
literature, 4:464
martyrdom, 4:629
miracles, 5:196–197
missionaries, 1:41, 5:205–206
monotheism, 5:269–270
moral philosophy, 6:254
mysticism, 5:352
Nietzsche, Friedrich, 5:502, 503
orthodoxy, 6:78–79
Ottoman Empire, 6:84
pogroms, 6:286–287
political cartoons, 1:452
reconciliation, 7:110
as religion, 7:159–161
Roman Catholic Church, 7:280
secular, 7:377–379
sin, 7:519, 520
slave culture, 1:40
supreme being, 8:230
theism, 8:341
theocracy, 8:342
universities, 8:532
virgins, 8:629
worship, 9:155
See also Jesus Christ
Christians, Clifford, 2:39
Chromosomes, 3:461
The Chrysanthemum and the Sword (Benedict), 1:120, 282, 2:195
Chrysler Corporation, 1:218, 219
The Church, 1:**532–534**
  Christianity, 1:530–532
  Coptic Christian Church, 2:132
  Lynd, Robert and Helen, 4:527

Roman Catholic Church, 7:280

Church, Frank, 1:484–485

Church and state, 1:**534–536**

    Burke, Edmund, 1:396–397

    Christian Democracy, 2:276

    Christianity, 1:531

    Church's role, 1:534

    clash of civilizations, 1:559

    communalism, 2:30

    creationism, 2:162–163

    divine right, 2:421

    fundamentalism, 3:235

    Hussein, Saddam, 3:534

    Israel, 4:277

    Jefferson, Thomas, 4:180

    Lebanese civil war, 4:396

    left wing, 4:403

    legal systems, 4:406

    religiosity, 7:163

    schooling, 7:352

    Scopes trial, 7:366

    secular, 7:377–379

    sovereignty, 8:39

Church Committee inquiry (1975–1976), 1:484–485

Church of England. *See* Anglicanism

Churchill, Ward, 1:336

Churchill, Winston, 1:**537–538**, 4:150

    architecture, 1:170

    Chamberlain, Neville, 1:490

    Cold War, 2:4

    conservatism, 2:84

    leaders, 4:376

    Treasury view, 8:444–445

    United Nations, 8:522

    World War II, 9:149

Ci, Jiwei, 2:36

Cicero, 1:495, 7:188, 237

Cicourel, Aaron, 2:98

CIG (Central Intelligence Group), U.S. *See* Central Intelligence Agency, U.S. (CIA)

Cigány. *See* Roma

Cigarettes. *See* Smoking; Tobacco industry

Cincinnatus, 8:323

CIO (Congress of Industrial Organizations), 4:302

CIO (Congress of Industrial Unions), 8:515–516

Circuit Court Act (1801), 4:223

Circular flow, 5:400, *400*

    See also Quesnay, François

Circular tie. *See* Majority rule

Circulating capital. *See* Capital

Circumplex model. *See* Leary, Timothy

Cirrhosis, 1:71

CIS (Commonwealth of Independent States), 2:30, 68, 8:513

CIT (Correspondence inference theory), 1:205

Citations, 1:**538–540**, 4:216

Cities, 1:**540–542**

    assimilation, 3:574

    backwash effects, 1:236–237

    black immigrants, 3:565

    caste, 1:459

    The Church, 1:532–533

    clientelism, 1:579

    community networks, 5:476

    ethnic diversity, 2:343

    human ecology, 3:510

    Ibn Khaldūn, 3:545–546

    Jacobs, Jane, 4:165

    metropolis, 5:118

    Moses, Robert, 5:296

    Multi-City Study of Urban Inequality, 5:314–315

    neighborhoods, 5:463–464

    poverty, 5:461–463

    representative and participatory democracy, 2:284

    resegregation of schools, 7:201–202

    rural to urban migration, 5:159–160

    settlement, 7:465

    suburbs, 8:210–211

    terrorism, 8:329

    underclass, 8:5–7

    xenophobia, 9:160–161

    See also City-state; *entries begining with* Urban; Metropolitan regions; Towns

Cities and the Wealth of Nations (Jacobs), 4:165

Citizens' Clearinghouse for Hazardous Wastes. *See* Center for Health, Environment, and Justice

Citizenship, 1:**542–544**

    Chinese Americans, 1:514–515

    Church and state, 1:535, 536

    civil rights, 1:549

    confederations, 2:68

    Constitution, U.S., 2:91

    cultural rights, 2:197

    democracy, 2:273–276, 7:191

    Dred Scott v. Sanford, 2:446

    East Indian diaspora, 2:475

    involuntary, 3:354

    Jewish diaspora, 4:190–193

    judicial activism, 1:19

    Latinos, 4:359

    liberty, 4:439–441

    Mexican Americans, 5:121

    negro terminology, 5:459

    patriotism, 6:175–176

    polyarchy, 6:366

    race, 7:4

    representative and participatory democracy, 2:284–285

    social, 9:67

    social exclusion, 7:587–588

    transnationalism, 8:433

    See also Naturalization

Citizenship Act (India 1955), 2:475

Citizenship and Immigration Services, U.S. (USCIS), 5:499

City of Boerne v. Flores (1997), 1:496, 535–536

City of Cleveland, International Association of Firefighters v. (1986), 3:373

The City of God (Augustine), 4:235

City of New York, Clinton v. (1998), 1:496

City of Women (Stansell), 3:483

City-state, 1:**544–545**

    citizenship, 1:542

    democracy, 2:273

    liberty, 4:439

    representative and participatory democracy, 2:283

    republic, 7:184

    as state, 8:102–104

The Civic Culture: Political Attitudes and Democracy in Five Nations (Almond and Verba), 1:83, 6:301, 327, 8:606

Civil Aeronautics Authority (1938). *See* Aviation industry

Civil Code (France 1804), 5:364

Civil disobedience, 1:**545–546**

    direct action, 2:372

    Gandhi, Mohandas K., 3:254–255

    Indian National Congress, 3:611

    moral suasion, 5:283

    Nehru, Jawaharlal, 5:460

    passive resistance, 6:166–168

    Thoreau, Henry David, 8:357

Civil Disobedience (Thoreau), 1:545, 2:372, 8:357

Civil disorders. *See* Riots

Civil engagement. *See* Volunteerism

Civil law, 4:227, 364, 405–406

Civil liberties, 1:**546–547**
  Bill of Rights, 1:298
  bioterrorism, 1:302
  Constitution, U.S., 2:91, 92
  democracy, 2:273
  due process, 2:461
  Japanese American incarceration, 3:599–601
  liberty and, 4:440
  political tolerance, 8:386
  Tolman, Edward, 8:387
  See also Civil rights

Civil Liberties Act (U.S. 1988), 3:601

Civil-military relation, 1:**547–548**, 4:172, 7:391–392

Civil rights, 1:**548–550**
  affirmative action, 1:31
  benign neglect, 1:283
  Bill of Rights, 1:298
  Birth of a Nation (film), 1:304, 305
  California Civil Rights Initiative, 1:416
  children's rights, 1:512–513
  citizenship, 1:542–544
  civil rights movement, U.S., 1:551–552
  Coloreds (South Africa), 2:15
  conflict, 2:70
  Congress of Racial Equality, 2:75
  Constitution, U.S., 2:91, 92
  constitutionalism, 2:94
  constitutions, 2:94, 95
  cultural rights, 2:197–198
  Democratic Party (U.S.), 2:287
  disability, 2:377–378
  Dixiecrats, 2:428–431, 430
  due process, 2:461
  gay, lesbian, transgender, and bisexual politics, 6:330–331
  gender inequality, 3:626–627
  Great Society, 3:372, 373, 374
  Hernandez v. Texas, 3:464–466
  indigenous rights, 3:614–616
  Jim Crow, 4:198–201
  Malcolm X, 4:563–564
  minorities, 5:191–192
  NAACP, 5:384–385
  Nazism, 5:449
  poll tax, 6:352–353
  race-conscious policies, 7:37
  Reconstruction Era, U.S., 7:112–115

Republican Party (U.S.), 7:186, 187
  Roosevelt, Franklin D., 7:283
  Southern politics, 6:340–343
  third world, 8:352
  Truth, Sojourner, 8:462
  untouchables, 1:90–92
  White, Walter, 9:81
  women, 9:108–109, 110–111
  women's suffrage, 8:214–217
  See also Civil liberties

Civil rights, Cold War, 1:**550–551**

Civil Rights Act (U.S. 1866), 7:112–113

Civil Rights Act (U.S. 1875), 1:551

Civil Rights Act (U.S. 1957), 1:551, 3:138–139

Civil Rights Act (U.S. 1964), 4:268, 6:650, 671
  affirmative action, 1:31
  black liberalism, 1:312
  Brimmer, Andrew, 1:371
  civil rights movement, U.S., 1:552
  Congress of Racial Equality, 2:75
  desegregation, 2:314, 315
  Great Society, 3:372
  international impact, 1:550
  judicial activism, 1:19
  NAACP, 5:384
  racial discrimination, 2:394–395
  sexual harassment, 6:474–475
  Southern politics, 6:342
  Title VII, 3:121, 123, 5:408–409
  wage discrimination, 2:401

Civil Rights Act (U.S. 1968), 1:552, 4:347

Civil Rights Cases (1883)
  Birth of a Nation (film), 1:305
  civil rights movement, U.S., 1:551
  equal protection, 2:614

Civil rights movement, U.S., 1:**551–552**
  African Americans, 1:35
  black conservatism, 1:311
  black middle class, 1:313
  black nationalism, 1:316, 317
  Black Panthers, 1:318
  black politics, 6:324
  Black Power, 1:320–321
  blackness, 1:328–329
  Brown v. Board of Education (1954), 1:374–375
  Chávez, César, 1:494
  Chicago *Defender* (newspaper), 1:501

civil disobedience, 1:545, 546
  Cold War, 1:550
  collective action frames, 7:605
  Congress of Racial Equality, 2:75
  desegregation, 2:313–315
  direct action, 2:372
  Forman, James, 3:174–175
  Hoover, J. Edgar, 3:501
  Houston, Charles Hamilton, 3:505
  integration, 4:57–60
  jazz, 4:178
  Jim Crow, 4:201
  Johnson, Lyndon B., 4:210
  Kennedy, John F., 4:254
  Kerner Commission Report, 4:257, 258
  King, Martin Luther, Jr., 4:267–269
  Ku Klux Klan, 4:294
  law, 4:362, 369–371
  liberation, 4:430
  Lynd, Staughton, 4:528–529
  Marshall, Thurgood, 4:625–626
  Mexican Americans, 5:123–124
  moral suasion, 5:283
  Muhammad Ali, 1:74
  multiracial movement, 5:331
  mutiracials, 5:332–333
  passive resistance, 6:167
  Pettigrew, Thomas F., 6:234–235
  quotas, 6:670–671
  race relations, 7:29–31
  revolution of rising expectations, 7:232
  school desegregation, 2:316–318
  separate-but-equal, 7:447
  Southern bloc, 8:34–35
  Southern politics, 6:342–343
  Southern strategy, 8:35–38
  Student Nonviolent Coordinating Committee, 8:183–184
  Thurmond, Strom, 8:360–361

Civil society, 1:**552–554**
  Christian Democracy, 2:277
  citizenship, 1:542–544
  civil-military relation, 1:547–548
  conservatism, 2:84
  consociational democracy, 2:278
  described, 7:651
  hegemony, 3:456
  political sociology, 8:3, 4
  primitive communism, 2:38

Civil union. *See* Marriage

Civil War, Mexican. *See* Mexican Revolution (1910–1920)

Civil War, U.S. *See* U.S. Civil War

Civil wars, 1:554–557
    Chinese Revolution, 1:519, 520
    civil, 9:34
    Darfur, 2:226–227
    disaster management, 2:382
    elites, 2:566
    just war, 4:236
    latifundia, 4:354
    Lebanon, 4:396–398
    national defense, 2:260
    political neutrality, 5:489
    Spanish Civil War, 1:112, 3:186, 8:42–44, 9:51
    Taliban, 8:263
    Tito, Josip, 8:376
    Yugoslavia, 9:168–169
    See also U.S. Civil War

Civilian Conservation Corps (CCC), 5:413, 494

Civilization, 1:557–559
    agricultural industry, 1:62
    alienation, 1:75
    ancient
        human sacrifice, 3:515
        Jewish diaspora, 4:190
    classical music, 1:575
    collapse, 3:241
    communalism, 2:30
    convergence theory, 2:117–118
    cradle of, 3:125–126
    culture, 2:202–203
    development theory, 2:339
    deviance, 2:352–354
    Muslims, 5:347
    Oedipus complex, 6:29
    plumbing, 6:281–282
    primitive communism, 2:37–38
    sanitation, 7:322
    tyranny of the majority, 8:478
    Veblen, Thorstein, 8:595
    See also names of specific civilizations

Civilization, Roman. *See* Roman civilization

Civilization (Mill), 8:478

Civilization and Its Discontents (Freud), 3:211, 213, 214, 8:627

Civilizations, clash of, 1:**559–560**
    Clark, Kenneth B., 1:558
    classical music, 1:575
    described, 1:558

Huntington, Samuel P., 3:525–526
    reciprocity, 7:105–107
    secular, 7:378
    triumphalism, 8:455–456

The Civilizing Process (Elias), 2:412

Claims, land. *See* Land claims

Clans. *See* Kinship

The Clansman (Dixon), 1:304, 3:347

Clapp, Robert, 9:103

Clapton, Eric, 1:343

Clark, Anna, 3:483

Clark, Colin, 5:400, 541

Clark, John Bates, 3:150
    accumulation of capital, 1:13
    capital, 1:430
    marginal product of labor, 4:305, 306, 307
    marginal productivity, 4:595

Clark, Kenneth B., 1:93, **560–561**, 9:24, 25
    Brown v. Board of Education (1954), 1:374, 376
    child development, 1:507
    litigation, 4:465
    race and psychology, 7:22

Clark, Mamie Phipps, 1:507, 560

Clark, Mark, 1:322

Clark, William, 4:182

Clark Plan, 1:561

Clarke, Charles, 9:46

Clarke, John Henrik, 1:309

Clash of civilizations, 1:**559–560**
    classical music, 1:575
    described, 1:558
    Huntington, Samuel P., 3:525–526
    reciprocity, 7:105–107
    secular, 7:378
    triumphalism, 8:455–456

The Clash of Civilizations and the Remaking of World Order (Huntington), 1:557, 559, 3:525, 7:163

Class, 1:**561–565**
    African socialism, 7:640–641
    authority, 1:214–215
    blue collar and white collar, 1:340
    Bonacich, Edna, 1:352
    burial grounds, 1:393
    Chinese diaspora, 1:517
    citizenship, 1:542–543
    communism, 2:34–35
    constructs, 7:579
    consumption, 2:107

coups d'etat, 2:156

credentialism, 2:166–167

Creole, 2:167

crime and criminology, 2:170

critical race theory, 2:175

cultural capital, 2:189, 190

cultural distinctions, 2:412–413

Davis, Angela, 2:243

dependency theory, 2:299

deviance, 2:354

distinctions, 2:412

false consciousness, 3:81–83

French Revolution, 3:205

global hierarchies, 8:542–543

identity politics, 6:335–336

Jewish diaspora, 4:191–192

knowledge society, 4:285

labeling theory, 4:300

landlords, 4:346

lateral mobility, 5:212

left wing, 4:403

Lewis, Oscar, 4:418–419

lifestyles, 4:445–446

lumpenproletariat, 4:516–517

managerial, 4:577–579
    bureaucracy, 1:390
    bureaucrat, 1:392
    capitalism, 1:442–443
    described, 1:563
    petty bourgeoisie, 1:361

meritocracy, 5:99

mobility, 5:208–211

mode of production, 5:220

mulatto escape hatch, 5:310–312

neocolonialism, 5:467

The New Class, 5:492–493

organic intellectuals, 4:66–67

patricians, 6:174–175

peasantry, 6:195

Pettigrew, Thomas F., 6:235

petty bourgeoisie, 1:361–362

political attitudes, 1:103

popular culture, 6:373–374

post-Parsonian American sociology, 8:5

Poulantzas, Nicos, 6:404–405

professional-managerial, 5:492, 9:130

schooling, 7:350, 352, 354–355

social constructs, 7:579

socioeconomic status, 7:655–659

sociology, 7:662

solidarity, 8:23–24

subaltern, 8:190–192

Class, *continued*
  surplus labor, 4:311–312
  towns, 8:405
  transitional conjunctures, 2:77–78
  tyranny of the majority,
    8:478–479
  upward mobility, 8:533–535
  urbanity, 8:544
  vulnerability, 8:657
  wealth, 9:44
  See also Bourgeoisie; Caste; Middle
    class; Underclass; Working class
Class, leisure, 1:**565–566**, 9:46
  conspicuous consumption, 2:88
  lifestyles, 4:445
  Veblen, Thorstein, 8:595–596,
    597
  wealth, 9:46
Class, managerial. *See* Managerial class
Class, productive. *See* Physiocracy
Class, proprietary. *See* Physiocracy
Class, rentier, 1:**566–568**, *567*
  inflation, 4:25
  managerial capitalism, 1:442–443
Class, sterile. *See* Physiocracy
*Class and Class Conflict in Industrial
  Society* (Dahrendorf), 1:214–215
Class conflict, 1:**568–571**
  capitalist mode of production,
    1:447
  cities, 1:541, 542
  class consciousness, 1:571
  cleavages, 1:578
  communism, 2:34–35, 36
  conspicuous consumption, 2:88
  consumerism, 2:105
  convergence theory, 2:117
  described, 1:561–564
  discrimination, 2:391
  elite theory, 2:562–564
  exploitation, 3:63–65
  Haiti, 3:407
  hegemony, 3:455
  labor, 4:300–301, 302
  leisure class, 1:571
  liberation, 4:430
  lynchings, 4:526
  Russian Revolution, 7:303–304
  taste for discrimination, 2:399
  totalitarianism, 8:395
  unequal education, 2:537–538
Class consciousness, 1:**571–572**,
  3:482–483
  class conflict, 1:569–571
  communism, 2:34

Class intervals, 3:206
Class struggle
  mode of production, 5:220
  predator-prey system, 5:524
  Thompson, Edward P., 8:354–356
Classes in Contemporary Capitalism
  (Poulantzas), 6:405
Classic, United States v., 9:84–85
Classical archaeology, 1:165–166
Classical competition. *See* Long period
  analysis
Classical conditioning, 1:**572–575**,
  6:43
  behaviorism, 1:276, 277
  learned helplessness, 4:387–389
  Pavlov, Ivan, 6:177–179
  phobia, 6:263
  reinforcement theories, 7:147
  shock experiments, 3:62
  Skinner box, 7:528
Classical economics, 2:**502–505**
  banana parable, 1:247
  capital, 1:430
  capitalism, 1:439
  consumption, 2:106
  equilibrium, 2:619–620
  full employment, 3:225
  Heilbroner, Robert, 3:456–457
  history, 2:498
  Jajmani matrix, 4:167
  Keynes, John Maynard, 4:260
  laissez-faire, 4:335–338
  long period analysis, 4:490
  long run, 4:491
  macroeconomics, 4:540–541
  markets, 4:607–608
  natural rate of unemployment,
    5:435, 437
  neo-Ricardian economics,
    2:519–521
  new classical economics, 2:522
  prices, 6:455–456
  quantity theory of money,
    6:659–660
  race, 7:13, 14
  Ricardian vice, 7:242
  surplus, 8:235
  violence, 8:627
  zero population growth, 9:174
Classical experiment, 1:425–426
Classical music, 1:**575–576**
Classical realism. *See* Political realism
Classical statistical analysis, 1:**576–577**
  law of large numbers, 4:372–373
  ordinary least squares, 4:391–394

Classical test theory. *See* Psychometrics
Classical unemployment, 8:503
Classicism
  humanism, 3:517
  Jefferson, Thomas, 4:182–183
Classics, University of Oxford, 8:528
Classics in Austrian Economics
  (Kirzner), 1:211
Classification
  consciousness disorders, 2:81
  data, 2:236
  emotion and affect, 2:571
  ideal type, 3:547
  industry, 3:622
  mental retardation, 5:89
  occupational, 7:656–657
  symbols, 8:250
Classification, racial. *See* Racial
  classification
Classification, self. *See* Self-
  classification
Classification, social. *See* Social
  categorization
The Classless Society (Kingston), 1:564
Classroom environment,
  underachievers, 8:484
Classrooms, jigsaw, 1:181
Clausewitz, Carl von, 9:17
Clay, Cassius Marcellus. *See* Ali,
  Muhammad (US boxer)
Clay, Henry, 1:497
Clay-clay models. *See* Vintage models
Clayton Antitrust Act (U.S. 1914),
  1:143, 144, 4:303
Clean Air Act Amendments (U.S.
  1970-), 6:359, 360, 362
Cleaning of money. *See* Money
  laundering
Cleansing, ethnic. *See* Ethnic conflict
CLEAR (Council on Licensure,
  Enforcement and Regulation), 6:23
Clearing, market. *See* Market clearing
Clearinghouse, market. *See* Market
  clearinghouse
*Cleavage Structures, Party Systems, and
  Voter Alignments* (Lipset and
  Rokkan), 1:577–578, 6:162
Cleavages, 1:**577–578**
  competitive party systems, 6:162
  constitutions, 2:95
  dependency theory, 2:298–300
  ethnic fractionalization, 3:7
Cleaver, Eldridge, 1:319
Cleaver, Harry, 4:330
Clericism, conservatism, 2:84
Clichy-sous-Bois riots (France), 8:539

Clientelism, 1:**578–579**, 6:176–177

Clifford, Clark, 1:481

Climate change
    greenhouse effect, 3:377–378
    natural disasters, 5:433
    urbanization, 8:548
    See also Global warming

Clinton, Bill, 1:**579–581**, 2:384
    Brimmer, Andrew, 1:372
    Bush, George H. W., 1:398
    California Civil Rights Initiative, 1:416
    Chávez, César, 1:494
    Church and state, 1:535
    computers, 2:60
    conservatism *vs.*, 2:86
    Democratic Party (U.S.), 2:288
    Great Society programs, 3:373
    impeachment, 3:585
    law and order, 4:371
    lying, 4:524
    managed competition, 2:54
    Nader, Ralph, 5:360
    nanotechnology, 5:361
    national health insurance, 5:395–396
    national service programs, 5:414
    Republican Party (U.S.), 7:187
    unequal education, 2:538
    urban renewal, 8:537

Clinton, Hillary, 1:579, 580, 581

Clinton, William J. *See* Clinton, Bill

Clinton v. City of New York (1998), 1:496

Cliometric Society, 1:582

Cliometrica: Journal of Historical Economics and Econometric History (periodical), 1:583

Cliometrics, 1:**581–583**
    Chicago School, 1:502
    Engerman, Stanley, 2:592–593
    Fogel, Robert, 3:161–162
    Tawney, R. H., 8:272
    Time on the Cross, 4:366–367

Cliques, 5:476, 478

Cliques, peer. *See* Peer cliques

Clock time, 1:**583–584**, 8:363

Clomipramine, 6:19

Closed-list systems, 8:655

Closed shop. *See* Labor law

Closed-shop agreements, 4:303, 316

Closure, social. *See* Social exclusion

Clotfelter, Charles T., 7:201

Cloture rule, 3:139

Cloward, Richard A., 9:24, 25

Clower, Robert W., 1:255–256, 6:454

Club of Rome, 1:**584–585**
    Limits to Growth, 3:241, 6:95
    nonrenewable natural resources, 5:437–438

Clubs, Jacobinism, 4:164

Cluster analysis, 1:**585–586**

Clustering Algorithms (Hartigan), 1:586

CMA (Critical medical anthropology), 1:131

CMP (Capitalist mode of production). *See* Capitalist mode of production (CMP)

CNN, 4:215

Co-evolution, organization theory, 6:69

Co-operation Act (Finland 1978), 1:593

Coal mining
    industrial accidents, 1:8
    See also Appalachia; Mining industry

Coale, Ansley J., 9:48, 174

Coalition, 1:**586–587**
    Congress Party, India, 2:76
    Riker, William, 7:249
    Russian Revolution, 7:304
    Southern bloc, 8:34–35
    urban politics, 6:351

Coalition government, 3:357, 4:277

Coalition theory, 1:**587–588**

Coard, Bernard. *See* Grenadian Revolution

Coase, Ronald, 1:502, **589–590**, 3:148
    Coase theorem, 1:590
    externality, 3:70
    law and economics, 4:367
    social cost, 7:583
    transaction cost, 8:427

Coase theorem, 1:**590–591**
    Coase, Ronald, 1:589
    social cost, 7:583
    Tragedy of the Commons, 8:422–423, 423
    transaction cost, 8:427

Coatsworth, J. Douglas, 7:204–205

Cobb, Jonathan, 9:132

Cobb-Douglas function, 3:155, 5:522

Cobden, Richard, 2:134

Cobweb cycles, 1:*591*, **591–592**, 3:53

Cocaine. *See* Drugs of abuse

Cochrane, Glynn, 1:124

Cochrane, John, 1:407

Code of Hammurabi. *See* Retaliation

Code of the Street (Anderson), 8:264

Codes of conduct. *See* Ethics

Codes of Manu. *See* Brahmins

Codetermination, 1:**592–594**

Codex Alimentaris Commission, 1:247

Coefficients
    Gini, 3:320, 320*t*, *321, 321t, 322, 322t*
        Deininger and Squire World Bank Inequality Database, 2:268
        equality, 2:617–618, *618*
        Fields' index of economic inequality, 3:137–138
        income distribution, 3:605
        income inequality, 4:1–2
        University of Texas Inequality Project, 8:50
        variation, 8:591–592
        wealth inequality, 4:9–11
    input, 3:155
    standardized, 3:76
    of variation, 8:591

Coercion
    annexation, 1:115
    libertarianism, 4:437–439
    liberty, 4:440
    national security, 5:413
    organization-environment theory, 6:71
    organization theory, 6:70
    violence, 8:622–623, 627

Coexistence, peaceful. *See* Peaceful coexistence

Coffee, Linda, 7:271

Coffee industry, 1:**594–596**

COFRAT (Committee on Freedom in Research and Teaching), 1:105–106

Cognition, 1:**596–599**
    attitudes, 7:573–574
    behaviorism, 1:280
    butterfly effect, 1:414
    children, 1:506–507, 511
    Chomsky, Noam, 1:527, 529
    consciousness, 2:78–79, 81–82
    constructivism, 2:96, 97
    contempt, 2:113
    cultural relativism, 2:195
    Darwin, Charles, 2:229–232
    Dawes, Robyn, 2:244–245
    dementia, 2:271–272
    equilibrium, 2:622–623
    habits, 3:403

Cognition, *continued*
    intelligence, 4:71–73
    knowledge, 4:278
    learned helplessness, 4:387–389
    life events and stress, 4:444
    loneliness, 4:486, 487
    mood, 5:275–276
    mood congruent recall, 5:277
    music, 5:345–346
    need for, 5:452
    neuroscience research, 5:484–485
    psychological depression, 2:307
    rituals, 7:260, 262–264
    self-system, 7:430
    Skinner, B. F., 7:527
    social
        attitudes, 7:573–574
        Bandura, Albert, 1:248–249
        bias, 7:570–572
        comparison, 7:576–577
        described, 1:598
        dual systems, 7:572–573
        errors, 7:570–572
        habitus, 3:404–406
        history, 7:569–570
        influence, 7:575
        intelligence, 4:74–75
        leaning perspective,
          7:602–603
        person memory, 6:215
        reciprocal determinism,
          2:331–332
        schemata, 7:570
        theory of mind, 8:346–348
    social psychology, 7:609–610
    talent, 8:262
    teachers, 8:294
Cognitive agnosticism, 1:57
Cognitive archaeology, 1:169
Cognitive atheism, 1:194–195
Cognitive balance. *See* Cognitive
    dissonance; Equilibrium in
    psychology
Cognitive-behavior therapy. *See*
    Learned helplessness; Psychotherapy
Cognitive-behavioral therapy,
    obsessions, 6:18
Cognitive development, adolescent,
    1:25
Cognitive-developmental perspective.
    See Developmental psychology
Cognitive dissonance, 1:599–601,
    3:132–133
    Aronson, Elliot, 1:180–181
    attitude change, 1:201

child development, 1:507
equilibrium, 2:623
reactance theory, 7:86
religiosity, 7:163
self-affirmation theory, 7:396–397
self-justification, 7:420–421
self-perception theory, 7:422–423
self-representation, 7:426–427
social judgment theory, 7:602
Cognitive distortions. *See*
    Psychotherapy
Cognitive egocentrism, 1:507
Cognitive map, social. *See* Social
    cognitive map
Cognitive mapping. *See* Social
    cognitive map
Cognitive matrix. *See* Rituals
Cognitive neuroscience, 1:599
Cognitive Psychology (Neisser), 1:598
Cognitive Psychology (periodical), 1:598
Cognitive science, 1:598–599
Cognitivism, 5:15
Cohabitation, 2:1–2
    gender differences, 3:128
    marriage, 4:615
    miscegenation, 5:199–200
    poverty-based, 3:84
    statistics, 3:91–92, 91*t*
Cohen, G. A., 3:166–167, 177, 8:577
Cohen, Jacob, 3:180
Cohen, Lizabeth, 4:445
Cohen, Mark, 1:358
Cohen, Stanley, 9:167–168
Cohesion, group, 3:388
Cohn, Bernard, 1:462
Cohort effects. *See* Period effects
Coincident indicators. *See* Lagging,
    leading, and coincident indicators
Cointegration, 2:2–4, 627
    See also Integration
Cointegration regression, 8:517–520
COINTELPRO, 7:175
Coker v. Georgia (1977), 7:65
Colbert, Stephen, 6:149
Cold War, 2:4–5
    alliances, 1:79, 81
    appeasement, 1:153
    arms control, 1:176
    arms race, 1:178
    Asian immigrants, 3:563–564
    Berlin Wall, 1:289
    bilateralism, 1:297
    birth control, 1:303
    Brezhnev, Leonid, 1:370

Bush, George H. W., 1:398
Central Intelligence Agency, U.S,
    1:483, 484
civilization, 1:558
communism, 2:35–36
conservatism, 2:85, 86
Cuban Missile Crisis, 2:183–185
Cuban Revolution, 2:186
decolonization, 2:256
defense, 2:258
deterrence, 2:333–334
disarmament, 2:380
domino theory, 2:434–435
Eisenhower, Dwight D., 2:555
food diplomacy, 3:166
iron curtain, 4:150
isolationism, 4:161
Kennedy, John F., 4:254
Korean War, 4:289
liberalism, 4:425
Macmillan, Harold, 4:538
modernization, 5:233
mutual deterrence, 2:334–335
NATO, 5:545
nuclear weapons, 9:31–32, 48, 49
peaceful coexistence, 6:185–188
refugees, 7:126
retaliation, 7:216
technology transfer, 8:308
terrorism, 8:328, 329
Thant, U., 8:334
third world, 8:351
weapons industry, 9:50
World War II and, 9:151
Cold War, civil rights, 1:550–551
Cole, Faye-Cooper, 1:345
Cole, G. D. H., 3:73–74
Cole, Harold, 3:370
Cole, Johnnetta, 1:133
Coleman, David A., 3:128
Coleman, Havens Realty Corporation v.,
    1:209
Coleman, James
    Almond, Gabriel A., 1:82
    race and education, 2:540, 7:17,
      565, 566
    social capital, 8:7
    See also Unequal education
Coleman Report. *See Equality of
    Educational Opportunity* (Coleman)
Collaboration, negotiation, 5:457
Collaborative ethnography, 1:123
Collateral damage, just war, 4:235,
    236
Collective action, 2:5–6

Asian American politics, 6:323
   mobilization, 5:213–215
   pluralistic ignorance, 3:560–561
   political sociology, 8:4
   post-Parsonian American sociology, 8:7
   rational choice theory, 7:75
   riots, 7:250
   rituals, 7:259–264
   self-efficacy, 7:410
   social movements, 7:603–607
   social relations, 7:612–613
   voluntary associations, 1:193
Collective action games, 2:**6–7**
Collective agriculture, 1:61
Collective bargaining. *See* Negotiation
Collective injury, terrorism, 8:624
Collective memory, 2:**7–8**
   concentration camps, 2:64
   described, 5:74–76
   Holocaust, 3:497
   trauma, 8:440
Collective wisdom, 2:**9–10**
   Durkheim, Émile, 2:466
   Jung, Carl, 4:229
   rumors, 7:295
   solidarity, 8:24
   tradition, 8:420–422
Collectivism, 2:**10–11**
   class conflict, 1:571
   common land, 2:26–28, 28
   communism, 2:34
   communitarianism, 2:39
   community power studies, 2:45
   conformity, 2:72
   individualism, 3:618, 619–620
   land reform, 4:341, 342, 343
   landlords, 4:345
   liberty, 4:439
   lying, 4:524
   lynchings, 4:526
   rotating savings and credit associations, 7:286–287
   socialism, 7:635–637
Collectivization. *See* Collectivism
Colleges, 1:32, 8:532
   See also Universities
Collegiate universities, 8:527
Colley, Linda, 8:355–356
Colligan, Robert C., 1:198
Collins, Michel, 3:395
Collins, Patricia Hill, 1:324
Collins, Randall, 6:649, 8:6, 7
Collins, Steven, 5:504–505

Collusion. *See* Imperfect competition
Colombia
   civil wars, 1:554
   clientelism, 1:579
   coffee industry, 1:594, 595
   drug traffic, 2:450, 451
   land reform, 4:343
Colombo, Cristoforo. *See* Columbus, Christopher
Colón, Christóbal. *See* Columbus, Christopher
Colón, Diego, 2:146
Colón, Jesús, 1:330
Colonial archaeology, 1:167
Colonial gaze, 3:**260–262**, 264
   Cook, James, 2:121–122
   exoticism, 3:46–47
Colonialism, 2:**11–13**
   absentee landlords, 4:348
   African socialism, 7:638, 639
   American Revolution, 1:103
   Arabs, 1:160
   Bourdieu, Pierre, 1:358
   bourgeoisie, 1:361
   British
      Bentham, Jeremy, 1:286
      Burke, Edmund, 1:396
      caste, 1:461, 462, 463
      Hall, Stuart, 3:408–409
      Jordan, 3:530–531
      Nasser, Gamal Abdel, 5:376
      Nehru, Jawaharlal, 5:460
   capitalist mode of production, 1:446, 447
   Caribbean, 1:448
   Cherokees, 1:497
   civil wars, 1:555
   civilization, 1:557, 558
   Coloreds (South Africa), 2:15–16
   colorism, 2:18
   Columbus, Christopher, 2:19–21
   communalism, 2:31
   communism, 2:34, 35
   concentration camps, 2:64
   constructivism, 2:97
   Cook, James, 2:121–122
   cooperation, 2:122
   Cortés, Hernán, 2:146–148
   Cox, Oliver C., 2:157–158
   Creole, 2:167
   creolization, 2:169
   democracy, 2:274
   dependency theory, 2:299–300
   development economics, 2:345

   development in sociology, 2:347
   development theory, 2:338–339
   diaspora, 2:356
   Diop, Cheikh Anta, 2:368–370
   East Indian diaspora, 2:471–475
   East Indies, 2:476
   empire, 2:575, 576
   ethnic conflict, 3:1
   ethnicity, 3:10
   exploitation, 3:65
   Fanon, Frantz, 3:99–100
   Frank, Andre Gunder, 3:187
   French
      Bourdieu, Pierre, 1:358, 359
      Haiti, 3:406–408
   Garvey, Marcus, 3:258
   gentility, 3:300–301
   going native, 3:338–339
   hybridity, 3:535, 536
   immigrants, 3:568, 577
   imperialism, 3:586–589
   indigenismo, 3:613
   indirect rule, 3:617–618
   internal colony, 2:13–15
   Inuit, 4:125
   Iroquois, 4:151
   Islamic fundamentalism, 3:237
   land claims, 4:340
   latifundia, 4:352–353
   Latinos, 4:358, 359
   legal systems, 4:405, 406
   Lenin, Vladimir Ilitch, 4:411
   liberalism, 4:425
   liberation, 4:429, 430
   liberation movements, 4:433
   loyalists, 4:508–509
   Lumumba, Patrice, 4:517–518
   Mexican Americans, 5:119–120
   Mill, James, 5:177
   modern, 3:260–262
   Monroe Doctrine, 5:272
   NAACP, 5:384
   nationalism, 5:417
   otherness, 6:83
   overconsumption, 8:8
   Pan-Caribbeanism, 6:119–120
   queer studies, 6:664–665
   race, 7:2–3
   race mixing, 7:26–27
   racial classification, 7:38, 39
   Raj, 7:55–57
   reciprocity, 7:106–107
   regions, 7:132
   representation, 7:172–173

Colonialism, *continued*
Resolution 1514 (UN), 8:524
Rhodes, Cecil, 7:240
Rodney, Walter, 7:269–270
self-determination, 7:405–406
servitude, 7:463
Spanish
Boricua, 1:355–356
Chiapas, 1:500
state, 8:104
Stolen Generations, 8:158–159
sugar industry, 8:218–219
surplus labor, 4:309
terrorism, 8:628–629
Thant, U., 8:334
third world, 8:352
travel and travel writing,
8:443–444
tribe, 8:450
tribes, 8:449
underconsumption, 8:488
violence, 8:623–624, 625–626
weapons industry, 9:49
white supremacy, 9:85
whiteness, 9:93
zombies, 9:181
See also Anticolonial movements;
Decolonization;
Neocolonialism; Postcolonialism
Colonialism, internal. *See* Internal
colony
Colonization
indigenous rights, 3:614–615
Mexican Americans, 5:119
Colony, internal, 2:**13–15**
Color-blind policies. *See* Race-blind
policies
Color preference, 6:**432–433**
Coloreds. *See* African Americans;
Blackness; Coloreds (Haiti);
Coloreds (South Africa); Negro
Coloreds (Haiti), 3:406–408
Coloreds (South Africa), 2:**15–17**
blackness, 1:328
desegregation, 2:315
townships, 8:405–407
Colorism, 2:**17–19**
mulattos, 5:312–313
phenotype, 6:243–245
race, 7:8–11
Colson, Anthony, 1:131
Columbus, Christopher, 2:**19–22**,
4:212, 5:423
Boricua, 1:355
cannibalism, 1:427

cotton industry, 2:152
East Indies, 2:476
pre-Columbian peoples, 6:426,
427
Colvin, Claudette, 1:311
Combahee River Collective. *See*
Intersectionality
Combatants, enemy, 3:393–394
Comeco, 2:137
COMECON (Council for Mutual
Economic Assistance), 9:149
Comedy, 2:**22–23**
parody, 6:148–149
rituals, 7:262
satire, 7:330
See also Theater
Comic books, 1:452, 2:**23–25**
*Comic Strips and Consumer Culture,
1890–1945* (Gordon), 2:23
Comics as Culture (Inge), 2:23
*Coming Out: Homosexual Politics in
Britain, from the Nineteenth Century
to the Present* (Weeks), 6:329
The Coming Race War? (Delgado),
2:175
Comintern, 3:364
Comisión Económica para América
Latina (CEPAL). *See* Economic
Commission for Latin America and
the Caribbean (ECLAC)
Comix. *See* Comic books
Commandos, 1:349, 350
Commentaries on the Laws of England
(Blackstone), 1:285
Commerce. *See* Trade
Commerce Department, U.S. *See* U.S.
Department of Commerce
Commercial banks. *See* Banking
industry
Commission for Conventional
Armaments, 9:52
Commission of Meditation,
Conciliation and Arbitration, 6:63
Commission on the Social Studies in
Schools, 1:268
Commission on the Status of Women
(U.S. 1963), 3:121, 123
Commission on Wartime Relocation
and Internment of Civilians, U.S.
(CWRIC), 3:601
Committee of Colored Citizens
(CCC), 9:99
Committee of Defense Ministers
(CDM), 9:35
Committee on Academic Freedom and
Academic Tenure, 1:105

Committee on Freedom in Research
and Teaching (COFRAT),
1:105–106
Committee to Reelect the President
(CREEP), 5:506
Commodified welfare, 9:68
Commodities
economic value, 8:575–577
objective value, 8:577–578
social values, 8:582
subjective value, 8:578–581
Commodities market. *See* Forward and
futures markets
Commodity, exchange value. *See*
Exchange value
Commodity fetishism, 3:82
Commodity Futures Trading
Commission, corporate fraud, 6:73
Commodity markets. *See* Forward and
futures markets
Commodity riots. *See* Riots
Commodity terms of trade (CTT). *See*
Terms of trade
Commodization, 5:15
Common Article 3 (Geneva
Convention), 9:22
Common Cause. *See* Public interest
advocacy
Common factor analysis, 3:75
Common good, 2:25
communitarianism, 2:39
community economic
development, 2:40
prisoner's dilemma, 6:472–474
Common knowledge rationality
games, 2:**25–26**
Common land, 2:**26–28**
land reform, 4:343
landlords, 4:345
primitive accumulation, 6:464
resource economics, 7:210–211
Tragedy of the Commons,
8:422–423
Common law
Declaration of Independence,
U.S., 2:254
judiciary, 4:227
jurisprudence, 4:232
jury selection, 4:233–234
legal systems, 4:405, 406
Common market, 2:**28–29**
customs union, 2:215
euro, 3:22–23
European Union, 3:23–25
Common property, fishing industry,
6:92

Common Rule (U.S.), 3:61, 4:43
Common School, 7:352–353
Common sense, hegemony, 3:364
Common Sense (Paine), 1:104
Common value model, 1:207
Common Vulnerability Scoring System, 8:656
Commonilization, automobile industry, 1:222–223
Commonplace Book (Tawney), 8:272
Commons. *See* Common land; *The Tragedy of the Commons* (Hardin)
Commons, John R., 4:44, 337
Commonwealth, 2:29–30
    Nyerere, Julius, 5:554
    Royal Commissions, 7:291–292
Commonwealth of Independent States (CIS), 2:30, 68, 8:513
Communal riots. *See* Riots
Communalism, 2:30–31
    Church and state, 1:535
    collectivism, 2:11
    common good, 2:25
    communism, 2:34
    communitarianism, 2:39–40
    community power studies, 2:42–46
    Jews, 4:190–193, 194
    primitive communism, 2:37, 38
    Raj, 7:56
    shtetlekh, 7:503–504
Communication, 2:31–34
    business, 1:402
    cellular technology, 8:306–308
    censorship, 1:475–476
    collective wisdom, 2:9–10
    consensus, 2:82
    conversational analysis, 2:118–120
    critical theory, 2:177–178
    cyberspace, 2:216–217
    destabilization, 2:320–321
    determinism, 2:323
    deterrence, 2:333
    digital divide, 2:366–367
    discourse, 2:387
    economic rhetoric, 2:495–496
    ethnography of, 1:129
    everyday life, 3:337–338
    Habermas, Jürgen, 3:401–402
    hermeneutics, 3:463
    hybridity, 3:535–536
    Lasswell, Harold, 4:351
    Lazarsfeld, Paul Felix, 4:375
    linguistic turn, 4:457–458
    material culture, 5:14–15

    medium is the message, 5:68–69
    message-based persuasion, 6:228–229
    microanalysis, 5:132–133
    nonverbal, 2:32, 33, 5:529–531
        contempt, 2:113
        lying, 4:524–525
    persuasion, 6:227–228
    primacy/recency effects, 6:457–458
    radio talk shows, 7:51–53
    relationship satisfaction, 7:151, 152
    sleeper effects, 7:550
    social system, 7:626–627
    speech act theory, 8:56–57
    storytelling, 8:160–161
    symbols, 8:251–253
    technological determinism, 2:332
    telecommunications industry, 8:313–316
Communication networks, 5:478, **479–481**, *480*
Communications Act (U.S. 1934), 1:476
Communicative freedom, 3:197–198
Communion, Holy. *See* Sacraments
Communism, 2:34–37
    Almond, Gabriel A., 1:82
    Bahro, Rudolf, 1:237–238
    Bay of Pigs, 1:262
    Berlin Wall, 1:289
    black Marxism, 4:642
    bolshevism, 1:351
    Brezhnev, Leonid, 1:370
    Bunche, Ralph Johnson, 1:388
    bureaucracy, 1:391
    Castro, Fidel, 1:465–466
    Central Intelligence Agency, U.S, 1:481, 483
    centrism, 1:488
    Chiang Kai-shek, 1:499
    Chinese diaspora, 1:516
    Chinese Revolution, 1:519, 520–521
    Churchill, Winston, 1:537
    civil rights, 1:550
    civil society, 1:553
    clash of civilizations, 1:559
    coffee industry, 1:595
    Cold War, 2:4–5
    collectivism, 2:11
    concentration camps, 2:63, 64
    Congress Party, India, 2:76
    conservatism, 2:85

    Conservative Party (U.K.), 2:87
    convergence theory, 2:117–118
    Croats, 2:179
    Cuba, 2:186
    Davis, Angela, 2:242, 243
    decolonization, 2:256
    developing countries, 2:335
    dialectical materialism, 5:21–23
    dictatorship, 2:359
    dissidents, 2:411
    domino theory, 2:434–436
    factory system, 3:77
    Ho Chi Minh, 3:492
    Hoover, J. Edgar, 3:501
    Hussein, Saddam, 3:532, 533–534
    iron curtain, 4:150
    Khmer Rouge, 4:262–263
    Khrushchev, Nikita, 4:264–265
    Korean War, 4:289
    Ladejinsky, Wolf, 4:327–328
    land reform, 4:342, 343
    Le Duc Tho, 4:398
    left wing, 4:403, 404
    legal systems, 4:406
    Lenin, Vladimir Ilitch, 4:411
    Leninism, 4:411–412
    Levellers, 4:414, 415
    Little Red Book, 4:467–468
    Lukacs, Georg, 4:515
    Lynd, Robert and Helen, 4:528
    Malthusian trap, 4:573
    Mao Zedong, 4:588–590
    Maoism, 4:590–591
    Marxian economics, 2:517
    Marxism, 4:638–641
    McCarthyism, 5:43–44
    mode of production, 5:219–220
    nationalization, 5:419
    New Class, 5:492
    one-party states, 6:41–42
    organic intellectuals, 4:66–67
    peaceful coexistence, 6:186–188
    Pol Pot, 6:289
    political correctness, 6:299–300
    political sociology, 8:4
    Reagan, Ronald, 7:88, 89
    repression, 7:175
    revolution, 7:229
    revolution of rising expectations, 7:232
    Robeson, Paul, 7:265, 266
    Roma, 7:279
    Russian economics, 7:299
    Russian Federation, 7:302, 303

Communism, *continued*
  Russian Revolution, 7:304
  Sartre, Jean-Paul, 7:327
  social history, 3:482
  socialism, 7:637, 638
  Solidarność, 8:25–26
  Spanish Civil War, 8:43–44
  Stalin, Joseph, 8:86
  Stalinism, 8:87
  state capitalism, 1:443–444
  Thatcher, Margaret, 8:335
  Thompson, Edward P., 8:353–356
  Tito, Josip, 8:375–376
  totalitarianism, 8:395
  transitional conjunctures, 2:77
  Truman, Harry S., 8:460
  Warsaw Pact, 9:34–36
  Yeltsin, Boris, 9:163–164
  zero population growth, 9:175
Communism, Conformity, and Civil Liberties (Stouffer), 8:386
Communism, primitive, 2:37–38, 5:19
Communism: The Story of the Idea and Its Implementation (Ozinga), 2:35
Communist Manifesto (Marx and Engels), 1:559, 568, 569, 570, 9:131
  communism, 2:34
  convergence theory, 2:117
  lumpenproletariat, 4:516
Communist Party (Africa), African National Congress, 1:42
Communist Party (China)
  Chinese Revolution, 1:520
  Little Red Book, 4:467, 468
  Maoism, 4:591
Communist Party (Cuba), 2:36
Communist Party (East Germany)
  Bahro, Rudolf, 1:237–238
  Luxemburg, Rosa, 4:522
Communist Party (U.S.), 2:242, 243
Communist Party (U.S.S.R.), 8:511
  Brezhnev, Leonid, 1:370
  dialectical materialism, 5:21–23
  Gorbachev, Mikhail, 2:36
  Lenin, Vladimir Ilitch, 4:411
  Leninism, 4:412
  Marx, Karl, 2:35
Communist Party (Vietnam), 4:398
Communist Party (Yugoslavia), 2:35
Communist Party Historian's Group (U.K.), 3:482, 483
Communitarianism, 2:38–40
  citizenship, 1:543

city-state, 1:544–545
common good, 2:25
communalism, 2:30–31
community economic development, 2:40–41
consensus, 2:82
freedom, 3:198
justice, 4:238
liberalism, 4:425–426
society, 7:651
Community action. *See* War on Poverty
Community Development Block Grants (CDBG), 8:537, 9:28
Community economic development, 1:542, 2:40–42
Community life, urban studies, 8:542
Community networks, 5:476
Community Partnership Act (U.S. 1975), 9:28
Community Power Structure: A Study of Decision Makers (Hunter), 3:524
Community Power Structure (Hunter), 2:42, 4:528
Community power studies, 2:42–47
  Hunter, Floyd, 3:524–525
  Lynd, Robert and Helen, 4:528
Community Power Succession: Atlanta's Policy-Makers Revisited (Hunter), 3:525
Community service
  national service programs, 5:413–415
  volunteerism, 8:642
  well-being, 3:293
Community Services Administration, U.S., 1:440, 9:28
Community Services Organization (CSO), 1:493
Community standards. *See* Censorship; Obscenity
Commutative justice, 4:237
Commute time, 9:128
Commuting, metropolitan regions, 7:133, 134, 135
Compact discs (CD), 8:622
Compagnie des Indes. *See* Mississippi Company
Companies. *See* Business; Corporations; Firms
Company of the West. *See* Mississippi Company
Comparative advantage, 1:5–6, 3:199–200
  bilateral trade, 8:414
  Corn Laws, 2:134

Dornbusch-Fischer-Samuelson model, 2:437–438
  export penetration, 3:66
  Heckscher-Ohlin-Samuelson model, 3:448–449
  infant industry, 4:11–12
  international economics, 2:508–509
  microelectronics industry, 5:138–139
  sharecropping, 7:491
  trade, 8:412
Comparative dynamics, 2:47–48
Comparative politics, 6:326–329
  Almond, Gabriel A., 1:82
  described, 6:321
  left and right, 4:401–402
  left wing, 4:402–404
  political culture, 6:301
Comparative statics, 2:48, 48–49
  comparative dynamics, 2:47
  Samuelson, Paul A., 7:318
Comparison, social. *See* Social comparison
Comparison method, paired. *See* Scales
Compassionate conservatism. *See* Benign neglect; Neoconservatism
Compensating variation. *See* Compensating wages
Compensating wages, 9:6
Compensation
  externality, 3:70
  land claims, 4:341
Compensation, unemployment, 2:49–50
Compensation criterion, 9:62
Compensatory equalization of treatments, 8:574
Competition, 2:50–51
  antitrust, 1:144
  banana industry, 1:245
  business, 1:402
  cities, 1:540
  Cold War, 2:4–5
  community power studies, 2:44, 45
  consumer protection, 2:102
  consumerism, 2:104
  consumption, 2:107, 108
  cooperation, 2:122
  corporate strategy, 2:138
  corporations, 2:139
  credentialism, 2:166

cultural group selection, 2:191, 192

currency devaluation and revaluation, 2:211

democratization, 2:288

discrimination, 2:389–391

distortions, 2:414

economic growth, 2:491

economics of information, 4:30–31

entrepreneurship, 2:605

export penetration, 3:66

flexibility, 3:156–157

group, 3:387

immigration, 3:581

import substitution, 3:593

increasing returns, 7:219–220

industry, 3:622–623

journalism, 4:213–214

laissez-faire, 4:338

liberation movements, 4:433

limited, 2:52

liquidity trap, 4:462

management, 4:574, 575

marginal revenue, 7:227–228

markup pricing, 4:610–612

monopsony, 5:267

nationalization, 5:419

oligopolistic, 2:50

prices, 6:456

privatization, 5:419

race, 7:13, 14

race relations cycle, 7:32

racial discrimination, 2:395

railway industry, 7:54

Russian economics, 7:299–300

School of Lausanne, 4:362

social status, 8:596

spatial theory, 8:44–45

steel industry, 8:128, 129

tâtonnement, 8:270–271

technology, 8:302

technology transfer, 8:309

telecommunications industry, 8:316

textile industry, 8:333–334

transportation industry, 8:438–439

unequal exchange, 8:505–506

Veblen, Thorstein, 8:596

wage discrimination, 2:400–401

Competition, imperfect, 2:50, 51, **51–54**

asymmetric information, 4:28–30

Kahn, Richard F., 4:245

monopsony, 5:267–268

predatory pricing, 6:428–429

price discrimination, 2:392–393

strategic behavior, 8:162–163

Competition, managed, 2:**54–55**, 5:395–396

Competition, Marxist, 2:**55–56**

Competition, monopolistic, 2:50, 51, **56–57**, 6:654

Competition, perfect, 2:50, 56, **57–58**, 9:4

imperfect competition *vs.*, 2:51–52

monopoly, 5:263–264

satiation, 7:328

surplus labor, 4:309

Competition law. *See* Antitrust

Competitive advantage. *See* Absolute and competitive advantage

Competitive advantage, Microsoft, 5:142–143

Competitive party systems, 6:**161–163**

ballots, 1:242

dealignment, 2:246–247

majorities, 4:560

plurality, 6:285–286

political parties, 6:306–308

Southern politics, 6:345–349

See also Multiparty systems; One-party states

Complementary/attraction theory. *See* Similarity/attraction theory

Complete Life of General George A. Custer (Whittaker), 1:258

Complete observers, 6:14–15

Complete participants, 6:14–15

Complex identity, 3:551

Complexes (psychology), 4:229, 231

Complexity theory. *See* System analysis

Compliance-based accountability, 1:10

Component analysis, 3:75

Components, prinicipal. *See* Principal components

Comprehensive System. *See* Rorschach test

Compromise, centrism, 1:488–489

Compromise of 1850, 7:545

Compulsion

defined, 6:18

obsessions *vs.*, 6:17

repetition, 3:210

Compulsory voting, 2:**58–59**

Computational states, 3:231

Computer games. *See* Video games

Computer simulation. *See* Computers

Computer-supported cooperative work (CSCW), 2:61

Computers

behaviorism, 1:278–279

blue collar and white collar, 1:339

cognition, 1:598

cyberspace, 2:216–217

Internet, 4:104–107

microelectronics industry, 5:138

Microsoft, 5:142–143

rentier class, 1:566–567

technocracy, 8:297

technological change, 1:491

vulnerability, 8:656

Computers, science and society, 2:**59–62**

Computing, human-centered, 2:61

Comstock, Anthony, 1:303, 3:89, 6:13

Comstock Law. *See* Act of the Suppression of Trade in and Circulation of Obscene Literature and Articles of Immoral Use

Comte, Auguste, 1:359, 2:62, 6:9

empiricism, 2:578

epistemology, 2:609

European sociology, 7:670

modernity, 5:231

positive social science, 6:387

positivism, 6:390

social statics, 7:620

sociology, 7:660

technotopia, 8:312

voluntaristic *vs.* structuralist sociology, 8:17

Conant, James Bryant, 7:237

Conceiving the New World Order: The Global Politics of Reproduction (Ginsburg and Rapp), 7:178

Concentration, flow (psychological), 3:158

Concentration camps, 2:**63–65**, 3:396

Bettelheim, Bruno, 1:290

Boer War, 1:349–350

Nazi, 5:450

See also Holocaust; Japanese American incarceration

Concentration ratios (CR), 2:53

A Concept of Agribusiness (Goldberg and Davis), 1:58

The Concept of Law (Hart), 4:363

The Concept of Representation (Pitkin), 6:273

Concerning Human Understanding (Locke), 1:137

Concert of Europe, 4:385

Concientization, 3:202

Concordat of 1801 (France), 5:364

Concurrence, groupthink, 3:388

Concurrent validity, 8:572, 573

Condillac, Étienne Bonnot de, 1:429

The Condition of Postmodernity (Harvey), 3:305

Conditionality, 2:**65**, 6:482

Conditioned response. *See* Classical conditioning

Conditioned stimulus, 1:572–573

Conditioning, classical, 1:**572–575**, 6:43
  behaviorism, 1:276, 277
  learned helplessness, 4:387–389
  Pavlov, Ivan, 6:177–179
  phobia, 6:263
  reinforcement theories, 7:147, 148
  shock experiments, 3:62
  Skinner box, 7:528

Conditioning, operant, 6:**43–44**
  behaviorism, 1:276, 277
  classical conditioning, 1:574
  reinforcement theories, 7:147, 148
  Skinner, B. F., 7:526
  Skinner box, 7:528

Conditions for optimal growth, 6:52

The Conditions of the Working Class in England (Engels), 3:77

Condoms, 1:64, 2:114, 115

Condon, Nixon v. (1932), 9:84

Condorcet, Marquis de, 2:**65–66**
  choice in economics, 1:524
  liberalism, 4:425
  majoritarianism, 4:558–559
  paradox of voting, 6:127
  scientific revolutions, 7:236

Condorcet method, 2:66, 6:127

Condorcet winner, 2:66, 4:562, 6:127

Condorcet's paradox. *See* Paradox of voting

Cone, James H., 4:435

Confederacy, U.S. *See* Confederate States of America

Confederate States of America, 2:**66–68**, 8:549–551
  Benjamin, Judah P., 1:284–285
  confederations, 2:68
  Davis, Jefferson, 2:243–244
  Democratic Party (U.S.), 2:287
  Lee, Robert E., 4:399–400
  Lincoln, Abraham, 4:451
  Reconstruction Era, U.S., 7:111
  Southern politics, 6:344–345
  vindication movements, 8:618–619

See also The South, U.S.; U.S. Civil War

Confederations, 2:**68–69**, 90–91

Conference Board, lagging, leading and coincident indicators, 4:331–332

Conference on Disarmament (1979), 1:176

Confidence intervals. *See* Statistics in the social sciences

Confidence limits. *See* Limits in probability

Configurations of Cultural Growth (Kroeber), 4:290

Confiscation, 2:**69–70**
  counterterrorism, 2:154, 155
  Jews, 2:21
  landlords, 4:347
  rentier class, 1:568

Conflict, 2:**70–71**
  bigotry, 1:295–296
  civil society, 1:553
  class, 9:132–133
  cognitive dissonance, 1:599–601
  community power studies, 2:43
  consensus, 2:82–83
  consociational democracy, 2:278
  disaster management, 2:382
  diversity, 2:419–420, 420
  economic value, 8:576
  exchange, 3:385
  leaders, 4:375–376
  left and right, 4:402
  neorealism, 9:14
  peace, 6:181
  petroleum industry, 6:232–233
  Pettigrew, Thomas F., 6:234
  political realism, 7:96–97
  post-Parsonian American sociology, 8:5, 6
  race relations, 7:29
  race relations cycle, 7:32, 33
  regions, 7:131–132
  religiosity, 7:163
  role, 7:272–273
  superordinate goals, 8:226–227
  teacher-child relationships, 8:292
  two-state solution, 8:476–478
  water resources, 9:41–42

See also Ethnic conflict; Revolution

Conflict, class. *See* Class conflict

Conflict, Decisions and Dissonance (Festinger), 3:133

Conflict, ethnic. *See* Ethnic conflict

Conflict, marital. *See* Marital conflict

Conflict, role. *See* Role conflict

Conflict, social. *See* Political sociology

Conflict management, African Crisis Response Initiative, 1:37–38

Conflict resolution. *See* Conflict; Negotiation

Conflict-spirals, arms race, 1:178

Conflict theory. *See* Political sociology

Conformity, 1:202, 2:**71–73**
  Asch, Solomon, 1:186–187, 217
  collective wisdom, 2:10
  collectivism, 2:10–11
  cults, 2:188
  habitus, 3:404, 405
  herd behavior, 3:459
  individualism, 3:619–620
  melting pot, 5:72
  organization theory, 6:70
  pluralistic ignorance, 3:560–561
  reactance theory, 7:85–86
  role theory, 7:275–276
  social influence, 7:598
  The Stepford Wives (film), 8:134–135

Confucianism
  Chinese diaspora, 1:516
  Chinese Revolution, 1:519
  divine right, 2:422
  hell, 3:458
  legal systems, 4:406
  middle way, 5:145–146
  welfare state, 9:68

Conglomerates, Chinese diaspora, 1:517

Congo
  Bunche, Ralph Johnson, 1:387
  Central Intelligence Agency, U.S, 1:484
  Lumumba, Patrice, 4:517–518
  Mobutu, Joseph, 5:215–217
  United Nations role, 8:524

Congregation for the Doctrine of the Faith, 8:594

Congress, U.S., 2:**73–74**
  agenda setting, 1:48
  bicameralism, 1:294
  black politics, 6:324
  Central Intelligence Agency, U.S, 1:484–485
  checks and balances, 1:496
  Chisholm, Shirley, 1:522
  Clinton, Bill, 1:580
  coalition, 1:587
  constituency, 2:89–90

Constitution, U.S., 2:91
Democratic Party (U.S.), 2:287, 288
Diet, 2:360, 361
Fenno, Richard F., Jr., 3:124–125
impeachment, 3:584, 585–586
Jefferson, Thomas, 4:180
judicial review, 4:223, 224
Kefauver, Estes, 4:251–252
lobbying, 4:474, 475
presidency, 6:442
primaries, 6:458–459
Reconstruction Era, U.S., 7:112
roll calls, 7:277
Southern politics, 6:345
See also House of Representatives, U.S.; Senate, U.S.
Congress of Industrial Organizations (CIO), 4:302
Congress of Industrial Unions (CIO), 8:515–516
Congress of Racial Equality (CORE), 2:**75**, 5:384–385
black nationalism, 1:317
civil rights movement, U.S., 1:552
Congress of Vienna (1814–1815), 2:84, 5:369, 9:145
Congress Party, India, 2:**75–77**
Bose, Subhas and Sarat, 1:356
Janata Party, 4:170, 171
See also Indian National Congress (INC)
Congressional Black Caucus, 1:522
Congressmen in Committees (Fenno), 3:124–125
Conjectural history, 1:127
Conjunctures, transitional, 2:77–78, **77–78**
Conkey, Margaret, 1:168–169
Conley, Dalton, 8:533
Connally, John, 9:33
Connecticut, abortion, 1:2
Connecticut, Cantwell v. (1940), 1:534
Connecticut, Griswold v. (1965), 2:461, 3:90, 7:271
Connectionism, 1:280, 8:358
Connelly, Thomas, 4:399
Connerly, Ward, 1:311, 416, 7:35, 36
See also Race-blind policies
Connolly, William E., 2:82
Connor, Eugene "Bull," 1:550
Connor, Melissa A., 1:259
Conquests for Gold, God and Glory, 3:340–341
Conrad, Alfred, 1:581

Conscience
consciousness, 2:78, 79–80
Dawes, Robyn, 2:245
Conscience of a Conservative (Goldwater), 2:85
Conscientious objectors. *See* Pacifism
Conscientious refusal, 1:545
See also Civil disobedience
Consciousness, 2:**78–82**
class, 1:569
communism, 2:34
conflict, 1:569–570
dreaming, 2:444–445
false, 3:81–83
Freud, Sigmund, 3:211–212
genetic determinism, 2:329–330
hallucinogens, 3:410–411
Jung, Carl, 4:228, 229–230
optimal state of, 3:157–158
race, 3:192
shamans, 7:486–488
theory of mind, 8:346–348
See also Self-consciousness
Consciousness, double. *See* Veils, in African American culture
Consciousness, self. *See* Self-consciousness
Consciousness, stream of. *See* Stream of consciousness
Conscription. *See* Selective Service; Servitude
Conscription, military. *See* Napoléon Bonaparte; Selective Service
Conseil d'Etat, 1:23
Consensus, 2:**82–83**
common good, 2:25
conflict, 2:70
Congress, U.S., 2:73
consociational democracy, 2:279
constitutions, 2:95
corporatism, 2:141
Consent, informed. *See* Informed consent
Consequences, consideration of future. *See* Consideration of future consequences
Consequences, operant conditioning, 6:43
The Consequences of Modernity (Giddens), 3:314
Consequentalism, utilitarianism, 8:553
Conservation. *See* Environment
Conservatism, 2:**83–87**
black, 1:310–311, 2:86
black liberalism, 1:312

Burke, Edmund, 1:396–397
centrism, 1:488
compassionate, 2:86
Conservative Party (U.K.), 2:87–88
Daughters of the American Revolution, 2:242
Dixiecrats, 2:428–431
Fahrenheit 9/11 (film), 3:80
freedom, 3:198
race-blind policies, 7:35
Reagan, Ronald, 7:88–89
Republican Party (U.S.), 7:186–187
social movements, 7:606
Southern politics, 6:339–349
Southern strategy, 8:35–38
Tolstoy, Leo, 9:20
welfare state, 9:68, 71
See also Neoconservatism; Right wing
Conservatism, religious. *See* Fundamentalism
Conservative Judaism. *See* Judaism
The Conservative Mind from Burke to Eliot (Kirk), 2:85
Conservative Party (Canada), 8:650
Conservative Party (U.K.), 2:**87–88**, 8:650
Chamberlain, Neville, 1:489–490
Churchill, Winston, 1:537–538
cleavages, 1:578
conservatism, 2:83, 86
jingoism, 4:201–202
Liberal Party (U.K.), 4:423, 428
Macmillan, Harold, 4:538
Thatcher, Margaret, 8:335
Consideration of future consequences, 8:368
Consistency. *See* Properties of estimators (asymptotic and exact)
Consociational democracy, 2:**277–280**, 3:332
elites, 2:566
ethnicity, 3:10
Lebanon, 4:396
Consolidated Stock and Petroleum Exchange (CSPE), 9:7
Consolidation. *See* Corporate strategies
Consortia
bauxite industry, 1:261
bourgeoisie, 1:361
Conspicuous consumption, 2:**88–89**, 9:46
consumerism, 2:104–105

Conspicuous consumption, *continued*
  described, 2:107
  hidden persuaders, 3:472–473
  leisure class, 1:566
  lifestyles, 4:445
  social distinctions, 2:412
Conspiracy
  Central Intelligence Agency, U.S,
    1:484
  Illuminati, 3:562
Constant, Benjamin, 4:439
Constant capital, 1:446
  See also Capital
The Constant Flux (Erikson and
  Goldthorpe), 8:533
Constantine, Emperor of Rome,
  1:532–533
Constantinople (city), 1:532–533,
  8:593
Constituency, 2:**89–90**
  Congress, U.S., 2:73–74
  conservatism, 2:83
  corruption, 2:144
  Internet, 4:107–108
  leaders, 4:375–376
  term limits, 8:323–324
Constitution, U.S., 2:**90–92**
  apportionment, 1:154–155
  appropriations, 1:155
  Beard, Charles, 1:268
  checks and balances, 1:495
  Church and state, 1:534–536
  civil liberties, 1:546–547, 548
  civil rights, 1:548, 549
  civil rights movement, U.S., 1:551
  Confederate States of America,
    2:66
  confederations, 2:68
  Congress, U.S., 2:73
  constitutional courts, 2:93
  corporations, 2:139–140
  crime and criminology, 2:172
  democracy, 2:273
  Douglass, Frederick, 2:439, 440
  Dred Scott v. Sanford, 2:446
  due process, 2:461
  electoral college, 2:559
  equal protection, 2:614–615
  First Amendment, 1:18
  Fourteenth Amendment, 5:444,
    8:652
    abortion, 1:4
    judicial activism, 1:19
    white primary, 9:84

Fifteenth Amendment, 8:651,
  9:84
  federalism, 3:113–114, 358–359
  Hamilton, Alexander, 3:413
  history, 1:104
  impeachment, 3:584–586
  judicial activism, 1:18–19
  judicial review, 4:223–225
  judiciary, 4:225
  liberty, 4:440
  Madison, James, 4:547–548
  naturalization, 3:578
  poll tax, 6:353
  presidency, 6:440–441
  private interests, 6:479
  referendum, 7:121
  Southern politics, 6:340
  Supreme Court, U.S., 8:232–234
  term limits, 8:323, 324
  women's suffrage, 8:216–217
  See also Bill of Rights, U.S.
Constitution, Weimer, 5:482
The Constitution of Liberty (Hayek),
  4:338
The Constitution of Society (Giddens),
  3:314
Constitutional Amendments, U.S. *See*
  Constitution, U.S.
Constitutional Code (Bentham), 1:286
Constitutional courts, 2:**92–93**,
  4:227–228
Constitutional monarchy, 5:**240–241**
  described, 5:240
  French Revolution, 3:203
  Magna Carta, 4:556–557
  monarchism, 5:237, 238
Constitutionalism, 2:**93–94**
  Kariel, Henry S., 4:249
  social justice, 4:241
Constitutionalism, treaty. *See* Treaty
  federalism
Constitutions, 2:**94–95**
  caste, 1:458, 459–460
  civil liberties, 1:546
  Condorcet, Marquis de, 2:66
  constitutional courts, 2:92–93
  constitutional monarchy, 5:241
  constitutionalism, 2:93–94
  dalits, 2:221
  De Gaulle, Charles, 2:264
  India, 2:75
  Japan, 2:360
  Juárez, Benito, 4:218
  law, 4:364
  Mexico, 5:131

Quebecois movement, 6:662, 663
  Reconstruction Era, U.S., 7:114
  republicanism, 7:188
  revolution, 7:229
  separation of powers, 7:449
  structure and function, 3:355
Constrained choice, 2:**95–96**
  choice in economics, 1:524–525
  Lagrange multipliers, 4:332–333
Constrained maximization. *See*
  Maximization
Construct validity, 8:570, 570t, 572,
  573–574
The Construction of Reality in the Child
  (Piaget), 1:506
Constructionism, social. *See* Social
  constructionism
Constructivism, 2:**96–99**
  empiricism, 2:579
  international relations, 4:100
  knowledge, 4:280
  meaning, 5:51, 52
  peace movements, 6:183
  personal constructs, 6:217
  scientism, 7:365
Constructs, personal. *See* Personal
  constructs
Constructs, social. *See* Social
  constructs
Consultative Group on International
  Agricultural Research, 2:342
Consume, marginal propensity to. *See*
  Marginal propensity to consume
Consumer, 2:*99,* **99–102**
  advocacy, 5:359–360
  cooperatives, 2:123–124
  demand, 2:268–271
  deregulation, 2:308–309
  discrimination, 2:389
  Exit, Voice, and Loyalty
    (Hirschman), 3:43
  imports, 3:594
  lexicographic preferences,
    4:422–423
  market, 3:282–283
  overlapping generations model,
    6:92–94
  price discrimination, 2:392–393
  product quality, 6:652, 654
  quality controls, 6:651
  racial discrimination, 2:395
  satisfaction, 6:56–57
  sovereignty, 9:62
  tastes, 8:268–269
  wage discrimination, 2:400–401

want creation, 9:14–15

wants, 9:15–17

Consumer Culture and Modernity (Slater), 4:446

Consumer Price Index (CPI). *See* Price indices

Consumer protection, 2:**102–103**, 3:372–373

Consumer sovereignty. *See* Value, subjective

Consumer spending. *See* Consumerism; Consumption

Consumer surplus, 2:**104**, 4:623–624

Consumerism, 2:**104–105**
  class consciousness, 1:572
  conspicuous consumption, 2:88–89
  consumption, 2:109
  consumption function, 2:109–110
  convergence theory, 2:117
  development theory, 2:339
  Lagrange multipliers, 4:332–333
  Latinos, 4:360–361
  lifestyles, 4:445, 446
  Lynd, Robert and Helen, 4:527–528
  rentier class, 1:566

A Consumer's Republic (Cohen), 4:445

Consumption, 2:**105–109**
  absolute income hypothesis, 1:6–7
  bubbles (economics), 1:378, 379
  class consciousness, 1:572
  coffee industry, 1:594
  conspicuous, 2:88–89, 9:46
    consumerism, 2:104–105
    described, 2:107
    hidden persuaders, 3:472–473
    leisure class, 1:565–566
    lifestyles, 4:445
    social distinctions, 2:412
  consumer, 2:99–102
  consumerism, 2:104–105
  consumption function, 2:109–110
  cotton industry, 2:152–153, 154
  demand, 2:270–271
  diminishing returns, 7:218–219
  distributed lags, 4:333–334
  economic growth, 2:486, 489
  elasticity, 2:556
  energy industry, 2:588
  energy sector, 2:591–592
  entertainment industry, 2:601–602
  Friedman, Milton, 3:217

Galbraith, John Kenneth, 3:246–247

global warming, 3:330

Green Revolution, 3:378

household sample survey, 5:409–410

indifference curve, 8:555–556

interest rates, 4:85

life-cycle hypothesis, 1:7, 4:441–443

lifestyles, 4:445–446

loans, 4:473

long period analysis, 4:489

marginal product of labor, 4:307

metropolitan regions, 7:134

national income accounts, 5:397–399

North-South models, 5:546–547

per capita, 3:346

permanent income hypothesis, 6:211–214

popular culture, 6:373–375

post Keynesian economics, 2:528–529

relative income hypothesis, 7:153–154, 154

soft drink industry, 1:595

subjective utility, 8:558–560

technophobia, 8:311

trade deficit, 8:416

trade-offs, 8:419

vectors, 8:600

wealth, 1:7

See also Underconsumption

Consumption function, 2:**109–111**
  consumer, 2:99–102
  Keynes, John Maynard, 4:261

Contact hypothesis, 2:**111–112**, 6:439–440, 9:136–137

Containment
  Cold War, 2:4
  defense, 2:258

Contango, 1:450, 2:**112–113**

A Contemporary Critique of Historical Materialism (Giddens), 3:314

Contemporary human biology, 1:118

Contempt, 2:**113–114**

Content analysis of verbatim explanations (CAVE), 6:54

Content validity, 8:570, 570*t*, 571*t*, 572, 574
  See also Validity, statistical

Contextual archaeology, 1:169

Contingency models of leadership, 4:379, 380, **384–385**

Contingency theory, 6:69, 72
  See also Organization theory

Contingent valuation (CV), 2:150

Continuity theories. *See* Stages of development

Contraception, 2:**114–115**, 115*t*, 3:88–90
  Catholic Church, 8:594
  out-of-wedlock births, 1:308
  reproduction, 7:178, 179
  reproductive politics, 7:180, 181, 182
  reproductive rights, 7:182, 183
  See also Birth control; Family planning

Contraception and Religion, a Short History (O'Grady), 2:114

Contract Air Mail Act (U.S. 1925), 1:232

Contract curve. *See* Welfare economics

Contracts, forward, 3:142

Contracts, social. *See* Social contracts

Contrality, 5:480

Contrapunteo cubano del tabaco y el azucar (Ortiz), 6:80

Contras. *See* Sandinistas

Contribution-based funding, 9:71

Control, arms. *See* Arms control

Control, birth. *See* Birth control

Control, capital. *See* Capital controls

Control, economics of. *See* Economics of control

Control, flow (psychological), 3:158

Control, locus of. *See* Locus of control

Control, population. *See* Population control

Control, price. *See* Wage and price controls

Control, quality. *See* Quality controls

Control, rent. *See* Rent control

Control, wage. *See* Wage and price controls

Control Board, Washington D.C., 1:372

Control consciousness. *See* Consciousness

Control groups, awareness, 8:574

Control groups, in social experiments, 7:590–591

Controlled breeding. *See* Eugenics

Controlled experiments, 3:**58–59**
  causality, 1:473
  developmental psychology, 2:350
  experimental realism, 7:93–95

Controls, price. *See* Inflation

Conundrum, 2:**116**

Convention for the Prevention and Punishment of the Crime of Genocide, 3:296–297, 298, 9:21–22

Convention on the Elimination of All Forms of Discrimination Against Women, 9:108, 110

Convention on the Rights of the Child (United Nations), 1:511, 512

Conventional Forces in Europe Treaty (1990), 1:176–177

Conventional neutrality, 5:487, 488

Conventions, political. *See* Political conventions

Conventions, social. *See* Norms

Conventions vs. norms, 5:536

Convergence theory, 2:**117–118**
  large sample properties, 4:349, 350
  limits in probability, 6:489

Convergent validity. *See* Validity, statistical

Conversational analysis (CA), 2:**118–121**

Converse, Philip E., 1:100, 425

Conversion (Religion)
  caste, 1:458, 459–460
  Columbus, Christopher, 2:20, 21
  infidels, 4:23
  missionaries, 5:205–206

Conversos, 2:21

Convex polyhedral cones (CPC), 8:563

Convexity, optimal growth, 6:52

Cook, James, 2:**121–122**, 7:309

Cook, Thomas, 8:443, 565

Cooke, Janet, 7:442–443

Cooley, Charles Horton, 3:85
  Blumer, Herbert, 1:344
  groups, 3:385
  looking-glass effect, 4:495
  Oedipus complex, 6:29

Coontz, Stephanie, 3:96

Cooper, Anna Julia, 1:324

Cooper, John Sherman, 9:33

Cooper, Russell, 2:127

Cooper, William W., 2:240

Cooper v. Aaron (1958), 2:316

Cooperation, 2:**122–123**
  coalition, 1:586–587
  codetermination, 1:592–593
  collective action, 2:5–6
  collective action games, 2:6
  collectivism, 2:10–11
  common land, 2:28

common market, 2:28–29

community power studies, 2:45

consociational democracy, 2:278

coordination failure, 2:128

cultural group selection, 2:191

Darwin, Charles, 2:229

Dawes, Robyn, 2:245

difference principle, 2:363

diplomacy, 2:370–371

group, 3:387

Keohane, Robert, 4:256–257

League of Nations, 4:385

multilateralism, 5:320–321

prisoner's dilemma, 6:471–474

stratification economics, 2:531

superordinate goals, 8:226–227

teachers, 8:295

trans-disciplinary research, 7:198

Cooperation Under the Security Dilemma (Jervis), 4:185

Cooperative games, 3:250
  general equilibrium, 3:284–285
  nonzero-sum games, 5:532–533

Cooperative learning, 8:295

Cooperatives, 2:**123–127**
  business, 1:401–402
  communalism, 2:31
  peasant, 6:74
  rural development, 2:341

Coopersmith, Stanley, 7:412

Coordination failure, 2:**127–128**, 127t

Copeland, Brian, 5:547

Copernicus, 8:532

Coping, 2:**128–130**
  diathesis-stress model, 2:358
  drought, 2:448
  emotion and affect, 2:572
  emotion regulation, 2:572–573
  John Henryism, 4:207–208
  life events and stress, 4:443–444
  locus of control, 4:478
  loneliness, 4:487
  optimism/pessimism, 6:54
  paranoia, 6:129
  social anxiety, 7:563
  stress, 8:174
  stress-buffering model, 4:444, 8:175–176

Copper industry, 2:**130–132**, 4:250, 251

Coptic Christian Church, 2:**132–133**

Coptic Orthodox Church. *See* Coptic Christian Church

Copyright infringement. *See* Intellectual property rights

Coquery-Vidrovitch, Catherine, 1:188

Corcoran, Kevin, 8:571

CORE (Congress of Racial Equality), 2:**75**, 5:384–385
  black nationalism, 1:317
  civil rights movement, U.S., 1:552

Core-periphery. *See* Dependency theory

Core theory, 2:347

Corn, 5:424, 425, 540

Corn Laws, 2:**133–134**, 3:200, 5:177

Corn syrup, high-fructose, 6:4

Cornelius Sulla, 2:359

Corner solutions, 1:475

Cornman, John M., 9:26

Corporal punishment, 2:**134–136**

Corporate Average Fuel Efficiency Standards (CAFE), 1:223

Corporate culture, organization man, 6:61–62

Corporate debt, leverage, 4:415–416

Corporate ethics. *See* Business ethics; Corporate social responsibility (CSR)

Corporate finance. Modigliani-Miller theorems, 5:235

Corporate fraud, 6:72–73

Corporate governance. *See* Managerial capitalism

Corporate income tax, 3:**607–608**

Corporate mergers. *See* Corporate strategies

Corporate misconduct, whistle-blowers, 9:79–81

Corporate owners, New Class, 5:492

Corporate social responsibility (CSR), 2:**136–138**
  coffee industry, 1:596
  cooperatives, 2:124
  corruption, 2:143
  See also Business ethics

Corporate strategies, 2:**138–139**
  Chinese diaspora, 1:517–518
  described, 2:139
  Tobin's Q, 8:380

Corporation for National and Community Service, 5:414, 8:638

Corporations, 2:**139–140**
  bourgeoisie, 1:361
  business ethics, 2:633–635
  codetermination, 1:592–593
  corporate social responsibility, 2:136–138
  corporate strategy, 2:138–139
  crime and criminology, 2:171–172
  defined, 1:400–401

demand creation, 3:246

economic control by, 3:247

enterprise, 2:599

finance, 3:141

Galbraith, John Kenneth, 3:246–247

large, 3:149

Lindblom, Charles Edward, 4:452–453

management, 4:574–575

managerial capitalism, 1:442–443

multidivisional, 6:72

multilevel-subsidiary, 6:72–73

Nader, Ralph, 5:359

petroleum industry, 6:230–231

petty bourgeoisie, 1:362

private sector, 6:480–481

stakeholders, 8:85–86

stock exchanges, 8:150–151

stock exchanges in developing countries, 8:152

stocks, 8:155–156

structure, 6:72

tax inequalities, 6:73

transnational, 2:139–140

vertically integrated, 3:78

See also Firms; Organizations

Corporatism, 2:**140–141**

bourgeoisie, 1:361

Christian Democracy, 2:277

community economic development, 2:41

Jewish diaspora, 4:190

left wing *vs.,* 4:403

Lindblom, Charles Edward, 4:452

Mussolini, Benito, 5:350

Partido Revolucionario Institucional, 6:157

pluralism, 6:283

socialization of investment, 7:649–650

state capitalism, 1:444

Correction, market. *See* Market correction

Correctional institutions. *See* Prisons

Correctional mental health. *See* Prison psychology

Correlates of War Project, 1:554

Correlations

factor analysis, 3:75

illusory, 7:571

serial, 3:289–290, 7:455–457, 8:372

Correspondence bias. *See* Over-attribution bias

Correspondence inference theory (CIT), 1:205

Correspondence principle. *See* Comparative dynamics; Comparative statics

Correspondence tests, 2:**141–143**

Correspondent inference theory. *See* Jones, Edward Ellsworth

Corruption, 2:**143–146**

capital flight, 1:434, 435, 436

Central Intelligence Agency, U.S, 1:484–485

clientelism, 1:579

Congress Party, India, 2:76

corporate social responsibility, 2:137–138

corporations, 2:140

crony capitalism, 2:180

diamond industry, 2:355–356

Duvaliers, 2:468–469

Gilded Age, 3:319

Hussein, Saddam, 3:533

lying, 4:524

Mafia, 4:550–553

money laundering, 5:263

Partido Revolucionario Institucional, 6:158

patronage, 6:176–177

Ponzi schemes, 6:368–369

restricted and unrestricted stocks, 8:157

sports industry, 8:67

stock options, 8:154

See Also Bribery; Fraud

Corso, Philip, 8:507

Cortés, Hernán, 2:**146–149**

Cortés, Hernando, 2:20

Corvée. *See* Servitude

Cosby, Bill, 1:310

Cosmides, Leda, 2:329, 3:33, 5:440

Cosmopolitanism, 2:149

Enlightenment, 2:597

internationalism, 4:103

laissez-faire, 5:493

transnationalism, 8:433–434

Cost, average. *See* Average and marginal costs

Cost, carrying. *See* Carrying cost

Cost, marginal. *See* Average and marginal costs

Cost, social. *See* Social costs

Cost, transaction. *See* Transaction cost

Cost-benefit analysis (CBA), 2:**150–151**

Bentham, Jeremy, 1:286

collective action, 2:5–6

collective action games, 2:6

consumer surplus, 2:104

social cost, 7:581–583

statistical discrimination, 2:397

technological change, 1:490

utilitarianism, 8:554

Cost function. *See* Loss functions

Cost of living

hedonic prices, 3:451

quantity index, 6:657

Cost of living indices. *See* Price indices

Costa, Dora, 9:127

Costa, Mariarosa Dalla, 1:447

Costa, Paul, 5:486, 487

Costa Rica, banana industry, 1:245

Costello, Tim, 5:540

Costs

accounting, 6:47

AIDS/HIV, 1:66

average, 1:230–231, *231*

competition, 2:50–51

marginal, 1:230–231, *231*

opportunity, 6:47

specialization, 1:6

wants, 9:16

social movements, 7:606

transaction, 8:426–427

capital flight, 1:435

Coase, Ronald, 1:589

Coase theorem, 1:590

diplomacy, 2:371

externality, 3:70

import penetration, 3:590

user, 8:551–552

variable, 1:230–232

See also Social costs

Cote d'Ivoire, African Crisis Response Initiative, 1:38

Cotto-Thorner, Guillermo, 5:552

Cotton industry, 2:**151–154**, 7:547–549

Egypt, 1:73

slavery, 1:34

Cottrell, Leonard S., Jr., 9:24

Coubertin, Pierre de, 6:40

Council for Mutual Economic Assistance (COMECON), 9:149

Council of Carthage (397), 1:532

Council of Chalcedon (451), 2:132

Council of Constantinople (381), 1:533, 2:132

Council of Economic Advisers, Okun's law, 6:35

Council of Ephesus (431), 1:533

Council of Europe, 1:546

Council of Hippo (393), 1:532

Council of Nicea (325), 1:533

Council of Nicea (787), 1:533

Council of State Governments, occupational regulation, 6:23

Council on Environmental Quality. *See* Environmental impact assessment

Council on Licensure, Enforcement and Regulation (CLEAR), 6:23

Council on Wage and Price Stability (COWPS), 9:3

Counsel to the President (Clifford), 1:481

Counseling, underachievers, 8:484

Counterconditioning, 1:574

Counterculture

comic books, 2:24

conservatism, 2:83

hallucinogens, 3:411

hippie, 9:120–121

jazz, 4:178

Leary, Timothy, 4:390–391

resistance, 7:208–209

rock 'n' roll, 7:268

vagabonds, 8:567

Counterfeiting. *See* Intellectual property rights

Counterforce, nuclear weapons, 9:31

Counterintelligence

Central Intelligence Agency, U.S, 1:482, 483

repression, 7:175

Counterterrorism, 2:154–156

Central Intelligence Agency, U.S, 1:483, 484, 485

Clinton, Bill, 1:580

domino theory, 2:435

national defense, 2:260, 261, 262

terrorists, 8:331

urban, 8:329

See also Terrorism

Countervalue, nuclear weapons, 9:31, 32

Countries. *See* Nation; Nation-state; State

Countries, developed. *See* Developed countries

Countries, developing. *See* Developing countries

The Country and the City (Williams), 2:192

Country and western music. *See* Music

Country Life Commission, U.S., 8:8

County School Board of New Kent County, Green v. (1968), 2:314

Coupland, Douglas, 3:292

Coups d'etat, 2:**156**

Castro, Fidel, 1:464–465

Chávez, Hugo, 1:494

civil wars, 1:554–556

dictatorship, 2:359

Hussein, Saddam, 3:532

Qadhafi, Muammar al, 6:647

Courbet, Gustave, 7:91, 92, 93

Cournot, Antoine Augustin, 2:57, 3:172, 7:219

Nash equilibrium, 5:373

noncooperative games, 5:517

Cournot-Nash Equilibrium, 3:172

Course of Positive Philosophy (Comte), 2:62

Court packing. *See* Roosevelt, Franklin D.; Supreme Court, U.S.

Courts. *See* Judiciary; Legal systems

Courts, constitutional. *See* Constitutional courts

Courtship, gentility, 3:301

Cov(). *See* Variance-covariance matrix

Covariance, 1:205–206, 2:**156–157**, *157*

factor analysis, 3:75

variance-covariance matrix, 8:589–590

Covariation theory. *See* Covariance

Covering law model. *See* Prediction

Covert action

Central Intelligence Agency, U.S, 1:482, 483–484

civil-military relation, 1:547

Cuban Missile Crisis, 2:183

defense, 2:259

terrorists, 8:330–331

See also Secrecy

Cow protectors, Vaisyas, 8:568

Cowboys, 1:470

Cowdry, E. V., 3:306

Cowles, Alfred, 1:403, 502, 2:548–549, 3:221

Cowles approach, 1:181

Cowles Commission, 1:403, 502, 3:529, 530, 4:287–288

COWPS (Council on Wage and Price Stability), 9:3

Cows, 1:121

Cox, Oliver C., 1:95–96, 324, 325, 2:**157–159**, 5:354, 7:30

CPC (Convex polyhedral cones), 8:563

CPEE (Centre Polytechnicien d'Études Économiques). *See* X-Crise

CPI (Consumer Price Index). *See* Price indices

CPS (Current Population Survey). *See* Current Population Survey (CPS)

CR (Concentration ratios), 2:53

Cradle of civilization, 3:125–126

Craft industries, factory system, 3:77

Craft unions. *See* Labor unions

Craftsmen, labor unions, 8:485, 486

Craik, Kenneth, 1:597

Cramer's rule. *See* Determinants

Crane, Diana, 1:539

Crania Americana (Morton), 2:325

Crary, Jonathan, 3:263

Crashes, market. *See* Economic crises

Crazy Horse, 2:**159–160**

Creaming, 2:**160–161**

Creamy layer, 2:**161**

Creation myths, Navajos, 5:446–447

Creation science. *See* Creationism

Creationism, 2:**161–163**

anti-intellectualism, 4:65

Church and state, 1:536

Scopes trial, 7:366

teleology, 8:318

Creative destruction, 2:**163–164**, 8:299

Creativity, 2:**164–166**

capitalism, 1:438

computers, 2:60

conformity, 2:72

creative destruction, 2:163–164

destabilization, 2:321

Drucker, Peter, 2:449–450

economic growth, 8:298–299

egalitarianism, 2:550

engineering, 2:595

entrepreneurship, 2:605

long run, 4:493, 493*t*, 494

paradigm, 6:126

process, 1:490–491

product, 1:490–491

recording industry, 7:116

talent, 8:261–262

technological change, 1:490

technology, 8:302–303, 304–305

technology adoption, 8:305

tradition, 8:420

The Credential Society: An Historical Sociology of Education and Stratification (Collins), 6:649

Credentialism, 2:**166–167**

Berg, Ivar E., 1:288

crowding hypothesis, 2:182
  mobility, 5:210–211
  qualifications, 6:649–650
  skill, 7:523–524
Credibility limits. *See* Limits in
  probability
Credit. *See* Finance; Loans
Credit, overlending, 6:94–95
Credit-Anstalt, 1:252
Credit market, adverse selection, 1:28
Credits, tax. *See* Tax credits
CREEP (Committee to Reelect the
  President), 5:506
Cremers, Emily, 6:93–94
Crenshaw, Kimberlé W., 2:174–175,
  3:121
  See also Critical race theory (CRT)
Creole, 2:**167–169**
  calypso, 1:417, 418
  liberation, 4:429
Creolization, 2:**169–170**
  Caribbean, 1:448
  described, 2:168, 169
  hybridity, 3:536
  language, 2:167
Crick, Bernard, 6:320
Crick, Francis, 3:461
Crick, Nicki R., 1:56, 7:599–600
Crime, hate. *See* Hate crimes
Crime, organized. *See* Crime and
  criminology; Mafia
Crime, white collar. *See* Crime and
  criminology
Crime and criminology, 2:**170–174**
  Becker, Gary S., 1:270, 271
  biological determinism, 2:326
  capital flight, 1:434, 435
  colorism, 2:17
  confiscation, 2:69, 70
  constructivism, 2:97
  counterterrorism, 2:155
  deviance, 2:352
  drug traffic, 2:450–452
  eugenics, 3:21–22
  Hoover, J. Edgar, 3:501
  human sterilization, 8:141
  identity, 3:552
  impeachment, 3:585
  imprisonment, 3:596–597
  integration, 4:61
  interrogation, 4:112
  Jefferson, Thomas, 4:180–181
  Kefauver, Estes, 4:252
  labeling theory, 4:299–300
  law, 4:363, 364, 369–372

longitudinal data, 2:238, 239
  lynchings, 4:526
  Mafia, 4:550–553
  money laundering, 5:263
  murder, 5:338–340
  narcissism, 5:370
  national defense, 2:260, 262
  Ortiz, Fernando, 6:80
  out-of-wedlock births, 1:307
  pimps, 6:271–273
  Ponzi schemes, 6:368–369
  prison industry, 6:468–469
  prison psychology, 6:470–471
  prisons, 6:475–477
  race-conscious policies, 7:37–38
  rape, 7:64–66
  self-constrained behavior, 1:274
  social values, 8:581–582
  Southern politics, 6:348
  tax evasion and avoidance,
    8:275–276
  terrorists, 8:330
  underclass, 8:5, 6
  vagabonds, 8:567
  violence, 8:623
  See also Hate crimes; War crimes
Crimes against humanity. *See*
  Genocide
Criminal Justice Act (U.K. 1988),
  2:69
Criminal Justice Act (U.K. 1993),
  2:69
Criminal law
  death-qualified jurors, 4:233
  judiciary, 4:227
Criminality, inherited, 3:248
Criminology. *See* Crime and
  criminology
Criminology, positive. *See* Ortiz,
  Fernando
Crises. *See* Economic crises
Crises, economic. *See* Economic crises
Crisis, Choice, and Change (Almond et
  al), 1:82
Crisis, identity. *See* Identity crisis
Crisis, midlife. *See* Midlife crisis
Crisis (periodical). *See* Du Bois, W. E.
  B.; National Association for the
  Advancement of Colored People
  (NAACP)
*The Crisis of European Sciences and
  Transcendental Phenomenology*
  (Husserl), 6:10–11
*The Crisis of the Dictatorships: Spain,
  Portugal, Greece* (Poulantzas), 6:405
Criteria, information, 8:598

Criterion validity, 8:570, 570*t*, 572,
  573
Critical awareness, 3:202
Critical legal studies. *See* Critical race
  theory
Critical medical anthropology (CMA),
  1:131
Critical race theory (CRT),
  2:**174–176**, 5:372
Critical realism. *See* Realist theory
Critical theory, 2:**176–179**
  archaeology of slave lives, 7:536
  constructivism, 2:97
  deviance, 2:353
  Habermas, Jürgen, 3:401
  international relations, 4:100–101
  praxis, 6:421–422
  schools in sociology, 8:11
  social theory, 7:628
Critical white studies. *See* Critical race
  theory; Whiteness
Critique de la view quotidienne
  (Lefebvre), 4:400
Critique of Daily Life (Lefebvre). *See*
  Critique de la view quotidienne
  (Lefebvre)
Critique of Judgment (Kant), 1:30
CRM (Cultural resource
  management), 2:**196–197**
Croatia. *See* Croats
Croats, 2:**179**, 9:168
  clash of civilizations, 1:559
  concentration camps, 2:64
  ethnic conflict, 3:2
  Serbs, 7:455
  Tito, Josip, 8:375–376
  Yugoslavian civil war, 9:168
Croce, Benedetto, 3:453, 455
Crockett, Davy. *See* Mexican-
  American War
Croly, Herbert, 5:500
Cromartie, Easley v., 8:653
Cromwell, Oliver, 9:153
Cromwell, William Nelson, 2:139, 9:8
Cronbach, Lee J., 8:572, 573
Cronbach's alpha. *See* Validity,
  statistical
Cronbach's coefficient. *See*
  Psychometrics
Cronkite, Walter, 4:214–215
Cronon, William, 2:193
Crony capitalism, 2:**180**
Crook, George, 2:159
Crops
  banana industry, 1:245–247

Crops, *continued*

    Boserup, Ester, 1:357

    fertile crescent, 3:125–126

    Green Revolution, 3:378

    land fertility, 3:130–132

    See also Agricultural industry

Cross-cultural analysis. *See* Ethnology

Cross-Cultural Sample, Standard. *See* Standard Cross-Cultural Sample (SCCS)

Cross-disciplinary research. *See* Trans-disciplinary research

Cross of gold, 2:**180–181**

Cross-sectional research, 7:**189–190**

    Chow test, 1:529

    Latino National Political Survey, 4:355

    longitudinal data, 2:238

    longitudinal research, 7:194

    pooled time series, 6:369–371, *370, 371,* 371*t*

    pseudopanel data, 2:239–240

    quantitative methods, 5:113

    time series regression, 8:371

Crosscutting Social Circles (Blau and Schwartz), 1:332

Crossley, Archibald, 6:358

Croswell, Harry, 3:414

Croushore, Dean, 5:403

Crow, Hugh, 4:468, 469

Crow (Native Americans), 5:424

Crowd behavior. *See* Herd behavior

Crowding hypothesis, 2:**181–183**

    discrimination, 2:390–391

    wage discrimination, 2:400–401, 404, 405

The Crowding Hypothesis (Bates and Fusfield), 2:182

Crowe, Ellen, 6:85

Crowley, Aleister, 4:554, 555

    See also Magic

CRT (Critical race theory), 2:**174–176**, 5:372

The Crucible (play), 5:44

Crude birth rate (CBR), 3:127

Crude oil. *See* Petroleum industry

Crummell, Alexander, 5:459

Crusades, 1:533

    See also Church

Cruse, Harold, 1:309, 2:14

Crypto-Jews, 2:21

CSCW (Computer-supported cooperative work), 2:61

Csikszentmihalyi, Mihaly, 3:157

CSO (Community Services Organization), 1:493

CSPE (Consolidated Stock and Petroleum Exchange), 9:7

CTC (Child Tax Credit, U.K.), 8:274–275

CTC (Child Tax Credit, U.S.), 8:274

CTT (Commodity terms of trade). *See* Terms of trade

CTW (Change To Win) coalition, 8:516

Cuba

    Bay of Pigs, 1:262

    blackface, 1:327

    blackness, 1:329

    Castro, Fidel, 1:463–467

    Central Intelligence Agency, U.S, 1:483

    Columbus, Christopher, 2:19, 20

    communism, 2:36

    concentration camps, 2:64

    Cortés, Hernán, 2:146

    Cuban Missile Crisis, 2:183–185

    Cuban Revolution, 2:185–187

    Guantánamo Bay, 3:393–394

    Kennedy, John F., 4:254

    Lafargue, Paul, 4:328–330

    land reform, 4:343, 344

    Latin American immigrants, 3:271

    Latin American revolutions, 7:234

    Latino/Latina studies, 4:356–357

    Latino National Political Survey, 4:354–356

    Latinos, 4:358, 359–360

    left wing, 4:404

    miscegenation, 5:200

    one-party state, 6:41–42

    Ortiz, Fernando, 6:80–81

    refugees, 7:126

    Santería, 7:324–326

    socialism, 7:638

    War of 1898 (Spanish-American), 8:619, 9:23–24

Cuban Americans, assimilation, 1:189

Cuban Counterpoint (Marliowski), 6:80

Cuban missile crisis, 2:**183–185**, 9:31

    Castro, Fidel, 1:466

    Cold War, 2:5

    Cuban Revolution, 2:186

    foreign policy, 3:170–171, 171

    Kennedy, John F., 4:254

    Khrushchev, Nikita, 4:264, 265

Cuban Revolution, 2:**185–187**

    Castro, Fidel, 1:465

Latin American revolutions, 7:234

    liberation theology, 4:434

    Monroe Doctrine, 5:272

Cue competition. *See* Reinforcement theories

Cues. *See* Priming

Cues, food, 6:3

Cuhel, Franz, 6:57

Culinary culture, 3:163

Cullen, Lisa, 6:22

Cult of personality, 6:**221–223**

    communism, 2:36

    dictatorship, 2:360

    Diop, Cheikh Anta, 2:369

    Hussein, Saddam, 3:531–535

    leaders, 4:376, 377

    leadership, 4:381–382

    Little Red Book, 4:467

    Mussolini, Benito, 5:349–350

Cults, 2:**187–189**

    defined, 6:20

    reincarnation, 7:145

Cultural and Natural Areas of Native North America (Kroeber), 4:290

Cultural anthropology, 1:119–124, 2:202–203

    landscape, 2:192–193

    relativism, 2:193–196

    United States, 1:137–138

    See also Ethnography

Cultural capital, 2:**189–191**, *190*

    conspicuous consumption, 2:89

    consumption, 2:107

    cultural distinctions, 2:412–413

    curriculum, 2:214

    gentility, 3:301

    habitus, 3:404–406

    leisure class, 1:566

    low and high culture, 2:204–205

    nouveaux riches, 5:548

    practice theory, 6:419

    tracking in schools, 8:410

    urbanity, 8:544

Cultural change, 1:122

Cultural determinism. *See* Culture; Determinism

Cultural distinctions, 2:**412–414**

    classical music, 1:575

    cultural tourism, 2:201–202

Cultural diversity. *See* Multiculturalism

Cultural ecology, 1:120

Cultural equivalence model. *See* Parent-child relationships

Cultural evolution, 1:137

Cultural group selection, 2:**191–192**, 3:292, 414–415

Cultural identity, neighborhoods, 5:464

Cultural integration
  Benedict, Ruth, 1:282
  Caribbean, 1:448
  citizenship, 1:543

Cultural landscape, 2:**192–193**

Cultural materialism, 1:120–121

Cultural norms, 5:537

Cultural pluralism. *See* Pluralism

Cultural preservation, Appalachia, 1:150

Cultural relativism, 1:123, 138, 2:**193–196**
  Benedict, Ruth, 1:282
  Boas, Franz, 1:119–120, 344, 345
  communication, 2:32
  cultural rights, 2:198
  culture and, 2:203
  deviance, 2:352, 353–354
  ethnomethodology, 3:19
  Herskovits, Melville J., 3:466, 467
  Huntington, Samuel P., 3:525–526
  out-of-wedlock births, 1:306–307
  primitivism, 6:465–466
  sanitation, 7:322
  tastes, 8:267–268

Cultural resource management (CRM), 2:**196–197**

Cultural retention, Native Americans, 5:428

Cultural Revolution
  Little Red Book, 4:467–468
  Mao Zedong, 4:589
  repression, 7:175

Cultural rights, 2:**197–198**
  colonial gaze, 3:260–262
  indigenous rights, 3:614–616

Cultural studies, 2:**198–201**
  African American, 1:32
  cultural distinctions, 2:413
  cultural relativism, 2:193–196
  Hall, Stuart, 3:408–410
  Veblen, Thorstein, 8:597

Cultural tourism, 2:**201–202**, 8:443–444

Cultural validity, 8:571

Cultural values. *See* Values (cultural)

Culture, 2:**202–204**
  advertising, 1:28
  Afro-Cuban, 6:80
  Arab, 1:159, 161

assimilation, 1:188–191

The Battle of Algiers (film), 1:257–258

Benedict, Ruth, 1:282

black
  Black Arts Movement, 1:309–310
  burial grounds, 1:393–394
  Diop, Cheikh Anta, 2:368–370
  Hurston, Zora Neale, 3:526, 527

black nationalism, 1:315

blackness, 1:328–330

borders, 1:354–355

Brahmins, 1:366–367

burial grounds, 1:392–393

as capital, 2:189–190

capital controls, 1:432

capitalism, 1:437

Caribbean, 1:448–449

caste, 1:457–460, 461–463

cellular technology, 8:309

characteristics of, 1:122

Cherokees, 1:496–498

child development, 1:506–507

child labor, 1:508, 509

children, 1:511

Chinese diaspora, 1:516, 517–518, 518

civil wars, 1:555

civilization, 1:557–558

cognitive dissonance, 1:601

collective memory, 2:8

color preference, 6:432, 433

colorism, 2:18

comic books, 2:23–24

communalism, 2:30

conformity, 2:71, 72

conspicuous consumption, 2:89

constructivism, 2:96, 97

consumption, 2:107

cooperation, 2:122–123

corporal punishment, 2:135–136

corporate, 6:61–62

Creole, 2:168–169

creolization, 2:169

culinary, 3:163

dance, 2:223–225

death and dying, 2:247–248

decolonization, 2:257

defined, 1:121–122, 127

dependency, 2:298

determinism, 2:323

deviance, 2:352

disability, 2:376

Disney, Walt, 2:410

diversity, 2:419–420

dowry and bride price, 2:440–441

East Indian diaspora, 2:474

emotion, 2:569

essentialism, 2:631

ethnic fractionalization, 3:6–8

ethnicity, 3:9

ethnocentrism, 3:11–12

ethnographic research, 7:192–194

ethnology and folklore, 3:17–18

ethnomethodology, 3:19

ethnomusicology, 3:20

exoticism, 3:46–47

folk, 3:192
  Black Arts Movement, 1:309
  Harlem Renaissance, 3:426, 427
  Hurston, Zora Neale, 3:526, 527, 528

freedom, 3:198–199

gay, lesbian, transgender, and bisexual politics, 6:330

Geertz, Clifford, 3:265–266

gender preference, 6:433–434

globalization, 3:331–332

Great Society programs, 3:372–373

habitus, 3:404–405

hegemony, 3:455, 456

high, 8:632–633

Hite, Shere, 3:485

Holocaust, 3:497

hybridity, 3:535–536

identity, 3:554–555

indigenismo, 3:613–614

indirect rule, 3:617–618

infidelity, 4:21

institutional development, 2:340

intelligence, 4:73

Internet, 4:105

Inuit, 4:124–125

Kinsey, Alfred, 4:270

kinship, 4:271–273

Kroeber, Alfred Louis, 4:290–291

labor supply, 4:320, 321

Latino/Latina studies, 4:356–357

lay theories, 4:374

learning, 1:122

left and right, 4:402

left wing, 4:403

legal systems, 4:407

leisure, 1:565–566, 4:408–409

Culture, *continued*

Lévi-Strauss, Claude, 4:416–417, 417

Lewis, Oscar, 4:418–419

lifestyles, 4:446

linguistic anthropology, 1:129–130

linguistic turn, 4:458

literature, 4:463–464

The Lonely Crowd (Riesman), 4:487

Lowie, Robert, 4:507

lying, 4:524

lynchings, 4:526–527

Lynd, Robert and Helen, 4:527–528

magic, 4:554–555

marriage, 4:612–616

masculinity, 5:1

maturation, 5:36

media, 5:60

medium is the message, 5:68–69

mental illness, 5:87–88

middleman minorities, 5:147–148

midlife crisis, 5:149–150

midwifery, 5:151–154

militarism, 5:165

misogyny, 5:203–204

moral domain theory, 5:279–280

morality, 5:283–286

motivation, 5:301

multiplural, 3:256

narcissism, 5:369, 370

Native Americans, 1:394–395, 5:424–426

neighborhood effects, 5:462

nonverbal communication, 5:530

norm of reciprocity, 7:107–108

nutrition, 5:551–552

oppositional, 6:48

Palestinian diaspora, 6:110

Pan-Africanism, 6:115–117

parent-child relationships, 6:133

parenting styles, 6:137–138

political, 3:408–410

polytheism, 6:367–368

post-Parsonian American sociology, 8:6–7

of poverty, 1:134, 8:582, 9:25

primitivism, 6:465–466

race, 7:3, 6–7, 9, 11, 15

race mixing, 7:26–28

racial identification, 3:548

racialization, 7:43

Radcliffe-Brown, A. R., 7:47

reciprocity, 7:105–107

regions, 7:130, 131

reincarnation, 7:145–146

religion, 7:159–161

religiosity, 7:162–163

repatriation, 7:168–169

replicator dynamics, 7:169–170

representation, 7:170–172, 172–173

reproduction, 7:178–179

research methods, 5:114

residential segregation, 7:383

resistance, 7:208–209

rites of passage, 7:256–259

rituals, 7:259–264

Roma, 7:278, 279

Roman Catholic Church, 7:280

romance, 7:281–282

Sahlins, Marshall, 7:308, 309

Sambo, 7:312–314

sellouts, 7:434–435

slaves, 1:40

social classification, 7:567

social pathology, 6:170

South, U.S., 8:32–33

Standard Cross-Cultural Sample, 8:88–92

stare, 8:101

storytelling, 8:160–161

street, 9:167

sublimate, 8:200

synergy in, 5:455

taboos, 8:259–260

Taino, 8:260–261

talent, 8:262

tastes, 8:267–268

technophobia, 8:311

television, 8:320

terror, 8:326

terror management theory, 8:327–328

terrorism, 8:329

theater, 8:336–338

theory of mind, 8:347

Thompson, Edward P., 8:353–354

time, 8:362

totalitarianism, 8:396

trade barriers, 1:255

tradition, 8:420–422

transnationalism, 8:433

trauma, 8:440–441

travel and travel writing, 8:443–444

Turner, Victor, 8:468–471

undereating, 8:491

unequal education, 2:537–538

unidentified flying objects, 8:507

universalism, 8:526–527

urban

case method, 1:453

communalism, 2:31

Ibn Khaldūn, 3:545–546

video technology, 8:309, 310

wage discrimination, 2:404

warlike, 3:102

Western

black nationalism, 1:315

Caribbean, 1:447–448

civilization, 1:557, 558

clash of civilizations, 1:559–560

death and dying, 2:248

development theory, 2:339

exoticism, 3:46–47

globalization, 3:334

undereating, 8:491

world music, 9:142

world-system, 9:10–11, 153

youth, 9:167–168

See also Acculturation; Counterculture; Hip hop; Multiculturalism; Transculturation

Culture, low and high, 2:**204–205**

classical music, 1:575

cultural distinctions, 2:412–413

cultural studies, 2:199

described, 2:203

literature, 4:464

minstrelsy, 5:194

popular culture, 6:373–375

Culture, material. *See* Material culture

Culture, political. *See* Political culture

Culture, popular. *See* Popular culture

Culture, street. *See* Street culture

Culture, youth. *See* Youth culture

Culture and Anarchy (Arnold), 4:463

Culture and Ethnology (Lowie), 4:507

Culture and Practical Reason (Sahlins), 7:309

Culture and Society (Williams), 2:199

Culture industry, 3:189

The Culture of Narcissism (Lasch), 5:369

Culture of poverty, 2:**206–207**

benign neglect, 1:283–284

black conservatism, 1:311

Clark, Kenneth B., 1:561

distributive justice, 4:240

Lewis, Oscar, 4:418–419
lifestyles, 4:445
morality, 5:285–286
Moynihan, Daniel Patrick,
5:304–305
Moynihan Report, 5:305–306
race relations, 7:30
racial inequality, 4:5–6
social demography, 2:296
social exclusion, 7:588–589
social pathology, 6:170, 171
street culture, 8:172–173
Tally's Corner, 8:263–264
urban poverty, 6:410, 411
Culture of the poor. *See* Culture of
poverty
Culture studies, popular. *See* Cultural
studies
Culture-writing. *See* Ethnography
Cummings, Milton C., 4:262
Cumulative causation, 1:94, 236–237,
2:**207–208**
Cumulative probability distribution
function. *See* Probability
distributions
Cumulative voting. *See* Bloc vote
Cunctator, Fabius, 3:73
Cuomo, Chris, 9:93
Curran, Patrick, 3:391
Currency, 2:**208–209**
bimetallic, 3:151, 344
carrying cost, 1:449–450
central banks, 1:477
contango, 2:112
cross of gold, 2:180–181
euro, 3:22–23
gold standard, 3:340, 343,
344–345
international economics, 2:509
liquidity, 4:459
monetary base, 5:243–245
See also Exchange rates; Money
Currency appreciation and
depreciation, 2:**209–211**
Dutch disease, 2:467–468
foreign reserves, 2:210, 7:202–203
money illusion, 5:261–262
Currency board, 3:39
Currency devaluation and revaluation,
2:**211–212,** 211*t*
Beggar-thy-neighbor, 1:272–273
central banks, 1:480
currency appreciation and
depreciation, 2:209
exchange rates, 3:37–40

foreign reserves, 2:211–212
J-Curve, 4:179
money, 5:251
money illusion, 5:261–262
Currency unions. *See* Monetary unions
Current account. *See* Balance of trade;
Trade deficit; Trade surplus
Current Population Survey (CPS),
2:**212–213,** 580
Current Population Survey (U.S.),
8:492
Curriculum, 2:**213–215**
sociology, 1:106
universities, 8:531
Currie, Janet, 3:437, 4:302
Currie, Laughlin, 3:370
Curse of dimensionality, 5:526
Curtin, Philip, 4:37, 7:546–547
See also Slave trade
Custer, Elizabeth Bacon, 1:258
Custer, George Armstrong, 1:258,
2:159, 7:522
Custer Died for Your Sins (Deloria),
1:259, 5:426–427
Custer Victorious (Urwin), 1:258
Custer's Last Stand. *See* Battle of the
Little Big Horn (1876)
*Custer's Last Stand: The Anatomy of an
American Myth* (Dippie), 1:259
Custis, Martha, 9:36
Customary law, 4:407
Customer. *See* Consumer
Customers, goodwill, 3:349–350
Customs, folk. *See* Culture; Tradition
Customs, social. *See* Culture; Tradition
Customs union, 2:**215–216**
common market, 2:29
confederations, 2:68
Meade, James, 5:49
Custred, Glynn, 1:416, 7:11
Cut flower industry. *See* Flower
industry
Cuts, tax. *See* Tax relief
Cutteridge, J. O., 9:97
Cuvier, Georges, 1:126
CWRIC (U.S. Commission on
Wartime Relocation and Internment
of Civilians), 3:601
Cyber-terrorism, 8:629
Cyberspace, 2:**216–217**
bigotry, 1:296
digital divide, 2:366–367
The Matrix (film), 5:31–32
microelectronics industry, 5:137,
139

Cycles
of poverty, 7:32–33
voting, 8:648
Cycles, business. *See* Business cycles
Cyclical unemployment, 3:227, 8:502
Cyclones, 5:432–434
Cyprus, 2:63
Cyril of Alexandria, Saint, 2:132
Czech Republic, state capitalism,
1:444
Czechoslovakia
communism, 2:35
Hitler, Adolf, 1:489
Sudetenland, 1:153
Warsaw Pact, 9:35
World War II, 9:147–148

D

Dahl, Robert Alan, 2:**219–221**
cleavages, 1:578
community power studies,
2:42–46
compulsory voting, 2:58
democracy, 2:275
democratization, 2:288
indices of democracy, 2:280
Lindblom, Charles Edward, 4:452
Lowi, Theodore J., 4:506
Lynd, Robert and Helen, 4:528
nondecision-making, 5:518
pluralism, 6:283
polyarchy, 6:366
power, 6:413
republic, 7:185
republicanism, 7:188
urban studies, 8:542
Dahrendorf, Ralf, 1:214–215, 563
Daily life, 3:79, 9:106
*Daily Summary. See President's Daily
Brief*
Daimler, Gottlieb, 1:217
Daimler Chrysler, 1:219
Dalai Lama, 1:384, 7:125
Dale, Tom, 1:62
Dalen, Hendrik van, 1:539
Dalits, 1:457–460, 462–463,
2:**221–222**
Ambedkar, B. R., 1:90–92
Buddhism, 1:383
creamy layer, 2:161
Dalmazzo, Alberto, 6:77
Daly, Markate, 2:38, 39
Daly, Mary, 9:106
Damas, Leon, 3:336
Danaid jar, 9:96

Dance, 2:**223–225**, 3:480, 7:522

Dances of the Tewa Pueblo Indians (Sweet), 2:224

Daniels, Arlene Kaplan, 9:122, 123

Daniels, Josephus, 9:99

Dann, Graham, 8:565

Les Danses Exotiques en France, 1880–1940 (Décoret-Ahiha), 2:224–225

Dante Alighieri. *See* Purgatory

Dantzig, George, 4:288, 6:5–6

Daoism. *See* Taoism

DAR (Daughters of the American Revolution), 2:**241–242**

Darby, H. C., 3:304

Darfur, 2:**226–227**

Darity, William, 1:442, 2:207
    discrimination, 2:390, 391
    full employment, 3:226
    lateral mobility, 5:212
    North-South models, 5:547
    overlending, 6:95
    race, 7:14
    railway industry, 7:53–54
    taste for discrimination, 2:399
    Theil index, 8:339, 340
    underclass, 8:485–486
    wage discrimination, 2:405

Dark Age Ahead (Jacobs), 4:165

Dark Ghetto, Dilemmas of Social Power (Clark), 1:561

Darrow, Clarence, 2:162, 7:366
    See also Scopes Trial

Darwin, Charles, 2:**227–232**, *230*, *231t*
    anthropology, 1:117
    archaeology, 1:166
    biological determinism, 2:325–326
    cultural anthropology, 1:119
    cultural relativism, 2:194
    environmental determinism, 2:327
    evolution, 1:126, 137
    genetic determinism, 2:329
    Hamilton's rule, 3:414
    Malthus, Thomas Robert, 4:571
    Malthusian trap, 4:573
    Marx, Karl, 4:629–630
    natural selection, 5:440
    naturalism, 5:442
    Nietzsche, Friedrich, 5:503
    race, 7:13
    racial classification, 1:126
    Scopes trial, 7:366
    sexual selection theory, 7:479
    sociobiology, 7:654
    Spencer, Herbert, 8:58
    supreme being, 8:231
    teleology, 8:318
    See also Darwinism, social

Darwin on Trial (Johnson), 2:162

Darwinism, social, 2:**232–234**
    behaviorism, 1:276
    biological determinism, 2:326
    environmental determinism, 2:327
    eugenics, 3:21–22
    Nazism, 3:495
    race, 7:13
    Spencer, Herbert, 8:58
    wealth and poverty, 5:495
    World War I, 9:146

Darwish, Adel, 9:42

Dasein, 3:43

Data, 2:**234–237**
    case method, 1:453
    census, 1:476–477
    descriptive statistics, 2:311–312
    Integrated Public Use Microdata Series, 4:53–56
    left and right censoring, 1:473–474
    quantification, 6:655–656
    real-time, 5:403
    sample censoring, 1:474–475
    self-report method, 7:424–426
    social demography, 2:296
    statistics, 8:121–122
    vintage of, 5:403

Data, longitudinal, 2:**238–239**
    pseudopanel, 2:239–240
    sample attrition, 7:315–316
    temporal priority, 7:194–196

Data, pseudopanel, 2:**239–240**

Data envelopment analysis (DEA), 1:354, 2:**240–241**, 4:350

Date rape. *See* Rape

Dating techniques
    processualism, 1:167
    radiocarbon, 1:164
    relative, 1:164
    seriation, 1:166

Datura stramonium. See Jimsonweed

Daughters of the American Revolution (DAR), 2:**241–242**

Davenant, Charles, 2:101

David, Jacques-Louis, 5:364

Davidoff, Constantino, 3:81

Davidson, Donald, 1:275

Davidson, Paul, 1:478

Davidson, Thomas, 3:73

Davidson, William V., 3:257

Davies, Christopher, 2:23

Davies, James C., 7:152–153, 232

Davis, Angela, 1:343, 2:**242–243**

Davis, David, 1:60

Davis, Gray, 7:102

Davis, Jefferson, 1:284–285, 2:66, 67, **243–244**

Davis, John A., 1:58

Davis, Katherine Bement, 7:481

Davis, Kingsley, 6:77
    class, 1:562–563
    demography, 2:293
    social demography, 2:295
    See also Demographic transition

Davis, Kiri, 1:376

Davis, Lewis S., 2:207, 5:547

Davis, Mike, 8:543

Davis, Miles, 4:177, 178

Davis, Nancy J., 7:206–207

Davis, Natalie Zemon, 5:371

Davis, Wade, 9:181

Davis-Floyd, Robbie, 7:259

Dawes, Robyn, 2:**244–245**

Dawes Act (U.S. 1887), 6:82

Dawes Plan (1924), 1:152

Dawkins, Richard, 3:352–353

The Dawn of European Civilization (Childe), 1:167

Dawson, Michael, 1:312

Day, work. *See* Work day

Day care, 2:**245–246**, 7:341

A Day in the Life of Ivan Denisovich (Solzhenitsyn), 3:396

Daysh, Henry, 3:304

DC Comics, 2:24

DCI (Director of Central Intelligence), U.S. *See* Central Intelligence Agency, U.S. (CIA)

DD (Dysthymic disorder), 2:306

De Anima (Aristotle), 1:275

de Beauharnais, Josephine, 5:363

De Beauvoir, Simone. *See* Beauvoir, Simone de; Feminism

De Beers Mining Company, 2:354, 355, 7:239, 240
    See also Diamond industry

de Boisguillebert, Pierre, 5:399

de Bry, Theodor. *See* Bry, Theodor de

De Cive (Hobbes), 3:493

De Corpore (Hobbes), 3:493

de Gaulle, Charles, 2:**264–266**, 374, 5:544

de Grey, Aubrey, 3:308

De Gustibus Non Est Disputandum (Becker and Stigler), 1:502

De Homine (Hobbes), 3:493

De Klerk, F. W., 1:147, 4:581

De la Garza, Rodolfo O., 6:337, 338

De Lauretis, Teresa, 5:371–372

De Man, Paul, 2:310

De Mille, Richard, 1:456

De Motu Animal (Aristotle), 1:275

de Pizan, Christine. *See* Pizan, Christine de

De Saussure, Ferdinand. *See* Linguistic anthropology; Saussure, Ferdinand de; Semiotics

De Soto, Hernando, 1:497, 2:28, **319–320**, 4:346

De Vader, Christy, 4:379

De Vany, Arthur, 2:601–602

De Wet, Christiaan, 1:349

DEA (Data envelopment analysis), 1:354, 2:**240–241**, 4:350

DEA (U.S. Drug Enforcement Agency), 2:455, 455*t*

Deacon, Bob, 9:68

Deadheads, 9:121

Deadly Identities (Maalouf), 3:**551**

Dealerships, automobile, 1:220

See also Automobile industry

Dealignment, 2:246–247, 431, 7:19

Democratic Party, 2:287

political parties, 6:308

populism, 6:384

Republican Party (U.S.), 7:187

Southern strategy, 8:35–38

Death, Black. *See* Disease; Nursery rhymes; Public health

Death and dying, 2:**247–249**

African burial grounds, 1:393–394

assisted, 1:191–192

bioethics, 1:301

morality, 2:248

burial grounds, 1:392–393

heaven, 3:445–446

hell, 3:457–459

human sacrifice, 3:515–516

murder, 5:338–340

Native American burial grounds, 1:394–395

reincarnation, 7:145–146

suicide, 8:221–223

taboos, 8:260

terror, 8:326–327

terror management theory, 8:327–328

See also Morbidity and mortality

The Death and Life of Great American Cities (Jacobs), 4:165, 8:536

Death camps. *See* Concentration camps

Death instinct, 3:211

The Death of White Sociology (Ladner), 1:324

Death penalty. *See* Capital punishment

Death-qualified jurors, 4:**233**, 234

Debray, Jules R., 3:395

Debreu, Gerard, 1:181–182, 2:**249–250**, 3:283, 8:108

Debriefing, 2:636, 3:58

Debs, Eugene, 9:17

Debt

corporate debt, 4:415–416

developing countries, 9:138

overlending, 6:94–95

third world, 1:28

Debt, foreign. *See* Loans

Debt, government. *See* National debt

Debt, national. *See* National debt

Debt, personal. *See* Personal debt

Debt crisis. *See* Herd behavior; Loan pushing

Debt market, 3:146

Debt peonage. *See* Servitude

Debt securities. *See* Bonds

Decade for Women (UN), 9:108, 110

The Decembrists (Tolstoy), 9:19, 20

Decentralization, 2:**250–251**

cities, 1:541

communalism, 2:30

conservatism, 2:84

convergence theory, 2:117

democratic centralism, 2:285, 286

empire, 2:576

energy industry, 2:589

informal economy, 4:27–28

Jefferson, Thomas, 4:182, 183

metropolitan regions, 7:132–135

representative and participatory democracy, 2:283–285

social work, 7:634

urban sociology, 8:16

Deception. *See* Lying

DeCicca, Philip, 5:391

Deciding What's News (Gans), 3:256

Decimalization, 8:70

Decision-making, 2:**251–253**

adaptive expectations, 1:19–20

bureaucracy, 1:390

business, 1:401–402

choice in economics, 1:524–525

choice in psychology, 1:525–526

codetermination, 1:592–593

cognitive dissonance, 1:599–600

collective wisdom, 2:9

communism, 2:34

community power studies, 2:42–46

computers, 2:60

confederations, 2:68–69

conformity, 2:72

consensus, 2:82–83

constrained choice, 2:95

consumer, 2:99–102

corporate strategy, 2:138–139

cost-benefit analysis, 2:150–151

Dawes, Robyn, 2:244–245

decentralization, 2:250

democracy, 2:273

dictatorship, 2:359–360

economic, 5:483–484, 6:47

environmental impact assessment, 2:605–607

firms, 3:149

groupthink, 3:387–388

incrementalism, 3:608–610

microeconomics, 5:133–136

mood, 5:276

mood congruent recall, 5:277

Nash equilibrium, 5:373

nondecision-making, 5:518

organizations, 6:71

policy analysis, 6:296–297

power, 5:518, 6:413

preferences, 6:435–436

rational expectations, 3:51–52

rationality, 7:81–82

risk neutrality, 7:253–254

Simon, Herbert A., 7:515

social cognition, 7:570–571

social judgment theory, 7:601–602

strategic behavior, 8:162–163

student's T-statistic, 8:185

technotopia, 8:312

trade-offs, 8:418–419

uncertainty, 8:482

Von Neumann-Morgenstern utility, 8:560–561

voting, 8:648

Decisive events, 2:**253–254**

Declaration of Independence, U.S., 1:104, 2:**254–255**, 4:180, 440

"Declaration of Jihad" (bin Laden), 1:299

Declaration of Philadelphia (1944), 4:303

Declaration of Principles (DOP). *See* Oslo Accords

Declaration of the Rights of Man and Citizen, 3:203

Declaration of the Rights of the Child 1924 (Geneva Declaration), 1:512

Decline, population. *See* Depopulation

Declining marginal utility, 8:558–559

The Declining Significance of Race (Wilson), 9:100

Decoding, 5:530

Decolonization, 2:255–257

    Bentham, Jeremy, 1:286

    colonialism and, 2:12

    commonwealth, 2:29

    coup d'etat, 2:156

    development economics, 2:344

    Indian National Army, 3:610–611

    indirect rule, 3:617–618

    Jinnah, Mohammed Ali, 4:203–204

    Kaunda, Kenneth, 4:250

    Kimathi, Dedan, 4:266

    land claims, 4:340–341

    land reform, 4:342

    Mobutu, Joseph, 5:215–217

    nationalism, 5:417–418

    Nkrumah, Kwame, 5:507–508

    Nyerere, Julius, 5:553–554

    Organization of African Unity, 6:62

    Pan-Africanism, 6:116

    postcolonialism, 6:392–393

    refugees, 7:126

    Rodney, Walter, 7:269–270

    rural development, 2:342

    United Nations role, 8:524

    violence, 8:626

Decomposition, Blinder-Oaxaca. *See* Blinder-Oaxaca decomposition technique

Decomposition, Cholesky. *See* Cholesky decomposition

Decomposition, econometric. *See* Econometric decomposition

Deconstruction. *See* Derrida, Jacques; Postmodernism

Decorative arts, 8:630

Décoret-Ahiha, Anne, 2:224–225

Dedomena, 2:235

Deduction. *See* Logic

Dee, Thomas, 5:391

Deeds and titles (property rights), 4:340, 343–344, 345–346

Deejays. *See* Hip hop

Deetz, James, 1:169

Defectives. *See* Human sterilization

Defense, 2:257–259

    deterrence, 2:333–334

    preemptive strike, 6:431–432

    spending, 9:50

Defense, national, 1:489, 2:257–259, **259–262**, 6:431

Defense, psychological. *See* Napoleon complex

Defense Department, U.S. *See* U.S. Department of Defense

Defense mechanisms. *See* Psychoanalytic theory

Defense of Marriage Act (DOMA) (1996), 2:426, 4:620

Defensive jihad, 1:70

Deficit, budget, 5:386–387

Deficit, national. *See* National debt

Deficit, trade. *See* Trade deficit

Deflation. *See* Inflation

Defoliants, Vietnam War, 8:614

Deforestation, 2:**262–264**, 605–606, 6:360

Degler, Carl, 5:310–311

Degradation, 6:14

Degrees of freedom, 2:**266–267**

DeGroot, Morris, 8:580

Deindustrialization

    Dutch disease, 2:468

    industrialization *vs.*, 3:622

    industry, 3:623

    social and economic aspects, 3:312–313

    unemployability, 8:497

    welfare state, 9:72

Deininger, Klaus, 2:268, 8:530

Deininger and Squire World Bank Inequality Database, 2:**267–268**

Deism. *See* Monotheism

Deities, 9:154–156

    See also Supreme being

DeJong, Gordon, 2:295

Del Monte, 1:245

Delaney, Martin, 1:315

Delay conditioning, 1:573

Delayed gratification. *See* Time orientation

Deleuze, Gilles, 1:447, 6:29, 398, 399

Delgado, Richard, 2:174–175

Deliberation, 2:25

Delinquency, juvenile. *See* Juvenile delinquency

Delinquency and Opportunity (Cloward and Ohlin), 9:24

Delle, James, 3:262

Delli Carpini, Michael, 2:238

Deloria, Vine, Jr., 1:98, 259, 5:426–427

Delusional disorder, 6:17–18

Demand, 2:**268–271**

    Barro-Grossman model, 1:256

    choice in economics, 1:524

    cobweb cycles, 1:591

    coffee industry, 1:595

    consumerism, 2:105

    consumption, 2:106

    creation, 3:246

    economic depression, 2:302–303

    elasticity, 2:555–556

    energy sector, 2:591–592

    entertainment industry, 2:601–602

    full capacity, 3:224

    health economics, 3:440

    Kalecki, Michał, 4:246–247

    labor, 4:308, 309, 312–314, 318

    Law, John, 4:366

    long period analysis, 4:490

    long run, 4:492

    marginal revenue, 7:227

    Marshall, Alfred, 4:623

    overproduction, 6:97

    point of effective, 1:51

    prices, 6:455–456

    regulation, 7:144

    revealed preference, 7:224–225

    Say's Law, 7:336–337

    technological change, 1:490

    unemployment, 8:498–499, 502

    utility function, 8:555

    wants, 9:16

    work day length, 9:127

    See also Aggregate demand

Demand, excess. *See* Excess demand

Demand for money, 5:**253–256**

    central banks, 1:478

    currency appreciation and depreciation, 2:209

    Law, John, 4:366

    liquidity trap, 4:461–462

    monetary base, 5:244

Demand-pull inventions, 1:490

Demand shock, 5:438

Dementia, 1:89, 2:**271–272**

D'Emilio, John, 6:329

Democide, 3:297

Democracy, 2:**272–276**

    Arrow possibility theorem, 1:184

black liberalism, 1:312

bourgeoisie, 1:361

bureaucracy, 1:391

Burke, Edmund, 1:396–397

centrism, 1:489

checks and balances, 1:495

Church and state, 1:536

citizenship, 1:542, 543

civil disobedience, 1:545

civil-military relation, 1:547

civil rights, 1:549, 550

civil wars, 1:555

civilization, 1:557

clash of civilizations, 1:559–560

cleavages, 1:578

clientelism, 1:579

coalition, 1:587

communalism, 2:30

communitarianism, 2:38, 39

community power studies, 2:42–43, 46

comparative politics, 6:327

competitive party systems, 6:161, 162

compulsory voting, 2:58

Congress Party, India, 2:76

conservatism, 2:83, 84

constituency, 2:90

constitutional courts, 2:92–93

constitutions, 2:94–95, 3:355, 5:241

convergence theory, 2:117

cooperatives, 2:124

corporatism, 2:140–141

corruption, 2:144

critical theory, 2:177, 178

Dahl, Robert Alan, 2:220

democratic centralism, 2:285–286

description, 3:354–355

direct, 6:36

dissidents, 2:411

distributive justice, 4:239

Durkheim, Émile, 2:466–467

economic growth, 2:487

elections, 2:556–557, 558, 562

electoral college, 2:559–560

elite theory, 2:562, 563, 564

elites, 2:565–566

freedom, 3:197–199

happiness, 3:418

Hartz, Louis, 3:429

human rights, 3:513

individualism, 3:618–619

inegalitarianism, 3:624

interest groups and interests, 4:82–83

journalism, 4:211–212

judicial review, 4:225

justice, 4:237–239

Key, V. O., Jr., 4:258

leaders, 4:375–376

left and right, 4:401

left wing, 4:404

Leninism, 4:412

liberal, 2:274, 4:423, 7:84–85

liberalism, 4:425

liberation movements, 4:432

liberty, 4:439

Magna Carta, 4:557

majorities, 4:559–560

majority rule, 4:560–561

majority voting, 4:562

mobilization, 5:215

monarchies, 5:241

Moore, Barrington, 5:278

national defense, 2:261

nationalism, 5:417

Neumann, Franz, 5:482

normal, 2:275

oligarchy *vs.*, 6:36, 37–38

Pakistan, 2:76

parent-child relationships, 6:131

peace, 6:180

pluralism, 6:283–284

political inequality, 4:3–4

political participation, 8:606

political parties, 6:308

political power, 6:415–416

political stability, 8:73–74

political tolerance, 8:385–386

politics, 6:319–320

polyarchy, 6:366

populism, 6:385

recall, 7:102–103

repression, 7:175

republicanism, 7:184, 188

Riker, William, 7:249

science policy, 5:362

secular, 7:378

social, 2:274

    black liberalism, 1:312

    convergence theory, 2:117

social justice, 4:242

social relations, 7:612–613

state capitalism, 1:444

technocracy, 8:296, 297

Tocqueville, Alexis de, 8:382–383

totalitarianism, 8:395–396

tyranny of the majority, 8:478–479

underrepresentation, 8:495

USSR dissolution, 8:513

voting schemes, 8:654–655

Yeltsin, Boris, 9:163–164

See also Democratization; Voting

Democracy, Christian, 2:276–277

Democracy, consociational, 2:277–280, 3:332

Democracy, direct. *See* Representative and participatory democracy

Democracy, indices of, 2:280–281

Democracy, participatory. *See* Democracy, representative and participatory

Democracy, racial, 2:282–283

Democracy, representative and participatory, 2:283–285

    Bentham, Jeremy, 1:285–286

    city-state, 1:545

    Congress, U.S., 2:73–74

    consensus, 2:82

    referendum, 7:120–122

Democracy, strong. *See* Representative and participatory democracy

Democracy and Education (Dewey), 2:284

Democracy and Its Critics (Dahl), 2:58

Democracy and the News (Gans), 3:256

Democracy in America (Tocqueville), 2:84, 3:618–619, 8:382, 383, 478–479

Democracy in Deficit (Buchanan and Wagner), 4:338

Democracy research, 7:**190–192**

Democratic centralism, 2:285–286

Democratic National Committee (U.S.), 9:43

Democratic Party (U.S.), 2:**286–288**

    African Americans, 5:497

    Bay of Pigs, 1:262

    California Civil Rights Initiative, 1:416

    Chávez, César, 1:493

    Clinton, Bill, 1:578–580

    Congress, U.S., 2:73–74

    dealignment, 2:246–247

    Dixiecrats, 2:428–431

    Great Society programs, 3:374

    law and order, 4:369, 370, 371–372

    left wing, 4:404

    military-industrial complex, 5:173–174

Democratic Party (U.S.), *continued*
  political business cycles, 1:406, 407
  political conventions, 6:297–299
  political parties, 6:306–308
  populism, 6:383–384
  race, 7:19
  Reconstruction Era, U.S., 7:115
  reproductive politics, 7:181
  Republican Party (U.S.), 7:186–188
  Roosevelt, Franklin D., 7:283
  Southern bloc, 8:34–35
  Southern politics, 6:339–349, 8:32–33
  Southern strategy, 8:35–38
  Thurmond, Strom, 8:360–361
  Truman, Harry S., 8:459–460
  voting patterns, 8:649–650
  white primary, 9:83–84
  Wilmington Riot of 1898, 9:99
  work day, 9:127
Democratic-Republican Party (U.S.) (U.S.). *See* Democratic Party (U.S.)
Democratization, 2:**288–290**
  civil society, 1:553
  Coloreds (South Africa), 2:16–17
  comparative politics, 6:327, 328
  direct action, 2:372
  domino theory, 2:434–436
  indices of democracy, 2:280–281
  Partido Revolucionario Institucional, 6:158
  recognition, 7:109–110
  research, 7:190–192
  Russian Federation, 7:303
  social relations, 7:612–613
  Yeltsin, Boris, 9:164
Demographic transition, 2:**290–292**
  Becker, Gary S., 1:270
  Harlem, 3:423–424
  immigration, 3:581
  morbidity and mortality, 5:291
  population studies, 6:381–382
  Russian Federation, 7:302
  zero population growth, 9:174
Demography, 2:**292–295**
  baby boomers, 1:235–236
  birth control, 1:303
  census, 1:476–477
  cities, 1:540–542
  cluster analysis, 1:585
  corporal punishment, 2:135
  cross-sectional research, 7:189–190

  depopulation, 2:301–302
  differential equations, 2:364
  drugs of abuse, 2:455–456
  East Indies, 2:476
  Graunt, John, 3:366–367
  lifestyles, 4:445, 446
  litigation, 4:465
  The Lonely Crowd (Riesman), 4:487
  lotteries, 4:503
  lying, 4:524
  marriage, 4:613–614
  metropolitan regions, 7:132–135
  Mexican Americans, 5:124–125
  migration, 5:156, 158
  niche, 1:29
  population studies, 6:381–382
  real business cycles, 1:409
  regions, 7:130
  religion, 7:161
  Roma, 7:278, 279
  rural to urban migration, 5:159
  suicide, 8:222–223
  Survey of Income and Program Participation, 8:243–244
  zero population growth, 9:173–176
  See also Demographic transition; Demography, social
Demography, social, 2:293, **295–297**
Demonstrations. *See* Protest
Demsetz, Harold, 1:502
Denaturalization, 5:444
The Denial of Death (Solomon, Greenberg and Pyszczynski), 8:326–327
Denison, Edward, 3:390
Denmark
  regressive taxes, 8:284–285
  state capitalism, 1:444
  tax revolts, 8:278, 279
Dennett, Daniel, 1:275, 5:40–41
Denney, Nancy, 6:85
Denney, Reuel, 4:487
Denny's (restaurant), 7:314
DeNora, Tia, 2:204
Densensitization, 1:574
Density, nonparametric estimation, 5:524–525
Density, population. *See* Population studies
Density, posterior. *See* Bayesian econometrics
Denton, Nancy, 5:462, 463, 6:48
Deoband movement, 8:624

Deontology. *See* Moral philosophy; Philosophy, moral
Deoxyribonucleic acid (DNA), 1:336, 3:460–461
Department of Agriculture (USDA). *See* U.S. Department of Agriculture
Department of Commerce, U.S. *See* U.S. Department of Commerce
Department of Commerce v. United States House of Representatives 1999), 1:154
Department of Defense, U.S. *See* U.S. Department of Defense
Department of Education, U.S., Carter, Jimmy, 1:451
Department of Energy, U.S., Carter, Jimmy, 1:451
Department of Health and Human Services, U.S. (DHHS), 4:33, 5:551
Department of Homeland Security, U.S., 2:155, 260, 384
Department of Housing and Urban Development, U.S. (HUD), 1:440, 5:302–303
Department of Justice, U.S. (DOJ), 2:53, 3:600, 601
Department of Labor, U.S., 4:303
Department of State, U.S., 1:481, 482, 2:184
Department of the Interior, U.S., 1:504
DePaulo, Bella, 4:524–525, 5:530
Dependence, serial. *See* Serial dependence
Dependency, 2:**297–298**
  benign neglect, 1:283–284
  black liberalism, 1:312
  culture of poverty, 2:206
  Moynihan Report, 5:305–306
  physical, 1:20–21
  psychological, 1:21
  psychological depression, 2:307
  relationship satisfaction, 7:151
Dependency, drug. *See* Addiction
Dependency theory, 2:**298–301**
  butterfly effect, 1:413–414
  capitalist mode of production, 1:447
  Cold War, 2:4
  democratization, 2:289–290
  developing countries, 2:335–336
  development in sociology, 2:346, 347
  development theory, 2:338–339
  Economic Commission for Latin America and the Caribbean, 2:482

economic inequality, 9:47
Frank, Andre Gunder, 3:187
import substitution, 3:592–593
industrialization, 3:621
internal colony, 2:14–15
international relations, 4:101
Latin American sociology, 7:676–677
political sociology, 8:4
Prebisch, Raúl, 6:422–423
Rodney, Walter, 7:269–270
Dependent variables, 3:286–291
Depersonalization, 2:113, 3:263
Depopulation, 2:**301–302**
demographic transition, 2:291–292
demography, 2:293
rural development, 2:341
social demography, 2:295–297
Deportation. *See* Immigration
Deposits, banking, 1:249, 251
Depreciation, currency. *See* Currency appreciation and depreciation
Depressants, 2:452, 454
Depression, economic, 2:**302–306**, *303, 305*
business cycle theories, 1:412
cross of gold, 2:181
decisive events, 2:254
diamond industry, 2:354
recession *vs.,* 7:103
Depression, Great. *See* Great Depression
Depression, psychological, 2:**306–308**
learned helplessness, 4:388–389
manic depression, 4:583–584
serotonin, 7:457–459
vulnerability, 8:656–657
weight, 9:59
Deprivation, relative. *See* Relative deprivation
Deregulation, 2:**308–309**
business, 1:402
Carter, Jimmy, 1:451
casino capitalism, 1:455
free trade, 3:196
informal economy, 4:27
NAFTA, 5:540–541
privatization, 6:481–482
railway industry, 7:54
transportation industry, 8:438
See also Regulation
Derivatives, 3:142, 146–147, 450
Derrida, Jacques, 2:**309–311**
critical theory, 2:178

Habermas, Jürgen, 3:401
linguistic turn, 4:457
postmodernism, 6:395–396
poststructuralism, 6:398–400
reciprocity, 7:105
sovereignty, 8:38
Derryberry, Douglas, 8:321
Dervin, Daniel, 9:105
Desai, Morarji, 3:253, 4:170–171
Descartes, René
behaviorism, 1:275–276, 277
consciousness, 2:79–80
functionalism, 3:231
knowledge, 4:278
objectivity, 6:8
supreme being, 8:231
Descending-bid auctions, 1:206
Descent. *See* Kinship
The Descent of Man (Darwin), 1:126
Description de l'Egypte (Commission of Arts and Science), 1:165, 6:75
Descriptive linguistics, 1:118
Descriptive statistics, 2:**311–313**, *312, 312t*
classical statistical analysis, 1:576–577
measures of central tendencies, 1:488
probability distributions, 6:493
randomness, 7:63
statistics in the social sciences, 8:123
student's T-statistic, 8:185
Desegregation, 2:**313–315**
contact hypothesis, 2:111
Eisenhower, Dwight D., 2:555
integration, 4:57
liberation, 4:430
See also Resegregation of schools; Segregation
Desegregation, school, 2:**316–319**
Brown v. Board of Education (1955), 1:377, 6:342, 7:16
civil rights, 1:550
Clark, Kenneth B., 1:560, 561
described, 2:313–314
judiciary, 4:227
race, 7:16–18
race-conscious policies, 7:37
resegregation, 2:316, 317–318, 7:201–202, 387–388
integration, 4:49–60
race, 7:18
Southern politics, 6:342

See also Brown v. Board of Education (1954); Civil rights movement, U.S.; Separate-but-equal
Desensitization, systemic. *See* Psychotherapy
Desertification, 6:360
Deshpande, Ashwini, 8:339, 340
Design, mechanism. *See* Mechanism design
Designer babies. *See* Eugenics; Mendel's Law
Designing Social Inquiry (Verba et al), 8:606
DeSilva, Luiz Ignatio "Lula," 8:517
Desires
needs *vs.,* 5:451, 453
as wants, 9:15–17
The Desis. *See* East Indian diaspora
Despotism. *See* Dictatorship
Dessalines, Jean-Jacques, 1:330, 3:408
Destabilization, 2:**320–321**
civil wars, 1:555
Marxist competition, 2:55
terrorism, 8:328–329, 330–331
d'Estaing, Valéry Giscard, 3:244
Destalinization. *See* Stalinism
Destruction, creative. *See* Creative destruction
Destruction, mutually assured, 9:31
Destructive obedience, 1:260, 6:**2–3**
Detainee Mission of the War on Terror, Guantánamo Bay, 3:393–394
Detente, 2:5
Determinants, 2:**321–323**
The Determinants of Political Knowledge in Comparative Perspective (Grönlund and Milner), 2:59
Determination, self. *See* Self-determination
Determinism, 2:**323–325**
caste, 1:461
chaos theory, 1:492
critical theory, 2:176
Lewis, Oscar, 4:418–419
multiple, 5:486
prediction, 6:429–430
regions, 7:131
Determinism, biological, 2:**325–327**, 329, 3:353
cultural group selection, 2:191–192
essentialism, 2:630–631
evolutionary psychology, 3:33

Determinism, biological, *continued*
    intelligence, 4:72–73
    race, 7:2–7, 8–11, 23
    racialization, 7:43
    Scarr, Sandra Wood, 7:340–341
    temperament, 8:321–322
Determinism, environmental, 2:323,
    327–328, 3:304
    cultural landscape, 2:192
    disease, 2:408
    Scarr, Sandra Wood, 7:340–341
    smoking, 7:559–560
Determinism, genetic, 2:327,
    329–330, 331
    cultural group selection,
      2:191–192
    Darwin, Charles, 2:229–232, 231*t*
    intelligence, 7:21–23
    slavery hypertension hypothesis,
      7:546–547
Determinism, nonadditive,
    2:**330–331**, 5:486
Determinism, reciprocal, 2:330–331,
    331–332, 5:486
Determinism, technological, 2:323,
    332–333, 8:296
Deterrence, 2:**333–334**
    alliances, 1:78
    Cold War, 2:5
    defense, 2:258
    Jervis, Robert, 4:186
    national defense, 2:259–262
    preemptive strike, 6:431–432
Deterrence, mutual, 2:**334–335**, 7:216
Detroit (MI), school desegregation in,
    2:317
Deutsch, André, 9:98
Deutsch, Morton, 2:72, 7:597–598
*Les Deux Indiens. Episode de la
    Conquéte de Borinquen* (Betances),
    1:355
Devaluation, currency. *See* Currency
    devaluation and revaluation
DeVault, Marjorie, 9:123
Developed countries, 2:335
    birth control, 1:303
    brain drain, 1:367–368
    capitalist mode of production,
      1:447
    class conflict, 1:570
    consumerism, 2:105
    consumption, 2:89, 107–109
    contraception, 2:114
    corporate income tax, 3:608
    corruption, 2:144

cumulative causation, 2:207
democracy, 2:274–275
dependency theory, 2:298–300
energy sector, 2:591–592
import penetration, 3:591, *591*
Kuznets hypothesis, 4:295–297
The North (global), 5:542–544
population control, 6:378
returns to scale, 7:223, 224
stagnation, 8:84–85
state capitalism, 1:444
tax evasion and tax avoidance,
    8:276
technological change, 1:492
trade liberalization, 4:428
unequal exchange, 8:505–506
urbanization, 8:547
wealth inequality, 4:10*t*
women's movement, 9:118
Developing countries, 2:**335–337**
    AIDS/HIV, 1:64, 65–67
    banana industry, 1:245–247
    Basic Needs Approach, 5:456
    birth control, 1:303
    brain drain, 1:367–368
    bribery, 1:371
    capital flight, 1:434, 435, 436
    capitalist mode of production,
      1:447
    central banks, 1:479–480
    Central Intelligence Agency, U.S,
      1:483
    class conflict, 1:570
    clientelism, 1:579
    common land, 2:26–27, 28
    communism, 2:35, 36
    compulsory voting, 2:59
    conditionality, 2:65
    consumerism, 2:105
    contraception, 2:114
    corporate income tax, 3:608
    corporations, 2:140
    corporatism, 2:141
    corruption, 2:144, 145
    crony capitalism, 2:180
    Cuba, 2:186–187
    cumulative causation, 2:207
    De Soto, Hernando, 2:319–320
    debt, 9:138
    demand for money, 5:254, 255
    democracy, 2:275
    democratization, 2:289
    demography, 2:291, 293–294
    dependency theory, 2:298–300

development economics,
    2:344–346
development in sociology,
    2:346–348
development theory, 2:337–339
digital divide, 2:367
emerging markets, 3:147
employment, 2:580, 581
energy sector, 2:592
ethnic diversity and, 2:343
ethnic enterprises, 3:6
export promotion, 3:67
flower industry, 3:159
food diplomacy, 3:166
gender, 3:272–277
General Motors, 3:286
Green Revolution, 3:378
happiness, 3:416
hate crimes, 3:431
health, 3:441–444, 7:321
herd behavior, 3:459–460
homelessness, 3:499
human rights, 3:286, 512–513
immigration, 3:581
immiserizing growth, 3:584
import penetration, 3:590–591
import substitution, 3:592–594
industrial accidents, 1:9
industrialization, 3:621
International Monetary Fund,
    4:95–96
international nongovernmental
    organizations, 4:97
Kaunda, Kenneth, 4:250–251
Kuznets hypothesis, 4:295–297
labor force participation,
    4:314–315
labor supply, 4:320–322
labor unions, 8:517
liquidity premium, 4:460–461
loans, 4:473
malnutrition, 4:567–568
microfinance, 5:140
midwifery, 5:152–154
militarism, 5:165
population control, 6:377–378
poverty, 6:405–407
Prebisch, Raúl, 6:422–423
representation, 7:173
resources, 7:212
returns to scale, 7:223, 224
revolution of rising expectations,
    7:231–232
rotating savings and credit
    associations, 7:286

rural development, 2:342
schizophrenia, 7:345
Singer, Hans, 7:520
The South (global), 5:542–544
stagflation, 8:83
stagnation, 8:84–85
stock exchanges, 8:151–153
structural adjustment, 8:176–178
surplus labor, 4:308–309
tax evasion and tax avoidance, 8:275, 276
taxes, 8:280, 281
Taylor, Lance, 8:285
technology, 1:492, 8:299, 309
telecommunications industry, 8:316
textile industry, 8:333–334
third world *vs.,* 8:12, 351–353
tobacco industry, 8:377–378
tourism, 8:399, 400
toxic waste, 8:408
trade liberalization, 4:428
unequal exchange, 8:505–506
urbanization, 8:546–547
Verdoorn's law, 8:608
want creation, 9:15
Washington Consensus, 9:38–40
water pollution, 6:365
water resources, 9:40–42
women's movement, 9:118
World Bank, 9:137–139
zero population growth, 9:174
See also Third World
Development, 2:**337–340**
aggression, 1:55–56
Appalachia, 1:150–151
black capitalism, 1:439
Boserup, Ester, 1:358
bribery, 1:371
capital controls, 1:432, 433
central banks, 1:479–480
civil wars, 1:555
civilization, 1:557–558
clash of civilizations, 1:560
classical economics, 2:503–504
Club of Rome, 1:585
community, 1:542, 2:40–41
cooperatives, 2:123–126, 124
corruption, 2:145
crony capitalism, 2:180
cumulative causation, 2:207
demand for money, 5:254
democracy, 2:274–275
democratization, 2:289–290

dependency theory, 2:298–300
developing countries, 2:335–337
Economic Commission for Latin America and the Caribbean, 2:482–483
energy industry, 2:589
ethnic fractionalization, 3:7–8
export promotion, 3:66–67
human ecology, 3:510, 511
import substitution, 3:592–594
in-wired, 1:505
industry, 3:623
Jacobs, Jane, 4:165
legacy effects, 4:404
Lundberg, Erik, 4:518–519
Mahathir Mohamad, 4:557–558
maquiladoras, 4:591–594
Meiji Restoration, 5:69–70
microfinance, 5:140
military regimes, 5:174–176
moral, 4:286–287
multisector models, 5:333–335
political sociology, 8:4
prison industry, 6:469
process, 1:490
product, 1:490
regions, 7:130, 132
state capitalism, 1:444
subsistence agriculture, 8:206
suburbs, 8:210–211
tax relief, 8:277–278
technology, 8:302–303
theory, 2:337–339
threshold effects, 8:359–360
toilets, 8:383–384
tourism industry, 8:399
See also Child development; Development economics
Development, human (Psychology). *See* Developmental psychology
Development, institutional, 2:**340–341**, 348
Development, political. *See* Democracy research
Development, research and. *See* Research and development (R&D)
Development, rural, 2:**341–342**
backwash effects, 1:236–237
cooperatives, 2:124
development economics, 2:346
Harris-Todaro model, 3:428
irrigation, 4:152–154
land reform, 4:341–345
rural sociology, 8:8–9
Development, stages of, 8:77–79

child, 1:505–508, 511–512
Comte, Auguste, 2:62
convergence theory, 2:117
developmental psychology, 2:349–351
Erikson, Erik, 2:625–626
identity, 3:552, 553–554
identity crisis, 3:556–557
maturation, 5:34–36
midlife crisis, 5:149
moral, 4:286–287
personality, 6:219
perspective-taking, 6:226–227
Piaget, Jean, 6:268–271
rites of passage, 7:256–259
self-representation, 7:426–427, 427*t*
theory of mind, 8:347
Development agencies, 9:139
Development and ethnic diversity, 2:**342–343**, 3:7–8
Development and gender, 2:348, 3:**272–277**
Development as Freedom (Sen), 2:348
Development banks, 9:139
Development economics, 2:**344–346**
backwash effects, 1:236–237
Chicago School, 1:502
coordination failure, 2:128
De Soto, Hernando, 2:319–320
dependency theory, 2:298–300
developing countries, 2:335–337
ethnic diversity, 2:342–343
gender, 3:272–277
Harris-Todaro model, 3:428
industrialization, 3:621–622
informal economy, 4:26–28
International Monetary Fund, 4:95–96
land reform, 4:341, 342
Lewis, W. Arthur, 4:420–421
modernization, 5:233
planning, 6:274–276
Prebisch-Singer hypothesis, 6:423–425
rural development, 2:341–342
Russian, 7:300, 301
stock exchanges in developing countries, 8:151–153
structuralist macroeconomics, 4:543–545
surplus labor, 4:308–309
Taylor, Lance, 8:285
theory, 2:337–339

Development in sociology, 2:62, **346–349**

Development induced displacement, 1:124

The Development of Capitalism in Russia (Lenin), 3:134

Developmental psycholinguistics. *See* Psycholinguistics

Developmental psychology, 2:**349–352**
   adolescent psychology, 1:24–27
   Ainsworth, Mary, 1:67–68
   Brazelton, T. Berry, 1:368–369
   children, 1:511–512
   equilibrium, 2:622–623
   Erikson, Erik, 2:625–626
   freedom, 3:196–197
   Freud, Sigmund, 3:213–214
   human ecology, 3:511
   maturation, 5:34–36
   midlife crisis, 5:148–150
   personality, 6:219
   Piaget, Jean, 6:268–271
   rites of passage, 7:256–259
   stability in psychology, 8:74–75
   See also Child development; Stages of development

Developmental regulations, 1:24

Deverson, Jane, 3:291

Deviance, 2:**352–354**
   conformity, 2:71
   constructivism, 2:97
   crime and criminology, 2:170
   culture of poverty, 2:206
   labeling theory, 4:299–300
   lifestyles, 4:445
   longitudinal data, 2:238, 239
   lynchings, 4:526–527
   peer influence, 6:201–202
   social values, 8:582, 583

Deviancy training. *See* Deviance; Peer effects

Deviation
   mean absolute, 8:585
   standard, 5:51, 8:94–95, *95*, 585, 591
   variance-covariance matrix, 8:589

Dewey, George, 9:23

Dewey, John
   aesthetics, 1:30
   behaviorism, 1:276
   curriculum, 2:214
   freedom, 3:198
   functionalism, 3:233
   habits, 3:402

Hegel, Georg Wilhelm Friedrich, 3:453
   James, William, 4:170
   New School for Social Research, 5:500
   organization man, 6:61
   pragmatism, 6:420
   representative and participatory democracy, 2:284
   science policy, 5:362

Dewey, Thomas, 9:32

DFTT (Double factorial terms of trade). *See* Terms of trade

DHHS (U.S. Department of Health and Human Services), 4:33, 5:551

Diabetes, 2:408, 3:307

Diaghilev, Sergei, 2:225

Diagnostic and Statistical Manual of Mental Disorders (DSM), 1:504
   addiction, 1:21
   alcoholism, 1:71
   attention-deficit/hyperactivity disorder, 1:197–198
   narcissism, 5:369
   obsessions, 6:17

Diagnostic testing, prenatal, 3:294–295

Diagrams, phase. *See* Phase diagrams

Dialectic of Enlightenment (Horkheimer and Adorno), 2:177, 203, 3:189, 496, 5:371

Dialectic of the Chinese Revolution (Ci), 2:36

Dialectical materialism, 5:**21–23**
   constructivism, 2:96
   Lefebvre, Henri, 4:400–401
   Marxism, 4:640
   scientific *vs.*, 5:19
   See also Primitive communism

Dialectical Materialism (Lefebvre), 4:400

Dialects. *See* Language

Dialogue with Trypho (Martyr), 6:79

Diamond, Douglas, 1:251

Diamond, Jared, 3:125, 126

Diamond, Peter A., 6:93

Diamond industry, 2:**354–356**, 7:239–240, 8:406

Diamond Trading Company (DTC), 2:355, 356

Diamond-water paradox, 1:210

Diamond Way. *See* Buddhism

Diaspora, 2:**356–357**
   African, 1:38–41
      African burial grounds, 1:393–394

      archaeology of slave lives, 7:530–531
   black immigrants, 3:565–566
   black Marxism, 4:642
   black nationalism, 1:317
   blackness, 1:328, 330
   dance, 2:223
   Diop, Cheikh Anta, 2:369
   Drake, St. Clair, 2:442
   Du Bois, W. E. B., 2:460
   Herskovits, Melville J., 3:466–467
   Hurston, Zora Neale, 3:527, 528
   Inikori, Joseph, 4:37–38
   Pan-African Congresses, 6:112–115
   Rastafari, 7:66–68
   Caribbean, 1:448–449
   Chinese, 1:515–519, 3:563
   dalits, 2:221
   East Indian, 2:471–475, 476
   hybridity, 3:536
   Jewish, 4:189–193, 193–196, 9:179, 180
   Latin American immigrants, 3:570
   Palestinian, 6:103–104, 107–110
   repatriation, 7:168–169
   Trouillot, Michel-Rolph, 8:457
   video technology, 8:310
   See also Immigration; Migration

Diasporic citizenship. *See* Immigrants

Diathesis-stress model, 2:**358–359**

Díaz, Porfirio, 4:219, 5:130, 7:233

Dicey, Albert Venn, 3:354–355, 7:292

Dichter, Ernest, 3:473

Dick-Read, Grantly, 5:431, 432

Dickens, Charles, 3:137, 301, 4:335, 8:553

Dickey, David, 1:228, 2:3

Dickey-Fuller distribution, 8:518

Dictatorship, 2:**359–360**
   corruption, 2:144
   description, 3:354
   Duvaliers, 2:468–469
   fascism, 3:102–105
   Hitler, Adolf, 3:486–488
   Hussein, Saddam, 3:531–535
   left wing *vs.*, 4:403
   liberalism, 4:425
   Mussolini, Benito, 5:349–350
   Pol Pot, 6:289
   revolution, 7:229
   socialism, 7:638
   Stalinism, 8:87

state capitalism, 1:444

See also Totalitarianism

Dictionnaire philosophique (Voltaire), 8:635, 636

Did Monetary Forces Cause the Great Depression? (Temin), 3:370

Diderot, Denis, 2:232, 8:635

Diebold, Francis, 4:499–500

Diegesis, 5:370

Diego de Mazariegos, 1:499

Dien Bien Phu, 1:140

Diener, Ed, 3:418

Diet, hypertension and, 3:539, 540

The Diet (Japan), 2:**360–361**

Dietary guidelines, 5:551

Dietary restraint. *See* Dieting

Dietary taboos. *See* Taboos

Dieting, 5:552, 6:3, 5

Dietrich, Jason, 5:212

Diewert, W. Erwin, 4:459

Difference equations, 2:**361–362**, 363

Difference principle, 2:**362–363**

Differential equations, 2:**363–366**, 4:455–457

Differentiation, 6:653–654

Diffused monotheism, 8:633

Diffusion of knowledge, 4:**281–282**

    material culture, 5:14

    technology, 1:490–492, 8:302, 305–306, 620

DiFinetti's theorem, 3:41–42

Diggers (faction). *See* Levellers

Digital divide, 2:60, **366–368**, *367*, 4:107

Dilemma, prisoner's (Economics). *See* Prisoner's dilemma (Economics)

Dilemma, prisoner's (Psychology). *See* Prisoner's dilemma (Psychology)

Dilemma, Samaritan's. *See* Bequests

Dilemmas, nonzero-sum games, 5:533

Dilemmas of Urban America (Weaver), 9:53

Dilthey, Wilhelm

    constructivism, 2:96

    epistemology, 2:609–610

    hermeneutics, 3:462

    linguistic turn, 4:457

    naturalism, 5:443

    objectivity, 6:11

    Weltanschauung, 9:78

DiMaggio, Paul, 2:205, 6:70

Dimensionality, curse of, 5:526

Diminishing returns, 7:**218–219**

    asymmetric returns to scale, 7:223, 224

described, 7:217, 218

Malthus, Thomas Robert, 4:570

returns to scale, 7:222–223

Ricardo, David, 7:244

Dimorphism, sexual, 1:84

Ding (concept of object), 6:9

Diop, Cheikh Anta, 1:558, 2:**368–370**

Diplomacy, 2:**370–372**

    bilateralism, 1:297

    Bunche, Ralph Johnson, 1:387

    Bush, George H. W., 1:398

    Carter, Jimmy, 1:451

    Chamberlain, Neville, 1:489

    civil wars, 1:554, 556

    Cold War, 2:5

    commonwealth, 2:29

    conflict, 2:70

    counterterrorism, 2:155

    Cuban Missile Crisis, 2:183–185

    Cuban Revolution, 2:186–187

    defense, 2:257–259

    European Union, 3:25

    food, 3:165–166

    Kissinger, Henry, 4:274–275

    League of Nations, 4:385–386

    legal systems, 4:407

    Monroe Doctrine, 5:272

    peace process, 6:185–186

    reconciliation, 7:110–111

    Thant, U., 8:334

    Trilateral Commission, 8:452–453

    trilateralism, 8:453–454

    See also Foreign policy; International relations

Dippie, Brian, 1:259

Direct, intensive, systematic, early, and comprehensive instruction (DISEC), 7:87

Direct action, 2:283–285, **372**

Direct democracy. *See* Representative and participatory democracy

Direct taxation. *See* Taxation

Director of Central Intelligence, U.S. (DCI). *See* Central Intelligence Agency, U.S. (CIA)

Director of National Intelligence, U.S. (DNI). *See* Central Intelligence Agency, U.S. (CIA)

Dirigisme. *See* Dirigiste

Dirigiste, 2:**372–374**, *373*, 414

Dirks, Nicholas, 1:462

Dirty float, 2:**375**

    currency appreciation and depreciation, 2:209

    exchange rates, 3:39

foreign reserves, 7:202

Disability, 2:**375–379**

    civil rights, 1:549

    correspondence tests, 2:142

    intelligence, 4:73

    mental retardation, 5:88–90

    unemployment, 8:21

Disabled People's International (DPI), 2:377

Disagreements. *See* Conflict

Disarmament, 2:**379–381**

    civil wars, 1:556

    League of Nations, 4:385

    Thompson, Edward P., 8:355

    United Nations Security Council, 9:52

    See also Arms control

Disaster management, 2:**381–385**, 447–448

Disasters, natural. *See* Natural disasters

Disc jockeys (DJ), 8:622

Discipline. *See* Corporal punishment

Discipline and Punish (Foucault), 3:182, 262, 263

A Discipline Divided (Almond), 1:82

Disclosure, law and economics, 4:367

Discontinuity theories. *See* Stages of development

Discounted present value, 2:**385–386**

Discounting. *See* Time preference

Discouraged unemployment. *See* Discouraged workers

Discouraged workers, 2:**386–387**, 4:315

    underemployment rate, 8:494

    unemployment, 8:497

    unemployment rate, 8:501

Discourse, 1:129, 2:177–178, **387–388**

Discourse on Method (Descartes), 1:275

The Discourse on the Origins of Inequality (Rousseau), 7:291

Discourses on Livy (Machiavelli), 4:533, 534

Discretion, rules versus, 7:**293–295**

Discriminant validity, 8:573–574

Discrimination, 2:**388–392**

    age, 3:308

      civil rights, 1:549

      race, 2:406

      wage, 2:401–402

    audits, 1:208–210

    Becker, Gary S., 1:270–271

    bigotry, 1:295–296

    caste, 1:90–92, 460, 463

Discrimination, *continued*
colonialism, 2:12
cultural rights, 2:197–198
customs union, 2:214, 215
dalits, 2:221, 222
disability, 2:377–378
distributive justice, 4:240
East Indian diaspora, 2:474
economic, 1:94
employment
age, 2:401–402
Body Mass Index, 1:348
buraku, 1:388–389
Chinese diaspora, 1:517
civil rights, 1:549
correspondence tests,
2:141–143
crowding hypothesis,
2:181–182
glass ceiling, 3:325–326
Glazer, Nathan, 3:327
marginal product of labor,
4:306
Myrdal, Gunnar, 1:94
racial, 2:393–396, 404, 5:384
statistical, 2:396–398
wage, 2:400–401, 404
women, 5:408–409, 9:117
equal opportunity, 2:611–613
ethnicity, 3:9
housing, 2:317, 4:347
immigrants, 3:578, 579
institutional, 4:92
intergenerational transmission,
4:89–90
intergroup relations, 4:91
litigation, 4:465
meritocracy, 5:99
nonblacks, 5:513–514
phenotype, 1:36
philanthropy, 6:246
reverse, 1:31
sexism, 7:473–474
sexual orientation, 7:478
social dominance orientation,
7:583–584
stereotypes, 8:136–139
stigma, 8:146–148
Sudras, 8:212–213
tariffs, 8:265, 266
trade barriers, 1:254–255
trade quotas, 6:672–673
transgender, 8:432
workplace, 5:408–409
xenophobia, 9:158–161

See also Gender gap
Discrimination, price, 2:**392–393**
monopsony, 5:267–268
product dumping, 2:462
revenue, 7:226–227
Discrimination, racial, 2:388–389,
390–392, **393–396**
affirmative action, 3:392–393
Arrow, Kenneth J., 1:182
audits, 1:208–210
biased policing, 6:289–291
black immigrants, 3:567
blackness, 1:328–329
Brimmer, Andrew, 1:371, 372
buraku, 1:388–389
Chinese Americans, 1:513–515
Chinese diaspora, 1:516
cities, 1:542
civil rights, 1:549, 550
civil rights movement, U.S.,
1:551–552
color-blind, 9:87
Coloreds (South Africa), 2:15
colorism, 2:17
Congress of Racial Equality, 2:75
Constitution, U.S., 2:92
contact hypothesis, 2:111–112
correspondence tests, 2:141–143
critical race theory, 2:175
Du Bois, W. E. B., 2:458–460
economics, 7:13–15
education, 7:16–18
educational achievement, 1:16
employment, 2:404, 5:384
engineering, 2:593–594
equal protection, 2:615
Hernandez v. Texas, 3:464–466
imprisonment, 3:596–597
interracial sex, 7:469–470
Japanese Americans, 3:599–601,
4:173–175
Jim Crow, 4:198–201
labor law, 4:303
Latino National Political Survey,
4:354–356
liberation, 4:429–430
life events and stress, 4:444
low and high culture, 2:205
Mexican Americans, 5:123
mulatto escape hatch, 5:310–312
Myrdal, Gunnar, 1:93–96
NAACP, 5:383–386
phenotype, 1:36
poll tax, 6:352

qualifications, 6:649–650
quota systems, 6:668–670
quotas, 6:670–671
racial democracy, 2:282
racism *vs.,* 7:44
reparations, 7:166–168
residential segregation, 7:384–385
restitution principle, 7:213–215
Roma, 7:278–279
separate-but-equal, 7:445–447
South, U.S., 8:32–33
Southern politics, 6:339–349
statistical, 2:395
Tally's Corner (Liebow), 8:264
taste for, 7:14
townships, 8:405–407
upward mobility, 8:534
Voting Rights Act (U.S. 1965),
8:653
wages, 9:4
white primary, 9:83–85
whiteness, 9:92–93
Wilson, William Julius,
9:100–101
working class, 9:131–133
Discrimination, statistical, 2:**396–398**
age, 2:402
described, 2:390
racial, 2:395
wage, 2:401, 403
Discrimination, taste for, 2:388–389,
390, **398–400,** 402
racial, 7:14
wage, 2:405
Discrimination, wage, 2:**400–401**
buraku, 1:388–389
econometric decomposition,
2:478–479
marginal product of labor, 4:306
occupation, 2:404
race, 2:17, 389–391, 400–401,
405–406
taste for, 2:405
Discrimination, wage, by age,
2:**401–402**
Discrimination, wage, by gender,
2:389–391, 400–401, **402–404,**
3:626
Blinder-Oaxaca decomposition
technique, 1:333–334
crowding hypothesis, 2:181
gender preference, 6:434
taste for discrimination, 2:399
Discrimination, wage, by occupation,
2:**404–405**

Discrimination, wage, by race, 2:17, 389–391, 400–401, **405–406**, 9:4
  Blinder-Oaxaca decomposition technique, 1:333–334
  Burakmin, 1:388–389
  econometric decomposition, 2:478–479
  restitution principle, 7:214–215
Disease, 2:**406–409**
  bioterrorism, 1:302
  burial grounds, 1:393
  Columbus, Christopher, 2:20–21
  disaster management, 2:382
  ethno-epidemiological methodology, 3:12–13
  John Henryism, 4:207–208
  malnutrition, 4:567–568
  medical anthropology, 1:130–132
  refugee camps, 7:125
  tobacco settlement, 7:466–467
  Tuskegee syphilis study, 8:472–473
  water pollution, 6:365
  See also names of specific diseases or disorders; Health; Morbidity and mortality
DISEC (Direct, intensive, systematic, early, and comprehensive instruction), 7:87
Diseconomies of scale, average costs, 1:232
Disenfranchisement. *See* Civil rights; Franchise; Voting
Disequilibrium economics. *See* Barro-Grossman model; Equilibrium in economics; New Keynesian economics; Patinkin, Don
Disfranchisement. *See* Civil rights; Voting
Disguised unemployment, 8:492, 497–498
Disgust. *See* Sanitation
Dishion, Thomas J., 6:201–202
Disinvestment. *See* Divestiture
Disney, Walt, 2:203, **409–410**
Disobedience. *See* Obedience
Disorders, psychiatric. *See* Psychiatric disorders
Dispensationalism, 2:162
Dispersion. *See* Variation
Displaced persons. *See* Refugees
Displacement, development induced, 1:124
Display rules, 5:530
Dispositional factors, altruism, 1:88

Disproportionality theory. *See* Accumulation of capital
Dispute Settlement Body, 9:144
Disputes. *See* Conflict
Disraeli, Benjamin, 2:83, 84, 87, 4:201, 202
Dissatisfaction. *See* Satisfaction
Dissidents, 2:**411–412**
  civil wars, 1:555
  imprisonment, 3:597
  repressive tolerance, 7:176–177
  terrorists, 8:330–331
Dissociative identity disorder. *See* Multiple personalities
Dissonance, 1:180–181, 9:136–137
  See also Cognitive dissonance
Distance, social. *See* Political tolerance; Social isolation
Distinction: A Social Critique of the Judgement of Taste (Bourdieu), 1:359, 2:107, 412, 8:565
Distinctions, social and cultural, 2:**412–414**
  classical music, 1:575
  cultural tourism, 2:201–202
Distortions, 2:**414–415**
  immiserizing growth, 3:583
  theory of second best, 8:350–351
Distributed lags, 4:**333–335**
  error-correction mechanisms, 2:627
  time series regression, 8:371
Distribution
  bimodal, 1:488
  classical economics, 1:447–448
  coffee industry, 1:595
  descriptive statistics, 2:311–313
  income
    agricultural economics, 1:58–59
    bubbles, 1:379
    Cambridge capital controversy, 1:419, 420
    class conflict, 1:571
    corporate social responsibility, 2:136
    corruption, 2:145
    Deininger and Squire World Bank Inequality Database, 2:267–268
    democracy, 2:275–276
    difference principle, 2:363
    equality, 2:617–618, *618*
    long period analysis, 4:490
    Luxembourg Income Study, 4:519–521, 521*t*

    marginal product of labor, 4:304, 305
    rentier class, 1:567
    utilitarianism, 9:63–64
    working class, 9:132
  marginal product of labor, 4:305–306, 307
  multimodal, 1:488
  nonparametric estimation, 5:524
  power, 6:415–416
  randomness, 7:63
  Ricardo, David, 7:244–246
  variation, 8:591–593
  wealth
    difference principle, 2:363
    School of Lausanne, 4:361–362
  See also Frequency distributions; Probability distributions
Distribution, beta. *See* Probability distributions
Distribution, Cauchy. *See* Probability distributions
Distribution, exponential. *See* Probability distributions
Distribution, gamma. *See* Probability distributions
Distribution, Gaussian. *See* Normal distribution
Distribution, Laplace. *See* Probability distributions
Distribution, logistic. *See* Probability distributions
Distribution, lognormal. *See* Probability distributions
Distribution, normal, 2:*415,* **415–417**
  central limit theorem, 1:486
  chi-square, 1:523
  measures of central tendencies, 1:487–488
  probability distributions, 6:494
  Z-test, 9:182–183
Distribution, Pareto. *See* Probability distributions
Distribution, Poisson, 2:*417,* **417–418**
Distribution, posterior. *See* Statistical inference
Distribution, prior. *See* Bayesian inference
Distribution, rectangular. *See* Normal distribution
Distribution, uniform, 2:*418,* **418–419**, 6:494
Distribution, Weibull. *See* Probability distributions

The Distribution of Wealth (Clark), 1:13

Distributions, probability. *See* Probability distributions

Distributive justice, 4:**239–241**
  consociational democracy, 2:279
  difference principle, 2:362–363
  as justice, 4:237
  marginal product of labor, 4:306
  restitution principle, 7:213–215
  social justice, 4:242

District of Columbia Financial Responsibility and Management Assistance Authority, 1:372

Districts, electoral. *See* Electoral districts

Divergent thinking, 2:165

Diversity, 2:**419–420**, 3:196
  biological anthropology, 1:125–127
  Blau, Peter M., 1:332
  Brown v. Board of Education (1954), 1:376
  bureaucracy, 1:391
  cleavages, 1:578
  collective wisdom, 2:9
  cultural rights, 2:197–198
  cultural studies, 2:200
  Dahl, Robert Alan, 2:220
  development and, 2:342–343
  elites, 2:565
  empire, 2:575
  multiculturalism, 5:316–318
  national defense, 2:260
  pluralism, 6:283–284
  Social Darwinism, 2:234
  variation, 8:591–593

Divestiture, 2:**420–421**, 8:315

Divided government, 2:74

Divine right, 2:**421–422**, 5:239

Divinity. *See* Supreme being

Divisia, François, 4:459

Divisia monetary index, 2:**422–423**, 5:261, 491, 6:658

Division of labor, 2:**423–426**
  Boserup, Ester, 1:358
  capitalist mode of production, 1:445–446
  class, 1:563, 571
  classical music, 1:575
  consumption, 2:106
  cooperation, 2:122, 123
  credentialism, 2:167
  dependency theory, 2:299, 300
  described, 4:302

Durkheim, Émile, 2:466
  economics, 2:490, 496–497
  ethnic diversity, 2:342, 343
  factories, 3:76, 77, 79
  free trade, 3:194
  gender differences, 9:72
  imports, 3:595
  Incas, 3:602
  increasing returns, 7:219
  inegalitarianism, 3:623
  labor, 4:301
  machinery, 4:535–536
  primitive accumulation, 6:463–464
  primitive communism, 2:38
  social statics, 7:620
  society, 7:651–652
  surplus labor, 4:311
  Taylorism, 8:287
  technological change, 1:491
  time and motion studies, 8:365
  towns, 8:404–405
  women's work, 9:124
  world-system, 9:153

The Division of Labor (Durkheim), 2:465

Divisive clustering, 1:585

Divorce and separation, 2:**426–428**
  childlessness, 1:510
  cohabitation, 2:1, 2
  family structure, 3:84–85, 93
  increase, 4:615
  Maccoby, Eleanor, 4:531–532
  out-of-wedlock births, 1:307
  sibling relationships, 7:506

Dixiecrats, 2:**428–431**
  civil rights movement, U.S., 1:551
  Democratic Party (U.S.), 2:287
  Republican Party (U.S.), 7:187
  Southern strategy, 8:36
  Thurmond, Strom, 8:360–361
  Truman, Harry S., 8:460

Dixit, Avinash, 2:56–57

Dixon, Thomas, 1:304, 306, 3:347

DJ (Disc jockeys), 8:622

Djilas, Milovan, 5:492
  See also New Class

Dmitriev, Vladimir K., 7:299–300

DNA (Deoxyribonucleic acid), 1:336, 3:460–461

DNA sequencing, 3:299

DNI, U.S. (Director of National Intelligence). *See* Central Intelligence Agency, U.S. (CIA)

Do Machines Make History? (Heilbronner), 2:332

Do the Right Thing (film), 1:243

Dobb, Maurice, 2:77, 3:134, 482

Dobrynin, Anatoly, 2:183, 184, 185

Dobzhansky, Theodosius, 2:**432–433**

Doctor Zhivago (Pasternak), 9:20

Documentary studies, 2:**433–434**, 3:140–141

Dodge, Harold F., 6:651

Dodge, Kenneth A., 7:599–600

Doe v. Bolton, 1:4

Doeringer, Peter, 6:77

Does Technology Drive History? (Smith and Marx), 2:332

Dogs, classical conditioning, 1:572–573

Doha Round, 3:281, 9:144

DOJ (U.S. Department of Justice), 2:53, 3:600, 601

Dolchstosslegende, 9:148

Dole, 1:245

Doll study. *See* Clark, Kenneth B.

Dollar (currency), 2:209, 211, 211*t*
  euro, 3:22, 23
  exchange rates, 3:39
  See also Currency

Dollarization, 3:39

DOMA (Defense of Marriage Act) (U.S. 1996), 2:426, 4:620

Domain fallacy, 8:574

Domar, Evsey, 5:464, 8:488–489

Domes, geodesic, 3:228–229

Domesday Book. See Census

Domestic affairs, international law, 3:360

Domestic Distortions, Tariffs, and the Theory of Optimum Subsidy (Bhagwati and Ramaswami), 1:293

Domestic work
  description, 9:123
  occupational hazards, 6:22–23
  societal definition, 9:108–109
  unpaid, 3:167
  wages, 9:124–125
  women's liberation, 9:113
  See also Servants

Domesticated animals
  fertile crescent, 3:125–126
  history, 3:162–163
  Native Americans, 5:424
  See also Animals

Dominance, inclusionary. *See* Assimilation

Dominance, social. *See* Social dominance orientation

Dominant strategy. *See* Zero-sum games

Dominican Republic, blackness and, 1:329

Domino theory, 2:256, **434–436**

Doña Marina. *See* Malinchistas

Donald, Michael, 4:527

Donner Party, 1:428

Donors, nongovernmental organizations, 5:520

Dooley, Michael, 2:212

Doonesbury (comic strip), 1:452

The Doors of Perception (Huxley), 3:411

DOP (Declaration of Principles). *See* Oslo Accords

Dopamine, 2:**436–437**, 6:18
  drugs of abuse, 2:453
    nonadditive determinism, 2:330, 331
    self-constrained behavior, 1:274
    serotonin, 7:457

Doré, 3:343

Dorfman, Robert, 2:117, 3:151, 6:51

Dornbusch, Rudiger, 6:98

Dornbusch-Fischer-Samuelson model, 2:**437–438**

Dorsey, Thomas A., 1:342

Dostoyevsky, Fyodor, 5:502

Double consciousness. *See* Veils, in African American culture

Double factorial terms of trade (DFTT). *See* Terms of trade

Douglas, Mary. *See* Sanitation

Douglas, Paul H., 2:103

Douglas, Stephen A., 4:451

Douglas, William O., 3:585

Douglas-Hume, Alex, 5:507

Douglass, Frederick, 1:310, 2:**438–440**, 9:113

Down, John Langdon H., 7:21

Down syndrome. *See* Race and psychology

Downey, Douglas, 6:48

Downs, Anthony, 2:59, 6:128, 8:44–45
  See also Spatial theory

Downsizing. *See* Employment

Dowry and bride price, 2:**440–442**, 3:83, 84, 4:613, 614–615

Doxa, 1:359, 564, 3:404, 405, 406, 6:79

Doxastic agnosticism, 1:57

Doxastic atheism, 1:194

Doyal, Len, 5:453

Draft, military. *See* Selective Service

Draft-board examinations, Flynn effect, 3:160

Drake, Jennifer, 9:115

Drake, St. Clair, 1:324, 2:181, **442–443**, 7:9, 10

Drake, W. Avon, 1:312

Drama. *See* Literature; Theater

Dramas, Fields, and Metaphors (Turner), 8:470

Drams, 3:136–137

Draper, Patricia, 9:109

Dravidians, 2:**443–444**

Drazen, Allan, 1:406

Dream, American, 1:**96–97**
  energy sector, 2:592
  immigrants, 3:575
  Japanese Americans, 4:173

Dreaming, 2:**444–445**, 3:209, 214, 4:231

The Dreams of Affliction (Turner), 8:470

Dred Scott v. Sanford (1857), 2:**445–447**
  black nationalism, 1:315
  federalism, 3:114
  judicial activism, 1:19
  Supreme Court, U.S., 8:234

Dreiser, Theodore, 1:96

Dresher, Melvin, 6:473

Drexler, K. Eric, 5:361–362

Drèze, Jacques, 1:256

Drought, 2:**447–449**, 3:97, 5:433

Drucker, Peter, 2:**449–450**, 4:285

Druckman, Daniel, 5:530

Drug addiction. *See* Addiction

Drug Enforcement Agency, U.S. (DEA), 2:455, 455t

Drug therapy
  depression, 2:307, 308
  hallucinogens, 3:411, 412
  hypertension, 3:540

Drug tolerance, 7:559–560, 8:**384–385**

Drug traffic, 2:**450–452**
  confiscation, 2:69–70
  deviance, 2:354
  hallucinogens, 3:412
  Mafia, 4:551
  money laundering, 5:263

Drug Trafficking Act (U.K. 1994), 2:69

Drug Trafficking Offences Act (U.K. 1986), 2:69

Drugs
  antianxiety, 1:147, 147t
  antihypertensive, 3:540
  infertility, 4:19–20
  See also specific drugs and classes of drugs; Drugs of abuse; Psychotropic drugs

Drugs of abuse, 2:**452–456**, 453t, 455t
  addiction, 1:20–22
  AIDS/HIV, 1:63, 66
  crime and criminology, 2:172, 173
  dopamine, 2:437
  drug traffic, 2:450–452
  lifestyles, 4:445
  steroids, 8:142–143
  tolerance, 8:384–385
  Woodstock, 9:121
  See also Hallucinogens

Drummond, Eric, 4:385

DSM. *See* Diagnostic and Statistical Manual of Mental Disorders

DSM *(Diagnostic and Statistical Manual of Mental Disorders). See Diagnostic and Statistical Manual of Mental Disorders* (DSM)

Du Bois, W. E. B., 2:**457–461**
  African American studies, 1:32
  Black Arts Movement, 1:309
  black liberalism, 1:312
  black middle class, 1:313
  Black Reconstruction, 9:77
  as black sociologist, 1:323, 325
  blackness, 1:330
  Boas, Franz, 1:345
  civil rights, 1:550, 551
  Clark, Kenneth B., 1:561
  colorism, 2:18
  diaspora, 2:356, 357
  Garvey, Marcus, 3:258
  Harlem, 3:424, 425
  Harris, Abram L., Jr., 3:427
  Jim Crow, 4:198, 200
  NAACP, 5:383
  negro terminology, 5:459
  Pan-African Congresses, 6:112–115
  The Philadelphia Nego, 5:389
  race relations, 7:10, 30
  school desegregation, 1:375
  slavery, 7:544–545
  social demography, 2:296
  sociology, 7:661
  Tally's Corner, 8:264
  urban studies, 8:541–542

Du Bois, W. E. B., *continued*
  veils, 8:602
  vindication, 8:618
  Weltanschauung, 5:372
  whiteness, 9:87, 91–92
Dual citizenship. *See* Citizenship
Dual economy, 2:**456–457**
  dependency theory, 2:298–300
  development economics, 2:344
  development in sociology, 2:347
  development theory, 2:338
  labor supply, 4:320
  surplus labor, 4:308–309
Dualism
  Giddens, Anthony, 3:314
  optimal growth, 6:52
  See also Functionalism; Reality
Dualism, economic. *See* Dual
  economy
Dubey, Pradeep, 3:284
Dubner, Stephen J., 2:326
Duc, Quang, 8:614
Due process, 2:**461–462**
  black nationalism, 1:315
  checks and balances, 1:496
  children's rights, 1:512
  civil liberties, 1:547
  Constitution, U.S., 2:92
  death-qualified jurors, 4:233
  equal protection, 2:614–615
  hearsay, 3:444–445
  Hernandez v. Texas, 3:465
  interrogation, 4:110, 112
  Jim Crow, 4:200
  jury selection, 4:233–234
  lynchings, 4:527
  repression, 7:174
  rule of law, 7:292–293
Duesenberry, James, 2:107, 109–110,
  3:417, 7:153
Dügü ceremony, 3:258
Dühring, Eugen, 8:627
Dukakis, Michael, 1:398, 4:371
Duke, David, 1:296
Duke Power Company, Griggs v.
  (1971), 1:288, 2:615, 6:671
Dulles, Allen W., 9:33
Dulles, John Foster, 2:334
Dumbarton Oaks, 9:150
Dummy variable trap. *See*
  Econometrics
Dumont, Louis, 1:461–462
Dumping, product, 2:**462**
Dunant, Henry, 5:509

Duncan, Otis Dudley, 1:563, 2:296,
  462–463
  Blinder-Oaxaca decomposition
    technique, 1:332
  intergenerational transmission,
    4:88
  socioeconomic status, 7:657, 658
Duncan, Starkey, 5:530
Dunham, Katherine, 2:223
Dunkel, Arthur, 8:548
Dunleavy, Patrick, 2:45
Dunning, William A., 1:304, 305
Duopoly, 5:517, 6:453, *453*
Dupuit, Jules, 2:104
Dupuy de Lome, Enrique, 9:23
Duration models, 1:385, 2:**463–464**,
  464
Durham Report, 3:587
Durkheim, Émile, 2:**465–467**
  alienation, 1:75
  altruism, 3:293
  anthropology, 1:137
  cities, 1:540
  class, 1:561, 562, 563
  collective memory, 2:7
  conformity, 2:71
  consensus, 2:82
  constructivism, 2:96
  cultural distinctions, 2:413
  cultural landscape, 2:192
  determinism, 2:324
  economic sociology, 7:668
  empiricism, 2:578–579
  epistemology, 2:609
  European sociology, 7:670
  functionalism, 3:232
  Goffman, Erving, 3:337–338
  groups, 3:385
  individualism, 3:620
  institutional analysis in sociology,
    7:673
  knowledge in sociology, 7:674
  labeling theory, 4:299
  labor, 4:300
  Lévi-Strauss, Claude, 4:416
  natural rights, 5:439
  objectivity, 6:9, 9:57
  political culture, 6:300–301
  political sociology, 8:4
  religion, 7:160
  religiosity, 7:162
  schools in sociology, 8:11
  scientific method, 7:363
  social pathology, 6:170
  social statics, 7:620

  social structure, 7:623
  social theory, 7:627, 628
  society, 7:651–652
  sociology, 7:660
  solidarity, 8:23–24
  suicide, 8:221–222
  theory, 8:345
  values, 8:581–582
Durkin, Kevin, 1:249
Duryea, Charles, 1:217
Duryea, Frank, 1:217
Dutch disease, 2:**467–468**
Dutch Tulipmania. *See* Great Tulip
  Mania
Dutchman (Baraka), 1:309
Duties, natural rights, 5:439
Duties (Trade). *See* Tariffs
Dutt, Amitava Krishna, 2:207, 5:547
Dutty, Boukman, 8:634
Duvalier, François (Papa Doc). *See*
  Duvaliers
Duvalier, Jean-Claude (Baby Doc). *See*
  Duvaliers
Duvalier, Michele. *See* Duvaliers
Duvalier, Simone. *See* Duvaliers
Duvaliers, 2:**468–469**
Duverger's law. *See* Political parties
Dvijas, 8:567–568
Dworkin, Ronald, 3:234, 4:239
Dwyer, Toom, 1:8
Dyad, 4:253
Dybvig, Philip, 1:251
Dye, Thomas R., 4:506
Dyer, Reginald, 5:460
Dyer Anti-Lynching Bill (U.S.), 5:384
Dying. *See* Death and dying
A Dying Colonialism (Fanon), 3:100
Dylan, Bob, 9:121
Dymaxion (DYnamic MAXimum
  tensION), 3:229
Dynamic games, 3:32
Dynamics
  chaos theory, 1:492–493
  comparative, 2:47
  replicator, 3:32, 7:169–170
Dynamics, group. *See* Intergroup
  relations
Dynamics, social. *See* Social relations
Dynastic state, 8:596–597
Dynasties. *See* Blood and bloodline
Dysfunctional families. *See* Family
  functioning
Dysthymic disorder (DD), 2:306
Dystopian literature, 8:396
Dystopianism, 8:561

E

E-business, 1:402–403, 5:245

E-commerce. *See* E-business

Eames, Edwin, 4:419, 5:462

Earl, Peter, 4:422

Earned income tax credit (EITC), 5:457

  described, 8:274

  hard-core unemployed, 3:422

  income maintenance experiments, 3:607

  social policy interventions, 4:118

Earnings. *See* Income; Wages

Earnings, individual. *See* Wages

Earthquakes, 5:432–434

  See also Natural disasters

Easley v. Cromartie, 8:653

East Africa, anticolonial movements, 1:139

East Asia. *See* Asia

East Germany

  Bahro, Rudolf, 1:237–238

  Berlin Wall, 1:289

  Communist Party, 1:237–238, 4:522

East Germany Communist Party. *See* Communist Party (East Germany)

East India Company (EIC), 1:396, 7:55

  See also Opium Wars

East Indian diaspora, 2:471–475

East Indies, 2:476

Easterlin, Richard, 3:415, 416–417, 7:153–154

Easterlin paradox. *See* Happiness

Easterly, William, 9:138

Eastern Band of Cherokee Indians (EBCI), 1:496, 498

Eastern Europe

  AIDS/HIV, 1:65

  Bahro, Rudolf, 1:237

  civil society, 1:553

  civilization, 1:558

  clash of civilizations, 1:559

  Cold War, 2:4

  communism, 2:34, 35, 36

  convergence theory, 2:117

  land reform, 4:342

  market socialism, 7:645

  Marxian economics, 2:516

  partitioning, 9:147, 149

  shtetlekh, 7:503–504

  socialism, 7:638

  state capitalism, 1:444

  USSR decine, 8:512–513

  Warsaw Pact, 9:34–36

  white supremacy, 9:86

  See also specific Eastern European countries; Europe

Eastern Orthodox Church. *See* Greek Orthodox Church

Easton, David, 2:476–477

  political science, 6:313

  political stability, 8:73

Eating disorders, 6:3, 17–18

  See also Overeating; Undereating

Eating Disorders Inventory, 6:3

The Eatonville Anthology (Hurston), 3:527

Eatonville (FL), 1:325, 3:526

eBay, 1:207–208

Ebbinghaus, Hermann, 1:597

EBCI (Eastern Band of Cherokee Indians), 1:496, 498

EC (European Commission). *See* European Commission (EC)

ECHR (European Convention on Human Rights), 1:546

ECLA (Economic Commission for Latin America). *See* Economic Commission for Latin America and the Caribbean (ECLAC)

ECLAC (Economic Commission for Latin America and the Caribbean). *See* Economic Commission for Latin America and the Caribbean (ECLAC)

ECM (Equilibrium correction models), 2:1–3

Eco-feminism, 9:113

Ecocire system, 3:222

École Polytechnique, 9:157, 158

Ecological systems theory. *See* Developmental psychology

Ecology

  cultural, 1:120

  human, 3:510–511

    Bahro, Rudolf, 1:238

    cultural landscape, 2:192–193

    deforestation, 2:262–264

    developmental psychology, 2:350–351

    drought, 2:447–448

    energy sector, 2:591–592

    environmental impact assessment, 2:605–607

    limits of growth, 4:448–450

    metropolitan regions, 7:134

    Park School, 6:142–143

    political theory, 6:318

    regions, 7:130

    resources, 7:212

  Occam's razor, 6:20

  population, 6:69

  social, 2:449–450

Econometric decomposition, 2:478–480

  bootstrap method, 1:353–354

  Cholesky decomposition, 1:526–527

Econometric Society. *See* Schumpeter, Joseph Alois

Econometrics, 2:480–482

  Bayesian, 1:262–265

  business cycle theories, 1:410

  business cycles, 1:403–405

  causality, 1:471–473

  Chicago School, 1:502

  Chow test, 1:529–530

  cliometrics, 1:581, 582

  cointegration, 2:2–3

  comparative statics, 2:48

  consumption function, 2:109–110

  demand for money, 5:255

  economic growth, 2:486–487

  exchangeability, 3:42

  Frisch, Ragnar, 3:221–222

  Hausman tests, 3:432–434

  heteroskedasticity, 3:470–471

  identification problem, 3:550

  income inequality, 4:1–2

  Keynes, John Maynard, 4:261

  Klein, Lawrence, 4:275–276

  Koopmans, Tjalling, 4:287–288

  labor economics, 2:514–515

  left and right censoring, 1:473–474

  loss functions, 4:495–502

  Lucas critique, 4:511

  nonlinear regression, 5:522

  nonparametric, 5:526

  normalization, 5:534

  Occam's razor, 6:20

  real business cycles, 1:407–409

  sample censoring, 1:474–475

  Sargent, Thomas, 7:326–327

  semiparametric estimation, 7:438–439

  specification, 8:48–50

  specification error, 8:50–52

  specification tests, 8:52–53

  supply, 8:229

  Tinbergen, Jan, 8:374–375

  Tobin, James, 8:378–379

  trends, 8:447–448

Econometrics, *continued*
See also Economic model
Economic and Social Council (UN),
3:275, 8:523
The Economic Basis of Politics (Beard),
1:268
Economic boom. *See* Economic
growth
Economic capital
gentility, 3:301
nouveaux riches, 5:548
venture, 8:604–605
vintage models, 8:619–621
Economic choice. *See* Choice in
economics
Economic Commission for Latin
America and the Caribbean
(ECLAC), 2:298–300, 347,
482–483, 4:543, 8:285
The Economic Consequences of Peace
(Keynes), 1:152, 4:261
Economic crises, 2:**483–485**
accumulation of capital, 1:12
banking, 1:250, 251, 252–253
bubbles (economics), 1:378–379
bull and bear markets, 1:385–386
business cycle theories, 1:409–410
capital flight, 1:434–436
central banks, 1:478, 480
decisive events, 2:253–254
drought, 2:447–448
economic depression, 2:302
foreign reserves, 7:203
herd behavior, 3:459–460
lender of last resort, 4:409–410
Lombard Street (Bagehot), 4:485
long run, 4:493
maquiladoras, 4:592–593
national defense, 2:260, 261
overproduction, 6:97
panics, 6:124–125
recession, 7:103–105
Soros, George, 8:31
South Sea Bubble, 8:33–34
speculation, 8:54–56
structural adjustment, 8:176–178
underconsumption, 8:488
X-Crise, 9:157–158
Economic decision-making,
5:483–484, 6:47
Economic depression, 2:**302–306**,
303, 305
business cycle theories, 1:412
decisive events, 2:254
diamond industry, 2:354

hobos, 3:494
long run, 4:493, 494
recession *vs.,* 7:103
See also Great Depression
Economic development
Appalachia, 1:150–151
black capitalism, 1:439–442
Boserup, Ester, 1:358
bribery, 1:371
capital controls, 1:432
central banks, 1:479–480
civil wars, 1:555
clash of civilizations, 1:560
classical economics, 2:503–504
Club of Rome, 1:585
community, 1:542, 2:40–41
cooperatives, 2:123–126
corruption, 2:145
crony capitalism, 2:180
cumulative causation, 2:207
demand for money, 5:254
democracy, 2:274–275
democratization, 2:289–290
dependency theory, 2:298–300
developing countries, 2:335–337
Economic Commission for Latin
America and the Caribbean,
2:482–483
ethnic fractionalization, 3:7–8
export promotion, 3:66–67
import substitution, 3:592–594
industry, 3:623
International Monetary Fund,
4:95–96
Lewis, W. Arthur, 4:420–421
Lundberg, Erik, 4:518–519
maquiladoras, 4:591–594
Meiji Restoration, 5:69–70
microfinance, 5:140
military regimes, 5:174–176
multisector models, 5:333–335
political sociology, 8:4
prison industry, 6:469
rural development, 2:341–342
state capitalism, 1:444
subsistence agriculture, 8:206
suburbs, 8:210–211
tax relief, 8:277–278
theory, 2:337–339
third-world sociology, 8:12–14
threshold effects, 8:359–360
tourism industry, 8:399
See also Underdevelopment

Economic Development
Administration (Puerto Rico), 6:44
Economic Development
Administration (U.S.), 1:440
*The Economic Development of Latin
America and Its Principal Problems*
(Prebisch), 2:299, 482
*Economic Development with Unlimited
Supplies of Labour* (Lewis), 4:320,
420
Economic Discomfort Index. See
Misery Index
Economic discrimination, 1:94
*Economic Essays on Value, Competition,
and Utility* (Dmitriev), 7:299–300
*Economic Fluctuations in the United
States, 1921-1941* (Klein), 4:276
Economic forecasting. *See*
Autoregressive models
The Economic Future of the Caribbean
(Williams and Frazer), 9:97
Economic geography, 7:130
Economic growth, 2:**485–492**, *488*
Arrow, Kenneth J., 1:182
backwash effects, 1:236–237
Becker, Gary S., 1:270
bubbles (economics), 1:378
capital controls, 1:432
capital flight, 1:434, 436
capitalism, 1:438
Chávez, Hugo, 1:495
Chinese diaspora, 1:518
Club of Rome, 1:585
consumerism, 2:104–105
corruption, 2:145
creative destruction, 2:163
Cuba, 2:187
cumulative causation, 2:207
development economics,
2:344–346
development theory, 2:337–339
dirigiste, 2:*373*, 373–374
Dutch disease, 2:467–468
endogenous, 8:621
Engerman, Stanley, 2:592–593
ethnic diversity, 2:342–343
ethnic fractionalization, 3:7–8
fundamentals, 2:490–491
golden rule in, 3:346
greenhouse effect, 3:378
history, 2:485–486, 491–492
immiserizing growth, 3:583–584
income inequality, 4:2
industrialization, 3:621
inflation, 4:25, 26

Kuznets hypothesis, 4:295–297
life-cycle hypothesis, 4:442, 443
limits, 4:448–450
long run, 4:493–494
measurement, 2:486
models, 2:487–489
multisector models, 5:333–335
neoclassical model, 5:464–466
North-South models, 5:547
optimal, 2:489–490, 6:51–53
physical capital, 6:264–265
population growth, 6:379
poverty, 6:406
private sector, 6:480
real income, 2:486–487
slavery, 1:34
Solow residual, 8:27–28
stages, 8:79–81
    developing countries, 2:335
    development in sociology,
        2:346–348
    development theory, 2:339
state capitalism, 1:443, 444
stationary state, 8:117–118
suburban sprawl, 8:208–209
technological progress, 8:298–300
    computers, 2:60
    Silicon Valley, 7:510–511
third-world sociology, 8:12–14
threshold effects, 8:359–360
trade deficit, 8:416
trade liberalization, 4:428
two-sector neoclassical
    endogenous, 8:563–564
underdevelopment, 8:489–491
University of Texas Inequality
    Project, 8:529–530
Verdoorn's law, 8:606–608
*Economic Growth in France and
    Britain: 1851-1950* (Kindleberger),
    4:267
Economic history. *See* Cliometrics
Economic inequality
    Fields' index of, 3:137–138
    globalization, 9:46–47
    health status, 8:592
    neoimperialism, 5:471
    University of Texas Inequality
        Project, 8:529–530
    welfare economics, 9:67
    welfare state, 9:67
    whiteness, 9:87, 91–92
Economic integration
    banking industry, 1:253, 254
    bull and bear markets, 1:386

business, 1:402
    cointegration and, 2:3
    common market, 2:28–29
    corporations, 2:139
    customs union, 2:215–216
*An Economic Interpretation of the
    Constitution* (Beard), 1:267
Economic liberalization
    capitalist mode of production,
        1:447
    export penetration, 3:66
    globalization, 3:334
Economic methodology, 2:**492–494**
    causality, 1:471–473
    Chicago School, 1:502
    comparative statics, 2:48, 49
    economic rhetoric, 2:495–496
    maximum likelihood regression,
        5:41–43
    neoclassical economics, 2:517–519
Economic model, 2:**494**
    business cycle theories, 1:410–412
    business cycles, 1:403–405
    causality, 1:471–473
    Chow test, 1:529
    cointegration, 2:2–3
    comparative statics, 2:48, 49
    consumption function, 2:109–110
    described, 5:226
    equilibrium, 2:620–621
    exchangeability, 3:41–42
    Hausman tests, 3:432–434
    IS-LM model, 4:158–160
    Klein, Lawrence, 4:276
    Lagrange multipliers, 4:333–335
    left and right censoring, 1:475
    mathematics in the social sciences,
        5:26–28
    maximum likelihood regression,
        5:41–43
    McFadden, Daniel L., 5:44–45
    microfoundations, 5:141
    monopolistic competition, 2:57
    multisector models, 5:333–335
    political business cycles, 1:406
    rational expectations, 3:51, 52
    real business cycles, 1:407–409
    representative agent, 7:173–174
    semiparametric estimation,
        7:438–439
    specification, 8:48–50
    surplus labor, 4:308–309
    threshold effects, 8:359–360
    time trends, 8:373
    Tinbergen, Jan, 8:374–375

two-sector models, 8:475–476
    X-Crise, 9:157–158
    See also Econometrics; Plantation
        economy model
Economic Opportunity Act (U.S.
    1964), 3:372, 9:28
Economic order, international. *See*
    International economic order
*Economic Origins of Jeffersonian
    Democracy* (Beard), 1:268
*Economic Policy and Democratic
    Thought: Pennsylvania, 1776-1860*
    (Hartz), 3:429
Economic psychology, 1:269,
    2:**494–495**
Economic recession. *See* Recession
Economic restructuring, 5:468
Economic rhetoric, 2:**495–496**
Economic sociology, 2:495,
    7:**668–670**
Economic status. *See* Socioeconomic
    status
Economic sterilization, 8:**139–140**
*Economic Theory and Under-Developed
    Regions* (Myrdal), 2:207
Economic Theory of Democracy
    (Downs), 2:59
Economic value. *See* Value
    (economics)
Economic zones, 5:466–467
Economics, 2:**496–499**
    Arrow, Kenneth J., 1:182
    Beard, Charles, 1:268
    capitalist mode of production,
        1:446–447
    chaos theory, 1:492–493
    circular flow of, 5:400, *400*
    citations, 1:538–539
    cliometrics, 1:581–583
    cognitive dissonance, 1:599
    cointegration, 2:2–3
    consumer, 2:99–102
    conundrum, 2:116
    cooperatives, 2:123–126
    corporate strategy, 2:138–139
    cost-benefit analysis, 2:150–151
    critical theory, 2:176–178
    exchange rates, 3:37
    fascism, 3:103
    freedom, 2:372–374, *373*
    health, 3:440–441, 442
    Hurwicz, Leonid, 3:529–530
    imprisonment, 3:597
    indices of poverty, 6:408–410
    industrial, 1:502
    inefficiency in, 8:148–149

Economics, *continued*

Internet, 4:105

knowledge, 4:278

lagging, leading and coincident indicators, 4:331–332

law, 4:367–369

Becker, Gary S., 1:271

Chicago School, 1:502

Marx, Karl impact, 4:634–635

Misery Index, 5:200–201

money, 5:249–252

multilateralism, 5:321

nonlinear, 5:523–524

nonprofit organizations, 3:324

optimizing behavior, 6:55

periodization, 6:210–211

political science, 6:311–312

positive social science, 6:389

postclassical, 7:13–14

prices, 6:455–456

principal-agent models, 6:467–468

prisoner's dilemma, 2:27, 6:471–472

professional journals, 4:216–217

regulation, 7:143–144

rent, 7:163–164

resource, 2:605–607, 7:210–211

restitution principle, 7:212–215

returns, 7:217–218, 218–219

risk, 7:251, 252–253

Russian, 2:117–118, 7:299–301

scarcity, 7:339–340

selection bias, 7:390

shocks, 7:500

social, 1:502

social science, 7:616

social system, 7:625

Standard Cross-Cultural Sample, 8:90

structural transformation, 8:181

subsitutability, 8:207–208

supply, 8:227–229

supply-side, 2:85

tax relief, 8:277–278

transaction cost, 6:69

transnationalism, 8:433

trust, 8:461

universalism, 8:526–527

urban, 5:183

utility function, 8:554

welfare analysis, 9:62–63

women, 9:108–109

yield, 9:164–166

zero-sum game, 9:177

See also Macroeconomics; Microeconomics

Economics, agricultural, 1:**58–59**

Boserup, Ester, 1:357–358

Chicago School, 1:502

civil wars, 1:554

cobweb cycles, 1:591

collectivism, 2:11

development economics, 2:344

dual economy, 2:457

farm quota system, 6:667–668

farm subsidies, 8:203–204

knowledge society, 4:283, 284

Kuznets hypothesis, 4:295, 297

Ladejinsky, Wolf, 4:327–328

land reform, 4:341–345

landlords, 4:345, 346

latifundia, 4:352–354

Lenin, Vladimir Ilitch, 4:411

loans, 4:472

NAFTA, 5:541

peasantry, 6:195–196

plantation economy model, 6:278–279

populism, 6:383

primitive communism, 2:37–38

slavery, 3:131, 161–162

subsistence agriculture, 8:204–206

Economics, Austrian, 1:**210–212**, 9:94–95

capitalism, 1:439

competition, 2:51

conservatism, 2:84

gold standard, 3:345

Hayek, Friedrich August von, 3:435

libertarianism, 4:438

Mises, Ludwig Edler von, 5:202–203

neoliberalism, 5:474

Wicksell effects, 9:94–95

Economics, behavioral, 2:**499–502**

Becker, Gary S., 1:270–271

economic psychology, 2:495

Hamilton's rule, 3:414, 415

happiness, 3:415–419

lexicographic preferences, 4:422–423

microeconomics, 5:133–136

neuroeconomics, 5:483–484

poverty, 6:407

strategic behavior, 8:162–163

Economics, choice in, 1:**524–525**

choice in psychology, 1:525–526

constrained, 2:95–96

consumer, 2:101

decision-making, 2:249–251

happiness, 3:416

lexicographic preferences, 4:422–423

lifestyles, 4:445, 446

McFadden, Daniel L., 5:44–45

revealed preference, 7:224–225

Tobin, James, 8:378

trade-offs, 8:418–419

Economics, classical, 2:**502–505**, 3:225

banana parable, 1:247

Cantillion, Richard, 1:428–429

capital, 1:430

capitalism, 1:439

consumption, 2:106

equilibrium, 2:619–620

full employment, 3:225

Heilbroner, Robert, 3:456–457

history, 2:498

Jajmani matrix, 4:167

Keynes, John Maynard, 4:260

laissez-faire, 4:335–338

long period analysis, 4:490

long run, 4:491

macroeconomics, 4:540–541

markets, 4:607–608

natural rate of unemployment, 5:435, 437

neo-Ricardian economics, 2:519–521

new classical economics, 2:522

prices, 6:455–456

quantity theory of money, 6:659–660

race, 7:13, 14

Ricardian vice, 7:242

surplus, 8:235

violence, 8:627

zero population growth, 9:174

Economics, development, 2:**344–346**

backwash effects, 1:236–237

Chicago School, 1:502

coordination failure, 2:128

De Soto, Hernando, 2:319–320

dependency theory, 2:298–300

developing countries, 2:335–337

ethnic diversity, 2:342–343

gender, 3:272–277

Harris-Todaro model, 3:428

industrialization, 3:621–622

informal economy, 4:26–28

International Monetary Fund, 4:95–96

land reform, 4:341, 342

Lewis, W. Arthur, 4:420–421

modernization, 5:233

planning, 6:274–276

Prebisch-Singer hypothesis, 6:423–425

rural development, 2:341–342

stock exchanges in developing countries, 8:151–153

structuralist macroeconomics, 4:543–545

surplus labor, 4:308–309

Taylor, Lance, 8:285

theory, 2:337–339

Economics, environmental. *See* Resource economics

Economics, equilibrium in, 2:**619–621**, 8:143–144

Arrow-Debreu model, 1:182–183

balance of payments, 1:238–240

Barro-Grossman model, 1:255–256

Beveridge curve, 1:292

business cycle theories, 1:410–412

capital, 1:431

chaos theory, 1:493

Chicago School, 1:502

cointegration, 2:2–3

comparative dynamics, 2:47

comparative statics, 2:48

competition, 2:50, 51

cumulative causation, 2:207

currency devaluation and revaluation, 2:211–212

decisive events, 2:253–254

economic depression, 2:303–304

Fisher, Irving, 3:151

full employment, 3:225–226

general, 3:283, 4:471–472

Hume, David, 3:519, 520

Hurwicz, Leonid, 3:529–530

immigration, 3:581, 582

involuntary unemployment, 4:137–138

Kalecki, Michał, 4:247

Keynes, John Maynard, 4:261

labor market, 4:318–319

liquidity trap, 4:461–462

long period analysis, 4:489–491

long run, 4:491–492

manifolds, 4:585

marginalism, 4:597

Marxist competition, 2:55

mathematical economics, 5:24

money, 5:252

multiple equilibria, 5:324–325

multiplier, 5:329–330

Nash, 1:479

neo-Ricardian economics, 2:521

neoclassical economics, 2:518

neoclassical growth model, 5:465

neutral rate of interest, 4:79

new classical economics, 2:522–524

Pareto, Vilfredo, 6:138–139

partial, 4:491

Patinkin, Don, 6:171–172

prices, 8:576

real business cycles, 1:407, 408

Rybczynski theorem, 7:305–306

School of Lausanne, 4:362

stability in economics, 8:76–77

stable nodes, 5:510–511

steady state, 8:126–127

sticky prices, 8:143–144

tâtonnement, 8:270–271

theory of second best, 8:350–351

topology, 8:390–391

transitional economies, 2:533

Z-D model, 9:172

Economics, experimental, 2:**505–506**, 514, 7:558–559

Economics, institutional, 2:**506–507**

Coase, Ronald, 1:589

development in sociology, 2:348

Galbraith, John Kenneth, 3:246–247

history, 2:498

institutional development, 2:340–341

institutionalism, 4:44–45

Myrdal, Gunnar, 5:351

transaction cost, 8:426–427

Economics, international, 2:**507–510**

bilateralism, 1:297

borders, 1:354–355

bull and bear markets, 1:386

capital, 1:431

Chicago School, 1:502

conditionality, 2:65

customs union, 2:215–216

dirty float, 2:375

economic sterilization, 8:139–140

international economic order, 4:92–94

International Monetary Fund, 4:95–96

Kindleberger, Charles Poor, 4:267

Meade, James, 5:48–49

overshooting, 6:98–99

Economics, Islamic, 2:**510–511**

Economics, Keynesian, 2:**511–513**

aggregate supply, 1:53–54

beauty contest metaphor, 1:269

carrying cost, 1:449–450

casino capitalism, 1:455, 456

central banks, 1:478

conservatism, 2:85

consumption function, 2:109

economics of control, 2:532

Great Depression, 3:370

Hicks, John R., 3:471–472

history, 2:499

inflation, 4:24

involuntary unemployment, 4:137–138

IS-LM model, 4:158–160

Kahn, Richard F., 4:245

Keynes, John Maynard, 4:259–262

Klein, Lawrence, 4:276

laissez-faire, 4:337

liberalism, 4:425

life-cycle hypothesis, 4:441

liquidity, 4:459

liquidity trap, 4:461–462

long run, 4:492

Lucas, Robert E., Jr., 4:510

macroeconomics, 4:541

macrofoundations, 4:546

Meade, James, 5:49

microfoundations, 5:141

minimum wage, 5:187

modernism, 5:230

monetarism, 5:242–243

multiplier, 5:329–330

new Keynesian economics, 2:524, 525

Patinkin, Don, 6:171–172

Phillips, A. W. H., 6:247–248

price *vs.* quantity adjustment, 6:453–454

quantity theory of money, 6:660

rate of profit, 7:74

relative income hypothesis, 7:153

rules *vs.* discretion, 7:293–294

Say's Law, 7:336–337

socialization of investment, 7:649–650

unemployment, 8:503

user costs, 8:552

wage and price controls, 9:2

War on Poverty, 9:25, 29

Economics, Keynesian, *continued*
    X-Crise, 9:158
    Z-D model, 9:172–173
    zero population growth, 9:174
Economics, labor, 2:**513–515**
    Blinder-Oaxaca decomposition technique, 1:332–334
    blue collar and white collar, 1:339
    Chicago School, 1:502
    Ginzberg, Eli, 3:323
    Harris, Abram L., Jr., 3:427
    labor demand, 4:312–314
    labor market, 4:318–319
    labor supply, 4:320–322
    marginal product of labor, 4:304–307
    Parnes, Herbert, 6:147–148
Economics, Marxian, 2:**515–517**
    Cambridge capital controversy, 1:420, 421
    capitalism, 1:439
    capitalist mode of production, 1:445–447
    class, 1:562, 563
    communism, 2:35–36
    competition, 2:50–51
    consumption, 2:106
    Hilferding, Rudolf, 3:476
    labor theory of value, 4:322–324
    Leontief, Wassily, 4:413
    long period analysis, 4:490
    long run, 4:491
    Luxemburg, Rosa, 4:522–523
    marginal product of labor, 4:307
    Marxist competition, 2:55–56
    mathematics in the social sciences, 5:27–28
    political economy, 6:303
    primitive communism, 2:37–38
    rate of exploitation, 7:70–71
    rate of profit, 7:73
    surplus labor, 4:309–312
    transitional conjunctures, 2:77, 78
Economics, mathematical, 5:**23–25**
    differential equations, 2:364
    economic rhetoric, 2:495–496
    equilibrium, 2:620
    Hurwicz, Leonid, 3:529–530
    Jacobian matrix, 4:163
    Keynes, John Maynard, 4:261
    matrix algebra, 5:32–34
    minimization, 5:185
    Potron, Maurice, 6:403–404
    School of Lausanne, 4:362
    Tinbergen, Jan, 8:374–375

Economics, neo-Ricardian, 2:**519–522**, 4:307, 8:235–236
Economics, neoclassical, 2:**517–519**
    agricultural economics, 1:59
    Cambridge capital controversy, 1:419–421
    capitalism, 1:439
    central banks, 1:478, 479
    common land, 2:27
    competition, 2:50
    cumulative causation, 2:207
    economic depression, 2:304
    endogenous preferences, 2:586
    equilibrium, 2:619, 620
    exchange value, 3:40–41
    Fisher, Irving, 3:150–152
    full capacity, 3:224
    history, 2:498
    immiserizing growth, 3:583
    institutional economics, 2:506
    Keynesian economics, 2:511–512
    Lagrange multipliers, 4:332–333
    liquidity trap, 4:461–462
    long period analysis, 4:490
    long run, 4:491
    marginal product of labor, 4:305, 306, 307
    markup pricing, 4:610
    Marxist competition, 2:55
    migration, 5:157
    neo-Ricardian economics, 2:520–521
    North-South models, 5:547
    optimizing behavior, 6:55
    political economy, 6:303
    price *vs.* quantity adjustment, 6:453–454
    prices, 6:456
    quantity theory of money, 6:660
    Robinson, Joan, 7:267
    surplus labor, 4:308–309
    unemployment, 8:503
    user costs, 8:552
    welfare analysis, 9:62–63
Economics, new classical, 2:**522–524**
    business cycles, 1:403
    central banks, 1:479
    involuntary unemployment, 4:138
    Keynesian economics, 2:512
    Lucas, Robert E., Jr., 4:510
    Lucas critique, 4:511
    monetarism, 5:242–243
    new Keynesian economics, 2:524, 525

Economics, New Keynesian, 2:**524–526**
    Barro-Grossman model, 1:256
    full employment, 3:226–227
    involuntary unemployment, 4:138
    Keynes, John Maynard, 4:260
    new classical economics, 2:524
    Say's Law, 7:337
    sticky prices, 8:143–144
Economics, Nobel Prize in, 2:**526–528**, 527*t*
    Becker, Gary S., 1:270
    Coase, Ronald, 1:589
    Debreu, Gerard, 2:249
    Fogel, Robert, 1:582
    Hicks, John R., 3:471–472
    Kahneman, Daniel, 2:251
    Koopmans, Tjalling, 4:287
    Kydland, Finn, 1:407
    Lucas, Robert E., Jr., 4:510
    McFadden, Daniel L., 5:44
    Meade, James, 5:48
    Modigliani, Franco, 5:234
    North, Douglass, 1:582
    Prescott, Edward, 1:407
    Selten, Reinhard, 2:506
    Simon, Herbert A., 7:515
    Smith, Vernon L., 2:506–506, 7:558–559
    Solow, Robert M., 8:26
    Stigler, George Joseph, 8:144
    Tobin, James, 8:378
Economics, Post Keynesian, 2:**528–529**
    casino capitalism, 1:455–456
    central banks, 1:478, 480
    full employment, 3:226–227
    inflation, 4:24–26
    involuntary unemployment, 4:138
    Kahn, Richard F., 4:245
    Kalecki, Michał, 4:246
    Keynes, John Maynard, 4:260
    marginal product of labor, 4:307
    markup pricing, 4:610–612
    Minsky, Hyman, 5:193–194
    uncertainty, 8:482
Economics, public, 2:**529–530**
Economics, race, 7:**13–16**
    hard-core unemployed, 3:421, 422
    Harris, Abram L., Jr., 3:426–427
    Latino National Political Survey, 4:355
    research, 5:389
Economics, stability in, 8:**76–77**
    demand for money, 5:255

fiscal policy, 6:292
Hurwicz, Leonid, 3:530
monetarism, 5:242–243
multiple equilibria, 5:324
phase diagrams, 6:240, 242
speculation, 8:54–55
steady state, 8:126–127
tâtonnement, 8:270–271
Economics, stratification, 2:**530–531**
crowding hypothesis, 2:181–182
race, 7:13–15
Economics, welfare, 9:**63–67**
Coase, Ronald, 1:589
Coase theorem, 1:590
customs union, 2:215
distributive justice, 4:240
Hicks, John R., 3:471
maximization, subjective utility,
8:578
Meade, James, 5:49
merit goods, 5:97–98
Pareto optimum, 6:139–140
Sen, Amartya Kumar, 7:440
social cost, 7:581–583
social welfare functions,
7:629–630
theory of second best, 8:350–351
welfare analysis, 9:62–63
Economics (Samuelson), 7:319
Economics of control, 2:372–374,
531–533
The Economics of Control (Lerner),
2:531, 532
The Economics of Discrimination
(Becker), 2:388–389, 398, 400,
5:389
The Economics of Imperfect Competition
(Robinson), 4:245
Economics of information, 4:**30–32**
Internet, 4:106
signals, 7:507–508
Stiglitz, Joseph E., 8:146
Economics of Input-Output Analysis
(Raa), 3:154
*The Economics of Slavery in the Ante-
Bellum South* (Conrad and Meyer),
1:581
The Economics of the Short Period
(Kahn), 4:245
The Economics of Welfare (Pigou),
1:590, 9:63
Économie-monde, 9:151–152
Economies, transitional, 2:**533–534**
development economics,
2:344–346
development in sociology, 2:347

ethnic diversity and, 2:342–343
Russian Federation, 7:302–303
state capitalism, 1:444
transitional conjunctures, 2:77–78
Yeltsin, Boris, 9:164
Economies of scale
average costs, 1:232
factories, 3:76
Verdoorn's law, 8:607
Economy
dual, 2:456–457
dependency theory,
2:298–300
development economics,
2:344
development theory, 2:338
labor supply, 4:320
Prebisch, Raúl, 6:422–423
surplus labor, 4:308–309
global
G7 countries, 3:243–244
Great Depression, 3:370
offshore banking, 6:32–33
herding, 5:447, 9:109
informal, 4:26–28
De Soto, Hernando,
2:319–320
deviance, 2:353
drug traffic, 2:449–451
dual economy, 2:457
employment, 2:581
multisector models,
5:334–335
rotating savings and credit
associations, 7:286–287
market, 2:274, 4:604–605
air pollution, 6:362
business, 1:400, 401
civil society, 1:552
codetermination, 1:592–593
common land, 2:28
conservatism, 2:85
Conservative Party (U.K.),
2:87
consumerism, 2:105
consumption, 2:106
convergence theory, 2:117
corporations, 2:140
development in sociology,
2:347
dirigiste, 2:372–374
governmentality, 3:362
marginal productivity,
4:595–596
market socialism, 7:644–646

monetarism, 5:242–243
NAFTA, 5:540–541
racial discrimination, 2:395
Ricardian equivalence, 7:241
Russian economics, 7:301
Russian Federation,
7:302–303
statistical discrimination,
2:396–398
taste for discrimination,
2:398–399
transitional economies, 2:533
private sector, 6:480–481
social, 4:361–362, 7:584–585
nonprofit organizations,
1:401, 3:324
School of Lausanne,
4:361–362
Economy, information. *See* Knowledge
society
Economy, knowledge. *See* Knowledge
society
Economy, political, 6:**302–304**
capitalist mode of production,
1:445–447
comparative politics, 6:327
decentralization, 2:250
dirigiste, 2:372–374
Heilbroner, Robert, 3:456–457
international relations, 4:101
Marxian economics, 2:515–517
media, 5:59
petroleum industry, 6:232
political business cycles,
1:406–407
political sociology, 8:3
slave trade, 7:538–539
subsistence agriculture, 3:98
trade quotas, 6:673
urban poverty, 6:411
Wall Street, 9:8–9
Economy, world. *See* World-system
Economy and Society (Weber), 1:214,
391–392, 3:474, 5:548, 9:54, 56,
57
The Economy of Cities (Jacobs), 4:165
Ecosystems, organization theory, 6:69
ECSC (European Coal and Steel
Community), 3:23, 24
See also European Union (EU)
Ecstasy (drug), 2:453
Ecuador, 1:245–246, 6:65
Ecumenism, 1:531
Eddy, E. M., 1:137
Eden, Anthony, 1:153

Edgeworth, Francis Ysidro, 2:181, 405, 3:150, 247
    allocation of goods, 9:64–65
    utility function, 8:555
    See also Crowding hypothesis; Probability theory
Edgeworth, Robert, 6:57
Edgeworth-Bowley box. *See* Welfare economics
Edin, Kathryn, 3:116
Edipe (Voltaire), 8:635
Edith Green Amendment, 9:27
EDLA (United Nations Economic Commission for Latin America). *See* Economic Commission for Latin America and the Caribbean (ECLAC)
EDM (Electronic dance music) DJs, 8:622
Edo Period, 3:134, 8:632
Education
    accountability, 1:9–11
    assessment, 5:381–382
    Berg, Ivar E., 1:288
    brain drain, 1:367
    Cambridge University, 1:421–423
    children, 1:511
    children's rights, 1:512
    coordination failure, 2:128
    creativity, 2:165
    critical race theory, 2:174–176
    day care, 2:245–246
    engineering, 2:594
    fertility rate, 6:57–60, *58, 60*
    gender equality, 9:114–115
    gifted and talented, 3:*316,* 316–318, 316*t*, 8:483–485
    Great Society programs, 3:372
    higher, 1:96
    institutional development, 2:340
    Jefferson, Thomas, 4:180
    jigsaw classrooms, 1:181
    leadership, 4:381
    Little Red Book, 4:468
    longitudinal data, 2:239
    merit goods, 5:97, 98
    multicultural, 3:327
    music, 5:345–346
    oppositionality, 6:49–51
    pedagogy, 6:196–197
    private, 2:314, 317
    qualifications, 6:649–650
    representative and participatory democracy, 2:284
    rhetoric, 7:237–239

    school readiness, 7:87–88
    separate but equal, 1:19, 3:316, 9:81
    Sequoyah, 7:454–455
    social demography, 2:296
    social work, 7:634
    special
        mental retardation, 5:89–90
        tracking in schools, 8:409–410
    teacher-child relationships, 8:291–292
    teacher expectations, 8:290–291
    teachers, 8:293–295
    time, 8:363
    tracking in schools, 8:409–410
    upward mobility, 8:533–535
    Veblen, Thorstein, 8:596
    wage variations, 9:4
    welfare state, 9:67
    See also Race and education; Resegregation of schools; School desegregation; Schooling
Education, higher. *See* Universities
Education, informal, 2:**534–535**
Education, returns to, 2:**535–537**
Education, unequal, 1:94, 2:**537–539**
    Brown v. Board of Education (1954), 1:373–376
    Brown v. Board of Education (1955), 1:377
    California Civil Rights Initiative, 1:416
    civil rights, 1:549
    civil rights movement, U.S., 1:551
    Clark, Kenneth B., 1:560, 561
    creaming, 2:160
    curriculum, 2:214–215
    digital divide, 2:366–367
    Houston, Charles Hamilton, 3:505
    Jencks, Christopher, 4:184–185
    Jim Crow, 4:200, 201
    mobility, 5:210–211
    qualifications, 6:649–650
    quotas, 6:671
    race, 7:16–18
    returns, 7:66
    teacher expectations, 8:290–291
    tracking in schools, 8:409–410
    Wells-Barnett, Ida B., 9:76
Education, U.S., 2:**539–546**, 541*t*, 543*t*, 544*t*
    anti-intellectualism, 4:65
    Blau, Peter M., 1:332

    blue collar and white collar, 1:338–339
    Brown v. Board of Education (1954), 1:373–376
    Brown v. Board of Education (1955), 1:377
    California Civil Rights Initiative, 1:416
    Church and state, 1:535, 536
    civil rights, 1:550
    civil rights movement, U.S., 1:551
    conservatism, 2:86
    contemporary, 3:540–542
    creationism, 2:162–163
    credentialism, 2:166–167
    Current Population Survey, 2:213
    curriculum, 2:213–215
    Department of Education, 1:451
    engineering, 2:594
    equal opportunity, 2:612–613
    Head Start, 3:437–438
    Head Start experiments, 3:438–440
    history, 3:539–540
    immigrants, 3:575, 576
    implications, 3:543–545
    Jefferson, Thomas, 4:180
    Latino/Latina studies, 4:354–355
    race, 7:16–18
    reforms, 2:542–543
    resegregation of schools, 7:201–202
    residential segregation, 3:540–542
    returns, 7:65–66
    rural development, 2:341
    school readiness, 7:87–88
    school segregation, 7:386–388
    school vouchers, 7:347–349
    standardized tests, 8:95–98
    unequal, 2:537–539
Education Amendment, Title IX, 3:121
Education and Jobs: The Great Training Robbery (Berg), 1:288
Education and race, 2:174–176, 7:**16–18**
Education for All Handicapped Children Act (U.S. 1968). *See* Mental retardation
Education in the British West Indies (Williams), 9:98
Education segregation. *See* School segregation; Unequal education
Educational achievement, 1:14–15
    acting white, 1:17
    African Americans, 6:33–34

assessment, 5:381–382

Gautreaux residential mobility program, 3:259–260

gender gap, 3:279

human fertility, 3:128

National Education Longitudinal Study, 5:390–392

oppositional culture, 6:48

racial achievement gap, 1:15–17

school vouchers, 7:348

schooling oppositionality, 6:50

underachievers, 8:484

Educational games, 8:612

Educational quality, 2:**546–548**, 7:348

Educational tracking. *See* Tracking in schools

Edwards, Alba, 7:656–657

Edwards, John, 3:374

Edwards, Michael, 5:520

Edwards, Ward, 5:519

EEC (European Economic Community), 3:23, 24, 5:488

See also European Union (EU)

EEG (Electroencelphalogram), 5:485

EEOC (Equal Employment Opportunity Commission), U.S., 3:420, 5:408–409, 6:671

EEZs (Exclusive Economic Zones), 3:153

The Effect on White Incomes of Discrimination in Employment (Bergmann), 2:181

Effect sizes, 3:180

Effectiveness. *See* Performance

Efficiency, mean square. *See* Properties of estimators (asymptotic and exact)

Efficiency, statistical. *See* Properties of estimators (asymptotic and exact)

Efficiency studies. *See* Time and motion studies

Efficiency vs. equity. *See* Distortions

Efficiency wages

Akerlof, George A., 1:69

description, 9:4

nominal wages, 5:512

noncompeting wage, 5:515

o-ring theory, 6:77

Efficient bargaining hypothesis. *See* Labor unions

Efficient market hypothesis (EMH), 2:**548–549**, 3:143, 4:131–132, 609

Effort justification, 1:600

Effort-shape notation. *See* Dance

Efron, Bradley, 1:353

Egalitarianism, 2:**550**

black liberalism, 1:312

citizenship, 1:543

consensus, 2:82–83

Dahl, Robert Alan, 2:220

distributive justice, 4:239–240

equal opportunity, 2:611–613

equality, 2:616–618

justice, 4:238

left wing, 4:403, 404

Rawls, John, 7:84–85

republicanism, 7:188

See also Inegalitarianism

Egalization, 3:522

Ego, 3:212–213, 4:229

See also Psychoanalytic theory

The Ego and the Id (Freud), 3:211, 212

Ego-involvement. *See* Social judgment theory

Egocentric networks, 5:479–480

Egoism

children, 1:511

civil society, 1:553

consumerism, 2:105

Durkheim, Émile, 2:466–467

ethical, 6:7

Egypt

abortion, 1:1

Arab-Israeli War of 1967, 1:156–159

Ben-Gurion, David, 1:283

Carter, Jimmy, 1:451

Coptic Christian Church, 2:132

cotton, 1:73

coups d'etat, 2:156

Diop, Cheikh Anta, 2:368–370

gender gap, 3:278

heaven, 3:445

hell, 3:458

Hussein, Saddam, 3:532

monotheism, 5:270

Muhammad Ali (Memet), 1:73

Nasser, Gamal Abdel, 5:375–377

Pyramids, 8:631

Sadat, Anwar, 7:307–308

slavery, 1:38

Suez Crisis, 8:213–214

United Arab Republic, 5:376–377, 8:520–522

veiling, 8:603

wealth, 9:44

Egypt and the Fertile Crescent (Holt), 3:126

Egyptian Orthodox Church. *See* Coptic Christian Church

Egyptology, 1:165

Ehrenberg, Israel. *See* Montagu, Ashley

Ehrenberg, Ronald G., 5:391

Ehrenreich, Barbara, 4:578, 5:492, 9:130, 133

Ehrenreich, John, 4:578, 5:492, 9:130, 133

Ehrlich, Paul R., 4:448, 449, 6:95

Ehrlichman, John, 9:42, 43

EIA (Environmental impact assessment), 2:**605–607**

EIC (East India Company), 1:396, 7:55

See also Opium Wars

Eichengreen, Barry, 2:212, 3:370

Eichmann, Karl, 1:173

Eichmann in Jerusalem (Arendt), 1:173

Eigen-values and eigen-vectors, 2:**551–554**

Eigenvector. *See* Eigen-values and eigen-vectors

Eight London Households (Wallman), 1:135

Eighteenth Brumaire of Louis Bonaparte (Marx), 1:571, 4:316–317

Eightfold Path. *See* Buddha; Buddhism

Einstein, Albert, 1:584, 2:164, 7:125

EIS (Environmental impact statements). *See* Environmental impact assessment (EIA)

Eisenhower, Dwight D., 2:**554–555**

Bay of Pigs, 1:262

Castro, Fidel, 1:465

civil rights, 1:550

civil rights movement, U.S., 1:551

desegregation, 2:314

domino theory, 2:434

Franco, Francisco, 3:186

Hungarian Revolution, 3:523

Khrushchev, Nikita, 4:264

militarism, 5:165

military-industrial complex, 5:173–174

Nasser, Gamal Abdel, 5:376

Nixon, Richard M., 5:506

Republican Party (U.S.), 7:186

Suez Crisis, 8:214

urban renewal, 8:536

Vietnam War, 8:613

wage and price controls, 9:2

weapons industry, 9:50

Eisenstadt v. Baird (1972), 3:90, 7:271

EITC (Earned income tax credit). *See* Earned income tax credit (EITC)

Ejército Zapatista de Liberación Nacional (EZLN). *See* Zapatistas

Ekman, Paul, 2:32, 33, 329, 5:530
El Salvador
    civil wars, 1:554
    land reform, 4:342, 343
    latifundia, 4:354
    Latin American immigrants, 3:572
Elam, Itzchak, 9:109
Elasticity, 2:52, **555–556**
Elasticity of substitution. *See*
    Production function; Separability;
    Utility function
Elder, Glen, Jr., 2:350
Elderly
    death and dying, 2:248
    depopulation, 2:302
    loneliness, 4:487
    suicide, 8:222
    volunteering, 3:293
    wage discrimination, 2:401–402
    See also Age and aging;
    Gerontology
Eldredge, Niles, 3:352
Elections, 2:**556–559**
    American National Election
      Studies, 1:100
    bloc vote, 1:334–335
    Burr, Aaron, 1:397
    Bush, George W., 1:399, 400
    business cycles, 1:403
    campaigning, 1:423–424
    Campbell, Angus, 1:424–425
    Carter, Jimmy, 1:451
    caste, 1:458, 460
    central banks, 1:479
    Central Intelligence Agency, U.S,
      1:483, 484
    Chisholm, Shirley, 1:522
    civil rights movement, U.S., 1:552
    Clinton, Bill, 1:578–579, 581
    coalition, 1:587
    community power studies, 2:42,
      43, 44
    competitive party systems,
      6:161–163
    compulsory voting, 2:58–59
    Congress, U.S., 2:73, 74
    Congress Party, India, 2:76
    conservatism, 2:85–86
    Conservative Party (U.K.), 2:87
    constituency, 2:89
    cross of gold, 2:180, 181
    Dahl, Robert Alan, 2:220
    democracy, 2:273
    Democratic Party (U.S.),
      2:287–288

Dixiecrats, 2:429–431
elections, 2:560–562
electoral college, 2:559–560
event studies, 3:30
exit poll, 3:45–46
Indian National Congress,
    3:611–612
Internet, 4:108
Israel, 4:276–277
Key, V. O., Jr., 4:258, 259
Labour Party (U.K.), 4:327
Latinos, 6:338*t*
law and order, 4:369, 370, 371
Liberal Party (U.K.), 4:423–424
Lincoln, Abraham, 4:450, 451
majority voting, 4:562–563
Miller, Warren, 5:180–181
mobilization, 5:213–214, 215
monarchism, 5:237–238
multiparty systems, 5:322–323
non-voting, 3:351
Palestinian Authority, 6:106–107
paradox of voting, 6:127–128
Partido Revolucionario
    Institucional, 6:156–159
Phalangists, 6:236
plurality, 6:285–286
political conventions, 6:297–299
political parties, 6:307–308
political psychology, 6:309
polling, 6:353–354
polyarchy, 6:366
populism, 6:383, 384
primaries, 6:458–459
primary, 9:83–85
Raj, 7:56
recall, 7:102–103
representative and participatory
    democracy, 2:285
Republican Party (U.S.), 7:187
Southern politics, 6:342–343,
    345–346
spatial theory, 8:45
whites, 6:338*t*
Electoral college, 2:284, **559–560,**
    4:223
Electoral districts
    apportionment, 1:154–155
    gerrymandering, 3:308–310
    single-member, 8:647
    Supreme Court decisions, 8:652,
      9:33
Electoral Engineering (Norris), 2:59
Electoral systems, 2:**560–562**
    ballots, 1:242

elections, 2:557–558
majority rule, 8:655
plurality, 6:285–286
voting, 8:647
voting schemes, 8:654–656
winner-take-all, 8:655
Electoral systems, first-past-the-post,
    2:561, 3:**149–150,** 8:655
Electoral Systems (Farrell), 2:59
Electra complex, 6:28–30
    See also Stages of development
Electric cars, 3:286
Electric shocks, destructive obedience,
    6:2
Electricity industry. *See* Energy
    industry
Electrification, rural. *See* Rural
    development
Electroencelphalogram (EEG), 5:485
Electronic business. *See* E-business
Electronic dance music (EDM) DJs,
    8:622
*The Elementary Forms of the Religious
    Life* (Durkheim), 2:7, 324, 465,
    3:385, 6:9
The Elementary Structures of Kinship
    (Lévi-Strauss), 4:417
Elements de la philosophie de Newton
    (Voltaire), 8:635
Éléments d'économique politique pure
    (Walras). *See Elements of Pure
    Economics* (Walras)
*Elements of Human Statistics or
    Comparative Demography* (Guillard),
    2:293
Elements of Law (Hobbes), 3:492
Elements of Pure Economics (Walras),
    4:361, 9:12
Elements of the Philosophy of Right
    (Hegel), 1:552
Elias, Norbert, 2:412
Eliminative behaviorism, 1:275
Eliot, T. S., 2:202, 4:464, 5:228
Elite, power. *See* Power elite
Elite theory, 2:**562–564,** 4:506
Elites, 2:**564–566**
    anarchism, 1:112
    Arab, 1:161
    aristocracy, 1:173–174
    bureaucracy, 1:390
    business
      public policy, 6:72
      Veblen, Thorstein, 8:596,
      597
    civilization, 1:558
    class, 1:562, 563

colonialism, resistance to, 8:623–624
Comte, Auguste, 2:62
corporatism, 2:141–142
cultural distinctions, 2:413
democratization, 2:290
entrepreneurship, 2:605
feminine beauty, 3:118–119
gentility, 3:301
hierarchy, 3:475
leisure class, 1:566
managerial capitalism, 1:442–443
middle class gap, 9:101
neocolonialism, 5:467
nouveaux riches *vs.*, 5:548
Republican Party (U.S.), 8:606
social distinctions, 2:412
social pathology, 6:170–171
technotopia, 8:312–313
University of Oxford, 8:528
urban politics, 6:350
Veblen, Thorstein, 8:595–596
welfare state, 9:71
whiteness, 9:92
See also Power elite
Elitism, 2:**566–567**
burial grounds, 1:392
civil society, 1:553
credentialism, 2:166–167
Fields' index of economic inequality, 3:138
Elizabeth II, Queen of England, 5:240, 241
Elizabeth Bacon Custer and the Making of a Myth (Leckie), 1:258
Elkins, Stanley, 2:64, 6:277, 7:314
Ellington, Duke, 4:176, 177
Ellis, Albert. *See* Psychotherapy
Ellis, Havelock, 5:369
Ellis, Lesa K., 8:321–322
Ellis, Susan, 8:638
Ellis Island, 2:**567–569**, 3:573
Ellison, Ralph, 1:310, 3:424, 9:91
Ellsberg, Daniel, 5:519, 9:42
Ellul, Jacques, 2:332
Elmore, Richard, 1:9
The Eloquent Body: Dance and Humanist Culture in Fifteenth-Century Italy (Nevile), 2:224
ELSI (Ethical, legal and societal implications), 5:362–363
The Elusive Quest for Growth (Easterly), 9:138
Ely, Richard T., 1:97

EM (Ethnomethodology). *See* Ethnomethodology
Emancipation. *See* Freedom; Liberation
Emancipation Edict (Japan 1871), 1:389
Emancipation Proclamation (1863), 4:429, 451
Embargoes
bilateral trade, 8:415
Carter, Jimmy, 1:451
Castro, Fidel, 1:465, 466, 467
Cuba, 2:186
Cuban Missile Crisis, 2:183, 184
Embarrassment. *See* Humiliation
Ember, Carol, 2:136
Ember, Melvin, 2:136
Embodied labor, 8:575
Emergency management. *See* Disaster management
Emergency powers
dictatorship, 2:359
repression, 7:175
Emerging markets, 3:147
Emerson, Richard, 3:386–387
Emerson, Rupert, 5:507
Emery, Henry Crosby, 1:449
EMH (Efficient market hypothesis), 2:**548–549**, 3:143, 4:131–132, 609
Emigrants. *See* Immigrants
Emigration. *See* Immigration
Émile (Rousseau), 2:284
Emirbayer, Mustafa, 5:476–477
Emissions, vehicle, 1:223
Emmanuel, Arghiri, 8:505–506
Emmons, Delos, 3:600
Emotion, 2:**569–570**
classical conditioning, 1:574
color preference, 6:432, 433
contempt, 2:113
coping, 2:129
Darwin, Charles, 2:229–232
infertility drugs, 4:19–20
infidelity, 4:20
James, William, 4:169
mood, 5:275
mood congruent recall, 5:277
romance, 7:281–282
Schachter, Stanley, 7:342
self-discrepancy theory, 7:393
self-system, 7:430
shock experiments, 3:62
social psychology, 7:609
sympathy, 8:253
Emotion and affect, 2:**571–572**

Emotion regulation, 2:**572–573**
emotion and affect, 2:572
equilibrium, 2:621
self-control, 7:402–404
shame, 7:489
temperament, 8:321–322
Emotional intelligence. *See* Multiple intelligences theory; Social intelligence
Empathy, 2:**573–574**
emotion and affect, 2:572
perspective-taking, 6:226–227
tastes, 8:267
Emperors. *See* Empire
Empire, 2:**574–577**
colonialism, 2:12
commonwealth, 2:29
decolonization, 2:255–257
imperialism, 3:586
state, 8:103–104
world, 9:152
See also Holy Roman Empire
Empire (Hardt and Negri), 1:447, 7:209
Empire and Emancipation: Power and Liberation on a World Scale (Nederveen Pieterese), 2:336
Empirical Exchange Rate Models of the Seventies: Do They Fit Out of Sample? (Meese and Rogoff), 2:209–210
Empirical literature—business cycles, 1:**403–405**
Empirical tests, natural experiments, 5:434–435
Empiricism, 2:**577–580**
consciousness, 2:80
constructivism, 2:96
existentialism, 3:42
genetic determinism, 2:329
James, William, 4:169
Kant, Immanuel, 4:248
Kuhn, Thomas, 4:292–294
Employee contributions, 9:72
Employer of last resort program. *See* Job guarantee
Employment, 2:**580–583**
aggregate supply, 1:53–54
capitalist mode of production, 1:445
codetermination, 1:592–593
common market, 2:29
creamy layer, 2:161
Current Population Survey, 2:213
equal opportunity, 2:612

Employment, *continued*
full, 3:225–228
central banks, 1:480
conundrum, 2:116
economic depression, 2:302
full capacity, 3:224
job guarantee, 4:205
labor market clearing, 8:498
gender equality, 9:114–115
gender gap, 3:274–275, 278
glass ceiling, 3:325–326
hazardous, 9:4–5
home-based, 9:125
interest rates, 4:85
job guarantee, 4:204–206
Kahn, Richard F., 4:245
Kalecki, Michał, 4:247
Keynes, John Maynard, 4:259
Keynesian economics, 2:511–513
labor demand, 4:314
labor force participation,
4:314–316
labor law, 4:316–317
labor market, 4:318–319
litigation, 4:465
maquiladoras, 4:591–594
metropolitan regions, 7:134
minimum wage, 5:186–187
Multi-City Study of Urban
Inequality, 5:314–315
multiple jobs, 9:129
NAFTA, 5:540–541
neighborhood effects, 5:462
neutral rate of interest, 4:79
oppositional culture, 6:48
qualifications, 6:649–650
quotas, 6:668–670, 670–671
right to, 3:227
self-employment, 1:517,
7:410–411
suboptimal, 8:20–21
surplus labor, 4:308
temporary, 1:220
time-and-a-half, 8:374
Treasury view, 8:444–445
women
female-headed families, 3:115
feminism, 3:120–121
history, 3:93
work week, 9:128–129
Z-D model, 9:172–173
See also Underemployment;
Unemployment
Employment, self. *See* Self-
employment

Employment, white collar, 2:583–586,
584t
black middle class, 1:314
blue collar and white collar,
1:337–340
credentialism, 2:166
crime and criminology, 2:171–172
crowding hypothesis, 2:182
workers, 9:130
Employment Act (U.S. 1946), 3:112,
227
Employment benefits, 8:565, 9:128
Employment discrimination
age discrimination, 2:401–402
Body Mass Index, 1:348
buraku, 1:388–389
Chinese diaspora, 1:517
civil rights, 1:549
correspondence tests, 2:141–143
crowding hypothesis, 2:181–182
described, 2:388–391
glass ceiling, 3:325–326
Glazer, Nathan, 3:327
marginal product of labor, 4:306
Myrdal, Gunnar, 1:94
racial, 5:384
racial discrimination, 2:393–396,
404, 405–406
statistical discrimination,
2:396–398
taste for discrimination,
2:398–399
wage discrimination, 2:400–401,
402–403, 404
women, 5:408–409, 9:117
Employment Division v. Smith (1990),
1:535–536
Empowerment, women, 3:274
gender mainstreaming, 3:275
NGOization, 5:521
Empowerment and Poverty Reduction
(World Bank), 3:274
The Empty Fortress (Bettelheim), 1:290
Enchanting a Disenchanted World
(Ritzer), 2:107
Enclosure movement. *See* Primitive
accumulation
Encoding, 5:530
*Encoding and Decoding in the Media
Discourse* (Hall), 3:409
Enculturation, 1:122
Encyclopedia Africana (Du Bois), 2:460
Encyclopedia of Creativity (Nickles),
6:126
*The Encyclopedia of Rural America: The
Land and People* (Goreham), 8:9

END (Europeans for Nuclear
Disarmament), 8:355
The End of Economic Man (Drucker),
2:449
The End of Liberalism (Lowi), 4:506
End-of-life care, assisted death,
1:191–192
The End of the World as We Know It
(Wallerstein), 9:10
Endangered Species Act (U.S. 1973),
6:360
Endogamy, 1:459, 460, 461
Endogeneity, 1:472
Endogenous economic growth, 8:621
Endogenous money, 1:478,
5:256–258, 258–259
Endogenous preferences, 2:586–587
Endogenous regression, 8:587–588
Endogenous uncertainty, 1:269
Endogenous variables. *See*
Predetermined variables
Enemy combatants, Guantánamo Bay,
3:393–394
Energy, 2:587–588
Carter, Jimmy, 1:451
solar, 3:378–379, 8:22–23
tax credits, 8:273
Energy consumption, 3:330
Energy expenditure (metabolic),
5:551, 8:491–492
Energy industry, 2:112, 588–591,
6:360
Energy sector, 2:591–592, 8:22–23
Enfranchisement. *See* Civil rights;
Voting
Engaged Buddhism. *See* Buddhism
Engel, Charles, 2:210
Engel v. Vitale (1962), 9:33
Engels, Friedrich, 1:360, 362, 3:177
Asiatic mode of production, 1:187
cities, 1:541
class, 1:563
class conflict, 1:569, 570
class consciousness, 1:571
communism, 2:34
communitarianism, 2:40
determinism, 2:324
dialectical materialism, 5:22–23
factory system, 3:77
feudal mode of production,
3:133–134
The German Ideology, 3:82
ideology, 3:559
import substitution, 3:592–593
liberation, 4:430

lumpenproletariat, 4:516, 517

matriarchy, 5:28, 29

neighborhoods, 5:463

primitive communism, 2:38

race, 7:13

Russian economics, 7:301

utopianism, 8:561

working class, 9:129–130, 131

Engendering Development (World Bank), 3:273

Engerman, Stanley, 2:**592–593**, 3:161–162

    cliometrics, 1:582

    railway industry, 7:53, 54

    Time on the Cross, 4:366–367

Engineering, 2:**593–595**, 8:365–366

The Engineers and the Price System (Veblen), 1:442

Engines of Creation (Drexler), 5:361

England

    Anglo-Portuguese trade, 8:413

    Bentham, Jeremy, 1:285–286

    blackface, 1:326, 327

    bubbles (economics), 1:378

    burial grounds, 1:393

    Burke, Edmund, 1:396–397

    Cambridge University, 1:421–423

    census, 1:476

    central banks, 1:477

    cities, 1:541

    colonialism, 3:568, 569

    common land, 2:27

    commonwealth, 2:29

    conservatism, 2:83

    Cook, James, 2:121–122

    divine right, 2:421

    factory system, 3:78–79

    feminism, 3:120

    feudal mode of production, 3:134

    gentility, 3:300

    impeachment, 3:584

    Jefferson, Thomas, 4:180

    journalism, 4:212

    labor, 4:301

    land claims, 4:340–341

    Law, John, 4:366

    legal systems, 4:406

    lender of last resort, 4:410

    Levellers, 4:413–414

    Liverpool slave trade, 4:468–469

    loyalists, 4:508–509

    Magna Carta, 4:556–557

    Parliament, 6:144

    Quebecois movement, 6:661

    rape, 7:65

    Ricardo, David, 7:241–243

    riots, 7:251

    South Sea Bubble, 8:33–34

    Thompson, Edward P., 8:354, 355

    Victorian Period, 8:528

    See also United Kingdom (U.K.)

England, Paula, 3:116

Engle, Robert, 1:229–230, 2:3, 8:587

English School, 4:100

Enlightened One. *See* Buddha

Enlightened ones. *See* Illuminati

Enlightenment, 2:**595–598**

    behaviorism, 1:275

    bureaucracy, 1:390, 391

    Cantillion, Richard, 1:429

    civil society, 1:552, 553

    communalism, 2:30

    communitarianism, 2:38, 39

    Condorcet, Marquis de, 2:66

    constructivism, 2:96

    cultural relativism, 2:195–196

    defense, 2:258

    French Revolution, 3:203

    humanism, 3:517

    Illuminati, 3:561–562

    Jefferson, Thomas, 4:179, 180, 181

    Jews, 4:195

    Kant, Immanuel, 4:249

    liberalism, 4:425–426

    rationalism, 7:77

    totalitarianism, 8:395

    University of Oxford, 8:528

    Voltaire, 8:635

Enlistment, military. *See* Military

Enrichment Triad Model, 8:485

Enriquez, Juan, 1:58

Enron, 1:455, 2:180, 6:72–73

Entauberung, 1:75

Enterprise, 2:**598–600**

Enterprise, black. *See* Black capitalism; Ethnic enterprises

Enterprise, free. *See* Market economy

Enterprise, state. *See* State enterprise

Enterprises, ethnic. *See* Ethnic enterprises

Entertainment industry, 2:**600–604**, 5:195, 7:115–116

Entfremdung, 1:75

Entheogens. *See* Hallucinogens

Enthoven, Alain C., 2:54

Entitlement, social justice, 4:241, 242

Entrepreneurship, 2:**604–605**

Bonacich, Edna, 1:351

Brimmer, Andrew, 1:372

capitalism, 1:438

Chinese diaspora, 1:517

cooperatives, 2:124

corruption, 2:145

creative destruction, 2:163–164

enterprise, 2:598–599

firms, 3:148–149

institutional, 6:70

labor, 4:302

middleman minorities, 5:147–148

Schumpeter, Joseph Alois, 7:356–357

self-employment, 7:411

surplus labor, 4:308

widow's cruse, 9:96

zombies, 9:181

Enumerations, population. *See* Census

Environment

    agricultural industry, 1:59, 62–63

    automobiles, 1:223

    banana industry, 1:246

    bauxite industry, 1:261

    Boas, Franz, 1:344, 345

    capitalist mode of production, 1:447

    Carter, Jimmy, 1:451

    child development, 1:506

    Club of Rome, 1:585

    common land, 2:27, 28

    cultural resource management, 2:197

    cultural tourism, 2:202

    Darwin, Charles, 2:227–232

    deforestation, 2:262–264

    development theory, 2:339

    diamond industry, 2:356

    diathesis-stress model, 2:358

    drought, 2:447–448

    energy sector, 2:591–592

    environmental Kuznets curves, 2:607–609

    free trade, 8:506

    Galton, Francis, 3:247–248

    globalization, 3:333

    gold mining, 3:342–343

    Great Society programs, 3:372–373

    legacy effects, 4:404–405

    limits of growth, 4:448–450

    Love Canal, 4:504–505

    maquiladoras, 4:594

    mining industry, 5:189–190

    NAFTA, 5:541

Environment, *continued*
North-South models, 5:547
nutrition, 5:551–552
obesity, 6:4
optimizing behavior, 6:56
organizations, 6:71–73
overpopulation, 6:95
petroleum industry, 6:232
plumbing, 6:281–282
pollution, 6:359–360
resource economics, 7:210–211
shipping industry, 7:498–499
silver industry, 7:512
steel industry, 8:130
technological change, 1:491–492
tourism, 8:399, 402
toxic waste, 8:407–409
trade liberalization, 4:428
underachievers, 8:484
urban sprawl, 8:540
urbanization, 8:547
Environmental determinism,
2:**327–328**, 3:304
cultural landscape, 2:192
described, 2:323
disease, 2:408
priming, 6:462
Scarr, Sandra Wood, 7:340–341
smoking, 7:559–560
twin studies, 8:473–475
Environmental economics. *See*
Resource economics
Environmental hazards, 8:656
Environmental impact assessment
(EIA), 2:**605–607**
Environmental impact statements
(EIS). *See* Environmental impact
assessment (EIA)
Environmental Kuznets curves,
2:**607–609**, *608*
Environmental Protection Agency,
U.S. (EPA). *See* U.S. Environmental
Protection Agency
Environmental responsibility,
corporate. *See* Corporate social
responsibility (CSR)
EPA (U.S. Environmental Protection
Agency). *See* U.S. Environmental
Protection Agency (EPA)
Eparchy, 3:376
Ephemeralization, 3:229
The Epic of America (Adams), 1:96
Epic poetry, 3:136–137
Epidemics
AIDS/HIV, 1:64, 65–66

Native Americans, 5:426
progress of, 1:65
See also Disease; Morbidity and
mortality
Epidemiological transition theory. *See*
Disease; Morbidity and mortality
Epidemiology. *See* Ethno-
epidemiological methodology
Epigamic selection, 1:84
Episcopal Church. *See* Anglicanism
Epistemological behaviorism, 1:275
Epistemology, 2:**609–611**, 4:278
Campbell, Donald, 1:425, 426
consciousness, 2:78–79
constructivism, 2:96
cooperation, 2:122–123
idealism, 3:547
James, William, 4:169
Kant, Immanuel, 4:248
Mannheim, Karl, 4:587
philosophy, 6:251
scientism, 7:364–365
universalism, 8:526
Epithets, racial. *See* Racial slurs
EPQ-R (Eysenck Personality
Questionnaire-Revised), 5:486–487
Epstein, Edward Jay, 4:215, 9:34
Epstein, Gerald, 1:480
Epstein, Mark, 1:385
Equal Employment Opportunity
Commission, U.S. (EEOC), 3:420,
5:408–409, 6:671
Equal opportunity, 2:**611–614**
California Civil Rights Initiative,
1:416
creaming, 2:160
creamy layer, 2:161
credentialism, 2:166–167
critical race theory, 2:175
democracy, 2:272
disability, 2:378
Jencks, Christopher, 4:184–185
quotas, 6:671
Rawls, John, 7:84–85
unequal education, 2:537
Equal Opportunity Act (U.S. 1964),
9:26
Edith Green Amendment, 9:27
Kennedy-Javits Amendment, 9:27
Nixon, Richard M., 9:28
Reagan, Ronald, 9:28
Equal Pay Act (U.S. 1963), 2:401,
3:123
Equal protection, 2:**614–616**

Brown v. Board of Education
(1954), 1:374
checks and balances, 1:496
children's rights, 1:512
civil liberties, 1:546–547, 547
civil rights, 1:549
Constitution, U.S., 2:92
Fourteenth Amendment, 8:652,
9:84
jury selection, 4:234
Equal Rights Amendment, U.S.
(ERA), 2:86, 3:121, 123, 5:409
See also National Organization for
Women
Equality, 2:**616–619**, *617, 618*
Benedict, Ruth, 1:282
Bourdieu, Pierre, 1:358
children's rights, 1:512
citizenship, 1:542–543
civil-military relation, 1:548
civil rights movement, U.S.,
1:551–552
Constitution, U.S., 2:92
democracy, 2:272, 273, 275
difference principle, 2:362–363
digital divide, 2:366–367
distributive justice, 4:239–240
equal opportunity, 2:611–613
gender
gender gap *vs.*, 3:279
global, 3:270, 279
macroeconomics, 3:275
poverty, 3:274
women's liberation,
9:114–115
inegalitarianism, 3:623–624
justice, 4:238
Kant, Immanuel, 4:248
left wing, 4:403, 404
liberty, 4:441
Rawls, John, 7:84–85
social justice, 4:242
Tawney, R. H., 8:272
Tocqueville, Alexis de, 8:382–383
See also Egalitarianism; Inequality
Equality (Tawney), 8:272
Equality of educational opportunity.
See Equal opportunity; Unequal
education
Equality of Educational Opportunity
(Coleman), 2:537–538, 540
Equality of opportunity. *See* Equal
opportunity
"Equality of what" debate, 3:233

Equations, 2:361–362, 363–365, 4:455–457

Equi-finality, 5:319–320

Equilibration. *See* Equilibrium in psychology

Equilibria, multiple. *See* Multiple equilibria

Equilibrium, 3:172
Cournot-Nash, 3:172
functionalism, 3:232
Nash, 3:252, 5:208, 373, 374–375, *375*
central banks, 1:479
common knowledge rationality games, 2:26
mechanism design, 5:58
screening and signaling games, 7:372
subgame perfection, 8:193–194
noncooperative, 3:284
nonzero-sum games, 5:532–533
partial, 6:151–153
long run, 4:491
Marshall, Alfred, 4:623
rational expectations, 3:172, 173
See also Equilibrium in economics; Equilibrium in psychology; Multiple equilibria

Equilibrium, general, 3:**283–285**
Arrow, Kenneth J., 1:181–182
Chicago School, 1:502
cobweb cycles, 1:592
Debreu, Gerard, 2:249
Hicks, John R., 3:471–472
Leontief, Wassily, 4:412–413
long run, 4:491
microeconomics, 5:134–135
microfoundations, 5:141
new classical economics, 2:522, 523
optimal growth, 6:51, 52
real business cycles, 1:408
School of Lausanne, 4:362
Uzawa, Hirofumi, 8:563
Walras' law, 9:11–13

Equilibrium, punctuated, 1:48, 3:352–353, 609–610, 6:**629–631**

Equilibrium correction models (ECM), 2:1–3

Equilibrium in economics, 2:**619–621**, 4:585, 8:143–144
Arrow-Debreu Model, 1:182–183
balance of payments, 1:238–240
Barro-Grossman model, 1:255–256

Beveridge curve, 1:292
business cycle theories, 1:410–412
capital, 1:431
chaos theory, 1:493
Chicago School, 1:502
cointegration, 2:2–3
comparative dynamics, 2:47
comparative statics, 2:48
competition, 2:50, 51
cumulative causation, 2:207
currency devaluation and revaluation, 2:211–212
decisive events, 2:253–254
economic depression, 2:303–304
Fisher, Irving, 3:151
full employment, 3:225–226
general, 3:283, 471–472
Hume, David, 3:519, 520
Hurwicz, Leonid, 3:529–530
immigration, 3:581, 582
involuntary unemployment, 4:137–138
Kalecki, Michał, 4:247
Keynes, John Maynard, 4:261
labor market, 4:318–319
liquidity trap, 4:461–462
long period analysis, 4:489–491
long run, 4:491–492
manifolds, 4:585
marginalism, 4:597
Marxist competition, 2:55
mathematical economics, 5:24
money, 5:252
multiple equilibria, 5:324–325
multiplier, 5:329–330
Nash, 1:479
neo-Ricardian economics, 2:521
neoclassical economics, 2:518–519
neoclassical growth model, 5:465
neutral rate of interest, 4:79
new classical economics, 2:522–524
Pareto, Vilfredo, 6:138–139
partial, 4:491
Patinkin, Don, 6:171–172
prices, 8:576, 577
real business cycles, 1:407, 408
Rybczynski theorem, 7:305–306
School of Lausanne, 4:362
stability in economics, 8:76–77
stable nodes, 5:510–511
steady state, 8:126–127
sticky prices, 8:143–144
tâtonnement, 8:270–271

theory of second best, 8:350–351
topology, 8:390–391
transitional economies, 2:533
Z-D model, 9:172
See also General equilibrium

Equilibrium in psychology, 2:**621–623**, 8:74–75

Equipossibility. *See* Probability theory

Equity, social. *See* Equality

Equity markets, 2:**623–624**, 3:146
beauty contest metaphor, 1:269
bid-ask spreads, 8:69–70
bourgeoisie, 1:360
bubbles (economics), 1:378
bull and bear markets, 1:385–386
casino capitalism, 1:455
corporations, 2:139
crash (1929), 3:367–369, 5:493, 9:8
institutional investors, 4:135–136
international trade, 3:147
investors, 4:133–134
lagging, leading and coincident indicators, 4:331
random walk, 7:61–63
risk-return tradeoff, 7:255–256
South Sea Bubble, 8:33–34
Tobin's Q, 8:380
Wall Street, 9:7–9

Equity *vs.* efficiency. *See* Distortions

Equivalence, Ricardian. *See* Ricardian equivalence

ERA, U.S. (Equal Rights Amendment). *See* Equal Rights Amendment, U.S. (ERA)

Erdal, David, 2:125

Eretz Israel. *See* Israel

Erickson, Robert, 8:533

Erikson, Erik, 2:**625–626**, 8:535
child development, 1:507
Gilligan, Carol, 3:319
identity, 3:553–554
identity crisis, 3:556–557
stages of development, 8:78

Eritrea, 1:355, 554

Erklèren, 5:443

Eros, 3:211

Eros and Civilization (Marcuse), 2:177

Erosion, soil, 1:62, 3:130–131

Eroticism, 2:**626–627**

ERPs (Event-related potentials), 5:485

Error, measurement. *See* Measurement error

Error, specification. *See* Specification error

Error-correction mechanisms,
 2:**627–628**, 6:652–653
Error term, in regression. *See*
 Generalized linear models (GLM)
Error terms. *See* Residuals
Errors
 fundamental attribution, 5:452
 Likert scale, 4:447
 litigation, 4:466
 nonspherical, 3:287
 social cognition, 7:570–572
 specification, 8:50–52
  Hausman tests, 3:432–434
  regression analysis, 7:139
Errors, standard, 2:**628–629**
Errors in variables. *See* Measurement
 error
Ervin, Sam, 9:43
Escape from Freedom (Fromm),
 3:222–223
Eskimos. *See* Inuit
Esping-Anderson, Gøsta, 7:631,
 9:67–68, 72
Espionage. *See* Counterintelligence;
 Intelligence
ESS (Explained sum of squares), 6:60
*Essai sur la nature du commerce en
 général* (Cantillon), 1:428–429,
 4:489
Essai sur le calcul intégral (Condorcet),
 2:66
Essai sur les moeurs (Voltaire), 8:635
Essai sur l'inegalite des races humaines
 (Gobineau). *See Essay on the
 Inequality of Human Races*
 (Gobineau)
*An Essay Concerning Human
 Understanding* (Locke), 4:476
Essay on Integral Calculus (Condorcet).
 See Essai sur le calcul intégral
 (Condorcet)
An Essay on Liberation (Marcuse),
 2:177
*Essay on the Application of Analysis to
 the Probability of Majority Decisions*
 (Condorcet), 2:66
*Essay on the Generative Principle of
 Political Constitutions* (Maistre),
 2:83
Essay on the History of Civil Society
 (Ferguson), 1:552
Essay on the Inequality of Human Races
 (Gobineau), 2:325, 3:335, 336
*An Essay on the Nature and Significance
 of Economic Science* (Robbins),
 8:554

*Essay on the Nature of Commerce in
 General* (Cantillon). *See Essai sur la
 nature du commerce en général*
 (Cantillon)
An Essay on the Principle of Population
 (Malthus), 1:358, 2:66, 3:164,
 4:448
 environmental determinism, 2:327
 Malthus, Thomas Robert, 4:569,
  570, 571
 Malthusian trap, 4:572–573
Essay Upon the Civil Wars of France
 (Voltaire), 8:635
Essence of Decision (Allison and
 Zelikow), 2:185
Essentialism, 2:**630–632**
 sexism, 7:473
 slavery hypertension hypothesis,
  7:546
Essentials of Behavior (Hull), 3:506
Establishment clause, 1:535, 536
Estate tax. *See* Inheritance tax
Estates (bequests). *See* Inheritance
 (economics)
Estates (land). *See* Feudalism;
 Latifundia
Estates (social divisions). *See* Caste
Esteem, 5:455
Estimation
 autoregressive models, 1:228–229
 central limit theorem, 1:486
 fixed effects regression, 3:155–156
 growth curve analysis, 3:390–391
 loss functions, 4:498–499
 Nadarya-Watson, 5:528–529
 nonparametric, 5:524–527, *525,
  526*
  Bayesian econometrics,
   1:262–264
  data envelopment analysis,
   2:239–240
  large sample properties,
   4:348–350
  left and right censoring,
   1:474
 parametric, 5:524–525
  large sample properties,
   4:348–350
  randomness, 7:63–64
 semiparametric, 1:474, 5:526,
  7:438–440
 standard errors, 2:629
Estimators, properties of. *See*
 Properties of estimators (asymptotic
 and exact)
Estimé, Durarsais, 2:468

Estonia, NATO and, 5:546
Estrangement. *See* Alienation
Estrich, Susan, 7:66
Eternal Vigilance (Jeffreys-Jones),
 1:481
Ethical, legal and societal implications
 (ELSI), 5:362–363
Ethical egoism, 6:7
Ethics, 2:**632–633**
 abortion rights, 1:4
 Baumrind, Diana, 1:260
 Bentham, Jeremy, 1:286
 Castaneda, Carlos, 1:456–457
 civil disobedience, 1:545, 546
 computers, 2:60
 consumerism, 2:104–105
 critical theory, 2:178
 data, 2:237
 ethnography, 3:15
 eugenics, 3:21–22
 euthanasia and assisted suicide,
  3:26–28
 hierarchy of needs, 5:451
 international relations, 4:101
 interrogation, 4:110
 Kant, Immanuel, 4:248
 legal systems, 4:406
 of listening, 5:371
 moral philosophy, 6:254–256
 moral realism, 7:95
 nanotechnology, 5:362–363
 Nietzsche, Friedrich, 5:502–503
 particularism, 6:155–156
 philosophy, 6:252
 professional journals, 4:216–217
 slave trade, 7:539
 social science, 7:615–616
 subliminal suggestion, 8:201–202
 universalism, 8:526–527
 utilitarianism, 8:554
 work, 9:101
 See also Bioethics
Ethics, business, 2:**633–635**
 bribery, 1:370–371
 bubbles (economics), 1:379
 corruption, 2:143
 crony capitalism, 2:180
 Ponzi schemes, 6:368–369
 See also Corporate social
  responsibility (CSR)
Ethics, corporate. *See* Business ethics;
 Corporate social responsibility
 (CSR)
Ethics, research. *See* Ethics in
 experimentation; Informed consent;

Institutional review board; Shock experiments
Ethics in experimentation, 2:**635–637**
    controlled experiments, 3:59
    described, 3:57–58
    human experiments, 3:60–61
    informed consent, 4:33
    institutional review board, 4:42–43
    lobotomy, 4:475–476
    Milgram, Stanley, 5:161–162
    qualitative methods, 5:111–112
    shock experiments, 3:62–63
    stem cells, 8:133–134
    Tuskegee syphilis study, 8:472–473
Ethiopia
    African Crisis Response Initiative, 1:38
    African socialism, 7:641
    annexation by Italy, 1:115
    borders, 1:355
    civil wars, 1:554, 555
    coffee industry, 1:594
    drought, 2:448
    feudal mode of production, 3:134
    League of Nations, 4:386
    Rastafari, 7:66–68
Ethiopian Delineators, 1:326
Ethiopian Orthodox Church, 7:67–68
Ethnic Chinese. *See* Chinese diaspora
Ethnic cleansing. *See* Ethnic conflict
Ethnic conflict, 2:70, 3:**1–2**
    civil wars, 1:554–555
    clash of civilizations, 1:559
    cleansing, 3:298
    cleavages, 1:578
    Clinton, Bill, 1:580
    comparative politics, 6:327–328
    concentration camps, 2:63–64
    contact hypothesis, 2:111–112
    Croats, 2:179
    crony capitalism, 2:180
    Darfur, 2:226–227
    democratization, 2:290
    development and, 2:343
    discrimination, 2:391
    essentialism, 2:631
    ethnic fractionalization, 3:6, 7–8
    ethnicity, 3:9–10, 11
    ethnocentrism, 3:11–12
    Milosevic, Slobodan, 5:184
    nation-states, 5:422–423
    national defense, 2:260

    partition, 6:159–161
    refugee camps, 7:124–125
    refugees, 7:126
    separatism, 7:450–451
    Serbs, 7:455
    terrorism, 8:628–629
    Tito, Josip, 8:376
    tribalism, 8:448–449
    violence, 8:623–624
Ethnic Conflict (Forbes), 2:112
Ethnic diversity. *See* Diversity; Ethnicity; Multiculturalism
Ethnic enclave, 3:**2–4**
    immigrants, 3:577
    Mafia, 4:552–553
    middleman minorities, 5:147–148
Ethnic Enterprise in America (Light), 1:516
Ethnic enterprises, 3:**4–6**, 5:147–148
Ethnic fractionalization, 3:**6–8**, 6:159–161
Ethnic minorities. *See* Minorities
Ethnicity, 3:**8–11**, 196
    addiction, 1:21
    American Sociological Association research, 1:106–107
    assimilation, 1:188–191
    blood and bloodline, 1:335–336
    census, 1:476, 477
    cleavages, 1:578
    color preference, 6:432
    comedy, 2:23
    cooperatives, 2:125
    corporal punishment, 2:135
    correspondence tests, 2:141–143
    Creole, 2:167–169
    crime and criminology, 2:173
    crony capitalism, 2:180
    cultural tourism, 2:201
    development and, 2:342–343
    essentialism, 2:630–631
    ethnomethodology, 3:19
    family structure, 3:93, 93*t*
    imprisonment, 3:596
    income inequality, 4:3
    intelligence, 4:73
    Latino National Political Survey, 4:354–356
    Latinos, 4:357–361
    liberation movements, 4:432, 433
    low and high culture, 2:205
    multiculturalism, 5:316–318
    nation and, 5:378
    naturalization, 5:444
    occupational status, 6:27

    psychology, 7:21
    race, 7:5, 10–11, 13
    racial democracy, 2:282–283
    racial discrimination, 2:394
    religion, 7:160
    role models, 7:273, 274
    Roma, 7:277–278
    schooling oppositionality, 6:49–51
    self-disclosure, 7:408
    servitude, 7:463
    socialization, 7:648
    stratification, 8:167
    symbolic, 3:256
    teacher-child relationships, 8:292
    tracking in schools, 8:410
    tribalism, 8:448–449
    underrepresentation, 8:495
    upward mobility, 8:534
    voting, 8:646
    whiteness, 9:85–86
    working class, 9:131–133
Ethno-epidemiological methodology, 3:**12–13**, 8:472–473
Ethnoarchaeology, 1:163–164
Ethnocentrism, 1:123, 3:**11–12**
    bigotry, 1:295
    Hitler, Adolf, 3:486–488
    liberation movements, 4:432
    Quebecois movement, 6:661–663
    race, 7:2–7
    tribalism, 8:448–449
Ethnogenesis, Garifuna, 3:256
Ethnographic research, 7:**192–194**
Ethnography, 3:**14–17**
    Benedict, Ruth, 1:281–282
    Boas, Franz, 1:137–138, 344, 345
    cannibalism, 1:427–428
    case method, 1:453
    Castaneda, Carlos, 1:456–457
    of communication, 1:129
    cultural relativism, 2:193, 194
    dance, 2:223–225
    description, 1:123
    ethnomusicology, 3:20
    globalization, 3:331, 332
    Hurston, Zora Neale, 3:527
    Jefferson, Thomas, 4:181
    Lowie, Robert, 4:507
    magic, 4:554–555
    Malinowski, Bronislaw, 4:566–567
    medical anthropology, 1:131
    primitivism, 6:465–466
    public anthropology, 1:133
    reflexivity, 7:122–123

Ethnography, *continued*
    reincarnation, 7:145–146
    research, 7:192–194
    research methods, 5:114
    Standard Cross-Cultural Sample,
      8:88–92
    street culture, 8:172–173
    Tally's Corner, 8:263–264
    tribalism, 8:448–449
    urban studies, 8:541–542
    See also Ethnology and folklore
Ethnological Society of London, 1:127
Ethnology and folklore, 1:123,
    3:**17–19**
    Croats, 2:179
    dance, 2:224
    ethnomusicology, 3:20
    Lowie, Robert, 4:507
    magic, 4:554–555
    music, 5:342–345
    nursery rhymes, 5:549–551
    reflexivity, 7:122–123
    South, U.S., 8:32–33
    storytelling, 8:160–161
    tradition, 8:420–422
    See also Ethnography
Ethnomethodology, 3:19
    conversational analysis, 2:118,
      119–120
    ethnographic research, 7:192–194
    phenomenology, 6:243
    research method, 5:114
    sociology, 7:663
Ethnomusicology, 3:**19–20,**
    5:342–345
Ethnonationalism. *See* Ethnocentrism;
    Liberation movements; Nationalism
    and nationality
Ethological attachment theory. *See*
    Attachment theory; Separation
    anxiety
Ethyl Corporation, 5:540
Études d'économie politique appliquée
    (Walras), 4:362
Études d'économie sociale (Walras),
    4:362
Etzioni, Amitai, 2:31, 39
Etzioni-Halevi, Eva, 2:564
EU (European Union). *See* European
    Union (EU)
Eucharist. *See* Sacraments
Euclid of Alexandria, 5:54
Eugene Lang College, 5:501
Eugenics, 3:**21–22**
    biological determinism, 2:326

birth control, 1:303, 3:89
blood and bloodline, 1:335–336
Galton, Francis, 3:247–248
genetic testing *vs.,* 3:295
heredity, 3:461
human sterilization, 8:140–141
Mendel's law, 5:83
Mexican Americans, 5:122
nativism, 5:430
nature *vs.* nurture, 5:446
Nazism, 3:495
Pearson, Karl, 6:192, 193
race, 7:10, 14
Spencer, Herbert, 8:58
surplus population, 8:238
zero population growth, 9:174
    See also Population control
Eugenides, Jeffrey, 3:272
Euhemerism, 5:549
Eukiyo-e, 8:632
Euler equation, 6:51
Euphrates River Basin, 9:41–42
Euro, 3:**22–23**
    as currency, 2:209
    currency appreciation and
      depreciation, 2:209
    European Union, 3:24–25
    exchange rates, 3:39
Euro barometer. *See* Pollsters
Euro-currency Standing Committee,
    6:33
Eurobonds, 3:147
Eurocentrism, 1:43–44, 47
Euromissiles, 6:184
Europe
    administrative law, 1:23
    anticolonial movements,
      1:139–141
    antitrust law, 1:145
    archaeology, 1:166
    architecture, 1:170
    banana industry, 1:245, 246
    blackness, 1:328
    borders, 1:355
    bourgeoisie, 1:361
    bull and bear markets, 1:386
    cattle industry, 1:470
    central banks, 1:477–478
    checks and balances, 1:495
    Christian Democracy, 2:276, 277
    Christian socialism, 7:642–643
    Christianity, 1:530
    The Church, 1:533–534
    Church and state, 1:536

civil liberties, 1:546
civilization, 1:557, 558
clash of civilizations, 1:559
classical music, 1:575
cleavages, 1:578
codetermination, 1:593
coffee industry, 1:594
Cold War, 2:4–5
colonial gaze, 3:261–262
colonialism, 2:12
Columbus, Christopher, 2:19–22
confederations, 2:68
conservatism, 2:83–84, 86
consumer protection, 2:102
convergence theory, 2:117
corporatism, 2:141
cosmopolitanism, 2:149
cotton industry, 2:152
coups d'etat, 2:156
cults, 2:188
day care, 2:245–246
decolonization, 2:255, 256
democracy, 2:273
democratic centralism, 2:285–286
developing countries, 2:336
divine right, 2:421–422
domino theory, 2:435
drought, 2:448
east-west partitioning, 9:147, 149
Enlightenment, 2:595–598
euro, 3:22–23
European Union, 3:23–25
fascism, 3:103–105
feudal mode of production, 3:134
feudalism, 3:135–136
flower industry, 3:158
ghettos, 3:311–312, 313
global warming effects, 3:330
gold standard, 3:343
hate crimes, 3:431
Holy Roman Empire, 3:498
imperialism, 3:586–589
international law, 3:360–361
interwar years, 4:121–122
Jews, 4:195–196
judiciary, 4:227–228
labor, 4:301–302
labor law, 4:317
land fertility, 3:131
land reform, 4:342
landlords, 4:345, 346
latifundia, 4:352–354
legal systems, 4:405
literature, 4:463–464

monarchism, 5:237–238

nation-states, 5:421

nationalism, 5:417

nationalization, 5:419

neoimperialism, 5:471

neutral states, 5:487–488

pacifism, 6:101–102

parliaments and parliamentary systems, 6:145–146

petty bourgeoisie, 1:362

political participation, 8:606

reproductive politics, 7:181

Roman Catholic Church, 7:280

Rothschilds, 7:289

slave-gun cycle, 7:540–542

socialism, 7:636–637

sociology, 7:670–671

    advertising, 1:29

    aristocracy, 1:173–174

    childlessness, 1:510

    Chinese diaspora, 1:517

    civil society, 1:552, 553

    common land, 2:27

    communalism, 2:30

    demographic transition, 2:292

    depopulation, 2:301

    fatherhood, 3:107

    migration, 3:567–569

    out-of-wedlock births, 1:308

    population aging, 3:306

    Roma, 7:277–279

state, 8:104

state capitalism, 1:444

state enterprise, 8:106–107

telecommunications industry, 8:315

textile industry, 8:333–334

theater, 8:338

time-and-a-half, 8:373–374

towns, 8:404

trade barriers, 1:255

unemployment, 8:18

urban, 1:135

vagabonds, 8:567

Verdoorn's law, 8:608

visual arts, 8:631

voter turnout, 8:645

voting, 8:646

voting patterns, 8:650

voting rights, 3:185

war, 1:554

weapons industry, 9:49–50

Wholesale Price Index, 9:94

women's work, 9:125

world-system, 9:153

xenophobia, 9:158, 159, 160–161

    See also specific countries; Eastern Europe; Western Europe

Europe and the People Without History (Wolf), 9:106

European Central Bank, 3:25

European Coal and Steel Community (ECSC), 3:23, 24

    See also European Union (EU)

European Coalition of Cities, 9:160–161

European Commission (EC), 7:54

European Community Household Panel, 3:107

European Convention on Human Rights (ECHR), 1:546

European Court of Human Rights, 1:546

European Economic Community (EEC), 3:23, 24, 5:488

    See also European Union (EU)

European immigrants, 3:**567–570**

    Ellis Island, 2:567–569

    Mafia, 4:552–553

    New York City immigrants, 3:572–573

    settlement, 3:577–578

European Parliament, Liberal Party (U.K.), 4:423

European sociology, 7:**670–671**

European Union (EU), 3:**23–26**

    automobile industry, 1:221–222

    banana industry, 1:245, 246

    banking industry, 1:253

    borders, 1:355

    bourgeoisie, 1:361

    cattle industry, 1:471

    citizenship, 1:543–544

    civilization, 1:558

    clash of civilizations, 1:559

    codetermination, 1:593

    coffee industry, 1:594

    common market, 2:28–29

    confederations, 2:69

    cotton industry, 2:153

    currency, 2:209

    customs union, 2:215

    euro, 3:22–23

    globalization, 3:334

    neutral states, 5:488

    Nkrumah, Kwame, 5:508

    occupational regulation, 6:24

    predatory pricing, 6:428

Thatcher, Margaret, 8:335

volunteerism, 8:638

welfare state, 9:73

xenophobia, 9:159

Europeans for Nuclear Disarmament (END), 8:355

Euthanasia and assisted suicide, 1:192, 3:**26–29**, 8:222

    bioethics, 1:301

    death and dying, 2:248

    morality, 2:248

Evaluation research. *See* Research methods

Evangelicalism, 1:534, 2:114, 277, 3:234, 236, 7:606, 9:69–70

Evans, Charles, 2:210

Evans, George, 1:20

Evans, John, 8:582

Evans-Pritchard, E. E., 1:128, 3:**29–30**, 6:367–368

Evasion, tax. *See* Tax evasion and tax avoidance

Eveleth Taconite Company, Jensen et al. v. (1997), 7:475

Event-related potentials (ERPs), 5:485

Event studies, 3:**30–31**

Evers, Medgar, 4:369

Every Man His Own Broker, or, A Guide to Exchange Alley (Mortimer), 1:385

Every Tongue Got to Confess (Hurston), 3:527

Everyday life, 3:337–338

Evidence

    hearsay, 3:444–445

    litigation, 4:465–466

Evidential behaviorism, 1:275

Evil, atheism and, 1:194

EVL model. *See Exit, Voice, and Loyalty* (Hirschman)

EVLN model. *See Exit, Voice, Loyalty and Neglect* (Hirschman)

Evolution

    anthropology, 1:117

    biological anthropology, 1:117–118, 125–127

    Church and state, 1:536

    creationism *vs.*, 2:162

    cultural, 1:137

    cultural anthropology, 1:119

    cultural group selection, 2:191

    Darwin, Charles, 2:227–232

    Dobzhansky, Theodosius, 2:432–433

    essentialism, 2:630

    naturalism, 5:442

Evolution, *continued*
  prosocial behavior, 1:89
  Scopes trial, 7:366
  Social Darwinism, 2:232–234
  of society, 8:595
      Boserup, Ester, 1:358
      emotion, 2:570
  See also Natural selection
The Evolution of the International Economic Order (Lewis), 4:420
Evolutionary biology, 3:352–353, 5:367
Evolutionary economics. *See* Schumpeter, Joseph Alois
Evolutionary games, 3:**31–33**
  Hamilton's rule, 3:415
  mixed strategy, 5:207–208
  replicator dynamics, 7:169–170
Evolutionary psychology, 3:**33–34**
  cultural group selection, 2:191–192
  Darwin, Charles, 2:229–232, *230, 231t*
  determinism, 2:323
  evolutionary theory of kinship, 4:273–274
  genetic determinism, 2:329–330
  natural selection, 5:440–441
  sex and mating, 7:470–471
  Social Darwinism, 2:233
  sociobiology, 7:653
Evolutionary socialists, 4:403
Evolutionary theory of kinship, 1:119, 4:**273–274**
  Darwin, Charles, 2:229
  Hamilton's rule, 3:414–415
Evolutionary theory of technological change, 1:491
Ewen, Stuart, 3:473
Exact estimators. *See* Properties of estimators (asymptotic and exact)
Excavations, 1:164
Exceptionalism, 1:107, 5:490
Excess demand, 3:**34–36**, *35, 36,* 4:24
Excess supply, 3:34–35, *35,* **36**
Exchange, mutual. *See* Reciprocity
Exchange, social. *See* Social exchange theory
Exchange, unequal. *See* Unequal exchange
Exchange and Power in Social Life (Blau), 1:332
Exchange Rate and Fundamentals (Engel and West), 2:210
Exchange rates, 3:**37–40**
  balance of payments, 1:238–240

beggar-thy-neighbor, 1:272–273
  bubbles (economics), 1:378
  capital controls, 1:432
  central banks, 1:478, 480
  chaos theory, 1:493
  cost-benefit analysis, 2:150–151
  currency appreciation and depreciation, 2:209–210
  currency devaluation and revaluation, 2:211–212
  dirty float, 2:375
  euro, 3:22–23
  fixed, 3:112
  flexible, 3:218
  foreign reserves, 7:202–203
  interest rates, 4:85–86
  international economics, 2:508–509, 4:92–94
  J-Curve, 4:179
  market fundamentals, 4:606
  Mundell-Fleming model, 5:335–336
  overshooting, 6:98
  Penn World Table, 6:204–205
  stagflation, 8:83
  transaction taxes, 8:427–428
Exchange value, 3:**40–41**
  barter *vs.,* 6:97
  labor theory of value, 4:323, 324
  surplus value, 8:240–241
  unequal, 8:505–506
  Walras, Léon, 9:12
  wealth, 9:46
Exchange value commodity. *See* Exchange value
Exchangeability, 3:**41–42**
  norm of reciprocity, 7:107–108
  reciprocity, 7:105–107
Exchanges, stock. *See* Stock exchanges; Stock exchanges in developing countries
Exchanges (social)
  conflict, 3:385
  groups, 3:386–387
Exclusion, social. *See* Social exclusion
Exclusion Acts. *See* Asian immigrants
Exclusive Economic Zones (EEZs), 3:153
ExComm (National Security Council Executive Committee), 2:183, 184
Executive branch. *See* Presidency
Executive Order 8802, 5:384, 9:81
Executive Order 10308, 5:384
Executive Order 11246, 3:373
Executive privilege, 9:43

Exhaustible resources. *See* Nonrenewable natural resources
Exhilaration. *See* Stagnation
Exiled persons. *See* Refugees
Existentialism, 3:**42–43**
  humanism, 3:518
  Lukacs, Georg, 4:516
  Sartre, Jean-Paul, 7:327
Exit, Voice, and Loyalty (Hirschman), 3:**43–45**
Exit, Voice, Loyalty and Neglect (Hirschman), 3:44–45
Exit polls, 3:**45–46**
Exner, John, 7:284
Exodusters, 1:325
Exogeneity, 1:472, 473, 2:3
Exogenous money, 1:478, 4:24, 5:**258–260**
Exogenous variables. *See* Predetermined variables
Exoticism, 3:**46–47**
Expansion, for Gold, God and Glory, 3:340–341
  See also Imperialism; Territorial expansion
Expansion, voluntary import. *See* Import promotion
Expansionism. *See* Imperialism; Territorial expansion
Expectancies. *See* Expectations
Expectancy X value theory, 1:14–15
Expectations, 3:**47–50**
  central banks, 1:478
  life-cycle hypothesis, 4:441–443
  locus of control, 4:477–478
  luck, 4:512–513
  optimism/pessimism, 6:54
  Rotter's Internal-External Locus of Control Scale, 7:289–290
  state theory, 3:386
  yield curve, 9:166
  See also Self-fulfilling prophecies
Expectations, adaptive, 1:**19–20**
Expectations, implicit, 3:**50–51**
Expectations, rational, 1:20, 3:**51–53**
  central banks, 1:479
  cobweb cycles, 1:591–592
  decribed, 3:49
  efficient market hypothesis, 2:548–549
  implicit expectations, 3:51
  Lucas, Robert E., Jr., 4:510
  Lucas critique, 4:511
  Sargent, Thomas, 7:326–327
  static, 3:53

Expectations, revolution of rising, 5:233, 7:**231–233**

Expectations, static, 3:**53**

Expectations, teacher, 8:**290–291**

Expected utility theory, 3:**54**, 5:519, 8:79
  expectations, 3:48
  lotteries, 4:503
  St. Petersburg paradox, 8:560
  subjective, 8:559, 560

Expenditure. *See* Spending

Expenses, national income accounts, 5:400

Experiential consciousness. *See* Consciousness

Experiential learning, 2:534, 3:202

Experiment, Stanford Prison. *See* Prison psychology; Zimbardo, Philip

Experimental economics, 2:**505–506**, 514, 7:558–559

Experimental methodology, 3:55–58

Experimental psychology, 2:80

Experimental realism, 3:56, 7:**93–95**

Experimentation, ethics in. *See* Ethics in experimentation

Experiments, 3:**55–58**
  classical, 1:425–426
  cognition, 1:597
  income maintenance, 3:605–607
  Monte Carlo, 5:274–275
    cointegration regression, 8:518–519
    uniform distribution, 2:418
    unit root regression, 8:517–518
  natural, 5:434–435, 7:591–592
  quasi-experiments, 1:425–426
  social, 7:590–592
    Campbell, Donald, 1:425–426
    moving to opportunity, 5:302–304
  Thorndike, Edward, 8:358

Experiments, controlled, 3:**58–59**, 5:434–435
  causality, 1:473
  developmental psychology, 2:350
  experimental realism, 7:93–95
  learned helplessness, 4:387–389

Experiments, human, 3:**59–61**
  cognitive dissonance, 1:599–600
  conformity, 2:71–72
  ethics, 2:635–637
  experimental realism, 7:93–95
  gender preference, 6:434

informed consent, 4:33
  institutional review board, 4:42–43
  Lewin, Kurt, 4:417–418
  luck, 4:512
  Milgram, Stanley, 5:161–162
  shock experiments, 3:62–63
  social influence, 7:594–598
  Zimbardo, Philip, 9:178

Experiments, policy. *See* Social experiments

Experiments, shock, 2:636, 3:**62–63**, 4:387–388

Expert witnesses, 4:465–467

Expiatory sacrifice, 9:155

Explained sum of squares (ESS), 6:60

Explanation in Geography (Harvey), 3:305

Exploitation, 3:**63–65**
  capitalism, 1:446, 8:576
  caste, 1:461
  child labor, 1:508–509
  class, 1:562, 563, 571
  colonialism, 2:12
  Columbus, Christopher, 2:19–21
  common land, 2:27, 28
  consumption, 2:106
  convergence theory, 2:117
  corporations, 2:140
  developing countries, 2:335–336
  East Indian diaspora, 2:471–475
  internal colony, 2:14
  labor, 4:301
  leisure class, 1:566
  liberation theology, 4:434
  marginal product of labor, 4:306
  Marxism, 4:638–641
  nonrenewable natural resources, 5:437–438
  rate, 7:70–71
  restitution principle, 7:213–215
  state capitalism, 1:444
  surplus labor, 4:310, 311
  sweatshops, 8:247–248

Exploitation, rate of. *See* Rate of exploitation

Exploration, space. *See* Space exploration

Exploration for Gold, God and Glory, 3:340–341
  See also Imperialism; Territorial expansion

Explorations in Economic History (periodical), 1:582

Explorations in Entrepreneurial History (periodical). *See Explorations in Economic History* (periodical)

Explorations in Personality (Murray), 1:14

Exploring the City (Hannerz), 1:134, 135

Exponential distribution. *See* Probability distributions

Export penetration, 3:**65–66**

Export promotion, 2:345, 3:**66–68**, 592

Export restraints, voluntary. *See* Import promotion

Exports, 3:**68–69**
  absolute advantage, 1:5–6
  automobile, 1:221–222
  balance of payments, 1:238–240
  banana industry, 1:245–246
  bauxite industry, 1:261
  beggar-thy-neighbor, 1:272–273
  cattle industry, 1:471
  currency appreciation and depreciation, 2:210
  economic growth, 2:486
  free trade, 3:194
  immiserizing growth, 3:583, 584
  industrialization, 3:621–622
  J-Curve, 4:179
  Leontief, Wassily, 4:413
  maquiladoras, 4:591–594
  product dumping, 2:462
  slave-gun cycle, 7:540–542
  terms of trade, 8:324–326
  toxic waste, 8:408–409
  in trade, 8:411–412
  trade deficit, 8:415–416
  trade liberalization, 4:427–428
  trade quotas, 6:672, 673
  trade surplus, 8:417–418
  transnational corporations, 3:594*t*

Exposure and response prevention, 6:18, 19

Exposure therapy, 1:573–574, 4:388
  See also Psychotherapy

Expropriation. *See* Confiscation

Expulsion, 3:1–2

Extended case method, 1:453, **454–455**

Extended family, 3:**86–87**
  black middle class, 1:314
  description, 3:83
  out-of-wedlock births, 1:306

External validity, 7:591, 8:573

Externality, 3:**70–71**

Externality, *continued*
distortions, 2:414
obese, 6:3, 4–5
theory of second best, 8:350, 351
Externalization, 1:75
Extinction, of humankind, 3:241
Extinction (Psychology), 1:573
Extinguishment, title. *See* Deeds and titles (property rights)
Extortion, 1:370–371
Extraterrestrials. *See* Unidentified flying objects (UFOs)
Extreme situations, 1:290
Extremism. *See* Radicalism
Extremists, Islamic, 3:237
Extrinsic values, 8:557
Ey, Henri, 2:81
Eye contact, 4:525
Eyeblink conditioning, 1:573, 574
Eysenck, Hans, 5:486–487
Eysenck, Sybil B. G., 5:486–487
Eysenck Personality Questionnaire-Revised (EPQ-R), 5:486–487
Ezili, 8:634
EZLN (Ejército Zapatista de Liberación Nacional). *See* Zapatistas
EZLN (Zapatista Army of National Liberation). *See* Zapatistas

F

F-Test. *See* Test statistics
Fabianism, 3:73–74, 4:403, 420–421
The Fable of the Bees (Mandeville), 4:489
Fabrega, Horacio, 1:131
Face validity. *See* Content validity
Faces at the Bottom of the Well (Bell), 2:175
Facial expressions, 5:530–531
Facilitation, social. *See* Social facilitation
Facing Mount Kenya (Kenyatta), 4:255
Fackler, P. Mark, 2:39
Facsimile machines, 1:490
Fact, stylized. *See* Stylized fact
Factor analysis, 3:75–76, 8:590
Factor-loading, matrix, 3:76
Factorial terms of trade. *See* Terms of trade
Factorial validity. *See* Construct validity
Factories, 3:76–78
development economics, 2:344–345
division of labor, 2:423–425
labor, 4:301

Taylorism, 8:287
time and motion studies, 8:365
Factors, fixed. *See* Returns to a fixed factor
Factors of production. *See* Capital; Labor; Land
Factory system, 3:78–79
African Americans, 1:34–35
blue collar and white collar, 1:337, 338, 339, 340
history, 3:76–78
labor, 4:301
textile industry, 8:333
working class, 9:130
Factory trawlers, 3:152–153
Facts, social. *See* Social facts
Facultative traits, 2:228
Faden, Arnold, 5:26
FAE (Fundamental attribution error), 1:206, 2:252, 5:452
Fahrenheit 9/11 (film), 3:79–80
Failed states, 7:126, 8:104, 105
Fair Employment Act (U.S. 1938), 4:303
Fair Housing Act (U.S. 1968), 2:317, 615, 4:210, 347, 5:384, 8:537
Fair Labor Standards Act (FLSA) (U.S. 1938), 4:303, 6:99, 100, 8:373–374, 9:127, 129
Fair Trade Labelling Organisation (FLO), 1:247
Fairfax, Thomas, 9:36
Falcon, Angelo, 4:354–356
Faletto, Enzo, 2:299
Falkland Islands War, 2:87, 3:80–81, 171, 8:335
Fallacy, 8:574
Fallon, April, 2:329
Fallout, radioactive, 9:30
False beliefs. *See* Lay theories
False Claims Act (U.S 1863.), 9:80
False consciousness, 3:81–83
False uniqueness, 3:388
Families, female-headed. *See* Female-headed families
Family, 3:83–86
affinal, 3:86, 87
African American, 1:314, 3:191–192
alcoholism, 1:71
average size, 6:96
Becker, Gary S., 1:270, 271
blended, 3:93
childlessness, 1:510
children, 1:511–512

children's rights, 1:512
Chinese diaspora, 1:517
cities, 1:540
civil society, 1:553
cohabitation, 2:1–2
conflict, 2:70
corporal punishment, 2:135
cultural capital, 2:189–190
cultural distinctions, 2:412
culture of poverty, 2:206
Darwin, Charles, 2:227–232
day care, 2:245–246
demographic transition, 2:291
disaster management, 2:384
dowry and bride price, 2:440–441
economic psychology, 2:495
formation, 3:83, 84
gay, lesbian, transgender, and bisexual politics, 6:331
Hamilton's rule, 3:414–415
households, 3:91
kinship, 4:271–273
labeling theory, 4:300
loneliness, 4:486–487
lying, 4:524
Mafia, 4:550–553
Oedipus complex, 6:29
out-of-wedlock births, 1:306, 308
Panel Study of Income Dynamics, 6:121–122
schizophrenia, 7:345–346
sibling relationships, 7:505–507
single-adult, 3:94
slaves, 1:40
social statics, 7:620
social system, 7:625
Family, extended, 3:86–87
black middle class, 1:314
description, 3:83
out-of-wedlock births, 1:306
Family, female-headed. *See* Female-headed families
Family, nuclear, 3:87
description, 3:83
history, 3:96
patriarchal, 3:96
Family and Medical Leave Act (U.S. 1993), 1:580
Family farms, 1:61, 150
Family functioning, 3:87–88
description, 3:85–86
divorce and separation, 2:428
Moynihan Report, 5:305–306
population growth, 6:379–380

transition to parenthood, 6:134–135

urban poverty, 6:411

Family Limitation (Sanger), 3:89

Family of origin, 3:86

Family planning, 3:**88–90**

    birth control, 1:303

    contraception, 2:115

    population control, 6:377–378

    zero population growth, 9:174–175

Family structure, 3:**90–95**, 91*t*, 92*t*, 93*t*

    description, 3:83

    family values, 3:96

    female-headed, 3:115–117

    matriarchy, 5:30

    neighborhood effects, 5:462

    out-of-wedlock births, 1:306, 308

    reproduction, 7:179

    school readiness, 7:87

    sibling relationships, 7:505–507

Family Support Act (U.S. 1988), 3:105–106

Family values, 2:30, 114, 3:**95–97**

Famine, 3:**97–99**, 164

    geography, 3:165

    malnutrition, 4:567–568

    morbidity and mortality, 5:291

    rural development, 2:342

    See also Food crisis

Fannie Lou Hamer, Rosa Parks, and Coretta Scott King Voting Rights Reauthorization and Amendments Act (U.S. 2006), 8:650

    See also Voting Rights Act (U.S. 1965)

Fanning, Shawn, 7:115–116

Fanon, Frantz, 1:330, 3:**99–100**, 513, 4:430

    Black Power, 1:321

    colonial gaze, 3:262, 264

    colonialism, 2:12

    decolonization, 2:257

    lumpenproletariat, 4:517

    narratives, 5:372

    neoimperialism, 5:471

    postcolonialism, 6:392

    racialization, 7:43

    resistance, 7:208

    violence, 8:625–626

    Wallerstein, Immanuel, 9:9

FAO (Food and Agriculture Organization), 1:246

Farber, Bernard, 3:86

Fard, W. D., 5:379–380

Fard Muhammad, 5:309–310, 348

A Farewell to Arms (Hemingway), 9:18

Faria, João Ricardo, 1:539

Farm quota system, 6:**667–668**

Farm subsidies, 6:667–668, 8:**203–204**

Farmer, James, 2:75

Farmer, Paul, 1:133

Farmers' Alliance, 6:383

Farmer's Home Administration (FmHA), 2:341

Farmers' Institutes, 6:74

Farmers *vs.* peasantry, 6:74

Farming. *See* Agricultural industry

Farming, tenant. *See* Agricultural industry

Farms, family, 1:61, 150

Farmworkers. *See* Agricultural industry; Migrant labor

Farrakhan, Louis, 5:310

    black nationalism, 1:317–318

    Nation of Islam, 5:381

    vindication movements, 8:619

Farrell, David, 2:59

Farrell, Michael, 2:240

Farsightedness, 3:**100–102**

Fascism, 3:**102–105**

    Bracero Program, 1:364

    bureaucracy, 1:391

    centrism, 1:488

    conformity, 2:72

    conservatism, 2:84

    corporatism, 2:140

    Croats, 2:179

    dictatorship, 2:359

    Drucker, Peter, 2:449

    Franco, Francisco, 3:186–187

    hegemony, 3:455

    Hitler, Adolf, 3:486–488

    Holocaust, 3:496

    left wing *vs.*, 4:403

    Michels, Robert, 5:132

    Mussolini, Benito, 5:349–350

    Peronism, 6:214

    political sociology, 8:4

    populism, 6:385

    revolution, 7:229

    Spanish Civil War, 8:43–44

    state capitalism, 1:443, 444

    totalitarianism, 8:395

    See also Nazism

Fascism and Dictatorship (Poulantzas), 6:405

Fascist Party (Italy), 3:104

Fashion, 3:118–119, 8:269

Fasle II (2004), 6:30

Fast food, 5:552, 6:4

Fasting, 9:155

Fatah, 1:323, 6:103, 104, 105–106, 107

Fatality rates. *See* Morbidity and mortality

Father Direct, 3:107

Fatherhood, 3:**105–108**

    female-headed families, 3:116

    out-of-wedlock births, 1:306, 307

FatherLit Database, 3:106

Fatimids, 1:160

Fatwa, 1:70–71

Faubus, Orval, 1:550, 551, 2:314, 316

Faúndex, Julio, 1:78

Faust, Katherine, 5:477

Faux, Geoffrey P., 9:26

Fax machines, 1:490

Fayol, Henri, 6:69

FBI. *See* Federal Bureau of Investigation

FCC (U.S. Federal Communications Commission), 1:475–476

FDA. *See* U.S. Food and Drug Administration (FDA)

FDI (Foreign direct investment). *See* Foreign investment

FDIC (Federal Deposit Insurance Corporation), 5:494

Feagin, Clairece Booher, 4:359

Feagin, Joseph, 3:**109**

    Latinos, 4:359

    racial slurs, 7:41, 42

    racialization, 7:43, 44

    school desegregation, 2:317

    whiteness, 9:91, 93

Fear

    conditioning, 1:573

    genetic determinism, 2:329, 330

    technophobia, 8:311

Fearon, James, 3:7–8

Febvre, Lucien, 3:482

FECA (Federal Election Campaign Act) (U.S. 1971), 1:423

Fechner, Gustav Theodor, 2:80

Fecundity, 3:126–127

Fedayeen, 1:322

Federal Bureau of Investigation (FBI)

    Black Panthers, 1:319

    Central Intelligence Agency, U.S, 1:481

    corporate fraud, 6:73

    counterterrorism, 2:155

Federal Bureau of Investigation (FBI),
continued
Disney, Walt, 2:410
hate crimes, 3:431
Hoover, J. Edgar, 3:500–501
McCarthyism, 5:44
national defense, 2:260
repression, 7:175
Federal Communications
Commission, U.S. (FCC),
1:475–476
*The Federal Communications
Commission* (Coase), 1:589, 590
Federal Convention (1787), 1:267
Federal Deposit Insurance
Corporation (FDIC), 5:494
Federal Election Campaign Act
(FECA) (U.S. 1971), 1:423
Federal Emergency Management
Agency (FEMA), 2:384
Federal government, 3:**357–359**
central banks, 1:478
Central Intelligence Agency, U.S,
1:480–482
Cherokees, 1:498
Confederate States of America,
2:66–67
Congress, U.S., 2:73–74
Constitution, U.S., 2:90–91
constitutional courts, 2:93
decentralization, 2:250–251
democratic centralism, 2:286
Democratic Party (U.S.), 2:286
divided, 2:74
electoral college, 2:559
politics, 6:321
See also Federalism
Federal Housing Administration, U.S.,
1:97
Federal Housing Authority (FHA),
8:536, 9:53
Federal National Mortgage
Administration (U.S.), 1:97
Federal Open Market Committee
(FOMC), 3:111, 380
Federal Regulation of Lobbying Act
(U.S. 1946), 4:475
Federal Reserve Act (U.S. 1913),
3:110–111, 112–113, 9:102
Federal Reserve Banks, 3:110–111,
112
Federal Reserve System, U.S.,
3:**110–111**
black capitalism, 1:441
Brimmer, Andrew, 1:372
bull and bear markets, 1:386

central banks, 1:478
Chicago School, 1:502
currency, 2:209
foreign reserves, 7:202–203
full capacity, 3:224
Great Depression, 3:368, 369
Greenspan, Alan, 3:379, 380
lender of last resort, 4:410
monetary policy, 6:294
natural rate of unemployment,
5:436
open market operations, 6:42
quantity index, 6:658
rules *vs.* discretion, 7:293
Taylor rule, 8:286
Federal Reserve System, U.S., analysis,
3:**112–113**
Federal Tax Credit for Energy
Efficiency, U.S., 8:273
Federal Trade Commission (FTC)
consumer protection, 2:103
imperfect competition, 2:53
Nader's Raiders, 5:360–361
Federal Trade Commission Act (U.S.
1914), 1:144–145, 9:102
Federal Writers Project (FWP), 3:528,
529
Federalism, 3:**113–115**
Bill of Rights, 1:297
checks and balances, 1:496
confederations, 2:68
Constitution, U.S., 2:91
constitutional limits, 3:113–114,
358–359
decentralization, 2:250–251
democratic centralism, 2:286
Democratic Party (U.S.), 2:286
description, 3:355–356
electoral college, 2:559
ethnicity, 3:10
Hamilton, Alexander, 3:413–414
Jefferson, Thomas, 4:182
job guarantee, 4:204–206
judicial review, 4:223–225
judiciary, 4:225
New Deal, 5:497–498
Pan-Caribbeanism, 6:119–120
politics, 6:321
republic, 7:184–185
Republican Party (U.S.), 7:185,
186
Russian Federation, 7:302–303
sovereignty, 8:39
voting schemes, 8:655
Washington, George, 3:114, 9:37

welfare, 9:61
Federalism, treaty. *See* Treaty
federalism
The Federalist Papers (Hamilton, Jay
and Madison), 1:495–496, 2:91,
3:413, 4:548, 9:37
Federalist Party (U.S.), 2:286, 287,
4:223, 7:189, 9:37, 38
Federation of Southern Cooperatives,
2:126
Federations
confederations *vs.,* 2:68–69
consociational democracy, 2:278
Solidarność, 8:25–26
Feedback, flow (psychological), 3:158
Feenstra, Robert C., 6:86
Feld, Steven, 9:142
Feldman, Fred, 8:557
Feldman, Robert, 4:525
Fellowship of the New Life, 3:73
Felt, Mark, 9:43
Felton, Agostini v. (1997), 1:535
FEMA (Federal Emergency
Management Agency), 2:384
Female-headed families, 3:**115–117**
Moynihan Report, 5:305–306
neighborhood effects, 5:462
out-of-wedlock births, 1:308
poverty, 3:274
Females
alpha, 1:83
women *vs.,* 3:267
The Feminine Mystique (Friedan),
3:121, 123, 216, 279, 5:408, 9:113
Femininity, 3:**117–119**
sexism, 7:473
social values, 8:582
work, 9:122
Feminism, 3:**119–122**
Beard, Mary, 1:268
black, 9:119
blackness, 1:330
capitalist mode of production,
1:447
childlessness, 1:510
class, 1:563–564
class consciousness, 1:572
critical race theory, 2:175
development in sociology, 2:348
Douglass, Frederick, 2:439–440
equal opportunity, 2:613
feminist sociology, 7:671–672
first wave, 3:119–120, 9:112–113,
116
gender politics, 6:333–334

Hite, Shere, 3:485
international relations, 4:101
intersectionality, 4:114–115
Kinsey, Alfred, 4:270
motherhood, 5:298, 299
neoconservative, 9:115
post-Parsonian American
   sociology, 8:5–6
postmodernism, 9:115, 117
privacy, 6:478
radical, 9:113
reproduction, 7:178–179
sexism, 7:473–474
social history, 3:483
social welfare system, 7:632
Standard Cross-Cultural Sample,
   8:91
stare, 8:101
Steinem, Gloria, 8:132–133
The Stepford Wives (film),
   8:134–135
Stowe, Harriet Beecher,
   8:161–162
subject/self, 8:195
third wave, 3:121, 269–270,
   9:115, 117
Truth, Sojourner, 8:462
utopianism, 8:561
Veblen, Thorstein, 8:596
vindication, 8:618
women's studies, 9:119
work, 9:122
See also Women's movement
Feminism, second wave, 3:120–121,
   122–124, 9:113–115, 116–117
gender politics, 3:267–268,
   6:333–334
intersectionality, 4:114
Feminism without Borders (Mohanty),
   3:270
Feminist anthropology, 1:121
Feminist Majority Foundation, 1:416,
   5:409
Feminist sociology, 7:**671–673**
constructivism, 2:96, 97
described, 7:663
development, 2:348
Fenno, Richard F., Jr., 2:89,
   3:**124–125**
Ferber, New York v. (1982), 6:13
Ferdinand, Franz, 8:628, 9:145
Ferdinand, King of Aragon, 2:19, 20,
   21
Ferguson, Adam, 1:552, 553
Ferguson, Faith I., 3:116

Ferguson, Plessy v. (1896), 1:19, 305,
   3:316, 505, 4:198
   Birth of a Nation (film), 1:305
   Brown v. Board of Education
      (1954), 1:373–374
   civil rights movement, U.S., 1:551
   equal protection, 2:614–615
   race, 7:16
   separate-but-equal, 7:446
   Supreme Court, U.S., 8:234
   unequal education, 2:537
Ferguson, Ronald, 1:17
Fernand Bruadel Center for the Study
   of Economics, 9:10, 153
Fernández, Sortero Figueroa, 1:356
Ferre, John P., 2:39
Ferrera, Maurizio, 9:68
Ferri, Enrico, 6:80
Ferrie, Joseph, 4:302
Fertile crescent, 3:**125–126**
The Fertile Crescent (Issawi), 3:126
Fertility, human, 3:**126–130**
baby boomers, 1:235
Becker, Gary S., 1:270
birth control, 1:302–303
childlessness, 1:510
demographic transition,
   2:291–292
demography, 2:293–294
depopulation, 2:301–302
population aging, 3:306
population control, 6:377–378
population growth, 6:378–379
population studies, 6:382
reproduction, 7:178–179
reproductive politics, 7:180–182
sexual selection theory, 7:479–480
social demography, 2:296–297
Fertility, land, 3:**130–132**
Fertility drugs, psychosocial issues,
   4:19–20
Fertility rate
education and, 6:57–60, *58, 60*
overpopulation, 6:96
The South, 5:542
total, 3:85
See also Human fertility
Fertilizers, 3:131–132, 377
Festinger, Leon, 3:**132–133**
Aronson, Elliot, 1:180
cognitive dissonance, 1:599–600
conformity, 2:72
dissonance theory, 9:136–137
Lewin, Kurt, 4:418
self-justification, 7:420–421

social comparison, 7:576, 577
Fetal rights, 1:4
Fetishism, 3:82
Feudal mode of production,
   3:**133–135**, 136, 9:126
class, 1:559
class conflict, 1:571
labor, 4:301
latifundia, 4:352–354
primitive communism, 2:37
transitional conjunctures, 2:77–78
Feudal rent, 3:133
Feudalism, 3:**135–136**
agricultural industry, 1:60
Anderson, Perry, 1:113
Chinese Revolution, 1:521
civil society, 1:552
class, 1:562
clientelism, 1:579
common land, 2:27
exploitation, 3:64, 65
French Revolution, 3:203
Hartz, Louis, 3:430
labor, 4:301
landlords, 4:345, 346
latifundia, 4:352–354
leaders, 4:376
leisure class, 1:565
Lenin, Vladimir Ilitch, 4:411
loans, 4:472
Magna Carta, 4:556
mobility, 5:209
peasantry, 6:195
servitude, 7:462
transitional conjunctures, 2:77–78
Feuerbach, Ludwig, 1:75, 2:34
*Fewer: How the New Demography of
   Depopulation Will Shape Our Future*
   (Wattenberg), 2:302
Feyerabend, Paul, 4:338, 339–340
Feynman, Richard P., 5:361
FHA (Federal Housing Authority),
   8:536, 9:53
Fiat money, 2:208–209, 5:251–252
Fichte, Johann Gottlieb, 1:359, 3:547,
   548
Fiction, 3:**136–137**
Alger, Horatio, 1:72
Arab, 1:161
as narratives, 5:371
naturalism, 5:442
science, 3:241
utopian, 8:561
War and Peace (Tolstoy), 9:20
See also Science fiction

Fiction, science. *See* Science fiction

Fiction, speculative. *See* Science fiction

Fictional characters, 3:137

Fictitious income, 3:98

Fiedler, Fred E., 4:379–380, 384

Field, Don, 8:9

Field theory, 4:417

Fields, Gary, 3:137–138

Fields' index of economic inequality, 3:**137–138**

Fieldwork
    cultural anthropology, 1:119
    ethnography, 3:14–16, 7:193

Fifteenth Amendment (U.S. Constitution), 8:651, 9:84

Fifty-three stages of the Tokaido (Hiroshige), 8:632

Figini, Paolo, 3:138

Figlio, David, 1:9

Figueroa v. Canada (2003), 3:309

FIH (Financial instability hypothesis). *See* Financial instability hypothesis

Fiji, East Indian diaspora and, 2:472, 473, 474

Filibuster, 3:**138–139**

Film industry, 3:**139–141**, 8:633
    Bamboozled (film), 1:243–245
    The Battle of Algiers (film), 1:257–258
    Battle of the Little Big Horn, 1:258–259
    Birth of a Nation (film), 1:304–306
    blackface, 1:327
    comic books, 2:24
    Disney, Walt, 2:409–410
    documentary studies, 2:434
    entertainment industry, 2:600–601, 602, 603
    Internet, 4:106–107
    law and order, 4:372
    Mafia, 4:552
    The Matrix (film), 5:31–32
    militarism, 5:165
    Robeson, Paul, 7:265
    Star Wars (film), 8:100–101
    stare, 8:101
    The Stepford Wives (film), 8:134–135
    totalitarianism, 8:296
    video industry, 8:310
    video technology, 8:309

Filmmakers, independent, 3:140–141

Filter theory. *See* Marriage

Final solution. *See* Holocaust

Finance, 3:**141–143**
    bid-ask spreads, 8:69–70
    capital flight, 1:434–436
    conditionality, 2:65
    discounted present value, 2:385–386
    initial public offering, 4:38–39
    international economics, 2:508–509, 4:92–94
    investment, 4:130–133
    investors, 4:133–134
    lender of last resort, 4:409–410
    leverage, 4:415–416
    loan pushing, 4:469–471
    loans, 4:472–473
    Minsky, Hyman, 5:193–194
    money, 5:251–252
    money laundering, 5:263
    Mundell-Fleming model, 5:335–336
    personal
        life-cycle hypothesis, 4:441–443
        metropolitan regions, 7:134
    Ponzi schemes, 6:368–369
    risk, 7:251
    risk neutrality, 7:254
    risk-return tradeoff, 7:255–256
    risk takers, 7:254–255
    rotating savings and credit associations, 7:286–287
    Rothschilds, 7:289
    Samuelson, Paul A., 7:318–319
    selling long and selling short, 7:432–433
    settlement, 7:464
    signals, 7:507–508
    speculation, 8:54–56
    spread, 8:68–69
    structural adjustment, 8:176–178
    yield, 9:164–166
    See also Microfinance

Finance, functional. *See* Keynesian economics

Finance, public, 3:**143–145**
    central banks, 1:480
    conservatism, 2:85
    consumption, 2:106, 108
    contraception, 2:114
    corporations, 2:140
    corporatism, 2:140, 141
    corruption, 2:144, 145
    cost-benefit analysis, 2:150–151
    cultural rights, 2:197
    development economics, 2:345

economic growth, 2:486–487

import substitution, 3:593

macroeconomics, 4:542

metropolitan regions, 7:134

offshore, 6:30, 32

public economics, 2:529–530

Ricardian equivalence, 7:241

sports industry, 8:66

Finance and Growth: Theory and Evidence (Levine), 1:253

Finance Capital (Hilferding), 1:446, 3:476

Financial capital. *See* Money

Financial crises. *See* Economic crises

Financial economics. *See* Finance

Financial instability hypothesis, 3:**145–146**
    beauty contest metaphor, 1:269
    business cycle theories, 1:410–412
    casino capitalism, 1:455–456
    economic depression, 2:304
    lender of last resort, 4:410

Financial markets, 3:**146–148**
    banking, 1:250
    beauty contest metaphor, 1:269
    bubbles (economics), 1:378–379
    bull and bear markets, 1:385–386
    capital controls, 1:433
    casino capitalism, 1:455
    central banks, 1:478–479, 480
    development economics, 2:345
    efficient market hypothesis, 2:548–549
    hedging, 3:450
    institutional investors, 4:135–136
    interest rates, 4:83–86
    investment, 4:131–132
    investors, 4:133–134
    Kindleberger, Charles Poor, 4:267
    liquidity, 4:459
    Lombard Street, 4:485
    market clearinghouse, 4:602–603
    market correction, 4:603–604
    market fundamentals, 4:605–606
    Minsky, Hyman, 5:193–194
    money, 5:252
    random walk, 7:61–63
    rentier class, 1:566–567
    selling long and selling short, 7:432–433
    Soros, George, 8:31
    spot market, 8:67–68
    stocks, 8:150–151, 151–153, 155–156
    Tobin, James, 8:378–379

transaction taxes, 8:427–428
  Wall Street, 9:7–9
Financial networks, 5:476
Financial Services Modernization Act
  (U.S. 1999), 1:253
Financial statements, 6:72–73
Finches, 2:228
Findlay, Ronald, 5:546
Fines. *See* Punishment
Fingerprints, 3:248
Finite Mixture Models (McLachlan and
  Peel), 1:586
Finite state grammar, 1:528
Finkbine, Sherri, 1:3
Finland
  codetermination, 1:593
  neutral states, 5:488
  voting rights, 3:185
Finnis, John, 4:365
Fiorina, Morris, 1:548
*Firefighters Local Union No. 1784 v.
  Stotts* (1984), 3:373, 6:671
Firms, 3:**148–149**
  data envelopment analysis, 2:240
  enterprise, 2:599
  national income accounts, 5:400
  skills specific to, 5:515
  statistical discrimination,
    2:396–398
  transaction cost, 8:427
  See also Corporations
First Amendment (U.S. Constitution),
  1:18
First Carib War (1772-1773),
  3:257–258
First Gulf War (1990-1991). *See* Gulf
  War of 1991
First New Deal (1933-1934), 5:493,
  494
First-order autoregressive serial
  correlation, 3:287
First-past-the-post, 2:561, 3:**149–150**,
  8:655
First-price sealed bid auctions,
  1:206–207
First wave feminism, 3:119–120,
  9:112–113, 116
  See also Women's suffrage
First world. *See* Developed countries
Firth, Raymond, 3:162–163
Fiscal policy, 6:**291–293**
  balance of payments, 1:238–240
  business cycles, 1:403
  capital flight, 1:434
  decentralization, 2:250

democratic centralism, 2:286
  employment, 2:583
  happiness, 3:418
  health economics, 3:441
  Keynes, John Maynard,
    4:259–262
  Lucas, Robert E., Jr., 4:510
  Lucas critique, 4:511
  macroeconomics, 4:542
  monetarism, 5:242–243
  moral suasion, 5:283
  political business cycles, 1:406
  real business cycles, 1:408
  Ricardian equivalence, 7:241
  Treasury view, 8:444–445
*Fiscal Sociology and the Theory of
  Public Finance* (Wagner), 3:144
Fischer, Claude, 5:476, 478
Fishbein, Martin, 3:403
Fisher, Franklin, 1:529
Fisher, Irving, 3:**150–152**, 5:261
  carrying cost, 1:449
  casino capitalism, 1:455
  economic depression, 2:303
  Frisch, Ragnar, 3:221
  Lagrange multipliers, 4:334
  lender of last resort, 4:410
  mathematical economics, 5:24
  neutrality of money, 5:490
  price indices, 6:447
  quantity index, 6:658
  quantity theory of money, 6:660
  real rate of interest, 4:81–82
  test statistics, 8:331, 332
  time preference, 8:369
Fisher, Mark E, 5:490
Fisher, Ronald Aylmer, 5:526, 7:590
Fisher, Sethard, 4:299
Fisher diagram, 3:151
Fisher equation. *See* Real rate of
  interest
Fisher ideal indexes, 5:398
Fishing, excessive. *See* Overfishing
Fishing industry, 3:**152–154**, 6:91–92,
  92
Fishkin, James, 2:285
Fiske, Donald W., 1:426, 5:530
Fisson, nuclear, 9:48, 52
Fitness, reproductive. *See* Sociobiology
Fitzgerald, Ella, 4:177
Fitzgerald, Ross, 5:454
Fitzpatrick, Frank, 3:301
*Five Families: Mexican Case Studies in
  the Culture of Poverty* (Lewis),
  1:134, 2:206, 4:418

Five Lectures on Psychoanalysis (Freud),
  3:211
Fixed capital. *See* Capital
Fixed coefficients production function,
  3:*154*, **154–155**, 8:601
Fixed effects regression, 3:**155–156**,
  7:58–59
Fixed exchange rates, 3:112
Fixed factor, returns to. *See* Returns to
  a fixed factor
Fixed-income securities. *See* Bonds
Fixed prices, aggregate demand, 1:50
Flags, 6:344–345
Flanagan, Scott C., 1:82
Flannery, Kent, 1:168
Flash, Grandmaster. *See* Grandmaster
  Flash
Flashbacks, 1:146
Flat taxes, 8:285
Flatt, Lester, 1:341
Flaubert, Gustave, 5:442, 7:92
Flavin, Marjorie, 2:110
Flavor industry, 8:583–584
Fleischmann, Robert David, 3:299
Fleming, J. Marcus, 5:335–336
Flex time, 9:129
Flexibility, 3:**156–157**, 218
Flexible pricing. *See* Price
  discrimination
Flexible specialization. *See* Just in time
  manufacturing (JIT)
Flexner, Abraham, 7:634
Flight, capital. *See* Capital flight
Flight behavior, 6:123
FLN (National Liberation Front),
  1:139, 140, 257–258, 8:613–614,
  625–626
FLO (Fair Trade Labelling
  Organisation), 1:247
Float, dirty. *See* Dirty float
Floating world, 8:632
Flood, Merrill, 6:473
Flooding (Psychology). *See*
  Psychotherapy
Floods, 5:432–434
  See also Natural disasters
Flores, City of Boerne v. (1997), 1:496,
  535–536
Flores, Guillermo, 2:15
Florida
  Bush, George W., 1:399
  Confederate States of America,
    2:66
  Cuban immigrants, 2:187
  Latin American immigrants, 3:571
  Osceola, 6:81–82

Flow, 3:**157–158**
  circular, 5:400, *400*
  saving rate, 7:334
  two-sided, 5:400–401
Flow, circular. *See* Quesnay, François
Flower industry, 3:**158–159**, 375
Flows (Economics). *See* Stocks and
  flows
Floyd, Jay, 7:271
FLP (Front de Libération du Quebec),
  6:662
FLSA (Fair Labor Standards Act) (U.S.
  1938). *See* Fair Labor Standards Act
  (FLSA) (U.S. 1938)
Flying saucers. *See* Unidentified flying
  objects (UFOs)
Flynn, James, 3:159–161
Flynn effect, 3:**159–161**
FmHA (Farmer's Home
  Administration), 2:341
fMRI (Functional magnetic resonance
  imaging), 5:483–484, 485
Foco insurgency, 3:395
Focus on the Family, 3:96
Fogel, Robert, 1:502, 2:592,
  3:**161–162**, 7:54
  cliometrics, 1:582
  North, Douglass, 5:539
  Time on the Cross, 4:366–367
Foggy Mountain Boys (musical
  group), 1:341
FOIA. *See* Freedom of Information
  Act (U.S. 1966)
Folk arts, 8:632–633
Folk culture, 3:192
  Black Arts Movement, 1:309
  Harlem Renaissance, 3:426
  Hurston, Zora Neale, 3:526, 527,
    528
Folk customs. *See* Culture; Tradition
Folk music, 9:142
Folk psychology. *See* Theory of mind
Folklore. *See* Ethnology and folklore
Folkman, Susan, 2:129
FOMC (Federal Open Market
  Committee), 3:111, 380
Foner, Philip, 9:126
Fonseca, Carlos, 7:235
Fontainebleau Memorandum, 1:152
Food, 3:**162–164**
  banana industry, 1:245–247
  Boserup, Ester, 1:357, 358
  caste, 1:459
  classical conditioning, 1:572–573
  Columbus, Christopher, 2:21

conundrum, 2:116
cooperatives, 2:123–124
cultural distinctions, 2:413
Green Revolution, 3:164–165
limits of growth, 4:448
malnutrition, 4:567–568
Malthusian trap, 4:572–573
peanut industry, 6:188–189
Sambo, 7:313–314
symbols, 8:250
taboos, 8:259
urban sprawl, 8:540
Food and Agriculture Organization
  (FAO), 1:246
Food and Drug Administration, U.S.
  (FDA). *See* U.S. Food and Drug
  Administration (FDA)
Food consumption, 3:377
Food crisis, 3:163, **164–165**
Food cues, 6:3
Food diplomacy, 3:**165–166**
Food Guide Pyramid, 5:551
Food safety, 1:58, 3:164, 165
Food stamps, 4:118, 119
Food supply
  agricultural industry, 1:59–60
  globalization, 3:163–164
  surplus, 1:62
Foot, Michael, 4:327
Foot-and-mouth disease, 1:471
For the New Intellectual (Rand), 6:8
Forbes, H. D., 2:112
Force, military. *See* War
Force (violence). *See* Violence
Force Acts (U.S. 1870-1871), 4:294
Forced labor camps. *See* Concentration
  camps
Forces, organization theory, 6:70, 71
Forces of production, 3:**166–167**
Ford, Gerald R., 5:506
  Carter, Jimmy, 1:451
  Central Intelligence Agency, U.S,
    1:484
  impeachment, 3:585
  law and order, 4:370
  Republican Party (U.S.), 7:187
  urban renewal, 8:537
  wage and price controls, 9:3
  War on Poverty, 9:28
  Warren Report, 9:33
  Watergate, 9:43
Ford, Harold, Jr., 6:344
Ford, Henry, 1:217–218, 3:167,
  8:287, 299
  division of labor, 2:424, 425

mass production, 3:77
Ford, Henry, II, 3:168
Ford, Thomas, 2:295
Ford, William, Jr., 3:169
Ford Foundation, 3:184, 9:27
Ford Motor Company, 1:217–221,
  223, 3:**167–169**
  mass production, 8:287–288
  technological change, 1:490
Ford of Europe, 3:169
Fordham, Signithia, 6:34
  acting white, 1:17
  oppositional culture, 6:48
Fordice, United States v. (1992), 6:650
Fordism, 8:287–288, 365
  See also Ford, Henry
Forecasting. *See* Autoregressive models;
  Prediction
Foreign-born workers, occupational
  hazards, 6:22
Foreign direct investment (FDI). *See*
  Foreign investment
Foreign-exchange market, 3:146
  See also Exchange rates
Foreign exchange rates. *See* Exchange
  rates
Foreign investment, 1:402
  business, 1:402
  Chinese diaspora, 1:518
  corporations, 2:140
  corruption, 2:145
  decentralization, 2:250–251
  divestiture, 2:421
  enterprise, 2:599
  liquidity premium, 4:460–461
  loan pushing, 4:469–471
  loans, 4:473
  rural development, 2:342
  structuralist macroeconomics,
    4:544
  technology transfer, 8:309
  trade deficit, 8:416
  trade liberalization, 4:428
Foreign labor. *See* Migrant labor
Foreign policy, 3:**169–172**
  alliances, 1:78–81
  analysis, 3:169–170
  appeasement, 1:152–154
  Ben-Gurion, David, 1:283
  capital controls, 1:432
  Castro, Fidel, 1:466–467
  Central Intelligence Agency, U.S,
    1:484
  Chamberlain, Neville, 1:489
  Cold War, 2:4

Conservative Party (U.K.), 2:87
Cuba, 2:186–187
  defense, 2:257–259
  food diplomacy, 3:165–166
  imperialism, 3:586–589
  internationalism, 4:102
  isolationism, 4:160–161
  jingoism, 4:201–202
  Kissinger, Henry, 4:274–275
  Latinos, 4:360
  League of Nations, 4:385
  Monroe Doctrine, 5:272
  neoconservatism, 5:469
  Nixon, Richard M., 5:505–506
  non-alignment, 5:513
  political realism, 7:96–97
  Thatcher, Margaret, 8:335
  Tito, Josip, 8:376
  Truman, Harry S., 8:459
  unilateralism, 8:509–510
  Vatican, 8:594
  vindication movements, 8:619
  See also Diplomacy; International
    relations
Foreign relations. *See* International
  relations
Foreign reserves, 7:**202–203**
  central banks, 1:478
  currency appreciation and
    depreciation, 2:210
  currency devaluation and
    revaluation, 2:211–212
  monetary base, 5:245
*Foreign Trade Regimes and Economic
  Development: India* (Bhagwati and
  Srinivasan), 1:293
Foreman, George, 1:74
Foresight, perfect, 3:**172–174**
Forests, 2:262–264
Forfeiture. *See* Confiscation
Forgiveness, 7:110–111
Form, William, 2:59
Formal authority, 1:215
Formal demography. *See* Demography
Formal rationality, 6:68
Formal volunteerism, 8:641–642
Forman, James, 3:**174–175**
Formation, racial, 3:**175–176**,
  548–550, 575
Formation, social, 3:**176–178**
Formative models, latent variables,
  8:585
Forms of Talk (Goffman), 3:338
Formulas, 3:**178–180**
Forrester, Jay, 3:241, 4:494

Forten, James, 1:311
Fortress Falklands policy, 3:81
Fortunati, Leopoldina, 1:447
Forum (newspaper), 1:237
Forward and futures markets,
  3:**180–182**
  carrying cost, 1:449–450
  central banks, 1:479
  cobweb cycles, 1:591
  coffee industry, 1:594
  contango, 2:112
  cotton industry, 2:152, 153
  description, 3:142
  hedging, 3:450
  nonrenewable natural resources,
    5:438
  transitional conjunctures, 2:77–78
Fosdick, Raymond, 4:527
Fossil fuels, 5:437–438, 6:359
Fossils, 1:118
Foster, George, 1:130, 4:290
Foster, Susan Leigh, 2:224
Foster, Vincent, 1:580
Foster, William T., 8:488
Foucault, Michel, 3:**182–183**
  bourgeoisie, 1:361
  capitalist mode of production,
    1:447
  constructivism, 2:97
  Davis, Angela, 2:243
  deviance, 2:353
  discourse, 1:129, 2:387
  gaze, 3:263
  governmentality, 3:361–362
  Habermas, Jürgen, 3:401
  hermeneutics, 3:464
  humanism, 3:518
  liberalism, 4:425
  linguistic turn, 4:457
  madness, 4:549
  modernity, 5:231
  objectivity, 6:11
  Oedipus complex, 6:29
  otherness, 6:83
  panoptic gaze, 3:262
  postmodernism, 6:395, 396
  poststructuralism, 6:398, 399
  power, 6:414
  resistance, 7:209
  sanitation, 7:323
  social values, 8:582
  sovereignty, 8:38
  violence, 8:623
Foundation Center, 3:184

Foundations, charitable, 3:**183–185**,
  4:96–99, 134
The Foundations of Capitalism (Cox),
  2:158
*The Foundations of Econometric
  Analysis* (Hendry and Morgan), 2:3
Foundations of Economic Analysis
  (Samuelson), 2:48, 7:318
Foundations of Social Theory
  (Coleman), 8:7
*The Foundations of the Nineteenth
  Century* (Chamberlain), 1:185
The Fountainhead (Rand), 6:7
Four-field anthropology, 1:116–122,
  124
Four Little Girls (film), 1:243
Fourier, Charles, 7:636–637, 8:561
Fourier, Joseph, 3:378
Fourteenth Amendment (U.S.
  Constitution)
  abortion, 1:4
  Bill of Rights, 1:298
  equal protection clause, 8:652,
    9:84
  judicial activism, 1:19
  naturalization, 5:444
  Supreme Court decisions, 9:33
  white primary, 9:84
*The Fourth Great Reawakening and the
  Future of Egalitarianism* (Fogel),
  3:162
Fourth Reich, 1:186
Fourth World Conference on Women,
  3:275
Fox, Richard A. Jr., 1:259
Fox, Richard G., 1:134
Fox Quesada, Vicente, 6:158, 159
Fractals, 1:492
Fractionalization, ethnic. *See* Ethnic
  fractionalization
A Fragment on Government (Bentham),
  1:285
Frame Analysis (Goffman), 3:338
Framing effects, 2:252
France
  administrative law, 1:23
  Algeria, 8:625–626
  American Revolution, 1:104
  annexation of Madagascar, 1:115
  anticolonial movements, 1:139,
    140
  architecture, 1:170
  aristocracy, 1:174
  banking industry, 1:251
  The Battle of Algiers (film),
    1:257–258

France, *continued*

blue collar and white collar, 1:340

Bourdieu, Pierre, 1:358–359

bubbles (economics), 1:378

burial grounds, 1:393

Burke, Edmund, 1:396

centrism, 1:488

Church and state, 1:536

cliometrics, 1:583

coffee industry, 1:594

colonialism, 1:358, 359, 3:406–408, 568

common market, 2:28–29

concentration camps, 2:63

Condorcet, Marquis de, 2:66

confiscation, 2:69

Congress of Vienna (1814-1815), 9:145

conservatism, 2:83, 84

conspicuous consumption, 2:89

correspondence tests, 2:142

dance, 2:224–225

De Gaulle, Charles, 2:264–265

decentralization, 2:250

decolonization, 2:256, 257

democratic centralism, 2:286

desegregation, 2:315

dirigiste, 2:374

divine right, 2:421–422

engineering education, 2:594

equal opportunity education, 2:612

fascism, 3:103

feudal mode of production, 3:134

feudalism, 3:136, 203

fishing industry, 3:152

immigrants, 8:539

integration, 4:62–63

Jacobinism, 4:164–165

Jefferson, Thomas, 4:181

Jewish diaspora, 4:191

Jews, 4:195, 196

judiciary, 4:227–228

Lafargue, Paul, 4:329, 330

laissez-faire, 4:335

Law, John, 4:366

Le Duc Tho, 4:398

Lefebvre, Henri, 4:400

left and right, 4:401–402

left wing, 4:402–403

monarchism, 5:237

Napoléon Bonaparte, 5:363–366

national debt, 5:386

Native Americans, 5:426

NATO, 5:544–546

neocolonialism, 5:467–468

petty bourgeoisie, 1:362

physiocracy, 6:266–267

Quebecois movement, 6:661

Quesnay, François, 6:666–667

racism, 7:45

resistance, 7:208

right wing, 7:247

schools, 8:11

social history, 3:482

socialism, 7:636–637

state enterprise, 8:106–107

Suez crisis, 5:376–377, 8:213–214

tariffs, 2:133–134

technotopia, 8:312–313

Turgot, Jacques, 8:466–467

unemployment compensation, 2:49

urban riots, 8:539

Vietnam War, 8:612–613

voting rights, 3:185

World War I, 9:145–147

World War II, 9:148–149

X-Crise, 9:157–158

xenophobia, 9:161

See also French Revolution

Franchise, 3:**185–186**

elections, 2:560–562

history, 8:646

polyarchy, 6:366

Supreme Court decisions, 9:84–85

white primary, 9:83–85

women, 3:120

See also Voting Rights Act (U.S. 1965)

Franciso Villa ante la historia (Herrera), 8:617

Franco, Francisco, 3:**186–187**

anarchism, 1:112

Spanish Civil War, 8:43–44

Francophone Africa. *See* Africa

Frank, Andre Gunder, 3:**187–188**

capitalist mode of production, 1:447

dependency theory, 2:299

developing countries, 2:335–336

development economics, 2:345

industrialization, 3:621

latifundia, 4:353

metropolis-satellite model, 9:153

unequal exchange, 8:505

Wallerstein, Immanuel, 9:10

Frank, Robert H., 2:108, 110, 9:15

Frank, Thomas, 9:168

Frankenberg, Ruth, 9:87

Frankfurt School, 1:424, 3:**188–189**

alienation, 1:75

capitalist mode of production, 1:446–447

class consciousness, 1:572

constructivism, 2:97

critical theory, 2:176–178

culture, 2:203

Fromm, Erich, 3:222–223

Habermas, Jürgen, 3:401

Hegel, Georg Wilhelm Friedrich, 3:453

political psychology, 6:309

praxis, 6:421–422

schools in sociology, 8:11

Frankl, Viktor, 2:63

Franklin, Benjamin, 3:**190–191**

charitable foundation, 3:183

cooperatives, 2:123

Declaration of Independence, U.S., 2:254

journalism, 4:212

political cartoons, 1:452

war, 9:18

Fraser, Nancy, 3:454, 9:132

Frasier, Mary M., 3:317

Fraternal organizations, 6:21

Fraud

bubbles (economics), 1:379

Castaneda, Carlos, 1:456–457

corporate, 6:72–73

corruption, 2:143, 144

landlords, 4:346

whistle-blowers, 9:79–81

Frazier, E. Franklin, 1:324, 3:**191–193**

black middle class, 1:313

Herskovits, Melville J., 3:467

Myrdal, Gunnar, 1:93

urban studies, 8:541

Williams, Eric, 9:97

Frazier, James, 1:119

Freakonomics (Dubner and Levitt), 2:326, 3:21–22

Frederick II, 8:635

Free coloreds, Haiti, 3:406–408

Free economy. *See* Market economy

Free enterprise. *See* Market economy

Free exercise clause (U.S. Constitution), 1:535–536

Free market economy. *See* Market economy

Free Officers, 5:376

Free rider, 3:**193–194**

collective action, 2:5–6, 6–7

common land, 2:28

cultural group selection, 2:191–192

multilateralism, 5:321

rational choice theory, 7:75

Free Soil Party, 7:186

Free speech. *See* Freedom of speech

Free Speech Coalition, Ashcroft v. (2002), 6:13

Free trade, 3:**194–196**

  Bentham, Jeremy, 1:286

  Bhagwati, Jagdish, 1:293

  bilateral trade, 8:414–415

  Corn Laws, 2:133–134

  customs union, 2:215

  environmental impact, 8:506

  European Union, 3:24

  exports, 3:68

  GATT, 3:281–282

  Hamilton, Alexander, 3:414

  international economics, 2:507–508

  labor, 4:302

  laissez-faire, 4:335

  Liberal Party (U.K.), 4:423, 424

  NAFTA, 3:196, 5:540–541

  Rand, Ayn, 6:8

  School of Lausanne, 4:362

  social costs, 8:506

  Tobin, James, 8:379

  unequal exchange, 8:505–506

  unilateralism, 8:510

Free will, 1:121, 3:196

Freed slaves, 8:618, 646

Freedom, 3:**196–200**

  academic, 1:105–106, 8:532

  Benedict, Ruth, 1:282

  Bill of Rights, 1:297–298

  bureaucracy, 1:391

  Burke, Edmund, 1:396–397

  cities, 1:540

  citizenship, 1:543

  civil liberties, 1:546–547, 548

  civilization, 1:557

  constitutions, 2:95

  critical theory, 2:176, 177, 178

  Declaration of Independence, U.S., 2:254–255

  development in sociology, 2:348

  economic, 2:372–374, *373*

  egalitarianism, 2:550

  intellectual, 6:8

  laissez-faire, 4:335–338

  liberalism, 4:425

  liberation, 4:428–430

  libertarianism, 4:437–439

  liberty and, 4:439, 440, 441

  natural rights, 5:439

  Rand, Ayn, 6:8

  Rawls, John, 7:84–85

  reactance theory, 7:85–86

  republicanism, 7:188

  state of nature, 8:110–111

  technophobia, 8:311

  from threat, 5:412

  tyranny of the majority, 8:478–479

Freedom, degrees of. *See* Degrees of freedom

Freedom Charter (ANC 1956), 1:42, 148

Freedom of expression. *See* Freedom of speech

Freedom of Information Act (U.S. 1966), 3:**201**, 8:435

Freedom of religion, 1:531, 534–536, 4:180, 547

Freedom of speech

  censorship, 1:475–476

  children's rights, 1:512

  critical race theory, 2:174, 175

  harassment, 3:420

  political tolerance, 8:385–386

  racial slurs, 7:42

Freedom of the press

  censorship, 1:475

  conservatism, 2:84

  corruption, 2:144

  Defender, 1:501

  Hamilton, Alexander, 3:414

Freedom Party (Austria), 9:160

Freedom Quilting Bee, 2:125

Freedom Riders, 1:551–552, 2:75, 314–315

  See also Student Nonviolent Coordinating Committee (SNCC)

Freely floating exchange rates. *See* Exchange rates

Freeman, Derek, 5:47–48

Freeman, Douglas, 4:399, 400

Freeman, Linton, 5:476

Freeman, Walter, 4:475–476

Freemasons, 3:561, 562, 6:21

Frege, Gottlob, 4:481, 5:503

Freire, Paulo, 2:12, 214, 3:**201–202**

French, John, 1:359

French Canadians. *See* Quebecois movement

French Cliometric Association, 1:583

French Enlightenment. *See* Enlightenment

French Indochina War, 8:613

French Revolution, 3:**203–205**

  Bentham, Jeremy, 1:285

  Burke, Edmund, 1:396

  centrism, 1:488

  conservatism, 2:83

  feudalism, 3:136

  Jacobinism, 4:164

  Jefferson, Thomas, 4:181, 182

  left and right, 4:401

  left wing, 4:402–403, 403

  liberalism, 4:425

  liberation movements, 4:432

  liberty, 4:439

  Napoléon Bonaparte, 5:363–364

  nation, 5:379

  patriotism, 6:176

  rationalism, 7:77

  right wing, 7:247

  terrorism, 8:328

  Tocqueville, Alexis de, 8:382–383

Frente Negra Brasileira, 1:329

Frente Sandinista para la Liberación Nacional (FSLN). *See* Sandinistas

Frequency distributions, 3:**205–209**, 206*t, 207, 208*

  bootstrap method, 1:353–354

  classical statistical analysis, 1:576–577

  probability distributions, 6:491

Freshwater resources. *See* Water resources

Freud, Sigmund, 3:**209–216**

  anxiety, 1:145

  basic needs, 5:455

  behaviorism, 1:276

  child development, 1:507

  comedy, 2:22

  consciousness, 2:81

  critical theory, 2:176, 177

  developmental psychology, 2:350

  dreaming, 2:444–445

  emotion regulation, 2:572

  equilibrium, 2:622

  Frankfurt School, 3:188

  hermeneutics, 3:463

  Jung, Carl, 4:228, 229, 230

  Kinsey, Alfred, 4:270

  Kohlberg, Lawrence, 4:286

  masculinity studies, 5:5–6

Freud, Sigmund, *continued*
  memory, 5:74
  Moore, Barrington, 5:278
  narratives, 5:370
  Oedipus complex, 6:28–30
  paranoia, 6:129
  polytheism, 6:367
  self-hatred, 7:416
  stages of development, 8:78
  subjectivity, 8:198
  sublimate, 8:200
  symbols, 8:250
  taboos, 8:259
  trauma, 8:440
  violence, 8:627
  Weltanschauung, 9:78
Freyer, Hans, 3:496
Freyre, Gilberto, 2:282
Frictional unemployment, 3:225, 227, 8:498, 502
Fried, Joel, 6:93
Friedan, Betty, 3:121, 123, **216–217**
  gender roles, 3:268
  gender studies, 3:279
  NOW, 5:408–409
  women's liberation, 9:113
Friedman, Benjamin, 6:95
Friedman, David, 4:438
Friedman, Meyer, 6:223
Friedman, Milton, 3:**217–220**
  adaptive expectations, 1:20
  bank failures, 1:252
  Chicago School, 1:502
  conservatism, 2:85
  consumption function, 2:109, 110
  corporate strategy, 2:138
  dirigiste, 2:373
  economic depression, 2:304
  economic methodology, 2:492–493
  expectations, 3:48
  free trade, 3:196
  full employment, 3:226
  Galbraith, John Kenneth, 3:247
  Great Depression, 3:368, 370
  Harris, Abram L., Jr., 3:427
  imperfect competition, 2:52
  income, 5:456
  income maintenance experiments, 3:605–606
  Keynes, John Maynard, 4:261
  Keynesian economics, 2:512
  Koopmans, Tjalling, 4:288
  laissez-faire, 4:336, 337–338

libertarianism, 4:437, 438
life-cycle hypothesis, 4:442
liquidity, 4:459
long run, 4:492
monetarism, 5:242
money, 5:252
natural rate of unemployment, 5:435
neoclassical economics, 2:519
neoliberalism, 9:38
new classical economics, 2:523
permanent income hypothesis, 6:211–214
Phillips curve, 6:248
quantity theory of money, 6:660
racial discrimination, 2:395
risk takers, 7:255
rules *vs.* discretion, 7:293, 294
school vouchers, 7:348
Stigler, George Joseph, 8:144, 145
trade-offs, 8:419
unemployment, 8:503
War on Poverty, 9:28
Friedman, Stanton, 8:507
Friedmann, George, 6:649
The Friend of Man (Mirabeau). *See L'ami des hommes* (Mirabeau)
Friendliness, 9:123
Friendship, 3:**220–221**
  peer cliques, 6:197–198
  peer effects, 6:198–200
  peer influence, 6:201–202
  similarity/attraction theory, 7:513–514
  social cognitive map, 7:575–576
Friesen, W. V., 2:32, 33
Frisch, Ragnar, 1:412, 3:**222**, 4:287
Fritsvold, Erik D., 2:354
From Columbus to Castro (Williams), 9:98
From Is to Ought: How to Commit the Naturalistic Fallacy and Get Away with It (Kohlberg), 4:286
From Social History to the History of Society (Hobsbawm), 3:483
Fromm, Erich, 3:**223**
  critical theory, 2:176
  Frankfurt School, 3:189, 222–223
  needs, 5:453
  Oedipus complex, 6:29
Front de Libération du Quebec (FLP), 6:662
Frontier, production. *See* Production frontier

Frontier analysis, stochastic. *See* Stochastic frontier analysis
Fructose, 6:4
Fry, E., 2:142
Frye, Northrop, 5:371
Fryer, Roland, 1:17
FSLA (Frente Sandinista para la Liberación Nacional). *See* Sandinistas
FTC (Federal Trade Commission)
  consumer protection, 2:103
  imperfect competition, 2:53
  Nader's Raiders, 5:360–361
Fuel efficiency, 1:223
Fuentes, Marta, 3:187
Fugitive Slave Act (U.S. 1850), 1:315, 8:482
Fuhrman, Susan, 1:9
Fukuyama, Francis, 2:117, 7:109
Fulbright, William, 2:183, 8:614
Fulfillment, 5:452
Full capacity, 3:**224–225**
Full employment, 3:**225–228**
  central banks, 1:480
  conundrum, 2:116
  economic depression, 2:302
  full capacity, 3:224
  job guarantee, 4:205
  neutral rate of interest, 4:79
Full Employment and Balanced Growth Act (U.S. 1978), 3:227
Full Employment in a Free Society (Beveridge), 3:227
Fuller, Buckminster, 3:**228–230**
Fuller, Wayne, 1:228, 2:3
Function, consumption. *See* Consumption function
Function, cost. *See* Loss functions
Function, cumulative probability distribution. *See* Probability distributions
Function, loss. *See* Loss functions
Function, moment generating. *See* Moment generating function
Function, partial autocorrelation. *See* Time series regression
Function, production. *See* Production function
Function, survivor. *See* Duration models
Function, utility. *See* Utility function
Functional finance. *See* Keynesian economics
Functional form, 3:**230–231**
Functional genomics, 3:299

Functional magnetic resonance imaging (fMRI), 5:483–484, 485
Functionalism, 1:279, 3:**231–233**
   class, 1:561, 563
   class conflict, 1:571
   consciousness, 2:81
   cultural anthropology, 1:119
   Malinowski, Bronislaw, 1:127, 3:232
   material culture, 5:14
   Merton, Robert K., 5:102–103
   modernization, 5:232–233
   political sociology, 8:4
   post-Parsonian American sociology, 8:5–7
   Radcliffe-Brown, A. R., 7:47
   religion, 7:160
   schooling, 7:353–354
   social exclusion, 7:589
   sociology, 3:231
   sports, 8:63
Functionalism, structural. *See* Structural functionalism
Functionings, 3:**233–234**
Functions
   impulse-response, 8:599
   latent, 3:232
   manifest, 3:232
   objective, 6:5–6
   See also Production function
Fundamental attribution error (FAE), 1:206, 2:252, 5:452
Fundamental values. *See* Market fundamentals
Fundamentalism, 3:**234–236**
   Almond, Gabriel A., 1:82
   clash of civilizations, 1:559
   religiosity, 7:162–163
   secular, 7:378–379
Fundamentalism, Christian, 3:**236–237**
   anti-intellectualism, 4:65
   conservatism, 2:86
   contraception, 2:114
   corporal punishment, 2:135
   creationism, 2:162
   right wing, 7:248
   Scopes trial, 7:366
   Southern politics, 6:347, 348, 349
   Truth, Sojourner, 8:462
Fundamentalism, Islamic, 3:**237–238**
   bin Laden, Osama, 1:298–300
   domino theory, 2:436
   jihad, 4:196–197

Khomeini, Ayatollah Ruhollah, 4:263–264
   suicide bombers, 8:224–225
   Taliban, 8:262–263
   terrorism, 8:329
   theocracy, 8:343
Fundamentals, market. *See* Market fundamentals
Funding
   appropriations, 1:155
   contribution-based, 9:71
   national service programs, 5:414
   nongovernmental organizations, 5:520
   Social Security, 9:129
   welfare, 9:71–72
Funeral homes, 3:239
Funerals, 2:247–248, 3:**238–240**
Fungibility, 2:495, 8:267
Fusfield, Daniel, 2:182
Fusion, 2:85
Fusionists. *See* Populism
Futagami, Ritsuko, 1:287
Future consequences, consideration of, 8:368
The Future Lasts Forever (Althusser), 1:87
The Future of Intellectuals and the Rise of the New Class (Gouldner), 5:492
Future shock, 3:**240–241**
Future Shock (Toffler), 3:240
The Future Tasks of the Alliance, 5:544
Futures markets. *See* Forward and futures markets
Futurology, 3:**241–242**
   adaptive expectations, 1:19–20
   computers, 2:60–61
   perfect foresight, 3:172–174
   uncertainty, 8:481–482
FWP (Federal Writers Project), 3:528, 529
Fyffes, 1:245

G

G. D. Searle, 1:303
G7 countries, 3:**243–244**, 591, *591*
G8 countries, 3:243, **244**
   bourgeoisie, 1:361
   global warming, 3:329
G20 countries, 3:243
Gable, Clark, 3:347
Gabon, OPEC, 6:65
Gabriel, Peter, 9:142
Gabriel (Prosser), 3:**244–246**, 7:534, 535

GAD (Gender and development). *See* Gender and development (GAD)
Gadamer, Hans-Georg
   collective memory, 2:8
   constructivism, 2:96
   hermeneutics, 3:462, 463, 464
   linguistic turn, 4:457–458
   objectivity, 6:11
   Weltanschauung, 9:78
Gage, Thomas, 1:103
Gain-loss hypothesis, 1:181
Gainful worker framework, 8:500
Gains. *See* Profits
Gaitskell, Hugh, 2:87, 4:327
Galanter, Marc, 7:258
Galbraith, John Kenneth, 2:507, 3:**246–247**
   advertising, 1:28
   bureaucracy, 1:390
   consumption, 2:106, 108
   convergence theory, 2:117
   economic inequality, 9:47
   entrepreneurship, 2:605
   full employment, 3:226
   hidden persuaders, 3:473
   scarcity, 7:340
   University of Texas Inequality Project, 8:530
   want creation, 9:14
   War on Poverty, 9:25
Gale, David, 6:51
Galí, Jordi, 1:408
Galileo, 6:20, 8:532
Gallatin, Albert, 1:92
Gallet, Craig, 4:296
Gallows Humor, a Sociological Phenomenon (Obrdlik), 2:23
Gallup, George, 6:358
Gallup, Gordon, 4:495
Gallup poll, 8:638
   See also Pollsters
Galor, Oded, 6:93
Galtieri, Leopoldo, 3:81
Galton, Francis, 3:**247–248**
   blood and bloodlines, 1:335
   eugenics, 3:21
   human sterilization, 8:140–141
   leadership, 4:378
   measures of central tendencies, 1:487
   Mendel's law, 5:83
   nature *vs.* nurture, 5:446
   Pearson, Karl, 6:192, 193–194
   race and psychology, 7:21–22

Galton, Francis, *continued*
    regression, 4:393, 7:136, 138,
      141–142
    Standard Cross-Cultural Sample,
      8:88–93
    talent, 8:261
    twin studies, 8:473
Gambino family, 4:553
Gambling, 3:**248–250**
    Cherokees, 1:498
    crime and criminology, 2:172
    entertainment industry, 2:601
    lotteries, 4:502–504
    Native Americans, 5:428
Game theory, 3:**250–252**
    central banks, 1:479
    coalition theory, 1:587–588
    competition, 2:50
    constrained choice, 2:95
    conundrum, 2:116
    coordination failure, 2:127–128
    diplomacy, 2:371
    dirigiste, 2:374
    Hamilton's rule, 3:414–415
    imperfect competition, 2:53
    labor force participation, 4:316
    logic, 4:480
    mathematical economics, 5:24–25
    maximin principle, 5:38–39
    mechanism design, 5:58
    microeconomics, 5:135
    mixed strategy, 5:207–208
    mutual deterrence, 2:334
    Nash equilibrium, 5:373, *374,*
      374–375
    neuroeconomics, 5:483–484
    perfect competition, 2:57–58
    prisoner's dilemma, 6:471–474
    rationality, 7:81
    replicator dynamics, 7:169–170
    screening and signaling games,
      7:371–372
    social constructs, 7:579
    strategic behavior, 8:162–163
    strategic games, 8:163–164
    strategy and voting games,
      8:165–166
    subgame perfection, 8:193–194
    topology, 8:391
    zero-sum game, 9:176–177
Games
    collective action, 2:6–7
    common knowledge rationality,
      2:25–26

    cooperative, 3:250, 284–285,
      5:532–533
    dynamic, 3:32
    educational, 8:612
    evolutionary, 3:31–33
      Hamilton's rule, 3:415
      mixed strategy, 5:207–208
      replicator dynamics,
        7:169–170
    noncooperative, 5:517–518,
      532–533
    nonzero-sum, 5:532–533
    screening and signaling,
      7:371–372
    separation and pooling,
      7:371–372
    strategy and voting, 8:165–166
    two-play ultimatum, 5:483–484
    video, 1:249, 8:310, 611–612
    See also Olympic Games; Strategic
      games
Gamio, Manuel, 1:345
Gamma distribution. *See* Probability
    distributions
Gamson, William, 7:604
Gandhi, Feroze, 3:252
Gandhi, Indira, 3:**252–253**
    Congress Party, India, 2:76–77
    Indian National Congress, 3:612
    Janata Party, 4:170, 171
    Vajpayee, Atal Bihari, 8:569
Gandhi, Mahatma. *See* Gandhi,
    Mohandas K.
Gandhi, Mohandas K., 3:**253–255**
    African National Congress, 1:42
    anticolonial movements, 1:139
    Boer War, 1:350
    Bose, Subhas and Sarat, 1:356
    caste, 1:462, 463
    civil disobedience, 1:545
    civil rights movement, U.S., 1:551
    civilization, 1:558
    Congress of Racial Equality, 2:75
    Congress Party, India, 2:76
    East Indian diaspora, 2:473
    Hinduism, 3:480
    Indian National Congress, 3:611
    Jinnah, Mohammed Ali, 4:203,
      204
    King, Martin Luther, Jr., 4:268
    liberation, 4:429
    Nehru, Jawaharlal, 5:460
    Nyerere, Julius, 5:554
    passive resistance, 6:167
    Raj, 7:56

    resistance, 7:208
    Thoreau, Henry David, 8:357
Gandhi, Priyanka, 2:77
Gandhi, Rahul, 2:77
Gandhi, Rajiv, 2:77, 3:252, 253, 612
Gandhi, Sanjay, 3:252, 253
Gandhi, Sonia, 2:77, 3:253, 612
Ganja. *See* Marijuana
Gans, Herbert J., 1:540, 3:**255–256**
    gemeinschaft, 3:267
    low and high culture, 2:204, 205
Gaon, Vilna, 3:323
Garbarino, Merwyn S., 1:136
Garber, Peter, 2:212
GARCH (Generalized Autoregressive
    and Conditional Heteroscedastic)
    models. *See* Autoregressive models
Garcia, F. Chris, 4:354–356
Garcia, Jerry, 9:121
Garcia, John A., 4:354–356
Gardner, Gerald, 6:21
Gardner, Howard, 4:72, 5:326, 327,
    8:262
Garegnani, Piero, 1:419, 420
Garfinkel, Harold, 2:98, 3:403
    conversational analysis, 2:118, 119
    ethnomethodology, 3:19
    gender, 3:268
    interpretive anthropology, 3:265
    linguistic anthropology, 1:129
    post-Parsonian American
      sociology, 8:7
Garifuna, 3:**256–257**
Garinagu. *See* Garifuna
Garland, Judy, 9:104
Garment industry. *See* Textile industry
Garmezy, Norman, 7:205
Garner, Catherine, 5:461–462
Garner, John H., 7:283
Garrett, Henry E., 1:186
Garrison, James, 9:34
Garrison, William Lloyd, 2:439, 5:383
Garvey, Marcus, 3:**258–259**
    back to Africa movement, 1:41
    black nationalism, 1:315–316
    Black Power, 1:320, 321, 322
    blackness, 1:330
    colorism, 2:18
    diaspora, 2:356
    Harlem, 3:424
    Harris, Abram L., Jr., 3:427
    Nation of Islam, 5:379
    Nkrumah, Kwame, 5:506–507
    Rastafari, 7:66–67

Williams, Eric, 9:97

Garza, Rodolfo de la, 4:354–356

Gas, natural. *See* Natural gas

Gasoline additives, 5:540

Gates, Bill, 5:142–143

Gates, Henry Louis Jr., 1:309

Gates, Robert, 3:394

GATT 1994 (General Agreement of Tariffs and Trade), 3:243–244, **281–282**

Gauchos, 1:470

Gaudet, Helen, 1:202

Gaullism. *See* De Gaulle, Charles

Gauss, Carl Friedrich
  measurement, 5:54
  measures of central tendencies, 1:487
  normal distribution, 2:416, 9:182
  ordinary least squares, 4:392–393, 6:60

Gauss linear model, 8:49*t*

Gauss-Markove theorem, 5:521, 522

Gaussian distribution. *See* Normal distribution

Gautama, Siddhārtha. *See* Buddha

Gauthier, David, 6:256

Gautreaux residential mobility program, 3:**259–260**, 5:303

Gay, lesbian, transgender, and bisexual politics, 6:**329–332**
  blackness, 1:330
  civil rights movement, U.S., 1:552
  critical race theory, 2:175
  deviance, 2:353–354
  left wing, 4:403
  queer studies, 6:663–665
  reproduction, 7:179
  same-sex marriage, 4:619–621
  sexual orientation, 7:479
  women's movement, 3:269

Gay, Peter, 8:636

Gayle v. Browder (1956), 2:615

Gays. *See* Gay, lesbian, transgender, and bisexual politics; Sexual orientation

Gaza Strip
  Arab-Israeli War of 1967, 1:156–159
  Palestine Liberation Organization, 6:103–104
  Palestinian Authority, 6:104–107
  Palestinian diaspora, 6:108, 109
  Palestinians, 6:111–112
  Rabin, Yitzhak, 7:1

Gaze, 3:46–47, **263–265**, 8:101

Gaze, colonial, 2:121–122, 3:46–47, **260–262**, 264

Gaze, panoptic, 3:**262–263**

GCC (Gulf Cooperation Council), 3:397

GDI (Gender-Related Development Index), 3:278

GDN (Global Development Network), 9:139

GDP (Gross domestic product). *See* Gross domestic product (GDP)

GDR (German Democratic Republic). *See* East Germany

GEAR (Growth, Employment and Redistribution), 1:43

Gearing ratio, 1:571

Geary Act (U.S. 1892), 1:513, 3:579

Ged, William, 4:212

Geddes, Andrew, 9:72

Geertz, Clifford, 1:121, 3:**265–266**
  hermeneutics, 3:464
  interpretive anthropology, 1:122
  narratives, 5:371
  objectivity, 6:11
  symbols, 8:250, 252

Gegenstand, 6:9

Gehry, Frank, 1:172

Geiger, Theodor, 3:496

Gelera Genomics, 3:299

Gell, Monday, 8:609

Gellner, Ernest, 5:378–379

GEM (Gender-Empowerment Measure), 3:278

Gemayel, Bashir, 4:396, 397

Gemayel, Pierre, 6:236

Gemeinschaft und gesellschaft (Toennies), 3:**266–267**, 385

Gender, 3:**267–270**
  African sociology, 7:665–666
  biological, 3:268, 9:107–110
  Boserup, Ester, 1:357
  citizenship, 1:542–543
  civil rights, 1:549
  class, 1:563–564
  constructivism, 2:97
  cross-cultural comparison, 3:268–269
  development economics, 3:272–277
  divorce and separation, 2:427–428
  empathy, 2:574
  essentialism, 2:630, 631
  factory system, 3:79
  gentility, 3:301
  Gilded Age, 3:318

Hamilton's rule, 3:414–415

heredity, 3:460

heteronormativity, 3:470

Hite, Shere, 3:485

lateral mobility, 5:213

lying, 4:524

masculinity, 3:269, 5:1–4

maturation, 5:36

men, 5:80–81

mental health, 5:85

midlife crisis, 5:149–150

misogyny, 5:203–204

morbidity and mortality, 5:291

performance, 6:208

political theory, 6:318

poverty, 3:273–274

reproduction, 7:179

role models, 7:274

schooling, inequality, 7:351

sex and mating, 7:470–472

sex *vs.,* 9:116

sexual selection theory, 7:479

social constructs, 7:579

social history, 3:483

socialization, 7:648

Standard Cross-Cultural Sample, 8:90

transgender, 8:431–432

Gender, alternatives to binary, 3:**270–272**, 6:663

Gender and development (GAD), 2:348, 3:**272–277**

Gender bending, 3:269

Gender differences
  aggression, 1:55–56
  attachment, 6:29
  division of labor, 9:72
  feminism, 3:121
  friendship, 3:221
  Gilligan, Carol, 3:319–320
  natural selection, 5:440–441
  occupational status, 6:27
  political attitudes, 1:103
  voting patterns, 8:650
  wages, 6:1
  weight, 9:59
  See also Gender gap

Gender discrimination. *See* Gender gap

Gender-Empowerment Measure (GEM), 3:278

Gender equality
  education, 9:114–115
  employment, 9:114–115

Gender equality, *continued*
    gender gap *vs.,* 3:279
    gender mainstreaming, 3:275
    global, 3:270, 279
    macroeconomics, 3:275
Gender gap, 3:**277–279**
    age discrimination, 2:402
    American Sociological Association, 1:106
    architecture, 1:172
    audits, 1:208–210
    Blinder-Oaxaca decomposition technique, 1:333–334
    civil rights, 1:549
    correspondence tests, 2:141–143
    crowding hypothesis, 2:181–182
    curriculum, 2:214
    Davis, Angela, 2:243
    demography, 2:294
    as discrimination, 2:388–392, 389–390
    distributive justice, 4:240
    engineering, 2:593–594
    equal opportunity, 2:612
    equal protection, 2:615
    labor force participation, 4:315–316
    labor market segmentation, 4:319
    labor supply, 4:320–321
    liberation, 4:430
    naturalization, 5:444
    paid employment, 3:274–275
    political participation, 9:108–109, 110–111, 117
    qualifications, 6:649
    quotas, 6:670–671
    sexism, 7:473–474
    sexuality, 7:483
    Smeal, Eleanor, 5:409
    standardized tests, 8:97
    talent, 8:261
    taste for discrimination, 2:399
    unpaid employment, 3:274–275
    unpaid work, 9:123, 125
    wage discrimination, 2:181, 389–391, 399, 400–401, 402–403, 405–406
    wages, 9:4
    welfare state, 9:68
    women's movement, 9:117
    women's studies, 9:119
    women's work, 9:125–126
    work, 9:122–123
    work week, 9:128
    working class, 9:131–133

Gender identity
    advertising, 1:28
    femininity, 3:119
    gender bending, 3:269
Gender inequality, 3:**624–627**
    Blinder-Oaxaca decomposition technique, 1:333–334
    California Civil Rights Initiative, 1:416
    civil rights, 1:549
    clash of civilizations, 1:560
    correspondence tests, 2:141–143
    crowding hypothesis, 2:181–182
    curriculum, 2:214–215
    development in sociology, 2:348
    inegalitarianism, 3:624
    intersectionality, 4:114–115
    liberation, 4:430
    patriarchy, 6:173–174
    pimps, 6:271–273
    Sen, Amartya Kumar, 7:440–441
    sexism, 7:473–474
    sports, 8:65
    See also Gender gap
Gender mainstreaming, 3:275, 5:521
Gender oppression. *See* Gender inequality
Gender politics, 6:**332–334**
    Chisholm, Shirley, 1:522
    Mankiller, Wilma, 4:586
    Mill, John Stuart, 5:179
Gender preference, 6:**433–435**
Gender-Related Development Index (GDI), 3:278
Gender studies, 3:**279–281**
    dependency, 2:298
    empiricism, 2:579
    infidelity, 4:21
    intelligence, 4:73
    masculinity studies, 5:5–8
    post-Parsonian American sociology, 8:5–6
    primates, 6:461
Gender Trouble (Butler), 3:269
Gendered language, 3:258
Genders, multiple, alternatives, 3:270–272, 6:663
Gene-mapping, 3:299
General Agreement of Tariffs and Trade (GATT 1994), 3:243–244, **281–282**
    customs union, 2:215–216
    import promotion, 3:592
    international economic order, 4:93, 94

    peasant organizations, 6:75
    trade liberalization, 4:428
    Uruguay Round, 3:281–282, 8:548–549, *549*
    World Trade Organization, 9:143–144
General Allotment Act (U.S. 1887), 5:427
General Assembly (UN), 8:522–523
    Resolution 242, 1:159
    Resolution 1514, 8:524
    See also United Nations (UN)
General aviation, 1:232–233
General Electric, 2:356, 3:**282–283**
General equilibrium, 3:**283–285**
    Arrow, Kenneth J., 1:181–182
    Chicago School, 1:502
    cobweb cycles, 1:592
    Debreu, Gerard, 2:249
    Hicks, John R., 3:471–472
    Leontief, Wassily, 4:412–413
    long run, 4:491
    microeconomics, 5:134–135
    microfoundations, 5:141
    new classical economics, 2:522, 523
    optimal growth, 6:51, 52
    real business cycles, 1:408
    School of Lausanne, 4:362
    Uzawa, Hirofumi, 8:563
    Walras' law, 9:11–13
General fertility rate (GFR), 3:127
    See also Human fertility
General Laws Amendment Acts (South Africa 1960), 1:148
General Method of Moments (GMM), 5:522
General Motors, 1:218, 219, 220–221, 3:167, **285–286**, 8:516
General Revenue Sharing (GRS), 8:537
General Social Survey (GSS), 6:27
General systems theory. *See* Systems theory
General Theory of Employment, Interest and Money (Keynes), 3:145, 172–173, 200
    aggregate demand, 1:49–51
    aggregate demand and supply price, 1:51–52
    banana parable, 1:247–248
    beauty contest metaphor, 1:269
    carrying cost, 1:450
    casino capitalism, 1:455
    full employment, 3:225–226

involuntary unemployment, 4:137–138
IS-LM model, 4:158
Kahn, Richard F., 4:245
Keynes, John Maynard, 4:259, 261
Keynesian economics, 2:511
life-cycle hypothesis, 4:441
long run, 4:492
Lundberg, Erik, 4:518
macroeconomics, 4:541
market clearing, 4:601–602
national income accounts, 5:400
neutral rate of interest, 4:79
nominal wages, 5:512
own rate of interest, 4:80
post Keynesian economics, 2:528
subjective probability, 6:490
unemployment, 8:502
voluntary unemployment, 8:637
Z-D model, 9:172–173
A General Theory of Exploitation and Class (Roemer), 8:577
General-to-specific methodology, 3:230
Generalized anxiety disorder, 1:146
Generalized Autoregressive and Conditional Heteroscedastic (GARCH) models. *See* Autoregressive models
Generalized least squares (GLS), **3:286–291**
Generalized linear models (GLM), 3:289, 4:484–485
Generalized method of moments. *See* Method of moments
Generalized reciprocity. *See* Reciprocity
Generalized system of preferences, 9:143
Generating Inequality: Mechanisms of Distribution in the U.S. Economy (Thurow), 3:508
Generation X, 3:**291–292**
Generation X (Coupland), 3:292
Generations, Stolen (Australia). *See* Stolen Generations (Australia)
Generosity, 3:**292–294**
The Genesis Flood (Morris), 2:162
Genetic code, testing, 3:295
Genetic determinism, 2:**329–330**
    biological determinism, 2:325–326
    cultural group selection, 2:191–192
    Darwin, Charles, 2:229–232, 231*t*

environmental determinism, 2:327
eugenics, 3:21–22
intelligence, 7:21–23
IQ controversy, 4:139–142
nonadditive determinism, 2:331
slavery hypertension hypothesis, 7:546–547
See also Heredity
Genetic testing, 1:300, 301, 3:**294–296**, 7:178, 179
Genetics
    adolescent psychology, 1:24
    alpha-males, 1:84
    Alzheimer's disease, 1:89–90
    behavioral, 5:446
    biological anthropology, 1:126
    evolutionary, 3:352–353
    natural selection, 5:441
    See also Genetic determinism; Heredity
Genetics and the Origin of Species (Dobzhansky), 2:432
Genette, Gérard, 5:371
Geneva Accords, Vietnam War, 8:613
Geneva Conference (1954), 8:613
Geneva Convention (1929), 9:21
Geneva Convention on the Prevention and Punishment of the Crime of Genocide (1949), 3:512, 514, 9:21–22
Geneva Declaration 1924 (Declaration of the Rights of the Child), 1:512
Geneva Protocol (1925), 1:176, 9:52
Genocide, 3:**296–298**
    concentration camps, 2:63–64
    Darfur, 2:227
    ethnic conflict, 3:2
    ethnicity, 3:10
    Hitler, Adolf, 3:487–488
    human rights, 3:512
    humiliation, 3:522
    just war, 4:236
    Khmer Rouge, 4:262
    Killing Fields, 4:265
    Milosevic, Slobodan, 5:184
    Pol Pot, 6:289
    Roma, 7:279
    Rwanda, 3:298, 8:524
    Stalin, Joseph, 8:86
    United Nations role, 8:524
    violence, 8:624
    World War II, 9:150–151
    See also Holocaust
Genocide Convention. *See* Convention for the Prevention and

Punishment of the Crime of Genocide
Genomics, 3:295, **298–299**
    heredity, 3:461–462
    Mendel's law, 5:83
    race, 7:23
Genotype. *See* Heredity
Genovese, Eugene, 3:483, 6:277–278
Genteel. *See* Gentility
Gentile, Giovanni, 3:453
Gentility, 3:**300–302**
Gentrification, 3:**302–303**, 5:463–464
    Chinese diaspora, 1:517
    cities, 1:542
    Harlem, 3:424
    towns, 8:405
Gentz, Friedrich, 2:84
Geo-economics, 3:23
Geocoding, 4:465, 466
Geodesic domes, 3:228–229
Geographical information systems (GISs), 3:305
Geographically weighted regression (GWR), 3:305
Geography, 3:**303–306**
    Columbus, Christopher, 2:19–22
    constituency, 2:89
    Cook, James, 2:121–122
    cultural landscape, 2:192–193
    East Indies, 2:476
    economic, 7:130
    environmental determinism, 2:327, 328
    famine, 3:165
    human, 3:303–305, 7:130
    regions, 7:130–132
    spatial theory, 8:44–45
    topography, 8:389–390
    transitional conjunctures, 2:77
Geopolitics, 3:23, 304
George, David Lloyd, 1:152
George, Henry, 4:346, 5:419, 7:164
George, Lloyd, 1:537
George Mason University, 4:439
Georgia, Cherokee Nation v. (1831), 1:497
Georgia, Coker v. (1977), 7:65
Georgia, Worcester v. (1832), 1:497
Georgia (country)
    commonwealth, 2:30
    nationalism, 5:418
Georgia (U.S. state)
    Cherokees, 1:497
    Confederate States of America, 2:66

Georgia v. Ashcroft (2003), 8:653

Gerard, Harold, 2:72, 7:597–598

Geras, Norman, 4:523

Gerber, Theodore, 8:534

Gerhardt, Michael, 3:585

Geriatrics. *See* Gerontology

Germ warfare. *See* Biological weapons; Bioterrorism

German Civil Code, 4:405

German Democratic Republic (GDR). *See* East Germany

German History in the Nineteenth Century (Treitschke), 2:84

The German Ideology (Marx and Engels), 1:187, 571, 2:324, 3:82, 559, 4:430

German Social Democratic Party, 6:36, 38

Germans, in Poland, 5:418

Germany
    administrative law, 1:23
    annexation of Austria, 1:115, 153
    appeasement, 1:152–153
    Aryans, 1:185–186, 3:335–336
    Austria annexation, 1:115
    automobile industry, 1:221
    banking industry, 1:252
    Berlin Wall, 1:289
    blood and bloodline, 1:336
    blue collar and white collar, 1:340
    Boer War, 1:349
    Bush, George H. W., 1:398
    central banks, 1:477
    Chamberlain, Neville, 1:489
    Churchill, Winston, 1:537–538
    city-state, 1:544
    cliometrics, 1:582
    cobweb cycles, 1:591
    codetermination, 1:593
    coffee industry, 1:594
    Cold War, 2:4, 5
    collective memory, 2:8
    common market, 2:28–29
    concentration camps, 2:63
    Congress of Vienna (1814-1815), 9:145
    conservatism, 2:83–84
    corporations, 2:140
    corporatism, 2:140
    Cuban Missile Crisis, 2:184
    dictatorship, 2:359
    Drang nach Osten, 9:145–146
    ethnic conflict, 3:2
    euthanasia and assisted suicide, 3:28
    fascism, 3:104
    ghettos, 3:312
    Great Depression, 3:367, 368, 369–370, 5:449, 9:148
    humanism, 3:517
    Illuminati, 3:561
    interwar years, 4:121
    judiciary, 4:227, 228
    Kuznets hypothesis, 4:295, 296
    latifundia, 4:353
    militarism, 5:164
    Molotov-Rubbentrop Pact (1939), 9:149
    Napoleonic Wars, 5:365
    national defense, 2:262
    NATO, 5:545
    negative income tax, 5:457
    New York City immigrants, 3:573
    pogroms, 6:288
    repression, 7:175
    schools, 8:11
    Social Darwinism, 2:233–234
    social welfare system, 7:632
    state capitalism, 1:443
    territorial expansion, 9:147–148
    totalitarianism, 8:394, 395
    Treaty of Versailles terms, 9:148
    unemployment compensation, 2:49
    United Nations membership, 8:522
    USSR agreement, 8:511
    Veblen, Thorstein, 8:596–597
    voting patterns, 8:650
    weapons industry, 9:49–50
    weapons of mass destruction, 9:51, 52
    See also East Germany; Hitler, Adolf; Holocaust; Nazism; West Germany

Gerontology, 2:271–272, 3:**306–308**

Gerontophobia. *See* Age and aging

Gerrymandering, 3:**308–310**, 8:646
    black politics, 6:325
    litigation, 4:465, 466
    Southern politics, 6:345–346
    Supreme Court decisions, 8:652–653
    See also Electoral districts

Gesell, Arnold, 1:506

Gestalt psychology, 3:**310**
    Asch, Solomon, 1:186
    consciousness, 2:81
    Tolman, Edward, 8:386–387

Gestalt therapy, 3:**310–311**

Getting a Job (Granovetter), 5:476, 478

Gettysburg, Battle of (1863), 4:399

GFR (General fertility rate), 3:127
    See also Human fertility

Ghana
    African Crisis Response Initiative, 1:38
    anticolonial movements, 1:139, 140
    blackness, 1:330
    Drake, St. Clair, 2:442
    Du Bois, W. E. B., 2:460
    Nkrumah, Kwame, 5:506–508

Gharbzadegi, 8:604

Ghettos, 3:**311–314**
    Chinese diaspora, 1:516
    cities, 1:541
    Clark, Kenneth B., 1:561
    culture of poverty, 2:206
    ethnic conflict, 3:1
    internal colony, 2:14
    Nazism, 5:450
    oppositional culture, 6:48
    slums, 7:551–552
    Tally's Corner, 8:263–264

Ghost Dance, 5:426

Gibbard, Allan, 1:525

Gibbs, Josiah Williard, 3:150

Gibbs, Lois, 4:505

Gibson, David, 2:33

Gibson, Eleanor, 1:506

Gibson, James, 2:97

Gibson, Mel, 3:516

Gibson, William, 2:216, 5:31, 32

Giddens, Anthony, 3:**314–315**
    class, 1:564
    constructivism, 2:97
    Durkheim, Émile, 2:465, 466
    institutional analysis in sociology, 7:673
    lifestyles, 4:446
    meaning, 5:52
    state capitalism, 1:444

Gideon v. Wainwright (1963), 8:233

Giere, Ronald, 2:494

Gift exchange. *See* Reciprocity

Gifted and talented, 3:**315–318**, *316, 316t*
    creativity, 2:165
    low and high culture, 2:204
    tracking in schools, 8:409–410
    underachievers, 8:483–485
    See also Talent

Gilbert, Martin, 1:152

Gilbert, Nigel, 2:61

Gilboa, Itzhak, 5:519

Gilbreth, Frank B., 8:365

Gilbreth, Lillian, 8:365

Gilded Age, 1:268, 3:**318–319**

Gilens, Margin, 9:72

Gilliam, Terry, 1:391

Gillies, Donald, 1:262

Gilligan, Carol, 3:**319–320**

Gilman, Charlotte Perkins, 8:561

Gilroy, Paul, 1:32, 3:410

Gine, Corrado, 3:320

Gingles, Thornburg v. (1986), 3:309, 8:652

Gingrich, Newt, 1:580, 2:74

Gini coefficient, 3:**320–323**, 320*t*, *321, 321t, 322, 322t*

    Deininger and Squire World Bank Inequality Database, 2:268

    equality, 2:617–618, *618*

    Fields' index of economic inequality, 3:137–138

    income distribution, 3:605

    income inequality, 4:1–2

    University of Texas Inequality Project, 8:530

    variation, 8:591–592

    wealth inequality, 4:9–11

Ginsberg, Allen, 1:384

Ginsburg, Faye, 7:178

Ginzberg, Carlo, 5:371

Ginzberg, Eli, 3:**323–324**, 9:27

Gioja, Melchiorre, 2:424

Giovanni, Nikki, 1:309

Giraud, Henri, 2:264

Girls, aggression and, 1:55–56

Girondist Party (France), 2:66, 4:401–402

Girvan, Norman, 6:278

GISs (Geographical information systems), 3:305

Giuliani, Rudy, 8:545

Giving birth. *See* Childbirth

Giza pyramids, 8:631

Gladstone, W. E., 1:153, 4:428, 8:428

Glaeser, Edward L., 9:72

Glasnost, 3:**324–325**, 351, 8:512

Glass, Gene V., 5:104

Glass ceiling, 3:**325–326**

Glass-Steagall Act (U.S. 1933), 1:252

Glazer, Nathan, 3:**327**, 5:221–222

    The Lonely Crowd (Riesman), 4:487

    Moynihan, Daniel Patrick, 5:304

    multiculturalism, 5:317

Glazer, Nona, 9:123

Glissant, Édouard, 2:169

Global Development Network (GDN), 9:139

Global economy

    G7 countries, 3:243–244

    Great Depression, 3:370

    offshore banking, 6:32–33

Global Fund, G8 countries, 3:244

Global justice movement. *See* Globalization

Global marketing and Advertising (de Mooij), 1:29

Global politics, world government and, 3:360

Global Pop (Taylor), 9:141, 142

Global Programme on AIDS, 9:140

Global trade. *See* Trade

Global warming, 3:**327–330**

    agricultural industry, 1:62–63

    air pollution, 6:362

    deforestation, 2:263

    disaster management, 2:384

    food supply, 3:164

    greenhouse effect, 3:377–378

    insurance industry, 4:53

    limits of growth, 4:449–450

    natural disasters, 5:433

    pollution, 6:360

    urbanization, 8:548

    vulnerability, 9:93

    water resources, 9:42

Globalization

    advertising, 1:29

    anarchism, 1:112

    automobile industry, 1:220

    class hierarchies, 8:542–543

    corporations, 2:139–140

    cultural change, 1:122

    cultural relativism, 2:195–196

    cultural studies, 2:200

    cyberspace, 2:217

    democracy research, 7:192

    development in sociology, 2:347

    development theory, 2:337

    diaspora, 2:357

    Disney, Walt, 2:410

    economic inequality, 9:46–47

    employment, 2:581

    exploitation, 3:65

    export penetration, 3:66

    Great Depression, 3:369

    immigrants, 9:126

    interest rates, 4:86

international economic order, 4:92–94

international nongovernmental organizations, 4:96–99

internationalism, 4:103

interwar years, 4:121–122

journalism, 4:214, 215

labor, 4:302

labor demand, 4:314

labor unions, 8:516–517

legal systems, 4:406

liberation movements, 4:433–434

linguistic anthropology, 1:118

mining industry, 5:188

mobility, 5:211

NAFTA, 5:540–541

nation-states, 5:421

national defense, 2:260

neoliberalism, 5:475

outsourcing, 6:86–87

political economy, 6:303–304

political sociology, 8:5

popular culture, 6:375

postnationalism, 6:398

poverty, 6:407, 9:46–47

powerlessness, 6:30

race, 7:11

relative surplus value, 7:155

rural sociology, 8:9

Seattle protests, 9:144–145

social movements, 7:607

social values, 8:582

society, 7:650

sociology, 7:662

state, 8:105

state power, 3:332

steel industry, 8:129

stratification, 8:167

surplus labor, 4:312

Taylorism, 8:288

third-world sociology, 8:13–14

Tobin, James, 8:379

tourism, 8:399, 400

tourism industry, 8:400–401

trade liberalization, 4:427, 428

transitional economies, 2:533

transnationalism, 8:433–434

trilateralism, 8:454

trust, 8:461

underclass, 9:100–101

underdevelopment, 1:110, 8:490–491

undereating, 8:491

underemployment, 8:492

Globalization, *continued*
    unemployment, 8:502
    urban poverty, 6:411
    urban studies, 8:542–543
    visual arts, 8:633
    wage discrimination, 2:403
    wealth, 9:46–47
    welfare, 9:73
    winner-take-all society, 9:103
    women's work, 9:125–126
    World Health Organization, 9:141
    World Trade Organization,
      9:144–145
    See also Transnationalism
Globalization, anthropological aspects
    of, 3:**330–332**
    hybridity, 3:535, 536
    Islamic fundamentalism, 3:237
    nation-states, 3:332
Globalization, social and economic
    aspects of, 3:**332–335**
    Blair, Tony, 1:285
    Bonacich, Edna, 1:352
    Bourdieu, Pierre, 1:359
    bourgeoisie, 1:361
    bubbles (economics), 1:378
    bull and bear markets, 1:386
    business, 1:402
    capital, 1:431
    capitalist mode of production,
      1:447
    Caribbean, 1:448–449
    Chinese diaspora, 1:518
    cities, 1:541
    citizenship, 1:543–544
    civilization, 1:557
    class conflict, 1:570
    community economic
      development, 2:41
    consumer protection, 2:103
    consumerism, 2:105
    cooperatives, 2:124
    corporate social responsibility,
      2:136
    cosmopolitanism, 2:149
    credentialism, 2:166–167
    entrepreneurial firms, 3:148
    finance, 3:143
    food supply, 3:163–164, 166
    gambling, 3:248
    gender development, 3:273
    gender equality, 3:270, 279
    ghettos, 3:312–313
    human rights, 3:512–513
    humiliation, 3:521, 522

Glorious Revolution (1688), 1:396,
    5:545
Glory Hunter (Van de Water), 1:258
GLS. *See* Generalized least squares
Gluckman, Max, 1:128
    extended case method, 1:454
    urban anthropology, 1:134
Glutamate, 2:272
Gluts. *See* Market gluts
GMM (General Method of
    Moments), 5:522
GNI (Gross national income),
    3:**384–385**, 5:399
GNP (Gross national product). *See*
    Gross national income (GNI)
Goals
    alienation, 1:75
    flow (psychological), 3:158
    needs *vs.,* 5:453
    social equilibrium, 3:232
    superordinate, 7:495, 8:226–227
Gobineau, Comte de, 3:**335–336**
    Aryans, 1:185
    biological determinism, 2:325
    liberation, 4:430
    race, 7:9
    whiteness, 9:90
Gobineau, Joseph Arthur de. *See*
    Gobineau, Comte de
Gochfeld, Michael, 6:22
God. *See* Supreme being
Gödel, Kurt, 4:481
Godelier, Maurice, 1:188, 8:450
Gods and goddesses. *See* Myth and
    mythology; Supreme being
God's Trombones (Johnson), 3:426
Godwin, William, 1:111, 4:569, 570
Goebbels, Joseph, 4:150
Goffman, Erving, 1:129, 3:**337–338**
    communication, 2:32
    conversational analysis, 2:118
    identity, 3:553
    intersubjectivity, 4:116
    labeling theory, 4:299
    performance, 6:207–208
    post-Parsonian American
      sociology, 8:7
    resistance, 7:208
    self-hatred, 7:416
    self-presentation, 7:423–424
    shame, 7:488–489
    social identification, 7:593
    society, 7:652
    stigma, 8:146–147

Going long. *See* Selling long and
    selling short
Going native, 2:201, 3:**338–339**
Going negative. *See* Campaigning
Gokhale, Gopal Krishna, 2:473
Golan Heights, 1:156–159
Gold, 1:349, 516, 3:**339–340**
Gold, God and Glory, 3:**340–341**
Gold, R., 6:14
Gold Coast. *See* Ghana
Gold industry, 3:**342–344**
Gold standard, 3:340, 343, **344–345**
    beggar-thy-neighbor, 1:273
    central banks, 1:478
    cross of gold, 2:180–181
    currency devaluation and
      revaluation, 2:211
    Great Depression, 3:369, 370
    interwar years, 4:121
    money, 5:251
    Ricardo, David, 7:243
Goldberg, Ray A., 1:58
Golden Age of Black Nationalism
    (Moses), 1:315
Golden Fetters (Eichengreen), 3:370
Golden rule in growth models, 3:**346**
Golden rule of accumulation, 3:346
Golden rule or flow, 3:157
Goldenweiser, Alexander, 1:345
Goldhaber, Daniel D., 5:391
Goldhagen, Daniel, 3:497
Goldman, Emma, 1:111
Goldmark, Josephine, 4:465
Goldstone, Jack, 8:6
Goldthorpe, John, 8:533, 534
Goldwater, Barry
    conservatism, 2:85
    Dixiecrats, 2:430
    Republican Party (U.S.), 7:186,
      187
    Southern politics, 6:342–343
    Southern strategy, 8:36
    Thurmond, Strom, 8:360
Golen, Steven, 2:32
Golliwogs. *See* Blackface
Golwalkar, M. S., 3:478
Gombrich, Richard, 5:504
Gomez, Michael, 1:41, 5:459
Gomillion v. Lightfoot (1960), 3:309,
    5:384
Gompers, Samuel, 5:430, 8:515
Gone with the Wind (book and film),
    3:**346–348**
    Birth of a Nation (film), 1:304

Confederate States of America, 2:67
   plantation, 6:277
Gonzalez, Abraham, 8:617
González, Juan, 4:360
González Casanova, Pablo, 7:677
González-Rivera, Gloria, 4:501
Good, I. J., 6:490
Goodbye Yellow Brick Road (John), 9:105
Goode, Eslanda Cardoza, 7:265
Goode, Judith, 4:419, 5:462
Goode, William J., 8:6, 7
Goodin, Robert, 4:453
Goodman, Andrew, 4:527
Goodman, Benny, 4:176, 177
Goodman, Paul, 3:311
Goodnow, Frank J., 6:312
Goods
   aggregate supply, 1:53–55
   allocation of, 9:64–65
   capital, 8:619–621
   conspicuous consumption, 2:89
   consumer, 2:99–102
   consumerism, 2:104–105
   consumption, 2:105–109
   cooperatives, 2:123–124
   final, 5:401
   gross national income, 3:384–385
   internal colony, 2:13
   luxury, 9:44–45, 46
   marginal rate of substitution, 8:555–556
   merit, 5:97–98
   public *vs.* private, 3:144
   social, underrepresentation, 8:495
   time preference, 8:369–370
   traded, 3:349
   wants for, 9:15–17
   wealth, 9:44
Goods, lumpy. *See* McFadden, Daniel L.
Goods, nontraded, 3:**349**
Goods, public. *See* Public goods
Goodwill, 2:137, 3:**349–350**
Goodwin, Richard M., 1:412, 5:524
Goolsbee, Austan, 2:366
Goose Green, Battle of (1982), 3:81
GOP (Grand Old Party). *See* Republican Party (U.S.)
Gorbachev, Mikhail, 3:**350–351**, 8:512–513
   Berlin Wall, 1:289
   Brezhnev, Leonid, 1:370
   Castro, Fidel, 1:466

Cold War, 2:5
   communism, 2:36
   decolonization, 2:256
   glasnost, 3:324–325, 351
   NATO, 5:546
   Reagan, Ronald, 7:89
   Russian economics, 7:301
   Russian Federation, 7:302
   Warsaw Pact, 9:35
   Yeltsin, Boris, 3:351, 9:163–164
Gordon, Avery, 2:64
Gordon, Bruce S., 5:383
Gordon, H. Scott, 7:210–211, 8:422
Gordon, Ian, 2:23
Gordon, Linda, 7:632–633
Gordon, Randall, 5:530
Gordon Nembhard, Jessica, 1:432, 2:125
Gore, Al, Jr.
   Bush, George W., 1:399
   Clinton, Bill, 1:579, 581
   Democratic Party (U.S.), 2:288
Goreham, Gary, 8:9
Gornick, Janet, 4:519
Gorres, Joseph von, 2:83
Gorz, André, 9:131
Gosling, Samuel, 1:597
Gosnell, Harold, 3:**351–352**
Gospels. *See* Bible
Gossip. *See* Rumors
Gottdiener, Mark, 1:541
Gottfried, Paul, 4:403
Gottman, John, 4:600
Göttner-Abendroth, Heide, 5:29–30
Gough, Ian, 5:453
Gould, Mark, 9:101
Gould, Stephen Jay, 2:326, 3:**352–353**
Gouldner, Alvin, 4:285, 7:107, 8:5
Gouveia, Elsa, 9:98
Government, 3:**353–357**
   autocratic, 3:354
   bureaucracy, 1:389–391
   business, 1:400, 401
   business relationship, 5:495–496
   capital controls, 1:431–433
   caste, 1:458
   censorship, 1:475–476
   Church and state, 1:534–536
   cities, 1:542
   civil liberties, 1:546–547
   civil rights, 1:549
   coalition theory, 1:588
   common land, 2:27–28
   commonwealth, 2:29

community power studies, 2:42–46
conflict, 2:70
conservatism, 2:84, 85, 86
Conservative Party (U.K.), 2:87
constitutions, 2:94–95
consumer protection, 2:102–103
corruption, 2:143–145
counterterrorism, 2:155
critical theory, 2:177
crony capitalism, 2:180
Dahl, Robert Alan, 2:219–220
day care, 2:246
decentralization, 2:250–251
Declaration of Independence, U.S., 2:254–255
development economics, 2:346
dirigiste, 2:372–374
documentary studies, 2:433
due process, 2:461
environmental impact assessment, 2:605–607
federalism, 3:113–115
fiscal policy, 6:291–293
impeachment, 3:584–586
indirect rule, 3:617–618
institutional economics, 2:506–507
Israel, 4:276–277
judiciary, 4:225–228
laissez-faire, 4:335–338
land claims, 4:340–341
leaders, 4:376–377
left and right, 4:402
left wing, 4:403, 404
liberalism, 4:425–426
libertarianism, 4:437, 438
liberty, 4:439
Locke, John, 4:476–477
merit goods, 5:97–98
military regimes, 5:174–176
mobilization, 5:214–215
monetary policy, 6:293–296
multiparty systems, 5:321–323
national defense, 2:259–262
parliaments and parliamentary systems, 6:145–147
Partido Revolucionario Institucional, 6:157–158
political business cycles, 1:406
political system, 6:316–317
polyarchy, 6:365–366
presidential, 1:216, 3:355, 9:37
private interests, 6:478–479

Government, *continued*
  private sector, 6:480–481
  privatization, 6:481–482
  public economics, 2:529–530
  racial discrimination, 2:395
  Raj, 7:55–56
  Rawls, John, 7:84
  regions, 7:130
  regulation, 7:143–144
  repression, 7:174–175
  republic, 7:184–185
  republicanism, 7:188
  role calls, 7:276–277
  Royal Commissions, 7:291–292
  Russian Revolution, 7:304
  semipresidential, 3:355
  separation of powers, 7:448–449
  socialization, 7:647
  Southern politics, 6:343
  state
      abortion laws, 1:2–3
      federalism, 3:113–115
      New Deal, 5:497–498
      welfare, 9:61
  state capitalism, 1:443–445
  surveillance, 3:263
  technocracy, 8:296–297
  technological change, 1:491–492
  technology, 8:303, 304
  technotopia, 8:312–313
  term limits, 8:323–324
  terrorism, 8:328–329
  terrorists, 8:330–331
  theocracy, 8:342–343
  totalitarian, 3:354
  transparency, 8:434–435
  tribal, 5:427–428
Government, coalition, 3:357, 4:277
Government, federal, 3:**357–359**
  central banks, 1:478
  Central Intelligence Agency, U.S,
      1:480–482
  Cherokees, 1:498
  Confederate States of America,
      2:66–67
  Congress, U.S., 2:73–74
  Constitution, U.S., 2:90–91
  constitutional courts, 2:93
  decentralization, 2:250–251
  democratic centralism, 2:286
  Democratic Party (U.S.), 2:286
  divided, 2:74
  electoral college, 2:559
  politics, 6:321

Government, self. *See* Self-
  determination
Government, unitary, 3:355, **359**
  decentralization, 2:250
  democratic centralism, 2:285, 286
  politics, 6:321
  voting schemes, 8:655
Government, world, 3:**360–361**
Government Accountability Project
  (U.S. 1966), 9:80
Government assistance. *See* Public
  assistance
Government of India Act (1935),
  5:460
Government programs. *See* Social
  programs
Government regulation. *See*
  Regulation
Government subsidies. *See* Public
  finance
Governmentality, 3:**361–362**
Governors of the Group of Ten, 6:33
Graburn, Nelson, 2:201
Gradgrind, Thomas, 8:553
Gradient method, 8:563
Graduate Faculty of Political and
  Social Science, 5:501
Graham, Benjamin, 1:455
Graham, Billy, 3:236
Graham, Pauline, 2:142
Grain
  food diplomacy, 3:166
  Green Revolution, 3:164–165
Grameen Bank, 3:**362–363**, 513
  loans, 4:473
  microfinance, 5:140
  poverty, 6:407
Grammar, 1:528, 598
The Grammar of Science (Pearson),
  6:191, 193
Gramsci, Antonio, 3:**363–364**
  Anderson, Perry, 1:112
  Black Arts Movement, 1:309
  capitalist mode of production,
      1:446
  civil society, 1:553
  class consciousness, 1:572
  cultural studies, 2:199
  culture, 2:203
  discourse, 2:387
  false consciousness, 3:82
  Hall, Stuart, 3:409, 410
  hegemony, 3:455–456
  international relations, 4:101
  organic intellectuals, 4:66

  postcolonialism, 6:392
  public intellectuals, 4:68, 69
  resistance, 7:208–209
  subaltern, 8:191
  vernacular intellectuals, 4:70
Grand Old Opry (radio program),
  1:341
Grand Old Party (GOP). *See*
  Republican Party (U.S.)
Grand Theft Auto (game), 8:612
Grand utility possibility frontier, 9:65
Grandmaster Flash, 3:480, 481
Granger, Clive, 1:472
  cointegration, 2:3
  loss functions, 4:496, 497, 499,
      501–502
Granger causality. *See* Causality
Granovetter, Mark, 5:476, 478, 7:669,
  8:6
Grant, Madison, 1:336, 5:430
Grant, Ulysses S., 3:**365–366**
  Chief Joseph, 1:503–504
  Ku Klux Klan, 4:294
  U.S. Civil War, 3:365, 8:550–551
Grants, land. *See* Rural development
Graphic arts, 8:632
  See also Visual arts
Graphic novels. *See* Comic books
Grassroots activity, 1:587, 2:40, 85,
  4:434, 505
Grateful Dead, 9:121
Gratification, delayed. *See* Time
  orientation
Gratification, instant. *See* Time
  orientation
Gratz v. Bollinger. *See* Grutter decision
  (1978)
Graunt, John, 3:**366–367**, 5:289
Graves, Joseph L., Jr., 2:326
Graziani, Augusto, 5:257
GRB (Gross reproduction rate), 3:127
Great Basin Native Americans, 5:424
Great Britain. *See* United Kingdom
  (U.K.)
Great Britain, 1801-. *See* United
  Kingdom (U.K.)
Great Britain, pre-1801. *See* England
Great Depression, 3:**367–371**
  agriculture, 5:494
  baby boomers, 1:235
  banking failures, 3:370,
      5:483–485, 496
  beggar-thy-neighbor, 1:273
  bubbles (economics), 1:378
  casino capitalism, 1:455

central banks, 1:478

Chamberlain, Neville, 1:489

dealignment, 2:247

Democratic Party (U.S.), 2:287

as economic depression, 2:302, 303, 304

fascism, 3:103

Federal Reserve System, 3:112

feminism, 3:120

Friedman, Milton, 3:218

full employment policy, 3:227

Germany, 3:367, 368, 369–370, 5:449, 9:148

human toll, 5:493–494

immigration, 3:573

jazz, 4:176

Keynes, John Maynard, 4:260, 261

labor unions, 8:35–36

laissez-faire, 4:338

lender of last resort, 4:410

macroeconomics, 4:541

national service programs, 5:413

Nazism, 5:449

real business cycles, 1:408

recession, 7:103

Republican Party (U.S.), 5:493–494, 497, 7:187

Roosevelt, Franklin D., 7:283

unemployment, 3:367, 369, 5:494, 8:500, 502, 503

voting patterns, 8:649

Wall Street, 9:8

welfare state, 9:69

See also New Deal

Great Leap Forward, 4:589

Great Lyre, 8:630

Great Schism (1054), 1:533

Great Society, 3:**371–375**

benign neglect, 1:283–284

futurology, 3:241

Glazer, Nathan, 3:327

Johnson, Lyndon B., 4:210

social welfare system, 7:631, 633

urban renewal, 8:536–537

The Great Transformation (Polanyi), 1:437

Great Tulip Mania, 1:378, 3:158, **375**, 7:433

Great Zimbabwe, 1:167

Greece

abortion, 1:1

archaeology, 1:165

architecture, 1:171

citizenship, 1:542

city-state, 1:544

class conflict, 1:569

communism, 2:34

confederations, 2:68

coups d'etat, 2:156

democracy, 2:273

freedom, 3:196

hell, 3:458

human sacrifice, 3:515

Jewish diaspora, 4:190

land fertility, 3:130–131

literature, 4:462–463

monotheism, 5:270

Muhammad Ali (Memet), 1:73

myth and mythology, 5:356–357

NATO, 5:545

reincarnation, 7:145, 146

representative and participatory democracy, 2:283

republic, 7:184

slave mode of production, 7:531–532

slavery, 1:38

state capitalism, 1:444

theater, 8:337

visual arts, 8:631

wealth, 9:44

Greek Orthodox Church, 1:531, 3:**375–376**

Christianity, 1:531

contraception, 2:114

history, 1:533

Roman Catholic Church, 7:280

Greeley, Horace, 4:213

Green, Joyce, 1:310

Green, T. H., 4:440

Green architecture, 1:172

Green belts, 8:540

The Green Book (Qadhafi), 3:**377**, 6:647, 648, 7:644

Green Corn Ceremony, 5:425

Green national income accounts, 6:52

Green Pamphlet (Gandhi), 3:254

Green parties, 4:403

Green Party (West Germany), 1:237–238

Green Revolution, 2:342, 3:164–165, **377–378**

Green Revolution Modern Varieties (GRMV), 3:378

Green v. County School Board of New Kent County (1968), 2:314

Greenaway, Kate, 5:550

Greenbacks, 2:181

Greenberg, Jeff, 8:326, 327

Greenhouse effect, 3:**378–379**

air pollution, 6:362

pollution, 6:360

urbanization, 8:548

Greensboro (NC), 2:75

Greenspan, Alan, 3:**379–381**

bubbles (economics), 1:379

long run, 4:494

Gregory, Chris, 7:106

Gregory the Great, 8:593

Gregory XIV, Pope, 1:2

Greider, William, 5:360

Grenadian Revolution, 3:**381–383**

Griffith, D. W., 1:304–306, 3:347

Griggs v. Duke Power Company (1971), 1:288, 2:615, 6:671

Grijalva, Juan de, 2:146–147

Griliches, Zvi, 1:490, 502, 3:389

Grillo, Ralph D., 1:134

Grim, Clarence, 7:546–547

Grimm, Jacob, 3:17–18

Grimm, Wilhelm, 3:17–18

Griswold v. Connecticut (1965), 2:461, 3:90, 7:271

GRMV (Green Revolution Modern Varieties), 3:378

Grodzins, Morton, 3:358

Grönlund, Kimmo, 2:59

Groom price. *See* Dowry and bride price

Gross, James, 2:572–573

Gross domestic product (GDP), 3:**383–384**, 6:52

aggregate supply price, 1:51

capital flight, 1:434

construction of, 5:401–403, 402*t*

economic growth, 2:486, 487

employment, 2:582

insurance, 4:49*t*

macroeconomics, 4:539–540

national debt, 5:386

national income accounts, 5:398–399

nominal, 5:401, 401*t*, 511

Penn World Table, 6:204–205

per capita, 5:399

pollution increase, 5:541

quantity index, 6:658–659

quantity theory of money, 6:660

recession, 7:103

Gross national income (GNI), 3:**384–385**, 5:399

Gross national product (GNP). *See* Gross national income

Gross reproduction rate (GRB), 3:127

Grossman, Gene, 2:605, 606
Grossman, Herschel I., 1:255–256, 9:13
Grossman, Sanford, 5:134–135
Grossman, Vasily, 9:20
Grosvenor, Gilbert H., 5:394
Grotian tradition, 5:489
Grotius, Hugo, 4:102, 5:489
Group Areas Act (South Africa 1950), 1:147–148, 2:15
Group cohesion, 3:388
Group dynamics. *See* Intergroup relations
Group identity, 3:385–386, 387
Group knowledge. *See* Collective wisdom
Group marriage, 3:83
Group of 20, 3:243
Group of 77, 5:542
Group of Eight. *See* G8 countries
Group of Seven. *See* G7 countries
Group polarization, 3:388
Group processes
    description, 3:385
    groupthink, 3:388
Group selection. *See* Cultural group selection
Groups, 3:**385–387**
    bigotry, 1:295–296
    Blumer, Herbert, 1:343–344
    citizenship, 1:543
    cognitive dissonance, 1:600
    collective action, 2:5–6
    collective action games, 2:6–7
    collective memory, 2:7
    collective wisdom, 2:9–10
    collectivism, 2:10–11
    comedy, 2:23
    common good, 2:25
    communitarianism, 2:39
    consensus, 2:82–83
    contact hypothesis, 2:111–112
    contempt, 2:113
    control, 8:574
    Creole, 2:168–169
    cultural group selection, 2:191–192
    Dahl, Robert Alan, 2:219–220
    experiments, 3:55
    herd behavior, 3:459–460
    identity, 1:30–32
    individualism, 3:619–620
    lynchings, 4:526–527
    noncompeting, 5:514–516
    pluralistic ignorance, 3:560–561

pressure, 2:74
primary, 3:85, 385
public opinion, 1:103
reactance theory, 7:85–86
rituals, 7:259–264
rumors, 7:297
sellouts, 7:434–435
social classification, 7:567
social dominance orientation, 7:583–584
social exchange theory, 7:585–586
social identity, 3:556, 7:593
sociology, 7:663
sociometry, 8:18–20
underrepresentation, 8:495–496
work, 9:136–137
    See also Interest groups and interests; Intergroup relations
Groupthink, 3:**387–388**
    collective wisdom, 2:9–10, 10–11
    conformity, 2:71–72
    cults, 2:188
    pluralistic ignorance, 3:560–561
Grovey v. Townsend (1935), 9:84, 85
Growers. *See* Agricultural industry
Grown, Caren, 3:274, 275
Growth, Distribution, and Uneven Development (Dutt), 5:547
Growth, economic. *See* Economic growth
Growth, Employment and Redistribution (GEAR), 1:43
Growth, immiserizing. *See* Immiserizing growth
Growth, limits of. *See* Limits of growth
Growth, neoclassical model for. *See* Neoclassical growth model
Growth, optimal. *See* Optimal growth
Growth, population. *See* Population growth
Growth, stunted, 8:**187–189**
Growth accounting, 3:**389–390**, 5:399, 8:27–28
Growth curve analysis, 3:**390–392**, *391*
Growth models, economic. *See* Economic growth
GRS (General Revenue Sharing), 8:537
Gruber, Howard, 2:165
Grünbaum, Adolf, 3:214
Grundgesetz, 1:23
Grundrisse (Marx), 1:187, 445, 2:106, 9:133
Grunge, 7:268

Grusky, David, 1:564
Grutter decision (1978), 2:317, 420, 3:373, **392–393**, 6:671, 8:234
Grutter v. Bollinger. See Grutter decision (1978)
GSS (General Social Survey), 6:27
Guano, 3:131
Guantánamo Bay, 3:**393–394**, 9:23–24
Guatemala
    banana industry, 1:246
    civil wars, 1:554
    Garifuna, 3:257–258
    land reform, 4:343
    latifundia, 4:354
    Latin American immigrants, 3:572
    Latin American revolutions, 7:234
Guattari, Felix, 1:447, 6:29
Guernica (Picasso), 8:630
Guerrilla marketing, 1:29
Guerrilla warfare, 3:**394–396**
    Boer War, 1:349
    Castro, Fidel, 1:464–465
    Chinese Revolution, 1:520
    dissidents, 2:411
    Latin American revolutions, 7:234
    liberation, 4:429
    Mau Mau, 5:36–38
    terrorists, 8:328, 330–331
Guevara, Ernesto "Che," 3:395
    Black Power, 1:321
    Cuban Revolution, 2:186
    Latin American revolutions, 7:234
Guha, Ranajit, 8:191
Guibernau, Montserrat, 5:421–422
Guicciardini, Francesco, 7:188
Guildford Four, 4:111
Guilds. *See* Labor unions
Guilkey, David K., 5:212
Guillard, Achille, 2:293
Guillaume, François, 9:157–158
Guillaume, Georges, 9:157–158
Guilt, hierarchy of needs, 5:451
Guinea-Bissau
    African Crisis Response Initiative, 1:38
    bauxite industry, 1:261
    Cabral, Amílcar, 1:415
Guinier, Lani, 1:580
Guizot, Francois, 4:401
Gulag Archipelago (Solzhenitsyn), 3:396
Gulags, 3:**396**, 8:29
    See also Concentration camps

Gulf Cooperation Council (GCC), 3:397

Gulf of Tonkin, 8:614

Gulf States, 3:**397**

Gulf Stream, 3:330

Gulf War of 1991, 3:**397–398**, 9:18
  bin Laden, Osama, 1:299
  Bush, George H. W., 1:398
  Hussein, Saddam, 3:534–535
  Iraq-U.S. War, 4:145–146
  just war, 4:236
  oil prices, 6:67

Gumperz, John J., 1:129

Gunder Frank, Andre. *See* Frank, Andre Gunder

Gungwu, Wang, 1:516

Guns, Germs and Steel (Diamond), 3:125, 126

Guomindang, 1:499
  Chinese Revolution, 1:520–521
  communism, 2:35

Gupta, Geeta Rao, 3:274

Gurr, Ted Robert, 5:422, 7:153

Gurwitsch, Aron, 5:501

Guryan, Jonathan, 2:366

Guthrie, Edwin, 1:275, 277

Gutierrez, Gustavo, 4:435

Gutman, Herbert, 3:483

Guttentag, Jack M., 6:94–95

Guttman, Louis, 3:398, 4:447

Guttman scale, 3:**398–399**

Guy, Buddy, 1:343

Guyana
  blackness, 1:328, 330
  East Indian diaspora, 2:474
  Rodney, Walter, 7:269–270

GWR (Geographically weighted regression), 3:305

Gyn/Ecology (Lorde), 9:106

Gypsies. *See* Roma

H

Ha'am, Ahad, 9:180

Haavelmo, Trygve, 3:222

Habeas corpus, 3:394, 7:292

Haber-Bosch process, 3:131

Habermas, Jürgen, 2:39, 82, 97, 3:**401–402**
  authority, 1:214
  critical theory, 2:177–178
  Frankfurt School, 3:189
  hermeneutics, 3:463–464
  intersubjectivity, 4:116–117
  schools in sociology, 8:11
  scientism, 7:365

separation of powers, 7:449

structural transformation, 8:180–181

universalism, 8:526

Habitat (United Nations Centre for Human Settlements), 3:499

Habitat for Humanity, 1:451

Habits, 3:**402–404**, 4:375

Habitus, 3:**404–406**
  Bourdieu, Pierre, 1:359
  class, 1:564
  cultural capital, 2:190
  practice theory, 6:419

Habshis, 1:39

Haciendas. *See* Latifundia

Hackett, David, 9:25, 26

Hacking, Ian. *See* Probability theory

Haddad, Carol, 2:60

Hades. *See* Hell

Hagan, John, 4:299, 300

Haganah, 1:283

Hagen, Edward, 2:329, 330

Hagen, Everett E., 8:562

Hagopian, Mark, 1:213

Hague, William, 2:88

Hague Conference (1899), 1:176, 4:385

Hague Conference (1907), 1:176, 4:385

Hague Conventions
  neutral states, 5:488
  political neutrality, 5:489
  See also War crimes

Hahid, Zaha, 1:172

Hahn, Frank, 3:218

Haider, Jörg, 9:160

Haidt, Jonathan, 3:293

Haig, Alexander, 3:81

Haiti
  blackness, 1:330
  Carter, Jimmy, 1:451
  Clinton, Bill, 1:580
  Duvaliers, 2:468–469
  Hurston, Zora Neale, 3:527
  Jacobinism, 4:165
  Latin American revolutions, 7:233
  liberation, 4:429
  refugees, 7:126
  religion, 7:161
  slavery, 3:204–205, 406–408, 5:364–365
  Toussaint-Louverture, 8:402–403
  Trouillot, Michel-Rolph, 8:457–458
  vodou, 8:633–634

zombies, 9:181
  See also Haitian Revolution

Haitian Diaspora. *See* Trouillot, Michel-Rolph

Haitian Revolution, 3:**406–408**
  Latin American revolutions, 7:233
  Toussaint-Louverture, 8:402–403
  voudou, 8:634

Hajj, 5:57

Halbwachs, Maurice, 2:7–8, 5:74

Haldeman, H. R., 9:43

Hale, Grace Elizabeth, 9:91

Hale, Matthew, 2:172

Haley, Alex, 4:564

Half-Man-Half-Woman, 3:271

Hall, Catherine, 3:483

Hall, Edward T., 1:171, 5:530

Hall, Elaine, 9:122

Hall, Granville Stanley, 1:102, 7:22

Hall, Kim, 9:93

Hall, Peter, 9:68

Hall, Robert, 2:110, 8:552

Hall, Rodney Bruce, 5:421

Hall, Stuart, 1:32, 3:**408–410**
  class, 1:564, 572
  cultural studies, 2:199–200
  diaspora, 2:357
  popular culture, 6:374
  representation, 7:171, 172
  resistance, 7:209
  Thompson, Edward P., 8:353, 354

Halley, Edmund, 1:487, 3:366

Hallford, James, 7:271

Hallo, William, 3:125–126

Hallucinogens, 3:**410–412**
  Castaneda, Carlos, 1:456–457
  drugs of abuse, 2:452, 454
  Leary, Timothy, 4:390–391
  See also Psychotropic drugs

Halpin, Andrew, 4:379

Ham, John, 8:14

Hamada, Koichi, 1:368

Hamas, 6:104, 105, 106, 107
  See also Intifada

Hamblett, Charles, 3:291

Hamdan, Salim Ahmed, 3:394

Hamdan v. Rumsfeld (2006), 3:394

Hamer, Dean, 2:163

Hamer, Fannie Lou, 3:216

Hamermesh, Daniel, 6:99

Hamilton, Alexander, 3:200, **413–414**
  apportionment, 1:154
  Burr, Aaron, 1:397
  checks and balances, 1:495–496

Hamilton, Alexander, *continued*
  conservatism, 2:84
  Constitution, U.S., 2:91
  constitutional courts, 2:92
  Democratic Party (U.S.), 2:286
  infant industry, 4:11, 12
  Jefferson, Thomas, 4:181
  Washington, George, 9:37, 38
Hamilton, Charles
  black nationalism, 1:317
  internal colony, 2:13
  race relations, 7:30
Hamilton, David, 1:539
Hamilton, Edward K., 9:28
Hamilton, Gary, 1:516
Hamilton, Gilbert, 7:481–482
Hamilton, James, 5:534
Hamilton, Walton, 4:44
Hamilton, William D. *See* Hamilton's
  rule; Kinship, evolutionary theory
  of
Hamilton's rule, 3:**414–415**,
  4:273–274
Hammarskjöld, Dag, 8:524
Hammond, Barbara, 4:420
Hammond, J. L., 4:420
Hammond, James Henry, 2:243,
  7:544
Hammurabi's Code. *See* Retaliation
Hampa afro-cubana: Los negros esclavos
  (Ortiz), 6:80
Hampton, Carl, 1:322
Hampton, Fred, 1:322
Hanau, Arthur, 1:591
Handbook of Adolescent Psychology
  (Lerner and Steinberg), 1:26
Handbook of Social Psychology
  (Aronson), 1:180
Handbook of South American Indians
  (Lowie), 4:507
Handy, W. C., 1:342–343
Hanemann, Michael, 9:63
Hanna, Judith Lynne, 2:224
Hannerz, Ulf, 1:134, 135
Hansen, Gary, 1:404
Happiness, 3:**415–419**, *417*
  altruism, 3:292–293
  conspicuous consumption, 2:89
  consumerism, 2:104–105
  decision-making, 2:252
  luck, 4:512
  mood, 5:276
  objective utility, 8:557
  positive psychology, 6:386
  real income, 7:90–91

  relative income hypothesis,
    7:153–154
  self-determination theory, 7:407,
    408
  wealth inequality, 4:8
The Happiness Hypothesis (Haidt),
  3:293
Harassment, 3:**420–421**
  racial slurs, 7:41–42
  sexual, 3:420–421, 7:474–475
  transgender, 8:432
Harberger, Arnold, 1:502, 8:277
Harburg, E. Y. "Yip," 9:105
Hard-core unemployed, 3:**421–423**
Hard Times (Dickens), 8:553
Hardie, James Keir, 4:327
Hardin, Garrett, 2:27, 245
  resource economics, 7:211
  Tragedy of the Commons, 8:422
Hardin, Russell, 2:94
Hardt, Michael, 1:447, 7:209
Hardy, Leroy C., 3:308–309
Hare, Nathan, 1:32
Harijans. *See* Dalits
Harlem, 3:**423–424**
  black Marxism, 4:642
  Clark, Kenneth B., 1:561
  See also Black Arts Movement
    (BAM); Harlem Renaissance
Harlem Is Nowhere (Ellison), 3:424
Harlem Renaissance, 1:35,
  3:**424–426**, 527
  See also Black Arts Movement
    (BAM); Harlem
Harlem Youth Opportunities
  Unlimited (HARYOU), 1:561, 9:25
Harmel Report, 5:544
Harmon, Dick, 1:259
Harmony of interest, 4:336
Harper v. Canada, 3:309
Harper's Weekly (periodical), 1:452
Harriman, W. Averell, 9:24
Harrington, Michael, 5:468, 9:25
Harris, Abram L., Jr., 1:312,
  3:**426–428**, 5:389
Harris, Angela, 2:174–175
Harris, Cheryl, 9:86, 87
Harris, Christine, 5:530
Harris, John, 3:428–429
  development economics, 2:344
  dual economy, 2:457
Harris, Joseph, 2:357
Harris, Judith Rich. *See* Peer effects
Harris, Marvin, 1:120–121, 122, 358
Harris, T. Robert, 6:77

Harris, Tirril, 8:656–657
Harris, Zellig, 1:527
Harris-Todaro model, 3:**428–429**
  development economics, 2:344
  dual economy, 2:457
  rural to urban migration, 5:160
Harrison, Bennett, 1:236, 2:14
Harrison, George, 9:142
Harrison, John, 1:583
Harrod, Roy Forbes, 5:464
  business cycle theories, 1:411
  competition, 2:51
  underconsumption, 8:488–489
Harrod-neutral technological change,
  1:491
Harsanyi, John C., 1:525, 5:208, 9:67
Hart, H. L. A., 4:363, 365
Hart, Mickey, 9:142
Hart-Celler Act (U.S. 1965). *See*
  Immigration and Naturalization Act
  (U.S. 1965)
Harter, Susan, 7:399, 427
Hartigan, John, 1:586
Hartman, Geoffrey, 2:310
Hartmann, Heidi, 1:447
Hartshorne, Hugh, 4:523–524
Hartshorne, Richard, 3:304
Hartwell, Steven, 6:2
Hartz, Louis, 2:84, 3:**429–430**
Harvard Civil Rights Project (2006),
  1:375
Harvard Law School, 2:174, 175
Harvard University, 8:11–12
*Harvest of Empire: A History of Latinos
  in America* (González), 4:360
Harvey, David, 3:305, 331
  capitalist mode of production,
    1:447
  class, 1:564
  neoliberalism, 5:474
HARYOU (Harlem Youth
  Opportunities Unlimited), 1:561,
  9:25
Hassan, Khwaja, 1:130
Hastings, Warren, 1:396
Hatch Act (U.S. 1887), 2:341, 8:8
Hate Crime Statistics (Federal Bureau
  of Investigation), 3:431
Hate crimes, 3:**430–432**
  bigotry, 1:296
  Chinese Americans, 1:514
  critical race theory, 2:175
  harassment, 3:420
Hate Crimes Statistics Act (1990),
  3:430

Hatred, self, 7:**416–417**, 488–489

Hatt, Paul K., 6:27, 7:657

Hauser, Philip, 2:296, 8:492

Hausman, Daniel, 2:494

Hausman, Jerry, 3:432–434, 9:63

Hausman tests, 3:**432–434**

Havana, Cuba, 6:80

Havas, Charles-Louis, 4:213

Havemann, Robert, 1:237

Havens Realty Corporation v. Coleman, 1:209

Hawaii
  annexation of, 1:115
  Cook, James, 2:122
  Pearl Harbor attack, 9:149

Hawley, Amos, 3:510

Hawthorne effect, 8:574

Hawtrey, Ralph G., 1:450

Hay-Herran Treaty (1903), 9:8

Hayek, Friedrich August von, 3:**434–436**
  banana parable, 1:248
  business cycle theories, 1:411, 412
  business cycles, 1:403
  capital, 1:430–431
  conservatism, 2:84, 85
  cultural group selection, 2:191
  free trade, 3:196
  Hurwicz, Leonid, 3:529
  laissez-faire, 4:336, 337–338
  liberalism, 4:426
  libertarianism, 4:437, 438
  Lundberg, Erik, 4:518
  Mont Pelerin Society, 5:272–273
  neoclassical economics, 2:519
  neoliberalism, 5:473–474, 9:38
  neutral rate of interst, 4:79
  ordinality, 6:57
  prices, 6:455
  scientism, 7:365

Hayflick, Leonard, 3:307

Haymarket Square riot, 3:**436**, 4:302, 8:515, 9:127

Hays, Peter L., 2:258

Hazard, moral. *See* Moral hazard

Hazard function. *See* Duration models; Probability distributions

Hazardous waste. *See* Toxic waste

Hazards
  environmental, 8:656
  occupational, 6:22–23
    compensating wages, 9:6
    industrial accidents, 1:8–9
    wages, 6:24–25

whistle-blowers, 9:80
vulnerability, 8:656–657
See also Moral hazard

Hazing. *See* Rites of passage

HCC (Human-centered computing), 2:61

HCI (Human-computer interaction), 2:61

HDI (Human Development Index), 3:278

HDTV (High-definition television), 3:141

Head Start, 3:**437–438**, 438–440, 9:28
  benign neglect, 1:283
  school readiness, 7:87

Head Start experiments, 3:**438–440**

Headlam, Cuthbert, 4:376

Healing, vodou, 8:634

Health
  addiction, 1:22
  adolescents, 5:405–407
  air pollution, 6:362
  cross-sectional research, 7:190
  defined, 9:140
  economic inequality, 8:592
  gender gap, 3:279
  labeling theory, 4:299
  life events and stress, 4:443–444
  lifestyles, 4:445
  loneliness, 4:486, 487
  malnutrition, 4:567–568
  marital conflict, 4:600
  medical anthropology, 1:130–132
  National Family Health Surveys, 5:392–394
  Navajos, 5:448
  noise pollution, 6:363
  objective utility, 8:557–558
  pollution, 6:359, 360
  population studies, 6:382
  racial discrimination, 2:394
  right to, 9:140
  risk assessment, 8:656–657
  sanitation, 7:321–323
  sensationalism, 7:443
  shamans, 7:486–488
  social isolation, 7:600
  stress, 8:173–175
  volunteerism, 8:642
  See also Disease

Health, Culture and Community (Paul), 1:131

Health, mental. *See* Mental health

Health, public. *See* Public health

Health care. *See* Medicine

Health economics, 3:**440–441**, 442

Health for All initiative, 9:140

Health in developing countries, 3:**441–444**, 7:321

Health insurance
  Current Population Survey, 2:213
  Medicare, 5:62–63
  pay-or-play, 5:396
  single-payer, 5:396

Health insurance, national. *See* National health insurance

Health maintenance organizations (HMOs), 5:396

Healthy People 2010, 5:407

Hearsay, 3:**444–445**, 7:295–298

Hearst, William Randolph, 4:212, 213, 9:23

Heart disease. *See* Cardiovascular disease

Heath, Edward, 2:87

Heaven, 2:248, 3:**445–446**
  See also Hell

Heaven and Hell (Huxley), 3:411

Heaven's Gate, 2:188

Heavy metal music, 7:268

Hebdige, Dick, 1:572

Hebert v. Louisiana (1926), 1:298

Hebrews. *See* Jews

Heckit. *See* Tobit

Heckman, James J., 2:143, 3:446

Heckman selection correction procedure, 3:**446–448**

Heckscher, Eli F., 3:448, 5:93, 94

Heckscher-Ohlin-Samuelson model, 3:**448–450**
  Dornbusch-Fischer-Samuelson model, 2:438
  exports, 3:69
  international economics, 2:508
  North-South models, 5:547
  Rybczynski theorem, 7:305, 306

Hedgewar, K. V., 3:478

Hedging, 3:**450–451**
  coffee industry, 1:594–595
  contango, 2:112
  institutional investors, 4:134
  Ponzi schemes, 6:368–369
  stock options, 8:153–154
  yield curve, 9:167

Hedonic prices, 3:**451–452**, 7:485

Hedonism, 8:558
  See also Farsightedness

Hedström, Peter, 2:72

Hefferline, Ralph, 3:311

Hegel, Georg Wilhelm Friedrich,
    3:452–453
    aesthetics, 1:30
    alienation, 1:75
    civil society, 1:552
    class consciousness, 1:571
    collective memory, 2:8
    communalism, 2:30
    communism, 2:34
    critical theory, 2:176, 177
    Frankfurt School, 3:188
    Hegelians, 3:453–454
    hegemony, 3:456
    idealism, 3:547–548
    Lefebvre, Henri, 4:400
    materialism, 5:19
    Neumann, Franz, 5:482
    objectivity, 6:9–10
    otherness, 6:82
    recognition, 7:109
    scientific method, 7:362, 363
Hegelians, 3:453–455
    critical theory, 2:176, 177, 178
    realist theory, 7:98
Hegemony, 3:455–456
    civil society, 1:553
    class consciousness, 1:572
    colonialism, 2:12
    cultural studies, 2:199
    culture, 2:203
    curriculum, 2:214
    decolonization, 2:257
    developing countries, 2:336
    empire, 2:575
    Gramsci, Antonio, 3:364
    Hall, Stuart, 3:410
    Hussein, Saddam, 3:533
    Iran-Iraq War, 4:143
    Jacobinism, 4:165
    Kindleberger, Charles Poor, 4:267
    liberalism, 4:425–426
    masculinity studies, 5:7–8
    multilateralism, 5:321
    organic intellectuals, 4:66, 67
    Pax Britannica, 6:179
    plantation, 6:277–278
    racial identification, 3:549
    resistance, 7:208–209
    social justice, 4:241
    transitional conjunctures, 2:78
    unilateralism, 8:509
Hegemony and Socialist Strategy (Laclau
    and Mouffe), 6:396
Heidegger, Martin

existentialism, 3:43
gaze, 3:263
hermeneutics, 3:463
humanism, 3:518
linguistic turn, 4:457
Lukacs, Georg, 4:515
modernity, 5:231
objectivity, 6:11
positivism, 7:98
poststructuralism, 6:399, 400
Weltanschauung, 9:78
Heider, Fritz, 1:205
    See also Equilibrium in psychology
Heighton, William, 9:126
Heilbroner, Robert, 2:332,
    3:456–457, 5:501
Heinen, Tom, 8:585
Heinlein, Robert, 7:361
Held, David, 5:421
Heliocentric theory, 8:532
Hell, 2:248, 3:457–459
    See also Heaven
Heller, Walter W., 9:25–26
Helms, Jesse, 6:343–344
Help America Vote Act (2000), 8:654
Helplessness, learned. *See* Learned
    helplessness
Hemings, Sally, 4:181, 7:468
Hemingway, Ernest, 9:18
Hempel, Carl, 1:275, 278, 279, 280
Hemphill, John, 4:379
Henderson, Fletcher, 4:176
Henderson, Lawrence, 7:237
Hendry, David, 2:3
Henle, Mary, 5:501
Henotheism. *See* Monotheism
Henry, John, 4:207
Hensley, Albert, 1:457
Henslin, James M., 1:214
Henson, Josiah, 8:482–483
Herb, Michael, 2:360
Herc, Kool, 3:480
Herculaneum, 1:165
Herd behavior, 3:459–460
    bubbles (economics), 1:378–379
    bull and bear markets, 1:385–386
    conformity, 2:71–72
    entertainment industry, 2:602
    jingoism, 4:201–202
    lynchings, 4:526–527
    majorities, 4:560
    panics, 6:123, 124–125
    pluralistic ignorance, 3:560–561
    race riots, 7:33–35

Herder, Johann Gottfried von, 5:378
    cultural relativism, 2:194, 195
    culture, 2:202–203
    determinism, 2:323
    nation-states, 5:421
Herding economy, 5:447, 9:109
Hereditary Genius (Galton), 3:247,
    4:378, 8:261
Hereditary monarchy. *See*
    Monarchism; Monarchy
Heredity, 3:460–462, 5:445
    biological determinism,
        2:325–326
    blood and bloodline, 1:335–336
    caste, 1:457, 458, 460, 461
    Darwin, Charles, 2:*230*, 231*t*
    diathesis-stress model, 2:358
    Dobzhansky, Theodosius,
        2:432–433
    eugenics, 3:21–22
    evolutionary theory of kinship,
        4:273–274
    Galton, Francis, 3:247–248
    Hamilton's rule, 3:414–415
    hypertension, 3:539
    intelligence, 4:72–73, 7:22–23
    IQ controversy, 4:139–142
    Mendel's law, 5:82–83
    obesity, 6:5
    ordinary least squares, 4:393
    path analysis, 6:168, 169
    personality, 6:219–220
    psychological depression, 2:306,
        307
    race, 7:6–7, 8–11
    religion, 2:163
    self-constrained behavior, 1:274
    sexual orientation, 7:476–477
    sibling relationships, 7:506
    talent, 8:261–262
    temperament, 8:321
    twin studies, 8:473–475
    See also Genetic determinism; Trait
        theory
Heresy, 4:22–23, 6:78–79
Herfindahl-Hirschman Index (HHI),
    2:53
Heritage. *See* Culture; Tradition
Heritage Foundation, 1:311
Heritage management. *See* Cultural
    resource management (CRM)
Herland (Gilman), 8:561
Herman, C. Peter, 6:3
Herman, Edward, 8:320
Herman, Nancy J., 4:300

Hermaphrodites, 3:272

Hermeneutics, 3:462–464, 4:457, 458

Hermeneutics and the Human Sciences
(Ricoeur), 3:462

Hernandez, Aileen, 3:121

Hernández, Pete, 3:464–465

Hernandez v. Texas (1954), 3:464–466

Herndon, Nixon v. (1927), 9:84

Hero, Rodney E., 6:337
    community power studies, 2:44
    Latino politics, 6:339

Herodotus, 1:119
    auctions, 1:206
    cannibalism, 1:427

Heroin, 3:412

Herrera, Celia, 8:617

Herrick, John J., 8:614

Herring, Cedric, 2:17

Herring, Richard J., 6:94–95

Herrnstein, Richard J., 1:15–16,
2:326, 3:160, 4:73, 7:22

Hersey, Paul, 4:379, 380

Hersh, Seymour, 4:275

Hershey, Marjorie R., 2:246–247

Herskovits, Frances S., 3:466, 467

Herskovits, Melville J., 3:466–467
    Boas, Franz, 1:345
    dance, 2:224
    Hurston, Zora Neale, 3:527

Hertz, Robert, 3:239

Hertz, Rosanna, 3:116

Hertz, Tom, 8:533

Herzl, Theodor, 1:282, 9:180

Hess, Gregory, 1:406

Hesse, Ludwig Otto, 3:467–468

Hessian matrix, 3:467–468, 4:163

Heterarchy, 3:468–469

Heterodoxy
    habitus, 3:404, 405, 406
    inflation, 4:23, 24–26
    See also Orthodoxy

Heterogenous agents. *See* Principal-
agent models

Heterogloss. *See* Linguistic
anthropology

Heteronomy, 4:248
    See also Kant, Immanuel

Heteronormativity, 3:470, 4:194,
6:663–665

Heterosexuality. *See* Sexual orientation

Heteroskedasticity, 3:470–471
    generalized least squares, 3:287,
289–290
    left and right censoring, 1:474
    regression analysis, 7:138, 139

Heterotypic stability. *See* Psychological
stability

Hetrick, Ronald, 6:99

Heywood, Andrew, 1:294

Heywood, Leslie, 9:115

Hezbollah, 1:579, 4:397–398

HFCS (High-fructose corn syrup), 6:4

HHI (Herfindahl-Hirschman Index),
2:53

HHS (U.S. Department of Health and
Human Services), 4:33, 5:551

Hickman, Larry, 3:167

Hicks, John R., 2:270, 3:471–472
    Arrow, Kenneth J., 1:181
    capital, 1:431
    compensation criterion, 9:62
    Hayek, Friedrich August von,
3:435
    IS-LM model, 4:158–159
    Kaldor-Hicks compensation test,
9:65
    liquidity, 4:459, 461
    market clearing, 4:602
    ordinality, 6:57
    short period, 7:501
    tâtonnement, 8:270–271
    two-sector models, 8:475
    utility function, 8:555

Hicks-Kaldor compensation. *See*
Public interest; Welfare economics

Hicks-neutral technological change,
1:491

Hidalgos, 2:146, 147

The Hidden Dimension (Hall), 1:171

Hidden persuaders, 3:472–473

The Hidden Persuaders (Packard),
2:107–108, 3:473, 8:201

Hierarchy, 3:473–475
    Benedict, Ruth, 1:282
    biological determinism, 2:325
    blackness, 1:328–329
    Brahmins, 1:366–367
    bureaucracy, 1:390
    caste, 1:457–460, 461
    civilization, 1:558
    class conflict, 1:571
    clientelism, 1:579
    cluster analysis, 1:585, 586
    Coloreds (South Africa), 2:15
    colorism, 2:18
    Comte, Auguste, 2:62
    contempt, 2:113
    conversational analysis, 2:118–120
    dalits, 2:221–222
    developing countries, 2:335–336

discrimination, 2:391, 399
    heterarchy, 3:468–469
    immigrants, 3:565, 580
    ingratiation, 4:34
    Jajmani matrix, 4:167
    Kshatriyas, 4:291–292
    labor, 4:301
    leaders, 4:376, 377
    left and right, 4:401
    low and high culture, 2:205
    marginalization, 4:599
    Maslow, Abraham, 5:11–12
    matriarchy, 5:28–30
    Meiji Restoration, 5:70
    Mexican Americans, 5:119–120
    miscegenation, 5:199–200
    patricians, 6:174–175
    phenotype, 6:243–244
    primates, 6:461
    race, 7:2–7, 9, 13–15, 23, 25, 27,
38, 44–45
    racial democracy, 2:282–283
    racial identification, 3:548–550
    racial inequality, 4:6
    right wing, 7:247
    self-actualization, 7:394–395
    social dominance orientation,
7:583–584
    social status, 7:621–622
    sports, 8:63–65
    subaltern, 8:190–192
    Sudras, 8:212–213
    system analysis, 8:257
    unequal education, 2:538–539

Higgins, E. Tory, 6:85, 7:415, 416

Higgins, Edward, 3:127

Higgs, Henry, 1:429

High blood pressure. *See* Hypertension

High culture. *See* Low and high
culture

High-definition television (HDTV),
3:141

High-fructose corn syrup (HFCS), 6:4

High Plains culture, 5:425

High-powered money. *See* Monetary
base

High technology. *See* Microelectronics
industry

Higham, John, 5:430

Higher education, American dream,
1:96

Higher Education Act (U.S. 1965),
3:372

Higher-order beliefs, 1:269

Highway Safety Act (U.S. 1966), 3:373

Hijab. See Veils, in Middle Eastern and North African cultures

Hijras, 3:271

Hilbert, David, 8:643

Hilferding, Rudolf, 1:12, 360, 361, 446, 3:476–477

Hill, Anita, 3:121, 7:474

Hill, Barney, 8:508

Hill, Betty, 8:508

Hill, Christopher, 3:482

Hill, Walter B., 9:53

Hillman, James, 1:391

Hilton, Rodney, 3:134

Hima tribe, 9:109

Hin-mut-too-yah-lat-kekht. *See* Chief Joseph

Hindenburg, Paul von, 3:487, 5:449

Hindess, Barry, 1:188, 3:134

Hindsight, 3:173

Hinduism, 3:477–480
    affirmative action, 1:31
    Ambedkar, B. R., 1:90–92
    Aryans, 1:185
    Brahmins, 1:366–367
    Buddha, 1:380, 381
    Buddhism, 1:383
    clash of civilizations, 1:559
    cows, 1:121
    dalits, 2:221–222
    demography, 7:161
    funerals, 3:239
    gold industry, 3:343
    hell, 3:458
    Jainism, 4:166
    Jajmani matrix, 4:167
    Jinnah, Mohammed Ali, 4:203–204
    Kshatriyas, 4:291–292
    legal systems, 4:406
    martyrdom, 4:629
    missionaries, 5:205
    monotheism, 5:271
    polytheism, 5:271, 6:367, 368
    reincarnation, 7:145
    Sikhism, 7:508–509
    sin, 7:519–520
    slave culture, 1:40
    Sudras, 8:212–213
    theism, 8:341
    Vaisyas, 8:567–568
    worship, 9:154, 155
    See also Caste

Hinkley, Wiersma, 3:206

Hip hop, 3:480–481, 7:269, 8:172–173

Hippie counterculture, Woodstock, 9:120–121

Hippocrates, occupational hazards, 6:22

Hirohito, 9:148

Hiroshima (Japan), 9:30, 52, 150

Hirsch, Alan, 4:524

Hirsch, Sam, 8:653

Hirschfeld, Magnus, 7:44

Hirschman, Albert O., 3:43–45, 5:535

Hirschman, Charles, 2:296

Hirst, Paul, 1:188, 3:134

Hispanics. *See* Latinos

Hispaniola, 2:19, 20, 146

Hiss, Alger, 2:85

Histadrut, 1:282, 283

Histograms, 3:207, *207*
    See also Statistical inference

Histoire de Charles XII (Voltaire), 8:635

Historical archaeology, 1:117

Historical economics. *See* Cliometrics

Historical institutionalism. *See* Neoinstitutionalism

Historical Judaism. *See* Judaism

Historical linguistics, 1:118

Historical particularism, 1:120

Historical sociology, 3:483

Historical time, uncertainty, 8:481–482

Historicism, 7:291

History
    Beard, Charles and Mary, 1:268–269
    The Church, 1:532–534
    cliometrics, 1:581–583
    conjectural, 1:127
    death and dying, 2:247–248
    drought, 2:448
    Jews, 4:193–196, 219–222
    natural, 1:136–137
    revisionist, 3:187–188
    revolution, 7:228–229
    Rousseau, Jean-Jacques, 7:291
    taxation, 8:280–281
    War and Peace (Tolstoy), 9:19

History, economic. *See* Cliometrics

History, social, 3:482–485
    case method, 1:453
    collective memory, 2:7–8
    memory, 5:74–75
    See also specific events, countries and policies

History and Class Consciousness (Lukacs), 1:572

History of Ancient Art (Winckelmann), 1:165

History of consciousness. *See* Consciousness

History of England (Hume), 3:519

History of Ethnological Theory (Lowie), 4:507

A History of Marxian Economics (Howard and King), 8:576

A History of National Accounting (Vanoli), 3:384

History of Rome (Livy), 6:20

History of Sexuality (Foucault), 3:182

A History of the English-Speaking Peoples (Churchill), 1:538

A History of the Guyanese Working People, 1881-1905 (Rodney), 7:270

History of the Indies (Las Casas), 2:146, 147

History of the People of Trinidad and Tobago (Williams), 9:98

History of the Russian Empire Under Peter the Great (Voltaire), 8:635

History Will Absolve Me (Castro), 2:186

Hitchens, Christopher, 4:275

Hite, Shere, 3:485–486, 7:482–483

Hite Report. *See* Hite, Shere

Hitler, Adolf, 3:486–488, 6:190
    appeasement, 1:153
    Arendt, Hannah, 1:173
    Aryans, 1:185–186
    bigotry, 1:296
    blood and bloodline, 1:336
    Chamberlain, Neville, 1:489, 490
    Churchill, Winston, 1:537
    concentration camps, 2:63
    ethnic conflict, 3:2
    fascism, 3:104
    ghettos, 3:312
    humiliation, 3:522
    Jung, Carl, 4:231
    League of Nations, 4:386
    Mussolini, Benito, 5:350
    Olympic Games, 6:40
    race, 7:5, 21
    relativism, 7:156, 157
    rise of, 9:148
    Social Darwinism, 2:233–234
    Spanish Civil War, 8:43
    state capitalism, 1:444
    Treaty of Versailles, 9:148
    USSR, 8:511

See also Holocaust; Nazism

Hitler's Willing Executioners
(Goldhagen), 3:497

Hittites, 3:394

HIV (Human immunodeficiency
virus), 1:63–65, 3:**488–490**
contraception, 2:115
developing countries, 1:65–67,
3:442
reproductive politics, 7:182
self-constrained behavior, 1:274
World Health Organization, 9:140
See also AIDS (Acquired
immunodeficiency syndrome)

Hizbollah. *See* Hezbollah

Hmong, 3:**490–491**
Chinese Americans, 1:514
funerals, 3:239

HMOs (Health maintenance
organizations), 5:396

Ho Chi Minh, 3:**491–492**
anticolonial movements, 1:139
Le Duc Tho, 4:398
Vietnam War, 8:612, 613

Ho Chi Minh Trail, 8:614

Hobbes, Thomas, 3:**492–493**
behaviorism, 1:275
constitutionalism, 2:93
cooperation, 2:122
defense, 2:258
distributive justice, 4:240
freedom, 3:196
hierarchy, 3:475
justice, 4:237
liberalism, 4:425
long period analysis, 4:489
moral philosophy, 6:255, 256
national security, 5:411
natural rights, 5:439
Neumann, Franz, 5:482
objectivity, 6:8
political realism, 7:96
politics, 6:319–320
property rights, 8:627
Rawls, John, 7:84
recognition, 7:109
social contract, 7:581
sovereignty, 8:38
state of nature, 8:110

Hobbies vs. work, 9:123

Hobhouse, Emily, 1:350

Hobhouse, Leonard, 4:424

Hobos, 3:**494**
See also Homelessness; Vagabonds

Hobsbawm, Eric, 3:482, 483

class consciousness, 1:572

collective memory, 2:8

liberation movements, 4:432, 433

Hobson, John Atkinson
Boer War, 1:350
bubbles (economics), 1:378
goodwill, 3:349
imperialism, 3:587–588
inventories, 4:128, 202
Leninism, 4:412
marginal product of labor,
4:306–307
rentier class, 1:567, 568
underconsumption, 8:488
world-system, 9:153

Hochschild, Arlie, 8:6

"Hockey stick" graph, 3:329

Hodder, Ian, 1:168

Hodge, Robert, 6:27

Hofmann, Albert, 3:411

Hofstadter, Richard, 2:232, 567

Hoggart, Richard, 2:199

Holbach, Paul-Henri Thiry, Baron d',
1:275

Holding companies, 6:72

Holiday, Billie, 4:177

Holidays, 8:565–566

Holism
anthropology, 1:138
disease, 2:407
individualism, 3:619–620
public anthropology, 1:133
trans-disciplinary research, 7:198

Hollander, Edwin, 4:380, 381

Hollerith, Herman, 2:61

Hollingshead, August B., 7:657

Hollister, Robinson G., 9:26

Holly, James T., 1:315, 316

Hollywood. *See* Entertainment
industry; Film industry

Holmes, John Haynes, 5:383

Holmes, Oliver Wendell, Jr., 4:223,
6:420

Holmes, Sherlock, 3:137

Holocaust, 3:**494–498**
Arendt, Hannah, 1:173
critical race theory, 2:175
cultural relativism, 1:123
destructive obedience, 6:2
ethnic conflict, 3:2
genocide, 3:296
humiliation, 3:522
Jewish diaspora, 4:190, 192
Jewish history, 4:196

memory, 5:75
xenophobia, 9:158
See also Anti-Semitism;
Concentration camps; Hitler,
Adolf; Jews; Nazism

Holstein, Gen. H.L. Villaume
Ducoudray, 1:355

Holsti, Kalevi J., 2:259

Holt, Edwin, 1:276

Holt, P. M., 3:126

Holy Communion. *See* Sacraments

Holy Land. *See* Palestine

Holy Roman Empire, 3:**498**

Holy Spirit, 1:531

Holy Trinity, 1:531, 533

Homagium, 3:135

Homans, George, 7:585, 8:7

Home-based employment, 9:125

Home care workers, 9:122

Home ownership
American Dream, 1:96–97
loans, 4:473

Home Rule League movement, 5:460

Home to Harlem (McKay), 3:426

Homeland Security Department, U.S.,
2:155, 260, 384

The Homeless (Jencks), 4:184

Homelessness, 3:**498–500**
case method, 1:453
census, 1:477
cities, 1:542
Jencks, Christopher, 4:184
See also Hobos; Vagabonds

Homeostatis. *See* Social system

Homer, 3:130–131

Homer Plessy v. John H. Ferguson
(1896). *See Plessy v. Ferguson* (1896)

Homestead Act (U.S. 1862), 1:61

Homesteading, 4:344, 346

Homicide. *See* Murder

Homo economicus. *See* Theory

Homo floresiensis, 1:126–127

Homo Hierarchicus (Dumont),
1:461–462

Homo neanderthalensis, 1:126–127

Homo psychologicus. *See* Theory

Homo sapiens, 1:126

Homosexual: Oppression and Liberation
(Altman), 6:329

The Homosexual Matrix (Tripp), 6:434

Homosexuality, AIDS/HIV, 1:63, 64,
66

Homosocial reproduction, 3:325–326

Homotypic stability. *See* Psychological
stability

Honda, 1:223

Honduras
    banana industry, 1:246
    Garifuna, 3:257–258

Honecker, Erich, 1:289

Hong Kong
    Chinese diaspora, 1:518
    film industry, 3:140
    Kuznets hypothesis, 4:297
    legal systems, 4:406
    Treaty of Nanking (1842), 6:46

Honneth, Axel, 3:189, 454, 7:628

Hoodoo. *See* Vodou

Hooker, John Lee, 1:342, 343

Hooker Chemical Corporation. *See* Occidental Chemical Corporation (OxyChem)

Hoover, Herbert
    conservatism, 2:85
    Dixiecrats, 2:429
    New Deal, 5:493, 494, 497
    Republican Party (U.S.), 7:187

Hoover, J. Edgar, 3:**500–501**, 7:175, 9:174
    Black Panthers, 1:319
    Garvey, Marcus, 3:258
    King, Martin Luther, Jr., 4:269
    McCarthyism, 5:44

Hope, 3:**501–503**, 4:477–478
    See also Optimism; Positive psychology

Hopi, 2:194–195, 5:424, 426, 447

Hopkins, Budd, 8:508

Hopkins, Samuel, 4:409

Hopkins, Terence K., 9:153

Hopwood, Texas v. (1996), 3:373

Horizontalist money approach. *See* Exogenous money

Horkheimer, Max
    critical theory, 2:176, 177
    culture, 2:203
    Enlightenment, 2:596, 597
    Frankfurt School, 3:188, 189
    narratives, 5:371
    praxis, 6:422
    social theory, 7:628

Hormones, alpha-males, 1:83, 84

Horn, Bobbie L., 6:95

Horney, Karen, 6:29

Horowitz, David, 3:109, 7:166

Horrace, William, 2:479

Hortacsu, Ali, 1:207–208

Horticulture, fertile crescent, 3:125

Horton, Willie, 4:371, 7:38

Horwitz, Morton, 2:139

Hostadter, Richard, 4:64

Hostages, 1:451, 4:142

Hostility, Cold War, 2:4

Hostos, Eugenio María de, 1:356

Hot money, 3:**504**
    capital flight, 1:434
    trade liberalization, 4:428

Hotelling rule. *See* Resource economics

Hotz, Henry, 3:336

Hourani, Akram, 8:521

House, Robert, 4:382

House of Commons, U.K. *See* Parliament, U.K.

House of Councillors, Japan, 2:360–361

House of Lords, U.K. *See* Parliament, U.K.

House of Peers, Japan, 2:360

House of Representatives, Japan, 2:360–361

House of Representatives, U.S.
    apportionment, 1:154–155
    appropriations, 1:155
    Chisholm, Shirley, 1:522
    Congress, U.S., 2:73–74
    lynchings, 4:527
    repression, 7:175

House of Youth Black Faith (HYBF), 7:67

House Select Committee on Assassinations (HSCA), 9:34

Household production accounts, 5:403–404

Households
    defined, 3:91
    family structure, 3:84
    household sample survey, 5:409–411
    national income accounts, 5:400
    production, 5:397, 403–404
    unpaid domestic work, 3:167

Housework. *See* Domestic work

Housing
    audits, 1:109–210
    black middle class, 1:314
    cities, 1:541, 542
    civil rights movement, U.S., 1:552
    Gautreaux residential mobility program, 3:259–260
    hedonic prices, 3:451
    landlords, 4:347
    loans, 1:97, 3:363
    market, 3:380

Multi-City Study of Urban Inequality, 5:314–315
    neighborhoods, 5:463–464
    school desegregation, 2:317
    socioeconomic status, 7:655–656
    tax credits, 8:273–274
    urban sprawl, 8:540

Housing Act (U.S. 1949), 8:536

Houston, Charles Hamilton, 3:**505**, 5:384
    black liberalism, 1:312
    Brown v. Board of Education (1954), 1:374
    Marshall, Thurgood, 4:625

Hout, Michael, 8:534

Houthakker, Hendrik, 8:562, 563

How Class Works (Aronowitz), 4:302

How Democratic Is the American Constitution? (Dahl), 2:220

How Europe Underdeveloped Africa (Rodney), 7:269–270

How to Live (Fisher), 3:152

Howard, Michael, 2:88, 8:576

Howard, T. R. M., 3:501

Howell, Leonard P., 7:67

Howlin' Wolf, 1:343

Hoxby, Caroline, 5:391

HPI (Human Poverty Index), 3:278

Hrappans, 2:443

HSCA (House Select Committee on Assassinations), 9:34

Hua, 9:108

Hubbert, M. King, 4:448

Huber, Evelyne, 3:185, 9:70

Huber, Joel, 8:369–370

Huber, P., 1:83

HUD (U.S. Department of Housing and Urban Development)
    black capitalism, 1:440
    Moving to Opportunity, 5:302–303

Hudson, Valerie, 3:170

Huerta, Dolores, 1:493

Huerta, Victoriano, 5:130–131

Huffing, 2:454–455

Hufton, Olwen, 8:567

Hughes, Everett, 3:497

Hughes, Langston, 3:424, 425, 426, 527

Hughes, Sarah, 1:514

Huichols, 1:457

Huis Clos (Sartre), 3:43

Hukumat-i Islami (Khomeini), 4:264

Hull, Belden, 9:28

Hull, Clark, 3:**505–506**

behaviorism, 1:275, 277, 278
  equilibrium, 2:623
  reinforcement theories, 7:147
  Thorndike, Edward, 8:358
Hulme, David, 5:520
Human Action (Mises), 1:211
Human behavior. *See* Behavior
Human capital, 3:**506–510**
  Becker, Gary S., 1:270, 271
  Berg, Ivar E., 1:288
  blue collar and white collar, 1:337
  Castro, Fidel, 1:466
  described, 1:429
  health economics, 3:440–441
  intergenerational transmission, 4:89
  Jencks, Christopher, 4:184
  labor economics, 2:514
  managerial capitalism, 1:442–443
  mobility, 5:210
  population studies, 6:382
  returns to education, 7:65–66
  soft skills, 8:21–22
  unemployability, 8:496
  wealth, 9:44
  winner-take-all society, 9:102–103
  workplace relations, 9:136
Human Capital (Becker), 1:270
Human-centered computing (HCC), 2:61
Human-computer interaction (HCI), 2:61
The Human Connection (Montagu and Matson), 5:529–530
Human development. *See* Developmental psychology; Physiology
Human Development Index (HDI), 3:278
Human Dignity and Humiliation Studies network, 3:521
Human ecology, 3:**510–511**
  Bahro, Rudolf, 1:238
  cultural landscape, 2:192–193
  deforestation, 2:262–264
  developmental psychology, 2:350–351
  drought, 2:447–448
  energy sector, 2:591–592
  environmental impact assessment, 2:605–607
  limits of growth, 4:448–450
  metropolitan regions, 7:134
  Park School, 6:142–143
  political theory, 6:318

regions, 7:130
  resources, 7:212
Human experiments, 3:**59–61**
  cognitive dissonance, 1:599–600
  conformity, 2:71–72
  ethics, 2:635–637
  experimental realism, 7:93–95
  gender preference, 6:434
  informed consent, 4:33
  institutional review board, 4:42–43
  Lewin, Kurt, 4:417–418
  luck, 4:512
  Milgram, Stanley, 5:161–162
  shock experiments, 3:62–63
  social influence, 7:594–598
  Zimbardo, Philip, 9:178
Human fertility, 3:**126–130**
  baby boomers, 1:235
  Becker, Gary S., 1:270, 271
  birth control, 1:302–303
  childlessness, 1:510
  demographic transition, 2:291–292
  demography, 2:293–294
  depopulation, 2:301–302
  infertility drugs, 4:19–20
  population aging, 3:306
  population control, 6:377–378
  population growth, 6:378–379
  population studies, 6:382
  reproduction, 7:178–179
  reproductive politics, 7:180–182
  social demography, 2:296–297
Human Genome Project, 3:295, 299
  ELSI, 5:362
  Mendel's law, 5:83
  nature *vs.* nurture, 5:446
  race, 7:11
Human geography, 3:303–305, 7:130
Human immunodeficiency virus (HIV). *See* HIV (Human immunodeficiency virus)
Human intelligence. *See* Intelligence
The Human Legacy (Festinger), 3:133
Human Nature and the Social Order (Cooley), 4:495
Human Poverty Index (HPI), 3:278
Human rights, 3:**512–515**
  abortion, 1:3–4
  Carter, Jimmy, 1:451
  census, 1:477
  child labor, 1:508–509
  children's rights, 1:512–513
  citizenship, 1:543–544

civil liberties, 1:546
  civil rights *vs.*, 1:548–549
  concentration camps, 2:63–64
  Condorcet, Marquis de, 2:66
  conflict, 2:70
  cultural rights, 2:197–198
  diamond industry, 2:356
  disability, 2:377
  fetal, 1:4
  free trade, 8:506
  General Motors, 3:286
  genocide, 3:296
  gesellschaft, 3:267
  health, 9:140
  humiliation, 3:522
  inalienable, 5:439
  indigenous rights, 3:614–615
  interrogation, 4:110–113
  left wing, 4:404
  liberty, 4:439
  moral suasion, 5:283
  Native Americans, 5:428
  natural, 5:438–439
  overpopulation, 6:96
  refugees, 7:125–126
  repression, 7:174–175
  reproductive, 3:120–121, 9:114, 117
  reproductive rights, 7:182, 183
  self-determination, 1:225
  slavery, 7:542–545
  trade liberalization, 4:428
  universalism, 8:526–527
  White, Walter, 9:81
  women, 9:109–110, 111–112, 117
  See also Basic needs
Human Rights Commission (UN), 8:524
Human Rights First, 3:431
Human Rights Watch, 1:547, 3:286
Human sacrifice, 3:**515–516**, 9:154
Human science, 9:78
Human Society (Davis), 2:293
Human sterilization, 8:**140–142**
  biological determinism, 2:326
  birth control, 1:302, 303
  blood and bloodline, 1:336
  contraception, 2:114
  eugenics, 3:21
  reproductive rights, 7:182
  surplus population, 8:238–239
Humanism, 3:**517–519**
  Althusser, Louis, 1:87

Humanism, *continued*
  equilibrium, 2:622
  Kaunda, Kenneth, 4:250
  Lefebvre, Henri, 4:400
  Lukacs, Georg, 4:515–516
  Machiavelli, Niccolò, 4:533–534
  Maslow, Abraham, 5:11–12
  positive psychology, 6:385
  Said, Edward, 7:309–310
Humanism and Democratic Criticism
  (Said), 7:310
Humanism in Zambia and a Guide to
  Its Implementation (Kaunda), 4:250
Humanitarianism, 1:451
Humankind, extinction of, 3:241
Humboldt, Alexander von, 3:303, 304
Humboldt, Wilhelm von, 4:424
Hume, David, 3:**519–520**
  Cantillion, Richard, 1:429
  empiricism, 2:578
  exogenous money, 5:258, 259
  Kant, Immanuel, 4:248–249
  laissez-faire, 4:337
  libertarianism, 4:437
  logic, 4:480
  Malthus, Thomas Robert, 4:570
  money, 5:252
  moral philosophy, 6:256
  neutrality of money, 5:490
  normative social sciences,
    5:534–535
  objectivity, 6:8–9
  polytheism, 6:367
  Popper, Karl, 6:371–372
  positive social science, 6:387
  quantity theory of money, 6:659
  race, 7:13
  relativism, 7:156
  Scottish moralists, 7:367–368
  supreme being, 8:231
  sympathy, 8:254
Hume process, 3:**520–521**
Humiliation, 3:**521–523**
  racial slurs, 7:41–42
  See also Shame
Humint. *See* Intelligence
Hummel, Ralph, 1:391, 392
Hummingbirds, 8:583
Humor, satire as, 7:330
Humor and Society (Koller), 2:23
Humphrey, Hubert, 2:288, 429, 430,
  5:505
Humphrey, Margo, 1:310
Humpty Dumpty, 5:549

Hungarian Revolution, 3:**523–524**
Hungary
  communism, 2:35
  latifundia, 4:353
  Warsaw Pact, 9:35
  See also Hungarian Revolution
Hunger. *See* Famine
Hunt, E. Howard, 9:43
Hunt, George, 1:345
Hunt, James, 4:378
Hunter, Alberta, 1:343
Hunter, Floyd, 3:**524–525**, 8:542
  community power studies, 2:42,
    45
  Dahl, Robert Alan, 2:219
  Lynd, Robert and Helen, 4:528
Hunter, James Davison, 3:96,
  7:162–163
Hunter, Walter, 1:276
Hunter-gatherers, 1:59–60, 9:109
Hunting
  Inuit, 4:125–126
  Native Americans, 5:424
Huntington, Samuel P., 1:108,
  3:**525–526**
  arms race, 1:178
  clash of civilizations, 1:557,
    559–560
  classical music, 1:575
  coups d'etat, 2:156
  democratization, 2:289
  religiosity, 7:163
  secular, 7:378
Huntington's disease, 3:294, 537
Hurd v. Hodge (1948), 3:505
Hurricane Katrina, 5:433
  See also Disaster management;
    Natural disasters
Hurston, Zora Neale, 3:**526–529**
  Black Arts Movement, 1:309
  black conservatism, 1:310
  black towns, 1:325
  Boas, Franz, 1:345
  Harlem Renaissance, 3:424, 426
Hurwicz, Leonid, 3:**529–530**, 8:562,
  563
Hussein, King of Jordan, 3:**530–531**
  Arab-Israeli War of 1967, 1:157
  Black September, 1:322, 323
  water resources, 9:42
Hussein, Saddam, 1:216, 3:**531–535**,
  8:521
  appeasement, 1:153
  autocracy, 1:216
  Bush, George H. W., 1:398

  Bush, George W., 1:399, 400
  Clinton, Bill, 1:580
  coalition, 1:587
  Gulf War of 1991, 3:397–398
  Iran-Iraq War, 4:143
  Iraq-U.S. War, 4:145–148
  just war, 4:236
  neoimperialism, 5:471
  September 11, 2001, 7:453
Husserl, Edmund, 2:80, 96
  objectivity, 6:10–11
  otherness, 6:82
  phenomenology, 6:242
  Weltanschauung, 9:78
Hutcheson, Francis, 1:495, 7:367, 368
Hutchinson, Ray, 1:541
Hutchinson affair. *See* Franklin,
  Benjamin
Hutterites, 2:40
Hutton, Bobby, 1:319
Hutus, 3:2, 10, 298
Huxley, Aldous, 1:391, 3:411, 8:561
Huxley, Julian, 2:233, 4:409
Huxley, Thomas H., 2:62, 233
HYBF (House of Youth Black Faith),
  7:67
Hybridity, 2:167, 168, 169,
  3:**535–537**
Hyde Amendment (U.S. 1976), 1:4
Hydraulic model, 3:151
Hydrogen cyanide, 9:52
Hygiene. *See* Sanitation
Hygiene, race. *See* Eugenics
Hymes, Charles, 6:85
Hymes, Dell, 1:129
Hynek, J. Alen, 8:507
Hyperactivity, 3:**537–538**
  See also Attention-
    deficit/hyperactivity disorder
    (ADHD)
Hypergamy. *See* Dowry and bride
  price
Hypernationalism, 5:420
Hyperopia. *See* Farsightedness
Hypertension, 3:**538–541**
  John Henryism, 4:207–208
  slavery hypertension hypothesis,
    7:546–547
Hypnosis, 3:213
Hypnosis and Suggestibility (Hull),
  3:506
Hypogamy. *See* Dowry and bride price
Hypothalamic-pituitary-adrenal axis,
  6:5

Hypothesis and hypothesis testing, 3:**541–543**
 Bayesian statistics, 1:265–266
 case method, 1:453
 experiments, 3:55–58
 functional form, 3:230
 logic, 4:480
 randomness, 7:64
 social demography, 2:297
 standard errors, 2:629
 statistics in the social sciences, 8:125–126
 structural equation models, 8:180
 test statistics, 8:331–333
 Z-test, 9:181–183
 See also Scientific method
Hypothesis and hypothesis testing, nested, 3:**543–544**
Hyppolite, Jean, 3:453
Hysteresis, unemployment, 2:514, 8:496, 502

I

IAEA (International Atomic Energy Agency), 1:176–177, 8:525
IARC (International Agricultural Research Centers), 3:377
IBFs (International banking facilities), 6:31
IBM, 1:402–403
 See also Microelectronics industry
Ibn Khaldūn, 1:119, 3:**545–546**
 African sociology, 7:664
 economic growth, 2:486, 490–491
Ibo. *See* Negro
IBRD (International Bank for Reconstruction and Development). *See* World Bank
ICBMs (Intercontinental ballistic missiles), 1:177, 9:31, 49
ICC (International Criminal Court), 3:297–298, 361, 512, 514, 9:22–23
Ice Age, Native Americans, 5:424
Iceberg Slim. *See* Pimps
Icecaps, melting, 3:328
Iceland
 gender gap, 3:278
 NATO, 5:544–546
Ickes, Harold, 5:497
ICO (International Coffee Organization), 1:595
ICOMOS (International Congress on Monuments and Sites), 2:197
ICSID (International Centre for Settlement of Investment Disputes), 9:137

Id, 3:212–213, 4:230
 See also Equilibrium in psychology; Freud, Sigmund; Psychoanalytic theory
IDA (International Development Association), 9:137, 139
The Idea of a University (Newman), 8:528–529
Ideal self, 6:85
Ideal type, 3:**546–547**, 9:55–56
Idealism, 3:**547–548**
 behaviorism, 1:276
 Disney, Walt, 2:410
 Hegel, Georg Wilhelm Friedrich, 3:451, 452, 453
 international relations, 4:100
 realist theory, 7:98
 reality, 7:100–101
Identification, racial, 3:**548–550**
 blackness, 1:328–330
 blood and bloodline, 1:335–336
 Coloreds (South Africa), 2:16–17
 Creole, 2:168
 described, 7:2–7, 8–11
 Diop, Cheikh Anta, 2:369–370
 discrimination, 2:391
 miscegenation, 5:199–200
 mulatto escape hatch, 5:310–312
 Multidimensional Inventory of Black Identity, 5:318–319
 multiracial movement, 5:331
 pardo, 6:130
 passing, 6:165–166
 psychology, 7:23
 race relations cycle, 7:31–33
 racial classification, 7:38–40
 racial democracy, 2:282
 racialization, 7:43–44
 religion, 7:25–26
 self-hatred, 7:416–417
 sellouts, 7:434–435
 wage discrimination, 2:405
Identification problem, 3:**550–551**, 7:121–122
Identification Problems in the Social Sciences (Manski), 7:121
Les identités meurtrières (Maalouf). *See Identities, Deadly* (Maalouf)
Identities, Deadly (Maalouf), 3:551
Identity, 3:**551–555**
 Boricua, 1:355–356
 Cherokees, 1:496, 498
 child development, 1:507
 Chinese Americans, 1:514–515
 Chinese diaspora, 1:517, 518

 civil wars, 1:555
 Clark, Kenneth B., 1:560
 clash of civilizations, 1:559–560
 cleavages, 1:577–578
 cognitive dissonance, 1:599
 collective memory, 2:7–8
 Coloreds (South Africa), 2:16–17
 Croats, 2:179
 cultural neighborhoods, 5:464
 Darfur, 2:226
 deadly, 3:551
 destabilization, 2:321
 Diop, Cheikh Anta, 2:369–370
 discrimination, 2:391, 399
 functionalism, 3:231
 gender, 1:28, 3:119, 269
 group, 1:30–32, 3:385–386, 387
 Huntington, Samuel P., 3:525
 hybridity, 3:535–536
 Jewish diaspora, 4:190–191
 Jews, 4:194–196, 222
 Latinos, 4:358
 liberation movements, 4:431–432, 433
 masculinity, 5:2–3, 5–6
 meaning, 5:51–52
 motherhood, 5:299
 nation-states, 5:420, 422
 nationalism, 5:417
 oppositional, 6:49–51
 Quebecois movement, 6:661–663
 queer studies, 6:664
 role conflict, 7:272–273
 self-classification, 7:397–398
 self-concept, 7:398–400
 social identification, 7:593–594
 tribalism, 8:448–449
 veiling, 8:603
 wage discrimination, 2:405
 whiteness, 9:87–89
 See also Self-identity
Identity, complex. *See* Complex identity
Identity, national. *See* Nationalism and nationality
Identity, racial. *See* Race; Racial identification
Identity, self. *See* Self-identity
Identity, social, 3:**555–556**
 caste, 1:457–460
 conformity, 2:71
 constructivism, 2:97
 Dawes, Robyn, 2:245
 Deadly Identities (Maalouf), 3:551

Identity, social, *continued*
  described, 3:552
  identification, 7:593–594
  identity politics, 6:334–336
  realist theory, 7:99
  stereotypes, 8:136–139
  stratification economics, 2:531
  violence, 8:623
  See also Self-concept; Self-identity
Identity crisis, 3:556–557
  adolescent, 3:554
  Erikson, Erik, 2:625
Identity matrix, 3:557–558,
  7:575–576
Identity politics, 6:334–336
  caste, 1:458, 460, 462–463
  Coloreds (South Africa), 2:15–17
  described, 3:554
  race-conscious policies, 7:38
  racial identification, 3:549, 550
  Roma, 7:279
  self-determination, 7:407
Identity theft, 3:552
Ideological State Apparatuses (ISAs),
  1:87
*Ideologies and Institutions in Urban
  France* (Grillo), 1:134
Ideology, 1:87, 3:558–560
  centrism, 1:488–489
  civil wars, 1:554
  class conflict, 1:569–570
  class consciousness, 1:572
  corruption, 2:145
  futurology, 3:241
  ideologies *vs.*, 1:87
  language, 1:130
  Marx, Karl, 3:82
  political correctness, 6:300
  prejudice, 6:440
  race, 7:3, 44–45
  radicalism, 7:48–51
Idiosyncratic credit, 4:380
Idol, Billy, 3:291
IDP (Internally displaced persons). *See*
  Refugees
Idris (King), 3:378
IE (Islamic economics), 2:510–511
IETF (Internet Engineering Task
  Force), 4:105
IFC (International Finance
  Corporation), 9:137
IFI (International financial
  institutions), 4:93–94, 5:468, 474
Ignatiev, Noel, 9:87–88, 92
Ignatius the Martyr, 1:532

Ignorance, pluralistic, 2:72, 3:388,
  560–561
IGOs (Intergovernmental
  organizations), 3:333–334, 8:5
IIALC (International Institute of
  African Languages and Cultures),
  1:44, 3:617–618
IIPUMS (Integrated Public Use
  Microdata Series), 6:26
Ikhwan Muslemin, 8:604
ILD (Institute for Liberty and
  Democracy), 2:319–320
Iliad (Homer), 3:130–131
Illegal aliens. *See* Immigrants
Illegitimate births. *See* Out-of-wedlock
  births
Illinois, Witherspoon v. (1968), 4:233
Illiteracy, 6:59, *60*
Illness, mental. *See* Mental illness
Illness, physical. *See* Disease
Illuminati, 3:561–562
Illusion, money. *See* Money illusion
Illusory correlation, 7:571
ILO (International Labour
  Organization). *See* International
  Labour Organization (ILO)
Image, body, 1:28
Images of Organization (Moore), 1:390
Imagination, 3:137, 8:561
Imani, Nikitah, 2:317
IMF. *See* International Monetary Fund
  (IMF)
Imitation. *See* Social learning
  perspective
Immigrants
  Appalachia, 1:149
  assimilation, 1:188–191
  Boas, Franz, 1:345
  Bonacich, Edna, 1:351, 352
  Caribbean, 1:448–449
  census, 1:477
  cities, 1:541
  cosmopolitanism, 2:149
  cultural anthropology, 1:120
  ethnic enclave, 3:4
  ethnic enterprises, 3:4–6
  globalization, 9:126
  illegal, 5:430–431
  New Deal coalition, 5:498
  New Immigrant Survey,
    5:499–500
  petty bourgeoisie, 1:362
  refugees, 7:125–127
  urban riots, 8:539
  whiteness, 9:86, 88, 90, 92

Immigrants, Asian, 3:562–564, 566t
  Chinese Americans, 1:513–515
  Chinese diaspora, 1:515–519
  cultural identity, 5:464
  ethnic enterprises, 3:4–5
  Japanese Americans, 4:173–175
  railway industry, 7:53
Immigrants, black, 1:36, 3:564–567,
  566t
  black nationalism, 1:316
  middle class, 1:313
  nationalism, 1:315
Immigrants, European, 3:567–570,
  9:86
  Ellis Island, 2:567–569
  Mafia, 4:552–553
  whiteness, 9:86, 88, 90, 92
Immigrants, Latin American, 2:187,
  3:566t, 570–572, 4:358
  Bracero Program, 1:364–365
  Chávez, César, 1:493–494
  Latino/Latina studies, 4:356–357
  law and order, 4:372
  Mexican Americans, 5:121–122,
    124–125
  Operation Bootstrap, 6:45
Immigrants, New York City,
  3:572–576, 574t
  Boricua, 1:356
  Ellis Island, 2:567–569
  Harlem, 3:423
  Latin American, 3:571, 4:359
Immigrants to North America,
  3:576–580
  African burial grounds, 1:393–394
  blackface, 1:327
  blood and bloodline, 1:336
  brain drain, 1:367–368
Immigration, 3:581–583
  Americanism, 1:108
  blood and bloodline, 1:336
  Bonacich, Edna, 1:351, 353
  brain drain, 1:367–368
  caste, 1:460
  Chinese Americans, 1:513–515
  citizenship, 1:543
  civil rights, 1:549
  Daughters of the American
    Revolution, 2:241, 242
  demography, 2:292, 294
  depopulation, 2:302
  Ellis Island, 2:567–569
  globalization, 3:334
  gold mining, 3:339–340
  labor market, 4:318–319

law and order, 4:372

left wing, 4:403

melting pot, 5:71–73

Mexican Americans, 5:121–122, 124–125

middleman minorities, 5:147–148

migration, 5:156–158

national defense, 2:260

nativism, 5:430–431

race, 7:14

race-conscious policies, 7:38

race relations, 7:29, 32–33

restitution principle, 7:213

transnationalism, 8:433–434

wage variations, 9:4

welfare state, 9:72–73

xenophobia, 9:159, 160, 161

zero population growth, 9:174

Zionism, 9:180

Immigration, New. *See* New Immigration

Immigration Act (U.S. 1892). *See* Asian immigrants; Chinese Americans

Immigration Act (U.S. 1917), 3:579

Immigration and Naturalization Act (U.S. 1965), 3:372, 564, 574, 579

Immigration Commission, U.S., 1:345

Immigration Reform Act (U.S. 1965). *See* Black immigrants

Immigration Reform and Control Act (U.S. 1986), 3:580

Immigration Reform and Control Act (U.S. 1990), 3:580

Immigration Restriction Act (U.S. 1924), 1:313, 336, 3:574, 599

Immiserizing growth, 1:293, **3:583–584**

Immiserizing Growth: A Geometrical Note (Bhagwati), 1:293

Immorality Amendment Act (South Africa 1950), 2:15

Immortality. *See* Afterlife

Immortalization, cell line, 3:307

The Impact of Exchange Rate Movements on U.S. Foreign Debt (Tille), 2:210

Impeachment, 1:580–581, **3:584–586**, 7:113

Imperfect competition, 2:50, **51–54**

  asymmetric information, 4:28–30

  Kahn, Richard F., 4:245

  monopsony, 5:267–268

  predatory pricing, 6:428–429

  price discrimination, 2:392–393

  strategic behavior, 8:162–163

Imperial Diet (Japan). *See* The Diet (Japan)

Imperial Germany and the Industrial Revolution (Veblen), 8:596–597

Imperial Gospel speech, 9:23–24

Imperialism, 3:**586–590**

  Boer War, 1:349, 350

  bourgeoisie, 1:361

  capitalism, 8:489

  capitalist mode of production, 1:446, 447

  Caribbean, 1:448

  Chomsky, Noam, 1:529

  colonialism and, 2:12

  Columbus, Christopher, 2:19–20

  commonwealth, 2:29

  communism, 2:35

  decolonization, 2:255–257

  developing countries, 2:335, 336

  diaspora, 2:356

  empire, 2:574–577

  environmental determinism, 2:327

  exploitation, 3:65

  gentility, 3:300–301

  Hilferding, Rudolf, 3:476

  import substitution, 3:593

  Indian National Army, 3:610–611

  land claims, 4:340

  Lenin, Vladimir Ilitch, 4:411

  Leninism, 4:412

  liberation, 4:429, 433

  Luxemburg, Rosa, 4:522

  Macmillan, Harold, 4:538

  Marxist competition, 2:55

  Mexican-American War, 5:126–129

  Pax Britannica, 6:179

  Raj, 7:55–57

  Rhodes, Cecil, 7:240

  self-determination, 7:405–406

  state, 8:104

  Wall Street, 9:8

  Wallerstein, Immanuel, 9:10

  See also Neoimperialism

Imperialism: The Highest Stage of Capitalism (Lenin), 1:350, 4:411, 412

Imperialism (Hobhouse), 1:350

Implicit expectations, 3:**50–51**

Import, marginal propensity to. *See* Marginal propensity to import

Import expansion, voluntary. *See* Import promotion

Import penetration, 3:**590–591**, *591*

Import promotion, 3:**592**

Import quota. *See* Trade quotas; Wage and price controls

Import substitution, 3:**592–594**

  development economics, 2:345

  development in sociology, 2:347

  Economic Commission for Latin America and the Caribbean, 2:482, 483

  export promotion, 3:66–67

  infant industry, 4:12

  Prebish, Raúl, 6:422–423

Imports, 3:**594–596**, 594*t*

  automobile, 1:221–222

  balance of payments, 1:238–240

  banana industry, 1:245–246

  beggar-thy-neighbor, 1:272–273

  currency appreciation and depreciation, 2:210

  free trade, 3:194

  J-Curve, 4:179

  Leontief, Wassily, 4:413

  product dumping, 2:462

  protection, 3:66

  slave-gun cycle, 7:540–542

  terms of trade, 8:324–325

  in trade, 8:411–412

  trade deficit, 8:415–416

  trade liberalization, 4:427–428

  trade quotas, 6:672

  trade surplus, 8:417–418

Impossibility theorem. *See* Arrow possibility theorem

Impression management. *See* Survey

Imprisonment, 3:**596–597**

  concentration camps, 2:63–64

  Mafia, 4:551

  prison psychology, 6:470–471

  See also Japanese American incarceration; Prisons

Improving America's Schools Act (1994), 2:538

Impulse control disorders, 3:248–249

Impulse-response functions, 8:599

In a Different Voice (Gilligan), 3:319–320

In Athena's Camp: Preparing for Conflict in the Information Age (Arquilla and Ronfeldt), 2:259

In Defense of Globalization (Bhagwati), 1:293

In-groups, 1:296, 9:136

In re Rodriguez (1897), 5:121

In Small Things Forgotten (Deetz), 1:169

In the Wake of the Plague (Cantor), 5:550

In-vitro fertilization (IVF), 7:178, 181
In vivo transfers, 1:287, 3:**597–598**
In-wired development, 1:505
INA (Indian National Army), 1:357, 3:**610–611**
Inada, Ken-Ichi, 3:599
Inada conditions, 3:**598–599**, *599*
INC (Indian National Congress), 1:139, 3:252, **611–612**, 5:460
Incarceration. *See* Imprisonment
Incarceration, Japanese American, 3:**599–601**, 4:174–175, 5:513
    Asian American politics, 6:322
    Asian immigrants, 3:563
    census, 1:477
    concentration camps, 2:63–64
    critical race theory, 2:175
    described, 4:174–175
    judiciary, 4:227
    Pearl Harbor, 6:190
Incas, 3:**601–602**
    archaeology, 1:166
    human sacrifice, 3:516
    pre-Columbian peoples, 6:427
Incentive. *See* Motivation
Incest, genetics, 2:229, *230*
Incest taboo. *See* Oedipus complex; Taboos
The Inclusion of the Other (Habermas), 3:401
Inclusionary dominance. *See* Assimilation
Inclusive suffrage, 2:58
Income, 3:**603–604**, 603*t*
    absolute, 1:6–7, *7*
    consumption function, 2:109–110
    diminishing returns, 7:218–219
    earned, 3:225–226
    economic growth, 2:486–487
    education in the U.S., 2:543–545
    educational quality, 2:546–547
    environmental Kuznets curves, 2:605–607
    fictitious, 3:98
    gross domestic product, 3:383–384
    happiness, 3:415–418, *417*
    liberalism, 9:68
    life-cycle hypothesis, 4:441–443
    measuring, 5:402–403
    national, 7:74
        balance of payments, 1:238–240
        economic growth, 2:486–487

national income accounts, 5:397–405
        rate of profit, 7:74
        restitution principle, 7:213
    nominal, 5:399, 511
    OCCSCORE, 6:26
    overlapping generations model, 6:92
    per capita, 3:346
    permanent, 1:7, 3:217, 6:211–214
    post-Keynesian economics, 2:528–529
    real, 2:486–487, 3:98, 5:399, 7:89–91
    returns to education, 7:65–66
    Stolper-Samuelson theorem, 8:159–160
    Survey of Income and Program Participation, 8:243–244
    tax credits, 8:273
    University of Texas Inequality Project, 8:489–491
    War on Poverty, 9:28
    See also Gross national income
Income, nominal. *See* Nominal wages
Income, Saving and the Theory of Consumer Behavior (Duesenberry), 7:153
Income distribution, 3:**604–605**
    agricultural economics, 1:58–59
    baby boomers, 1:235–236
    bequests, 1:286
    blue collar and white collar, 1:340
    bubbles (economics), 1:379
    Cambridge capital controversy, 1:419, 420
    class conflict, 1:571
    corporate social responsibility, 2:136
    corruption, 2:145
    Deininger and Squire World Bank Inequality Database, 2:267–268
    democracy, 2:275–276
    difference principle, 2:363
    equality, 2:617–618, *618*
    Fabianism, 3:73–74
    Kahn, Richard F., 4:245
    Kuznets hypothesis, 4:295–297
    long period analysis, 4:490
    long run, 4:491
    Luxembourg Income Study, 4:519–521, 521*t*
    marginal product of labor, 4:304, 305
    poverty, 6:407
    rentier class, 1:567

    social exclusion, 7:588
    Tinbergen, Jan, 8:374–375
    utilitarianism, 9:63–64
    working class, 9:132
Income Dynamics, Panel Study of. *See* Panel Study of Income Dynamics (PSID)
Income hypothesis, absolute. *See* Absolute income hypothesis
Income hypothesis, permanent. *See* Permanent income hypothesis
Income hypothesis, relative. *See* Relative income hypothesis
Income inequality, 4:**1–3**
    bequests, 1:286
    black liberalism, 1:312
    black middle class, 1:313–314
    blue collar and white collar, 1:338, 340
    cohabitation, 2:1
    crowding hypothesis, 2:181
    Deininger and Squire World Bank Inequality Database, 2:267–268
    democracy, 2:275
    deregulation, 2:309
    difference principle, 2:363
    discrimination, 2:388–391
    distributive justice, 4:239–240
    gender inequality, 3:626
    Gini coefficient, 3:320–323, 320*t*, *321*, 321*t*, *322*, 322*t*
    happiness, 3:415–418
    immigrants, 3:580
    income distribution, 3:604–605
    indices of poverty, 6:408–410
    intersectionality, 4:115
    Jencks, Christopher, 4:184–185
    King, Martin Luther, Jr., 4:269
    Kuznets hypothesis, 4:295–297
    Luxembourg Income Study, 4:519–521
    New York City immigrants, 3:575
    sexual orientation, 7:478
    social demography, 2:296
    stratification economics, 2:530, 531
    wealthy *vs.* workers, 6:73
Income maintenance experiments, 3:**605–607**
Income policy. *See* Inflation; Wage and price controls
Income tax
    conservatism, 2:85
    described, 8:281
    negative, 5:456–457

Income tax, corporate, 3:**607–608**

Income terms of trade (ITT). *See* Terms of trade

Incongruity effect. *See* Person memory

Increasing returns, 7:**219–221**
    asymmetric returns to scale, 7:223, 224
    cumulative causation, 2:207–208
    described, 7:217, 218
    returns to scale, 7:222–223

Increasing Returns and Economic Progress (Young), 2:207, 7:220

Incrementalism, 3:**608–610**, 4:452–453, 596

Incumbents, 6:458–459

Indebtedness, 1:282

Indecency, 6:13
    See also Obscenity

Indentured migration, 2:471–475

Indentured servitude. *See* Servitude

Independence, political. *See* Self-determination

Independence movements. *See* Liberation movements

Independent filmmakers, 3:140–141

Independent living, 2:377–378

Independent private value model, 1:207

Independent variables, 3:155–156

Independent voters. *See* Political parties; Voting

Index, quantity. *See* Quantity index

Index, time. *See* Time trends

Index Visible, 3:152

Indexes. *See* Indices

India
    affirmative action, 1:31
    AIDS/HIV, 1:65, 66
    Ambedkar, B. R., 1:90–92
    anticolonial movements, 1:139
    Asiatic mode of production, 1:187
    automobile industry, 1:221
    bauxite industry, 1:261
    binary gender alternatives, 3:271
    blue collar and white collar, 1:339
    borders, 1:355
    Bose, Subhas and Sarat, 1:356–357
    Brahmins, 1:366–367
    Buddha, 1:379–381
    Buddhism, 1:381–383
    bull and bear markets, 1:386
    caste, 1:457–459, 461–463, 3:254
    China, 5:542
    civil disobedience, 1:546, 5:460

coffee industry, 1:594
colorism, 2:18
commonwealth, 2:29
Congress Party, 2:75–77
creamy layer, 2:161
dalits, 2:221–222
democratization, 2:289
direct action, 2:372
dowry and bride price, 2:441
Dravidians, 2:443–444
East Indian diaspora, 2:471–475
East Indies, 2:476
education, 2:612
film industry, 3:140
Five-year Plans, 5:393
Gandhi, Indira, 3:252–253, 253–255
global warming, 3:330
Hinduism, 3:477, 478, 479, 480
history, 5:460–461
household sample survey, 5:409–411
human sacrifice, 3:516
Indian National Army, 3:610–611
Indian National Congress, 3:611–612
integration, 4:61
Jainism, 4:166–167
Jajmani matrix, 4:167
Janata Party, 4:170–171
Jinnah, Mohammed Ali, 4:203–204
job guarantee, 4:206
Kshatriyas, 4:291–292
land reform, 4:342, 343, 344, 5:460–461
latifundia, 4:353
legal systems, 4:406
microelectronics industry, 5:139
National Family Health Surveys, 5:392–394
Nehru, Jawaharlal, 5:460–461
nonrenewable natural resource use, 5:438
nuclear weapons, 9:32
partition, 6:160
primitive communism, 2:35–36
quotas, 6:669, 670
Raj, 7:55–57
reincarnation, 7:145, 146
Sanskritization, 7:323–324
Sikhism, 7:508–509
Singh, V. P., 7:521
slavery, 1:38, 39
state, 8:103

Sudras, 8:212–213
surplus labor, 4:309
trade quotas, 6:672
tribe, 8:450–451
tribes, 8:449
Vajpayee, Atal Bihari, 8:568–569
water resources, 9:41
wealth, 9:45
zero population growth, 9:174

Indian Appropriation Act (U.S. 1871), 5:427

Indian caste system. *See* Caste

Indian Currency and Finance (Keynes), 4:261

Indian Independence Act (India 1947), 3:255

Indian National Army (INA), 1:357, 3:**610–611**

Indian National Congress (INC), 1:139, 3:252, **611–612**, 5:460

Indian Removal Act (U.S. 1830), 1:497–498, 5:427

Indian Removal Act (U.S. 1838), 2:64

Indian Reorganization Act (U.S. 1934), 5:427

Indians, American. *See* Native Americans

Indians (Asian people), 2:141–142

Indians of All Tribes, 1:98

Indicative planning. *See* Convergence theory

Indicators, lagging, leading, and coincident, 4:**331–332**

Indices, price. *See* Price indices

Indices, time. *See* Time trends

Indices of democracy, 2:**280–281**

Indices of political instability, 6:**304–306**
    destabilization, 2:320–321
    political stability, 8:72–74

Indices of poverty, 6:**408–410**

Indies Company. *See* Mississippi Company

Indifference curves. *See* Ordinality

Indifference principle. *See* Ordinality

Indigenismo, 3:**612–614**, 5:429

Indigenous peoples. *See* Natives

Indigenous rights, 3:**614–617**
    Boricua, 1:355–356
    buraku, 1:388–389
    Cherokees, 1:497–498
    Chiapas, 1:499
    citizenship, 1:543
    class conflict, 1:570
    cultural rights, 2:197

Indigenous rights, *continued*
    cultural tourism, 2:202
    indigenismo, 3:612–614
    internal colony, 2:14
    land claims, 4:340–341
    Means, Russell, 5:53
    Native American burial grounds,
      1:395
    sovereignty, 8:39
    Stolen Generations, 8:158–159
    Taino, 8:261
    treaty federalism, 8:445–446
Indirect aggression. *See* Social
    aggression
Indirect rule, 3:**617–618**
    internal colony, 2:13
    representative and participatory
      democracy, 2:283
Indirect taxation. *See* Taxation
Individual liberty, 5:439
Individual psychology, 4:18, 19
Individual rights
    common good, 2:25
    communitarianism, 2:39
    Constitution, U.S., 2:91–92
    cultural rights, 2:198
Individual selection, 3:414–415
Individual transferable quotas, fishing
    industry, 3:153
Individualism, 3:**618–620**
    business ethics, 2:634–635
    choice in economics, 1:524–525
    cities, 1:540
    citizenship, 1:543
    civil liberties, 1:547
    civil society, 1:552, 553
    collectivism, 2:10–11
    common good, 2:25
    communalism, 2:30–31
    communitarianism, 2:38–40
    community power studies, 2:45
    conservatism, 2:84
    defense, 2:258
    democracy, 2:274, 275
    destabilization, 2:321
    distributive justice, 4:240
    Durkheim, Émile, 2:465, 466
    freedom, 3:196–197
    Hayek, Friedrich August von,
      3:435
    Hegel, Georg Wilhelm Friedrich,
      3:453
    Hegelians, 3:454
    justice, 4:237–238
    laissez-faire, 4:335–336

    liberalism, 4:425–426
    liberation, 4:429
    libertarianism, 4:437–439
    liberty, 4:439–441
    lifestyles, 4:446
    lying, 4:524
    marginalism, 4:596
    methodological, 1:210
    neoclassical economics, 2:516–518
    neoliberalism, 5:473, 474
    organization man, 6:61
    petty bourgeoisie, 1:362
    rational choice theory, 7:74–76
    social relations, 7:611–613
    Tocqueville, Alexis de, 8:383
    tyranny of the majority,
      8:478–479
Individualism and the Intellectuals
    (Durkheim), 2:465
Indivisibilities, 7:222–223
Indochina, 1:139–140, 8:612–613
Indonesia
    anticolonial movements, 1:139
    Chinese diaspora, 1:516, 518
    coffee industry, 1:594
    interpretive anthropology, 3:265
    land reform, 4:343, 344
    nonrenewable natural resource
      use, 5:438
    OPEC, 6:65
Induced abortion. *See* Abortion
Induced compliance, 1:600
Induction. *See* Logic
Indulgence, 3:101–102
Indus Basin, 9:41
Indus River Basin Treaty, 9:41
Industrial accidents, 1:**8–9,** 9*t*
Industrial archaeology, 1:117
Industrial Areas Foundation, 1:493
Industrial capitalism, 1:238, 3:300
Industrial Crises in Contemporary
    England (Tugan-Baranovsky), 7:299
Industrial Democracy (Webb), 3:74
Industrial economics, 1:502
Industrial organization. *See* Industry
Industrial Revolution
    agricultural industry, 1:61
    factory system, 3:78–79
    feudalism, 3:136
    nouveaux riches, 5:548
    visual arts, 8:632
    weapons industry, 9:49
    welfare state, 9:69
    work day, 9:126

    See also Industrialization
Industrial slavery. *See* Slavery industry
Industrial Workers of the World
    (IWW), 4:302, 8:515
Industrialization, 3:**620–622**
    agriculture, 1:61–62
    Appalachia, 1:150–151
    capitalist mode of production,
      1:446
    children's rights, 1:512
    cities, 1:542
    cleavages, 1:578
    clientelism, 1:579
    conspicuous consumption, 2:89
    cotton industry, 2:152
    cumulative causation, 2:208
    demography, 2:291, 294
    dependency theory, 2:299, 300
    development economics,
      2:344–345
    division of labor, 2:423–425
    Dutch disease, 2:467–468
    export promotion, 3:66–67
    future shock, 3:240
    global warming, 3:330
    hypertension, 3:538
    import substitution, 3:592–594
    industrial accidents, 1:8–9
    industry, 3:623
    knowledge society, 4:283–284
    Kuznets hypothesis, 4:295, 297
    labor, 4:301
    latifundia, 4:353
    legacy effects, 4:404
    Lewis, W. Arthur, 4:420–421
    long run, 4:493
    Luddites, 4:513–515
    maquiladoras, 4:591–594
    mobility, 5:209
    monopoly capitalism, 5:266–267
    noncompeting groups, 5:514–515
    nutrition, 5:552
    Operation Bootstrap, 6:44–45
    popular music, 6:376
    populism, 6:383–384
    post-Parsonian American
      sociology, 8:6
    Prebisch, Raúl, 6:422–423
    Prebisch-Singer hypothesis,
      6:423–425
    quality controls, 6:651
    railway industry, 7:53–54
    rural development, 2:341
    schooling, 7:353
    slavery industry, 7:547–549

socialism, 7:635–637

technological progress, 8:299

textile industry, 8:333

time and motion studies, 8:365

totalitarianism, 8:395

towns, 8:404

underdevelopment, 8:489–491

upward mobility, 8:534

urban poverty, 6:410

urbanization, 8:546

water pollution, 6:364–365

weapons industry, 9:49–50

welfare state, 9:69

women's work, 9:124–125

work day, 9:126–128

working class, 9:130

Industrialized nations. *See* Developed
countries

Industry, 3:**622–623**

codetermination, 1:592–593

culture, 3:189

fatality rates, 9:4

infant, 3:200

labor, 4:301

organization, 3:324

value added by, 3:383–384, 5:402

See also names of specific industries

Inefficiency, economics, 8:148–149

Inegalitarianism, 3:**623–624**

citizenship, 1:543–544

distributive justice, 4:240

See also Egalitarianism

Inequality

Blau, Peter M., 1:332

community power studies, 2:43,
44

computers, 2:60

crime and criminology, 2:170

digital divide, 2:366–367

economic

Fields' index of, 3:137–138

globalization, 9:46–47

health status, 8:592

neoimperialism, 5:471

University of Texas Inequality
Project, 8:529–530

welfare economics, 9:67

welfare state, 9:67

whiteness, 9:87, 91–92

equal opportunity, 2:611–613

exploitation, 3:63–65

left wing, 4:403

Multi-City Study of Urban
Inequality, 5:314–315

regressive taxes, 8:284–285

reproduction, 7:178

Rousseau, Jean-Jacques,
7:290–291

schooling, 7:351, 352–353,
354–355

slavery, 7:542–545

social status, 7:621–622

social welfare functions,
7:629–630

stratification, 8:166–167

tax, 6:73

Theil index, 8:339–340

third-world sociology, 8:12–14

variation, 8:591–593

See also Equality; Inegalitarianism

*Inequality: A Reassessment of the Effect
of Family and Schooling in America*
(Jencks et al.), 4:184

Inequality, gender, 3:**624–627**

Blinder-Oaxaca decomposition
technique, 1:333–334

California Civil Rights Initiative,
1:416

civil rights, 1:549

clash of civilizations, 1:560

correspondence tests, 2:141–143

crowding hypothesis, 2:181–182

curriculum, 2:214–215

development in sociology, 2:348

inegalitarianism, 3:624

intersectionality, 4:114–115

liberation, 4:430

patriarchy, 6:173–174

pimps, 6:271–273

Sen, Amartya Kumar, 7:440–441

sexism, 7:473–474

sports, 8:64–65, 65

Inequality, income, 4:**1–3**

bequests, 1:286

black liberalism, 1:312

black middle class, 1:313–314

blue collar and white collar, 1:338,
340

cohabitation, 2:1

crowding hypothesis, 2:181

Deininger and Squire World Bank
Inequality Database, 2:267–268

democracy, 2:275

deregulation, 2:309

difference principle, 2:363

discrimination, 2:388–391

distributive justice, 4:239–241

gender inequality, 3:626

Gini coefficient, 3:320–323, 320*t*,
321, 321*t, 322,* 322*t*

happiness, 3:415–418

immigrants, 3:580

income distribution, 3:604–605

indices of poverty, 6:408–410

intersectionality, 4:115

Jencks, Christopher, 4:184–185

King, Martin Luther, Jr., 4:269

Luxembourg Income Study,
4:519–521

New York City immigrants, 3:575

sexual orientation, 7:478

social demography, 2:296

stratification economics, 2:530,
531

wealthy *vs.* workers, 6:73

Inequality, political, 4:**3–5**

Bentham, Jeremy, 1:285

caste, 1:458, 463

citizenship, 1:542–543

civil wars, 1:554–555

creaming, 2:160

creamy layer, 2:161

dalits, 2:221–222

democracy, 2:273, 7:192

distributive justice, 4:240

gender inequality, 3:626–627

stratification, 8:168–170

underrepresentation, 8:495

Inequality, racial, 4:**5–8**

biological determinism,
2:325–326

black middle class, 1:314

black politics, 6:325

Brimmer, Andrew, 1:372

California Civil Rights Initiative,
1:416

civil rights, 1:549

Congress of Racial Equality, 2:75

constructivism, 2:97

correspondence tests, 2:141–143

critical race theory, 2:174–176

crowding hypothesis, 2:182

disease, 2:408

distributive justice, 4:240

economics, 7:13–15

Engerman, Stanley, 2:592–593

hard-core unemployed, 3:421,
422, 423

Harris, Abram L., Jr., 3:427

imprisonment, 3:596–597

income inequality, 4:3

intersectionality, 4:114–115

Jim Crow, 4:198–201

Inequality, racial, *continued*
John Henryism, 4:207–208
post-Parsonian American
sociology, 8:5
prisons, 6:476
qualifications, 6:649–650
quota systems, 6:668–670
quotas, 6:670–671
race-conscious policies, 7:36–38
racial classification, 7:39
racial democracy, 2:282–283
reparations, 7:166–168
restitution principle, 7:213–215
social demography, 2:296
Southern politics, 6:339–349
sports, 8:64–65
wage discrimination, 2:404,
405–406
whiteness, 9:87
Inequality, wage. *See* Income
inequality
Inequality, wealth, 4:8–11, 9*t*, 10*t*
African Americans, 1:34, 35
bequests, 1:286
black middle class, 1:314
consumerism, 2:105
Deininger and Squire World Bank
Inequality Database, 2:267–268
human rights, 3:513–514
income inequality, 4:3
inegalitarianism, 3:624
inheritance, 4:35–36
landlords, 4:346
neocolonialism, 5:467–468
political sociology, 8:3
Inequality and Heterogeneity (Blau),
1:332
Inequality and morality, 5:286–288
Inequality of exchange. *See* Unequal
exchange
Inequality Reexamined (Sen), 5:535
Inequity. *See* Inequality
Infancy in Uganda (Ainsworth), 1:67
Infant development. *See* Child
development
Infant industry, 3:200, 593, 4:11–13
Infant mortality. *See* Morbidity and
mortality
Infants
development, 1:25
infant-mother attachment, 1:67,
195–196
See also Children
Infecundity. *See* Human fertility
Inference

archaeology, 1:168
correspondence inference theory,
1:205
rationality, 7:80
Inference, Bayesian, 1:263, 4:13–14,
14, 8:122
Inference, statistical, 4:15–18
Bayesian inference, 4:13–14
bootstrap method, 1:353–354
central limit theorem, 1:486
classical statistical analysis,
1:576–577
controlled experiments, 3:58–59
correspondence tests, 2:143
data envelopment analysis, 2:241
large sample properties,
4:348–350
method of moments, 5:105–107
random samples, 7:60–61
randomness, 7:63–64
social sciences, 8:123
specification tests, 8:52–53
Inference, trait. *See* Trait inference
Inferential statistics. *See* Hypothesis
and hypothesis testing
Inferiority, black. *See* White supremacy
Inferiority complex, 4:18–19, 5:366
Infertility drugs, psychosocial issues,
4:19–20
Infidelity, 4:20–22
Infidels, 4:22–23
Infinite horizon model, 6:52
Inflation, 4:23–26, 6:*451*
central banks, 1:478, 479
conundrum, 2:116
currency devaluation and
revaluation, 2:211
decisive events, 2:254
development economics, 2:345
dirigiste, 2:373
dowry and bride price, 2:441
economic crises, 2:484
economic depression, 2:302–304,
303, 305
exchange rates, 3:37, 38–39
Federal Reserve System,
3:112–113
Greenspan, Alan, 3:380
happiness, 3:418
Kahn, Richard F., 4:245
life-cycle hypothesis, 4:442–443
long run, 4:493, 494
Lundberg, Erik, 4:519
macroeconomics, 4:540
monetary policy, 6:294–295

national income accounts, 5:398
natural rate of unemployment,
5:436
neutral rate of interest, 4:79
nominal income, 5:511
nominal interest rates, 4:87
Phillips curve, 6:248–250
price indices, 6:449, *451*
rate, 5:398
real income, 7:89–91
real rate of interest, 4:81
real wages, 5:511–512
rules *vs.* discretion, 7:294
stable nodes, 5:510
stagflation, 8:82–83
static expectations, 3:53
structuralist macroeconomics,
4:544
surprise, 5:436
trade-offs, 8:419
unemployment, 3:226
wage and price controls, 9:3
Influence, peer. *See* Peer influence
Influence, social. *See* Social influence
*The Influence of Tobacco Smoking on
Mental and Motor Efficiency* (Hull),
3:506
Influences of Geographic Environment
(Semple), 2:328
Informal economy, 4:26–28
De Soto, Hernando, 2:319–320
deviance, 2:353
drug traffic, 2:449–451
dual economy, 2:457
employment, 2:581
immigrants, 3:575, 576
multisector models, 5:334–335
rotating savings and credit
associations, 7:286–287
Informal education, 2:534–535
Informal sector. *See* Informal economy
Informal volunteerism, 8:641–642
Information, asymmetric, 1:68–69,
4:28–30
distortions, 2:414
predatory pricing, 6:428–429
signals, 7:507–508
trade barriers, 1:255
zero-sum game, 9:177
Information, economics of, 4:30–32
Arrow, Kenneth J., 1:182
citations, 1:538–539
Hurwicz, Leonid, 3:529–530
Internet, 4:106
signals, 7:507–508

Stiglitz, Joseph E., 8:146

Information criteria. *See* Model selection tests

Information economy. *See* Knowledge society

Information processing. *See* Reinforcement theories

Information processing, social. *See* Social information processing

Information society. *See* Knowledge society

Information technology, cyberspace, 2:217

    See also Computers

Informed consent, 4:32–34

    bioethics, 1:301

    ethics, 2:632, 636

    ethnography, 3:15

    experiments, 2:636, 3:58

    Tuskegee syphilis study, 8:472–473

Infosys (company), 2:137

Infringement, copyright. *See* Intellectual property rights

Inge, M. Thomas, 2:23

Inglehart, Ronald, 9:69

INGOs (International nongovernmental organizations), 1:293, 4:96–99

Ingratiation, 4:34–35, 211, 7:423–424

Inhalants, 2:454–455

Inheritance (economics), 4:35–36

    bequests, 1:286–287

    intergenerational transmission, 4:89

    primogeniture, 1:174, 3:86

    in vivo transfers, 3:597–598

Inheritance (genetics). *See* Heredity

Inheritance tax, 4:36–37

    bequests, 1:287

    in vivo transfers, 3:598

Inikori, Joseph, 4:37–38

Initial public offering (IPO), 3:142, 4:38–39

Initiation rites. *See* Rites of passage

Initiative (political science), 4:39–40

Injury, collective, 8:624

Injustice. *See* Inequality; Justice

Inkblot test. *See* Rorschach test

Innis, Roy, 2:75

Innocence, presumption of, 7:292

Innocent II, Pope, 4:556

Innovation. *See* Creativity; Progress; Technological change

Innovation and Entrepreneurship (Drucker), 2:449–450

Input coefficients, 3:155

Input-output matrix, 4:40–41

    fixed coefficients production function, 3:154

    Leontief, Wassily, 4:412–413

    Potron, Maurice, 6:403

    social accounting matrix, 7:562–563

    vectors, 8:601

Inputs, production. *See* Capital; Labor; Land

Inquest (Epstein), 9:34

Inquiries into Human Faculty and Its Development (Galton), 3:247–248

Inquiry and Change (Lindblom), 4:453

An Inquiry into the Nature and Causes of the Wealth of Nations (Smith). *See The Wealth of Nations* (Smith)

Inquisition, 1:530, 2:21, 7:280

    See also Roman Catholic Church

Inside money, 5:260–261

Insider trading, 1:379

Insko, Chester, 7:598

INSNA (International Network for Social Network Analysis), 5:481

Instability, political, indices of. *See* Political instability, indices of

Instability and Economic Growth (Lundberg), 4:519

Instant gratification. *See* Time orientation

Instant runoff voting, 8:655

Instincts, 3:210–211, 211, 8:595

Institut fur Sozialforschung. *See* Frankfurt School

Institute for Environment and Human Security, 8:656

Institute for Liberty and Democracy (ILD), 2:319–320

Institute for Research on Poverty, 9:26–27

Institute for Retired Professionals, 5:501

Institute of Social Research. *See* Frankfurt School

Institutional analysis in sociology, 2:348, 7:673–674

Institutional change, 5:545

Institutional development, 2:340–341, 348

Institutional discrimination, 4:92

Institutional economics, 2:506–507

    Coase, Ronald, 1:589

    development in sociology, 2:348

Galbraith, John Kenneth, 3:246–247

    history, 2:498

    institutional development, 2:340–341

    institutionalism, 4:44–45

    Myrdal, Gunnar, 5:351

    transaction cost, 8:426–427

Institutional investors, 4:135–137

Institutional review board (IRB), 4:42–43

    ethics in experimentation, 2:636–637

    experiments, 3:57–58

    human experiments, 3:61

    informed consent, 4:33

    shock experiments, 3:63

Institutional Revolutionary Party. *See* Partido Revolucionario Institucional (PRI)

Institutional theory. *See* Institutionalism

Institutionalism, 4:44–45, 6:162

    Chicago School, 1:502

    credentialism, 2:166–167

    ethics, 2:632–633

    institutional development, 2:340–341

    institutional economics, 2:506–507

    Mitchell, Wesley Clair, 5:206–207

    organization theory, 6:70

    race relations, 7:30

    social relations, 7:611–613

    See also Neoinstitutionalism

Institutions

    cultural anthropology, 1:124

    defined, 5:472–473

    in neoinstitutionalism, 5:472

    North, Douglass, 5:538–539

Institutions, Institutional Change and Economic Performance (North), 5:538

Instituto per le Opere di Religione (IOR), 8:593

Instrumental aggression, 1:55, 83

Instrumental conditioning. *See* Operant conditioning

Instrumental variables regression, 4:45–48, 394

Instrumentalism. *See* Theory

Instrumentally-rational action, 9:56

Insulating factors. *See* Stress-buffering model

Insurance, 4:48–50, 49*t*

    health, 5:395–396

Insurance, *continued*
  law and economics, 4:367
  managed competition, 2:54–55
  moral hazard, 5:280–281
  risk, 3:143, 7:251
Insurance, national health. *See*
  National health insurance
Insurance, unemployment. *See*
  Unemployment compensation
Insurance industry, 4:**50–53**,
  5:280–281, 7:371
Insurgency. *See* Revolution
Intangible assets, 5:398–399
Integrated Public Use Microdata Series
  (IPUMS), 4:**53–56**, 54*t*, 55*t*, 56*t*,
  6:26
Integration, 4:**56–63**
  black nationalism, 1:317
  cross-national context, 4:61–63
  decline, 4:59–61
  described, 4:56–57
  ethnicity, 3:11
  evaluation, 4:59
  Jews, 4:190, 191–193, 196
  labor, 4:303
  military, 1:501, 2:315, 5:169
  organizational, 1:480–482
  policy, 4:57–59
  political, 2:278
  role theory, 7:276
  school, 2:313–314
      Brown v. Board of Education
        (1954), 1:373–376
      Brown v. Board of Education
        (1955), 1:377
      civil rights movement, U.S.,
        1:551
      Clark, Kenneth B., 1:560,
        561
      desegregation, 2:316–318
      resegregation, 7:201–202
  social equilibrium, 3:232
  See also Cointegration
Integration, cultural. *See* Cultural
  integration
Integration, economic. *See* Economic
  integration
*The Intellectual Crisis in American
  Public Administration* (Ostrom),
  3:144
Intellectual freedom, 6:8
The Intellectual History of Laissez-Faire
  (Viner), 4:335
Intellectual property. *See* Property
Intellectual property rights,
  6:555–556

entertainment industry,
  2:602–603
Internet, 4:106–107
monopoly, 5:264, 265
NAFTA, 5:541
pharmaceutical industry,
  6:237–238, 239
recording industry, 7:115–116
technological progress, 8:299
technology, 8:304–305
trade liberalization, 4:428
World Trade Organization, 9:143
Intellectualism, anti-, 4:**64–66**
Intellectuals, organic, 4:**66–67**
Intellectuals, public, 4:**68–69**
Intellectuals, vernacular, 4:**70**
Intelligence, 4:**70–74**
  artificial
      behaviorism, 1:278–279
      cognition, 1:598
      computers, 2:61
      social intelligence, 4:75
      theory of mind, 8:348
  biological determinism, 2:326
  Comte, Auguste, 2:62
  creativity, 2:165
  dementia, 2:272
  genetic determinism, 2:329
  heredity, 7:21–23
  IQ controversy, 4:139–142
  leadership, 4:378, 379
  Piaget, Jean, 6:268–271
  political
      Central Intelligence Agency,
        U.S, 1:480–485
      conservatism, 2:85
      counterterrorism, 2:154–155
      repression, 7:175
  talent, 8:261–262
  See also Counterintelligence
Intelligence, adaptive. *See* Social
  intelligence
Intelligence, emotional. *See* Multiple
  intelligences theory; Social
  intelligence
Intelligence, multiple types of. *See*
  Multiple intelligences theory
Intelligence, social, 4:**74–75**, 5:327
Intelligence (IQ) tests
  Flynn effect, 3:159–161
  gifted and talented education,
    3:317
  normal distribution, 2:416
  underachievers, 8:484

The Intelligence of Democracy
  (Lindblom), 4:452–453
Intelligence Reform and Terrorism
  Prevention Act (U.S. 2004), 1:485
Intelligent design. *See* Creationism
Intentionality, 2:78, 80, 3:264, 6:419,
  486
Interaction, group. *See* Intergroup
  relations
Interaction, social. *See* Social relations
Interaction process analysis (IPA),
  3:386
Interaction Ritual (Goffman), 3:337
Interactionism, symbolic, 1:343–344,
  4:**75–76**, 495
  conversational analysis, 2:118
  emotion, 2:569
  identity, 3:553
  microsociology, 7:678
  post-Parsonian American
    sociology, 8:7
  role theory, 7:276
  schools in sociology, 8:10
  self-presentation, 7:423–424
  social constructionism, 7:578
  social identity, 3:558
  society, 7:653
  sociology, 7:661
  voluntaristic *vs.* structuralist
    sociology, 8:17
Intercontinental ballistic missiles
  (ICBMs), 1:177, 9:31, 49
Interdependence, 3:70–71, 4:253,
  8:256–257, 257–258
Interdependent preferences, 2:586,
  6:**437–438**
Interdisciplinary research. *See* Trans-
  disciplinary research
Interest, natural rate of, 4:*77*, **77–78**
Interest, neutral rate of, 4:**78–80**
Interest, own rate of, 4:**80–81**
Interest, public. *See* Public interest
Interest, real rate of, 1:449–450,
  4:**81–82**
Interest, self. *See* Self-interest
Interest and Prices (Wicksell), 4:78–79
Interest-based bargaining, 5:457
Interest groups and interests, 4:**82–83**
  children's rights, 1:513
  cleavages, 1:578
  collective action, 2:5–6
  community power studies,
    2:43–46
  Congress, U.S., 2:74
  constituency, 2:89–90
  corporatism, 2:140–141

corruption, 2:144

Dahl, Robert Alan, 2:219–220

deviance, 2:353

identity politics, 6:334–336

lobbying, 4:474–475

Lowi, Theodore J., 4:506

military-industrial complex, 5:173–174

pluralism, 6:282–284

pressure groups, 6:443

regulation, 7:143–144

roll calls, 7:277

tariffs, 8:265–266

third world, 8:352

Interest rates, 4:**83–87**

central banks, 1:478, 480

Chamberlain, Neville, 1:489

demand for money, 5:254

development economics, 2:345

discounted present value, 2:385–386

Fisher equation, 3:151

investment, 4:132–133

Islamic economics, 2:510

life-cycle hypothesis, 4:443

liquidity, 4:459, 461–462

loans, 4:472, 473

monetary policy, 6:293, 295, 296

rentier class, 1:567

spread, 8:68–69

Tobin, James, 8:378

yield, 9:164–166, 166–167

Interest rates, nominal, 4:**87–88**

Interests, private. *See* Private interests

Intergenerational mobility, 4:88–90, 5:209, 8:533

Intergenerational transmission, 4:**88–90**

bequests, 1:286–288

inheritance, 4:35–36

lateral mobility, 5:212–213

in vivo transfers, 3:597–598

Intergovernmental organizations (IGOs), 3:333–334, 8:5

Intergovernmental Panel on Climate Change (IPCC), 3:328–329

Intergroup relations, 3:385, 4:**90–92**, 5:476

bigotry, 1:295–296

Blau, Peter M., 1:332

Blumer, Herbert, 1:343–344

collective action, 2:5–6, 6–7

collective wisdom, 2:9

collectivism, 2:10–11

consensus, 2:82–83

contact hypothesis, 2:111–112

contempt, 2:113

Dawes, Robyn, 2:245

ethnocentrism, 3:11–12

identity, 3:554

Kelley, Harold, 4:253

Lewin, Kurt, 4:417–418

microsociology, 7:678

norm of reciprocity, 7:108

prejudice, 6:439–440

race relations, 7:28–31

race relations cycle, 7:31–33

racial identification, 3:548

reactance theory, 7:85–86

rituals, 7:259

Sherif, Muzafer, 7:495

stereotypes, 8:136–139

stratification economics, 2:531

superordinate goals, 8:226–227

wage discrimination, 2:405

Interior Department, U.S., 1:504

Intermediate range nuclear weaponry, 5:544

Internal colony, 2:12, **13–15**, 3:570, 6:337, 339

Internal conflicts. *See* Civil wars

Internal market. *See* Common market

Internal Revenue Service, U.S. (IRS), 2:86, 8:428

Internal review board. *See* Institutional review board

Internal validity, 7:591, 8:573, 574

Internally displaced persons (IDP). *See* Refugees

International affairs. *See* International relations

International Agricultural Research Centers (IARC), 3:377

International Aluminum Institute, 1:261

International Association for Research in Income and Wealth, 3:384

International Association of Firefighters v. City of Cleveland (1986), 3:373

International Atomic Energy Agency (IAEA), 1:176–177, 8:523

International Bank for Reconstruction and Development. *See* World Bank

International banking facilities (IBFs), 6:31

International Centre for Settlement of Investment Disputes (ICSID), 9:137

International Coffee Organization (ICO), 1:595

International Competition Network, 1:145

International Congress on Monuments and Sites (ICOMOS), 2:197

International Cooperative Alliance, 2:123

International Cotton Advisory Committee (ICAC), 2:153

International Court of Justice, 3:360, 8:523

International Covenant on Civil and Political Rights (UN), 1:546, 9:108, 110

International Covenant on Economic, Social and Cultural Rights (UN 1966), 1:225

International Criminal Court (ICC), 3:297–298, 361, 512, 514, 9:22–23

International Development Association (IDA), 9:137, 139

International economic order, 4:**92–94**

International economics, 2:**507–510**

bilateralism, 1:297

borders, 1:354–355

bull and bear markets, 1:386

capital, 1:431

Chicago School, 1:502

conditionality, 2:65

customs union, 2:215–216

dirty float, 2:375

economic sterilization, 8:139–140

international economic order, 4:92–94

International Monetary Fund, 4:95–96

Kindleberger, Charles Poor, 4:267

Meade, James, 5:48–49

overshooting, 6:98–99

International Electric Association, 3:282

International Federation of Agricultural Producers, 6:74–75

International Finance Corporation (IFC), 9:137

International financial institutions (IFI), 4:93–94, 5:468, 474

International General Medical Society for Psychotherapy, 4:231

International Institute of African Languages and Cultures (IIALC), 1:44, 3:617–618

International Labour Organization (ILO), 3:274, 512

Bhagwati, Jagdish, 1:293

cooperatives, 2:124

employment, 2:581

employment gender gap, 3:274

International Labour Organization
(ILO), *continued*
founding, 4:303
underemployment, 8:492
unemployment, 8:500
working poor, 9:122
See also Sweatshops
International law
abortion, 1:3
antitrust, 1:145
history, 3:360–361
war crimes, 9:21–22
See also Internationalism
International Military Tribunal for the
Punishment of War Criminals,
3:361
International Monetary Fund (IMF),
4:**95–96**
balance of payments, 1:238, 240
beggar-thy-neighbor, 1:273
capital controls, 1:432–433
conditionality, 2:65
currency devaluation and
revaluation, 2:211
developing countries, 2:336
development theory, 2:338
establishment, 9:150
free trade, 3:195–196
G8 countries, 3:244
international economic order, 4:93
loans, 4:473
neocolonialism, 5:468
overlending, 6:95
role, 9:8
structural adjustment, 8:176, 178
underdevelopment, 8:491
International Network for Social
Network Analysis (INSNA), 5:481
International nongovernmental
organizations (INGOs), 1:293,
4:**96–99**
International Olympic Committee,
6:40
International order, economic. *See*
International economic order
International Organization for
Standardization (ISO 14001), 1:246
International Phonetic Alphabet,
1:118
International politics. *See* International
relations
International relations, 4:**99–101**
alliances, 1:78–81
Anglo-Portuguese trade, 8:413
beggar-thy-neighbor, 1:272–273
bilateral trade, 8:414–415

bilateralism, 1:297
borders, 1:354–355
Bracero Program, 1:364–365
Bunche, Ralph Johnson, 1:387
Castro, Fidel, 1:465, 466–467
Chiang Kai-shek, 1:499
Chinese Revolution, 1:519–520,
521
civil-military relation, 1:547–548
civil rights, 1:550
civil wars, 1:554
coalition, 1:587
Cold War, 2:4–5
comparative politics, 6:327–328
conflict, 2:70–71
Conservative Party (U.K.), 2:87
Cuban Missile Crisis, 2:183–185
Cuban Revolution, 2:185–187
cultural resource management,
2:196–197
De Gaulle, Charles, 2:265
defense, 2:257–259
deterrence, 2:333–334
developing countries, 2:336
disarmament, 2:379–380
European Union, 3:25
exploitation, 3:65
game theory, 3:251
international economic order,
4:92–94
isolationism, 4:160–161
Jervis, Robert, 4:185
just war, 4:235–237
Keohane, Robert, 4:256–257
Kissinger, Henry, 4:274–275
Korean War, 4:289
landlords, 4:345
League of Nations, 4:385–386
Lebanese civil war, 4:397–398
legal systems, 4:407
Mahathir Mohamad, 4:557–558
Monroe Doctrine, 5:272
multilateralism, 5:320–321
mutual deterrence, 2:334–335
nation-states, 5:420–421
national defense, 2:260, 261
negotiation, 5:458
neocolonialism, 5:466–467
non-alignment, 5:513
Pax Britannica, 6:179
peace, 6:180–182, 185–186
political realism, 7:96–97
politics, 6:321
Reagan, Ronald, 7:89

religiosity, 7:163
retaliation, 7:216
space exploration, 8:40–42
superordinate goals, 8:226–227
tariffs, 8:266
Thatcher, Margaret, 8:335
Tito, Josip, 8:376
trade deficit, 8:415–416
Trilateral Commission, 8:452–453
trilateralism, 8:453–454
unilateralism, 8:509–510
Waltz, Kenneth, 9:14
See also Diplomacy; Foreign policy
International Rorschach Society. *See*
Rorschach Test
International Rural Sociology
Association (IRSA), 8:9
International studies. *See* International
relations
International trade. *See* Trade
International Trade Organization
(ITO), 9:143
Internationalism, 4:**101–104**
civil-military relation, 1:547
cosmopolitanism, 2:149
international economic order,
4:92–94
international relations, 4:99–101
interwar years, 4:121–122
left wing, 4:403
transnationalism, 8:433
trilateralism, 8:453–454
Internet, 4:**104–107**
activism, 1:18
advertising, 1:29
auctions, 1:207–208
bigotry, 1:296
business, 1:402–403
computers, 2:60, 61
digital divide, 2:366–367
disability, 2:378
documentary studies, 2:434
entertainment industry, 2:602,
603
journalism, 4:215
microelectronics industry, 5:136,
139
mobilization, 5:214
political cartoons, 1:452
recording industry, 7:115–116
teachers, 8:295
technocracy, 8:297
technological determinism, 2:332
technology, 8:304
youth culture, 9:168

Internet, impact on politics, 1:423–424, 2:60, 61, 285, 4:**107–109**

Internet bubble, 4:**109–110**

Internet Engineering Task Force (IETF), 4:105

Internment, Japanese American. *See* Japanese American incarceration

The Interpersonal Diagnosis of Personality: A Functional Theory and Methodology for Personality Evaluation (Leary), 4:390

Interpersonal relations. *See* Social relations

Interpretation. *See* Hermeneutics; Meaning

The Interpretation of Culture (Geertz), 3:265–266

The Interpretation of Dreams (Freud), 2:444, 3:209

Interpretive anthropology, 1:121, 3:265–266

Interpretivism, 4:99

Interracial marriage, 4:**616–619**, *617, 619*
    blood and bloodline, 1:335–336
    buraku, 1:389
    Coloreds (South Africa), 2:15
    miscegenation, 5:199–200
    race mixing, 7:26, 28
    racial democracy, 2:283

Interracial sex, 7:**467–470**
    Coloreds (South Africa), 2:15
    mulattos, 5:312–313
    race mixing, 7:26–28

Interrogation, 4:**110–114**, 8:233

Interrole conflict. *See* Role conflict

Intersectionality, 3:121, 4:**114–116**, 6:335

Interstate Commerce Commission. *See* Progressive movement

Interstate system, 9:153

Interstate wars. *See names of specific interstate wars;* War

Interstimulus interval, 1:573

Intersubjectivity, 2:178, 4:**116–117**

Interteaching, 8:295

Intertemporal substitution. *See* Elasticity; Time preference

Interval scores, 3:206

Intervals, confidence. *See* Statistics in the social sciences

Interventions, social policy, 4:**117–119**

Interventions, social skills, 4:**119–120**

Interviewing
    ethnographic research, 7:193–194

qualitative methods, 5:110–112

respondent-related validation, 8:571

Rorschach test, 7:285

sample surveys, 8:245

survey methods, 5:116–117, 7:197

Interwar years, 4:**121–122**, 8:444–445

Intifada, 4:**122–124**, 6:103, 105–106

Intimacy. *See* Friendship

Intragenerational mobility, 8:533

Intrarole conflict. *See* Role conflict

Intrinsic values, 8:557

Introduction to Black Studies (Karenga), 1:47

Introduction to History (Ibn Khaldūn). *See Muqaddimah: An Introduction to History* (Ibn Khaldūn)

An Introduction to the Principles of Morals and Legislation (Bentham), 1:285, 8:552–553

Introduction to the Study of the Law of the Constitution (Dicey), 7:292

Introductory Lectures on Psychoanalysis (Freud), 3:211

Introspection. *See* Consciousness

Intuitive criterion. *See* Screening and signaling games

Inuit, 4:**124–126**, 5:429, 9:108

Invention. *See* Creativity; Technological progress

Inventories, 4:**126–129**, 7:338–339

Inventory of father involvement. *See* Fatherhood

Inverse matrix, 4:**129–130**, 163

Inversion, matrix. *See* Inverse matrix

Inversion, symbolic. *See* Rites of passage

Investigations into the Method of the Social Sciences (Menger), 1:210

Investigative methods. *See* Research methods

Investitures, 3:135

Investment, 4:**130–133**
    aggregate demand price, 1:53
    banana parable, 1:247–248
    beauty contest metaphor, 1:269
    bequests, 1:287
    black capitalism, 1:439–442
    black middle class, 1:314
    bubbles (economics), 1:378–379
    bull and bear markets, 1:385–386
    Cantillion, Richard, 1:429
    capital controls, 1:432
    casino capitalism, 1:455
    Chinese diaspora, 1:518

cognitive dissonance, 1:599

competition, 2:50, 51

coordination failure, 2:128

corruption, 2:145

development economics, 2:344–345

economic depression, 2:302–303

economic growth, 2:486, 487, 488

energy, 2:587

energy industry, 2:589–590

foreign, 2:140
    business, 1:402
    Chinese diaspora, 1:518
    corporations, 2:140
    corruption, 2:145
    decentralization, 2:250–251
    divestiture, 2:421
    liquidity premium, 4:460–461
    rural development, 2:342

hedging, 3:450

herd behavior, 3:459–460

human capital, 3:507

institutional investors, 4:135–136

Internet Bubble, 4:109–110

investors, 4:133–134

Kahn, Richard F., 4:245

Kalecki, Michał, 4:246, 247

Keynes, John Maynard, 4:260–261

liquidity, 4:459

Markowitz, Harry M., 4:609–610

Minsky, Hyman, 5:193–194

national income accounts, 5:398–399

nationalization, 5:419

net, 5:398–399

overlapping generations model, 6:93

perfect foresight, 3:172

post Keynesian economics, 2:528–529

random walk, 7:61–63

rentier class, 1:566–567, *567*

research and development, 7:199–200

risk neutrality, 7:253–254

risk-return tradeoff, 7:255–256

risk takers, 7:254–255

rumors, 7:296

selling long and selling short, 7:432–433

socialization, 7:649–650

stock exchanges, 8:150–151

stocks, 8:155–156

Investment, *continued*
surplus labor, 4:309, 310
technology, 8:620–621
Tobin, James, 8:378–379
Tobin's Q, 8:379–381
trade-offs, 8:419
transaction taxes, 8:427–428
widow's cruse, 9:96
yield curve, 9:166–167
Z-D model, 9:172–173, *173*
Investment banking. *See* Banking
Investment banks, 8:605
Investors, 4:**133–135**
managerial capitalism, 1:442–443
rentier class, 1:566–567
state capitalism, 1:444
stock exchanges, 8:150–151
stock options, 8:153–154
Investors, institutional, 4:**135–137**
Invisibility, whites, 9:87
Invisible hand. *See* Cantillon, Richard;
Laissez-faire; Smith, Adam
Involuntary unemployment,
4:**137–139**, 8:498
full employment, 3:226
Keynes, John Maynard, 4:260
unemployment rate, 8:502–504
Inward Hunger (Williams), 9:98
IOR (Instituto per le Opere di
Religione), 8:593
IPA (Interaction process analysis),
3:386
IPCC (Intergovernmental Panel on
Climate Change), 3:328–329
IPO (Initial public offering), 3:142,
4:**38–39**
IPUMS (Integrated Public Use
Microdata Series), 4:**53–56**, 54*t*,
55*t*, 56*t*, 6:26
IQ controversy, 4:71–73, **139–142**,
7:21–23
IQ tests. *See* Intelligence (IQ) tests
IRA (Irish Republican Army),
4:**148–149**
guerrilla warfare, 3:395
Loyalists, 4:509
Iran
Carter, Jimmy, 1:451
Central Intelligence Agency, U.S,
1:483–484
Hussein, Saddam, 3:534
Iran-Contra affair, 4:142
Iran-Iraq War, 4:143
Iranian Revolution, 4:143–145

Khomeini, Ayatollah Ruhollah,
4:263–264
Mossadegh, Mohammad,
5:296–297
oil production, 6:67
OPEC, 6:65
veiling, 8:602, 604
Iran-Contra affair, 4:**142–143**
Central Intelligence Agency, U.S,
1:483, 484
Iran-Iraq War, 4:143
Reagan, Ronald, 7:89
Iran-Iraq War, 4:**143**
Arab League, 1:156
Hussein, Saddam, 3:534
Iran-Contra affair, 4:142
Khomeini, Ayatollah Ruhollah,
4:264
OPEC, 6:66
Iranian Revolution, 4:**143–145**
Iran-Iraq War, 4:143
Khomeini, Ayatollah Ruhollah,
4:264
OPEC, 6:66
veiling, 8:603
Iraq
Bush, George H. W., 1:398
Central Intelligence Agency, U.S,
1:484
civil-military relation, 1:547
Clinton, Bill, 1:580
counterterrorism, 2:155
ethnic conflict, 3:2
Gulf War of 1991, 3:397–398
Hussein, Saddam, 3:531–535
Iran-Contra affair, 4:142
Iran-Iraq War, 4:143
Iranian Revolution, 4:145
Kuwait invasion, 1:70, 159, 8:524
national defense, 2:260
oil production, 6:67
Palestinian diaspora, 6:109
partition, 6:161
UN sanctions, 8:524
United Arab Republic, 8:521, 522
water resources, 9:41–42
Iraq-U.S. War, 4:**145–148**
Al Jazeera, 1:69–70
Al-Qaeda, 1:86
bin Laden, Osama, 1:300
Blair, Tony, 1:330
Bush, George W., 1:399–400
ethnic conflict, 3:2
Fahrenheit 9/11 (film), 3:80
guerrilla warfare, 3:395

mercenaries, 9:51
military-industrial complex, 5:174
neoconservatism, 5:469
neoimperialism, 5:471
OPEC, 6:65
Republican Party (U.S.), 7:187
September 11, 2001, 7:453
vindication movements, 8:619
IRB (Institutional review board). *See*
Institutional review board (IRB)
Ireland
commonwealth, 2:29
gerrymandering, 3:309
Irish Republican Army, 4:148–149
latifundia, 4:353
Liberal Party (U.K.), 4:424
loyalists, 4:508, 509
naturalization, 5:444
New York City immigrants,
3:572–573
postcolonialism, 6:392–393
See also Northern Ireland
Irenaeus, 1:532, 6:78
Ireton, Henry, 4:414
Irish immigrants, 9:86, 88, 90, 92
Irish Republican Army (IRA),
4:**148–149**
guerrilla warfare, 3:395
Loyalists, 4:509
Iron Curtain, 4:**150**
Churchill, Winston, 1:538
Cold War, 2:5
communism, 2:35–36
Iron industry. *See* Steel industry
Iron Lady. *See* Thatcher, Margaret
Iron law of oligarchy, 3:474, 6:36,
37–39
Iroquois, 4:**151–152**, 5:425, 426,
9:108–109
Appalachia, 1:149
Cherokees, 1:496
consensus, 2:82–83
matriarchy, 5:28, 29
Seneca, 7:442
Irrationality. *See* Rationality
Irredentism, 5:418
See also Nationalism and
nationality
Irrigation, 3:126, 4:**152–154**, 9:40
IRS (Internal Revenue Service, U.S.),
2:86, 8:428
IRSA (International Rural Sociology
Association), 8:9
IRT (Item response theory), 1:10–11
Irving, James, 4:468, 469

Irving, Washington, 2:21–22
Irwin, Douglas A., 8:510
IS-LM-BP model. *See* Mundell-Fleming model
IS-LM model, 4:*158*, **158–160**
    Hicks, John R., 3:471–472
    Keynes, John Maynard, 4:259, 261
    liquidity, 4:459
    liquidity trap, 4:461
    stable nodes, 5:510
Isabella, Queen of Castile, 2:19, 20, 21
Isard, Walter, 3:304–305, 8:541
ISAs (Ideological State Apparatuses), 1:87
Ishi. *See* Kroeber, Alfred Louis
Islam, 4:**154–158**
    Arabs, 1:159–160
    black nationalism, 1:316, 317
    Christianity, 1:530
    The Church, 1:533
    clash of civilizations, 1:559–560
    communalism, 2:30
    contraception, 2:114
    Darfur, 2:226–227
    demography, 7:161
    divorce and separation, 2:427
    economics, 2:510
    euthanasia and assisted suicide, 3:28
    gender gap, 3:278
    The Green Book, 3:377
    heaven, 3:446
    hell, 3:458
    Hussein, Saddam, 3:533, 534
    Ibn Khaldūn, 3:545–546
    infidels, 4:22, 23
    Iranian Revolution, 4:144
    Iraq-U.S. War, 4:145, 147–148
    Islamic socialism, 7:643–644
    Jews, 4:195
    jihad, 4:196–197
    Jinnah, Mohammed Ali, 4:203–204
    Judaism, 4:221, 222
    Lebanese civil war, 4:396, 397
    legal systems, 4:406
    loans, 4:472
    Malcolm X, 4:563, 564
    martyrdom, 4:628
    Mecca, 5:57
    missionaries, 5:206
    monotheism, 5:270
    Muhammad, 5:308–309

    Muhammad, Elijah, 5:309–310
    Ottoman Empire, 6:84
    politics, 7:160
    Salafism, 1:70–71
    Sikhism, 7:508–509
    sin, 7:519
    slavery, 1:38–39, 40
    social movements, 7:606–607
    social relations, 7:613
    supreme being, 8:231–232
    taboos, 8:259
    theism, 8:341
    theocracy, 8:342, 343
    veil, 3:118, 8:602–604
    wealth, 9:45
    worship, 9:155
    xenophobia, 9:158, 161
    See also Muslims; Qur'an
Islam, Nation of. *See* Nation of Islam
Islam and Capitalism (Robinson), 4:472
Islamic economics (IE), 2:**510–511**
Islamic extremists, 3:237
Islamic fundamentalism, 3:**237–238**
    Al-Qaeda, 1:86
    bin Laden, Osama, 1:298–300
    domino theory, 2:436
    Iranian Revolution, 4:145
    jihad, 4:196–197
    Khomeini, Ayatollah Ruhollah, 4:263–264
    Muslims, 5:348
    Sadat, Anwar, 7:307–308
    suicide bombers, 8:224–225
    Taliban, 8:262–263
    terrorism, 8:329
    theocracy, 8:343
    veiling, 8:603
    violence, 8:624
Islamic Government (Khomeini). *See Hukumat-i Islami* (Khomeini)
Islamic socialism, 6:647–648, 7:**643–644**
Islamophobia, 9:158, 161
Isle of Man, 2:63
ISO 14001 (International Organization for Standardization), 1:246
Isolation, social. *See* Social isolation
Isolationism, 4:**160–162**
    Beard, Charles, 1:268
    League of Nations, 4:385
    linguistic, 5:462
    neutrality, 5:490
    unilateralism *vs.*, 8:509

Israel
    Amin, Idi, 1:109
    Arab-Israeli War of 1967, 1:156–159, 3:531, 533, 5:377
    Arafat, Yasir, 1:162
    Ben-Gurion, David, 1:282–283
    bigotry, 1:296
    bin Laden, Osama, 1:299
    Black September, 1:322–323
    Bonacich, Edna, 1:351–352
    borders, 1:355
    Bunche, Ralph Johnson, 1:387
    Carter, Jimmy, 1:451
    constitutions, 2:94
    defense, 2:258
    divestiture, 2:421
    ethnic conflict, 3:1
    ethnicity, 3:10
    Holocaust, 3:497
    Hussein, King of Jordan, 3:531
    Hussein, Saddam, 3:532, 533
    intifada, 4:122–124
    Jewish diaspora, 4:189–193
    Judaism, 4:219–220, 222
    Knesset, 4:276–277
    Lebanese civil war, 4:396, 397, 398
    Meir, Golda, 5:70–71
    naturalization, 5:444
    Palestine Liberation Organization, 1:159, 6:103–104
    Palestinian Authority, 6:104–107
    Palestinians, 6:111–112
    preemptive strike, 6:431
    Rabin, Yitzhak, 7:1–2
    Sharon, Ariel, 7:493
    Suez Crisis, 5:376–377, 8:213–214
    two-state solution, 8:476–478
    water resources, 9:41–42
    Zionism, 9:178–180
    See also Jews; Palestine
Israeli-occupied territories. *See* Gaza Strip; West Bank
Israelites. *See* Jews
Issawi, Charles, 3:126
Issei. *See* Asian immigrants
Issue advocacy, 1:424
IT (Information technology), cyberspace, 2:217
    See also Computers
Italian immigrants, 9:86, 90
Italian Renaissance
    architecture, 1:171
    freedom, 3:196

Italian Renaissance, *continued*
humanism, 3:517
visual arts, 8:631, 632–633
Italy
annexation of Ethiopia, 1:115
banking industry, 1:251
The Battle of Algiers (film),
1:257–258
central banks, 1:477
Chamberlain, Neville, 1:489
coffee industry, 1:594
concentration camps, 2:63
cooperatives, 2:125
corporatism, 2:140
dictatorship, 2:359
fascism, 3:103–104, 5:449
ghettos, 3:313
hegemony, 3:455
humanism, 3:517
interwar years, 4:122
latifundia, 4:353, 354
League of Nations, 4:386
left wing, 3:363–364
Mafia, 4:550–551
Medicis, 5:66–68
Mussolini, Benito, 5:349–350
national debt, 5:386
NATO, 5:544–546
regions, 7:131–132
territorial expansion, 9:147–148
voting patterns, 8:650
xenophobia, 9:160
Item response theory. *See*
Psychometrics
Item response theory (IRT), 1:10–11
ITO (International Trade
Organization), 9:143
ITT (Income terms of trade). *See*
Terms of trade
IVF (In-vitro fertilization), 7:178, 181
IWW (Industrial Workers of the
World), 4:302, 8:515
Iyad, Abu Ali, 1:323

J

J-Curve, 4:**179**
Jabotinsky, Vladimir, 1:283, 9:180
Jabotinsky, Ze'ev. *See* Jabotinsky,
Vladimir
Jackman, Richard, 8:637
Jackson, Andrew
anti-intellectualism, 4:64–65
Cherokees, 1:497
Democratic Party (U.S.), 2:286
Trail of Tears, 8:423–424

veto, 8:610, 9:37
Jackson, Cecile, 3:274
Jackson, Frank, 3:231
Jackson, George, 1:319
Jackson, Margot, 2:238
Jackson, Michael, 9:104
Jackson, Susan, 3:157
Jackson, Thomas "Stonewall," 8:550
Jackson Board of Education, Wygant v.
(1986), 6:671
Jacksonian Democrats, 9:92
JACL (Japanese American Citizens
League), 4:175
Jacob K. Javits Gifted and Talented
Students Education Program, 3:315
Jacobi, Carl Gustav Jacob, 4:163
Jacobian matrix, 4:**163**
Jacobini, H. B., 1:23
Jacobinism, 4:**164–165**, 402–404
Jacobs, David, 8:508
Jacobs, James B., 3:431
Jacobs, Jane, 4:**165–166**, 5:296, 8:542
Jacobs, T. Owens, 4:378
Jacobsen, Carlyle, 4:475
Jacobson, Lenora, 7:414–415
Jacobson, Matthew Frye, 9:88, 91
Jainism, 1:185, 3:458, 478,
4:**166–167**
Jains. *See* Jainism
Jajmani matrix, 4:**167**
Jakobson, Roman, 4:416, 417
Jam bands, 9:121
Jamaica
bauxite industry, 1:261
blackness, 1:329, 330
Hall, Stuart, 3:408
Pan-Caribbeanism, 6:119–120
People's Political Party (PPP),
7:67, 69
People's Political Party (PPP),
3:258
Rastafari, 7:66–70
reggae, 7:127–129
Rodney, Walter, 7:269
James, C. L. R., 4:**168**, 9:97
Black Arts Movement, 1:309
blackness, 1:330
Pan-African Congresses, 6:113
Robeson, Paul, 7:266
state capitalism, 1:443–444
Toussaint-Louverture, 8:403
James, Harvey, 1:370
James, Henry, 9:20
James, Sherman. *See* John Henryism
James, William, 4:**169–170**

behaviorism, 1:276
cognition, 1:597
consciousness, 2:80, 81
emotion and affect, 2:571
empiricism, 2:578
functionalism, 3:233
genetic determinism, 2:329
on habits, 3:402–403
looking-glass effect, 4:495
mysticism, 5:353
pragmatism, 6:420
self-esteem, 3:179, 7:412
self-representation, 7:426
self-system, 7:430
stream of consciousness,
8:170–172
James II, King of England, 1:396
Jamestown Island, 7:106–107
Janata Party, 3:253, 4:**170–171**,
7:521, 8:569
Jane Crow. *See* Jim Crow
Janis, Irving, 3:387–388
Janjaweed, 2:226, 227
Janowitz, Morris, 4:**171–173**
Jäntti, Markus, 4:519
Japan
annexation of Korea, 1:115
anticolonial movements, 1:139
arms control, 1:176
automobile industry, 1:219,
221–222
banana industry, 1:245, 246
Benedict, Ruth, 1:282
bequests, 1:286
biological weapons, 9:52
bioterrorism, 1:302
Bose, Subhas and Sarat, 1:357
bubbles (economics), 1:378, 379
Buddhism, 1:383, 384
buraku, 1:388–389
cannibalism, 1:427
caste, 1:461
cellular technology, 8:306, 307
Chamberlain, Neville, 1:489
Chiang Kai-shek, 1:499
Chinese diaspora, 1:518
Chinese Revolution, 1:520, 521
clash of civilizations, 1:559
coffee industry, 1:594
cognitive dissonance, 1:601
colorism, 2:18
consumption, 2:107
corporations, 2:140
dance, 2:224

decentralization, 2:250
decolonization, 2:256
dictatorship, 2:360–361
divine right, 2:422
division of labor, 2:425
economic depression, 2:302, 304, *305*
factory system, 3:78
feudal mode of production, 3:134
fishing industry, 3:152
flower industry, 3:158
Great Depression, 3:370
import promotion, 3:592
Indian National Army, 3:610–611
Korean War, 4:289
Ladejinsky, Wolf, 4:327–328
land reform, 4:342
landlords, 4:346
Le Duc Tho, 4:398
League of Nations, 4:386
life-cycle hypothesis, 4:443
liquidity trap, 4:462
Meiji Restoration, 5:69–70
merit, 5:96
microelectronics industry, 5:138–139
militarism, 5:164
oligarchy, 6:37
Pearl Harbor, 6:190
population aging, 3:306
reproductive politics, 7:181
rice cuisine, 3:163
saving rate, 2:108
Shinto, 7:496–497
state capitalism, 1:444
theater, 8:337
toxic waste, 8:409
Veblen, Thorstein, 8:596–597
visual arts, 8:632
weapons industry, 9:49–50
Wholesale Price Index, 9:94
World War II, 9:148, 149
Japan, Inc. *See* Orientalism; Xenophobia
Japanese American Citizens League (JACL), 4:175
Japanese American incarceration, **3:599–601**, 4:174–175, 5:513
Asian American politics, 6:322
Asian immigrants, 3:563
census, 1:477
concentration camps, 2:63–64
critical race theory, 2:175
described, 4:174–175
judiciary, 4:227

Pearl Harbor, 6:190
Japanese-American Reparation Act (U.S. 1988), 2:63
Japanese Americans, 4:**173–175**
Chinese Americans, 1:514
critical race theory, 2:175
incarceration, 3:599–601
model minority, 5:220–221, 220–222
Pearl Harbor, 6:190
race, 7:5
settlement, 3:563
See also Japanese American incarceration
Jaques, Elliot, 4:378
Jargowsky, Paul, 8:486
Jarvis, Edward, 3:241
Jary, D., 1:202
Jary, J., 1:202
Jaspers, Karl, 2:81
Jasso, Guillermina, 5:499
Jatis, 1:458, 461, 462, 7:324
Javits, Jacob, 3:315, 9:27
Jaworski, Leon, 9:43
Jay, John, 2:91
Jay, Martin, 3:263
Jay Treaty (1794), 9:37
Jazz, 4:**176–178**
blues, 1:342
cooperation, 2:123
Harlem Renaissance, 3:425
interwar years, 4:121
popular music, 6:376
See also Bop music; Bossa nova; Swing music
Jazz Age. *See* Interwar years
Jealousy, 5:440
Jean and Dinah (song), 1:418
Jefferson, Gail, 2:118
Jefferson, Thomas, 4:**179–184**
archaeology, 1:165–166
Burr, Aaron, 1:397
checks and balances, 1:495
Declaration of Independence, U.S., 1:104, 2:254
federalism, 3:114
Hamilton, Alexander, 3:414
interracial sex, 7:468
Jesus Christ, 4:187
judicial review, 4:223, 224
liberty, 4:440
panoptic gaze, 3:262
representative and participatory democracy, 2:284, 285
republicanism, 7:188

slavery, 7:544, 545
zero population growth, 9:174
The Jefferson Bible (Jefferson). *See The Life and Morals of Jesus of Nazareth* (Jefferson)
Jefferson County Board of Education, Meredith v. (2006), 1:375–376
Jefferson County Board of Education, United States v. (1966), 2:314
Jeffreys-Jones, Rhondri, 1:481
Jellal, Mohamed, 1:287
JEM (Justice and Equality Movement), 2:226–227
Jemmy, 7:533, 534, 535
Jencks, Christopher, 4:**184–185**
Jenkins, Gwilym M., 8:518
autoregressive models, 1:229
cointegration, 2:3
white noise, 9:82
Jenkins, Roy, 4:427
Jenkins Activity Survey. *See* Type A/Type B personality
Jensen, Arthur. *See* Race and psychology
Jensen, Leif, 8:14
Jensen et al. v. Eveleth Taconite Company (1997), 7:475
Jerusalem, Israel, 1:156–159, 533
Jervis, Robert, 4:**185–186**
Jesus Christ, 4:**186–189**
Christianity, 1:530–532
The Church, 1:532–534
heaven, 3:445–446
liberation theology, 4:435–436
Nietzsche, Friedrich, 5:502, 503
worship, 9:155
Jevons, William Stanley
Austrian economics, 1:210–211
Bentham, Jeremy, 1:286
Cantillion, Richard, 1:429
Congress Party, India, 2:76
Fabianism, 3:74
human capital, 3:507
marginal product of labor, 4:305
race, 7:14
utility function, 8:555
Walras, Léon, 9:11
The Jew in the Lotus: A Poet's Rediscovery of Jewish Identity in Buddhist India (Kamenetz), 1:385
Jewelry, gold, 3:343
Jewish diaspora, 2:356–357, 4:**189–193**, 193–196, 9:179, 180
Jewish nationalism. *See* Zionism
The Jewish State (Herzl), 9:180

Jews, 4:**193–196**
  Ashkenazi, 3:295
  Ben-Gurion, David, 1:282–283
  Benjamin, Judah P., 1:284–285
  bigotry, 1:296
  biological determinism, 2:326
  Christianity, 1:530
  Columbus, Christopher, 2:21, 22
  communalism, 2:30
  concentration camps, 2:63, 64
  critical race theory, 2:175
  ethnic conflict, 3:1, 2
  European immigrants, 3:568
  genocide, 3:296
  ghettos, 3:311, 313
  Hitler, Adolf, 3:487–488
  loans, 4:472
  migration, 3:573
  model minority, 5:221–222
  race, 7:6
  racial slurs, 7:42
  repression, 7:175
  Roman Catholic Church, 7:280
  self-hatred, 7:416
  Sharon, Ariel, 7:493
  shtetlekh, 7:503–504
  Social Darwinism, 2:233–234
  two-state solution, 8:477
  whiteness, 9:92
  See also Anti-Semitism; Holocaust;
    Israel; Jewish diaspora; Judaism;
    Palestine; Pogroms; Zionism
JFK (film), 9:34
Jhelum River, 9:41
Jiang Jieshi. *See* Chiang Kai-shek
Jíbaros, 1:355
Jigsaw classrooms, 1:181
Jihad, 4:**196–198**
  bin Laden, Osama, 1:298–299
  defensive, 1:70
  Hartz, Louis, 3:430
  veiling, 8:604
  See also Islamic fundamentalism
Jim Crow, 4:**198–201**, 199
  black politics, 6:324
  Brown v. Board of Education
    (1954), 1:373, 375
  citizenship, 1:543
  civil rights movement, U.S., 1:551
  critical race theory, 2:175
  Dixiecrats, 2:428–431
  Dred Scott v. Sanford (1857),
    2:446
  Harlem, 3:424

  Hernandez v. Texas (1954),
    3:464–466
  Houston, Charles Hamilton,
    3:505
  imprisonment, 3:596
  jazz, 4:176
  lynchings, 4:526
  minstrelsy, 5:195
  NAACP, 5:384
  negro terminology, 5:459
  passing, 6:165–166
  race-conscious policies, 7:36–37
  racism, 7:44, 46
  Sambo, 7:313
  separate-but-equal, 7:445–447
  South, U.S., 8:32–33
  Southern politics, 6:340–341, 341
  Voting Rights Act (U.S. 1965)
    (U.S. 1965), 8:651
  white primary, 9:83–85
  white supremacy, 9:86
  Wilmington Riot of 1898, 9:99
Jimsonweed, 1:456
Jingoism, 4:**201–203**
Jinnah, Mohammed Ali, 4:**203–204**
Jipangu. *See* Japan
JIT (Just in time manufacturing),
  1:218, 2:425, 3:78
J.M. Kaplan Center for New York
  City Affairs, 5:501
Job Corps, 1:283
Job guarantee, 4:**204–206**
Job Placement and Unemployment
  Insurance Act (Germany 1927),
  2:49
Job search, networks, 5:476, 478
Job security. *See* Employment
Job segregation, 3:326
Job Training Partnership Act (U.S.
  1982), 2:160
Job vacancy rates. *See* Vacancy rates
Jobs. *See* Employment; Work
Jobs Study (OECD), 8:504–505
Johannesburg (South Africa), 1:517
Johansen, Søren, 2:3, 8:514
Johanson, Donald, 4:**206–207**
John, Elton, 9:105
John, King of England, 4:556
John Birch Society, 7:248
John Henryism, 3:540, 4:**207–209**,
  444, 6:87–88
John Law's Essay on a Land Bank
  (Law), 4:366
John Paul II, Pope, 7:280, 8:594
Johnson, Andrew

  Davis, Jefferson, 2:244
  impeachment, 3:585
  Lincoln, Abraham, 4:451
  Reconstruction Era, U.S.,
    7:112–113, 114
Johnson, Bertram, 1:548
Johnson, Charles S., 1:93, 324
Johnson, Colleen Leahy, 3:86
Johnson, D. Gale, 1:502
Johnson, Harry M., 1:502, 3:559–560
Johnson, Jack, 1:74
Johnson, James Weldon, 3:423, 424,
  425, 426, 5:383, 9:81
Johnson, Lyndon B., 4:**209–210**
  affirmative action, 1:31
  Appalachian Regional
    Development Act, 1:151
  benign neglect, 1:283–284
  Brimmer, Andrew, 1:372
  culture of poverty, 2:206
  Democratic Party (U.S.),
    2:287–288
  Dixiecrats, 2:430
  domino theory, 2:434
  Federal Reserve System, 3:112
  freedom, 3:200
  Great Society, 3:371–375
  hard-core unemployed, 3:421
  Head Start, 3:437
  Kennedy, John F., 4:254, 255
  Kerner Commission Report,
    4:257, 258
  King, Martin Luther, Jr., 4:268
  Kissinger, Henry, 4:274
  law and order, 4:370
  national service programs, 5:413
  quotas, 6:670, 671
  Selective Service, 7:392
  social welfare system, 7:631, 633
  Southern strategy, 8:36
  urban renewal, 8:536–537
  Vietnam War, 1:153, 4:210, 8:614
  Voting Rights Act (U.S. 1965),
    8:651
  War on Poverty, 9:24, 25–26
  Warren Report, 9:33–34
Johnson, Phillip E., 2:162
Johnson-Forest Tendency, 4:168
Johnson-Reed Act (U.S. 1924), 2:568
Johnston, Joseph E., 8:550
*Jokes and Their Relation to the
  Unconscious* (Freud). *See Der Witz
  und sein Beziehung zum
  Unbewussten* (Freud)
Jolson, Al, 1:327

Jonas, Hans, 5:501
Jones, Bryan, 1:48, 3:609–610
Jones, Catherine, 9:68
Jones, Charles, 6:77
Jones, Edward Ellsworth, 4:**210–211**
Jones, Gareth Stedman, 3:483, 484
Jones, James A., 9:25
Jones, James Warren, 2:188
Jones, Jim. *See* Jones, James Warren
Jones, Paula, 1:580
Jones, William, 1:345
Jones Act (U.S. 1917), 1:356
Jonsson, Jan, 8:535
Jordan
    Arab-Israeli War of 1967,
      1:156–159
    Arafat, Yasir, 1:162
    Black September, 1:322, 323
    Hussein, King of Jordan,
      3:530–531
    Hussein, Saddam, 3:533
    Palestinian diaspora, 6:109
    social relations, 7:613
    veiling, 8:604
Jordan, Antoinette, 2:142
Jordan, Barbara, 3:584
Jordan, James, 3:173
Jordan River, 1:154, 9:41–42
Jorgenson, Dale, 3:389, 5:399, 8:552
Joseph, Chief. *See* Chief Joseph
Joseph, Keith, 2:87
*Joseph Conrad and the Fiction of
    Autobiography* (Said), 7:310
Josephson, Matthew, 3:318
Josephus, Flavius, 8:342
Jourard, Sidney, 7:408–409
Journal of Economic History
    (periodical), 1:582
Journalism, 4:**211–216**
    censorship, 1:475
    comic books, 2:23
    Defender, 1:501
    political cartoons, 1:452
    sensationalism, 7:442–444
    Wells-Barnett, Ida B., 9:76
Journals, professional, 4:**216–217**
    bias, 5:105
    citations, 1:538–539
    cliometrics, 1:582, 583
    cognition, 1:598
    Latino National Political Survey,
      4:355
    Thompson, Edward P., 8:353, 355
Journey of Reconciliation (1947), 2:75
Journeymen, 8:514

Jowell, Roger, 2:141–142
Jowett, Benjamin, 8:528
Joyce, Patrick, 3:483–484
Juan Carlos I, King of Spain, 3:186
Juan the Chamula (Pozas), 7:262
Juárez, Benito, 4:**217–219**
Judaism, 4:**219–223**
    Arabs, 1:159
    Buddhism, 1:385
    Christianity, 1:530
    The Church, 1:532
    communalism, 2:30
    contraception, 2:114
    demography, 7:161
    divorce and separation, 2:427
    euthanasia and assisted suicide,
      3:28
    funerals, 3:239
    heaven, 3:445
    hell, 3:457–458
    infidels, 4:22, 23
    Jesus Christ, 4:186–187
    Jewish diaspora, 4:189–193
    legal systems, 4:406
    loans, 4:472
    martyrdom, 4:628
    missionaries, 5:205
    monotheism, 5:268, 269
    mysticism, 5:352
    orthodoxy, 6:78–79
    Ottoman Empire, 6:84
    sin, 7:519
    supreme being, 8:230
    taboos, 8:260
    theism, 8:341
    worship, 9:155
    See also Jews; Zionism
Judeocide. *See* Holocaust
Judges. *See* Judiciary
Judgment, social. *See* Social judgment
    theory
Judgment (wisdom). *See* Decision-
    making
*Judgments of Responsibility: A
    Foundation for a Theory of Social
    Conduct* (Weiner), 4:478
Judicial activism, 1:**18–19,**
    4:223–225, 226–228
Judicial appointments, filibuster,
    3:139
Judicial branch. *See* Judiciary
Judicial restraint, 1:19
Judicial review, 4:**223–225**
    Constitution, U.S., 2:92
    constitutional courts, 2:93

    constitutionalism, 2:94
    judiciary, 4:225, 227–228
    jurisprudence, 4:231–233
    Supreme Court, U.S., 8:232–234
Judiciary, 4:**225–228**
    Brown v. Board of Education
      (1955), 1:377
    checks and balances, 1:496
    civil liberties, 1:546–547
    confiscation, 2:69
    conflict, 2:70
    conservatism, 2:84
    constitutional courts, 2:92–93
    corruption, 2:144
    crime and criminology, 2:173–174
    impeachment, 3:585, 586
    judicial review, 4:223–225
    jurisprudence, 4:231–233
    jury selection, 4:233–234
    law, 4:363, 364, 365
    legal systems, 4:405–407
    litigation, 4:464–467
    lobbying, 4:474
    presidency, 6:442
    Royal Commissions, 7:291–292
    separation of powers, 7:448–449
    Supreme Court, U.S., 8:232–234
Juhn, Chinhui, 2:478, 479
Julian Rosenwald Fund, 3:183
Julius Caesar, 2:359
Julius Caesar (Shakespeare), 1:495
June War. *See* Arab-Israeli War of 1967
Jung, Carl, 4:**228–231**
    basic needs, 5:455
    creativity, 2:165
    equilibrium, 2:622
    Freud, Sigmund, 3:215
    Holocaust, 3:496, 497
    midlife crisis, 5:149
The Jungle (Sinclair), 1:8
Junker, Buford, 6:14
Junta. *See* Dictatorship; Military
    regimes
Juries, 4:465, 525
Jurisdiction, 4:224, 225
Jurisprudence, 4:226–228, **231–233,**
    363, 405–407, 6:390–391
Jurors, death-qualified, 4:**233,** 234
Jury selection, 4:**233–235**
Jus sanguinis, 5:444
Jus soli, 5:444
Just in time manufacturing (JIT),
    1:218, 2:425, 3:78
Just-in-time production. *See* Just in
    time manufacturing (JIT)

Just-in-time teaching, 8:295
Just war, 4:196–197, **235–237**
Justice, 4:**237–239**
    civil disobedience, 1:545
    commutative, 4:237
    crime and criminology, 2:170,
      173–174
    equality, 2:616–617
    exploitation, 3:63–65
    imprisonment, 3:596–597
    judiciary, 4:225–228, 226–228
    law, 4:363
    liberalism, 4:426
    Love Canal, 4:504, 505
    lynchings, 4:526–527
    maximin principle, 5:39
    peace, 6:181
    political philosophy, 6:258–259
    procedural, 4:241
    Rawls, John, 7:84–85
    reconciliation, 7:110
    reparations, 7:166–168
    reproductive rights, 7:183
    retaliation, 7:215–216
    social exclusion, 7:588
    substantive, 4:241
Justice, distributive, 4:237, **239–241**
    consociational democracy, 2:279
    difference principle, 2:362–363
    marginal product of labor, 4:306
    restitution principle, 7:213–215
    social justice, 4:242
Justice, social, 4:**241–243**
    Chávez, César, 1:494
    class conflict, 1:570–571
    digital divide, 2:366–367
    Feagin, Joseph, 3:109
    functionings, 3:233–235
    Lynd, Staughton, 4:528–529
    social movements, 7:603–607
    Vajpayee, Atal Bihari, 8:569
    Woodstock, 9:121
Justice and Equality Movement
    (JEM), 2:226–227
Justice as Fairness: A Restatement
    (Rawls), 4:238, 5:39
Justification, self. *See* Self-justification
Juvenile delinquency, 1:25, 9:25
Juvenile Deliquency and Youth
    Offenses Act (U.S. 1961), 9:25
Juveniles. *See* Children

K

Kachin, 1:128
Kádár, János, 3:523

Kaeppler, Adrienne, 2:224, 225
Kafka, Franz, 1:391
Kagan, Robert, 8:509
Kagel, John H., 1:207, 9:103
Kahana, Eva, 3:293
Kahn, Herman, 3:241
Kahn, Richard F., 4:**245–246**, 492,
    7:501
Kahn, Robert, 4:379
Kahneman, Daniel
    behavioral economics, 2:500
    Cholesky decomposition, 1:526
    decision-making, 2:251
    happiness, 3:418
    liberalism, 4:425
    maximization, 5:40–41
    non-expected utility theory, 5:519
    objective utility, 8:557
    otimizing behavior, 6:56
    See also Rationality
Kain, John, 8:542–543, 9:101
Kaine, Timothy, 4:371
Kaiser Wilhelm. *See* Wilhelm II,
    German Emperor
Kaldor, Nicholas
    asymmetric returns to scale,
      7:223–224
    compensation criterion, 9:62
    cumulative causation, 2:207–208
    foresight, 3:173
    Kaldor-Hicks compensation test,
      9:65
    markup pricing, 4:611
    neoclassical growth model, 5:465
    nonlinear systems, 5:523–524
    returns, 7:217
    speculation, 8:55
    stylized fact, 8:189–190
    Verdoorn's law, 8:607
    widow's cruse, 9:96
Kaldor-Hicks compensation test, 9:65
Kaldor-Hicks efficiency, 8:556
Kaldor's Law. *See* Verdoorn's Law
Kalecki, Michał, 4:**246–248**
    business cycles, 1:406, 411–412
    difference equations, 2:362
    economic crises, 2:484–485
    Luxemburg, Rosa, 4:522
    underconsumption, 8:489
    unemployment, 8:503
    widow's cruse, 9:96
Kalman filter, 4:78
Kamenetz, Rodger, 1:385
Kammatic Buddhism, 5:504

Kanaya, Tomoe, 3:160
Kansas-Nebraska Act (U.S. 1854),
    4:450
Kant, Immanuel, 4:**248–249**
    aesthetics, 1:30
    autonomy, 1:224–225
    consciousness, 2:80
    consensus, 2:82
    constructivism, 2:96
    cosmopolitanism, 2:149
    critical theory, 2:176, 178
    cultural relativism, 2:194
    Frankfurt School, 3:188
    Hegel, Georg Wilhelm Friedrich,
      3:452
    idealism, 3:547
    internationalism, 4:102
    liberalism, 4:425
    linguistic turn, 4:457
    merit, 5:95
    moral philosophy, 6:255–256, 256
    morality, 5:285
    naturwissenchaft, 9:78
    objectivity, 6:9, 10
    physical geography, 3:304
    Popper, Karl, 6:372
    race, 7:3
    relativism, 7:156
    representative and participatory
      democracy, 2:284
    social justice, 4:241
    supreme being, 8:231
    time orientation, 8:368
    universalism, 8:526
Kanter, Rosebeth Moss, 5:3
Kantorovich, Leonid, 4:287, 288
Kanuri society, 8:630
Das Kapital (Marx). *See Capital: A
    Critique of Political Economy* (Marx)
Kaplan, Howard, 2:238
Karenga, Maulana, 1:47, 317
Karhunen-Loève transform, 8:590
Kariel, Henry S., 2:220, 4:**249–250**
Karl, Barry, 3:183
Karl Marx's Theory of History (Cohen),
    8:577
Karlin, Jennifer, 2:60
Karma. *See* Reincarnation
Karush-Kuhn-Tucker conditions. *See*
    Linear and nonlinear programming;
    Maximization
Kasavuba, Joseph, 4:517, 518
Kashf al-Asrar (Khomeini), 4:263–264
Kashmir, 5:434, 9:41
Kast, Ludwig, 3:306

Katsushika Hokusai, 8:632
Katusic, Slavica K., 1:198
Katz, Cindi, 8:390
Katz, Daniel, 4:379
Katz, Lawrence F., 9:4
Katz, Michael, 4:419, 8:487
Katz, Richard, 3:309
Katz, Stan, 3:183
Katznelson, Ira, 9:87
Kaufmann, Daniel, 2:145
Kaufmann, Franz-Xaver, 9:73
Kaunda, Kenneth, 4:**250–251**
Kautilya, Chanakya, 9:45
Kautsky, Karl
    class consciousness, 1:572
    imperialism, 3:588–589
    latifundia, 4:353
    underconsumption, 8:488
Kawai, Masao, 1:83
Kawamura, Syunzo, 1:83
Kazakhstan, 2:30
Kealiinohomoku, Joann, 2:224
Kean, Thomas H., 1:485
Kean Commission, U.S., 1:485
Kebede, Ashenafi, 1:342
Keeler, Scott, 2:238
Kefauver, Estes, 4:**251–252**
Kehoe, Patrick J., 5:491
Keinan, Anat, 3:101
Keith, Verna, 2:17
Keller, Fred, 8:294
Kelley, Harold, 1:205–206,
    4:**252–253**
Kelly, George Alexander, 6:216–217
Kelly, John, 7:612
Kelly, R. E., 4:381
Kemet, Afrocentricity, and Knowledge
    (Asante), 1:47
Kenc, Turalay, 6:94
Kendall, Willmoore, 2:85
Kendler, Kenneth, 2:306
Kendrick, John, 3:390
Kenkel, Donald, 5:391
Kennedy, Charles, 4:427
Kennedy, John F., 4:**253–255**
    affirmative action, 1:31
    Alliance for Progress, 6:45
    Bay of Pigs, 1:262
    Brimmer, Andrew, 1:371
    campaigning, 1:423
    Castro, Fidel, 1:465–466
    Central Intelligence Agency, U.S,
      1:484
    civil rights, 1:550

Cold War, 2:5
    Cuban Missile Crisis, 2:183–185
    Democratic Party (U.S.), 2:287
    domino theory, 2:434
    Great Society, 3:372
    Johnson, Lyndon B., 4:210
    journalism, 4:214
    Khrushchev, Nikita, 4:264
    King, Martin Luther, Jr., 4:268
    Kissinger, Henry, 4:274
    law and order, 4:369
    Macmillan, Harold, 4:538
    Mafia, 4:552
    national service programs, 5:413
    Nixon, Richard M., 5:505
    Okun's law, 6:35
    quotas, 6:670–671
    Vietnam War, 8:614
    wage and price controls, 9:2–3
    War on Poverty, 9:24, 25
    Warren Report, 9:33–34
Kennedy, Paul, 1:153
Kennedy, Robert F., 2:184, 4:214,
    9:25, 27
Kennedy-Javits Amendment, 9:27
Kennewick Man, 5:427
Kent State University, Vietnam War
    protests, 8:616
Kentucky, 1:2
Kenya, 4:255–256
    concentration camps, 2:63
    crony capitalism, 2:180
    Harris-Todaro model, 3:428
    Kimathi, Dedan, 4:266
    Leakey, Richard, 4:386–387
    Mau Mau, 5:36–38
    urbanization, 8:546, 547
Kenyatta, Jomo, 1:128, 4:**255–256**
Keohane, Robert, 4:**256–257**, 8:606
Kerensky, Alexander, 7:304
Kernel function, 5:528–529
Kernels, 5:527
Kerner, Otto J., Jr., 4:257–258
Kerner Commission Report (1968),
    4:257–258, 8:538
Kerouac, Jack, 1:384, 4:177
Kerry, John, 1:400
Kershaw, Joseph A., 9:26
Kessler, Gladys, 7:467
Key, V. O., Jr., 4:**258–259**, 8:648
    Dixiecrats, 2:430
    Southern politics, 6:339–340
Key, Wilson Bryan, 3:473
Keyes, Alan, 1:311

Keynes, John Maynard, 3:145,
    4:**259–262**
    absolute income hypothesis, 1:6–7
    aggregate demand, 1:49–51
    aggregate demand and supply
      price, 1:51–52
    aggregate supply, 1:53–54
    appeasement, 1:152
    banana parable, 1:247
    basic needs, 5:455
    beauty contest metaphor, 1:269
    business cycle theories, 1:411
    business cycles, 1:403
    capital controls, 1:432
    carrying cost, 1:449–450
    casino capitalism, 1:455, 456
    central banks, 1:478
    consumption function, 2:109
    demand for money, 5:253–254
    economic crises, 2:484
    economic depression, 2:302, 303
    economic history, 2:499
    endogenous money, 5:257
    expectations, 3:48
    free trade, 3:195
    Frisch, Ragnar, 3:222
    full capacity, 3:224
    full employment, 3:225–226
    individualism, 3:619
    interest rates, 4:84–85
    International Monetary Fund,
      4:95
    involuntary unemployment,
      4:137–138
    IS-LM model, 4:158
    Kahn, Richard F., 4:245
    Kalecki, Michał, 4:246
    Keynesian economics, 2:511–513
    laissez-faire, 4:337
    leisure, 4:409
    liberalism, 4:425
    life-cycle hypothesis, 4:441
    liquidity, 4:459
    liquidity trap, 4:461–462
    long run, 4:491–492
    Lundberg, Erik, 4:518
    macroeconomics, 4:541
    Malthus, Thomas Robert, 4:571
    market clearing, 4:601–602
    mathematical economics, 5:24
    multiplier, 5:329–330
    national income accounts, 5:400
    natural rate of interest, 4:77
    neutral rate of interest, 4:79

Keynes, John Maynard, *continued*
    new Keynesian economics, 2:525
    nominal wages, 5:512
    normative social sciences,
        5:534–535
    overconsumption, 8:488
    own rate of interest, 4:80
    perfect foresight, 3:172–173
    post Keynesian economics, 2:528
    price *vs.* quantity adjustment,
        6:453–454
    rentier class, 1:567, 568
    risk, 7:252, 255
    Say's Law, 7:336–337
    scarcity, 7:340
    short period, 7:501
    Singer, Hans, 7:520
    socialization of investment,
        7:649–650
    speculation, 8:55
    Sraffa, Piero, 8:70–71
    subjective probability, 6:490
    Tinbergen, Jan, 8:374
    Tobin, James, 8:378–379
    Tobin's Q, 8:379–380
    Treasury view, 8:444–445
    uncertainty, 8:481–482
    unemployment, 8:18, 22, 503,
        9:13
    voluntary unemployment, 8:637
    wealth, 9:45
    widow's cruse, 9:96
    Z-D model, 9:172–173
    zero population growth, 9:174
Keynes-Hansen secular stagnation
    theory, 3:217
Keynesian consumption function. *See*
    Absolute income hypothesis
Keynesian economics, 2:*511,* 511–513
    aggregate supply, 1:53–54
    beauty contest metaphor, 1:269
    carrying cost, 1:449–450
    casino capitalism, 1:455, 456
    central banks, 1:478
    conservatism, 2:85
    consumption function, 2:109
    economics of control, 2:532
    Great Depression, 3:370
    Hicks, John R., 3:470–471
    history, 2:499
    inflation, 4:24
    involuntary unemployment,
        4:137–138
    IS-LM model, 4:158–160
    Kahn, Richard F., 4:245

Keynes, John Maynard,
    4:259–262
    Klein, Lawrence, 4:276
    laissez-faire, 4:337
    liberalism, 4:425
    life-cycle hypothesis, 4:441
    liquidity, 4:459
    liquidity trap, 4:461–462
    long run, 4:491–492
    Lucas, Robert E., Jr., 4:510
    macroeconomics, 4:541
    macrofoundations, 4:546
    Meade, James, 5:49
    microfoundations, 5:141
    minimum wage, 5:187
    monetarism, 5:242–243
    multiplier, 5:329–330
    new Keynesian economics, 2:524,
        525
    Patinkin, Don, 6:171–172
    Phillips, A. W. H., 6:247–248
    price *vs.* quantity adjustment,
        6:453–454
    quantity theory of money, 6:660
    rate of profit, 7:74
    relative income hypothesis, 7:153
    rules *vs.* discretion, 7:293–294
    Say's Law, 7:336–337
    socialization of investment,
        7:649–650
    unemployment, 8:503
    user costs, 8:562
    wage and price controls, 9:2
    War on Poverty, 9:25, 29
    X-Crise, 9:158
    Z-D model, 9:172–173
    zero population growth, 9:174
The Keynesian Revolution (Klein),
    4:276
Keyserling, Leon, 9:25
Khaldūn, Ibn. *See* Ibn Khaldūn
Khalid Sheikh Mohammed, 1:299
Khama, Seretse, 2:274
Khanh, Nguyen, 8:614–615
Khartoum Resolution, 1:159
Khmer Rouge, 4:262–263
    concentration camps, 2:64
    ethnic conflict, 3:2
    Killing Fields, 4:265
    Pol Pot, 6:289
Khoisans. *See* Coloreds (South Africa)
Khomeini, Ayatollah Ruhollah,
    4:263–264
    Hussein, Saddam, 3:534
    Iranian Revolution, 4:144, 145

theocracy, 8:343
Khrushchev, Nikita, 4:264–265,
    8:511–512
    Berlin Wall, 1:289
    Brezhnev, Leonid, 1:370
    Cold War, 2:5
    Cuban Missile Crisis, 2:183–185
    cult of personality, 6:222–223
    glasnost, 3:325
    gulags, 3:396
    Hungarian Revolution, 3:523–524
    peaceful coexistence, 6:187
    Russian Federation, 7:302
Kibbutzim, 1:351–352, 2:31
Kibera, Kenya, 8:546, 547
Kickbacks. *See* Corruption
Kidder, Alfred V., 1:167
Kierkegaard, Søren, 3:43, 453
Kihlstrom, John, 4:74–75
Kikuyu, 5:37
The Killer Angels (Shaara), 4:399
Killing Fields, 4:265–266
    Khmer Rouge, 4:263
    Pol Pot, 6:289
Kim Il Sung, 4:289
Kimathi, Dedan, 4:266
Kin selection. *See* Sociobiology
Kinder, Donald R., 1:103
Kindleberger, Charles Poor, 1:252,
    4:266–267
Kindness. *See* Altruism
Kinds of Power (Hillman), 1:391
Kinesics, 5:530
Kinesics and Context (Birdwhistell),
    5:530
King, Albert, 1:343
King, B. B., 1:343
King, Eugene, 1:345
King, Freddie, 1:343
King, Gary, 8:606
King, Gregory, 5:399
King, John E., 8:576
King, Mackenzie, 2:473–474
King, Martin Luther, Jr., 4:267–269
    black conservatism, 1:311
    black liberalism, 1:312
    Black Power, 1:321
    blackness, 1:330
    Bunche, Ralph Johnson, 1:388
    civil disobedience, 1:545, 546
    civil rights movement, U.S.,
        1:551–552
    Hoover, J. Edgar, 3:501
    Johnson, Lyndon B., 4:210

journalism, 4:214
Kennedy, John F., 4:254
Kerner Commission Report, 4:258
Malcolm X, 4:563–564
Nation of Islam, 5:380
Nobel Peace Prize, 1:550
race-blind policies, 7:35–36
Thoreau, Henry David, 8:357
urban riots, 8:538
Voting Rights Act (U.S. 1965),
8:651
King, Robert G., 5:490, 491
Kingdon, John, 1:48, 3:609
Kings. *See specific monarchs*
Kingston, Pau, 1:564
Kinnock, Neil, 2:88, 4:326, 327
Kinsey, Alfred, 4:**269–270**, 7:482
Kinship, 3:182, 4:*271*, **271–273**, 271*t*
alliances, 1:128
blood and bloodline, 1:335–336
British anthropology, 1:127
cities, 1:540
dictatorship, 2:360
female-headed families, 3:116
Lévi-Strauss, Claude, 4:416
Mafia, 4:550–553
marriage, 4:615
matriarchy, 5:28–30
networks, 5:478
nuclear family, 3:87
primates, 6:461
race, 7:4
reincarnation, 7:145, 146
reproduction, 7:179
See also Family
Kinship, evolutionary theory of,
1:119, 2:229, 3:414–415,
4:**273–274**
Kirchheimer, Otto, 2:176
Kirk, Russell, 2:85
Kirkpatrick, Jeane, 8:395
Kirkpatrick, Shelley, 4:379
Kirsanow, Peter N., 4:317
Kirzner, Israel, 1:211, 6:57
Kissinger, Henry, 4:**274–275**
Allende, Salvador, 1:77–78
Le Duc Tho, 4:398
Vietnam War, 8:616
Kiswahili, 5:554
Kitab al-'Ibar (Ibn Khaldūn), 3:545
Kitchen Debate. *See* Khrushchev,
Nikita; Nixon, Richard M.
Kitchener, Herbert, 1:349
Kitchin cycle. *See* Real business cycles

Kivetz, Ran, 3:101
KKK (Ku Klux Klan). *See* Ku Klux
Klan (KKK)
Klamer, Arjo, 1:539, 2:495
Klein, Lawrence, 4:**275–276**, 6:389
Klein, Melanie, 3:215
Kleindeutschland, 3:573
Knesset, 4:**276–277**
Knight, Frank, 1:502
Caribbean, 1:448
Harris, Abram L., 3:427
laissez-faire, 4:335
risk, 7:252
risk takers, 7:255
subjective probability, 6:490
Knights of Labor, 3:436, 4:302,
8:523–524
Know-Nothing Party, 3:578, 5:430
Knowledge, 4:**277–281**
Afrocentrism, 1:47
cognition, 1:598
collective wisdom, 2:9–10
common knowledge rationality
games, 2:25–26
consciousness, 2:78–79
constructivism, 2:96, 97
creation, 3:148
data, 2:234–237
diminishing returns, 7:219
empiricism, 2:577–578
epistemology, 2:609–610
informal education, 2:534–535
Kuhn, Thomas, 4:292–294
Mannheim, Karl, 4:587
objectivism, 6:6–8
objectivity, 6:8–11
philosophy, 6:251
Rand, Ayn, 6:6–8
self-perception theory, 7:422–423
sociology, 1:426, 7:674–676
universalism, 8:526
Knowledge, diffusion of, 1:490, 491,
492, 4:**281–282**
Knowledge, group. *See* Collective
wisdom
Knowledge, self. *See* Self-perception
theory
Knowledge and Human Interests
(Habermas), 2:177, 3:401
Knowledge economy. *See* Knowledge
society
Knowledge in sociology, 7:674–676
Knowledge society, 4:**283–286**
computers, 2:60
credentialism, 2:166

cyberspace, 2:217
digital divide, 2:366–367
Drucker, Peter, 2:449
industrialization, 3:622
qualifications, 6:649
skill, 7:523–524
Knowledge workers, 5:493
Knox, John, 1:531
Knox, Robert, 3:336
Koch, Edward, 9:24–25
Koffka, Kurt, 3:310, 311
Kohl, Helmut, 2:84
Kohlberg, Lawrence, 3:319,
4:**286–287**
Köhler, Wolfgang, 1:186, 3:310, 311,
8:358, 388
Kohnken, Gunter, 4:525
Kohut, Heinz, 1:290
Koinonia, 3:196
Kojève, Alexandre, 3:453
Koller, Marvin R., 2:23
Kolmogorov, Andrey, 8:588
Kondratief, Nikolai
long run, 4:492, 493, 494
Russian economics, 7:300
Kondratief cycles. *See* Long waves
Kondratief wave. *See* Long waves
Konjunkturer och ekonomisk politik
(Lundberg), 4:519
Koopmans, Tjalling, 1:502,
4:**287–288**, 6:51
Korea, 4:**288–289**
annexation by Japan, 1:115
Buddhism, 1:383
partition, 6:160–161
United Nations role, 8:523–524
See also North Korea; South Korea
Korean Americans. *See* Asian
immigrants
Korean War, 4:**288–289**
mortality, 9:17–18
wage and price controls, 9:2
Kornbluh, Karen, 6:99
Korpi, Walter, 9:68, 69, 70, 72
Korsch, Karl, 1:571
Kossina, Gustav, 1:167, 185
Kothari, Rajni, 2:76
Kotlikoff, Laurence, 4:35, 6:93
Koustas, Zisimos, 5:491
Koyce lags. *See* Distributed lags
Koyck, L. M., 4:334
Kozol, Jonathan, 2:316
Kraftwerk, 9:142
Kratochwil, Friedrich, 5:421
Krauthammer, Charles, 8:509

Kremer, Michale, 6:76–77

Krenz, Egon, 1:289

Kreps, David. *See* Screening and signaling games

Kreuger, Alan, 2:605, 606

Kristeva, Julia, 6:82–83

Kristol, Irving. *See* Neoconservatism

Kroeber, Alfred Louis, 1:345, 4:**289–291**

Kroeber, Ursula. *See* Le Guin, Ursula K.

Kropotkin, Petr, 1:111, 2:233

Kropotkin, Pyotr Alekseyevich. *See* Kropotkin, Petr

Krueger, Alan, 9:5

Kruger, Paul, 1:349

Krugman, Paul, 2:208, 212

Kshatriyas, 4:**291–292**
    Brahmins, 1:366
    caste, 1:457–458, 461
    Vaisyas, 8:568

Ku Klux Klan (KKK), 4:**294–295**
    bigotry, 1:296
    Birth of a Nation (film), 1:305
    black nationalism, 1:316
    Jim Crow, 4:200
    Reconstruction Era, U.S., 7:113–114
    right wing, 7:248
    Wilson, Woodrow, 9:102

Kuhlman, Charles, 1:258

Kuhn, Peter, 9:128

Kuhn, Thomas, 4:**292–294**, 480
    economic methodology, 2:493
    empiricism, 2:579
    Lakatos, Imre, 4:338–339
    modernity, 5:231
    paradigm, 6:125, 126
    philosophy of science, 6:261
    scientific revolutions, 7:235, 236–237
    triumphalism, 8:455

Kuhn-Tucker conditions. *See* Linear and nonlinear programming; Maximization

!Kung, 9:109–110

Kuomintang. *See* Guomindang

Kurath, Gertrude P., 2:224, 225

Kurds, 3:534, 8:630

Kurtosis. *See* Descriptive statistics

Kurtzman, Lemon v. (1971), 1:535

Kürwille, 3:266–267

Kurz, Heinz, 3:154, 8:577

Kurzweil, Ray, 2:60–61

Kuwait

Gulf Cooperation Council, 3:397

Gulf War of 1991, 3:397–398

Hussein, Saddam, 3:534

Iraq invasion, 1:70, 159, 8:524

OPEC, 6:65

Palestinian diaspora, 6:109

Kuwatli, Shukri al-, 8:521

Kuznets, Simon, 4:295–297
    dual economy, 2:456
    Fogel, Robert, 3:161
    Freidman, Milton, 3:217
    national income accounts, 5:397, 400
    University of Texas Inequality Project, 8:529–530

Kuznets' curve. *See* Kuznets hypothesis

Kuznets hypothesis, 2:607–609, 4:**295–297**, *296*, 5:541

Kwame Ture. *See* Black nationalism; Black Power

Kwan, Michelle, 1:514–515

Ky, Nguyen Cao, 8:614

Kydland, Finn, 1:404, 407, 408, 479

Kymlicka, Will, 9:72

Kyoto Protocol, 1:543, 3:330, 333, 378

Kyrgyzstan, 2:30, 137

L

La Barre, Weston, 1:457

La Mettrie, Julien de, 1:275

La Venta, 6:39

La Vida (Lewis), 1:202

Laban, Rudolf von, 2:223
    See also Dance

Labanotation. *See* Dance

Labeling theory, 4:**299–300**, 8:582
    crime and criminology, 2:170
    deviance, 2:352–353
    mental retardation, 5:90
    post-Parsonian American sociology, 8:7

Labor, 4:**300–304**
    abstract, 9:122
    capital, 1:430
    capitalist mode of production, 1:445–446
    Chinese Americans, 1:513
    Christian socialism, 7:643
    class conflict, 1:569
    cooperatives, 1:402
    direct action, 2:372
    East Indian diaspora, 2:471–475
    embodied, 8:575
    exploitation, 3:64–65, 7:70–71

Haymarket Square riot, 3:436

human capital, 3:506–509

Incas, 3:602

internal colony, 2:13, 14

Lafargue, Paul, 4:330

leisure, 4:408–409

Luddites, 4:513–515

machinery, 4:535–536

management science, 4:576–577

maquiladoras, 4:591–594

Marxian economics, 2:515–517, 4:630

mining industry, 5:188–189

mobility, 5:208–211

monopsony, 5:267–268

populism, 6:383–384

primitive communism, 2:37

principal-agent models, 6:467–468

prison, 7:462–463

real business cycles, 1:408–409

Ricardo, David, 7:244–246

Rybczynski theorem, 7:305–306

silver industry, 7:512

social relations, 7:611–612

subsistence agriculture, 8:205

sweatshops, 8:247–248

Taylorism, 8:287–288

Thompson, Edward P., 8:354–355
    See also Division of labor; Employment; Work

Labor, child. *See* Child labor

Labor, division of. *See* Division of labor

Labor, foreign. *See* Migrant labor

Labor, marginal product of, 4:**304–307**, *305*, 421

Labor, migrant. *See* Migrant labor

Labor, prison. *See* Servitude

Labor camps. *See* Concentration camps

Labor demand, 4:**312–314**
    involuntary unemployment, 4:137–138
    labor market, 4:318
    marginal productivity, 4:595–596
    surplus labor, 4:308, 309

Labor Department, U.S., 4:303

Labor economics, 2:**513–515**
    Blinder-Oaxaca decomposition technique, 1:332–334
    blue collar and white collar, 1:339
    Chicago School, 1:502
    Ginzberg, Eli, 3:323
    Harris, Abram L., Jr., 3:427

labor demand, 4:312–314

labor market, 4:318–319

labor supply, 4:320–322

marginal product of labor, 4:304–307

Parnes, Herbert, 6:147–148

Labor force

agricultural industry, 1:60–61

geographical immobility, 8:497

National Longitudinal Survey of Youth, 5:407–408

quotas, 6:671

unemployment framework, 8:500, *500*

Labor force participation, 4:**314–316**

codetermination, 1:592–593

day care, 2:245–246

discouraged workers, 2:386–387

education in the U.S., 2:543

labor supply, 4:321–322

See also Hard-core unemployed

Labor law, 4:303, **316–318**

employment, 2:581, 582

factory system, 3:79

flexibility, 3:157

Neumann, Franz, 5:482

sweatshops, 8:247–248

U.S., 4:303

Labor-Management Relations Act (U.S. 1947). *See* Taft-Hartley Act (U.S. 1947)

Labor Management Reporting and Disclosure Act (U.S. 1959), 4:303

Labor market, 4:**318–319**

balkanization of, 5:515

banana industry, 1:245

Berg, Ivar E., 1:288

Beveridge curve, 1:292

Blinder-Oaxaca decomposition technique, 1:332–334

blue collar and white collar, 1:337–340

Bonacich, Edna, 1:352, 353

Bracero Program, 1:364–365

capitalism, 1:437–438

clearing, 8:498

corruption, 2:145

credentialism, 2:166–167

crowding hypothesis, 2:181–182

discrimination, 2:388–391

employment, 2:580–583

flexibility, 3:157

full employment, 3:225–228

gold industry, 3:343

Harris-Todaro model, 3:428–429

involuntary unemployment, 4:137

labor economics, 2:513–515

labor supply, 4:320–322

migration, 5:157

natural rate of unemployment, 5:435–437

noncompeting groups, 5:514–516

outsourcing, 6:86

perfect competition, 9:4

population studies, 6:382

primary, 8:637

qualifications, 6:649

secondary, 8:637

skill, 7:523–524

transnationalism, 8:433

underemployment, 8:492–493

wage discrimination, 2:400–401, 402–403

winner-take-all, 9:102–103

women's work, 9:124–126

work day length, 9:134–135

Labor market segmentation (LMS), 4:**319–320**

blue collar and white collar, 1:337–340

described, 4:302

dual economy, 2:456–457

ethnic enclave, 3:3

marginal product of labor, 4:306

Taylorism, 8:287

Labor market segregation, 2:389

Labor Party (Israel), 1:283

Labor productivity. *See* Productivity

Labor relations. *See* Workplace relations

Labor-saving technological change, 1:491

Labor supply, 4:**320–322**

agricultural industry, 1:60–61

foreign, 4:303

immigration, 3:581, 582

involuntary unemployment, 4:137–138

labor market, 4:318

marginal productivity, 4:595–596

overemployment, 6:90

overlapping generations model, 6:92–94

surplus labor, 4:308–309, 309

wage discrimination, 2:403

work day, 9:127

Labor surplus

development economics, 2:344

exploitation, 3:64–65

factory system, 3:77

Lewis, W. Arthur, 4:420–421

technological progress, 8:300

transitional conjunctures, 2:77, 78

Labor surplus, conventional economics, 4:**308–309**

Labor surplus, Marxist and radical economics, 1:562, 4:**309–312**

Labor theory of value, 3:40, 4:**322–324**

Amin, Samir, 1:110

Cambridge capital controversy, 1:420

capital, 1:430

capitalist mode of production, 1:445–446

class, 1:562

comparative advantage, 1:5–6

consumption, 2:106–107

exchange value, 3:40

exploitation, 3:64–65

Leontief, Wassily, 4:413

Marxist theory, 3:155

relative surplus value, 7:155

surplus labor, 4:309–312

surplus value, 8:240–241

technological change, 1:491

transformation problem, 8:429–431

Labor unions, 4:**325–326**, 8:513–517

automobile industry, 1:220, 3:168, 285–286

black middle class, 1:314

blue collar and white collar, 1:340

Bonacich, Edna, 1:352, 353

Bracero Program, 1:364

Chávez, César, 1:493–494

Chinese diaspora, 1:516

Christian Democracy, 2:277

clientelism, 1:578

codetermination, 1:593

film industry, 3:140

Gilded Age, 3:318

gold industry, 3:343

Haymarket Square riot, 3:436

history, 4:301–303

industrial accidents, 1:8

labor law, 4:303, 316, 317

Labour Party (U.K.), 4:326

left wing, 4:403

Lindblom, Charles Edward, 4:452–453

Mexican Americans, 5:123

mining industry, 5:188–189

natural rate of unemployment, 5:435, 436

Labor unions, *continued*
real income, 7:90
social relations, 7:611–612
Solidarność, 8:25–26
state capitalism, 1:444
steel industry, 8:128–129
sweatshops, 8:247–248
syndicalism, 8:254–256
white collar employment, 2:585
Labor utilization framework (LUF), 8:492
Labour Party (Britain), 4:**326–327**
Blair, Tony, 1:330–331
centrism, 1:489
cleavages, 1:578
Conservative Party (U.K.), 2:88
Fabianism, 3:73, 74
Hall, Stuart, 3:410
left wing, 4:404
Liberal Party (U.K.), 4:423, 424
Tawney, R. H., 8:272
Thatcher, Margaret, 8:335
Lacan, Jacques, 3:453
gaze, 3:264
Oedipus complex, 6:29
subjectivity, 8:199
Laclau, Ernesto, 2:299, 6:396
Ladaique, Maxime, 9:70
Ladejinsky, Wolf, 4:**327–328**
Ladino, 1:500
Ladson-Billings, Gloria, 2:176
The Lady's Guide to Perfect Gentility (Thornwell), 3:301
Lafargue, Catalina, 4:328–329
Lafargue, Paul, 4:**328–331**
Laffer, Arthur, 2:85
Lagging, leading, and coincident indicators, 4:**331–332**
Lagour Representation Committee, 3:73
Lagrange, Joseph-Louis, 6:6
Lagrange multiplier test. *See* Specification tests
Lagrange multipliers, 4:**332–333**
Lags, distributed, 2:627, 4:**333–335**, 8:371
Lags, Koyce. *See* Lags, distributed
Laguna de los Cerros, 6:39
Laicite, 1:536
Laine, James, 4:292
Laissez-faire, 4:**335–338**
Conservative Party (U.K.), 2:87
cosmopolitism, 5:493
dirigiste, 2:372–374
individualism, 3:619

libertarianism, 4:438
long period analysis, 4:489, 490
parent-child relationships, 6:131
Turgot, Jacques, 8:466
Laitin, David, 3:7–8
Laity, Jainism, 4:166–167
Lakatos, Imre, 4:**338–340**, 6:261
Lake, David, 5:412
Lakota (Native Americans), 1:258, 259, 2:159
Lakota Noon (Michno), 1:259
Lalonde, Robert, 9:4
Lamaze, Fernand, 5:432
Lamb, Brian, 2:142
Lamb, Michael, 3:106
Lambton, John, 3:587
Lamont, Michelle, 8:7
Lampman, Robert J., 9:25, 26
Lamy, Pascal, 9:143
Land
agricultural industry, 1:59–62
annexation, 1:115–116
aristocracy, 1:174
Boserup, Ester, 1:357
class conflict, 1:569
latifundia, 4:352–354
nationalization, 5:419
Native Americans, 5:427
population growth, 8:546
rent, 7:163–164
resource economics, 7:210–211
rural development, 2:341
subsistence agriculture, 3:98, 8:205
tenure, 4:345
urbanization, 8:546
See also Property; Territorial expansion
Land, common. *See* Common land
Land claims, 4:**340–341**
borders, 1:354–355
Cherokees, 1:497, 498
Chiapas, 1:500
Chief Joseph, 1:503–504
common land, 2:26–28
Iroquois, 4:152
Mugabe, Robert, 5:307–308
Navajos and Hopis, 5:447
treaty federalism, 8:445–446
Land fertility, 3:**130–132**
Land grants. *See* Rural development
Land of Israel. *See* Israel
Land redistribution. *See* Land reform
Land reform, 4:**341–345**

indigenismo, 3:613
Ladejinsky, Wolf, 4:327–328
landlords, 4:346
latifundia, 4:354
Land-to-the-tiller programs. *See* Land reform
Landauer, Gustav, 2:31
Landefeld, J. Steven, 5:399
Länderkunde, 3:304
Landlord-peasant relations, 9:20
Landlordism, 4:346
Landlords, 4:**345–347**
Ladejinsky, Wolf, 4:328
land reform, 4:343
latifundia, 4:352
rent, 7:163–164
rent control, 7:165
sharecropping, 7:490–492
Landlords, absentee, 4:346, **347–348**
Landmines, 1:176
Landowners. *See* Landlords
Landry, Bart, 1:313
Landscape, 3:303, 304
Landscape, cultural. *See* Cultural landscape
Landslides, 5:433
Lane, Mark, 9:34
Lang, Michael, 9:121
Lang, Sabine, 5:521
Lange, Carl, 2:571, 4:169
Lange, Oskar, 1:502, 3:529, 7:645, 8:108–109
Langlois, Richard, 3:148
Langman, Lauren, 6:30
Langston, John Mercer, 1:326
Language
Arabic, 1:159
behaviorism, 1:277–278
blackness, 1:330
Boas, Franz, 1:344, 345
body, 5:530
Cherokees, 1:497
child development, 1:506
Chomsky, Noam, 1:527–529
cognition, 1:598
constructivism, 2:97
conversational analysis, 2:118–120
Creole, 2:167–168, 169
Croats, 2:179
cultural relativism, 2:194–195
data, 2:236–237
discourse, 2:387
Dravidians, 2:443–444
everyday life, 3:338

gendered, 3:258
ideology, 1:130
linguistic anthropology,
    1:118–119, 129–130
linguistic turn, 4:457–458
message-based persuasion, 6:229
Native American, 1:129
pidgin, 1:40
race relations cycle, 7:33
representation, 7:170–172
Skinner, B. F., 7:527
as social action, 1:129–130
theory of mind, 8:347
world, 1:118
    See also Communication;
    Psycholinguistics
Language acquisition. *See*
Psycholinguistics
The Language of Chartism (Jones),
    3:483
Lansdale, Edward G., 8:613
Laos, 2:118, 3:491
Lapid, Yosef, 5:421
Laplace, Pierre-Simon, 2:416, 6:429,
    486
Laplace distribution. *See* Probability
    distributions
Laplacian determinism. *See* Prediction
Lapps, 3:83
Lapwai Reservation, 1:503–504
Large numbers, law of. *See* Law of
    large numbers
Large sample properties, 4:**348–350**
Larsen, Nella, 3:424, 425, 426
Las Casas, Bartolomé de, 2:20, 146,
    147
Lasch, Christopher, 1:28, 5:369
Lashley, Karl, 1:276
Laslett, Peter, 3:83, 306
Laspeyre's index, 3:151, 5:398
    See also Quantity index
Lasswell, Harold, 4:**351**, 6:309, 312
The Last Bar-B-Que (Humphrey),
    1:310
Last stands, 1:258–259
LAT (Living apart together), 3:84
Latané, Bibb, 3:179
Late Capitalism (Mandel), 4:579, 580
Latent functions, 3:232
Latent learning, 1:597
Latent pattern maintenance-tension
    management, 3:232
Latent trajectory analysis, 3:391
Latent variables, 8:585, **586**
Lateral mobility, 5:**212–213**

Latifundia, 3:136, 4:346, **352–354**
Latin America
    aboriginal peoples, 5:423
    AIDS/HIV, 1:65
    banana industry, 1:245–247
    blackness, 1:328, 329
    blood and bloodline, 1:336
    Bracero Program, 1:364–365
    Caribbean, 1:447–449
    Castro, Fidel, 1:463–467
    Christian Democracy, 1:472,
        2:277
    Christian socialism, 7:643
    cities, 1:541
    civil wars, 1:554
    clash of civilizations, 1:559
    clientelism, 1:579
    coffee industry, 1:594
    colorism, 2:18
    communism, 2:36
    concentration camps, 2:64
    corporatism, 2:141
    coups d'etat, 2:156
    creolization, 2:169
    dance, 2:224
    decolonization, 2:255
    dependency theory, 2:298–300
    developing countries, 2:335–337
    development economics, 2:344
    development in sociology, 2:347
    domino theory, 2:434, 435
    drug traffic, 2:450–452
    Economic Commission for Latin
        America and the Caribbean,
        2:482–483
    feudalism, 3:136
    flower industry, 3:158–159
    Frank, Andre Gunder, 3:187
    imperialism, 3:589
    import substitution, 3:593
    indigenismo, 3:612–614
    international relations, 2:187
    land reform, 4:342–343, 344
    landlords, 4:346
    latifundia, 4:352, 354
    Latino/Latina studies, 4:356–357
    Latino National Political Survey,
        4:354–356
    legal systems, 4:405
    liberation, 4:429
    liberation theology, 4:434–436
    Memín Pinguín, 5:73–74
    mining industry, 5:189
    Monroe Doctrine, 5:272

    moreno/morena, 5:293–294
    negro terminology, 5:458–459
    neocolonialism, 5:467
    overlending, 6:94–95
    phenotype, 6:245
    populism, 6:384–385
    positivism, 6:390
    Prebisch, Raúl, 6:422–423
    privatization, 5:420
    race, 7:19
    race mixing, 7:26–27
    reproductive politics, 7:181–182
    revolutions, 7:233–235
    self-employment, 7:411
    servitude, 7:463
    socialism, 7:638
    structuralist macroeconomics,
        4:543–545
    telecommunications industry,
        8:316
    trade barriers, 1:255
    trigueño, 8:452
    underdevelopment, 8:490–491
    urban anthropology, 1:135
    urban sprawl, 8:540
    Verdoorn's law, 8:608
    Washington Consensus, 9:38–39
    whitening, 9:90
    working class, 9:132
Latin American Dependency school,
    5:466
Latin American immigrants,
    3:570–572, 4:358
    Bracero Program, 1:364–365
    Chávez, César, 1:493–494
    Latino/Latina studies, 4:356–357
    Latino National Political Survey,
        4:354–356
    law and order, 4:372
    Mexican Americans, 5:121–122
    settlement, 3:578
    socioeconomic status, 3:566*t*
Latin American revolutions,
    4:217–219, 7:**233–235**
Latin American sociology, 7:**676–677**
Latin Americans. *See* Latinos
*Latin Journey: Cuban and Mexican
    Immigrants in the United States*
    (Portes and Bach), 4:359
Latino immigrants. *See* Latin
    American immigrants
Latino/Latina studies, 4:**356–357**
Latino National Political Survey
    (LNPS), 4:**354–356**

Latino National Survey (LNS), 4:355–356

Latino politics, 6:**337–339**, 338*t*
    Latino National Political Survey, 4:354–356
    Mexican Americans, 5:125–126
    public opinion, 7:20–21

Latinos, 3:566*t*, 4:**357–361**
    addiction, 1:21
    affirmative action, 1:31
    Black Panthers, 1:319
    Bonacich, Edna, 1:352
    Bracero Program, 1:365
    California Civil Rights Initiative, 1:416
    cities, 1:541
    civil rights movement, U.S., 1:552
    colorism, 2:17
    crime and criminology, 2:173
    critical race theory, 2:175
    crowding hypothesis, 2:182
    digital divide, 2:366
    discrimination, 5:513
    drugs of abuse, 2:455
    female-headed families, 3:116–117
    hip hop, 3:480, 481
    illegal immigrants, 5:430–431
    interracial marriage, 4:616–619
    jazz, 4:177–178
    Latino National Political Survey, 4:354–356
    liberation theology, 4:436
    lynchings, 4:526
    metropolitan regions, 7:135
    minorities, 5:191
    occupational status, 6:27
    out-of-wedlock births, 1:307
    phenotype, 6:244
    political science, 7:20–21
    race, 7:6, 7
    racial discrimination, 2:394
    racial identification, 3:549
    resegregation of schools, 7:201–202
    returns to education, 7:66
    role models, 7:274
    school desegregation, 2:318
    sellouts, 7:434
    socioeconomic status, 3:566*t*
    Southern politics, 6:347–348
    upward mobility, 8:534
    urban renewal, 8:537
    wage discrimination, 2:400
    whiteness, 9:93

    See also Boricua; Mexican Americans

Latinos and the Changing Face of America (Saenz), 4:359

Latitudes. *See* Social judgment theory

Laughlin, J. Laurence, 3:151

Laughter. *See* Comedy

Laughter: An Essay on the Meaning of the Comic (Bergson), 2:22

Laumann, Edward, 7:483

Laundering, money. *See* Money laundering

Lausanne, school of, 4:**361–362**, 9:11

Lausanne Conference (1932), 1:152

Laviera, Tato, 5:553

Lavoisier, Antoine-Laurent, 5:399, 7:236

Law, 4:**362–365**
    abortion, 1:3–4
    absentee landlords, 4:348
    Bentham, Jeremy, 1:285
    bioterrorism, 1:302
    blood and bloodline, 1:336
    censorship, 1:475–476
    children, 1:511
    Chinese Americans, 1:513–514, 515
    Church and state, 1:534–536
    civil, 4:227, 364, 405–406
    civil disobedience, 1:545–546
    civil liberties, 1:548
    civil rights movement, U.S., 1:551–552
    compulsory voting, 2:58
    confiscation, 2:69–70
    constitutionalism, 2:93–94
    constitutions, 2:94–95
    consumer protection, 2:102–103
    Corn Laws, 2:133–134
    corporations, 2:139
    crime and criminology, 2:170–171
    critical race theory, 2:174–176, 178
    cultural resource management, 2:196
    customary, 4:407
    deviance, 2:352
    divorce and separation, 2:426–427
    equal protection, 2:614–615
    euthanasia and assisted suicide, 3:26–28
    habitus, 3:405
    hate crimes, 3:430, 431
    human sterilization, 8:141
    inheritance, 1:174, 3:86
    international, 3:360–361
    interracial sex, 7:469, 470
    interrogation, 4:110
    Israel, 4:276
    judiciary, 4:226–228
    jurisprudence, 4:231–233
    labor, 4:303, 316–318
    landlords, 4:346–347
    legal systems, 4:405–407
    litigation, 4:464–467
    Magna Carta, 4:556–557
    marriage, 4:613, 615
    miscegenation, 5:199–200
    natural, 5:438–439, 442
    negotiated settlement, 7:465–466
    norms *vs.*, 5:536
    occupational, 6:23–34
    positivism, 6:390–391
    privacy, 6:477–478
    race mixing, 7:26–28
    rape, 7:65–66
    referendum, 7:120
    retaliation, 7:215–216
    same-sex marriage, 4:619–621
    secrecy, 6:32
    settlement, 7:464
    social psychology, 7:610
    Supreme Court, U.S., 8:232–234
    tobacco settlement, 7:466–467
    universalism, 8:526
    war crimes, 9:21–22

    See also names of specific types of law; International law

Law, administrative, 1:**22–23**

Law, canon. *See* Roman Catholic Church

Law, common. *See* Common law

Law, international. *See* Internationalism

Law, John, 1:251, 428, 4:**366–367**, 5:259

Law, natural. *See* Natural law

Law, rule of. *See* Rule of law

Law and economics, 1:271, 502, 4:**367–369**

Law and order, 4:**369–372**
    biased policing, 6:289–291
    discrimination, 2:390
    drugs of abuse, 2:455
    due process, 2:461
    national defense, 2:260
    race-conscious policies, 7:37
    Southern politics, 6:348

Law enforcement. *See* Law and order

Law of diminishing product, 4:305

Law of Economy. *See* Occam's razor

Law of effect, 1:574, 8:358, 359

Law of exercise, 8:358

Law of large numbers, 1:486,
4:**372–374**, *373*, 409

Law of mortality. *See* Morbidity and
mortality

Law of one price. *See* Purchasing
power parity

The Law of Peoples (Rawls), 7:84

Law of readiness, 8:358

Law of Return (Isreal), 5:444

Law of variable proportions, 4:305,
305

Lawrence, Frederick M., 3:431

Lawrence, Paul, 6:69

Laws (Plato), 6:280

The Laws and Customs of War on Land
(Hague Convention), 9:21

Laws of Manu, 8:568

Laws of nature, 3:230

Lawyers Committee for Human
Rights, 3:431

Lay persons, Jainism, 4:166–167

Lay theories, 4:**374**
lying, 4:525
theism, 8:340–341
theory of mind, 8:346–347

Layard, Henry, 1:165

Layard, Richard, 3:418, 8:637

Layne, Lancelot, 1:419

Layoffs, 1:339

Lazarsfeld, Paul Felix, 1:202,
4:**374–375**

Lazarus, Richard S., 2:128–129
See also Coping

Lazear, Edward, 9:128–129

LCH (Life-cycle hypothesis). *See* Life-
cycle hypothesis (LCH)

Le Bon, Gustave, 2:9, 7:21, 33
See also Race and psychology

Le Corbeiller, Philippe, 5:524

Le Courbisier, 1:171

Le Duc Tho, 4:275, **398–399**, 8:616

Le Guin, Ursula K., 3:272, 4:290,
407–408, 7:360–361

Le Pen, Jean-Marie, 1:296

Leach, Edmund, 1:128

Leaders, 4:291–292, **375–377**, 376*t,*
377–382

Leadership, 4:375–377, **377–384**
alpha-males, 1:83, 84
Congress, U.S., 2:73–74
coups d'etat, 2:156
definition, 4:377–378

elitism, 2:566–567
Hunter, Floyd, 3:524–525
narcissism, 5:369
oligarchy, 6:36, 38
theories, 4:378–382

Leadership, contingency model of,
4:**384–385**

*Leadership and Performance Beyond
Expectations* (Bass), 4:377

Leading indicators. *See* Lagging,
leading, and coincident indicators

League of Arab States. *See* Arab League

League of Nations, 1:297, 4:**385–386**
arms control, 1:176
disarmament, 2:380
Kant, Immanuel, 4:249
Wilson, Woodrow, 9:102

League of Revolutionary Black
Workers, 1:321, 3:175

League of the South (LoS), 8:619

League of United Latin American
Citizens (LULAC), 3:465

Leakage, 5:530

Leakey, Louis, 4:386, 387

Leakey, Mary, 4:386

Leakey, Meave, 4:386

Leakey, Richard, 4:207, **386–387**

Lean production, 1:218, 222, 3:78,
8:365–366

Lear, Jonathan, 3:215

Lear, Martha, 3:120

Learned helplessness, 4:**387–389**, 6:54
locus of control, 4:477–478
self-defeating behavior, 7:404
Seligman, Martin, 7:431–432
shock experiments, 3:62

Learned optimism. *See* Learned
helplessness; Seligman, Martin

Learning
active, 8:293–294
behaviorism, 1:276, 277
child development, 1:506–507
collective wisdom, 2:9
cooperative, 8:295
cultural, 1:122
experiential, 3:202
Hull, Clark, 3:506
latent, 1:597
neuroscience research, 5:484–485
Pavlov, Ivan, 6:178–179
shock experiments, 3:62
Thorndike, Edward, 8:358–359
Tolman, Edward, 8:386–387
See also Developmental
psychology; Education;

Intelligence; Learned
helplessness; Reinforcement
theories; Social learning
perspective

Learning, experiential. *See* Experiential
learning

Learning, observational. *See* Models
and modeling

Learning, social. *See* Social learning
perspective

Learning disorders, 1:198, 199
See also specific disorders

Learning to Labor (Willis), 6:48

Leary, Timothy, 3:411, 4:**390–391**

Leasing, 4:345, 346–347, 7:163–164,
165

Leasor, James, 5:550

Least developed countries,
overlending, 6:95

Least squares, ordinary (OLS),
4:**391–394**
instrumental variables regression,
4:45–47
recursive models, 7:117
serial correlation, 7:455–457
Tobin, James, 8:379
two-stage least squares *vs.,* 4:395

Least squares, three-stage, 4:**394–395**

Least squares, two-stage, 4:394,
395–396

Leavis, F. R., 4:464

Lebanese Civil War, 1:554, 4:**396–398**

Lebanese Forces (LF), 4:396, 397

Lebanese National Movement (LNM),
4:397

Lebanese Phalanges Party. *See*
Phalangists

Lebanon
Arafat, Yasir, 1:162
borders, 1:355
civil-military relation, 1:547
civil war, 4:396–398
civil wars, 1:554
clientelism, 1:579
Palestinian diaspora, 6:108, 109
Phalangists, 6:236

Lebensraum, 3:304

Lebenswelt, 9:78

Leboyer, Frederick, 5:432

Leckie, Shirley, 1:258

Lectures on Fine Art (Hegel), 1:30

Leder, K., 5:454

Lederer, Emil, 5:501

Lee, Don L., 1:309

Lee, Henry, 9:38

Lee, Kuan Yew, 3:74

Lee, Richard, 4:415, 8:536
Lee, Robert E., 2:67, 3:365, 4:**399–400**, 8:550–551
Lee, Shelton Jackson. *See* Lee, Spike
Lee, Spike, 1:243–245, 2:18, 7:314
Lee, Tae-Hwy, 4:499, 501
Lee, Young-joo, 8:638–640, *639*
Lee (Freeman), 4:399
Lefebvre, Henri, 1:569, 4:**400–401**, 8:545
Left and right, 4:**401–402**
　centrism, 1:488–489
　cleavages, 1:578
　coalition theory, 1:588
　Democratic Party (U.S.), 2:286–288
　Hegelians, 3:454
　identity politics, 6:335–336
　Jacobinism, 4:164–165
　left wing, 4:402–404
　moderates, 5:226–227
　political correctness, 6:300
　Republican Party (U.S.), 7:185–187
　resistance, 7:208
　right wing, 7:247–248
　spatial theory, 8:44–45
Left and right censoring, 1:**473–474**, 2:464
The Left Hand of Darkness (Le Guin), 3:272, 4:407
Left wing, 4:**402–404**
　centrism, 1:488–489
　Christian Democracy, 2:276
　class, 1:564
　conservatism, 2:83
　Gramsci, Antonio, 3:363–364
　Hall, Stuart, 3:410
　journalism, 4:214
　Lynd, Robert and Helen, 4:528
　Lynd, Staughton, 4:528–529
　political business cycles, 1:406
　political tolerance, 8:386
　repression, 7:175
　repressive tolerance, 7:176–177
　right wing, 7:247–248
　technophobia, 8:311
　terrorism, 8:629
　See also Left and Right; Liberalism
Legacy effects, 4:**404–405**
Legal authority, 1:214
Legal Defense and Education Fund, Inc, 5:384
Legal precedents, 4:405–406
Legal systems, 4:**405–407**

citizenship, 1:542
crime and criminology, 2:173–174
critical race theory, 2:174–176
Jefferson, Thomas, 4:180–181
judiciary, 4:227–228
jurisprudence, 4:231–232
jury selection, 4:233–234
law, 4:363, 365
litigation, 4:464–467
lynchings, 4:526–527
Ottoman Empire, 6:84
rule of law, 7:292–293
Legalism, 7:292
Legend into History (Kuhlman), 1:258
The Legendary Topography of the Holy Land (Halbwachs), 2:7
Legendre, Adriene Marie, 4:392, 393
Legends. *See* Storytelling
Legends, urban. *See* Rumors
Legibility, 8:583
Legislation
　Diet, 2:361
　lynchings, 4:527
Legislative branch. *See names of specific legislative bodies;* Parliaments and parliamentary systems
Legislative districts. *See* Apportionment
Legislatures, 8:647
Legitimate authority, 1:214, 3:353–354
　destructive obedience, 6:2–3
　nationalism, 5:417
Legitimation
　groups, 3:386
　nationalism, 5:417
Legitimation Crisis (Habermas), 3:401
Legum, Colin, 5:507
Legumes, 3:131–132
Leibenstein, Harvey, 2:500, 4:313
Leiber, Fritz, 7:361
Leibfried, Stephan, 9:68, 69, 73
Leibniz, Gottfried Wilhelm, 1:114
Leijonhufvud, Axel, 1:256, 6:454
　See also Price vs. quantity adjustment
Lein, Laura, 3:116
Leisure, 4:**408–409**
　conspicuous, 1:566
　consumerism, 2:104
　lifestyles, 4:445
　tourism, 8:398
Leisure class, 1:**565–566**, 5:548, 8:595–596
　conspicuous consumption, 2:88

lifestyles, 4:445
Veblen, Thorstein, 8:595–596, 597
wealth, 9:46
Leisure time
　family functioning, 3:85
　standard of living, 9:129
　vacations, 8:565–566
　work day length, 9:134, 135
　work week, 9:128
Leisure work, 9:123
Lemert, Edwin M., 4:299
Lemkin, Raphael, 3:296, 494–495
Lemon v. Kurtzman (1971), 1:535
Lemons. *See* Akerlof, George A.
Lender of last resort, 4:**409–410**, 485
Lending (finance). *See* Loans
Leñero-Otero, Luis, 3:87
Length of working day. *See* Work day
Leniency programs, 1:145
Lenin, Vladimir Ilitch, 4:**410–411**
　Asiatic mode of production, 1:187
　bolshevism, 1:350–351
　bourgeoisie, 1:361
　capitalist mode of production, 1:446
　career, 8:511
　Castro, Fidel, 1:464
　Chinese Revolution, 1:520
　class conflict, 1:569
　class consciousness, 1:572
　communism, 2:35
　convergence theory, 2:117
　dialectical materialism, 5:19
　Fabianism, 3:74
　feudal mode of production, 3:133–134
　Hilferding, Rudolf, 3:476
　imperialism, 1:350, 3:587, 588–589, 8:489
　Leninism, 4:411–412
　Lukacs, Georg, 4:515, 516
　primitive accumulation, 6:464
　rentier class, 1:568
　Rivera, Diego, 8:632
　Russian economics, 7:299
　Russian Federation, 7:302
　Russian Revolution, 7:303, 304
　self-determination, 7:406
　social theory, 7:628
　socialism, 7:637–638
　Stalin, Joseph, 8:86
　Stalinism, 8:87
　Trotsky, Leon, 8:456

Lenin and Philosophy (Althusser), 3:82
Leninism, 4:**411–412**
    bolshevism, 1:350–351
    class consciousness, 1:572
    communism, 2:35, 36
    conservatism, 2:85
    convergence theory, 2:117
    democratic centralism, 2:285
    legal systems, 4:406
    Lenin, Vladimir Ilitch, 4:410–411
    Lukacs, Georg, 4:515, 516
    Trotsky, Leon, 8:456
Lenski, Gerhard, 1:358
Leo III, Pope, 8:593
Leo XIII, Pope, 2:277, 8:594
Leonard, Robert, 5:517
Leonardo da Vinci, 8:633
Leone, Mark, 1:169
Leontief, Wassily, 3:154, 4:**412–413**
    cobweb cycles, 1:591
    Heckscher-Ohlin-Samuelson
        model, 3:449
    Russian economics, 7:301
    separability, 7:444
    social accounting matrix,
        7:562–563
    vectors, 8:600
Leontief function. *See* Fixed
    coefficients production function
Leontief matrix. *See* Input-output
    matrix
Leontief-Sono separability condition.
    See Separability
The Leopard's Spots (Dixon), 1:304
Lerner, Abba, 1:51–52, 2:531–532
    See also Economics of control
Lerner, Richard M., 1:26
Lerner index. *See* Imperfect
    competition
Lesbianism. *See* Gay, lesbian,
    transgender, and bisexual politics;
    Sexual orientation
Lesbians. *See* Gay, lesbian, transgender,
    and bisexual politics; Sexual
    orientation
Less-developed countries. *See*
    Developing countries
Lesser, William, 1:470
A Letter Concerning Toleration (Locke),
    4:476
Letter from Birmingham Jail (King),
    1:552, 4:268
Letters Concerning the English Nations
    (Voltaire), 4:336–337, 8:635

Lettres philosphiques sur les Anglais
    (Voltaire). *See Letters Concerning the
    English Nations* (Voltaire)
Leuchtenburg, William E.,
    5:493–494, 495–496
Levassor, Emile, 1:217
Leveling norms, 5:536–537
Levellers, 4:**413–415**
Levels of analysis framework,
    3:170–172
Leverage, 4:**415–416**, 459, 6:368–369
Lévesque, René, 6:662
Levhari, David, 6:163–164
Levi, Margaret, 7:613
Lévi-Strauss, Claude, 1:120,
    4:**416–417**
    British anthropology, 1:128
    cultural studies, 2:199
    dance, 2:225
    reciprocity, 7:106
    structuralism, 8:182
    symbols, 8:250, 252
    totemism, 8:397
The Leviathan (Hobbes), 3:493,
    4:237, 5:411, 439
Levin, Dan, 9:103
Lévinas, Emmanuel, 6:82–83, 399,
    400
Levine, David, 2:124–125, 5:391
Levine, Robert A., 9:26
Levine, Ross, 1:253
Levine, Timothy, 4:524–525
Levinson, Daniel, 6:220–221
Levinson, Jerrold, 1:29–30
Levitt, Steven D., 1:502, 2:326,
    3:21–22
The Levittowners (Gans), 3:256, 267
Levy, Paul, 9:135
Lewin, Kurt, 4:**417–418**, 9:135
    Aronson, Elliot, 1:180
    management science, 4:576–577
    parent-child relationships, 6:131,
        132
    time orientation, 8:368
Lewinsky, Monica, 1:580
Lewis, Bernard, 1:559
Lewis, C. S., 8:231
Lewis, Catherine, 6:137
Lewis, David, 3:173, 5:520
Lewis, H. Gregg, 1:270, 502
Lewis, Jane, 9:68
Lewis, Meriwether, 4:182
Lewis, Nolan, 4:476
Lewis, Oscar, 4:**418–420**, 5:462, 9:25,
    109

    culture of poverty, 1:134, 202,
        2:206
    Tally's Corner, 8:264
Lewis, W. Arthur, 4:**420–422**, 421,
    6:411, 9:136
    crowding hypothesis, 2:181–182
    development economics, 2:344
    development theory, 2:338
    dual economy, 2:456
    Kuznets hypothesis, 4:295
    labor supply, 4:320
    surplus labor, 4:308–309
Lewis-Beck, Michael, 6:58
Lexicographic preferences, 4:**422–423**
Lexicon, mental. *See* Psycholinguistics
LF (Lebanese Forces), 4:396, 397
Liabilities. *See* Wealth
Liars, 5:530
Liberal corporatism. *See* Corporatism
Liberal democracy, 2:274, 7:84–85
Liberal Democrats (Britain). *See*
    Liberal Party (U.K.)
Liberal feminism, 3:121
Liberal Party (U.K.), 1:537, 2:87,
    4:**423–424**
The Liberal Tradition in America
    (Hartz), 3:429–430
Liberal Unionist Party (U.K.). *See*
    Conservative Party (U.K.)
Liberalism, 4:**425–427**
    Bentham, Jeremy, 1:286
    black, 1:312
    Black Panthers, 1:319
    centrism, 1:488
    Christian Democracy, 2:276, 277
    common good, 2:25
    communitarianism, 2:38
    conservatism, 2:83, 84–85
    cooperation, 2:122
    critical theory, 2:177, 178
    defense, 2:258
    Enlightenment, 2:595–598
    feminism, 9:113
    freedom, 3:196–197
    Hartz, Louis, 3:429–430
    Hayek, Friedrich August von,
        3:434, 435
    humanism, 3:518
    Huntington, Samuel P., 3:526
    international relations, 4:99–100
    libertarianism, 4:437, 438
    liberty, 4:425
    Locke, John, 4:476–477
    Lowi, Theodore J., 4:506

Liberalism, *continued*
    Mises, Ludwig Edler von, 5:202–203
    modernization, 5:232–234
    Mont Pelerin Society, 5:272–273
    national security, 5:412
    New Deal, 5:497
    Rawls, John, 7:84–85
    repressive tolerance, 7:176–177
    Shklar, Judith, 7:499
    social contract, 7:581
    socialism, 7:636–637
    welfare state, 9:68, 70
    See also Left wing; Neoliberalism
Liberalization, economic
    capitalist mode of production, 1:447
    export penetration, 3:66
    globalization, 3:334
Liberalization, order of. *See* Trade liberalization
Liberalization, trade, 4:**427–428**
    assessment, 8:411, 412–413
    Bhagwati, Jagdish, 1:293
    bilateral, 8:414–415
    capital controls, 1:432–433
    classical economics, 2:504
    Corn Laws, 2:133–134
    exports, 3:69
    physiocracy, 6:266
    tariffs, 8:265–266
    textile industry, 8:333–334
    transitional economies, 2:533
Liberation, 4:**428–431**
    children's rights, 1:512
    liberation movements, 4:431–434, 434–436
    See also Women's liberation
Liberation, women's. *See* Women's liberation
Liberation movements, 4:**431–434**
    black Marxism, 4:642
    Black Power, 1:321
    buraku, 1:389
    Cabral, Amílcar, 1:415–416
    calypso, 1:418
    Chiapas, 1:500
    class conflict, 1:570–571
    developing countries, 2:335
    direct action, 2:372
    Indian National Army, 3:610–611
    internal colony, 2:13, 15
    Le Duc Tho, 4:398
    as liberation, 4:429
    Lumumba, Patrice, 4:517–518

Machel, Samora, 4:532–533
    Mau Mau, 5:36–38
    Mexican-American, 5:126–129
    Mexican-Americans, 5:120
    Palestinian Liberation Organization, 6:103–104
    Raj, 7:55–57
    Rastafari, 7:68
    revolution of rising expectations, 7:231–232
    self-determination, 7:405–406
    separatism, 7:450–451
    Zionism, 9:180
Liberation theology, 4:**434–437**
    Christian socialism, 7:643
    social justice, 4:242
    socialism, 7:638
Liberia, 3:504, 8:618
Libertarianism, 4:**437–439**
    Boricua, 1:355
    Church and state, 1:535
    justice, 4:238–239
    left wing, 4:403
    Rand, Ayn, 6:8
    right wing, 7:248
    social justice, 4:241–242
Liberties, civil. *See* Civil liberties
Liberty, 4:**439–441**
    Burke, Edmund, 1:396–397
    choice in economics, 1:525
    conservatism, 2:83, 84, 85
    Constitution, U.S., 2:91
    Declaration of Independence, U.S., 2:254–255
    defense, 2:258
    democracy, 2:273
    egalitarianism, 2:550
    individual, 5:439
    justice, 4:238
    laissez-faire, 4:335–338
    liberalism, 4:425
    libertarianism, 4:437–439
    moral sentiments, 5:282
    Rawls, John, 7:84–85
    representative and participatory democracy, 2:283
    right wing, 7:248
    Tocqueville, Alexis de, 8:382–383
Liberty, civil. *See* Civil liberties
Libido, 3:213, 4:228, 229
    See also Psychoanalytic theory
Libya
    counterterrorism, 2:155
    The Green Book, 3:377

Islamic socialism, 7:644
    OPEC, 6:65, 66
    Qadhafi, Muammar al, 6:647–648
Licensure, occupational, 6:23–34
Liddle, Roger, 4:326
Liddy, G. Gordon, 9:43
Lieber, Francis, 6:311
Liebman, Wilma B., 4:317
Liebmann, New State Ice Co. v., 3:114
Liebow, Elliot, 8:263–264
Lies. *See* Lying
Lievrouw, Leah, 2:60
Life
    artificial, 6:20
    biological, gender, 3:268, 9:107–110
    instincts, 3:210–211
    satisfaction, 3:292–293
    value of, 6:25
    work *vs.,* 9:126
    See also Quality of life
Life, pro-. *See* Pro-choice/pro-life
Life and Fate (Grossman), 9:20
The Life and Morals of Jesus of Nazareth (Jefferson), 4:183
The Life and Times of Pancho Villa (Katz), 8:617
Life course perspective. *See* Developmental psychology
Life-cycle hypothesis (LCH), 4:**441–443**
    consumption, 1:7
    consumption function, 2:109, 110
    inheritance, 4:35
    Modigliani, Franco, 5:234
    relative income hypothesis, 7:153, 154
    saving rate, 7:335
    in vivo transfers, 3:597–598
Life event model. *See* Life events, stress
Life events, stress, 4:**443–444**
    hypertension, 3:538, 539–540
    relationship satisfaction, 7:152
Life expectancy, 3:306–307
    AIDS/HIV, 1:66
    life-extension research, 3:308
    tables, 3:366
    See also Morbidity and mortality
Life-extension research, 3:307–308
Life in a Haitian Valley (Herskovits), 3:467
Life of Jesus (Strauss), 5:502
Life of Turgot (Condorcet), 2:66
Life of Voltaire (Condorcet), 2:66
Life Orientation Test (LOT), 6:54

Life span, human. *See* Morbidity and mortality

Life-sustaining treatment, 1:191

Life-world *(lebenswelt),* 9:78

Lifespan development. *See* Developmental psychology

Lifestyles, 4:445–446
  alternative, 8:583
  corporate culture, 6:61
  cross-sectional research, 7:190
  diathesis-stress model, 2:358
  energy sector, 2:591–592
  Gautreaux residential mobility program, 3:259–260
  globalization, 3:334
  hypertension, 3:538, 539–540
  morbidity and mortality, 5:291
  New Deal, 5:496–497
  overeating, 6:89
  sedentary, 6:4
  type A/type B personality, 6:222–223

Light, Ivan, 1:516

Lightfoot, Gomillion v. (1960), 3:309, 5:384

LIHTC (U.S, Low Income Housing Tax Credit), 8:273–274

Lijphart, Arend, 1:578, 2:278

Likelihood, 5:534, 8:519

Likelihood ratio test. *See* Specification tests

Likert, Jeffrey, 2:60

Likert, Rensis, 1:424, 4:447

Likert scale, 4:447–448, 7:196–197, 338

Lilburne, John, 4:414

Lima, Almeida, 4:475

Liminality. *See* Turner, Victor

Limited competition, 2:52

Limited liability, 1:400–401, 2:140

Limited sovereignty, Native Americans, 5:428

Limited voting. *See* Bloc vote

Limits, confidence. *See* Limits in probability

Limits, term. *See* Term limits

Limits in probability, 6:486–489

Limits of growth, 4:448–450

The Limits of Growth (Meadows), 4:448–451

The Limits of Liberty (Buchanan), 2:374, 4:338

The Limits to Capitalism (Harvey), 3:305

The Limits to Growth: A Report for the Club of Rome's Project on the

Predicament of Mankind (Meadows, Meadows, Randers, and Behrens), 1:585, 2:61, 3:241, 6:95, 7:211

Lin, Cheng-Hsien, 2:238

Lin, Nan, 5:476

Lin, Shoukang, 6:93

Lin Biao, 4:467, 468

Lincoln, Abraham, 4:450–452
  Birth of a Nation (film), 1:305
  Davis, Jefferson, 2:243–244
  Grant, Ulysses S., 3:365
  liberation, 4:429
  Selective Service, 7:392
  U.S. Civil War, 8:549–551

Lincoln, C. Eric, 1:309, 5:379

Lindahl, Erik, 1:431, 4:79

Lindbergh, Charles, 1:232

Lindblom, Charles Edward, 4:452–454
  community power studies, 2:45
  incrementalism, 3:608–609, 610
  polyarchy, 6:366

Lindsay, John V., 9:27

Line, poverty. *See* Indices of poverty

Lineage. *See* Kinship

Lineages of the Absolutist State (Anderson), 1:113

Linear and nonlinear programming, 6:527–531
  Hurwicz, Leonid, 3:530
  Koopmans, Tjalling, 4:288
  mathematical economics, 5:24
  objective functions, 6:5–6

Linear regression, 4:454–455, *455,* 8:589
  description, 5:521
  log-linear models, 4:484–485
  regression analysis, 7:138–141

Linear systems, 4:455–457, 5:523
  catastrophe theory, 1:468–469
  heterarchy, 3:469

Linguistic anthropology, 1:118–119, 129–130
  Chomsky, Noam, 1:527–529
  consciousness, 2:78
  conversational analysis, 2:118–120
  Creole, 2:167–168
  creolization, 2:169
  cultural relativism, 2:194–195
  dance, 2:224
  Diop, Cheikh Anta, 2:369, 370
  discourse, 2:387
  Dravidians, 2:442–443
  ethnicity, 3:9
  hybridity, 3:536

race, 7:8–11
  Roma, 7:277–279
  semiotics, 7:436–438

Linguistic behaviorism, 1:278

Linguistic isolation, 5:462

Linguistic turn, 4:457–458
  constructivism, 2:97
  conversational analysis, 2:118, 119
  cultural relativism, 2:194–195
  post-Parsonian American sociology, 8:6–7
  Rorty, Richard, 7:286

Linguistics
  Chomsky, Noam, 1:527–529
  Creole, 2:167–168
  creolization, 2:169
  determinism, 2:323
  discourse, 2:387
  sociolinguistics, 1:118, 2:117–119
  structuralism, 8:181–182
  See also Linguistic anthropology; Psycholinguistics

Linnaeus, Carolus, 1:126, 2:325, 7:21, 38–39

Lintner, John, 3:141

Linville, Patricia, 7:399–400

Linz, Juan, 1:213

Lion-Human (sculpture), 8:630

Lipinski, Tara, 1:514

Lippmann, Walter, 5:412

Lipset, Seymour Martin, 1:107–108
  class, 1:561, 562, 563
  cleavages, 1:577–578
  competitive party systems, 6:162
  democracy, 2:273, 289

Lipsey, Richard G., 7:222, 8:351

Lipsitz, George, 9:86

Liquidity, 4:459–460
  central banks, 1:478
  effect, 4:459
  Kahn, Richard F., 4:245
  lender of last resort, 4:409–410
  leverage, 4:415–416
  life-cycle hypothesis, 4:442, 443
  preference framework, 4:459
  premium, 4:460
  trap, 4:461–462

Liquidity premium, 4:459, 460–461, 9:166–167

Liquidity trap, 4:459, 461–462

Liquor industry. *See* Spirits industry

LIS (Luxembourg Income Study). *See* Luxembourg Income Study (LIS)

The Lisbon Earthquake (Voltaire), 8:635

List, Friedrich, 4:11, 12, 8:413

List, John, 4:296

Listening, ethics of, 5:371

Liston, Sonny, 1:74

Literature, 4:**462–464**
 citations, 1:538–539
 dystopian, 8:396
 ethnology and folklore, 3:17–18
 Harlem Renaissance, 3:425
 indigenismo, 3:613
 Kshatriyas, 4:291
 Le Guin, Ursula K., 4:407–408
 militarism, 5:165
 modernism, 5:228–230
 primitivism, 6:466
 realism, 7:91–93
 Sambo, 7:313
 Sartre, Jean-Paul, 7:327
 satire, 7:330
 science fiction, 7:360–362
 travel and travel writing,
  8:443–444

Lithuania, NATO, 5:546

Litigation, social science role in,
 4:**464–467**

Little, Malcolm. *See* Malcolm X

Little Big Horn, Battle of the (1876),
 1:**258–259**, 5:426, 7:522

Little Big Man (film), 1:258

Little Red Book, 4:**467–468**, 589

Little Rock (AK), 1:550, 551

Little Rock Nine. *See* Civil rights;
 Cold War

"Little Steel Formula," 9:2

Little Walter, 1:343

Littlefield, Henry M., 9:105

Liver disease, alcoholic, 1:71

Liverpool, Hollis, 1:418

Liverpool slave trade, 4:**468–469**

Livestock, 3:162–163, 5:447

Living, standard of. *See* Standard of
 living

Living apart together (LAT), 3:84

Livingston, Robert R., 2:254

Livius, Titus, 7:188

Livre de la Cité des Dames (Pizan),
 3:119–120

Livy, 6:20

Lloyd George, David, 4:428

LMS (Labor market segmentation).
 See Labor market segmentation
 (LMS)

LNM (Lebanese National Movement),
 4:397

LNS (Latino National Survey),
 4:**355–356**

Loan pulling. *See* Loan pushing

The Loan Pushers (Darity and Horn),
 6:95

Loan pushing, 4:**469–472**, *470, 471*
 capital flight, 1:435–436
 herd behavior, 3:459–460

Loans, 1:428, 4:**472–473**
 banking, 1:249–250, 251
 central banks, 1:478, 480
 conditionality, 2:65
 discounted present value,
  2:385–386
 economic depression, 2:304
 herd behavior, 3:459–460
 housing, 1:97, 3:363
 international nongovernmental
  organizations, 4:96–99
 lender of last resort, 4:409–410
 leverage, 4:415–416
 loan pushing, 4:469–471
 monetary policy, 6:293
 money, 5:251–252
 overlending, 6:94–95
 redlining, 2:317
 rotating savings and credit
  associations, 7:286–287
 structural adjustment, 9:138
 structuralist macroeconomics,
  4:544–545
 trade liberalization, 4:428
 World Bank, 9:138
 yield, 9:164–165, 166–167
 See also Foreign investment;
  Microfinance

Lobby Disclosure Act (U.S. 1995),
 4:475

Lobbying, 4:**474–475**
 corporations, 2:140
 interest groups and interests, 4:83
 mobilization, 5:213–215
 pressure groups, 6:442–443

Lobotomy, 4:**475–476**

LOC (Locus of control). *See* Locus of
 control (LOC)

Local Color Movement, 1:150

Local government, 3:359

Local networks, 5:479–480

Local stability (economic), 8:563

Locality, globalization, 3:332

Location theory. *See* Spatial theory;
 Urban economics

Locke, Alain, 1:35, 309, 9:97

Locke, Edwin, 4:379

Locke, John, 4:**476–477**
 anthropology, 1:137
 consciousness, 2:80
 constitutionalism, 2:93
 cooperation, 2:122
 Declaration of Independence,
  U.S., 2:254, 255
 distributive justice, 4:240
 egalitarianism, 2:550
 empiricism, 2:577–578
 executive power, 3:413
 exogenous money, 5:258–259
 feminism, 3:120
 freedom, 3:196
 Hartz, Louis, 3:429–430
 Hobbes, Thomas, 3:493
 justice, 4:237
 knowledge, 4:280
 Levellers, 4:414
 liberalism, 4:425
 libertarianism, 4:437, 439
 liberty, 4:440
 moral philosophy, 6:255
 natural rights, 5:438–439
 objectivity, 6:8
 private interests, 6:478
 Rawls, John, 7:84
 republicanism, 7:184, 188
 semiotics, 7:436
 separation of powers, 7:449
 social contract, 7:581
 social justice, 4:241
 sovereignty, 8:38
 state of nature, 8:110–111
 Two Treatise of Government, 3:120
 universalism, 8:526

Locus of control (LOC), 4:**477–478**
 learned helplessness, 4:387–389
 motivation, 5:300–301
 Rotter's Internal-External Locus of
  Control Scale, 7:289–290
 social comparison, 7:576–577

Locusts, 5:433

Lodge, Henry Cabot, 9:102

Löfgren, Orvar, 8:566

Loft living, 3:302

Log-linear models, 4:**484–485**

Logan, Frank, 1:277

Logic, 4:**479–481**
 Aristotle, 1:174
 conundrum, 2:116
 discourse analysis, 1:129
 knowledge, 4:278
 symbols, 8:250–251

Logic, symbolic, 4:**481–482**

Logic (Hegel). *See Science of Logic* (Hegel)

The Logic of Collective Action (Olson), 2:219–220, 7:611–612

The Logic of Health-Care Reform (Starr), 2:54

The Logic of Images in International Relations (Jervis), 4:185

The Logic Political Survival (de Mesquita et al), 6:37

Logical behaviorism, 1:275, 277–279, 3:231

　See also Behaviorism

Logical positivism. *See* Positivism

Logik der Rettung (Bahro), 1:237–238

Logistic distribution. *See* Probability distributions

Logistic regression, 4:**482–483**, 7:139–140

Logit regression. *See* Logistic regression

Lognormal distribution. *See* Probability distributions

Logotherapy, 2:63

Lombard Street (Bagehot), 1:478, 4:410, **485–486**

Lombroso, Cesare, 6:80

London Diamond Syndicate, 2:355

Loneliness, 4:**486–488**

The Lonely Crowd (Riesman), 4:488

Long-distance telephone service. *See* Telecommunications industry

Long March. *See* Chinese Revolution

Long period analysis, 4:**489–491**
　classical economics, 2:502–503
　long run, 4:491–492
　partial equilibrium, 6:152
　Z-D model, 9:172

Long period prices. *See* Long period analysis

Long run, 4:**491–492**
　cointegration, 2:2, 3
　long period analysis, 4:489–491
　partial equilibrium, 6:152

Long run prices. *See* Long period analysis

Long-selling. *See* Selling long and selling short

Long-term memory. *See* Mood congruent recall

Long waves, 4:**492–494**, 493t, 9:153
　business cycle theories, 1:410
　economic crises, 2:485
　Mandel, Ernest, 4:580

Longevity, 3:306

　See also Morbidity and mortality

Longfellow, Henry Wadsworth, 1:72

Longitudinal data, 2:**238–239**
　pseudopanel data, 2:239–240
　sample attrition, 7:315–316
　temporal priority, 7:194–196

Longitudinal research, 7:**194–196**
　cross-sectional research, 7:189
　longitudinal data, 2:238–239
　panel studies, 6:120–121
　path analysis, 6:168, 169
　pseudopanel data, 2:239–240
　quantitative methods, 5:113

Longitudinal surveys. *See* Panel studies

Longstreet, James, 4:399

Looking Backward (Bellamy), 8:312, 561

Looking-glass effect, 4:**494–495**, 7:416, 488

López, Ian Haney, 9:88

Lophophora williamsii. *See* Mescaline

Lord, Robert, 4:379

Lord Invader (musician), 1:417

Lord Shorty (musician). *See* Blackman, Garfield

Lorde, Audre, 9:106

Lords, feudalism and, 3:135

Lord's Resistance Army, 1:110

Lorenz, Edward, 1:413, 492

Lorenz curve, 3:138, 320–323, 604–605

Lorsch, Jay, 6:69

LoS (League of the South), 8:619

Los Angeles (CA), 4:372
　Black Power, 1:321
　Bonacich, Edna, 1:352
　school desegregation, 2:316–317

Lösch, August, 8:541

Loss functions, 4:**495–502**, 499t
　asymmetry, 4:497–498
　binary forecast and maximum score, 4:499
　density forecasts, 4:500–501
　described, 4:495–496
　estimation and evaluation, 4:498
　Granger-causality testing, 4:501–502
　interval forecasts, 4:500
　probability forecasts, 4:499–500
　regression functions, 4:496–497
　return prediction, 4:498
　risk, 4:496
　volatility forecasts, 4:501

Lost cause. *See* Vindication

Lost Counties of Bunyoro, 6:12

LOT (Life Orientation Test), 6:54

Lotka-Volterra equation, 2:365

Lotman, Yuri, 5:371–372

Lott, Trent, 2:431

Lotteries, 1:524, 4:**502–504**

Louis XIV, King of France, 2:421–422

Louis XVI, King of France, 3:203–204
　See also French Revolution

Louisiana
　civil rights movement, U.S., 1:551
　Confederate States of America, 2:66
　Creole, 2:168
　creolization, 2:169

Louisiana, Hebert v. (1926), 1:298

Louisiana Purchase, 4:182

Louison, George, 3:383

Loury, Glenn, 7:564

Love, romantic. *See* Romance

Love Canal, 4:**504–505**, 6:359

Loving v. Virginia (1967), 7:28

Low and high culture, 2:**204–205**
　classical music, 1:575
　cultural distinctions, 2:412–413
　cultural studies, 2:199
　described, 2:203
　literature, 4:464
　minstrelsy, 5:194
　popular culture, 6:373–375
　visual arts, 8:632–633

Low Income Housing Tax Credit, U.S. (LIHTC), 8:273–274

Low-income lifestyles. *See* Lifestyles

Lowe, Adolph, 1:411, 2:532
　See also Economics of control

Lower triangularization, 8:599

Lowi, Miriam R., 9:42

Lowi, Theodore J., 1:48, 2:219, 220, 4:**506–507**

Lowie, Robert, 1:345, 4:**507–508**

Loyal Orange Order, 4:509

Loyalists, 4:**508–510**

Loyalty
　clientelism, 1:578–579
　communitarianism, 2:39
　Daughters of the American Revolution, 2:242
　Exit, Voice, and Loyalty (Hirschman), 3:43–45
　political parties, 6:306, 308
　white collar employment, 2:585

Lozano, Fernando, 9:128

LSD (Lysergic acid diethylamide), 3:410, 411, 412

LSD (Lysergic acid diethylamide),
continued
See also Drugs of abuse;
Hallucinogens
Lubbock, John, 2:38
Lucas, Robert E., Jr., 4:**510–511**,
5:490
adaptive expectations, 1:19, 20
Chicago School, 1:502
consumption function, 2:110
labor supply, 4:321
law and economics, 1:271
long run, 4:492
Lucas critique, 4:511
new classical economics, 2:522,
523
voluntary unemployment, 8:637
Lucas, Scott, 4:252
Lucas critique, 1:472, 4:510, **511–512**
Luck, 4:**512–513**, 554–555
Luckmann, Thomas, 2:96, 3:403,
6:69–70
Lucy. See Johanson, Donald
Lucy: The Beginnings of Humankind
(Johanson), 4:207
*Lucy's Child: The Discovery of a Human
Ancestor* (Johanson), 4:207
Luddites, 4:**513–515**, 536, 8:311
Ludic dimension. See Rituals
LUF (Labor utilization framework),
8:492
Luftwaffe, 9:51
Lugard, Frederick, 1:43–44
Luhmann, Niklas, 7:626–627
Lukacs, Georg, 3:82, 4:**515–516**
class conflict, 1:569
class consciousness, 1:572
Frankfurt School, 3:188
Mannheim, Karl, 4:586
narratives, 5:371
Lukes, Steven, 6:412, 413
Lula. See Integration
LULAC (League of United Latin
American Citizens), 3:465
Lumet, Sidney, 9:104
Lumpenproletariat, 4:**516–517**, 599,
8:485
Lumpy goods. See McFadden, Daniel
L.
Lumumba, Patrice, 1:321, 484,
4:**517–518**
Lundberg, Erik, 4:**518–519**, 8:154
Lundy, Garvey, 6:48
Lust. See Romance
Luther, Martin, 1:452, 531

Lutheranism, 1:531, 533, 534
Luxembourg
common market, 2:28
Luxembourg Income Study,
4:519–521
NATO, 5:544–546
permanent neutrality, 5:488
Luxembourg Income Study (LIS),
4:**519–522**, 521*t*
Luxemburg, Rosa, 4:**522–523**, 8:488,
9:131
accumulation of capital, 1:12–13
capitalist mode of production,
1:446
class consciousness, 1:572
primitive accumulation, 6:464
world-system, 9:153
Luxury Fever (Frank), 2:108
Luxury goods, 9:44–45, 46
Lvov, Georgii, 7:304
Lyceum, 1:174
Lyell, Charles, 1:166
Lying, 4:**523–525**
cognitive dissonance, 1:600
experimental realism, 7:94
interrogation, 4:111
shock experiments, 3:63
Lyman, Stanford, 7:29
Lynch, Owen, 1:462
Lynchings, 4:**526–527**
black towns, 1:325, 326
Jim Crow, 4:200
race-conscious policies, 7:37
Wells-Barnett, Ida B., 1:323,
9:76–77
Lynd, Helen, 4:**527–528**, 7:656,
8:542
Lynd, Robert, 4:**527–528**, 7:656,
8:542
Lynd, Staughton, 4:**528–529**
Lyons, Richard, 2:210
Lyotard, Jean-François, 2:97, 6:398,
399, 400
Lysergic acid diethylamide (LSD),
3:410, 411, 412

M
MA (Moving average), 1:227–228
Maalouf, Amin. See Deadly identities
Maastricht Treaty, 3:24–25
MacAloon, John, 6:40
MacArthur, Douglas, 4:289, 5:505,
8:460
MacCannell, Dean, 8:399
Macchu Picchu, 1:166

Maccoby, Eleanor, 1:260, 4:**531–532**,
6:136
MacDonald, Ramsay, 4:327
Mach, Ernest, 1:212
Machado, Gerardo, 2:186
Machel, Samora, 4:**532–533**
Machiavelli, Niccolò, 1:495, 2:359,
4:**533–534**
hegemony, 3:456
Medicis, 5:67
modernity, 5:230
political realism, 7:96
political science, 6:310–311
politics, 6:319, 320
republicanism, 7:188, 189
Machiavellianism. See Machiavelli,
Niccolò; Political realism
Machine functionalism, 3:231
See also Functionalism
Machine politics. See Political
machines
Machine Politics (Gosnell), 3:352
Machinery, 4:**534–536**
blue collar and white collar, 1:337
division of labor, 2:423–425
labor, 4:301, 302
Luddites, 4:513–515
machinery question, 4:536–537
mining industry, 5:189
relative surplus value, 7:155
rentier class, 1:566–567
Machinery question, 4:**536–538**
Machtpolitik. See Political realism
MacIntyre, Alasdair, 2:39
MacKay, Charles, 3:375
Mackinder, Halford, 3:304
MacLeod, Arene, 8:603
Macmillan, Harold, 4:**538–539**
Macon County (AL), 8:472–473
MacQueen, James, 1:586
Macro-sociology, 7:**677–678**
described, 7:662
microanalysis, 5:132–133
Parsonian sociology, 8:1–2
Macroeconomics, 4:**539–543**
adaptive expectations, 1:20
aggregate demand, 1:50–51,
51–52
automobile industry, 1:221–222
banking industry, 1:252–253
Barro-Grossman model, 1:256
Beveridge curve, 1:292
business cycles, 1:403–405
capital, 1:431
central banks, 1:478

cliometrics, 1:582
conditionality, 2:65
consumption, 2:106–109, 110
coordination failure, 2:128
description, 3:142–143
economic sterilization, 8:139–140
energy industry, 2:590
energy sector, 2:591–592
expectations, 3:47–49
exports, 3:69
Friedman, Milton, 3:219
full capacity, 3:224
gender equality, 3:275
general equilibrium, 3:285
globalization, 3:331
investment, 4:130–133
IS-LM model, 4:158–160
Keynes, John Maynard,
　4:259–262
Klein, Lawrence, 4:276
Lucas, Robert E., Jr., 4:510
macrofoundations, 4:545–547
microeconomics, 5:135
microfoundations, 5:141
multiplier, 5:329–330
Mundell-Fleming model,
　5:335–336
neutrality of money, 5:490–491
New Classical, 3:226
optimal growth, 6:52
overshooting, 6:98–99
petroleum industry, 6:230
real business cycles, 1:407–408
representative agent, 7:173–174
screening and signaling games,
　7:371–372
social accounting matrix,
　7:562–563
Solow, Robert M., 8:26–27
stocks and flows, 8:157–158
Tinbergen, Jan, 8:374–375
Tobin, James, 8:378–379
trade surplus, 8:417–418
underconsumption, 8:488
vector autoregression, 8:598–600
want creation, 9:15
X-Crise, 9:157–158
Macroeconomics, new open economy.
　See New open economy
　macroeconomics (NOEM)
Macroeconomics, structuralist,
　4:**543–545**, 8:285
Macroeconomics (Galbraith and
　Darity), 3:226–227

*Macroeconomics and the Theory of
　Rational Behavior* (Klein), 4:276
Macrofoundations, 3:331, 4:**545–547**
Macurdy, Thomas, 4:322
MAD (Mutual assured destruction),
　2:5, 9:31
Mad cow disease. *See* Bovine
　spongiform encephalopathy (BSE)
Madagascar, 1:115, 8:583–584
Maddison, Angus, 5:399
Maddox (ship), 8:614
Madeira, slavery, 1:39
Madero, Francisco, 5:130, 7:233,
　9:171
Madison, James, 4:**547–548**
　Bill of Rights, 1:298
　Castro, Fidel, 1:467
　checks and balances, 1:495
　Constitution, U.S., 2:91
　Democratic Party (U.S.), 2:286
　Hamilton, Alexander, 3:414
　Jefferson, Thomas, 4:180
　judicial review, 4:223–224
　referendum, 7:120–121
　representative and participatory
　　democracy, 2:284
　republic, 7:184–185
　republicanism, 7:188
　separation of powers, 7:449
Madison, Marbury v. (1803), 1:496
Madness, 4:**548–550**
　dementia, 2:271–272
　deviance, 2:353
　manias, 4:582–583
　See also Mental illness; Psychiatric
　　disorders; Psychopathology
Madness and Civilization (Foucault),
　2:353, 3:182
Madonna, 3:270
Mafeje, Archie, 7:665
Mafia, 2:172, 4:252, **550–554**
Magic, 4:**554–556**
　Castaneda, Carlos, 1:456
　luck, 4:512
　Malinowski, Bronislaw, 4:566–567
　medicine, 5:63
　myth and mythology, 5:355–357
　shamans, 7:486–488
　taboos, 8:260
　zombies, 9:181
Magic Sam, 1:343
*The Magical Number Seven, Plus or
　Minus Two: Some Limits on our
　Capacity for Processing Information*
　(Miller), 1:597

Magliocco, Sabina, 6:21
Magna Carta, 4:406, **556–557**
Magnes, Juday, 9:180
Magnetic resonance imaging (MRI),
　5:483–484, 485
Magnetoencephalography (MEG),
　5:485
Magnusson, David, 1:25
Mahathir Mohamad, 4:**557–558**
Mahavira, 4:166
Mahāyanā Buddhism, 5:504, 505
Mahinda, 1:383
Mahuri Vaisyas, 8:568
Maier, Steven, 4:387, 388
Main, Darren John, 9:105
Main, Mary, 1:196
Maine, Henry, 1:127, 2:38
Mainstream economics. *See*
　Neoclassical economics
Mainstreaming, 2:378, 3:275, 5:521
Maistre, Joseph de, 2:83, 84, 86
Maize. *See* Corn
Major, John, 2:87
Major depressive disorder (MDD),
　2:306
Majoritarianism, 4:**558–559**
　consociational democracy, 2:278,
　　279
　majority rule, 4:560–561
　pluralism, 6:284
　plurality, 6:286
　repression, 7:175
　Tocqueville, Alexis de, 8:383
　tyranny of the majority,
　　8:478–479
Majorities, 4:**559–560**
　coalition theory, 1:588
　Condorcet, Marquis de, 2:66
　conformity, 2:71, 72
　consensus, 2:82
　elite theory, 2:562–564
　ethnic fractionalization, 3:6–8
　leaders, 4:376
　majoritarianism, 4:558–559
　plurality, 6:285–286
　social justice, 4:242
　tyranny of the majority,
　　8:478–479
Majority, tyranny of. *See* Tyranny of
　the majority
Majority rule, 4:**560–562**
　Condorcet, Marquis de, 2:66
　Constitution, U.S., 2:91
　majoritarianism, 4:558
　majorities, 4:559

Majority rule, *continued*
    representative and participatory
        democracy, 2:284
    with runoff, 8:655
    tyranny of the majority,
        8:478–479
Majority voting, 4:**562–563**
    Congress, U.S., 2:74
    democracy, 2:273
    elections, 2:557, 560, 561
    electoral college, 2:559
    majority rule, 4:560–561
    referendum, 7:121
*The Making and Unmaking of
    Whiteness* (Conference, 1977), 9:86
The Making of Black Revolutionaries
    (Forman), 3:174
The Making of Index Numbers (Fisher),
    3:151
*The Making of the English Working
    Class* (Thompson), 1:564, 2:199,
    3:482–483, 8:354, 355, 356
Malan, D. F., 1:147
Malawi, zombies, 9:181
Malaysia
    Chinese diaspora, 1:516, 518
    ethnicity, 3:10
    legal systems, 4:406
    Mahathir Mohamad, 4:557–558
Malcolm X, 4:**563–564**
    Black Arts Movement, 1:309
    black conservatism, 1:310
    black liberalism, 1:312
    black nationalism, 1:316–317
    Black Panthers, 1:318
    Black Power, 1:321
    blackness, 1:330
    civil rights movement, U.S., 1:552
    King, Martin Luther, Jr., 4:269
    Muhammad, Elijah, 5:310
    Muslims, 5:348
    Nation of Islam, 5:380, 381
Malcomson, James M., 8:620
*Male Interracial Wage Differentials:
    Competing Explanations* (Mason),
    2:182
Mali, African Crisis Response
    Initiative, 1:38
La Malinche. *See* Malinchistas
Malinchistas, 4:**564–566**
Malingering. *See* Lying
Malinowski, Bronislaw, 4:**566–567**
    British anthropology, 1:127
    cultural anthropology, 1:119
    functionalism, 1:127, 3:232

    funerals, 3:238
    magic, 4:554
    Oedipus complex, 6:29
    Ortiz, Fernando, 6:80
    participant observation, 6:14
    reincarnation, 7:145
    religion, 7:160
Malinvaud, Edmond, 1:256, 6:52
Malnutrition, 4:**567–569**
Malone, Paul, 1:336
Malone, Philip, 1:336
Malthus, Thomas Robert, 4:**569–572**
    accumulation of capital, 1:12
    Bentham, Jeremy, 1:286
    birth control, 1:303
    Boserup, Ester, 1:357, 358
    Club of Rome, 1:585
    Condorcet, Marquis de, 2:66
    diminishing returns, 7:218
    economic depression, 2:303
    economic value, 8:576
    environmental determinism, 2:327
    limits of growth, 4:448, 449
    Malthusian trap, 4:572–573
    morbidity and mortality, 5:291
    overpopulation, 6:95
    overproduction, 6:97
    population growth, 3:164, 165
    population studies, 6:381–382
    rent, 7:164
    Ricardo, David, 7:243, 244, 245
    surplus population, 8:237–239
    zero population growth, 9:174,
        175
Malthusian trap, 2:116, 4:**572–574**
Mamgain, Vaishali, 8:608
Man, Economics and State (Rothbard),
    1:211
Man, the State and War (Waltz), 9:14
Man a Machine (La Mettrie), 1:275
Man and His Works (Herskovits),
    3:467
The Man-Eating Myth (Arens), 1:427
Man for Himself (Fromm), 3:223
Managed care, 2:54
Managed competition, 2:54–55,
    5:395–396, 396
Managed float exchange rates. *See*
    Dirty float
Management, 4:**574–576**
    capitalism, 1:438
    cooperatives, 1:402
    disaster, 2:381–384
    firms, 3:148
    inventories, 4:128

    rumors, 7:297–298
    scienctific, 1:8
    technological progress, 8:299–300
    volunteer programs, 8:640
Management, cultural resource. *See*
    Cultural resource management
    (CRM)
Management, scientific. *See* Taylorism
Management science, 2:449–450,
    4:**576–577**
Managerial capitalism, 1:**442–443**
    corporate social responsibility,
        2:136
    leisure class, 1:570–572
    leverage, 4:415–416
    rentier class, 1:566–568
Managerial class, 4:**577–579**
    bureaucracy, 1:390
    bureaucrat, 1:392
    described, 1:563
    managerial capitalism, 1:442–443
    petty bourgeoisie, 1:362
    underclass, 8:485–486
The Managerial Revolution (Burnham),
    1:390
Managerial society. *See* Managerial
    class
Managers
    control of, 6:71
    New Class, 5:492
Managing Existence in Naples (Pardo),
    1:135
Manchester School, 1:128
Manchuria, 1:520, 521
Mandel, Ernest, 4:492, **579–580**
Mandela, Nelson, 4:**580–581**
    African National Congress,
        1:42–43
    apartheid, 1:148
    civil disobedience, 1:545
    humiliation, 3:522
    liberation, 4:430
    Mandela, Winnie, 4:581, 582
    repression, 7:174
    segregation, 7:382
Mandela, Winnie, 4:**581–582**
Mandelbrot, Benoit, 1:492
Mandelson, Peter, 4:326
Mandeville, Bernard, 4:489
Maneopause, 9:108
Manet, Edouard, 7:92–93
Manga, 2:24
Manhattan Project, 9:47–48
Manian, Nanmathi, 6:85
Manias, 4:**582–583**, 583–584

Manias, Panics, and Crashes: A History of Financial Crises (Kindleberger), 4:267

Manic depression, 2:306, 4:582–583, **583–585**

Manifest destiny. *See* Americanism; Annexation; Mexican-American War

Manifest functions, 3:232

Manifolds, 4:**585–586**

Mankiller, Wilma, 4:**586–587**

Mankiw, Gregory, 2:110

Manley, Michael, 7:68–69

Manly, Alex, 9:99

Mann, Horace, 7:352

Mann, Jonathan, 3:490

Mann, Michael, 3:329, 8:6

Mann, Richard, 4:379

Mannheim, Karl, 2:96, 4:**587**
   false consciousness, 3:82
   ideology, 3:560
   knowledge in sociology, 7:674–675
   Lukacs, Georg, 4:515
   triumphalism, 8:455

Manning, Nick, 9:68

Manorialism. *See* Feudalism

Manski, Charles, 7:121–122
   See also Identification problem; Reflection problem

Manu, Codes of. *See* Brahmins

Manu Smriti, 1:185

Manufacturing, 1:34–35
   build-to-order, 1:223
   decline, 3:312–313
   economies of scale, 3:76, 8:607
   family structure changes, 3:93–94
   just-in-time, 1:218, 3:78
   lean, 3:78
   maquila, 3:283, 286, 5:540
   mass production, 3:76–77, 168
   NAFTA, 5:540
   overtime, 6:99
   scientific, 3:77–78
   work day, 9:126
   See also Factories; Factory system

Manufacturing Content: The Political Economy of the Mass Media (Herman and Chomsky), 8:320

Manure, 3:131–132

Manusmriti, 1:366

Manza, Jeff, 9:71

Mao Tse-tung. *See* Mao Zedong

Mao Zedong, 4:**587–590**
   Black Arts Movement, 1:309

Chiang Kai-shek, 1:499

Chinese Revolution, 1:519, 520–521
   communism, 2:35–36
   guerrilla warfare, 3:395
   Khmer Rouge, 4:263
   Korean War, 4:289
   Little Red Book, 4:467–468
   Maoism, 4:590–591
   socialism, 7:638
   upward mobility, 8:534
   working class, 9:132

Maoism, 4:**590–591**
   Little Red Book, 4:467–468
   Pol Pot, 6:289

Maps, Dymaxion, 3:229

Maquiladoras, 4:**591–594**
   General Electric, 3:283
   General Motors, 3:286
   NAFTA, 5:540

MAR (Missingness is at random), 3:391

Marble cake system, 3:358

Marble Man (Connelly), 4:399

Marbury, William, 4:223–224

Marbury v. Madison (1803), 1:496, 4:223–224, 8:232–233
   See also Supreme Court, U.S.

MARC (Metropolitan Applied Research Center), 1:561

Marcel, Jesse, 8:507

Marches (demonstrations). *See* Protest

Marcia, James, 3:556

Marcus, George, 8:386

Marcuse, Herbert, 4:**594–595**, 5:482
   capitalist mode of production, 1:447
   class consciousness, 1:572
   critical theory, 2:176, 177
   Davis, Angela, 2:242
   lumpenproletariat, 4:517
   repressive tolerance, 7:176–177
   social theory, 7:628
   work day, 9:127

Mare, Robert, 2:238

Marginal and average costs, 1:**230–232**, *231*

Marginal principle. *See* Marginalism

Marginal product analysis, 3:150

Marginal product of labor (MPL), 4:**304–308**, *305*
   Lewis, W. Arthur, 4:421
   surplus labor, 4:308–309, *309*

Marginal productivity, 1:430, 4:304–307, **595–596**

Marginal propensity to consume (MPC), 1:6–7, 2:109, 110, 6:**544–546**

Marginal propensity to import, 6:**546**

Marginal propensity to save, 6:**546–547**

Marginal q. *See* Tobin's Q

Marginal rate of substitution, 8:555–556

Marginal revenue, 7:226, **227–228**

Marginal theory of distribution, 4:305–306, 307

Marginal utility. *See* Marginalism

Marginalism, 4:**596–598**, 8:558–559
   capital, 1:430
   economic history, 2:498
   Ricardian vice, 7:242
   Sraffa, Piero, 8:71–72
   underrepresentation, 8:495–496
   unemployment, 8:501
   value, objective, 8:578
   Walras, Léon, 9:11

Marginalist Revolution, 8:555

Marginalization, 4:**598–599**
   affirmative action, 1:30–32
   Boer War, 1:350
   Coloreds (South Africa), 2:15–17
   creolization, 2:169–170
   Hall, Stuart, 3:409, 410
   heteronormativity, 3:470
   immigrants, 3:565, 575
   land claims, 4:340–341, 341
   lumpenproletariat, 4:516–517
   Mexican Americans, 5:123
   Roma, 7:278–279
   See also Social exclusion

Mariátegui, José Carlos, 3:613

Marielitos, 3:571, 4:359–360

Mariette, Auguste, 1:165

Marighela, Carlos, 3:395

Marijuana
   hallucinogens, 3:411, 412
   Rastafari, 7:67
   See also Drugs of abuse

Marín, Louis Munoz, 6:44

Marín y Shaw, Francisco Gonzalez, 1:356

Mariners, Renegades, and Castaways: Herman Melville and the World We Live In (James), 4:168

Marinho, E. Luis Lemos, 8:608

Maritain, Jacques, 2:277

Marital conflict, 4:**599–601**
   contempt, 2:113
   divorce and separation, 2:426–428

Marital conflict, *continued*
  infidelity, 4:20–21
  relationship satisfaction, 7:151, 152
  sibling relationships, 7:506
Marital rape. *See* Rape
Maritime Arhaice peoples, 5:424
Mark Antony, 2:359
Market, labor. *See* Labor market
Market, spot. *See* Spot market
Market-based accountability, 1:9–11
Market clearing, 4:**601–603**
Market clearinghouse, 4:**602–603**
Market correction, 4:**603–604**
  bubbles (economics), 1:378–379
  bull and bear markets, 1:385–386
Market economy, 4:**604–605**
  air pollution, 6:362
  business, 1:400, 401
  civil society, 1:552
  codetermination, 1:592–593
  common land, 2:28
  conservatism, 2:85, 86
  Conservative Party (U.K.), 2:87
  consumerism, 2:105
  consumption, 2:106
  convergence theory, 2:117
  corporations, 2:140
  democracy, 2:274
  development in sociology, 2:347
  dirigiste, 2:372–374
  entrepreneurship, 2:604–605
  financial instability hypothesis, 3:145–146
  full employment, 3:225–226
  governmentality, 3:362
  Hayek, Friedrich August von, 3:435
  laissez-faire, 4:335–338
  latifundia, 4:353
  leisure, 4:408
  long period analysis, 4:489–491
  marginal productivity, 4:595–596
  market socialism, 7:644–646
  markets, 4:606–608
  monetarism, 5:242–243
  NAFTA, 5:540–541
  racial discrimination, 2:395
  Ricardian equivalence, 7:241
  Russian economics, 7:301
  Russian Federation, 7:302–303
  statistical discrimination, 2:396–398
  taste for discrimination, 2:398–399

  transitional economies, 2:533
  See also Public sector
Market fundamentals, 4:**605–606**
Market gluts, 6:96–97
Market power. *See* Imperfect competition
Market price. *See* Exchange value
Market prices. *See* Spot market
Market segmentation, 1:585
Market signaling, 1:288
Market socialism, 7:**644–646**
  convergence theory, 2:117
  economics of control, 2:532
  transitional economies, 2:533
The Market System (Lindblom), 4:453
Marketing
  cattle industry, 1:470, 471
  cluster analysis, 1:585
  coffee industry, 1:595–596
  color preference, 6:433
  consumption, 2:107–108
  corporate social responsibility, 2:137
  corporate strategy, 2:138–139
  corporations, 2:140
  cultural tourism, 2:201
  guerrilla, 1:29
  Latinos, 4:360–361
  lexicographic preferences, 4:422–423
  lifestyles, 4:445
  prestige, 6:444
  price discrimination, 2:392–393
  role models, 7:274
  subjective value, 8:579
  See also Advertising
Markets, 4:**606–609**
  adverse selection, 1:27–28, 9:103
  asymmetric information, 4:28–30
  bubbles (economics), 1:379
  capitalism, 1:437–439
  imperfect competition, 2:51–53
  industry, 3:622–623
  market economy, 4:604–605
  perfect competition, 2:57–58
  power, 2:51–53
  reform, 2:346, 347
  sports industry, 8:66
  spot, 1:449–450, 8:67–68
  technological change, 1:490, 491
  trust, 8:461
Markets, bear. *See* Bull and bear markets
Markets, bull. *See* Bull and bear markets

Markets, commodities. *See* Forward and futures markets
Markets, common. *See* Common market
Markets, equity. *See* Equity markets
Markets, financial. *See* Financial markets
Markets, futures. *See* Forward and futures markets
Markets, internal. *See* Common market
Markets, labor. *See* Labor market
Markets, protected. *See* Protected markets
Markets, securities. *See* Equity markets
Markets, single. *See* Common market
Markets, spot. *See* Spot market
Markets, stock. *See* Equity markets
Markets and Hierarchies (Williamson), 3:474, 5:515
Markov Chain Monte Carlo algorithms (MCMC), 1:263–264
Markowitz, Harry M., 3:141, 4:**609–610**
  risk-return tradeoff, 7:255, 256
  Tobin, James, 8:378
Markup pricing, 4:**610–612**
Márkus, György, 5:454
Marley, Bob, 7:68, 128–129
Maroons, 1:328
Marr, Wilhelm, 1:141
Marriage, 4:**612–616**
  caste, 1:459
  childlessness, 1:510
  Chinese Americans, 1:513
  Chinese diaspora, 1:516
  cohabitation, 2:1–2
  crime and criminology, 2:172
  Darwin, Charles, 2:229
  divorce and separation, 2:426–428
  dowry and bride price, 2:440–441
  family structure, 3:83, 84, 93
  femininity, 3:118
  gender differences, 3:128
  group, 3:83
  infidelity, 4:20–21
  kinship, 4:271, 272
  loneliness, 4:487
  out-of-wedlock births, 1:306–308
  property law, 3:120
  rape, 7:65
  relationship satisfaction, 7:151–152
  romance, 7:282
  sexuality, 7:481–482

social, 3:83

statistics, 3:91, 91*t*, 92, 92*t*

The Stepford Wives (film), 8:134–135

taboos, 8:259–260

See also Marital conflict

Marriage, interracial, 4:**616–619**, *617, 619*

blood and bloodline, 1:335–336

buraku, 1:389

Coloreds (South Africa), 2:15

miscegenation, 5:199–200

race mixing, 7:26, 28

racial democracy, 2:283

Marriage, same-sex, 4:**619–621**

gay, lesbian, transgender, and bisexual politics, 6:331

increase, 4:615–616

law, 2:426

relationship satisfaction, 7:151–152

sexual orientation, 7:478–479

Marriage squeeze hypothesis. *See* Dowry and bride price

Marriott, McKim, 1:461

Marris, Robin Lapthorn, 1:442

Marryshow, Theophilus A., 9:97

Mars, 4:**621–622**

Marsalis, Wynton, 4:177, 178

Marschak, Jacob, 1:502, 8:580

Marshall, Alfred, 4:**622–624**

aggregate demand, 1:50

aggregate demand and supply price, 1:51

Austrian economics, 1:211

Bentham, Jeremy, 1:286

classical economics, 2:502

comparative statics, 2:48

consumer surplus, 2:104

cumulative causation, 2:207

goodwill, 3:349

Hicks, John R., 3:472

increasing returns, 7:219–220

interest rates, 3:151

labor demand, 4:312

long run, 4:491

marginal product of labor, 4:305

markets, 4:608

mathematical economics, 5:24

neoclassical economics, 2:516

noncompeting groups, 5:515

partial equilibrium, 6:151–152

race, 7:14

rent, 7:164

representative agent, 7:174

returns, 7:218

sharecropping, 7:490–491

short period, 7:501

social cost, 7:582

supply, 8:229

utility function, 8:555

welfare analysis, 9:62–63

Marshall, F. Ray, 9:26

Marshall, George Catlett, 1:521

Marshall, Irving, 1:449

Marshall, John, 1:397, 3:114, 4:223, 224

See also Supreme Court, U.S.

Marshall, T. H., 1:543, 9:67

Marshall, Thurgood, 4:**624–626**

black liberalism, 1:312

Brown v. Board of Education (1954), 1:374, 375

Houston, Charles Hamilton, 3:505

NAACP, 5:384

Nation of Islam, 5:380

War on Poverty, 9:24

Marshall Plan, 9:149

Marston, John, 4:523

Marten, Gerald, 3:510

Martí, José

Castro, Fidel, 1:464, 467

communism, 2:36

Cuban Revolution, 2:185, 186, 187

Martin, John, 1:260, 6:136

Martin, William McChesney, Jr., 3:112

Martingale, 3:53

Martinique

blackness, 1:330

Fanon, Frantz, 3:99

Martyr, Justin, 6:78, 79

Martyrdom, 4:**626–629**

The Church, 1:532

terrorism, 8:329

Marvel Comics, 2:24

Marx, Karl, 4:**638–641**

accumulation of capital, 1:12

agricultural industry, 1:61

alienation, 1:75

Asiatic mode of production, 1:187–188

bourgeoisie, 1:361

capital, 1:429, 430

Capital: A Critique of Political Economy, 1:12, 3:79, 82, 133, 8:489, 576

capitalism, 1:437

capitalist mode of production, 1:445–447

Castro, Fidel, 1:464, 467

civil society, 1:553

class, 1:561, 562, 563

class conflict, 1:568, 570

class consciousness, 1:571–572

class-struggle cycle, 5:524

classical economics, 2:502

communism, 2:34–35, 36

communitarianism, 2:40

competition, 2:50–51

constructivism, 2:96

consumption, 2:106

convergence theory, 2:117

cooperation, 2:122, 123

critical theory, 2:176, 177

cult of personality, 6:222

determinism, 2:324

dialectical materialism, 5:22–23

economic crises, 2:484

economic depression, 2:303

egalitarianism, 2:550

elite theory, 2:562

exchange value, 3:40

factory system, 3:79

false consciousness, 3:81–83

feudal mode of production, 3:133, 136, 9:126

forces of production, 3:166–167

The German Ideology, 3:82

groups, 3:386

Harris, Abram L., Jr., 3:427

Hegel, Georg Wilhelm Friedrich, 3:452, 453

Hegelians, 3:453, 454

hegemony, 3:455–456

hermeneutics, 3:463

humanism, 3:518

ideology, 3:559

immiserizing growth, 3:583

imperialism, 3:588, 589

internationalism, 4:102

irrigation, 4:152

Kalecki, Michał, 4:246

labor, 4:300

labor theory of value, 4:322–324

Lafargue, Paul, 4:329–330

laissez-faire, 4:337

land fertility, 3:131

Latin American revolutions, 7:233

Lefebvre, Henri, 4:400

leisure class, 1:566

Leninism, 4:411–412

Marx, Karl, *continued*
  liberalism, 4:425
  liberation, 4:430
  long period analysis, 4:490
  long run, 4:491
  Lukacs, Georg, 4:515–516
  lumpenproletariat, 4:516–517
  Luxemburg, Rosa, 4:522
  Mandel, Ernest, 4:579–580
  Marxist competition, 2:55–56
  materialism, 5:19
  mathematics in the social sciences, 5:27–28
  middle class, 5:143–144
  mode of production, 5:218–220
  modernity, 5:231
  Moore, Barrington, 5:278
  mystification, 5:353–355
  national income accounts, 5:399
  needs, 5:453
  objectivity, 6:10, 9:57
  otherness, 6:83
  overproduction, 6:97
  Perron-Froebenius theorem, 2:552, 554
  petty bourgeoisie, 1:362
  political sociology, 8:3, 4
  political stratification, 8:168
  Popper, Karl, 6:372
  post-Parsonian American sociology, 8:5
  power elite, 6:417–418
  praxis, 6:421
  primitive accumulation, 6:463–464
  primitive communism, 2:37–38
  prisons, 6:476
  production, 9:94
  Quesnay, François, 6:666, 667
  race, 7:13–14, 15
  rate of exploitation, 7:70–71
  rationalism, 7:77
  relative deprivation, 7:152
  relative surplus value, 7:154–155
  religiosity, 7:162
  repressive tolerance, 7:176
  reproduction model, 8:600
  resistance, 7:208
  Russian economics, 7:299, 301
  Schumpter, Joseph, 2:163
  science, 7:358
  scientific method, 7:363
  self-determination, 7:406
  slave mode of production, 7:531–532

social change, 7:568–569
social formation, 3:177
social structure, 7:623
social theory, 7:628
socialism, 7:637
sociology, 7:660, 661, 662
state enterprise, 8:106, 107, 108
stratification, 8:166
subjectivity, 8:198–199
surplus, 8:235
surplus labor, 4:309–312
surplus population, 8:237–238
surplus value, 8:240–241
Taylorism, 8:287
technological change, 1:491
transformation problem, 8:429–431
Trouillot, Michel-Rolph, 8:457
two-department model of reproduction, 8:563
underclass, 8:485
underconsumption, 8:488
underdevelopment, 8:489
urban sociology, 8:15
utopianism, 8:561
value, objective, 8:575–577, 578
wages, 9:122
wealth, 9:44, 45–46
work day, 9:126, 127
working class, 9:129–130, 131
See also Marxian economics; Marxism
Marx, Karl, impact on anthropology, **4:631–633**
Marx, Karl, impact on economics, **4:634–635**
Marx, Karl, impact on sociology, **4:635–638**
Marx, Leo, 2:332
Marx After Sraffa (Steedman), 8:576
Marxian economics, **2:515–517**
  Cambridge capital controversy, 1:420, 421
  capitalism, 1:439
  capitalist mode of production, 1:445–447
  class, 1:562, 563
  communism, 2:35–36
  competition, 2:50–51
  consumption, 2:106
  Hilferding, Rudolf, 3:476
  labor theory of value, 4:322–324
  Leontief, Wassily, 4:413
  long period analysis, 4:490
  long run, 4:491

Luxemburg, Rosa, 4:522–523
marginal product of labor, 4:307
mathematics in the social sciences, 5:27–28
political economy, 6:303
primitive communism, 2:37–38
rate of exploitation, 7:70–71
rate of profit, 7:73
surplus labor, 4:309–312
transitional conjunctures, 2:77, 78
See also Marx, Karl; Marxism
Marxism, **4:638–641**
  accumulation of capital, 1:13
  African socialism, 7:641
  Bahro, Rudolf, 1:237–238
  bourgeoisie, 1:360
  British anthropology, 1:128
  capitalist mode of production, 1:445–447
  Christian socialism, 7:642–643
  cities, 1:541
  civil society, 1:553
  class, 1:562, 563, 564
  class conflict, 1:569, 571
  class consciousness, 1:571–572
  communism, 2:34–36, 36
  consumption, 2:106
  convergence theory, 2:117
  critical theory, 2:176–178
  Cuba, 2:186
  curriculum, 2:214
  democratic centralism, 2:285
  dependency theory, 2:299
  dialectical materialism, 5:21–23
  exploitation, 3:64–65
  false consciousness, 3:81
  feminism, 3:122, 9:113
  Frank, Andre Gunder, 3:187
  Frankfurt School, 3:188
  French Revolution, 3:205
  Fromm, Erich, 3:222–223
  geography, 3:305
  Hegel, Georg Wilhelm Friedrich, 3:452
  hegemony, 3:455–456
  Hilferding, Rudolf, 3:476
  ideology, 3:559
  immigration, 3:581
  intersectionality, 4:114
  knowledge in sociology, 7:674–675
  labor, 4:300
  labor theory of value, 3:155
  Lafargue, Paul, 4:329–330

Lefebvre, Henri, 4:400

left wing, 4:403

legal systems, 4:406

Lenin, Vladimir Ilitch, 4:410–411

Leninism, 4:411–412

liberation, 4:430

liberation theology, 4:436

Lukacs, Georg, 4:515–516

lumpenproletariat, 4:516–517

managerial class, 4:578

Mandel, Ernest, 4:579

Mao Zedong, 4:588–590

Maoism, 4:590–591

marginalization, 4:599

military regimes, 5:174–176

mode of production, 5:218–220

monopoly capitalism, 5:266

petty bourgeoisie, 1:362

political economy, 6:303

political science, 6:313–314

political sociology, 8:3, 4

post-Parsonian American sociology, 8:5

Poulantzas, Nicos, 6:404–405

power, 6:413–414

praxis, 6:421

primitive communism, 2:37–38

Russian Revolution, 7:303

schools in sociology, 8:11

social change, 7:568–569

social formation, 3:176–178

social history, 3:482, 484

socialism, 7:637–638

Thompson, Edward P., 8:353–354

transformation problem, 8:429–431

Trotsky, Leon, 8:455–456

Trouillot, Michel-Rolph, 8:457

underconsumption, 8:488

underdevelopment, 8:489

unequal education, 2:538

war, 9:17

working class, 9:131, 132–133

world-system, 9:153

zombies, 9:181

See also Austro-Marxism; Marx, Karl; Marxian economics; Neo-Marxism

Marxism, black, 4:**641–643**

black liberalism, 1:312

Harlem Renaissance, 3:426

Harris, Abram L., Jr., 3:426–427

James, C. L. R., 4:168

Marxism and Philosophy (Korsch), 1:569

Marxism-Leninism. *See* Leninism; Marxism

Marxist competition, 2:**55–56**

Marx's Notes on Method (Hall), 3:409

Mary (Virgin), 1:533

Maryland, Murray v. (1936), 3:505

Mas-Colell, Andreau, 9:95

Masalit, 2:226–227

Masculinity, 3:117, 269, 5:**1–5**

men, 5:80–81

social values, 8:582

work, 9:122

Masculinity studies, 5:**5–11**, 8:142–143

Maslow, Abraham, 5:**11–12**

hierarchy of needs, 5:451, 453, 454, 455

mysticism, 5:353

positive psychology, 6:385

self-actualization, 7:394–395

Mason, Charlotte Osgood, 3:527

Mason, Patrick L., 2:182, 3:96

discrimination, 2:390, 391

taste for discrimination, 2:399

wage discrimination, 2:405

Mason, William, 1:83

Mass communication. *See* Communication

Mass media. *See* Media

Mass production

automobile industry, 1:217–218

Ford Motor Company, 3:168

history, 3:77

See also Factories; Industrialization; Manufacturing

Mass violence, as genocide, 3:296–297

Massachusetts

abortion, 1:2

American Revolution, 1:103–104

gerrymandering, 3:308–309

Massachusetts Institute of Technology (MIT), 1:419

Massey, Douglas, 5:462, 463, 499, 6:48, 8:5

Massive resistance. *See Brown v. Board of Education* (1955)

Masten, Ann, 7:204–205

Master-servant relationship. *See* Servitude

Masters of Deceit: The Story of Communism in America and How to Fight It (Hoover), 3:501

Mastery orientation, 1:15

Mata Mathurashani Devi, 8:568

Matching, pattern. *See* Campbell, Donald

Material culture, 1:155, 2:200, 5:**12–18**

Material wealth, 9:44, 45

See also Wealth

Materialism, 5:**18–21**

central state, 1:278

civil society, 1:553

communism, 2:34

constructivism, 2:96

cultural, 1:120

functionalism, 3:231

Giddens, Anthony, 3:314

idealism, 3:547

leisure class, 1:565–566

Marxist competition, 2:55–56

mystification, 5:355

primitive communism, 2:37, 38

reality, 7:100

Tocqueville, Alexis de, 8:383

visual arts, 8:632

Materialism, dialectical, 5:**21–23**

constructivism, 2:96

Lefebvre, Henri, 4:400–401

Marxism, 4:640

scientific *vs.*, 5:19

Le matérialisme dialectique (Lefebvre), 4:400

Materials, raw, 5:438

Mathematical economics, 5:**23–25**

differential equations, 2:364

economic rhetoric, 2:495–496

equilibrium, 2:620

Hessian matrix, 3:467–468

Hurwicz, Leonid, 3:529–530

Jacobian matrix, 4:163

Keynes, John Maynard, 4:261

matrix algebra, 5:32–34

Potron, Maurice, 6:403–404

School of Lausanne, 4:362

Tinbergen, Jan, 8:374–375

Mathematical formulas. *See* Formulas

Mathematical Investigations in the Theory of Value and Prices (Fisher), 3:150

Mathematical models, 3:230–231

See also Models and modeling

Mathematics in the social sciences, 5:**25–28**

chi-square, 1:523

Condorcet, Marquis de, 2:65–66

differential equations, 2:364

heterarchy, 3:468–469

Lazarsfeld, Paul Felix, 4:375

Mathematics in the social sciences, *continued*
   measures of central tendencies, 1:486, 487–488
   optimizing behavior, 6:55
   quantification, 6:655–656
   symbolic logic, 4:481–482
   topology, 8:390–391
Mathios, Alan, 5:391
Mating. *See* Sex and mating
Matriarchy, 5:**28–31**
   Native Americans, 5:424, 425, 426
   primitive communism, 2:37, 38
Matrix
   factor-loading, 3:76
   variance-covariance, 8:590–591
Matrix, inverse. *See* Inverse matrix
Matrix, Jacobian. *See* Jacobian matrix
Matrix, Jajmani. *See* Jajmani matrix
The Matrix (film), 5:**31–32**
Matrix algebra, 5:**32–34**
   Cholesky decomposition, 1:526–527
   determinants, 2:321–323
   Hessian matrix, 3:467–468
   identity matrix, 3:557–558
   Jacobian matrix, 4:163
   Jajmani matrix, 4:167
   linear systems, 4:455–457
   Potron, Maurice, 6:403
Matrix inversion. *See* Inverse matrix
Matson, Floyd, 5:529–530
Maturation, 5:**34–36**
   child development, 1:505–509
   rites of passage, 7:256–259
   stages of development, 8:77–79
Mau, Steffen, 9:69, 71, 73
Mau Mau, 5:**36–38**
   Bamboozled, 1:243, 244
   Kenyatta, Jomo, 4:255
   Kimathi, Dedan, 4:266
Maurice, F. D., 7:642
Mauritius, 2:169
Maurras, Charles, 2:84, 86
Mauss, Marcel, 2:223, 4:416, 7:105–106
   See also Dance
Maximand, 6:6
Maximin expected utility theory, 5:519
Maximin principle, 5:**38–39**
Maximization, 5:**39–41**, 41*t*
   behavioral economics, 2:501
   demand, 2:269

Hamilton's rule, 3:414–415
   Lagrange multipliers, 4:332–333
   mechanism design, 5:58
   neoclassical economics, 2:516–517, 519
   objective functions, 6:5–6
   rationality, 7:81–82
   welfare, 8:558
Maximum likelihood regression, 5:**41–43**, 534
   duration models, 2:464
   three-stage least squares, 4:395
   two-stage least squares, 4:395
Maximum sustainable yield (MSY), 6:91, *92*
May, Mark, 4:523–524
May Fourth movement, 1:520
Mayall, John, 1:343
Mayans, 1:166, 3:516, 6:427
   See also Pre-Columbian peoples
Maybach, Wilhelm, 1:217
Mayer, Alfred, 2:34
Maynard Smith, John, 3:415
Mbeki, Thabo, 1:43
MBTI (Myers-Briggs Type Indicator), 4:230
MC (Member of Congress). *See* Congress, U.S.
MCA, 1:441
McAdoo, Orpheus M., 1:327
MCC (Mondragon Cooperative Corporation), 1:112, 2:125
McCabe, Edward P., 1:326
McCarran-Walter Immigration and Nationality Act (U.S. 1952), 1:513, 3:563–564
McCarthy, Danielle, 2:252
McCarthy, Joseph Raymond, 2:85, 3:501, 4:214, 5:43–44, 8:613
McCarthyism, 5:**43–44**
   conservatism, 2:85
   Hoover, J. Edgar, 3:501
   journalism, 4:214
   Lynd, Robert and Helen, 4:528
   repression, 7:175
McClelland, David, 1:14
McCloskey, Deidre, 1:502, 2:495–496
McCloud, Scott, 2:23
McCloy, John, 9:33
McCombie, John, 8:608
McCone, John, 2:184
McCord, James W., Jr., 9:43
McCormick, Katharine, 1:303
McCorvey, Norma, 7:271, 272
McCrae, Robert, 5:486, 487

McDaniel, Hattie, 3:347–348
McDougall, Gay, 3:514
McDougall, William, 1:276
McDowell, John, 5:443
McFadden, Daniel L., 5:**44–45**
McGee, R. John, 1:138, 6:428
McGee, W. J., 1:92
McGlowan, Angela, 1:311
McGovern, George, 5:359
McGregor, Douglas, 5:455
McIntosh, Peggy, 9:87
McKay, Claude, 3:424, 426
McKendrick, Neil, 2:89
McKenzie, Lionel
   general equilibrium, 3:283
   optimal growth, 6:51, 52
McKenzie, Roderick D., 7:132, 8:541
McKinley, William
   cross of gold, 2:181
   Cuba, 2:185
   War of 1898, 9:23–24
   Wilmington Riot of 1898, 9:99
McKinney, Karyn, 9:91, 92
McKinney Act (1987). *See* Stewart B. McKinney Homeless Assistance Act (1987)
McKissick, Floyd, 2:75
McKusick, Victor A., 3:298–299
McLachlan, Geoff, 1:586
McLaurin v. Oklahoma (1950), 3:505
McLennan, J. F., 1:127
McLoyd, Vonnie, 2:135
McLuhan, Marshall, 5:**45–46**
   media, 5:60
   medium is the message, 5:68–69
   technological determinism, 2:332
MCMC (Markov Chain Monte Carlo algorithms), 1:264–265
McNamara, Robert, 2:184, 9:138
McNatt, D. Brian, 4:381
McPhail, Clark, 7:251
MCSUI (Multi-City Study of Urban Inequality). *See* Multi-City Study of Urban Inequality (MCSUI)
MCTR (Missile Technology Control Regime), 1:177
MDD (Major depressive disorder), 2:306
MDMA (Methylenedioxymethamphetamine). *See* Ecstasy (drug)
Mead, George Herbert, 5:**46–47**
   Blumer, Herbert, 1:344
   cultural anthropology, 1:120
   groups, 3:385

intersubjectivity, 4:116
looking-glass effect, 4:495
Oedipus complex, 6:29
role theory, 7:275, 276
self-hatred, 7:416–417
self-representation, 7:427
social identity, 3:556
sociology, 7:661
symbolic interactionism, 4:76
Mead, Margaret, 5:**47–48**
    Boas, Franz, 1:345
    determinism, 2:323
    feminity, 3:117
    public anthropology, 1:133
    sensationalism, 7:443
Meade, James, 5:**48–50**
Meadowcroft, Michael, 4:427
Meadows, Donella, 2:61, 4:449–451
Mean (mathematics), 5:**50–51**
    absolute deviation, 8:585
    descriptive statistics, 2:312
    measures of central tendencies,
        1:487–488
    normal distribution, 2:415–416
    regression toward, 7:141–142,
        8:574
Mean square efficiency. *See* Properties
    of estimators (asymptotic and exact)
Meaning, 5:**51–52**
    behaviorism, 1:274–280
    communication, 2:32
    cultural studies, 2:199
    data, 2:234–237
    linguistic turn, 4:457–458
    material culture, 5:15
    Pitkin, Hanna, 6:273
    poststructuralism, 6:398–399
    representation, 7:170–172
    social constructs, 7:578–580
The Meaning of the Nuclear Revolution
    (Jervis), 4:186
Means, Gardiner, 1:442
Means, Russell, 1:98, 5:**53**
Means-end theory, 1:211
Means of production. *See* Forces of
    production; Mode of production
Mearsheimer, John, 5:420
Measurement, 5:**53–55**
    Cambridge capital controversy,
        1:419, 420
    census, 1:476–477
    central tendencies, 1:487–488
    cliometrics, 1:581
    cluster analysis, 1:585–586
    discrimination, 2:391

employment, 2:580
    income inequality, 4:1–2
    IQ controversy, 4:139
    philosophy of science, 6:260
    prejudice, 6:439
    quality controls, 6:651
    quantification, 6:655–656
    scales, 7:338–339
    statistical reliability, 7:157–158
    time, 1:583–584
    validation, 8:569–572, 570*t*, 571*t*
    wage discrimination, 2:400
Measurement, economic. *See*
    Econometrics
Measurement, psychological. *See*
    Psychometrics
Measurement error, 5:**55–57**, 8:50–52
Measures of central tendencies,
    1:**487–488**, 5:51, 217–218
Meatpacking, 1:470
Mecca, 5:**57**
Mechanism (philosophy)
    bureaucracy, 1:390
    bureaucrats, 1:392
    capitalist mode of production,
        1:447
    checks and balances, 1:495–496
    consciousness, 2:79, 80
    Descartes, René, 1:275, 276
    theory, 8:343–344
Mechanism design, 5:**58**
Mechanism for Conflict Prevention,
    Management and Resolution, 6:62,
    63
Mechanization. *See* Machinery
Media, 5:**59–61**
    Bandura, Albert, 1:248–249
    body image, 1:346–347
    business ethics, 2:634
    campaigning, 1:423–424
    Chomsky, Noam, 1:529
    Christian fundamentalism, 3:236
    colonial gaze, 3:261
    consumption, 2:108
    critical theory, 2:177
    journalism, 4:211–216
    Lasswell, Harold, 4:351
    Latino National Political Survey,
        4:355
    Lazarsfeld, Paul Felix, 4:375
    literature, 4:464
    McLuhan, Marshall, 5:45–46
    medium is the message, 5:68–69
    political attitudes, 1:202–203
    political cartoons, 1:452

political parties, 6:308
    popular culture, 6:374
    radio talk shows, 7:51–53
    repression, 7:174
    sensationalism, 7:442–444
    social system, 7:626
    social values, 8:582
    stare, 8:101
    television, 8:320
    terrorism, 8:329
    Vietnam War, 8:615
    violence, 1:56
    whistle-blowers, 9:79
Median (mathematics)
    descriptive statistics, 1:487–488
    measures of central tendencies,
        1:487–488
Mediated stability. *See* Psychological
    stability
Mediation. *See* Negotiation
Medicaid, 3:374, 5:**61–62**
    Current Population Survey, 2:213
    history, 5:396
    social policy interventions, 4:118,
        119
Medical anthropology, 1:**130–132,**
    3:12–13
Medical care industry. *See* Medicine
Medical ethics, 1:300–301
Medical-industrial complex,
    5:395–396
Medical services industry. *See*
    Medicine
Medicalization, 5:431
Medicare, 5:**62–63**
    baby boomers, 1:236
    Great Society, 3:374
    history, 5:396
    socialized medicine, 5:66
Medicine, 5:**63–65**
    bioethics, 1:300–301
    conversational analysis, 2:119
    Cuba, 2:187
    Current Population Survey, 2:213
    death and dying, 2:248
    dementia, 2:271–272
    disease, 2:406–408
    drug tolerance, 8:385
    ethics in experimentation, 2:635
    Great Society programs, 3:372
    health economics, 3:440–441
    Hinduism, 3:479
    imperfect competition, 2:53
    infertility drugs, 4:19–20
    insurance industry, 4:51

Medicine, *continued*
   lobotomy, 4:475–476
   medicine, 5:63–65
   mental health, 5:84–86
   merit goods, 5:98
   microelectronics industry, 5:139
   midwifery, 5:151–154
   National Longitudinal Study of
     Adolescent Health, 5:406–407
   pharmaceutical industry,
     6:236–239
   population aging, 3:307
   prevention science, 6:445–446
   primary health care, 3:443
   private, 9:61
   socialized medicine, 5:65–66
   spending, 5:395
   stem cells, 8:133–134
   tourism, 8:400
Medicine, Magic and Religion (Rivers),
   1:130
Medicine, social. *See* Public health
Medicine, socialized, 5:**65–66**
   Clinton, Bill, 1:580
   health economics, 3:440
   managed competition, 2:54–55
Medicis, 5:**66–68**
Medieval times. *See* Middle Ages
Meditation
   nirvāna, 5:504
   worship, 9:155
   See also Buddhism
*The Mediterranean and the
   Mediterranean World in the Age of
   Philip II* (Braudel), 9:152
Medium is the message, 4:214, 5:60,
   68–69
Meehl, Paul, 2:244
Meek, Ronald, 8:576
Meese, Richard, 2:209–210
MEG (Magnetoencephalography),
   5:485
Mehmet Ali. *See* Ali, Muhammad
   (Egyptian military leader)
Mehrabian, Albert, 5:530
Meigs, Anna, 9:108
Meiji Restoration, 2:360, 5:**69–70**,
   6:37
Mein Kampf (Hitler), 2:233, 3:486,
   7:175
Meir, Golda, 5:**70–71**, 7:1
Melanesians, 3:238
Mellor, William, 2:372
Melting pot, 5:**71–73**
   Latin American immigrants, 3:570

Moynihan, Daniel Patrick, 5:304
   New York City immigrants, 3:575
   See also Assimilation
Melucci, Alberto, 1:563
Memantine, 2:272
Member of Congress (MC). *See*
   Congress, U.S.
Memín Pinguín, 1:327, 5:**73–74**
Memories of the Battle of Algiers
   (Saadi). *See Souvenirs de la bataille
   d'Alger* (Saadi)
Memory, 5:**74–76**
   collective, 3:497
   mood, 5:276
   mood congruent recall, 5:277
   primacy/recency effects,
     6:457–458
   script models, 7:372–373
   semantic, 7:435–436
   unidentified flying objects, 8:507
Memory, collective. *See* Collective
   memory
Memory, person. *See* Person memory
Memory, semantic. *See* Semantic
   memory
Memory, social. *See* Collective
   memory
Memory in psychology, 5:**76–80**
   cognition, 1:597, 598
   dementia, 2:271–272
   trauma, 8:439–440
Memphis (TN), 9:76
Men, 5:**80–82**
   blue collar and white collar, 1:337
   body image, 1:346
   contraception, 2:114
   dependency, 2:298
   divorce and separation, 2:427–428
   fertility, 3:128–129
   infidelity, 4:21
   Jews, 4:194
   labor force participation, 4:315
   labor supply, 4:321
   lying, 4:524
   marriage statistics, 3:92, 92*t*
   masculinity, 5:1–4, 5–8
   Napoleon complex, 5:366–367
   patriarchy, 6:173–174
   pimps, 6:271–273
   relationship satisfaction, 7:151
   sex and mating, 7:470–472
   weight, 9:59
Menarche, 9:108
Mendel's law, 5:**82–83**

Dobzhansky, Theodosius,
   2:432–433
Pearson, Karl, 6:193
Mendleson, Barbara, 2:33
Mendoza, Sally, 1:83
Menger, Carl, 4:305
   Austrian economics, 1:210–211
   gold standard, 3:345
   ordinality, 6:57
   utility function, 8:555
   Walras, Léon, 9:11
Mensheviks, 1:351, 7:303, 304
Menstruation, 9:108
Mental depression. *See* Psychological
   depression
Mental health, 5:**83–86**
   Cherokees, 1:496
   Child Behavior Checklist,
     1:504–505
   coping, 2:128–129
   Galton, Francis, 3:247
   Jung, Carl, 4:230–231
   labeling theory, 4:299
   locus of control, 4:477–478
   loneliness, 4:486–487
   military, 5:170–171
   positive psychology, 6:385–386
   post-traumatic stress, 6:401–403
   prison psychology, 6:470–471
   psychopathology, 6:594*t*
   self-esteem, 7:412–414
   self-representation, 7:426–427
   shamans, 7:488
   socioeconomic status, 7:357
   suicide, 8:221–223
   type A/type B personality,
     6:222–223
   weight, 9:59
Mental illness, 5:**86–88**
   dementia, 2:271–272
   diathesis-stress model, 2:358
   disease, 2:408
   Foucault, Michel, 3:182
   Goffman, Erving, 3:337
   infertility drugs, 4:19–20
   lobotomy, 4:475–476
   manias, 4:582–583
   manic depression, 4:583–584
   mental health, 5:83–86
   multiple personalities, 5:327–328
   paranoia, 6:128–130
   personality, 6:220
   schizophrenia, 7:344–346
   social anxiety, 7:563–564

suicide, 8:221–223

transgender, 8:432

trauma, 8:439–441

See also Madness; Psychiatric disorders; Psychopathology

Mental lexicon. *See* Psycholinguistics

Mental retardation, 4:75, 5:**88–91**

Mental states, 3:231

Mentalizing. *See* Theory of mind

Mento, 7:127

Mentoring, 5:**91–93**, 7:273

Mercantilism, 5:**93–94**

absolute advantage, 1:5–6, 5*t*

bilateral trade, 8:414

caste, 1:457, 461

Chinese diaspora, 1:515–516, 517

Corn Laws, 2:134

De Soto, Hernando, 2:319–320

Hume process, 3:520–521

Jainism, 4:166, 167

petty bourgeoisie, 1:361–362

Postlethwayt, Malachy, 6:394

quantity theory of money, 6:659–660

Smith, Adam, 5:474

Mercenaries, 9:51

Merchant banks, 6:31

Merchants. *See* Mercantilism

Meredith, Crystal, 1:376

Meredith, John, 4:369

Meredith v. Jefferson County Board of Education (2006), 1:375–376

Mergers and acquisitions. *See* Corporate strategies

Merit, 2:166–167, 5:**94–97**

Merit goods, 5:**97–98**

Meritocracy, 5:**98–100**

credentialism, 2:166

egalitarianism, 2:550

merit, 5:94–96

mobility, 5:209

race-blind policies, 7:35, 36

schooling, 7:351

upward mobility, 8:533

Meritocracy, multiracial, 5:**100–101**

Merleau-Ponty, Maurice, 3:264, 403, 453

Mernissi, Fatima, 8:603

Merriam, Charles Edward, Jr., 3:351, 5:**101–102**, 6:312

Merton, Robert K., 3:142, 5:**102–103**, 8:5

alienation, 1:75

conformity, 2:71

functionalism, 3:232

post-Parsonian American sociology, 8:5

science, 7:359

self-fulfilling prophecies, 7:414–415

sociology, 7:661

Veblen, Thorstein, 8:596

Merton, Thomas, 1:384

MESBIC (Minority Enterprise Emall Business Investment Companies), 1:440, 441

See also Black capitalism

Mescaline, 1:456–457, 3:410, 411, 412

Mesmer, Franz Anton. *See* Psychotherapy

Meso-American civilization. *See* Aztecs; Incas; Mayans; Olmecs; Pre-Columbian peoples

Mesopotamia, 1:544

agricultural industry, 1:62

archaeology, 1:165

fertile crescent, 3:126

heaven, 3:445

slavery, 1:38, 39

visual arts, 8:630

wealth, 9:44

Message-based persuasion, 6:227–228, **228–230**, 7:550

Messianism, 4:194, 7:66–67

Messias, Deanne, 9:123

Messick, Samuel, 8:571–572, 573

Mestizaje. *See* Blackness; Racial classification; Racial identification

Mestizo. *See* Blackness; Racial classification; Racial identification

Mestrovic, Stjepan G., 8:597

Meta-analysis, 5:**104–105**

Metabolism, 5:551

Metadata, 2:236

Metaethics, 2:632, 6:252

Metainformation, 2:236

Metallgesellschaft Refining and Marketing (MGRM), 2:112

Metalwork, 8:631

Metaphor. *See* Symbols

Metaphysics. *See* Philosophy; Reality

Metapreferences, 5:535

Metcalf, Robert, 5:137

Metchnikoff, Elie, 3:306

Meteorology, 1:413, 414

Methamphetamine, 2:453, 3:412

Methane, greenhouse effect, 3:378

Method, scientific. *See* Scientific method

Method of moments, 3:156, 5:**105–107**, 6:191–192

Method of Successive Approximation, 6:43

Method variance. *See* Self-report method

Methodological behaviorism, 1:275, 279

Methodological holism. *See* Holism

Methodological individualism, 1:210

See also Individualism

Methodological naturalism, 5:442–443

Methodological subjectivity, 1:210

Methodology, 5:**107–110**

behavioral political science, 6:316

Campbell, Donald, 1:425–426

Cantillon, Richard, 1:429

census, 1:477

child development, 1:508

cliometrics, 1:581–583

empiricism, 2:578–579

ethics, 2:632–633

experimental, 3:55–58

Hume, David, 3:519–520

ideal type, 3:546–547

longitudinal data, 2:238–239

microanalysis, 5:132–133

philosophy of science, 6:260–261

political science, 6:311, 312

pseudopanel data, 2:239–240

quality controls, 6:651

social science, 7:615

temperament, 8:321–322

twin studies, 8:473–475

value free social science, 7:618–619

See also Ethnomethodology

Methodology, economic. *See* Economic methodology

Methodology, ethno-epidemiological. *See* Ethno-epidemiological methodology

The Methodology of Positive Economics (Friedman), 1:502

Methods

interrogation, 4:110–111

research

citations, 1:538–539

comparative politics, 6:327

developmental psychology, 2:351

documentary studies, 2:433–434

empiricism, 2:578–579

Methods, *continued*
    ethics, 2:632–633
    ethnography, 3:14–16
    experimental realism,
        7:93–95
    methodology, 5:107–109
    scientific, 4:338–340
    self-report method,
        7:424–426
    Thorndike, Edward, 8:358
Methods, qualitative, 5:**110–112**
    hypothesis and hypothesis testing,
        3:542–543
    methodology, 5:109
    quantitative methods *vs.,* 5:113
    survey methods, 5:116–117
Methods, quantitative, 5:**112–113**
    behavioral political science,
        6:315–316
    case method, 1:453
    cliometrics, 1:581–583
    cluster analysis, 1:585–586
    Duncan, Otis Dudley, 2:462–463
    empiricism, 2:578–579
    event studies, 3:30–31
    Frisch, Ragnar, 3:221–222
    hypothesis and hypothesis testing,
        3:541–542, 543
    Lasswell, Harold, 4:351
    longitudinal data, 2:238–239
    Merton, Robert K., 5:105–106
    meta-analysis, 5:104–105
    methodology, 5:109
    probability, 6:484–486
    quantification, 6:655–656
    as research methods, 5:113–115
    standard errors, 2:628–629
    survey, 8:241–242
    test statistics, 8:331–333
Methods, research in sociology,
    1:323–325, 359, 3:485, 5:**113–115,**
    7:661
    bigotry, 1:295–296
    case method, 1:453, 454
    hermeneutics, 2:462–463
    longitudinal data, 2:238–239
    microsociology, 7:678
    pseudopanel data, 2:239–240
    sample surveys, 8:244–245
Methods, survey, 5:**116–118**
    Campbell, Angus, 1:424–425
    Current Population Survey,
        2:212–213
    Head Start experiments, 3:438

    hypothesis and hypothesis testing,
        3:542
    survey research, 7:196–197
Methuen Treaty. *See* Corn laws
Methylcyclopentadienyl manganeses
    tricarbonyl (MMT), 5:541
Methylenedioxymethamphetamine
    (MDMA). *See* Ecstasy (drug)
Métis, 5:429
Metonym. *See* Symbols
Metropolis, 1:541, 5:**118–119,**
    7:132–135, 9:9–10
Metropolis-Hastings algorithm (MH),
    1:264
Metropolis-satellite model, 9:153
Metropolitan Applied Research Center
    (MARC), 1:561
The Metropolitan Community
    (McKenzie), 7:132
Metropolitan Life Insurance
    Company, 1:347
Metropolitan regions, 2:44–45,
    7:**132–135,** 8:546
    See also Cities
Metropolitan Statistical Areas (MSA),
    7:134, 135
Metternich, Clemens von, 2:84
Metz, Robert, 4:494
Metzner, Ralph, 4:390, 391
Mexican-American War, 5:**126–129,**
    8:549
    Lee, Robert E., 4:399
    Mexican Americans, 5:126
Mexican Americans, 5:**119–126**
    assimilation, 1:189
    Bracero Program, 1:365
    Chávez, César, 1:493–494
    citizenship, 5:121
    civil rights movement, 5:123–124
    colonization, 5:119
    critical race theory, 2:175
    Hernandez v. Texas, 3:464–466
    Huntington, Samuel P.,
        3:525–526
    immigration, 5:124–125
    independence, 5:120
    Latino/Latina studies, 4:356–357
    Latino National Political Survey,
        4:354–356
    Latinos, 4:358–359
    malinchistas, 4:564–565
    migrant labor, 5:154–155
    politics, 5:125–126
    sellouts, 7:435
    social change, 5:120–121
    World War II, 5:122–123

Mexican Civil War. *See* Mexican
    Revolution (1910–1920)
Mexican Revolution (1910–1920),
    5:**129–131**
    Latin American revolutions,
        7:233–234
    Mexican Americans, 5:121–122
    Zapata, Emiliano, 9:171–172
Mexican-Texas War (1836), 5:120
Mexican-U.S. Program of the Loan of
    Laborers. *See* Bracero Program
Mexico
    African burial grounds, 1:393
    authoritarianism, 1:214
    automobile industry, 1:221
    banana industry, 1:246
    banking industry, 1:253
    blackface, 1:327
    Bracero Program, 1:364–365
    Castaneda, Carlos, 1:457
    class conflict, 1:570–571
    clientelism, 1:579
    coffee industry, 1:594
    corporatism, 2:141
    Cortés, Hernán, 2:146–148
    cotton industry, 2:151
    cultural tourism, 2:201–202
    drug traffic, 2:451
    immigrants, 1:494
    imperialism, 2:20
    Juárez, Benito, 4:217–219
    labor, 4:302
    labor market, 4:318, 319
    land reform, 4:342, 344
    latifundia, 4:353, 354
    Latin American immigrants, 3:570
    Latin American revolutions,
        7:233–234
    Latino/Latina studies, 4:356–357
    Latino National Political Survey,
        4:354–356
    Latinos, 4:358–359
    Lewis, Oscar, 4:418, 419
    malinchistas, 4:564–565
    maquiladoras, 4:591–594
    Mexican-American War,
        5:126–129
    Mexican Americans, 5:119–126
    Mexican Revolution, 5:129–131
    NAFTA, 5:540–541
    Partido Revolucionario
        Institucional, 6:156–159
    phenotype, 6:244
    pollution, 5:541
    populism, 6:384

trade barriers, 1:255
vanilla industry, 8:583–584
Villa, Francisco (Pancho),
    8:617–618
volunteerism, 8:638
Zapata, Emiliano, 9:171–172
See also Chiapas
Meyer, John, 1:581
Meyer, Max, 1:276
MFA (Multifibre Arrangement),
    6:672–673
Mfume, Kweisi, 5:383
MGRM (Metallgesellschaft Refining
    and Marketing), 2:112
MH (Metropolis-Hastings algorithm),
    1:264
MI-5 (U.K.), 2:155
Miao. *See* Hmong
MIBI (Multidimensional Inventory of
    Black Identity). *See*
    Multidimensional Inventory of
    Black Identity (MIBI)
Miceli, Marcia P., 9:79
Michelangelo, 8:633
Michels, Robert, 2:43, 283, 5:**132**
    elite theory, 2:562, 563
    elites, 2:565
    oligarchy, 3:474, 6:36, 37–38
    political sociology, 8:3
Michigan, racial identification, 3:549
Michigan Election Studies. *See*
    American National Election Studies
Michno, Gregory, 1:259
Micro loans, 3:362–363
    See also Microfinance
Microanalysis, 5:**132–133**
Microcredit. *See* Microfinance
Microcultures, 1:122
Microeconomics, 5:**133–136**
    choice in economics, 1:524
    constrained choice, 2:95
    consumption, 2:107–109
    description, 3:143
    expectations, 3:48
    full capacity, 3:223–224
    general equilibrium, 3:285
    macroeconomics, 4:539
    macrofoundations, 4:545
    managed competition, 2:54
    microfoundations, 5:141
    optimizing behavior, 6:55
    Solow, Robert M., 8:26–27
    stocks and flows, 8:158
Microelectronics industry, 5:**136–139**,
    7:510–511

Microfinance, 5:**140–141**
    human rights, 3:513
    loans, 4:473
    poverty, 6:407
Microfoundations, 5:**141**
    Barro-Grossman model, 1:256
    cultural group selection, 2:191
    Lucas, Robert E., Jr., 4:510
    macrofoundations, 4:546
    representative agent, 7:173–174
Microloans. *See* Microfinance
Microprocessors. *See* Microelectronics
    industry
Microsociology, 7:**678–679**
    constructivism, 2:98
    described, 7:662–663
    macro-sociology *vs.,* 7:678
    microanalysis, 5:132–133
    post-Parsonian American
        sociology, 8:6–7
    social constructionism, 7:578
Microsoft, 2:52, 5:**142–143**
Middle Ages
    abortion, 1:2
    agricultural industry, 1:60
    architecture, 1:171
    census, 1:476
    The Church, 1:533–534
    conservatism, 2:83–84
    freedom, 3:196
    landlords, 4:346
    loans, 4:472
    minstrelsy, 5:194
    Roman Catholic Church, 7:280
Middle class, 5:**143–145**
    cities, 1:541, 542
    class conflict, 1:569
    class consciousness, 1:572
    creamy layer, 2:161
    Cuba, 2:186
    cultural capital, 2:190
    democracy, 2:273
    elites, 9:101
    family structure changes, 3:93–94
    female-headed families, 3:116
    gentility, 3:301
    gentrification, 3:302–303
    managerial class, 4:577, 578–579
    popular culture, 6:373, 374
    social history, 3:483
    social welfare system, 7:631–632
    urbanity, 8:545
    See also Black middle class;
        Bourgeoisie; Petty bourgeoisie

Middle class, black. *See* Black middle
    class
Middle East
    AIDS/HIV, 1:65
    Central Intelligence Agency, U.S,
        1:484, 485
    clientelism, 1:579
    domino theory, 2:435–436
    European Union, 3:25
    interwar years, 4:122
    Islamic fundamentalism,
        3:237–238
    Kissinger, Henry, 4:275
    land fertility, 3:130–131
    Rabin, Yitzhak, 7:1–2
    United Nations role, 8:525
    veils, 8:602–604
    virgins, 8:629
Middle Range theory, 1:168
Middle way, 1:488–489, 5:**145–147**
Middleman minorities, 5:**147–148**
    Bonacich, Edna, 1:351, 352, 353
    Chinese diaspora, 1:515, 516
Middlesex (Eugenides), 3:272
Middletown. *See* Community power
    studies; Lynd, Helen; Lynd, Robert
Middletown (Lynd and Lynd),
    4:527–528, 7:656
Middletown in Transition (Lynd and
    Lynd), 4:527–528
Midlarsky, Elizabeth, 3:293
Midlife crisis, 5:**148–151**
Midwifery, 5:**151–154**
Mieno, Yasushi, 1:379
Mies, Maria, 1:447
MIGA (Multilateral Investment
    Guarantee Agency), 9:137
Mighty Chalkdust (musician). *See*
    Liverpool, Hollis
Mighty Sparrow (musician), 1:418,
    419
Migrant labor, 4:318–319, 5:**154–156**
    Bonacich, Edna, 1:352
    Bracero Program, 1:364–365
    Chávez, César, 1:493–494
    civil rights movement, U.S., 1:552
    domestic labor *vs.,* 4:302
    Hamilton's rule, 3:415
    Latinos, 3:570, 4:358–359
    melting pot, 5:73
    townships, 8:405–407
    xenophobia, 9:159, 160
Migrants, political. *See* Refugees
Migration, 5:**156–159**
    African Americans, 1:501

Migration, *continued*
African diaspora, 1:38, 40–41
Asian immigrants, 3:562–564
black towns, 1:325–326
Bracero Program, 1:364–365
Caribbean, 1:448–449
caste, 1:460
census, 1:477
Chinese diaspora, 1:515–519
demography, 2:293, 294
depopulation, 2:302
European immigrants, 3:567–569
forced, 3:1–2
globalization, 3:332
hedonic prices, 3:451
Hmong, 3:491
hybridity, 3:536
in immigration, 3:582–583
indentured, 2:471–475
Jim Crow, 4:200
labor market, 4:318–319
Latin American immigrants, 3:570
Latinos, 4:358, 359, 360
New York City immigrants, 3:573
population growth, 6:378–379
population studies, 6:382
settlement, 7:464–465
suburbs, 8:210–211
transnationalism, 8:433–434
urbanization, 8:547
See also Diaspora
Migration, rural to urban, 5:**159–161**
African Americans, 1:34–35
Appalachia, 1:151
backwash effects, 1:236–237
black middle class, 1:313
cities, 1:540
Harlem Renaissance, 3:425
Harris-Todaro model, 3:428
metropolitan regions, 7:132
rural development, 2:341–342
Milano School of Management and
Urban Policy, 5:501
Miles, Nelson, 1:504
Miles, Robert, 7:43, 45
Milgram, Stanley, 5:**161–163**, 6:2,
7:571
authority, 1:215
Baumrind, Diana, 1:260
conformity, 2:72
ethics in experimentation,
2:635–636
Holocaust, 3:497
human experiments, 3:60

institutional review board, 4:42
shock experiments, 3:62–63
social influence, 7:595–596
Milgrom, Paul R., 1:207
Miliband, Ralph
capitalist mode of production,
1:447
political science, 6:313–314
Poulantzas, Nicos, 6:404
Milieu therapy, 1:290
Militants, 5:**163–164**
Black Panthers, 1:317, 318–320
Black Power, 1:321, 322
civil rights movement, U.S., 1:552
internal colony, 2:13
Militarism, 5:**164–166**
African socialism, 7:640
civil-military relation, 1:548
communism, 2:36
conservatism, 2:84
coups d'etat, 2:156
law and order, 4:369
military regimes, 5:174–176
neocolonialism, 5:467–468
neoimperialism, 5:470–471
Veblen, Thorstein, 8:597
Military, 5:**166–173**
African Americans, 1:501
alliances, 1:78–81
cognition, 1:597–598
Confederate States of America,
2:67
consequences of service,
5:170–171
counterterrorism, 2:155
desegregation, 2:315
deterrence, 2:333–334
dictatorship, 2:359–360
Huntington, Samuel P., 3:526
Indian National Army, 3:610–611
Janowitz, Morris, 4:171, 172
Jim Crow, 4:201
Lee, Robert E., 4:399–400
Levellers, 4:414
lying, 4:524
militarism, 5:164–165
military regimes, 5:174–176
mobilization, 5:214–215
morale, 5:170
motivation, 5:170
national defense, 2:259–262
power elite, 6:417, 418
preemptive strike, 6:431–432
recruitment, 5:168–169

rites of passage, 7:258
Selective Service, 7:391–392
servitude, 7:463
socialization, 5:169–170
society and, 5:166–167
Southern politics, 6:348
space arms race, 1:178–179
subaltern, 8:190–191
technology, 5:167–168
training, 5:169–170
women, 5:169
See also Civil-military relation
Military authoritarianism, 1:213–214
Military aviation industry, 1:232–233
Military Commissions Act (U.S.
2006), 3:394
Military draft. *See* Selective service
Military force. *See* War
Military Government in Europe
(Lemkin), 3:296
Military-industrial complex, 5:168,
173–174, 9:50–51
Eisenhower, Dwight D., 2:555
militarism, 5:165
power elite, 6:417
Military Reconstruction Act (U.S.
1867), 7:111, 113
Military regimes, 5:**174–177**
civil-military relation, 1:548
Duvaliers, 2:468–469
Khmer Rouge, 4:262–263
Killing Fields, 4:265
militarism, 5:165
repression, 7:174–175
Military spending
opportunity costs, 6:47
weapons industry, 9:50
See also Public finance
Military tribunals, Guantánamo Bay,
3:394
Militias
right wing, 7:248
white supremacy, 9:86
Mill, James, 3:200, 4:424, 5:**177–178**,
7:336, 8:488
Mill, John Stuart, 5:**178–180**
Austrian economics, 1:210
autonomy, 1:225
blue collar and white collar, 1:339
Campbell, Donald, 1:426
Comte, Auguste, 2:62
exchange value, 3:40
freedom, 3:198
happiness, 3:415
Harris, Abram L., Jr., 3:427

increasing returns, 7:219, 220
interest rates, 3:151
justice, 4:237–238
laissez-faire, 4:335
liberalism, 4:425
liberation, 4:429
libertarianism, 4:437
liberty, 4:440
merit goods, 5:97
noncompeting groups, 5:514–515
objective utility, 8:557
Ricardo, David, 7:243
scientific method, 7:363
social justice, 4:241, 242
stationary state, 8:117–118
subjective utility, 8:558
tyranny of the majority,
8:478–479
utilitarianism, 8:553
welfare economics, 9:63
zero population growth, 9:174
Mille Lacs Band of Chippewa Indians et
al., Minnesota et al. v., 5:428
Millenarianism, 8:561
Millennium Development Goals
(UN), 3:273, 8:525, 9:39–40
Millennium Ecosystem Assessment,
2:263
Miller, Arthur, 5:44
Miller, George A., 1:597
Miller, J. Hillis, 2:310, 4:464
Miller, Jon D., 5:362
Miller, Mark J., 3:581, 582
Miller, Merle, 1:481
Miller, Merton, 2:549, 5:235
Miller, Neal, 1:277
Miller, Warren, 1:100, 425,
5:**180–181**
Miller, William Ian, 7:321–322
Miller v. California, 6:13, 8:652–653
Millet, Kate, 7:473
Milliken v. Bradley (1974), 2:314, 317,
7:17, 201
Million Man March (1996),
1:317–318
Mills, C. Wright, 5:**181–183**
corporations, 2:140
Dahl, Robert Alan, 2:219
elites, 2:565
elitism, 2:567
labor unions, 8:516
Lazarsfeld, Paul Felix, 4:375
Lowi, Theodore J., 4:506
Lynd, Robert and Helen, 4:528
political parties, 6:307

power elite, 6:417–418
Veblen, Thorstein, 8:597
Weimar Constitution, 5:482
white collar employment,
2:584–585
Mills, Edwin, 3:50–51, 5:**183–184**
Milner, Alfred, 1:349
Milner, Henry, 2:59
Milosevic, Slobodan, 5:**184**,
9:168–169
Milton, Friedman, 1:270
Mimesis, 5:370
See also Representation
Mimetic forces
organization-environment theory,
6:71
organization theory, 6:70
Mincer, Jacob, 1:271, 3:507–508, 9:4
Mind. *See* Consciousness
Mind, Self, and Society (Mead), 3:385
Mind, theory of. *See* Theory of mind
Mind-body connection
consciousness, 2:79–80, 81–82
functionalism, 3:231–232
mood, 5:276
Mind-body dichotomy. *See*
Knowledge; Psychoanalytic theory
The Mind of Primitive Man (Boas),
1:345
Mind reading. *See* Theory of mind
Minerals, 5:437–438
Mines, land. *See* Landmines
Minh, Duong Van, 8:614
Mini-systems, 9:152
Minimand, 6:6
Minimax theorem. *See* Zero-sum
games
Minimization, 5:**185–186**, 6:5–6
Minimum wage, 5:**186–187**
description, 9:5
excess supply, 3:36
labor, 4:303
labor demand, 4:314
labor economics, 2:514
labor law, 4:317
natural rate of unemployment,
5:435, 436
Mining industry, 5:**187–190**
bauxite, 1:261
Boer War, 1:349, 350
coal
Appalachia, 1:151
industrial accidents, 1:8
common market, 2:28–29
copper, 2:130–131

diamond, 2:355–357
gold, 3:339–340, 342–343
Rhodes, Cecil, 7:239, 240
silver, 7:512–513
townships, 8:406
Ministry of Health and Family Welfare
(India), 5:392–394
Ministry of International Trade and
Industry (MITI Japan), 1:444
Minnesota, Near v. (1931), 1:475
Minnesota et al. v. Mille Lacs Band of
Chippewa Indians et al., 5:428
Minnesota Population Center,
6:25–26
Minorities, 5:**190–193**
agenda setting, 1:48
assimilation, 1:188–191
baby boomers, 1:235, 236
banking, 1:250
buraku, 1:388–389
California Civil Rights Initiative,
1:416
cities, 1:541
citizenship, 1:542–543
coalition, 1:587, 588
colonialism, 2:12
colorism, 2:17
Columbus, Christopher, 2:21
Congress, U.S., 2:74
cooperatives, 2:125
crony capitalism, 2:180
cultural rights, 2:197–198
digital divide, 2:366–367
discrimination audits, 1:208–210
elite theory, 2:562–564
ethnic fractionalization, 3:6–8
ethnomethodology, 3:19
ghettos, 3:311–314
gifted and talented education,
3:*316*, 316–317, 316*t*
glass ceiling, 3:325–326
hard-core unemployed, 3:421, 422
Latinos, 4:357–361
low and high culture, 2:205
mobility, 5:211
multiracial meritocracy,
5:100–101
neighborhood effects, 5:461–463
neighborhoods, 5:463
New Deal coalition, 5:498
race, 7:5
racial discrimination, 2:393–396
realist theory, 7:99
repression, 7:175
schooling oppositionality, 6:49–51

Minorities, *continued*
  social science, 7:317–318
  voting, 8:646
  voting rights, 8:651–654
  welfare, 9:60–61
  xenophobia, 9:158–161
  See also names of specific minority groups; Model minority
Minorities, middleman. *See* Middleman minorities
Minorities, model. *See* Model minority
Minority, model. *See* Model minority
Minority Education and Caste (Ogbu), 6:34
Minority Enterprise Small Business Investment Companies (MESBIC), 1:440, 441
Minsky, Hyman, 1:252, 3:145–146, 5:193–194
  casino capitalism, 1:455–456
  economic depression, 2:304
  lender of last resort, 4:410
  Wall Street, 9:8
Minstrelsy, 5:194–195
  Bamboozled, 1:243, 244, 245
  blackface, 1:326–327
  Jim Crow, 4:198–199
  Sambo, 7:312, 313, 314
Minty Alley (James), 4:168
Mintz, Sidney W., 3:163, 5:195–196
  Caribbean, 1:448
  materialism, 5:19
Minutemen Civil Defense Corps, 1:365
Mirabeau, Marquis de. *See* Quesnay, François
Miracles, 5:196–197
Miranda rights. *See* Interrogation
Miranda v. Arizona (1966), 2:461, 8:233, 9:33
Mirrlees, James, 5:465
Mirror representation. *See* Constituency
The Mirth of Nations (Davies), 2:23
MIRVs (Multiple independently targeted reentry vehicles), 9:31, 49
Misanthropy, 5:198–199
Misattribution, 1:600
Miscarriage, 1:3
Miscegenation, 5:199–200
  biological determinism, 2:326
  blackness, 1:328, 329
  blood and bloodline, 1:335–336
  Coloreds (South Africa), 2:15–16
  colorism, 2:18

hybridity, 3:535
interracial marriage, 4:616–619
interracial sex, 7:467–470
phenotype, 6:243–244
race mixing, 7:26–28
racial democracy, 2:282
Thurmond, Strom, 8:361
whitening, 9:90
Misconduct, whistle-blowers, 9:79–81
Misery index, 5:200–202, *201*
Mises, Ludwig Edler von, 5:202–203
  bureaucracy, 1:390, 392
  business cycles, 1:211
  conservatism, 2:84, 85
  Hayek, Friedrich August von, 3:435
  Hurwicz, Leonid, 3:529
  libertarianism, 4:437, 438
  neoliberalism, 5:474
  ordinality, 6:57
  voluntary unemployment, 8:637
Mishan, Edward J., 2:150
Mishnah, 6:78
Mishra, Santosh, 4:501
Misogyny, 5:203–205, 7:473
Misrecognition, 1:359
Missile Technology Control Regime (MCTR), 1:177
Missiles, 1:177, 6:184, 9:31, 49
Missingness is at random (MAR), 3:391
Missionaries, 1:41, 5:205–206
  East Indian diaspora, 2:473
  travel and travel writing, 8:443–444
Mississippi
  civil rights movement, U.S., 1:551, 552
  Confederate States of America, 2:66
  voting rights, 8:651–652
Mississippi Bubble (1719-1720), 1:378, 428
Mississippi Company, 4:366
Mississippi River, flood control, 5:433
Missouri Compromise, 7:545
Missouri ex. rel. Gaines v. Canada (1938), 3:505
Misspecification tests. *See* Specification tests
Mitchell, Clarence, 5:384
Mitchell, Deborah, 9:68
Mitchell, Margaret, 1:304, 3:346–348
Mitchell, Wesley Clair, 4:518, 5:206–207, 500

business cycle theories, 1:410
  Koopmans, Tjalling, 4:288
Mitchell, Wisconsin v. (1993), 3:431
MITI (Ministry of International Trade and Industry, Japan), 1:444
Mitterrand, François, 2:374
Mixed race persons. *See* Multiracials
Mixed races. *See* Race mixing
Mixed strategy, 5:207–208, 9:177
Mixtecs, 6:426
MKULTRA, 4:111
MLM (Multilevel modeling), 3:390–391
MM theorems, 3:141–142
MMT (Methylcyclopentadienyl manganeses tricarbonyl), 5:541
MNC (Mouvement National Congolais), 4:517–518
Mnemohistory, 2:8
MNR (Movimiento Nacionalista Revolucionario), 7:234
Mnrovia Group, 6:62
Moa, Pío, 3:186
Mob psychology. *See* Herd behavior
Mobile telephones. *See* Cellular technology
Mobility, 5:208–212
  Blau, Peter M., 1:332
  Caribbean, 1:448–449
  caste, 1:460
  cities, 1:540
  credentialism, 2:166–167
  destabilization, 2:320
  Gautreaux residential mobility program, 3:259–260
  glass ceiling, 3:325–326
  intergenerational transmission, 4:88–90
  Japanese Americans, 4:174
  social
    family values, 3:96
    fascism, 3:103
    intergenerational, 8:533
    intragenerational, 8:533
    schooling oppositionality, 6:49
    upward, 8:533–535
Mobility, intergenerational. *See* Intergenerational mobility
Mobility, lateral, 5:212–213
Mobility, upward. *See* Upward mobility
Mobilization, 5:213–215, 214*t*
  Asian American politics, 6:322
  caste, 1:458, 460

Castro, Fidel, 1:466, 467
Chinese Revolution, 1:520, 521
Christian Democracy, 2:276
civil disobedience, 1:546
class conflict, 1:570
collective action, 2:5–6
Coloreds (South Africa), 2:17
communism, 2:35–36
community economic development, 2:41
community power studies, 2:43, 44
conservatism, 2:85
dictatorship, 2:360
elites, 2:565–566
Indian National Congress, 3:611–612
liberation movements, 4:433
lobbying, 4:474
peace movements, 6:182–183, 184
political participation, 6:154
Roma, 7:279
social movements, 7:603–607
Mobilization for Youth, 9:24, 25
Mobilization of bias, 5:518
Mobs. *See* Herd behavior
Mobutu, Joseph, 4:518, 5:215–217
Moch, François, 9:157, 158
Moche, 8:631
Mode (mathematics), 5:*217*, 217–218
measures of central tendencies, 1:487–488
See also Descriptive statistics
Mode of production, 5:218–220
Asiatic
described, 5:219
primitive communism, 2:35–36
capitalist, 1:445–447
convergence theory, 2:117
described, 5:220
primitive communism, 2:37
rate of exploitation, 7:70–71
transitional conjunctures, 2:77–78
class, 1:562, 563
class conflict, 1:571
collectivism, 2:11
corporate social responsibility, 2:137–138
exploitation, 3:65
feudal, 1:562
labor, 4:301
latifundia, 4:352–354

primitive communism, 2:37
transitional conjunctures, 2:77–78
lumpenproletariat, 4:516, 517
primitive accumulation, 6:463–464
primitive communism, 2:37–38
slave, 1:562, 7:531–533
class conflict, 1:569
cliometrics, 1:581, 582
internal colony, 2:13–14
primitive communism, 2:37
Time on the Cross, 8:366–367
transitional conjunctures, 2:77
Model, economic. *See* Economic model
Model minority, 5:220–222
Asian American politics, 6:322–323
Asian immigrants, 3:564
Chinese Americans, 1:514
Japanese Americans, 4:173, 174, 175
A Model of Balance-of-Payments Crises (Krugman), 2:212
Model selection tests, 5:222–224, 8:598
Model T, 1:218, 3:77
Modeling (social science). *See* Models and modeling
Models and modeling, 5:224–226
cognition, 1:597
developmental psychology, 2:350
disability, 2:375–376, 377
exchangeability, 3:41–42
mathematics in the social sciences, 5:25–28
maximum likelihood regression, 5:41–43
model selection tests, 5:222–224
peer influence, 6:202
phobia, 6:263
quantitative methods, 5:113
social leaning perspective, 7:602–603
socialization, 7:647
See also names of specific models; Economic model
Moderates, 1:488–489, 5:226–228
Modern liberty, 4:439
Modern Politics (James), 4:168
Modern portfolio theory. *See* Risk-return tradeoff
Modern racism. *See* Racism

The Modern World System (Wallerstein), 5:466, 9:9, 153
Modernism, 5:228–230
literature, 4:463–464
postmodernism, 6:395–397
primitivism, 6:465, 466
subjectivity, 8:198
underdevelopment, 8:490–491
Modernity, 5:230–232
Afro-Cuban culture, 6:80
alienation, 1:75
Caribbean, 1:447–448
Christian fundamentalism, 3:236
civilization, 1:557
class, 1:562–563
collective memory, 2:8
comedy, 2:23
communalism, 2:30
consumption, 2:106, 107
destabilization, 2:320–321
development in sociology, 2:346–347, 348
fundamentalism, 3:234
Jews, 4:195–196
lifestyles, 4:446
race and religion, 7:24–26
Rand, Ayn, 6:8
reflexive, 3:314–315
religiosity, 7:162
socialism, 7:638
tradition, 8:420
Veblen, Thorstein, 8:595–596
vulnerability, 8:657
Wallerstein, Immanuel, 9:10–11
Wolf, Eric, 9:106
Modernity and Self-Identity: Self and Society in the Late Modern Age (Giddens), 4:446
Modernity and the Holocaust (Bauman), 3:496
Modernization, 5:232–234
caste, 1:459
clash of civilizations, 1:560
conformity, 2:72
democracy research, 7:191
democratization, 2:289–290
demography, 2:294
developing countries, 2:335
development economics, 2:344–345
development theory, 2:337, 339
plumbing, 6:281–282
telecommunications industry, 8:316
zero population growth, 9:174

Modigliani, Franco, 5:**234–235**
  consumption function, 2:109, 110
  demand, 2:270
  efficient market hypothesis, 2:549
  inheritance, 4:35
  IS-LM model, 4:159
  life-cycle hypothesis, 4:441–442
  Modigliani-Miller theorems, 5:235
  rules *vs.* discretion, 7:293
Modigliani-Miller theorems,
  5:**235–236**
  capital structure, 3:141
  dividend policy, 3:141–142
  efficient market hypothesis, 2:549
  leverage, 4:416
  Markowitz, Harry M., 4:609
  Modigliani, Franco, 5:234
Mogensen, Vernon, 6:22
Mohamed, A. Rafik, 2:354
Mohammed. *See* Muhammad
Mohanty, Chandra Talpade, 3:270
Moivre, Abraham de, 1:486, 2:416
Moldova, 2:30
Moles (spies). *See* Intelligence
Mollenkoph, John, 8:543
Möller, F. Max, 1:185
Molotov-Rubbentrop Pact (1939),
  9:149
Moment generating function,
  5:**236–237**
Moments. *See* Descriptive statistics
Monaco, 1:544
Monarchism, 5:**237–238**
  conservatism, 2:83, 84
  Hamilton, Alexander, 3:413
  left wing *vs.,* 4:403
Monarchy, 1:396–397, 5:**238–240**
  American Revolution, 1:103
  Aristotle, 1:175
  checks and balances, 1:495
  Chinese Revolution, 1:519
  democracy, 2:273
  dictatorship, 2:360
  divine right, 2:421–422
  feudalism, 3:135
  Hussein, King of Jordan,
    3:530–531
  Kshatriyas, 4:291
  Magna Carta, 4:556–557
  monarchism, 5:237–238
  sovereignty, 8:38
Monarchy, absolute. *See* Monarchism;
  Monarchy
Monarchy, constitutional, 3:203,
  4:556–557, 5:**240–241**

Monarchy, heredity. *See* Monarchism;
  Monarchy
Mondragon Cooperative Corporation
  (MCC), 1:112, 2:125
Monet, Claude, 7:93
Monetarism, 5:**242–243**
  central banks, 1:477–480
  Chicago School, 1:502
  conservatism, 2:85
  endogenous money, 5:256–257
  inflation, 4:24
  Keynesian economics, 2:512
  microfoundations, 5:141
  money, 5:252
  quantity theory of money, 6:660
  rules *vs.* discretion, 7:293–294
  Thatcher, Margaret, 8:335
Monetary base, 5:**243–246**, 260–261
Monetary History of the United States
  (Friedman and Schwartz), 3:368,
  370
Monetary policy, 6:**293–296**, 294*t*
  balance of payments, 1:238–240
  bull and bear markets, 1:386
  business cycles, 1:403
  capital flight, 1:434
  central banks, 1:477–480
  Chamberlain, Neville, 1:489
  conditionality, 2:65
  conservatism, 2:85
  cross of gold, 2:180–181
  currency, 2:209
  currency devaluation and
    revaluation, 2:211–212
  demand for money, 5:255
  dirty float, 2:375
  economic sterilization, 8:139–140
  employment, 2:582–583
  euro, 3:22–23
  exchange rates, 3:37–40
  exogenous money, 5:258–259
  Friedman, Milton, 3:218–219
  interest rates, 4:85–86
  international economics, 2:509
  Keynes, John Maynard, 4:261
  liquidity, 4:459
  loans, 4:473
  Lucas, Robert E., Jr., 4:510
  Lucas critique, 4:511
  macroeconomics, 4:542
  monetarism, 5:242–243
  monetary base, 5:244
  monetary theory, 5:246–249
  money, 5:249–252
  moral suasion, 5:283

natural rate of interest, 4:77, 78
  nominal interest rates, 4:87
  Phillips curve, 3:112
  political business cycles, 1:406
  real business cycles, 1:407, 408
  Ricardian equivalence, 7:241
  rules *vs.* discretion, 7:293–294
  supply of money, 5:260–261
  Treasury view, 8:444–445
Monetary production economy. *See*
  Production
Monetary theory, 5:**246–249**
  bimetallic controversy, 3:151
  classical economics, 2:504
  Divisia monetary index,
    2:422–423
  Hayek, Friedrich August von,
    3:434, 435
  Law, John, 4:366
  liquidity, 4:459
  money, 5:249–252
  Patinkin, Don, 6:171–172
  Taylor rule, 8:286
  Tobin, James, 8:378–379
  See also Quantity theory of money
*Monetary Trends in the United States
  and the United Kingdom* (Friedman),
  3:217
Monetary unions, 3:39, 5:251
Money, 5:**249–253**
  cost-benefit analysis, 2:150–151
  currency appreciation and
    depreciation, 2:209–210
  currency devaluation and
    revaluation, 2:211–212
  Divisia monetary index,
    2:422–423
  euro, 3:22–23
  hot, 3:504
  interest rates, 4:84–85
  liquidity, 4:459
  monetary base, 5:243–245
  monetary policy, 6:293
  monetary theory, 5:246–249
  neutrality of, 5:490–491
  peasantry, 3:98
  purchasing power of, 3:151
  quantity theory, 6:659–660
    Fisher, Irving, 3:151
    Friedman, Milton,
      3:217–218, 219
    Hume, David, 3:520
    Hume process, 3:521
  soft, 1:424
  Tobin, James, 8:378–379

See also Currency; Exchange rates

Money, demand for, 5:**253–256**
central banks, 1:478
currency appreciation and depreciation, 2:209
Law, John, 4:366
liquidity trap, 4:461–462

Money, Employment, and Inflation (Barro and Grossman), 1:255

Money, endogenous, 1:478, 5:**256–258**, 258–259

Money, exogenous, 5:**258–260**
central banks, 1:478
inflation, 4:24

Money, high-powered. *See* Monetary base

Money, hot. *See* Hot money

Money, inside. *See* Inside money

Money, Interest, and Prices (Patinkin), 6:171

Money, neutral. *See* Neutrality of money

Money, quantity theory of. *See* Quantity theory of money

Money, supply, 5:**260–261**
central banks, 1:478, 480
cross of gold, 2:180–181
currency, 2:209
currency appreciation and depreciation, 2:209
economic depression, 2:304, *305*
endogenous money, 5:256–257
exogenous money, 5:258–259
inflation, 4:24
liquidity, 4:459
monetarism, 5:242–243
monetary base, 5:243–245
rules *vs.* discretion, 7:293–294

Money, time value. *See* Discounted present value

Money and Trade Considered (Law), 4:366

Money growth rule, 3:218–219

Money illusion, 3:151, 4:81–82, 5:**261–263**

Money laundering, 5:**263**
See also Hot money

Money market instruments, 4:134

Money markets, 3:147

Money multiplier. *See* Multiplier

Monism. *See* Monotheism

Monitoring, self. *See* Self-monitoring

Moniz, António Moniz, 4:475

Monkey trial. *See* Scopes trial

Monks, 4:166–167

Monnet, Jean, 2:28–29

Monocentric models. *See* Spatial theory

Monogenesis, 7:39

Monophysite churches. *See* Oriental Orthodox churches

Monopolistic competition, 2:**56–57**
as competition, 2:50, 51, 52–53
price setting and price taking, 6:452, *452*
product quality, 6:654

Monopoly, 5:**264–265**
antitrust, 1:144
bubbles (economics), 1:378
capitalist mode of production, 1:446
consumer protection, 2:103
creative destruction, 2:163
credentialism, 2:166
deregulation, 2:309
distortions, 2:414
economic growth, 2:491
Fabianism, 3:73
imperfect competition, 2:52–53
increasing returns, 7:219–220
internal colony, 2:14
Kalecki, Michał, 4:247
Leninism, 4:412
loan pushing, 4:470
Microsoft, 5:142–143
monopolistic competition, 2:56–57
price setting and price taking, 6:*451*, 451–452
prices, 6:456
privatization, 5:419
technological change, 1:491
Tobin's Q, 8:379, 380
trade quotas, 6:672
underdevelopment, 1:110, 8:489–490
Wall Street, 9:7–8, 8

Monopoly capitalism, 5:**266–267**

Monopsony, 5:**267–268**
discrimination, 2:391
imperfect competition, 2:52
monopoly *vs.*, 5:264
price setting and price taking, 6:452, *452*

Monotheism, 5:**268–271**, 8:340
diffused, 8:633
Judaism, 4:219, 220–222
polytheism, 6:367
theism, 8:341

Monroe, Bill, 1:341

Monroe, James
Gabriel (Prosser), 3:245
Monroe Doctrine, 5:272, 470

Monroe Doctrine, 5:272, 470

Mont Pelerin Society, 3:435, 5:**272–273**, 473–474, 9:38

Montagnard Constitution (France), 2:66

Montagu, Ashley, 2:326, 5:**273–274**, 529–530

Montalva, Eduardo Frei, 1:77

Montana, United States Department of Commerce v., 1:154

Monte Carlo experiments, 5:**274–275**
cointegration regression, 8:518–519
uniform distribution, 2:418
unit root regression, 8:517–518

Monte Verde, 1:170

Montelius, Oscar, 1:166

Montesquieu, Charles Louis de Secondat, Baron de, 1:119, 127, 495
Cantillion, Richard, 1:429
civil society, 1:553
laissez-faire, 4:337
political sociology, 8:3
republicanism, 7:188
separation of powers, 7:448, 449

Montezuma II, 2:147, 148

Montgomery, Isaiah T., 1:325

Montgomery (AL), 1:551

Monumental sculpture, Olmecs, 6:39

Mood, 5:**275–277**, 277

Mood congruent recall, 5:**277–278**

Mood dependent recall. *See* Mood congruent recall

Moody, Dwight, 3:234

Moon, Sun Myung, 7:258

Moonies, 7:258

Moore, Barrington, 5:**278–279**, 8:6

Moore, Gareth, 1:390

Moore, George Edward, 4:259, 8:553

Moore, Gordon, 5:136, 137

Moore, Michael Francis, 3:79–80

Moore, Richard B., 1:330

Moore, Robert, 8:542

Moore, Wilbert, 1:562–563, 6:77

Moore's law. *See* Moore, Gordon

Moral development, 4:286–287

Moral domain theory, 5:**279–280**

The Moral Economy of the English Crowd in the Eighteenth Century (Thompson), 4:301, 8:254

Moral entrepreneurs, 2:353

The Moral Equivalent of War (James), 4:169
Moral hazard, 5:**280–282**
  insurance, 4:50
  insurance industry, 4:41
  lender of last resort, 4:410
  overlending, 6:94, 95
  sharecropping, 7:491
Moral Majority, 2:86, 3:96
Moral panic theory, 9:167–168
Moral philosophy, 6:**254–257**
  common good, 2:25
  moral sentiments, 5:282
  Scottish moralists, 7:367–370
  social science, 7:615
Moral psychology, 4:286–287
Moral realism, 7:**95–96**
Moral sentiments, 5:**282–283**
Moral suasion, 5:**283**
Moral universalism. *See* Universalism
Morales, Evo, 1:570, 2:451
Morality, 5:**283–286**
  business ethics, 2:635
  civil disobedience, 1:545, 546
  communitarianism, 2:39
  conflict, 2:70
  conservatism, 2:84, 85
  crime and criminology, 2:170
  death and dying, 2:248
  Durkheim, Émile, 2:465–467
  euthanasia and assisted suicide, 3:26–28
  hierarchy of needs, 5:451
  jurisprudence, 4:232–233
  just war, 4:235–237
  Kohlberg, Lawrence, 4:286–287
  law, 4:363, 364
  legal systems, 4:406
  moral domain theory, 5:279–280
  moral realism, 7:95
  moral suasion, 5:283
  relativism, 7:156–157
  slave trade, 7:539
  slavery, 7:542–545
  terrorists, 8:330
  values, 5:469
  zombies, 9:181
Morality and inequality, 5:**286–288**
Morbidity and mortality, 5:**288–293**
  changes in, 8:657
  civil wars, 1:556
  crude, 3:127
  demographic transition, 2:291
  demography, 2:293–294

hypertension, 3:538–539
  industrial accidents, 1:9
  industry-based, 9:4
  natural disasters, 5:433–434
  obesity, 9:58
  population growth, 6:378–379
  population studies, 6:381, 382
  wars, 9:17–18
  See also Death and dying
More, Thomas, 2:40, 4:239, 8:561
Moreno, Jacob, 5:476
Moreno/Morena, 1:328, 329, 5:**293–295**
Morgan, Augustus de, 4:481
Morgan, Gareth, 1:392
Morgan, J. P., 9:8
Morgan, Lewis Henry, 1:92, 4:272
  archaeology, 1:166
  determinism, 2:323
  matriarchy, 5:28, 29
  primitive communism, 2:38
Morgan, Mary, 2:3
Morgan, Thomas Hunt, 2:432
Morgenstern, Oskar
  choice in economics, 1:524
  game theory, 3:250, 8:556, 643, 9:176–177
  risk, 7:252
  subjective utility, 8:557
  zero-sum game, 9:176–177
  See also Von Neumann-Morgenstern utility
Morgenthau, Hans, 5:**295**, 420
Morning-after pill. *See* U.S. Food and Drug Administration (FDA)
Morocco, 1:139, 6:62–63
Morrell, Robert, 3:106–107
Morrill Land-Grant College Act (U.S. 1862), 2:341, 8:8
Morrill Land-Grant College Act (U.S. 1890), 8:8
Morris, Amandad Sheffield, 1:25–26
Morris, Henry M., 2:162
Morris, William, 8:561
Morrison, Toni, 2:17
Morrow, James, 6:37
Mortality. *See* Morbidity and mortality
Mortality bias, 8:574
Mortality salience, 7:**311–312**, 8:327
Mortgages, 1:97, 3:146, 4:473
Mortimer, Thomas, 1:385
Morton, A. L., 3:482
Morton, Samuel, 2:325
Mosca, Gaetano, 2:562, 563, 8:3
Moscoso, Teodoro, 6:44, 45

Moses, Robert, 5:**296**, 8:536
Moses, Wilson, 1:315
Mosher, Clelia, 7:480–481
Moskos, Charles C., 5:414
Moss, Carlton, 3:347
Moss, John E., 3:200
Mossadegh, Mohammad, 1:483–484, 4:144, 5:**296–297**
Mossadeq, Mohammed. *See* Mossadegh, Mohammad
Mossin, Jan, 3:141
Most-favored-nation status, 3:281, 9:143
Motherhood, 5:**297–300**
  attachment theory, 1:67, 195–196
  Bowlby, John, 1:363
  Brazelton, T. Berry, 1:369
  day care, 2:245–246
  fertility, 3:128–129
  matriarchy, 5:29
  out-of-wedlock births, 1:306, 307
  rites of passage, 7:258
  Scarr, Sandra Wood, 7:341
  single, 3:116
  wage penalty, 3:116–117
Mothers of the Plaza del Mayo, 9:110, 112
Motion Picture Association of America, 3:140
Motion picture industry. *See* Film industry
Motion studies. *See* Time and motion studies
Motivation, 5:**300–302**
  achievement, 1:14–15
  altruism, 1:88–89
  caste, 1:460
  choice in psychology, 1:526
  collective action, 2:5–6
  creativity, 2:164–165
  Freud, Sigmund, 3:211
  ideal type, 3:546–547
  leaders, 4:377
  leadership, 4:377, 378, 381
  military, 5:170
  personality, 6:219
  relativism, 7:156–157
  self-determination theory, 7:407–408
  social comparison, 7:576–577
  Taylorism, 8:287
Mott, Lucretia, 9:113
Mouffe, Chantal, 6:396
Mound Bayou, MI, 1:325
Mounds, archaeology, 1:165–166

Mount Auburn Cemetery (MA), 1:393

Mountain Meadows massacre (1857), 2:188

Mountain people, Appalachia, 1:150

Mountbatten, Louis, 4:203, 204

Mourides, 1:41

Mourning, 3:239

Mouvement National Congolais (MNC), 4:517–518

Mouzelis, Nicos, 3:314

Movement of the Fifth Republic, 1:494–495

Movie industry. *See* Film industry

Movimento Negro Unificado, 1:329

Movimiento Nacionalista Revolucionario (MNR), 7:234

Moving average (MA), 1:227–228

Moving average model. *See* Autoregressive models

Moving equilibria. *See* Social system

Moving to Opportunity, 3:260, **5:302–304**

Mowrer, O. H, 1:277

Moynihan, Daniel Patrick, 3:191, **5:304–305**
  benign neglect, 1:283–284
  black dysfunctionality hypothesis, 3:327
  culture of poverty, 2:206
  Lewis, Oscar, 4:419
  Moynihan Report, 5:305–306
  urban poverty, 6:411

Moynihan Report, **5:305–307**
  culture of poverty, 2:206
  education in the U.S., 2:540
  Lewis, Oscar, 4:419
  lifestyles, 4:445
  matriarchy, 5:30
  Moynihan, Daniel Patrick, 5:304
  Tally's Corner, 8:264
  urban poverty, 6:411

Mozambique
  African socialism, 7:641
  blackness, 1:330
  civil wars, 1:554
  Machel, Samora, 4:532–533

Mozetic, Gerald, 1:212

MPC (Marginal propensity to consume), 1:6–7

MPL (Marginal product of labor). *See* Marginal product of labor (MPL)

MRI (Magnetic resonance imaging), 5:483–484, 485

MSA (Metropolitan Statistical Areas), 7:134, 135

MSY (Maximum sustainable yield), 6:91, *92*

Muddy Waters, 1:343

Mugabe, Robert, 5:**307–308**

Muhammad, 1:533, 5:**308–309,** 9:155
  Islam, 4:154–155
  jihad, 4:197
  legal systems, 4:406
  Mecca, 5:57

Muhammad, Elijah, 5:**309–310,** 380, 381, 8:619
  black conservatism, 1:311
  black nationalism, 1:316, 317
  Malcolm X, 4:563, 564
  Muslims, 5:348

Muhammad, Wallace, 5:381

Muhammad, Warith Deen, 1:317

Muhammad Ali (boxer). *See* Ali, Muhammad (US boxer)

Muhammad Ali (Memet). *See* Ali, Muhammad (Egyptian military leader)

Mulatto escape hatch, 5:**310–312**

Mulattos, 5:**312–314**
  blackness, 1:328, 329
  Boricua, 1:355
  Coloreds (South Africa), 2:15–16
  mulatto escape hatch, 5:310–312
  mutiracials, 5:332
  race, 7:4
  race mixing, 7:27, 28

Mullainathan, Sendhil, 2:142

Müller, F. Max, 2:194

Mulroney, Brian, 6:662

Multi-City Study of Urban Inequality (MCSUI), 5:**314–315**

Multi-site research, 1:123

Multicollinearity, 5:**315–316,** 7:138–141

Multiculturalism, 5:**316–318**
  Boricua, 1:355
  citizenship, 1:543
  Creole, 2:168–169
  creolization, 2:169–170
  cultural rights, 2:197–198
  cultural studies, 2:200
  education, 3:327
  ethnicity, 3:10–11
  feminist sociology, 7:672
  Gans, Herbert J., 3:256
  Harlem, 3:423
  Harlem Renaissance, 3:425
  identity, 3:555
  Latinos, 4:360

majoritarianism, 4:558
melting pot, 5:71–73
nonblacks, 5:514
pluralism, 6:283–284
race-conscious policies, 7:38
race relations, 7:29
tradition, 8:421
working class, 9:132
xenophobia, 9:158–161

Multidimensional Inventory of Black Identity (MIBI), 5:**318–319**

Multidisciplinary research. *See* Transdisciplinary research

Multidivisional corporations, 6:72

Multifibre Arrangement (MFA), 6:672, 673

Multifinality, 5:**319–320**

Multilateral Investment Guarantee Agency (MIGA), 9:137

Multilateralism, 1:296, 297, 5:**320–321,** 8:452–453, 509–510

Multilevel modeling (MLM), 3:390–391

Multilevel-subsidiary corporations, 6:72–73

Multimedia. *See* Microelectronics industry

Multimodal distribution, 1:488

Multinational corporations. *See* Transnationalism

Multiparty systems, 5:**321–323**
  Democratic Party (U.S.), 2:286–288
  democratization, 2:288
  Liberal Party (U.K.), 4:423–424
  plurality, 6:285–286
  political parties, 6:307
  Republican Party (U.S.), 7:185–187
  See also One-party states

Multiple births, 5:**323–324**

Multiple determinism, 5:486

Multiple equilibria, 2:127–128, 5:**324–326**

Multiple-factors theory, 3:75

Multiple genders, alternatives, 3:270–272, 6:663

Multiple independently targeted reentry vehicles (MIRVs), 9:31, 49

Multiple intelligences theory, 5:**326–327**
  described, 4:72
  talent, 8:262

Multiple personalities, 5:**327–329**

Multiple price lists, 8:579, 580

Multiplex. *See* Symbols

Multiplier, 4:245, 5:**329–330**

Multipliers, Lagrange. *See* Lagrange multipliers

Multiracial meritocracy, 5:**100–101**

Multiracial movement, 5:**331–332**

Multiracials
    classification, 5:514
    Coloreds (South Africa), 2:15–16
    creolization, 2:169
    critical race theory, 2:175
    multiracial meritocracy, 5:100–101
    race mixing, 7:26–28

Multiracials in the United States, 5:**332–333**
    blood and bloodline, 1:336
    colorism, 2:17–18
    mulatto escape hatch, 5:311–312
    mulattos, 5:312–313
    multiracial movement, 5:331
    racial classification, 7:40
    racial identification, 3:549

Multisector models, 5:**333–335**

Multivocality. *See* Symbols

Mumford, Lewis, 2:332
    urban studies, 8:541
    urbanization, 8:546

Mummery, Albert Frederick, 1:378, 4:128, 8:488

Muncie, IN, 4:527–528

Mundell, Robert, 2:209, 5:335–336

Mundell-Fleming model, 5:**335–337**, 8:417

Mundial Upheaval Society. *See* Wolf, Eric

Mundt, Robert J., 1:82

Munich Pact, 9:149

Municipalization, 5:419

Münsterberg, Hugo, 5:**337**

Muqaddimah: An Introduction to History (Ibn Khaldūn), 2:486, 491, 3:545

Murder, 5:**338–341**
    See also Genocide

Murdock, George P., 3:83, 8:88, 92

Murphy, Antoin, 1:428, 429

Murphy, Kevin, 1:502, 2:478, 479, 6:56

Murray, Charles, 3:160, 7:22
    biological determinism, 2:326
    intelligence, 4:73
    racial achievement gap, 1:15–16
    social exclusion, 7:588–589
    underclass, 8:486

Murray, Henry, 1:14

Murray, Pauli, 3:121, 4:199, 5:408–409

Murray v. Maryland (1936), 3:505

Murray v. Pearson (1935), 4:625

Murrow, Edward R., 4:214

Murth, John F., 3:173

Murthy, Narayana, 2:137

Museveni, Yoweri, 5:**341–342**, 6:12

Musgrave, Richard, 3:144

Musgrave, Robert A., 5:97

Mushrooms, sacred. *See* Psilocybin

Music, 5:**342–345**, 9:103
    African diaspora, 1:40
    Arab, 1:161
    Black Arts Movement, 1:310
    Black Power, 1:321
    bluegrass, 1:341–342
    blues, 1:342–343, 3:425, 426
    bop, 4:177
    bossa nova, 4:178
    calypso, 1:417–419
    Celtic, 9:142
    classical, 1:575–576
    entertainment industry, 2:601, 602–603
    ethnomusicology, 3:19–20, 5:342–345
    folk, 9:142
    Internet, 4:106–107
    modernism, 5:230
    popular, 9:141–142
        jazz, 4:177–178
        Rastafari, 7:68–69
        youth culture, 9:167
    recording industry, 7:115–116
    reggae, 7:127–129
    rock 'n' roll, 7:268–269
    rock steady, 7:127, 128
    ska, 7:127–128
    soul, 7:268
    swing, 4:176–177
    theater, 8:338
    Woodstock, 9:120–121
    world, 9:141–142
        jazz, 4:177–178
        popular music, 6:377
    See also Hip hop; Jazz

Music, psychology of, 5:**345–346**

Music and Dance of the Tewa Pueblos (Kurath and Garcia), 2:224

Muslim Brotherhood, 1:299

Muslim League (Pakistan), 2:76

Muslims, 5:**346–349**
    biased policing, 6:290

bin Laden, Osama, 1:298–300
    caste, 1:459, 462
    Christianity, 1:530
    The Church, 1:533
    clash of civilizations, 1:559, 560
    cleavages, 1:578
    concentration camps, 2:64
    Coptic Christian Church, 2:132
    ethnic conflict, 3:2
    gold industry, 3:343
    hate crimes, 3:431
    Hinduism, 3:478–479
    Hussein, Saddam, 3:534
    Islamic economics, 2:510
    jihad, 4:196–197
    Jinnah, Mohammed Ali, 4:203–204
    missionaries, 5:206
    Muhammad, 5:308–309
    Muhammad, Elijah, 5:309–310
    Raj, 7:56
    Roman Catholic Church, 7:280
    sin, 7:519
    social movements, 7:606–607
    women
        femininity, 3:118
        veils, 3:118, 8:602–604
    xenophobia, 9:158, 161
    See also Islam

Muslims, black. *See* Nation of Islam (NOI)

Musselwhite, Charlie, 1:343

Mussolini, Benito, 5:**349–350**
    Facism, 3:103–104
    hegemony, 3:455
    Michels, Robert, 5:132
    Nazism, 5:449
    World War II, 9:148

Mutesa, Edward, 6:12

Muth, John F., 1:20, 2:110, 3:50, 51

Mutual assured destruction (MAD), 2:5, 9:31

Mutual deterrence, 1:177, 2:**334–335**, 7:215, 216

Mutual exchange. *See* Reciprocity

Mutual funds, 4:135–136, 6:73

Mutual UFO Network, 8:507

Mutually assured destruction. *See* Mutual deterrence; Retaliation

My Lai massacre, 8:614–615

My Struggle (Hitler). *See Mein Kampf* (Hitler)

Myanmar
    AIDS/HIV, 1:65
    anticolonial movements, 1:139

Thant, U., 8:334

Myers-Brigg Type Inventory. *See* Equilibrium in psychology; Jung, Carl; Myers-Briggs Type Indicator (MBTI)

Myers-Briggs Type Indicator (MBTI), 4:230

Myerson, Roger B., 1:207

Myint, Hla, 1:5, 4:309

Myopia. *See* Farsightedness

Myopia, alcohol. *See* Steele, Claude M.

Myrdal, Gunnar, 5:350–352
   An American Dilemma, 1:93–96, 3:467, 5:389
   backwash effects, 1:236
   benign neglect, 1:283
   Bunche, Ralph Johnson, 1:388
   charitable foundations, 3:184
   Clark, Kenneth B., 1:560, 561
   Cox, Oliver C., 2:158
   cumulative causation, 2:207
   Green Revolution, 3:164
   Herskovits, Melville J., 3:467
   neutral rate of interest, 4:79
   research, 5:389
   Stockholm School, 8:154
   underdevelopment, 8:490
   wage discrimination, 2:405
   welfare state, 9:73

The Mystery of Capital: Why Capitalism Triumphs in the West and Fails Everywhere Else (De Soto), 2:28, 319, 4:346

Mysticism, 5:352–353
   cults, 2:188
   death and dying, 2:248
   magic, 4:554–555
   Sitting Bull, 7:522
   Turner, Nat, 8:467–468

Mystics and Zen Master (Merton), 1:385

Mystification, 5:353–355

Myth and mythology, 5:355–358
   Battle of the Little Big Horn, 1:258–259
   cognitive dissonance, 1:599
   Confederate States of America, 2:67
   creation, 5:446–447
   death and dying, 2:247
   diaspora, 2:356–357
   hope, 3:501
   Lévi-Strauss, Claude, 4:417
   lost cause, 2:67

malinchistas, 4:564–565
Malinowski, Bronislaw, 4:566–567
matriarchy, 5:28
racial democracy, 2:282–283
self-, 5:371
unidentified flying objects, 8:507
zombies, 9:181

The Myth of the Negro Past (Herskovits), 3:466, 467

Mythologiques (Lévi-Strauss), 4:417

N

N-dimensional vectors, 8:600

N-person theory, 3:250

NAACP. *See* National Association for the Advancement of Colored People

NAC (Native American Church), 1:457

NAC (North Atlantic Council), 5:545

Nadarya-Watson Estimation, 5:528–529

Nader, Ralph, 5:359–360

Nader's Raiders, 5:359, 360–361

Nadle, 3:271

NAEP (National Assessment of Educational Progress), 1:10, 15, 5:381–382

NAFTA (North American Free Trade Agreement). *See* North American Free Trade Agreement (NAFTA)

Nāgārjuna, 5:146

Nagasaki, 9:30, 52, 150

NAGB (National Assessment Governing Board), 5:381

NAGC (National Association for Gifted Children), 3:317

Nagel, Ernest, 7:118

NAGPRA (Native American Graves Protection and Repatriation Act) (U.S. 1990), 1:395, 5:427

Nagy, Imre, 3:523, 524

NAICU (Nonaccelerating inflation capacity utilization rate), 3:224

Nail, John E., 3:424

Nairobi, Kenya, 8:546

NAIRU (Nonaccelerating inflation rate of unemployment). *See* Natural rate of unemployment

Naive psychology. *See* Theory of mind

Nakao, Keiko, 6:27

Nakosteen, Robert, 8:589

NAM (Non-Aligned Movement), 1:466, 5:513, 541–542

Namenang, A. Bame, 3:107

Namibia, 2:63

Naming fallacy, 8:574

Nanak, 7:508–509

Nancy, Jean-Luc, 6:398, 399, 400

Nanotechnology, 3:241, 5:361–363

Napalm, 8:614

Napoléon Bonaparte, 3:408, 4:516–517, 5:363–366
   coups d'etat, 2:156
   dictatorship, 2:359
   Egyptian archaeology, 1:165
   French Revolution, 3:204

Napoleon complex, 5:366–367

Napoleonic Code (1804), 4:405

Napoleonic Wars, 5:365–366, 367–369, 417

Napster, 7:115–116

NARAL Pro-Choice America, 3:216

Narayan, Jaya Prakash, 4:170

Narayanan, K. R., 1:458

Narcisse, Clairvus, 9:181

Narcissism, 3:213, 5:369–370, 453, 8:597

Narrative of the Life of Frederick Douglass, an American Slave, Written by Himself (Douglass), 2:439

Narratives, 5:370–372
   abduction, 8:508
   critical race theory, 2:175–176
   Douglass, Frederick, 2:439
   myth and mythology, 5:355–357
   personality, 6:219
   qualitative methods, 5:111
   realist theory, 7:98
   rumors, 7:296
   sociology, 7:663
   storytelling, 8:160–161

NARS (National Agricultural Research Systems), 3:377

Narula, Smita, 1:463

NASA (National Aeronautical and Space Administration), 3:388

Nash, Adam, 3:294

Nash, John F., Jr., 5:373–374
   mixed strategy, 5:207
   noncooperative games, 5:517

Nash equilibrium, 5:374–375, *375*
   bargaining solution, 5:373
   central banks, 1:479
   common knowledge rationality games, 2:26
   game theory, 3:252
   noncooperative games, 5:517
   prisoner's dilemma, 6:473
   screening and signaling games, 7:372
   subgame perfection, 8:193–194

Nash equilibrium, *continued*
  upward mobility, 5:208
Nasser, Gamal Abdel, 1:299,
  5:**375–377**, 7:307
    Arab-Israeli War of 1967, 1:154,
      5:377
    coups d'etat, 2:156
    Hussein, Saddam, 3:532
    Lebanese civil war, 4:396
    nationalism, 1:160
    United Arab Republic, 8:521–522
Nast, Thomas, 1:452, 5:**377–378**,
  7:186
Nation, 5:**378–379**
  civil wars, 1:554
  communalism, 2:31
  defined, 5:416, 420, 421
  ethnicity, 3:10
  Huntington, Samuel P.,
    3:525–526
  liberation, 4:429
  most-favored, 9:143
  national defense, 2:259–260
  postnationalism, 6:397–398
  society, 7:650
  See also Nation-state
Nation building
  Caribbean, 1:448
  decolonization, 2:256
  Gilded Age, 3:318–319
  land claims, 4:340
  nation-states, 5:421–422
Nation of Islam (NOI), 5:**379–381**
  black capitalism, 1:439
  black nationalism, 1:316–318
  blackness, 1:328
  civil rights movement, U.S., 1:552
  Malcolm X, 4:563–564
  Muhammad, Elijah, 5:309–310
  Muhammad Ali, 1:74
  Muslims, 5:348
  vindication movements, 8:619
*The Nation-State and Nationalism in
  the Twentieth Century* (Guibernau),
  5:421–422
The Nation-State and Violence
  (Giddens), 3:314
Nation-states, 5:**420–423**
  citizenship, 1:542, 543, 544
  city-state *vs.*, 1:544
  civil liberties, 1:546
  collective memory, 2:8
  colonialism, 2:11–12
  communalism, 2:31
  confederations, 2:68–69

defined, 5:379, 412, 422
democracy, 2:273
European Union, 3:23
gesellschaft, 3:266–267
globalization, 3:332
land claims, 4:340–341
legal systems, 4:406
liberation movements, 4:431, 432,
  433–434
liberty, 4:439
markets, 4:607
national defense, 2:260
nationalism and nationality,
  5:416–417
one-party, 6:41–42
political neutrality, 5:489–490
postnationalism, 6:397–398
representative and participatory
  democracy, 2:284
security, 5:411–413
as state, 8:104–105
statelessness, 8:112–114
world-system, 9:153
See also State
National Advisory Commission on
  Civil Disorders, U.S. *See Kerner
  Commission Report* (1968)
National Aeronautical and Space
  Administration (NASA), 3:388
National Agricultural Research
  Systems (NARS), 3:377
National American Graves Protection
  and Repatriation Act (U.S. 1990),
  7:169
National and Community Service
  Trust Act (U.S. 1993), 5:414
National Asian Pacific American Legal
  Consortium, 3:431
National Assembly (France)
  left and right, 4:400–401
  left wing, 4:402
  right wing, 7:247
National Assessment Governing Board
  (NAGB), 5:381
National Assessment of Educational
  Progress (NAEP), 1:10, 15,
  5:**381–382**
National Association for Gifted
  Children (NAGC), 3:317
National Association for the
  Advancement of Colored People
  (NAACP), 5:**382–386**
    Birth of a Nation (film), 1:304
    black nationalism, 1:316
    blackness, 1:328
    Boas, Franz, 1:345

Brown v. Board of Education
  (1954), 1:374, 375
California Civil Rights Initiative,
  1:416
civil rights, 1:550
civil rights movement, U.S., 1:551
Congress of Racial Equality, 2:75
Du Bois, W. E. B., 2:459–460
Garvey, Marcus, 3:258
Harris, Abram L., Jr., 3:427
Houston, Charles Hamilton,
  3:505
Jim Crow, 4:200
King, Martin Luther, Jr.,
  4:268–269
lynchings, 4:526
White, Walter, 9:81–82
National Association of Broadcasters,
  1:441
National Bureau of Economic
  Research (NBER), 6:658–659,
  7:103–104, 103*t*
National Center on Fathers and
  Families (NCOFF), 3:106
National Coalition of Anti-Violence
  Programs, 3:431
National Collective Identity (Hall),
  5:421
National Committee for Buraku
  Liberation (Japan), 1:389
National Committee to Combat
  Fascism. *See* Black Panthers
National Committee to End the War
  in Vietnam, 8:614–615
National Compensation Survey, 9:128
National Consumer Cooperative
  Bank, 9:28
National Council on Women's Rights
  (Brazil), 9:109, 111
National debt, 5:**386–387**
  central banks, 1:480
  Hamilton, Alexander, 3:413
  loan pushing, 4:469–471
  loans, 4:473
  Ricardian equivalence, 7:241
  Ricardian vice, 7:241–242
  Ricardo, David, 7:243
National defense, 2:257–259,
  259–262
    Chamberlain, Neville, 1:489
    preemptive strike, 6:431
National deficit. *See* National debt
National Democratic Alliance (NDA),
  8:569
National Diet (Japan). *See The Diet
  (Japan)*

National Economic Association, 5:**387–390**

National Education Longitudinal Study (NELS), 5:**390–392**

National Environmental Policy Act (U.S. 1969), 2:606

National Excellence Report (1993), 3:315

National Family Health Surveys (India), 5:**392–394**

National Farm Workers of America (NFWA). *See* United Farm Workers of America (UFWA)

National Federation of Coffee Growers of Colombia, 1:595

National Flood Insurance Program (NFIP), 5:432

National Foundation on the Arts and Humanities Act (U.S. 1965), 3:372

National Geographic (periodical), 5:**394**

National Geographic Society, 5:394

National Guard, U.S., Kent State University shooting, 8:615

National Head Start Association, U.S., 3:437

National Head Start/Public School Early Childhood Transition Development Study (1991-98), 3:439–440

National Health and Nutrition Examination Survey (NHANES), 1:347, 7:190, 9:59

National health insurance, 5:**395–396**
managed competition, 2:54–55
Medicare, 5:62–63
socialized medicine, 5:65–66

National Health Service, U.K. (NHS), 2:54

National Heart, Lung, and Blood Institute, 1:347

National identity, 5:417, 420, 422

National income accounts, 5:**397–405**, *400*, 401*t*, 402*t*
balance of payments, 1:238–240
economic growth, 2:486–487
green, 6:52
input-output matrix, 4:41
nominal income, 5:511
rate of profit, 7:74
restitution principle, 7:213

National Income and Outlay (Clark), 5:400

National Indian Youth Council, 1:98

National Industrial Recovery Act (U.S. 1935), 5:494

National Infrastructure Advisory Council, U.S., 8:656

National Institute for Occupational Safety and Health Act (U.S.), 1:8–9

National Institute for Standards and Technology, 1:583

National Institute of Child Health and Human Development, 5:406–407, 499

National Institute of Mental Health (NIMH), 3:323, 9:27

National Institute on Aging, 3:292, 5:499

National Institute on Mental Health, 3:292

National Institutes of Health (NIH), 1:347, 5:499

National Labor Relations Act (U.S. 1935), 4:302, 303, 316–317, 5:494–495, 496, 8:516

National Labor Relations Board (NLRB), 4:303, 317

National Labor Union (NLU), 4:302

National Levelers Association (Japan). *See* National Committee for Buraku Liberation (Japan)

National Liberation Army (China), 1:520

National Liberation Front (FLN), 1:139, 140, 257–258, 8:613–614, 625–626

National Longitudinal Study of Adolescent Health, 5:**405–407**

National Longitudinal Survey of Labor Market Experience, 5:407

National Longitudinal Survey of Youth (NLSY), 2:238, 5:**407–408**, 6:148

National Minority Purchasing Council (NMPC), 1:441

National Movement for the Establishment of the Forty-ninth State, 1:320

National Museum of the American Indian Act (U.S. 1989), 7:169

National Nanotechnology Initiative (NNI), 5:361–362

National Opinion Research Center (NORC), 5:407, 6:27

National Organization for Women (NOW), 3:120–121, 123, 216, 5:**408–409**

National Origins Act (U.S. 1924), 3:579, 5:430

National Party (South Africa), 1:42, 147

National policy. *See* Public policy

National product, 6:52

National Republican Congressional Committee (NRCC), 7:187

National Republican Senatorial Committee (NRSC), 7:187

National Research Act (U.S. 1974), 3:60, 63, 4:33

National Review, 2:85

National Rural Center, 9:28

National Sample Survey (India), 5:**409–411**

National Science Foundation, U.S.
American National Election Studies, 1:100
nanotechnology, 3:241
New Immigrant Survey, 5:499

National security, 5:**411–413**
Central Intelligence Agency, U.S, 1:480–485
civil liberties, 1:547
Cold War, 2:4
counterterrorism, 2:154–155
death and dying, 2:248
defense, 2:257–259
Huntington, Samuel P., 3:526
international relations, 4:101
Japanese American incarceration, 3:600
Jervis, Robert, 4:185–186
Kissinger, Henry, 4:274–275
League of Nations, 4:385
militarism, 5:165
national defense, 2:259–262
political realism, 7:96–97
privatization, 9:51
terrorists, 8:331

National Security Act (U.S. 1947), 1:481–482

National Security Council, U.S., 2:155, 4:142

National Security Council Executive Committee, U.S. (ExComm), 2:183, 184

National service programs, 5:**413–415**

National Service Trust Fund, 5:414

National Socialism. *See* Nazism

National Socialist German Workers' Party, 5:448–450
fascism, 3:104
genocide, 3:296
Lebensraum, 3:304
See also Nazism

National Survey of American Life (NSAL), 5:415

National Survey of Black Americans, 5:**415–416**

National Survey of Children's Health (U.S. 2003), 1:198

National Survey on Drug Use and Health (NSDUH), 1:21, 2:173

National Teachers Corps., 3:372

National Telecommunications and Information Administration (NTIA), 2:366

National Trades' Union (NTU), 8:514

National Union for People of African Descent, 1:320

National values, 9:70

National Water Carrier project (Isreal), 1:154

National Woman Suffrage Association, 3:120

National Women's Political Caucus, 3:216

National Women's Studies Association (NWSA), 9:119

Nationalism, African. *See* Pan-Africanism

Nationalism, Arab. *See* Pan-Arabism

Nationalism, Caribbean. *See* Pan-Caribbeanism

Nationalism, Jewish. *See* Zionism

Nationalism and nationality, 5:**416–418**

  Algeria, 8:625–626

  Americanism, 1:108

  Arab

    history, 1:160

    Hussein, King of Jordan, 3:531

  bigotry, 1:296

  black, 1:315–318, 4:168

    back to Africa movement, 3:258

    black liberalism, 1:312

    blackness, 1:329

    Garvey, Marcus, 3:258–259

  calypso, 1:418

  Castro, Fidel, 1:465

  centrism, 1:488

  Chinese Revolution, 1:519–521

  classical music, 1:575

  communalism, 2:31

  confederations, 2:68

  conservatism, 2:84, 86

  cosmopolitanism, 2:149

  Creole, 2:168

  creolization, 2:169–170

  Croats, 2:179

  Cuba, 2:186, 187

  Daughters of the American Revolution, 2:241–242

defined, 5:416–417, 421

democratization, 2:289, 290

diaspora, 2:356–357

ethnocentrism, 3:11–12

fascism, 3:103

GATT, 3:282

Hitler, Adolf, 3:486–488

Ho Chi Minh, 3:491–492

Huntington, Samuel P., 3:525–526

Hussein, Saddam, 3:533–534

identity, 3:555

imperialism, 3:587

India, 1:356, 3:611–612

Israel, 1:282–283

jingoism, 4:201–202

Judaism, 4:222

liberation, 4:429

liberation movements, 4:431–432, 433

literature, 4:463

loyalists, 4:508, 509

malinchistas, 4:565

Mau Mau, 5:36–38

Milosevic, Slobodan, 5:184

nation-states, 5:420

nation *vs.*, 5:378

national defense, 2:260

neo-Confederate, 8:619

Olympic Games, 6:40–41

Palestinian, 1:159, 161–162, 6:103–104, 104–107

patriotism, 6:175–176

political sociology, 8:4

Quebecois movement, 6:661–663

queer studies, 6:664–665

Raj, 7:56

reggae, 7:127, 129

religion, 7:160–161

self-determination, 7:405–407

separatism, 7:450–451

Serbs, 7:455

state, 8:104–105

statism, 8:119–120

third world, 8:352

Thompson, Edward P., 8:355–356

Tito, Josip, 8:376

tradition, 8:420–421

Veblen, Thorstein, 8:596–597

white supremacy, 8:618–619, 9:86

xenophobia, 9:161

See also Pan-Africanism; Pan-Arabism; Postnationalism; Transnationalism; Zionism

Nationality. *See* Nationalism and nationality

Nationalization, 5:**419–420**

  Bracero Program, 1:364–365

  Chávez, Hugo, 1:495

  Congress Party, India, 2:76

  copper industry, 2:131

  corporations, 2:140

  Cuba, 2:186

  dependency theory, 2:300

  dirigiste, 2:374

  Hussein, Saddam, 3:533

  Labour Party (U.K.), 4:326

  left wing, 4:403

  Mossadegh, Mohammad, 5:296–297

  Partido Revolucionario Institucional, 6:158

  petroleum industry, 6:231

  Qadhafi, Muammar al, 6:647

  telecommunications industry, 8:314

  transportation industry, 8:437–438

Nations and Nationalism in a Global Era (Smith), 5:422

Native American burial grounds, 1:**394–396**, 7:169

Native American Church (NAC), 1:457

Native American Graves Protection and Repatriation Act (NAGPRA) (U.S. 1990), 1:395, 5:427

Native Americans, 5:**423–428**

  addiction, 1:21

  affirmative action, 1:31

  Appalachia, 1:149

  Battle of the Little Big Horn, 1:258–259

  binary gender alternatives, 3:271

  Black Panthers, 1:319

  blood and bloodline, 1:336

  burial grounds, 1:394–395

  Castaneda, Carlos, 1:456–457

  census, 1:477

  Cherokees, 1:496–498

  Chief Joseph, 1:503–504

  colonialism, 2:12

  Columbus, Christopher, 2:19–21, 22

  concentration camps, 2:64

  confederations, 2:68

  consensus, 2:82–83

  Cortés, Hernán, 2:147–148

  Crazy Horse, 2:159–160

critical race theory, 2:175
cultural relativism, 2:194
dance, 2:223, 224
defined, 5:429–430
digital divide, 2:366
East Indies, 2:476
economics, 7:13
going native, 3:338–339
hallucinogens, 3:411, 412
immigrants *vs.*, 3:577
Incas, 3:601–602
indigenismo, 3:612–614
Inuit, 4:124–126
Iroquois, 4:151–152
Jefferson, Thomas, 4:181
Kroeber, Alfred Louis, 4:290
land claims, 4:340–341
landlords, 4:346
languages, 1:129
latifundia, 4:353
Lowie, Robert, 4:507
lynchings, 4:526
Mankiller, Wilma, 4:586
Means, Russell, 5:53
minorities, 5:191–192
monotheism, 5:271
mysticism, 5:352–353
occupational status, 6:27
oppression, 5:513
Osceola, 6:81–82
passing, 6:166
phenotype, 6:244
political science, 7:20–21
pre-Columbian peoples,
    6:426–427
race, 7:3, 4
race mixing, 7:26, 27
reciprocity, 7:106–107
reincarnation, 7:145, 146
religion, 7:161
repatriation, 7:169
role models, 7:274
schooling, 7:355
Seneca, 7:441–442
Sequoyah, 7:453–455
servitude, 7:463
Sitting Bull, 7:522
suicide, 8:222
Taino, 8:260–261
time, 8:362
totemism, 8:397
Trail of Tears, 8:423–424
treaty federalism, 8:446
tribalism, 8:448–449

unemployment, 5:448
women, 9:108
See also American Indian
    Movement
Native intellectual, 3:99
Natives, 5:**429–430**
    Boricua, 1:355–356
    buraku, 1:388–389
    Caribbean, 1:448
    caste, 1:462
    citizenship, 1:543
    Cook, James, 2:122
    cooperation, 2:123
    cooperatives, 2:123
    corporate social responsibility,
        2:137
    cultural tourism, 2:201–202
    decolonization, 2:257
    defined, 5:429
    desegregation, 2:315
    Diop, Cheikh Anta, 2:369
    ethnic conflict, 3:1
    ethnicity, 3:9
    going native, 3:338–339
    indigenismo, 3:612–614
    indirect rule, 3:617–618
    land claims, 4:340–341
    race, 7:11
    religion, 7:159, 160
    repatriation, 7:168–169
    Stolen Generations, 8:158–159
    totemism, 8:397–398
    treaty federalism, 8:445–446
    tribes, 8:449–451
    See also Indigenous rights
Nativism, 5:429, **430–431**
    Chinese Americans, 1:513
    Creole, 2:168
    ethnocentrism, 3:11–12
    genetic determinism, 2:329
    New York City immigrants, 3:573
    racial slurs, 7:41
    xenophobia, 9:158–161
NATO. *See* North Atlantic Treaty
    Organization
NATO-Russia Permanent Joint
    Council (PJC), 5:546
Natural childbirth, 5:**431–432**
Natural disasters, 5:**432–434**
    death and dying, 2:248
    drought, 2:447–448
    management, 2:381–384
    national defense, 2:260
    prediction, 6:430

race-blind policies, 7:36
refugee camps, 7:124, 125
refugees, 7:127
rumors, 7:295, 296, 297
Natural experiments, 5:**434–435**,
    7:591–592
Natural gas, 1:451
Natural gas industry. *See* Energy
    industry
Natural history, 1:136–137
Natural law, 4:238, 5:**438–439**
    crime and criminology, 2:170
    deviance, 2:352
    moral philosophy, 6:254–255, 256
    naturalism, 5:442
    physiocracy, 6:266–267
    universalism, 8:526
Natural Law and Natural Rights
    (Finnis), 4:365
Natural rate of interest, 4:*77,* 77–**78**,
    78–79
Natural rate of unemployment, 3:218,
    5:**435–437**, 8:499, 503, 9:2, 3
Natural resources
    agricultural economics, 1:58–59
    agricultural industry, 1:62
    air pollution, 6:361
    common land, 2:26–28
    consumption, 6:95
    deforestation, 2:262–264
    Dutch disease, 2:467–468
    nonrenewable, 5:437–438
        legacy effects, 4:404–405
        limits of growth, 4:448
        resource economics,
            7:210–211
    pollution, 6:360
    renewable, 5:437
    rentier class, 1:571
    as resources, 7:211–212
    silver industry, 7:512–513
    solar energy, 8:22–23
    violence and allocation of,
        8:626–628
Natural rights, 4:232, 5:**438–439**
    conservatism, 2:85
    Declaration of Independence,
        U.S., 2:254–255
    Hobbes, Thomas, 3:492–493
    justice, 4:237, 238
    liberty, 4:441
    Locke, John, 4:477
    rule of law, 7:292–293
Natural science, 9:78

Natural selection, 5:**440–441**
  alpha-males, 1:83–84
  biological determinism, 2:326
  Darwin, Charles, 2:227–232
  Dobzhansky, Theodosius,
    2:432–433
  environmental determinism, 2:327
  evolutionary psychology, 3:33–34
  evolutionary theory of kinship,
    4:273, 274
  genetic determinism, 2:329
  Gould, Stephen Jay, 3:352–353
  Mendel's law, 5:83
  model minority, 5:221
  murder, 5:339–340
  Pearson, Karl, 6:191, 192, 193
  race, 7:13
  racism, 7:45
  replicator dynamics, 7:169–170
  sex and mating, 7:471–472
  sexual selection theory, 7:479–480
  Social Darwinism, 2:233
  social system, 7:626
  sociobiology, 7:654
  supreme being, 8:230
  tastes, 8:268
  teleology, 8:318
  violence, 8:628
Natural will, 3:266–267
Naturalism, 5:**441–443**
  constructivism, 2:96, 97
  disease, 2:406, 407
  distributive justice, 4:240–241
  realism, 7:92
  theory, 8:343–344
Naturalistic case study. *See* Case
  method
Naturalization, 5:**444–445**
  Asian immigrants, 3:563
  Chinese Americans, 1:513, 514
  Constitution, U.S., 3:578
  Mexican Americans, 5:121
  See also Citizenship
Naturalization Act (U.S. 1790), 5:444
Nature
  laws of, 3:230
  state, 7:84
Nature, state of. *See* State of nature
Nature and nurture. *See* Nature vs.
  nurture
The Nature of Economies (Jacobs),
  4:165
The Nature of Geography (Hartshorne),
  3:304

The Nature of Peace (Veblen),
  8:596–597
The Nature of Prejudice (Allport), 1:81,
  2:111
The Nature of the Firm (Coase), 1:589
Nature vs. nurture, 3:461, 4:184,
  5:**445–446**
  biological determinism,
    2:325–326
  child development, 1:505–508
  children, 1:511–512
  family functioning, 3:88
  femininity, 3:118
  gender preference, 6:434
  genetic determinism, 2:329
  heredity, 3:461
  intelligence, 4:72–73
  IQ controversy, 4:139–142
  Jencks, Christopher, 4:184
  maturation, 5:34, 35
  Mead, Margaret, 5:48
  mental illness, 5:87–88
  meritocracy, 5:99
  Montagu, Ashley, 5:273
  paranoia, 6:128–129
  Scarr, Sandra Wood, 7:340–341
  sibling relationships, 7:506–507
  talent, 8:261
  trait theory, 8:425–426
  twin studies, 8:473–475
Naturwissenchaft, 9:78
Navajo-Hopi Land Settlement Act
  (U.S. 1974), 5:447
Navajos, 3:271, 5:425, 426, **446–448**
Naval power, U.K., 3:171
Nazi Party. *See* National Socialist
  German Workers' Party
Nazi-Soviet Nonaggression Pact
  (1939), 8:511
Nazism, 5:**448–450**
  Anti-Semitism, 9:148
  Arendt, Hannah, 1:173
  Aryans, 1:185–186
  blood and bloodline, 1:336
  census, 1:477
  centrism, 1:488
  Chamberlain, Neville, 1:489, 490
  Churchill, Winston, 1:537–538
  civil disobedience, 1:545
  concentration camps, 2:63, 64
  conservatism, 2:84
  corporatism, 2:140
  critical theory, 2:176
  cultural relativism, 1:123
  destructive obedience, 6:2

  dictatorship, 2:359
  ethics in experimentation, 2:635
  ethnic conflict, 3:2
  eugenics, 3:21, 495
  fascism, 3:104
  German academia, 5:500–501
  ghettos, 3:312, 313
  Gobineau, Comte de, 3:336
  iron curtain, 4:150
  Jung, Carl, 4:231
  Neumann, Franz, 5:482
  Olympic Games, 6:40
  pogroms, 6:288
  political sociology, 8:4
  race, 7:5, 10
  racial slurs, 7:42
  racism, 7:44, 9:148
  repression, 7:175
  Roma, 7:279
  Social Darwinism, 2:233–234
  totalitarianism, 8:295, 394
  Tuskegee syphilis study, 8:473
  weapons of mass destruction, 9:52
  white supremacy, 9:86
  See also Hitler, Adolf; Holocaust
NBAS (Neonatal Behavioral
  Assessment Scale), 1:369
NBTT (Net barter terms of trade). *See*
  Terms of trade
NCLB (No Child Left Behind Act)
  (U.S. 2001). *See* No Child Left
  Behind Act (U.S. 2001)
NCOFF (National Center on Fathers
  and Families), 3:106
NDA (National Democratic Alliance),
  8:569
Ndembu, 8:469–471
Neal, Larry, 1:309
Neanderthals. *See Homo*
  neanderthalensis
Near, Janet P., 9:79
Near v. Minnesota (1931), 1:475
Nebraska Press Association v. Stuart
  (1976), 1:475
Necessities, 5:**451–452**
Nederveen Pieterse, Jan, 2:336
Need for cognition, 5:**452–453**
Needham, Rodney, 1:128, 4:272
Needs, 5:**453–455**
  achievement, 1:14–15
  biological, 5:451, 455
  for cognition, 5:452
  consumerism, 2:104, 105
  consumption, 2:106
  functionalism, 3:232

hierarchy of, 5:451, 453, 454, 455
malnutrition, 4:567–568
Maslow, Abraham, 5:11–12
psychological, 5:451
relative, 5:455
scarcity, 7:340
self-actualization, 7:394–395
social, 5:451, 455
survival, 5:453
wealth *vs.*, 9:44–45
See also Necessities
Needs, basic, 4:567–568, 5:451,
455–456, 7:407–408
Negative campaigning. *See*
Campaigning
Negative Dialectics (Adorno), 2:177
Negative income tax, 3:605–607,
5:**456–457**, 7:590
Negative liberty, 4:439–440
Negative reciprocity. *See* Reciprocity
Negativity. *See* Pessimism
Neglect, 3:44, 6:132, 133
Negotiated settlement, 7:**465–466**
Negotiation, 5:**457–458**
civil wars, 1:554, 556
coalition theory, 1:587–588
Coase theorem, 1:590
codetermination, 1:593
conflict, 2:70
consensus, 2:82–83
diplomacy, 2:370–371
discrimination, 2:391
labor law, 4:303, 316, 317
labor union, 4:325
land claims, 4:341
Lindblom, Charles Edward,
4:452–453
peace process, 6:185–186
screening and signaling games,
7:371
social exchange theory, 7:585–586
social relations, 7:611–612
Negrete, Agustin Lopez, 8:617
Negri, Antonio, 1:447, 7:209
Negritude movement, 3:336
Negro Factories Corporation, 3:258
"The Negro Family: The Case for
National Action" (Moynihan). *See*
Moynihan Report
Negro Fellowship League, 9:77
The Negro Ghetto (Weaver), 9:53
The Negro in the Caribbean
(Williams), 9:97
Negro Labor (Weaver), 9:53
Negro Politicians (Gosnell), 3:351–352

Negros, 5:**458–459**
Fanon, Frantz, 3:99–100
race, 7:4
See also African Americans;
Blackness
Nehru, Jawaharlal, 5:**460–461**
anticolonial movements, 1:139
Congress Party, India, 2:75, 76, 77
democracy, 2:274
Fabianism, 3:74
Indian National Congress,
3:611–612
Jinnah, Mohammed Ali, 4:203,
204
Nasser, Gamal Abdel, 5:376
non-alignment, 5:513
Neighborhood effects, 5:**461–463**,
464
externality, 3:70
pollution, 6:360
slums, 7:551–552
social isolation, 7:601
Neighborhoods, 1:540, 4:445,
5:**463–464**
Neisser, Ulric, 1:598, 3:160, 7:426
*Neither Black nor White: Slavery and
Race Relations in Brazil and the
United States* (Degler), 5:310
Nelson, Charles, 1:228, 2:1
Nelson, Daniel, 8:587
Nelson, Margaret K., 3:116
Nelson, Richard, 1:491, 7:199–200
Nembhard, Jessica Gordon. *See*
Gordon Nembhard, Jessica
Nena, 9:142
*Neo-colonialism: The Last Stage of
Imperialism* (Nkrumah), 5:466, 507
Neo-Destour Party, 1:139
Neo-Malthusianism. *See* Birth control
Neo-Marxism, 2:176–178, 4:101
New Class, 5:492
occupational status, 6:27
Poulantzas, Nicos, 6:404–405
war, 9:17
Neo-Nazis, 5:450, 9:86
Neo-paganism, 6:21
NEO PI-R (Revised NEO Personality
Inventory), 5:487
Neo-Ricardian economics, 2:**519–522**
marginal product of labor, 4:307
surplus, 8:235–236
Neo-Shumpeterians, 4:494
Neobehaviorism, 1:277, 2:477, 8:386
Neoclassical competition. *See* Perfect
competition

Neoclassical economics, 2:**517–519**
agricultural economics, 1:59
business cycles, 1:403
Cambridge capital controversy,
1:419–421
capitalism, 1:439
central banks, 1:478, 479
common land, 2:27
competition, 2:50
cumulative causation, 2:207
economic depression, 2:304
endogenous preferences, 2:586
equilibrium, 2:619, 620
exchange value, 3:40–41
Fisher, Irving, 3:150–152
full capacity, 3:224
history, 2:498
immiserizing growth, 3:583
institutional economics, 2:506
Keynesian economics, 2:511–512
Lagrange multipliers, 4:332–333
liquidity trap, 4:461–462
long period analysis, 4:490
long run, 4:491
marginal product of labor, 4:305,
306, 307
markup pricing, 4:610
Marxist competition, 2:55
migration, 5:157
neo-Ricardian economics,
2:520–521
North-South models, 5:547
optimizing behavior, 6:55
political economy, 6:303
price *vs.* quantity adjustment,
6:453–454
prices, 6:456
quantity theory of money, 6:660
Robinson, Joan, 7:267
satiation, 7:328–329
surplus labor, 4:308–309
unemployment, 8:503
user costs, 8:562
welfare analysis, 9:62–63
Neoclassical growth model,
5:**464–466**
Inada conditions, 3:599
natural rate of interest, 4:77
Solow residual, 8:27–28
Neoclassical realism. *See* Political
realism
Neocolonialism, 5:**466–468**
developing countries, 2:336
development economics, 2:345
indirect rule, 3:617–618

Neocolonialism, *continued*
  internal colony, 2:13
  Lumumba, Patrice, 4:518
  Nkrumah, Kwame, 5:507
  underdevelopment, 8:489
  See also Colonialism
Neoconfederate nationalism, 8:619
Neoconservatism, 5:468–469
  benign neglect, 1:284
  communalism, 2:30
  feminism, 9:115
  left wing, 4:404
  Reagan, Ronald, 7:89
  Republican Party (U.S.), 7:187
  right wing, 7:248
  Thatcher, Margaret, 8:335
  unequal education, 2:538
  See also Conservatism
Neocorporatism. *See* Corporatism
Neoimperialism, 5:470–472, 6:375
  See also Imperialism
Neoinstitutionalism, 5:472–473
  institutional development,
    2:340–341
  organization-environment theory,
    6:71
  organization theory, 6:70
  post-Parsonian American
    sociology, 8:6
  See also Institutionalism
Neoliberalism, 5:473–475
  Bourdieu, Pierre, 1:359
  citizenship, 1:543
  class, 1:564
  Conservative Party (U.K.), 2:87
  cooperation, 2:122
  deregulation, 2:308–309
  developing countries, 2:336
  development theory, 2:338
  international relations, 4:100
  NAFTA, 5:541
  petty bourgeoisie, 1:362
  political economy, 6:304
  Washington Consensus, 5:474,
    9:38–40
  See also Liberalism
Neolithic Revolution
  fertile crescent, 3:125
  Native Americans, 5:424
Neonatal Behavioral Assessment Scale
  (NBAS), 1:369
Neoplatonism, 3:458
Neopluralism, 2:220
Neorealism, 7:97
  international relations, 4:100

national security, 5:412–413
  Waltz, Kenneth, 9:14
NeoRican Jetliner (Carrero), 5:552
Neorricans. *See* Nuyoricans
Neorrigquenco. *See* Nuyoricans
Neoteny, 5:273
Nepotism, 2:398, 405
Nesbitt, Richard, 6:4–5
Nested hypothesis, 3:543–544
Nestorian Church, 1:533
Net barter terms of trade (NBTT). *See*
  Terms of trade
Net exports. *See* Balance of trade
Net investments, 5:398–399
Net reproduction rate (NRR), 3:127
Nethercutt, Casey, 4:372
Netherlands
  bubbles (economics), 1:378
  codetermination, 1:593
  concentration camps, 2:63
  correspondence tests, 2:142
  Dutch disease, 2:467–468
  flower industry, 3:158–159
  international trade, 3:76
  NATO, 5:544–546
Network analysis, 5:475–477
  communication networks,
    5:479–480
  global, 5:480
  post-Parsonian American
    sociology, 8:6
  social capital, 5:481
Networks, 5:477–479
  Chinese diaspora, 1:517–518
  citations, 1:539
  cities, 1:541
  clientelism, 1:579
  communalism, 2:31
  community, 5:476
  crony capitalism, 2:180
  cultural capital, 2:189, 190
  defined, 5:475
  destabilization, 2:320
  egocentric, 5:479–480
  financial, 5:476
  globalization, 3:332–334
  job search, 5:476
  kinship, 5:478
  local, 5:479–480
  microelectronics industry,
    5:136–139
  migration, 5:157–158
  public policy, 5:476
  social exchange theory, 7:585–586

society, 3:240
  soladarity, 8:24
  spatial, 8:541
  thresholds, 5:481
  wage discrimination, 2:404
Networks, communication, 5:478,
  479–481, *480*
Neumann, Franz, 2:176, 5:**481–483**
Neumann, John von. *See* von
  Neumann, John
Neumann, William, 5:108–109
Neurath, Otto, 1:275
Neuroeconomics, 5:301, **483–484**
Neurology. *See* Neuroscience
Neuromancer (Gibson), 2:216, 5:31,
  32
Neuropeptides, 5:551
Neuroscience, 5:**484–485**
  classical conditioning, 1:572–574
  cognition, 1:598
  consciousness, 2:81
  dementia, 2:271–272
  dopamine, 2:436–437
  gender preference, 6:434
  hyperactivity, 3:537–538
  lobotomy, 4:475–476
  memory in psychology, 5:77
  mood, 5:276
  murder, 5:338–339
  personality, 6:219–220
  prejudice, 6:439
  reinforcement theories, 7:146–148
  selective attention, 7:391
  semantic memory, 7:435–436
  serotonin, 7:457–460
  sex and mating, 7:471–472
  sexual orientation, 7:476
  shyness, 7:505
  social psychology, 7:610–611
  stem cells, 8:133–134
  temperament, 8:321
  theory of mind, 8:346–348
Neuroscience, social, 2:330–331,
  5:**485–486**
Neuroticism, 1:145, 3:210, 213,
  5:**486–487**, 7:447–448
Neurotransmitters, addiction, 1:21
Neutral policies, racial. *See* Race-blind
  policies
Neutral rate of interest, 4:78–80
Neutral social science. *See* Value free
  social science
Neutral states, 2:265, 5:**487–489**
Neutrality, political, 5:487, **489–490**,
  513

Neutrality, risk. *See* Risk neutrality

Neutrality of money, 5:**490–491**

Nevile, Jennifer, 2:224

New ageism, 3:308

New Archaeology, 1:167–168

A New Challenge Model of a Volunteer Program (Lee and Brudney), 8:638–640, *639*

The New Class, 4:577, 578, 5:220, **492–493**

The New Class (Djilas), 5:492

New classical economics, 2:**522–524**
  business cycles, 1:403
  central banks, 1:479
  employment, 3:226
  involuntary unemployment, 4:138
  Keynesian economics, 2:512
  Lucas, Robert E., Jr., 4:510
  Lucas critique, 4:511
  monetarism, 5:242–243
  new Keynesian economics, 2:524, 525

New Deal, 5:**493–498**
  conservatism, 2:83, 84–85
  Democratic Party (U.S.), 2:287
  Dixiecrats, 2:429, 430
  federalism, 3:114
  Great Depression, 3:370
  James, William, 4:170
  job guarantee, 4:206
  judiciary, 4:227
  labor, 4:302
  Republican Party (U.S.), 7:187
  rural development, 2:341
  social welfare system, 7:631, 632–633
  social work, 7:634
  subjective utility, 8:557
  urban renewal, 8:536
  voting patterns, 8:648
  Wizard of Oz, 9:105
  See also Roosevelt, Franklin D.

New economic history. *See* Cliometrics

New Frontier, 3:241, 372

New genre theory, 4:381

New Guinea, 3:238, 9:108

New Hampshire, Chaplinsky v. (1942), 7:42

New Haven (CT), 2:42, 219

New History movement, 1:268

New Immigrant Survey, 5:**499–500**

New Immigration, 3:573–574, 575

The New Industrial State (Galbraith), 1:390, 3:246–247

New Jersey, corporations, 2:139, 140

New Jersey Income Maintenance Experiment, 7:590

New Jersey Plan, 2:91

New Jewel Movement (NJM), 3:381–383

New Keynesian economics, 2:**524–526**
  Barro-Grossman model, 1:256
  full employment, 3:226–227
  involuntary unemployment, 4:138
  Keynes, John Maynard, 4:260
  money, 5:252
  new classical economics, 2:524
  Say's Law, 7:337

New Labour (U.K.). *See* Labour Party (Britain)

New Lafayette Theatre, 1:309

New Left Review, 1:112, 8:353, 355

The New Men of Power (Mills), 8:516

New Model Army (NMA), 4:414

New Negro, 1:35

New open economy macroeconomics (NOEM), 8:417

New Orleans (LA)
  African burial grounds, 1:393
  jazz, 4:176

The New Reasoner (periodical), 8:353, 355

New reproductive technologies (NRT), 7:178, 179

New Right, 3:96, 9:114, 115

New Roles and Relevance (Lewis and Wallace), 5:520

New School for Social Research, 1:268, 5:**500–502**

New State Ice Co. v. Liebmann, 3:114

New Testament, 1:530, 532
  See also Bible

New World in the Tropics: The Culture of Modern Brazil (Freyre), 2:282

New York (state)
  abortion, 1:2
  Love Canal, 4:504–505
  Roosevelt, Franklin D., 7:283

New York Board of Trade (NYBOT), 2:153

New York (NY)
  African burial grounds, 1:393–394
  globalization, 8:543
  hip hop, 3:480–481
  labor unions, 8:513–514
  metropolitan area, 8:546
  Moses, Robert, 5:296
  Nuyoricans, 5:552–553
  rent control, 7:165

  urban renewal, 8:536
  urban riots, 8:538–539
  War on Poverty, 9:24–25, 27
  Woolworth Building, 8:631
  See also Harlem

New York (NY), immigrants to, 3:423, **572–576**, 574*t*
  Boricua, 1:356
  Ellis Island, 2:567–569
  Latin American, 3:571, 4:359
  Latinos, 4:359

New York Society for the Suppression of Vice, 1:303

New York Stock and Exchange Board (NYSEB), 9:7–9

New York Stock Exchange, 2:58

New York Times Co. v. United States (1971), 1:475

New York v. Ferber (1982), 6:13

New Zealand
  blood and bloodline, 1:336
  commonwealth, 2:29
  constitutions, 2:94
  Cook, James, 2:122
  cultural resource management, 2:196
  legal systems, 4:406
  urban sprawl, 8:540
  Vietnam War, 8:614

Newberry v. United States, 9:84, 85

Newbold, Paul, 2:3

Newborn development. *See* Child development

Newcomb, Theodore M., 7:596–597

Newell, William Wells, 5:550

Newly industrializing countries. *See* Developing countries

Newman, John Henry, 8:528–529

Newman, Katherine S., 5:462

News. *See* Journalism

News from Nowhere (Morris), 8:561

Newspapers. *See* Journalism

Newton, Huey P., 1:319

Newton, Isaac, 1:137, 4:292–294

Newton, John, 4:468–469

Newton-Raphson algorithm, 5:522

Newyorquino. *See* Nuyoricans

Neysmith, Sheila, 9:122

Nez Perce, 1:503–504

Nez Perce War (1877), 1:503, 504

NFIP (National Flood Insurance Program), 5:432

NFWA (National Farm Workers of America). *See* United Farm Workers of America (UFWA)

Ng, Yew-Kwang, 8:351

NGO. *See* Nongovernmental organizations

Ngo, Dinh Diem, 8:613–614

NGOization, 5:521

NGOs, States and Donors (Hulme and Edwards), 5:520

NGOs (Nongovernmental organizations). *See* Nongovernmental organizations (NGOs)

NHANES (National Health and Nutrition Examination Survey), 1:347, 7:190, 9:59

Nhat Hanh, Thích, 1:385

NHS (National Health Service, U.K.), 2:54

Niagara Falls (NY), 4:504–505

Niagara Movement, 5:383

Nicaragua
   Central Intelligence Agency, U.S, 1:483
   civil wars, 1:554
   Garifuna, 3:257–258
   Iran-Contra affair, 4:142
   land reform, 4:343
   latifundia, 4:354
   Latin American immigrants, 3:572
   Latin American revolutions, 7:235
   Latinos, 4:358, 360
   Sandinistas, 7:319–320

Nicene Creed, 1:533, 534

Niche demographics, 1:29

Nichiren Shōoshū. *See* Buddhism

Nicholas II, Tzar of Russia, 7:304, 8:511

Nichomachean Ethics (Aristotle), 1:175

Nichter, Mark, 1:131

Nickell, Stephen, 8:637

Nickles, Thomas, 6:126

Nicodemus, Kansas, 1:325–326

Nicolau, George, 9:27

Nicolaus, Martin, 9:133

Nicomachean Ethics (Aristotle), 1:275, 3:464, 4:237

Nie, Norman H., 8:606

Nietzsche, Friedrich, 3:182, 5:502–503
   aesthetics, 1:30
   classical music, 1:575
   collective memory, 2:8
   collective wisdom, 2:9
   cultural values, 8:578
   freedom, 3:198
   hermeneutics, 3:462–463

humanism, 3:518

Kariel, Henry S., 4:249

Lefebvre, Henri, 4:400

linguistic turn, 4:457

modernity, 5:231

objectivism, 6:7

objectivity, 6:11

otherness, 6:83

Nigeria
   AIDS/HIV, 1:66
   caste, 1:460
   civil wars, 1:554
   OPEC, 6:65
   quotas, 6:670

Nigger Heaven (Van Vechten), 3:425

Nightmares, 3:210

NIH. *See* National Institutes of Health

Nihilism, 5:502–503

Nikkei. *See* Japanese Americans

Nilotics, 6:12

NIMBY (Not In My Backyard). *See* Neighborhood effects

NIMH (National Institute of Mental Health), 3:323, 9:27

9/11/2001 attacks. *See* September 11, 2001

9/11 Commission, U.S. *See* Kean Commission, U.S.

1924 Declaration of the Rights of the Child, 1:512

1984 (Orwell), 1:390, 5:492, 8:561

Nintendo, 8:611

Nirvāna, 3:211, 5:504–505
   See also Buddhism

Nisbett, Richard, 2:252

Nisei. *See* Japanese Americans

Nishimura, Kazuo, 6:51–52

Nitrogen fertilizers, 3:131–132

Nitrogen fixation, 3:131

Nitrous oxide, 3:378

Nixon, L. A., 9:84

Nixon, Richard M., 5:505–506
   Allende, Salvador, 1:77–78
   benign neglect, 1:283
   campaigning, 1:423
   Chomsky, Noam, 1:529
   desegregation, 2:314
   Dixiecrats, 2:430–431
   Great Society programs, 3:373
   impeachment, 3:584, 585
   income maintenance experiments, 3:606
   journalism, 4:215
   Kerner Commission Report, 4:258
   Khrushchev, Nikita, 4:265

Kissinger, Henry, 4:274, 275
   law and order, 4:370, 371
   Le Duc Tho, 4:398
   Mao Zedong, 4:589
   Moynihan, Daniel Patrick, 5:305
   Nader's Raiders, 5:360
   national service programs, 5:413
   quotas, 6:671
   Rabin, Yitzhak, 7:1
   Republican Party (U.S.), 7:186, 187
   Selective Service, 7:392
   Southern strategy, 8:36–37
   urban renewal, 8:537
   Vietnam War, 8:614–615
   wage and price controls, 9:3
   War on Poverty, 9:28
   Watergate, 9:42–44

Nixon, United States v. (1974), 5:506, 9:43

Nixon, Walter, Jr., 3:586

Nixon v. Condon (1932), 9:84

Nixon v. Herndon (1927), 9:84

NJM (New Jewel Movement), 3:381–383

Nkomo, Joshua, 5:307

Nkrumah, Kwame, 5:506–508
   African socialism, 7:639, 640
   anticolonial movements, 1:139, 140
   Black Power, 1:321
   blackness, 1:330
   Drake, St. Clair, 2:442
   Du Bois, W. E. B., 2:460
   Kaunda, Kenneth, 4:250, 251
   Kenyatta, Jomo, 4:255
   neocolonialism, 5:466, 467
   Organization of African Unity, 6:62
   Pan-African Congresses, 6:113

NLRB (National Labor Relations Board). *See* National Labor Relations Board (NLRB)

NLSY (National Longitudinal Survey of Youth), 5:407–408, 6:148

NLU (National Labor Union), 4:302

NMA (New Model Army), 4:414

NMDA receptor antagonists, 1:90

NMPC (National Minority Purchasing Council), 1:441

NNI (National Nanotechnology Initiative), 5:361–362

NNWS (Non-Nuclear Weapons States), 1:176–177

No Child Left Behind Act (U.S. 2001), 1:10, 400, 2:538, 542–543, 7:201–202

No Exit (Sartre). *See Huis Clos* (Sartre)

The Nobel Memorial Prize for Clive W. J. Granger (Hendry), 2:3

Nobel Peace Prize, 5:**508–510**, 509*t*
    Borlaug, Norman, 2:342
    Bunche, Ralph Johnson, 1:387–388
    Carter, Jimmy, 1:451
    King, Martin Luther, Jr., 1:550
    Kissinger, Henry, 4:275, 8:615
    Le Duc Tho, 4:398, 8:615
    Mandela, Nelson, 4:580, 581
    Nkrumah, Kwame, 5:508

Nobel Prize (Economics), 2:**526–528**, 527*t*
    Becker, Gary S., 1:270
    Coase, Ronald, 1:589
    Debreu, Gerard, 2:249
    Fogel, Robert, 1:582
    Hicks, John R., 3:471–472
    Kahneman, Daniel, 2:251
    Koopmans, Tjalling, 4:287
    Kydland, Finn, 1:407
    Lucas, Robert E., Jr., 4:510
    McFadden, Daniel L., 5:44
    Meade, James, 5:48
    Modigliani, Franco, 5:234
    North, Douglass, 1:582, 5:538
    Prescott, Edward, 1:407
    Selten, Reinhard, 2:506
    Simon, Herbert A., 7:515
    Smith, Vernon L., 7:558
    Smith, Verson, 2:505
    Solow, Robert M., 8:26
    Stigler, George Joseph, 8:144
    Tobin, James, 8:378

Noble Truths. *See* Buddha; Buddhism

Nobles, feudalism, 3:135–136

Noboa, 1:245

Nodes, globalization, 3:332–334

Nodes, stable, 5:**510–511**

NOEM (New open economy macroeconomics), 8:417

Nogueira, Cládio André Gondim, 8:608

NOI (Nation of Islam). *See* Nation of Islam (NOI)

Noise, statistical, 8:**120–121**

Noise, white, 9:**82–83**

Noise Control Act (U.S. 1974), 6:363

Noise pollution, 6:360, **363–364**

Nominal gross domestic product, 5:401, 401*t*

Nominal income, 5:399, **511**

Nominal three-step estimation (NOMINATE), 7:277

Nominal wages, 5:**511–513**, 7:89

Nominalism, 2:406–407

NOMINATE (Nominal three-step estimation), 7:277

Non-Aligned Movement (NAM), 1:466, 5:513, 541–542

Non-alignment, 5:461, **513**
    Castro, Fidel, 1:466
    Cuba, 2:186–187
    neutrality, 5:487–488
    third world, 8:351–352
    Tito, Josip, 8:376

Non-expected utility theory, 3:54, 5:**519–520**

Non-Nuclear Weapons States (NNWS), 1:176–177

Non-voting, 3:351

Non-Voting (Gosnell), 3:351

Non-Walrasian economics. *See* Barro-Grossman model; Patinkin, Don

Nonaccelerating inflation capacity utilization rate (NAICU), 3:224

Nonaccelerating inflation rate of unemployment (NAIRU). *See* Natural rate of unemployment

Nonadditive determinism, 2:**330–331**, 5:486

Nonaggression, 6:7

Nonaligned movement, 5:488

Nonblacks, 5:**513–514**

Noncompeting groups, 5:**514–516**

Nonconformity. *See* Conformity

Nonconstant-sum games. *See* Nonzero-sum games

Nonconvexity, 6:52

Noncooperation movement, 5:460

Noncooperative equilibrium, 3:284
    See also Nash equilibrium

Noncooperative games, 5:**517–518**, 532–533, 6:471–474

Nondecision-making, 5:**518**, 6:413

Nonfamily households, 3:91

Nongovernmental organizations (NGOs), 5:**520–521**
    Bhagwati, Jagdish, 1:293
    business, 1:401
    Club of Rome, 1:584–585
    commonwealth, 2:29
    communalism, 2:31
    corruption, 2:143, 144, 145
    human rights, 3:513

moral suasion, 5:283
    peace, 1:584–585, 6:182
    political sociology, 8:5
    refugee camps, 7:124–125

Nonlinear programming. *See* Linear and nonlinear programming

Nonlinear regression, 5:**521–523**

Nonlinear systems, 5:**523–524**
    butterfly effect, 1:413–414
    catastrophe theory, 1:468–469
    heterarchy, 3:468, 469
    linear systems *vs.*, 4:457
    threshold effects, 8:359–360

Nonmarital births. *See* Out-of-wedlock births

Nonparametric estimation, 5:**524–527**, *525, 526*
    Bayesian econometrics, 1:262–264
    data envelopment analysis, 2:240–241
    large sample properties, 4:348–350
    left and right censoring, 1:474
    statistics in the social sciences, 8:124–125

Nonparametric regression, 2:266–267, 5:525–526, **527–529**, *528*

Nonprofit organizations, 1:401, 3:324

Nonprofit sector. *See* Social economy

Nonrenewable natural resources, 5:**437–438**
    legacy effects, 4:404–405
    limits of growth, 4:448
    resource economics, 7:210–211
    as resources, 7:211–212

Nonretroactivity, 7:292

Nonscalar varianc-covariance matrices, 3:287

Nonspherical errors, 3:287

Nontraded goods, 3:**349**

Nonverbal communication, 2:32, 33, 113, 4:524–525, 5:**529–531**

Nonverbal Communication (Druckman et al), 5:530

Nonverbal Communications (Mehrabian), 5:530

Nonviolent protest. *See* Passive resistance

Nonwhites, 5:**531–532**
    immigrants, 9:90
    racial inequality, 4:6

Nonzero-sum games, 3:250, 251, 5:**532–533**

Nora, Pierre, 2:8

NORC (National Opinion Research Center), 5:407, 6:27

Nordhaus, William D., 1:406, 479, 5:399

Norm of reciprocity, 7:**107–109**

Normal accident theory, 1:9

Normal capacity. *See* Full capacity

Normal democracy, 2:275

Normal distribution, 2:*415,* 415–417
- central limit theorem, 1:486
- chi-square, 1:523
- measures of central tendencies, 1:487–488
- probability distributions, 6:494
- Z-test, 9:182–183

Normalization, 5:**533–534**

Normative ethics, 2:632

Normative forces, 6:70, 71

Normative neutrality, 5:490

Normative social sciences, 2:70, 71, 72, 5:**534–536**

Norms, 5:**536–538**
- autokinetic effect, 1:216–217
- child development, 1:508
- conformity, 2:71, 72
- consensus, 2:82
- corporal punishment, 2:135–136
- critical theory, 2:178
- cultural, 5:537
- cultural distinctions, 2:412, 413
- cultural group selection, 2:192
- destabilization, 2:321
- deviance, 2:352
- dowry and bride price, 2:440–441
- habitus, 3:404, 405
- heteronormativity, 3:470
- institutional development, 2:340
- lay theories, 4:374
- morality, 5:283–286
- Moynihan Report, 5:305–306
- Parsons, Talcott, 6:149
- peer cliques, 6:197–198
- pluralistic ignorance, 3:560–561
- rational choice theory, 7:75
- reciprocity, 7:107–108
- role theory, 7:275–276
- Sherif, Muzafer, 7:495
- social, 1:216–217
- social exclusion, 7:589
- social structure, 7:624
- time, 8:363
- values, 8:581

Norris, Pippa, 2:59, 9:69

The North (global), 5:**542–544**
- gender inequality, 3:625
- Prebisch, Raúl, 6:422–423

Prebisch-Singer hypothesis, 6:424–425

North, Cecil C., 6:27, 7:657

North, Douglass, 1:582, 5:**538–539**

North, Oliver, 4:142, 143, 7:320

North Africa
- AIDS/HIV, 1:65
- anticolonial movements, 1:139
- Islamic fundamentalism, 3:237–238
- population aging, 3:306
- veils, 8:602–604

North America
- archaeology, 1:165–166
- cattle industry, 1:470–471
- day care, 2:245–246
- dependency theory, 2:298–300
- four-field anthropology, 1:116–122
- negro terminology, 5:459
- prehistory, 5:423–424
- Verdoorn's law, 8:608
- women's work, 9:124
- *See also specific countries*

North American Free Trade Agreement (NAFTA), 3:196, 5:**539–542**
- automobile industry, 1:222
- banking industry, 1:253
- bourgeoisie, 1:361
- Clinton, Bill, 1:580
- labor, 4:302
- maquiladoras, 4:593
- trade barriers, 1:255

North American immigrants, 3:**576–580**
- African burial grounds, 1:393–394
- blackface, 1:327
- blood and bloodline, 1:336
- brain drain, 1:367–368
- melting pot, 5:71–73

North Atlantic Council (NAC), 5:545

North Atlantic Treaty Organization (NATO), 5:**544–546**
- bioterrorism, 1:302
- defense, 2:258
- establishment, 9:149
- national defense, 2:261
- role, 9:151
- success, 1:79, 81
- Warsaw Pact, 9:34–35
- Yugoslavian civil war, 9:168–169

North Carolina
- Cherokees, 1:496, 498

Confederate States of America, 2:67

law and order, 4:372

North Korea
- concentration camps, 2:64
- convergence theory, 2:117–118
- democratization, 2:288
- Korean War, 4:288–289
- land reform, 4:343, 344
- left wing, 4:404
- nuclear weapons, 9:48
- one-party state, 6:41–42
- United Nations membership, 8:522

North Piegan, 9:109

North-South models, 5:**546–548**
- dependency theory, 2:298–300
- development economics, 2:345
- development theory, 2:339
- Economic Commission for Latin America and the Caribbean, 2:482
- exploitation, 3:65
- immigration, 3:581
- Prebisch-Singer hypothesis, 6:424–425
- returns, 7:217–218
- terms of trade, 8:325–326

North Star (newspaper), 2:439

North Vietnam. *See* Vietnam War

Northeast Native Americans, 5:425

Northern Alliance, 8:263

Northern Cheyenne (Native Americans), 1:258, 259

Northern Ireland, 2:63, 4:509
- *See also* Ireland

Northern League (Italy), 9:160

Northern Radical Republicans, 1:115

Northern Rhodesia. *See* Zambia

Northside Center for Child Development (New York, NY), 1:561

Northwest Coast Native Americans, 5:425

Norway
- annexation of Svalbard Islands, 1:115
- gender gap, 3:278
- NATO, 5:544–546
- state capitalism, 1:444
- voting rights, 3:185

Norwegian Nobel Committee, 5:508–509

Not In My Backyard (NIMBY). *See* Neighborhood effects

Notes on Social Measurement, Historical and Critical (Duncan), 2:463

Notes on the State of Virginia (Jefferson), 4:181

Notes Towards the Definition of Culture (Eliot), 2:202

Nott, Josiah, 3:336

Nouveaux riches, 5:**548–549**

Novack, Cynthia, 2:224

Nove, Alec, 7:645

Novels. *See* Fiction

Novels, graphic. *See* Comic books

NOW (National Organization for Women), 3:120–121, 123, 216, 5:**408–409**

Nozick, Robert, 2:613, 4:238–239, 240, 241, 424

NPT. *See* Nuclear Non-Proliferation Treaty

NRCC (National Republican Congressional Committee), 7:187

NRDC, Vermont Yankee v. (1978), 2:606

NRR (Net reproduction rate), 3:127

NRSC (National Republican Senatorial Committee), 7:187

NRT (New reproductive technologies), 7:178, 179

NSAL (National Survey of American Life), 5:415

NSDUH (National Survey on Drug Use and Health), 1:21, 2:173

NSS. *See* National Sample Survey (India)

NTIA (National Telecommunications and Information Administration), 2:366

An Introduction to Comparative Administrative Law (Jacobini), 1:23

NTU (National Trades' Union), 8:514

Nu, U., 1:139

Nuclear Non-Proliferation Treaty (1970), 1:176–177, 178, 9:52

Nuclear power industry. *See* Energy industry

Nuclear proliferation, 6:**540–543**, 9:30, 32, 48–49
  Cold War, 2:5
  Waltz, Kenneth, 9:14
  weapons of mass destruction, 9:52

Nuclear Test-Ban Treaty (1963), 2:5

Nuclear war, 1:179, 9:**30–32**

Nuclear weapons, 9:30–32, **47–49**, 52
  arms control, 1:176–177
  arms race, 1:178
  Bush, George H. W., 1:398

Cuban Missile Crisis, 2:183–185
Cuban Revolution, 2:186
defense, 2:258, 259
deterrence, 2:333–334
disarmament, 2:380
intermediate range, 5:544
Jervis, Robert, 4:186
mutual deterrence, 2:334
peace movements, 6:183
United Nations role, 8:525
World War II, 9:150

Nuclear Weapons States (NWS), 1:176–177

Null hypothesis, 8:331

Numbers, law of large. *See* Law of large numbers

Numdial Upheaval Society, 9:105

Nuns, Jainism, 4:166–167

Nuremberg Charter, 9:21

Nuremberg Code (1947), 4:33, 42

Nuremburg Laws (1935), 3:488, 495

Nursery rhymes, 5:**549–551**

Nurture, nature vs. *See* Nature vs. nurture

Nussbaum, Martha C., 4:239
  development in sociology, 2:348
  functionings, 3:234

Nutrient cycling, 3:131

Nutrition, 3:162, 5:**551–552**

Nuyoricans, 5:**552–553**
  Boricua, 1:356
  Latin American immigrants, 3:571
  Latinos, 4:359

NWS (Nuclear Weapons States), 1:176–177

NWSA (National Women's Studies Association), 9:119

NYBOT (New York Board of Trade), 2:153

Nye, Joseph, Jr., 2:259

Nyerere, Julius, 5:513, **553–554**
  African socialism, 7:640
  collectivism, 2:11
  Kaunda, Kenneth, 4:250, 251
  Pan-African Congresses, 6:113, 114

NYSEB (New York Stock and Exchange Board), 9:7–9

O

O-ring theory, 6:**76–77**

OAAU (Organization for Afro-American Unity), 1:317, 321

Oakes, Timothy, 2:201

Oakeshott, Michael, 7:293

OAS (Organization of American States)
  Cuban Missile Crisis, 2:184
  Cuban Revolution, 2:186

OAU (Organization of African Unity), 1:109, 5:554, 6:**62–63**

Oaxaca, Ronald, 1:333, 2:478, 479, 6:**1–2**

Oaxaca decomposition. *See* Blinder-Oaxaca decomposition technique

O'Barr, William M., 1:28

Obedience
  authority, 1:215
  experimental realism, 7:94
  Milgram, Stanley, 5:161–162
  shock experiments, 3:62–63
  social influence, 7:595–596

Obedience, destructive, 1:260, 6:**2–3**

Obese externality, 6:**3**, 4–5

Obesity, 5:552, 6:**4–5**
  body image, 1:346
  Body Mass Index, 1:347, 348
  description, 9:58–59
  as disease, 2:407
  food cues, 6:3
  overeating, 6:89–90
  Schachter, Stanley, 7:342

Obeyesekere, Gananath, 1:428

Obinger, Herbert, 9:70, 73

Object love, 3:213

Objective functions, 6:**5–6**

Objective probability. *See* Probability

Objective tests. *See* Psychometrics

Objective utility, 8:**557–558**

Objective value, 2:520, 8:**577–578**

Objectivism, 2:520, 4:438, 6:**6–8**, 7:95

Objectivity, 6:**8–11**
  Bourdieu, Pierre, 1:359
  choice in economics, 1:524, 525–526
  class conflict, 1:569, 570
  collective memory, 2:7, 8
  epistemology, 2:610
  ethnographic research, 7:193–194
  intersubjectivity, 4:116–117
  Kuhn, Thomas, 4:292–294
  quantification, 6:655
  realist theory, 7:98–99
  social constructs, 7:579
  social justice, 4:241
  universalism, 8:527
  Weber, Max, 9:54–55, 57
  See also Subjectivity

Objectivity in sociology. *See* Value free social science

Objects, women as, 3:118

Objekte, 6:9

Obote, Apollo Milton, 1:109–110, 6:12–13

Obrador, Andres Manuel Luis, 6:159

Obrador, Lopez, 1:571

Obrdlik, Antonin, 2:24

Obregón, Alvaro, 5:130, 131

O'Brien, Margaret, 3:107

Obscenity, 6:13–14
    censorship, 1:476
    conservatism, 2:86
    feminism, 3:121
    racial slurs, 7:41–42

Observation
    hyperactivity, 3:537–538
    hypothesis and hypothesis testing, 3:541, 542
    natural experiments, 5:434–435
    underachievers, 8:484

Observation, participant, 6:14–17
    ethnographic research, 7:193–194
    qualitative methods, 5:110
    reflexivity, 7:122–123

Observational learning. *See* Models and modeling

Obsessions, 6:17–18

Obsessive-compulsive disorder (OCD), 1:146, 6:18–19

Occam's razor, 1:229, 6:19–20

Occasional neutrality, 5:487

Occidental Chemical Corporation (OxyChem), 4:504–505

Occidental Petroleum, 4:505

OCCSCORE (Occupational Score Index), 6:25–26

Occult, 6:20–22

Occupation and Employment Survey, 6:23

Occupational crowding. *See* Crowding hypothesis

Occupational hazards, 6:22–23
    compensating wages, 9:6
    crime and criminology, 2:171–172
    industrial accidents, 1:8–9
    wages, 6:24–25
    whistle-blowers, 9:80

Occupational regulation, 6:23–24
    child labor, 1:509
    noise pollution, 6:364

Occupational safety, 6:24–25
    enforcement, 6:22
    industrial accidents, 1:8–9

    labor law, 4:317
    sweatshops, 8:247–248

Occupational Safety and Health Act (U.S. 1970), 6:25

Occupational Safety and Health Administration, U.S. (OSHA), 1:8–9, 6:22, 364

Occupational Score Index (OCCSCORE), 6:25–26

Occupational segregation. *See* Crowding hypothesis

Occupational status, 6:26–28
    black middle class, 1:313, 314
    Blau, Peter M., 1:332
    blue collar and white collar, 1:337, 339–340
    bureaucrat, 1:392
    Chinese diaspora, 1:517
    class, 1:564
    computers, 2:60
    credentialism, 2:166–167
    crowding hypothesis, 2:181–182
    discrimination, 2:391
    Duncan, Otis Dudley, 2:463
    engineering, 2:594, 595
    lateral mobility, 5:212–213
    socioeconomic status, 7:656–658
    underemployment, 8:493, 494
    wage discrimination, 2:404

Occupations
    classification, 6:26
    noncompeting groups, 5:514–516
    rewards, 6:25–26

Occupied territories (Israel). *See* Gaza Strip; West Bank

OCD (Obsessive-compulsive disorder), 1:146, 6:18–19

Oceania, cattle industry, 1:470

Ochlocracy, 2:284

Ochsner, Albert, 8:140

Ocoee, Florida, 1:328

O'Connor, James, 1:447

O'Connor, Sandra Day
    Grutter decision, 3:392
    Miller v. California, 8:652–653

Octoroons, 1:328, 5:333, 7:4

O'Dell, Jack, 2:13

Odent, Michel, 5:432

O'Donnell, Guillermo, 1:214, 2:290

OECD. *See* Organization for Economic Cooperation and Development

OECD Employment Outlook (2004), 8:504–505

Oedipal period, 3:212

Oedipus complex, 6:28–30

Oedipus Trilogy, 6:28

OEO (Office of Equal Opportunity), 9:26–27

Of Body (Hobbes). *See De Corpore* (Hobbes)

Of Man (Hobbes). *See De Homine* (Hobbes)

Of Mice and Men (Steinbeck), 5:366

Of the Balance of Trade (Hume), 3:520

OFCs (Offshore financial centers), 6:30, 32

Offering, initial public. *See* Initial public offering (IPO)

Offermann, Lynn, 4:380, 381

Office of Equal Opportunity, U.S. (OEO), 9:26–27

Office of Immigration Statistics, U.S. (OIS), 5:499

Office of Management and Budget, U.S. (OMB), 5:331, 333

Office of Price Administration, U.S. (OPA), 9:2

Office of Strategic Services, U.S. (OSS), 1:482

Offshore banking, 3:504, 6:30–33

Offshore financial centers (OFCs), 6:30, 32

Offshoring, 1:339, 6:86

Ogbu, John U., 6:33–34
    acting white, 1:17
    oppositional culture, 6:48
    racial achievement gap, 1:16
    schooling oppositionality, 6:49–50

Ogden, Suzanne, 2:35–36

Ogé, Vincent, 3:407

Ogou, 8:634

O'Grady, Kathleen, 2:114

Ohanian, Lee, 3:370

Ohlin, Bertil, 3:448

Ohlin, Lloyd, 9:24

Oikumenê, 1:448

Oil, crude. *See* Petroleum industry

Oil companies. *See* Petroleum industry

"Oil for Food" program, 8:524

Oil lease auctions, 9:103

Oil producing countries, Gulf Cooperation Council, 3:397

Oil shocks, 5:437

OIS (Office of Immigration Statistics), 5:499

Okin, Susan Moller, 4:239

Oklahoma
    black towns, 1:326
    Cherokees, 1:496, 498
    civil rights, 1:549

Tulsa Riot, 8:465–466

Oklahoma, Skinner v. (1942), 2:461

Okner, Benjamin, 8:277

Okun, Arthur, 5:200, 201, 6:35

Okun's law, 6:**35–36**, 8:608

The Old Curiosity Shop (Dickens), 3:301

The Old Regime and the French Revolution (Tocqueville), 8:383, 384

Old Testament, 1:530, 532

Older people. *See* Elderly

Olds, Ransom E., 3:285

Olds Motor Vehicle Company, 3:285

OLG model. *See* Overlapping generations model

Oligarchy, 6:**36–37**
    aristocracy, 1:173–174
    civil society, 1:553
    coups d'etat, 2:156
    description, 3:354
    Lenin, Vladimir Ilitch, 4:411
    managerial class, 4:578, 579

Oligarchy, iron law of, 3:474, 6:36, **37–39**

Oligopoly, 2:53, 57, 6:453, *453*
    competition, 2:50
    film industry, 3:140
    markup pricing, 4:610–611, 612
    stable nodes, 5:510

Oligopsony, 2:53

Oliver Brown, et al. v. Board of Education of Topeka, et al. 387 U.S. 483 (1954). *See Brown v. Board of Education* (1954)

Olmecs, 6:**39**
    human sacrifice, 3:516
    pre-Columbian peoples, 6:426

OLS (Ordinary least squares). *See* Ordinary least squares (OLS)

OLS regression. *See* Ordinary least squares regression

Olson, Mancur, Jr., 2:219–220, 4:83, 7:611–612

Olympic Games, 6:**39–41**
    Carter, Jimmy, 1:451
    Chinese Americans, 1:514–515
    sports industry, 8:67

Oman, Gulf Cooperation Council, 3:397

OMB (U.S. Office of Management and Budget), 5:331, 333

Omi, Michael, 3:175–176

Omnibus Budget Reconciliation Act (U.S. 1993), 1:580

Omnivores, 3:162–163

Omohundro, John T., 1:517

On Becoming a Person (Rogers), 2:31

On Democracy (Dahl), 2:220

On Formal Structures of Practical Actions (Garfinkel), 2:119

On Holiday (Löfgren), 8:566

On Liberty (Mill), 4:424, 440, 8:478, 479, 553

On the Admission of Women to the Rights of Citizenship (Condorcet), 2:66

On the Cunning of Imperialist Reason (Bourdieu), 1:359

On the Genealogy of Morals (Nietzche), 5:503

On the Natural Variety of Mankind (Blumenbach), 1:126

On the Origin of Species (Darwin), 1:126, 166, 2:233, 326, 327, 5:440, 7:13

On the Principles of Political Economy and Taxation (Ricardo), 4:536, 537, 7:243, 244, 245, 246

On the Relations between the Physical and the Moral Aspects of Man (Cabanis), 1:275

On the Scope and Method of Political Economy (Keynes), 5:534

On the Social Contract (Rousseau), 2:284, 3:618, 7:290

On the Theory of the Budget of the Consumer (Slutsky), 7:300

On War (Clausewitz), 9:17

One Continental Congress, 1:103–104

One-Dimensional Man (Marcuse), 2:177, 4:594, 595

One-party states, 6:**41–42**
    Brezhnev, Leonid, 1:370
    dictatorship, 2:358, 359
    first-past-the-post elections, 3:149–150
    Leninism, 4:412
    Mussolini, Benito, 5:350
    See also Competitive party systems; Multiparty systems

Oniki, Hajime, 1:6

Online auctions, 1:207–208

Online business. *See* E-business

Online environment. *See* Cyberspace; Internet

Ontogenetics, 1:25

Ontological naturalism, 5:442

Ontology, 5:502–503
    See also Philosophy; Reality

Oorschot, Wim van, 9:72

OPA (Office of Price Administration), U.S, 9:2

OPEC. *See* Organization of Petroleum Exporting Countries

Open access, fishing industry, 6:92

Open-list systems, 8:655

Open market operations, 6:**42–43**

Open Regular Board, 9:7

Operant conditioning, 6:**43–44**
    behaviorism, 1:276, 277
    reinforcement theories, 7:147, 148
    Skinner, B. F., 7:526
    Skinner box, 7:528

Operating surplus, national income accounts, 5:400–401

Operation Bootstrap, 2:326, 3:571, 4:359, 6:**44–45**

Operation Dodoma, 2:11

Operation Peter Pan, 3:571

Operation Wetback, 5:123

Operationalization, 3:55–56

Opiates, 2:452, 453

Opie, Iona, 5:550

Opie, Peter, 5:550

Opinion, public. *See* Public opinion

Opinion polls, 6:**355–358**
    cross-sectional research, 7:189–190
    happiness, 3:416, 418
    polling, 6:353–355
    pollsters, 6:358–359

Opium, 8:263

Opium Wars, 6:**45–46**

Oppenheim, Paul, 7:118–119

Oppenheimer, Ernest, 2:355

Oppenheimer, Franz, 4:345

Opportunity, Moving to. *See* Moving to Opportunity

Opportunity costs, 1:429, 6:**47**
    specialization, 1:6
    wants, 9:16

Opportunity Funding Corporation, 9:28

Oppositionality, 6:**48–49**

Oppositionality, schooling, 6:**49–51**

Oppression
    Fanon, Frantz, 3:99–100
    gender, 3:121
    nonblacks, 5:513–514

Optimal growth, economic, 2:489–490, 6:**51–53**

Optimism, 6:**53–55**
    baby boomers, 1:235
    black conservatism, 1:311
    locus of control, 4:477–478
    mood, 5:276
    positive psychology, 6:386

Optimism, *continued*
    See also Hope
Optimism, learned. *See* Learned
    helplessness; Seligman, Martin
Optimization. *See* Optimizing
    behavior
Optimizing behavior, 6:**55–56**
    consumer, 2:99–102
    golden rule in growth models,
        3:346
    loss functions, 4:495–502
    Lucas, Robert E., Jr., 4:510
    objective functions, 6:6
    tastes, 8:267
Optimum, Pareto. *See* Pareto
    optimum
Options, 1:163
Options, stock. *See* Stock options
Oral tradition. *See* Storytelling
Orangeism, 4:509
Oranges, 5:438
Orchids, vanilla, 8:583–584
Order, international economic. *See*
    International economic order
Order, law and. *See* Law and order
Order, spontaneous. *See* Hayek,
    Friedrich August von
*Order Flow and Exchange Rate
    Dynamics* (Evans and Lyons), 2:210
Order of Illuminists. *See* Illuminati
Order of liberalization. *See* Trade
    liberalization
Order of the Golden Dawn, 6:21
Ordeshook, Peter, 7:249
Ordinality, 6:**56–57**
    subjective utility, 8:558
    utility function, 8:555–556
    welfare economics, 9:*64,* 64–65
Ordinary least squares (OLS),
    4:**391–394**
    instrumental variables regression,
        4:45–47
    recursive models, 7:117
    serial correlation, 7:455–457
    Tobin, James, 8:379
    two-stage least squares *vs.,* 4:395
Ordinary least squares regression,
    3:286–291, 6:**57–61,** *58, 60*
    autoregressive models, 1:228–229
    cointegration regression, 8:518
    fixed effects regression, 3:155–156
    heteroskedasticity, 3:470
    linear regression, 4:454–455
    regression analysis, 7:138–141

simultaneous equation bias,
    7:515–518
three-stage, 4:394–395
Oregon, Chief Joseph, 1:503–504
Organ inferiority, 5:366
Organic agriculture, 9:41
Organic intellectuals, 4:**66–67**
Organic matter, 3:130, 132
Organization-environment theory,
    6:71–73
Organization for Afro-American Unity
    (OAAU), 1:317, 321
Organization for Economic
    Cooperation and Development
    (OECD)
    brain drain, 1:367–368
    corruption, 2:145
    economic inequality, 9:46–47
    gender gap, 3:279
    international economic order, 4:94
    Jobs Study, 8:504–505
    labor force participation, 4:315
    toxic waste, 8:408
    trade liberalization, 4:428
    transfer pricing, 8:428
    unemployment compensation,
        2:49
    welfare, 9:61
    welfare state, 9:67, 70
Organization for Security and
    Cooperation in Europe (OSCE),
    3:431
Organization man, 6:**61–62**
The Organization Man (Whyte),
    6:61–62
Organization of African Unity (OAU),
    1:109, 5:554, 6:**62–64**
Organization of American States
    (OAS)
    Cuban Missile Crisis, 2:184
    Cuban Revolution, 2:186
Organization of Petroleum Exporting
    Countries (OPEC), 6:*64,* 64–**68,**
    65, 66, 67
    crude oil prices, 5:438, 6:64–65,
        65
    energy industry, 2:588
    establishment, 5:542
    imperfect competition, 2:52
    oil shocks, 5:437
    petroleum industry, 6:230, 231
Organization theory, 6:**68–70**
    Blau, Peter M., 1:332
    bureaucracy, 1:389–391
    bureaucrat, 1:391–392
    leaders, 4:376, 377

leadership, 4:379, 380, 382–383
    transaction cost, 8:427
Organizational culture, 6:61–62
Organizational process model, 3:171
Organizations, 6:**71–74**
    business, 1:401–402
    institutional development,
        2:340–341
    intergovernmental, 3:333–334
    Mafia, 4:550–553
    management, 4:574–575
    nonprofit, economics, 3:324
    post-Parsonian American
        sociology, 8:6
    social economy, 7:583–584
    structure, 6:68–70
    voting, 8:647–648
Organizations, industrial. *See* Industry
Organizations, labor. *See* Labor unions
Organizations, peasant, 6:74–75
Organizations, self-help. *See*
    Volunteerism
Organized crime. *See* Crime and
    criminology; Mafia
Organized labor. *See* Labor unions
Organon (Aristotle), 1:174
Oriental Despostism (Wittfogel), 1:188
Oriental Orthodox churches, 1:533
Orientalism, 6:**75–76**
    caste, 1:461
    exoticism, 3:46–47
    representation, 7:173
    Said, Edward, 7:310
Orientalism (Said), 1:188, 2:203, 6:75,
    76, 7:173, 310
Origin of the Germans (Kossina), 1:167
Original accumulation, 8:627
Original sin. *See* Sin
*The Origins of Family, Private Property
    and the State* (Engels), 1:187, 3:134
The Origins of Totalitarianism
    (Arendt), 1:173
Orloff, Ann, 9:68
Ormsby, Hilda, 3:304
Orthodox economics. *See* Neoclassical
    economics
Orthodox Judaism. *See* Judaism
Orthodoxy, 1:531, 6:**78–79**
    in Church history, 1:532, 533
    clash of civilizations, 1:559
    constructivism, 2:96
    Coptic Christian Church, 2:132
    habitus, 3:404, 405, 406
    inflation, 4:23–24
    radicalism, 7:48–51

universities, 8:532

See also Heterodoxy

Orthogenic School (University of Chicago), 1:290–291

Orthopraxy, 6:78

Ortiz, Fernando, 2:170, 6:**80–81**

Ortodoxo Party. *See* Partido del Pueblo Cubano

Orwell, George, 1:390, 391, 8:561

OSCE (Organization for Security and Cooperation in Europe), 3:431

Osceola, 6:**81–82**

Osgood, Charles, 1:277

OSHA (U.S. Occupational Safety and Health Administration), 1:8–9, 6:22, 364

Oslo Accords, 1:162, 6:104, 105, 106

OSS (U.S. Office of Strategic Services), 1:482

Ossietzky, Carl von, 5:510

Osterman, Paul, 6:86

Ostner, Ilona, 9:68

Ostrom, Vincent, 3:144

Ostrower, Francie, 2:205

Oswald, James, 3:521

Oswald, Lee Harvey, 4:254, 255, 9:33, 34

OTC (Over-the-counter) market, 3:147, 180

Othello (Shakespeare), 1:326

The Other, 6:**82–83**

    ethnic fractionalization, 3:7

    ethnicity, 3:9

    ethnocentrism, 3:11–12

    exoticism, 3:46–47

    imprisonment, 3:597

    Mintz, Sidney W., 5:196

    poststructuralism, 6:399–400

    primitivism, 6:465

    racial slurs, 7:41

    representation, 7:173

The Other America (Harrington), 9:25

The Other Path: The Economic Answer to Terrorism (De Soto), 2:319, 320

Otherness. *See* The other

Otsuki, Hideaki, 1:286

Ottawa Landmines Convention (1997), 1:176

Otto, Rudolf, 9:154

Ottoman Empire, 6:**83–85**

    African diaspora, 1:39

    ethnic conflict, 3:2

    Muhammad Ali (Memet), 1:73

    Pan-Arabism, 6:117–118

    World War I, 9:145

Ouch, Hyoe, 8:562

Ought self, 6:**85**

Out-groups, 1:295, 296

Out-of-sample forecasting, 3:230

Out-of-wedlock births, 1:**306–308**, 4:615

    female-headed families, 3:115

    statistics, 3:91–92

Outcault, Richard, 2:23

Outline of a Theory of Practice (Bourdieu), 1:359, 6:79

Outlines of a Philosophy of the History of Men (Herder), 5:421

Output

    full capacity, 3:223–225

    growth accounting, 3:389–390

    Okun's law, 6:35–36

    per capita, 5:399

    Verdoorn's law, 8:606–608

    See also Input-output matrix

Outsiders: Studies in the Sociology of Deviance (Becker), 4:445

Outsourcing, 6:**86–87**

    automobile industry, 1:220

    blue collar and white collar, 1:339

    labor demand, 4:314

    labor unions, 8:517

Over-attribution bias, 6:**88–89**

Over-the-counter (OTC) market, 3:147, 180

Overachievers, 5:301, 6:**87–88**, 222–223

Overcapacity, automobile industry, 1:222

Overconsumption. *See* Consumption

Overeating, 1:274, 6:**89–90**

Overeducated workers, 8:494

Overemployment, 6:**90–91**

Overfishing, 6:**91–92**, *92*

    resource economics, 7:210–211

    Tragedy of the Commons, 8:422

Overlapping generations model, 6:**92–94**

Overlending, 6:**94–95**

    banking, 1:250

    leverage, 4:415–416

Overpopulation, 6:**95–96**

    Club of Rome, 1:585

    depopulation, 2:301

    limits of growth, 4:448

    population growth, 6:379

    population studies, 6:381–382

    zero population growth, 9:173–174

Overproduction, 6:**96–98**

capitalist mode of production, 1:446

coffee industry, 1:595

Oversaving. *See* Consumption; Saving rate

Overseas Chinese. *See* Chinese diaspora

Overshooting, 6:*98*, **98–99**

Oversight. *See* Accountability

The Overspent American (Schor), 2:108

Oversupply. *See* Surplus

Overtaking criterion, 6:51

Overtime, 6:**99–100**, 9:127

    fair Labor Standards Act (FLSA) (U.S. 1938), 9:129

    labor law, 4:303

    time-and-a-half, 8:373–374

    wages, 1:54

Overton, Richard, 4:414

Overweight. *See* Obesity

The Overworked American (Schor), 6:99

Ovington, Mary White, 5:383

Owen, David, 4:427

Owen, Robert, 8:561

Owen, Robert Dale, 4:239, 8:488

Owens, Major, 9:27

Own rate of interest, 4:**80–81**

Ownership

    absentee, 8:596

    agricultural industry, 1:60

    common land, 2:26–28

    communism, 2:34

    cooperatives, 2:123–126

    corporate, 5:492

    externality, 3:70–71

    firms, 3:149

    home, 1:96–97

    land claims, 4:340–341

    land reform, 4:341–345

    landlords, 4:345–347

    libertarianism, 4:437, 438

    television, 8:320

    user costs, 8:561–562

    working class *vs.*, 9:129

    See also Property rights

Oxford University. *See* University of Oxford

OxyChem (Occidental Chemical Corporation), 4:504–505

Ozinga, James, 2:35

P

Paasche index, 3:151

    See also Price indices

PAC (Pan-African Congresses), 1:42, 2:356–357, 6:**112–115**, 115–116

PAC (Political action committees), 1:424, 5:395–396

Pacifism, 6:**101–102**
    Christianity, 1:531
    civil rights movement, U.S., 1:552
    Congress of Racial Equality, 2:75
    just war, 4:235
    law and order, 4:370–371
    Lynd, Staughton, 4:528, 529
    passive resistance, 6:167
    peace movements, 6:182
    See also Peace

Packard, Vance, 2:107–108, 3:473, 8:201

Packing, court. *See* Roosevelt, Franklin D.; Supreme Court, U.S.

PAD (Postmodernism and development theory), 2:348

Paddling. *See* Corporal punishment

Padilla, Gilbert, 1:493

Padmore, George, 9:97

Paganism, 2:188

Page Act (U.S. 1875), 1:513

Pahl, R. E., 8:542

Paid employment, gender gap, 3:274–275

PAIGC (Partido Africano da Independéncia de Guinea e Cabo Verde), 1:415

Pain. *See* Psychosomatics

Paine, Thomas, 1:104, 4:415

Painter, Gary, 5:391

Painter, Sweatt v. (1950), 3:505

Painting. *See* Visual arts

Paired comparison method. *See* Scales

Pakistan
    bin Laden, Osama, 1:298
    borders, 1:355
    commonwealth, 2:29
    democracy, 2:76
    gender gap, 3:278
    Islamic socialism, 7:644
    Jinnah, Mohammed Ali, 4:203–204
    land reform, 4:343, 344
    nuclear weapons, 9:32
    partition, 6:160
    Raj, 7:55–57
    slavery, 1:39
    Taliban, 8:263
    water resources, 9:41

Palacio, Joseph, 3:257–258

Paleoanthropology, 1:118

Paleoconservatism, 7:248

Paleontology. *See* Archaeology; Johanson, Donald; Leakey, Richard

Palestine
    Ben-Gurion, David, 1:282–283
    Christianity, 1:530
    in Church history, 1:533
    Hussein, Saddam, 3:533
    Jewish diaspora, 4:190–191
    partition, 6:160
    Said, Edward, 7:310
    two-state solution, 8:476–478
    See also Israel; Jews; Palestinians

Palestine Liberation Organization (PLO), 6:**103–104**
    Arab-Israeli War of 1967, 1:154, 159
    Arab League, 1:156
    Arafat, Yasir, 1:161–162
    Black September, 1:322–323
    Hussein, King of Jordan, 3:531
    intifada, 4:123
    Lebanese civil war, 4:396, 397
    Phalangists, 6:236
    Rabin, Yitzhak, 7:1

Palestine War (1948), 1:160

Palestinian Authority, 1:161, 162, 4:123, 124, 6:**104–107**

Palestinian diaspora, 6:103–104, **107–110**

Palestinians, 6:**111–112**
    Arab-Israeli War of 1967, 1:159
    Arafat, Yasir, 1:161–162
    Ben-Gurion, David, 1:283
    bin Laden, Osama, 1:299
    Black September, 1:322–323
    diaspora, 6:107–110
    ethnic conflict, 3:1
    Hussein, King of Jordan, 3:531
    intifada, 4:122–124
    Lebanese civil war, 4:396
    liberation movements, 4:432
    Palestine Liberation Organization, 6:103–104
    Palestinian Authority, 6:104–107
    Rabin, Yitzhak, 7:1–2
    self-determination, 7:407
    Sharon, Ariel, 7:493
    two-state solution, 8:476–478
    Zionism, 9:180

Palladio, Andrea, 4:182–183

Palme, Joakim, 9:68

Palmer, Alexander Mitchell, 3:501, 4:302, 8:515

Palmer Raids (1918-1921), 4:302

Pan-African Congresses (PAC), 1:42, 2:356–357, 6:**112–115**, 115–116

Pan-African Telecommunications Network (Panaftel), 8:316

Pan-Africanism, 6:**115–117**
    African National Congress, 1:42
    African socialism, 7:639–640
    apartheid, 1:148
    black Marxism, 4:642
    black nationalism, 1:317
    diaspora, 2:356–357
    Diop, Cheikh Anta, 2:369
    Du Bois, W. E. B., 2:460
    James, C. L. R., 4:168
    Machel, Samora, 4:532–533
    Nkrumah, Kwame, 5:507, 508
    Pan-African Congresses, 6:112–115
    Robeson, Paul, 7:266
    Rodney, Walter, 7:269–270

Pan-Arabism, 6:**117–118**
    history, 1:161
    Hussein, King of Jordan, 3:531
    Hussein, Saddam, 3:531–533
    interwar years, 4:122
    Islamic socialism, 7:643–644
    Lebanese civil war, 4:396
    Phalangists, 6:236
    Qadhafi, Muammar al, 6:647
    United Arab Republic, 8:520–521, 522

Pan-Caribbeanism, 1:448–449, 6:**119–120**

Panaftel (Pan-African Telecommunications Network), 8:316

Panama
    Carter, Jimmy, 1:451
    hot money, 3:504

Panama Canal Treaty (1978), 1:451, 9:8

Pancho Villa. *See* Villa, Francisco

Panel data model, 3:287, 289

Panel studies, 6:**120–121**
    longitudinal, 2:238, 7:194–196
    pseudopanel data, 2:240
    random effects regression, 7:58–59
    sample attrition, 7:315–316
    Survey of Income and Program Participation, 8:243–244

Panel Study of Income Dynamics (PSID), 2:238, 6:**121–122**

Pangenesis, 1:335, 336

Panhard, Rene, 1:217

Panic (reaction), 1:146, 6:**122–124**

Panics (economics), 6:**124–125**
  central banks, 1:478
  decisive events, 2:254
  economic depression, 2:302
  South Sea Bubble, 8:33–34
  speculation, 8:54–56
Panoptic gaze, 3:**262–263**
Panopticon, 1:285, 3:262–263
Panopticon or The Inspection House
  (Bentham), 3:262
Pantheism. *See* Monotheism
Pantouflage, 8:313
Panzieri, Raniero, 1:447
Paoli, Pasquale, 5:363
Papacy
  abortion, 1:2
  Holy Roman Empire, 3:498
  See also names of specific popes;
    Roman Catholic Church;
    Vatican
Papadimitriou, Dimitri, 1:455–456
Paper Tangos (Taylor), 2:224
Paradigm, 6:**125–127**
  business cycles, 1:403
  Kuhn, Thomas, 4:292–293
  race relations, 7:29–31
Paradise. *See* Heaven
Paradox, Bertrand's. *See* Bertrand's
  paradox
Paradox, Pasinetti. *See* Pasinetti
  paradox
Paradox of thrift, widow's cruse, 9:96
Paradox of voting, 2:66, 6:**127–128**
  majoritarianism, 4:558–559
  majority voting, 4:562
  strategic games, 8:163–164
Paraguay
  coups d'etat, 2:156
  dictatorship, 2:359
Paralanguage, 5:530
Parameters
  estimation, 5:524–525
    large sample properties,
      4:348–350
    randomness, 7:63–64
  recursive, 8:599
  variables, 8:590
    probability distributions,
      6:493
    randomness, 7:64
    semiparametric estimation,
      7:438–439
Paramilitary operations. *See* Covert
  action
Paranoia, 6:**128–130**

Parapraxis. *See* Psychoanalytic theory
Pardo, 1:328, 329, 6:**130–131**
Pardo, Italo. *See* Urban anthropology
Parent-child relationships, 6:**131–134**
  attachment theory, 1:67
  Baumrind, Diana, 1:260
  bequests, 1:287
  Bettelheim, Bruno, 1:290–291
  Bowlby, John, 1:363
  Brazelton, T. Berry, 1:369
  children and, 1:511–512
  cohabitation, 2:1–2
  corporal punishment, 2:134–136
  day care, 2:245–246
  out-of-wedlock births, 1:306, 307
  Spock, Benjamin, 8:61–62
  in vivo transfers, 3:597–598
Parenthood, transition to, 6:**134–135**
  Brazelton, T. Berry, 1:369
  motherhood, 5:297–299
  rites of passage, 7:258
Parenting styles, 6:**135–138**, *136*
  Baumrind, Diana, 1:260
  Brazelton, T. Berry, 1:369
  class, 1:563
  corporal punishment, 2:134–136
  cultural capital, 2:190
  dependency, 2:297
  empathy, 2:574
  motherhood, 5:297–299
  parent-child relationships,
    6:131–133
  resiliency, 7:205–206
  socialization, 7:647–648
  Spock, Benjamin, 8:61–62
Parents
  attachment theory, 1:195–196
  fertility, 3:128–129
  ought self, 6:85
  parental uncertainty, 5:440
Parents Involved in Community Schools
  v. Seattle School District (2006),
  1:375–376
Pareto, Vilfredo, 6:**138–139**
  elite theory, 2:562, 563
  entrepreneurship, 2:605
  Hicks, John R., 3:472
  Lafargue, Paul, 4:330
  ordinality, 6:57
  Pareto optimum, 6:139–140
  School of Lausanne, 4:362
  utilitarianism, 9:63
Pareto distribution. *See* Probability
  distributions

Pareto optimum, 6:**139–140**, 9:63,
  64–65
  distortions, 2:414
  Pareto, Vilfredo, 6:138–139
  theory of second best, 8:350–351
Parfit, Derek, 8:370
Paris Peace Accords (1973), 4:398,
  8:615
Paris Peace Conference (1919), 1:519
Parity, codetermination, 1:593
Parity, purchasing power. *See*
  Purchasing power parity
Park, Robert E., 2:296, 3:266–267,
  6:14, **140–142**
  assimilation, 1:189–190
  Cox, Oliver C., 2:158
  Park School, 6:142–143
  race relations, 7:28–30, 31–32
Park Chung Hee, 1:443
Park School, 6:**142–143**
Parker, Henry C., 3:424
Parkin, Frank, 1:563
Parkinson's disease, Muhammad Ali,
  1:74
Parks, Rosa, 1:311, 551, 2:314, 4:268,
  5:384
Parliament, U.K., 6:**143–145**
  Bentham, Jeremy, 1:285–286
  bicameralism, 1:294
  Blair, Tony, 1:330
  Burke, Edmund, 1:396
  Chamberlain, Neville, 1:490
  Conservative Party (U.K.),
    2:87–88
  constituency, 2:90
  Levellers, 4:413–414
  Liberal Party (U.K.), 4:423, 424
  lobbying, 4:474
  political parties, 6:307
Parliamentary systems. *See* Parliaments
  and parliamentary systems
Parliaments and parliamentary
  systems, 6:**145–147**
  bicameralism, 1:294
  coalition, 1:588
  coalitions, 1:587, 3:357
  constitutions, 2:95, 5:241
  Diet, 2:360–361
  elections, 2:557, 561
  freedom, 3:198
  Knesset, 4:276–277
  monarchies, 5:238, 240, 241
  Parliament, U.K., 6:143–145
  separation of powers, 7:448–449
Parnes, Herbert, 6:**147–148**

Parochial education. *See* Private education
Parody, 6:**148–150**
Parrington, Vernon, 3:300
Parsimony. *See* Occam's razor
Parsimony, principle of. *See* Occam's razor
Parsonian sociology, 8:**1–2**
    Parsons, Talcott, 6:149–150
    political science, 6:313
    social system, 7:623–627
Parsons, Elsie Clews, 1:345
Parsons, Talcott, 1:563, 3:115, 6:**150–151**
    conformity, 2:71
    determinism, 2:323
    development in sociology, 2:346
    functionalism, 3:232
    Giddens, Anthony, 3:314
    modernization, 5:232
    Parsonian sociology, 8:1–2
    political science, 6:313
    political stability, 8:73
    post-Parsonian American sociology, 8:5
    role theory, 7:275
    schools in sociology, 8:11
    social statics, 7:620
    social system, 7:624–626
    sociology, 7:661
    system analysis, 8:256–257
    values, 8:581
Parsons School of Design, 5:501
Parti Québécois (PQ), 6:662, 663
Partial autocorrelation function. *See* Time series regression
Partial equilibrium, 6:**151–153**
    long run, 4:491
    Marshall, Alfred, 4:623
Participant observation, 6:**14–17**
    ethnographic research, 7:193–194
    reflexivity, 7:122–123
Participation, labor force, 4:303, **314–316**
    codetermination, 1:592–593
    day care, 2:245–246
    discouraged workers, 2:386–387
Participation, political, 6:**153–155**
    Asian American politics, 6:322
    authoritarianism, 1:213
    black politics, 6:324, 325–326
    citizenship, 1:542–544
    community power studies, 2:42, 43
    consensus, 2:82–83

    corruption, 2:144
    coups d'etat, 2:156
    Dahl, Robert Alan, 2:220
    democracy, 2:273, 8:606
    democratization, 2:288
    gender gap, 3:278–279, 9:108–109, 110–111, 117
    Habermas, Jürgen, 3:401–402
    happiness, 3:418
    Internet, 4:107–109
    labor, 4:303
    Latino politics, 6:337, 338
    liberty, 4:439
    mobilization, 5:213–214
    parliaments and parliamentary systems, 6:145–147
    political inequality, 4:4
    political system, 6:317
    polyarchy, 6:366
    representative and participatory democracy, 2:283–285
    Riker, William, 7:249
    socioeconomic status, 8:606
    Supreme Court decisions, 9:84–85
    Verba, Sidney, 8:606
Participation in American (Verba and Nie), 8:606
Participatory democracy. *See* Democracy, representative and participatory; Representative and participatory democracy
Particularism, 1:120, 6:**155–156**
Partido Africano da Independéncia de Guinea e Cabo Verde (PAIGC), 1:415
Partido del Pueblo Cubano, 1:464
Partido Independiente de Color, 1:329
Partido Revolucionario Cubano (PRC), 1:464
Partido Revolucionario Institucional (PRI), 5:130, 6:**156–159**
Parties, political. *See* Political parties
Partisans. *See* Political parties
Partition, 6:**159–161**
    Jinnah, Mohammed Ali, 4:203–204
    Korean War, 4:289
    separatism, 7:450–451
Partnership for Peace, 5:544
Partridge, W. L., 1:137
Parts suppliers, auto, 1:219–220
Party dealignment. *See* Dealignment
Party of God. *See* Hezbollah
Party Politics in the West Indies (James), 4:168
Party systems, competitive, 6:**161–163**

    ballots, 1:242
    majorities, 4:560
    multiparty systems, 5:321–323
    plurality, 6:285–286
    political parties, 6:306–308
    Southern politics, 6:345–349
    See also One-party states
PAS (Physician-assisted suicide). *See* Euthanasia and assisted suicide
Pasinetti, Luigi, 1:419, 420, 6:**163–164**, 164–165
Pasinetti paradox, 6:163, **164–165**
Passages from Antiquity to Feudalism (Anderson), 1:113
Passing, 1:328, 5:313, 6:**165–166**
Passing (Larsen), 3:426
The Passing of the Great Race (Grant), 1:336, 5:430
Passion, erotic. *See* Eroticism
Passion, romantic. *See* Romance
Passional Christi und Antichristi (Luther), 1:452
Passive resistance, 6:**166–168**
    black nationalism, 1:317
    Black Power, 1:321
    Bose, Subhas and Sarat, 1:356
    Brown v. Board of Education (1954), 1:374
    Chávez, César, 1:493
    civil disobedience, 1:545–546
    civil rights movement, U.S., 1:551–552
    Congress of Racial Equality, 2:75
    Congress Party, India, 2:77
    direct action, 2:372
    dissidents, 2:411
    Gandhi, Mohandas K., 2:76, 3:480, 4:268
    King, Martin Luther, Jr., 4:267, 268, 269
    liberation, 4:429
    Lynd, Staughton, 4:528–529
    moral suasion, 5:283
    Student Nonviolent Coordinating Committee, 8:183–184
    Thoreau, Henry David, 8:357
Passy, Frédéric, 5:509
Past and Present, 3:482
Pasternak, Boris, 9:20
Patel, Sardar Vallabhai, 2:76
Pateman, Carole, 2:220
Patents. *See* Intellectual property rights
Paterfamilias, 3:96
Paternalism, 4:352
Paterson, William, 4:224

Path analysis, 2:463, 6:**168–169**, 7:117–118

Pathology, psychiatric. *See* Mental illness; Psychiatric disorders; Psychopathology

Pathology, social, 6:**169–171**
  black liberalism, 1:312
  culture of poverty, 2:206
  Lewis, Oscar, 4:419
  murder, 5:338–339
  social isolation, 7:601
  urban poverty, 6:410–411

Pathos of Power (Clark), 1:561

Paths in Utopia (Buber), 2:31

Patinkin, Don, 3:218, 6:**171–173**

Patriarchy, 6:**173–174**
  crime and criminology, 2:172
  demographic transition, 2:292
  femininity, 3:119
  intersectionality, 4:114
  leaders, 4:376
  liberation, 4:430
  marriage, 4:614
  matriarchy, 5:29, 30
  men, 5:80–81
  Native Americans, 5:426
  nuclear family, 3:96
  primitive communism, 2:37, 38
  sexism, 7:474
  sexual harassment, 7:474–475
  Veblen, Thorstein, 8:596
  virgins, 8:630
  women's liberation, 9:115

Patricians, 6:**174–175**

Patrick, Hugh, 1:253

Patrimonial capitalism, 1:442

Patriot Act (U.S. 2001), 1:18

Patriotism, 6:**175–176**
  Americanism, 1:108
  consumption, 2:108
  Daughters of the American Revolution, 2:241–242
  jingoism, 4:201–202
  military, 5:168–169
  religion, 7:160
  September 11, 2001, 7:453
  statism, 8:119–120

Patronage, 6:**176–177**
  clientelism, 1:579
  competitive party systems, 6:162
  Congress Party, India, 2:76, 77
  dictatorship, 2:360
  political parties, 6:308
  visual arts, 8:631–632

Pattern matching. *See* Campbell, Donald

Pattern prediction. *See* Prediction

Patterns, voting. *See* Voting patterns

Patterns of Culture (Benedict), 1:282, 2:195

Patterns of Democracy (Lijphart), 1:578

Patterson, Floyd, 1:74

Paukert, Felix, 4:295–296

Paul IV, Pope, 3:312

Paul, Alice, 3:123

Paul, Benjamin, 1:131

Paul the Apostle, 4:187, 6:78

Pavlov, Ivan, 6:43, **177–179**
  behaviorism, 1:276
  classical conditioning, 1:572–573
  learned helplessness, 4:388
  reinforcement theories, 7:147, 148
  Skinner, B. F., 7:525, 526
  Skinner box, 7:528
  Thorndike, Edward, 8:358

Pavlovian conditioning. *See* Classical conditioning

Pax Americana, 5:470–471

Pax Britannica, 6:**179–180**

Pay. *See* Wages

Pay Advisory Committee, 9:3

Pay-or-play health insurance, 5:396

Payments, balance of. *See* Balance of payments

Payton, Philip A. Jr., 3:423–424

PCC (Political Consultative Committee), 9:35

PCJDYC (President's Conference on Juvenile Delinquency and Youth Crime), 9:25

Peabody, George, 3:183

Peace, 6:**180–182**
  common market, 2:28–29
  economic growth, 2:491
  famine, 3:98–99
  Kant, Immanuel, 4:249
  League of Nations, 4:385
  Pax Britannica, 6:179
  peace movements, 6:182–185
  United Nations role, 8:523–524
  Veblen, Thorstein, 8:596–597
  See also Nobel Peace Prize; Pacifism

Peace Corps, 5:414

Peace Movement of Ethiopia, 1:320

Peace movements, 6:101–102, **182–185**

Peace of Westphalia (1648), 3:360
  See also Westphalian order

Peace process, 6:**185–186**
  Bunche, Ralph Johnson, 1:387
  Carter, Jimmy, 1:451
  civil wars, 1:554, 556
  diplomacy, 2:370
  disarmament, 2:379
  European Union, 3:25
  Le Duc Tho, 4:398
  Palestine Liberation Organization, 6:103–104
  Palestinian Authority, 6:104–107
  Palestinians, 6:112
  Rabin, Yitzhak, 7:1–2
  Sharon, Ariel, 7:493

Peaceful coexistence, 4:264, 6:**186–188**

Peacekeeping, 1:37–38, 8:524

Peach, Ceris, 5:463

Peacock, James, 1:133

Peanut industry, 6:**188–190**

Pearce, C. Glenn, 2:32

Pearce, David G., 5:517

Pearl Harbor, 6:**190**, 9:149
  Central Intelligence Agency, U.S, 1:480–481
  Japanese American incarceration, 3:600
  Roosevelt, Franklin D., 7:283

Pearlin Personal Mastery Scale. *See* Motivation

Pearson, Karl, 3:247, 6:**190–194**
  autoregressive models, 1:228
  centrism, 1:488
  method of moments, 5:105
  nonparametric estimation, 5:526
  ordinary least squares, 4:393
  regression analysis, 7:138
  Spearman rank correlation coefficient, 8:47
  standard deviation, 8:94

Pearson, Lester, 6:662

Peasant movements. *See* Peasantry

Peasant organizations, 6:74–75

Peasant Road, 6:75

Peasant Wars of the Twentieth Century (Wolf), 9:106

Peasantry, 6:**195–196**
  bolshevism, 1:351
  Boricua, 1:355
  caste, 1:457
  Chinese Revolution, 1:520, 521
  civil wars, 1:554
  class conflict, 1:569
  common land, 2:27, 28
  communism, 2:35–36

Peasantry, *continued*
dance, 2:224
famine, 3:97–99
farmers *vs.*, 6:74
feudal mode of production, 3:133–135
feudalism, 1:60, 3:135–136
Gramsci, Antonio, 3:364
labor, 4:301
Ladejinsky, Wolf, 4:328
land reform, 4:342
latifundia, 4:352–354
Lenin, Vladimir Ilitch, 4:411
Lewis, W. Arthur, 4:420–421
Mau Mau, 5:36–38
Moore, Barrington, 5:278
Russian economics, 7:299, 300
Russian Revolution, 7:303–304
servitude, 7:462
socialism, 7:636
subsistence agriculture, 8:204–206
war, 9:20
Wolf, Eric, 9:106
Peattie, Lisa, 9:123
Pechman, Joseph, 8:277
Peculiar institution. *See* Slavery
Pedagogy, 6:**196–197**, 7:350–351
See also Teachers
Pedagogy, social. *See* Social pedagogy
Pedagogy of the Oppressed (Freire), 2:214, 3:202
Pedigrees, 3:461
Peel, David, 1:586
Peel, Robert, 2:133
Peer cliques, 6:**197–198**, 202–203
Peer effects, 6:**198–201**
peer relations research, 6:202–203
smoking, 7:560
social cognitive map, 7:575–576
socialization, 6:198–199
Peer influence, 6:**201–202**
acting white, 1:17
children, 1:511–512
communication networks, 5:480–481
conformity, 2:71–72
peer effects, 6:199
peer relations research, 6:202–203
pluralistic ignorance, 3:561
role models, 7:274
social cognitive map, 7:575–576
social skills interventions, 4:120
socialization, 7:647
underachievers, 8:484

Peer pressure. *See* Peer influence
Peer relations research, 6:197–198, **202–204**
Pegged exchange rates. *See* Exchange rates
Peirce, Charles Sanders, 4:169
behaviorism, 1:276
objectivity, 6:10
pragmatism, 6:420
symbolic logic, 4:481
See also Semiotics
Pekkarinen, Tuomas, 6:77
The Peloponnesian War (Thucydides), 4:235
Peltier, Leonard, 1:99
Peltzman, Sam, 1:502
Penalties. *See* Punishment
Pendlebury, David, 1:539
Penetration, export. *See* Export penetration
Penis envy. *See* Oedipus complex
Penitentiaries. *See* Prisons
Penn World Table (PWT), 6:**204–205**
Pen's parade. *See* Probability distributions
Pension plans, 4:134
Pensions, 3:307
Pentagon Papers, 9:42
Pentecostalism, 1:531, 7:163
People of Puerto Rico (Steward), 9:105
The People's Choice (Lazarsfeld), 1:202, 4:375
People's History of England (Morton), 3:482
People's Liberation Army, China (PLA), 1:520–521, 2:35, 4:467, 588, 589
People's National Movement (PNM), 9:98
People's National Party (PNP), 7:67, 68–69
People's Party (U.S.), 2:181
People's Political Party (PPP), 3:258, 259
People's Republic of China. *See* China
People's Revolutionary Government (Grenada PRG), 3:381–383
People's Temple, 2:188
Péquistes. *See* Parti Québécois (PQ)
Per capita consumption, 3:346
Per capita income, 3:346
Per capita output, 5:399
Per se rule, 1:143
Perception
cognition, 1:598
color preference, 6:432–433

colorism, 2:17–18
communication, 2:31, 32
consciousness, 2:81
constructivism, 2:97
cultural relativism, 2:194–195
diplomacy, 2:371
lay theories, 4:374
other, 6:82–83
social comparison, 7:577
teacher-child relationships, 8:292
See also Self-perception theory
Perception, person, 6:**205–207**
Jones, Edward Ellsworth, 4:210–211
Kelley, Harold, 4:252–253
person memory, 6:215–216
trait inference, 8:424
Perception and Misperception in International Politics (Jervis), 4:185
Perceptual development, 1:506
Père-Lachaise, 1:393
Perestroika. *See* Glasnost; Gorbachev, Mikhail
Perez v. Sharp (1948), 7:28
Perfect competition, 2:**57–58**
as competition, 2:50
imperfect competition *vs.*, 2:51–52
labor market, 9:4
monopoly, 2:56, 5:263–264
satiation, 7:328
surplus labor, 4:309
Perfect foresight, 3:**172–174**
Perfection, subgame. *See* Subgame perfection
Performance, 6:**207–209**
accountability, 1:11
achievement, 1:15
contingency models of leadership, 4:384
minstrelsy, 5:194–195
rewards, 9:103
rituals, 7:260–262
Performance anxiety, 3:179
Performance-based accountability, 1:9–11
Performance studies. *See* Performance
Performing Blackness: Enactments of African-American Modernism (Benston), 1:309
Perils of Dominance (Porter), 8:614
Period effects, 6:**209–210**
Periodicals, professional. *See* Professional journals
Periodization, 6:**210–211**

Peripheral capitalism, 1:516

Periphery, 2:347, 8:490, 9:9–10

Perls, Frederick S., 3:311

Perls, Laura, 3:311

Permanent income hypothesis (PIH), 6:**211–214**, *212*
   absolute income hypothesis, 1:7
   consumption function, 2:109, 110
   life-cycle hypothesis, 4:442
   quantity theory, 3:217
   relative income hypothesis, 7:153, 154

Permanent neutrality, 5:487, 488, 490, 513

Permanent Treaty (1934), 3:393

Permissiveness, 6:132–133, 135–136, 137

Perón, Eva. *See* Peronism

Perón, Juan. *See* Peronism

Peronism, 2:156, 6:**214–215**, 384

Perot, Ross, 1:398, 579, 5:540

Perpetual foreigner syndrome, 1:514–515

Perron-Frobenius theorem, 2:**551–554**, 6:403

Perrotta, Cosimo, 9:45

Perrow, Charles, 1:9

Persecution, religious. *See* Religious persecution

Persian Gulf War (1991). *See* Gulf War of 1991

Person memory, 6:**215–216**

Person perception, 6:**205–207**
   Jones, Edward Ellsworth, 4:210–211
   Kelley, Harold, 4:252–253
   person memory, 6:215–216
   trait inference, 8:424

Person-situation debate, 6:**225–226**
   prison psychology, 6:471
   trait inference, 8:424
   trait theory, 8:425–426

Personal capitalism, 1:442

Personal constructs, 6:**216–217**

Personal debt
   consumerism, 2:105
   consumption, 2:108, 109
   consumption function, 2:110
   servitude, 7:462

Personal finance
   life-cycle hypothesis, 4:441–443
   metropolitan regions, 7:134

Personal outcomes, 5:390–392

Personal relations. *See* Social relations

Personal space, 1:171

Personal spending. *See* Consumerism; Consumption

Personalist probability. *See* Subjective probability

Personality, 6:**217–220**
   Allport, Gordon W., 1:81
   Asch, Solomon, 1:186
   child-rearing, 1:120
   creativity, 2:164–165
   equilibrium, 2:622
   Erikson, Erik, 2:625–626
   identity, 3:553
   Jung, Carl, 4:228, 229–230
   leaders, 4:377
   Leary, Timothy, 4:390
   lying, 4:524
   multiple personalities, 5:327–328
   murder, 5:339–340
   neuroticism, 5:486–487
   person-situation debate, 6:225–226
   personal constructs, 6:216–217
   psychological depression, 2:307
   relationship satisfaction, 7:151
   resiliency, 7:204–207
   Rorschach test, 7:284–285
   Scarr, Sandra Wood, 7:340–341
   shyness, 7:504–505
   similarity/attraction theory, 7:513–514
   stability in psychology, 8:74–75
   stages of development, 8:77–79
   temperament, 8:321–322
   trait theory, 8:425–426
   urbanity, 8:544

Personality: A Psychological Interpretation (Allport), 1:81

Personality, authoritarian, 2:64, 6:**220–221**

Personality, cult of, 6:**221–223**
   communism, 2:36
   dictatorship, 2:360
   Diop, Cheikh Anta, 2:369
   leaders, 4:376, 377
   leadership, 4:381–382
   Little Red Book, 4:467

Personality, type A/type B, 6:218, **223–225**

Personality disorders, 6:220, 572
   See also specific disorders.

Perspective-taking, 2:573–574, 6:**226–227**

Persuasion, 6:**227–228**
   attitude change, 1:200–201
   campaigning, 1:423–424

consumption, 2:107–108
   diplomacy, 2:371
   economic rhetoric, 2:495–496
   moral suasion, 5:283
   primacy/recency effects, 6:457–458
   sleeper effects, 7:550
   social judgment theory, 7:602
   subliminal suggestion, 8:201–202
   See also Hidden persuaders

Persuasion, message-based, 6:**227–228, 228–230**, 7:550

Peru
   civil wars, 1:554
   De Soto, Hernando, 2:319–320
   guerrilla warfare, 3:395
   visual arts, 8:631

Pesaran, Hashem, 4:499

Pessimism, 6:**53–55**
   death and dying, 2:247–248
   locus of control, 4:477–478
   misanthropy, 5:198
   mood, 5:276
   personality, 6:218
   psychological depression, 2:307
   self-verification, 7:431

Pesticide poisonings, 3:159

PET (Positron emission tomography), 5:485

Pétain, Philippe, 2:264

Petersen, William, 5:220–221

Peterson, Chris, 6:54

Peterson, Dale, 1:84

Peterson, Paul, 1:548

Petioni, C. Augustin, 9:97

Petit Martinique, Grenadian Revolution, 3:381–383

Petrie, William Matthew Flinders, 1:165

Petroleum industry, 6:**230–234**
   Chávez, Hugo, 1:495
   crude oil
      OPEC capacity, 6:64, *64*
      price, 5:438, 6:64–65, *65, 66*
      reserves, 6:*66*
   energy sector, 2:587–588, 588, 591
   Hussein, Saddam, 3:533, 534
   limits of growth, 4:448
   Mossadegh, Mohammad, 5:296–297
   Seven Sister Companies, 6:65, 65t
   See also Organization of Petroleum Exporting Countries

Petronius, 6:149

Pettigrew, Thomas F., 6:**234–235**

Petty, Richard E., 5:452

Petty, William, 5:399

Petty bourgeoisie, 1:361–362, 563, 7:411

Peyote. *See* Mescaline

Pfeffer, Jeffrey, 1:11

PGD (Preimplantation genetic diagnosis), 3:294–295

Phalangists, 4:396, 397, 6:**236**

Phan Dinh Khai. *See* Le Duc Tho

Phantastica. *See* Hallucinogens

Pharmaceutical industry, 6:**236–239**
    drug tolerance, 8:385
    technological change, 1:490, 491
    trade liberalization, 4:428
    See also Drugs; Medicine

Pharmacogenomics, 3:295

Pharmacotherapy. *See* Drug therapy

Phase diagrams, 6:**240–242**, 240*t*, *241*

Phase-structure grammar, 1:528

PHC (Primary health care), 3:443
    See also Medicine

Phear, John, 2:38

Phelps, Edmund
    full employment, 3:226
    golden rule in growth models, 3:346
    natural rate of unemployment, 5:435
    new classical economics, 2:523
    Okun's law, 6:35
    Phillips curve, 6:248
    trade-offs, 8:419
    unemployment, 8:503

Phenomenal consciousness. *See* Consciousness

Phenomenology, 6:**242–243**
    consciousness, 2:78, 79–81
    constructivism, 2:96, 98
    determinism, 2:323
    existentialism, 3:43
    habits, 3:403
    knowledge, 4:278, 279, 280
    Sartre, Jean-Paul, 7:327
    theory, 8:344, 345

The Phenomenology of Mind (Hegel), 1:75, 3:452, 6:9–10

Phenomenology of Spirit (Hegel). *See* *The Phenomenology of Mind* (Hegel)

Phenotype, 5:445, 6:**243–245**
    blackness, 1:328
    colorism, 2:17–18
    discrimination, 1:36

Latino National Political Survey, 4:354, 355
    mulattos, 5:313

Phil, the Fiddler (Alger), 1:72

Philadelphia Convention, 2:91

The Philadelphia Negro (Du Bois), 1:323, 5:389

Philadelphia (PA), 1:394

Philanthropy, 6:**245–247**
    charitable foundations, 3:183–185
    institutional development, 2:340
    international nongovernmental organizations, 4:96–99
    Rothschilds, 7:289
    Social Darwinism, 2:233
    Soros, George, 8:31
    well-being, 3:292–293

Philippines
    AIDS/HIV, 1:65
    banana industry, 1:245, 246
    Chinese diaspora, 1:517, 518
    land reform, 4:343
    latifundia, 4:353

Philistines. *See* Palestinians

Phillips, A. W. H., 6:**247–248**, 248–250, 8:419

Phillips, Howard, 9:28

Phillips, Peter, 2:3

Phillips curve, 3:151, 6:**248–251**
    adaptive expectations, 1:20
    Federal Reserve System, 3:112
    natural rate of unemployment, 5:436, 437
    new Keynesian economics, 2:524, 525
    Phillips, A. W. H., 6:246, 247
    stagflation, 8:82
    Taylor rule, 8:286
    trade-offs, 8:419
    unemployment, 8:503
    unemployment and inflation, 3:226
    wage and price controls, 9:2

Philology, 2:194

Philosophical behaviorism, 1:274, 275, 277–279

The Philosophical Discourse of Modernity (Habermas), 3:401–402

A Philosophical Enquiry into the Origin and Our Ideas of the Sublime and Beautiful (Burke), 1:396

Philosophical naturalism, 5:442–443

Philosophy, 6:**251–254**
    African sociology, 7:664, 665
    consciousness, 2:78–82

Derrida, Jacques, 2:309–310

Hegel, Georg Wilhelm Friedrich, 3:451–452
    Hegelians, 3:453–454
    idealism, 3:547–548
    Judaism, 4:221
    jurisprudence, 4:232–233
    Kant, Immanuel, 4:248–249
    logic, 4:479–480
    materialism, 5:18–21
    rationality, 7:80
    supreme being, 8:231
    symbolic logic, 4:481–482
    systems theory, 8:257–258
    See also names of specific philosophies

Philosophy, moral, 6:**254–257**
    common good, 2:25
    moral sentiments, 5:282
    Scottish moralists, 7:367–370
    social science, 7:615

Philosophy, political, 6:**257–259**
    Davis, Angela, 2:243
    Habermas, Jürgen, 3:401–402
    individualism, 3:618–620
    justice, 4:237
    liberalism, 4:425–426
    libertarianism, 4:437–439
    liberty, 4:439–441
    moderates, 5:226–227
    political theory, 6:318
    politics, 6:321
    Popper, Karl, 6:372
    state of nature, 8:110–111

Philosophy of law. *See* Law

Philosophy of Mind and Cognition (Braddon-Mitchell and Jackson), 3:232

The Philosophy of Right (Hegel), 3:452, 453, 454

Philosophy of science, 6:**259–262**
    Campbell, Donald, 1:425, 426
    evolutionary psychology, 3:34
    Lakatos, Imre, 4:338–340
    methodology, 5:108–109
    Popper, Karl, 6:371–372
    reductionism, 7:118–119
    scientific revolutions, 7:236–237
    theory, 8:343

The Philosophy of the Revolution (Nasser), 5:376

Phish, 9:121

Phobia, 6:**262–263**, 262*t*
    genetic determinism, 2:329
    social, 1:146

specific, 1:146

technophobia, 8:310–311

Phoenix Program, 1:484

Phones, cellular. *See* Cellular technology

Phosphorus fertilizers, 3:131–132

Photography. *See* Visual arts

Physical aggression, 1:56

Physical anthropology. *See* Biological anthropology

Physical capital, 2:344–345, 3:506–509, **6:264–265**

Physical dependency, 1:20–21

Physical development, childhood. *See* Child development

Physical geography, 3:303–305

Physical quality of life index, **6:265–266**

Physician-assisted suicide (PAS). *See* Assisted death; Euthanasia and assisted suicide

Physics, reductionism, 7:118

Physiocracy, **6:266–268**

Cantillion, Richard, 1:429

laissez-faire, 4:335

latifundia, 4:353

Quesnay, François, 6:666, 667

Turgot, Jacques, 8:466

Physiological needs. *See* Biological needs

Physiology

alpha-males, 1:83–84

women, 9:107–110

See also Child development

The Physiology of Industry (Mummery and Hobson), 1:378

Piaget, Jean, **6:268–271**

child development, 1:506

constructivism, 2:97

developmental psychology, 2:350

equilibrium, 2:622–623

Kohlberg, Lawrence, 4:286

moral realism, 7:95

perspective-taking, 6:226

schemas, 7:344

stages of development, 8:78–79

Picard, Michel, 2:201

Picasso, Pablo, 3:425, 8:630, 632

Pickering, John, 3:585

Pidgin language, 1:40, 2:167

Piece rate systems, 9:128–129

Pierce, Brooks, 2:478, 479

Pierce, Jennifer, 9:122

Piercy, Marge, 8:561

Piereson, James, 8:386

Pierson, Paul, 9:71

Pietri, Pedro, 5:553

Piety, 3:118

Pigou, Arthur C., 4:462, 5:397

Coase theorem, 1:590

social cost, 7:582–583

welfare economics, 9:63

PIH (Permanent income hypothesis). *See* Permanent income hypothesis (PIH)

Pilgrimage, 5:57, 9:155

Piliavin, jane, 3:293

Pilot National Asian American Political Study (PNAAPS), 7:20

See also Race and political science

Pimps, **6:271–273**

Pinchot, Elizabeth, 1:391

Pincus, Gregory, 1:303

Pinderhughes, Dianne M., 6:283

Pinero, Miguel, 5:552–553

Pinheiro, Paulo, 2:135

Pinochet, Augusto, 1:502

authoritarianism, 1:214

concentration camps, 2:64

genocide, 3:298

Latin American revolutions, 7:234

neoliberalism, 9:38

rule of, 1:78

women, 9:110, 112

Pinsker, Leon, 9:179

Piore, Emanuel, 3:324

Piore, Michael, 6:77

Piore, Nora Kahn, 3:324

Piracy. *See* Intellectual property rights

Pirenne, Henri, 8:546

Pitkin, Hanna, **6:273–274**, 8:496

Pius IX, Pope, 1:2

Pius XI, Pope, 1:483, 2:277, 7:280

Pius VII, Pope, 5:364, 365

Pius XII, Pope, 7:280

Pizan, Christine de, 3:119–120

PJC (NATO-Russia Permanent Joint Council), 5:546

PLA, China (People's Liberation Army). *See* People's Liberation Army, China (PLA)

Placage. *See* Mulattos

Plagiarism, 4:216–217

Plague. *See* Disease; Nursery rhymes; Public health

The Plague and the Fire (Leasor), 5:550

A Plague on Your Houses (Wallace and Wallace), 4:445

Plagues. *See* Morbidity and mortality

Plain Speaking (Miller), 1:481

Plan of Ayala, 9:171

Plan of Parliamentary Reform (Bentham), 1:285–286

Planned Parenthood Federation of America, 3:89

Planned Parenthood of Southeastern Pennsylvania v. Casey (1992), 1:4

Planning, **6:274–277**

bioterrorism, 1:302

communism, 2:34

conservatism, 2:84

convergence theory, 2:117

coping, 2:129

dirigiste, 2:373

economics of control, 2:532

environmental impact assessment, 2:605–607

human ecology, 3:510, 511

left wing, 4:403

Moses, Robert, 5:296

optimal growth, 6:51–53

Russian economics, 7:300

Tinbergen, Jan, 8:375

urban, 4:165

Planning, indicative. *See* Convergence theory

Plant, Arnold, 1:589

Plantation, **6:277–278**

archaeology of slave lives, 7:530–531

Caribbean, 1:448

concentration camps, 2:64

Haiti, 3:407

land reform, 4:343, 344

landlords, 4:346

latifundia, 4:352, 353

Mintz, Sidney W., 5:195–196

plantation economy model, 6:278–279

settlement, 7:465

slavery, 1:39–40, 3:161–162

sugar industry, 8:218

Plantation economy model, **6:278–279**

described, 6:277

Engerman, Stanley, 2:592

Time on the Cross, 8:366–367

Plants (factories). *See* Factories

Plasticity, adolescent psychology, 1:24

Plato, **6:279–280**

aesthetics, 1:30

Alger, Horatio, 1:72

animism, 1:114

Aristotle, 1:174

Plato, *continued*
  communism, 2:34
  family values, 3:96
  freedom, 3:196
  hell, 3:458
  humanism, 3:517
  idealism, 3:547
  justice, 4:237
  knowledge, 4:278
  moral philosophy, 6:254
  narratives, 5:370
  politics, 6:319, 320
  Popper, Karl, 6:372
  reality, 7:101
  recognition, 7:109
  reincarnation, 7:146
  representation, 7:171
  representative and participatory
    democracy, 2:284
  The Republic, 3:96, 8:561
  social contract, 7:581
  utopianism, 8:561
  wealth, 9:45
Platt Amendment (U.S. 1901), 3:393
Playing Indian, 3:338
Pleasure, 3:209–210, 211, 213
  hedonism, 8:558
  objective utility, 8:557
  ordinality, 6:56–57
Pleasure principle. *See* Psychoanalytic
  theory
Plekhanov, Georgi Valentinovich,
  3:455
Plessy, Homer. *See* Separate-but-Equal
Plessy v. Ferguson (1896), 1:19, 3:316,
  505, 4:198
  Birth of a Nation (film), 1:305
  Brown v. Board of Education
    (1954), 1:373–374
  civil rights movement, U.S., 1:551
  equal protection, 2:614–615
  race, 7:16
  separate-but-equal, 7:446
  Supreme Court, U.S., 8:234
  unequal education, 2:537
Pliny the Elder, 4:352
PLO (Palestinian Liberation
  Organization). *See* Palestine
  Liberation Organization (PLO)
Plosser, Charles, 1:228, 2:1
Plotinus, 5:270
Plott, Charles R., 2:506
Plumb, J. H., 2:89
Plumbing, 6:**281–282**, 8:383–384
Pluralism, 6:**282–285**

clash of civilizations, 1:559
communalism, 2:31
community power studies,
  2:42–46
competitive party systems, 6:162
conformity, 2:72
consensus, 2:82
constitutions, 2:95
corporatism, 2:140, 142
cultural studies, 2:200
Dahl, Robert Alan, 2:219–220
ethnicity, 3:10–11
Hinduism, 3:479
interest groups and interests, 4:82
Kariel, Henry S., 4:249
Latino politics, 6:337, 338, 339
liberalism, 4:426
Lowi, Theodore J., 4:506
Lynd, Robert and Helen, 4:528
melting pot, 5:72
power, 6:413, 417
republic, 7:185
tyranny of the majority,
  8:478–479
urban politics, 6:350–351
xenophobia, 9:158–161
Pluralistic ignorance, 2:72, 3:388,
  560–561
Plurality, 6:**285–286**
  bloc vote, 1:334–335
  cleavages, 1:578
  elections, 2:557–558, 560–561,
    562
  majority rule, 4:561
Plutarch, 9:18
Plutocracy, 1:173
PNAAPS (Pilot National Asian
  American Political Study). *See* Race
  and political science
PNM (People's National Movement),
  9:98
PNP (People National Party), 7:67,
  68–69
Poalei Zion, 1:283
Poetry
  Arab, 1:161
  epic, 3:136–137
  See also Literature
Pogroms, 3:569, 6:**286–289**
  See also Anti-Semitism
Poincaré, Henri, 1:492, 5:524
Poindexter, John, 4:142, 143
Point of effective demand, 1:51
Point-set topology, 8:563
Poisons, 9:181

Poisson, Siméon Denis, 2:417, 4:484
Poisson distribution, 2:*417,* 417–418
Poisson models. *See* Generalized linear
  models (GLM)
Pol Pot, 2:64, 4:262, 263, 6:**289**
Poland
  communism, 2:35
  concentration camps, 2:63
  Germans in, 5:418
  ghettos, 5:450
  Hitler, Adolf, 1:490, 3:488
  Holocaust, 3:497
  Kalecki, Michał, 4:246
  land reform, 4:342
  latifundia, 4:352, 353
  Luxemburg, Rosa, 4:522–523
  repression, 7:175
  Solidarność, 8:25–26
  state capitalism, 1:443
  Warsaw Ghetto, 3:313
  Warsaw Pact, 9:35
  World War II, 1:153, 9:147–148
Polanyi, Karl, 1:437, 5:474
Policing, biased, 6:**289–291**
  discrimination, 2:390
  integration, 4:61
  racial democracy, 2:282
Policing the Crisis (Hall), 3:410
Policy
  race-blind, 7:35–36
    black conservatism,
      1:310–311
    described, 7:7
  race-conscious, 7:36–38
    critical race theory,
      2:174–176
  structural, 4:542
Policy, fiscal, 6:**291–293**
  balance of payments, 1:238–240
  business cycles, 1:403
  capital flight, 1:434
  decentralization, 2:250
  democratic centralism, 2:286
  employment, 2:583
  happiness, 3:418
  health economics, 3:441
  Keynes, John Maynard,
    4:259–262
  Lucas, Robert E., Jr., 4:510
  Lucas critique, 4:511
  macroeconomics, 4:542
  monetarism, 5:242–243
  moral suasion, 5:283
  political business cycles, 1:406

real business cycles, 1:408
Ricardian equivalence, 7:241
Treasury view, 8:444–445
Policy, foreign, 3:**169–172**
Ben-Gurion, David, 1:283
capital controls, 1:432
Castro, Fidel, 1:466–467
Central Intelligence Agency, U.S,
1:484
Chamberlain, Neville, 1:489
Cold War, 2:4
Conservative Party (U.K.), 2:87
Cuban Revolution, 2:186–187
defense, 2:257–259
imperialism, 3:586–589
international relations, 4:100
internationalism, 4:102
isolationism, 4:160–161
Latinos, 4:360
League of Nations, 4:385
Monroe Doctrine, 5:272
political realism, 7:96–97
Thatcher, Margaret, 8:335
Tito, Josip, 8:376
Truman, Harry S., 8:459
Policy, monetary, 6:**293–296**, *294*
balance of payments, 1:238–240
bull and bear markets, 1:386
business cycles, 1:403
capital flight, 1:434
central banks, 1:477–480
Chamberlain, Neville, 1:489
conditionality, 2:65
conservatism, 2:85
cross of gold, 2:180–181
currency, 2:209
currency devaluation and
revaluation, 2:211–212
demand for money, 5:255
dirty float, 2:375
economic sterilization, 8:139–140
employment, 2:582–583
euro, 3:22–23
exchange rates, 3:37–40
exogenous money, 5:258–259
Friedman, Milton, 3:218–219
interest rates, 4:85–86
international economics, 2:509
Keynes, John Maynard, 4:261
liquidity, 4:459
loans, 4:473
Lucas, Robert E., Jr., 4:510
Lucas critique, 4:511
macroeconomics, 4:542

monetarism, 5:242–243
monetary base, 5:244
monetary theory, 5:246–249
money, 5:249–252
moral suasion, 5:283
natural rate of interest, 4:77, 78
nominal interest rates, 4:87
political business cycles, 1:406
real business cycles, 1:407, 408
Ricardian equivalence, 7:241
rules *vs.* discretion, 7:293–294
supply of money, 5:260–261
Treasury view, 8:444–445
Policy, public, 6:**618–620**
agenda setting, 1:48–49
agribusiness, 1:58
bequests, 1:287
brain drain, 1:368
business elites, 6:72
consumption, 2:105
contraception, 2:114
corporatism, 2:140–141
cost-benefit analysis, 2:150–151
creative destruction, 2:164
culture of poverty, 2:206
Dahl, Robert Alan, 2:219–220
dalits, 2:221, 222
Darwin, Charles, 2:231–232, 231*t*
dirigiste, 2:372–374
disability, 2:377–378
disaster management, 2:384–385
economic depression, 2:304
employment, 2:582–583
ethnic diversity and, 2:343
federalism, 3:114
full employment, 3:227–228
GATT, 3:282
gender gap, 3:278
globalization, 3:334
happiness, 3:418–419
hard-core unemployed, 3:422, 423
herd behavior, 3:459
Hunter, Floyd, 3:524–525
immigration, 3:578–579, 580
incrementalism, 3:608–610
interest groups and interests,
4:82–83
interest rates, 4:85
Lasswell, Harold, 4:351
Latino National Political Survey,
4:355
legacy effects, 4:404–405
Lindblom, Charles Edward,
4:452–453

lobbying, 4:474–475
long run, 4:494
Lowi, Theodore J., 4:506
macroeconomics, 4:541–542
Nader, Ralph, 5:359
networks, 5:476
noise pollution, 6:363–364
Pettigrew, Thomas F., 6:234–235
planning, 6:274–276
policy analysis, 6:296–297
pressure groups, 6:442–443
prevention science, 6:446
referendum, 7:120–122
reparations, 7:166–168
rural sociology, 8:8
science, 5:362
social values, 8:582
stem cells, 8:133–134
technotopia, 8:313
theory of second best, 8:350–351
transnational, 9:73
underclass, 8:487
welfare analysis, 9:62–63
whiteness, 9:90
winner's curse, 9:104
Policy analysis, 3:608–610, 6:296–297
Policy experiments. *See* Social
experiments
The Policy-Making Process (Lindblom),
4:453
Policy process. *See* Public policy
Polisario Front, 6:63
Politburo (U.S.S.R.). *See* Presidium
(U.S.S.R.)
Politcs, Southern U.S., 8:32–33
Political action committees (PAC),
1:424, 5:395–396
Political asylum
Latin American immigrants,
3:571, 572
refugee camps, 7:124–125
refugees, 7:126
Political attitudes, 1:**202–204**
Political behavior, 8:606
Political bosses, 1:579
Political business cycles, 1:**406–407**,
479, 4:492–494
Political cartoons, 1:452, 5:377–378
Political clubs, 4:164
See also Political parties
Political Consultative Committee
(PCC), 9:35
Political conventions, 6:297–299
Political correctness, 6:**299–300**
racial slurs, 7:41–42

Political correctness, *continued*
   sexism, 7:473, 474
   women's liberation, 9:114
Political culture, 6:**300–302**
   British, 3:408–410
   bureaucracy, 1:389–391
   campaigning, 1:423–424
   clash of civilizations, 1:559–560
   corruption, 2:145
   political cartoons, 1:452
   political sociology, 8:4
Political development. *See* Democracy
   research
Political dissidents. *See* Dissidents
Political economy, 6:**302–304**
   capitalist mode of production,
     1:445–447
   comparative politics, 6:327
   decentralization, 2:250
   dirigiste, 2:372–374
   Heilbroner, Robert, 3:456–457
   international relations, 4:101
   Marxian economics, 2:515–517
   media, 5:59
   petroleum industry, 6:232
   political business cycles,
     1:406–407
   political sociology, 8:3
   slave trade, 7:538–539
   subsistence agriculture, 3:98
   trade quotas, 6:673
   urban poverty, 6:411
   Wall Street, 9:8–9
Political Economy in Macroeconomics
   (Drazen), 1:406
The Political Economy of Marx
   (Howard and King), 8:576
Political independence. *See* Self-
   determination
Political inequality, 4:**3–5**
   Bentham, Jeremy, 1:285
   caste, 1:458, 463
   creaming, 2:160
   dalits, 2:221–222
   democracy, 2:273, 7:192
   distributive justice, 4:240
   gender inequality, 3:626–627
   underrepresentation, 8:495
Political instability, indices of,
   6:**304–306**
   destabilization, 2:320–321
   political stability, 8:72–74
Political intelligence. *See* Intelligence
Political Justice (Godwin), 4:569

Political Liberalism (Rawls), 4:238,
   559, 7:84, 85
Political machines, 1:579
Political migrants. *See* Refugees
Political movements. *See* Social
   movements
Political neutrality, 5:**489–490**
Political participation, 6:**153–155**
   Asian American politics, 6:322
   authoritarianism, 1:213
   black politics, 6:324, 325–326
   citizenship, 1:542–544
   community power studies, 2:42,
     43
   consensus, 2:82–83
   corruption, 2:144
   coups d'etat, 2:156
   Dahl, Robert Alan, 2:220
   democracy, 2:273, 8:606
   democratization, 2:288
   gender gap, 3:278–279,
     9:108–109, 110–111, 117
   Habermas, Jürgen, 3:401–402
   happiness, 3:418
   Internet, 4:107–109
   labor, 4:303
   Latino politics, 6:337, 338
   liberty, 4:439
   mobilization, 5:213–214
   parliaments and parliamentary
     systems, 6:145–147
   political inequality, 4:4
   political system, 6:317
   polyarchy, 6:366
   representative and participatory
     democracy, 2:283–285
   Riker, William, 7:249
   socioeconomic status, 8:606
   Supreme Court decisions, 9:84–85
   Verba, Sidney, 8:606
   voting, 8:645
Political parties, 6:**306–308**, 8:655
   Asian American politics, 6:322
   authoritarianism, 1:214
   ban on, 8:646
   business cycles, 1:403
   campaigning, 1:423
   Campbell, Angus, 1:425
   centrism, 1:488–489
   checks and balances, 1:496
   Christian Democracy, 2:276–277
   cleavages, 1:577, 578
   clientelism, 1:578
   coalition, 1:587, 3:357
   communism, 2:34

   competitive party systems,
     6:161–163
   Confederate States of America,
     2:67
   Congress, U.S., 2:73–74
   consociational democracy, 2:279
   constituency, 2:90
   cross of gold, 2:181
   dealignment, 2:246–247
   democratization, 2:288
   dictatorship, 2:358, 359
   Diet, 2:361
   elections, 2:557–558, 560,
     561–562
   Hinduism, 3:478
   identification, 2:246
   India, 2:75–77, 3:611–612
   Israel, 4:277
   libertarianism, 4:439
   Mexican Americans, 5:125–126
   mobilization, 5:213–214
   multiparty systems, 5:321–323
   oligarchy, 6:36
   one-party states, 6:41–42
   political conventions, 6:297–299
   populism, 6:383–385
   primaries, 6:458–459
   race, 7:19
   roll calls, 7:277
   Schattschneider, E. E., 7:342–343
   Singh, V. P., 7:521
   Southern U.S., 6:345–346,
     8:32–33, 34–35, 35–38
   spatial theory, 8:44–45
   state capitalism, 1:444
   voting patterns, 8:648–650
   See also names of specific parties;
     Political clubs
Political Parties (Michels), 5:132, 6:36,
   37–38
Political philosophy, 6:**257–259**
   Davis, Angela, 2:243
   Habermas, Jürgen, 3:401–402
   individualism, 3:618–620
   justice, 4:237
   liberalism, 4:425–426
   libertarianism, 4:437–439
   liberty, 4:439–441
   moderates, 5:226–227
   political theory, 6:318
   politics, 6:321
   Popper, Karl, 6:372
   state of nature, 8:110–111
Political power, 6:320, **415–417**
   aristocracy, 1:174

bilateralism, 1:296–297
caste, 1:458, 460, 462–463
Catholic Church, 8:594
Central Intelligence Agency, U.S,
    1:480–485
checks and balances, 1:495–496
civil-military relation, 1:547–548
Cold War, 2:4–5
Congress, U.S., 2:73–74
Congress Party, India, 2:75–77
consociational democracy, 2:278
Constitution, U.S., 2:91
constitutional courts, 2:93
constitutionalism, 2:94
constitutions, 2:94
corporations, 2:136
corporatism, 2:141–142
corruption, 2:143–145
coups d'etat, 2:156
Dahl, Robert Alan, 2:219–220
defense, 2:258
democracy, 2:273, 275–276
democratization, 2:289
elite theory, 2:562–564
elites, 2:564–566
ethnicity, 3:10–11
indirect rule, 3:617–618
inegalitarianism, 3:623–624
Johnson, Lyndon B., 4:209
judicial review, 4:223–225
judiciary, 4:226–227
Key, V. O., Jr., 4:258–259
latifundia, 4:353
Lowi, Theodore J., 4:506
political parties, 6:306–307
political realism, 7:96–97
political sociology, 8:3
polyarchy, 6:366
presidency, 6:440–442
third world, 8:352
Political Power and Social Classes
    (Poulantzas), 1:563, 6:404
Political psychology, 6:**308–310**
    campaigning, 1:423–424
    Lasswell, Harold, 4:351
    Lazarsfeld, Paul Felix, 4:375
Political realism, 4:235, 274–275,
    7:**96–97**
Political representation. *See*
    Constituency; Democracy;
    Representation
Political rights, 1:543
    Congress Party, India, 2:76
    democracy, 2:273
    political inequality, 4:4

Political science, 6:**310–315**
    Almond, Gabriel A., 1:82, 8:606
    Aristotle, 1:174–175
    bureaucracy, 1:389–391
    Campbell, Angus, 1:424–425
    centrism, 1:488–489
    cleavages, 1:577–578
    clientelism, 1:578–579
    coalition, 1:586–587, 587–588
    Cold War, 2:4
    corporatism, 2:140–141
    coups d'etat, 2:156
    federalism, 3:113–115
    Fenno, Richard F., Jr., 3:124–125
    freedom, 3:196–198
    game theory, 3:251
    identity, 3:554
    international relations, 4:99–101
    Kariel, Henry S., 4:249–250
    Keohane, Robert, 4:256–257
    Key, V. O., Jr., 4:258–259
    Lindblom, Charles Edward,
        4:452–453
    opinion polls, 6:356
    political philosophy, 6:257
    political sociology, 8:2–3
    political theory, 6:318
    politics, 6:321
    polling, 6:355
    research, 3:351–352
    social science, 7:616
    spatial theory, 8:44–45
    zero-sum game, 9:177
Political science, behavioral,
    6:312–314, **315–316**
    Easton, David, 2:476–477
    Lasswell, Harold, 4:351
    Merriam, Charles Edward, Jr.,
        5:101–102
    Miller, Warren, 5:180–181
    opinion polls, 6:356
    spatial theory, 8:44–45
Political science and race, 7:**18–21**
    Birth of a Nation (film),
        1:304–306
    Hall, Stuart, 3:409–410
    Latino National Political Survey,
        4:354–356
Political sociology, 8:**2–5**
    conflict, 2:70–71
    democracy research, 7:190–192
    described, 7:662
    Hall, Stuart, 3:408–410
    Lasswell, Harold, 4:351
    Lazarsfeld, Paul Felix, 4:375

macro-sociology, 7:678
    post-Parsonian American
        sociology, 8:5, 6
    sports, 8:63
Political stability, 2:274–276, 421,
    8:**72–74**
Political stratification, 8:3, **168–170**
Political system, 6:**316–317**
    bureaucracy, 1:389–391
    citizenship, 1:542
    comparative politics, 6:327
    Congress, U.S., 2:73–74
    dissidents, 2:411
    economic growth, 2:491
    elites, 2:565–566
    Hamilton, Alexander, 3:413
    heterarchy, 3:468, 469
    indirect rule, 3:617–618
    multiparty systems, 5:321–323
    parliaments and parliamentary
        systems, 6:145–147
    political science, 6:313
    political theory, 6:318
    politics, 6:319, 320–321
    polyarchy, 6:365–366
    revolution, 7:228–231
    revolution of rising expectations,
        7:231–232
    Russian Federation, 7:303
    social system, 7:625
    technocracy, 8:296–297
    technotopia, 8:312–313
    theocracy, 8:342–343
    totalitarianism, 8:394–396
    See also Democracy; Republic
*The Political System: An Inquiry into
    the State of Political Science* (Easton),
    2:477
Political Systems of Highland Burma
    (Leach), 1:128
Political theory, 6:**318–319**
    Burke, Edmund, 1:396–397
    centrism, 1:488–489
    consensus, 2:82–83
    liberty, 4:439–441
    Shklar, Judith, 7:499
Political tolerance, 8:**385–386**
    Church and state, 1:536
    citizenship, 1:543
    xenophobia, 9:158–161
Political trust, 1:193
Politicians. *See* Government; Politics;
    Public sector
Politics, 6:**319–321**
    Beard, Charles, 1:268

Politics, *continued*
  biological determinism, 2:325,
    326
  borders, 1:354–355
  bureaucracy, 1:389–391
  business cycles, 1:403–405
  California Civil Rights Initiative,
    1:416
  census, 1:476
  centrism, 1:488–489
  cleavages, 1:577–578
  coalition, 1:586–587, 587–588
  coffee industry, 1:595
  communalism, 2:31
  community power studies,
    2:42–46
  conflict, 2:70
  Congress, U.S., 2:73–74
  Congress Party, India, 2:75–77
  consensus, 2:82–83
  constituency, 2:89–90
  corporatism, 2:140–141
  corruption, 2:143–145
  coups d'etat, 2:156
  cultural rights, 2:197
  cultural tourism, 2:201–202
  dealignment, 2:246–247
  democracy research, 7:190–192
  diplomacy, 2:370–371
  direct action, 2:372
  documentary studies, 2:434
  elections, 2:557–558
  elites, 2:565–566
  Exit, Voice, and Loyalty
    (Hirschman), 3:43–45
  global, 3:333–334, 360
  Illuminati, 3:562
  impeachment, 3:584–586
  imprisonment, 3:596, 597
  initiative, 4:39–40
  Internet, 4:107–109
  journalism, 4:211–212
  judiciary, 4:226–227
  labor, 4:302
  land reform, 4:344–345
  law and order, 4:369–372
  lobbying, 4:474–475
  metropolitan regions, 7:135
  military-industrial complex,
    5:173–174
  minorities, 5:192
  moderates, 5:226–227
  multiparty systems, 5:321–323
  patronage, 6:176–177
  pluralism, 6:282–284

  political cartoons, 1:452
  political sociology, 8:2–3
  political system, 6:316–317
  political theory, 6:318
  pressure groups, 6:442–443
  racial classification, 7:39
  religion, 7:160–161
  representation, 7:172
  Royal Commissions, 7:292
  Russian Federation, 7:302–303
  school vouchers, 7:348–349
  social movements, 7:603–607
  social relations, 7:612–613
  sports industry, 8:67
  subaltern, 8:191
  tariffs, 8:265–266
  tolerance, 8:385–386
  women, 1:522, 9:108–110
  See also specific countries
Politics, Asian American, 6:**321–323**,
  7:20–21
Politics, black, 6:**323–326**
  Chisholm, Shirley, 1:522
  Coloreds (South Africa), 2:15–17
  Defender, 1:501
  Harris, Abram L., Jr., 3:427
  public opinion, 7:18–20
Politics, comparative, 6:**326–329**
  Almond, Gabriel A., 1:82
  described, 6:321
  left and right, 4:401–402
  left wing, 4:402–404
  political culture, 6:301
Politics, Economics, and Welfare
  (Lindblom and Dahl), 4:452
Politics, gay, lesbian, transgender, and
  bisexual, 6:**329–332**, 663–665
  blackness, 1:330
  civil rights movement, U.S., 1:552
  critical race theory, 2:175
  deviance, 2:353–354
  left wing, 4:403
  same-sex marriage, 4:619–621
  sexual orientation, 7:479
Politics, gender, 6:**332–334**
  Chisholm, Shirley, 1:522
  Mankiller, Wilma, 4:586
  Mill, John Stuart, 5:179
Politics, identity, 6:**334–336**
  caste, 1:458, 460, 462–463
  Coloreds (South Africa), 2:15–17
  race-conscious policies, 7:38
  Roma, 7:279
  self-determination, 7:407

Politics, Latino, 6:**337–339**, 338*t*
  Latino National Political Survey,
    4:354–356
  Mexican Americans, 5:125–126
  public opinion, 7:20–21
Politics, Parties, and Pressure Groups
  (Key), 4:258–259
Politics, reproductive. *See*
  Reproductive politics
Politics, Southern, 6:**339–349**
  black, 6:343–346
  civil rights movement, 6:342–343
  Civil War, 6:340
  Democratic Party (U.S.),
    2:286–287
  Dixiecrats, 2:428–431
  Key, V. O., Jr., 4:258
  modern, 6:346–349
  race, 7:19
  Reconstruction Era, 6:340–341,
    7:111–115
  Southern bloc, 8:34–35
  Southern strategy, 8:35–38
  states' rights, 6:343
  studies, 6:339–340
  Thurmond, Strom, 8:360–361
  voting, 6:341
  See also Jim Crow; Segregation;
    U.S. Civil War
Politics, urban, 6:**349–351**, 350*t*
  clientelism, 1:579
  community power studies, 2:42,
    44–45
  Southern, 6:347
*Politics: Who Gets What, When, and
  How* (Lasswell), 4:351
Politics (Aristotle), 1:175
*Politics among Nations: The Struggle for
  Power and Peace* (Morgenthau),
  5:295, 420
Politics and Markets (Lindblom), 4:453
Politics and Society in the South (Black
  and Black), 6:339, 340
The Politics of the Developing Areas
  (Almond and Coleman), 1:82
Polivy, Janet, 6:3
Polk, James, 5:126, 127–129
Poll, Roper. *See* Pollsters
Poll tax, U.K. *See* Thatcher, Margaret
Poll tax, U.S., 1:552, 6:**351–353**
Polling, 6:**353–355**
  dealignment, 2:246, 247
  exit poll, 3:45–46
  pollsters, 6:358–359
Pollock, Friedrich, 1:446, 2:176

Polls, exit, 3:**45–46**

Polls, opinion, 6:**355–358**
    cross-sectional research,
        7:189–190
    polling, 6:353–355
    pollsters, 6:358–359

Polls, straw, 6:356

Pollsters, 6:**358–359**

Pollution, 6:**359–361**
    agricultural industry, 1:62
    Coase theorem, 1:590
    environmental impact assessment,
        2:605–607
    environmental Kuznets curves,
        2:607–609
    Kuznets hypothesis, 5:541
    legacy effects, 4:404
    light, 6:360
    limits of growth, 4:449
    Love Canal, 4:504–505
    NAFTA, 5:541
    technological change, 1:490
    urbanization, 8:547
    See also Environmental impact

Pollution, air, 6:360, **361–363**

Pollution, noise, 6:360, **363–364**

Pollution, water, 4:154, 6:**364–365**,
    9:41

Pollution taxes. *See* Air pollution

Polo, Marco, 1:119, 427

Polyarchy, 2:220, 6:282, **365–367**

Polyarchy (Dahl), 2:288

Polybius, 1:495

Polygamy. *See* Marriage

Polygenesis, 7:10

Polygons, 3:208, *208*

Polygraphs. *See* Interrogation; Lying

Polygyny. *See* Dowry and bride price

Polyhedrons, 8:563

Polytheism, 6:**367–368**
    monotheism, 5:268, 270
    theism, 8:340–341

Polyvinyl chloride (PVC), 8:621

Pompeii, 1:165

Pompidou, Georges, 2:265

Pontecorvo, Gillo, 1:257–258

Pontifical Commission for the Vatican
    State, 8:593

Ponzi, Charles, 6:368

Ponzi scheme, 6:**368–369**

Poole, Elijah. *See* Muhammad, Elijah

Pooled time series and cross-sectional
    data, 6:**369–371**, *370, 371,* 371*t,*
    7:455–457

Poor. *See* Poverty

Poor people. *See* Poverty

Poor Richard's Almanack (Franklin),
    3:190

"Pop Goes the Weasel," 5:549–550

Pop music, 9:141–142

Popes. *See names of specific popes;*
    Papacy; Roman Catholic Church;
    Vatican

Popper, Karl, 1:332, 6:**371–373**
    Campbell, Donald, 1:426
    communalism, 2:31
    economic methodology, 2:493
    Lakatos, Imre, 4:338–339
    liberalism, 4:425
    logic, 4:480
    philosophy of science, 6:260–261
    prediction, 6:429, 430
    science, 7:358, 359
    scientific method, 7:362–363

The Popular Arts (Hall), 3:409

Popular culture, 6:**373–376**
    Black Arts Movement, 1:309
    cultural studies, 2:199
    as culture, 2:203
    identity, 3:551
    lifestyles, 4:445
    literature, 4:464

Popular Culture and High Culture
    (Gans), 3:256

Popular culture studies. *See* Cultural
    studies

Popular Front movement, 5:497

Popular initiative. *See* Initiative

Popular music, 6:**376–377**
    bluegrass, 1:341–342
    jingoism, 4:201–202
    Rastafari, 7:68–69
    rock 'n' roll, 7:268–269
    See also Jazz

Popular sovereignty
    nation-states, 5:421
    nationalism, 5:417

Popular Unity (Chile), 1:77–78

Population, aging, 3:306–307, 6:93,
    94, 9:72

*Population: An Introduction to Concepts
    and Issues* (Weeks), 2:295

Population (Malthus). *See An Essay on
    the Principle of Population* (Malthus)

The Population Bomb (Ehrlich), 4:448,
    6:95

Population control, 6:**377–378**
    Club of Rome, 1:585
    depopulation, 2:301–302
    population growth, 6:380

zero population growth,
    9:173–176
See also Birth control;
    Contraception; Eugenics;
    Family planning; Reproduction

Population decline. *See* Depopulation

Population ecology, 6:69

Population growth, 6:**378–381**
    baby boomers, 1:235–236
    Boserup, Ester, 1:357, 358
    census, 1:476–477
    conundrum, 2:116
    deforestation, 2:264
    demographic transition,
        2:291–292
    demography, 2:293
    diminishing returns, 7:218
    doubling time, 3:366
    food crisis, 3:164–165
    land use, 8:546
    limits of growth, 4:448, 449
    Malthus, Thomas, 3:164
    Malthusian trap, 4:572–573
    morbidity and mortality, 5:291
    population studies, 6:381–382
    projections, 6:95–96
    slaves, 1:40
    stable nodes, 5:510
    Tragedy of the Commons, 8:422
    urbanization, 8:546, 547
    water resources, 9:40
    zero, 9:173–176
    See also Depopulation;
        Overpopulation

Population Reference Bureau, 6:95

Population Registration Act (South
    Africa 1950), 2:15

Population studies, 6:**381–383**
    butterfly effect, 1:414
    census, 1:476–477
    cities, 1:540
    Current Population Survey,
        2:212–213
    demographic transition,
        2:291–292
    demography, 2:292–295
    diversity, 2:419–420
    Graunt, John, 3:366–367
    Malthus, Thomas Robert,
        4:569–571
    Malthusian trap, 4:572–573
    mean, 5:51
    metropolitan regions, 7:132–135
    regions, 7:130
    social demography, 2:295–297

Population studies, *continued*
   See also Depopulation;
    Overpopulation
Population Studies (Hauser and
   Duncan), 2:296
Population surplus, 1:446, 8:**237–240**
Populism, 6:**383–385**, 9:99
   African socialism, 7:638, 640
   Chávez, Hugo, 1:494–495
   class conflict, 1:570–571
   Clinton, Bill, 1:579
   conservatism, 2:85, 86
   cross of gold, 2:181
   Democratic Party (U.S.), 2:286,
    287
   elitism, 2:567
   Hall, Stuart, 3:409, 410
   Peronism, 6:214
   Russian Revolution, 7:303
   Wizard of Oz, 9:105
Populists. *See* Populism
Pornography. *See* Obscenity
The Portable Voltaire (Redman), 8:635
Porter, Gareth, 8:614
Porter, Michael, 2:139
Porter, Theodore, 6:655
Portes, Alejandro, 4:359–360
   development in sociology, 2:347,
    348
   ethnic enclave, 3:3, 4
   Latin American sociology, 7:676
   social capital, 7:565–566
   See also Assimilation
Portfolio investment. *See* Investment
Portfolio management, 3:141
Portugal
   Anglo-Portuguese trade, 8:413
   Cabral, Amílcar, 1:415
   Columbus, Christopher, 2:19, 20
   Corn Laws, 2:133, 134
   coups d'etat, 2:156
   decolonization, 2:256
   judiciary, 4:227
   Napoleonic Wars, 5:365, 368
   NATO, 5:544–546
   overseas conquests, 3:341
   slavery, 1:39, 5:458
   state capitalism, 1:444
Positional bargaining, 5:457
Positive criminology. *See* Ortiz,
   Fernando
Positive liberty, 4:439–440
Positive psychology, 6:54, **385–386**
   flow, 3:157–158
   optimism, 6:55

Seligman, Martin, 7:432
   social psychology, 7:609
   See also Hope
Positive Psychology Center. *See*
   Positive psychology; Seligman,
   Martin
Positive social science, 6:**387–389**
   Comte, Auguste, 2:62
   normative social sciences *vs.,*
    5:534–536
   Riker, William, 7:249
   survey research, 7:196
Positivism, 6:**389–392**
   behaviorism, 1:277, 278
   Comte, Auguste, 2:62
   empiricism, 2:578
   epistemology, 2:609
   hermeneutics, 3:462
   international relations, 4:99
   internationalism, 4:102
   jurisprudence, 4:232
   logic, 4:481
   methodology, 5:108–109
   political science, 6:312
   positive social science, 6:387–389
   realist theory, 7:98–99
   rhetoric, 7:238
   Riker, William, 7:249
   theory, 8:343, 344
   value free social science,
    7:618–619
Positron emission tomography (PET),
   5:485
Posner, Gerald, 9:34
Posner, Richard, 1:270, 502, 4:367
Possessive individualism. *See*
   Individualism
Possibility theorem, Arrow. *See* Arrow
   possibility theorem
Post Keynesian economics, 2:**528–529**
   casino capitalism, 1:455–456
   central banks, 1:478, 480
   full employment, 3:226–227
   inflation, 4:24–26
   involuntary unemployment, 4:138
   Kahn, Richard F., 4:245
   Kalecki, Michał, 4:246
   Keynes, John Maynard, 4:260
   marginal product of labor, 4:307
   markup pricing, 4:610–612
   Minsky, Hyman, 5:193–194
   uncertainty, 8:482
Post-Parsonian American sociology,
   8:**5–8**

Post-processual archaeology,
   1:168–169
Post-traumatic stress, 1:146, 6:19,
   401–403, 8:174
   described, 8:440–441
   military, 5:170–171
   multiple personalities, 5:328
   phobia, 6:263
   torture, 8:393
Post-traumatic stress disorder (PTSD).
   See Post-traumatic stress
Postbellum period, 3:348
Postclassical economics, 7:13, 14, 15
Postcolonialism, 6:**392–393**
   African socialism, 7:638
   Caribbean, 1:448
   constructivism, 2:97
   decolonization, 2:257
   developing countries, 2:336–337
   ethnic enterprises, 3:6
   hybridity, 3:535, 536
   narratives, 5:372
   representation, 7:172–173
   underdevelopment, 8:489–491
   Zionism, 9:180
   See also Colonialism
Postdam Agreement (1945), 9:35
Posterior density. *See* Bayesian
   econometrics
Posterior distribution. *See* Statistical
   inference
Postfeminism, 9:117
Posthumus, Nicholaas, 3:375
Postindustrialism, 4:283–284
   future shock, 3:240
   industrialization, 3:622
   mobility, 5:210–211
   occupational hazards, 6:22
   technocracy, 8:296, 297
Postlethwayt, Malachy, 6:**394–395**
Postmodern Geographers (Soja), 3:305
Postmodernism, 6:**395–397**
   constructivism, 2:97
   cultural studies, 2:199
   development in sociology, 2:348
   feminism, 9:115, 117
   gender studies, 3:279
   Generation X, 3:292
   geography, 3:305
   Kariel, Henry S., 4:249
   media, 5:60
   political philosophy, 6:259
   political sociology, 8:5
   poststructuralism, 6:398
   realist theory, 7:97–98, 99

social change, 7:569

social science, 7:616–617

sociology, 7:663

subjectivity, 8:199

theater, 8:338

tourism, 8:399–400

urban studies, 8:542

Postmodernism and development theory (PAD), 2:348

Postnationalism, 1:543, 6:**397–398**

Postpositivist realism. *See* Realist theory

Poststructuralism, 6:**398–401**

Bourdieu, Pierre, 1:359

cultural studies, 2:199

Derrida, Jacques, 2:310

discourse, 2:387

Enlightenment, 2:595–596

international relations, 4:101

political sociology, 8:5

power, 6:414

social science, 7:616–617

Potassium fertilizers, 3:131–132

Potenital Pareto improvement, 9:65

Potron, Maurice, 6:**403–404,** 9:157–158

Potter, Kimberly, 3:431

Pottery, 8:630, 631

Pottier, Johan, 3:163

Poulantzas, Nicos, 6:**404–405**

bourgeoisie, 1:360

capitalist mode of production, 1:447

class, 1:563, 564

political science, 6:313–314

power, 6:413–414

surplus labor, 4:311

Pound (British currency), 2:211, 211*t*

Poverty, 6:**405–408**

attitudes, 1:202

benign neglect, 1:283–284

black capitalism, 1:439, 441–442

black liberalism, 1:312

child labor, 1:509

civil wars, 1:555

Congress Party, India, 2:76

consumerism, 2:105

conundrum, 2:116

corruption, 2:145

Current Population Survey, 2:213

dalits, 2:222

De Soto, Hernando, 2:319–320

democracy, 2:274

development theory, 2:337–339

discrimination, 2:391

ethnic diversity and, 2:343

female-headed families, 3:115–116, 274

freedom, 3:200

function of, 3:256

gender, 3:273–274

ghettos, 3:312–313

globalization, 3:332, 9:46–47

happiness, 3:416–418

Head Start, 3:437

Head Start experiments, 3:438–440

health in developing countries, 3:442

hierarchy of needs, 5:541

homelessness, 3:498, 499

household sample survey, 5:409–410

income inequality, 4:3

isolation of, 3:138

Jencks, Christopher, 4:184

King, Martin Luther, Jr., 4:269

laissez-faire, 4:335, 336, 337, 338

land reform, 4:341–345

latifundia, 4:353, 354

liberation theology, 4:434–436

low and high culture, 2:205

Luxembourg Income Study, 4:519–521

malnutrition, 4:567–568

Malthus, Thomas Robert, 4:570–571

marginalization, 4:599

Medicaid, 5:61–62

metropolitan regions, 7:134

minimum wage, 5:186

modernization, 5:233

Moving to Opportunity, 5:302–303

Moynihan Report, 5:305–306

Native Americans, 5:428

needs, 5:454

New Deal, 5:495

regressive taxes, 8:284–285

social Darwinism, 5:495

social policy interventions, 4:118, 119

social welfare system, 7:631–633

The South, 5:546

statistics, 3:92, 92*t*

street culture, 8:172–173

Tally's Corner, 8:263–264

third world, 5:541–542

urban anthropology, 1:134

urbanization, 8:547

vagabonds, 8:567

Venezuela, 1:495

water resources, 9:40

wealth, 9:45

working poor, 3:77, 9:122

World Bank, 9:138–139

See also Culture of poverty; Underclass; War on poverty; Welfare

Poverty, culture of. *See* Culture of poverty

Poverty, indices of, 6:**408–410**

Poverty, urban, 1:541, 542, 6:**410–412**

Lewis, Oscar, 4:418–419

Multi-City Study of Urban Inequality, 5:314–315

neighborhood effects, 5:461–463

slums, 7:551–552

Poverty and Depression in the United States (Keyserling), 9:25

Poverty line. *See* Indices of poverty

Povery and Famines (Sen), 3:164

Powell, Adam Clayton Powell, Jr., 1:321, 9:25

Powell, Colin, 2:371

Powell, Gladys, 9:81

Powell, John Wesley, 8:389

Powell, Lewis F., 3:392

Powell, Walter, 6:70

Power, 6:**412–414**

alliances, 1:79

baby boomers, 1:235

bureaucracy, 1:389–391

Clark, Kenneth B., 1:561

class, 1:563

coercive, 3:387

community, 2:42–46, 4:528

constructivism, 2:97

cultural capital, 2:189, 190

curriculum, 2:214

in decision-making, 5:518

destabilization, 2:320–321

deviance, 2:353

diplomacy, 2:371

emergency

dictatorship, 2:359

repression, 7:175

emotion, 2:570

executive branch, 3:355

firms, 3:149

groups, 3:386–387

hegemony, 3:455–456

heterarchy, 3:469

Power, *continued*
    Hunter, Floyd, 3:524–525
    Huntington, Samuel P., 3:525–526
    Kshatriyas, 4:291–292
    labeling theory, 4:300
    law, 4:363
    legitimate, 3:353–354
    market, 2:51–53
    material culture, 5:16
    minorities, 5:191
    Morgenthau, Hans, 5:295
    occupational status, 6:26–28
    patriarchy, 6:173–174
    prestige, 6:443–444
    racial discrimination, 2:394
    representation, 7:172–173
    social distinctions, 2:412
    social exchange theory, 7:585–586
    transparency, 8:434–435
    underrepresentation, 8:495
    urban studies, 8:542
    values, 8:582
    visual arts, 8:631–632
    See also Community power studies
Power, balance of. *See* Balance of power
Power, community. *See* Community power studies
Power, Marilyn, 5:213
Power, market. *See* Imperfect competition
Power, monopoly. *See* Monopoly
Power, political, 6:320, **415–417**
    aristocracy, 1:174
    bilateralism, 1:296–297
    caste, 1:458, 460, 462–463
    Catholic Church, 8:594
    Central Intelligence Agency, U.S, 1:480–485
    checks and balances, 1:495–496
    civil-military relation, 1:547–548
    Cold War, 2:4–5
    Congress, U.S., 2:73–74
    Congress Party, India, 2:75–77
    consociational democracy, 2:278
    Constitution, U.S., 2:91
    constitutional courts, 2:93
    constitutionalism, 2:94
    constitutions, 2:94
    corporations, 2:136
    corporatism, 2:141–142
    corruption, 2:143–145
    coups d'etat, 2:156
    Dahl, Robert Alan, 2:219–220

    defense, 2:258
    democracy, 2:273, 275–276
    democratization, 2:289
    elite theory, 2:562–564
    elites, 2:564–566
    ethnicity, 3:10–11
    indirect rule, 3:617–618
    inegalitarianism, 3:623–624
    Johnson, Lyndon B., 4:209
    judicial review, 4:223–225
    judiciary, 4:226–227
    Key, V. O., Jr., 4:258–259
    latifundia, 4:353
    Lowi, Theodore J., 4:506
    political parties, 6:306–307
    political realism, 7:96–97
    political sociology, 8:3
    polyarchy, 6:366
    presidency, 6:440–442
    third world, 8:352
Power elite, 6:**417–418**
    bureaucracy, 1:390, 391
    caste, 1:463
    community power studies, 2:42–46
    corporatism, 2:141–142
    corruption, 2:143–145
    crime and criminology, 2:170
    Dahl, Robert Alan, 2:219–220
    decolonization, 2:256
    democratization, 2:289
    hierarchy, 3:474–475
    knowledge society, 4:285
    Latino politics, 6:337
    leaders, 4:376
    Lowi, Theodore J., 4:506
    Lynd, Robert and Helen, 4:528
    Mills, C. Wright, 5:182
    political parties, 6:307
    state capitalism, 1:444
    See also Elites
The Power Elite (Mills), 2:567, 4:528, 5:182, 482, 8:597
The Power of the Purse (Fenno), 3:124–125
Power plants. *See* Energy industry
Power politics. *See* Political realism
Powerlessness, 3:196, 6:30
Powers, Joelle D., 8:572
Powers, separation of. *See* Separation of powers
Poyas, Peter, 8:609
PPO (Preferred provider organizations), 2:53, 54

PPP (People's Political Party), 3:258, 259
PPP (Purchasing power parity). *See* Purchasing power parity
PQ (Parti Québécois), 6:662, 663
Practice-related validation, 8:571–572
Practice theory, 6:**418–419**
Practicing anthropology. *See* Public anthropology
Praetorian polities, 2:156
Pragmatism, 6:**419–421**
    behaviorism, 1:276
    constructivism, 2:96
    habits, 3:402–403
    Hegel, Georg Wilhelm Friedrich, 3:453
    James, William, 4:169–170
    Janowitz, Morris, 4:172
    knowledge, 4:279–280
    Mead, George Herbert, 5:46
    Rorty, Richard, 7:285–286
Pragmatism: A New Name for Some Old Ways of Thinking (James), 4:169, 170
Pragmatism and Religion (James), 4:170
Prägnanz, 3:310
Prato, Giuliana B., 1:135
Pratt, John, 8:556
Praxeology, 1:211
Praxis, 6:**421–422**
    behaviorism, 1:276
    class conflict, 1:569
    constructivism, 2:96
Prayer, school, 1:536, 2:86, 3:236
Prayer Meeting, or, The First Militant Minister (Caldwell), 1:310
PRBA (Program for Research on Black Americans), 5:415–416
PRC (Partido Revolucionario Cubano), 1:464
Pre-Columbian peoples, 1:166, 3:515–516, 5:119, 423, 6:39, **426–427**
    See also Incas
Pre-historic Times, as Illustrated by Ancient Remains, and the Manners and Customs of Modern Savages (Lubbock), 1:166
Preadaptations, 2:228
    See also Adaptation
Prebisch, Raúl, 6:**422–423**
    dependency theory, 2:299
    developing countries, 2:335
    development economics, 2:345

Economic Commission for Latin America and the Caribbean, 2:482
economic inequality, 9:47
immiserizing growth, 3:583
industrialization, 3:621
Latin American sociology, 7:676
Prebisch-Singer hypothesis, 6:424
Singer, Hans, 7:520
structuralist macroeconomics, 4:543
terms of trade, 8:325–326
Prebisch-Singer hypothesis, 6:**423–426**, 8:505
development economics, 2:345
Singer, Hans, 7:520
terms of trade, 8:325–326
Precautionary motive. *See* Demand for money
Precedents, legal. *See* Legal precedents
Preconsciousness, 3:212
See also Consciousness
Predation, 8:596, 597
Predator-prey models. *See* Predatory pricing
Predator-prey system, 5:524
Predatory pricing, 2:462, 6:**428–429**
Predestination, 6:566–567
Predetermined variables, 4:47, 8:**586–588**
Prediction, 6:**429–431**
adaptive expectations, 1:19–20
Bayesian statistics, 1:265–266
bull and bear markets, 1:385–386
butterfly effect, 1:413–414
causality, 1:472
cointegration, 2:2–3
computers, 2:60–61
currency appreciation and depreciation, 2:209–210
decision-making, 2:252
econometrics, 2:480–482
economic model, 2:494
efficient market hypothesis, 2:548–549
futurology, 3:240–242
growth curve analysis, 3:392
imperfect competition, 2:52
implicit expectations, 3:50–51
lagging, leading and coincident indicators, 4:331
loss functions, 4:495–502
out-of-sample, 3:230
perfect foresight, 3:172–174
random walk, 7:61–63

rational expectations, 3:51–52
static expectations, 3:53
theory, 8:344–345
time trends, 8:373
trait theory, 8:425
Predictive genetic testing, 3:295–296
Predictive validity, 8:572
Preemptive strike, 2:258, 6:**431–432**
Preface to Democratic Theory (Dahl), 1:578, 2:220
Preference, color, 2:17, 6:**432–433**
Preference, gender, 6:**433–435**
Preferences, 6:**435–437**
Arrow possibility theorem, 1:183–184
choice in economics, 1:524–525
choice in psychology, 1:525–526
classical conditioning, 1:574
Condorcet, Marquis de, 2:66
conformity, 2:72
consumer, 2:99–102
consumption, 2:107
conversational analysis, 2:118, 119
demand, 2:269
generalized system of, 9:143
indifference curve, 9:64, 64–65
models, 5:519
ordinality, 6:56–57
over preferences, 5:535
rationality, 7:80
relative income hypothesis, 7:153, 154
revealed, 8:580
utilitarianism, 8:554, 9:63–64
utility function, 8:556
want creation, 9:14–15
See also Tastes
Preferences, endogenous, 2:**586–587**
Preferences, interdependent, 2:586, 6:**437–438**
Preferences, lexicographic. *See* Lexicographic preferences
Preferences, revealed. *See* Revealed preference
Preferences, time. *See* Time preference
Preferential bloc voting. *See* Bloc vote
Preferential boost systems, 6:668–670
Preferred provider organizations (PPO), 2:53, 54
Prehistoric archaeology, 1:117, 166
Preimplantation genetic diagnosis (PGD), 3:294–295
Preindustrial society, 1:8, 173–174
Prejudice, 6:**438–440**
Allport, Gordon W., 1:81

bigotry, 1:295–296
colorism, 2:17–18
constructivism, 2:97
contact hypothesis, 2:111–112
discrimination, 2:389
ethnicity, 3:9–10
ethnocentrism, 3:11–12
intergroup relations, 4:91
interracial sex, 7:468–470
marginal product of labor, 4:306
polling, 6:354–355
race, 7:2–7
race and psychology, 7:23
racial inequality, 4:6
racism, 7:44, 45
Rastafari, 7:67
social dominance orientation, 7:583–584
social science, 7:615–616
stereotypes, 8:136–139
stigma, 8:146–148
wage discrimination, 2:400–401, 404, 405–406
xenophobia, 9:158–161
Prejudice and Your Child (Clark), 1:561
Premack, David, 8:346
Premium, liquidity. *See* Liquidity premium
Premium wages, 6:24–25
Prenatal diagnostic testing, 3:294–295
Prescott, Edward, 1:404, 407, 408, 479
Prescott-Clarke, Patricia, 2:141–142
Present orientation. *See* Time orientation
Presentation, self. *See* Self-presentation
The Presentation of Self in Everyday Life (Goffman), 3:337
Preservation, cultural, 1:150, 2:197
Presidency, 3:355, 6:**440–442**, 8:610–611
autocracy, 1:216
Bush, George H. W., 1:398
Bush, George W., 1:399–400
business cycles, 1:403
Carter, Jimmy, 1:450–451
checks and balances, 1:496
Clinton, Bill, 1:579–581
Confederate States of America, 2:66
Congress, U.S., 2:74
Constitution, U.S., 2:91
constitutions, 2:95
Davis, Jefferson, 2:243–244

Presidency, *continued*
Democratic Party (U.S.),
2:287–288
Eisenhower, Dwight D.,
2:554–555
electoral college, 2:559–560
Hamilton, Alexander, 3:413
impeachment, 3:584, 585, 586
Jefferson, Thomas, 4:179–183
Johnson, Lyndon B., 4:209–210
Kennedy, John F., 4:253–255
Lincoln, Abraham, 4:450–451
lobbying, 4:474
Madison, James, 4:547–548
primary, 6:458–459
Reagan, Ronald, 7:88–89
Roosevelt, Franklin D., 7:282–283
separation of powers, 7:448–449
term limits, 8:323, 324, 9:37
Truman, Harry S., 1:480–482,
8:459–460
*See also names of specific U.S.
presidents*
*President Roosevelt and the Coming of
the War: A Study in Appearances and
Realities, 1941* (Beard), 1:268–269
President's Commission on the
Assassination of John F. Kennedy.
See Warren Report
President's Committee on Equal
Employment Opportunity, 1:31
President's Conference on Juvenile
Delinquency and Youth Crime
(PCJDYC), 9:25
President's Daily Brief, 1:481
Presidium (U.S.S.R.), 1:370
Press. *See* Journalism
Press, freedom of. *See* Freedom of the
press
Presser, Stanley, 8:571
Pressure, peer. *See* Peer influence
Pressure groups, 6:442–443
Congress, U.S., 2:74
interest groups and interests, 4:82
lobbying, 4:474–475
military-industrial complex,
5:173–174
Prestige, 6:443–445
Asch, Solomon, 1:186
occupational status, 6:26–28
socioeconomic status, 7:657–658
Preston, Lewis, 9:138
Preston, Paul, 3:186
Preston, Samuel, 8:592
Presumption of innocence, 7:292
Preto. *See* Pardo

Pretos, 1:328
Prevention science, 6:445–447
crime and criminology, 2:173–174
psychological depression, 2:308
risk assessment, 8:656, 657
Preventive action, 6:431–432
PRG (People's Revolutionary
Goverment (Grenada), 3:381–383
PRI (Partido Revolucionario
Institucional). *See* Partido
Revolucionario Institucional (PRI)
Price, bride. *See* Dowry and bride
price
Price, groom. *See* Dowry and bride
price
Price, market. *See* Exchange value
Price controls. *See* Inflation; Wage and
price controls
Price discrimination, 2:392–393
monopsony, 5:267–268
product dumping, 2:462
revenue, 7:226–227
Price-dividends ratio. *See* Market
fundamentals
Price-earnings ratio. *See* Market
fundamentals
Price-enhancing ratio. *See* Market
fundamentals
Price indices, 6:447–450, *450*
Fisher, Irving, 3:151
hedonic prices, 3:451
Laspeyres, 3:151, 5:398
national income accounts, 5:398
quantity index, 6:656–657
real income, 7:90
The Price of Power (Hersh), 4:275
Price setting and price taking,
6:450–453, *451, 452*
monopolistic competition, 2:56
predatory pricing, 6:428–429
price discrimination, 2:392–393
Price skimming. *See* Price
discrimination
Price-specie-flow mechanism. *See*
Hume process
Price taking. *See* Price setting and
price taking
Price theory, 1:502
Price vs. quantity adjustment,
6:453–454
Price Wicksell effects (PWE), 9:94–95
Prices, 6:455–457
aggregate demand, 1:50
aggregate supply, 1:51–53, 53–55
banana industry, 1:245

Barro-Grossman model,
1:255–256
bull and bear markets, 1:385–386
buying *vs.* selling, 8:580
Cambridge capital controversy,
1:420
capital, 1:430
carrying cost, 1:449
coffee industry, 1:594–595
competition, 2:50–51
consumer, 2:99–102, 104
contango, 2:112
cotton industry, 2:153, 154
cross of gold, 2:181
discrimination, 2:392–393
elasticity, 2:555–556
equilibrium, 8:576, 577
exchange value, 3:40–41
flexibility, 3:156–157
general equilibrium, 3:283–285
hedonic, 3:451–452, 7:485
Hilferding, Rudolf, 3:476
imperfect competition, 2:52
inflation, 4:23–26
liquidity trap, 4:461–462
long period analysis, 4:489–491
long run, 4:491
market, 1:449–450, 8:67–68
market-clearing, 1:183
market correction, 4:603–604
markup, 4:610–612
markup pricing, 4:610–612
microeconomics, 5:134–135
monetary policy, 6:294–295
monopoly, 5:264–265
monopsony, 5:267–268
natural resources, 5:438
partial equilibrium, 6:152
Phillips curve, 6:248–250
predatory, 2:462, 6:428–429
predatory pricing, 6:428–429
price setting and price taking,
6:450–453
price *vs.* quantity adjustment,
6:453–454
professional journals, 4:216
shadow, 6:456, 7:484–486
sticky, 8:143–144
subjective value, 8:578–581
tâtonnement, 8:270–271
trade, 6:672–673, 8:411–413
transfer, 8:428–429
value, objective, 8:577–578
water, 9:40–41

Wholesale Price Index, 9:93–94
Wicksell effects, 9:94–95
Prices, long period. *See* Long period analysis
Prices and Production (Hayek), 1:211, 3:434
Prices of production. *See* Long run
Pricing, transfer. *See* Transfer pricing
Pride. *See* Shame
Priestley, Joseph, 7:236
Priestley, M. B., 9:82–83
Primacy/recency effects, 6:457–458
Primaries, 6:458–459
    campaigning, 1:423
    political conventions, 6:298–299
    white, 9:83–85
Primary groups, 3:85, 385
Primary health care (PHC), 3:443
    See also Medicine
Primary labor markets, 8:637
    See also Labor market
Primates, 1:117–118, 6:459–462
    alpha-males, 1:83–84
    Johanson, Donald, 4:206–207
    Leakey, Richard, 4:386–387
    nonadditive determinism, 2:330
    theory of mind, 8:346
    tools, 8:388
Priming, 6:462–463, 7:344, 572
Primitive accumulation, 4:345, 6:463–465
Primitive communism, 2:37–38
Primitive Culture (Tylor), 1:114, 127
Primitive Marriage (McLennan), 1:127
Primitive religion, 1:114
Primitive Religion (Lowie), 4:507
Primitive societies. *See* Primitivism
Primitive Society (Lowie), 4:507
Primitivism, 6:465–466
    anthropology, 1:137
    civilization, 1:557
    Harlem Renaissance, 3:425, 426
Primogeniture, 1:174, 3:86
Primordialism, 2:631, 3:10, 5:378
Primus, Pearl, 2:223
The Prince (Machiavelli), 4:533, 534
Principal-agent models, 5:281, 6:467–468
Principal component analysis. *See* Factor analysis
Principal components, 6:466–467
The Principle of Hope (Bloch), 8:561–562

Principles (Ricardo). *See* On the Principles of Political Economy and Taxation (Ricardo)
Principles of Behavior (Hull), 3:506
Principles of Economics (Marshall), 2:48, 4:312, 608, 622, 623, 624, 7:174, 8:229, 555
Principles of Economics (Menger), 1:210
Principles of Geology, Being an Attempt to Explain the Former Changes of the Earth Surface by Reference to Causes Now in Operation (Lyell), 1:166
Principles of Morals and Legislation (Bentham), 8:554–556
Principles of Perceptual Learning and Development (Gibson), 1:506
Principles of Political Economy (Mill), 8:553
The Principles of Psychology (James), 2:80, 4:169
The Principles of Psychology (Miller), 1:597
The Principles of Scientific Management (Taylor), 3:77, 8:287, 365
Prior distribution. *See* Bayesian inference
Prior restraint. *See* Censorship
Priors. *See* Bayesian econometrics
Prison industry, 6:468–469
Prison labor. *See* Servitude
The Prison Notebooks (Gramsci), 3:364, 4:66
Prison psychology, 6:470–471
Prisoner's dilemma (Economics), 2:27, 6:471–472
Prisoner's dilemma (Psychology), 3:32, 6:256, 472–475, *473*
Prisons, 6:475–477
    AIDS/HIV, 1:65
    Bentham, Jeremy, 1:285
    crime and criminology, 2:173
    Davis, Angela, 2:242, 243
    out-of-wedlock births, 1:307
    panoptic gaze, 3:262, 263
    prison psychology, 6:470–471
    servitude, 7:462–463
    surplus population, 8:239
    Zimbardo, Philip, 9:178
    See also Imprisonment; Japanese American incarceration
Pritchard, Jack "Gullah," 8:609
Pritchett, Lant, 9:4
Privacy, 6:477–478
    Constitution, U.S., 2:92
    insurance industry, 4:53

    religiosity, 7:162
    reproductive rights, 7:182, 183
    Roe v. Wade, 7:271
    tastes, 8:267
    video industry, 8:309, 310
Private education, 2:314, 317
Private goods vs. public, 3:144
Private interests, 6:478–480
Private property, 6:551–553
    anarchism, 1:111–112
    Christian Democracy, 2:277
    conservatism, 2:83, 84
    convergence theory, 2:117
    economic growth, 2:491
    inegalitarianism, 3:624
    privatization, 6:481–482
    Tragedy of the Commons, 8:422–423
The Private Roots of Public Action (Verba et al), 8:606
Private schools. *See* Private education
Private sector, 6:480–481
    bureaucracy, 1:390
    bureaucrat, 1:392
    business, 1:400, 401
    consumption, 2:106
    engineering, 2:594–595
    general equilibrium, 3:283–285
    technological change, 1:490–491
Private value auctions, 1:208
Private vs. public self-consciousness, 7:397, **400–402**
Privatization, 6:481–482
    common land, 2:27
    Davis, Angela, 2:243
    deregulation, 2:309
    description, 5:419–420
    health care, 9:61
    land reform, 4:343
    managed competition, 2:54
    national security, 9:51
    private sector, 6:480–481
    railway industry, 7:54
    state capitalism, 1:443–444
    structural adjustment, 8:177
    telecommunications industry, 8:314, 316
    Thatcher, Margaret, 8:335
    transitional economies, 2:533
    transportation industry, 8:438
    water resources, 9:40–42
    welfare, 9:69–70, 72
Privilege, occupational status, 6:26–28

Pro-choice/pro-life, 5:439, 6:**501–503**
  reproductive politics, 7:180, 181
  Roe v. Wade, 7:271–272
Pro-choice/pro-life movement
  abortion rights, 1:4
  women's liberation, 9:115
Pro-life movement. *See* Pro-choice/pro-life
Proactive aggression, 1:55
Probabilistic prediction. *See* Prediction
Probabilistic regression, 6:**482–484,** 7:139–140
Probability, 6:**484–486**
  Bayesian statistics, 1:265–266
  central limit theorem, 1:486
  loss functions, 4:499–500
  prediction, 6:429–430
  variance, 8:589
Probability, limits in, 6:**486–489**
Probability, subjective, 5:519, 6:**489–491,** 7:252
Probability distributions, 6:**491–498,** 495*t*–496*t*
  associated functions, 6:492
  Bayesian inference, 4:13
  classical statistical analysis, 1:576–577
  continuous univariate, 6:494, 495*t*, 496*t*
  cumulants, 6:493
  described, 6:491–492
  distributional parameters, 6:493
  fixed coefficients production function, 3:155
  general equilibrium, 3:284
  kurtosis, 6:493
  large sample properties, 4:348–350
  mean, 6:493
  moments, 6:493
  skewness, 6:493
  subdistributions, 6:494
  subgroups, 6:493–494
  uniform distribution, 2:418–419
  utility function, 8:555, 556
  variance, 6:493
Probability theory, 6:**498–501**
  Bayes' theorem, 1:263
  Koopmans, Tjalling, 4:287
  quality controls, 6:651–652
Probability Theory and Statistical Inference: Econometric Modeling with Observational Data (Spanos), 4:350
Probit regression. *See* Probabilistic regression

The Problem of Social Cost (Coase), 1:589, 590
Problem-solving
  collective wisdom, 2:9, 10
  conundrum, 2:116
  creativity, 2:164
  tools, 8:388–389
Procedural justice, 4:241
Procedural rationality. *See* Rationality
Proceeds of Crime Act (U.K. 2002), 2:69
The Process (religious group), 2:188
Process development, 1:490, 491
Process innovation, 1:490–491
Processual archaeology, 1:167–168
Proclamation of 1763 (U.K.), 1:149
Proconsuls, 8:528
Procrastination. *See* Time orientation
Procreation. *See* Reproduction
Producer surplus, 6:**503–504**
Product development. *See* Research and development (R&D)
Product differentiation. *See* Imperfect competition
Product dumping, 2:**462**
Product innovation, 1:490–491
Product promotion. *See* Marketing
Product quality, 1:595–596, 3:43, 6:**652–654**
Production, 6:**504–507**
  Asiatic mode of, 1:187–188
  Austrian economics, 1:211
  blue collar and white collar, 1:337, 339
  Bohm-Bawerk's average period of, 3:151
  bourgeoisie, 1:360
  Cambridge capital controversy, 1:419–421
  capital, 1:429–431
  capitalism, 1:437
  cobweb cycles, 1:591–592
  consumption, 2:106, 107
  cotton industry, 2:152
  feudal mode of, 3:133–135, 136, 9:126
  forces of, 3:166–167
  full capacity, 3:223–225
  general equilibrium, 3:284
  households, 5:397, 403–404
  leadership, 4:379
  lean, 1:218, 222
  leisure class, 1:566
  petty bourgeoisie, 1:361, 362
  Quesnay, François, 6:666–667

technological change, 1:491
technology, 8:302–305
time and motion studies, 8:365–366
variable costs, 1:231–232
vector analysis, 8:600–601
Wicksell effects, 9:94
See also Mass production; Overproduction
Production, forces. *See* Forces of production
Production, lean. *See* Lean production
Production, mass. *See* Factories; Industrialization
Production, mode of, 5:**218–220**
  Asiatic, 2:35–36, 5:219
  capitalist, 1:445–447, 2:37, 77–78, 117, 3:176–178, 7:70–71
  class, 1:562, 563
  class conflict, 1:571
  collectivism, 2:11
  corporate social responsibility, 2:137–138
  exploitation, 3:65
  feudal, 1:562, 565, 2:37, 77–78, 4:301, 352–354
  lumpenproletariat, 4:516
  primitive accumulation, 6:463–464
  primitive communism, 2:37–38
  slave, 1:562, 566, 581, 582, 2:13–14, 37, 77, 592–593, 7:531–533
  Time on the Cross, 8:366–367
Production, prices of. *See* Long run
Production factors. *See* Capital; Labor; Land
Production frontier, 2:240–241, 6:**507–508**
Production function, 6:**508–512**
  aggregate, 8:619–620
  growth accounting, 3:389–390
  Inada conditions, 3:598–599
  o-ring theory, 6:76–77
  separability, 7:444–445
  Solow residual, 8:27–28
  technological progress, 8:300–302
  two-sector models, 8:475–476
  See also Fixed coefficients production function
Production inputs. *See* Capital; Labor; Land
Production of Commodities by Means of Commodities: Prelude to a Critique of

Economic Theory (Sraffa), 2:502, 504, 8:577
Productive class. *See* Physiocracy
Productive Thinking (Wertheimer), 3:310
Productivity, 1:5–6, 6:**513**
    absolute advantage, 1:5–6
    age discrimination, 2:402
    Berg, Ivar E., 1:288
    Boserup, Ester, 1:357–358
    citations, 1:539
    cooperatives, 2:124
    data envelopment analysis, 2:240–241
    discrimination, 2:390–391
    division of labor, 2:423–424
    ethnic diversity, 2:343
    Greenspan, Alan, 3:379
    growth accounting, 3:389–390
    labor, 1:5–6, 4:313–314, 5:399
    management science, 4:576
    marginal product of labor, 4:304–307
    national income accounts, 5:397–399, 399
    neoclassical growth model, 5:465
    o-ring theory, 6:77
    per capita output, 5:399
    product quality, 6:653
    rate of profit, 7:71–72, *72*
    Taylorism, 8:287–288
    technological change, 1:491
    time and motion studies, 8:365–366
    total factor, 5:399
    Verdoorn's law, 8:606–608
    wage discrimination, 2:403
    white collar employment, 2:585
    women, 9:108–109
    work day length, 9:134–135
    See also Output
Productivity, marginal, 1:430, 4:304–307, **595–596**
Productivity, total factor. *See* Growth accounting
Productivity and Rate of Return (Lundberg). *See* Produktivitet och räntabilitet (Lundberg)
Products, final, 5:402
Produktivitet och räntabilitet (Lundberg), 4:519
Profanity, 6:**514–515**
Professional journals, 4:**216–217**
    bias, 5:105
    citations, 1:538–539

cliometrics, 1:582, 583
cognition, 1:598
    Latino National Political Survey, 4:355
    Thompson, Edward P., 8:353, 355
Professional-managerial class, 5:492, 9:130
    See also Managerial class; New Class
Professional relations. *See* Workplace relations
Professionalization, 6:**515–517**
    classical music, 1:575
    credentialism, 2:166–167
    ethics, 2:632
    quantification, 6:655
Professoriate, 6:**517–521**, 8:527
The Professors (Horowitz), 3:109
Profiling, racial. *See* Biased policing; Racial discrimination
Profit, rate of. *See* Rate of profit
Profitability, 6:**521–522**
Profits, 6:**522–525**
    arbitrage, 1:162–163
    capital, 1:430
    capitalism, 1:437–438
    capitalist mode of production, 1:446
    competition, 2:50–51
    confiscation, 2:69–70
    corporate social responsibility, 2:137
    corporate strategy, 2:138–139
    discrimination, 2:390, 391
    economic growth, 2:490
    interest rates, 4:84
    labor theory of value, 4:323
    long period analysis, 4:489–490
    Pasinetti paradox, 6:164–165
    relative surplus value, 7:154–155
    rentier class, 1:567
    revenue *vs.,* 7:226
    Ricardo, David, 7:244–246
    short-term, 6:86
    statistical discrimination, 2:397
    surplus labor, 4:309–310
    time preference, 8:369
    Tobin's Q, 8:380
    transformation problem, 8:429–431
    violence, 8:627
    widow's cruse, 9:96
Program for Monetary Stability (Friedman), 3:218

Program for Research on Black Americans (PRBA), 5:415–416
Programmed retardation, 6:**525–527**
Programming, linear and nonlinear, 6:**527–531**
    Hoopmans, Tjalling, 4:288
    Hurwicz, Leonid, 3:350
    mathematical economics, 5:24
    objective functions, 6:5–6
Progresa program (Mexico), 6:407
Progress, 6:**531–533**
    anthropology, 1:137
    civilization, 1:557
    Kuhn, Thomas, 4:292–294
    Lakatos, Imre, 4:338–340
    primitive communism, 2:38
    Social Darwinism, 2:232, 233, 234
Progress, technological. *See* Technological progress
Progressive Era, 3:318
Progressive historians. *See* New History movement
Progressive Islam, 3:378
Progressive movement, 4:170, 6:**533–536**
Progressive taxes, 8:280, 282, **283–284**
Progressives, 6:**536–538**
    curriculum, 2:214
    left wing, 4:404
    referendum, 7:120
Progressivism. *See* Progressives
Prohibition, U.S.
    Constitution, U.S., 2:92
    crime and criminology, 2:172
    deviance, 2:353
    jazz, 4:176
Prohibition of Mixed Marriages Act (South Africa 1949), 2:15
Project Blue Book, 8:507
Project Head Start. *See* Head Start
Project Mogul, 8:508
Project South, 1:18
Projections, systems dynamics, 3:241
Projective tests. *See* Psychometrics
Proletariat, 6:**538–540**
    bourgeoisie, 1:360
    civil society, 1:553
    as class, 1:562, 563
    class conflict, 1:569
    class consciousness, 1:571–572
    communism, 2:34, 35
    consumption, 2:106
    convergence theory, 2:117

Proletariat, *continued*
  hegemony, 3:455
  landlords, 4:345
  latifundia, 4:353–354
  leisure class *vs.,* 1:565
  lumpenproletariat, 4:516–517
  mode of production, 5:220
  petty bourgeoisie, 1:362
  socialism, 7:637–638
  Trotsky, Leon, 8:456
Proliferation, nuclear, 6:**540–543,**
  9:30, 32, 48–49
  Cold War, 2:5
  Waltz, Kenneth, 9:14
  weapons of mass destruction, 9:52
Promotion, export. *See* Export
  promotion
Promotion, import. *See* Import
  promotion
Promotion, product. *See* Marketing
Promotion of Bantu Self Government
  Act (South Africa 1959), 1:148
Proof, burden of, 3:386
Propaganda, 6:**543–544**
  Central Intelligence Agency, U.S,
    1:482, 483
  civil rights, 1:550
  hegemony, 3:455, 456
  Hitler, Adolf, 3:486–488
  Lasswell, Harold, 4:351
  Levellers, 4:414
  television, 8:320
  visual arts, 8:631–632
Propaganda Technique in World War I
  (Lasswell), 4:351
Propensity score matching, 7:591
Propensity to consume, marginal,
  2:109, 110, 6:**544–546**
Propensity to import, marginal, 6:**546**
Propensity to save, marginal,
  6:**546–547**
Properties of estimators (asymptotic
  and exact), 4:348–350, 6:**547–549**
Property, 6:**549–551**
  class, 1:562, 563
  class conflict, 1:568–571
  collectivism, 2:11
  common, 6:92
  crime and criminology, 2:171
  cultural resource management,
    2:196–197
  landlords, 4:345
  latifundia, 4:352–354
  left and right, 4:402
  left wing, 4:403

Mises, Ludwig Edler von,
  5:202–203
  original accumulation, 8:627
  rent, 7:163–164
  rentier class, 1:566–568
  violence, 8:627
  whiteness as, 9:87
  See also Land
Property, private, 6:**551–553**
  anarchism, 1:111–112
  Christian Democracy, 2:277
  conservatism, 2:83, 84
  convergence theory, 2:117
  economic growth, 2:491
  inegalitarianism, 3:624
  privatization, 6:481–482
  Tragedy of the Commons,
    8:422–423
Property law, 3:120
Property rights, 6:**553–555**
  capitalism, 1:437, 439
  Coase, Ronald, 1:589
  Coase theorem, 1:590
  common land, 2:26–28
  confiscation, 2:69–70
  corporations, 2:139
  cultural rights, 2:197
  De Soto, Hernando, 2:319, 320
  desegregation, 2:314–315
  dirigiste, 2:373
  distributive justice, 4:240
  energy industry, 2:588–589
  Hobbes, Thomas, 8:627
  laissez-faire, 4:337
  land claims, 4:340–341
  land reform, 4:341–345
  landlords, 4:345–347
  legacy effects, 4:404
  libertarianism, 4:437, 438
  Locke, John, 4:476, 477
  natural rights, 5:439
  North-South models, 5:547
  primitive communism, 2:37, 38
  rape, 7:65
  Tragedy of the Commons,
    8:422–423
  urban studies, 8:542
  Washington Consensus, 9:39
  wealth, 9:45
  See also Ownership
Property rights, intellectual,
  5:540–541, 6:**555–556,** 9:143
  entertainment industry,
    2:602–603
  Internet, 4:106–107

monopoly, 5:264, 265
  NAFTA, 5:541
  pharmaceutical industry,
    6:237–238, 239
  recording industry, 7:115–116
  technological progress, 8:299
  technology, 8:304–305
  trade liberalization, 4:428
  World Trade Organization, 9:143
Property seizures. *See* Confiscation
Prophecies, self-fulfilling. *See* Self-
  fulfilling prophecies
Proportional representation, 3:357,
  8:647, 655
Proposition 2 (Michigan). *See*
  California Civil Rights Initiative
Proposition 187 (California),
  5:430–431
Proposition 209 (California). *See*
  California Civil Rights Initiative
Proprietary class. *See* Physiocracy
Proslavery arguments. *See* Slavery
Prospect theory, 6:**556–557**
Prosser, Ann, 3:245
Prosser, Gabriel, 3:**244–246**
Prosser, Thomas Henry, 3:245
Prostitution, 6:**557–559**
  AIDS/HIV, 1:66
  crime and criminology, 2:172
  pimps, 6:271–273
Protected markets, 4:11–12,
  6:**559–561**
Protection, consumer. *See* Consumer
  protection
Protection, equal. *See* Equal
  protection; Equality
Protection, import, 3:66
Protectionism, 6:**561–563**
  Bhagwati, Jagdish, 1:293
  bourgeoisie, 1:361
  children's rights, 1:512
  Corn Laws (U.K.), 3:200
  customs union, 2:215–216
  dependency theory, 2:300
  dirigiste, 2:373
  farm quota system, 6:667–668
  free trade *vs.,* 3:194
  outsourcing, 6:86–87
  textile industry, 8:333–334
Protein gap. *See* Malnutrition
Proteomics, 3:299
Protest, 6:**564–566**
  Black Power, 1:320–322
  Boer War, 1:350

Brown v. Board of Education (1954), 1:374–375
Carter, Jimmy, 1:451
Chávez, César, 1:493
Chinese Revolution, 1:520
civil disobedience, 1:545–546
civil rights movement, U.S., 1:551–552
Coloreds (South Africa), 2:15
comic books, 2:24
Congress of Racial Equality, 2:75
Congress Party, India, 2:77
critical race theory, 2:174–175
Davis, Angela, 2:242–243
desegregation, 2:314–315
direct action, 2:372
dissidents, 2:411–412
Haymarket Square riot, 3:436
indigenismo, 3:613
Jim Crow, 4:199–201
Kariel, Henry S., 4:249
labor law, 4:303
law and order, 4:369
Levellers, 4:413–415
Love Canal, 4:504–505
Luddites, 4:513–515
lynchings, 4:526
Lynd, Staughton, 4:528–529
Mandela, Nelson, 4:580–581
martyrdom, 4:627–628
Mexican Americans, 5:124, 125
mobilization, 5:213–214, 215
Moving to Opportunity, 5:302–303
peace movements, 6:182–185
revolution, 7:228, 229
riots, 7:250
rock 'n' roll, 7:268
social movements, 7:603–607
Southern politics, 6:342
Student Nonviolent Coordinating Committee, 8:183–184
tax revolts, 8:278–279
terrorists, 8:330, 331
townships, 8:406, 407
See also Activism; Passive resistance
Protest movements. *See* Social movements
The Protestant Ethic (Weber), 6:61, **566–569**, 655, 9:55–56, 57
Protestant Reformation, 1:530–531, 3:135–136
Protestantism, 6:**569–571**
Americanism, 1:108
Christianity, 1:530–531

in Church history, 1:533–534
civilization, 1:557, 558
communalism, 2:30
creationism, 2:161–163
cults, 2:188
evangelical, 9:69
fundamentalism, 3:234–235
liberation theology, 4:435
loyalists, 4:508–509
missionaries, 5:205–206
politics, 7:160
Protestant Ethic, 6:566–568
sin, 7:519
subject/self, 8:195
Weber, Max, 9:56, 57
Proto-state. *See* State
Prototypes, 6:**571–572**
Proudhon, Pierre-Joseph, 1:111
See also Anarchism
Proundhonists, 4:403
Proxemics, 5:530
Prügl, Elisabeth, 9:124–125
Prussia, Napoleonic Wars, 5:367–369
Pseudopanel data, **2:239–240**
PSID (Panel Study of Income Dynamics). *See* Panel Study of Income Dynamics (PSID)
Psilocin, 3:411, 412
Psilocybe mexicana. See Psilocybin
Psilocybin, 3:410, 411, 412
Castaneda, Carlos, 1:456–457
Leary, Timothy, 4:390
The Psychedelic Experience (Leary, Alpert and Metzner), 4:391
Psychedelics. *See* Hallucinogens
Psychiatric disorders, 6:**572–576**
consciousness, 2:81
disease, 2:408
Jung, Carl, 4:230–231
lobotomy, 4:475–476
locus of control, 4:477–478
manias, 4:582–583
manic depression, 4:583–584
multiple personalities, 5:327–328
paranoia, 6:128
psychological depression, 2:306–308
schizophrenia, 7:344–346
trauma, 8:439–441
See also Madness; Mental illness; Psychopathology
Psychiatry. *See* Mental health; Psychotherapy; Psychotropic drugs
Psychoanalytic theory, 1:507, 3:214, 6:**576–578**

Bowlby, John, 1:363
Brazelton, T. Berry, 1:369
class consciousness, 1:572
consciousness, 2:81
critical theory, 2:176
developmental psychology, 2:350
disease, 2:408
dreaming, 2:444–445
emotion regulation, 2:572
equilibrium, 2:622
Erikson, Erik, 2:625–626
Freud, Sigmund, 3:208–216
Jung, Carl, 4:230
loneliness, 4:486
marriage, 4:614
masculinity studies, 5:5–6
memory, 5:74
mental health, 5:86
midlife crisis, 5:148–150
paranoia, 6:129
positive psychology, 6:385, 386
self-system, 7:430
stages of development, 8:78
Weltanschauung, 9:78
Psychodynamic theory. *See* Equilibrium in psychology; Freud, Sigmund
Psychointegrators. *See* Hallucinogens
Psycholinguistics, 6:**578–580**
Chomsky, Noam, 1:527–529
consciousness, 2:78
linguistic turn, 4:457–458
speech act theory, 8:56–57
Psychological behaviorism, 1:274–275, 276–277
Psychological capital, 6:**580–582**
Psychological defense. *See* Napoleon complex
Psychological dependency, 1:21
Psychological depression, 2:**306–308**
diathesis-stress model, 2:358
learned helplessness, 4:388–389
serotonin, 7:457–459
See also Manic depression
Psychological needs, 5:451
Psychological stability, 8:*74,* **74–75**
Psychological therapy. *See* Psychotherapy
Psychology, 6:**582–586**
adolescent, 1:24–27, 3:552
body image, 1:346
child development, 1:505–508
developmental psychology, 2:349

Psychology, *continued*

Erikson, Erik, 2:625
hope, 3:502
identity, 3:552, 553–554, 555
loneliness, 4:486
maturation, 5:36
peers, 6:198–200, 201–202
psychological depression, 2:307, 308
Rosenberg's Self-Esteem Scale (RSES), 7:288
self-constrained behavior, 1:273–274
social cognitive map, 7:575–576
suicide, 8:222
teacher-child relationships, 8:291–292
youth culture, 9:167–168
choice, 1:525–526, 599–600
cognitive dissonance, 1:599–600
decision-making, 2:249–251
Lazarsfeld, Paul Felix, 4:375
lexicographic preferences, 4:422–423
rational choice theory, 7:74–76
reactance theory, 7:85–86
self-constrained behavior, 1:273–274
sociometry, 8:18–20
classical conditioning, 1:572–574
cognitive, 1:596–599
communication, 2:31–32
consciousness, 2:80
constructivism, 2:97
dependency, 2:297–298
developmental, 2:349–351
Ainsworth, Mary, 1:67–68
equilibrium, 2:622–623
Erikson, Erik, 2:625–626
freedom, 3:196, 197
Freud, Sigmund, 3:213–214
human ecology, 3:511
maturation, 5:34–36
midlife crisis, 5:148–150
personality, 6:219
Piaget, Jean, 6:268–271
rites of passage, 7:256–259
stability in psychology, 8:74–75
economic, 1:269, 599, 2:494–495
equilibrium, 2:621–623, 8:74–75

essentialism, 2:631
evolutionary, 3:33–34
cultural group selection, 2:191–192
Darwin, Charles, 2:229–232, 231t
determinism, 2:323
evolutionary theory of kinship, 4:273–274
natural selection, 5:440–441
sex and mating, 7:470–471
sociobiology, 7:653
functionalism, 3:231, 233
Gestalt, 3:310
Asch, Solomon, 1:186
consciousness, 2:81
Tolman, Edward, 8:386–387
habits, 3:402–404
identity, 3:553–554
individual, 4:18, 19
James, William, 4:169–170
Jung, Carl, 4:228–231
lying, 4:523–525
memory, 1:597, 2:271–272, 5:76–80
memory in, 1:598
mood, 5:275–276
moral, 4:286–287
Münsterberg, Hugo, 5:337
music, 5:345–346
bluegrass, 1:341–342
blues, 1:342–343
classical music, 1:575
jazz, 4:176–178
panic, 6:122–123
political, 6:308–310
campaigning, 1:423–424
Lasswell, Harold, 4:351
Lazarsfeld, Paul Felix, 4:375
positive, 6:55, 385–386
flow, 3:157–158
Seligman, Martin, 7:432
social psychology, 7:609
prison, 6:470–471
prisoner's dilemma, 3:32, 6:472–474, *473*
rape, 7:64–65
resiliency, 7:204–207
self-system, 7:430
separation anxiety, 7:447–448
social, 7:608–611
Aronson, Elliot, 1:180–181
Blumer, Herbert, 1:343–344
cognitive dissonance, 1:599–601

collective wisdom, 2:9–10
communication, 2:32–33
conformity, 2:71–72
decision-making, 2:251–253
evolutionary psychology, 3:33–34
evolutionary theory of kinship, 4:273–274
Festinger, Leon, 3:132–133
Fromm, Erich, 3:222–223
game theory, 3:251–252
habitus, 3:404–406
intergroup relations, 4:90–92
Jones, Edward Ellsworth, 4:210–211
Kelley, Harold, 4:252–253
Lazarsfeld, Paul Felix, 4:375
Lewin, Kurt, 4:417–418
looking-glass effect, 4:494–495
luck, 4:512–513
Marx, Karl, 4:630
primacy/recency effects, 6:457–458
race, 7:21–23
romance, 7:281–282
rumors, 7:295–298
script models, 7:372–373
self-consciousness, 7:400–402
self-guides, 7:415–416
self-presentation, 7:423–424
social cognition, 7:569–575
social influence, 7:594–598
social science, 7:616
stability, 8:74–75
stages of development, 8:77–79
stream of consciousness, 8:170–172
sublimate, 8:200
torture, 8:392–393
Zimbardo, Philip, 9:178
Psychology, agency in, 6:**586–587**
Psychology, emotional. *See* Emotion and affect
Psychology, folk. *See* Theory of mind
Psychology, naive. *See* Theory of mind
Psychology and race, 1:560, 7:**21–24**, 45
Psychology as the Behaviorist Views It (Watson), 1:276
Psychology flow. *See* Flow
The Psychology of Interpersonal Relations (Heider), 1:205
The Psychology of Jingoism (Hobson), 4:202

Psychology of music, 5:**345–346**

Psychology of teaching. *See* Teachers

Psychometrics, 6:**587–590**
  Bayesian statistics, 1:266
  intelligence, 4:71
  Likert scale, 4:447
  loneliness, 4:486
  polling, 6:353–354
  Rorschach test, 7:284–285
  Rosenberg's Self-Esteem Scale (RSES), 7:287–288
  self-consciousness, 7:401–402
  statistical reliability, 7:157–158

Psychoneuroendocrinology, 6:**590–591**, 7:457–460

Psychoneuroimmunology, 6:**591–592**

Psychopathology, 6:**592–595**, 592*t*, 593*t*, 594*t*
  dementia, 2:271–272
  dependency, 2:297–298
  emotion regulation, 2:573
  paranoia, 6:128–130
  trauma, 8:439–441
  See also Madness; Mental illness; Psychiatric disorders

Psychopharmogenomics. *See* Psychotropic drugs

Psychosexual development. *See* Psychoanalytic theory

Psychosomatics, 3:461, 6:**595–596**

Psychosomatics, social, 6:**596–598**

Psychosurgery. *See* Lobotomy

Psychosurgery (Freeman and Watts), 4:475

Psychotherapy, 6:**598–601**
  anxiety, 1:147
  Buddhism, 1:385
  classical conditioning, 1:573–574
  equilibrium, 2:622
  habits, 3:402
  hyperactivity, 3:538
  Jung, Carl, 4:228, 230–231
  learned helplessness, 4:388
  manias, 4:583
  manic depression, 4:584
  mental health, 5:86
  obsessions, 6:18
  panic, 6:123
  phobia, 6:263
  psychological depression, 2:307–308
  schizophrenia, 7:345
  self-defeating behavior, 7:405
  See also names of specific therapies

Psychotropic drugs, 6:**602–603**

  hyperactivity, 3:538
  manias, 4:583
  manic depression, 4:584
  mental health, 5:86
  panic, 6:123
  phobia, 6:263
  schizophrenia, 7:345
  serotonin, 7:458–460
  See also Hallucinogens

PTSD (Post-traumatic stress disorder). *See* Post-traumatic stress

Puberty, 1:25
  body image, 1:346
  maturation, 5:34–36

Public administration, 6:**603**
  metropolitan regions, 7:132–133
  regions, 7:130
  technotopia, 8:312–313

Public anthropology, 1:**132–134**

Public assistance, 6:**604–606**, 605*t*
  culture of poverty, 2:206
  democracy, 2:274
  Great Society, 3:372
  labor force participation, 4:315, 316
  labor supply, 4:322
  Medicaid, 5:61–62
  social policy interventions, 4:118–119
  social welfare system, 7:631–633
  subsidies, 8:202–203

Public Broadcasting System. *See* Television

Public choice theory, 6:**606–607**
  public economics, 2:529, 530
  Riker, William, 7:249

Public economics, 2:**529–530**

Public finance, 3:**143–145**
  central banks, 1:480
  conservatism, 2:85
  consumption, 2:106, 108
  contraception, 2:114
  corporations, 2:140
  corporatism, 2:140, 141
  corruption, 2:144, 145
  cost-benefit analysis, 2:150–151
  cotton industry, 2:153
  cultural rights, 2:197
  depopulation, 2:301–302
  development economics, 2:345
  digital divide, 2:*367*
  economic growth, 2:486–487
  import substitution, 3:593
  macroeconomics, 4:542

  metropolitan regions, 7:134
  public economics, 2:529–530
  Ricardian equivalence, 7:241
  sports industry, 8:66
  subsidies, 8:202–203
  trade liberalization, 4:428

Public Finance in Democratic Process (Buchanon), 3:144

Public goods, 6:*608*, **608–609**, *609*
  collection action games, 2:6
  collective action, 2:5–6
  deregulation, 2:308–309
  hedonic prices, 3:451
  merit goods, 5:97–98
  money, 5:249–252
  nationalization, 5:419
  nonzero-sum games, 5:*532*, 532–533
  private interests, 6:479
  private sector, 6:481
  private *vs.*, 3:144
  Samuelson, Paul A., 7:318

Public health, 6:**609–612**
  applied anthropology, 1:131
  bioterrorism, 1:302
  census, 1:476
  disaster management, 2:382
  disease, 2:408
  ethno-epidemiological methodology, 3:12–13
  health economics, 3:440–441
  HIV, 3:488–490
  Love Canal, 4:504–505
  malnutrition, 4:567–568
  managed competition, 2:54–55
  medicine, 5:63–65
  morbidity and mortality, 5:290
  national defense, 2:260
  plumbing, 6:281–282
  risk assessment, 8:656–657
  tobacco industry, 8:377–378
  toilets, 8:383–384
  Tuskegee syphilis study, 8:472–473
  water pollution, 6:364, 365
  World Health Organization, 9:139–141
  See also Health in developing countries

Public Health Service, U.S. (USPHS), 8:472–473

Public intellectuals, 4:**68–69**

Public interest, 6:**612–614**
  collective action, 2:5–6
  private interests, 6:478–479

Public interest, *continued*
  regulation, 7:143
  television, 8:320
Public interest advocacy, 6:**614–615**,
  7:664
Public interest anthropology. *See*
  Public anthropology
Public offering, initial. *See* Initial
  public offering (IPO)
Public officials. *See* Public sector
Public opinion, 6:**615–618**
  business elites, 6:72
  business ethics, 2:634
  Exit, Voice, and Loyalty
    (Hirschman), 3:43
  group differences, 1:103
  Guttman scale, 3:398–399
  herd behavior, 3:459
  judiciary, 4:226–227
  Key, V. O., Jr., 4:258, 259
  Lazarsfeld, Paul Felix, 4:375
  poll, 6:353–355
  polls, 6:355–357, 359–360
  sample surveys, 8:244–245
  See also Opinion polls; Political
    attitudes
*Public Opinion and American
  Democracy* (Key), 4:258, 259
Public opinion polls. *See* Opinion
  polls
Public policy, 6:**618–620**
  agenda setting, 1:48–49
  agribusiness, 1:58
  bequests, 1:287
  brain drain, 1:368
  business elites, 6:72
  consumption, 2:105
  contraception, 2:114
  corporatism, 2:140–141
  cost-benefit analysis, 2:150–151
  creative destruction, 2:164
  culture of poverty, 2:206
  Dahl, Robert Alan, 2:219–220
  dalits, 2:221, 222
  Darwin, Charles, 2:231–232, 231*t*
  dirigiste, 2:372–374
  disability, 2:377–378
  disaster management, 2:384–385
  economic depression, 2:304
  employment, 2:582–583
  ethnic diversity and, 2:343
  federalism, 3:114
  full employment, 3:227–228
  GATT, 3:282
  gender gap, 3:278

globalization, 3:334
happiness, 3:418–419, 418–419
hard-core unemployed, 3:422, 423
herd behavior, 3:459
Hunter, Floyd, 3:524–525
immigration, 3:578–579, 580
incrementalism, 3:608–610
interest groups, 4:82–83
interest rates, 4:85
Lasswell, Harold, 4:351
Latino National Political Survey,
  4:355
legacy effects, 4:404–405
Lindblom, Charles Edward,
  4:452–453
lobbying, 4:474–475
long run, 4:494
Lowi, Theodore J., 4:506
macroeconomics, 4:541–542
Nader, Ralph, 5:359
networks, 5:476
noise pollution, 6:363–364
Pettigrew, Thomas F., 6:234–235
planning, 6:274–276
policy analysis, 6:296–297
pressure groups, 6:442–443
prevention science, 6:446
referendum, 7:120–122
reparations, 7:166–168
rural sociology, 8:8
science, 5:362
social values, 8:582
stem cells, 8:133–134
technotopia, 8:313
theory of second best, 8:350–351
transnational, 9:73
underclass, 8:487
welfare analysis, 9:62–63
whiteness, 9:90
winner's curse, 9:104
Public relations. *See* Marketing
Public Religions in the Modern World
  (Casanova), 7:162
Public rights, 1:547, 551–552,
  6:**620–621**
Public schools. *See* Education
Public sector, 6:**621–623**
  bureaucracy, 1:390
  bureaucrat, 1:392
  business, 1:401
  consumption, 2:106
  corruption, 2:143–145
  crony capitalism, 2:180
  impeachment, 3:584–586

lobbying, 4:474–475
patronage, 6:176–177
planning, 6:275–276
policy analysis, 6:296–297
private sector, 6:480–481
public economics, 2:529–530
recall, 7:102–103
state enterprise, 8:105–109
technological change, 1:490–491
term limits, 8:323–324
transitional economies, 2:533
See also Market economy
Public Service Investigation Agency
  (Japan), 2:155
Public spending. *See* Public finance
Public sphere, 6:**623–625**
  critical theory, 2:177
  Habermas, Jürgen, 3:401–402
  privacy, 6:477, 478
  religiosity, 7:162
  society, 7:651
  structural transformation,
    8:180–181
Public utilities, 6:**625–626**
Public vs. private self-consciousness.
  See Private vs. public self-
  consciousness
Public welfare, 2:25, 4:337,
  6:**626–628**
Public Works Administration (PWA),
  5:494
Puebloan peoples, 5:425
Pueblos, 6:426
Puerto Rico
  blackness, 1:329, 330
  Columbus, Christopher, 2:19, 20
  immigrants, 6:45
  Latin American immigrants, 3:571
  Latino/Latina studies, 4:356–357
  Latino National Political Survey,
    4:354–356
  Latinos, 4:358, 359
  Nuyoricans, 5:552–553
  Operation Bootstrap, 6:44–45
  Taino, 8:260, 261
  See also Boricua
Pugno, Maurizio, 8:608
Pulitzer, Joseph, 4:213
Pulling, loan. *See* Loan pushing
Pullman porters, 6:**628–629**
Punch (periodical), 1:452
Punch-Out (game), 8:611
Punctuated equilibrium, 1:48,
  3:352–353, 609–610, 6:**629–631**
Punishment, 6:**631–634**

Baumrind, Diana, 1:260
Becker, Gary S., 1:270, 271
Bettelheim, Bruno, 1:290–291
collective action games, 2:7
colorism, 2:17
compulsory voting, 2:58
confiscation, 2:69–70
corporal, 2:134–136
deterrence, 2:333
dissidents, 2:411
divestiture, 2:420–421
drugs of abuse, 2:456
functionalism, 3:232
hell, 3:457–459
human sacrifice, 3:515
imprisonment, 3:596–597
Jefferson, Thomas, 4:180–181
law, 4:363
norm of reciprocity, 7:108
operant conditioning, 6:43
parent-child relationships, 6:131
race-conscious policies, 7:37–38
rape, 7:65
retaliation, 7:215–216
Zimbardo, Philip, 9:178
zombies, 9:181
See also Capital punishment
Punk music, 7:268
Purchasing power
baby boomers, 1:235
of money, 3:151
national income accounts, 5:398
The Purchasing Power of Money
(Brown), 3:151
Purchasing power parity, 2:508, 5:511,
6:204–205, **634–635**
Purdue University, 1:582
Pure competition. *See* Perfect
competition
The Pure Concept of Diplomacy (Calvet
de Magalhães), 2:370–371
Pure Economics (Walras), 9:12
Pure Land Buddhism. *See* Buddhism
Purgatory, 3:458, 6:**635–637**
Purification, 1:366, 458, 459, 461,
462, 6:**637–640**
Puritanism, 6:566–568, 8:342,
9:56–57
Puritans. *See* Puritanism
Puritans and the Poor (Hill), 3:482
Purnell Act (U.S. 1925), 8:8
Purposive behaviorism, 1:276
Push-pull effects. *See* Migration;
North American immigrants
Pushing, loan. *See* Loan pushing

Putin, Vladimir, 6:**640–641**, 7:303,
9:164
Putnam, Frederick Ward, 1:92
Putnam, Hilary, 3:231, 5:535, 6:388,
7:98, 118–119, 8:455
Putnam, Robert, 1:543, 5:476,
6:**641–642**, 7:565
Putnam, Samuel P., 8:321–322
Putting-in system, 3:76–77
Putting-out system, 3:76, 6:**642–643**
Putty-clay model, 8:620
Putty-clay models. *See* Vintage models
Putty-putty model, 8:620
Putty-putty models. *See* Vintage
models
Putty-semi-putty models. *See* Vintage
models
Puzzles, 2:116
PVC (Polyvinyl chloride), 8:621
PWA (Public Works Administration),
5:494
PWE (Price Wicksell effects), 9:94–95
PWT (Penn World Table). *See* Penn
World Table (PWT)
Pygmalion effects, 4:380–381,
6:**644–645**, 7:414–415
Pyramid schemes, 6:369
Pyramids, 8:631
Pyszczynski, Tom, 8:326–327, 327

Q

Q theory. *See* Tobin's Q
Qadhafi, Muammar Abu Minyar al-.
See Qadhafi, Muammar al
Qadhafi, Muammar al, 3:377–378,
6:66, **647–649**, 7:644
Qassem, Abdul-Karim, 3:531–532
Qatar, 1:69, 3:397, 6:65
QTM (Quantity theory of money).
See Quantity theory of money
(QTM)
Quadagno, Jill, 7:633
Quadregesimo Anno (Pius XI), 2:277
Quadroons, 1:328, 7:4
Quadruplets. *See* Multiple births
Quakers. *See* Religious Society of
Friends
Qualia. *See* Functionalism
Qualifications, 6:**649–650**
credentialism, 2:166–167
quota systems, 6:669
returns to education, 7:66
Qualitative methods, 5:**110–112**
hypothesis and hypothesis testing,
3:542–543
methodology, 5:109

quantitative methods *vs.*, 5:113
survey methods, 5:116–117
Quality, product, 1:595–596, 3:43,
6:**652–654**
Quality controls, 6:**650–652**
coffee industry, 1:595–596
hedonic prices, 3:451
product quality, 6:652
Quality of education. *See* Educational
quality
Quality of life
cooperatives, 2:125
development in sociology, 2:348
hedonic prices, 3:451
physical quality of life index,
6:265–266
rural development, 2:342
vacations, 8:566
Quality of life index, physical. *See*
Physical quality of life index
Quality of service. *See* Product quality
Qualla Boundary, 1:498
Quantification, 5:107–109,
6:**655–656**
Quantitative geography, 3:304–305
Quantitative methods, 5:**112–113**
behavioral political science,
6:315–316
case method, 1:453
cliometrics, 1:581–583
cluster analysis, 1:585–586
Duncan, Otis Dudley, 2:462–463
empiricism, 2:578–579
event studies, 3:30–31
Frisch, Ragnar, 3:221–222
hypothesis and hypothesis testing,
3:541–542, 543
Lasswell, Harold, 4:351
longitudinal data, 2:238–239
Merton, Robert K., 5:105–106
meta-analysis, 5:104–105
methodology, 5:109
probability, 6:484–486
quantification, 6:655–656
as research methods, 5:113–115
standard errors, 2:628–629
survey, 8:241–242
test statistics, 8:331–333
Quantity index, 6:**656–659**
Quantity theory of money (QTM),
6:**659–661**
currency, 2:209
described, 5:251–252
endogenous money, 5:256–257
exogenous money, 5:258–259

Quantity theory of money (QTM), *continued*
  Fisher, Irving, 3:151
  Friedman, Milton, 3:217–218, 219
  Hume, David, 3:520
  Hume process, 3:521
  monetarism, 5:242
Quantity vs. price adjustment. *See* Price vs. quantity adjustment
Quarantines (diplomacy). *See* Embargoes
Quasi-experimentation. *See* Campbell, Donald
Quasi-experiments, 1:425–426
Quasi-state. *See* State
Quebecois movement, 6:**661–663**
Queer studies, 6:330, **663–666**
Queer theory. *See* Gay, lesbian, transgender, and bisexual politics; Queer studies
Quesnay, François, 3:154, 6:**666–667**
  civilization, 1:558
  Leontief, Wassily, 4:413
  physiocracy, 6:266
The Question of Palestine (Said), 7:310
La Question Sociale, 4:361, 362
Questioning. *See* Interrogation
Questionnaires. *See* Sample surveys
Quetelet, Adolphe, 4:373
Qui tam, 9:80
Quicksand (Larsen), 3:426
The Quiet Don (Sholokhov), 9:20
Quiet option. *See* Covert action
Quiggin, John, 5:519
Quine, W. V., 1:275, 278, 279, 280, 5:443
Quintuplets. *See* Multiple births
Quit India Movement, 8:569
Quota Act (U.S. 1921), 2:568
Quota system, farm, 6:**667–668**
Quota systems, 6:**668–670**
  affirmative action, 1:31
  civil rights, 1:549
  Columbus, Christopher, 2:20
  creamy layer, 2:161
Quotas, 6:**670–672**
  affirmative action as, 3:392–393
  Asian immigrants, 3:563–564
  caste, 1:459
  Chinese Americans, 1:513–514
  elections, 2:561
  Ellis Island, 2:568
  European immigrants, 3:569
  fishing industry, 3:153

  immigrants, 3:579
  Mexican Americans, 5:122
  See also Quota systems
Quotas, trade, 6:**672–673**
  tariffs, 8:265–266
  trade barriers, 1:254–255
  trade liberalization, 4:427
Quotations from Chairman Mao (Mao Zedong), 4:**467–468**, 589
Qur'an, 1:533, 4:196–197, 5:347, 348
Qutb, Sayyid, 1:70, 299

R

Raa, Thijs ten, 3:154
Rabin, Yitzhak, 1:162, 7:**1–2**
Race, 1:116–125, 7:**2–8**
  addiction, 1:21
  benign neglect, 1:283–284
  Bourdieu, Pierre, 1:359
  caste, 1:460
  categories, 3:175–176
  census, 1:476
  citizenship, 1:542–543
  civil rights, 1:549
  colorism, 2:17–18
  comic books, 2:24
  crime and criminology, 2:173
  empiricism, 2:579
  essentialism, 2:630–631
  ethnicity, 3:10, 7:5
  history, 7:2–3
  ideology, 7:3
  imprisonment, 3:596–597
  intelligence, 4:73
  interracial marriage, 4:*619*
  IQ controversy, 4:140–141
  kinship, 7:4
  lateral mobility, 5:212–213
  liberation movements, 4:432
  low and high culture, 2:205
  measurement, 5:54–55
  Montagu, Ashley, 5:273
  Multi-City Study of Urban Inequality, 5:314–315
  naturalization, 5:444
  negro terminology, 5:458–459
  passing, 6:165–166
  racialization, 7:43–44
  schooling, 7:354–355
  social constructs, 7:6–7, 580
  social identification, 7:593
  social pathology, 6:170
  social relations, 7:3–4
  socialization, 7:648
  sociology

  defined, 9:91
  family structure, 3:93, 93*t*
  occupational status, 6:27
  underclass, 8:486–487
  upward mobility, 8:534
  urban riots, 8:538–539
  stratification, 8:167
  teacher-child relationships, 8:292
  tracking in schools, 8:410
  trigueño, 8:452
  weight, 9:59
  whiteness, 7:5–6
Race, critical theory. *See* Critical race theory (CRT)
Race: Science, and Politics (Benedict), 2:195
Race and anthropology, 7:**8–13**
  blackness, 1:328–330
  Boas, Franz, 1:344–345
  critical race theory, 2:174–176
  Du Bois, W. E. B., 2:458–460
  Herskovits, Melville J., 3:466–467
  Hurston, Zora Neale, 3:526–528
  Latino National Political Survey, 4:355
  slavery hypertension hypothesis, 7:546–547
Race and economics, 7:**13–16**
  hard-core unemployed, 3:421, 422
  Harris, Abram L., Jr., 3:426–427
  Latino National Political Survey, 4:355
  research, 5:389
Race and education, 2:174–176, 7:**16–18**
Race and Ethnicity in Chicago Politics: A Reexamination of Pluralist Theory (Pinderhughes), 6:283
Race and political science, 7:**18–21**
  Birth of a Nation (film), 1:304–306
  Hall, Stuart, 3:409–410
  Latino National Political Survey, 4:354–356
  political attitudes, 1:103
  voting patterns, 8:649–650
Race and psychology, 1:560, 7:**21–24**, 45
Race and religion, 7:4–5, 5, **24–26**, 45
Race-blind policies, 1:310–311, 7:7, 8–9, **35–36**
Race-conscious policies, 2:174–176, 5:331, 7:**36–38**
Race consciousness, 3:192
Race hygiene. *See* Eugenics

Race in the Schools (Blau), 2:318
Race mixing, 7:**26–28**
    blackness, 1:328
    blood and bloodline, 1:335–336
    Coloreds (South Africa), 2:15–17
    colorism, 2:18
    Creole, 2:168
    creolization, 2:169
    critical race theory, 2:175
    hybridity, 3:535, 536
    interracial sex, 7:467–470
    Mexican Americans, 5:119–120
    mulatto escape hatch, 5:310–312
    mulattos, 5:312–313
    multiracial movement, 5:331
    mutiracials, 5:332–333
    phenotype, 6:243–244
    racial democracy, 2:282–283
    See also Miscegenation
Race relations, 7:**28–31**
    assimilation, 1:188–191
    bigotry, 1:295–296
    Birth of a Nation (film),
      1:304–306
    black conservatism, 1:310–311
    black nationalism, 1:315
    Blumer, Herbert, 1:344
    Boer War, 1:350
    Bracero Program, 1:365
    Brown v. Board of Education
      (1954), 1:374
    Bunche, Ralph Johnson, 1:388
    case method, 1:453
    civil rights, 1:550
    civil rights movement, U.S.,
      1:551–552
    constructivism, 2:97
    contact hypothesis, 2:111–112
    Cox, Oliver C., 2:157–159
    critical race theory, 2:174–176
    crowding hypothesis, 2:182
    cumulative causation, 2:207
    cycle, 1:189–190
    desegregation, 2:313–315
    discrimination, 2:391
    Gilded Age, 3:318–319
    Haiti, 3:407
    Harris, Abram L., Jr., 3:427
    internal colony, 2:13–14
    interracial marriage, 4:616–619
    interracial sex, 7:467–470
    Jim Crow, 4:198–201
    Kerner Commission Report,
      4:257, 258

lynchings, 4:526–527
Malcolm X, 4:563–564
miscegenation, 5:199–200
Park, Robert E., 6:141, 142
Park School, 6:143
Pettigrew, Thomas F., 6:234–235
political science, 7:19–20
race and education, 7:17–18
race-conscious policies, 7:36–38
race mixing, 7:26–28
racial democracy, 2:282–283
racial slurs, 7:41–42
racialization, 7:43–44
Sambo, 7:312–314
school desegregation, 2:316–318
South, U.S., 8:32–33
Southern bloc, 8:34–35
wage discrimination, 2:405
Race Relations Act (U.S. 1968). *See*
  Integration
Race Relations Act (U.S. 1976). *See*
  Integration
Race Relations Amendment (U.S.
  2000). *See* Integration
Race relations cycle, 7:29–30, **31–33**
Race riots, United States, 7:**33–35**
    Birth of a Nation (film), 1:304
    black nationalism, 1:317
    Black Panthers, 1:319
    Black Power, 1:321
    black towns, 1:325
    blackness, 1:328
    Chicago, 1:501
    Chinese diaspora, 1:516
    Congress of Racial Equality, 2:75
    Jim Crow, 4:200
    Kerner Commission Report,
      4:257, 258
    law and order, 4:369–371, 372
    Mexican Americans, 5:122–123
    revolution of rising expectations,
      7:232
    Tulsa riot, 8:465–466
    Wilmington Riot of 1898, 4:200,
      9:98–100
Rachman, Stanley J., 1:145
Racial achievement gap, 1:**15–17**
    Clark, Kenneth B., 1:561
    educational, 6:33–34, 48
    IQ controversy, 4:140–141
    Jencks, Christopher, 4:184
    oppositional culture, 6:48
    qualifications, 6:649–650
    race and education, 7:17
    schooling oppositionality, 6:50

standardized tests, 8:96–98
Steele, Claude M., 8:130–131
stereotype threat, 8:135–136
teacher expectations, 8:290–291
tracking in schools, 8:409–410
unequal education, 2:537–539,
  540–545
Racial and Ethnic Relations (Feagin
  and Feagin), 4:359
Racial attitudes, 1:**204–205**
    colorism, 2:17–18
    political science, 7:19–20
    race-conscious policies, 7:37
Racial classification, 7:**38–40**
    anthropology, 7:9
    biological anthropology, 1:126
    biracial, 1:36
    blackness, 1:328–330
    blood and bloodline, 1:335–336
    Boas, Franz, 1:345
    census, 1:476, 477
    colonial gaze, 3:262
    Coloreds (South Africa), 2:16
    colorism, 2:17–18
    critical race theory, 2:175
    described, 7:2–7
    East Indies, 2:476
    equal protection, 2:615
    essentialism, 2:630–631
    fingerprints, 3:248
    Gobineau, Comte de, 3:335–336
    Latino National Political Survey,
      4:354–356
    Latinos, 4:358
    measurement, 5:55
    Mexican Americans, 5:121
    moreno/morena, 5:293–294
    mulatto escape hatch, 5:310–312
    multiracial movement, 5:331
    nonblacks, 5:513–514
    nonwhites, 5:531–533
    pardo, 6:130
    psychology, 7:21
    race mixing, 7:27, 28
    racial inequality, 4:6
    white supremacy, 9:85
*Racial Conflict and Economic
  Development* (Lewis), 2:182
Racial democracy, 2:**282–283**
Racial desegregation. *See*
  Desegregation
Racial discrimination, 2:**393–396**
    affirmative action, 3:392–393
    Arrow, Kenneth J., 1:182
    audits, 1:208–210

Racial discrimination, *continued*
　biased policing, 6:289–291
　black immigrants, 3:567
　blackness, 1:328–329
　Brimmer, Andrew, 1:371, 372
　buraku, 1:388–389
　Chinese Americans, 1:513–515
　Chinese diaspora, 1:516
　cities, 1:542
　civil rights, 1:549, 550
　civil rights movement, U.S.,
　　1:551–552
　color-blind, 9:87
　Coloreds (South Africa), 2:15
　colorism, 2:17
　Congress of Racial Equality, 2:75
　Constitution, U.S., 2:92
　contact hypothesis, 2:111–112
　correspondence tests, 2:141–143
　critical race theory, 2:175
　described, 2:388–392
　Dred Scott v. Sanford, 2:445–446
　Du Bois, W. E. B., 2:458–460
　econometric decomposition,
　　2:478–479
　economics, 7:13–15
　education, 7:16–18
　employment, 2:404, 5:384
　engineering, 2:593–594
　equal protection, 2:615
　Hernandez v. Texas, 3:464–466
　imprisonment, 3:596–597
　interracial sex, 7:469–470
　Japanese Americans, 3:599–601,
　　4:173–175
　Jim Crow, 4:198–201
　labor law, 4:303
　Latino National Political Survey,
　　4:354–356
　liberation, 4:429–430
　life events and stress, 4:444
　low and high culture, 2:205
　Mexican Americans, 5:123
　mulatto escape hatch, 5:310–312
　Myrdal, Gunnar, 1:93–96
　NAACP, 5:383–386
　poll tax, 6:352
　profiling, 2:390
　psychology, 7:23
　qualifications, 6:649–650
　quota systems, 6:668–670
　quotas, 6:670–671
　racial democracy, 2:282
　racism *vs.,* 7:44

reparations, 7:166–168
residential segregation, 7:384–385
restitution principle, 7:213–215
Roma, 7:278–279
separate-but-equal, 7:445–447
South, U.S., 8:32–33
Southern politics, 6:339–349
Tally's Corner, 8:264
townships, 8:405–407
Voting Rights Act (U.S. 1965),
　8:653
wage discrimination, 2:400–401,
　404, 405–406, 3:16–17
wages, 9:4
white primary, 9:83–85
whiteness, 9:92–93
Wilson, William Julius,
　9:100–101
working class, 9:131–133
Racial epithets. *See* Racial slurs
Racial formation, 3:**175–176,**
　548–550, 575
Racial identification, 3:**548–549**
　blackness, 1:328–330
　blood and bloodline, 1:335–336
　Coloreds (South Africa), 2:16–17
　Creole, 2:168
　Diop, Cheikh Anta, 2:369–370
　discrimination, 2:391
　immigrants, 3:575
　miscegenation, 5:199–200
　mulatto escape hatch, 5:310–312
　Multidimensional Inventory of
　　Black Identity, 5:318–319
　multiracial movement, 5:331
　pardo, 6:130
　passing, 6:165–166
　psychology, 7:23
　race, 7:2–7, 8–11
　race relations cycle, 7:31–33
　racial classification, 7:38–40
　racial democracy, 2:282
　racialization, 7:43–44
　religion, 7:25–26
　self-hatred, 7:416–417
　sellouts, 7:434–435
　wage discrimination, 2:405
　whiteness, 9:87–89
Racial inequality, 4:**5–8**
　biological determinism,
　　2:325–326
　black middle class, 1:314
　black politics, 6:325
　Brimmer, Andrew, 1:372

California Civil Rights Initiative,
　1:416
civil rights, 1:549
Congress of Racial Equality, 2:75
constructivism, 2:97
correspondence tests, 2:141–143
critical race theory, 2:174–176
crowding hypothesis, 2:182
disease, 2:408
distributive justice, 4:240
economics, 7:13–15
Engerman, Stanley, 2:592–593
hard-core unemployed, 3:421,
　422, 423
Harris, Abram L. Jr., 3:427
imprisonment, 3:596–597
income inequality, 4:3
intersectionality, 4:114–115
Jim Crow, 4:198–201
John Henryism, 4:207–208
post-Parsonian American
　sociology, 8:5
prisons, 6:476
qualifications, 6:649–650
quota systems, 6:668–670
quotas, 6:670–671
race-conscious policies, 7:36–38
racial classification, 7:39
racial democracy, 2:282–283
racial discrimination, 2:393–396
reparations, 7:166–168
restitution principle, 7:213–215
social demography, 2:296
Southern politics, 6:339–349
sports, 8:64–65
wage discrimination, 2:404,
　405–406
whiteness, 9:87
Racial Integrity Act (Virginia 1924),
　1:336
Racial minorities. *See* Minorities
Racial Oppression in America (Blauner),
　7:30
Racial profiling. *See* Biased policing
Racial resentment. *See* Racism
Racial segregation. *See* Segregation
Racial slurs, 7:**41–43**
Racialization, 7:**43–44**
　child development, 1:507–508
　East Indian diaspora, 2:474
　Hall, Stuart, 3:409–410
　immigrants, 3:565, 575
　Muslims, 5:346
　race and, 7:2–7, 8–11
　racial inequality, 4:5, 6

rape, 7:65
    sellout, 7:434–435
Racially mixed persons. *See*
    Multiracials
Racism, 7:**44**–**47**
    American Sociological Association
        research, 1:105–107
    Aryans, 1:185–186
    Bamboozled, 1:243–245
    benign neglect, 1:283–284
    biased policing, 6:289–291
    biological determinism, 2:325
    Birth of a Nation (film),
        1:304–306
    black conservatism, 1:310
    black liberalism, 1:312
    Black Power, 1:320
    black towns, 1:325
    blackface, 1:326–327
    blood and bloodline, 1:335–336
    Boas, Franz, 1:344
    Boer War, 1:350
    Bonacich, Edna, 1:351, 352
    Brown v. Board of Education
        (1954), 1:373–376
    Brown v. Board of Education
        (1955), 1:377
    buraku, 1:388–389
    Chinese Americans, 1:513, 514
    cities, 1:541
    civil rights movement, U.S.,
        1:551–552
    Clark, Kenneth B., 1:560, 561
    colonialism, 2:12
    colorism, 2:17–18
    constructivism, 2:97
    contact hypothesis, 2:111–112
    correspondence tests, 2:141–143
    Cox, Oliver C., 2:158
    cultural anthropology, 1:121
    Daughters of the American
        Revolution, 2:242
    Davis, Angela, 2:242, 243
    determinism, 2:323
    Disney, Walt, 2:410
    Dred Scott v. Sanford, 2:445–446
    Du Bois, W. E. B., 2:458–460
    environmental determinism,
        2:327–328
    eugenics, 3:21–22
    harassment, 3:420
    hate crimes, 3:430–431
    Hitler, Adolf, 3:486–488
    Hume, David, 3:520
    immigrants, 3:579–580

    intergroup relations, 4:91
    Jefferson, Thomas, 4:181
    Jim Crow, 4:198–201
    Kant, Immanuel, 4:248–249
    Ku Klux Klan, 4:294
    liberation, 4:429–430
    lynchings, 4:526–527
    Mexican Americans, 5:122–123
    model minority, 5:220–222
    Muslims, 5:346, 348
    Myrdal, Gunnar, 1:93–96
    Nazism, 9:148
    out-of-wedlock births, 1:307
    political science, 7:18–21
    polling, 6:354–355
    psychology, 7:21–23
    race, 7:2–7, 8–11
    race-blind policies, 7:35
    race-conscious policies, 7:36–38
    race relations, 7:30
    racial discrimination, 2:393–396
    racial slurs, 7:41–42
    racialization, 7:43–44
    right wing, 7:248
    Roma, 7:278–279
    South, U.S., 8:32–33
    sports, 8:64–65
    stigma, 8:147–148
    Tally's Corner, 8:264
    Trail of Tears, 8:423–424
    Tuskegee syphilis study,
        8:472–473
    wage discrimination, 2:405–406
    women's liberation, 9:114
    xenophobia, 9:158–161
    See also Prejudice; White
        supremacy
Racism, symbolic. *See* Racism
Radcliffe-Brown, A. R., 7:**47**–**48**
    African studies, 1:44
    British anthropology, 1:127
    everyday life, 3:337
    functionalism, 3:232
    network analysis, 5:475
Radhakrishnan, Sarvepalli, 3:480
Radical behaviorism, 1:277, 279
Radical churches. *See* Anabaptists
Radical feminism, 9:113
Radicalism, 7:**48**–**51**
    Black Arts Movement, 1:309, 310
    black Marxism, 4:641–642
    black nationalism, 1:316, 317
    Castro, Fidel, 1:465, 467
    centrism, 1:488

    Chinese Revolution, 1:520
    class consciousness, 1:572
    Coloreds (South Africa), 2:15
    conservatism, 2:84
    coups d'etat, 2:156
    Cuban Revolution, 2:186
    Davis, Angela, 2:242–243
    development economics, 2:345
    Du Bois, W. E. B., 2:459–460
    elites, 2:565–566
    feminism, 3:121–122
    French Revolution, 3:204
    Hartz, Louis, 3:430
    internal colony, 2:14
    Jacobinism, 4:164–165
    jazz, 4:178
    law and order, 4:369
    Le Duc Tho, 4:398
    left wing, 4:402, 403
    Levellers, 4:413–415
    liberation theology, 4:435–436
    Luxemburg, Rosa, 4:522–523
    Lynd, Staughton, 4:528–529
    peace movements, 6:184
    rationalism, 7:76–77
    repression, 7:175
    repressive tolerance, 7:176–177
    resistance, 7:208
    revolution, 7:230
    right wing, 7:248
    Robeson, Paul, 7:266
    Russian Revolution, 7:303–304
    scientific method, 7:362
    scientific revolutions, 7:236
    surplus labor, 4:309–312
    syndicalism, 8:254–256
    terrorism, 8:328–329
    theater, 8:338
Radio, popular music, 6:376
Radio Free Europe (RFE), 3:523
Radio news. *See* Journalism
Radio talk shows, 1:475–476, 4:375,
    7:**51**–**53**
Radioactive fallout, 9:30
Radiocarbon dating techniques, 1:164
Radiological weapons, 9:52
Radner, Roy, 3:173, 6:51
Ragged Dick (Alger), 1:72
The Ragged Trousered Philanthropists
    (Tressell), 4:517
Railroad industry. *See* Railway
    industry
*Railroads and American Economic
    Growth* (Fogel), 3:161

Railway industry, 7:**53–55**
Appalachia, 1:151
cliometrics, 1:582
Fogel, Robert, 3:161
Reconstruction Era, U.S., 7:114
transportation industry, 8:436–438
Rainbow/PUSH Coalition. *See* Coalition
Rainey, Gertrude, 1:343
Rainey, Ma. *See* Rainey, Gertrude
Rainwater, Lee, 9:70
The Raj, 7:**55–57**
Rajan, Rajuram, 3:148
Rajneeshees, 1:301, 9:52
RAM (Revolutionary Action Movement), 1:317, 321, 2:14
Ramadier, Thierry, 7:198
Ramaswami, V. K., 1:293
Ramey, Garey, 1:20
Ramey, Roger, 8:507
Ramsey, Frank P., 6:51, 52, 490
Ramseyer, J. Mark, 6:37
Ramus, Peter, 7:237–238
Ranch Rescue, 4:372
Rand, Ayn, 4:438, 8:526
See also Objectivism
Randall, Alice, 3:348
Randolph, A. Philip, 1:35, 312, 9:81
See also Pullman porters
Randolph, Edmund, 9:37
Random effects. *See* Generalized linear models (GLM)
Random effects regression, 7:**58–59**
Random samples, 7:**59–61**, *61*
controlled experiments, 3:58–59
experiments, 3:55
opinion polls, 6:356–357
probability, 6:484
sample surveys, 8:244–245
Random variables, 8:**588–589**
central limit theorem, 1:486
uniform distribution, 2:418–419
Random walk, 7:**61–63**
autoregressive models, 1:228
efficient market hypothesis, 2:548–549
time series regression, 8:372
Randomness, 7:**63–64**
Bayesian inference, 4:13
butterfly effect, 1:413–414
causality, 1:472, 473
chaos theory, 1:492
natural experiments, 5:434–435
probability, 6:484, 486

sampling, 7:316–317
in social experiments, 7:590–592
Range, 8:585, 591
Ranney, Austin, 3:354
Ransom, Michael R., 2:479, 6:1
Rao, P. V. Narasimha, 2:77
Rap music. *See* Hip hop
Rape, 7:**64–66**
crime and criminology, 2:172
interracial sex, 7:468
mulattos, 5:312
reproductive rights, 7:182
Rape of Nanking. *See* Chinese Revolution
Raphael, 8:633
Rapp, Rayna, 3:294, 7:178
Rapping, Leonard, 2:522, 4:321
Rappoport, David, 8:628
Rappoport, Peter, 3:368
Rapso, 1:419
Ras Tafari. *See* Selassie, Haile
Rastafari, 3:259, 7:**66–70**
blackness, 1:329
reggae, 7:128, 129
Rodney, Walter, 7:269
Rastafarianism. *See* Rastafari
Rastafarians. *See* Rastafari
Rastas. *See* Rastafari
Rasul v. Bush (2004), 3:394
Rate, response. *See* Survey
Rate of exploitation, 7:**70–71**
The Rate of Interest (Fisher), 3:151
Rate of profit, 7:**71–74**, *72, 73*
Mandel, Ernest, 4:580
markup pricing, 4:610–612
rate of exploitation, 7:70–71
Rate of returns. *See* Returns
Rate of surplus value. *See* Rate of exploitation
Rational actor model, 3:170–171
Rational addiction, 6:56
Rational choice theory (Economics). *See* Choice in economics; Constrained choice; Rationality
Rational choice theory (RCT), 7:**74–76**
choice in psychology, 1:525–526
coalition theory, 1:588
crime and criminology, 2:172
Cuban Missile Crisis, 2:185
distributive justice, 4:240–241
evolutionary games, 3:31–32
logic, 4:480
marriage, 4:614
maximin principle, 5:38–39

moral philosophy, 6:256
neuroeconomics, 5:484
post-Parsonian American sociology, 8:7
rationality, 7:81–82
satisficing behavior, 7:331–332
School of Lausanne, 4:362
self-constrained behavior, 1:273
Rational emotive therapy. *See* Psychotherapy
Rational expectations, 3:**51–53**
adaptive expectations *vs.,* 1:20
central banks, 1:479
cobweb cycles, 1:591–592
described, 3:49
efficient market hypothesis, 2:548–549
equilibrium, 3:172, 173
implicit expectations, 3:51
Lucas, Robert E., Jr., 4:510
Lucas critique, 4:511
Sargent, Thomas, 7:326–327
static expectations, 3:53
Rational-legal authority, 6:68
Rational will, 3:266–267
The Rationale of Reward (Mill), 8:553
Rationalism, 7:**76–79**
conservatism, 2:83
curriculum, 2:214
existentialism, 3:42
Judaism, 4:221
Kant, Immanuel, 4:248
Klein, Lawrence, 4:276
liberalism, 4:425
scientific method, 7:362
Weltanschauung, 9:78
Rationality, 4:286–287, 7:**79–83**
Becker, Gary S., 1:270, 271
behavioral economics, 2:500, 501
bounded, 5:473, 6:55–56, 71
bubbles (economics), 1:379
bull and bear markets, 1:385
bureaucracy, 1:390, 391
bureaucrat, 1:391–392
business cycles, 1:403
choice in psychology, 1:525–526
coalition theory, 1:587, 588
cognitive dissonance, 1:599
collective action, 2:5–6
collective wisdom, 2:10
common knowledge rationality games, 2:25–26
compulsory voting, 2:59
consensus, 2:82

consumption, 2:106
creative destruction, 2:163, 164
critical theory, 2:177, 178
Dawes, Robyn, 2:244–245
decision-making, 2:251
demand, 2:269
democracy, 2:275–276
   formal, 6:68
Habermas, Jürgen, 3:401–402
habits, 3:403
Hegel, Georg Wilhelm Friedrich,
   3:453
Hegelians, 3:454
ideal type, 3:546–547
leaders, 4:376, 377
logic, 4:479–480
microeconomics, 5:133–136
Mills, C. Wright, 5:181–182
modernity, 5:230
mystification, 5:353–355
neoclassical economics, 2:517–519
objective utility, 8:557
particularism, 6:155–156
petty bourgeoisie, 1:362
political sociology, 8:3
Popper, Karl, 6:371–372
prisoner's dilemma, 6:471–472
race, 7:13–14
rational choice theory, 7:75
rational expectations, 3:51–52
Riker, William, 7:249
satisficing behavior, 7:331–332
self-justification, 7:420–421
tastes, 8:267
time preference, 8:370
Weber, Max, 9:55, 57
Rationalization. *See* Rationality
Rationing. *See* Wage and price controls
Rationing models. *See* Barro-
   Grossman model
Ratzel, Friedrich, 2:192, 327, 328
Raudenbush, Stephen, 5:461–462
R.A.V. v. St. Paul, Minnesota (1992),
   7:42
Ravens Progressive Matrices, 3:160
Ravenstein, E. G., 5:159
Raw materials, 5:438
Rawls, John, 7:**84–85**
   choice in economics, 1:525
   civil disobedience, 1:545
   difference principle, 2:362–363
   distributive justice, 4:239
   equal opportunity, 2:613
   equality, 2:616, 617

functionalism, 3:233
   justice, 4:238–239
   liberalism, 4:426
   majoritarianism, 4:559
   maximin principle, 5:39
   political philosophy, 6:258–259
   recognition, 7:109
   social contract, 7:581, 9:67
   social justice, 4:241, 242
Ray, James Earl, 4:269
Raz, Joseph, 4:365
RBC (Real business cycles). *See* Real
   business cycles (RBC)
RCA, 8:516–517
RCT (Rational choice theory). *See*
   Rational choice theory (RCT)
R&D (Research and development).
   See Research and development
   (R&D)
Re-constructing Archaeology (Shanks
   and Tilley), 1:168
Re-sinification, 1:518
REA (Rural Electrification
   Administration), 2:341
Reactance theory, 7:**85–86**
Reactive aggression, 1:55
Reactive attachment disorder,
   1:196–197
Readiness, school, 7:**87–88**
Reading the Past (Hodder), 1:168
Reagan, Ronald, 7:**88–89**
   Berlin Wall, 1:289
   Bush, George H. W., 1:398
   casino capitalism, 1:455
   Central Intelligence Agency, U.S,
      1:483
   computers, 2:60
   conservatism, 2:86
   cost-benefit analysis, 2:150
   domino theory, 2:435
   free trade, 3:196
   G7 countries, 3:243
   Gorbachev, Mikhail, 8:512
   Grenadian Revolution, 3:382
   international relations, 1:451
   Iran-Contra affair, 4:142
   law and order, 4:370
   liberation theology, 4:435
   Muhammad Ali, 1:74
   Nader, Ralph, 5:360
   NAFTA, 5:541
   national service programs, 5:413
   neoconservatism, 5:469
   neoliberalism, 9:38
   progressive taxes, 8:284

Qadhafi, Muammar al, 6:648
   Republican Party (U.S.), 7:187
   Sandinistas, 7:320
   schooling, 7:353
   Southern strategy, 8:37
   Star Wars, 8:100
   state capitalism, 1:445
   Thatcher, Margaret, 8:335
   unequal education, 2:538
   wage and price controls, 9:3
   War on Poverty, 9:28
Reaganomics. *See* Reagan, Ronald
Real authority, 1:215
Real business cycles (RBC),
   1:**407–409**
   bubbles (economics), 1:378–379
   bull and bear markets, 1:385–386
   business cycle theories, 1:412
   economic depression, 2:304
   Keynesian economics, 2:512
   lagging, leading and coincident
      indicators, 4:331
   long run, 4:492–493
   models, 1:403–405
   political business cycles, 1:406,
      407
   quantity index, 6:658–659
Real estate. *See* Property
Real income, 2:486–487, 3:98, 5:399,
   7:**89–91**
*Real Rape: How the Legal System
   Victimizes Women Who Say No*
   (Estrich), 7:66
Real rate of interest, 1:449–450,
   3:151, 4:**81–82**, 5:491
Real-time data, 5:403
Real wages
   nominal wages *vs.,* 5:511–512
   unemployment rate, 8:503
   voluntary unemployment, 8:637
   See also Real income
Real Wages, Employment, and Inflation
   (Lucas and Rapping), 4:321
Real Wicksell effects (RWE), 9:94–95
Realignment. *See* Dealignment
Realism, 7:**91–93**
   constructivism, 2:96
   defense, 2:257–258
   Durkheim, Émile, 2:465
   idealism, 3:547
   knowledge, 4:278–279
   Morgenthau, Hans, 5:295
   peace, 6:180–181
   realist theory, 7:97–99
   reality, 7:100

Realism, *continued*
    theater, 8:338
    See also Neorealism
Realism, experimental, 3:56, 7:**93–95**
Realism, moral, 7:**95–96**
Realism, political, 4:235, 274–275,
    7:**96–97**
Realist theory, 4:99, 5:295, 7:**97–100**
Reality, 7:**100–102**
    culture, 2:203
    empiricism, 2:579
    idealism, 3:547–548
    The Matrix (film), 5:31–32
    relativism, 7:155–156
    representation, 7:170–172
    social constructs, 7:278–580
Reality, virtual. *See* Cyberspace
Reality anxiety, 1:145
Reality principle, 3:210
Realpolitik. *See* Kissinger, Henry;
    Political realism
Reason. *See* Rationality
Reason and Revolution (Marcuse),
    5:482
Reason of state. *See* Political realism
The Reasonableness of Christianity
    (Locke), 4:476
The Reasoner (periodical). *See The New
    Reasoner* (periodical)
Rebates, tax. *See* Tax relief
Rebellion (military conflict). *See*
    Revolution
Rebellions, slave
    Gabriel (Prosser), 3:244–246
    Vesey, Denmark, 8:609
    Wilmington Riot of 1898, 4:200,
       9:98–100
Recall, 7:**102–103**
Recall, mood congruent. *See* Mood
    congruent recall
Recall, mood dependent. *See* Mood
    congruent recall
Recency effects. *See* Primacy/recency
    effects
Recession, 7:**103–105**, 103*t*
    economic crises, 2:484
    economic depression *vs.,* 2:302
    inventories, 4:128
    lagging, leading and coincident
       indicators, 4:331–332
    long run, 4:493–494
    quantity index, 6:658–659
    yield curve, 9:167
Reciprocal altruism, 1:89

Reciprocal determinism, 2:330–331,
    331–332, 5:486
Reciprocity, 7:**105–106**
    externality, 3:70
    Jajmani matrix, 4:167
    labor demand, 4:314
    self-disclosure, 7:408
    social exchange theory, 7:585–586
    social identity, 3:556
    socialization, 7:647
    sociobiology, 7:654
    trust, 8:460–461
Reciprocity, norm of, 7:**107–108**
Recognition, 1:539, 2:197, 7:**109–110**
Reconciliation, 7:**110–111**, 111–115
Reconnection, 1:41
*Reconstruction, Political and Economic:
    1865-1877* (Dunning), 1:304
Reconstruction Act (U.S. 1867). *See*
    Military Reconstruction Act (U.S.
    1867)
Reconstruction Era, U.S., 7:**111–115**
    annexation, 1:115
    Birth of a Nation (film),
       1:304–306
    Jim Crow, 4:199
    separate-but-equal, 7:445–447
    South, U.S., 8:32
    Southern politics, 6:340–341
Reconstructionism, social, 2:213, 214
Recording industry, 2:601, 602–603,
    6:376–377, 7:**115–116**
Records, vinyl, 8:**621–622**
Recruitment, military. *See* Military
Recruitment, volunteers, 8:638–639
Rectangular distribution. *See* Normal
    distribution
Recursive models, 7:**116–118**, 8:599
Red Army (China). *See* People's
    Liberation Army, China (PLA)
Red Book (China). *See* Little Red
    Book
Red Guards (China). *See* People's
    Liberation Army, China (PLA)
Red Shirts, 4:372, 9:99
Red Vienna project, 1:212
Reddick, Lawrence D., 1:32
Redfield, Robert, 3:266, 4:418
Redish, Angela, 1:253
Redistribution, income. *See* Income
    distribution
Redistribution, land. *See* Land reform
Redistributive justice, 7:166–168
Redlich, Frederick, 7:657
Redlining, 2:317, 7:552

Redman, Ben Ray, 8:635
Reduced form equation. *See*
    Predetermined variables
Reduced rank regression, 8:518
Reductionism, 7:**118–120**
    political sociology, 8:3
    political system, 6:317
    rational choice theory, 7:74–76
    scientism, 7:364, 365
    theory, 8:345
Redundancy, 2:33
Reed, Jimmy, 1:343
Reed, Susan, 2:225
Reed v. Reed (1971), 1:19
Rees, Al, 1:502
Rees, Martin, 3:241
Reeves, Frank D., 9:27
*Reference re Provincial Electoral
    Boundaries* (Supreme Court of
    Canada, 1991), 3:309
Referendum, 1:416, 7:**120–121**, 8:647
Referential belief structures, 3:386
Reflation. *See* Inflation
Reflection, self. *See* Ethnography;
    Participant observation
Reflection problem, 7:**121–122**
*Reflections on the Production and
    Distribution of Wealth* (Turgot),
    8:466
Reflections on the Revolution in France
    (Burke), 1:396, 2:83
Reflective models, 8:585
Reflective thought, 3:214
Reflex Action and Theism (James),
    4:170
Reflexes, classical conditioning, 6:43
*Réflexions sur la formation et la
    distribution des richesses* (Turgot),
    4:489
Reflexive consciousness. *See*
    Consciousness
Reflexive inquiry. *See* Reflexivity
Reflexive turns. *See* Reflexivity
Reflexivity, 3:314–315, 7:**122–124**
    ethnography, 3:15, 16
    extended case method, 1:454
    religion, 7:161
Reforestation, 2:262
Reform
    Central Intelligence Agency, U.S,
       1:484–485
    Congress Party, India, 2:76–77
    conservatism, 2:86
    Constitution, U.S., 2:91
    Cuban Revolution, 2:186

curriculum, 2:214
education in the U.S., 2:542–543
Iranian Revolution, 4:144
land, 4:341–345
market, 2:346, 347
Partido Revolucionario
  Institucional, 6:157–158
patronage, 6:177
poll tax, 6:352–353
rape law, 7:66–67
Reconstruction Era, U.S.,
  7:113–115
referendum, 7:120
Russian economics, 7:301
Russian Federation, 7:302
schooling, 7:353
tax, 8:283, 284, 285
Thatcher, Margaret, 8:335
unequal education, 2:538
Reform Judaism. *See* Judaism
Reformation, Protestant. *See*
  Protestant Reformation
Reformed churches, 1:531, 533, 534
Refoulement, 7:126
Refugee Act (U.S. 1980), 7:125, 126
Refugee camps, 7:**124–125**
Refugees, 7:**125–127**
  Asian immigrants, 3:564
  European immigrants, 3:569
  Hmong, 3:491
  Jewish diaspora, 4:192
  Latin American immigrants,
    3:571, 572
  Latinos, 4:360
  Palestine Liberation Organization,
    6:103–104
  refugee camps, 7:124–125
  repatriation, 7:168–169
  statelessness, 8:112–114
  xenophobia, 9:159–160
Refutation of all Heresies (Martyr), 6:78
*Regents of the University of California v.
  Bakke. See Grutter* decision (1978)
Reggae, 1:419, 7:68–69, **127–129**
Regime theory. *See* Urban politics
Regimes, military. *See* Military regimes
Regional geography. *See* Human
  geography
Regional science. *See* Geography
Regions, 7:**130–132**
Regions, metropolitan, 2:44–45,
  7:**132–135**, 8:546
  See also Cities
Registration, occupational, 6:23
Regression, 7:**136–137**

audits *vs.,* 1:208
Bayesian econometrics, 1:264
Bayesian statistics, 1:265–266
cointegration, 2:3, 8:518–519
endogenous, 8:587–588
fixed effects, 3:155–156
geographically weighted, 3:305
loss functions, 4:496–497
multicollinearity, 5:315–316
multifinality, 5:319–320
reduced rank, 8:519
survival analysis, 8:*246,* 246–247
time trends, 8:373
Tobin, James, 8:378–379
tobit, 8:381–382
toward the mean, 8:574
two-stage least squares, 4:395
unit root, 1:228, 8:518
Regression, instrumental variables,
  4:**45–48**, 394
Regression, linear, 4:**454–455**, *455,*
  8:589
  description, 5:521
  log-linear models, 4:484–485
  regression analysis, 7:138–141
Regression, logistical, 4:482–483,
  7:139–140
Regression, maximum likelihood,
  5:**41–43**
  duration models, 2:464
  three-stage least squares, 4:395
  two-stage least squares, 4:395
Regression, nonlinear, 5:**521–523**
Regression, nonparametric,
  2:266–267, 5:525–526, **527–529**,
  528
Regression, ordinary least squares,
  3:286–291, 6:**57–61**, *58, 60*
  autoregressive models, 1:228–229
  cointegration regression, 8:518
  fixed effects regression, 3:155–156
  heteroskedasticity, 3:470
  linear regression, 4:454–455
  regression analysis, 7:138–141
  simultaneous equation bias,
    7:515–518
  three-stage, 4:394–395
Regression, probabilistic, 6:**482–484**,
  7:139–140
Regression, random effects, 7:**58–59**
Regression, seemingly unrelated,
  4:394, 7:117, **379–381**
Regression, time series, 8:**371–372**,
  518–519
  Chow test, 1:529–530

cointegation, 2:1–3
difference equations, 2:362
duration models, 2:463–464
loss functions, 4:495–502
serial correlation, 7:455–457
stationary process, 8:114–117
trends, 8:447–448
unit root and cointegration
  regression, 8:518–519
Regression analysis, 5:522, 7:**138–141**
  Bayesian econometrics, 1:264
  business cycles, 1:403, 405
  causality, 1:472
  Cholesky decomposition, 1:526
  degrees of freedom, 2:266–267
  functional form, 3:230
  Heckman selection correction
    procedure, 3:446–448
  inverse matrix, 4:130
  left and right censoring, 1:474
  multifinality, 5:319–320
  nested hypothesis, 3:544
  principal components, 6:466–467
  simultaneous equation bias,
    7:515–518
  trends, 8:447–448
Regression towards the mean,
  7:**141–143**, *142*
Regressive taxes, 8:280, **284–285**
Regret. *See* Farsightedness
Regulation, 7:**143–145**
  absentee landlords, 4:348
  air pollution, 6:362
  banking industry, 1:250, 251,
    252, 253–254
  Brimmer, Andrew, 1:371
  Cantillion, Richard, 1:429
  capital controls, 1:431–433
  casino capitalism, 1:455–456
  censorship, 1:475–476
  central banks, 1:477–480
  checks and balances, 1:496
  Church and state, 1:534–536
  Coase, Ronald, 1:589
  Coase theorem, 1:590
  common land, 2:27–28
  compulsory voting, 2:58
  concentration camps, 2:64
  Congress Party, India, 2:77
  conservatism, 2:85
  consumer protection, 2:102–103
  corporate social responsibility,
    2:137
  corporations, 2:139, 140
  corruption, 2:144

Regulation, *continued*
  credentialism, 2:166–167
  crime and criminology, 2:170–171
  developmental, 1:24
  dirigiste, 2:372–374
  distortions, 2:414
  drugs of abuse, 2:455
  Ellis Island, 2:567–569
  employment, 2:582
  energy industry, 2:589
  exchange rates, 3:37–40
  exogenous money, 5:258–259
  export promotion, 3:66–67
  hallucinogens, 3:411–412
  human experiments, 3:61
  immigration, 3:278–279,
    563–564, 569, 573–574, 580,
    581
  informal economy, 4:27–28
  informed consent, 4:33
  institutional review board,
    4:42–43
  insurance industry, 4:50, 52
  investment, 4:133
  labor law, 4:317
  land reform, 4:344
  loans, 4:473
  lobbying, 4:475
  Lowi, Theodore J., 4:506
  macroeconomics, 4:541–542
  metropolitan regions, 7:135
  Mexican Americans, 5:122
  midwifery, 5:152–154
  monetarism, 5:242–243
  monetary base, 5:245
  noise pollution, 6:363–364
  occupational, 6:23–34
  pharmaceutical industry,
    6:238–239
  pollution, 6:359
  predatory pricing, 6:428
  prices, 6:455–456
  private interests, 6:479
  privatization, 6:481–482
  racial discrimination, 2:395
  railway industry, 7:54
  rent control, 7:165
  selling long and selling short,
    7:433
  shipping industry, 7:498, 499
  smoking, 7:560–561
  state capitalism, 1:443
  statistical discrimination,
    2:397–398
  sticky prices, 8:143
  stock exchanges, 8:151, 152
  technological change, 1:491
  technophobia, 8:311
  telecommunications industry,
    8:314, 315
  time-and-a-half, 8:373–374
  tobacco industry, 8:377
  toxic waste, 8:408–409
  transportation industry,
    8:436–437
  water pollution, 6:365
  See also Deregulation
Regulation, antitrust. *See* Antitrust
  regulation
Regulation, emotional. *See* Emotion
  regulation
Regulation, occupational. *See*
  Occupational regulation
Regulation, self. *See* Self-control; Self-
  monitoring
Rehabilitation of criminals. *See* Prisons
Reich, Michael, 2:391
Reich, Robert, 4:284–285, 302,
  5:492–493, 6:86–87
Reich, Wilhelm, 1:569, 3:189
Reichard, Gladys, 1:345
Reid, Ira, 1:93
Reification, 2:177, 178, 4:516, 7:3–4,
  11
Reign of Terror. *See* French Revolution
Rein, Martin, 9:70
Reincarnation, 7:**145–146**
  Buddha, 1:380
  Buddhism, 1:382
  hell, 3:458
  Jainism, 4:166
  samsara, 5:504
  See also Afterlife
Reinert, Hans, 1:185
Reinforcement theories, 7:**146–149**
  behaviorism, 1:277
  classical conditioning, 1:573–574
  cognition, 1:597
  operant conditioning, 6:43
  Seligman, Martin, 7:431
  Skinner, B. F., 7:526
  Skinner box, 7:528
  talent, 8:262
  Thorndike, Edward, 8:358–359
Reinsel, Gregory C., 9:82
Reitman, Ben, 3:494
Rejection and acceptance, 7:**149–150**
  peer cliques, 6:197–198
  peer effects, 6:198–200
  peer influence, 6:202
Relational aggression. *See* Social
  aggression
Relations, foreign. *See* International
  relations
Relations, group. *See* Intergroup
  relations
Relations, international. *See*
  International relations
Relations, interpersonal. *See* Social
  relations
Relations, labor. *See* Workplace
  relations
Relations, parent-child. *See* Parent-
  child relationships
Relations, race. *See* Race relations
Relations, sibling. *See* Sibling
  relationships
Relations, social. *See* Social relations
Relations, teacher-child. *See* Teacher-
  child relationships
Relations, workplace. *See* Workplace
  relations
Relations in Public (Goffman), 3:337
Relationship satisfaction, 3:179,
  7:**151–152**
Relative dating techniques, 1:164
Relative deprivation, 7:**152–153**, 232
Relative income hypothesis,
  2:109–110, 4:442, 7:**153–154**
Relative needs, 5:455
Relative surplus population (RSP),
  4:311, 312
Relative surplus value, 7:**154–155**
Relatives. *See* Family; Kinship
Relativism, 7:**155–157**
  cultural, 1:119–120, 123, 138
  linguistic, 1:129
  moral realism, 7:95
  particularism, 6:156
Relativism, cultural. *See* Cultural
  relativism
Relativity, cultural. *See* Cultural
  relativism
Reliability
  probability, 6:485–486
  scales, 7:339
  self-report method, 7:425
Reliability, statistical, 7:**157–158**
  left and right censoring,
    1:473–474
  Likert scale, 4:447
  Rorschach test, 7:285
  sample censoring, 1:474–475
  self-report method, 7:425
  survey, 8:241–242
Relics. *See* Material culture

Relief Fund for South African Women and Children, 1:350

Relief tax. *See* Tax relief

Religion, 7:**159–162**
    African burial grounds, 1:393–394
    agnosticism, 1:57
    anarchism, 1:111–112
    belonging, 3:385
    Black Arts Movement, 1:309–310
    black nationalism, 1:315, 316
    black politics, 6:326
    Brahmins, 1:366
    Buddha, 1:379–381
    burial grounds, 1:392–393
    cannibalism, 1:428
    Castaneda, Carlos, 1:456–457
    caste, 1:457–460, 461
    census, 1:476–477
    charitable foundations, 3:183
    Cherokees, 1:497
    Christian Democracy, 2:276–277
    Christian socialism, 7:642–643
    Church and state, 1:534–536
    civilization, 1:558
    clash of civilizations, 1:559–560
    cleavages, 1:578
    cognitive dissonance, 1:599
    communalism, 2:30
    Comte, Auguste, 2:62
    conservatism, 2:83, 84, 86
    consumerism, 2:105
    contraception, 2:114
    creationism, 2:161–163
    cults, 2:187–189
    cultural relativism, 2:194
    death and dying, 2:248
    Durkheim, Émile, 2:465–466
    ethnicity, 3:9
    European immigrants, 3:569
    euthanasia and assisted suicide, 3:28
    family functioning, 3:85
    freedom of, 1:531, 534–536, 4:180
    hallucinogens, 3:411, 412
    heaven, 3:445–446
    hell, 3:457–459
    Hmong, 3:490
    human sacrifice, 3:515–516
    Incas, 3:602
    insurance industry, 4:53
    interracial sex, 7:469–470
    Jainism, 4:166–167
        Aryans, 1:185

    hell, 3:458
        Hinduism, 3:478
    James, William, 4:170
    jurisprudence, 4:232–233
    justice, 4:239
    Kant, Immanuel, 4:248
    Khomeini, Ayatollah Ruhollah, 4:263–264
    Kinsey, Alfred, 4:270
    Knesset, 4:277
    left wing, 4:403
    legal systems, 4:406
    liberation theology, 4:434–436
    loans, 4:472
    Lynd, Robert and Helen, 4:527
    magic, 4:554–555
    Malinowski, Bronislaw, 4:566–567
    markets, 4:607
    martyrdom, 4:626
    middle way, 5:145–146
    miracles, 5:196–197
    misogyny, 5:204
    missionaries, 5:205–206
    monotheism, 5:271
    Muhammad, 5:308–309
    Muhammad, Elijah, 5:309–310
    Muslims, 5:346–348
    mysticism, 5:352–353
    myth and mythology, 5:355–357
    national defense, 2:260
    Native American burial grounds, 1:394–395
    Oedipus complex, 6:29
    Ottoman Empire, 6:84
    pacifism, 6:101–102
    political theory, 6:318
    polytheism, 6:367–368
    primitive, 1:114, 6:466
    Protestant Ethic, 6:566–568
    Raj, 7:56–57
    Rastafari, 7:66–70
    reconciliation, 7:110–111
    reincarnation, 7:145–146
    religiosity, 7:162–163
    right wing, 7:247, 248
    rites of passage, 7:257, 258, 259
    Roman Catholic Church, 7:280
    saints, 5:270, 9:155
    Santería, 7:324–326
    schooling, 7:352
    secular, 7:377–379
    shamans, 7:486–488
    Shinto, 7:496–497

    Sikhism, 7:508–509, 508–510, 9:155
        caste, 1:459
        hell, 3:458
        martyrdom, 4:629
    sin, 7:518–520
    Sitting Bull, 7:522
    social system, 7:625
    Southern politics, 6:347, 348
    spirituality, 8:59–61
    suicide, 8:223
    symbols, 8:251
    taboos, 8:259–260
    Taoism
        Chinese diaspora, 1:516
        hell, 3:458
    technophobia, 8:311
    terrorism, 8:329
    theism, 1:194, 8:340–341, 9:154–155
    theocracy, 8:342–343
    time, 8:362
    totemism, 8:397–398
    tradition, 8:421
    Turner, Nat, 8:467–468
    unidentified flying objects, 8:507
    universities, 8:532
    welfare, 9:69–70
    white supremacy, 9:86
    worship, 9:154–156
    xenophobia, 9:158–159
    Zoroastrianism
        Aryans, 1:185
        hell, 3:458
        monotheism, 5:270–271
    See also Buddhism; Christianity; Hinduism; Islam; Jesus Christ; Judaism; Rituals; Supreme being

Religion and race, 7:5, **24–26**, 45

Religion and the Rise of Capital (Tawney), 8:272

Religion of Humanity, 2:62

Religion within the Limits of Reason Alone (Kant), 4:248

Religiosity, 7:**162–163**

Religious conservatism. *See* Fundamentalism

Religious conversion, 1:458, 459–460, 2:20, 21

Religious freedom. *See* Freedom of religion

Religious fundamentalism. *See* Christian fundamentalism; Fundamentalism; Islamic fundamentalism

Religious persecution
    Christianity, 1:531
    The Church, 1:532
    Columbus, Christopher, 2:21
    Coptic Christian Church, 2:132
    pogroms, 6:286–288
    Roman Catholic Church, 7:280
    See also Anti-Semitism
Religious reform movements,
    terrorism, 8:624, 629
Religious right. *See* Right wing
Religious Society of Friends, 2:83
Religious tolerance, 4:476, 477
Remarriage, 3:84–85
    See also Family; Marriage
Remedial tracks. *See* Tracking in
    schools
Remediation, 4:404, 405
*Remembering: A Study in Experimental
    and Social Psychology* (Bartlett),
    1:597
Remittances, 3:6
*A Remonstrance of Many Thousand
    Citizens* (Overton and Walwyn),
    4:414
Removal Act (U.S. 1830). *See* Indian
    Removal Act (U.S. 1830)
Renaissance, Harlem. *See* Harlem
    Renaissance
Renaissance, Italian. *See* Italian
    Renaissance
Renan, Ernest, 3:453
Renewable natural resources, 5:437
Renfrew, Colin, 1:168
Reno, Marcus, 1:258, 259
Reno, Shaw v., 8:652
Rent, 7:**163–165**
    feudal, 3:133
    landlords, 4:345, 346–347
    returns to a fixed factor, 7:221
    Ricardo, David, 7:243, 244, 246
    user costs, 8:551–552
Rent ceilings. *See* Rent control
Rent control, 7:**165–166**, 9:2
    See also Wage and price controls
Rent-seeking. *See* Rent
Rentier class, 1:**566–568**, *567*
    inflation, 4:25
    landlords, 4:346
    managerial capitalism, 1:442–443
Renzulli, Joseph, 8:4
ReOrient (Frank), 3:187–188
Reparations, 7:**166–168**
    Asian American politics, 6:323
    black towns, 1:325

critical race theory, 2:175
decolonization, 2:257
Germany, 9:148
Japanese American incarceration,
    3:601
Japanese Americans, 2:63, 4:175
land claims, 4:341
restitution principle, 7:213–215
slavery industry, 7:549
Tulsa Riot, 8:466
Repatriation, 7:**168–169**
    diaspora, 2:356–357
    Rastafari, 7:67
    refugees, 7:127
Repeal Act (U.K. 1846), 2:133, 134
Repetition compulsion, 3:210
Replication, 3:56
Replicative senescence, 3:307
Replicator dynamics, 3:32, 7:**169–170**
Report of the Warren Commission.
    See Warren Report
Representation, 7:**170–172**
    apportionment, 1:154–155
    black politics, 6:325
    codetermination, 1:592–593
    cognition, 1:598
    community power studies,
        2:42–43
    confederations, 2:68
    Congress, U.S., 2:73–74
    constituency, 2:89–90
    Constitution, U.S., 2:91
    Dahl, Robert Alan, 2:220
    digital divide, 2:366–367
    elections, 2:557–558, 560–562
    electoral college, 2:559
    liberation, 4:430
    minorities, 5:192
    parliaments and parliamentary
        systems, 6:146
    Pitkin, Hanna, 6:273
    polyarchy, 6:366
    proportional, 8:647, 655
    Rorty, Richard, 7:286
    Southern politics, 6:345–346
    term limits, 8:323–324
    underrepresentation, 8:495–496
    women, 9:108–109, 110–111,
        117
Representation, mirror. *See*
    Constituency
Representation, self. *See* Self-
    representation
Representation in postcolonial
    analysis, 7:**172–173**

Representative agent, 7:**173–174**
Representative and participatory
    democracy, 2:**283–285**
    Bentham, Jeremy, 1:285–286
    city-state, 1:545
    Congress, U.S., 2:73–74
    consensus, 2:82
    initiative, 4:39–40
    monarchism, 5:238
    oligarchy *vs.,* 6:36
    recall, 7:102–103
    referendum, 7:120–122
    republic, 7:184–185
    republicanism, 7:188
Representative design, 1:425
Repression, 7:**174–176**, *175*
    Black Power, 1:322
    Castro, Fidel, 1:467
    Chiang Kai-shek, 1:499
    civil wars, 1:554–555
    Coloreds (South Africa), 2:15
    dissidents, 2:411–412
    Haymarket Square riot, 3:436
    Hussein, Saddam, 3:533–534
    liberation theology, 4:434, 435
    mobilization, 5:215
    repressive tolerance, 7:176–177
    terrorists, 8:331
    totalitarianism, 8:294
Repressive tolerance, 4:594, 7:175,
    176–177
Repressive Tolerance (Marcuse),
    7:176–177
Reproduction, 7:**178–180**
    Darwin, Charles, 2:229
    family functioning, 3:85, 86, 88
    homosocial, 3:325–326
    reproductive politics, 7:180–182
    reproductive rights, 7:182–183
    two-department model of, 8:563
    vectors, 8:600
    See also Birth control;
        Contraception; Family
        planning; Population control
The Reproduction of Mothering
    (Chodorow), 8:5–6
Reproductive fitness. *See* Sociobiology
Reproductive Health Services, Webster v.,
    1:4
Reproductive politics, 7:**180–182**,
    8:133–134
Reproductive rights, 7:**182–184**
    biological determinism, 2:326
    history, 3:120–121
    reproduction, 7:178–179

women's liberation, 9:114

women's movement, 9:117

Republic, 7:**184–185**

  Chinese Revolution, 1:519–520

  constitutions, 5:241

  monarchies, 5:240, 241

  representative and participatory democracy, 2:284

  republicanism, 7:188–189

The Republic (Plato), 2:34, 284, 3:96, 4:237, 6:279–280, 7:146, 8:561

Republic of New Africa, 1:321

Republican National Committee (RNC), 7:186, 187

Republican Party (U.S.), 7:**185–187**

  Bay of Pigs, 1:262

  Birth of a Nation (film), 1:304, 305

  black conservatism, 1:311

  Bush, George H. W., 1:398

  Bush, George W., 1:399, 400

  California Civil Rights Initiative, 1:416

  Clinton, Bill, 1:580

  conservatism, 2:85, 86

  cross of gold, 2:181

  dealignment, 2:246–247

  Democratic Party (U.S.), 2:287, 288

  desegregation, 2:314

  Dixiecrats, 2:430–431

  elite participation, 8:606

  Great Depression, 5:493–494, 497

  law and order, 4:369, 370, 371–372

  Lincoln, Abraham, 4:451

  political business cycles, 1:406, 407

  political conventions, 6:297–299

  political parties, 6:306–308

  race, 7:19

  Reagan, Ronald, 7:88–89

  Reconstruction Era, U.S., 7:112–115

  reproductive politics, 7:181

  South, U.S., 8:33

  Southern bloc, 8:34–35

  Southern politics, 6:340–349

  Southern strategy, 2:430–431, 8:35–38, 360

  Thurmond, Strom, 8:360–361

  voting patterns, 8:649–650

  work day, 9:127

Republicanism, 7:**188–189**

  American Revolution, 1:103, 104

Bentham, Jeremy, 1:285–286

  citizenship, 1:543

  Constitution, U.S., 2:91

  critical theory, 2:178

  Hamilton, Alexander, 3:413

  Jacobinism, 4:164

  Jefferson, Thomas, 4:180, 181, 182, 183

  Machiavelli, Niccolò, 4:534

  republic, 7:184–185

Repulsion. *See* Similarity/attraction theory

Rerum Novarum (Leo XIII), 2:277

Rescorla, Robert A., 7:148

Research

  business cycles, 1:403–405

  cognition, 1:598

  Integrated Public Use Microdata Series, 4:53–56

  National Economic Association, 5:389

Research, cross-sectional, 7:**189–190**

  Latino National Political Survey, 4:355

  longitudinal, 2:238, 7:194

  pseudopanel data, 2:239–240

Research, democracy, 7:**190–192**

Research, ethnographic, 7:**192–194**

Research, interdisciplinary. *See* Trans-disciplinary research

Research, longitudinal, 2:238–239, 7:**194–196**

  cross-sectional research, 7:189

  path analysis, 6:169

  pseudopanel data, 2:239–240

Research, multidisciplinary. *See* Trans-disciplinary research

Research, peer relations. *See* Peer relations research

Research, qualitative. *See* Qualitative methods

Research, quantitative. *See* Quantitative methods

Research, survey, 1:424–425, 4:519–521, 7:**196–197**

Research, trans-disciplinary, 7:**197–199**

  music, 5:342–345

  myth and mythology, 5:357

  political sociology, 8:2–3

  theory, 8:345

Research and development (R&D), 1:490, 7:**199–201**

  monopoly, 5:265

  pharmaceutical industry, 6:238

  tax credits, 8:274

technological change, 1:491–492

  technological progress, 8:299

Research ethics. *See* Ethics in experimentation; Informed consent; Institutional review board; Shock experiments

Research methods, 5:113–115, 7:661

  archaeology, 1:168

  bigotry, 1:295–296

  biological anthropology, 1:126

  black sociologists, 1:323–325

  Boas, Franz, 1:137–138

  Bourdieu, Pierre, 1:359

  case method, 1:453

  citations, 1:538–539

  comparative politics, 6:327

  developmental psychology, 2:351

  documentary studies, 2:433–434

  Duncan, Otis Dudley, 2:462–463

  empiricism, 2:578–579

  ethics, 2:632–633

  ethnography, 3:14–16

  experimental realism, 7:93–95

  extended case method, 1:454

  formulas, 3:178–180

  functional form, 3:230–231

  general-to-specific, 3:230

  Hite, Shere, 3:485

  longitudinal data, 2:238–239

  methodology, 5:107–109

  microsociology, 7:678

  multi-site, 1:123

  natural experiments, 5:434–435

  network analysis, 5:475–477

  objectivity, 9:54–55

  pseudopanel data, 2:239–240

  sample surveys, 8:244–245

  science, 4:338–340

  self-report method, 7:424–426

  Thorndike, Edward, 8:358

  See also Hypothesis and hypothesis testing; Observation; Qualitative methods; Quantitative methods; Scientific method; Survey methods

Resegregation of schools, 7:**201–202**

  after school desegregation, 2:316, 317–318

  integration, 4:59–60

  race, 7:18

  school segregation, 7:387–388

Reservation wages, 4:315, 321

Reservations, Native American, 5:427–428

  See also Affirmative action

Reserves, foreign, 7:**202–203**
central banks, 1:478, 480
currency appreciation and depreciation, 2:210
currency devaluation and revaluation, 2:211–212
monetary base, 5:245
Resettlement. *See* Settlement
Residential segregation, 7:**383–386**
caste, 1:458
cities, 1:541
civil rights movement, U.S., 1:552
Coloreds (South Africa), 2:15
described, 7:381–382
education in the U.S., 2:542
resegregation of schools, 7:201
separate-but-equal, 7:446
slums, 7:551–552
suburbs, 8:210–211
towns, 8:405
townships, 8:405–407
urban poverty, 6:410–411
Residuals, 7:**203–204**
Residuum, 4:598–599
Resiliency, 7:**204–207**
learned helplessness, 4:387–389
luck, 4:512
role models, 7:273
Resistance, 7:**207–210**
Black Panthers, 1:318–320
Brown v. Board of Education (1954), 1:374–375
Brown v. Board of Education (1955), 1:377
bureaucracy, 1:391
Coloreds (South Africa), 2:15
Davis, Angela, 2:243
decolonization, 2:256
desegregation, 2:313–314
developing countries, 2:336
Ho Chi Minh, 3:491–492
Indian National Army, 3:610–611
intifada, 4:122–124
Le Duc Tho, 4:398
liberation movements, 4:433
liberation theology, 4:434
Luddites, 4:513–515
militants, 5:163–164
racial identification, 3:549
reactance theory, 7:85–86
school desegregation, 2:316
terrorists, 8:330, 331
violence, 8:623
Resistance, massive. *See Brown v. Board of Education* (1955)

Resistance, passive. *See* Passive resistance
Resistance, slave. *See* Slave resistance
Resistance to Civil Government (Thoreau). *See* Civil Disobedience (Thoreau)
Resnick, Stephen, 2:78
Resolution, conflict. *See* Conflict; Negotiation
Resolution 242 (U.N.), 1:159
Resolution 1514 (U.N.), 8:524
Resource allocation
agricultural economics, 1:58–59
comparative advantage, 1:5
indifference curve, 9:*64*, 64–65
Pareto optimal, 9:63
violence, 8:626–628
Resource economics, 2:605–607, 7:**210–211**
Resource management, cultural (CRM), 2:**196–197**
Resource mobilization, 7:604–605
Resources, 7:**211–212**
economics, 7:210–211
externality, 3:70–71
organization-environment theory, 6:72
Tragedy of the Commons, 8:422–423
See also Natural resources; Nonrenewable natural resources
Resources, natural. *See* Natural resources
Resources, nonrenewable. *See* Nonrenewable natural resources
Resources, water. *See* Water resources
Respondent-related validation, 8:571
Response, conditioned. *See* Classical conditioning
Response, unconditioned. *See* Classical conditioning
Response bias. *See* Bias; Survey
Response rate. *See* Survey
Responses (Psychology). *See* Stimuli and responses
Responsibility, corporate. *See* Corporate social responsibility (CSR)
The Responsible Electorate (Key and Cummings), 4:259
Responsiveness
constituency, 2:89
parent-child relationships, 6:131–133
political inequality, 4:5

Restitution principle, 2:69, 70, 7:**212–215**, 215–216
Restraint, judicial, 1:19
Restraint theory. *See* Weight
Restraints, voluntary export. *See* Import promotion
Restricted and unrestricted stocks, 8:**156–157**
Reswitching controversy, 1:13
Retail sales. *See* Consumption
Retaliation, 7:**215–216**
tariffs, 7:216
whistle-blowers, 9:80
Retardation, mental. *See* Mental retardation
Retardation, programmed. *See* Programmed retardation
Rethinking Social Policy (Jencks), 4:185
Retirement, 1:235, 236, 4:441–443
Retreatism, 1:75
Retribution. *See* Punishment
The Return of Culture and Identity in IR Theory (Lapid and Kratochwil), 5:421
Returns, 7:**217–218**
energy, 2:587
liquidity, 4:459
liquidity premium, 4:460
long period analysis, 4:489–490
loss functions, 4:498
risk-return tradeoff, 7:255–256
Returns, diminishing, 7:**218–219**
asymmetric returns to scale, 7:223, 224
described, 7:217, 218
rent, 7:164
returns to scale, 7:222
Ricardo, David, 7:244
Returns, increasing, 7:**219–221**
asymmetric returns to scale, 7:223, 224
cumulative causation, 2:207–208
described, 7:217, 218
returns to scale, 7:222–223
Returns to a fixed factor, 7:**221**
Returns to education, 2:**535–537**
Returns to scale, 7:**222–223**
described, 7:217
diminishing returns, 7:218
increasing returns, 7:219–220
Returns to scale, asymmetric, 7:**223–224**
Réunion island, Creoles, 2:169
Reuter, Paul Julius, 4:213

Revaluation, currency. *See* Currency devaluation and revaluation
Revanchist urbanity, 8:545
Revealed preference, 1:524, **7:224–226**, 8:580
Revenge. *See* Vindication
Revenue, **7:226–227**
    average, 7:226
    capital controls, 1:432
    lotteries, 4:503–504
Revenue, marginal, 7:226, **227–228**
Revenue equivalence theorem, 1:207
Reverse discrimination, 1:31
Review board, institutional. *See* Institutional review board
Revised NEO Personality Inventory (NEO PI-R), 5:487
Revisionism
    federal government, 3:358
    Frank, Andre Gunder, 3:187–188
    French Revolution, 3:205
    Lee, Robert E., 4:399–400
    Stalinism, 8:87
Revolt. *See* Revolution
Revolts, tax. *See* Tax revolts
Revolution, **7:228–231**
    Burke, Edmund, 1:396–397
    as civil war, 1:554
    communism, 2:34–36
    computers, 2:61
    conservatism, 2:83
    coups d'etat, 2:156
    De Soto, Hernando, 2:320
    decolonization, 2:257
    developing countries, 2:336
    foco theory, 3:395
    Hartz, Louis, 3:430
    Huntington, Samuel P., 3:526
    Irish Republican Army, 4:148–149
    land reform, 4:342, 343
    landlords, 4:345, 346
    latifundia, 4:353–354
    Lenin, Vladimir Ilitch, 4:411
    Locke, John, 4:477
    long run, 4:494
    Lukacs, Georg, 4:516
    lumpenproletariat, 4:517
    national defense, 2:260
    peasantry, 6:74, 196
    petty bourgeoisie, 1:362
    relative deprivation, 7:152
    Russian Federation, 7:303
    Skocpol, Theda, 7:529
    social movements as, 7:606

    socialism, 7:637–638
    transitional conjunctures, 2:77–78
    working class, 9:130, 131
    See also names of specific revolutions
Revolution, American. *See* American Revolution
Revolution, Latin American, 4:217–219, **7:233–235**
Revolution, scientific, **7:235–237**
    conundrum, 2:116
    Kuhn, Thomas, 4:292–294
    paradigm, 6:125–127
Revolution of rising expectations, 5:233, **7:231–233**
Revolutionary Action Movement (RAM), 1:317, 321, 2:14
Revolutionary Bolivarian Movement (Venezuela), 1:494
Revolutionary Council of al-Fatah. *See* Fatah
Revolutionary Nationalism and the Afro-American (Cruse), 2:14
Revolving-door transaction, 1:435–436
Rewards
    cognition, 1:597
    cognitive dissonance, 1:600
    dopamine, 2:436–437
    performance, 9:103
Rex, John, 8:542
RFE (Radio Free Europe), 3:523
Rhetoric, **7:237–239**
Rhetoric, economic, **2:495–496**
Rhodes, Cecil, 2:354, **7:239–240**
Rhodes, Eduardo, 2:240
Rhodesia. *See* Zambia; Zimbabwe
Rhodesia, Northern. *See* Zambia
Rhonda M. Williams Doctoral Dissertation Award, 5:390
Riach, Peter, 2:142–143
Ricardian equivalence, **7:240–241**, 242, 244
Ricardian vice, **7:241–243**
Ricardo, David, 7:241–242, **243–247**
    accumulation of capital, 1:12
    Anglo-Portuguese trade, 8:413
    Austrian economics, 1:210
    Bentham, Jeremy, 1:286
    bilateral trade, 8:414
    capital, 1:430
    capitalist mode of production, 1:446
    class, 1:562
    classical economics, 2:504
    consumption, 2:106

    Corn Laws, 2:134
    economic depression, 2:302–303
    economic value, 8:576
    exchange value, 3:40
    exploitation, 3:64
    exports, 3:68–69
    immiserizing growth, 3:583
    labor theory of value, 1:5–6, 4:323, 324
    long period analysis, 4:490
    long run, 4:491
    machinery, 4:535
    Machinery Question, 4:536–537
    Malthus, Thomas Robert, 4:570, 571
    marginalism, 4:597
    markets, 4:608
    Mill, James, 5:177
    North-South models, 5:546
    overproduction, 6:96–97
    quantity theory of money, 6:659–660
    rent, 7:164
    returns, 7:217
    Ricardian equivalence, 7:241
    Sraffa, Piero, 8:71
    surplus, 8:235–236
    Wicksell effects, 9:94
Ricci, Umberto, 1:591
Rice, 3:163, 377, 5:438
Rice, Thomas Dartmouth, 1:326, 4:198–199, 5:195
Rich, Denise, 1:581
Rich, Judith, 2:142–143
Rich, Marc, 1:581
Richards, Audrey, 9:108
Richardson, Eliott, 9:43
Richardson, Lewis Fry, 4:456
Richness. *See* Wealth
Richter, Linda, 3:106–107
Ricketts, Erol, 8:485, 486
Ricks, Willie, 1:320
Ricoeur, Paul, 2:96, 3:462–463, 4:457, 5:371
Riddick v. School Board of the City of Norfolk (1986), 7:201
Riddles, 2:116
Rieff, Phiip, 6:29–30
Riega, Celso Garcia de la, 2:22
Rieger, Elmar, 9:68, 69, 73
Riesman, David, 4:487, 8:596, 597
Rifai, Zaid al-, 1:323
Rifkin, Jeremy, 4:330
Rig Veda (sacred text), 1:185, 366, 457
The Right to Be Lazy (Lafargue), 4:330

Right to life. *See* Pro-choice/pro-life

Right to work laws. *See* Labor law

Right wing, 7:247–248
- centrism, 1:488–489
- conservative movement, U.S., 7:606
- jingoism, 4:201–202
- left wing *vs.*, 4:402–404
- multiculturalism, 5:317–318
- political business cycles, 1:406
- same-sex marriage, 4:620
- xenophobia, 9:160
- *See also* Conservatism; Left and Right

Right-wing authoritarianism. *See* Authoritarian personality; Authoritarianism

Rights, aboriginal. *See* Indigenous rights

Rights, abortion. *See* Abortion rights

Rights, children's. *See* Children's rights

Rights, civil. *See* Civil rights

Rights, cultural. *See* Cultural rights

Rights, human. *See* Human rights

Rights, indigenous. *See* Indigenous rights

Rights, individual. *See* Individual rights

Rights, natural. *See* Natural rights

Rights, political. *See* Political rights

Rights, property. *See* Property rights

Rights, public. *See* Public rights

Rights, reproductive. *See* Reproductive rights

Rights, social. *See* Social rights

Rights, states'. *See* States' rights

Rights, women's. *See* Women's movement

Riker, William, 1:588, 2:286, 4:562–563, 7:249

Riksbank (Sweden), 1:477

Riley, Amos, 8:482–483

Riley, J., 3:86

Riley, M., 3:86

Riley, Matilda White, 3:306

Ring around the Rosie, 5:550

Rinzai Zen. *See* Buddhism

Riot Act (England 1715), 7:251

Riotous Assemblies Act (South Africa 1914), 1:148

Riots, 7:249–251
- Kaunda, Kenneth, 4:250
- New York City immigrants, 3:573
- suburbs, 8:539
- urban, 7:34–35, 8:537–539

See also names of specific riots; Race riots, United States

Ripley, Alexandra, 3:348

Riqueti, Victor de. *See* Quesnay, François

Le Rire: Essai sur la signification deu comique (Bergson), 2:22

The Rise and Fall of the Confederate Government (Davis), 2:243

The Rise of American Civilization (Beard and Beard), 1:268

The Rise of the Meritocracy, 1870-2033: An Essay on Education and Equality (Young), 5:98

The Rise of the Western World: A New Economic History (North and Thomas), 1:582, 5:539

The Rising Curve (Neisser), 3:160

Risk, 7:251–253
- assessment, 8:656–657
- bureaucrat, 1:392
- capitalism, 1:438
- compensating wages, 9:6
- diathesis-stress model, 2:358
- entrepreneurship, 2:605
- expected utility theory, 3:54
- hypertension, 3:539–540
- institutional investors, 4:136
- insurance, 3:143, 4:48–50
- insurance industry, 4:50–53
- investors, 4:134
- Jervis, Robert, 4:186
- liquidity premium, 4:460–461
- loss functions, 4:496
- maximin principle, 5:38–39
- natural disasters, 5:432–433
- non-expected utility theory, 5:519
- overlending, 6:94
- overtime, 6:99
- sharecropping, 7:491
- social movements, 7:606
- stocks, 8:156
- subjective utility, 8:559–560
- utility function, 8:556
- Von Neumann-Morgenstern utility, 3:217, 5:374, 8:560
- vulnerability, 8:656–657

Risk aversion. *See* Maximin principle; Risk; Risk neutrality

Risk management, 8:656

Risk neutrality, 7:253–254

Risk-return tradeoff, 7:255–256

Risk Society (Beck), 8:657

Risk takers, 7:254–255

Rites of passage, 7:256–259

death and dying, 2:247–248

rituals, 7:263

Turner, Victor, 8:470

Ritter, Carl, 2:327, 3:304

Ritual driver. *See* Rituals

The Ritual Process (Turner), 8:470

Rituals, 7:259–264
- Black Arts Movement, 1:309–310
- Brahmins, 1:366
- burial grounds, 1:392–393
- cannibalism, 1:428
- Castaneda, Carlos, 1:456–457
- caste, 1:461–462
- Cherokees, 1:497
- community power studies, 2:43
- cults, 2:188
- death and dying, 2:248
- emotion, 2:569
- everyday life, 3:337
- hallucinogens, 3:411, 412
- Hinduism, 3:477–478, 479
- human sacrifice, 3:515–516
- Incas, 3:602
- Jews, 4:194
- lynchings, 4:526
- magic, 4:554–555
- Mecca, 5:57
- Muslims, 5:347
- mysticism, 5:352–353
- Native American burial grounds, 1:395
- religion, 7:159–161
- rites of passage, 7:256–259
- Santería, 7:325
- self-justification, 7:421
- shamans, 7:486–488
- social distinctions, 2:412
- Turner, Victor, 8:468–471
- vacations, 8:566
- vodou, 8:634
- womanhood, 9:108
- worship, 9:154–155

Ritzer, George, 2:107, 8:582

Rivalry, sibling. *See* Sibling relationships

Rivalry-specific arms control, 1:176, 177

Rivas, Carlos Lehder, 2:451

Rivera, Diego, 8:632

Rivers, W. H. R., 1:130, 166

RNC (Republican National Committee), 7:186, 187

The Road to Serfdom (Hayek), 2:84, 3:201, 4:338, 5:473

Robbe-Grillet, Alain, 3:518

Robber barons, 2:180, 3:318, 4:338

Robber cave experiment. *See* Sherif, Muzafer; Superordinate goals

Robbins, Lionel, 8:554, 9:127

Roberts, D. John, 1:207

Roberts, Frederick Sleigh, 1:349

Roberts, John, 9:121

Robertson, Dennis, 4:306

Robertson, James, 1:363

Robeson, Paul, 1:550, 7:**265–267**

Robespierre, Maximilien, 3:204, 4:164

Robideaux, Bob, 1:99

Robins, Richard, 1:597

Robinson, Cedric, 1:310

Robinson, James Harvey, 5:500

Robinson, Joan, 7:**267–268**

    accumulation of capital, 1:13

    Cambridge capital controversy, 1:419, 420, 421

    discrimination, 2:391

    Kahn, Richard F., 4:245

    Luxemburg, Rosa, 4:522

    monopolistic competition, 2:56

    monopsony, 5:267

    neoclassical growth model, 5:465

    underemployment, 8:492, 494

    Wicksell effects, 9:94

Robinson, Maxine, 4:472

Robinson, P. M., 5:526

Robusta coffee. *See* Coffee industry

Rochdale Equitable Pioneers Society, 2:124

Rochin v. California (1952), 2:461

Rock 'n' roll, 1:342, 6:375–376, 7:**268–269**

Rock steady music, 7:127, 128

Rockefeller, John D., Jr., 4:527

Rockefeller, John D., Sr., 8:632

Rockefeller, Nelson A., 4:274

Rockefeller Foundation, 1:303

Rockoff, Hugh, 1:253

Rockstar Games, 8:612

Roddick, Anita, 2:137

Rodgers, William III, 2:479

Rodham, Hillary. *See* Clinton, Hillary

Rodin, Judith, 1:346

Rodinson, Maxime, 1:188, 2:510

Rodney, Walter, 1:330, 7:**269–270**

The Rodrigo Chronicles (Delgado), 2:175

Rodríguez de Francis, José Gaspar, 2:359

Roe, Jane. *See* McCorvey, Norma

Roe v. Wade (1973), 1:2–3, 4, 7:**270–272**

due process, 2:461

history, 3:90

reproductive politics, 7:180, 181

Supreme Court, U.S., 8:234

Roediger, David, 9:86, 87–88, 91, 92, 126

Roemer, John, 3:65, 8:577

Rogers, Carl, 2:31, 622

    See also Psychotherapy

Rogers, Everett M., 8:305

Rogers, J. A., 9:97

Rogoff, Kenneth, 2:209–210, 5:545

Rohde, David, 8:610

Rohrer, Heinrich, 5:361

Rojek, Chris, 8:597

Rokkan, Stein, 1:577–578, 6:162, 9:73

Role conflict, 7:**272–273**

Role models, 1:310, 7:**273–275**

Role overload. *See* Role theory

Role theory, 7:**275–276**

    empathy, 2:573–574

    identity, 3:552, 553

    Parsons, Talcott, 6:150

    performance, 6:207–208

    perspective-taking, 6:226–227

    Zimbardo, Philip, 9:178

Role using. *See* Role theory

Roll, Jordan, Roll: The World the Slaves Made (Genovese), 6:277

Roll calls, 2:74, 7:**276–277**

Roma, 2:63, 7:**277–279**, 8:141, 630

Roman Catholic Church, 7:**280**

    abortion, 1:1–2, 8:594

    birth control, 1:303

    Christian Democracy, 2:276–277

    Christian socialism, 7:643

    Christianity, 1:530–531

    as Church, 1:532, 533, 534

    Church and state, 1:535–536

    civilization, 1:557

    cleavages, 1:578

    Columbus, Christopher, 2:20, 21, 22

    communalism, 2:30

    conservatism, 2:83

    contraception, 2:114, 8:594

    Croats, 2:179

    cults, 2:188

    divorce and separation, 2:426

    feudalism, 3:135–136

    funerals, 3:238

    infidels, 4:22–23

    latifundia, 4:353

legal systems, 4:406

liberation theology, 4:434–435, 436

loans, 4:472

loyalists, 4:509

Malthusian trap, 4:573

Medicis, 5:67–68

missionaries, 5:206

monotheism, 5:270

Napoléon Bonaparte, 5:364

political cartoons, 1:452

political power, 8:594

rituals, 9:155

Santería, 7:325

sin, 7:519

vodou, 8:634

    See also Papacy; Vatican

Roman civilization

    abortion, 1:1

    archaeology, 1:165

    architecture, 1:170, 171

    auctions, 1:206

    autocracy, 1:216

    Bacchanalia, 6:20

    checks and balances, 1:495

    Christianity, 1:530, 531

    The Church, 1:532–533

    class conflict, 1:569

    dictatorship, 2:359

    ghettos, 3:312

    hell, 3:458

    human sacrifice, 3:515

    Jesus Christ, 4:186–187

    Jewish diaspora, 4:190

    latifundia, 4:352

    monotheism, 5:270

    myth and mythology, 5:356–357

    Nietzche, Friedrich, 5:503

    patricians, 6:174–175

    republicanism, 7:188

    retaliation, 7:215

    slave mode of production, 7:531–532

    theater, 8:337–338

    Vatican, 8:593

Romance, 7:**281–282**, 470–472

Romani, 7:277–279

Romania, 4:353, 5:544, 9:35

Romanticism, 8:338

Rome, Club of. *See* Club of Rome

Rome, Italy, Church and, 1:533

Romer, Christina, 3:368

Romer, Paul, 2:208, 6:52, 8:350–351

Romero, Oscar Arnulfo, 4:435

Ronco, William, 9:123
Roney, Christopher R. J., 6:85
Ronfeldt, David, 2:259
Roosevelt, Eleanor
    feminism, 3:123
    liberalism, 5:497
    NAACP, 5:383
    White, Walter, 9:81
Roosevelt, Franklin D., 2:429, 430,
    7:**282–283**
    African Americans, 5:496
    Beard, Charles, 1:268–269
    Bracero Program, 1:364
    Churchill, Winston, 1:538
    Cold War, 2:4
    conservatism, 2:85
    Democratic Party (U.S.), 2:287
    Executive Order 8802, 5:384,
        9:81
    federalism, 3:114
    French Indochina War, 8:612–613
    Great Depression, 3:368
    Japanese American, 3:600
    Japanese Americans, 4:174–175
    judiciary, 4:227
    Keynes, John Maynard, 3:200
    labor, 4:302
    national service programs, 5:413
    Pearl Harbor, 6:190
    public persona, 5:497
    reelection, 5:497–498
    Republican Party (U.S.), 7:187
    right to employment, 3:227
    rural development, 2:341
    Selective Service, 7:392
    social welfare system, 7:631
    Supreme Court, U.S., 8:233
    term limits, 9:37
    Truman, Harry S., 8:459
    United Nations, 8:522
    urban renewal, 8:536
    voting patterns, 8:648, 649
    White, Walter, 9:81
    Wizard of Oz, 9:105
    See also New Deal
Roosevelt, Theodore
    Americanism, 1:108
    Monroe Doctrine, 5:272
    Nobel Peace Prize, 5:510
    Panama Canal, 9:8
    Wilson, Woodrow, 9:102
Roosevelt Corollary, 5:272
The Roots of Appeasement (Gilbert),
    1:152

Rope and Faggot (White), 9:81
Roper, Elmo, 6:358
Roper poll. *See* Pollsters
Rorschach, Herman. *See* Rorschach
    test
Rorschach test, 7:**284–285**
Rorty, Richard, 1:275, 4:457,
    7:**285–286**
Rosa, Antônio Lisboa da, 8:608
ROSCAs (Rotating savings and credit
    associations), 7:**286–287**
Rosch, Eleanor. *See* Prototypes
Roscher, Wilhelm, 1:210
Rosdolsky, Roman, 7:301
Rose, Andrew, 2:212
Rose, Robert, 1:83
Rose, Sandra, 1:563
Rose, Sonya, 3:483
Rosen, Sherwin, 1:502, 6:77
Rosenau, James, 3:170
Rosenbaum, Alissa Zinovievan. *See*
    Rand, Ayn
Rosenbaum, Yankel, 3:431
Rosenberg, Alfred, 1:185
Rosenberg, Morris, 7:287–288, 412,
    413
Rosenberg, Nathan, 1:491
Rosenberg, Sam, 5:213
Rosenberg's Self-Esteem Scale (RSES),
    7:**287–288**
Rosenbluth, Frances, 6:37
Rosenman, Joel, 9:121
Rosenman, Ray, 6:223
Rosenthal, Robert, 7:414–415
Rosenzweig, Marks R., 5:499
Rosetta Stone, 1:165
Rosewood (FL), 1:325, 328
Rosicrucians, 6:21
Ross, Diana, 9:104
Ross, John, 1:497
Ross, Stephen, 3:141
Rossi, Pellegrino. *See* Public rights
Rossi, Peter, 6:27
Rostow, Walt Whitman, 2:335, 339
    development in sociology, 2:346
    stages of economic growth,
        8:79–80, 79–81
Roswell Incident, 8:507–508
Rotating savings and credit
    associations (ROSCAs), 7:**286–287**
Roth, Alvin E., 1:208
Roth v. United States (1957), 6:13
Rothbard, Murray N., 4:438, 439
    Austrian economics, 1:211
    ordinality, 6:57

    universalism, 8:526
    See also Anarchism
Rothbart, Mary K., 8:321–322
Rothman, Barbara Katz, 3:294
Rothschild, K. W., 2:55–56
Rothschild family. *See* Rothschilds
Rothschilds, 7:**289**
Rothstein, Alexandra, 5:391
Rotten kid theorem. *See* Bequests
Rotter, Julian, 4:477–478, 7:289–290
    See also Locus of control
Rotter's Internal-External Locus of
    Control Scale, 4:477, 5:300,
    7:**289–290**
Round tripping, 1:435–436
Rountree, George, 9:99
Rouse, Cecilia, 1:9
Rousseau, Jean-Jacques, 7:**290–291**
    autonomy, 1:224–225
    civil society, 1:553
    civilization, 1:557
    collectivism, 2:11
    consensus, 2:82
    dictatorship, 2:359
    freedom, 3:197
    Hobbes, Thomas, 3:493
    individualism, 3:618
    Jervis, Robert, 4:185–186
    Lévi-Strauss, Claude, 4:416
    liberty, 4:440–441
    political culture, 6:300
    political sociology, 8:3
    representative and participatory
        democracy, 2:283, 284
    social contract, 7:581
    social theory, 7:627
    socialism, 7:636
    state of nature, 8:111
Rowlatt Act (1919 India), 5:460
Roy, Arundhati, 5:521
Royal Anthropological Institute. *See*
    Public anthropology
Royal Commissions, 7:**291–292**
Royce, Anya Peterson, 2:224
Royce, Josiah, 3:453
Rozelle, Richard, 5:530
Rozin, Paul, 2:329
RSES (Rosenberg's Self-Esteem Scale),
    7:**287–288**
RSP (Relative surplus population),
    4:311, 312
RSS (Rural Sociological Society), 8:8,
    9
RU-486. *See* U.S. Food and Drug
    Administration (FDA)

Rubb, Stephen, 8:494

Rubenstein bargaining. *See* Screening and signaling games

Ruby, Jack, 9:34

Ruddle, Frank H., 3:298–299

Rudebusch, Glenn, 4:499–500

Rudolph, Wilma, 5:366

Rueschemeyer, Dietrich, 3:185, 9:71

Rugged individualism. *See* Individualism

Rule, Hamilton's. *See* Hamilton's rule

Rule, indirect. *See* Indirect rule

Rule, majority. *See* Majority rule

Rule of anticipated reactions, 5:518

Rule of law, 7:**292–293**
    citizenship, 1:542
    civil-military relation, 1:547
    civil society, 1:553
    judiciary, 4:225–226
    law and order, 4:372

Rule utilitarianism, 8:553

Rules of Sociological Method (Durkheim), 2:465

Rules versus discretion, 7:**293–295**

Ruling class. *See* The New Class

Rum and Coca-Cola (song), 1:418

Rumbaut, Ruben. *See* Assimilation

Rumors, 7:**295–298**, 420, 8:307
    See also Hearsay

Rumsfeld, Donald H., 5:469, 8:509, 9:28

Rumsfeld, Hamdan v. (2006), 3:394

Run, short. *See* Short run

Rural and Urban Community Action Program, 9:26

Rural development, 2:**341–342**
    backwash effects, 1:236–237
    cooperatives, 2:124
    development economics, 2:346
    Harris-Todaro model, 3:428
    irrigation, 4:152–154
    land reform, 4:341–345
    rural sociology, 8:8–9

Rural Development Loan Fund, 9:28

Rural electrification. *See* Rural development

Rural Electrification Administration (REA), 2:341

Rural Sociological Society (RSS), 8:8, 9

Rural sociology, 8:**8–9**
    digital divide, 2:366, 367
    human ecology, 3:510
    Lefebvre, Henri, 4:401

Rural Sociology and the Environment (Field and Burch), 8:9

Rural to urban migration, 5:**159–161**
    African Americans, 1:34–35
    Appalachia, 1:151
    backwash effects, 1:236–237
    black middle class, 1:313
    cities, 1:540
    Harris-Todaro model, 3:428
    metropolitan regions, 7:132
    rural development, 2:341–342

Rusbult, Caryl, 3:179

Rush, Otis, 1:343

Rush to Judgment (Lane), 9:34

Rushdie, Salman, 3:137

Rushton, J. Philippe, 7:22–23

Rusk, Dean, 2:183

Russel Sage Foundation, 3:184

Russell, Bertrand, 3:454
    behaviorism, 1:275, 277
    objectivity, 6:9
    symbolic logic, 4:481
    war, 9:18

Russell, Daniel, 9:99

Russell, Richard B., 2:183, 9:33

Russia
    AIDS/HIV, 1:65
    automobile industry, 1:221
    banana industry, 1:245
    bolshevism, 1:350–351
    Chinese diaspora, 1:517
    Congress of Vienna (1814-1815), 9:145
    convergence theory, 2:117, 118
    economics, 7:299–301
    feudal mode of production, 3:134
    feudalism, 3:135
    gold mining, 3:339
    hegemony, 3:455, 456
    hot money, 3:504
    interwar years, 4:121–122
    Jewish diaspora, 4:191
    jingoism, 4:201–202
    judiciary, 4:227
    land reform, 4:342, 343, 344
    landlords, 4:346
    Napoleonic Wars, 5:365
    national defense, 2:260
    national income accounts, 5:400
    nationalism, 5:418
    petroleum industry, 6:233
    pogroms, 6:287–288
    political science
        bilateralism, 1:297

    civil disobedience, 1:545
    commonwealth, 2:30
    communism, 2:35
    dictatorship, 2:359
    G8 admission, 3:243
    Lenin, Vladimir Ilitch, 4:410–411
    NATO, 5:546
    one-party state, 6:41
    socialism, 7:638
    Russian Revolution, 7:303–304
    separatism, 7:450
    state capitalism, 1:444
    totalitarianism, 8:394, 395
    Trotsky, Leon, 8:455–456
    tzars, 1:216
    upward mobility, 8:534
    War and Peace (Tolstoy), 9:19–21
    weapons industry, 9:49–50
    World War I, 9:145–147, 146–147
    Yeltsin, Boris, 9:163–164
    See also Russian Federation; Union of Soviet Socialist Republics (U.S.S.R.)

Russian economics, 2:117, 118, 7:**299–302**, 302–303

The Russian Factory in the Nineteenth Century (Tugan-Baranovsky), 7:299

Russian Federation, 7:**302–303**
    See also Russia

Russian Revolution, 7:**303–305**
    bolshevism, 1:350–351
    Chinese Revolution, 1:520
    communism, 2:35
    hegemony, 3:455
    Lenin, Vladimir Ilitch, 4:410–411
    Leninism, 4:411–412
    liberation, 4:430
    Lukacs, Georg, 4:515
    socialism, 7:637–638
    Stalin, Joseph, 8:86
    Stalinism, 8:87

Russian Revolution, Second. *See* Russian Federation

Rustow, Dankwart A., 2:289

Rutter, Michael, 7:205

Rwanda
    Ad Hoc International Criminal Tribunals, 9:22
    civil wars, 1:555
    ethnic conflict, 3:2
    ethnicity, 3:10
    genocide, 3:298, 8:524
    humiliation, 3:522

Rwanda, *continued*
refugees, 7:126
RWE (Real Wicksell effects), 9:94–95
Rybczynski, Tadeusz M., 7:305
Rybczynski theorem, 3:449, 583,
7:**305–306**
Ryle, Gilbert, 1:275, 278, 280
Rytman, Helene, 1:87
Ryzhkov, Nikolai, 8:512

S

S-curve hypothesis. *See* Kuznets
hypothesis
Saadi, Yacef, 1:257
Saari, Donald, 1:184
Sachs, Curt, 1:575
Sachs, Jeffrey, 5:507
Sachs, Walter E., 5:383
Sacks, Harvey, 2:97, 98, 118, 119
Sacraments, 1:531, 534, 9:155
Sacred, 9:154
See also Symbols
Sacred thread ceremony, 8:567–568
Sacrifice
expiatory, 9:155
human, 3:515–516, 9:154
worship, 9:154–155
See also Rituals
Sadat, Anwar, 7:**307–308**, 9:42
Saddle point. *See* Phase diagrams;
Zero-sum games
Saenz, Rogelio, 4:359
Safety
agribusiness, 1:58
architecture, 1:170–171
basic needs, 5:455
food, 3:164
occupational, 6:24–25
enforcement, 6:22
industrial accidents, 1:8–9
labor law, 4:317
sweatshops, 8:247–248
Sagan, Scott D., 9:14
Saharan Arab Democratic Republic,
6:62–63
Sahlins, Marshall, 4:330, 7:105–106,
308–309
Said, Edward, 7:**309–311**
anti-Semitism, 1:142
Asiatic mode of production, 1:188
culture, 2:203
exoticism, 3:47
humanism, 3:518
liberation, 4:430
narratives, 5:372

orientalism, 6:75, 76
postcolonialism, 6:392
public intellectuals, 4:69
representation in postcolonial
analysis, 7:172–173
social status, 7:621
subaltern, 8:191
Saint-Domingue. *See* Haiti
Saint Hilda's College, 8:527
Saint Petersburg paradox, 5:519
Saint-Simon, Henri, compte de, 2:62,
7:637, 8:312
Saint Thomas Aquinas. *See* Thomas
Aquinas, Saint
Saints, 5:270, 9:155
See also Religion
Sakharov, Andrei, 1:545
Salaam, Kalamu ya, 1:309
Salafism, 1:70–71
Salamon, Lester M., 8:638
Salaried employees, 9:127
work week, 9:128
working class, 9:133
See also Wages
Salaries. *See* Wages
Salas Barraza, Jesús, 8:618
Saleeby, Dennis, 5:455
Salience, mortality, 7:**311–312**, 8:328
Salinas, Carlos, 5:540
Salinger, J. D., 9:167
Salivation, 6:43
Sallaz, Jeffrey, 6:87
Salop, Steven, 4:313
Salovey, Peter, 2:252
Salpingectomy. *See* Human
sterilization
SALs (Structural adjustment loans),
9:138
SALT (Strategic Arms Limitations
Talks), 1:176, 9:31–32
Carter, Jimmy, 1:451
Cold War, 2:5
Salt retention hypothesis. *See* Slavery
hypertension hypothesis
Salter, Mary. *See* Ainsworth, Mary
Salvadori, Neri, 3:154, 8:577
SAM (Social accounting matrix). *See*
Social accounting matrix (SAM)
Samaritan's dilemma. *See* Bequests
Samba. *See* Dance
Samba: Resistance in Motion
(Browning), 2:224
Sambo (stereotype), 6:277, 7:**312–315**
Sambo's (restaurant), 7:313–314
Same-sex marriage, 4:**619–621**

gay, lesbian, transgender, and
bisexual politics, 6:331
increase, 4:615–616
law, 2:426
relationship satisfaction,
7:151–152
sexual orientation, 7:478–479
Sami culture, family structure, 3:83
Samoa, Mead, Margaret, 5:47–48
Samora, Julian, 4:357
Sample. *See* Censoring, sample;
Sampling; Selection bias
Sample, Standard Cross-Cultural
(SCCS), 8:**88–93**
Sample attrition, 7:**315–316**
Sample censoring, 1:**474–475**
left and right censoring,
1:473–474
tobit, 8:381–382
Sample surveys, 8:**244–245**
cross-sectional research, 7:189
Current Population Survey,
2:211–212, 212–213, 580
Hite, Shere, 3:485
Latino National Political Survey,
4:354–356
longitudinal data, 2:239
opinion polls, 6:355–357
cross-sectional research,
7:189–190
happiness, 3:416, 418
polling, 6:353–355
pollsters, 6:358–359
standard errors, 2:628–629
survey research, 7:196–197
Campbell, Angus, 1:424–425
Luxembourg Income Study,
4:519–521
research methods, 5:115
survey methods, 5:116–117
Samples, random. *See* Random
samples
Sampling, 7:**316–318**
archaeology, 1:168
Campbell, Angus, 1:424–425
hypothesis and hypothesis testing,
3:542
large sample properties,
4:348–350
law of large numbers, 4:372–373
Monte Carlo experiments,
5:274–275
randomness, 7:64
sample censoring, 1:474–475
selection bias, 7:389–390
statistical noise, 8:120–121

Samsara (reincarnation), 5:504
See also Reincarnation
Samuelson, Paul A., 3:150–151,
7:**318–319**
  autoregressive models, 1:228
  Cambridge capital controversy,
    1:419, 420
  citations, 1:539
  comparative advantage, 1:6
  comparative statics, 2:48
  convergence theory, 2:117
  demand, 2:269, 270
  general equilibrium, 3:284
  Heckscher-Ohlin-Samuelson
    model, 3:448
  laissez-faire, 4:337
  mathematical economics, 5:24
  maximization, 5:39–40
  Okun's law, 6:35
  optimal growth, 6:51
  overlapping generations model,
    6:93
  revealed preference, 7:224–225
  state enterprise, 8:109
  Stolper-Samuelson theorem,
    3:449, 7:305, 306, 8:159–160
  tâtonnement, 8:270–271
  trade-offs, 8:418–419
  unequal exchange, 8:506
  utility function, 8:556
  Von Neumann-Morgenstern
    utility, 8:560
  welfare economics, 9:64
Samuelson, William F., 9:103
Sanchez, Rodrigo, 2:21
Sanchez, Sonia, 1:309
Sanctions
  norms, 5:537
  United Nations, 8:524
  See also Punishment
Sandel, Michael, 4:238
Sandinistas, 7:**319–321**
  Iran-Contra affair, 4:142
  Latin American revolutions, 7:235
Sandino, Augusto César, 7:235, 319
  See also Sandinistas
Sandwich Islands. See Hawaii
The Sane Society (Fromm), 3:223
Sanford, Dred Scott v. (1857). *See Dred
  Scott v. Sanford* (1857)
Sanford, R. Nevitt, 6:220–221
Sanger, Frederick, 3:299
Sanger, Margaret, 1:303, 3:89, 7:180
Sanitation, 2:329–330, 7:**321–323**
  plumbing, 6:281–282

toilets, 8:383–384
  water pollution, 6:364
Sanskritization, 7:**323–324**
  caste, 1:458–459
  dowry and bride price, 2:441
  Hinduism, 3:477
Santa Anna, Antonio Lopez de. *See*
  Mexican-American War
*Santa Clara v. Southern Pacific
  Railroad* (1886), 2:140
Santaella, Inocencia Martínez, 1:356
Santayana, George, 3:300
Santería, 7:**324–326**
Santo Domingo, 8:633
São Tomé
  slavery, 1:39
Sapir, Edward, 1:129, 345, 2:194, 323
Sapir-Whorf hypothesis, 1:129, 2:323
  See also Anthropology; Linguistic
    anthropology
Sapiro, Virginia, 1:103
Sapolsky, Robert M., 1:83
SAR (Sons of the American
  Revolution), 2:241
Sarbanes-Oxley Act (U.S. 2002), 9:80
Sargan, J. Denis, 2:3
Sargent, Thomas, 1:20, 7:**326–327**
SARP (Strong axiom of revealed
  preference), 7:224–225
Sartori, Giovanni, 6:38, 162, 8:2–3
  See also Political sociology
Sartre, Jean-Paul, 7:**327–328**
  anti-Semitism, 1:141
  class consciousness, 1:572
  existentialism, 3:42, 43
  gaze, 3:263–264
  Hegel, Georg Wilhelm Friedrich,
    3:453
  humanism, 3:518
  otherness, 6:82
Sassen, Saskia, 8:543
Satanic Verses (Rushdie), 3:137
Satanism, 2:188
  See also Magic; Religion; Taboos
Satellite accounts, 5:397, 403
Satellites, weapons, 1:178–179
Satiation, 5:551, 7:**328–330**
Satire, 7:**330–331**
  blackface, 1:326–327
  parody, 6:148–149
  political cartoons, 1:452
Satisfaction
  consumer, ordinality, 6:56–57
  Exit, Voice, and Loyalty
    (Hirschman), 3:43–45

life, altruism, 3:292–293
  relationship, 3:179, 7:151–152
Satisficing behavior, 7:**331–332**
  behavioral economics, 2:500
  rational choice theory, 7:74–76
Satisfiers, 5:454
Satterthwaite, Mark, 1:525
Saudi Arabia
  Al Jazeera, 1:69
  bin Laden, Osama, 1:298–299
  Gulf Cooperation Council, 3:397
  OPEC, 6:65, 66–67
  Taliban, 8:263
  veiling, 8:602
Sauer, Carl, 2:192
Saul of Tarsus. *See* Paul the Apostle
Saussure, Ferdinand de, 2:97, 3:518
  semiotics, 7:436–438
  structuralism, 8:181–182
Sauvy, Alfred. *See* Third world
Savage, Leonard J., 6:490
  choice in economics, 1:524
  risk takers, 7:255
Savage Inequalities (Kozol), 2:316
The Savage Mind (Lévi-Strauss), 4:416
Savages
  defined, 5:429
  Veblen, Thorstein, 8:595–596
Savarkar, Vir, 3:478
Save, marginal propensity to,
  6:**546–547**
Save More Tomorrow Plan (SMT),
  2:252–253
Savigliano, Marta, 2:224
Saving, Thomas, 2:601–602
Saving rate, 2:270, 7:**332–336**, 332t,
  333, 334
  banana parable, 1:247–248
  bequests, 1:287
  bubbles (economics), 1:378
  Cantillion, Richard, 1:429
  consumerism, 2:105
  consumption, 2:108–109
  consumption function, 2:109
  coordination failure, 2:128
  decision-making, 2:252–253
  development economics, 2:345
  economic growth, 2:488, 489
  investment, 4:132
  Kalecki, Michał, 4:246–247
  life-cycle hypothesis, 4:441–443
  loans, 4:473
  Pasinett paradox, 6:164–165

Saving rate, *continued*
    post Keynesian economics,
        2:528–529
    relative income hypothesis, 7:153,
        154
    rentier class, 1:571
    Ricardian equivalence, 7:241
    rotating savings and credit
        associations, 7:286–287
Savings
    aggregate demand price, 1:52–53
    overlapping generations model,
        6:92
Savings and credit associations,
    rotating (ROSCAs), 7:**286–287**
Savings and loan associations. *See*
    Banking industry
Savitch, H. V., 8:543
Sawhill, Isabel, 8:485, 486
Say, Jean-Baptiste
    Cantillion, Richard, 1:429
    economic depression, 2:302–303
    laissez-faire, 4:335
    underconsumption, 8:488
    See also Say's Law
Sayan, Serdar, 6:94
Sayers, Sean, 9:122
Say's Law, 7:**336–338**
    aggregate demand, 1:50, 52–53
    banana parable, 1:247
    consumption function, 2:109
    economic depression, 2:302–303
    Keynes, John Maynard, 4:260
    market clearing, 4:601
    Mill, James, 5:177
    overproduction, 6:96–97
    quantity theory of money, 6:659
    underconsumption, 8:488, 489
    unemployment, 8:503
SBIC (Small business investment
    companies), 1:440
Scalawags, 7:113
Scale, returns to. *See* Returns to scale
Scales, 7:**338–339**
    self-consciousness, 7:401–402
    statistics in the social sciences,
        8:126
    validation, 8:569–572, 570*t*, 571*t*
    See also names of specific scales
Scandals. *See* Corruption
Scandinavia, cohabitation in, 2:1
Scarcity, 7:**339–340**, 9:16
    Coase, Ronald, 1:589
    Coase theorem, 1:590
    consumption, 2:106

Malthus, Thomas Robert, 4:570
Scarf, Herbert, 3:284
Scarr, Sandra Wood, 7:**340–341**
SCCS (Standard Cross-Cultural
    Sample), 8:**88–93**
Schaar, John, 2:613
Schachter, Stanley, 2:571, 6:3, 4–5,
    7:**341–342**
Schadenfreude. *See* Sympathy
Schaefer, Milner B., 6:91, 7:210–211
Scharpf, Fritz, 9:73
Schattschneider, E. E., 3:185,
    7:**342–343**
    agenda setting, 1:48
    interest groups and interests, 4:82
Schaumber, Peter Carey, 4:317
Scheduled Castes and Tribes (India).
    See Caste
Schegloff, Emanuel, 2:117, 119
Scheier, Michael F., 6:54–55
Scheinkman, José, 6:51
Scheler, Max, 7:674–675
Schelling, Friedrich Wilhelm Joseph,
    3:547, 548
Schelling, Thomas, 5:535
Schemas, 7:**344**
    person memory, 6:215–216
    script models, 7:372–373
    self-schemata, 7:426–427, 428
    social cognition, 7:570
    social information processing,
        7:599–600
Schempp, Abington School District v.,
    9:33
Schenely Corporation, 1:493, 494
Schiff, Steven, 8:508
Schiller, Ferdinand C., 6:421
Schism, Great (1054), 1:533
Schizophrenia, 7:**344–346**
    diathesis-stress model, 2:358
    dopamine, 2:436
    madness, 4:548
    paranoia, 6:128
    psychopathology, 6:592*t*
    resiliency, 7:205
    See also Mental illness
Schjelderup-Ebbe, Thorleif, 1:83
Schleiermacher, Friedrich, 3:462
Schleiffen Plan, 9:146
Schliemann, Heinrich, 7:**346–347**
Schlozman, Kay Lehman, 8:606
Schmeeckle, Maria, 3:86
Schmeidler, David, 5:519
Schmidt, Manfred G., 9:70
Schmidt, Peter, 8:589

Schmidt, Vivien, 9:73
Schmitt, Carl, 2:359, 3:198
Schmitter, Philippe C., 2:290
Schneider, David, 4:272–273
Schneider, Hermann, 1:189
    See also Assimilation
Schneider, Tamera, 2:252
Schoenberg, Arnold, 1:575
Scholes, Myron, 3:142
Schomburg, Arturo A., 1:32, 330, 356
Schomburg Center for Research in
    Black Culture, 1:32
*School Board of the City of Norfolk,
    Riddick v.* (1986), 7:201
School Daze (film), 2:18
School desegregation, 2:**316–319**
    Brown v. Board of Education
        (1955), 1:377, 6:342, 7:16
    civil rights, 1:550
    Clark, Kenneth B., 1:560, 561
    described, 2:313–314
    judiciary, 4:227
    race, 7:16–18
    race-conscious policies, 7:37
    resegregation, 2:316, 317–318,
        7:201–202, 387–388
        integration, 4:59–60
        race, 7:18
    Southern politics, 6:342
    *See also Brown v. Board of
        Education* (1954); Civil rights
        movement, U.S.; Separate-but-
        equal
School of Lausanne, 4:**361–362**, 9:11
School prayer, 1:536, 2:86, 3:236
School readiness, 7:**87–88**
School resegregation. *See*
    Resegregation of schools
School segregation, 7:**386–389**
    Brown v. Board of Education
        (1955), 1:377, 6:342, 7:16
    civil rights, 1:549
    Clark, Kenneth B., 1:560, 561
    Houston, Charles Hamilton,
        3:505
    Jim Crow, 4:200, 201
    Marshall, Thurgood, 4:625–626
    Pettigrew, Thomas F., 6:234–235
    qualifications, 6:649–650
    race, 7:16–18
    racial attitudes, 1:204
    Reconstruction Era, U.S., 7:114
    resegregation, 2:316, 317–318,
        7:201–202, 387–388
        integration, 4:59–60

race, 7:18

schooling, 7:354–355

tracking in schools, 8:409–410

Warren, Earl, 9:32–33

See also Brown v. Board of Education (1954); Civil rights movement, U.S.; Education, U.S.; Separate-but-equal; Unequal education

School tracking

resegregation of schools, 7:201

school segregation, 7:388

U.S., 2:542

School vouchers, 7:**347–350**

Church and state, 1:535

conservatism, 2:85

desegregation, 2:314

resegregation of schools, 7:201–202

schooling, 7:354

Schooling, 7:**350–352**

Berg, Ivar E., 1:288

blue collar and white collar, 1:337, 339

credentialism, 2:166–167

cultural distinctions, 2:412

oppositionality, 6:49–51

public schools, prayer in, 3:236

school readiness, 7:87–88

social demography, 2:296

social work, 7:634

teacher expectations, 8:290–291

tracking in schools, 2:542, 8:409–411

resegregation, 7:201

segregation, 7:388

See also Education

Schooling in the USA, 7:69–75, **352–356**

curriculum, 2:213–215

school readiness, 7:87–88

tracking in schools, 2:542

unequal education, 2:537–539, 7:351

See also Education, U.S.; School segregation

Schools in sociology, 8:**9–12**

Schools tracking, 8:**409–411**

Schopenhauer, Arthur, 1:114, 5:502

Schor, Juliet, 2:108, 109, 6:99, 9:15

leisure, 4:409

multiple jobs, 9:129

work day length, 9:127, 135

work week, 9:128

Schröder, Ernst, 4:481

Schudson, Michael, 1:28–29

Schulman, Paul R., 4:453

Schultz, Henry, 1:591

Schultz, Theodore W., 1:502, 4:309, 9:28

agricultural economics, 1:59

Lewis, W. Arthur, 4:421

See also Subsistence agriculture

Schultze, Charles L., 9:26

Schumacher, E. F., 6:95

Schuman, Howard, 1:103

Schumpeter, Joseph Alois, 3:148, 221, 4:260, 7:**356–357**

business cycle theories, 1:412

Cantillon, Richard, 1:429

capitalism, 1:438, 439

creative destruction, 2:162–163, 163–164

economic depression, 2:304

elections, 2:556

endogenous growth theory, 8:621

Heilbroner, Robert, 3:457

Hilferding, 3:476–477

long run, 4:493

Ricardian vice, 7:241, 242

technological change, 1:491

technology, 8:303

Schumpeterian hypothesis, 1:491

Schütz, Alfred, 2:96

habits, 3:403

phenomenology, 6:242–243

Schwartz, Anna J., 3:218

bank failures, 1:252

economic depression, 2:304

Great Depression, 3:368, 370

Schwartz, Joseph, 1:332

Schwarzenegger, Arnold, 7:102

Schwerner, Michael, 4:527

Science, 7:**357–360**

cognitive, 1:598–599

computers, 2:59–61

creationism *vs.,* 2:161–163

Diop, Cheikh Anta, 2:369–370

Hinduism, 3:479–480

human, 9:78

knowledge, 4:277–279

Kuhn, Thomas, 4:292–294

Lakatos, Imre, 4:338–340

management, 2:449–450, 4:576–577

Merton, Robert K., 5:102–103

modernity, 5:231

natural, 9:78

paradigm, 6:125–127

prevention, 6:445–447

crime and criminology, 2:173–174

psychological depression, 2:308

risk assessment, 8:656, 657

public policy, 5:362

scientism, 7:364–365

Scopes trial, 2:162, 7:366

See also specific sciences; Philosophy of science; Political science; Social science

Science fiction, 3:241, 7:**360–362**

Le Guin, Ursula K., 4:407

The Matrix (film), 5:31–32

Star Trek, 8:99

Star Wars, 8:100–101

The Science of Living (Adler), 4:445

Science of Logic (Hegel), 3:452, 547–548

The Science of Muddling Through (Lindblom), 3:608, 4:452

Scientific management. *See* Management; Taylorism

Scientific manufacturing, 3:77–78

Scientific method, 7:**362–364**

behavioral political science, 6:315–316

Lakatos, Imre, 4:338–340

logic, 4:480

methodology, 5:107–109

theory, 8:344–345

See also Experiments; Hypothesis and hypothesis testing; Observation

Scientific racism. *See* Racism

Scientific Research and Experimental Development Tax Incentive Program, Canada (SRED), 8:274

Scientific revolutions, 7:**235–237**

conundrum, 2:116

Kuhn, Thomas, 4:292–294

paradigm, 6:125–127

Scientific socialism. *See* Islamic socialism

Scientism, 7:**364–365**

SCLC (Southern Christian Leadership Conference). *See* Southern Christian Leadership Conference (SCLC)

Scoon, Paul, 3:383

Scopes, John. *See* Scopes trial

Scopes trial, 2:162, 7:**366–367**

Scopolamine, 3:411

Scorched-earth policy, 1:349, 2:227

Scores

interval, 3:206

Scores, *continued*
    Occupational Score Index,
        6:25–26
    variance, 8:589–590
Scotch, Norman, 1:131
Scotland
    civil society, 1:552
    Scottish moralists, 7:367–370
    See also United Kingdom (U.K.)
Scott, Douglas D., 1:259
Scott, Howard, 8:296, 298
Scott, Joan, 3:269, 8:355
Scott, Winfield, 1:497, 5:128
Scott Act (U.S. 1888), 1:513
Scott-Brown, Denise, 1:172
Scottish Enlightenment. *See*
    Enlightenment
Scottish moralists, 7:**367–371**
Scoville, James G., 4:167
Scramble for Africa. *See* Imperialism
Screening and signaling games,
    7:**371–372**
Scripps, E. W., 4:212, 213
Script models, 7:**372–373**
Scripture
    Hinduism, 3:477, 479
    reading of, 9:155
    See also Bible; Qur'an
Scruggs, Earl, 1:341
Scullin, Matthew, 3:160
Sculpture
    history, 8:630
    monumental, Olmecs, 6:39
    See also Visual arts
SDS (Students for a Democratic
    Society), 4:529
SDT (Self-determination theory),
    7:**407–408**
SEA, European Union 1968 (Single
    European Act), 2:29
Seaga, Edward, 7:69
Seale, Bobby, 1:319
Seals, Son, 1:343
Search and seizure, hallucinogens,
    3:412
Search engines. *See* Computers
Searle, John J., 1:129
Seater, John J., 5:490
Seattle protests, 9:144–145
*Seattle School District, Parents Involved
    in Community Schools v.* (2006),
    1:375–376
Secession, 7:**373–375**
    Benjamin, Judah P., 1:284
    as civil war, 1:554

civil wars, 1:555
Davis, Jefferson, 2:243
Democratic Party (U.S.), 2:287
Lee, Robert E., 4:399–400
Quebecois movement, 6:661–663
Reconstruction Era, U.S.,
    7:111–112
separatism, 7:450–451
South, U.S., 8:32
See also Confederate States of
    America; U.S. Civil War
Second Battle of Ypres (1915), 9:52
Second best, theory of, 2:414,
    8:**350–351**
Second Carib War (1796-1796),
    3:257–258
Second Hague Convention, 5:489
Second Industrial Revolution, 3:282
Second International, 1:446
Second New Deal (1935-1936),
    5:493, 494–495
    See also New Deal
Second-price auctions, 1:206–207,
    8:579–580
Second Russian Revolution. *See*
    Russian Federation
The Second Sex (de Beauvoir), 3:120,
    267
Second sight. *See* Veils, in African
    American culture
Second Treatise of Government (Locke),
    2:254, 4:237
Second wave feminism, 3:120–121,
    122–124, 267–268, 9:113–115,
    116–117
    gender politics, 3:267–268,
        6:333–334
    intersectionality, 4:114
The Second World War (Churchill),
    1:538
Secondary labor markets, 8:637
Secondat, Charles de. *See*
    Montesquieu, Charles Louis de
    Secondat, Baron de
Secrecy, 7:**375–377**
    ballots, 1:242
    banking laws, 6:32
    fraternal societies, 6:21
    Illuminati, 3:561–562
    Mafia, 4:550–553
    magic, 4:554–555
    transparency, 8:435
    zombies, 9:181
    See also Covert action
The Secret of Hegel (Stirling), 3:453
Secret societies. *See* Secrecy

Secrets Revealed (Khomeini). *See Kashf
    al-Asrar* (Khomeini)
Sectionalism, regions, 7:131
Sector, energy, 8:22–23
Sector, informal. *See* Informal
    economy
Sector, nonprofit. *See* Social economy
Sector, private. *See* Private sector
Sector, public. *See* Public sector
Secular. *See* Secularism
Secular effects, 6:209–210
Secular humanism. *See* Humanism
Secularism, 7:**377–379**
    caste, 1:461, 462
    The Church, 1:534
    civilization, 1:558
    clash of civilizations, 1:560
    demographic transition, 2:292
    futurology, 3:241
    humanism, 3:518
    latifundia, 4:353
    left wing, 4:403
    religiosity, 7:162
    rituals, 7:259
    taboos, 8:259–260
    time, 8:362
Secularization. *See* Secularism
Secure base. *See* Attachment theory
Securities. *See* Bonds; Stocks
Securities and Exchange Commission,
    on corporate fraud, 6:73
Securities transaction tax. *See*
    Transaction taxes
Security
    defined, 5:412
    United Nations role, 8:523–524
    See also National security
Security, job. *See* Employment
Security Council (UN), 8:523–524
    Commission for Conventional
        Armaments, 9:52
    Resolution 242, 1:159
    Resolution 678, 8:524
Security through Regularized
    Immigration and a Vibrant
    Economy Act, U.S. 2007
    (STRIVE), 1:365
SED, East Germany (Socialist Unity
    Party), 1:289
SED (Sozialistische Einheitspartei
    Deutschlands). *See* Communist
    Party (East Germany)
Sedek, Grzegorz, 4:389
Sedentary lifestyle and obesity, 6:4

Seduction of the Innocent (Wertham), 2:23–24

Seeing vs. being seen, 3:263

Seemingly unrelated regressions (SUR), 7:**379–381**
  recursive models, 7:117
  three-stage least squares, 4:394

Sega, 8:611
  See also Video games

Segalen, Martine, 3:87

Segerfeldt, Fredrik, 9:40

Segmentation, labor market. *See* Labor market segmentation

Segregation, 7:**381–383**
  apartheid, 1:147–149, 9:86
  Birth of a Nation (film), 1:305, 306
  black towns, 1:326
  blackness, 1:328–329
  colonialism, 2:12
  Coloreds (South Africa), 2:15
  Congress of Racial Equality, 2:75
  crowding hypothesis, 2:181–182
  as discrimination, 2:390–391
  Dixiecrats, 2:429
  equal protection, 2:614–615
  ethnic conflict, 3:1
  Hernandez v. Texas, 3:464–466
  job, 3:326
  Mexican Americans, 5:122–123
  Nation of Islam, 5:380
  neighborhoods, 5:462, 463
  race-conscious policies, 7:37
  separate-but-equal, 7:445–447
  South, U.S., 8:32–33
  Southern politics, 6:339–349
  taste for discrimination, 2:399
  Thurmond, Strom, 8:360–361
  wage discrimination, 2:400–401, 404, 405–406
  Weaver, Robert C., 9:53–54
  Wilson, Woodrow, 9:102
  See also Civil rights movement, U.S.; Desegregation; Integration; Jim Crow

Segregation, occupational. *See* Crowding hypothesis

Segregation, residential, 7:**383–386**
  caste, 1:458
  cities, 1:541
  civil rights movement, U.S., 1:552
  Coloreds (South Africa), 2:15
  described, 7:381–382
  education in the U.S., 2:542
  resegregation of schools, 7:201

separate-but-equal, 7:446
slums, 7:551–552
suburbs, 8:210–211
towns, 8:405
townships, 8:405–407
urban poverty, 6:410–411

Segregation, school, 7:**386–389**
  Brown v. Board of Education (1955), 1:377, 6:342, 7:16
  civil rights, 1:549
  Clark, Kenneth B., 1:560, 561
  Houston, Charles Hamilton, 3:505
  Jim Crow, 4:200, 201
  Marshall, Thurgood, 4:625–626
  Pettigrew, Thomas F., 6:234–235
  qualifications, 6:649–650
  race, 7:16–18
  racial attitudes, 1:204
  Reconstruction Era, U.S., 7:114
  resegregation, 2:316, 317–318, 7:201–202, 387–388
    integration, 4:59–60
    race, 7:18
  schooling, 7:354–355
  tracking in schools, 8:409–410
  Warren, Earl, 9:32–33
  See also Brown v. Board of Education (1954); Civil rights movement, U.S.; Separate-but-equal; Unequal education

Seguino, Stephanie, 3:275

SEI (Socioeconomic Index), 6:27

SEIN (Societal and ethical implications of nanotechnology), 5:362–363

SEIU (Service Employees International Union), 8:516

Seizures (law), 3:412

Seizures of property. *See* Confiscation

Selassie, Haile, 3:258
  Organization of African Unity, 6:62
  Rastafari, 7:66–70

Selby, Karen, 1:131

Selection
  adverse selection effect, 1:27–28, 9:103
  cultural group, 2:190–191, 191–192
  epigamic, 1:85
  kin, 1:89
  sexual, 1:84–85
  See also Natural selection

Selection, natural. *See* Natural selection

Selection bias, 7:**389–390**, 8:574
  choice in psychology, 1:526
  creaming, 2:160
  Heckman selection correction procedure, 3:446–448
  jury selection, 4:233–234
  labor supply, 4:321, 322
  tobit, 8:381
  wage discrimination, 2:404

Selective attention, 7:**391**

Selective breeding. *See* Eugenics

Selective serotonin reuptake inhibitors (SSRIs), 1:147, 6:18, 19

Selective Service, 7:**391–393**
  Confederate States of America, 2:67
  Davis, Jefferson, 2:243–244
  draft cards, 9:114
  Lynd, Staughton, 4:529
  servitude, 7:463
  social experiments, 7:591
  social relations, 7:613
  Vietnam War, 7:591, 8:614–615

Selective Service Act (U.S. 1917), 7:392

Selective Training and Service Act (U.S. 1940), 7:392

Selectorate theory. *See* Political stability

Self, 7:209, 8:**194–196**
  ideal, 6:85
  Jung, Carl, 4:230
  ought, 6:85
  See also Self-concept

Self-actualization, 5:455, 7:**394–396**
  equilibrium, 2:622
  Maslow, Abraham, 5:11–12

Self-affirmation theory, 7:**396–397**, 8:130–131

Self-awareness theory, 7:**397**
  rejection and acceptance, 7:149–250
  self-consciousness, 7:400–402

Self-censorship. *See* Censorship

Self-centeredness. *See* Egoism

Self-classification, 7:**397–398**
  racial classification, 7:40
  racial identification, 3:548–550

Self-concept, 7:**398–400**
  children, 1:511, 512
  identity crisis, 3:556–557
  looking-glass effect, 4:494–495
  role conflict, 7:272–273
  self-affirmation theory, 7:396–397
  self-enhancement, 7:411–412

Self-concept, *continued*
  self-handicapping strategies,
      8:164–165
  self-representation, 7:426–427
  self-schemata, 7:428
  social identification, 7:593–594
  social identity, 3:557–558
  See also Self-esteem; Self-identity
Self-confidence and conformity, 2:71
Self-consciousness, 3:158
  as consciousness, 2:79, 80
  evolution of, 5:451
  private *vs.* public, 7:400–402
  self-awareness theory, 7:397
Self-consciousness scale, 7:397,
      400–402
Self-constrained behavior, 1:273–274
  emotion regulation, 2:572–573
  empathy, 2:574
Self-control, 7:402–404
  farsightedness, 3:100–102
  motivation, 5:300–301
  self-monitoring, 7:421–422
  time orientation, 8:368
  See also Self-constrained behavior
Self-defeating behavior, 7:404–405
Self-determination, 7:405–407
  anticolonial movements, 1:139
  autonomy, 1:224–225
  Bourdieu, Pierre, 1:358
  Cabral, Amílcar, 1:415–416
  Chinese Revolution, 1:519–520
  decolonization, 2:255–257
  democracy, 2:272, 273
  Ho Chi Minh, 3:492
  human rights, 3:513
  India, 1:356–357
  Jefferson, Thomas, 4:180
  liberation, 4:429
  Mexican Americans, 5:120
  Palestinian Authority, 6:104–107
  representative and participatory
      democracy, 2:283–285
  republicanism, 7:188
  separatism, 7:450–451
*Self-Determination and the African
    American People* (Forman), 3:175
Self-determination theory (SDT),
      7:407–408
Self-disclosure, 7:408–409
  friendship, 3:221
  Likert scale, 4:447–448
Self-discrepancy theory, 7:393
  self-guides, 7:415–416
  self-schemata, 7:428

Self-doubt, overachievers, 6:88
Self-efficacy
  Bandura, Albert, 1:248
  motivation, 5:301
  personality, 6:219
  positive psychology, 6:386
  reciprocal determinism,
      2:331–332
  Rotter's Internal-External Locus of
      Control Scale, 4:477, 5:300,
      7:289–290
  time orientation, 8:358
Self-employment, 1:517, 7:410–411
Self-enhancement, 7:411–412
  self-serving bias, 7:429
  self-verification, 7:430–431
Self-esteem, 3:179, 7:412–414
  attribution, 1:206
  Brown v. Board of Education
      (1954), 1:376
  child development, 1:507
  contempt, 2:113
  equilibrium, 2:622
  looking-glass effect, 4:495
  mortality salience, 7:311
  recognition, 7:109–110
  rejection and acceptance, 7:150
  role conflict, 7:273
  Rosenberg's Self-Esteem Scale,
      7:287–288
  rumors, 7:295, 297
  self-affirmation theory, 7:396–397
  self-awareness theory, 7:397
  self-defeating behavior, 7:405
  self-efficacy, 7:409
  self-enhancement, 7:411–412
  self-handicapping strategies,
      8:164–165
  self-representation, 7:427
  self-serving bias, 7:429
  self-verification, 7:430–431
  social comparison, 7:576–577
  terror, 8:326–327
  Veblen, Thorstein, 8:596
  See also Self-concept
Self-fulfilling prophecies, 3:172,
      7:414–415
  black conservatism, 1:311
  leadership, 4:381
  luck, 4:512
  reflexivity, 7:122
  stereotypes, 8:139
  teacher expectations, 8:290, 291
  See also Expectations

Self-government. *See* Self-
    determination
Self-guides, 7:415–416
  ought self, 6:85
  self-discrepancy theory, 7:393
  self-representation, 7:426–427
Self-handicapping strategies,
      8:**164–165**
Self-hatred, 7:416–417, 488–489
Self-help organizations. *See*
    Volunteerism
Self-identity, 7:417–420
  described, 3:552
  identity crisis, 3:556–557
  lifestyles, 4:446
  looking-glass effect, 4:494–495
  microsociology, 7:678
  social identity, 3:557–558
  third world, 8:352
  See also Self-concept
Self-image. *See* Body image; Self-
    concept
Self-interest, 3:196, 199–200
  collective action, 2:5–6
  Durkheim, Émile, 2:466–467
  individualism, 3:618–619
  interdependent preferences, 6:437
  laissez-faire, 4:335–336, 337
  leaders, 4:377
  League of Nations, 4:385
  moral philosophy, 6:254–255
  prisoner's dilemma, 6:473
  public benefits, 3:199
  rational choice theory, 7:75
  rationality, 7:79
Self-justification, 7:420–421
Self-knowledge. *See* Self-perception
    theory
Self-love. *See* Narcissism
Self-monitoring, 7:421–422
  consciousness, 2:80
  self-awareness theory, 7:397
  self-constrained behavior,
      1:273–274
  self-control, 7:402–404
  self-schemata, 7:428
Self-mythologizing, 5:371
Self-perception theory, 7:422–423
  cognitive dissonance, 1:600–601
  looking-glass effect, 4:494–495
  self-awareness theory, 7:397
  self-consciousness, 7:400–402
  self-representation, 7:426–427
  social comparison, 7:576–577
Self-presentation, 7:423–424

ethnographic research, 7:193
Jones, Edward Ellsworth, 4:211
performance, 6:207–208
self-control, 7:421–422
self-handicapping strategies,
8:164–165
Self-reflection. *See* Ethnography;
Participant observation
Self-regulation. *See* Self-monitoring
Self-report method, 7:424–426
Rorschach test, 7:285
self-classification, 7:397–398
Self-representation, 7:426–428, 427*t*
Self-respect, difference principle,
2:363
Self-restraint. *See* Self-constrained
behavior; Self-control
Self-rule. *See* Self-determination;
Sovereignty
Self-schemata, 7:426–427, **428–429**
Self-service shopping, 9:123
Self-serving bias, 1:206, 7:**429**
person perception, 6:206
self-enhancement, 7:411–412
self-report method, 7:425
Self/subject, 7:209, 8:**194–196**
Self-system, 7:**429–430**
Self-verification, 7:**430–431**
Self-worth. *See* Self-esteem
Selfish gene theory, 2:191
Selfishness, 3:**292–294**
Hamilton's rule, 3:414–415
Rand, Ayn, 6:7
Seligman, Martin, 7:**431–432**
happiness, 3:418
learned helplessness, 4:387–389
optimism/pessimism, 6:54, 55
shock experiments, 3:62
Sellars, Wilfrid, 1:275, 280
Sellers, Robert, 7:23
Selling long and selling short, 1:385,
7:**432–434**
Sellouts, 7:**434–435**
Selten, Reinhard, 2:506
Selznick, David O., 3:347
SEM (Structural equation models). *See*
Structural equation models (SEM)
Semantic behaviorism. *See* Logical
behaviorism
Semantic memory, 7:**435–436**
Semantics. *See* Language
Semi-authoritarianism, 1:213
Seminole Indians, 6:81–82
Semiotics, 2:97, 7:**436–438**

Semiparametric estimation, 1:474,
5:526, 7:**438–440**
Semipresidential government, 3:355
The Semisovereign People
(Schattschneider), 3:185
Semitic civilization, heaven, 3:445
Semple, Ellen Churchill, 2:328
Sen, Amartya Kumar, 3:164,
7:**440–441**
Arrow, Kenneth J., 1:182
Cambridge capital controversy,
1:420
capabilities, 5:511, 535
choice in economics, 1:524, 525
Deadly Identities, 3:551
development in sociology, 2:348
distributive justice, 4:240
happiness, 3:416
indices of poverty, 6:408–409
Lewis, W. Arthur, 4:421
needs, 5:454
objective utility, 8:557
real income, 7:91
surplus labor, 4:309
utilitarianism, 8:553–554
welfare analysis, 9:62
welfare economics, 9:67
Senate, U.S.
appropriations, 1:155
Central Intelligence Agency, U.S,
1:484
Congress, U.S., 2:73–74
Fenno, Richard F., Jr., 3:124–125
filibuster, 3:138–139
League of Nations, 4:385, 386
lynchings, 4:527
McCarthyism, 5:43–44
Senators on the Campaign Trail
(Fenno), 3:124–125
Sendero Luminoso, 3:395
Seneca, 7:**441–442**
Seneca Falls Convention (1848),
9:113
See also Women's suffrage
Senechal de la Roche, Roberta, 4:526
Senegal
African Crisis Response Initiative,
1:38
Diop, Cheikh Anta, 2:368
Senghor, Léopold Sédar, 2:369, 3:518,
5:513
Sengstacke, John H., 1:501
Senility, 1:89, 2:271–272
Senior citizens. *See* Elderly
Sennett, Richard, 8:544

Sensation, objectivity, 6:8
Sensationalism, 7:**442–444**
Sensenbrenner, Jim, 1:365
Sensitive dependence on initial
conditions. *See* Butterfly effect
Sensitivity training, 4:418
Sensory and perceptual development,
1:506
Sentience. *See* Consciousness
Sentiments, moral, 5:**282–283**
Separability, 7:**444–445**
Separate Amenities Act (South Africa
1953), 2:15
Separate-but-equal, 7:**445–447**
equal protection, 2:615
Jim Crow, 4:198
Marshall, Thurgood, 4:625
race and education, 7:16
*See also Brown v. Board of
Education* (1954); Civil rights
movement, U.S.; Desegregation;
Segregation; Unequal education
Separation, marital. *See* Divorce and
separation
Separation and pooling games,
7:371–372
Separation anxiety, 1:363, 7:**447–448**
Separation of church and state. *See*
Church and state
Separation of powers, 7:**448–449**
checks and balances, 1:495–496
Congress, U.S., 2:73
Hamilton, Alexander, 3:413
judicial review, 4:223–225
judiciary, 4:226–227
parliaments and parliamentary
systems, 6:146
Republican Party (U.S.), 7:185,
186
rule of law, 7:292
Supreme Court, U.S., 8:234
veto, 8:610–611
See also Presidency
Separationism, 1:535
See also Church and state
Separatism, 7:**450–451**
Sephardim. *See* Jews
September 11, 2001, 7:**451–453**
aviation industry, 1:233
bin Laden, Osama, 1:299–300
Bush, George W., 1:399
central banks, 1:298
Central Intelligence Agency, U.S,
1:483, 485
consumption, 2:108

September 11, 2001, *continued*
    counterterrorism, 2:155
    defense, 2:259
    disaster management, 2:382, 385
    Fahrenheit 9/11 (film), 3:79–80
    Hussein, Saddam, 3:535
    Muslims, 5:346, 348
    Republican Party (U.S.), 7:187
    terror management theory, 8:328
    Wall Street, 9:9
    xenophobia, 9:161
    See also Islamic fundamentalism;
        Terrorism
Sequoyah, 1:497, 7:**453–455**
Seraph on the Suwanee (Hurston),
    3:528
Serbia, 9:168–169
    Clinton, Bill, 1:580
    Milosevic, Slobodan, 5:184
    nationalism, 5:418
    World War I, 9:145
Serbs, 7:**455**
    clash of civilizations, 1:559
    concentration camps, 2:63, 64
    Croats, 2:179
    ethnic conflict, 3:2
    Milosevic, Slobodan, 5:184
    Tito, Josip, 8:376
    Yugoslavian civil war, 3:406–407
Serendipitous inventions, 1:490
Serfdom. *See* Servitude
Serfling, Robert J., 4:349
Serial correlation, 3:289–290,
    7:**455–457**, 8:372
Serial dependence, 8:371
Seriation dating, 1:166
    See also Anthropology
Serletis, Apostolos, 5:491
Serotonin, 6:18, 19, 7:**457–460**
    drugs of abuse, 2:454
    psychological depression, 2:307
Servants
    indentured, 3:254
    women's work, 9:125
    See also Servitude; Slaves
Service, community. *See* Community
    service
Service, Selective. *See* Selective Service
Service Employees International
    Union (SEIU), 8:516
Service industry
    blue collar and white collar, 1:338,
        339, 340
    employment, 2:580
    nontraded goods, 3:349

women, 3:93–94
Service learning programs, 8:642
Servitude, 3:254, 569, 7:**460–464**
Set point theory, 6:4–5
Setting, price. *See* Price setting and
    price taking
Settlement, 7:**464–465**
    Asian immigrants, 3:562–564
    black immigrants, 3:565, 566
    Cherokees, 1:497
    European immigrants, 3:568–569
    Hmong, 3:491
    Latin American immigrants, 3:570
    North American immigrants,
        3:577
    refugees, 7:124–125, 127
Settlements, negotiated, 7:**465–466**
Settlements, tobacco, 7:**466–467**
Seun, Wing, 2:478–479
Seven Sister Companies, 6:65, 65*t*
    See also Petroleum industry
Seven Years' War, 6:661–663
Sewell, Bill, 8:7
Sex, interracial, 7:**467–470**
    Coloreds (South Africa), 2:15
    mulattos, 5:312–313
    race mixing, 7:26–28
Sex (gender). *See* Gender
Sex and mating, 7:**470–473**
    Darwin, Charles, 2:229
    eugenics, 3:21
    family functioning, 3:85, 88
    family structure, 3:93
    Freud, Sigmund, 3:210–211
    gender politics, 6:332–334
    Hite, Shere, 3:485
    infidelity, 4:20–21
    pimps, 6:271–273
    primates, 6:461
    romance, 7:281–282
    sociobiology, 7:653–654
    taboos, 8:259–260
    virgins, 8:629–630
    See also Contraception;
        Miscegenation; Rape
Sex differences. *See* Gender differences
Sex discrimination. *See* Gender gap;
    Sexism
Sex ration at birth, 3:366
Sex stereotypes
    gender gap *vs.*, 3:277
    work, 9:122
Sex vs. gender, 9:116
Sexism, 7:**473–474**

Disney, Walt, 2:410
    pimps, 6:271–273
    women's liberation, 9:114
    See also Gender gap
Sexual abuse. *See* Rape; Torture
Sexual Behavior in the Human Female
    (Kinsey), 4:270
Sexual Behavior in the Human Male
    (Kinsey), 4:270
Sexual dimorphism, alpha-males, 1:83
Sexual harassment, 3:420–421,
    7:**474–475**
Sexual orientation, 6:434
    body image, 1:346
    clash of civilizations, 1:560
    critical race theory, 2:175
    Kinsey, Alfred, 4:270
    liberation, 4:430
    queer studies, 6:330, 663–665
    sexuality, 7:482
    transgender, 8:431–432
    See also Gay, lesbian, transgender,
        and bisexual politics
Sexual orientation, determinants of,
    3:470, 7:**475–477**
Sexual orientation, social and
    economic consequences, 1:549,
    7:**477–479**
*Sexual Politics, Sexual Communities:
    The Making of a Homosexual
    Minority in the United States, 1940-
    1970* (D'Emilio), 6:329
Sexual Politics (Millet), 7:473
Sexual selection theory, 1:84–85,
    7:**479–480**
Sexual trafficking. *See* Pimps;
    Prostitution
Sexuality, 7:**480–484**, 481*t*
    constructivism, 2:97
    contraception, 2:114–115
    Darwin, Charles, 2:229, *230*
    eroticism, 2:626–627
    gender politics, 6:332–334
    heteronormativity, 3:470
    Hite, Shere, 3:485
    Kinsey, Alfred, 4:269–270
    Mead, Margaret, 5:47
    out-of-wedlock births, 1:307
    queer studies, 6:663–665
    reproductive politics, 7:180–181,
        182
    romance, 7:281
    stages of development, 8:77–79
    transgender, 8:431–432

See also Gay, lesbian, transgender, and bisexual politics; Sexual orientation

Seychelles, Creole, 2:169

SFTT (Single factorial terms of trade). *See* Terms of trade

Shaara, Michael, 4:399

Shabazz, El-Hajj Malik. *See* Malcolm X

Shadow Open Market Committee, 1:502

Shadow prices, 6:456, 7:**484–486**

Shah, Mohammed Reza, 1:484, 4:143, 144, 145

Shaikh, Anwar, 4:324

Shakespeare, William, 1:326, 495

Shakti, 8:568

Shamans, 1:114, 7:**486–488**, 8:398

Shame, 3:521–522, 7:**488–490**

The Shame of the Cities (Steffens), 2:180

Shankarcharaya, Adi, 1:367

Shanks, Michael, 1:168

Shannon, Claude E., 2:32, 33, 4:31

SHAPE (Supreme Headquarters, Allied Powers Europe), 5:543

Shapiro, Carl, 4:313, 9:5

Shapiro, Robert Y., 9:71

Shapley, Lloyd, 3:284

Sharecropping, 1:34, 7:**490–492**
    cooperatives, 2:126
    land reform, 4:342
    principal-agent models, 6:468

Sharia, 4:406

Sharon, Ariel, 7:**493**
    Palestinian Authority, 6:106
    water resources, 9:42

Sharp, Granville, 7:**494**

Sharp, Perez v. (1948), 7:28

Sharpe, Sam, 1:330

Sharpe, William, 3:141

Sharpville Massacre of 1960, 1:148
    See also Apartheid

Shartle, Carroll, 4:378

Shastri, Lal Bahadur, 3:252

Shaw, George Bernard, 3:74

Shaw, Greg M., 9:71

Shaw v. Reno, 8:652

Shays' Rebellion, 2:91

Shell shock. *See* Post-traumatic stress

Shenouda III, Pope, 2:132

Shepard, Lorrie, 8:572

Shepard, Matthew, 1:296, 3:431

Sheppard's Lemma. *See* Separability

Shepperson, George, 2:357

Sherbert v. Verner (1963), 1:535

Sherif, Muzafer, 1:216–217, 7:**494–496**
    social influence, 7:595
    superordinate goals, 8:226–227

Sherman, Roger, 2:254

Sherman, William T., 8:551

Sherman Antitrust Act (U.S. 1890), 1:143, 144, 4:303

Shevardnadze, Eduard, 3:351

Shevky, Eshref, 8:541

Shewhart, Walter A., 6:651

Shia Islam. *See* Shi'ism

Shift work, 9:128

Shi'ism, 1:160, 4:**154–158**
    See also Islam

Shi'ite Islam. *See* Shi'ism

Shiller, Robert, 3:143

Shils, Edward, 3:558, 560, 4:171, 7:375, 376, 377

Shimono, Keiko, 1:286

Shingon Buddhism. *See* Buddhism

Shining Path, 2:319
    See also De Soto, Hernando

Shinto, 7:**496–497**

Shipping industry, 7:**497–499**, 8:436–438

Shipwrecks, 2:196–197

Shivaji: Hindu King in Islamic India (Laine), 4:292

Shklar, Judith, 7:**499–500**

Shock experiments, 3:**62–63**
    ethics in experimentation, 2:636
    learned helplessness, 4:387–388
    Milgram, Stanley, 5:161–162

Shocks, 7:**500–501**
    business cycles, 1:403, 404, 405, 412
    central banks, 1:479
    decisive events, 2:254
    economic depression, 2:303–304
    energy industry, 2:590
    fiscal policy, 6:292
    foreign reserves, 7:203
    real business cycles, 1:407–409
    recession, 7:104

Sholokhov, Mikhail, 9:20

Shop, closed. *See* Labor law

Shopping. *See* Consumption

Short message systems (SMS), 8:306–308

Short people, Napoleon complex, 5:366–367

Short period, 7:**501–502**
    Kahn, Richard F., 4:245

long run, 4:491–492
    partial equilibrium, 6:152
    Z-D model, 9:172, 173

Short run, 7:**502–503**
    cointegration, 2:2, 3
    long run, 4:491–492
    partial equilibrium, 6:152

Short-selling, 1:385, 7:432–434

Short-term profit, outsourcing and, 6:86

Shriver, Sargent, 9:26

Shtetl, 7:**503–504**

Shubik, Martin, 1:206, 3:284

Shudra. *See* Sudras

Shultz, T. W., 1:270

Shutdowns, 4:302

Shyness, 7:**504–505**, 9:178

Sibling relationships, 2:229, *230*, 5:446, 7:**505–507**

Sibling rivalry. *See* Sibling relationships

Sicily, Mafia and, 4:550–551

Sickness. *See* Disease

Siddartha, Nirvāna, 5:504
    See also Buddha

Sidgwick, Henry, 8:553

Sidis (Indian ethnic group), 1:39

Le Siécle de Louis XIV (Voltaire), 8:635

Siegel, Shepard, 8:385

Siegel Prestige Scale, 6:27

Sierra Leone
    African Crisis Response Initiative, 1:38
    crony capitalism, 2:180
    vindication movements, 8:618

Sieyès, Emmanuel, 3:203

Sigmund, Paul, 1:77

Sign, theory of the, 6:10

Signaling games, 7:**371–372**

Signals, 7:**507–508**

Significance, statistical
    formulas, 3:180
    validity, 8:574
    variance, 8:589–590

Significance testing. *See* Hypothesis and hypothesis testing

Signification structure, 3:265–266

Sik, Ota, 2:117

Sikhism, 7:**508–510**, 9:155
    caste, 1:459
    hell, 3:458
    martyrdom, 4:629

Silicon Valley, 5:136–139, 7:**510–511**

Silk Road, 7:**511–512**
    See also Trade

Silver-backed currency, 2:181

Silver industry, 3:344, 7:**512–513**

SIM (Subscriber identity modules). *See* Cellular technology

Simar, Léopold, 2:241

Similarity/attraction theory, 7:**513–514**
romance, 7:281–282
social psychology, 7:610

Simmel, Georg, 1:540, 2:96, 3:385, 4:515, 5:530, 7:376, 377
alienation, 1:75
communalism, 2:31
Oedipus complex, 6:29
post-Parsonian American sociology, 8:6

Simmons, Furnifold, 9:99

Simmons-Harris, Zelman v. (2002), 1:535, 7:348

Simon, Dennis, 8:610

Simon, Herbert A., 2:101, 3:148, 7:**515**
behavioral economics, 2:500
choice in psychology, 1:525–526
management science, 4:577
maximization, 5:40–41
optimizing behavior, 6:55–56
satisficing behavior, 7:331

Simon, Paul, 9:141, 142

Simonde de Sismond, J. C. L., 6:96
accumulation of capital, 1:12
underconsumption, 8:488

Simonie, Frank, 5:412

Simons, Henry C., 1:502
lender of last resort, 4:410
rules *vs.* discretion, 7:293, 294

Simonson, Itamar, 3:101

Simonton, Deborah, 9:124–125, 125

A Simplest Systematics for the Organization of Turntaking in Conversation (Sacks, Schegloff and Jefferson), 2:118

Simpson, O. J., 4:364

Simpson, William, 3:125–126

Sims, Christopher, 1:527, 8:598–600

Simulactra, 8:597

Simulation, computer. *See* Computers

Simulation for the Social Scientist (Gilbert and Troitzsch), 2:61

Simultaneity bias, 8:372

Simultaneous conditioning, 1:573

Simultaneous equation bias, 7:116, 118, **515–518**, *516, 517*

Simultanous equations, system of. *See* Linear systems; Nonlinear systems

Sin, 7:**518–520**
See also Religion

Sinai Peninsula
Arab-Israeli War of 1967, 1:156–159
Nasser, Gamal Abdel, 5:377

Sinclair, Barbara, 1:48

Sinclair, Upton, 1:8

Singapore
Chinese diaspora, 1:518
as city-state, 1:544
Kuznets hypothesis, 4:297
labor market, 4:319
multiracial meritocracy, 5:100–101

Singer, Hans, 7:**520–521**
development economics, 2:345
Prebisch-Singer hypothesis, 6:424
terms of trade, 8:325–326

Singer, Jerome, 2:571

Singer, Peter, 8:553

Singh, Charan, 4:170, 171

Singh, Manmohan, 2:77

Singh, Mohan, 3:610

Singh, V. P., 7:**521**

Single-adult family, 3:94

Single European Act, European Union 1968 (SEA), 2:29

Single factorial terms of trade (SFTT). *See* Terms of trade

Single market. *See* Common market

Single-member districts (SMD), 8:647

Single mothers. *See* Female-headed families

Single-object auctions, 8:579–580

Single-parent families. *See* Family structure; Female-headed families

Single-party states. *See* One-party states

Single-payer health insurance, 5:396

Single transferable vote system (STV), 8:647

Single transferable voting, 8:655

Singleton, Benjamin, 1:325

Sinitic Censorate, 1:23

Sinn Fein. *See* Irish Republican Army (IRA)

Sino-Indian War (1962), 5:461

Sino-Japanese War (1937-1945), 1:521

Sinsheimer, Robert, 3:299

Sioux, 5:426

SIPP (Survey of Income and Program Participation), 8:**243–244**

Sir Arthur Lewis Memorial Lecture, 5:390

Sir Lanka, national health insurance, 5:395

Sirica, John, 9:43

Sisterhood. *See* Second wave feminism; Women's liberation

Sisters. *See* Sibling relationships

Sistine Chapel, 8:633

Sisulu, Walter, 1:148

Sit-ins. *See* Civil rights movement, U.S.; Passive resistance

Sitting Bull, 5:426, 7:**522**

Situation-person debate. *See* Person-situation debate

Situational analysis, 1:454

Situational factors, altruism, 1:88–89

Situational leadership theory, 4:379, 380

Sivan, Emmanuel, 1:82

Siverson, Randolph, 6:37

Six Crises (Nixon), 5:506

Six-Day War. *See* Arab-Israeli War of 1967

Sixtus V, 1:2

Sjoberg, Gideon, 5:159

Ska, 7:127–128

Skeptics, 1:275

Sketch for a Historical Picture of the Progress of the Human Mind (Condorcet), 2:66

Skewness, 2:312
See also Descriptive statistics

Skill bias, technological progress, 8:**300–302**

Skills, 7:**523–525**
Berg, Ivar E., 1:288
blue collar and white collar, 1:337, 338
computers, 2:59
crowding hypothesis, 2:182
engineering, 2:593–594
ethnic diversity, 2:342, 343
firm-specific, 5:515
labor, 4:301–302, 302, 319
labor demand, 4:313
obsolescent, 8:503
qualifications, 6:649–650

Skills, soft, 8:**21–22**

Skimming, price. *See* Price discrimination

Skin color. *See* Blackness; Whiteness

Skin whitening, 9:**89–91**

Skinner, B. F., 7:**525–527**
behaviorism, 1:275, 277, 278, 280

Chomsky, Noam, 1:528
developmental psychology, 2:350
habits, 3:403
language, 1:528
operant conditioning, 1:574,
   6:43–44
prediction, 6:430
reinforcement theories, 7:147
Thorndike, Edward, 8:358, 359
Skinner box, 1:574, 6:44, 7:**528**
Skinner v. Oklahoma (1942), 2:461
Skinnerian behaviorism, 1:277
Skocpol, Theda, 7:**529**
hypotheses, 3:542–543
post-Parsonian American
   sociology, 8:6
social welfare system, 7:631, 632
welfare state, 9:69, 71
world-system, 9:153
Skolnick, Arlene, 3:87
SLA (Sudanese Liberation
   Movement/Army), 2:226–227
Slack, Tim, 8:494
Slapping. *See* Corporal punishment
Slash-and-burn agriculture, 3:130
Slater, Don, 4:446
Slater, Philip, 6:29
Slaughter, Anne-Marie, 3:333
Slaughterhouse Cases (1883), 2:614
Slave-gun cycle, 7:**540–542**
Slave lives, archaeology of, 7:**529–531**
   See also Slaves
Slave mode of production, 7:**531–533**
   class, 1:562
   class conflict, 1:572
   cliometrics, 1:581, 582
   Engerman, Stanley, 2:592–593
   internal colony, 2:13–14
   primitive communism, 2:37
   Time on the Cross, 8:366–367
   transitional conjunctures, 2:77
Slave resistance, 7:**533–536**
   liberation, 4:429
   rebellions
      Gabriel (Prosser), 3:244–246
      Vesey, Denmark, 8:609
      Wilmington Riot of 1898,
         9:98–100
   Turner, Nat, 8:468
Slave trade, 7:**537–540**
   Bentham, Jeremy, 1:286
   Confederate States of America,
      2:66
   Inikori, Joseph, 4:37–38
   Liverpool, 4:468–469

railway industry, 7:53–54
Rodney, Walter, 7:269–270
slave-gun cycle, 7:540–542
Slaveowners. *See* Slavery
Slavery, 7:**542–546**
   African American history, 1:34
   African burial grounds, 1:393–394
   African diaspora, 1:38–40
   agricultural industry, 1:60–61,
      3:131
   Appalachia, 1:150
   archaeology, 7:529–531
   Atlantic slave trade, 1:39–40
   Bentham, Jeremy, 1:286
   Birth of a Nation (film),
      1:304–305
   black nationalism, 1:315
   black politics, 6:323–324
   blackness, 1:328, 329
   blues, 1:342
   Caribbean, 1:448
   cliometrics, 1:581, 582
   colorism, 2:18
   Columbus, Christopher, 2:19–20
   concentration camps, 2:64
   Constitution, U.S., 2:91, 92
   cotton industry, 2:152
   Creole, 2:169
   Davis, Jefferson, 2:243
   Democratic Party (U.S.), 2:287
   diaspora, 2:356
   Douglass, Frederick, 2:438–440
   economic growth, 1:34, 2:491
   educational achievement, 6:34
   Engerman, Stanley, 2:592–593
   federalism, 3:114
   Fogel, Robert, 3:161–162
   Frazier, E. Franklin, 3:191
   Hume, David, 3:520
   immigration, 3:577
   ingratiation, 4:34
   internal colony, 2:13–14
   interracial sex, 7:468
   Jefferson, Thomas, 4:181
   Jim Crow, 4:198
   labor, 4:301
   Lafargue, Paul, 4:328–329
   latifundia, 4:352, 353
   Lee, Robert E., 4:399
   liberation, 4:429
   Lincoln, Abraham, 4:451
   Liverpool slave trade, 4:468–469
   Mintz, Sidney W., 5:196
   moral suasion, 5:283

Moynihan, Daniel Patrick, 5:304
mulattos, 5:312–313
Napoléon Bonaparte, 5:364–365
negro terminology, 5:458–459
out-of-wedlock births, 1:306–307
plantations, 1:39–40, 3:161–162,
   6:277–279
race, 7:2–3, 4, 13, 26, 27
racial classification, 7:39
racism, 7:45–46
rape, 7:65
Reconstruction Era, U.S.,
   7:111–112
reparations, 7:166–168
restitution principle, 7:213–215
Saint-Dominigue revolt,
   3:204–205
servitude, 7:461
settlement, 7:465
slave mode of production,
   7:531–533
slavery hypertension hypothesis,
   7:546–547
Stowe, Harriet Beecher,
   8:161–162
sugar industry, 8:218–219
Thoreau, Henry David, 8:357
Time on the Cross, 4:366–367
Tocqueville, Alexis de, 8:383
transitional conjunctures, 2:77
Truth, Sojourner, 8:462
Tubman, Harriet, 8:464–465
Uncle Tom, 8:482–483
Vesey, Denmark, 8:608–610
vodou, 8:633–634
wage, 9:126
zombies, 9:181
   See also Abolition of slavery;
      Confederate States of America;
      Dred Scott v. Sanford; Slaves;
      The South, U.S.; U.S. Civil
      War
*Slavery: A Problem in American
   Institutional and Intellectual Life*
   (Elkins), 6:277
Slavery, abolition of. *See* Abolition of
   slavery
Slavery and Capitalism (Williams),
   3:131
Slavery hypertension hypothesis,
   7:**546–547**
Slavery industry, 4:468–469,
   7:**547–549**
   See also Slave trade
Slaves
   Africville, 1:45–46

Slaves, *continued*
culture, 1:40
family, 1:40
freed, 8:618
Haiti, 3:406–407
population growth, 1:40
voting, 8:646
whitening, 9:89
See also Lynchings; Slave
resistance; Slavery
Slavs. *See* Croats; Serbs
Sleep, dreaming, 2:444–445
Sleeper effects, 7:**550**
Slidell, John, 5:128
Sloan, Alfred, 1:218
Slovakia, NATO and, 5:546
Slovenia, 5:544, 9:168
*The Slowing Down of the Engine of
Growth* (Lewis), 4:420
Slums, 7:**551–552**
clientelism, 1:579
Harlem, 3:424
landlords, 4:346
See also Housing; Poverty
Slurs, racial, 7:**41–43**
Slutsky, Eugen, 1:227, 7:300, 8:555
Small, William Stanton, 7:147
Small business, Chinese diaspora,
1:517
Small business investment companies
(SBIC), 1:440
Small is Beautiful (Schumacher), 6:95
Smallpox, 9:140
Smart, J. C., 8:553
Smart cards. *See* Microelectronics
industry
SMD (Single-member districts), 8:647
Smeal, Eleanor, 5:409
SMG (Strategic market game) model,
3:284
Smith, Adam, 7:**552–558**
accumulation of capital, 1:12
adverse selection, 1:28
altruism, 3:414
Anglo-Portuguese trade, 8:413
Austrian economics, 1:210
autonomy, 1:225
Bentham, Jeremy, 1:286
bilateral trade, 8:414
Cantillion, Richard, 1:429
capitalist mode of production,
1:446
civil society, 1:552, 553
class, 1:562
classical economics, 2:504

compensating wages, 9:4
conservatism, 2:84
Conservative Party (U.K.), 2:87
consumption, 2:106
convergence theory, 2:117
Corn Laws, 2:133, 134
cosmopolitanism, 2:149
cumulative causation, 2:207
dirigiste, 2:373
division of labor, 2:423–425
economic growth, 2:490, 491
economic value, 8:576
exchange value, 3:40
factory system, 3:76–77
free trade, 3:194
Hamilton, Alexander, 3:414
happiness, 3:415
human capital, 3:506–507
increasing returns, 7:219
industrialization, 3:620–621
labor, 4:301
labor theory of value, 4:323
laissez-faire, 4:335, 336, 337
liberalism, 4:425
libertarianism, 4:437, 438, 439
life, 7:552–553
long period analysis, 4:489
long run, 4:491
machinery, 4:535
Malthus, Thomas Robert, 4:570
Malthusian trap, 4:572
management science, 4:574
marginal product of labor, 4:307
markets, 4:607
mercantilism, 5:93, 474
moral sentiments, 5:282
national income accounts, 5:399
noncompeting groups, 5:514
North-South models, 5:546
occupational safety, 6:24
prices, 6:455
primitive accumulation, 6:163
rationalism, 7:76–77
returns, 7:217
rhetoric, 7:238
Ricardo, David, 7:243, 244, 245,
246
Scottish moralists, 7:368
tastes, 8:267
Taylorism, 8:287
technological change, 1:491
towns, 8:404–405
Verdoorn's law, 8:606
water/diamond paradox, 8:555

wealth, 9:45
writings, 7:553–557
Smith, Alfred E., 7:283
Smith, Alison, 3:107
Smith, Alistair, 6:37
Smith, Anthony D., 5:422
Smith, Bessie, 1:343
Smith, Employment Division v. (1990),
1:535–536
Smith, Iain Duncan, 2:88
Smith, James P., 5:499
Smith, John, 2:88, 4:326, 327
Smith, Julia, 2:135
Smith, Lonnie E., 9:85
Smith, Mamie, 1:343
Smith, Merritt, 2:332
Smith, Neil, 8:545
Smith, Peter B., 2:72
Smith, R., 3:87
Smith, Tommie, 6:40
Smith, Valene, 2:201
Smith, Vernon L., 7:**558–559**
behavioral economics, 2:501
experimental economics, 2:505,
506
Smith-Lever Act (U.S. 1914), 2:341,
8:8
Smith v. Allright, 9:85
Smithson, James, 3:183
Smoking, 7:**559–562**
addiction, 1:21
adolescents, 5:391
drug tolerance, 8:385
harassment, 3:420
prevalence, 8:376–377
Schachter, Stanley, 7:342
tobacco settlement, 7:466–467
See also Tobacco industry
Smoot-Hawley Tariff Act (U.S. 1930),
1:273
SMS (Short message systems),
8:306–308
SMT (Save More Tomorrow Plan),
2:252–253
Smuts, Jan Christen, 1:349, 2:474
apartheid, 1:147
Gandhi, Mohandas K., 3:254
SNA (System of National Accounts),
5:397, 398–401
SNCC (Student Nonviolent
Coordinating Committee). *See*
Student Nonviolent Coordinating
Committee (SNCC)
Sniping, 1:207–208
Snowden, David, 2:272

Snowden, Ethel, 4:150

Snyder, Gary, 1:384

Snyder, Mark, 7:421–422

Sober, Elliott, 2:631

Soca, 1:417, 418, 419

Social accounting matrix (SAM),
7:**562–563**
  Jajmani matrix, 4:167
  Leontief, Wassily, 4:412–413

Social action. *See* Behavior

Social activism. *See* Activism

Social aggression, 1:55, 56

Social and cultural distinctions,
2:**412–414**

Social and Liberal Democratic Party
(Britain). *See* Liberal Party (U.K.)

The Social Animal (Aronson), 1:180

Social anthropology. *See* Ethnography

Social anxiety, 1:146, 6:262,
7:**563–564**

Social capital, 7:**564–567**
  African Americans, 1:36
  cultural capital, 2:190
  described, 1:430
  habitus, 3:404–406
  network analysis, 5:481
  political sociology, 8:4
  voluntary associations, 1:193

Social categorization, 7:**567–568**
  cleavages, 1:577
  conformity, 2:71
  conversational analysis, 2:119
  cultural distinctions, 2:413
  essentialism, 2:631
  ethnicity, 3:9
  intergroup relations, 4:91
  mulatto escape hatch, 5:310–312
  racial identification, 3:548–550
  Raj, 7:56–57
  social identity, 3:557–558
  solidarity, 8:23–24
  stereotypes, 8:136–139
  taste for discrimination, 2:399
  teacher expectations, 8:290–291

Social change, 7:**568–569**
  activism, 1:18
  class, 1:561
  Conservative Party (U.K.), 2:87
  constitutional courts, 2:93
  cooperation, 2:122
  creolization, 2:169–170
  cyberspace, 2:217
  demographic transition,
    2:290–292
  direct action, 2:372

future shock, 3:240

globalization, 3:333

language and, 1:129–130

Lynd, Robert and Helen, 4:528

Mexican Americans, 5:120–121

modernization, 5:232–234

Park School, 6:143

primitive communism, 2:37–38

recognition, 7:109

revolution, 7:228–231

rituals, 7:264

social formation, 3:177

social pathology, 6:169–171

technological change, 1:490

Social choice, 1:524
  Arrow possibility theorem,
    1:183–184
  leaders, 4:376
  theory, 8:654
  topology, 8:391
  voting schemes, 8:654

Social Choice and Individual Values
(Arrow), 8:654

Social citizenship, 9:67

Social class. *See* Class

Social classification. *See* Social
categorization

Social closure. *See* Social exclusion

Social cognition, 7:**569–575**
  attitudes, 7:573–574
  Bandura, Albert, 1:248–249
  bias, 7:570–572
  comparison, 7:576–577
  described, 1:598
  dual systems, 7:572–573
  errors, 7:570–572
  habitus, 3:404–406
  history, 7:569–570
  influence, 7:575
  intelligence, 4:74–75
  leaning perspective, 7:602–603
  person memory, 6:215
  reciprocal determinism,
    2:331–332
  schemata, 7:570
  social comparison, 7:576–577
  social influence, 7:575
  social leaning perspective,
    7:602–603
  theory of mind, 8:346–348

Social cognitive map, 7:**575–576**
  cognition, 1:597
  social identity, 3:557–558

Social comparison, 7:**576–578**, 597

Social conflict theory. *See* Political
sociology

Social conservatism, Tolstoy, Leo, 9:20

The Social Construction of Reality
(Berger and Luckman), 2:96,
6:69–70

Social constructionism, 2:96–98,
7:**578**
  Darwin, Charles, 2:231*t*
  essentialism, 2:630
  gay, lesbian, transgender, and
    bisexual politics, 6:329
  personal constructs, 6:216–217
  phenomenology, 6:243
  queer studies, 6:663
  race, 7:8–11
  social constructs, 7:578–580
  voluntaristic *vs.* structuralist
    sociology, 8:17

Social constructs, 7:**578–580**
  comedy, 2:22–23
  economic sociology, 7:669
  empiricism, 2:579
  intelligence, 4:73
  measurement, 5:54–55
  performance, 6:207–208
  phenomenology, 6:243
  qualifications, 6:649, 650
  race, 7:2, 6–7, 8–11, 43
  representation, 7:173
  self/subject, 8:194–195
  social constructionism, 7:578
  subjectivity, 8:199

Social Contract (Rousseau). *See On the
Social Contract* (Rousseau)

Social contracts, 7:**581**, 9:67
  British anthropology, 1:127
  common land, 2:28
  communalism, 2:30
  constitutionalism, 2:93–94
  defense, 2:258
  Hobbes, Thomas, 3:492–493
  moral philosophy, 6:255, 256
  political philosophy, 6:258
  Rawls, John, 7:84–85
  Rousseau, Jean-Jacques, 3:197,
    7:290
  social justice, 4:241, 242
  state of nature, 8:110

Social conventions. *See* Norms

Social costs, 7:**581–583**
  absentee landlords, 4:348
  air pollution, 6:362, 363
  Coase, Ronald, 1:589
  Coase theorem, 1:590

Social costs, *continued*
    free trade, 8:506
    unemployment, 8:501
Social customs. *See* Culture; Tradition
Social Darwinism, 2:**232–234**
    behaviorism, 1:276
    biological determinism, 2:326
    environmental determinism, 2:327
    eugenics, 3:21–22
    Nazism, 3:495
    race, 7:13
    Spencer, Herbert, 8:58
    wealth and poverty, 5:495
    World War I, 9:146
Social Darwinism in American Thought
    (Hofstadter), 2:232
Social democracy, 2:274
    black liberalism, 1:312
    convergence theory, 2:117
Social Democratic parties
    cleavages, 1:578
    Germany, 4:522
    left wing, 4:403
    Liberal Party (U.K.), 1:537, 2:86,
        4:423–424
    Luxemburg, Rosa, 4:522
    Social Democratic Workers' Party
        (Russia), 7:303
    welfare state, 9:68
Social Democratic Party (Germany)
    (SPD), 4:522
Social Democratic Party (Britain),
    1:537, 2:86, 4:427–428
Social Democratic Workers' Party
    (Russia), 7:303
Social demography, 2:293, **295–297**
Social Demography (Ford and DeJong),
    2:295
Social deviance. *See* Deviance
Social dilemmas, nonzero-sum games,
    5:533
Social distance. *See* Political tolerance;
    Social isolation
Social distinctions, 2:**412–414**
Social dominance orientation,
    7:**583–584**
    authoritarian personality, 6:221
    cults, 2:188
    ethnic conflict, 3:1–2
    ethnicity, 3:6–8, 10
    hierarchy, 3:474
    immigrants, 3:580
    men, 5:80–81
    nonadditive determinism, 2:330

post-Parsonian American
    sociology, 8:5, 6
prestige, 6:443–444
primates, 6:461
race, 7:3, 7
race and religion, 7:25–26
racial identification, 3:549
racial slurs, 7:41
social distinctions, 2:412
social status, 7:622
Social dynamics. *See* Social relations
Social ecology, 2:449–450
Social economics, Chicago School,
    1:502
Social economy, 7:**584–585**
    nonprofit organizations, 1:401,
        3:324
    School of Lausanne, 4:361–362
    See also Market economy;
        Volunteerism
Social equilibrium, functionalism,
    3:232
Social evolution
    Boserup, Ester, 1:358
    emotion, 2:570
Social exchange theory, 7:**585–586**
    Blau, Peter M., 1:332
    emotion, 2:569–570
    marriage, 4:614
    norm of reciprocity, 7:107–108
    post-Parsonian American
        sociology, 8:7
    rational choice theory, 7:75
    reciprocity, 7:105–107
    trust, 8:460–461
Social exclusion, 7:**586–589**
    Asian immigrants, 3:563–564,
        579
    Blair, Tony, 1:331
    blood and bloodline, 1:335–336
    citizenship, 1:542–543
    cultural distinctions, 2:413
    ethnic fractionalization, 3:6
    Luxembourg Income Study,
        4:521*t*
    New York City immigrants, 3:573
    privacy, 6:477
    race relations, 7:29
    rejection and acceptance,
        7:149–150
    restitution principle, 7:213–215
    slums, 7:552
    social distinctions, 2:412
    taste for discrimination,
        2:398–399

wage discrimination, 2:404
    See also Marginalization;
        Unemployment
Social experiments, 7:**590–592**
    Campbell, Donald, 1:425–426
    moving to opportunity,
        5:302–304
Social facilitation, 7:**592–593**
Social facts, 2:465, 5:52
    empiricism, 2:579
    social constructs, 7:579
    theory, 8:345
Social formation, 3:**176–178**
The Social Frameworks of Memory
    (Halbwachs), 2:7
Social goods, underrepresentation,
    8:495
Social gospel movement, 7:667
Social history, 3:**482–485**
    case method, 1:453
    collective memory, 2:7–8
    memory, 5:74–75
    See also specific events, countries and
        policies
The Social History of an Indonesian
    Town (Geertz), 3:265
Social humanism. *See* Humanism
Social identification, 7:576–577,
    593–594
    See also Social identity
Social identity, 3:**555–556**
    caste, 1:457–460
    conformity, 2:71
    constructivism, 2:97
    Dawes, Robyn, 2:245
    Deadly Identities, 3:551
    described, 3:552
    identity politics, 6:334–336
    intergroup relations, 4:90
    realist theory, 7:99
    stereotypes, 8:136–139
    stratification economics, 2:531
    violence, 8:623
    See also Self-concept; Self-identity
Social impact theory, 3:179
Social indifference curve, 9:*65, 65*–66
Social influence, 7:**594–599**
    baby boomers, 1:235–236
    communication, 2:32
    community power studies, 2:43
    conformity, 2:71–72
    consumption, 2:105
    human ecology, 3:511
    hypertension, 3:539, 540
    Kelley, Harold, 4:253

leadership, 4:375–382
lifestyles, 4:445–446
looking-glass effect, 4:494–495
nutrition, 5:552
Parsonian sociology, 8:1
persuasion, 6:227–228
reactance theory, 7:85–86
rumors, 7:295–298
See also Herd behavior
Social information processing,
7:599–600
person memory, 6:215
script models, 7:372–373
Social intelligence, 4:**74–75**, 5:327
Social interaction. *See* Social relations
Social isolation, 7:**600–601**
cities, 1:541
colonialism, 2:12
loneliness, 4:486–487
looking-glass effect, 4:495
Park, Robert E., 6:141
Park School, 6:143
peer effects, 6:199–200
privacy, 6:477
taste for discrimination, 2:399
wage discrimination, 2:401
See also Intergroup relations;
Marginalization
Social judgment theory, 7:**601–602**
collective wisdom, 2:9–10
conformity, 2:71–72
Dawes, Robyn, 2:244–245
lay theories, 4:374
Social justice, 4:**241–243**
Chávez, César, 1:494
class conflict, 1:568–570
digital divide, 2:366–367
Feagin, Joseph, 3:109
functionings, 3:233–235
Lynd, Staughton, 4:528–529
social movements, 7:603–607
Vajpayee, Atal Bihari, 8:569
Woodstock, 9:121
Social Justice and the City (Harvey),
3:305
Social learning perspective, 6:43,
7:602–603
Bandura, Albert, 1:248–249
developmental psychology, 2:350
locus of control, 4:477–478
role models, 7:274
Rotter's Internal-External Locus of
Control Scale, 7:289–290
Social marriage, 3:83
Social medicine. *See* Public health

Social memory. *See* Collective memory
Social mobility
family values, 3:96
fascism, 3:103
intergenerational, 8:533
intragenerational, 8:533
schooling oppositionality, 6:49
See also Upward mobility
Social movements, 7:**603–608**
Black Arts Movement, 1:309–310
black nationalism, 1:315–318
Blau, Peter M., 1:332
citizenship, 1:543
class, 1:563, 572
coalition, 1:587
dalits, 2:221
direct action, 2:372
Love Canal, 4:504–505, 6:359
mobilization, 5:214, 7:604–606
peace movements, 6:101–102,
182–185
political sociology, 8:4
rock 'n' roll, 7:268
urban sociology, 8:16
See also Postmodernism; Social
change
Social needs, 5:451, 455
Social networks. *See* Networks
Social neuroscience, 2:330–331,
5:**485–486**
Social norms. *See* Norms
Social Organization (Lowie), 4:507
*The Social Origins of Dictatorship and
Democracy* (Moore), 8:6
The Social Origins of Private Life
(Coontz), 3:96
Social pathology, 6:**169–171**
black liberalism, 1:312
culture of poverty, 2:206
Lewis, Oscar, 4:419
murder, 5:338–339
social isolation, 7:601
urban poverty, 6:410–411
Social pedagogy, 2:535
Social phobia. *See* Social anxiety
Social policy interventions, 4:**117–119**
Social Problems as Collective Behavior
(Blumer), 1:344
Social programs
appropriations, 1:155
baby boomers, 1:235, 236
benign neglect, 1:283–284
distributive justice, 4:240
political science, 5:469
volunteerism, 8:641

See also Welfare
Social protest. *See* Protest
Social psychology, 7:**608–611**
Aronson, Elliot, 1:180–181
Blumer, Herbert, 1:343–344
cognitive dissonance, 1:599–601
collective wisdom, 2:9–10
communication, 2:32–33
conformity, 2:71–72
decision-making, 2:251–253
evolutionary psychology, 3:33–34
evolutionary theory of kinship,
4:273–274
Festinger, Leon, 3:132–133
Fromm, Erich, 3:222–223
game theory, 3:251–252
habitus, 3:404–406
intergroup relations, 4:90–92
Jones, Edward Ellsworth,
4:210–211
Kelley, Harold, 4:252–253
Lazarsfeld, Paul Felix, 4:375
Lewin, Kurt, 4:417–418
looking-glass effect, 4:494–495
luck, 4:512–513
Marx, Karl, 4:630
primacy/recency effects,
6:457–458
race, 7:21–23
romance, 7:281–282
rumors, 7:295–298
script models, 7:372–373
self-consciousness, 7:400–402
self-guides, 7:415–416
self-presentation, 7:423–424
social cognition, 7:569–575
social influence, 7:594–598
Social Psychology (Asch), 1:187
Social psychosomatics, 6:**596–598**
Social Readjustment Rating Scale
(SRRS), 4:443–444
Social reconstructionism, 2:214
Social Reform or Revolution?
(Luxemburg), 4:522
Social relations, 7:**611–614**
capitalist mode of production,
1:447
cellular technology, 8:307
children, 1:506–507, 511–512
cities, 1:540
civil society, 1:553
clientelism, 1:578–579
cohabitation, 2:1–2
collective action, 2:6
communalism, 2:31

Social relations, *continued*
computers, 2:60, 61
constructivism, 2:96, 97
consumerism, 2:105
contempt, 2:113
contingency models of leadership, 4:384
conversational analysis, 2:118
cooperation, 2:122–123
cultural distinctions, 2:413
cyberspace, 2:216, 217
dependency, 2:297–298
disease, 2:408
emotion, 2:569–570, 572
equilibrium, 2:623
ethnicity, 3:10–11
ethnomethodology, 3:19
Exit, Voice, and Loyalty (Hirschman), 3:44
extended case method, 1:454
factory system, 3:79
globalization, 3:332–334
hope, 3:502–503
identity, 3:554
ingratiation, 4:34
leaders, 4:377
Leary, Timothy, 4:390–391
Lewin, Kurt, 4:417–418
life events and stress, 4:444
loneliness, 4:486–487
mentoring, 5:91–92
migration, 5:157–158
misanthropy, 5:198
peers, 6:197–198, 201–202, 202–203
pluralistic ignorance, 3:560–561
practice theory, 6:419
psychological depression, 2:307
race, 7:3–4
racial identification, 3:548
rational choice theory, 7:74–76
reconciliation, 7:110–111
reflection problem, 7:121–122
reflexivity, 7:123
role theory, 7:275–276
romance, 7:281–282
rumors, 7:295, 297
self-disclosure, 7:409
self-presentation, 7:423–424
sex and mating, 7:470–472
shame, 7:488–489
shyness, 7:504–505
similarity/attraction theory, 7:513–514

social capital, 7:564–566
social skills interventions, 4:119–120
social system, 7:624–625
society, 7:652–653
sociometry, 8:18–20
teacher-child relationships, 8:291–293
television, 8:320
traumatic bonding, 8:441–442
trust, 8:460–461
See also Parent-child relationships; Workplace relations
Social responsibility, corporate. *See* Corporate social responsibility (CSR)
Social rights, 1:543–544
Social risk management (SRM), 8:656
Social science, 7:**614–618**
Becker, Gary S., 1:271
Bourdieu, Pierre, 1:359
butterfly effect, 1:414
case method, 1:453
catastrophe theory, 1:468–469
causality, 1:471–473
citations, 1:538–539
classical music, 1:575
clientelism, 1:578–579
communication, 2:31
computers, 2:60, 61
controlled experiments, 3:59
creationism, 2:163
cultural relativism, 2:193–196
cyberspace, 2:217
data, 2:237
development theory, 2:337–338
documentary studies, 2:433–434
empiricism, 2:578–579
Enlightenment, 2:595–598
epistemology, 2:609–610
ethics, 2:632–633
evolutionary psychology, 3:33–34
factor analysis, 3:75–76
hermeneutics, 3:462–464
Holocaust, 3:495–496
Hume, David, 3:519–520
hybridity, 3:535–536
hypothesis, 3:541–543
Ibn Khaldūn, 3:545–546
identity, 3:553–555
Janowitz, Morris, 4:171–172
litigation, 4:464–467
logic, 4:479–480
mathematics, 5:25–28
chi-square, 1:523

Condorcet, Marquis de, 2:65–66
differential equations, 2:364
heterarchy, 3:468–469
Lazarsfeld, Paul Felix, 4:375
measures of central tendencies, 1:486, 487–488
optimizing behavior, 6:55
quantification, 6:655–656
symbolic logic, 4:481–482
topology, 8:390–391
multifinality, 5:319–320
music, 1:575, 5:342–345
naturalism, 5:443
normative, 2:71, 72, 5:534–536
periodization, 6:210–211
philosophy, 6:252–253
philosophy of science, 6:259–261
positive, 6:387–389
Comte, Auguste, 2:62
normative social sciences *vs.*, 5:534–536
Riker, William, 7:249
survey research, 7:196
postmodernism, 6:395–397
prevention science, 6:445–446
privacy, 6:477–478
probability, 6:484–486
qualitative methods, 5:110–112
hypothesis, 3:542–543
methodology, 5:109
quantitative methods *vs.*, 5:113
survey methods, 5:116–117
reductionism, 7:118–119
political sociology, 8:3
political system, 6:317
rational choice theory, 7:74–76
scientism, 7:364, 365
theory, 8:345
reflexivity, 7:122–123
regions, 7:130–132
religion, 7:159–163
rhetoric, 7:237, 238–239
risk, 7:253
scales, 7:338–339
self-classification, 3:548–550, 7:40, 397–398
symbolic logic, 4:481–482
theory, 8:343–345
topology, 8:390–391
tradition, 8:420–422
zero-sum game, 9:177

See also specific subdisciplines, topics, and people
Social science, value free, 7:**618–620**
    methodology, 5:108
    positive social science, 6:387–389
Social science role in litigation, 4:**464–467**
Social Security
    baby boomers, 1:235, 236
    Bush, George W., 1:400
    demand, 2:270
    funding, 9:129
    Great Depression, 3:369
    labor force participation, 4:315, 316
    life-cycle hypothesis, 4:442, 443
Social Security Act (U.S. 1935), 2:49, 5:494–495, 8:536, 9:61
Social Security Act (U.S. 1965), 3:372, 5:396
Social situations, 1:454
Social skill interventions, 4:**119–120**
Social soundness analysis, 1:124
Social statics, 7:**620–621**
Social status, 7:**621–622**
    alpha-males, 1:83
    ascribed, 1:60
    beliefs, 3:386
    Blau, Peter M., 1:332
    caste, 1:457–460, 461–463
    children, 1:511
    Chinese diaspora, 1:517
    colorism, 2:18
    competition, 8:596
    conspicuous consumption, 2:88, 89
    consumption, 2:107
    Cox, Oliver C., 2:157–158
    criminology, 2:170, 171
    dalits, 2:222
    Duncan, Otis Dudley, 2:463
    emotion, 2:570
    groups, 3:386
    intergenerational transmission, 4:88–90
    leisure class, 1:570, 8:596, 597
    lifestyles, 4:445
    meritocracy, 5:99
    microsociology, 7:678–679
    mobility, 5:208–211
    nonadditive determinism, 2:330
    occupational, 6:26–28
    political participation, 8:606
    prestige, 6:443–444
    retaliation, 7:216

    servitude, 7:463
    Social Darwinism, 2:233
    social distinctions, 2:412
    wealth, 9:46
    workplace relations, 9:136
    See also Class; Stratification
Social stratification. *See* Stratification
Social structure, 7:**623–624**
    civil society, 1:552–553
    class conflict, 1:571
    conspicuous consumption, 2:89
    conversational analysis, 2:118–120
    cultural capital, 2:190
    heterarchy, 3:468–469
    hierarchy, 3:473–475
    Incas, 3:602
    institutional analysis in sociology, 7:673
    Jainism, 4:166–167
    kinship, 4:271–273
    knowledge society, 4:284–285
    Kshatriyas, 4:291–292
    The Lonely Crowd (Riesman), 4:487
    macrofoundations, 4:545–547
    Mafia, 4:551–552
    Parsonian sociology, 8:1–2
    post-Parsonian American sociology, 8:6, 7
    practice theory, 6:418–419
    role theory, 7:275–276
    social constructionism, 7:578
    structural transformation, 8:180–181
    system analysis, 8:256–257
    towns, 8:404–405
    Turner, Victor, 8:468–471
    See also Caste
Social Structure (Murdock), 3:83
Social Structures of the Economy (Bourdieu), 2:89
Social surplus, 2:520
Social system, 7:**624–627**
    common land, 2:26
    heterarchy, 3:468–469
    hierarchy, 3:473–475
    macro-sociology, 7:677–678
    mobility, 5:208–211
    Parsonian sociology, 6:149–150, 313, 7:624–627, 8:1–2
    post-Parsonian American sociology, 7:626–627, 8:5, 6
    primates, 6:460–461
    systems theory, 8:257–258
Social theory, 7:**627–629**

Bourdieu, Pierre, 1:358–359
    caste, 1:461–463
    constructivism, 2:96–98
    critical theory, 2:176–178
    Enlightenment, 2:595–598
    equilibrium, 2:622–623
    Marcuse, Herbert, 4:594–595
    Marx, Karl, 4:631–632
    Parsons, Talcott, 6:149–150
    social constructs, 7:578–580
Social Theory and Social Structure (Merton), 8:5
Social transformation. *See* Social change
Social values. *See* Values (cultural)
Social welfare functions, 7:**629–631**
    description, 9:*65*, 65–66
    excess demand, 3:35
    merit goods, 5:97–98
Social welfare system, 7:**631–633**
    Arrow possibility theorem, 1:183–184
    children's rights, 1:512
    common good, 2:25
    Great Society, 3:371–375
    Pareto efficiency, 8:76
    Sen, Amartya Kumar, 7:440
    Thatcher, Margaret, 8:335
    See also Welfare; Welfare state
Social work, 7:**633–635**
Socialism, 7:**635–638**
    Allende, Salvador, 1:77
    Althusser, Louis, 1:87
    Arab, 5:376
    Austro-Marxism, 1:212, 3:476
    Bay of Pigs, 1:262
    British, 1:113
    bureaucrat, 1:392
    capitalist mode of production, 1:446
    Castro, Fidel, 1:464, 467
    centrism, 1:488, 489
    Christian Democracy, 2:277
    Churchill, Winston, 1:537
    collectivism, 2:11
    communitarianism, 2:40
    conservatism, 2:84
    consociational democracy, 2:279
    convergence theory, 2:117
    critical theory, 2:176–177
    Cuba, 2:186–187
    dependency theory, 2:300
    distributive justice, 4:239
    Durkheim, Émile, 2:466

Socialism, *continued*
Fabianism, 3:73–74
feminism, 3:122, 9:113
The Green Book, 3:377
Harris, Abram L., Jr., 3:427
Hartz, Louis, 3:429, 430
Hayek, Friedrich August von, 3:434, 435
Hilferding, Rudolf, 3:476
Hitler, Adolf, 3:486, 487
humanism, 3:518
Hussein, Saddam, 3:533
James, C. L. R., 4:168
Jewish diaspora, 4:190
Keynes, John Maynard, 4:262
Labour Party (U.K.), 4:326, 327
Lafargue, Paul, 4:328, 329–330
left wing, 4:403
Lenin, Vladimir Ilitch, 4:410–411
Leninism, 4:411–412
Levellers, 4:415
liberalism, 4:425
Lynd, Staughton, 4:529
Machel, Samora, 4:532
Marxian economics, 2:516
Michels, Robert, 5:132
Mont Pelerin Society, 5:272–273
Mussolini, Benito, 5:349
primitive communism, 2:37
Robeson, Paul, 7:266
Russian economics, 7:299
Russian Revolution, 7:303–304
Social Darwinism, 2:233
Stalinism, 8:87
syndicalism, 8:254–256
Tawney, R. H., 8:272
totalitarianism, 8:395
transitional economies, 2:533
upward mobility, 8:534
utopian, 7:636–637, 8:561
world-system, 9:153
Zionism, 9:180
See also Communism; Marxism
Socialism, African, 7:**638–642**
collectivism, 2:11
Kaunda, Kenneth, 4:250
Socialism, Christian, 4:403, 7:**642–643**
Socialism, Islamic, 6:647–648, 7:**643–644**
Socialism, market, 7:**644–646**
convergence theory, 2:117
economics of control, 2:532
transitional economies, 2:533

Socialism, national. *See* Nazism
Socialism: Utopian and Scientific (Engels), 2:40, 3:134
Socialist Unity Party, East German (SED), 1:289
Socialization, 7:**646–649**
aggression, 1:56
child development, 1:507, 508
family functioning, 3:85, 88
femininity, 3:118–119
liberation, 4:430
Maccoby, Eleanor, 4:531
masculinity studies, 5:6–7
military, 5:169–170
peer cliques, 6:197–198
schooling, 7:350–351
self-hatred, 7:417
self-representation, 7:427
temperament, 8:321
Veblen, Thorstein, 8:595
Socialization of investment, 7:**649–650**
Socialized medicine, 5:**65–66**
Clinton, Bill, 1:580
health economics, 3:440
managed competition, 2:53–55
Medicare, 5:62–63
Socially Engaged Buddhism. *See* Buddhism
Societal and ethical implications of nanotechnology (SEIN), 5:362–363
Society, 7:**650–653**
cities, 1:540–541
civil, 1:552–553
Christian Democracy, 2:277
citizenship, 1:542–544
civil-military relation, 1:547–548
conservatism, 2:84
consociational democracy, 2:278
described, 7:651
hegemony, 3:456
political sociology, 8:3, 4
primitive communism, 2:38
community power studies, 2:42–46
community *vs.,* 2:30, 31
computers, 2:59–61
conformity, 2:71
consumption, 2:106
ethnographic research, 7:192–194
evolution of, 8:595
Boserup, Ester, 1:358
emotion, 2:570

gemeinschaft and gesellschaft, 3:266–267, 385
Hamilton's rule, 3:414–415, 4:273–274
Internet, 4:105
knowledge, 4:283–286
computers, 2:60
credentialism, 2:166
cyberspace, 2:217
digital divide, 2:366–367
Drucker, Peter, 2:449
industrialization, 3:622
qualifications, 6:649
skill, 7:523–524
macro-sociology, 5:132–133, 7:662, 677–678, 8:1–2
media, 5:59
network, 3:240
postindustrial, future shock, 3:240
preindustrial, aristocracy, 1:8, 173–174
primitive, 1:137, 557, 3:425, 426, 6:465–466
racial inequality, 4:5
social statics, 7:620
social structure, 7:623–624
social system, 7:625
sports, 8:63–65
types, 4:283–285
winner-take-all, 9:102–103
women defined by, 9:108–109
Society, managerial. *See* Managerial class
Society, secret. *See* Secrecy
Society for Medical Anthropology, 1:131
Society for Utopian Studies, 8:562
Society of Friends. *See* Religious Society of Friends
Society of the Friends of the Constitution. *See* Jacobinism
Sociobiology, 7:**653–655**
altruism and prosocial behavior, 1:89
cooperation, 2:122
Darwin, Charles, 2:229–232
eugenics, 3:21
evolutionary psychology, 3:33–34
evolutionary theory of kinship, 4:273–274
interracial sex, 7:469
Social Darwinism, 2:232–234
Standard Cross-Cultural Sample, 8:91
Sociocultural Theory in Anthropology (Garbarino), 1:136

Socioeconomic Index (SEI), 6:27

Socioeconomic status, 7:**655–660**

assimilation, 1:189

biological determinism, 2:326

black immigrants, 3:566–567, 566*t*

Blau, Peter M., 1:332

class conflict, 1:571

cleavages, 1:577

community power studies, 2:44, 45

consumption, 2:108

corporal punishment, 2:135

crime and criminology, 2:173

democracy, 2:273

demography, 2:293

diathesis-stress model, 2:358

digital divide, 2:366–367

education in the U.S., 2:540–542

immigrants, 3:566*t*

income inequality, 4:3

Jacobs, Jane, 4:165

John Henryism, 4:207–208

latent variables, 8:585

Latino politics, 6:337, 338, 339

Latinos, 4:360

low and high culture, 2:205

lying, 4:524

morbidity and mortality, 5:290, 291

multiracial meritocracy, 5:100

New York City immigrants, 3:574*t,* 575

occupational status, 6:26–28

phenotype, 6:244

political participation, 6:154, 8:606

racial discrimination, 2:395

relative income hypothesis, 7:153

schizophrenia, 7:345

school readiness, 7:87

talent, 8:261

tracking in schools, 8:410

vacations, 8:565

volunteerism, 8:642

voting patterns, 8:649–650

war, 9:17

See also Class; Market economy

The Sociogenesis of Lynching (Senechal de la Roche), 4:526

Sociogram. *See* Sociometry

Sociolinguistics, 1:118, 2:118–120

The Sociological Imagination (Mills), 4:375, 5:182

Sociologie de l'Algérie (Bourdieu), 1:358

Sociologists, black, 1:**323–325**

Sociology, 7:**660–664**

anthropology, 3:231

children, 1:511

cognitive dissonance, 1:599

comedy, 2:22–23

communication, 2:31–32

Comte, Auguste, 2:62

conformity, 2:71–72

conspicuous consumption, 2:89

consumption, 2:105–107

curriculum, 1:106

demography, 2:293, 294–295

development, 2:62, 346–349

Durkheim, Émile, 2:465–467

emotion, 2:569–570

Feagin, Joseph, 3:109

functionalism, 3:231, 232–233

habits, 3:402

historical, 3:483

India, caste, 1:457–460, 461–463

institutional analysis, 2:348, 7:673

Le Guin, Ursula K., 4:407

lifestyles, 4:445–446

loneliness, 4:486

Mannheim, Karl, 4:587

Merton, Robert K., 5:102–103

positivism, 6:389–390

practice of, 1:106

rational choice theory, 7:74–76

religion, 7:160

social demography, 2:296

social identity, 3:558

social science, 7:616

sociometry, 8:18–20

subaltern, 8:191

symbolic interactionism, 4:76

toilets, 8:384

U.K., caste, 1:460, 461, 462

See also specific topics, people and countries

Sociology, African, 7:**664–666**

black immigrants, 3:565–566

blackness, 1:328

census, 1:477

Creole, 2:168, 169

diaspora, 2:356–357

digital divide, 2:367

Turner, Victor, 8:468–471

Sociology, American, 7:**666–668**

Asian immigrants, 3:562–564, 566*t*

baby boomers, 1:235–236

bigotry, 1:295–296

biological determinism, 2:326

black immigrants, 3:564–567, 566*t*

black middle class, 1:313–314

black sociologists, 1:323–325

Blau, Peter M., 1:331–332

Bourdieu, Pierre, 1:359

caste, 1:460, 461

Cherokees, 1:496–498

childlessness, 1:510

Chinese Americans, 1:513–515

Chinese diaspora, 1:516

cities, 1:541–542

class, 1:563

class conflict, 1:570

cohabitation, 2:1

Creole, 2:168

crime and criminology, 2:173

culture of poverty, 2:206

Daughters of the American Revolution, 2:241–242

demographic transition, 2:292

deviance, 2:353

digital divide, 2:366–367

diversity, 2:420

Du Bois, W. E. B., 2:458–460

Duncan, Otis Dudley, 2:462–463

environmental determinism, 2:328

European immigrants, 3:566*t*

immigrants, 3:576–580

imprisonment, 3:596–597

integration, 4:57–61

intergenerational transmission, 4:88–90

interracial marriage, 4:616–619, *617*

Janowitz, Morris, 4:171–172

Latin American immigrants, 3:566*t,* 570–572

Latinos, 4:354–356, 357–361

Lewis, Oscar, 4:419

Lynd, Robert and Helen, 4:527–528

marriage, 4:612–616

Mexican Americans, 5:119–126

middleman minorities, 5:147–148

mulatto escape hatch, 5:310–312

multiracial, 5:331, 332–333

Panel Study of Income Dynamics, 6:121–122

phenotype, 6:244

political, 8:4

post-Parsonian, 8:5–7

Sociology, American, *continued*
    race, 7:3, 4, 5, 6, 7
    race-blind policies, 7:36
    race-conscious policies, 7:36–38
    race mixing, 7:27–28
    race relations, 7:28–31
    racial classification, 7:40
    racial discrimination, 2:394–395
    racial identification, 3:548–550
    racial inequality, 4:6, 7
    racism, 7:45–46
    residential segregation, 7:384–385
    rural, 8:8–9
    same-sex marriage, 4:619–621
    schools, 8:11–12
    social policy interventions,
      4:118–119
    social welfare system, 7:631–633
    wage discrimination, 2:401, 402
Sociology, economic, 2:495,
    7:668–670
Sociology, European, **7:670–671**
    advertising, 1:29
    aristocracy, 1:173–174
    childlessness, 1:510
    Chinese diaspora, 1:517
    civil society, 1:552, 553
    common land, 2:27
    communalism, 2:30
    demographic transition, 2:292
    depopulation, 2:301
    fatherhood, 3:107
    migration, 3:567–569
    out-of-wedlock births, 1:308
    population aging, 3:306
    Roma, 7:277–279
    schools, 8:11
Sociology, feminist, 7:663, **671–673**
    constructivism, 2:97
    development, 2:348
Sociology, knowledge in, 1:426,
    7:674–676
Sociology, Latin American, **7:676–677**
    Bracero Program, 1:364–365
    Caribbean, 1:447–449
    cities, 1:541
    colorism, 2:18
    Creole, 2:168, 169
    moreno/morena, 5:293–294
    positivism, 6:390
    trigueño, 8:452
Sociology, macro-, **7:677–678**
    described, 7:662
    microanalysis, 5:132–133

Parsonian sociology, 8:1–2
Sociology, micro-, **7:678–679**
    constructivism, 2:98
    described, 7:662–663
    macro-sociology *vs.,* 7:678
    microanalysis, 5:132–133
    post-Parsonian American
      sociology, 8:6–7
    social constructionism, 7:578
Sociology, objectivity in. *See* Value free
    social science
Sociology, Parsonian, **8:1–2**
    Parsons, Talcott, 6:149–150
    political science, 6:313
    social system, 7:623–627
Sociology, pioneers in. *See* Ibn
    Khaldūn
Sociology, political, **8:2–5**
    conflict, 2:70–71
    democracy research, 7:190–192
    described, 7:662
    Hall, Stuart, 3:408–410
    Lasswell, Harold, 4:351
    Lazarsfeld, Paul Felix, 4:375
    macro-sociology, 7:678
    post-Parsonian American
      sociology, 8:5, 6
    sports, 8:63
Sociology, post-Parsonian American,
    8:5–8
Sociology, rural, **8:8–9**
    digital divide, 2:366, 367
    human ecology, 3:510
    Lefebvre, Henri, 4:401
Sociology, schools in, **8:9–12**
Sociology, third world, **8:12–15**
    birth control, 1:303
    development in sociology,
      2:346–348
Sociology, urban, **8:15–17**
    cities, 1:540–542
    Feagin, Joseph, 3:109
    Gandhi, Indira, 3:256
    Harlem, 3:423–424
    human ecology, 3:510
    metropolitan regions, 7:132–135
    Multi-City Study of Urban
      Inequality, 5:314–315
    regions, 7:130
    social isolation, 7:600
    street culture, 8:173–174
    suburbs, 8:210–211
    towns, 8:404–405
Sociology, voluntaristic vs.
    structuralist, **8:17–18**

Sociometry, 5:480, **8:18–20,** *19, 20*
    peer relations research, 6:202–203
    rejection and acceptance, 7:150
    social status, 7:622
Sociomusical theory. *See* Music
Socrates, 1:73
Soft drink industry, 1:595, 6:4
Soft money, 1:424
Soft skills, **8:21–22**
Soil
    erosion, 1:62, 3:130–131
    fertility, 3:130–132
    tests, 3:130
Soja, Edward, 3:305
Sokal, Alan, 6:397
Sokolowski, S. Wojciech, 8:638
Solar energy, 3:378–379, **8:22–23**
*The Soldier and the State: The Theory
    and Politics of Civil-Military
    Relations* (Huntington), 3:526
Soldiers. *See* Militarism; Military
Solidarity, **8:23–25**
    class, 1:562
    Coloreds (South Africa), 2:15
    cooperatives, 2:125–126
    Jewish diaspora, 4:190–193
    social, 8:582
    social movements, 7:606–607
    third world, 8:352–353
    tribalism, 8:448
Solidarity (Poland). *See* Solidarność
Solidarność, **8:25–26**
Solomon, Judith, 1:196
Solomon, Sheldon, 8:326, 327
Solow, Robert M., **8:26–27**
    business cycles, 1:405
    Cambridge capital controversy,
      1:419
    convergence theory, 2:117
    Galbraith, John Kenneth, 3:247
    golden rule in growth models,
      3:346
    growth accounting, 3:399
    labor productivity, 5:399
    neoclassical growth model,
      5:464–466
    new Keynesian economics, 2:525
    optimal growth, 6:51
    Solow residual, 8:27–28
    Uzawa, Hirofumi, 8:563
Solow residual, **8:27–28**
Solow-Swan growth model. *See*
    Neoclassical growth model
Solzhenitsyn, Aleksandr, 3:396, **8:29**
Somalia

caste, 1:460

Clinton, Bill, 1:580

Islamic socialism, 7:644

refugees, 7:126

Sombart, Werner, 1:437, 438, 445, **8:29–30**

Some Principles of Stratification (Davis and Moore), 1:562–563

Some Thoughts Concerning Education (Locke), 4:476

Sommes, Battle of the (1916), 9:18

Somoza, Anastasio, 7:235, 319, 320

Sono, Masazo, 7:444

Sons of the American Revolution (SAR), 2:241

Sons of the Shaking Earth (Wolf), 9:105

Sophocles, Oedipus Trilogy, 6:28

Sorcery. *See* Magic

Sorel, Georges, 8:627

Sørensen, Jesper, 1:564

Sorger, Gerhard, 6:52

Soro, Bruno, 8:608

Sorokin, Pitirim, 1:575, 3:241, 8:10

Soros, George, **8:31–32**

SORT (Strategic Offensive Reduction Treaty), 9:32

Soskice, David, 9:68

Sōtō Zen. *See* Buddhism

Soul, animism, 1:113–114

Soul music, 7:268

The Souls of Black Folk (Du Bois), 1:323, 2:459–460, 3:425, 4:198, 8:602

Soulside (Hannerz), 1:135

The South (global), 5:**542–544**

    gender inequality, 3:625

    Prebisch, Raúl, 6:422–423

    Prebisch-Singer hypothesis, 6:424–425

    self-employment, 7:411

    third world, 8:352

    urban poverty, 6:411

The South, U.S., 8:**32–33**

    African American exodus, 1:501

    archaeology of slave lives, 7:530–731

    Benjamin, Judah P., 1:284–285

    Birth of a Nation (film), 1:304–306

    black middle class, 1:313

    black politics, 6:324

    Brown v. Board of Education (1955), 1:377

    caste, 1:461

civil disobedience, 1:546

Congress of Racial Equality, 2:75

contact hypothesis, 2:111–112

cooperatives, 2:125–126

corporal punishment, 2:136

creationism, 2:162

Davis, Jefferson, 2:243–244

Democratic Party (U.S.), 2:286–287

Dixiecrats, 2:428–431

    civil rights movement, U.S., 1:551

    Democratic Party (U.S.), 2:287

    Republican Party (U.S.), 7:187

    Southern strategy, 8:36

    Thurmond, Strom, 8:360–361

    Truman, Harry S., 8:460

Key, V. O., Jr., 4:258

King, Martin Luther, Jr., 4:268, 269

landlords, 4:346

law and order, 4:369, 371, 372

Lee, Robert E., 4:399–400

lynchings, 4:526–527

plantations, 6:277–279

poll tax, 1:552, 6:352–353

race, 7:19

race and education, 7:16

race-conscious policies, 7:36–37

race mixing, 7:27–28

Republican Party (U.S.), 7:186, 187

Roosevelt, Franklin D., 7:283

Southern bloc, 8:34–35

Thurmond, Strom, 8:360–361

Time on the Cross, 8:366–367

See also Brown v. Board of Education (1954); Civil rights movement, U.S.; Confederate States of America; Jim Crow; Reconstruction Era, U.S.; Segregation; Separate-but-equal; Southern politics; U.S. Civil War

South Africa

    African National Congress, 1:41–43

    AIDS/HIV, 1:66

    anticolonial movements, 1:140

    apartheid, 1:147–149, 9:86

    black middle class, 1:313, 314–315

    black nationalism, 1:318

blackface, 1:327

blackness, 1:328

Boer War, 1:349–350

Bonacich, Edna, 1:351–352

Chinese diaspora, 1:517

civil disobedience, 1:545

Coloreds (South Africa), 1:328, 2:15–17, 315, 8:405–407

commonwealth, 2:29

democratization, 2:288

desegregation, 2:315

diamond industry, 2:354–356

direct action, 2:372

divestiture, 2:421

East Indian diaspora, 2:473, 474

gold mining, 3:340, 342

indentured servants, 3:254

land reform, 4:343

legal systems, 4:406

liberation, 4:430, 431–432

Machel, Samora, 4:532–533

Mandela, Nelson, 4:580

Mandela, Winnie, 4:581–582

mining industry, 5:189

minorities, 5:192

nuclear weapons, 9:48

race, 7:5, 19–20

racial inequality, 4:6–7

reconciliation, 7:110

repression, 7:174

Rhodes, Cecil, 7:240

school segregation, 7:386

segregation, 7:382

townships, 8:405–407

truth and reconciliation commissions, 8:463

xenophobia, 9:159

zombies, 9:181

The South African War: Causes and Effects (Hobson), 1:350

South America

    cattle industry, 1:470, 471

    cotton industry, 2:151

    economics, dependency theory, 2:298–300

    gold mining, 3:339

    left wing, 4:404

    liberation theology, 4:436

    regions, 7:132

    terrorism, 8:628

    See also specific countries

South Asia

    caste, 1:461

    Central Intelligence Agency, U.S, 1:485

South Asia, *continued*
  Chinese diaspora, 1:516, 518
  See also Asia; *specific countries*
South Carolina
  Confederate States of America, 2:66
  Thurmond, Strom, 8:360, 361
South Dakota, referendum, 7:120
South Korea, 4:288–289
  automobile industry, 1:219
  capital controls, 1:432
  corporations, 2:140
  developing countries, 2:336
  Kuznets hypothesis, 4:297
  land reform, 4:342
  state capitalism, 1:443
  underdevelopment, 8:490
  United Nations membership, 8:522
South Ossetians, 5:418
South Sea Bubble, 1:378, 4:366, **8:33–34**
South Sea Company, 4:366
Southeast Native Americans, 5:425
Southern agrarianism, 2:85
Southern bloc, **8:34–35**
Southern Christian Leadership Conference (SCLC), 4:268, 269
  civil rights movement, U.S., 1:551
  King, Martin Luther, Jr., 4:268, 269
Southern Pacific Railroad, Santa Clara v. (1886), 2:140
Southern politics, **6:339–349**
  black politics, 6:324, 343–346
  civil rights movement, 6:342–343
  Civil War, 6:340
  Democratic Party (U.S.), 2:286–287
  Dixiecrats, 2:428–431
  modern, 6:346–349
  race, 7:19
  Reconstruction Era, 6:340–341, 7:111–115, 8:32
    annexation, 1:115
    Birth of a Nation (film), 1:304–306
    Jim Crow, 4:199
    separate-but-equal, 7:445–447
  Republican Party (U.S.), 7:186, 187
  Southern bloc, 8:34–35
  Southern strategy, 8:35–38
  states' rights, 6:343

studies, 6:339–340
Thurmond, Strom, 8:360–361
voting, 6:341
See also Jim Crow; The South, U.S.; U.S. Civil War
Southern Politics in State and Nation (Key), 4:258, 6:339–340
Southern states. *See* The South, U.S.
Southern strategy, **8:35–38**
  Dixiecrats, 2:430–431
  Southern bloc, 8:35
  Thurmond, Strom, 8:360
Southerners (U.S.). *See* White southerners (U.S.)
Southwest Native Americans, 5:425
Souvenirs de la bataille d'Alger (Saadi), 1:257
Sovereignty, **8:38–40**
  black nationalism, 1:315
  borders, 1:354–355
  capitalism, 1:437
  Cherokees, 1:496, 497, 498
  concentration camps, 2:63
  confederations, 2:68–69
  Constitution, U.S., 2:91
  decolonization, 2:255–257
  dictatorship, 2:359
  empire, 2:575, 576
  Hobbes, Thomas, 3:492–493
  just war, 4:235
  League of Nations, 4:385, 386
  liberation, 4:429
  limited, Native Americans, 5:428
  Magna Carta, 4:556–557
  patriotism, 6:176
  popular
    nation-states, 5:421
    nationalism, 5:417
  Quebecois movement, 6:661–663
  Rousseau, Jean-Jacques, 7:291
  secession, 7:373–374
  self-determination, 7:405–407
  separatism, 7:450–451
  social contract, 7:581
  state, 8:102–105
  tyranny of the majority, 8:478–479
Sovereignty, consumer. *See* Value, subjective
Sovereignty under Challenge (Glazer), 3:327
Soviet-Afghan War (1980s), 7:606–607
Soviet economics. *See* Russian economics

Soviet Union. *See* Union of Soviet Socialist Republics (U.S.S.R.)
Sowell, Thomas, 1:311
Soweto. *See* Townships
Soweto Uprising of 1976, 1:148
  See also Apartheid
Sozialistische Einheitspartei Deutschlands (SED). *See* Communist Party (East Germany)
Space, arms race, 1:178–179
Space, personal, 1:171
Space exploration, **8:40–42**
  Cold War, 2:5
  Kennedy, John F., 4:254
  Mars, 4:621–622
  tourism, 8:400
Space shuttles
  groupthink, 3:388
  o-ring theory, 6:76
Spaceship Earth. *See* Fuller, Buckminster
Spaemann, Robert, 2:38
Spain
  anarchism, 1:112
  automobile industry, 1:221
  Boricua, 1:355–356
  colonialism (Chiapas), 1:500
  Columbus, Christopher, 2:19–20, 21
  concentration camps, 2:64
  cooperatives, 2:125
  Cortés, Hernán, 2:146–148
  drought, 2:448
  fishing industry, 3:152
  Franco, Francisco, 3:186–187
  land reform, 4:342
  latifundia, 4:353, 354
  Napoleonic Wars, 5:365, 367–369
  Native Americans, 5:426
  overseas conquests, 3:341
  regions, 7:131
  Spanish Civil War, 8:42–44
  state capitalism, 1:444
  voting patterns, 8:650
  War of 1898, 2:185, 8:619, 9:23–24
Spance, Michael. *See* Screening and signaling games; Signals
Spanish-American War (1898). *See* War of 1898
Spanish Civil War (1936-1939), 1:112, 3:186, **8:42–44**, 9:51
Spanking. *See* Corporal punishment
Spanos, Aris, 4:350
Sparks, Colin, 2:198

Sparta, 1:544, 6:175

Spartacist League. *See* Communist Party (East Germany)

Spatial behavior, 5:530

Spatial mapping. *See* Geography

Spatial mismatch hypothesis, 9:101

Spatial networks, urban studies, 8:541

Spatial theory, 8:**44–46**
    metropolitan regions, 7:132–135
    Mills, Edwin, 5:183
    regions, 7:131

SPD (Social Democratic Party, Germany), 4:522

SPE (Stanford Prison Experiment), 9:178

Spearman, Charles, 4:71, 8:46
    See also Intelligence

Spearman rank correlation coefficient, 8:**46–48**, 47*t*

Special activities. *See* Covert action

Special education
    mental retardation, 5:89–90
    tracking in schools, 8:409–410

Special period (Cuba), 1:466–467
    See also Castro, Fidel

Specialization. *See* Division of labor

Speciesism, 8:553

Specific phobias, 1:146

Specification, 8:**48–50**, 49*t*

Specification error, 8:**50–52**
    Hausman tests, 3:432–434
    regression analysis, 7:139

Specification tests, 8:**52–54**, 52*t*
    See also Hausman tests

Spector, Janet, 1:168–169

Spectral Analysis and Time Series (Priestley), 9:82–83

Speculation, 8:**54–56**
    beauty contest metaphor, 1:269
    bubbles (economics), 1:379, 3:380
    casino capitalism, 1:455–456
    contango, 2:112
    coordination failure, 2:128
    efficient market hypothesis, 2:548–549
    random walk, 7:61–63
    rumors, 7:297
    selling long and selling short, 7:432–433
    South Sea Bubble, 8:33–34
    stocks, 8:156

Speculation on the Stock and Produce Exchanges of the United States (Emery), 1:449

Speculative fiction. *See* Science fiction

Speculative motive. *See* Demand for money

Speech, freedom of. *See* Freedom of speech

Speech act theory, 8:**56–57**

Speed of adjustment. *See* Flexibility

Spence, A. Michael, 6:649

Spence, Kenneth, 1:275, 277

Spence, Michael, 1:68

Spence, Thomas, 4:415, 5:419

Spencer, Herbert, 2:213, 326, 8:**57–59**
    assimilation, 1:189
    cultural evolution, 1:137
    determinism, 2:323
    environmental determinism, 2:327
    functionalism, 3:232
    hierarchy, 3:475
    libertarianism, 4:437, 439
    race relations, 7:29
    Social Darwinism, 2:232–233
    social statics, 7:620
    sociology, 7:661

Spencer, Margaret Beale, 1:376, 507
    See also Brown v. Board of Education (1954)

Spending
    campaign, 9:84
    health care, 5:395
    Kalecki, Michał, 4:246–247
    military
        defense, 9:50
        opportunity costs, 6:47
        weapons industry, 9:50
    real consumption, 5:397–398
    welfare, 9:60, 71–72
    See also Gross domestic product (GDP)

Spending, consumer. *See* Consumerism; Consumption

Spending, government. *See* Public finance

Spending, public. *See* Public finance

Spengler, Oswald, 1:575

Sphere, public. *See* Public sphere

Spier, Leslie, 1:345

Spies. *See* Intelligence

Spilerman, Seymour, 8:538

Spin-offs, 1:440, 441

Spingarn, Joel, 3:427

Spinning frame, 3:77

Spirit House, 1:309

Spirit of the Laws (Montesquieu), 1:119, 127

Spirits industry
    crime and criminology, 2:172

deviance, 2:353
    tariffs, 2:133–134

Spiritualism, 1:533, 6:21
    animism, 1:113–114
    women, 9:109
    See also Religion

Spirituality, 7:486–488, 8:**59–61**

Spiro, Melford, 5:504

Spivak, Gayatri, 7:173
    See also Representation in postcolonial analysis

Spock, Benjamin, 8:**61–63**
    Brazelton, T. Berry, 1:369
    parent-child relationships, 6:131, 132
    See also Child development

Spoils system. *See* Patronage

Spontaneous abortion, 1:1

Spontaneous order. *See* Hayek, Friedrich August von

Sports, 8:**63–65**
    steroids, 8:142–143
    television, 8:319

Sports industry, 8:**65–67**, 142–143

Spot market, 1:449–450, 8:**67–68**

Spot prices. *See* Spot market

Sprawl, suburban. *See* Suburban sprawl

Sprawl, urban. *See* Urban sprawl

The Spread of Nuclear Weapons (Waltz and Sagan), 9:14

Spreads, 8:**68–69**

Spreads, bid-ask, 8:**69–70**

Sprecher, Susan, 3:86

Spriggs, William, 5:540

Sprott, Julian, 1:492

Spying. *See* Hoover, J. Edgar; Intelligence

Spyridakis, Manos, 1:135

Squatters, 4:346, 348

Squire, Lyn, 2:268, 8:530

Sraffa, Piero, 8:**70–72**, 577
    Cambridge capital controversy, 1:419, 420
    capital, 1:429, 430
    classical economics, 2:502
    increasing returns, 7:220
    monopolistic competition, 2:56
    neo-Ricardian economics, 2:520
    own rate of interest, 4:80
    Perron-Froebenius theorem, 2:551, 552–554
    Quesnay, François, 6:667
    returns, 7:217
    Ricardo, David, 7:245–246

Sraffa, Piero, *continued*
    surplus, 8:235–236
Sraffian economics. *See* Neo-Ricardian
    economics
SRC (Survey Research Center),
    1:424–425
SRED (Scientific Research and
    Experimental Development Tax
    Incentive Program, Canada), 8:274
Sri Lanka
    civil wars, 1:554
    commonwealth, 2:29
Srinivas, M. N., 1:458, 461, 7:323
Srinivasan, T. N., 1:293
SRM (Social risk management), 8:656
SRRS (Social Readjustment Rating
    Scale), 4:443–444
SSR (Sum of squares of residuals),
    5:526–527
SSRIs (Selective serotonin reuptake
    inhibitors), 1:147, 6:18, 19
St. John, Henry, 8:635
St. Louis Post-Dispatch, 4:213
St. Paul, Minnesota, R.A.V. v. (1992),
    7:42
St. Petersburg paradox, 8:560
    See also Expectations; Von
        Neumann-Morgenstern utility
Staatswissenshaft. *See* State
Stability, mediated. *See* Psychological
    stability
Stability, political, 8:**72–74**
    democracy, 2:274–276
    divine right, 2:421
Stability, psychological, 8:*74,* 74–75
Stability in economics, 8:**76–77**
    demand for money, 5:255
    fiscal policy, 6:292
    Hurwicz, Leonid, 3:530
    local, 8:563
    monetarism, 5:242–243
    multiple equilibria, 5:324
    phase diagrams, 6:240, 242
    speculation, 8:54–55
    steady state, 8:126–127
    tâtonnement, 8:270–271
Stable nodes, 5:**510–511**
Stacey, Judith, 3:86
Stack, Carol, 3:116, 5:462
Staël, Madame de, 6:387
Stages of development, 8:**77–79**
    Comte, Auguste, 2:62
    convergence theory, 2:117
    Erikson, Erik, 2:625–626

identity, 3:552, 553–554,
    555–556
maturation, 5:34–36
midlife crisis, 5:149
moral, 4:286–287
personality, 6:219
perspective-taking, 6:226–227
Piaget, Jean, 6:268–271
rites of passage, 2:247–248,
    7:256–259, 263, 8:470
self-representation, 7:426–427,
    427*t*
theory of mind, 8:347
See also Child development;
    Developmental psychology
Stages of economic growth, 8:**79–82**
    developing countries, 2:335
    development in sociology,
        2:346–348
    development theory, 2:339
*The Stages of Economic Growth: A Non-
    Communist Manifesto* (Rostow),
    2:335, 346
Stagflation, 8:**82–83**
    Barro-Grossman model, 1:256
    conservatism, 2:85
    Keynes, John Maynard, 4:260
    long run, 4:493–494
Staggers Act (U.S. 1980), 7:54
Stagnation, 8:**83–85**
    consumption, 2:106
    monopoly capitalism, 5:266, 267
Stakeholders, 8:**85–86**
    institutional development, 2:340,
        341
    prevention science, 6:445
Stalemates, 1:556
Stalin, Joseph, 2:35, 8:**86–87**
    Arendt, Hannah, 1:173
    bolshevism, 1:351
    Brezhnev, Leonid, 1:369, 370
    career, 8:511
    Churchill, Winston, 1:538
    Cold War, 2:4, 5
    concentration camps, 2:64
    cult of personality, 6:222–223
    dictatorship, 2:359
    Gramsci, Antonio, 3:364
    gulags, 3:396
    Khrushchev, Nikita, 4:264
    Korean War, 4:289
    Lenin, Vladimir Ilitch, 4:411
    Leninism, 4:412
    Lukacs, Georg, 4:515, 516

Molotov-Rubbentrop Pact (1939),
    9:149
repression, 7:175
Russian economics, 7:300, 301
Russian Federation, 7:302
Solzhenitsyn, Aleksandr, 8:29
Spanish Civil War, 8:43
Stalinism, 8:87–88
state capitalism, 1:443–444
Tito, Josip, 8:376
totalitarianism, 8:394
Trotsky, Leon, 8:456
United Nations, 8:522
War and Peace, 9:20
See also Communism; Union of
    Soviet Socialist Republics
    (U.S.S.R.)
Stalinism, 8:**87–88**
    bolshevism, 1:351
    Khrushchev, Nikita, 4:264
    Lukacs, Georg, 4:515, 516
    Solzhenitsyn, Aleksandr, 8:29
    Stalin, Joseph, 8:86
    state capitalism, 1:443–444
    totalitarianism, 8:394, 395
    Trotsky, Leon, 8:456
Stalking. *See* Obsessions
Stamp Act (UK 1765), 1:103
Standard Cross-Cultural Sample
    (SCCS), 8:**88–93**
Standard deviation, 8:**94–95,** *95*
    defined, 8:585, 591
    mean, 5:51
Standard errors, 2:**628–629**
Standard of living
    American Dream, 1:96–97
    citizenship, 1:543
    economic growth, 2:486–487
    leisure time, 9:129
    quantity index, 6:657–658
    work week, 9:128
    See also Class; Market economy
Standard Oil, 4:527
Standardization. *See* Modernism
Standardized coefficients, 3:76
Standardized tests, 8:**95–98**
    education in the U.S., 2:543
    educational accountability,
        1:10–11
    educational quality, 2:547
    equal opportunity, 2:611–612
    intelligence, 4:71, 72
    racial achievement gap, 1:15–17
    school readiness, 7:87
    tracking in schools, 8:410

Standards, community. *See* Censorship; Obscenity

Standards for Educational and Psychological Testing, 8:570–571

Stanford, Max, 1:318

Stanford Prison Experiment (SPE), 9:178

See also Prison psychology; Zimbardo, Philip

Stanley, Carter, 1:341

Stanley, Ralph, 1:341

Stanley Brothers (musical group), 1:341

Stansell, Christine, 3:483

Stanton, Elizabeth Cady, 2:439, 440, 3:120, 9:113

See also Women's suffrage

Stanton, Max E., 3:86

Staples, Robert, 5:30

Star Trek (television program), 8:99

Star Wars (film), 8:**100–101**

The Stare, 8:**101–102**

Stark, Rodney, 1:558, 3:241

Stark, Tom, 5:403

Starr, Kenneth, 1:580

Starr, Paul, 2:54

START (Strategic Arms Reduction Treaty), 1:177

Stasi (East German security police), 1:237

State, 8:**102–105**

  anarchism, 1:111–112

  autocracy, 1:216

  borders, 1:354–355

  bourgeoisie, 1:361

  capitalism, 1:437, 443–445

  children's rights, 1:512

  citizenship, 1:542

  civil disobedience, 1:545–546

  civil-military relation, 1:547–548

  civil society, 1:552–553

  civil wars, 1:554–556

  civilization, 1:557

  clash of civilizations, 1:559

  communism, 2:34

  constitutions, 2:94, 95

  corporations, 2:139

  corporatism, 2:140–141

  critical theory, 2:177

  cultural rights, 2:198

  cultural tourism, 2:201–202

  defense, 2:257–259

  defined, 5:416, 420

  dirigiste, 2:372–374

  distributive justice, 4:240

  dynastic, 8:596–597

  entrepreneurship, 2:605

  exogenous money, 5:258–259

  failed, 7:126

  hegemony, 3:455–456

  industrialization, 3:620–621

  institutional analysis in sociology, 7:673

  Keohane, Robert, 4:256–257

  left wing, 4:403

  liberalism, 4:425

  liberty, 4:439–441

  nation *vs.,* 5:378, 379

  national defense, 2:259–262

  nationalism, 5:416

  neutral, 2:265, 5:487–489

  one-party, 6:41–42

    Brezhnev, Leonid, 1:370

    competitive party systems, 6:161, 162

    dictatorship, 2:358, 359

    first-past-the-post electoral systems, 3:149–150

    Leninism, 4:412

    Mussolini, Benito, 5:350

  outsourcing, 6:86–87

  political philosophy, 6:257–258

  political science, 6:310–314

  political sociology, 8:3–5

  political system, 6:316–317

  Poulantzas, Nicos, 6:404–405

  representative and participatory democracy, 2:283

  secession, 7:373–374

  secrecy, 7:376–377

  Skocpol, Theda, 7:529

  social justice, 4:242

  society, 7:651

  statelessness, 8:112–114

  statism, 8:119–120

  terrorism, 8:329, 628

  third world, 8:352

  two-state solution, 8:476–478

  violence, 8:622–623

  weak, 1:555, 2:156

  See also City-state; Nation-state; Welfare state

State, Church and. *See* Church and state

State, Power, Socialism (Poulantzas), 6:405

State, stationary. *See* Stationary state

State, steady, 8:**126–128**

State and Revolution (Lenin), 4:411, 412

State anxiety, 1:146

State Board of Elections, Allen v., 8:651

State capitalism, 1:**443–445**

  convergence theory, 2:117

  corporations, 2:140

  critical theory, 2:177

  entrepreneurship, 2:605

State-centered theory. *See* Neoinstitutionalism

State corporatism. *See* Corporatism

State Department, U.S.

  Central Intelligence Agency, U.S, 1:481, 482

  Cuban Missile Crisis, 2:184

State-dependent retrieval, 8:**111–112**

State enterprise, 8:**105–110**

  dirigiste, 2:374

  petroleum industry, 6:231, 232

State government

  abortion laws, 1:2–3

  federalism, 3:113–115

  New Deal, 5:497–498

  welfare, 9:61

  whistle-blowers, 9:80

State of nature, 7:84–85, 8:**110–111**

Statelessness, 4:189–193, 8:**112–114**

Statement by Experts on Problems of Race (U.N.), 9:86

States, one-party. *See* One-party states

States and Social Revolution: A Comparative Analysis of France, Russia, and China (Skocpol), 3:542–543

States' rights

  Bill of Rights, 1:297–298

  checks and balances, 1:496

  Confederate States of America, 2:67

  Constitution, U.S., 2:90–91

  Davis, Jefferson, 2:243

  Dixiecrats, 2:429–431

  due process, 2:461

  electoral college, 2:559

  Jefferson, Thomas, 4:182

  judicial review, 4:224

  Reconstruction Era, U.S., 7:112–115

  referendum, 7:120

  same-sex marriage, 4:619, 620

  Southern bloc, 8:34–35

  Southern politics, 6:342–344

States' Rights Democratic Party. *See* Dixiecrats

The Statesman (Plato), 6:280

Static expectations, 3:**53**

Statics, comparative. *See* Comparative statics

Statics, social, 7:**620–621**

Stationary process, 8:**114–117**, *115, 116*

Stationary state, 8:**117–118**

Statism, 8:**119–120**
> bourgeoisie, 1:361
> dirigiste, 2:372–374

Statistical analysis, classical. *See* Classical statistical analysis

Statistical bias, 4:348–350, 6:547–549

Statistical discrimination, 2:**396–398**
> age discrimination, 2:402
> described, 2:390
> racial, 2:395
> wage discrimination, 2:401, 403

Statistical efficiency, 4:348–350, 6:547–549

Statistical inference, 4:**15–18**
> Bayesian inference, 4:13–14
> bootstrap method, 1:353–354
> central limit theorem, 1:486
> classical statistical analysis, 1:576–577
> controlled experiments, 3:58–59
> correspondence tests, 2:143
> data envelopment analysis, 2:241
> large sample properties, 4:348–350
> method of moments, 5:105–107
> random samples, 7:60–61
> randomness, 7:63–64
> specification tests, 8:52–53
> statistics, 8:122, 123

Statistical life, value of, 6:25

Statistical noise, 8:**120–121**

Statistical reliability, 7:**157–158**
> left and right censoring, 1:474–475
> Likert scale, 4:447
> Rorschach test, 7:285
> sample censoring, 1:474–475
> self-report method, 7:425
> survey, 8:241–242

Statistical validity. *See* Validity, statistical

Statistics, 8:**121–123**
> Bayes' theorem, 1:262–263
> Bayesian, 1:266–267
>> Dawes, Robyn, 2:244
>> limits in probability, 6:487–488
> business cycles, 1:403–405
> census, 1:476–477

degrees of freedom, 2:266–267

descriptive, 2:311–313, *312,* 312*t*
> classical statistical analysis, 1:576–577
> measures of central tendencies, 1:488
> probability distributions, 6:493
> randomness, 7:63
> statistics in the social sciences, 8:123
> student's T-statistic, 8:185

generalized lease squares, 3:288–289

hate crimes, 3:431

mode, 5:218

model selection tests, 5:222–224

moment generating function, 5:236

Monte Carlo experiments, 5:274–275

Pearson, Karl, 6:190–194

probability, 6:484–486

quantification, 6:655–656

respondent-related validation, 8:571

sampling, 7:317

Spearman rank correlation coefficient, 8:46–48

standard deviation, 8:94–95

test, 8:331–333
> Chow test, 1:529–530
> formulas, 3:179–180
> quality control, 6:651
> reliability, 7:157–158
> variation, 8:592
> Z-test, 9:181–183

white noise, 9:82–83

See also Econometrics

Statistics, inferential. *See* Hypothesis and hypothesis testing

Statistics, test. *See* Test statistics

Statistics in the social sciences, 8:**123–126**
> Bayesian inference, 4:13–14
> Bayesian statistics, 1:265–266
> catastrophe theory, 1:468–469
> central limit theorem, 1:486
> chi-square, 1:523
> Duncan, Otis Dudley, 2:462–463
> event studies, 3:30–31
> exchangeability, 3:41–42
> mean, 5:50–51
> normal distribution, 2:415–416
> probability, 6:484–486

quantitative methods, 5:113

randomness, 7:63–64

regression, 7:136–137

selection bias, 7:389–390

statistical inference, 4:15, 17

survey, 8:241–242

uniform distribution, 2:418–419

See also Statistics

Stattin, Hakan, 1:25

Status. *See* Occupational status; Social status; Socioeconomic status

Status-behavior link. *See* Role theory

Status characteristics theory, 3:386, 6:26

Status quo
> rituals, 7:264
> social pathology, 6:169–171

Status symbols. *See* Prestige

Statutory rape. *See* Rape

Steady state, 8:**126–128**

Steamers, 2:152

Stearns, Elizabeth, 4:524

Steedman, Ian, 4:324, 8:576

Steel, David, 4:427

Steel industry, 8:**128–130**
> common market, 2:28–29
> price controls, 9:2–3

Steele, Claude M., 1:15, 16, 8:**130–132**
> cognitive dissonance, 1:601
> stereotype threat, 8:135–136

Steele, Shelby, 1:311
> *See also* Race-blind policies

Steering (discrimination), 2:317

Stefancic, Jean, 2:175

Steffens, Lincoln, 2:180

Stehr, Nico, 4:285

Stein, Stanley, 4:354

Steinbeck, John, 5:366

Steinbert, Laurence, 1:25–26

Steinbert, Stephen, 3:327

Steinem, Gloria, 3:123, 8:**132–133**
> *See also* Feminism

Steinmo, Sven, 9:73

Stem cells, 3:307, 8:**133–134**

Stepford Wives (film), 8:**134–135**

Stephens, Alexander, 2:67

Stephens, Evelyne. *See* Huber, Evelyne

Stephens, John D., 3:185, 9:70

Stereotype threat, 1:15, 8:**135–136**
> racial achievement gap, 1:16
> self-actualization, 7:396

Stereotypes, 8:**136–139**
> age discrimination, 2:402

ageism, 3:308
Asian immigrants, 3:564
Bamboozled, 1:243–245
bigotry, 1:295
blackface, 1:327
blood and bloodline, 1:336
caste, 1:461
child development, 1:507–508
Chinese Americans, 1:514–515
Coloreds (South Africa), 2:17
colorism, 2:18
constructivism, 2:97
ethnicity, 3:9–10
exoticism, 3:46–47
intergroup relations, 4:91
Jim Crow, 4:198–199
journalism, 4:212–213
lay theories, 4:374
metropolitan regions, 7:134–135
minorities, 5:191–192
minstrelsy, 5:195
model minority, 5:220–222
Muslims, 5:346, 348
neuroscience research, 5:485
otherness, 6:83
polling, 6:354–355
priming, 6:462
race, 7:6, 7, 23
racial democracy, 2:282
racial discrimination, 2:395
racism, 7:44, 45
Sambo, 6:277, 7:312–314
schemas, 7:344
sex, 3:277, 9:122
social cognition, 7:573
social psychology, 7:610
South, U.S., 8:33
Steele, Claude M., 8:131
stigma, 8:146–148
wage discrimination, 2:401, 404
women's work, 9:125
Sterile class. *See* Physiocracy
Sterilization, economic, 8:**139–140**
Sterilization, human, 3:88, 8:**140–142**
   biological determinism, 2:326
   birth control, 1:302, 303
   blood and bloodline, 1:336
   contraception, 2:114
   eugenics, 3:21
   reproductive rights, 7:182
   surplus population, 8:238–239
Stern, Nicholas, 4:450
Stern Report (2006), 3:329
Sternberg, Robert, 5:326, 327

See also Intelligence
Steroids, 8:**142–143**
Steroids, anabolic. *See* Anabolic
   steroids
Stevens, Thaddeus, 1:304, 305, 7:113
Stevenson, Adlai, 1:267, 2:184
Stevenson, Coke R., 1:364
Steward, Julian, 1:167, 9:105
Stewart, Dugald, 2:423–424
Stewart, Frances, 5:456
Stewart B. McKinney Homeless
   Assistance Act (1987), 3:499
Steyn, Melissa, 9:86
Sticky prices, 8:**143–144**
Stigler, George Joseph, 8:**144–145**
   Chicago School, 1:502
   Coase, Ronald, 1:589
   consumer protection, 2:103
   regulation, 7:144
Stiglitz, Joseph E., 1:68, 2:56–57,
   4:313, 7:491, 8:**145–146**, 9:5
Stigma, 8:**146–148**
   blackness, 1:328–329
   Body Mass Index, 1:348
   cannibalism, 1:427–428
   caste, 1:463
   childlessness, 1:510
   dementia, 2:271
   happiness, 3:419
   HIV, 3:490
   labeling theory, 4:299
   madness, 4:548–550
   mental retardation, 5:90
   race-blind policies, 7:36
   self-hatred, 7:416
   weight, 9:59
Stigma (Goffman), 3:337
Stilwell, Joseph, 1:499
Stimulants, 2:452, 453
   See also Psychotropic drugs
Stimuli and responses
   behaviorism, 1:276, 279
   classical conditioning, 1:572–574
   cognition, 1:598
   coping, 2:128–129
   habits, 3:402–403, 404
   Pavlov, Ivan, 6:178–179
   reinforcement theories, 7:146–148
   Thorndike, Edward, 8:358–359
Stimulus, unconditioned. *See* Classical
   conditioning
Stinchcombe, Arthur, 6:77
Stirling, James Hutchinson, 3:453
Stochastic frontier analysis, 8:**148–149**

Stochastic trend. *See* Unit root
   regression
Stochastic variable. *See* Random
   variables
Stock, Gregory, 3:308
Stock, James H., 1:229, 8:519
Stock exchanges, 8:**150–151**
   beauty contest metaphor, 1:269
   bull and bear markets, 1:385–386
   forward and futures markets,
      3:180–181
   perfect competition, 2:58
   See also Bonds; Equity markets;
      Stocks
Stock exchanges in developing
   countries, 8:**151–153**
Stock market. *See* Equity markets;
   Stock exchanges
Stock market crashes. *See* Economic
   crises
Stock options, 8:**153–154**
Stockholm School, 8:**154–155**
   Lundberg, Erik, 4:518–519
   Myrdal, Gunnar, 5:351
Stockholm syndrome. *See* Traumatic
   bonding
Stocks, 8:**155–156**
   beauty contest metaphor, 1:269
   bull and bear markets, 1:385–386
   business ethics, 2:634
   carrying cost, 1:450
   corporations, 2:139
   description, 3:142
   event studies, 3:30, 31
   Internet Bubble, 4:109–110
   investors, 4:134
   market correction, 4:603–604
   market fundamentals, 4:605–606
   random walk, 7:61–63
   risk-return tradeoff, 7:255–256
   South Sea Bubble, 8:33–34
   stock exchanges, 8:150–151
   Tobin's Q, 8:379–381
   transaction taxes, 8:427–428
   unrestricted, 8:156–157
   Wall Street, 9:7–9
Stocks, restricted and unrestricted,
   8:**156–157**
Stocks and flows, 8:*157,* **157–158**
Stogdill, Ralph, 4:378–379
Stoics, 1:275
Stokes, Donald, 1:100, 425
Stolen Generations (Australia),
   8:**158–159**
Stoll, Michael, 9:101

Stolper, Wolfgang, 1:6, 8:159–160
Stolper-Samuelson theorem,
  8:**159–160**
  Heckscher-Ohlin-Samuelson
    model, 3:449
  Rybczynski theorem, 7:305, 306
Stone, Harlan, 2:615
Stone, Lucy, 3:122
Stone, Oliver, 9:34
Stone, Richard, 5:397, 400
Stone Age Economics (Sahlins),
  7:308–309
Storytelling, 5:370–371, 8:**160–161**
  critical race theory, 2:175–176
  Rorty, Richard, 7:286
  rumors, 7:296
  See also Narratives
*Stotts, Firefighters Local Union No.
  1784 v.* (1984), 3:373, 6:671
Stouffer, Samuel, 8:386
  See also Political tolerance
Stowe, Harriet Beecher, 8:**161–162**,
  482–483
Strabo, 2:327
Strachan, Selwyn, 3:383
Strait of Tiran, 1:157
Strange, Susan, 1:455
*The Strange Death of Marxism: The
  European Left in the New
  Millennium* (Gottfried), 4:403
Strange Situation (child development),
  1:67–68, 195–196, 507, 508
Strangers in the Land (Higham), 5:430
Strategic Arms Limitations Talks
  (SALT), 1:176, 9:31–32
  Carter, Jimmy, 1:451
  Cold War, 2:5
Strategic Arms Reduction Treaty
  (START), 1:177
Strategic behavior, 8:**162–163**
  defense, 2:258
  deterrence, 2:333–334
  diplomacy, 2:371
  evolutionary games, 3:32
  Jervis, Robert, 4:185–186
  mixed strategy, 5:207–208
  mutual deterrence, 2:334–335
  preemptive strike, 6:431–432
  replicator dynamics, 7:169–170
  strategic games, 8:163–164
  subgame perfection, 8:193–194
Strategic games, 8:**163–164**
  common knowledge rationality
    games, 2:25–26
  coordination failure, 2:127–128

evolutionary games, 3:32
noncooperative games, 5:517
strategy and voting games,
  8:165–166
zero-sum games, 9:176–177
Strategic market game (SMG) model,
  3:284
Strategic Offensive Reduction Treaty
  (SORT), 9:32
Strategic planning. *See* Planning
Strategies, business. *See* Corporate
  strategies
Strategies, corporate. *See* Corporate
  strategies
Strategies, self-handicapping,
  8:**164–165**
Strategy, dominant. *See* Zero-sum
  games
Strategy and voting games,
  8:163–164, **165–166**
  See also Strategic games
A Strategy of Decision (Lindblom and
  Braybrooke), 4:452–453
Stratification, 8:**166–167**
  Berg, Ivar E., 1:288
  Blau, Peter M., 1:332
  Brahmins, 1:366–367
  caste, 1:457–460, 461
  civilization, 1:558
  class conflict, 1:571
  colorism, 2:18
  credentialism, 2:166–167
  cultural distinctions, 2:412–413
  dalits, 2:221–222
  ethnic conflict, 3:1
  feminist sociology, 7:672
  intergenerational transmission,
    4:88–90
  IQ controversy, 4:141–142
  Jajami matrix, 4:167
  knowledge society, 4:284–285
  Kshatriyas, 4:291–292
  labor, 4:301
  Latinos, 4:360
  low and high culture, 2:204
  mobility, 5:208–211
  o-ring theory, 6:77
  patricians, 6:174–175
  phenotype, 6:244
  qualifications, 6:649–650
  race, 7:2–7
  racial identification, 3:548–550
  sampling, 7:317
  schooling, 7:350–351
  social distinctions, 2:412–413

social statics, 7:620
social status, 7:621–622
socioeconomic status, 7:656, 658,
  659
sociology, 7:662
subaltern, 8:190–192
Sudras, 8:212–213
surplus labor, 4:311–312
wage discrimination, 2:403
See also Class; Marginalization
Stratification, political, 8:3, **168–170**
Stratification, social. *See* Stratification
Stratification economics, 2:**530–531**
  crowding hypothesis, 2:181
  race, 7:13–15
Stratigraphy, 1:166
Strauman, Timothy J., 6:85
Straus, Robert, 1:131
Strauss, David, 5:502
Strauss, Leo, 2:85
Stravinsky, Igor, 1:575
Straw polls, 6:356
Strayhorn, Billy, 4:177
Stream of consciousness, 8:**170–172**
Street children. *See* Children
Street culture, 8:**172–173**
  culture of poverty, 2:206
  lifestyles, 4:445
  low and high culture, 2:205
  youth culture, 9:167
  See also Urban sociology
Streeten, Oaul, 5:456
The Strength of Weak Ties
  (Granovetter), 5:478
Stress, 8:**173–175**
  anxiety, 1:146
  cognitive dissonance, 1:600
  coping, 2:128–129
  diathesis-stress model, 2:358
  hypertension, 3:539–540
  John Henryism, 4:207–208
  life events, 4:443–444
  mental health, 5:85
  motivation, 5:301
  population growth, 6:379–380
  psychological depression,
    2:306–307
  stress-buffering model, 8:175–176
  Type A/type B personality, 6:224
Stress-buffering model, 4:444,
  8:**175–176**
Stress disorder, traumatic. *See* Post-
  traumatic stress
Stride toward Freedom (King), 4:268
Strikes. *See* Labor unions; Protest

STRIVE (Security through Regularized Immigration and a Vibrant Economy Act, U.S. 2007), 1:365

Stroessner, Alfredo, 2:156

Strong axiom of revealed preference (SARP), 7:224–225

Strong democracy. *See* Representative and participatory democracy

Strong Religions (Almond, et al), 1:82

Strong separability. *See* Separability

Structural adjustment, 8:**176–178**

Structural adjustment loans (SALs), 9:138

Structural equation models (SEM), 3:390–391, 8:**178–180**
   discriminant validity, 8:573–574
   Duncan, Otis Dudley, 2:463
   identification problem, 3:550

Structural functionalism, 3:232, 6:150
   European sociology, 7:671
   macro-sociology, 7:678
   Parsonian sociology, 8:2
   schools in sociology, 8:11–12
   sociology, 7:661
   stratification, 8:166

Structural policy, 4:542

Structural realism. *See* Neorealism

Structural transformation, 2:344–346, 8:**180–181**

The Structural Transformation of the Public Sphere (Habermas), 2:176, 177, 3:401

Structural unemployed, 3:421–423

Structural unemployment, 3:227, 8:502

Structuralism, 8:**181–183**
   capitalist mode of production, 1:447
   class, 1:564
   constructivism, 2:97
   cultural studies, 2:199
   democratization, 2:290
   development economics, 2:344
   discourse, 2:387
   emotion, 2:570
   extended case method, 1:453
   humanism, 3:518
   Lefebvre, Henri, 4:401
   Lévi-Strauss, Claude, 4:416–417
   material culture, 5:15
   Parsons, Talcott, 6:149–150
   political culture, 6:301–302
   postmodernism, 6:395–397
   power, 6:413–414

racial inequality, 4:6

Radcliffe-Brown, A. R., 7:47

role theory, 7:275–276

Sahlins, Marshall, 7:308, 309

social relations, 7:611–613

social structure, 7:623

structuralist macroeconomics, 4:543–545

system analysis, 8:257

voluntarism *vs.*, 8:17–18

See also Poststructuralism

Structuralist macroeconomics, 4:**543–545**, 8:285

Structuralist vs. voluntaristic sociology, 8:**17–18**

Structuration, 8:17–18

Structure, social. *See* Social structure

Structure and Change in Economic History (North), 5:538

Structure and Function in Primitive Society (Malinowski), 1:127

Structure of American Economy (Leontief), 4:412

The Structure of Science (Nagel), 7:118

The Structure of Scientific Revolutions (Kuhn), 4:292, 294, 338–339, 6:125, 126

Structure of signification, 3:265–266

Structurism, 1:121

Strydom, J. G., 1:147

Stuart, Nebraska Press Association v. (1976), 1:475

Student Nonviolent Coordinating Committee (SNCC), 4:269, 8:**183–184**
   black nationalism, 1:317
   civil rights movement, U.S., 1:552
   Davis, Angela, 2:242
   Forman, James, 3:175
   Lynd, Staughton, 4:528–529
   NAACP, 5:384–385

Students, gifted. *See* Gifted and talented

Students for a Democratic Society (SDS), 4:529

Student's T-statistic, 8:**184–187**, *185,* 332

Studies in Linear and Non-Linear Programming (Hurwicz), 8:563

Studies in the Development of Capitalism (Dobb), 3:482

Studies in the Labor Theory of Value (Meek), 8:576

Studies in the Quantity Theory of Money (Friedman), 3:217–218

Studies in the Theory of Economic Expansion (Lundberg), 4:518

Studies on Hysteria (Freud), 3:209

A Study of Archaeology (Taylor), 1:167

Stumpf, Carl, 2:80

Stunted growth, 8:**187–189**

Stupid White Men (Moore), 3:80

Sturges v. Bridgman (U.K. 1879), 1:589

Stuyvesant, Peter, 9:7

STV (Single transferable vote system), 8:647

Stycos, J. Mayone, 2:295

Stylized fact, 8:**189–190**

Sub-Saharan Africa
   AIDS/HIV, 1:65, 66
   anticolonial movements, 1:140
   Green Revolution, 3:378
   population aging, 3:306

Subaltern, 8:**190–193**
   postcolonialism, 6:392
   reggae, 7:66–70, 127
   representation, 7:173

Subarctic Native Americans, 5:426

Subcaste. *See* Caste

Subculture lifestyles, 4:445

Subemployment, 8:493

Subfecundity. *See* Human fertility

Subgame perfection, 8:*193,* **193–194,** *194*

Subject/self, 7:209, 8:**194–196**

The Subjection of Women (Mill), 3:120, 8:553

Subjective probability, 6:**489–491**
   non-expected utility theory, 5:519
   risk, 7:252

Subjective utility, 8:**558–560**
   defined, 8:77
   expected utility theory, 3:54
   Hicks, John R., 3:472
   rational choice theory, 7:74–76

Subjective value. *See* Value, subjective

Subjectivity
   capitalist mode of production, 1:447
   choice in economics, 1:524
   choice in psychology, 1:525–526
   class conflict, 1:569, 570
   class consciousness, 1:572
   collective memory, 2:7, 8
   intersubjectivity, 4:116–117
   knowledge, 4:278–279
   methodological, 1:210
   probability, 6:486
   realist theory, 7:99

Subjectivity, *continued*
  social constructs, 7:579
  social justice, 4:241
  society, 7:653
  subject/self, 8:195
  universalism, 8:527
  See also Objectivity
Subjectivity, analysis, 8:**198–199**
Subjectivity, overview, 8:**196–198**
Sublimate, 8:**199–201**
Subliminal Seduction (Key), 3:473
Subliminal suggestion, 8:**201–202**
  hidden persuaders, 3:472–473
  priming, 6:462
Submarines, nuclear weapons, 9:49
Submissiveness. *See* Social dominance
  orientation
Suboptimal employment, 8:500–501
Subscriber identity modules (SIM). *See*
  Cellular technology
Subsidiaries, 6:72
  See also Corporations
Subsidies, 8:**202–203**
  bequests, 1:287
  Bhagwati, Jagdish, 1:293
  black capitalism, 1:441
  state capitalism, 1:443, 444
Subsidies, farm, 6:667–668,
  8:**203–204**
Subsidies, tax. *See* Tax relief
Subsistence agriculture, 8:**204–206**
  famine, 3:97–99
  Lewis, W. Arthur, 4:420–421
  See also Agricultural industry
Subsistence compromise, 3:97–99
Substance abuse, 1:20–22
Substantive justice, 4:241
Substantive rationality. *See* Rationality
Substitutability, 8:**207–208**
  elasticity, 2:555, 556
  returns, 7:217
  technological change, 1:491
Substitution, elasticity of. *See*
  Production function; Separability;
  Utility function
Substitution, import. *See* Import
  substitution
Substitution, intertemporal. *See* Time
  preference
Suburban sprawl, 8:**208–210**
  cities, 1:541
  metropolitan regions, 7:132–135
  Mills, Edwin, 5:183
  rural development, 2:341
Suburbs, 8:**210–212**

African American middle class,
  1:36
Gans, Herbert J., 3:256
Gautreaux residential mobility
  program, 3:259–260
metropolitan regions, 7:132–135
resegregation of schools, 7:201
riots, 8:539
suburban sprawl, 8:208–209
towns, 8:405
trends, 8:540
urban sprawl, 8:539–541
Successive approximation, 1:574
Successive limited comparison. *See*
  Incrementalism
Sudan
  bin Laden, Osama, 1:299
  Darfur, 2:226–227
  genocide, 8:524
  Muhammad Ali (Memet), 1:73
Sudanese Liberation Movement/Army
  (SLA), 2:226–227
Sudetenland, 1:153
Sudnow, David, 2:98
Sudras, 8:**212–213**
  Brahmins, 1:366
  caste, 1:457–458, 461
  Indian National Congress, 3:611
Suez Crisis, 8:**213–214**
  Ben-Gurion, David, 1:283
  Hungarian Revolution, 3:523–524
  Macmillan, Harold, 4:538
  Nasser, Gamal Abdel, 5:376–377
Suffrage
  inclusive, 2:58
  polyarchy, 6:366
  universal, 2:58, 288, 4:414
  See also Franchise; Voting
Suffrage, women's, 3:120, 8:**214–218**
  Condorcet, Marquis de, 2:66
  Mill, John Stuart, 5:179
  See also Franchise; Voting;
    Women's movement
Sufism. *See* Islam
Sugar Act (UK 1764), 1:103
Sugar industry, 3:163, 8:**218–221**
  Cuba, 2:186
  slavery, 1:40, 7:547–549
Sugden, Robert, 8:269
Suggestion, subliminal. *See* Subliminal
  suggestion
Sugrue, Thomas, 8:542–543
Suicide, 8:**221–223**
  assisted, 1:192
  cults, 2:188

Durkheim, Émile, 2:466
  See also Assisted death; Euthanasia
    and assisted suicide
Suicide, assisted. *See* Euthanasia and
  assisted suicide
Suicide (Durkheim), 2:465
Suicide bombers, 8:**224–225**
  See also Terrorism
Sukarno, Ahmed, 1:139, 5:376
Sullivan, Henry Stack, 6:29
Sullivan, John, 8:386
Sullivan, Patricia, 5:497
Sullivan and Cromwell (law firm),
  2:139
Sum of squares of residuals (SSR),
  5:526–527
Sumerians, 1:544
Summa Theologica (Aquinas), 4:235
*A Summary View of the Rights of British
  America* (Jefferson), 4:180
Summers, Lawrence, 4:35, 8:408
Summers, Robert, 6:204
Sumner, William Graham, 2:233,
  3:150, 4:437, 9:136
Sun King. *See* Louis XIV, King of
  France
Sun Yat-sen, 8:**225–226**
  Chiang Kai-shek, 1:499
  Chinese Revolution, 1:519, 520
Sundquist, James, 5:498
Sunnism, 4:**154–158**
  See also Islam
Super Mario Brothers, 8:611
  See also Video games
Superego, 3:212–213
  See also Equilibrium in
    psychology; Freud, Sigmund;
    Psychoanalytic theory
Superfund, pollution, 6:359–360
Superheroes, 2:24
Supermarkets, 1:58
Superordinate goals, 7:495,
  8:**226–227**
Superpowers. *See* Balance of power;
  Hegemony
Supervision. *See* Accountability
Supply, 8:**227–229**, *229*
  aggregate, 1:53–55, *54,*
    9:172–173
  cobweb cycles, 1:591
  coffee industry, 1:595
  conundrum, 2:116
  economic depression, 2:302–303
  excess, 3:34–35, *35, 36*
  farm quota system, 6:667–668

full capacity, 3:224

health economics, 3:440

long period analysis, 4:490

long run, 4:492

Marshall, Alfred, 4:623

overproduction, 6:97

prices, 6:455–456

regulation, 7:144

Say's Law, 7:336–337

technological change, 1:490

total, 5:401

unemployment, 8:499, 503

work day length, 9:127

See also Labor supply; Supply of money

Supply, labor. *See* Labor supply

Supply of money, 5:**260–261**

central banks, 1:478

cross of gold, 2:180–181

currency, 2:209

currency appreciation and depreciation, 2:209

economic depression, 2:304, *305*

endogenous money, 5:256–257

exogenous money, 5:258–259

inflation, 4:24

liquidity, 4:459

monetarism, 5:242–243

monetary base, 5:243–245

rules *vs.* discretion, 7:293–294

Support

coping, 2:129

life events and stress, 4:444

stress-buffering model, 8:176

transition to parenthood, 6:134–135

Suppresssion of Communism Act (South Africa 1950), 1:148

Supremacy, white. *See* White supremacy

Supreme being, 8:**230–232**

agnosticism, 1:57

atheism, 1:194–195

Brahmins, 1:366

Christianity, 1:531

The Church, 1:533

creationism, 2:161–163

existentialism, 3:43

Jews, 4:194, 220–221

liberation theology, 4:435–436

miracles, 5:196–197

monarchy, 5:239

monotheism, 5:271

mysticism, 5:352–353

Nietzsche, Friedrich, 5:502–503

philosophy, 6:251

polytheism, 6:367–368

religion, 7:159–161

sin, 7:519

theism, 8:340–341

See also Religion

Supreme Court, Canada and gerrymandering, 3:309

Supreme Court, U.S., 8:**232–235**

abortion, 1:2–3, 4

affirmative action, 3:373, 392–393

agenda setting, 1:48

antitrust, 1:143

apportionment, 1:154

Bill of Rights, 1:298

Birth of a Nation (film), 1:305

campaign spending, 9:84

censorship, 1:475

checks and balances, 1:496

Cherokees, 1:497

Church and state, 1:534, 535–536

civil rights, 1:549

civil rights movement, U.S., 1:551

confiscation, 2:69

conservatism, 2:86

Constitution, U.S., 2:91, 92

constitutional courts, 2:93

contraception, 3:90

corporations, 2:140

death-qualified jurors, 4:233

desegregation, 2:313–315

due process, 2:461

environmental impact assessment, 2:606

equal protection, 2:614–615

eugenics, 3:21

executive privilege, 9:43

federalism, 3:113, 114

film industry, 3:139

gerrymandering, 3:309

Guantánamo Bay, 3:394

hallucinogens, 3:412

hate crimes, 3:431

housing audits, 1:209

Houston, Charles Hamilton, 3:505

human sterilization, 8:141

interrogation, 4:112

Jim Crow, 4:198

judicial activism, 1:19

judicial review, 4:223–224

judiciary, 4:225, 226, 227

Marshall, Thurgood, 4:624–626

miscegenation, 5:199–200

naturalization, 5:444

obscenity, 6:13

Pentagon Papers, 9:42

poll tax, 6:352

predatory pricing, 6:428

public school prayer, 3:236

qualifications, 6:650

quotas, 6:671–672

race-conscious policies, 7:37

race mixing, 7:28

racial slurs, 7:42

rape, 7:65

reproductive politics, 7:180

research and development, 7:201–202

resegregation of schools, 7:201

retaliation, 7:216

school desegregation, 2:316–318

school segregation, 7:387, 388

school vouchers, 7:348

segregation, 3:464–466

separate-but-equal, 3:316, 7:446, 447

sexual harassment, 6:474–475

slavery, 2:445–446

Southern politics, 6:342, 345, 346

treaty rights, 5:428

unequal education, 7:16–17

voting rights, 5:384, 8:651–654

wage and price controls, 9:2

Warren, Earl, 9:32–33

Watergate, 5:506

See also names of specific cases

Supreme Headquarters, Allied Powers Europe (SHAPE), 5:543

SUR (Seemingly unrelated regressions), 7:**379–381**

recursive models, 7:117

three-stage least squares, 4:394

Surgery, psychiatric. *See* Psychosurgery

Suriname Folk-Lore (Herskovits and Herskovits), 3:467

Surowiecki, James, 2:9

Surplus, 8:**235–236**

capital, 1:430

coffee industry, 1:595

consumer, 2:104

world-system, 9:153–154

Surplus, producer. *See* Producer surplus

Surplus, trade. *See* Trade surplus

Surplus labor

conventional economics, 4:308–309

Surplus labor, *continued*
  development economics, 2:344
  exploitation, 3:64–65
  Lewis, W. Arthur, 4:420–421
  Marxist and radical economics,
    1:562, 4:309–312
  technological progress, 8:300
  transitional conjunctures, 2:77, 78
Surplus population, 1:446, 8:**237–240**
Surplus value, 8:**240–241**
  absolute, 7:155
  capitalist mode of production,
    1:445–446
  class, 1:563
  class conflict, 1:571
  consumption, 2:106
  exploitation, 3:64
  labor theory of value, 4:322, 323
  rate of exploitation, 7:70–71
  relative, 7:154–155
  surplus labor, 4:309
  technological change, 1:491
  transitional conjunctures, 2:77
Surplus value, rate of. *See* Rate of
  exploitation
Surprise inflation, natural rate of
  unemployment, 5:436
Surprises. *See* Shocks
Surveillance
  governmental, 3:263
  panoptic gaze, 3:262
  See also Counterintelligence;
    Intelligence
Survey methods, 5:**116–118**
  Campbell, Angus, 1:424–425
  Current Population Survey,
    2:212–213
  Head Start experiments, 3:438
  hypothesis and hypothesis testing,
    3:542
  survey research, 7:196–197
  See also Sampling
Survey of Income and Program
  Participation (SIPP), 8:**243–244**
Survey research, 7:**196–197**
  Campbell, Angus, 1:424–425
  Luxembourg Income Study,
    4:519–521
  research methods, 5:115
  survey methods, 5:116–117
Survey Research Center (SRC),
  1:424–425
Surveys, 8:**241–243**
  census, 1:476–477
  employment, 2:580

exit poll, 3:45–46
  longitudinal data, 2:239,
    7:194–196
  polling, 6:353–355
  self-classification, 7:397–398
  self-report method, 7:424–426
  sex, 7:481*t*
  sexuality, 7:480–483, 481*t*
  See also Panel studies
Surveys, opinion. *See* Opinion polls
Surveys, sample, 8:**244–245**
  Current Population Survey,
    2:212–213
  Latino National Political Survey,
    4:354–356
  opinion polls, 6:355–357
  survey research, 7:196–197
Surveys, time use. *See* Time allocation
Survival analysis regression, 8:*246*,
  246–247
Survival needs, 5:453
Survival of the fittest. *See* Natural
  selection
Survivor function. *See* Duration
  models
Susceptibility. *See* Vulnerability
Sussman, Marvin, 3:87
Sustainable systems
  architecture, 1:172
  overfishing, 6:91, *92*
  urban sprawl, 8:540–541
  urbanization, 8:546
  See also Ecology; Environment
Sutherland, Edwin, 2:171
Sutton, Robert, 1:11
Suzuki, Masao, 4:174
Svalbard Islands, 1:115
Sviridoff, Mitchell, 9:27
Swan, Trevor
  neoclassical growth model,
    5:464–466
  Uzawa, Hirofumi, 8:563
Swann, William B., Jr., 7:430
*Swann v. Charlotte-Meklenburg Board
  of Education* (1971), 2:314
Swastika. *See* Nazism; Rituals
Swatantra, 2:76
Sweatshops, 1:351, 352, 353,
  8:**247–249**, 9:125
Sweatt v. Painter (1950), 3:505
Sweden
  central banks, 1:477
  codetermination, 1:593
  corporal punishment, 2:134–135
  corporatism, 2:141

democracy, 2:273, 274
  gender gap, 3:278
  job guarantee, 4:206
  Lundberg, Erik, 4:518–519
  managed competition, 2:54
  market socialism, 7:645–646
  neutral states, 5:488
  social welfare system, 7:632
  socialization of investment,
    7:649–650
  state capitalism, 1:444
  Stockholm School, 8:154–155
  volunteerism, 8:638
Swedish School of Economics. *See*
  Stockholm School
Sweet, Jill, 2:224
Sweetness and Power (Mintz), 5:20,
  196
Sweezy, Paul, 2:77, 5:266
  capitalist mode of production,
    1:447
  feudal mode of production, 3:134
  Hilferding, Rudolf, 3:476
  overconsumption, 8:488
Swidden agriculture, 5:425
Swidler, Ann, 8:7
Swing music, 4:176–177
Switzerland
  banking industry, 1:252
  central banks, 1:477
  citizenship, 1:543
  compulsory voting, 2:58
  confederations, 2:69
  corporatism, 2:141
  hot money, 3:504
  permanent neutrality, 5:488, 513
  unemployment compensation,
    2:49
Sylla, Richard, 1:253
Sylvester, James Joseph, 3:467
Symbolic analysts, 5:492–493
  See also New Class
Symbolic capital, 1:359, 6:418
Symbolic ethnicity, 3:256
Symbolic Exchange and Death
  (Baudrillard), 2:203
*Symbolic Interaction: Perspective and
  Method* (Blumer), 1:343–344
Symbolic interactionism, 1:343–344,
  4:**75–76**, 495
  conversational analysis, 2:118
  emotion, 2:569
  identity, 3:553
  microsociology, 7:678

post-Parsonian American sociology, 8:7

role theory, 7:276

schools in sociology, 8:10

self-presentation, 7:423–424

social constructionism, 7:578

social identity, 3:558

society, 7:653

sociology, 7:661

voluntaristic *vs.* structuralist sociology, 8:17

Symbolic inversion. *See* Rites of passage

Symbolic logic, 4:**481–482**

Symbolic racism. *See* Racism

Symbols, 5:451, 8:**249–253**

Bandura, Albert, 1:248

Battle of the Little Big Horn, 1:258–259

borders, 1:354–355

burial grounds, 1:392–393

constructivism, 2:97, 98

creativity, 2:165

cultural, 1:122, 2:197, 203–204

distinctions, 2:413

relativism, 2:194

diaspora, 2:356–357

labeling theory, 4:300

law and order, 4:369

myth and mythology, 5:355–357

religion, 7:159–161

representation, 7:170–172

rites of passage, 7:256–259

rituals, 7:260

semiotics, 7:436–438

Southern politics, 6:344–345

Turner, Victor, 8:468–471

zombies, 9:181

Symbols, status. *See* Prestige

Sympathy, 8:**253–254**

emotion and affect, 2:572

tastes, 8:267

Syncretism

Creole, 2:169

Herskovits, Melville J., 3:467

religion, 7:161

Santería, 7:325

vodou, 8:634

Syndicalism, 8:**254–256**

labor unions, 8:515

left wing, 4:403

Michels, Robert, 5:132

Synergetics, Fuller, Buckminster, 3:229

Syntactic Structures (Chomsky), 1:527–528

Syntax. *See* Language

Syphilis, 8:472–473

Syria

agricultural industry, 1:62

Arab-Israeli War of 1967, 1:156–159

Hussein, Saddam, 3:532, 533

Lebanese civil war, 4:396, 397, 398

Palestinian diaspora, 6:109–110

United Arab Republic, 8:520–522

water resources, 9:41–42

System, self, 7:**429–430**

System analysis, 8:**256–257**

marginalism, 4:596

systems theory, 8:257–258

System of National Accounts (SNA), 5:397, 398–401

The System of Nature (Holbach), 1:275

System of Positive Policy (Comte), 2:62

Systematic desensitization. *See* Psychotherapy

Systematic geography, 3:304

Systematic processing. *See* Attitudes

Systems dynamics projections, 3:241

Systems of Survival (Jacobs), 4:165

Systems theory, 8:**257–258**

constructivism, 2:97

critical theory, 2:178

Easton, David, 2:477

heterarchy, 3:468–469

political system, 6:316–317

scientific method, 7:364

social system, 7:623–627

Systems theory, ecological. *See* Developmental psychology

Szasz, Thomas, 2:408

T

T-statistics

Dickey-Fuller distribution, 8:518

student's, 8:184–187, *185,* 332

Theil's, 8:592

Tabasco, Mexico, Olmec culture, 6:39

Tabb, William, 2:14

Tableau économique (Quesnay), 3:154, 6:666

See also Physiocracy; Quesnay, François

Taboos, 8:**259**

caste, 1:459

comic books, 2:24

deviance, 2:352

Kinsey, Alfred, 4:270

magic, 4:554–555

marriage, 4:615

sanitation, 7:322

toilets, 8:384

Tabula rosa, 2:578

Taft, Robert, 2:85

Taft, William H., 9:102

Taft-Hartley Act (U.S. 1947), 4:303, 317, 8:516

Taget sum, 3:98

Tahara (purification), 3:239

Ta'if Agreement (Lebanon, 1989), 4:397

Tailoring work, 9:123

Taine, Hippolyte, 3:453

Taino, 8:**260–261**

Boricua, 1:355–356

Columbus, Christopher, 2:19

pre-Columbian peoples, 6:427

Tait, Lawson, 8:140

See also Human sterilization

Taiwan

Chinese diaspora, 1:516, 518

corporations, 2:140

filibuster, 3:139

Kuznets hypothesis, 4:297

land reform, 4:342

landlords, 4:346

underdevelopment, 8:490

United Nations membership, 8:522

Tajikistan, commonwealth, 2:30

Takahashi, Korekiyo, 3:370

Talent, 8:**261–262**

gifted and talented education, 3:315–318

underachievers, 8:483–485

Talented. *See* Gifted and talented

Talented persons. *See* Gifted and talented

Tali, Wasif al-, 1:323

Taliban, 8:**262–263**

bin Laden, Osama, 1:299

Bush, George W., 1:399

Central Intelligence Agency, U.S, 1:483

counterterrorism, 2:155

deviance, 2:353

drug traffic, 2:451

femininity, 3:118

national defense, 2:261

theocracy, 8:343

violence, 8:624

Tally's Corner (Liebow), 8:**263–265**

Talmud, 4:193–194

Tambiah, Stanley, 5:505

Tambo, Oliver, 1:42, 148

Taming the Sovereigns: Institutional Change in International Politics (Holsti), 2:259

Tancred, Peta, 9:122

Taney, Roger Brook, 1:315, 3:114

TANF (Temporary Assistance for Needy Families). *See* Culture of poverty

Tango. *See* Dance

Tango and the Political Economy of Passion (Savigliano), 2:224

Tannenbaum, Frank, 4:299

Tantric Buddhism. *See* Buddhism

Tantrism, human sacrifice, 3:516

Tanzania
  African socialism, 7:640
  Amin, Idi, 1:109–110
  collectivism, 2:11
  Nyerere, Julius, 5:553–554

Taoism
  Chinese diaspora, 1:516
  hell, 3:458

Tarde, Gabriel, 2:107

Targeted Negative Income Tax (Germany), 5:457

Targeted pricing. *See* Price discrimination

Tariffs, 8:265–266
  banana industry, 1:246
  beggar-thy-neighbor, 1:272–273
  bilateral trade, 8:414, 415
  Chamberlain, Neville, 1:489
  common market, 2:29
  Corn Laws, 2:133–134
  customs union, 2:215
  product dumping, 2:462
  retaliation, 7:216
  trade barriers, 1:254–255
  trade liberalization, 4:427–428
  trade quotas, 6:672–673

Tarski, Alfred, 4:481

Taste for discrimination, 2:398–400
  age discrimination, 2:402
  described, 2:388–389, 390
  politics, 7:20
  race, 7:14
  wage discrimination, 2:405

Tastes, 8:266–270
  aesthetics, 1:30
  cultural distinctions, 2:413
  lifestyles, 4:446
  low and high culture, 2:204, 205

popular culture, 6:373–374
  sample surveys, 8:244–245
  See also Preferences

TAT (Thematic Apperception Test). *See* Achievement

Tate, William, 2:176

Tâtonnement, 8:270–271, 563, 9:12
  Arrow-Debreu Model, 1:183
  Patinkin, Don, 6:171, 172

Tattered Tom (Alger), 1:72

Tawney, R. H., 8:271–272

Tax, estate. *See* Inheritance tax

Tax, flat. *See* Flat taxes

Tax, income. *See* Corporate income tax; Income tax; Negative income tax

Tax, inheritance. *See* Inheritance tax

Tax, poll. *See* Poll tax, U.S.; Thatcher, Margaret

Tax, Sol, 2:224

Tax, Tobin. *See* Tobin, James; Transaction taxes

Tax, transaction. *See* Transaction taxes

Tax, value-added (VAT). *See* Value-added tax (VAT)

Tax avoidance. *See* Tax evasion and tax avoidance

Tax-based incomes policy. *See* Wage and price controls

Tax breaks. *See* Tax relief

Tax burden. *See* Tax incidence

Tax credits, 3:421, 422, 8:272–275
  See also Earned Income Tax Credit

Tax cuts. *See* Tax relief

Tax evasion and tax avoidance, 8:275–276
  described, 8:280, 282
  hot money, 3:504
  transfer pricing, 8:428–429

Tax exemptions, Operation Bootstrap, 6:44

Tax gap, 8:276

Tax havens. *See* Offshore banking

Tax incidence, 8:276, 276–277
  corporate income tax, 3:607–608
  described, 8:280, 281–282

Tax inequality, wealth, 6:73

Tax progressivity. *See* Progressive taxes

Tax rebates. *See* Tax relief

Tax Reform Act (U.S. 1969), 3:183

Tax relief, 3:380, 8:272–273, 277–278

Tax revolts, 8:278–279
  described, 8:280, 281
  Lynd, Staughton, 4:529

Tax subsidies. *See* Tax relief

Tax write-offs. *See* Tax relief

Taxation, 8:279–280
  black capitalism, 1:442
  capital controls, 1:432
  conservatism, 2:86
  Constitution, U.S., 2:91
  dirigiste, 2:373
  distortions, 2:414
  economic growth, 2:491
  employment, 2:582
  labor supply, 4:322
  lotteries, 4:503–504
  monopoly, 5:265
  Ricardian equivalence, 7:241
  Ricardian vice, 7:241–242
  Ricardo, David, 7:243, 246
  Thatcher, Margaret, 8:335

Taxes, 8:280–283
  air pollution, 6:362
  brain drain, 1:368
  bubbles (economics), 1:379
  Bush, George H. W., 1:398
  Bush, George W., 1:399, 400
  capital flight, 1:434
  hedonic prices, 3:451
  income, negative, 5:456–457
  indentured servants, 3:254
  inheritance, bequests, 1:287
  investment, 4:133
  landlords, 4:346, 347
  monetary base, 5:245
  poll, 1:552, 6:351–353
  transaction, 8:427–428
    Tobin, James, 8:378, 379
    transfer pricing, 8:428–429
  in vivo transfers, 3:598
  welfare economics, 9:63
  welfare funding, 9:71
  See also Income tax; Tariffs

Taxes, pollution. *See* Air pollution

Taxes, progressive, 8:280, 282, 283–284

Taxes, regressive, 8:280, 284–285

Taylor, Barbara, 3:483

Taylor, Charles, 3:454, 463, 464, 7:109, 9:132

Taylor, Craig Barr, 1:248

Taylor, Frederick Winslow, 1:390, 3:77, 8:287
  division of labor, 2:424–425
  industrial accidents, 1:8
  management, 4:574, 576
  organization theory, 6:69

time and motion studies, 8:365
Taylor, Grant, 8:369
Taylor, Harriet, 5:179
Taylor, John B., 7:294, 8:286
Taylor, Julie, 2:224
Taylor, Lance, 4:544, 8:**285–286**
Taylor, Rufus, 1:482
Taylor, Scott, 5:547
Taylor, Timothy D., 9:141, 142
Taylor, Walter, 1:167
Taylor curve. *See* Taylor rule
Taylor-Gooby, Peter, 9:72
Taylor rule, 7:293, 294, 8:**286–287**
Taylorism, 8:**287–288**
   division of labor, 2:424–425
   industrial accidents, 1:8
   management, 4:574, 576
   time and motion studies,
     8:365–366
TCE (Transaction cost economics),
   6:69
Tea industry, 8:**288–290**
Teacher-child relationships,
   8:**291–293**
Teacher expectations, 8:**290–291**
Teachers, 8:**293–295**
   pedagogy, 6:196–197
   schooling, 7:350–351
Teaching theories. *See* Teachers
Teams and teambuilding
   leadership, 4:377, 381
   work, 9:136–137
Teamsters Union, 1:494
Teasdale, John, 4:388
Teatro bufo. *See* Blackface
Technical change. *See* Technological
   change
Technocracy, 8:**296–297**
   engineering, 2:595
   managerial class, 4:578
   rites of passage, 7:259
   social values, 8:582
   technocrats, 8:297–298
   technotopia, 8:312–313
Technocracy, Inc., 8:296, 298
Technocrats, 8:**297–298**
   bureaucracy, 1:390
   described, 8:296
   engineering, 2:595
   New Class, 5:492–493
   technotopia, 8:312–313
   urbanity, 8:545
Technological change, 1:**490–492**,
   8:619
   checks and balances, 1:496

described, 8:302
determinism, 2:332
division of labor, 2:423–425
labor demand, 4:313
legacy effects, 4:405
Luddites, 4:513–515
Machinery Question, 4:536–537
progress, 8:298–302
rentier class, 1:566–567
social aspects, 1:490
surplus labor, 4:310–311
technological determinism, 2:332
technological progress, 8:298–302
vintage models, 8:619–621
Technological determinism,
   2:**332–333**
   described, 2:323
   technocracy, 8:296
Technological diffusion curve. *See*
   Technology, adoption of
Technological progress
   asymmetric returns to scale, 7:223
   diminishing returns, 7:219
   employment, 2:580–581
   engineering, 2:595
   Internet, 4:104–107
   long run, 4:493, 493*t*
   machinery, 4:534–536
   microelectronics industry,
     5:136–139
   modernity, 5:230
   popular culture, 6:375
   telecommunications industry,
     8:314–315
Technological progress, economic
   growth, 2:486–490, 8:**298–300**
   computers, 2:60
   Silicon Valley, 7:510–511
Technological progress, skill bias, 2:59,
   8:**300–302**
Technology, 8:**302–305**
   bioethics, 1:300
   blue collar and white collar, 1:339
   bubbles (economics), 1:379
   business, 1:402
   business cycles, 1:403, 405
   cellular, 8:306–308
   change, 1:490–492
   communalism, 2:30
   critical theory, 2:177
   cyberspace, 2:216–217
   diffusion, 8:620
   disaster management, 2:382
   forces of production, 3:167
   future shock, 3:240

investments, 8:620–621
journalism, 4:212–213, 214
knowledge society, 4:283, 284
Luddites, 4:513–515
material culture, 5:13–14
media, 5:60
memory, 5:75
military, 5:167–168
mining industry, 5:189
neoclassical growth model, 5:465
networks, 5:478
nonrenewable natural resources,
   5:437–438
optimal growth, 6:52
post-World War II development,
   9:150
real business cycles, 1:407,
   408–409
religion, 7:161
representative and participatory
   democracy, 2:285
reproduction, 7:178, 179
research and development,
   7:199–200
teachers, 8:295
technocracy, 8:296–297, 297–298
technophobia, 4:513–515,
   8:310–312
transfer, 8:308–309
   described, 8:303–304
   technological progress, 8:299
transparency, 8:435
unemployment, 8:502
video, 8:309–310
vintage models, 8:619–621
vulnerability, 8:657
war, 9:18
winner-take-all society, 9:103
See also Microelectronics industry
Technology, adoption of, 8:**305–306**
   digital divide, 2:366–367
   economic growth, 8:298
   teachers, 8:295
   technological change, 1:490
   technological progress, 8:299
Technology, cellular, 8:**306–308**
Technology, video, 8:**309–310**
Technology transfer, 8:**308–309**
   described, 8:303–304
   North-South models, 5:547
   technological progress, 8:299
Technophobia, 4:513–515, 8:**310–312**
Technotopia, 8:**312–313**
Teenagers. *See* Adolescents

Telecommunications Act (U.S. 1996), 1:476, 8:315

Telecommunications industry, 8:**313–317**
> cellular technology, 8:306–308
> microelectronics industry, 5:138–139
> *See also* Communication

Telegraph. *See* Telecommunications industry

Teleology, 8:**317–318**
> development theory, 2:339
> forces of production, 3:167

Telephone. *See* Telecommunications industry

Teles da Rosa, Antônio Lisboa. *See* Rosa, Antônio Lisboa da

Television, 8:**318–321**
> Al Jazeera, 1:69–70
> campaigning, 1:423–424
> censorship, 1:475–476
> films, 3:140
> high-definition, 3:141
> journalism, 4:214–215
> parody, 6:149
> Sambo, 7:313
> *Star Trek,* 8:99
> video technology, 8:309, 310

Television: Technology and Cultural Form (Williams), 2:332

Television networks, 3:140

Tell My Horse (Hurston), 3:527

Telser, Lester, 1:502

Temin, Peter, 3:370

Temperament, 8:**321–322**
> mood, 5:275
> personality, 6:217–218, 219–220
> shyness, 7:504–505
> trait theory, 8:425–426

Temple University, Latino National Political Survey, 4:354–356

Temporality bias. *See* Cross-sectional research; Research, cross-sectional

Temporary Assistance for Needy Families (TANF). *See* Culture of poverty

Temporary Assistance for Needy Families (TANF) (1997). *See* Culture of Poverty

Temporary employment, 1:220

Temptation. *See* Sin

Tenancy system, 1:34

Tenant farming. *See* Agricultural economics

Tenants. *See* Leasing

Tendai Buddhism. *See* Buddhism

Tendencies. *See* Trait theory

Tennessee, Confederate States of America, 2:67

Tennessee Valley Authority (TVA), 5:494

The Tentative Pregnancy (Rothman), 3:294

Teosinte, 5:424

Term limits, 8:**323–324,** 9:37

Term structure of interest rates. *See* Interest rates

Terms of trade, 6:423–425, 8:**324–326**

Terraces, 3:130–131

Territorial expansion
> annexation, 1:115–116
> pre-World War II, 9:147–148

Terroism Act (South Africa 1966), 1:148

Terror, 8:**326–327**

Terror management theory, 8:326, **327–328**

Terrorism, 8:**328–330,** 330–331
> aviation industry, 1:233
> biased policing, 6:290
> bin Laden, Osama, 1:298–300
> Black September, 1:322–323
> Central Intelligence Agency, U.S, 1:483, 484, 485
> citizenship, 1:544
> collective injury, 8:624
> cyber, 8:629
> defense, 2:259
> disaster management, 2:382, 385
> *Fahrenheit 9/11* (film), 3:79–80
> Guantánamo Bay, 3:393–394
> history, 8:628–629
> Islamic, 1:70–71
> just war, 4:236
> militants, 5:163–164
> Muslims, 5:346, 348
> narcissism, 5:369
> national defense, 2:260, 261, 262
> nuclear weapons, 9:32
> petroleum industry, 6:233
> Qadhafi, Muammar al, 6:648
> suicide bombers, 8:224–225
> totalitarianism, 8:394
> tourism industry, 8:402
> USSR dissolution, 8:513
> violence, 1:299–300, 8:328–331, 624, 628–629
> *See also* Bioterrorism; Counterterrorism; September 11, 2001

Terrorists, 8:**330–331**
> bin Laden, Osama, 1:298–300
> bioterrorism, 1:301–302
> Black September, 1:322–323
> suicide bombers, 8:224–225
> *See also* September 11, 2001

Tertullian, 1:532

Test experience, 8:574

Test statistics, 8:**331–333**
> Chow test, 1:529–530
> formulas, 3:179–180
> quality control, 6:651
> reliability, 7:157–158
> variation, 8:592
> Z-test, 9:181–183

Testimony
> hearsay, 3:444–445, 7:295–298
> litigation, 4:465–466
> lying, 4:525

Testing, genetic. *See* Genetic testing

Testing, hypothesis. *See* Hypothesis and hypothesis testing

Testing, significance. *See* Hypothesis and hypothesis testing

Testing effect, 8:294

Testing Women, Testing the Fetus (Rapp), 3:294

Testosterone
> aggression, 1:56
> alpha-males, 1:83, 84

Tests, correspondence. *See* Correspondence tests

Tests, empirical, 5:434–435

Tests, intelligence. *See* Intelligence (IQ) tests

Tests, objective. *See* Psychometrics

Tests, projective. *See* Psychometrics

Tests, standardized. *See* Standardized tests

Tet Offensive, 8:614

Tetrodotoxin, 9:181

Tewa (Native Americans), 2:224

Texas
> annexation of, 1:115
> Bracero Program, 1:364
> Bush, George W., 1:399
> civil rights, 1:549
> Confederate States of America, 2:66
> filibuster, 3:138–139
> *Hernandez v. Texas,* 3:464–466
> Mexican-American War, 5:126–129
> referendum, 7:120
> *Roe v. Wade,* 7:270–271

white primary, 9:84

Texas Democratic Party, 9:84

Texas-Mexican War (1836), 5:120

Texas v. Hopwood (1996), 3:373

Text messaging. *See* Cellular technology

Textile industry, 8:**333–334**
   Bonacich, Edna, 1:351, 352
   cotton industry, 2:152–154
   labor unions, 8:514
   Luddites, 4:513–515

TFR (Total fertility rate), 3:85

Thailand
   AIDS/HIV, 1:65
   Chinese diaspora, 1:518
   Hmong, 3:491

Thaler, Richard, 2:252–253

Thalidomide, 1:3, 2:635

Thanatophobia. *See* Death and dying

Thanatos, 3:211

Thant, U., 8:**334–335**

Thatcher, Margaret, 8:**335–336**
   Blair, Tony, 1:285
   conservatism, 2:84, 86
   Conservative Party, 2:87–88
   Falkland Islands war, 3:81
   free trade, 3:196
   Hall, Stuart, 3:410
   individualism, 3:619
   Liberal Party, 4:423
   Macmillan, Harold, 4:538
   neoliberalism, 9:38
   poll tax, 6:353
   progressive taxes, 8:284
   tax revolts, 8:278, 279

Theater, 8:**336–339**
   Black Arts Movement, 1:309–310
   blackface, 1:326–327
   performance, 6:207–208
   realism, 7:91–92
   Robeson, Paul, 7:265–266

Theil, Henri, 4:394
   See also Theil index

Theil index, 3:605, 8:**339–340**, 530

Theil's T statistics, 8:592

Their Eyes Were Watching God (Hurston), 3:426, 527, 528

Theism, 1:194, 8:**340–341**, 9:154–155

Thematic Apperception Test. *See* Achievement

Theme parks, 2:410, 8:400

Theocracy, 8:**342–343**
   Church and state, 1:534–536

Iranian Revolution, 4:145

Theology, liberation, 4:**434–437**
   Christian socialism, 7:643
   social justice, 4:242
   socialism, 7:638

Théorie de la spéculation (Bachelier), 2:548

Theories, 8:**343–345**
   praxis, 6:421–422
   reductionism, 7:118–119
   religion, 7:159–161
   See also names of specific theories; Social theory

The Theory of Business Enterprise (Veblen), 8:596

Theory of Capitalist Development (Sweezy), 1:447

A Theory of Cognitive Dissonance (Festinger), 3:132–133

The Theory of Communicative Action (Habermas), 2:177, 178, 3:401

A Theory of Critical Elections (Key), 4:259

Theory of Economic Development (Schumpeter), 1:438

Theory of Games and Economic Behavior (Neumann and Morgenstern), 3:250, 8:556, 643, 9:176–177

The Theory of Interest (Fisher), 3:151, 4:81

Theory of International Politics (Waltz), 9:14

A Theory of Justice (Rawls), 1:545, 4:238, 424, 5:39, 7:84

Theory of mind, 8:**345–349**
   consciousness, 2:78–82
   evolutionary psychology, 3:33–34
   Marx, Karl, 4:629–630
   perspective-taking, 6:226

Theory of Money and Credit (Mises), 1:211

The Theory of Moral Sentiments (Smith), 5:282, 283, 284

The Theory of Political Coalitions (Riker), 7:249

Theory of Production (Kurz and Salvadori), 8:577

Theory of Public Finance (Musgrave), 3:144

Theory of second best, 2:414, 8:**350–351**

A Theory of the Calculus of Voting (Riker and Ordeshook), 7:249

A Theory of the Consumption Function (Friedman), 3:217, 4:260

The Theory of the Leisure Class (Veblen), 1:565–566, 2:88, 107, 412, 4:445, 5:548, 8:595–596

Theory of the Sign, 6:10

Theory of Value (Debreu), 2:249, 3:283

The Theory of Wages (Hicks), 3:471

Theory Y, 5:455

Therapy, drug. *See* Drug therapy

Therapy, psychological. *See* Psychotherapy

Theravada Buddhism, 5:504

There Ain't No Black in the Union Jack (Gilroy), 3:410

Thernstrom, Abigail, 8:651

They Died with Their Boots On (film), 1:258–259

Thích Nhat Hanh. *See* Nhat Hanh, Thích

Thieu, Nguyen Van, 8:614

Think tanks, 1:584–585, 9:157–158

Thinking
   cognition, 1:598
   consciousness, 2:78, 79
   conundrum, 2:116
   divergent, 2:165

Thinness, 9:59

Third Bauxite Mine Rehabilitation Survey (International Aluminum Institute), 1:261

Third Estate, 5:541

Third International, 3:455

Third Reich. *See* Germany; Nazism

The Third Wave (Huntington), 2:289

Third Wave Agenda (Heywood and Drake), 9:115

Third wave feminism, 3:121, 269–270, 9:115, 117

The Third Way (Giddens), 3:315

Third world, 5:541–542, 8:**351–353**
   birth control, 1:303
   Castro, Fidel, 1:466
   civil wars, 1:554, 555
   communism, 2:34, 35, 36
   critical race theory, 2:174, 175
   crony capitalism, 2:180
   debt crisis (1980s), 1:28
   dependency theory, 2:299
   development in sociology, 2:346–348
   European Union, 3:25
   International Monetary Fund, 4:95–96
   labor unions, 8:517
   sociology, 1:303, 2:346–348, 8:12–14

Third world, *continued*
  urban sprawl, 8:540
  zero population growth, 9:174,
    175
  See also Developing countries
Thirlwall, Anthony P., 8:607, 608
Thirty-six View of Mount Fugi
  (Hikusai), 8:632
Thirty Years' War (1618-1648),
  3:135–136, 9:18
Thom, Mel, 1:98
Thom, René, 1:468
Thomas, Clarence, 3:121, 7:474
Thomas, Duncan, 3:437
Thomas, J. J., 9:97
Thomas, Robert P., 5:545
Thomas Aquinas, Saint
  abortion, 1:2
  Aristotle, 1:175
  just war, 4:235
  politics, 6:319
  supreme being, 8:230, 231
Thompson, E. P. *See* Thompson,
  Edward P.
Thompson, Edward P., 8:353–357
  Anderson, Perry, 1:113
  class, 1:564
  class conflict, 1:570
  class consciousness, 1:572
  cultural studies, 2:199
  humanism, 3:518
  labor, 4:301
  social history, 3:482–483
  work day, 9:126
  working class, 9:131
Thomsen, Christian, 1:166
Thoreau, Henry David, 1:545, 2:9,
  372, 8:357
Thornburg v. Gingles (1986), 3:309,
  8:652
Thorndike, Edward, 8:358–359
  behaviorism, 1:276
  operant conditioning, 1:574
  reinforcement theories, 7:146, 147
  social intelligence, 4:74
Thorndike, Robert L., 8:4
Thornton, Henry, 4:410
Thornwell, Emily, 3:301
Thought
  cognition, 1:598
  history, Foucault, Michel,
    3:182–183
  reflective, 3:214
Threat
  freedom from, 5:412

  stereotype, 1:15, 16
  of violence, 8:627–628
Threat, stereotype. *See* Stereotype
  threat
Three Age System, 1:166
Three-stage least squares, 4:394–395,
  395
The Three Worlds of Welfare Capitalism
  (Esping-Anderson), 7:531–632,
  9:67–68
Threshold effects, 8:359–360
Thrift, paradox of, 9:96
Thucydides, 2:82, 4:235
Thunder Rolling in the Mountains.
  See Chief Joseph
Thurman, Wallace, 2:17
Thurmond, Strom, 3:138–139,
  8:360–361
    civil rights movement, U.S., 1:551
    Democratic Party (U.S.), 2:287
    Dixiecrats, 2:429–431
    Republican Party (U.S.), 7:187
    Southern strategy, 8:36
    Truman, Harry S., 8:460
Thurow, Lester, 3:508–509, 7:166
Thurstone, L. L., 3:75, 4:447
TI (Transparency International). *See*
  Transparency International (TI)
Tibet
  Buddhism, 1:383–384
  regions, 7:131
  water resources, 9:41
Tibetan Buddhism, 9:155
  See also Buddhism
Tiebour choice, 5:391
Tiebout, Charles M., 3:451
Tiebout effects. *See* Hedonic prices
Tijerina, Reies López, 5:124
Tilak, Bal Gangadhar, 3:254
Till, Emmett, 1:551, 4:527
Tille, Cédric, 2:210
Tilley, Christopher, 1:168
Tilly, Charles, 4:599, 8:6
Timberlake, William, 7:147–148
Time, 8:361–363
  clock, 1:583–584
  commute, 9:128
  flex, 9:129
  historical, 8:481
  leisure, 3:!75, 8:565–566, 9:128,
    129, 134, 135
  narratives, 5:371
  overemployment, 6:90–91
  short period, 7:501–502
  short run, 7:502–503

  survival analysis regression,
    8:246–247
  work day, 9:126–127, 134–135
*Time, Work-Discipline, and Industrial
  Capitalism* (Thompson), 8:354–355
Time allocation, 1:270, 271,
  8:363–365, 364t
Time-and-a-half, 8:373–374
Time and motion studies, 8:365–366
  chaos theory, 1:492
  management, 4:574, 576
  Taylorism, 8:287
Time and Narrative (Ricoeur), 5:371
Time domain techniques, 9:82–83
Time indices. *See* Time trends
Time on the Cross (Engerman and
  Fogel), 3:161–162, 8:366–368
  cliometrics, 1:582
  Engerman, Stanley, 2:592
Time orientation, 8:368–369
  decision-making, 2:252–253
  self-control, 7:402–404
Time preference, 2:385–386,
  8:369–371
Time Series Analysis (Box, et al), 9:82
Time series regression, 8:371–372
  Chow test, 1:529–530
  cointegration, 2:2–3
  difference equations, 2:362
  duration models, 2:463–464
  loss functions, 4:495–502
  serial correlation, 7:455–457
  stationary process, 8:114–117
  trends, 8:447–448
  unit root and cointegration
    regression, 8:518–519
Time series studies
  statistical validity, 8:574
  white noise, 9:82–83
Time-space compression, 3:331
Time transformation, 3:158
Time trends, 8:373
Time use surveys. *See* Time allocation
Time value of money. *See* Discounted
  present value
Timms, Duncan, 8:541
Tín Bùi. *See* Bùi, Tín
Tinbergen, Jan, 8:374–375
  cobweb cycles, 1:591
  convergence theory, 2:117
  Koopmans, Tjalling, 4:287
  Lagrange multipliers, 4:334
  positive social science, 6:389
Tirole, Jean, 1:215
Tiruneh, Gizachew, 2:275–276, 6:416

Titchener, Edward B., 3:233
Title I-D, Equal Opportunity Act (U.S. 1964), 9:27
Title II, Equal Opportunity Act (U.S. 1964), 9:26
Title VII, Civil Rights Act (U.S. 1964), 3:121, 123, 5:408–409
Title IX, Education Amendment (U.S.), 3:121
Title XVIII, Social Security Act (U.S. 1965), 5:396
Titles (property rights). *See* Deeds and titles (property rights)
Tito, Josip Broz, 2:35, 5:513, **8:375–376**
Titoism, 8:376
To Secure These Rights (1947), 9:81
Tobacco addiction, 1:21
Tobacco industry, **8:376–378**
    Columbus, Christopher, 2:21
    drugs of abuse, 2:455
    tobacco legal settlements, 7:466–467
    See also Smoking
Tobacco settlements, 7:**466–467**
Tobago, Williams, Eric and, 9:96–98
    See also Trinidad
Tobin, James, 3:219, 6:35, **8:378–379**
    income, 5:456
    Koopmans, Tjalling, 4:288
    left and right censoring, 1:474
    risk takers, 7:255
    Tobin's Q, 8:379–381
    tobit, 8:381–382
    two-sector models, 8:475
Tobin tax. *See* Tobin, James; Transaction taxes
Tobin's Q, 8:378, **379–381**
Tobit, 8:**381–382**
    left and right censoring, 1:474
    regression analysis, 7:140
    Tobin, James, 8:379
Tocqueville, Alexis de, 8:**382–383**
    American exceptionalism, 1:107
    civil society, 1:553
    conservatism, 2:84
    corporations, 2:139
    democratic centralism, 2:285
    freedom, 3:197–198
    Gobineau, Comte de, 3:335–336
    individualism, 3:618–619
    left and right, 4:401
    liberation, 4:429
    majorities, 4:560
    patriotism, 6:176

relative deprivation, 7:152
religiosity, 7:163
representative and participatory democracy, 2:284
revolution of rising expectations, 7:231
social theory, 7:628
tyranny of the majority, 8:478–479
urban sociology, 8:16
Todaro, Michael, 3:428–429
    development economics, 2:344
    dual economy, 2:457
Todorov, Tzvetan, 5:371
Toennies, Ferdinand, 3:266–267
Toffler, Alvin, 3:240
Toilets, 8:**383–384**
    plumbing, 6:281–282
    sanitation, 7:323
Tokenism, 2:14
Tokugawa (period). *See* Edo Period
Tokugawa (shogun), 5:69–70
Tokyo tribunals, 9:21
Tolerance
    religious, Locke, John and, 4:476
    smoking, 7:559–560
Tolerance, drug, 8:**384–385**
Tolerance, political, 8:**385–386**
    church and state, 1:536
    citizenship, 1:543
    xenophobia, 9:158–161
Tolerance, repressive. *See* Repressive tolerance
Tolman, Edward, 8:**386–387**
    behaviorism, 1:275, 276, 277
    Campbell, Donald, 1:425
    cognition, 1:597
    reinforcement theories, 7:147
    Thorndike, Edward, 8:358, 359
Tolman v. Underhill (1955), 8:387
Tolnay, Stewart, 2:296, 4:526
Tolstoy, Leo, 1:545, 9:19–21
Toltecs, 6:427
    See also Pre-Columbian peoples
Tomming. *See* Uncle Tom
Tönnies, Ferdinand, 3:385
    communalism, 2:30
    groups, 3:385
    urban studies, 8:541
    welfare state, 9:69
Tooby, John, 2:329, 5:440
Tools, 8:**387–389**
Toomer, Jean, 3:426
Topel, Robert, 9:4

Topology, 8:**390–391**
    manifolds, 4:585
    point-set, 8:563
Topophilia, 8:389–390
Töppfer, Rudolphe, 2:23
Topsoil, 3:130
Torah, 4:219–220, 221
Tories. *See* Conservative Party (U.K.)
Tornadoes, 5:433
    See also Natural disasters
Torres, Luis de, 2:20
Torts, 4:364, 7:216
Torture, 8:**391–394**, 392*t*
    Geneva Convention, 9:22
    interrogation, 4:112
Total factor productivity. *See* Growth accounting
Total fertility rate (TFR), 3:85
Total revenue. *See* Revenue
Total sum of squares (TSS), 6:60
Total supply, 5:401
Totalitarianism, 8:**394–397**
    Arendt, Hannah, 1:173
    authoritarianism *vs.*, 1:213
    civil-military relation, 1:547–548
    conservatism, 2:85
    cult of personality, 6:221–223
    description, 3:354
    Hitler, Adolf, 3:486–488
    Holocaust, 3:496
    liberalism, 4:425
    political sociology, 8:4
    Solzhenitsyn, Aleksandr, 8:29
    Stalinism, 8:87
    terrorism, 8:628
    world government, 3:360
    See also Dictatorship
Totem and Taboo (Freud), 3:211–212, 212
Totemism, 8:**397–398**
Touraine, Alain, 3:240, 6:649
Touré, Ahmed Sékou, 1:321, 3:408, 5:508
Touré, Ali Farka, 1:342
Touré, Sékou. *See* African socialism
Tourette's disorder, 3:537
Tourgée, Albion, 1:115
Tourism, 8:**398–400**, 565
Tourism, cultural. *See* Cultural tourism
Tourism industry, 8:**400–402**
    Cherokees, 1:498
    described, 8:399
The Tourist As a Metaphor of the Social World (Dann), 8:565

Toussaint-Louverture, 8:**402–403**
    Black Power, 1:321
    blackness, 1:330
    Jacobinism, 4:165
    liberation, 4:429
    slave resistance, 3:407–408, 7:535
Toward the African Revolution (Fanon),
    3:100
Toward Understanding Germany
    (Lowie), 4:507
Towards the Year 2000 (Bell), 3:241
Tower, John, 4:142
Towns, 8:**404–405**
    black, 1:325–326
    gemeinschaft, 3:266–267
    Lynd, Robert and Helen,
      4:527–528
    representative and participatory
      democracy, 2:283
    shtetlekh, 7:503–504
    suburbs, 8:210–211
    See also Cities
Townsend, Grovey v. (1935), 9:84, 85
Townshend Acts (UK 1767), 1:103
Townships, 8:**405–407**
Toxic waste, 8:**407–409**, 408–409
    air pollution, 6:361
    Love Canal, 4:504–505
    maquiladoras, 4:594
    pollution, 6:359–360
    water pollution, 6:364–365
Toynbee, Arthur, 2:247–248
Toyota Motor Corporation, 1:218,
    219, 220–221
Trace conditioning, 1:573
Traceability, 1:471
Tracking in schools, 8:**409–411**
    education in the U.S., 2:542
    resegregation of schools, 7:201
    school segregation, 7:388
A Tract on Monetary Reform (Keynes),
    1:449, 4:261
Tractatus (Wittgenstein), 6:9
Tracy, Antoine Destutt de, 3:559–570
Trade, 3:98, 6:97, 8:**411–413**
    automobile industry, 1:221–222
    beggar-thy-neighbor, 1:272–273
    Bhagwati, Jagdish, 1:293
    bourgeoisie, 1:361
    Castro, Fidel, 1:465–467
    cattle industry, 1:470–471
    Chinese diaspora, 1:515–516, 518
    Chinese Revolution, 1:519–520
    coffee industry, 1:594
    cosmopolitanism, 2:149

cotton industry, 2:152, 153
cumulative causation, 2:207
currency appreciation and
    depreciation, 2:210
currency devaluation and
    revaluation, 2:211
dependency theory, 2:299–300
development economics, 2:345
dirigiste, 2:373
Dornbusch-Fischer-Samuelson
    model, 2:437–438
Economic Commission for Latin
    America and the Caribbean,
    2:482–483
event studies, 3:30
exchange rates, 3:37–40
exoticism, 3:46
exports, 3:65–69
factory system, 3:76–77
financial markets, 3:147
Heckscher-Ohlin-Samuelson
    model, 3:448–449
imperfect competition, 2:53
imports, 3:590–591, 592,
    594–595
international economics,
    2:507–508, 4:92–94
Leontief, Wassily, 4:412, 413
macroeconomics, 4:540
mercantilism, 5:93–94
microelectronics industry, 5:138
Mundell-Fleming model,
    5:335–336
North-South models, 5:546–547
overlapping generations model,
    6:93–94
Postlethwayt, Malachy, 6:394
Prebisch, Raúl, 6:422–423
product dumping, 2:462
reciprocity, 7:105
retaliation, 7:216
Ricardo, David, 7:246
shipping industry, 7:198
Silk Road, 7:511
state capitalism, 1:444
steel industry, 8:130
subsistence agriculture, 8:206
sugar industry, 8:218–220
tariffs, 8:265–266
technological progress, 8:299
terms of, 6:423–425, 8:324–326
textile industry, 8:333–334
toxic waste, 8:408
urbanization, 8:546
wants, 9:16

    See also Exports; Imports; Slave
      trade
Trade, Anglo-Portuguese, 8:**413–414**
Trade, bilateral, 8:**414–415**
    Anglo-Portuguese trade, 8:413
    import promotion, 3:592
Trade, free. *See* Free trade
Trade, slave. *See* Slave trade
Trade, terms of. *See* Terms of trade
Trade agreements. *See* Trade
Trade agreements, neoimperialism,
    5:471
Trade associations, 8:513–514
Trade balance, 1:**241–242**
    balance of payments, 1:238–240
    central banks, 1:478
    currency appreciation and
      depreciation, 2:210
    described, 8:411–412
    exports, 3:67, 68–69
    Hume process, 3:520–521
    J-Curve, 4:179
    trade surplus, 8:417–418
Trade barriers, 1:**254–255**
    automobile industry, 1:221–222
    bilateral trade, 8:414–415
    common market, 2:29
    customs union, 2:215
    export penetration, 3:66
    exports, 3:68
    import penetration, 3:590, 591
    tariffs, 8:265–266
    tea industry, 8:289
    trade liberalization, 4:427–428
    trade quotas, 6:672–673
Trade creation. *See* Customs union
Trade cycle, nonlinear systems,
    5:523–524
Trade deficit, 8:**415–417**
    balance of payments, 1:238–240
    balance of trade, 1:241–242
    central banks, 1:480
    Corn Laws, 2:133–134
    Hume process, 3:520–521
    J-Curve, 4:179
Trade diversion. *See* Customs union
Trade liberalization, 4:**427–428**
    assessment, 8:411, 412–413
    Bhagwati, Jagdish, 1:293
    bilateral trade, 8:414–415
    capital controls, 1:432
    classical economics, 2:504
    convergence theory, 2:118
    Corn Laws, 2:133–134

exports, 3:69
physiocracy, 6:266
tariffs, 8:265–266
textile industry, 8:333–334
transitional economies, 2:533
Trade-offs, 8:**418–420**
inegalitarianism, 3:623–624
scarcity, 7:340
self-defeating behavior, 7:404–405
sex and mating, 7:471–472
Trade quotas, 6:**672–673**
tariffs, 8:265–266
trade barriers, 1:254–255
trade liberalization, 4:427
Trade surplus, 8:**417–418**
balance of payments, 1:238–240
balance of trade, 1:241–242
Hume process, 3:520–521
Trade unions. *See* Labor unions;
Unions
Traded goods, from nontraded goods,
3:349
Tradition, 8:**420–422**
conservatism, 2:83, 85, 86
Conservative Party (U.K.), 2:87
cultural rights, 2:197–198
ethnology and folklore, 3:17–18
leaders, 4:376
Lee, Robert E., 4:399
literature, 4:463
The Lonely Crowd (Riesman),
4:487
medicine, 5:63, 64–65
memory, 5:75
midwifery, 5:151–154
morality, 5:285
right wing, 7:247–248
storytelling, 8:160–161
Traditional action, 9:56
Traditional authority, 1:214, 6:68
Traditional societies, hallucinogens
and, 3:411, 412
Trafficking, drug. *See* Drug traffic
Trafficking, sexual. *See* Pimps;
Prostitution
The Tragedy of the Commons (Hardin),
8:**422–423**
common land, 2:27
laissez-faire, 4:337–338
legacy effects, 4:404
prisoner's dilemma, 6:472–474
resource economics, 7:211
Trager, Frank, 5:412
Trail of Broken Treaties (1973), 1:99
Trail of Tears, 1:497–498, 8:**423–424**

Training. *See* Education
Trait anxiety, 1:146
Trait inference, 8:**424**
Trait-situation controversy. *See* Person-
situation debate
Trait theory, 1:200, 8:**425–426**
crime and criminology, 2:172
Darwin, Charles, 2:228–229
identity, 3:553
leadership, 4:378–379
lying, 4:524
Mendel's law, 5:82–83
motivation, 5:301
person-situation debate,
6:225–226
personality, 6:217–218
self-esteem, 7:413
similarity/attraction theory, 7:514
stability in psychology, 8:75
temperament, 8:321–322
twin studies, 8:473–475
The Traitor (Dixon), 1:304
Trajectory analysis. *See* Growth curve
analysis
Trans-Atlantic cables, 2:152
Trans-Atlantic Slave Trade Database.
See Slave trade
Trans-disciplinary research, 7:**197–199**
music, 5:342–345
myth and mythology, 5:357
political sociology, 8:2–3
theory, 8:345
Transaction cost economics (TCE),
6:69
Transaction costs, 8:**426–427**
capital flight, 1:435
Coase, Ronald, 1:589
Coase theorem, 1:590
diplomacy, 2:371
externality, 3:70
import penetration, 3:590
Transaction taxes, 8:**427–428**
Tobin, James, 8:378, 379
transfer pricing, 8:428–429
Transactional leadership, 4:376, *376*,
380, 381
Transactions motive. *See* Demand for
money
Transcendentalism. *See* Buddhism
Transciptomics, 3:299
Transculturation, 2:170, 6:80, 81
Transfer of technology. *See* Technology
transfer
Transfer pricing, 8:**428–429**
Transfers, in vivo. *See* In vivo transfers

Transflective displays. *See* Symbols
Transformation, social. *See* Social
change
Transformation, structural,
2:344–346, 8:**180–181**
Transformation problem, 8:**429–431**
labor theory of value, 4:323–324
loss functions, 4:497
mathematics in the social sciences,
5:28
Transformational leadership, 4:376,
376, 381, 382
Transgender, 8:**431–432**
See also Gay, lesbian, transgender,
and bisexual politics
Transgression. *See* Sin
Transition, demographic. *See*
Demographic transition
Transition rituals. *See* Rites of passage
Transition theory, epidemiological. *See*
Disease; Morbidity and mortality
Transition to parenthood, 6:**134–135**
Brazelton, T. Berry, 1:369
motherhood, 5:297–299
rites of passage, 7:258
Transitional class, 1:362
Transitional economies, 2:**533–534**
development economics,
2:344–346
development in sociology, 2:347
ethnic diversity and, 2:342–343
Russian Federation, 7:302–303
state capitalism, 1:444
transitional conjunctures, 2:77–78
Yeltsin, Boris, 9:164
Transitions from Authoritarian Rule
(O'Donnell, Schmitter, and
Whitehead), 2:290
Transitory income, 4:442
Transjordan. *See* Jordan
Transmission, intergenerational. *See*
Intergenerational transmission
Transmission mechanism, 1:404, 407
Transnationalism, 8:**433–434**
banana industry, 1:245
Caribbean, 1:448–449
Chinese diaspora, 1:515, 516,
517, 518
citizenship, 1:543–544
codetermination, 1:593
coffee industry, 1:594
cooperatives, 2:124
corporations, 2:139–140
cosmopolitanism, 2:149
development economics, 2:345

Transnationalism, *continued*
  diaspora, 2:357
  energy industry, 2:590
  enterprise, 2:599
  exploitation, 3:65
  exports, 3:594*t,* 595
  growth, 2:139–140
  hybridity, 3:536
  immigration, 3:570, 575, 582
  imports, 3:594–595, 594*t*
  international nongovernmental
    organizations, 4:96–99
  interwar years, 4:121–122
  mining industry, 5:189
  national defense, 2:260, 262
  petroleum industry, 6:230, 231
  plantation economy model, 6:278
  political sociology, 8:5
  public policy, 9:73
  social movements, 7:606–607
  technology transfer, 8:309
  terrorism, 8:329–330
  transfer pricing, 8:428–429
  See also Globalization
Transparency, 8:**434–435**
  bureaucracy, 1:391, 392
  central banks, 1:479
  common land, 2:28
  cooperatives, 2:125
  corruption, 2:144
  institutional investors, 4:136
  League of Nations, 4:385
  managerial capitalism, 1:442
  monetary policy, 6:295
Transparency International (TI)
  bribery, 1:371
  corruption, 2:144, 145
  lying, 4:524
Transportation industry, 8:**435–439**
  Carter, Jimmy, 1:451
  civil rights movement, U.S., 1:551
  Congress of Racial Equality, 2:75
  cotton industry, 2:152
  desegregation, 2:314–315
  equal protection, 2:615
  Great Society programs,
    3:372–373
  metropolitan regions, 7:132, 134
  railway industry, 7:53–55
  tourism, 8:398
  tourism industry, 8:401
  trade barriers, 1:255
Transsexuals. *See* Transgender
Transvaal. *See* South Africa

Trauma, 8:**439–441**
  Holocaust, 3:497
  memory, 5:75
  stress, 8:173–175
  torture, 8:391–394
  zombies, 9:181
  See also Post-traumatic stress
Traumatic bonding, 8:**441–442**
Traumatic neuroses, 3:210
Traumatic stress disorder. *See* Post-
  traumatic stress; Trauma; Traumatic
  bonding
Travel and travel writing, 8:**442–444**
  Cook, James, 2:121–122
  tourism, 8:398–402
Trawlers, 3:152–153
Treas, Judith, 6:27
Treason, 1:397, 483, 2:244
Treasury Department, U.S., 3:413
Treasury view, 8:**444–445**
Treaties
  human rights, 3:512
  land claims, 4:341
  See also names of specific treaties
A Treatise on Money (Keynes), 1:247,
  450, 4:261
A Treatise on Probability (Keynes),
  4:260, 6:490
A Treatise on the Family (Becker),
  1:270, 271
Treaty constitutionalism. *See* Treaty
  federalism
Treaty federalism, 8:**445–446**
Treaty of 1855, 1:503
Treaty of 1863, 1:503
Treaty of Friendship, Co-operation
  and Mutual Assistance. *See* Warsaw
  Pact
Treaty of Guadalupe Hidalgo, 5:120,
  121, 128–129, 447
Treaty of London (1841), 1:73
Treaty of Nanking (1842), 6:46
Treaty of New Echota (1835), 1:497
Treaty of Paris (1783), 1:104
Treaty of Paris (1898), 9:23
Treaty of Rome (1957), 2:29
Treaty of Schönbrunn (1809), 5:365
Treaty of Tientsin (1858), 6:46
Treaty of Tordesillas (1494), 2:20
Treaty of Vereeniging (1902), 1:350
Treaty of Versailles (1919), 3:486,
  488, 4:385, 386, 9:147, 148
  See also Interwar years
Treaty of Westphalia (1648), 4:235
Treaty rights, 5:428

Treiman, Donald, 6:27
Treitschke, Heinrich von, 2:84
Trench war, 9:146
Trends, 8:**447–448**
Trends, time. *See* Time trends
Tressell, Robert, 4:517
Trevelyan, George Macaulay, 3:482
Trial and error learning. *See* Operant
  conditioning
The Trial of Henry Kissinger
  (Hitchens), 4:275
Triangularization, lower, 8:599
Triarchic theory of intelligence. *See*
  Intelligence; Multiple intelligences
  theory
Tribalism, 5:427–428, 8:**448–449**
  Deadly Identities, 3:551
  Hussein, Saddam, 3:533
  Ibn Khaldun, 3:545–546
  state, 8:104
  Turner, Victor, 8:470–472
Tribble, Romie, 4:297
Tribes, 8:**449–451**
  autocracy, 1:216
  caste, 1:458
  creamy layer, 2:161
  urbanization, 1:134
  Wolf, Eric, 9:106
Tribunals, military, 3:394
Tricyclic antidepressants, 1:147
Trigger, Bruce, 1:167
Trigueño, 8:**451–452**
Trilateral Commission, 8:**452–453,**
  454
Trilateralism, 8:452, 453–**454**
Trinidad
  blackness, 1:328, 330
  calypso, 1:417–419
  Cox, Oliver C., 2:157–158
  Creole, 2:169
  creolization, 2:170
  East Indian diaspora, 2:474
  James, C. L. R, 4:168
  Pan-Caribbeanism, 6:119–120
  Williams, Eric, 9:96–98
Trinidad Village (Herskovits and
  Herskovits), 3:467
Trinity, Holy. *See* Holy Trinity
Trinity (bomb), 9:48
Triplets. *See* Multiple births
Tripp, C. A., 6:434
TRIPS (Agreement on Trade-Related
  Aspects of Intellectual Property
  Rights), 9:143
Tristes tropiques (Lévi-Strauss), 4:416

Triumphalism, 8:454–455

Trobriand Islands, 1:127, 6:14, 29

Troglodytes (de Castelnau), 1:44

Troitzsch, Klaus, 2:61

Tronti, Mario, 1:447

Tropico en Manhattan (Cotto-Thorner), 5:552

Trostel, Philip, 8:369

Trotsky, Leon, 8:455–456
    Asiatic mode of production, 1:188
    managerial class, 4:579
    Mandel, Ernest, 4:579
    Russian Revolution, 7:304
    Stalin, Joseph, 8:86
    Stalinism, 8:87

Trotskyists. *See* Neoconservatism; Trotsky, Leon

Troubles. *See* Irish Republican Army (IRA)

Trouillot, Michel-Rolph, 8:457–458

Trubetzkoy, Nikolai, 4:417

Trucking industry. *See* Transportation industry

Trudeau, Pierre Elliott, 6:662
    See also Quebecois movement

True Levellers. *See* Levellers

Trujillo, Rafael Leónidas, 1:464

The Truly Disadvantaged (Wilson), 7:600

Truman, Harry S., 8:459–460, 613
    Central Intelligence Agency, U.S, 1:480–481, 485
    civil rights, 1:550
    Democratic Party (U.S.), 2:287
    desegregation, 2:315
    development in sociology, 2:346
    Dixiecrats, 2:428, 429, 430
    domino theory, 2:435
    Executive Order 10308, 5:384
    Jim Crow, 4:201
    Kefauver, Estes, 4:252
    Korean War, 4:289
    New Deal legacy, 5:498
    Nixon, Richard M., 5:505
    wage and price controls, 9:2
    White, Walter, 9:81

Truncation, left and right censoring, 1:473

Trust (economics), 4:330

Trust (psychology), 8:460–462
    child development, 1:507
    codetermination, 1:593
    Giddens, Anthony, 3:314–315
    leaders, 4:375–376
    political, 1:193

rotating savings and credit associations, 7:287
    rumors, 7:297–298
    social, voluntary assocations, 1:193

Trust in Numbers: The Pursuit of Objectivity in Science and Public Life (Porter), 6:655

Trustee Council (UN), 8:523

Trusteeship model, 1:476

Trusts, business, 1:144

Les trusts américains (Lafargue), 4:330

Truth. *See* Reality

Truth, Sojourner, 4:114–115, 8:462

Truth and Method (Gadamer), 3:462, 9:78

Truth and reconciliation commissions, 8:462–464
    described, 7:110
    Machel, Samora, 4:532–533
    segregation, 7:382

Truth in Lending Act (U.S. 1968), 2:103

Tryptophan. *See* Serotonin

Tsalagi, 1:497

Tse-Tung, Mao. *See* Mao Zedong

Tsebelis, George, 9:71

Tsigani. *See* Roma

TSS (Total sum of squares), 6:60

Tsunamis, 5:433
    See also Disaster management; Natural disasters

Tuan, Mia, 1:514

Tubman, Harriet, 8:464–465

Tucker, Josiah, 3:521

Tuekakas, 1:503

Tugan-Baranovsky, Mikhail I., 1:12, 7:299

Tulip Mania. *See* Great Tulip Mania

Tulips, 3:158, 375

Tulsa, Oklahoma, 1:328

Tulsa Riot (1921), 4:200, 8:465–466

Tumin, Melvin, 1:563

Tunisia, 1:139, 8:602

Ture, Kwame. *See* Black nationalism; Black Power; Carmichael, Stokely

Turgot, Jacques, 8:466–467
    Cantillion, Richard, 1:429
    Condorct, Marquis de, 2:66
    long period analysis, 4:489
    marginal product of labor, 4:305

Turing, Alan, 1:278–279

Turing test, 1:278–279

Turkey
    Church and state, 1:536

civilization, 1:558
    Cuba, 2:184
    ethnic conflict, 3:2
    gender gap, 3:278
    genocide, 3:296
    land fertility, 3:130–131
    NATO, 5:545
    veiling, 8:602

Turkmenistan, 2:30

Turn, linguistic. *See* Linguistic turn

Turner, Bryan S., 2:510

Turner, John C., 2:71

Turner, Nat, 8:467–468
    Black Power, 1:321
    slave resistance, 7:534, 536

Turner, Ralph H., 7:276

Turner, Victor, 7:257, 8:468–471, 470
    midlife crisis, 5:149
    rites of passage, 7:257
    symbols, 8:252

Turnpike theorems, 6:51

Turntablism. *See* Hip hop

Turntaking, 2:118, 119

Tuskegee syphilis study, 8:472–473
    ethics in experimentation, 2:635
    human experiments, 3:60
    informed consent, 4:33
    institutional review board, 4:42

Tutors, 8:527

Tutsis, 3:2, 10, 298

Tutu, Desmond, 1:148
    See also Apartheid; Mandela, Winnie

TVA (Tennessee Valley Authority), 5:494

Tversky, Amos, 1:526, 2:251, 5:519, 6:56
    behavioral economics, 2:500
    maximization, 5:40–41
    See also Rationality

Tweed, Boss. *See* Tweed, William

Tweed, William, 1:452, 5:377

Twelve-step model, 1:22

Twenty-First Century Nanotechnology Research and Development Act (U.S. 2003), 5:362

Twi culture, virgins, 8:630

Twice-born *(dvijas)*, 8:567–568

Twin studies, 8:473–475
    heredity, 3:461
    intelligence, 7:22
    IQ controversy, 4:139–140
    nature *vs.* nurture, 5:446
    psychological depression, 2:307
    Scarr, Sandra Wood, 7:340–341

Twin studies, *continued*
 sexual orientation, 7:476–477
Twins. *See* Multiple births
Two-department model of
 reproduction, 8:563
Two-dimensional vectors, 8:600–601
Two-party system, voting, 8:647
Two-person theory, game theory,
 3:250
Two-play ultimatum games,
 5:483–484
Two-sector models, 8:475–476,
 563–564
 See also Harris-Todaro model
Two-sided flow, 5:400–401
Two-stage least squares (2SLS), 4:394,
 395–396
Two-state solution, 8:476–478
Two Treatises of Government (Locke),
 3:120, 4:476, 5:439, 8:526
A Two-Year-Old Goes to Hospital
 (film), 1:363
2SLS (Two-stage least squares). *See*
 Two-stage least squares (2SLS)
Tylor, Edward B., 1:114, 119,
 121–122, 127
 archaeology, 1:166
 culture, 2:203
 Standard Cross-Cultural Sample,
 8:88–92
Type, ideal. *See* Ideal type
Type A/type B personality, 6:218,
 223–225
Typhoons, 5:433
Tyranny. *See* Totalitarianism
Tyranny of the majority, 8:478–479
 individualism, 3:619
 majoritarianism, 4:558–559
 majorities, 4:560
 majority rule, 4:560–561
 representative and participatory
 democracy, 2:284
Tyson, Karolyn, 6:48
Tyson, Laura D'Andrea, 2:124–125
Tyson, Mike, 8:611
Tzars, 1:216

U

U-curves, environmental. *See*
 Environmental Kuznets curves
UAR (United Arab Republic),
 5:376–377, 8:**520–522**
UAW (United Auto Workers), 1:220,
 493, 3:285–286, 4:302
Übermensch. *See* Nietzsche, Friedrich

UC Regents v. Bakke (1978). *See*
 Grutter decision (1978)
UDC (United Daughters of the
 Confederacy), 8:619
UDHR (Universal Declaration of
 Human Rights). *See* Universal
 Declaration of Human Rights
UDV (União de Vegetal), 3:412
UFOs (Unidentified flying objects),
 8:**506–509**
UFWA (United Farm Workers of
 America), 1:493–494, 552, 5:155
Uganda
 African Crisis Response Initiative,
 1:38
 Ainsworth, Mary, 1:67
 Amin, Idi, 1:109–110
 coffee industry, 1:594
 Museveni, Yoweri, 5:341
 Obote, Apollo Milton, 6:12–13
Uganda National Liberation Army
 (UNLA), 1:110
Uganda People's Congress (UPC),
 6:12
UGCC (United Gold Coast
 Convention), 1:140
Uhle, Max, 1:166
Ujamaa, villagization. *See* Socialism,
 African
U.K. *See* United Kingdom (U.K.)
Ukraine
 commonwealth, 2:30
 judicial review, 4:225
 land reform, 4:343, 344
Ulbricht, Walter, 1:289
Ulianov, Vladimir. *See* Lenin, Vladimir
 Ilitch
Ullman, Richard, 5:412
Umayyad caliphate, 1:159–160
Umkhonto we Sizwe (African National
 Congress), 1:148
UN (United Nations). *See* United
 Nations (UN)
UN Emergency Force (UNEF I),
 8:524
UN-Habitat, 8:546
Unanimity, 1:525
The Uncertainties of Knowledge
 (Wallerstein), 9:10
Uncertainty, 8:481–482
 choice in economics, 1:524, 525
 conformity, 2:72
 constrained choice, 2:95
 Dawes, Robyn, 2:245
 destabilization, 2:320

environmental impact assessment,
 2:606–607
 expectations, 3:47, 48
 general equilibrium, 3:284
 liquidity premium, 4:460–461
 maximin principle, 5:38–39
 parental, 5:440
 risk, 7:252, 254–255
 rumors, 7:295, 297
 shocks, 7:500
 statistical inference, 4:16
 technological change, 1:491
 time preference, 8:370
*Uncertainty and the Welfare Economics
 of Medical Care* (Arrow), 3:440
Uncle Tom, 8:**482–483**
 Bamboozled, 1:244
 ingratiation, 4:34
 malinchistas, 4:565
 self-hatred, 7:416
Uncle Tom's Cabin (Stowe),
 8:161–162, 482–483
Unconditioned response. *See* Classical
 conditioning
Unconditioned stimulus. *See* Classical
 conditioning
Unconscious
 creativity, 2:165
 Freud, Sigmund, 3:211–212, 215
 See also Consciousness;
 Psychoanalytic theory;
 Psychotherapy
Underachievers, 8:**483–485**
 defined, 6:87
 motivation, 5:301
Underclass, 8:**485–488**
 Gans, Herbert J., 3:256
 globalization, 9:100–101
 IQ controversy, 4:141–142
 Jencks, Christopher, 4:184
 lumpenproletariat, 4:516–517
 Marx, Karl, 3:82
 neighborhood effects, 5:462
 social exclusion, 7:588
 vagabonds, 8:567
 Wilson, William Julius, 8:485,
 486, 9:100
Underconsumption, 1:110, 2:106,
 109, 8:**488–489**
Underdeveloped countries. *See*
 Developing countries
Underdevelopment, 1:110, 8:**489–491**
 dependency theory, 2:298–300
 development economics, 2:344,
 346

development in sociology, 2:347

Economic Commission for Latin
America and the Caribbean,
2:482

ethnic diversity and, 2:343

Prebisch, Raúl, 6:422–423

Rodney, Walter, 7:269–270

third world, 8:352

See also Developing countries

Undereating, 8:**491–492**

body image, 1:346

malnutrition, 4:567–568

self-constrained behavior, 1:274

Underemployment, 8:**492–493**

defined, 8:494

self-employment, 7:411

surplus labor, 4:308

total, 8:500–501

See also Unemployment

Underemployment rate, 8:**493–495**

See also Unemployment rate

Underground economy. *See* Informal
economy

Underground Railroad, 1:545,
8:464–465

Underhill, Tolman v. (1955), 8:387

Underinsured persons, 5:396

Undernutrition. *See* Malnutrition

Underrepresentation, 8:**495–496**

Undersaving. *See* Saving rate

Understanding Comics (McCloud),
2:23

Underwater archaeology, 1:117

Underworld. *See* Hell

Undiscounted case, 6:51

UNDP. *See* United Nations
Development Program (UNDP)

UNEF I (UN Emergency Force),
8:524

Unemployable, 8:**496–497**

Unemployment, 8:**497–499**

aggregate supply, 1:54

banana parable, 1:247

Barro-Grossman model,
1:255–256

Beveridge curve, 1:292

blue collar and white collar, 1:339

carrying cost, 1:450

causes, 8:501–504

central banks, 1:478

Chamberlain, Neville, 1:489

cities, 1:541, 542

classical, 8:503

crowding hypothesis, 2:182

cyclical, 3:227, 8:502

dalits, 2:222

defined, 8:493

development economics, 2:344

disguised, 8:492, 497–498

economics of control, 2:532

frictional, 3:225, 227, 8:498, 502

Great Depression, 3:367, 369,
5:494, 8:500, 502, 503

happiness, 3:418–419

hard-core unemployed, 3:421–423

Harris-Todaro model, 3:428

human fertility, 3:128

inflation, 3:226, 4:25–26

involuntary, 3:226, 4:137–139,
259, 8:18, 498, 502–504

Kahn, Richard F., 4:245

Keynes, John Maynard, 4:260,
9:13

Keynesian economics, 2:511–512

labor economics, 2:514

labor force participation,
4:314–315

macroeconomics, 4:540

Malthus, Thomas Robert, 4:571

mass, 8:503

Moynihan Report, 5:305–306

Native Americans, 5:448

natural rate of, 3:218, 5:435–437,
8:499, 503

neighborhoods, 5:462, 463

neutral rate of interest, 4:79

New Deal, 5:495

Okun's law, 6:35–36

Operation Bootstrap, 6:45

Phillips curve, 6:248–250

racial discrimination, 2:405

rate of, 1:292, 8:499–505, *500*

stable nodes, 5:510

stagflation, 8:82

stocks and flows, 8:158

structural, 3:227, 8:502

subsidies, 8:203

surplus labor, 4:308

tariffs, 8:265

technological change, 1:490

trade-offs, 8:419

Treasury view, 8:444–445

underclass, 8:485–487

unemployability, 8:496–497

voluntary, 3:225, 4:259, 8:498,
502–504, 636–637

Walras' law, 9:13

See also Discouraged workers;
Social exclusion

Unemployment compensation,
2:49–50

Unemployment rate, 1:292,
8:**499–505**, *500*

UNEP (United Nations Environment
Programme), 8:408

Unequal development. *See* Unequal
exchange

Unequal education, 1:94, 2:**537–539**,
7:351

Brown v. Board of Education
(1954), 1:373–376

Brown v. Board of Education
(1955), 1:377

California Civil Rights Initiative,
1:416

civil rights, 1:549

civil rights movement, U.S., 1:551

Clark, Kenneth B., 1:560, 561

creaming, 2:160

curriculum, 2:214–215

digital divide, 2:366–367

education in the U.S., 2:539–545

Houston, Charles Hamilton,
3:505

Jencks, Christopher, 4:184–185

Jim Crow, 4:200, 201

mobility, 5:210–211

qualifications, 6:649–650

quotas, 6:671

race, 7:16–18

returns to education, 7:66

teacher expectations, 8:290–291

tracking in schools, 8:409–410

U.S., 7:351

Wells-Barnett, Ida B., 9:76

See also School desegregation;
School segregation

Unequal exchange, 8:**505–506**

dependency theory, 2:299, 300

development economics, 2:345

Economic Commission for Latin
America and the Caribbean,
2:482

industrialization, 3:621

Prebisch, Raúl, 6:422–423

Prebisch-Singer hypothesis,
6:423–425

structuralist macroeconomics,
4:544

terms of trade, 8:325–326

UNESCO (United Nations
Educational, Scientific, and Cultural
Organization), 3:512

Unexpected inflation, natural rate of
unemployment, 5:436

UNHCR (United Nations High Commissioner for Refugees), 7:124, 126, 168

UNIA (Universal Negro Improvement Association and African Communities League), 1:315–316, 320, 321, 328, 3:258, 259

União de Vegetal (UDV), 3:412

Unicameralism. *See* Bicameralism

UNICEF (United Nations Children's Fund)
    homelessness, 3:499
      National Family Health Surveys, 5:392

Unidentified flying objects (UFOs), **8:506–509**

UNIDO (United Nations Industrial Development Organization), 8:50

Uniform Bertrand's Paradox. *See* Uniform distribution

Uniform distribution, 2:*418*, **418–419**, 6:494

Unilateralism, 1:296, 297, **8:509–510**

Unilinealism, 1:137

Uninsured persons, 5:396

Unintended treatments, 8:574

Union, European. *See* European Union (EU)

Union of Soviet Socialist Republics (U.S.S.R.), **8:510–513**
    Afghan war, 7:606–607
    agricultural industry, 1:61
    appeasement, 1:153
    Arab-Israeli War of 1967, 1:154
    arms control, 1:176
    arms race, 1:178
    Bahro, Rudolf, 1:237
    Bay of Pigs, 1:262
    Berlin Wall, 1:289
    bilateralism, 1:297
    bin Laden, Osama, 1:298
    Brezhnev, Leonid, 1:369–370
    Bush, George H. W., 1:398
    Carter, Jimmy, 1:451
    Castro, Fidel, 1:465–466
    Central Intelligence Agency, U.S, 1:481, 483
    Chiang Kai-shek, 1:499
    Chinese Revolution, 1:520, 521
    Churchill, Winston, 1:538
    civil disobedience, 1:545
    civilization, 1:558
    Cold War, 2:4–5
    collectivism, 2:11
    commonwealth, 2:30
    concentration camps, 2:64
    conservatism, 2:85, 86
    convergence theory, 2:117
    corporations, 2:140
    Cuban Missile Crisis, 2:183–185
    Cuban Revolution, 2:186–187
    cult of personality, 6:222–223
    decolonization, 2:255, 256
    defense, 2:258
    deterrence, 2:333–334
    dialectical materialism, 5:21–23
    dictatorship, 2:359
    dissidents, 2:411
    distributive justice, 4:239
    domino theory, 2:434–436
    drought, 2:448
    fall of, 3:241, 350–351, 5:417–418, 8:512–513
    glasnost, 3:324–325, 351, 8:512
    gulags, 3:396, 8:29
    hegemony, 3:455
    history, 8:510–513
    Hungarian Revolution, 3:523–524
    Hussein, Saddam, 3:532, 534
    iron curtain, 1:538, 2:5, 35–36, 4:150
    James, C. L. R., 4:168
    Kennedy, John F., 4:254, 255
    Khrushchev, Nikita, 4:264–265
    Kissinger, Henry, 4:274, 275
    Korean War, 4:289
    Ladejinsky, Wolf, 4:327–328
    legal systems, 4:405, 406
    Lenin, Vladimir Ilitch, 4:410–411
    Leninism, 4:411–412
    managerial class, 4:578, 579
    market socialism, 7:644–646
    Marxism, 4:638–639
    Molotov-Rubbentrop Pact, 9:149
    mutual deterrence, 2:334–335
    nationalism, 5:417–418
    NATO, 5:546
    nuclear weapons, 9:30, 31–32, 48, 49
    peaceful coexistence, 6:186–188
    petroleum industry, 6:231
    propaganda and civil rights, 1:550
    Russian Federation, 7:302–303
    separatism, 7:450
    socialism, 7:638
    sociology, Moore, Barrington, 5:278
    Solzhenitsyn, Aleksandr, 8:29
    Spanish Civil War, 8:43–44
    Stalin, Joseph, 8:86
    Stalinism, 8:87–88
    state capitalism, 1:443–444
    state enterprise, 8:106–107
    third world, 8:351
    totalitarianism, 8:395
    United Nations membership, 8:522
    Vietnam War, 8:612–613
    visual arts, 8:632
    Warsaw Pact, 9:34–36
    weapons industry, 9:50
    World War II, 9:149
    Yeltsin, Boris, 9:163–164
    Zionism, 9:180
    See also Communism; Russia

Union shop. *See* Labor law

Unions, **8:513–517**
    agricultural, 6:74
    common market, 2:28–29
    Confederate States of America, 2:66–67
    crowding hypothesis, 2:181, 182
    customs, 2:215–216
      common market, 2:29
      confederations, 2:68
      Meade, James, 5:49
    monetary, 3:39, 5:251
    See also European Union (EU); Labor unions

Uniqueness, false, 3:388

Unit root regression, 1:228, **8:517–520**

Unit rule, 2:559

Unitarianism, Alger, Horatio, 1:72

Unitary government, 3:355, **359**
    decentralization, 2:250
    democratic centralism, 2:285, 286
    politics, 6:321
    voting schemes, 8:655

United Arab Emirates
    Gulf Cooperation Council, 3:397
    OPEC, 6:65

United Arab Republic (UAR), 5:376–377, **8:520–522**

United Arab States, 8:521, 522

United Auto Workers (UAW), 1:220, 493, 3:285–286, 4:302

United Black Movement. *See* Movimento Negro Unificado

United Daughters of the Confederacy (UDC), 8:619

United Empire Loyalists, 4:508–509

United Farm Workers of America (UFWA), 1:493–494, 552, 5:155

United Farm Workers Organizing Committee. *See* United Farm Workers of America (UFWA)

United Gold Coast Convention (UGCC), 1:140

United Irishmen, 4:509

United Keetoowah Band, 1:496, 497

United Kingdom (U.K.)

abortion, 1:2

agriculture, 3:164

American Revolution, 1:103–104

Amin, Idi, 1:109

Anglo-Portuguese trade, 8:413

anthropology, 1:127–128

appeasement, 1:152–153

architecture, 1:170

aristocracy, 1:174

arms control, 1:176

banana parable, 1:247–248

banking industry, 1:251

Bentham, Jeremy, 1:285–286

bequests, 1:286

bioterrorism, 1:302

blackface, 1:326, 327

blue collar and white collar, 1:340

Boer War, 1:348–350

calypso, 1:417, 418

Cambridge University, 1:419, 421–423

capitalist mode of production, 1:446

caste, 1:460, 461, 462

census, 1:476–477

centrism, 1:489

cleavages, 1:578

colonialism

Bentham, Jeremy, 1:286

Burke, Edmund, 1:396

caste, 1:461, 462, 463

Hall, Stuart, 3:408–409

Jordan, 3:530–531

Nasser, Gamal Abdel, 5:376

Nehru, Jawaharlal, 5:460

commonwealth, 2:29–30

concentration camps, 2:63

confiscation, 2:69

Congress of Vienna (1814-1815), 9:145

conservatism, 2:83, 84, 86

constituency, 2:90

constitutions, 2:94, 5:238

Corn Laws, 2:133–134, 3:200, 5:177

correspondence tests, 2:141–142

cotton industry, 2:152

cultural resource management, 2:196, 197

cultural studies, 2:199, 200

currency devaluation and revaluation, 2:211

decentralization, 2:250

democracy, 2:273, 274

democratic centralism, 2:286

desegregation, 2:315

East Indian diaspora, 2:471–475

empire, 2:575, 576

engineering education, 2:594

ethnicity, 3:10–11

Fabianism, 3:73, 74

factory system, 3:77

Falkland Islands war, 2:87, 3:80–81, 171, 8:335

first-past-the-post electoral systems, 3:150

gender gap, 2:142–143

gerrymandering, 3:309

goodwill, 3:350

Great Depression, 3:367, 368, 369

Hall, Stuart, 3:408–410

health economics, 3:440, 441

hot money, 3:504

humanism, 3:517–518

imperialism, 3:589

Indian National Army, 3:610–611

indirect rule, 3:617–618

industrial accidents, 1:8

industrialization, 3:620

integration, 4:62

jingoism, 4:201–202

Jinnah, Mohammed Ali, 4:203–204

judiciary, 4:227

jury selection, 4:233, 234

Kenyatta, Jomo, 4:256

Kuznets hypothesis, 4:295, 296

land claims, 4:340–341

landlords, 4:345, 346

lender of last resort, 4:410

Liberal Party, 1:537, 2:87, 4:423–424

liberalism, 4:425

literature, 4:463

lobbying, 4:474

Lombard Street (Bagehot), 4:485

loyalists, 4:509

Luddites, 4:513–515

Macmillan, Harold, 4:538

managed competition, 2:54

Marxian economics, 2:516

Mau Mau, 5:36–38

monarchies, 5:237, 238, 240, 241

Napoleonic Wars, 5:365, 366, 367–369

national defense, 2:260

Native Americans, 5:426

NATO, 5:544–546

naval supremacy, 3:171

neoimperialism, 5:470

nouveaux riches, 5:548

Opium Wars, 6:45–46

Pan-Caribbeanism, 6:119–120

Pax Britannica, 6:179

pluralism, 6:282

political parties, 6:307

poll tax, 6:353

postcolonialism, 6:392–393

qualifications, 6:650

Quebecois movement, 6:661

Radcliffe-Brown, A. R., 7:47

railway industry, 7:53–54

Raj, 7:55–57

repression, 7:175

Ricardo, David, 7:242–243

Royal Commissions, 7:291–292

social history, 3:482

socialism, 1:113

socialized medicine, 5:65–66

Stolen Generations, 8:158–159

Suez Crisis, 5:376–377, 8:213–214

Tawney, R. H., 8:272

tax credits, 8:274–275

tax revolts, 8:278

taxes, 8:281

telecommunications industry, 8:315

television, 8:320

Thompson, Edward P., 8:353–356

Treasury view, 8:444–445

treaty federalism, 8:446

unemployment compensation, 2:49

unitary government, 3:359

United Nations membership, 8:522

University of Oxford, 1:421, 422, 8:527–529

urban sprawl, 8:540

voting patterns, 8:650

welfare state, 9:69

Wholesale Price Index, 9:94

women's work, 9:125

World War I, 9:145–147

World War II, 9:148–149

xenophobia, 9:161

United Kingdom (U.K.), *continued*
    See also names of prime ministers,
    political parties and specific
    countries
United Nations (UN), **8:522–525**
  anticolonial movements, 1:140,
    2:256
  bilateralism, 1:297
  Bush, George W., 1:399
  Castro, Fidel, 1:467
  census, 1:477
  children, 1:511, 512–513
  citizenship, 1:543
  civil rights, 1:546, 550
  civil wars, 1:554, 556
  clash of civilizations, 1:559
  cooperatives, 2:124
  corporal punishment, 2:135
  cultural rights, 2:198
  Darfur, 2:226, 227
  Decade for Women, 9:108, 110
  decolonization, 2:256
  defense, 2:259
  deforestation, 2:262–263
  depopulation, 2:301
  development theory, 2:338
  diamond industry, 2:355–356
  diplomacy, 2:370, 371
  disarmament, 2:379, 380
  enterprise, 2:599
  General Assembly, 8:522–523,
    524
  genocide convention, 3:296–297,
    298
  Gulf War of 1991, 3:398
  health in developing countries,
    3:442
  history, 3:361, 9:149–150
  human rights, 1:548–549, 3:512,
    513, 514, 8:524
  Human Rights Commission,
    8:524
  input-output matrix, 4:41
  International Court of Justice,
    3:360, 8:523
  International Covenant on Civil
    and Political Rights, 1:546,
    9:108, 110
  International Covenant on
    Economic, Social and Cultural
    Rights (1966), 1:225
  internationalism, 4:102–103
  Iraq-U.S. War, 4:145, 146
  just war, 4:235
  Khmer Rouge, 4:263
  Killing Fields, 4:263

  Korean War, 4:289
  League of Nations, 4:386
  liberation, 4:429
  malnutrition, 4:567–568
  membership, 5:378
  Millennium Development Goals,
    3:273, 8:525, 9:39–40
  multisector models, 5:334
  "Oil for Food" program, 8:524
  peace, 6:181–182
  positivism, 6:389, 390
  poverty, 6:405–407
  Qadhafi, Muammar al, 6:648
  refugee camps, 7:124–125
  refugees, 7:125–127
  repatriation, 7:168, 169
  reproductive rights, 7:183
  Resolution 678, 8:524
  Resolution 1514, 8:524
  Secretariat, 8:523
  Statement by Experts on Problems of
    Race, 9:86
  System of National Accounts,
    5:397
  technology transfer, 8:308–309
  Thant, U., 8:334
  torture, 8:392
  Trustee Council, 8:523
  two-state solution, 8:477
  "Uniting for Peace" resolution,
    8:524
  urbanization, 8:546
  USSR, 8:511
  Washington Consensus, 9:39
  as world government, 3:360
  xenophobia, 9:160, 161
  Yugoslavian civil war, 9:168
United Nations Centre for Human
  Settlements (Habitat), 3:499
United Nations Children's Fund
  (UNICEF)
  homelessness, 3:499
  National Family Health Surveys,
    5:392
United Nations Conference on
  International Organizations, 9:150
United Nations Convention on the
  Rights of the Child (1989), 1:511,
  512
United Nations Declaration of
  Human Rights (1948), 5:456
United Nations Declaration on the
  Rights of Indigenous Peoples
  (1994), 5:429
United Nations Development Program
  (UNDP), 7:91

  economic inequality, 9:46–47
  gender gap, 3:278
  Washington Consensus, 9:39
  water resources, 9:40
  women, 9:110, 112
United Nations Economic and Social
  Council
  gender mainstreaming, 3:275
  role, 8:523
United Nations Economic
  Commission for Latin America
  (EDLA). *See* Economic
  Commission for Latin America and
  the Caribbean (ECLAC)
United Nations Educational,
  Scientific, and Cultural
  Organization (UNESCO), 3:512
United Nations Environment
  Programme (UNEP), 8:408
United Nations Framework on
  Climate Change, 3:378
United Nations High Commissioner
  for Refugees (UNHCR), 7:124,
  126, 168
United Nations Industrial
  Development Organization
  (UNIDO), 8:530
United Nations International Labour
  Organization (ILO). *See*
  International Labour Organization
  (ILO)
United Nations Millennium
  Declaration (2000), 3:442
United Nations Monetary and
  Financial Conference. *See* Bretton
  Woods Agreement
United Nations Office on Drugs and
  Crime (UNODC), 3:412
United Nations Security Council,
  8:523, 524
  Commission for Conventional
    Armaments, 9:52
  Resolution 242, 1:159
United Nations University, 8:656
United Nations World Conference on
  Human Rights, 3:431
United Nations World Health
  Organization. *See* World Health
  Organization (WHO)
United States, New York Times Co. v.
  (1971), 1:475
United States (U.S.), 3:309, 4:1, 2–3
  abortion law, 1:2–3, 3–4
  accountability, 1:10
  activism, 1:18
  administrative law, 1:23
  advertising, 1:28–29

affirmative action, 1:31
African burial grounds, 1:393–394
African Crisis Response Initiative, 1:37–38
agenda setting, 1:48
air pollution, 6:362
Allende, Salvador, 1:77–78
Alzheimer's disease, 1:89
American National Election Studies, 1:100
annexation of Texas, 1:115
anthropology, 1:136–138
    Benedict, Ruth, 1:282
    Boas, Franz, 1:344–345
    Castaneda, Carlos, 1:456–457
    Herskovits, Melville J., 3:466–467
    Hurston, Zora Neale, 3:526–528
    Lévi-Strauss, Claude, 4:416–417
    Lowie, Robert, 4:507–508
    Mad, Margaret, 5:47
    Mintz, Sidney W., 5:195–196
    Montagu, Ashley, 5:273–274
    natives, 5:429–430
    urban, 1:135
anti-intellectualism, 4:64–65, 65
antitrust law, 1:143, 144–145
apportionment, 1:154–155
appropriations, 1:155
architecture, 1:170
arms control, 1:176
arms race, 1:178
Aryan Nations movement, 1:185–186
Asian American politics, 6:321–323
assimilation, 1:188–191
automobile industry, 1:218–219, 220, 221–222, 3:167–169
balance of payments, 1:*239t*
ballots, 1:242
banana industry, 1:245, 246
banking industry, 1:251, 252–253
Battle of the Little Big Horn, 1:258–259
bauxite industry, 1:261
Bay of Pigs, 1:262
beggar-thy-neighbor, 1:273
Benjamin, Judah P., 1:284–285
bequests, 1:286
bilateralism, 1:297
Bill of Rights, 1:297–298

bioterrorism, 1:301–302
birth control, 1:303
Black Arts Movement, 1:309–310
black capitalism, 1:439–442
black conservatism, 1:310–311
black liberalism, 1:312
black nationalism, 1:315
Black Panthers, 1:318–320
Black Power, 1:320–322
black towns, 1:325–326
blackface, 1:326–327
blackness, 1:328–329
Blau, Peter M., 1:331–332
blood and bloodline, 1:336
blue collar and white collar, 1:338, 340
bourgeoisie, 1:361
Bracero Program, 1:364–365
brain drain, 1:367–368
Brown v. Board of Education (1954), 1:373–376
Brown v. Board of Education (1955), 1:377
bubbles (economics), 1:378, 379
Buddhism, 1:384
bull and bear markets, 1:386
burial grounds, 1:393
Burr, Aaron, 1:397–398
California Civil Rights Initiative, 1:416
Campbell, Angus, 1:424–425
Carter, Jimmy, 1:451
casino capitalism, 1:455
Castro, Fidel, 1:465, 466–467
cattle industry, 1:470
censorship, 1:475–476
census, 1:476–477
Central Intelligence Agency, U.S, 1:480–485
centrism, 1:489
checks and balances, 1:495–496
Chiang Kai-shek, 1:499
Chicago School, 1:502–503
Chinese Revolution, 1:520, 521
Chomsky, Noam, 1:529
Church and state, 1:534–536
Churchill, Winston, 1:538
civil disobedience, 1:545, 546
civil liberties, 1:548
civil rights, 1:549, 550
civil rights movement, 1:551–552
clash of civilizations, 1:559
class structure, 9:133
cleavages, 1:578
clientelism, 1:578–579

cliometrics, 1:581–582
coalition, 1:587
coffee industry, 1:594, 595
cognition, 1:597–598
cognitive dissonance, 1:601
Cold War, 2:4–5
colonialism, 2:12
colorism, 2:17–18
Columbus, Christopher, 2:21–22
comic books, 2:23–24
commonwealth, 2:29
competition, 2:52
computers, 2:60
concentration camps, 2:63–64
Confederate States of America, 2:66–67
confederations, 2:68
confiscation, 2:69
Congress, U.S., 2:73–74
Congress of Racial Equality, 2:75
conservatism, 2:83, 84–86, 3:80, 7:606
constituency, 2:89–90
Constitution, 2:90–92
constitutional courts, 2:93
consumer protection, 2:103
consumption, 2:107–109
contact hypothesis, 2:111–112
contraception, 2:114–115, 3:89, 90
copper industry, 2:130–131
corporations, 2:139–140
correspondence tests, 2:142
cotton industry, 2:151, 152
counterterrorism, 2:155
creationism, 2:161–163
credentialism, 2:166–167
crime and criminology, 2:173
crony capitalism, 2:180
cross of gold, 2:180–181
Cuban Missile Crisis, 2:183–185
Cuban Revolution, 2:185–186
cults, 2:188–189
cultural resource management, 2:196, 197
cultural studies, 2:200
culture of poverty, 2:206
cumulative causation, 2:207
currency, 2:209
currency appreciation and depreciation, 2:210
currency devaluation and revaluation, 2:211
Current Population Survey, 2:212–213, 213

United States (U.S.), *continued*

curriculum, 2:213–215

Dahl, Robert Alan, 2:219–220

Daughters of the American Revolution, 2:241–242

dealignment, 2:246–247

death and dying, 2:248

death-qualified jurors, 4:233

decentralization, 2:250

Declaration of Independence, U.S., 2:254–255

decolonization, 2:255, 257

defense, 2:258

defense spending, 9:50

democracy, 2:273–274

democratic centralism, 2:286

Democratic Party (U.S.), 2:286–288

desegregation, 2:313–315

deterrence, 2:333–334

developing countries, 2:335, 336

development and ethnic diversity, 2:343

direct action, 2:372

dirty float, 2:375

disaster management, 2:381–382

discouraged workers, 2:386–387

divestiture, 2:421

divorce and separation, 2:426–427

Dixiecrats, 2:428–431

documentary studies, 2:433–434

domino theory, 2:434–436

Dred Scott v. Sanford, 2:445–446

drought, 2:448

drug traffic, 2:450–452

drugs of abuse, 2:452–456, 453*t*, 455*t*

due process, 2:461

East Indian diaspora, 2:474–475

economic crises, 2:483, 484, 485

economic depression, 2:302, *303*

education, 7:69–75, 71*t*, 73*t*, 74*t*

Ellis Island, 2:567–569

empire, 2:574, 576, 577

employment, 2:580, 581

energy industry, 2:588–590

engineering, 2:594

entertainment industry, 2:600–603

environmental impact assessment, 2:605–607

equal opportunity, 2:612–613

equity markets, 2:624

ethnic enterprises, 3:4–5

eugenics, 3:21, 22

exit poll, 3:45–46

exports, 3:594*t*

family farms, 1:61

family structure, 3:90–94, 91*t*, 92*t*, 93*t*

family structure changes, 3:93–94

fatherhood, 3:105–106

Federal Reserve System, 3:110–111, 112–113

federalism, 3:113–115, 358–359

female-headed families, 3:116

feminism, 3:120–121, 122–124

filibuster, 3:138–139

fishing industry, 3:152

flower industry, 3:158–159

foreign reserves, 7:202–203

full capacity, 3:224

full employment, 3:227–228

gay, lesbian, transgender, and bisexual politics, 6:330–331

gender gap, 3:278

gerrymandering, 3:308–309

ghettos, 3:312–313

Gilded Age, 3:318–319

going native, 3:338–339

gold mining, 3:342

gold standard, 3:343

goodwill, 3:350

Great Depression, 3:367–369, 370

Gulf War of 1991, 3:397–398

hallucinogens, 3:411–412

Hartz, Louis, 3:429–430

hate crimes, 3:430–431

Head Start, 3:437–438

Head Start experiments, 3:438–440

health care, 5:395–396

health care coverage, 9:61

health economics, 3:440–441

homelessness, 3:498–499

hot money, 3:504

human experiments, 3:60–61

human rights, 3:513–514

human sterilization, 8:141

Hungarian Revolution, 3:523, 524

Huntington, Samuel P., 3:525–526

Hussein, Saddam, 3:532, 533, 534–535

impeachment, 3:584–586

import promotion, 3:592

imprisonment, 3:596–597

income maintenance experiments, 3:605–607

individualism, 3:618–619

industrial accidents, 1:8–9

inflation, 6:*450*

inheritance, 4:35–36

inheritance tax, 4:36–37

internal colony, 2:13–15

international economic order, 4:93

international relations Iran-Iraq War, 4:143

internationalism, 4:102, 103

interwar years, 4:121, 122

Iran-Contra affair, 4:142–143

isolationism, 4:160–161

Jacobinism, 4:164

Janowitz, Morris, 4:171–172

Japanese American incarceration, 3:599–601

Jefferson, Thomas, 4:180

Jews, 4:191, 195, 196, 222

judicial activism, 1:18–19

judiciary, 4:225, 227–228

jurisprudence, 4:232–233

jury selection, 4:234

Kuznets hypothesis, 4:295, 296, 297

labor, 4:302, 303

labor law, 4:316–317

labor market, 4:318, 319

labor unions, 4:326, 8:513–517

Lafargue, Paul, 4:330

lagging, leading and coincident indicators, 4:331–332

land claims, 4:340–341

land fertility, 3:131

land reform, 4:342

landlords, 4:346–347

law and order, 4:369–372

Le Duc Tho, 4:398

League of Nations, 4:385–386

Lebanese civil war, 4:397

left wing, 4:404

legal systems, 4:406

leisure, 4:409

lender of last resort, 4:410

Leontief, Wassily, 4:413

liberation, 4:429, 430

liberation theology, 4:435

libertarianism, 4:438, 439

life-cycle hypothesis, 4:442, 443

liquidity trap, 4:461–462

literature, 4:463–464

loans, 4:472–473

lobbying, 4:474

Locke, John, 4:476, 477

longitudinal data, 2:238

lotteries, 4:503–504
Lowi, Theodore J., 4:506
loyalists, 4:508, 509
lynchings, 4:526–527
macroeconomics, 4:541
Mafia, 4:552
managed competition, 2:53–54
managerial capitalism, 1:442–443
maquiladoras, 4:591–594
McCarthyism, 5:43–44
Medicaid, 5:61–62
Medicare, 5:62–63
mercenaries, 9:51
metropolitan regions, 7:133–135
microelectronics industry, 5:138
migrant labor, 5:154–155
militarism, 5:164–165
miscegenation, 5:199–200
monetary base, 5:243–245
Monroe Doctrine, 5:272
mutual deterrence, 2:334–335
NAFTA, 5:540–541
national debt, 5:386
national defense, 2:261–262
national income accounts, 5:400
Native Americans
    burial grounds, 1:395
    Chief Joseph, 1:503–504
    law, 5:427–428
nativism, 5:430–431
NATO, 5:544–546
natural resources consumption,
    6:95
naturalization law, 5:444
Navajos, 5:448
negative income tax, 5:456–457
neighborhoods, 5:463–464
neoconservatism, 5:468–469
neoimperialism, 5:470–471
noise pollution, 6:363–364
nonblacks, 5:513–514
nuclear weapons, 9:30, 31–32,
    47–48, 49
obesity, 6:4
obscenity law, 6:13
occupational regulation, 6:23, 25
out-of-wedlock births, 1:307–308
overemployment, 6:90
overtime, 6:99, 100
Pearl Harbor, 6:190
pharmaceutical industry,
    6:236–239
philanthropy, 6:245–247
pluralism, 6:283

political participation, 8:606
political parties, 6:306–308
political science, 6:383–384
political tolerance, 8:386
poll tax, 6:352–353
pollution, 6:359–360
popular culture, 6:374, 375
population aging, 3:306
power elite, 6:417–418
predatory pricing, 6:428
preemptive strike, 6:431
presidency, 6:440–442
    Bush, George H. W., 1:398
    Bush, George W., 1:399–400
    business cycles, 1:403
    Carter, Jimmy, 1:450–451
    checks and balances, 1:496
    Clinton, Bill, 1:579–581
    Eisenhower, Dwight D.,
        2:554–555
    Lincoln, Abraham,
        4:450–451
    Madison, James, 4:547–548
    Reagan, Ronald, 7:88–89
    Roosevelt, Franklin D.,
        7:282–283
    Truman, Harry S.,
        1:480–482
price indices, 6:447–449, *450*
primaries, 6:458–459
prisons, 6:475–476
psychological depression, 2:306
public intellectuals, 4:68–69
qualifications, 6:649–650
quotas, 6:669, 670–671
race riots, 7:33–35
racial attitudes, 1:204
racial slurs, 7:41–42
railway industry, 7:53–55
rape, 7:64–66
rate of profit, 7:71–74, *72, 73*
real business cycles, 1:407–409
recession, 7:103–105, 103*t*
Reconstruction Era, U.S.,
    7:111–115
referendum, 7:120–122
refugees, 7:126
regulation, 7:143–144
religion, 7:159–161, 163
reparations, 7:166–168
repatriation, 7:169
representative and participatory
    democracy, 2:284, 285
repression, 7:175
reproductive politics, 7:180–181

reproductive rights, 7:182, 183
republic, 7:184
Republican Party (U.S.),
    7:185–187
residential segregation, 7:384–385
restitution principle, 7:213–215
retaliation, 7:216
returns, 7:65–66
riots, 7:250, 251
rock 'n' roll, 7:268–269
Roe v. Wade, 7:270–272
Roman Catholic Church, 2:22
rules *vs.* discretion, 7:293
rural development, 2:341–342
school desegregation, 2:316–318
school readiness, 7:87–88
school segregation, 7:386–388
schools, 8:11–12
slavery, 1:34, 39–40, 60, 3:131
social policy interventions,
    4:118–119
social science, 7:617
sociology
    Asian immigrants,
        3:562–564, 566*t*
    baby boomers, 1:235–236
    bigotry, 1:295–296
    biological determinism, 2:326
    black immigrants,
        3:564–567, 566*t*
    black middle class,
        1:313–314
    black sociologists, 1:323–325
    Bourdieu, Pierre, 1:359
    caste, 1:460, 461
    Cherokees, 1:496–498
    childlessness, 1:510
    Chinese Americans,
        1:513–515
    Chinese diaspora, 1:516, 518
    cities, 1:541–542
    class, 1:563
    class conflict, 1:570
    cohabitation, 2:1
    Creole, 2:168
    crime and criminology,
        2:171–172
    culture, 8:362
    Darfur, 2:227
    demographic transition,
        2:292
    deviance, 2:353
    digital divide, 2:366–367
    diversity, 2:420

United States (U.S.), *continued*

Du Bois, W. E. B., 2:458–460

Duncan, Otis Dudley, 2:462–463

environmental determinism, 2:328

European immigrants, 3:566*t*

immigrants, 3:575, 576–580

imports, 3:594*t*

integration, 4:57–61

intergenerational transmission, 4:88–90

interracial marriage, 4:616–619, *617*

Jacobinism, 4:165

Latin American immigrants, 3:566*t*, 570–572

Latinos, 4:354–355, 354–356, 357–361, 6:337–339

Lewis, Oscar, 4:419

Lynd, Robert and Helen, 4:527–528

marriage, 4:612–616

Mexican-American War, 5:126–129

Mexican Americans, 5:119–126

middleman minorities, 5:147–148

mulatto escape hatch, 5:310–312

multiracial, 5:331, 332–333

Panel Study of Income Dynamics, 6:121–122

phenotype, 6:244

political, 8:4

post-Parsonian, 8:5–7

race, 7:3, 4, 5, 6, 7, 16–18, 18–21

race-blind policies, 7:36

race-conscious policies, 7:36–38

race mixing, 7:27–28

race relations, 7:28–31, 32–33

racial classification, 7:40

racial discrimination, 2:394–395

racial identification, 3:548–550

racial inequality, 4:6, 7

racism, 7:45–46

resegregation of schools, 7:201–202

rural, 8:8–9

same-sex marriage, 4:619–621

school vouchers, 7:347–349

slavery, 7:542–545

social welfare system, 7:631–633

Southern politics, 6:339–349

standardized tests, 8:95–98

state capitalism, 1:444–445

statistics

addiction, 1:21

HIV, 1:63

industrial accidents, 1:9*t*

obesity, 6:4

occupational hazards, 6:22

occupational regulation, 6:23

overemployment, 6:90

underclass, 8:486

underemployment rate, 8:494

volunteerism, 8:638

working class, 9:133

Suez Crisis, 8:213–214

Supreme Court, 8:232–234

surplus labor, 4:312

tariffs, 2:134

tax credits, 8:273–274

tax evasion and tax avoidance, 8:276

tax incidence, 8:277

tax revolts, 8:278, 279

taxes, 8:281, 282, 283

technology, 8:304–305

technology transfer, 8:308

telecommunications industry, 8:314–315

television, 8:320

term limits, 8:323–324

textile industry, 8:333–334

time-and-a-half, 8:373–374

Tinbergen, Jan, 8:374–375

tobacco industry, 8:376, 377

Tocqueville, Alexis de, 8:382–383

towns, 8:404, 405

toxic waste, 8:408–409

trade deficit, 8:416

tradition, 8:420–421

transfer pricing, 8:428–429

transportation industry, 8:438–439

Uncle Tom, 8:482–483

underclass, 8:485–487

underdevelopment, 8:491

underemployment rate, 8:494

unemployment, 8:498

unemployment compensation, 2:49, 50

unequal, 7:67–69

United Nations membership, 8:522

See also names of political parties, specific agencies, cities and states

United States, Bonnichsen v. (2004), 1:395

United States, Newberry v., 9:84–85

United States, Roth v., 6:13

United States Agency for International Development (USAID), 1:124, 5:392

United States Constitution. *See* Constitution, U.S.

United States Department of Commerce v. Montana, 1:154

United States House of Representatives, Department of Commerce v. (1999), 1:154

United States v. Carolene Products (1938), 2:615

United States v. Classic, 9:84–85

United States v. Fordice (1992), 6:650

United States v. Jefferson County Board of Education (1966), 2:314

United States v. Nixon, 5:506, 9:43

United Steelworkers of America v. Weber (1979), 3:373, 6:671

"Uniting for Peace" resolution (UN), 8:524

Univariate autoregressive processes. *See* Time series regression

Universal Declaration of Human Rights (UDHR), 1:548–549, 3:512, 8:524

universalism, 8:526

women, 9:108, 110

See also Human rights

The Universal Dictionary of Trade and Commerce (Postlethwayt), 6:394

Universal Negro Improvement Association and African Communities League (UNIA), 1:315–316, 320, 321, 328, 3:258, 259

Universal suffrage, 2:58, 288, 4:414

Universalism, 8:**526–527**

Arrow possibility theorem, 1:184

norm of reciprocity, 7:107

realist theory, 7:99

Universities, 8:527, **531–533**

affirmative action, 3:392–393

American sociology, 7:667–668

diversity, 2:420

education in the U.S., 2:543–545

engineering, 2:594–595
equal opportunity, 2:612–613
ethics, 2:632–633
history, 8:527–528, 531–532
institutional investors, 4:134
Newman, John Henry, 8:528–529
political correctness, 6:300
race-blind policies, 7:35
rhetoric, 7:237, 238
rural development, 2:341
rural sociology, 8:8
*See also names of specific universities
or colleges*
University in Exile, 5:501
University in Turmoil (Wallerstein), 9:9
University of California, 1:416
University of California-Berkeley,
2:174
University of Cambridge. *See*
Cambridge University
University of Chicago
Bettelheim, Bruno, 1:290–291
black sociologists, 1:324
Harris, Abram L., Jr., 3:427
human ecology, 3:510
Janowitz, Morris, 4:171, 172
See also Chicago School
University of Lausanne, 4:361–362
University of Michigan, 1:424,
3:392–393
University of Oxford, 1:421, 422,
8:527–529
University of Texas Inequality Project,
8:529–531
University of Virginia, Jefferson,
Thomas, 4:183
UNLA (Uganda National Liberation
Army), 1:110
UNODC (United Nations Office on
Drugs and Crime), 3:412
Unpaid work, gender gap, 3:274–275,
9:123, 125
Unrestricted stocks. *See* Restricted and
unrestricted stocks
Unsafe at Any Speed (Nader), 5:359
Untouchables. *See* Dalits; Sudras
UPC (Uganda People's Congress),
6:12
Upper class, African American, 3:192
Upward mobility, **8:533–535**
class, 1:563
creamy layer, 2:161
described, 5:208–211
development in sociology, 2:347
lateral mobility, 5:212–213

Latinos, 4:359
Urban anthropology, 1:**134–136**
case method, 1:453
human ecology, 3:511
metropolitan regions, 7:132–135
street culture, 8:173–174
Urban Anthropology (Fox), 1:134
Urban areas. *See* Cities
Urban bias, 3:593
The Urban Complex (Weaver), 9:53
Urban culture
case method, 1:453
communalism, 2:31
Ibn Khaldun, 3:545–546
See also Street culture
Urban design, 8:542
Urban ecology. *See* Human ecology
Urban economics, 5:183
Urban foundation. *See* Townships
Urban legends. *See* Rumors
Urban Mass Transportation Act (U.S.
1964), 3:372–373
Urban planning and development
cooperatives, 2:124
development economics, 2:346
Jacobs, Jane, 4:165
metropolitan regions, 7:132–135
rural development *vs.,* 2:341–342
studies, 8:542
Urban politics, 6:**349–351**, 350*t*
clientelism, 1:579
community power studies, 2:42,
44–45
Southern politics, 6:347
Urban poverty, 6:**410–412**
described, 1:541, 542
Lewis, Oscar, 4:418–419
Multi-City Study of Urban
Inequality, 5:314–315
neighborhood effects, 5:461–463
slums, 7:551–552
Urban renewal, 8:**536–537**
described, 1:542
gentrification, 3:302–303,
5:463–464
ghettos, 3:313
Harlem, 3:424
Jacobs, Jane, 4:165
Weaver, Robert C., 9:53
Urban riots, 7:34–35, 8:**537–539**
Urban sociology, 8:**15–17**
cities, 1:540–542
Feagin, Joseph, 3:109
Gandhi, Indira, 3:256

Harlem, 3:423–424
human ecology, 3:510
metropolitan regions, 7:132–135
Multi-City Study of Urban
Inequality, 5:314–315
regions, 7:130
social isolation, 7:600
street culture, 8:173–174
suburbs, 8:210–211
towns, 8:404–405
Urban sprawl, 8:**539–541**
described, 1:541, 542
metropolitan regions, 7:132–135
Urban studies, 8:**541–544**
case method, 1:453
cities, 1:540–542
community power studies, 2:42,
44–45
dual economy, 2:457
human ecology, 3:510
Jacobs, Jane, 4:165
metropolitan regions, 7:132–135
Multi-City Study of Urban
Inequality, 5:314–315
neighborhood effects, 5:461–463
urban sociology, 8:15–16
Urban underclass. *See* Underclass
The Urban Villagers (Gans), 1:540,
3:256
Urban warfare, guerrilla, 3:395
Urbanism as a Way of Life (Wirth),
1:540
Urbanity, 8:**544–545**
Urbanization, 8:**545–548**
alienation, 3:222–223
civilization, 1:557
development economics, 2:344,
346
history, 8:546
human ecology, 3:510
metropolitan regions, 7:132–135
rural to urban migration,
5:159–160
socialism, 7:636
towns, 8:404–405
trends, 8:540
tribes, 1:134
Ure, Andrew, 2:424
Uruguary Round, 3:281–282,
8:**548–549**, *549,* 9:143–144
Uruguay, cattle industry, 1:471
Urwin, Gregory J., 1:258
U.S. (United States). *See* United States
(U.S.); *See also entries beginning with
U.S.*

U.S. Advanced Research Projects Agency (ARPA), 4:104

U.S. Alliance for Progress, 1:303, 6:45

U.S. Army Corps of Engineers, 5:433

U.S. Army Medical Research Institute of Infectious Diseases (USAMRIID), 1:302

U.S. Bureau of Economic Analysis (BEA), 4:331–332, 6:658

U.S. Bureau of Labor Statistics (BLS), 5:407
  Current Population Survey, 2:212
  discouraged workers, 2:386
  employment, 2:580
  industry fatality rates, 9:4
  labor data, 4:303
  multiple jobs, 9:129
  Wholesale Price Index, 9:94
  work week, 9:128

U.S. Census Bureau, 2:212, 296, 7:40
  apportionment, 1:154
  family structure, 3:91
  multiculturalism, 5:514

U.S. Citizenship and Immigration Services (USCIS), 5:499

U.S. Civil War, 8:**549–551**
  Appalachia, 1:150
  Benjamin, Judah P., 1:284–285
  Birth of a Nation (film), 1:304–306
  cotton industry, 2:152
  creationism, 2:162
  Davis, Jefferson, 2:66, 67, 243–244
  Grant, Ulysses S., 3:365, 8:550–551
  Lee, Robert E., 3:365, 4:399–400, 8:550–551
  Lincoln, Abraham, 4:451
  Nast, Thomas, 5:377
  regions, 7:131
  Southern politics, 6:340
  vindication movements, 8:618–619
  See also Confederate States of America; Reconstruction Era, U.S.

U.S. Commission on Wartime Relocation and Internment of Civilians (CWRIC), 3:601

U.S. Congress. *See* Congress, U.S.

U.S. Country Life Commission, 8:8

U.S. Department of Agriculture (USDA)
  black capitalism, 1:440
  Food Guide Pyramid, 5:551

Rural Development, 2:341–342
  rural sociology, 8:8

U.S. Department of Commerce
  black capitalism, 1:441
  Brimmer, Andrew, 1:371
  product dumping, 2:462

U.S. Department of Defense
  Central Intelligence Agency, U.S, 1:481, 482, 485
  national defense, 2:260

U.S. Department of Education, Carter, Jimmy, 1:451

U.S. Department of Energy, Carter, Jimmy, 1:451

U.S. Department of Health and Human Services (DHHS), 4:33, 5:551

U.S. Department of Homeland Security, 2:155, 260, 384

U.S. Department of Housing and Urban Development (HUD)
  black capitalism, 1:440
  Moving to Opportunity, 5:302–303

U.S. Department of Justice (DOJ), 2:53, 3:600, 601

U.S. Department of Labor, 4:303

U.S. Department of State
  Central Intelligence Agency, U.S, 1:481, 482
  Cuban Missile Crisis, 2:184

U.S. Department of the Interior, 1:504

U.S. Department of War. *See* U.S. Department of Defense

U.S. Drug Enforcement Agency (DEA), 2:455, 455*t*

U.S. Environmental Protection Agency (EPA)
  air pollution, 6:362
  Love Canal, 4:505
  noise pollution, 6:363–364
  pollution, 6:359, 360

U.S. Food and Drug Administration (FDA), 2:455, 6:237, 238–239

U.S. Immigration Commission, 1:345

U.S. Internal Revenue Service (IRS), 2:86, 8:428

U.S.-Iraq War. *See* Iraq-U.S. War

U.S. National Guard, Kent State university shooting, 8:615

U.S. National Head Start Association, 3:437

U.S. National Infrastructure Advisory Council, 8:656

U.S. National Security Council, 2:155, 4:142

U.S. Occupational Safety and Health Administration (OSHA), 1:8–9, 6:22, 364

U.S. Office of Management and Budget (OMB), 5:331, 333

U.S. Office of Strategic Services (OSS), 1:482

U.S. Public Health Service (USPHS), 8:472–473

U.S. South. *See* The South, U.S.

U.S. Steel Corporation, 5:494

U.S. Supreme Court. *See* Supreme Court, U.S.

U.S. War Relocation Authority (WRA), 3:600–601

USA Freedom Corps, 5:414

Usable Knowledge (Lindblom and Cohen), 4:453

USAID (United States Agency for International Development), 1:124, 5:392

USAMRIID (U.S. Army Medical Research Institute of Infectious Diseases), 1:302

USCIS (U.S. Citizenship and Immigration Services), 5:499

USDA. *See* U.S. Department of Agriculture

The Use of Pleasure (Foucault), 3:182

Use value. *See* Exchange value

User costs, 8:**551–552**

The Uses of Literacy (Hoggart), 2:199

USPHS (U.S. Public Health Service), 8:472–473

USS Maine, 9:23

U.S.S.R. (Union of Soviet Socialist Republics). *See* Union of Soviet Socialist Republics (U.S.S.R.)

Usury. *See* Loans

Utagawa Hiroshige, 8:632

Utilitarianism, 8:**552–554**
  Bentham, Jeremy, 1:285, 286
  choice in economics, 1:524, 525
  common good, 2:25
  justice, 4:237–238
  liberalism, 4:425
  liberty, 4:440, 441
  majority rule, 4:561
  Mill, James, 5:177
  Mill, John Stuart, 5:178–179
  moral philosophy, 6:255, 256
  political philosophy, 6:258
  post-Parsonian American sociology, 8:7

rational choice theory, 7:74–76
social justice, 4:241, 242
tastes, 8:266
welfare economics, 9:63–64, 67
Utilitarianism (Mill), 4:237–238,
8:553
Utilities, public. *See* Public utilities
Utility
cardinal, 6:57, 8:558
Choquet expected, 5:519
defined, 8:554
maximin expected, 5:519
maximizing, 6:47
non-expected, 3:54, 5:519–520
ordinal, 6:56–57, 8:556, 558
See also Expected utility theory
Utility, marginal. *See* Marginalism
Utility, objective, 8:557–558
Utility, subjective, 8:77, **8:558–560**
defined, 8:77
expected utility theory, 3:54
Hicks, John R., 3:472
rational choice theory, 7:74–76
Utility, Von Neumann-Morgenstern,
3:217, 5:374, **8:560–561**, 643
choice in economics, 1:524, 525
expected utility theory, 3:54
risk, 7:252
vectors, 8:601
Utility function, **8:554–556**
choice in economics, 1:524
consumer, 2:99–102
consumption function, 2:110
discounted present value,
2:385–386
exchange value, 3:40
interdependent preferences, 6:437
labor force participation, 4:315
Lagrange multipliers, 4:332–333
neoclassical economics, 2:516–517
rationality, 7:79–82
relative income hypothesis, 7:153
revealed preference, 7:224–225
risk neutrality, 7:254
separability, 7:444–445
UTIP. *See* University of Texas
Inequality Project
Utopia (More), 2:40, 8:561
Utopianism, **8:561–562**
Castro, Fidel, 1:464
communalism, 2:30, 31
communitarianism, 2:40
conservatism, 2:83, 85
distributive justice, 4:239

Maoism, 4:591
Plato, 6:279–280
social, 1:171–172
socialism, 7:636–637, 8:561
technotopia, 8:312–313
vacations, 8:566
Uunk, Wilfred, 9:72
Uzawa, Hirofumi, **8:562–564**
comparative advantage, 1:6
separability, 7:444
Uzbekistan, 2:30
Uzoka, Azubike, 3:87

V

Vacancy rates, 1:292
Vacations, 2:201, **8:565–566**
Vagabonds, **8:566–567**
See also Hobos; Homelessness
Vaisyas, **8:567–568**
Brahmins, 1:366
caste, 1:457–458, 461
Vajpayee, Atal Bihari, **8:568–569**
Vajrayāna Buddhism. *See* Buddhism
Valenze, Deborah, 3:483
Validation, **8:569–572**, 570*t*, 571*t*
practice-related, 8:571–572
respondent-related, 8:571, 571*t*
Validity, content. *See* Validity,
statistical
Validity, convergent. *See* Validity,
statistical
Validity, statistical, **8:572–575**
concurrent, 8:572, 573
construct, 8:570, 570*t*, 572,
573–574
content, 8:570, 570*t*, 571*t*, 572,
574
convergent, 8:573
criterion, 8:570, 570*t*, 572, 573
cultural, 8:571
defined, 8:570
discriminant, 8:573–574
experimental realism, 7:94
experiments, 3:57
external, 7:591, 8:573
internal, 7:591, 8:573, 574
Likert scale, 4:447
predictive, 8:572
Rorschach test, 7:285
Rosenberg's Self-Esteem Scale,
7:288
scales, 7:339
self-report method, 7:425
statistical reliability, 7:158
survey, 8:242

Vallance, Brenda J., 2:258
Valuation, contingent. *See* Contingent
valuation (CV)
Value, exchange. *See* Exchange value
Value, fundamental. *See* Market
fundamentals
Value, labor theory of. *See* Labor
theory of value
Value, objective, 2:520, **8:577–578**
See also Value (economics)
Value, rate of surplus. *See* Rate of
exploitation
Value, subjective, **8:578–581**
auctions, 1:206–208, 8:579–580
consumption, 2:106–107
exchange value, 3:41
Hicks, John R., 3:472
See also Value (economics)
Value (economics), **8:575–577**
absolute surplus, 7:155
added by industry, 3:383–384,
5:402
aggregate, 9:12–13
bourgeoisie, 1:360–361
bubbles (economics), 1:378–379
Cambridge capital controversy,
1:419, 420
classical economics, 1:447–448
cost-benefit analysis, 2:150–151
currency appreciation and
depreciation, 2:209–210
currency devaluation and
revaluation, 2:211–212
discounted present, 2:385–386
distortions, 2:414
exchange, 6:97, 8:505–506, 9:12
Hilferding, Rudolf, 3:476
labor theory of, 1:5–6, 110, 3:155
Law, John, 4:366
liquidity premium, 4:460
objective, 8:577–578
relative surplus, 7:154–155
Ricardo, David, 7:244–246
surplus, 9:153–154
capitalist mode of
production, 1:445–446
class, 1:563
class conflict, 1:571
consumption, 2:106
labor theory of value, 4:322,
323
rate of exploitation, 7:70–71
technological change, 1:491
transitional conjunctures,
2:77

Value (economics), *continued*
    Tobin's Q, 8:379–381
    wealth, 9:46
    work, 9:122
Value-added accountability, 1:10–11
Value-added tax (VAT), 8:284–285
Value elicitation. *See* Value, subjective
Value free social science, 7:**618–620**
    methodology, 5:108
    positive social science, 6:387–389
Value-loss model, 6:51
Value of statistical life (VSL), 6:25
Value-rational action, 9:56
Values (cultural), 8:578, **581–583**
    achievement, 1:14–15
    conflict, 2:70
    conformity, 2:71
    consumerism, 2:105
    cultural distinctions, 2:412, 413
    cultural relativism, 1:123
    extrinsic, 8:557
    family, 2:30, 114, 3:95–97
    identity, 3:552
    intrinsic, 8:557
    national, 9:70
    Nietzsche, Friedrich, 5:502
    norms *vs.,* 5:536
    objective, 8:578
    organization theory, 6:70
    rites of passage, 7:256–259
    rituals, 7:259–264
    social exclusion, 7:589
    social structure, 7:623–624
    subsistence, 3:97
    tradition, 8:420–421
    vindication movements, 8:619
    wealth, 9:44–45
    Weber, Max, 9:55–56
    women's studies, 9:120
Van Balen, Frank. *See* Balen, Frank van
Van de Kaa, Dirk, 2:292
Van de Water, Frederic, 1:258
Van den Boom, C. Dymphna, 3:116
Van Gennep, Arnold, 3:239, 8:469, 470
Van Gogh, Vincent, 8:632
Van Horne's Lessee v. Dorrance (1795), 4:224
Van Langendonck, Jef, 9:72
Van Look, Paul, 2:115
van Oorschot, Wim. *See* Oorschot, Wim van
Van Tassel, Alan R., 2:258

Van Vechten, Carl, 3:425
Van Velsen, Jaap, 1:454
Vance, Zebulon, 2:67
Vancouver's Chinatown (Anderson), 5:464
Vanilla industry, 8:**583–584**
Vanity. *See* Narcissism
Vanoli, Andre, 3:384
VAR models. *See* Vector autoregression
Varga, Evgenij, 1:188
Vargas, Jose Antonio, 8:612
Variability, 8:**584–585**
    average, 8:590
    costs, average, 1:230–232
    variance, 8:589–590
    variance-covariance matrix, 8:589
Variable, stochastic. *See* Random variables
Variable capital. *See* Capital
Variables
    causality, 1:471–473
    cointegration, 2:2–3
    controlled experiments, 3:58–59
    covariance, 2:156–157
    dependent, 3:286–291
    experiments, 3:55–58
    factor analysis, 3:75–76
    independent, fixed effects regression, 3:155–156
    left and right censoring, 1:473–474
    logistic regression, 4:482–483
    measures of central tendencies, 1:487–488
    ordering, 8:599
    parametric, 8:590
    sample censoring, 1:474–475
Variables, latent, 8:**586**
Variables, predetermined, 4:47, 8:**586–588**
Variables, random, 8:**588–589**
    central limit theorem, 1:486
    uniform distribution, 2:418–419
Variance, 8:585, **589–590**, 591
Variance, method. *See* Self-report method
Variance-covariance matrix, 8:**590–591**
Variation, 8:591, **591–593**
Variation, compensating. *See* Compensating wages
Varick, Cesar, 7:533–534
The Varieties of Religious Experience (James), 4:170

Varieties of the Human Species (Buffon), 1:126
Varnas, 1:457–458, 461
Vascular dementia. *See* Dementia
Vassals, 3:133–134
VAT (Value-added tax), 8:284–285
Vatican, 8:**593–595**
    Christian Democracy, 2:277
    Christian socialism, 7:643
    Christianity, 1:530–531
    Church history, 1:533
    vodou, 8:634
    See also Roman Catholic Church
Vatican City, 1:544
Vattimo, Gianni, 3:463
Vauban, Sébastien Le Prestre de, 5:399
Vaughan, Stevie Ray, 1:343
Vaughn, Sarah, 4:177
Veblen, Thorstein, 1:442, 3:167, 8:**595–597**
    aesthetics, 1:30
    conspicuous consumption, 2:88, 89
    consumption, 2:107
    economic psychology, 2:495
    enterprise, 2:599
    epistemology, 2:610
    goodwill, 3:349–350
    institutional economics, 2:507
    institutionalism, 4:44
    laissez-faire, 4:337
    leisure, 4:408
    leisure class, 1:565–566
    lifestyles, 4:445
    Lynd, Robert and Helen, 4:527
    neoclassical economics, 2:517
    New School for Social Research, 5:500
    nouveaux riches, 5:548
    rentier class, 1:568
    science, 7:358
    social distinctions, 2:412
    Tobin's Q, 8:379
    wealth, 9:46
Vector autoregression, 1:229, 8:**598–600**, 601
    error-correction mechanisms, 2:627
    real business cycles, 1:408–409
Vector error correction model. *See* Unit root regression
Vectors, 2:551–554, 8:*600*, **600–601**, *601*
Vedas. *See* Brahmins
Vedic culture, 3:477, 9:154

See also India

Vega, Bernardo, 1:356

Veghte, Benjamin, 9:71, 72

Vehicle accidents, 9:4

Vehicle emissions, 1:223

Veigh, Vivian, 3:347

Veils, in African American culture, **8:602**

Veils, in Middle Eastern and North African cultures, 3:118, **8:602–604**

Veinho, Joseph, 2:20

Velázquez, Diego, 2:146–147

Velez, Raymon, 9:24–25

Venables, Anthony, 2:208

Venditti, Alain, 6:52

Venditti, Nishimura, 6:52

Venezuela
    Castro, Fidel, 1:466
    Chávez, Hugo, 1:494–495
    class conflict, 1:570–571
    Cuba, 2:187
    developing countries, 2:336–337
    Latin American revolutions, 7:235
    oil production, 6:67
    OPEC, 6:65
    populism, 6:384

Venice, Italy and ghettos, 3:313

Venirepersons. *See* Jury selection

Venter, Craig, 3:299

Venture capital, 1:440–441, **8:604–605**

Venturi, Robert, 1:172

VER (Voluntary export restraints). *See* Import promotion

Vera, Bush v. (1996), 8:653

Vera, Hernán, 2:317, 9:91

Veracruz, Mexico, 6:39

Verba, Sidney, **8:605–606**
    comparative politics, 6:327
    political culture, 6:301

Verbal Behavior (Skinner), 1:277, 7:527

Verdoorn, P. J., 8:607

Verdoorn's law, **8:606–608**

Verification, mutual, 1:177

Verification, self. *See* Self-verification

Vermont Yankee v. NRDC (1978), 2:606

Vernacular intellectuals, 4:**70**

Verner, Sherbert v. (1963), 1:535

Vernon, James, 3:483–484

Vernon, William T., 1:326

Vers une Architecture (Jenneret), 1:171

Versailles Treaty (1919). *See* Treaty of Versailles (1919)

Versailles Treaty (1920). *See* Interwar years

Verstehen, 5:443

Verticalist money approach. *See* Endogenous money

Vertically integrated corporations, 3:78

Vertovec, Steven, 2:357

Verwoerd, H. F., 1:147

Vesey, Denmark, 3:408, 7:534, 535–536, 8:**608–610**

Vesey, Joseph, 8:608–609

Vespucci, Amerigo, 2:21

Veterans, Chinese Americans, 1:513

Veterans Administration, U.S., mortgages, 1:97

Veto, 8:**610–611**
    checks and balances, 1:496
    Confederate States of America, 2:66
    Congress, U.S., 2:74
    consensus, 2:83
    Reconstruction Era, U.S., 7:112
    Washington, George, 9:37

Via Campesina, 6:75

Via chilena, 1:78

Vicary, James, 3:473

Vice, Ricardian. *See* Ricardian vice

Vickrey, William S., 1:207

Vico, Giambattista, 2:96

Victim, blaming. *See* Culture of poverty

Victim blame analysis, 6:33–34

Victorian Period, University of Oxford, 8:528

The Victory of Reason: How Christianity Led to Freedom, Capitalism, and Western Success (Stark), 1:558

Victory without War (Nixon), 5:506

Vidal de La Blache, Paul, 3:304

Video games, 8:**611–612**
    Bandura, Albert, 1:249
    video technology, 8:310

Video technology, 8:**309–310**

Vienna Declaration and Programme of Action (1993), 3:431

Viet Cong, 4:398

Viet Minh. *See* Ho Chi Minh

Viet Minh Front, 3:492

Vietnam
    borders, 1:355
    Chinese diaspora, 1:516, 518
    coffee industry, 1:594, 595
    conformity, 2:72
    decolonization, 2:256
    Hmong, 3:491

    Ho Chi Minh, 3:491–492
    Ladejinsky, Wolf, 4:328
    land reform, 4:343
    latifundia, 4:353
    Le Duc Tho, 4:398
    Pol Pot, 6:289
    refugees, 7:126
    socialism, 7:638
    working class, 9:132

Vietnam War, 8:**612–616**
    anticolonial movements, 1:139
    appeasement, 1:153
    Central Intelligence Agency, U.S, 1:484
    Chomsky, Noam, 1:529
    Clinton, Bill, 1:579
    guerrilla warfare, 3:395
    Johnson, Lyndon B., 1:153, 4:210, 8:614
    journalism, 4:214–215
    Kariel, Henry S., 4:249
    Kennedy, John F., 4:255
    King, Martin Luther, Jr., 1:552
    Kissinger, Henry, 4:275
    Le Duc Tho, 4:398
    Lynd, Staughton, 4:529
    Mexican Americans, 5:124
    modernization, 5:233
    mortality, 9:18
    Nixon, Richard M., 5:506
    peace movements, 6:183–184
    Pentagon Papers, 9:42
    Selective Service, 7:591, 8:614–615
    wage and price controls, 9:3
    Woodstock, 9:121

Vietnamization, 8:614–615

Vietorisz, Thomas, 1:236

The View from Afar (Lévi-Strauss), 4:417

Vigilantism, 4:372, 526

Villa, Francisco, 8:**617–618**
    Latin American revolutions, 7:233
    Zapata, Emiliano, 9:171

Villa, Pancho. *See* Villa, Francisco

Village studies, 1:123, 135

Villages, gemeinschaft, 3:266–267

Villard, Oswald Garrison, 5:383

Vindication, 8:**618–619**

Vindication of the Rights of Women (Wollstonecraft), 3:120, 8:618

Viner, Jacob, 1:502, 3:370, 4:335, 336

Vinson, Fred, 9:32

Vintage models, 8:**619–621**

Vintage of data, 5:403

Vinyl recordings, 8:621–622
Violence, 8:**622–625**
 absolute, 8:626
 Bandura, Albert, 1:249
 Black September, 1:323
 civil disobedience, 1:545–546
 civil wars, 1:555
 colonialism, 8:623–624, 625–626
 compensating wages, 9:4
 contempt, 2:113
 corporal punishment, 2:134–136
 crime and criminology, 2:171, 172
 cults, 2:188–189
 decolonization, 2:257
 direct action, 2:372
 drug traffic, 2:450–451
 East Indian diaspora, 2:474
 ethnic diversity and, 2:343
 ethnic fractionalization, 3:7–8
 ethnicity, 3:9
 Fanon, Frantz, 8:625–626
 humiliation, 3:522
 Jim Crow, 4:200
 law and order, 4:369–371
 lynchings, 4:526–527
 masculinity, 3:269
 mass, as genocide, 3:296–297
 media, 1:56
 militants, 5:163–164
 peace movements, 6:184
 pimps, 6:273
 race riots, 7:33–34
 Reconstruction Era, U.S.,
  7:113–114
 repression, 7:174–175
 resource allocation, 8:626–628
 riots, 7:249–251
 self-constrained behavior,
  1:273–274
 socialization, 1:56
 suicide bombers, 8:224–225
 television, 8:319–320
 threats of, 8:627–628
 torture, 8:391–394
 video games, 8:611–612
 women's movement, 9:117
 See also Hate crimes
Violence, Fanon, Frantz on,
 8:**625–626**
Violence, in terrorism, 1:299–300,
 8:328–331, 624, **628–629**
Violence, role in resource allocation,
 8:**626–628**
Virchow, Rudolf, 1:131
Virgin Mary. *See* Mary (Virgin)

Virgin of Guadalupe. *See* Symbols
Virginia
 blood and bloodline, 1:336
 civil rights, 1:549
 Confederate States of America,
  2:67
 desegregation, 2:313–314
 Jefferson, Thomas, 4:180, 181,
  183
 Lee, Robert E., 4:399–400
 voting rights, 8:652
 Washington, George, 9:36, 37
Virginia, Loving v. (1967), 7:28
Virginia Military Institute, 1:549
Virginia Plan, 2:91
Virgins, 8:**629–630**, 9:108
Virtual reality. *See* Cyberspace
Virtue, 5:502, 6:256
Virus, human immunodeficiency. *See*
 HIV (Human immunodeficiency
 virus)
Viscusi, W. Kip, 8:369–370, 557
Vision, gaze, 3:263–265
VISTA (Volunteers in Service to
 America), 5:413
Visual arts, 8:**630–633**
 Black Arts Movement, 1:309–310
 material culture, 5:14
 modernism, 5:229
 primitivism, 6:465, 466
 realism, 7:91–93
 sculpture, 6:39, 8:630
 stare, 8:101
Visual behavior, 5:530
Visual cliff method, 1:506
Visualization, 5:476
Vitale, Engel v., 9:33
Vitalism, 1:114
Vivekananda, Swami, 3:480
Vlastos, Gregory, 5:95
Vodou, 8:**633–634**
 demography, 7:161
 Santería, 7:326
 zombies, 9:181
Voegelin, Eric, 2:85
Vogel, Ronald, 8:543
Voir dire, 4:234
Voisin, Charles, 1:232
Voisin, Gabriel, 1:232
Vojta, George, 3:324
Volcker, Paul, 3:112
Voloshinov, Valentin, 1:130
Voltaire, 8:**634–636**
 laissez-faire, 4:336–337
 liberalism, 4:425

Voltaire: Historian (Brumfitt), 8:636
Voltaire's Politics (Gay), 8:636
Voluntarism, 8:17–18
Voluntaristic vs. structuralist sociology,
 8:**17–18**
Voluntary associations, 1:**193–194**
 cooperatives, 2:123
 international nongovernmental
  organizations, 4:96–99
 social theory, 7:628
 See also Nongovernmental
  organizations
Voluntary export agreements,
 1:221–222
Voluntary export restraints (VER). *See*
 Import promotion
Voluntary import expansion (VIE). *See*
 Import promotion
Voluntary unemployment, 3:225,
 8:498, **636–637**
 Keynes, John Maynard, 4:260
 unemployment rate, 8:502–504
Volunteer programs, 8:**638–641**, *639*
Volunteer Protection Act (U.S. 1997),
 8:640
Volunteerism, 8:638, 640, **641–643**
 elderly, 3:293
 national service programs,
  5:413–415
Volunteers in Service to America
 (VISTA), 5:413
Von Mises, Ludwig, 7:645
Von Neumann, John, 8:**643**
 capital, 1:429
 choice in economics, 1:524
 game theory, 3:250, 8:556, 643
 Nash equilibrium, 5:373
 noncooperative games, 5:517
 nonlinear systems, 5:524
 optimal growth, 6:51
 Perron-Froebenius theorm, 2:554
 risk, 7:252
 utility function, 8:556
 vectors, 8:600
 zero-sum game, 9:176–177
Von Neumann-Morgenstern utility,
 3:217, 5:374, 8:**560–561**, 643
 choice in economics, 1:524, 525
 expected utility theory, 3:54
 risk, 7:252
 vectors, 8:601
Voodoo. *See* Vodou
Vorster, B. J., 1:147
Voss, D. Stephen, 1:548
Vote, alternative, 8:**643–645**, *644t*

Vote, women's right to. *See* Women's suffrage

Voter turnout, 8:645

Voting, 8:**645–648**, 646

    approval, 8:655

    ballots, 1:242

    Birth of a Nation (film), 1:304, 305

    campaigning, 1:423–424

    Campbell, Angus, 1:424–425

    caste, 1:458

    centrism, 1:488–489

    citizenship, 1:542, 543

    civil rights movement, U.S., 1:551, 552

    Coloreds (South Africa), 2:15

    compulsory, 2:58–59

    Condorcet, Marquis de, 2:66

    Constitution, U.S., 2:91, 92

    cooperatives, 2:124

    cumulative, 8:655

    cycles, 8:648

    dealignment, 2:247

    democratization, 2:288

    differential equations, 2:365

    Dred Scott v. Sanford, 2:446

    electoral systems, 2:559–560, 560–562

    exit polls, 3:45–46

    instant runoff, 8:655

    Internet, 4:108

    Jim Crow, 4:201

    Latinos, 6:338*t*

    patterns, 8:649–650

    plurality, 6:285–286

    political conventions, 6:297–299

    political parties, 6:307–308

    political psychology, 6:309

    polling, 6:353–354

    polyarchy, 6:366

    primaries, 6:458–459

    recall, 7:102–103

    referendum, 7:120–122

    rights, 3:185

    Riker, William, 7:249

    roll calls, 7:276–277

    single transferable, 8:655

    Southern politics, 6:341, 342

    strategy and voting games, 8:165–166

    Whites, 6:338*t*

    women's suffrage, 8:214–217

    See also Majority voting; Paradox of voting

Voting, bloc. *See* Bloc vote

Voting, women's rights. *See* Women's suffrage

Voting patterns, 8:**648–650**

    ballots, 1:242

    Congress, U.S., 2:73–74

    constituency, 2:90

    dealignment, 2:247

    elections, 2:558

    Key, V. O., Jr., 4:259

    litigation, 4:466

    metropolitan regions, 7:135

    middle class, 5:145

    referendum, 7:121

Voting rights. *See* Franchise

Voting Rights Act (U.S. 1965), 1:552, 3:309, 372, 8:646, **650–654**

    black liberalism, 1:312

    Black Power, 1:321

    Congress of Racial Equality, 2:75

    Johnson, Lyndon B., 4:210

    King, Martin Luther, Jr., 4:268

    NAACP, 5:384

    Southern politics, 6:342

Voting schemes, 8:**654–656**

    ballots, 1:242

    bloc vote, 1:334–335

    choice in economics, 1:525

Vouchers, school. *See* School vouchers

VSL (Value of statistical life), 6:25

Vulnerability, 8:**656–657**

    diathesis-stress model, 2:358

    disaster management, 2:382–383

    learned helplessness, 4:387–389

    peer influence, 6:202

    schizophrenia, 7:345

Vygotsky, Lev, 1:506–507, 2:623

W

Wacquant, Loïc, 1:359

Waddell, Alfred M., 9:99

Waddington, Samuel, 4:415

Wade, Henry, 7:271

Wade, John, 1:591

Wade, Robert, 2:145

Wade, Roe v. (1973). *See* Roe v. Wade (1973)

Wage, minimum. *See* Minimum wage

Wage and price controls, 2:108, 9:**1–4**

    Barro-Grossman model, 1:255–256

    Cantillon, Richard, 1:429

    Hurwicz, Leonid, 3:529, 530

    landlords, 4:346

    loan pushing, 4:470

    rent control, 7:165

Wage discrimination, 2:**400–401**

    described, 2:389–391

    marginal product of labor, 4:306

Wage discrimination, by age, 2:**401–402**

Wage discrimination, by gender, 2:389–391, 400–401, **402–404**, 3:626

    Blinder-Oaxaca decomposition technique, 1:333–334

    crowding hypothesis, 2:181

    gender preference, 6:434

    taste for discrimination, 2:399

Wage discrimination, by occupation, 2:**404–405**

Wage discrimination, by race, 2:17, 389–391, 400–401, **405–406**, 9:4

    Blinder-Oaxaca decomposition technique, 1:333–334

    Burakmin, 1:388–389

    econometric decomposition, 2:478–479

    restitution principle, 7:214–215

Wage inequality. *See* Income inequality

Wages, 9:**4–5**

    aggregate supply, 1:54

    banana parable, 1:247–248

    basic real, 3:218

    Blinder-Oaxaca decomposition technique, 1:332–334

    blue collar and white collar, 1:337, 338, 338*t*

    Bracero Program, 1:364

    capitalist mode of production, 1:445

    class conflict, 1:569, 571

    codetermination, 1:593

    compensating, 9:4

    development economics, 2:344

    economic depression, 2:304

    efficiency, 5:512, 515, 9:4

        Akerlof, George A., 1:69

        o-ring theory, 6:77

    factory system, 3:79

    flexibility, 3:157

    Ford Motor Company, 3:168

    gender differences, 6:1

    globalization, 3:334

    Harris-Todaro model, 3:428

    human capital, 3:506–509

    inflation, 4:25, 26

    involuntary unemployment, 4:137–138

    job guarantee, 4:205

    Kahn, Richard F., 4:245

Wages, *continued*
  Kalecki, Michał, 4:246, 247
  Keynesian economics, 2:511–513
  labor, 4:300, 301
  labor demand, 4:312, 313–314
  labor economics, 2:514–515
  labor law, 4:303
  labor market, 4:318, 319–320
  labor supply, 4:320–322
  labor union, 4:325
  Lewis, W. Arthur, 4:420, 421
  low, overconsumption and, 8:488
  maquiladoras, 4:593
  marginal product of labor, 4:306
  marginal productivity, 4:595–596
  Marx, Karl, 9:122
  monopsony, 5:267–268
  national income accounts, 5:400
  nominal, 5:511–512
  Oaxaca wage decomposition
    technique, 6:1–2
  occupational hazards, 6:24–25
  occupational regulation, 6:24
  penalty, motherhood, 3:116–117
  premium, 6:24–25
  rate of profit, 7:71–72, *72*
  real
      nominal wages *vs.,*
        5:511–512
      unemployment rate, 8:503
      voluntary unemployment,
        8:637
  reservation, 4:315, 321
  Ricardian vice, 7:242
  Ricardo, David, 7:244–246
  slavery to, 9:126
  surplus labor, 4:308–309,
    309–312
  time-and-a-half, 8:373–374
  unemployment compensation,
    2:49, 50
  women's work, 9:124–125
  work day, 9:126
  work week, 9:128–129
  See also Minimum wage;
    Overtime; Wage discrimination
The Wages of Whiteness (Roediger),
  9:87
Waggoner, Daniel, 5:534
Wagner, Allan R., 7:148
Wagner, Richard, 1:575, 3:144, 145,
  4:338
  Gobineau, Comte de, 3:335
  Nietzsche, Friedrich, 5:502
Wagner, Robert, 9:24, 27

Wagner Act (U.S. 1935). *See* National
  Labor Relations Act (U.S. 1935)
Wahlbeck, Östen, 2:357
Wain, Mark, 3:318
Wainwright, Gideon v. (1963), 8:233
Wainwright v. Witt (1984), 4:233
Waitresses, 9:122–123
Wakefield, Edward Gibbon, 2:424,
  3:587
Wal-Mart, labor unions and, 8:516
Walden (Thoreau), 8:357
Walden Two (Skinner), 6:44
Waldner, Ilmar, 4:453
Walker, Aaron Thibeaux (T-Bone),
  1:343
Walker, Alice, 9:115
Walker, David, 8:618, 619
Walker, Francis Amasa, 1:97
Walker, Madame C. J., 1:311
Walker, Rebecca, 3:121, 123–124,
  9:115
Walkowitz, Judith, 3:483
Wall Street, 9:7–9
Walla, Graham, 3:74
Wallace, Alfred Russel, 2:233, 327
Wallace, Anthony F. C., 1:93
Wallace, Deborah, 4:445
Wallace, George, 1:551, 2:430–431,
  6:343
Wallace, Neil, 1:20
Wallace, Rodrick, 4:445
Wallace, Tina, 5:520
Wallach, Hans, 1:186
Wallerstein, Immanuel, 2:336, 5:466,
  9:9–11
  capitalist mode of production,
    1:447
  development in sociology, 2:347
  post-Parsonian American
    sociology, 8:6
  third-world sociology, 8:12, 13–14
  transitional conjunctures, 2:78
  world-system, 9:10–11, 152–153
Wallis, John, 5:545
Wallman, Sandra, 1:135
Wallowa Valley, 1:503–504
Walras, Léon, 3:150, 9:11–12
  Arrow-Debreu Model, 1:182–183
  Austrian economics, 1:211
  capital, 1:430
  Debreu, Gerard, 2:249
  demand, 2:269, 270
  equilibrium, 2:620, 3:283
  Leontief, Wassily, 4:413
  markets, 4:608

  multiple equilibria, 5:324–325
  neoclassical economics, 2:518
  Pareto, Vilfredo, 6:138, 139
  Patinkin, Don, 6:171, 172
  Ricardian vice, 7:242
  School of Lausanne, 4:361–362
  state enterprise, 8:107–108
  tâtonnement, 8:270
  utility function, 8:555
Walras' identity. *See* Walras' law
Walras' law, 9:11, **12–13**
Walsh, Dennis P., 4:317
Walt Disney Company, 2:409–410
Walter, Eugene V., 8:390
Walter, Rodney, 7:**269–270**
Walters, Richard, 1:248
Waltz, Kenneth, 3:170, 9:14
  Keohane, Robert, 4:256–257
  nation-states, 5:420
  political realism, 7:97
Walwyn, William, 4:414
Walzer, Michael, 2:613, 4:235
Wang, NIng, 8:399
Wanniski, Jude, 2:85
Want creation, 9:**14–15**
  consumerism, 2:105
  consumption, 2:107
Wants, 9:**15–17**
  needs *vs.,* 5:453
  satiation, 7:328–329
War, 9:**17–19**
  alliances, 1:79
  arms control, 1:175
  arms race, 1:178
  civil-military relation, 1:548
  civil war *vs.* interstate, 1:554,
    555–556
  conflict, 2:70–71
  contempt, 2:113
  democratic centralism, 2:286
  democratization, 2:290
  disaster management, 2:382
  economic growth, 2:491
  famine, 3:98
  fascism, 3:102
  guerrilla, 3:394–396
  Hobbes, Thomas, 3:492–493
  interrogation, 4:112–113
  jihad, 4:196–197
  just, 4:235–237
  Lenin, Vladimir Ilitch, 4:411
  Leninism, 4:412
  long run, 4:494
  Marxist competition, 2:55

national defense, 2:260

Native Americans, 5:424–425, 426

neutral states, 5:487–489

nuclear, 1:179, 9:30–32

peace, 6:181

political neutrality, 5:489–490

post-traumatic stress, 6:402

preemptive strike, 6:431–432

refugee camps, 7:124–125

slave-gun cycle, 7:540–542

trench, 9:146

urban, 3:395

Veblen, Thorstein, 8:596–597

violence, 8:622–624

See also names of specific wars; Civil wars; Cold War; Pacifism; Revolution

War, civil. *See* Civil wars

The War against the Poor (Gans), 3:256

War and Peace (Tolstoy), 9:**19–21**

War between the States. *See* U.S. Civil War

War Brides Act (U.S. 1945), 1:513

War crimes, 9:**21–22**

civil-military relation, 1:547

concentration camps, 2:64

conformity, 2:72

history, 3:361

informed consent, 4:33

interrogation, 4:112–113

Khmer Rouge, 4:263

Killing Fields, 4:265

terrorists *vs.,* 8:330

Yugoslavian civil war, 9:168

War Department, U.S. *See* U.S. Department of Defense

War fatigue. *See* Post-traumatic stress

War neurosis. *See* Post-traumatic stress

War of 1812, 5:470

War of 1898 (Spanish-American), 2:185, 8:619, 9:23–24, **23–24**

War of Independence (U.S. 1775-1783). *See* American Revolution

War of the Bavarian Successsion (1778-1779), 9:17

War on poverty, 3:372, 374, 9:**24–30**

Appalachia, 1:151

black capitalism, 1:439

culture of poverty, 2:206

Lewis, Oscar, 4:419

race, 7:19

War on terror, Guantánamo Bay, 3:393–394

See also Terrorism; Terrorists

War Powers Act (U.S. 1973), 5:506

War Relocation Authority, U.S. (WRA), 3:600–601

Ward, Joe, 1:585

Ward, Robin, 2:143

Waring, Marilyn, 3:625

Warlords

Chinese Revolution, 1:519–520

defense, 2:259

Warms, Richard L., 1:138

Warner, Charles Dudley, 3:318

Warner, Lloyd, 7:258

Warner, Michael, 1:482, 3:470

Warner, William Lloyd, 7:656

WARP (Weak axiom of revealed preference), 7:224–225

Warren, Austin, 4:463

Warren, Earl, 9:**32–33**

Brown v. Board of Education (1954), 1:374, 375

Brown v. Board of Education (1955), 1:377

Hernandez v. Texas, 3:464, 465–466

judiciary, 4:227

school desegregation, 2:316

Supreme Court, U.S., 8:233–234

Warren Report, 9:**33–34**

Warrior, Clyde, 1:98

Warsaw Ghetto, 3:313

Warsaw Pact, 2:5, 9:**34–36**, 149, 151

Washington, Booker T., 3:427, 4:200, 7:29

Birth of a Nation (film), 1:305

black conservatism, 1:311

black towns, 1:325, 326

Garvey, Marcus, 3:258

NAACP, 5:383

Washington, D.C.

Brimmer, Andrew, 1:372

Clark, Kenneth B., 1:561

Tally's Corner, 8:263–264

Washington, Dinah, 4:177

Washington, George, 9:**36–38**

apportionment, 1:154

Burr, Aaron, 1:397

federalism, 3:114, 9:37

Hamilton, Alexander, 3:413

Jefferson, Thomas, 4:181–182

segregation, 2:315

unilateralism, 8:509

Washington, Jesse, 4:526

Washington Consensus, 5:474, 9:**38–40**

Washington Naval Treaty (1922), 1:176, 177

Wason selection tasks, 3:33

Wasserman, Stanley, 5:477

Wassermann, Lew, 3:139

Wasson, R. Gordon, 1:456

Waste, toxic. *See* Toxic waste

Waste disposal. *See* Sanitation

Water

diamond paradox, 8:555

objective utility, 8:557

prices, 9:40–41

Water pollution, 4:154, 6:**364–365**, 9:41

Water resources, 9:**40–42**

drought, 2:447–448

Jordan River, 1:154

plumbing, 6:281–282

water pollution, 6:364–365

Watergate, 9:**42–44**

journalism, 4:215

Nixon, Richard M., 5:506

Warren Report, 9:34

Waterloo, Battle of (1815), 5:366, 368

Waters, Mary, 1:191

Waters, Muddy. *See* Muddy Waters

Watson, James, 3:461

Watson, John

behaviorism, 1:274, 275, 276, 278

developmental psychology, 2:350

habits, 3:403

Watson, Mark W., 1:229, 5:490, 491, 8:519

Watson, Tom, 6:383, 384

Wattenberg, Ben, 2:302

Watts, Alan, 1:384, 385

Watts, Harold W., 9:26

Watts, James, 4:475–476

Watts riot (Los Angeles, CA 1965), 4:372

Wave, Kondratief. *See* Long waves

Waves, long. *See* Long waves

Waves (economics), 1:410

WBI (World Bank Institute), 9:139

We Are All Multiculturalists (Glazer), 3:327

We Righteous Bombers (Bullins), 1:309

We the Living (Rand), 6:7

Weak axiom of revealed preference (WARP), 7:224–225

Weak states

civil wars, 1:555

coups d'etat, 2:156

Weak ties, strength of, 5:478

Wealth, 6:73, 9:**44–47**

Wealth, *continued*
    aggregate demand, 1:50
    baby boomers, 1:235–236
    bequests, 1:286–287
    Blau, Peter M., 1:332
    caste, 1:461
    commonwealth, 2:29–30
    conspicuous consumption, 2:88, 89
    consumption, 1:7, 2:107, 108
    consumption function, 2:110
    distribution, 2:363, 4:361–362, 9:44, 45–47
    elitism, 3:138
    inheritance, 4:35–36
    life-cycle hypothesis, 4:442, 443
    Luxembourg Income Study, 4:520
    material, 9:44, 45
    nouveaux riches, 5:548
    Rothschilds, 7:289
    saving rate, 7:334
    social Darwinism, 5:495
    in vivo transfers, 3:597–598
    whiteness, 9:87
Wealth (Carnegie), 3:183
Wealth inequality, 4:8–11, 9*t*, 10*t*
    African Americans, 1:34, 35
    bequests, 1:286
    black middle class, 1:314
    consumerism, 2:105
    Deininger and Squire World Bank Inequality Database, 2:267–268
    human rights, 3:513–514
    income inequality, 4:3
    inegalitarianism, 3:624
    inheritance, 4:35–36
    landlords, 4:346
    neocolonialism, 5:467–468
    political sociology, 8:3
The Wealth of Nations (Smith), 1:429, 3:76–77, 199
    Corn Laws, 2:133
    dirigiste, 2:373
    division of labor, 2:423–425
    economic growth, 2:490, 491
    increasing returns, 7:219
    laissez-faire, 4:335
    liberalism, 4:425
    libertarianism, 4:437
    long period analysis, 4:489
    markets, 4:607
    rational choice theory, 7:76–77
    returns, 7:217
    Smith, Adam, 7:552–557

Weapons
    antisatellite, 1:178–179
    arms control, 1:175–180
    arms race, 1:175, 177–179
    biological, 9:52
    chemical, 9:52–53, 146
    Iran-Contra affair, 4:142
    post-World War II development, 9:150
    slave-gun cycle, 7:540–542
    technological advances, 9:18
Weapons, nuclear, 9:47–49, 52
    Bush, George H. W., 1:398
    Cuban Missile Crisis, 2:183–185
    Cuban Revolution, 2:186
    defense, 2:258, 259
    deterrence, 2:333–334
    disarmament, 2:380
    intermediate range, 5:544
    Jervis, Robert, 4:186
    mutual deterrence, 2:334
    peace movements, 6:183
    United Nations role, 8:525
    World War II, 9:150
Weapons industry, 9:49–51
Weapons of mass destruction (WMD), 9:51–53
    Bush, George W., 1:399, 400
    Central Intelligence Agency, U.S, 1:485
    chemical, 3:411
    defense, 2:258, 259
    description, 9:18
    Iraq-U.S. War, 4:145–148
    just war, 4:236
    mutual deterrence, 2:334
Weather, 1:413, 414, 5:433
Weaver, Robert C., 9:53–54
Weaver, Warren
    communication, 2:32
    prediction, 6:430
Webb, Beatrice, 3:74
Webb, Sydney, 3:74
Weber, Alfred, 3:304
Weber, Max, 9:54–58
    alienation, 1:75
    American sociology, 7:668
    authority, 1:214, 6:68
    bureaucracy, 1:389–392, 3:263
    capitalist mode of production, 1:445
    class, 1:561, 562, 563
    class conflict, 1:569, 571
    constructivism, 2:96

    corporations, 2:139
    cultural values, 8:578
    dictatorship, 2:360
    elite theory, 2:562, 563
    epistemology, 2:610
    European sociology, 7:670
    Frankfurt School, 3:188
    freedom, 3:198
    government, 3:353–354
    hierarchy, 3:474
    ideal type, 3:546–547
    ideology, 3:559
    individualism, 6:61
    industrial accidents, 1:8
    institutional analysis in sociology, 7:673
    irrigation, 4:152–153
    Islamic economics, 2:510
    labor, 4:300–301
    leadership, 4:376–377, 381–382
    leisure, 4:408
    lifestyles, 4:445
    management science, 4:577
    meaning, 5:51
    methodological individualism, 1:210
    middle class, 5:143, 144
    Mills, C. Wright, 5:181
    Moore, Barrington, 5:278
    naturalism, 5:443
    neoinstitutionalism, 5:472
    Nietzsche, Friedrich, 5:502
    nirvāna, 5:504
    nouveaux riches, 5:548
    political culture, 6:300
    political sociology, 8:3, 4
    power elite, 6:417–418
    Protestant Ethic, 6:61, 566–568, 655, 9:55–56, 57
    qualifications, 6:649
    quantification, 6:655
    rationalism, 7:77
    religion and religiosity, 7:160, 162
    scientific method, 7:363
    secrecy, 7:376
    social distinctions, 2:412
    social structure, 7:623–624
    social theory, 7:628, 629
    sociology, 7:660–661
    state, 1:547
    stratification, 8:166
    subject/self, 8:195
    subjectivity, 8:196
    triumphalism, 8:455

urban studies, 8:541

value free social science, 7:618–619

violence, 8:622–623

Weber, Robert J., 1:207

Weber, United Steelworkers of America v. (1979), 3:373, 6:671

Websites. *See* Internet

Webster, Daniel, 1:497

Webster, Frank, 2:217

Webster, Yehudi, 7:43

Webster v. Reproductive Health Services, 1:4

Wechsler Adult Intelligence Scale, 3:160

Wechsler Intelligence Scale for Children (WISC), 3:160

WED (Women, environment, and development theory), 2:348

Wedderburn, Robert, 4:415

Weddington, Sarah, 7:271

Week, work. *See* Work week

Weeks, Jeffrey, 6:329

Weeks, John, 2:295

Weeks, work, 9:**128–129**

WEF. *See* World Economic Forum

WEF (World Economic Forum), 3:278

Wei Jingsheng, 1:546

Weibull distribution. *See* Probability distributions

Weichselbaumer, Doris, 2:142

Weight, 9:**58–60**

> body image, 1:346
>
> Body Mass Index, 1:347–348
>
> management, 5:551–552

Weil, Felix, 3:188

Weimar Triangle, 8:454

Weimer Constitution, 5:482

Weinberger, Caspar, 4:143

Weiner, Bernard, 1:15, 4:388, 478

Weingast, Barry, 5:545

Weir, Margaret, 9:71

Weirich, Paul, 8:370

Weis, Nancy, 5:496–497

Weisberg, Harold, 9:34

Weisbrod, Burton A., 3:324

Weishaupt, Adam, 3:561–562

Weiss, Albert, 1:276

Weiss, Andrew, 4:313–314

Weiss, Eric M., 8:612

Weitzman, Martin, 6:52

Weizäcker, Carl C. von, 6:51

Weizmann, Chaim, 1:282

Welfare, 9:**60–62**

Arrow possiblity theory, 1:181–182

benign neglect, 1:283–284

black conservatism, 1:311

Clinton, Bill, 1:581

cognitive dissonance, 1:599

commodified, 9:68

conservatism, 2:85

culture of poverty, 2:206

economic growth, 2:486–487

funding, 9:71–72

globalization, 9:73

history, 9:68–71

income maintenance experiments, 3:605–607

Jencks, Christopher, 4:184

labor force participation, 4:315, 316

labor supply, 4:322

Medicaid, 5:61–62

out-of-wedlock births, 1:307, 308

privatization, 9:69–70, 72

race-conscious policies, 7:37

socialization of investment, 7:649

Solow, Robert M., 8:26–27

spending, 9:60, 71–72

state capitalism, 1:444, 445

Thatcher, Margaret, 8:335

want creation, 9:15

See also Social welfare system

Welfare, public. *See* Public welfare

Welfare, social. *See* Social welfare system

Welfare (well-being). *See* Happiness

Welfare analysis, 9:**62–63**

> excess demand, 3:35
>
> price discrimination, 2:393
>
> social cost, 7:581–583

Welfare economics, 9:**63–67**

> Coase, Ronald, 1:589
>
> Coase theorem, 1:590
>
> customs union, 2:215
>
> distributive justice, 4:240
>
> Hicks, John R., 3:471
>
> maximization, subjective utility, 8:578
>
> Meade, James, 5:49
>
> merit goods, 5:97–98
>
> Pareto optimum, 6:139–140
>
> Sen, Amartya Kumar, 7:440
>
> social cost, 7:581–583
>
> social welfare functions, 7:629–630
>
> theory of second best, 8:350–351
>
> welfare analysis, 9:62–63

Welfare functions, social. *See* Social welfare functions

Welfare Reform Act (U.S. 1996), 1:580

Welfare state, 9:**67–76**

> children's rights, 1:512
>
> citizenship, 1:543
>
> communalism, 2:30
>
> conservatism, 2:84–85
>
> Conservative Party (U.K.), 2:87
>
> convergence theory, 2:117
>
> description, 9:60–61
>
> equality, 2:617
>
> governmentality, 3:362
>
> Great Society programs, 3:374
>
> informal economy, 4:27
>
> liberalism, 4:425
>
> managed competition, 2:54–55
>
> private interests, 6:479
>
> Social Darwinism, 2:233
>
> social justice, 4:242
>
> social welfare system, 7:631–633
>
> state capitalism, 1:444
>
> underclass, 8:486
>
> unemployment, 8:504

Welfare system, social. *See* Social welfare system

Well-being

> altruism, 3:292–293
>
> commonwealth, 2:29–30
>
> cost-benefit analysis, 2:150
>
> gender gap, 3:279
>
> wealth, 9:44
>
> *See also* Happiness

Wellek, René, 4:463

Wellesley, Arthur, 5:368

Wellman, Barry, 5:476

Wells, Heather, 8:608

Wells-Barnett, Ida B., 4:200, 5:383, 9:**76–77**

> as black sociologist, 1:323
>
> lynchings, 4:526

Weltanschauung, 5:372, 9:**77–79**

Weltfish, Gene, 1:345

Welthild, 9:78

Wernicke-Korsakoff syndrome, 1:71

Wertham, Frederic, 2:23–24, 9:24

Wertheimer, Max

> Asch, Solomon, 1:186
>
> Gestalt psychology, 3:310, 311

Wesenwille, 3:266–267

> *See also* Will

Wesolowski, Wlodzimierz, 2:564

West, Cornel, 1:312

West, Kenneth, 2:210

West Africa, 4:168

West Bank, 9:41–42
  Arab-Israeli War of 1967, 1:156–159
  Palestine Liberation Organization, 6:103–104
  Palestinian Authority, 6:104–107
  Palestinian diaspora, 6:108, 109
  Palestinians, 6:111–112
  Rabin, Yitzhak, 7:1

West Germany
  Bahro, Rudolf, 1:237–238
  Berlin Wall, 1:289
  common market, 2:28–29
  Habermas, Jürgen, 3:401, 402

West Indian Federation, 6:119–120

West Indies, 4:168

Westerfield, Samuel Z., 5:389

Westerfield Award, 5:389–390

Western culture, 1:70–71
  black nationalism, 1:315
  Caribbean, 1:447–448
  civilization, 1:557, 558
  clash of civilizations, 1:559–560
  death and dying, 2:248
  development theory, 2:339
  exoticism, 3:46–47
  globalization, 3:334
  undereating, 8:491
  world music, 9:142
  See also specific countries

Western Europe
  capitalist mode of production, 1:446
  cleavages, 1:578
  coffee industry, 1:595
  Corn Laws, 2:133–134
  partitioning, 9:147, 149
  saving rate, 2:108
  transitional conjunctures, 2:77–78
  See also specific Western European countries; Europe

Westley, Robert, 2:174, 175

Westminster model, 3:150

Westmoreland, William, 8:614

Westphalian order, 3:360–361, 4:235
  national security, 5:411–412
  nationalism and nationality, 5:416

Wet, Christiaan de. *See* de Wet, Christiaan

Weyler y Nicolau, Valeriano, 9:23

WHA (World Health Assembly), 9:140

What is Property (Proudhon), 1:111

What Is to Be Done? (Lenin), 4:410–411

Wheare, K. C., 3:113

Wheat, 3:377

Wheeler, R. E. M., 1:166

When Affirmative Action Was White (Katznelson), 9:87

When the Levees Broke (film), 1:243

Whewell, William, 7:363

Whig Party (U.S.), 2:286, 287, 7:186

Whig Party (England), 1:396

Whigs and Hunters: The Origin of the Black Art (Thompson), 8:355

Whiskey Rebellion (1794), 9:38

Whistle-blowers, 9:**79–81**, 80

Whitcomb, John C., 2:162

White, Burlington Northern and Santa Fe Railway v. (2006), 7:216

White, Douglas R., 8:88, 92

White, Eugene, 3:368

White, Gilbert Fowler, 5:433

White, Harrison, 5:476, 8:6

White, Hayden, 5:371

White, Leslie, 1:167, 2:203, 323

White, Walter, 5:384, 9:**81–82**
  civil rights, 1:550
  Harris, Abram L., Jr., 3:427

White by Law (Lopez), 9:88

White collar. *See* Blue collar and white collar

White Collar: The American Middle Classes (Mills), 5:182

White Collar (Wright), 8:597

White collar employment, 2:583–585, **583–586**, 584*t*
  black middle class, 1:314
  blue collar and white collar, 1:337–340
  credentialism, 2:166
  crime and criminology, 2:171–172
  crowding hypothesis, 2:182
  workers, 9:130

White flight, 2:314, 316–317, 6:235, 7:17, 201

White House. *See* Presidency

White noise, 9:**82–83**

White primary, 9:**83–85**

White Privilege (McIntosh), 9:87

White Sands Missile Range, 9:48

White southerners (U.S.)
  nationalism, 8:618–619
  New Deal coalition, 5:498
  slavery, 1:34
  white primary, 9:83–85

White studies. *See* Whiteness

White supremacy, 9:**85–87**
  agricultural industry, 1:61
  biological determinism, 2:325, 326
  Birth of a Nation (film), 1:304–306
  black nationalism, 1:315, 316
  Black Power, 1:321
  blackness, 1:328–329
  blood and bloodline, 1:335–336
  Clark, Kenneth B., 1:561
  Cox, Oliver C., 2:158
  cultural relativism, 1:123
  Dixiecrats, 2:429–431
  Dred Scott v. Sanford, 2:446
  gentility, 3:300–301
  Hitler, Adolf, 3:486–488
  Jim Crow, 4:198–200
  law and order, 4:372
  lynchings, 4:526, 527
  race, 7:2–7, 8–11, 13
  race mixing, 7:27
  racial democracy, 2:282
  separate-but-equal, 7:445–447
  South, U.S., 8:32–33
  Southern politics, 6:342, 343
  whitening, 9:89–91
  See also Aryans; Ku Klux Klan; Racism

White Women, Race Matters (Frankenberg), 9:87

Whitehead, Alfred North
  supreme being, 8:231
  symbolic logic, 4:481

Whitehead, Laurence, 2:290

Whiteman, Paul, 4:176

Whiteman, Unison, 3:383

Whiteness, 9:**87–89**, 90, 91–93
  blackface, 1:327
  blackness, 1:328
  blood and bloodline, 1:336
  colorism, 2:17–18
  ethnicity, 9:85–86
  immigrants, 3:579–580, 9:86, 88, 90
  Latino National Political Survey, 4:355
  Mexican Americans, 5:121
  moreno/morena, 5:293–294
  mulatto escape hatch, 5:310–312
  mulattos, 5:312–313
  mutiracials, 5:332–333
  passing, 6:165–166
  phenotype, 6:243–245
  public policy, 9:90

race, 7:2–7, 8–11
research, 9:86, 88
Whitening, 9:**89–91**
blood and bloodline, 1:336
Creole, 2:168
racial inequality, 4:7
Whites, 9:**91–93**
addiction, 1:21
Black Panthers, 1:319
Black Power, 1:321
body image, 1:346
burden of acting white, 6:49–50
choice in psychology, 1:526
civil rights movement, U.S.,
1:551, 552
colorism, 2:17–18
crime and criminology, 2:173
critical race theory, 2:175
dominance, 5:513–514
ethnic enterprises, 3:5
hypertension, 3:538–539
immigrants, 3:566*t*
invisibility, 9:87
minorities, 5:192
out-of-wedlock births, 1:307
passing, 6:166
psychology, 7:21
race, 7:3
racial classification, 7:39
urbanity, 8:545
See also Acting white
Whitman, Walt, 9:126
Whitney, Eli, 2:152
Whitney, William Dwight, 2:194
Whittaker, Frederick, 1:258
WHO (World Health Organization).
See World Health Organization
*Who Are We? The Challenges to
America's National Identity*
(Huntington), 3:525
*Who Gets Ahead? The Determinants of
Economic Success in America* (Jencks
et al.), 4:184
Who Governs? (Dahl), 2:219, 220,
4:528
Who Killed the Electric Car (film),
3:286
Wholesale Price Index (WPI),
9:**93–94**
Whorf, Benjamin Lee, 1:129,
2:194–195, 323
Why England Slept (Kennedy), 4:254
Whyte, William Hollingsworth,
6:61–62, 8:542
Wiccans, 2:188

Wickenden, William, 2:425
Wicksell, Knut, 4:78–79, 518, 9:94
interest rates, 4:84
machinery, 4:535
marginal product of labor, 4:305
quantity theory of money, 6:660
Stockholm School, 8:154
Wicksell effects, 9:**94–96**
Wicksteed, Philip H., 4:305
WID (Women in development
theory), 2:348
Widdowson, Peter, 4:464
WIDER (World Institute for
Development Economics Research),
2:267, 268, 9:47
Widow's cruse, 9:**96**
Wiener, Anthony J., 3:241
Wiggins, David, 5:453
WIID (World Income Inequality
Database), 2:268
Wildavsky, Aaron, 3:609, 610
Wilder, David A., 2:71
Wilensky, Harold, 9:67, 70
Wilhelm II, German Emperor, 1:349,
3:77
Wilkins, Roy, 4:268–269, 5:384, 385
Wilkinson, J. Harvie III, 1:377
Will
free, 1:121, 3:196
natural, 3:266–267
rational, 3:266–267
*The Will to Believe, and Other Essays in
Popular Philosophy* (James), 4:169,
170
William II, German Emperor. *See*
Wilhelm II, German Emperor
*William Morris: From Romantic to
Revolutionary* (Thompson), 8:353
William of Ockham, 6:20
Williams, Aubrey, 5:497
Williams, Christine, 8:6
Williams, Drid, 2:224
Williams, Eric, 3:131, 4:168, 7:53,
54, 9:**96–98**
Williams, John Burr, 1:455
Williams, Patricia, 5:372
Williams, Raymond, 2:192, 198, 199,
332, 3:63
class, 1:564
culture, 2:202
Thompson, Edward P., 8:353, 354
Williams, Rhonda, 2:405
Williams, Robert F., 1:318, 5:385
Williams, Walter, 9:26
Williams, William Carlos, 1:356

Williamson, Jeffrey, 4:309
Williamson, John, 9:38
Williamson, Oliver
firms, 3:148
hierarchy, 3:474–475
noncompeting groups, 5:515
transaction cost economics, 6:69
Williamson, Sonny Boy, 1:343
Willig, Robert, 9:63
Willingness to pay, 9:62
Willis, Gordon B., 8:571
Willis, Paul, 6:48
Willmott, Peter, 8:542
Willowbrook hepatitis studies, 4:33,
8:473
Wilmington (NC), 4:372
Wilmington Riot of 1898, 4:200,
9:**98–100**
Wilson, Charles Z., 5:387, 389
Wilson, Edith, 9:102
Wilson, Edward O., 2:234
Wilson, Harold, 4:327
Wilson, James, 4:485
Wilson, Paul, 2:241
Wilson, Pete, 1:416
Wilson, Richard, 1:99
Wilson, William Julius, 4:419,
9:**100–101**
black liberalism, 1:312
as black sociologist, 1:324, 325
neighborhood effects, 5:462
post-Parsonian American
sociology, 8:5
social isolation, 7:600–601
underclass, 8:485, 486, 9:100
urban studies, 8:542
Wilson, Woodrow, 9:**101–102**
Birth of a Nation (film), 1:306
Democratic Party, 2:287
League of Nations, 4:385
militarism, 5:165
popular sovereignty, 5:421
self-determination, 1:139, 7:406
Villa, Francisco (Pancho), 8:617,
618
women's suffrage, 8:217
work day length, 9:127
World War I, 9:146
Winant, Howard, 3:175–176
Winckelmann, Johann J., 1:165
The Wind Done Gone (Randall), 3:348
Windstorms, 5:433
Windward Islands, 3:257–258
Wine. *See* Spirits industry
Winer, Ben, 4:379

Winkelman, Michael, 7:486–487
Winner, Langdon, 2:217, 332
Winner-take-all elections, 8:655
Winner-take-all society, 9:**102–103**
Winner's curse, 1:207, 9:**103–104**
Winter, Johnny, 1:343
Winter, Nicholas, 1:103
Winter, Sidney, 1:491
Winthrop, John, 1:108
Wireless communications. *See* Telecommunications industry
Wirth, Louis, 1:540, 7:130, 8:541, 546
WISC (Wechsler Intelligence Scale for Children), 3:160
Wisconsin v. Mitchell (1993), 3:431
Wisconsin v. Yoder (1972), 1:535
Wisdom, collective. *See* Collective wisdom
Withdrawal, sexual, 2:114
Withdrawal of life-sustaining treatment, 1:192
Witherspoon v. Illinois (1968), 4:233
Witholding life-sustaining treatment, 1:191–192
Without Consent or Contract: The Rise and Fall of American Slavery (Engerman and Fogel), 8:367
Witness (Chambers), 2:85
Witnesses
    hearsay, 3:444–445
    lying, 4:525
Witnesses, expert. *See* Expert witnesses
Witt, Shirley, 1:98
Witt, Wainwright v. (1984), 4:233
Witte, Dryden, 8:589
Wittfogel, Karl, 1:188, 4:153
Wittgenstein, Ludwig, 3:463
    behaviorism, 1:275, 277–278, 280
    objectivity, 6:9
Der Witz und sein Beziehung zum Unbewussten (Freud), 2:23, 3:214
The Wiz (play), 9:104
Wizard of Oz, 9:**104–105**
WMA (World Medical Association), 8:392
WMD. *See* Weapons of mass destruction
Wohlforth, William C., 8:510
Wolcott, Harry, 6:14
Wold, Herman, 1:227–228
Wolf, Charles, 4:524
Wolf, Eric, 9:**105–106**
Wolfe, John, 1:586
Wolfer, Arnold, 5:412

Wolff, Francois-Charles, 1:287
Wolff, Richard, 2:78
Wolfowitz, Paul, 9:138
Wollstonecraft, Mary, 3:120, 8:618
Wolpe, Harold, 1:447
Woman on the Edge of Time (Piercy), 8:561
The Woman Rebel (Sanger), 3:89
Womanhood
    defined, 9:107
    rituals, 9:108
Woman's Role in Economic Development (Boserup), 1:357
Women, 9:**107–110**
    advertising, 1:28
    age discrimination, 2:402
    agenda setting, 1:48
    architecture, 1:172
    biological determinism, 2:326
    birth control, 1:303
    black, 9:125–126
        economists, 5:387–390
        gender, 3:268
        women's studies, 9:119
    body image, 1:346
    Boserup, Ester, 1:358
    California Civil Rights Initiative, 1:416
    calypso, 1:418–419
    caste, 1:458
    childlessness, 1:510
    Chinese Americans, 1:513
    Chinese diaspora, 1:516, 517
    citizenship, 1:542–543
    civil rights, 1:549
    Confederate States of America, 2:67
    contraception, 2:114–115
    corporate culture, 6:61
    correspondence tests, 2:141–143
    crime and criminology, 2:172, 173
    cultural tourism, 2:201
    Daughters of the American Revolution, 2:241–242
    dependency, 2:298
    depopulation, 2:301
    development in sociology, 2:348
    deviance, 2:353
    Disney, Walt, 2:410
    distributive justice, 4:240
    divorce and separation, 2:427–428
    economic role, 9:108–109
    employment discrimination, 5:408–409
    empowerment, 3:274

    female *vs.,* 3:267
    femininity, 3:117–119
    feminist sociology, 7:671–672
    gender politics, 6:332–334
    glass ceiling, 3:325–326
    history, 9:109–110
    history of, 1:268
    identity politics, 6:335
    immigration, 3:581
    infidelity, 4:21
    jazz, 4:177
    Jews, 4:194
    Jim Crow, 4:199, 200
    labor force participation, 4:315–316
    labor supply, 4:320, 321
    labor unions, 8:514
    lateral mobility, 5:213
    leisure class, 1:566
    litigation, 4:465
    lying, 4:524
    marriage statistics, 3:92, 92t
    matriarchy, 5:28–30
    military, 5:169
    misogyny, 5:203–204
    motherhood, 5:297–299
    Muslim, veil, 3:118
    Muslim, veils, 8:602–604
    NGOization, 5:521
    nirvāna, 5:504
    as objects, 3:118
    out-of-wedlock births, 1:306, 307–308
    patriarchy, 6:173–174
    phenotype, 6:245
    pimps, 6:271–273
    politics, 9:108–110, 110–112, 117
    prisons, 6:476
    psychological depression, 2:306
    qualifications, 6:649, 650
    quotas, 6:670
    rape, 7:64–66
    relationship satisfaction, 7:151
    rites of passage, 7:258
    science fiction, 7:361
    Selective Service, 7:392
    self-disclosure, 7:408
    self-hatred, 7:417
    sex and mating, 7:470–472
    sexism, 7:473–474
    sexuality, 7:480–483
    stratification, 8:166–167
    Taliban, 8:263

toilets, 8:384
University of Oxford, 8:527
Veblen, Thorstein, 8:596
virgins, 8:629–630
wage discrimination, 2:181,
   389–391, 399–403, 405–406
weight, 9:59
work, 9:108–109, 122–123,
   124–126
working class, 9:125
   See also Feminism; Gender
      differences; Gender gap; Work
      and women
Women, environment, and
   development theory (WED), 2:348
Women and Human Development
   (Nussbaum), 2:348
Women and politics, 9:**110–112**
   See also Gender politics
Women as Force in History (Beard),
   1:268
Women-headed families. *See* Female-
   headed families
Women in development theory
   (WID), 2:348
Women's Equity Action League, 3:121
Women's liberation, 4:315, 430,
   9:**112–116**
   See also Feminism
Women's movement, 9:112–115,
   116–118
   civil rights movement, U.S., 1:552
   contraception, 2:114
   Douglass, Frederick, 2:439–440
   Friedan, Betty, 3:121, 123, 216,
      268
   gender inequality, 3:626–627
   gender studies, 3:279
   legal rights, 9:117
   lesbians, 3:269
   NGOization, 5:521
   obscenity, 6:14
   political rights, 9:109–110,
      111–112
   reproduction, 7:178–179,
      180–182, 182–183
   Roe v. Wade, 7:270–272
   Truth, Sojourner, 8:462
   women's suffrage, 2:66, 5:179,
      8:214–217
   See also Feminism
Women's studies, 9:**118–120**
   Hite, Shere, 3:485
   Kinsey, Alfred, 4:270
Women's suffrage, 8:**214–218**
   Condorcet, Marquis de, 2:66

Mill, John Stuart, 5:179
   See also Franchise; Voting;
      Women's movement
Women's Worlds: International
   Interdisciplinary Congress on
   Women, 9:119
Wood, B. Dan, 1:145
Wood, Charles, 3:582
Wood, Robert, 2:201
Wood, Stuart, 3:150
Wood, Thomas E., 1:416
Woodblock prints, 8:632
Woodruff, Guy, 8:346
Woods, Rose Mary, 9:43
Woodson, Carter G., 1:345, 3:425
   African American studies, 1:32
   Black Power, 1:322
Woodstock, 9:**120–121**
Woodward, Bob, 4:215, 9:43
Woolley, Leonard, 1:165
Woolley, Michael E., 8:571
Woolworth Building, New York City,
   8:631
Worcester, Samuel, 1:497
Worcester v. Georgia (1832), 1:497
Work, 9:**121–124**
   alienated, 3:79
   ethic, 3:301
   gender gap, 3:274–275
   job guarantee, 4:204–206
   Lafargue, Paul, 4:330
   lay theories, 4:374
   leisure, 4:408, 9:123
   life *vs.,* 9:126
   overtime, 6:99–100
   role conflict, 7:273
   shift, 9:128
   tayloring, 9:123
   Taylorism, 8:287
   unpaid, 9:123, 125
   See also Domestic work;
      Employment
Work and women, 9:108–109,
   122–123, **124–126**
   black middle class, 1:314
   capitalist mode of production,
      1:447
   consumption, 2:108
   crowding hypothesis, 2:181–182
   day care, 2:245–246
   demographic transition, 2:291
   discrimination, 2:389–391
   employment, 2:580
   gender inequality, 3:625–626

labor force participation,
   4:315–316
labor supply, 4:320, 321
leadership, 4:381
maquiladoras, 4:592, 593, 594
marriage, 4:613–614
motherhood, 5:298
Scarr, Sandra Wood, 7:341
taste for discrimination, 2:399
wage discrimination, 2:400–401,
   402–403
Work day, 9:**126–128**, 134–135
   blue collar and white collar, 1:337
   labor law, 4:303
   labor supply, 4:322
   leisure, 4:408–409
   length, 9:126–127, 134–135
      class conflict, 1:569
      consumption function, 2:110
      labor law, 4:303
      leisure, 4:408–409
   rate of exploitation, 7:70
   surplus labor, 4:310
   Taylorism, 8:287
   time-and-a-half, 8:373–374
The Work of Nations (Reich), 4:302
Work teams/groups, 9:136–137
Work week, 9:**128–129**
   labor law, 4:317
   time-and-a-half, 8:373–374
Workers, 9:133
   blue-collar, 9:130
   cooperatives, 2:123–126
   discouraged, 2:386–387, 8:497
      underemployment rate, 8:494
      unemployment, 8:501
   exploitation, in flower industry,
      3:159
   foreign-born, occupational
      hazards, 6:22
   gainful, 8:500
   income inequality, 6:73
   knowledge, 5:493
   marginal, 8:501
   migrant, 4:318–319
   outsourcing, 6:86–87
   overeducated, 8:494
   poor, 3:77, 9:122
   salaried, 9:127, 128, 133
   Taylorism, 8:287–288
   whistle-blowers, 9:79–81
   white-collar, 9:130
   See also Labor; Proletariat;
      Working class
Workers' compensation, 6:25

Workers of Zion. *See Poalei Zion*

Workfare programs. *See* Welfare

Workforce Investment Act (1998), 3:422

Working, Holbrook, 1:228

Working capital. *See* Capital

Working class, 1:563, 9:**129–134**, 133
  blue collar and white collar, 1:337–340
  Bonacich, Edna, 1:352
  capitalist mode of production, 1:445–446, 447
  Christian socialism, 7:643
  cities, 1:541
  citizenship, 1:542–543
  class conflict, 1:569, 570, 571
  class consciousness, 1:571–572
  cleavages, 1:578
  communism, 2:34
  Conservative Party (U.K.), 2:87
  critical theory, 2:176
  cultural capital, 2:190
  cultural studies, 2:199
  described, 1:564
  factory system, 3:77
  fascism, 3:103
  gentrification, 3:302
  hegemony, 3:455
  history, 9:129–130
  labor, 4:300–301, 303
  leisure, 4:408
  Lenin, Vladimir Ilitch, 4:410–411
  liberation, 4:430
  Luddites, 4:513–515
  Lynd, Staughton, 4:529
  Marxism, 4:638–641
  middle class, 5:143–145
  mutual fund investments, 6:73
  neocolonialism, 5:467
  oppositional culture, 6:48
  organic intellectuals, 4:66–67
  Peronism, 6:214–215
  petty bourgeoisie, 1:362
  Russian Revolution, 7:303–304
  social history, 3:482–483
  social welfare system, 7:631–632
  Solidarność, 8:25–26
  surplus labor, 4:311–312
  Thompson, Edward P., 8:353–356
  transformation, 1:562
  University of Oxford, 8:528
  upward mobility, 8:533–535
  Veblen, Thorstein, 8:595–596
  women, 9:125

work day length, 9:134–135
  See also Proletariat

Working conditions
  Chávez, César, 1:493–494
  codetermination, 1:593

Working day. *See* Work day

Working Tax Credit, U.K. (WTC), 8:274–275

Working women. *See* Work and women

Workload, female-headed families, 3:116

Workplace relations, 9:**135–137**
  alcoholism, 1:71
  codetermination, 1:592–593
  contingency models of leadership, 4:384
  cooperatives, 2:124–125
  defined, 6:22–23
  discrimination, 5:408–409
  division of labor, 2:424–425
  industrial accidents, 1:8–9
  ingratiation, 4:34
  labor, 4:303
  preindustrial, 1:8
  sexual harassment, 6:474–475
  Solidarność, 8:25–26
  See also Social relations

Works and Lives (Geertz), 3:265

Works Progress Administration (WPA), 5:413, 494–495

Workshops, 8:514

The World, the Text, and the Critic (Said), 7:310

World Accumulation, 1492-1789 (Frank), 3:187

The World and Africa (Du Bois), 8:618

World Bank, 9:**137–139**
  Basic Needs Approach, 5:456
  beggar-thy-neighbor, 1:273
  bribery, 1:371
  conditionality, 2:65
  crony capitalism, 2:180
  Deininger and Squire World Bank Inequality Database, 2:267–268
  developing countries, 2:336
  development theory, 2:338
  economics, underdevelopment, 8:491
  Empowerment and Poverty Reduction, 3:274
  Engendering Development, 3:273
  establishment, 9:150
  free trade, 3:195–196
  G8 countries, 3:244

international economic order, 4:93
  loans, 4:473
  nominal income, 5:511
  rural development, 2:342
  water resources, 9:40–42

World Bank Institute (WBI), 9:139

World Civilizations (Schneider), 1:189

World Commission on Environment and Development, 4:404

World Community of Islam, 5:381

World Court. *See* International Court of Justice

World Disarmament Conference (1932-1936), 1:176

World Economic Forum (WEF), 3:278

World economy. *See* Global economy; World-system

World-empire, 9:152

World government, 3:**360–361**

World Health Assembly (WHA), 9:140

World Health Organization (WHO), 9:139–141
  AIDS/HIV, 1:65
  banana industry, 1:246
  bioterrorism, 1:302
  contraception, 2:114, 115
  disease, 2:407
  health in developing countries, 3:441, 442, 443
  HIV, 3:490
  sanitation, 7:321
  tobacco industry, 8:377

World Health Report 2003 (World Health Organization), 3:442, 443

The World in Depression, 1929-1939 (Kindleberger), 4:267

World Income Inequality Database (WIID), 2:268

World Institute for Development Economics Research (WIDER), 2:267, 268, 9:47

World language, 1:118

World Medical Association (WMA), 8:392

World music, 9:**141–142**
  jazz, 4:177–178
  popular music, 6:377
  reggae, 7:129

World-picture *(welthild)*, 9:78

World Population and Housing Census Program, 1:477

World Revolution 1917-1936: The Rise and Fall of the Communnist International (James), 4:168

World Social Forum, 3:513

World-system, 9:**151–154**
  colonialism, 2:12
  corporations, 2:139
  Cox, Oliver C., 2:158
  democratization, 2:289
  developing countries, 2:336
  development in sociology, 2:346, 347
  immigration, 3:581
  international relations, 4:101
  Marx, Karl, 4:637
  migration, 5:157
  political sociology, 8:4
  schools in sociology, 8:10–11
  stratification, 8:167
  Wallerstein, Immanuel, 9:10–11
  welfare state, 9:73

World trade. *See* International trade

World Trade Center, 1:233, 9:9

World Trade Organization (WTO), 3:281–282, 9:**143–145**
  banana industry, 1:246
  Bhagwati, Jagdish, 1:293
  bilateralism, 1:297
  corporations, 2:140
  cotton industry, 2:153
  critics, 3:282
  Doha Round, 3:281, 9:144
  economic inequality, 9:46–47
  economics, underdevelopment, 8:491
  establishment, 3:244, 8:548, 549
  free trade, 3:195–196
  game theory, 3:251
  intellectual property rights, 5:540–541
  international economic order, 4:94
  neocolonialism, 5:468
  peasant organizations, 6:75
  product dumping, 2:462
  retaliation, 7:216
  tariffs, 8:266
  textile industry, 8:334
  trade liberalization, 4:428
  unilateralism, 8:510
  Uruguay Round, 3:281–282, 8:548–549, *549*, 9:143–144

A World View of Race (Bunche), 1:388

World War I, 9:**145–147**
  alliances, 1:79
  appeasement, 1:152
  aviation industry, 1:232
  bilateralism, 1:297
  Chinese Revolution, 1:519–520

Churchill, Winston, 1:537
concentration camps, 2:63
decisive events, 2:254
interwar years, 4:121–122
Keynes, John Maynard, 4:260
League of Nations, 4:385
mortality, 9:18
Ottoman Empire, 6:84
refugee camps, 7:124
reparations, 9:148
wage and price controls, 9:1
weapons industry, 9:50
weapons of mass destruction, 9:52
Wilson, Woodrow, 9:102

World War II, 9:**147–151**
  alliances, 1:79
  appeasement, 1:152–153
  Asian immigrants, 3:563
  aviation industry, 1:232
  baby boomers, 1:235
  census, 1:477
  Central Intelligence Agency, U.S, 1:480–481, 482
  Chinese Revolution, 1:521
  Churchill, Winston, 1:537–538
  cognition, 1:597–598
  Cold War, 2:4
  concentration camps, 2:63–64
  De Gaulle, Charles, 2:264
  decisive events, 2:254
  democratization, 2:289
  Eisenhower, Dwight D., 2:555
  ethnic conflict, 3:2
  genocide, 9:150–151
  India, 1:356–357
  Indian National Army, 3:610–611
  interwar years, 4:121–122
  Japanese Americans, 3:600–601, 4:174–175
  jazz, 4:177
  Jewish diaspora, 4:190
  Jewish history, 4:196
  Keynes, John Maynard, 4:259, 260
  League of Nations, 4:386
  legacy of, 9:149–150
  martyrdom, 4:628
  Mexican Americans, 5:122–123
  mortality, 9:18
  Mussolini, Benito, 5:349–350
  nuclear weapons, 9:30, 48
  Pearl Harbor, 6:190
  petroleum industry, 6:233
  refugee camps, 7:124

Roosevelt, Franklin D., 7:283
Truman, Harry S., 8:459
USSR, 8:511
wage and price controls, 9:1–2
war crimes, 9:21
weapons industry, 9:50
weapons of mass destruction, 9:52
women's employment, 3:120
Zionism, 9:180
See also specific topics and people connected to the war; Hitler, Adolf; Holocaust; Nazism

World Water Development Report (2003), 9:40

World Wide Web (WWW). *See* Internet

World3, 4:448–449

The Worldly Philosophers (Heilbroner), 3:456–457

Worldview, Weltanschauung, 9:**77–79**

Worsaae, Jens, 1:166

Worship, 9:**154–156**
  monotheism, 5:269
  polytheism, 6:367–368
  religiosity, 7:162–163
  See also Religion

Worth, self. *See* Self-esteem

Wounded Knee, 5:426

Wovoka, 5:426

WPA (Works Progress Administration), 5:413, 494–495

WPI (Wholesale Price Index), 9:**93–94**

WRA (U.S. War Relocation Authority), 3:600–601

Wrangham, Richard, 1:84

Wray, L. Randall, 1:455–456, 480

The Wretched of the Earth (Fanon), 1:321, 2:257, 3:99, 513, 4:517, 8:626

Wright, Eric Olin, 8:5

Wright, Erik Olin, 1:563, 3:65, 5:144, 6:27, 9:133

Wright, Fielding, 2:429

Wright, John, 1:48

Wright, Louis T., 5:383

Wright, Orville, 1:232

Wright, Quincy, 9:17

Wright, Randall, 1:404

Wright, Richard, 1:330

Wright, Sewell, 2:463

Wright, Wilbur, 1:232

Write-offs, tax. *See* Tax relief

Writer's Guild of America, 3:140

Writing, travel. *See* Travel and travel writing
Writing to learn, 8:294
WTO. *See* World Trade Organization
Wu, Frank, 1:514
Wundt, Wilhelm, 2:80, 3:233
Würzburg school, 2:80, 81
WWW (World Wide Web). *See* Internet
Wygant v. Jackson Board of Education (1986), 6:671
Wythe, George, 4:180

X

X-Crise, 9:**157–158**
Xenophobia, 8:119–120, 9:**158–161**
Xie He, 8:631

Y

Yajñas, 1:366
Yajnopavita, 8:567–568
Yakovlev, Aleksandr, 3:351
Yalta Conference (1945), 2:4, 8:522
Yamazaki, Kazuko, 2:224
Yang, Weiping, 4:501
Yang, Yang, 4:499
Yarlung Zangbo River, 9:41
Yasgur, Max, 9:121
Yates, Frances A., 6:21
Yeang, Ken, 1:172
The Year 2000 (Kahn and Wiener), 3:241
Yellow journalism. *See* Journalism
The Yellow Kid (Outcault), 2:23
Yellow River Basin, 9:41
Yeltsin, Boris, 3:351, 7:302, 303, 8:512, 9:**163–164**
Yemen, 8:521, 522
Yew, Lee Kuan. *See* Lee, Kuan Yew
Yield, 9:**164–166**
    liquidity premium, 4:460
    maximum sustainable, 6:91, *92*
    spread, 8:68–69
Yield curve, 9:165, **166–167**
Yntema, Theodore O., 3:529
Yoder, Wisconsin v. (1972), 1:535
Yoon, Yong J., marginal product of labor, 4:307
Yoruba. *See* Negro; Santería
Young, Allyn A.
    increasing returns, 2:207, 7:217, 220, 8:607
    marginal product of labor, 4:307
Young, Iris Marion, 2:82, 9:132
Young, Kate, 3:273
Young, Michael, 5:98–99, 8:542

Young adults, National Longitudinal Survey of Youth, 5:407–408
    See also Adolescents; Youth culture
Young Plan (1929), 1:152
Youth Conservation Corps, 5:413
Youth culture, 9:**167–168**
    comic books, 2:24
    rock 'n' roll, 7:268
    See also Adolescents
Youth risk behavior survey. *See* Cross-sectional research
Youth Risk Behavior Survey (YRBS), 7:190
Youths. *See* Adolescent psychology
Yuan, Shikai and the Chinese Revolution, 1:519
Yugoslavia, 9:168–169
    Ad Hoc International Criminal Tribunals, 9:22
    breakup, 5:418
    civil-military relations, 1:547
    clash of civilizations, 1:559
    communism, 2:35
    concentration camps, 2:64
    conformity, 2:72
    Croats, 2:179
    ethnic conflict, 3:2
    genocide, 3:298
    Milosevic, Slobodan, 5:184
    NATO, 5:545–546
    Serbs, 7:455
    Tito, Josip, 8:375–376
    United Nations role, 8:524
    Warsaw Pact, 9:35
Yugoslavian civil war, 9:**168–169**
Yule, Udny, 1:226–227
Yumans, 5:425
Yunus, Muhammad, 3:362–363, 513, 4:473, 5:140, 6:407
Yuroks, 5:424

Z

Z-D model, 9:**172–173**, *173*
Z-test, 9:**181–183**
Zacharias, 8:593
Zahn-Waxler, Carolyn, 1:56
Zaibatsu, 2:140
Zambia, 4:250–251, 7:239–240
Zan, Ni, 8:631
Zanzibar and Nyerere, Julius, 5:554
Zapata, Emiliano, 9:**171–172**
    Latin American revolutions, 7:233, 235
    Mexican Revolution, 5:130, 131

Zapatista Army of National Liberation (EZLN). *See* Zapatistas
Zapatistas, 1:500, 7:235
    See also Zapata, Emiliano
Zapotecs, 6:426
Zartman, William, 1:556
Zasulich, Vera, 1:446
al-Zawahiri, Ayman, 1:299
Zeigler, L. Harmon, 4:506
Zelan, Karen, 1:290
Zelikow, Philip, 2:185
Zelizer, Viviana, 8:7
Zellner, Arnold, 4:394
Zelman v. Simmons-Harris (2002), 1:535, 7:348
Zen. *See* Buddhism
Zen Buddhism. *See* Buddhism
Zend-Avesta, 1:185
Zeno of Citium, 1:111
Zero marginal product of labor. *See* Lewis, W. Arthur; Surplus labor
Zero population growth, 9:**173–176**
Zero-sum games, 1:587, 3:250, 9:**176–177**
Zerowork, 4:330
Zha, Tao, 5:534
Zheng, Yuhuang, 3:101
Zhou, Enlai, 6:188
Zhu, De, 1:520, 521
Zimbabwe
    land reform, 4:343
    Mugabe, Robert, 5:307–308
    Rhodes, Cecil, 7:239–240
Zimbardo, Philip, 9:**178**
    human experiments, 3:60
    prison psychology, 6:471
    social influence, 7:596
Zimmer, Michael, 8:589
Zimmerman, Michael, 8:577
Zingales, Luigi, 3:148
Zingg, Robert, 7:443
Zionism, 9:**178–180**
    Ben-Gurion, David, 1:282–283
    bigotry, 1:296
    black nationalism, 1:316
    Bonacich, Edna, 1:351–352
    Jewish diaspora, 4:190–193
    Jewish history, 4:195–196
    liberation movements, 4:432
    Meir, Golda, 5:70–71
    pogroms, 6:288
    Sharon, Ariel, 7:493
    two-state solution, 8:477
    See also Jews; Judaism